Seventh Edition

Readings in Canadian History
POST-CONFEDERATION

Seventh Edition

Readings in Canadian History
POST-CONFEDERATION

R. DOUGLAS FRANCIS
University of Calgary

DONALD B. SMITH
University of Calgary

Australia   Canada   Mexico   Singapore   Spain   United Kingdom   United States

THOMSON

NELSON

**Readings in Canadian History: Post-Confederation
Seventh Edition**

by R. Douglas Francis and Donald B. Smith

**Associate Vice President,
Editorial Director:**
Evelyn Veitch

Executive Editor:
Anne Williams

Marketing Manager:
Laura Armstrong

Developmental Editor:
Linda Sparks

Permissions Coordinator:
Paula Joiner

Production Editor:
Lara Caplan

Copy Editor:
Karen Rolfe

Proofreader:
Shirley Corriveau

Indexer:
Elizabeth Bell

Production Coordinator:
Ferial Suleman

Design Director:
Ken Phipps

Cover Design:
Peter Papayanakis

Compositor:
Interactive Composition Corporation

Printer:
Transcontinental

**Library and Archives Canada
Cataloguing in Publication Data**

Readings in Canadian History / [edited by] R. Douglas Francis, Donald B. Smith.—7th ed.

Includes bibliographical references and index.

ISBN 0-17-641537-8 (v. 2.)

1. Canada–History–Textbooks.
I. Francis, R. D. (R. Douglas), 1944–
II. Smith, Donald B., 1946–

FC165.R42 2005   971
C2005-905052-7

For information about the photographs featured on the cover, see the Photo Credits (page 617).

CONTENTS

PREFACE

In this seventh edition of our two-volume *Readings in Canadian History*, as in previous editions, our aim has been to provide a collection of articles suitable for introductory Canadian history tutorials. This has meant selecting topics related to the major issues that are explored in such history courses, and providing valuable readings of a general nature. We have included articles that deal with the various regions of the country and, whenever possible, those that reflect new research interests among Canadian historians. Consequently, we have changed some of the readings. Unfortunately, because of space limitations, the addition of new articles meant that several worthwhile readings in the sixth edition had to be dropped. This new edition, however, will better meet the needs of introductory students in Canadian history today.

This volume includes two or three selections on each of 15 Topics, thereby affording instructors flexibility in choosing readings. Short introductions to each Topic set the readings in a historical context and offer suggestions for further reading. It is our hope that this reader will contribute to increased discussion in tutorials, as well as complement course lectures and, where applicable, textbooks. In particular, *Readings in Canadian History* can be used effectively in conjunction with the textbooks *Origins: Canadian History to Confederation*, 5th ed. (Toronto: Thomson Nelson, 2004), and *Destinies: Canadian History since Confederation*, 5th ed. (Toronto: Thomson Nelson, 2004), both by R. Douglas Francis, Richard Jones, and Donald B. Smith. As a new feature for this edition, we have provided for each Topic weblinks to primary sources on the World Wide Web. We have also provided suggestions of appropriate secondary sources.

Important reference works for students preparing essays and reports on different aspects of Canadian history include *Dictionary of Canadian Biography*, vols. 1–14, with additional volumes in preparation (Toronto: University of Toronto Press, 1966–); *Historical Atlas of Canada*, vols. 1–3 (Toronto: University of Toronto Press, 1987–1993); and the annotated bibliographical guides by M. Brook Taylor, ed., *Canadian History: A Reader's Guide*, vol. 1, *Beginnings to Confederation* (Toronto: University of Toronto Press, 1994); and Doug Owram, ed., *Canadian History: A Reader's Guide*, vol. 2, *Confederation to the Present* (Toronto: University of Toronto Press, 1994).

ACKNOWLEDGMENTS

We wish to thank the following individuals who offered valuable suggestions for changes in the seventh edition of *Readings in Canadian History: Post-Confederation*: Cynthia Comacchio of Wilfred Laurier University, Ernest Levos of Grant MacEwan College, Catherine Wilson of the University of Guelph, Brent McIntosh of North Island College, Graham Broad of the University of Western Ontario, Catherine Briggs of the University of Waterloo, Karen Dubinsky of Queen's University, Mark Leier of Simon Fraser University, and Ross Fair of Ryerson University.

In preparing past editions of the readers, we and the publisher sought advice from a number of Canadian historians. Their comments were generously given and greatly improved the original outlines of the collections. We would like to thank, in particular, Douglas Baldwin of Acadia University, Robert A. Campbell of Capilano College, Roger Hall of the University of Western Ontario, and Brent McIntosh of North Island College for their valuable reviews of the fifth edition. Thanks, too, for comments on earlier editions to Douglas Baldwin of Acadia University, Olive Dickason of the University of Alberta, Carol Wilton-Siegel of York University, John Eagle of the University of Alberta, Roger Hall of the University of Western Ontario, Hugh Johnston of Simon Fraser University, and Wendy Wallace and Paul Whyte of North Island College. Many other individuals made valuable suggestions; we are indebted to John Belshaw of the University of the Cariboo, Margaret Conrad of Acadia University, Beatrice Craig of the University of Ottawa, Chad Gaffield of the University of Ottawa, Marcel Martel of Glendon College — York University, Thomas Socknat of the University of Toronto, Robert Sweeny of Memorial University, Duncan McDowell of Carleton University, and Peter Ward of the University of British Columbia.

Heartfelt thanks also go to Anne Williams, Rebecca Rea, Lara Caplan, and Linda Sparks of Thomson Nelson, for their help and constant encouragement toward the completion of this seventh edition, and to Karen Rolfe, who copy edited the book. A special thanks goes to David Smith who researched the World Wide Web for sources, particularly primary sources, appropriate for each Topic. Finally, we wish to thank those Canadian historians who consented to let their writings be included in this reader. Their ideas and viewpoints will greatly enrich the study and appreciation of Canadian history among university and college students taking introductory courses in Canadian history.

Douglas Francis
Donald Smith
Department of History
University of Calgary

Topic One

An Era of Nation Building

The construction of the Canadian Parliament buildings in 1863. The buildings were completed in 1866, in time for Confederation the following year.

English-speaking Canadian historians, writing within the National School of Canadian historiography in the interwar years, looked upon the achievement of Confederation, the establishment of a national policy, and the building of the Canadian Pacific Railway as great nation-building events. The union of the three colonies of the United Canadas, Nova Scotia, and New Brunswick into Confederation in 1867 was seen as the political nucleus around which a transcontinental nation was formed within six years. The national policy of a high tariff, railway building, and settlement of the West provided the rationale for this new transcontinental nation to remain viable economically and independent of the United States by fostering east-west trade. The completion of the Canadian Pacific Railway (CPR) in 1885 provided the means for east-west trade to take place. But equally important, the herculean effort required to complete the railway provided the mythology of nation building. It reinforced the belief that with the railway, Canada would thrive as a transcontinental nation.

The following three readings both reinforce and challenge this well-established English-Canadian historiography. Writing in the context of the divisive Canadian constitutional debate of the 1980s and 1990s, and from the perspective of an American observer, John Rohr examines the debates in the Parliament of the United Canadas in 1865 on the 72 Resolutions passed at the Quebec Conference in October 1864. Eventually they became the British North America (BNA) Act of 1867—Canada's constitution. Rohr focuses on the differing opinions among the Fathers of Confederation on such issues as: a legislative versus a federal union; imperial ratification of the constitution versus seeking the people's consent; the inclusion or exclusion of the Intercolonial Railway in the constitution; and close or distant relations with the United States. Rohr explains why the BNA Act often evolved differently than the way the advocates of Confederation intended. By contrasting the actions and ideas of the Canadian Fathers of Confederation with the American founding fathers, Rohr also notes important differences in the Canadian and American political traditions.

Craig Brown reinforces the perspective of the English-Canadian national school of historiography with regards to the national policy by explaining its popularity in the late 19th century. He notes that it was seen as a step towards greater autonomy from Britain within the British Empire, and to increasing Canadian economic independence from the United States. As well, the national policy was presented as a means of uniting Canada when the traditional forms of national unity—a common language, religion, or ethnic composition—and a common geography and history, were absent.

Andy den Otter challenges the mythology that the CPR colonized the West, established Canadian independence from the United States, and created a national identity. Instead, he argues that as an expression of the latest communication and transportation technology, the CPR enhanced the centralizing and metropolitan dominance of central Canada over the hinterland regions of the Maritimes and the West. This led to resentment, alienation, and inequities within the country rather than unity. As well, he argues, the CPR was never meant to offer an alternative to American railways and hence to establish Canadian economic independence from the United States but, instead, the exact opposite: a means to exploit the dynamic American economy. Hence the mythology of the CPR is simply that—a myth, perpetuated by its builders and supporters because it worked to their advantage to have such a perspective.

What was the traditional national historical perspective on Confederation, the national policy and the CPR in English-Canadian historiography, and how do these three historians either reinforce or challenge that perspective? In what ways do the three authors share common assumptions about Canada despite their differing conclusions? Which perspective—the nationalist or what might be called the antinationalist—do you find most convincing and why? What relevance do these three readings have to the current political and economic situation in Canada?

The traditional nationalist perspective on Confederation can be found in the following three general texts: Donald Creighton, *The Road to Confederation: The Emergence of Canada, 1863–1867* (Toronto: Macmillan, 1964); W.L. Morton, *The Critical Years: The Union of British North America, 1857–1873* (Toronto: McClelland and Stewart, 1964); and P.B. Waite, *The Life and Times of Confederation, 1864–1867: Politics, Newspapers, and the Union of British North America* (Toronto: University of Toronto Press, 1962). Christopher Moore takes a more recent look at the topic of Confederation in the context of the current constitutional debate in *1867: How the Fathers Made a Deal* (Toronto: McClelland & Stewart, 1997). See as well the readings by A.I. Silver, "Confederation and Quebec," and Paul Romney, "Confederation: The Untold Story," in R. Douglas Francis and Donald B. Smith, eds., *Readings in Canadian History: Pre-Confederation*, 7th ed. (Toronto: Thomson Nelson, 2006). A more critical view of Confederation can be found in Paul Romney, *Getting It Wrong: How Canadians Forgot the Past and Imperiled Confederation* (Toronto: University of Toronto Press, 1999). A good primary source is P.B. Waite, ed., *The Confederation Debates in the Province of Canada, 1865* (Toronto: McClelland & Stewart, 1963).

On the Maritime provinces and Confederation, see Phillip A. Buckner, "The 1860s: An End and a Beginning," in *The Atlantic Region to Confederation: A History*, eds. Phillip A. Buckner and John G. Reid, (Toronto: University of Toronto Press,1994), pp. 360–86. See as well, Phillip Buckner, with P.B. Waite and William M. Baker, "CHR Dialogue: The Maritimes and Confederation: A Reassessment," *Canadian Historical Review*, 71, 1 (March 1990): 1–45.

On the American influence on Confederation, consult Robin Winks, *Canada and the United States: The Civil War Years* (Montreal: Harvest House, 1971 [1960]), and Greg Marquis, *In Armageddon's Shadow: The Civil War and Canada's Maritime Provinces* (Montreal/Kingston: McGill-Queen's University Press, 1998). Studies of Britain's influence include C.P. Stacey, *Canada and the British Army, 1841–1871*, rev. ed. (Toronto: University of Toronto Press, 1963 [1936]) and Ged Martin, *Britain and the Origins of Canadian Federation, 1837–67* (Vancouver: University of British Columbia Press, 1995).

Craig Brown presents his analysis of the national policy in greater detail in *Canada's National Policy, 1883–1900: A Study in Canadian–American Relations* (Princeton: Princeton University Press, 1964). For a critical view of the national policy, see John Dales, *The Protective Tariff in Canada's Development* (Toronto: University of Toronto Press, 1966). Donald Creighton's works contain the traditional defence of the National Policy; see, for example, *Canada's First Century* (Toronto: Macmillan, 1970). Ben Forster analyzes the events leading up to the adoption of the National Policy in *A Conjunction of Interests: Business, Politics, and Tariffs, 1825–1879* (Toronto: University of Toronto Press, 1986). The negative impact of the National Policy on developments in the hinterlands of the Maritimes and the West can be found in D. Bercuson ed., *Canada and the Burden of Unity*, (Toronto: Macmillan, 1977). T.W. Acheson's "The National Policy and the Industrialization of the Maritimes, 1880–1910," *Acadiensis* 1, 2 (Spring 1972): 3–28, is also of interest. Kenneth Norrie's "The National Policy and Prairie Economic Discrimination, 1870–1930," in *Canadian Papers in Rural History*, ed. Donald Akenson (Gananoque, ON: Langdale Press, 1978), pp. 13–33, questions whether western farmers had legitimate grievances against the National Policy. Michael Bliss looks at the connection between the National Policy and the spread of American branch plants in Canada in "Canadianizing American Business: The Roots of the Branch Plant," in *Close to the 49th Parallel etc.: The Americanization of Canada*, ed. I. Lumsden (Toronto: University of Toronto Press, 1970), pp. 26–42. The Fall 1979 issue of the *Journal of Canadian Studies* (vol. 14) is devoted to "The National Policy, 1879–1979."

Andy den Otter presents a more detailed look at the role of railways in the formation of Canada in *The Philosophy of Railways: The Transcontinental Railway Idea in British North America* (Toronto: University of Toronto Press, 1997). An insightful article on the role of technology, especially railways, in the formation of Canadian nationalism is Maurice Charland, "Technological Nationalism," *Canadian Journal of Political and Social Theory*, 10, 1–2 (1986): 196–220. A popular account of the CPR can be found in Pierre Berton's two-volume study, *The National Dream: The Great Railway, 1871–1881* (Toronto: McClelland & Stewart, 1970) and *The Last Spike: The Great Railway, 1881–1885* (Toronto: McClelland & Stewart, 1974). See as well David Cruise and Alison Griffiths, *Lords of the Line: The Men Who Built the Railway* (New York: Viking, 1988). In *The Canadian Pacific Railway and the Development of Western Canada* (Montreal/Kingston: McGill-Queen's University Press, 1989), John A. Eagle examines the CPR's contributions to western Canadian economic growth between 1896 and 1914. Suzanne Zeller's *Inventing Canada: Early Victorian Science and the Idea of a Transcontinental Nation* (Toronto: University of Toronto Press, 1987) examines the role of scientists in shaping the idea of a transcontinental nation.

WEBLINKS

Sir John A. Macdonald
http://www.collectionscanada.ca/primeministers/h4-3025-e.html
A biography of Canada's first prime minister. Also included are a selection of his speeches.

British North America Act
http://www.ola.bc.ca/online/cf/documents/constitution1867.html
The full text of the British North America Act, 1867.

Orders-in-Council, 1867–1882
http://www.collectionscanada.ca/archivianet/020157_e.html
A searchable database of orders-in-council submitted to the Privy Council from 1867 to 1882. Suggested search terms include the "Canadian Pacific Railway" and "Louis Riel."

History of the Federal Electoral Ridings since 1867
http://www.parl.gc.ca/information/about/process/house/hfer/hfer.asp?Language=E
This site is a database of federal election results since 1867, and is searchable by riding, candidate, and election year.

Canadian Pacific Railway Charter
http://www.canadahistory.com/sections/documents/canadian_pacific_railway_charter.htm
The charter of the Canadian Pacific Railway, as written in 1880.

Canadian Pacific Railway Essay
http://www.canadiana.org/ECO/PageView/07451/0003?id=ed2a214957bac8b7
An essay written in 1885 by George M. Grant, Principal of Queen's University, regarding the merit of the Canadian Pacific Railway.

CN Images of Canada Gallery
http://imagescn.technomuses.ca/railways/index_in.cfm?id=18&index=1
A gallery of Canadian railway images mostly from the late 19th century.

Article One

Current Canadian Constitutionalism and the 1865 Confederation Debates

John A. Rohr

Tantae molis erat
Romanam condere gentem.

Aeneid: I, 33

The purpose of this article is to examine the Confederation debates of 1865 in the hope of illuminating some dark corners of the exhausting constitutional quarrels that have dominated Canadian politics for the past two decades. By the "Confederation debates of 1865," I mean the debates of the 8th Provincial Parliament of Canada, which were held during February and March of 1865 in Quebec City. These debates focused on a set of resolutions adopted by delegates from Canada, New Brunswick, Newfoundland, Nova Scotia, and Prince Edward Island at a conference also held in Quebec City during the previous October. These resolutions led eventually to the British North America (BNA) Act of 1867.

The reader might wonder why I turn — of all places — to the Confederation debates for enlightenment on a contemporary crisis. Having read all 1,032 pages of these debates, I harbour the suspicion that I belong to a very exclusive club of North American academic eccentrics and, as an American, I expect that mine is a very small subset of this club. My most recent work has analyzed contemporary problems in terms of certain themes evident in the founding periods of the United States and of the Fifth French Republic.[1] Following the lead of Hannah Arendt, I believe that, for many western nations, founding periods are normative and that those who study such periods often discover events, arguments, and principles that illuminate a nation's subsequent development.[2]

To apply this idea to Canada presents a problem I did not encounter in studying the United States or the Fifth Republic. Despite the importance of the Declaration of Independence in American history, it is the drafting of the Constitution of the United States in 1787 and the subsequent debates over its ratification that define the founding of the present American Republic. Although the origins of France itself trail off into some dim and distant past, there can be no doubt that the Fifth Republic was founded in 1958. In studying the founding of the present regimes in France and the United States, I knew at once where to turn. With Canada, it was not as simple. The Proclamation Act, the Quebec Act, and the Act of Union present worthy challenges to Confederation as the founding period of Canada and, even if these challengers are ultimately exposed as impostors, the Confederation period itself harbors enough important events — most notably, the crucial meeting in Quebec City in October 1864 — to make the Confederation debates something less than the sole contender for serious study of Canada's founding.[3] Despite these methodological problems, I shall focus exclusively on the Confederation debates of 1865.[4] I do so because no other event from the Confederation period

Source: John Rohr, Canadian Constitutionalism and the 1865 Confederation Debates, *American Review of Canadian Studies* 28, 4 (Winter 1988): 413–444.

has records as complete as these and, more importantly, because these records reveal a sustained level of serious — and at times profound — public argument which, I believe, is unequalled in Canadian constitutional history.

In the months preceding the 1995 Quebec Referendum, considerable attention was lavished upon the precise wording of the text to be submitted to the people. At first, the debate focused on the speculative question of what it would be and, once this was known, what it should have been.[5] Federalists argued that their opponents had deliberately muddied the waters, misleading Quebeckers into thinking that they could live in a sovereign Quebec that somehow remained part of Canada. The federalist strategy was to reduce the question to a stark dichotomy: either you are in or you are out — a formulation sovereigntists wisely ignored. Both sides invoked such powerful symbols as Canadian passports and currency to support their respective positions. Post-election analysis revealed that substantial numbers of Yes voters thought that a sovereign Quebec would in some way or other remain part of Canada, despite the scoldings they received from stern federalists for being so illogical. Although no end to the crisis is in sight, I cannot help thinking that when the end comes, it will appear — much to the chagrin of ideologues of all stripes — in some hopelessly illogical compromise, whose sole merit will be that it works. If so, the Confederation debates on Canadian federalism offer an illuminating precedent. Perhaps Justice Holmes had it right when he said that a page of history is worth a volume of logic. Following the texts of the debates, this article has four substantive sections: the distribution of powers in Canadian federalism; the need for popular consent to constitutional change; the central role of public administration; and the image of the United States throughout the Confederation debates. The paper concludes with some brief unsolicited advice for my neighbors to the north, the musings of one who has thought long and often on these foundational matters.

CANADIAN FEDERALISM AND THE DISTRIBUTION OF POWERS

Americans who study Canadian constitutional history feel right at home when they get around to examining the regulation of commerce, because both countries impose an interprovincial or interstate limitation on the regulatory powers of their respective federal governments. Thus, in principle, neither Ottawa nor Washington may regulate commercial affairs that are strictly intraprovincial or intrastate. Despite this similarity in principle, Washington's writ, in fact, runs much further and deeper into the economic life of the United States than does Ottawa's in Canada. Noting this difference, a widely used textbook on Canadian constitutional law states that "ironically, the express restrictions in the American constitution have proved to be far less of a barrier to the development of national economic policies than have the judicially created restrictions in Canada."[6] This is "ironic" because the Constitution of the United States explicitly limits its federal government's regulatory power to "commerce among the states," whereas article 91 of the BNA Act of 1867 imposes no such limitation. Among the explicitly enumerated powers entrusted to "the exclusive Legislative Authority of the Parliament of Canada," one finds quite simply "the Regulation of Trade and Commerce." The "judicially created restrictions" mentioned in the text quoted above refer primarily to a series of late-nineteenth and early-twentieth century decisions by the Judicial Committee of the Privy Council (JCPC) — the British institution which, despite the creation of the Supreme Court of Canada in 1875, de facto exercised the ultimate judicial authority in Canadian affairs until 1949.

In the late 1920s and early 1930s, Canadian constitutional scholars who favored a more active role for their federal government subjected the JCPC decisions limiting Ottawa's power over commerce to a withering attack. The gist of their argument was neatly captured in a pithy and oft-quoted sentence written by the distinguished jurist William Kennedy: "Seldom have statesmen more deliberately striven to write their purposes into law, and seldom have these more signally failed before the judicial technique of statutory interpretation."[7] Kennedy's complaint finds considerable support in the unadorned text of the BNA Act, which the JCPC had construed quite narrowly. Article 91 confers upon Parliament a sweeping power "to make Laws for the Peace, Order and good Government of Canada in relation to all Matters not coming within the Classes of Subjects by this Act assigned exclusively to the Legislatures of the Provinces." Then, for good measure, it specifies a long list of explicit federal powers that are added "for greater Certainty, but not so as to restrict the Generality of the foregoing Terms of this Section"— that is, of the peace, order, and good government or "POGG" clause, as it came to be known. Among these enumerated powers one finds "the Regulation of Trade and Commerce." Jurisprudentialists of a federalist persuasion held that POGG was the sole grant of power to the federal government and the specific enumerations were merely concrete examples of the broader, more comprehensive power. The practical point of their position was that the federal government enjoyed plenary power to regulate trade and commerce.

The JCPC had interpreted the text differently, finding in the exclusive grant to the provinces in article 92 of a power to "make laws in relation to . . . Property and civil Rights in the Province" an impressive limitation on the federal government's power over trade and commerce. Much of the jurisprudence of the late-nineteenth and early-twentieth centuries centered on JCPC's effort to find the right balance between these texts, with most of the decisions favoring the provinces.[8] This line of reasoning culminated in a series of opinions authored by Lord Haldane which restricted POGG to an "exceptional" power to be used only in an "emergency" or in the face of "sudden danger to the social order" or in "special circumstances such as a great war."[9]

Canadian nationalists, like William Kennedy, seem to be on target when they find JCPC's interpretation of the BNA Act crabbed and strained. Although the Quebec Resolutions, the text debated in 1865, differed somewhat from the BNA Act of 1867, it was close enough to provide evidence suggesting that a good number of the delegates favored expansive powers for the federal government.[10] The 29th Resolution, anticipating what would eventually emerge as the POGG clause in the BNA Act, provided: "The General Parliament shall have power to make Laws for the peace, welfare, and good government of the Federated Provinces (saving the Sovereignty of England) and especially laws respecting the following subjects." It then went on to enumerate a long list of specific powers, most of which reappeared in the BNA Act. Among them was the "Regulation of Trade and Commerce."

During the Confederation debates, support for a broad interpretation of federal power came first and foremost from John A. Macdonald. Warming to one of his favorite topics — how to avoid the fatal flaws in the Constitution of the United States — Macdonald celebrated the superior wisdom of the Quebec Resolutions as follows:

> [The Americans] commenced, in fact, at the wrong end. They declared by their Constitution that each state was a sovereignty in itself, and that all the powers incident to a sovereignty belonged to each state, except those powers which, by the Constitution, were conferred upon the General Government and Congress. Here we have adopted a different system. We have strengthened the General Government. We have given the General Legislature all the great subjects of legislation. We have conferred on them, not only specifically and in detail, all the powers which are incident to sovereignty, but we have expressly declared that all subjects of general interest not distinctly and exclusively conferred upon the local governments and local legislatures, shall be conferred upon the General Government and Legislature.[11]

Variations on this theme can he found throughout the debates. Following Macdonald's lead, Isaac Bowman contrasts the Quebec Resolutions favorably with the Constitution of the United States, and then goes on to assert: "In the scheme submitted to us, I am happy to observe, that the principal and supreme power is placed in the hands of the General Government, and that the powers deputed to local governments are of a limited character."[12]

David Jones sees in the American doctrine of states' rights "the cause of the bloodshed and civil war" that has ravaged that unhappy land for the last four years." He then points out that "our case is exactly the reverse," in that instead of having the provinces delegate powers to the proposed central government, the central government "gives to these provinces just as much or as little as it chooses." He then quotes in full the centralizing language of Quebec Resolution 45: "In regard to all subjects over which jurisdiction belongs to both the General and Local Legislatures, the laws of the General Parliament shall control and supersede those made by the Local Legislature, and the latter shall be void so far as they are repugnant to, or inconsistent with, the former."[13] Richard Cartwright is pleased to report that "every reasonable precaution seems to have been taken against leaving behind us any reversionary legacies of sovereign state rights to stir up strife and discord among our children."[14] Finally, John Scoble advises his colleagues that a "careful analysis of the scheme convinces me that the powers conferred on the General or Central Government secure it all the attributes of sovereignty, and the veto power which its executive will possess and to which all local legislation will be subject, will prevent a conflict of laws and jurisdictions in all matters of importance, so that I believe in its working it will be found, if not in form yet in fact and practically, a legislative union."[15]

Scoble's reference to a "legislative union" is particularly significant because throughout the debates many delegates from Canada West who supported the Quebec Resolutions added that their only disappointment lay in the federal character of the proposed union. They would have preferred a legislative union — that is, an even more centralized regime than the one they were approving. Nevertheless, they would support the Quebec Resolutions because they bid fair to bring about a unified structure close enough to the legislative union they really desired.[16] Such statements, combined with those cited above, go a long way toward supporting William Kennedy's remark that "seldom have statesmen more deliberately striven to write their purposes into law" and that these purposes included an extremely vigorous federal government.

Upon closer examination, however, the federalist case is not as strong as it might at first appear. The friends of Confederation from Canada East seemed at times to be reading a text quite different from the strongly centralized document revealed in the passages we have just quoted. Take, for example, the following comments from four of the most prominent members of the Quebec delegation supporting Confederation:

> Etienne Pascal Taché: ". . . for all questions of a general nature would be reserved for the General Government, and those of a local character to the local governments, who would have the power to manage their domestic affairs as they deemed best."[17]

> George Cartier: "Questions of commerce, of international communication, and all matters of general interest, would be discussed and determined in the General Legislature."[18]

> Hector-Louis Langevin: "All local interests will be submitted and left to the decision of the local legislatures."[19]

> Joseph Cauchon: "But if no mention was made of divorce in the Constitution, if it was not assigned to the Federal Parliament, it would of necessity belong to the local parliaments as it belongs to our Legislature now, although there is not one word respecting it in the Union Act."[20]

What these remarks have in common is an exceedingly broad interpretation of provincial power under the Quebec Resolutions and one that finds little support in the text. Their argument seems to rely inordinately upon clause 18 of Resolution 43, which gives the provincial legislatures power to make laws respecting "generally all matters of a private or local nature, not assigned to the General Parliament." This passage is no match for the sweeping power of the General Parliament "to make laws for the peace, welfare, and good government of the Federated Provinces."[21] As noted above, this sweeping power was supplemented with the power to legislate "especially" in a long list of substantive areas which concludes with the power to legislate "generally respecting all matters of a general character, not specially and exclusively reserved for Local Government and Legislatures." The distinction drawn by the Quebec delegates between general and local matters was too neat and simple. They seemed to assume that the distinction between the two spheres was almost self-evident. Such an assumption is at odds with the language of the Quebec Resolutions. As we saw above, Resolution 45 anticipated that there would be jurisdictional conflicts between general and local legislation and that they should be resolved in favor of the federal government.[22]

The highly centralized character of the proposed confederation did not escape its opponents from Quebec. Unlike Taché, Cartier, et al., anticonfederationists, like the Dorions (Antoine-Aimé and Jean Baptiste Eric), Joseph Perrault, and L.A. Olivier, agreed entirely with John A. Macdonald's strongly federalist interpretation of the proposed constitution and for that very reason voted against it. Consider the following:

> J.B.E. Dorion: "I am opposed to this scheme of Confederation, because we are offered local parliaments which will be simply nonentities, with a mere semblance of power on questions of minor importance."[23]

> Joseph Perrault: "Local governments . . . will be nothing more than municipal councils, vested with small and absurd powers, unworthy of a free people, which allow us at most the control of our roads, our schools, and our lands."[24]

> A.A. Dorion: "I find that the powers assigned to the General Parliament enable it to legislate on all subjects whatsoever. It is an error to imagine that these powers are defined and limited, by the 29th clause of the resolutions. Were it desirous of legislating on subjects placed under the jurisdiction of the local legislatures, there is not a word in these resolutions which can he construed to prevent it, and if the local legislatures complain, Parliament may turn away and refuse to hear their complaints, because all the sovereignty is vested in the General Government, and there is no authority to define its functions and attributes and those of the local governments."[25]

If we look only at the *Franco-Français* debate on the Resolutions, it seems clear that the opponents of Confederation read the text more accurately but the Quebec supporters read it more wisely. It is inconceivable that men as sophisticated as Taché, Cartier, and Langevin did not understand the meaning of the text before them. They understood it only too well, but imposed a strained interpretation upon it that would sufficiently obfuscate its clear meaning so as to make it politically possible for Quebec to enter the Confederation. Further, their point of view prevailed when, some years later, the JCPC found in the tiny acorn of provincial power over property and civil rights the origins of what eventually became the mighty oak of decentralization that overshadowed POGG and the rest of Macdonald's carefully laid plans. Events proved that there was too little political support, not just in Quebec but in all of Canada for Macdonald's grand vision ever to become a reality. The Quebec Confederationists were poor exegetes but great statesmen. They knew that at times confusion is the friend of compromise. Perhaps there is a lesson in all this for the contemporary and possibly salutary confusion over the meaning of sovereignty.

CONSENT OF THE GOVERNED

Peter H. Russell begins his widely read *Constitutional Odyssey* by recalling what he describes as "perhaps the most haunting lines in Canadian history." He refers to a letter written in 1858 by three prominent fathers of Confederation, George-Etienne Cartier, Alexander Galt, and John Ross, to Sir Edward Bulwer-Lytton, the British colonial secretary at that time. The "haunting lines" are as follows: "It will be observed that the basis of Confederation now proposed differs from that of the United States in several important particulars. It does not profess to be derived from the people but would be the constitution provided by the imperial parliament, thus remedying any defect."[26]

Russell then contrasts this statement with a comment by Newfoundland premier Clyde Wells in 1990: "The Constitution belongs to the *people* of Canada — the ultimate source of sovereignty in the nation." Russell assures his reader that "between the two passages quoted lies much more than the gulf of years."[27] Indeed, the "constitutional odyssey" on which he embarks is the fascinating story of how Canadians made their way from the first statement to the second.

Although the Confederation debates provide many passages echoing the sentiments of the authors of the letter to Bulwer-Lytton, they also provide, however illogically, many passages anticipating Clyde Wells's statement as well. Despite the nearly universal support among the delegates for the monarchy and the no less universal rejection of both republicanism and democracy, the issue of whether the Quebec Resolutions should somehow be ratified by the people of Canada revealed a curious commitment to the notion that the legitimacy of a major constitutional change requires some sort of popular consent.

Naturally, the opponents of the Quebec Resolutions pressed this argument ceaselessly. They hoped that some sort of referendum, or even a new election, focused exclusively on confederation, would open the proposed text to a careful public scrutiny, which its most controversial measures could not withstand. They knew, for instance, that the confederation document was exceedingly vulnerable on the grounds that it called for a legislative council — later to be renamed the Senate — whose members were to be appointed for life by the Crown and whose number could not be increased. This measure was a concession to the Maritime provinces and enjoyed little support in Canada where, as of 1865, the members of the upper house of Parliament, the "legislative council," were elected. The opponents of Confederation knew that if they could rivet the attention of the people on the appointive senate and other unpopular measures, the supporters of the constitution might have to accept some amendments to the proposed Quebec Resolutions. This, they surmised, would set off a chain reaction in the Maritime provinces, which would demand further changes and thereby unravel the whole scheme. Thus the question of the need for recourse to the people was of considerable strategic importance throughout the debates. It was a point on which the friends of Confederation could not yield an inch. The interesting point for our purposes is to review the arguments both sides made in support of their respective positions.

The argument of the anticonfederationists was straightforward. Consider the following:

James O'Halloran: "I remarked at the outset, that I must deny to this House the right to impose on this country this or any other Constitution, without first obtaining the consent of the people. Who sent you here to frame a Constitution? You were sent here to administer the Constitution as you find it."[28]

J.B.E. Dorion: "I am opposed to the scheme of Confederation, because I deny that this House has the power to change the political constitution of the country, as it is now proposed to do, without appealing to the people and obtaining their views on a matter of such importance.[29]

Matthew Cameron: "Sir, I cannot conceive it to be possible that any body of men sent here by the people under the constitution will make changes in that Constitution which were not contemplated by those who sent them here, without submitting those changes first to the people."[30]

One could hardly ask for clearer statements affirming the principle that constitutions derive their just powers from the consent of the governed. Similar statements abound throughout the debates.[31]

The friends of Confederation were clearly embarrassed by this call for a recourse to the people. Their determination to reject it was thoroughly justified strategically, as the almost disastrous results of an election in New Brunswick, held as the Canadian Confederation debates were in progress, amply demonstrated.[32] The problem for the Confederationists was that their objections were merely strategic. They struggled in vain to find a principled response to the demand that the people of the two Canadas approve the proposed massive constitutional revision. The best they could do was to make tradition do the work of principle by arguing that recourse to the people was not the British way of doing things. Typical of this approach was the following comment from John Ross, one of the authors of Peter Russell's "haunting lines": "I will add that this mode of appealing to the people is not British but American, as under the British system the representatives of the people in Parliament are presumed to be competent to decide all the public questions submitted to them."[33] The problem with this argument was that it was easily defeated by recalling that there were ample precedents for Canadians and other colonists adapting British practices to local circumstances. Recourse to the people, like Confederation itself, would be such an adaptation.[34]

Throughout the debates, the Confederationists were reluctant to challenge directly the call for recourse to the people, preferring instead to dismiss it on procedural grounds. For example, when James Currie, an articulate anticonfederationist, introduced a resolution that the Legislative Council should not make a decision on the Quebec Resolutions "without further manifestation of the public will than has yet been declared," he met a host of procedural objections.[35] Alexander Campbell queried him on just how this "further manifestation of the public will" would come about. Transforming Currie's resolution into a man of straw, he dismissed as absurd the notion — a notion never proposed by Currie — that "the nearly four millions of people who comprise the provinces to be affected by the union should meet together *en masse*."[36] He also rejected the possibility of a special election on Confederation because such an election would require that Parliament first be dissolved, an impossible precondition since a majority of the members in both houses supported the government's commitment to Confederation and, therefore, there was no basis for dissolution. "Receiving the support of more than two-thirds of the representatives of the people as the present Government does," Campbell asked, "how is it possible that Parliament could be dissolved to suit the views of a small minority?"[37]

Timing was another procedural roadblock the Confederationists placed in the path of recourse to the people. On the very first day of the debates, 3 February 1865, Confederationist Fergusson Blair said that submitting the plan to the electors at that time "would involve a delay which could not be compensated for by any benefit proposed to be derived from such a course." He allowed, however, that "the subject would present a different aspect" in the event that at a later date there should be "numerous petitions in favor of an appeal to the people."[38]

As the debates drew to a close, however, the Confederationists changed their position on timing. On Saturday, 11 March 1865, the Legislative Assembly finally voted to approve the Quebec Resolutions. When the same body reconvened the following Monday, John Cameron, a supporter of the text, surprised his colleagues by offering a resolution requesting the Governor General to "be pleased to direct that a constitutional appeal shall be made to the people" before the text is dispatched to London for "the consideration of the Imperial Parliament."[39]

Thomas Parker, who, like Cameron, had voted for the Resolutions on the previous Saturday, opposed the Monday morning resolution to submit the text to the people before it went to London. Timing was his principal concern. "If the resolutions were to be referred to the people at all," he said, "it should have been before they received the sanction of the House." He asked rhetorically, "Are we to turn round today and reverse what we did on Saturday last?" He would have favored recourse to the people earlier, "but not now, after their [the Resolutions'] deliberate sanction by the House; to do so would stultify the Legislature."[40] Thus Parker opposed recourse to the people at the end of the debates because it was too late, whereas his fellow Confederationist, Fergusson Blair, opposed it at their beginning because it was too early.

The Confederationists' reluctance to answer directly the argument for consulting the people was underscored in their determination to expand the variety of procedural considerations they relied upon to sidestep the intrinsic merits of the issue. These additional procedural matters included: efforts to have resolutions calling for consultation ruled out of order; complaints about the expense such consultations would involve; and, most importantly, a constantly recurring theme that there was no need to consult the people in a formal referendum or an election because they had already been consulted in countless informal ways that made their overwhelming support for Confederation abundantly clear.[41]

Throughout the debates the participants frequently went out of their way to proclaim their loyalty to the British monarchy and their widespread contempt for republicanism and democracy, especially in their American incarnations. Despite these commitments, both sides in the Confederation debates revealed a surprising acceptance of the liberal principle demanding popular consent for major constitutional change. Political strategy governs the manner in which this acceptance becomes manifest. The anticonfederationists shout it from the rooftops, while their opponents grumble discreetly about the practical problems of implementing in deed the doctrine they will not condemn in principle.

THE CENTRALITY OF PUBLIC ADMINISTRATION

Americans following recent constitutional vagaries in Canada were surprised to learn that less than a month after the 1995 Quebec Referendum, Prime Minister Chrétien delivered himself of the opinion that "the real problems in Canada are economic growth and the creation of jobs and good solid administration."[42] That the Prime Minister of Canada would mention "good solid administration" as one of the nation's three "real" problems in the immediate aftermath of a referendum that nearly destroyed his country must surely have struck interested Americans as extraordinary and perhaps even as bizarre. Public administration is not prestigious activity in the United States. It is inconceivable that an American president in the midst of a great constitutional crisis would turn to administration — good and solid or otherwise — as the path to political salvation. Not so in Canada. Chrétien's remark was part of a national chorus that evoked the muse of administration to inspire politicians to achieve the high statesmanship needed to bind up the nation's wounds. Constitutional debates over the very survival of the regime moved effortlessly into detailed discussions of such classic administrative themes as environmental management, immigration policy, public finance, civil service pensions, education, manpower and training, unemployment benefits, control of natural resources, and, of course, that hardy perennial of Canadian Federalism, equalization of payments. Federalists were not alone in enlisting administration to support their cause. Quebec sovereigntists, most notably Premier Lucien Bouchard, frequently tempered the high rhetoric of sovereignty with the mundane details of education, employment, health care, civil service reform, and financial management that would make it all possible and worthwhile.[43]

The striking variation in the value Canadians and Americans assign to public administration marks an important difference in the political cultures of the two countries. Some have traced it back to the American Revolution, arguing that refugee Loyalists brought to their new country an affection for government that was quite literally alien to their erstwhile rebellious neighbors to the south.[44] This affection, so the argument goes, was reinforced by the warm welcome they found in what remained of British North America. Whatever the explanation, the phenomenon itself is clear enough today among both federalists and sovereigntists. It was also true in 1865 when both friends and foes of the Quebec Resolutions enlisted detailed questions of administration as weapons in defending their respective positions. The Confederation debates reveal a host of administrative questions that absorbed the attention of the delegates. The topics ranged from broad generalizations on the hopes for improved administration that Confederation was expected to provide, to more focused attention to public works, and, finally, to very specific discussions on canals and schools.[45] Woven into the fabric of these arguments was a curious debate over the provision in Resolution 64 that the "General Parliament" would make "an annual grant in aid" to each province "equal to eighty cents per head of the population, as established by the census of 1861." Subsequent resolutions provided special benefits for New Brunswick, Newfoundland, and Prince Edward Island. These provisions triggered debates foreshadowing later controversies over the equalization payments that would play so important a role in the administration of Canadian federalism.[46]

Among the many administrative questions debated in 1865, however, none can match the importance of the Intercolonial Railway. In rehearsing the debates over this immensely controversial innovation, I have no intention of weighing the merits of the issue. I examine the railroad question, which was to dominate the early development of Canadian administration, only to give a very specific example of the salience of administration in the debates. I do this to establish a link between past and present, thereby suggesting that when contemporary Canadians link mundane questions of administration to the high statesmanship of saving a great nation, they echo sentiments harking back to the beginnings of Confederation.

Quebec Resolution 68 proposed an "Intercolonial Railway" to extend "from Rivière du Loup, through New Brunswick, to Truro in Nova Scotia." Its importance in the debates for friend and foe alike of the resolutions is textually demonstrable. Speaking before the Legislative Council, William Macmaster, an opponent of Confederation, denounced the proposed railroad as "a very questionable part of the project" and then elevated its importance by adding "indeed to my mind it is the most objectionable of the whole."[47] Echoing these sentiments, anticonfederationist Matthew Cameron saw the railroad as nothing less than the "leading feature" of the proposed constitutional change and one of the main reasons why it should be rejected."[48]

Not to be outdone, the friends of Confederation were no less outspoken in supporting the railroad than their adversaries were in condemning it. For Antoine Harwood, "the building of the Intercolonial Railway" was "the most important consideration of all for everyone, and one which would of itself be sufficient to make us desire the union of the provinces."[49] Raising his sights beyond the railway proposed in the text before him, Colonel Arthur Rankin proclaimed it but the first step toward "that still more important and magnificent project, the Atlantic and Pacific Railway." Seeing the embryo of this grander project in the proposed Intercolonial Railway, Rankin assured his colleagues that "it would be impossible to overestimate the advantages which any country must derive from being possessed of a line of communication destined to become the highway from Europe to Asia."[50]

With such strong statements both in its favor and against it, the Intercolonial Railway became, of course, the subject of considerable controversy. At the very outset of the debates in the Legislative Assembly, Luther Holton, a prominent anticonfederationist, went to the heart of the matter when he registered his surprise at finding in a constitutional text a proposal to build a railway. He ridiculed this provision as "a novelty that, perhaps might not be found in the constitution of any country."[51] To this John A. Macdonald replied: "The railroad was not, as stated by Mr. Holton, a portion of the Constitution, but was one of the conditions on which the Lower Provinces agreed to enter into the constitutional agreement with us."[52]

Macdonald's distinction between "a portion of the Constitution" and a "condition" for accepting the constitution was no shallow legalism. It produced an immediate and most unwelcome reaction in New Brunswick where the friends of Confederation were facing an imminent election that focused on the Quebec Resolutions. For Samuel Tilley, the leading New Brunswick Confederationist, the Intercolonial Railway was absolutely essential. It was, as Donald Creighton puts it, "Tilley's biggest political asset."[53] Albert J. Smith, Tilley's principal opponent, seized on Macdonald's unfortunate comment that the railway was not a "portion of the Constitution" to argue that the commitments in the Quebec Resolutions most favorable to New Brunswick, above all the Intercolonial Railway, meant nothing at all. Frantically, Macdonald sent a telegram to Tilley assuring him that the provision for the Railway — regardless of its status as part of the constitution — would appear in the text of the imperial act which was the ultimate goal of the Quebec Resolutions. His remarks helped to reassure the "terrified Unionists" in New Brunswick, but mistrust and hard feelings remained.[54]

The prominent place given to the railway provision in the proposed constitution brought a technical dimension to the Confederation debates conspicuously absent from the comparable debates in the United States in 1787 or in France in 1958. The railroad clause prompted extremely lengthy and detailed discussions of what we might call today financial management. The wearisome detail in the two excerpts that follow capture nicely the technical flavor of much of the debate over the railroad:

> Hon. Mr. RYAN—[speaking in favor of the resolutions on 20 February] . . . I want to shew by this [a lengthy discussion he had just finished on the economics of transporting a barrel of flour] that the carrying of flour over the Intercolonial Railway will not be so difficult of accomplishment as people who have not gone into the calculation closely may be disposed to imagine. (Hear, hear.) I have here, too, a statement of the imports of flour into New Brunswick, Nova Scotia, and Newfoundland. It is as follows:

Imports of Flour	Barrels
New Brunswick	243,000
Nova Scotia	328,000
Newfoundland	226,000
[Total]	797,000

> Mr. A. MACKENZIE—[speaking against the resolutions on 23 February] . . . Major Robinson estimates the cost of the road at about £7,000 Pounds per mile, or about £2,800,000 altogether. I do not think, judging from the statement he gives of the grades in the road, the bridges to be built, and the material to be found along the line, that it is a fair inference that the cost would equal the amount he sets down. The character of the ground over which the road will pass is very similar to the railways of Canada. It is represented to be very much of the nature of the country through which the Great Western runs westward of Hamilton over a great portion of the line. The best portion of the line is equal to the worst portions of the Great Western. Even at the cost of £7,000 per mile the expense of constructing the entire road would be a little over fifteen millions of dollars.[55]

Statements of this nature abound throughout the Confederation debates.[56] As noted above, there is nothing like them in the French or American debates. Luther Holton was right. To insert a clause about a specifically named railroad into a constitution was an innovation, but it underscores a blending of administration and constitutionalism in a distinctively Canadian way.

Before concluding our study of the railroad as an example of administration in the Confederation debates, we should note the theme of technology driving constitutional reform. Speaking in favor of the resolutions, John Ross invoked Lord Durham's famous (or infamous) *Report* of 1839 in which he argued that a railroad "between Halifax and Quebec would, in fact, produce relations between these provinces that would render a general union absolutely necessary."[57] This same passage is cited by Anselme Paquet, an opponent of Confederation, as a reason for rejecting the Quebec Resolutions.[58] The curious fact that the same author is cited verbatim, first for Confederation and then against it, is explained by the diametrically opposed memories of Lord Durham in the two Canadas as of 1865. Generally loved and admired in Ontario, in Quebec he was, quite simply, despised.[59] What is interesting for our purposes, however, is that both friends and foes of Lord Durham agree with his prediction that an Intercolonial Railway would be a particularly apt means for achieving political unity. Logically enough, Ross and Paquet cite Lord Durham's argument, each to his own end of bringing about Confederation (for Ross) or of stopping it (for Paquet.) For the latter the railroad should be opposed because it would lead to political union as the *mal-aimé* Durham had correctly surmised. For the former, the railroad should be supported for precisely the same reason. For our study of the administrative-constitutional link, however, the important point is that Lord Durham had the wit to foresee technological innovation as a sure path to constitutional reform and that men on both sides of the 1865 debate recognized that he was right.

The Confederation fathers of 1865 had no need of promptings from Lord Durham to see the connection between the Intercolonial Railway and Confederation. Thus, anticonfederationist James Currie, noting that "some leading men in Halifax had said 'the Railway first, and Confederation next,'" argues that the simplest way to defeat Confederation would be to reject the railway proposal. He was satisfied that "if the Intercolonial Railway project were taken out of the scheme [that is, the proposed constitution], we would not hear much about it afterwards."[60] Although Currie, like Lord Durham, saw a close connection between the railway and Confederation, he did not fear the railway as simply a means to Confederation. His argument was that the Confederationists in the Maritime provinces cared only about the railway but would cynically embrace Confederation as a necessary evil. This position was expanded by A.A. Dorion who attributed to Samuel Tilley, the prominent New Brunswick Confederationist, the sentiment "no railway, no Confederation." Indeed, A.A. Dorion went on to denounce the entire Confederation plan as nothing but an elaborate scheme to rescue the financially troubled Grand Trunk Railroad.[61]

Confederationist Hector-Louis Langevin candidly acknowledges that his cause would be doomed without the Intercolonial Railway, "for it is almost impossible that so great an enterprise [as the Intercolonial Railway] should succeed unless it is in the hands of a great central power.[62] Thus Langevin joins his opponents Currie and Dorion in acknowledging, albeit for very different reasons, the close link between the proposed railroad and Confederation itself. In the passage just cited, however, Langevin seems to reverse Lord Durham's timetable because he envisions Confederation ("a great central power") preceding the railroad. Langevin's priorities differ sharply from those of his fellow Confederationist A.M. Smith who, rather surprisingly, concedes that "as a commercial undertaking, the Intercolonial Railway presents no attraction." He then adds, however, that "for the establishing of those intimate social and commercial relations indispensable to political unity between ourselves and the sister provinces, the railway is a necessity."[63]

Although there are many variations on the theme, the theme itself is clear and unambiguous.[64] Regardless of how they might differ on the merits of the Quebec Resolutions, the men of 1865 were at one in seeing a close connection between Confederation and the great public enterprise of the Intercolonial Railway. That is, they found in railroads, the "high tech" of their day, a path to meaningful compromise that created a great nation. Today there is no dearth of technological innovation; it is the hallmark of our time. Perhaps some bright statesmen in Quebec City or Ottawa will seize upon it to restore that nation.

THE IMAGE OF THE UNITED STATES IN THE CONFEDERATION DEBATES

The United States has played a muted role throughout the present constitutional crisis of its neighbor to the north. The official position of the U.S. government has been to encourage Canadians of all stripes to patch up their differences, while it maintains a low profile to avoid aggravating a situation that is already volatile enough. Some attention has been given to the likely impact of an independent Quebec upon the North American Free Trade Agreement, but this question tends to be readily subsumed under the larger question of the economic viability of Quebec as a nation in its own right. Howard Galganov, an outspoken defender of Anglophone rights in Quebec, had little to show for his ill-advised trip to Wall Street to discourage American investment in his province because of its language policies. Traditional trade disputes between Canada and the United States continue apace, but this is simply business as usual with little relevance to Quebec's claims of sovereignty.

This subdued role contrasts sharply with the dark shadow cast by the United States upon the Confederation debates of 1865 which took place during the closing months of the American Civil War. One of the major arguments for Confederation was the need to prepare for a possible attack from the United States once the war was over. Canadian statesmen of all persuasions knew that the government of the United States was greatly displeased with the sympathetic position of the British Empire toward the southern states throughout the war. Several minor but exceedingly unpleasant border skirmishes had not escaped the attention of thoughtful Canadians. The record of the debates reveals a serious concern that the victorious Union armies might soon invade Canada to settle some scores with the British Empire and even to annex certain sections of British North America.

American influence on the Confederation debates was not limited to the fear of armed invasion. American ideas and institutions made their mark as well. Although the Confederation fathers outbid one another in condemning American republicanism, the republican Constitution of the United States fared better at their hands, playing, as it were, to mixed reviews, while top billing was reserved for the framers of the American Constitution. Let us examine more closely how the Confederation fathers regarded these three crucial elements of the American founding: republicanism, the constitutional text, and the authors of that text.

We have already had occasion to note the pervasive commitment to monarchy among the participants in the Confederation debates. Consequently, their pejorative references to American republicanism come as no surprise, being simply the opposite side of the monarchist coin. Thus Benjamin Seymour can refer to "all the wild republican theories of our neighbor," while Philip Moore rejects the proposed constitution because "the engrafting of this system of government upon the British Constitution has a tendency to at least introduce the republican system."[65] Alexander Vidal, one of the few Confederationists who favored referring the proposed text to the people, warned his fellow Confederationists that "I am not to be deterred from expressing my views by the taunt of republicanism."[66] J.O. Bureau, an opponent of Confederation, professed to detect "republican sentiments" among members of the government who had introduced the Quebec Resolutions, whereas Colonel Frederick Haultain, a staunch Confederationist, suspected some of his opponents of being "men with annexation tendencies . . . who are inclined toward republican institutions."[67] Thus, both friends and foes of Confederation used republicanism as a club to beat their opponents. At times American republicanism was identified with democracy, as when David Macpherson predicted that failure to approve the Confederation plan would put Canada on an inclined plane leading inevitably to its incorporation into the American union. Canadians would find themselves "plunged into a malstrom [sic] of debt, democracy and demagogism." To which his listeners shouted "Hear, Hear."[68]

The American Constitution itself fared better at the hands of the Confederation fathers than the republican principles that underlay it. For every John Sanborn labeling it as "that horror of our constitution-makers," there was a David Christie ready to celebrate "the wonderful fabric of the American constitution."[69] As noted above, John A. Macdonald took the lead in singling out the decision to leave residual power with the states as the great flaw in the constitution of the United States. Learning from this American mistake, the Confederationists proposed to confer on the "General Parliament" the sweeping power "to make Laws for the peace, welfare and good government of the Federated Provinces"—the forerunner of the POGG clause of the BNA Act. Although Macdonald was unrelenting in condemning this fundamental flaw in the American Constitution, he also found in it much to admire. At the very outset of the Confederation debates, he made it clear that he would not follow "the fashion to enlarge on the defects of the Constitution of the United States," adding that he was "not one of those who look upon it as a failure." On the contrary, he considered it "one of the most skillful works which human intelligence ever created" and "one of the most perfect organizations that ever governed a free people." To recognize "that it has some defects is but to say that it is not the work of Omniscience, but of human intellects." Canadians are "happily situated in having had the opportunity of watching its operation, seeing its working from its infancy till now." Consequently, "we can now take advantage of the experience of the last seventy-eight years, during which that Constitution has existed, and I am strongly of the belief that we have, in a great measure, avoided in this system which we propose for the adoption of the people of Canada, the defects which time and events have shown to exist in the American Constitution."[70] This is a rather generous assessment, coming as it did near the end of the fourth year of the dreadful civil war fought to preserve the Constitution of the United States.

Not everyone agreed with Macdonald's analysis that the tragic flaw in the American Constitution lay in its defective federalism, which failed to give adequate power to the national government. Leonidas Burwell found no fault with American federalism. Indeed, he thought that "as a principle of free government it has been successful" and he doubted "whether history records a like example, under ordinary circumstances, of such great success and prosperity." For Burwell, the failure to come to terms with slavery was the great American tragedy. Slavery "was the cause of the war. It was opposed to the spirit of the age and had to be eradicated."[71] David Christie echoed Burwell's sentiments. The American Constitution "has stood many rude tests and but for the existence . . . of an element in direct antagonism to the whole genius of their system — negro slavery — the Constitution would have continued to withstand — yes, and after the extinction of that element, will continue to withstand — all the artillery which their own or foreign depotism can array against it."[72]

For the most part, references to the Constitution of the United States came in general statements on its spirit and institutions with little attention to specific textual provisions. There were some interesting exceptions, however. The partial veto of the American president over acts of Congress struck anticonfederationist Philip Moore as an attractive alternative to Parliament's power of disallowance over provincial legislation.[73] J.B.E. Dorion praised the complex procedure Americans required for constitutional change and contrasted it pointedly with the willingness of the Confederationists to adopt the Quebec Resolutions by a simple act of the Canadian Parliament with no recourse to the people.[74] John A. Macdonald cited the proposal in the Quebec Resolutions to subject criminal offenses to federal jurisdiction as a marked improvement over the American constitutional practice of leaving such matters to the states.[75] On the other hand, in a somewhat confused reference to the contracts clause — that is, the clause in the American Constitution which forbids states from impairing the obligation of contracts — John Sanborn lauded the Americans for providing greater protection for property against state governments than the Quebec Resolutions offered against provincial governments.[76]

Despite its republican foundations, the Constitution of the United States received, on balance, rather high marks from the monarchist Canadian Parliamentarians of 1865. The rave reviews, however, were saved for the framers of the American Constitution and appeared in such statements as Joseph Cachon's reference to "the illustrious founders of the Union" and Isaac Bowman's salute to the American founding fathers as "some of the wisest and ablest statesmen."[77] Even when George-Etienne Cartier condemns George Washington's "insidious offer" to Quebeckers to join the American Revolution, the context makes clear that the target of his contempt is the offer itself but not the man from whom it issued.[78] The most remarkable encomium, however, came from John Ross, who suggested that opponents of Confederation might overcome their narrow provincialism if they would take the trouble to "read the debates which preceded the establishment of the American Constitution." He singled out the debates in Virginia, "which at that time, by reason of its wealth and population, bore a similar relation to the other colonies to that which Canada now bears to the Lower Provinces." By reading the great speeches of "the Madisons, the Marshalls, the Randolphs, the Henrys, the Lees and others," opponents of Confederation would see that "those great patriots," setting aside the small-village feelings and animosities tending to embarrass and to destroy harmony, "acted like great men, true and noble men as they were, and applied themselves to their task with the purpose of bringing it to a successful issue."[79]

In view of the high esteem in which the Confederation fathers held the framers of the American Constitution, it seems fitting that we examine the extent to which they used ideas, strategies, and arguments similar to those employed by their American predecessors. Here we meet at once an embarrassment of riches. The founding fathers in both countries

- insisted that the time for constitutional reform was "now or never," with the Americans threatening the grim spectre of civil war or foreign invasion and the Canadians the inevitable slide down the inclined plane leading to annexation to or conquest by the United States;[80]
- maintained that the new constitution would provide better public administration;[81]
- congratulated their fellow citizens on having the rare opportunity to choose their destiny freely;[82]
- answered arguments from their opponents to the effect that enhanced military readiness would provoke attacks from potential enemies;[83]
- endured severe attacks from their opponents on alleged procedural irregularities and outright illegalities in their innovations;[84] and
- weighed the merits of invoking divine intervention on behalf of their efforts.[85]

Although the topics from which to choose are many and varied, I shall develop only one of them here: the constructive use of ambition by statesmen. Perhaps the most famous line in American political science appears in *Federalist 51*, where James Madison looks to the ambition of statesmen to safeguard the cardinal constitutional principle of separation of powers. Although the Canadian Confederation is not grounded in the principle of separation of powers, the broader implications of the creative possibilities of political ambition were not lost on the Confederation fathers. In his opening address to the Legislative Assembly, John A. Macdonald suggested that Confederation would enhance the prestige of Canada to such an extent that the representative of Queen Victoria in Canada would always be a man of the highest quality, perhaps even "one of her own family, a Royal Prince." Although Canadians could put no restrictions on Her Majesty's prerogative to appoint whomever she wished, he added that once Confederation is in place, "it will be an object worthy of the ambition of the statesmen of England to be charged with presiding over our destinies."[86]

Canadian statesmen would also feel the attraction of ambition once they have a broader political field for their actions. Lord Durham had anticipated this development when he wrote that the union he envisioned in 1839 "would elevate and gratify the hopes of able and aspiring men. They would no longer look with envy and wonder at the great arena of the bordering Federation, but see the means of satisfying every legitimate ambition in the high office of the judicature and executive government of their own union."[87] Charles Alleyn echoed Lord Durham's sentiments when he predicted that with Confederation a "worthy field will be opened for the ambition of our young men and our politicians will have a future before them, and may fairly aspire to the standing and rewards of statesmen. (Cheers.)"[88]

The release of creative energy occasioned by Confederation was felt as far away as British Columbia. Although British Columbia was not a party to the Quebec Resolutions, many people in that part of British North America felt — correctly as it turned out — that the proposed Confederation would soon include them as well. Hector-Louis Langevin read aloud an editorial from a British Columbia newspaper, which included the following consideration among the advantages of Confederation:

> Instead of seeing the talent of our statesmen fettered, harassed and restrained within the narrow limits of local politics, we shall find its scope extended to a whole continent, while a more vast and more natural field will be thrown open to the active and enterprising spirit of the North American Provinces.[89]

Participants in the Confederation debates felt that the seriousness of the topic under consideration was bringing out the best in them. Colonel Arthur Rankin allowed that "it is to me a matter of congratulation to observe that, at last, something has arisen which has given a higher tone to the debates in this House, and to the utterances of our public men." He attributed this improvement "to the fact that we are discussing a question of greater importance than has ever before been brought under our consideration." Finally, he added, the Legislative Assembly has turned its attention "to something worthy of the consideration of gentlemen who aspire to establish for themselves the reputation of statesmen."[90]

In a remarkably eloquent address, Thomas D'Arcy McGee celebrated the capacity of the Confederation question to elevate the tone of public life throughout British North America. "The provincial mind, it would seem, under the inspiration of a great question, leaped at a single bound out of the Slough of mere mercenary struggle for office, and took post on the high and honorable ground from which alone this great subject can be taken in all its dimensions." He congratulated the "various authors and writers" on Confederation because they seem "to be speaking or writing as if in the visible presence of all the colonies." No longer are such public men merely "hole-and-corner celebrities." They now write and speak as though "their words will be scanned and weighed afar off as well as at home." He was pleased to observe that "many men now speak with a dignity and carefulness which formerly did not characterize them, when they were watched only by their own narrow and struggling section, and weighed only according to a stunted local standard." He hoped that the proposed Confederation would "supply to all our public men just ground for uniting in nobler and more profitable contests than those which have signalized the past."[91] Thomas D'Arcy McGee's high-minded sentiments challenge serious statesmen on both sides of today's Quebec separation issue to maintain a level of public argument worthy of their subject. The subject itself merits the best efforts of ambitious men and women, for on one side there is the creative exhilaration of founding a new nation and on the other the patriotic duty of saving an old one.

CONCLUSION

To conclude this article, I shall revisit John Ross's extraordinary advice to his fellow legislative councilors that they read the Virginia debates on the ratification of the Constitution of the United States. He mentioned specifically James Madison, John Marshall, Edmund Randolph, Patrick Henry, and Richard Henry Lee. Anyone who followed Ross's advice might have been surprised to discover that two of these five men, Henry and Lee, opposed ratification of the Constitution and a third, Edmund Randolph, somewhat characteristically, straddled the issue by refusing to sign it as a delegate to the Constitutional Convention in Philadelphia and then reluctantly supporting it during the crucial debates in Richmond. Henry, Lee, and, to a lesser extent, Randolph were "Anti-Federalists"; that is, they formed part of the broad, articulate, and very able opposition to the proposed constitution. Like most backers of losing causes, the Anti-Federalists were not treated kindly by history.[92] This began to change, however, as Americans prepared to celebrate the bicentennial of their constitution in 1987. Thanks to the prodigious scholarly efforts of Herbert J. Storing, the writings and speeches of the Anti-Federalists were compiled in a seven-volume work entitled *The Complete Anti-Federalist*.[93] Storing made a powerful argument that the Anti-Federalists should be included among the founding fathers of the Republic even though they opposed the Constitution that still governs that Republic. His reason was that they contributed substantially to "the dialogue of the American founding." That is, the Constitution of the United States was a product of a great public argument, as befits the origins of a free society, and the Anti-Federalists formed an essential, though ultimately unsuccessful, part of that founding argument. Today American constitutional scholars take the Anti-Federalists far more seriously than they did just two decades ago, crediting them with initiating the movement for the Bill of Rights and for pointing out serious flaws in the Constitution that are still with us today. Contemporary Americans familiar with the Anti-Federalist literature bring a much richer understanding to their country's constitutional problems than those unfamiliar with it.

I am not prepared to repeat Ross's advice today; but, in the spirit of his comments, I shall take the liberty of urging contemporary Canadians to familiarize themselves not with the Virginia statesmen of 1788, but with their own Canadian statesmen of 1865, including those who opposed Confederation — the Canadian version of the American Anti-Federalists. Etienne Taché urged those "honorable members" of the Legislative Council "who objected to any particular measure" to make their objections part of the record "and so secure the advantage of placing their views before the country."[94] The "honorable members" were not bashful about airing their dissenting views nor were the members of the Legislative Assembly. Perceptive contemporary statesmen may find in these anticonfederationist arguments considerable insight into the flaws of Canadian federalism. The same holds for the arguments of many of those Quebeckers who supported Confederation but did so with a far more guarded interpretation of the extent of federal power over the provinces than a literal reading of the Confederation text would suggest. Here they will find Canadian public argument at its best.[95]

Robert Vipond surely had it right when he said that the Confederation debates of 1865 lack the depth of the American debates of 1787–88. Events did not force the Canadians of 1865 to examine "first political principles" as they did for the Americans who had recently emerged from a revolution that had made a definitive "self-conscious break with the past."[96] Consequently, when compared with their American counterparts, the Canadian debates may seem forbidding, burdened as they are with admittedly tedious discussions on how to finance railroads, canals, and other public works. But in this very tedium, with its meticulous attention to exquisite administrative detail, contemporary Canadians may learn something about themselves and what their history tells them of how they go about solving their problems, even problems of the highest questions of state such as those that Quebec asks today.

NOTES

The research for this article was made possible through generous support from the Canadian Studies Research Grant Program of the Canadian Embassy in Washington. I am particularly grateful to Ms. Judy Meyer, Chief Librarian at the Embassy, and her competent staff for their gracious help and encouragement.

1. John A. Rohr, *To Run a Constitution: The Legitimacy of the Administrative State* (Lawrence, KS: University Press of Kansas, 1986); John A. Rohr, *Founding Republics in France and America: A Study in Constitutional Governance* (Lawrence, KS: University Press of Kansas, 1995).
2. Hannah Arendt, *On Revolution* (New York: Viking Press, 1963), 214.
3. Unfortunately, the records of the Quebec Conference of October 1864 are fragmentary at best. See A.G. Doughty, "Notes on the Quebec Conference, 1864," *Canadian Historical Review* (March 1926): 26–47. For informative accounts of what is known about this conference, see Donald Creighton, *The Road to Confederation: The Emergence of Canada, 1863–1867* (Toronto: Macmillan, 1964), chapters 5–6; W.L. Morton, *The Critical Years: The Union of British North America, 1857–1873* (Toronto: McClelland and Stewart, 1964), 155–162; Robert Rumilly, *Histoire de la Province de Quebec*, 2 vols. (Montreal: Editions Bernard Valiquette, 1940), 22–26; P.B. Waite, *The Life & Times of Confederation 1864–1867* (Toronto: University of Toronto Press, 1962), chapter 7.
4. *Parliamentary Debates on the Subject of the Confederation of the British North American Provinces*, 3d Session, 8th Provincial Parliament of Canada (Quebec: Hunter, Rose & Co., 1865). Hereafter *Debates*. In referencing the *Debates*, I will give the page or pages and, where appropriate, I will also insert parenthetically the numbers 1 or 2 and the letters a, b, and c to indicate the column from which the citation was taken and its position within the column. Thus (2c) means the text cited can be found in the lowest third of the second column; (1a) means the top third of the first column; (1b) the middle third of the first column, etc.
5. The wording of the referendum text was ". . . new economic and political partnership within the scope of the Bill respecting the future of Quebec and of the agreement signed on June 12, 1995?"
6. Peter H. Russell, Rainer Knopff, and Ted Morton, *Federalism and the Charter: Leading Constitutional Decisions* (Ottawa: Carleton University Press, 1993), 38. The statement remains true today despite the recent decision of the Supreme Court of the United States in *U.S. v. Lopez* 115 S. Ct. 1624 (1995).
7. Richard Risk, "The Scholars and the Constitution: P.O.G.G. and the Privy Council," *Manitoba Law Journal* 23 (1996): 509.
8. The story is told with admirable clarity in Robert P. Vipond, *Liberty and Community: Canadian Federalism and the Failure of the Constitution* (Albany: SUNY Press, 1991), chapter 2.
9. Risk, 500–501, citing *Board of Commerce Reference* [1922] 1 A.C. 191 at 197–8 and *Fort Frances Pulp and Power v. Manitoba Free Press* [1923] A.C. 696 at 703 and 704.
10. The differences between the two texts can be traced to a conference in London where certain changes were introduced into the text approved in the colonies to meet objections from the mother country. See Donald Creighton, *The Road to Confederation*, chapter 14.
11. *Debates*, 33(2b.) For further development of this theme by John A. Macdonald, see pages 40(1c)–42(2c).
12. Ibid., 807(2b).
13. Ibid., 818(1c).
14. Ibid., 823(1b).
15. Ibid., 911(2a).
16. For examples of statements supporting legislative union, see ibid., 75(2); 425(1a); 465(1a); 749(2c); 806(2c); 818(2c); 918(1a); 976(2).
17. Ibid., 9(2c).
18. Ibid., 55(1b).
19. Ibid., 373(1a).
20. Ibid., 702(2b).
21. Resolution 29.
22. For a discussion of the Confederationists' studied efforts to avoid clarifying jurisdictional questions, see Vipond, chapter 2.

23. *Debates*, 859(2a).
24. Ibid., 623(2b).
25. Ibid., 689(2c). For similar statements, see 690 and 176(1c–2b).
26. Peter H. Russell, *Constitutional Odyssey: Can Canadians Become a Sovereign People?* 2nd ed. (Toronto: Univ. of Toronto Press, 1993), 1.
27. Ibid., 2.
28. *Debates*, 797(2b).
29. Ibid., 864(1a).
30. Ibid, 985 (1b).
31. See, for example, 12(2c); 120(1b); 277(2b); 733(2a); 883(1b); 894(2c); 934(1b).
32. See Creighton, 246–252.
33. *Debates*, 77(2c.) For similar statements, see 471(2)–472(1); 579(2c); and 1004.
34. *Debates*, 330(1b).
35. Ibid., 269(1b).
36. Ibid., 292(2c).
37. Ibid., 295(1c–2a). Currie's proposal was received favorably by some supporters of the Quebec Resolutions. See the remarks of Alexander Vidal and Walter Dickson, *Debates*, 284–290 and 301–309.
38. Ibid., 11(2c). For another statement anticipating a later appeal to the people, see *Debates*, 840(2b).
39. Ibid., 962(2c).
40. Ibid., 1019(2b).
41. Ibid., 327(2b,) 769–770, 990(1b,) 110–115 *passim*, 432(1c), 765(2a), 809(1 c), 888(1), 891(2c), 995(2b).
42. "PM Eyes Way to Improve Federation," *Toronto Star* (22 November 1995), reprinted in NEWSCAN of 24 November 1995.
43. See especially Premier Bouchard's remarks of 6 December 1995 at Laval in what *L'Actualité* called "*un veritable discours du trône.*" Michel Vestel, "Bouchard l'énigme," *L'Actualité* 21 (février 1996): 17–25 at 20. See also "A l'écoute du Quebec," *L'Actualité* 21 (1er mars 1996): 13; Jean Pare, "Le Grand theatre de Quebec," *L'Actualité* 21 (1er mai 1996): 8; Jean Chartier, "Plan O: l'opération secrète de Parizeau," *L'Actualité* 21 (1er juin 1996): 11–12; Michel Vastel, "Le Bilan de Fernand Dumont," *L'Actualité* 21 (15 septembre 1996): 86–96; "Lucien Bouchard and the Weekend Psychodrama," *The Globe and Mail* (28 November 1996), reprinted in NEWSCAN of 29 November 1996.)
44. David V.J. Bell, "The Loyalist Tradition in Canada," *Journal of Canadian Studies* 5 (1970): 22–33.
45. For the general statements, see Debates, 30(1c) and 131(2c); on public works, see 366(1a) and 920(1b); on education, see 95(1) and 411 (1b–2b). The discussion of canals was pervasive throughout the debates. To sample some of the main arguments, see 79(1c), 639(1b–2c), 680(2c).
46. Ibid., 69(2), 93(2h), 377(1c)–379, 158(2c)–159, 178(1a), 258(2c)–259, 280(2b), 758(1b), 861(2a), 945(2b)–947(2b).
47. Ibid., 229(2c).
48. Ibid., 979(2a).
49. Ibid., 832(2c).
50. Ibid., 920(2b).
51. Ibid., 17(2h).
52. Ibid., 18(1c).
53. Creighton, 250.
54. Ibid., 250–251.
55. *Debates*, 336(1c) and 430(2c)–431(1a).
56. Ibid., 109(1c), 201(2a), 377–379, 386(2b), 415(2c)–416, 467–469, 512(1b–c), 553, 677(2), 681(2), 693(2)–694(1), 702(1h), 703(1a), 751–757, 762(1c), 791, 812–814, 901(1a).
57. Debates, 77(1 a).
58. Ibid., 790(1h).
59. French Canadians have tended to look upon Durham as an unmitigated racist with nothing but contempt for the French way of life in British North America. For a convincing statement of a more generous interpretation, see Janet Ajzenstat, *The Political Thought of Lord Durham* (Montreal/Kingston: McGill-Queen's University Press, 1988). For examples of French Canadian resentment of Lord Durham, see 789, 844(1h), 850(2b)–852(2b); for a defense of Lord Durham, see 908(1c)–910(1a).
60. *Debates*, 52(1b).
61. Ibid., 251(2a).

62. Ibid., 356(2a).
63. Ibid., 901(2c).
64. For other statements linking railroads to confederation, see 896(1a), 227(1a), 132(2a), 297(1b).
65. Ibid., 205(1b) and 228(2c).
66. Ibid., 304(1b).
67. Ibid., 190(1a) and 636(1a).
68. Ibid., 152(1b). The "inclined plane" metaphor was originally introduced by Etienne Taché at the very beginning of the debate in the Legislative Council and became a standard rhetorical weapon of the confederationists throughout the debates. See *Debates*, 6(1c), 343(1a), 82(2b), 152(2b), 155(2a), 206(2a), 325(1c), 326(1c), 332, 342(2c), 741(2c), 746(2b), 826(1a). The metaphor was rejected as inappropriate at 46(1b) and 60(1c). For examples of antirepublican statements in addition to those provided in the text, see 129(2b), 143(1b), 189(2c), 209(2b), 241(2c)–242(1a), 288(1a).
69. Ibid., 122(2b) and 219(2c).
70. Ibid., 32(2c). Macdonald's assessment of the constitution was echoed by Thomas D'Arcy McGee; see *Debates*, 145(1b).
71. Ibid., 446(2a–b).
72. Ibid., 212(1c).
73. Ibid., 238(2c).
74. Ibid., 228(2c)–229(1a). Dorion does not have the American system for amending the constitution quite right, but his description is close enough to support the point he was making when he introduced it into the debates.
75. Ibid., 41(1).
76. Ibid., 123(1c). Sanborn correctly refers to "the celebrated Dartmouth College decision in which Webster so distinguished himself." He mistakenly states that the case turned on a clause in the Constitution of the United States "provides that no law could be passed which would affect the rights of property." The case actually involved the clause in the tenth section of the first article, which prohibits the states from passing laws "impairing the Obligation of Contracts."
77. Ibid., 565(2b) and 804(2b).
78. Ibid., 57(2c).
79. Ibid., 74(1b).
80. For the origins of the inclined Plane metaphor, see the remarks of Etienne Taché at 152 (1h). For examples of the use of the "now or never" argument at the time of the founding of the American Republic, see Rohr, *Founding Republics*, 184–189.
81. *Debates*, 30(1c) and 131(2c); for the American position on this point, see Rohr, *To Run a Constitution*, 1–3.
82. *Debates*, 363(1c); Federalist 1.
83. *Debates*, 621(2a); John A. Rohr, "Constitutional Foundations of the United States Navy: Text and Context," *Naval War College Review* 45 (1992): 68–83.
84. *Debates*, 704(16), 705(1b), 857(1b); Forrest MacDonald, *Novus Ordo Seclorum: The Intellectual Origins of the Constitution* (Lawrence, KS: University Press of Kansas, 1985), 279–284.
85. *Debates*, 648(1a); on Benjamin Franklin's call for prayer at the convention, see Max Farrand, ed., *The Records of the Federal Convention of 1787*, 4 vols. (New Haven: Yale University Press, 1966), 1, 450–452.
86. *Debates*, 34(2a).
87. Ibid., 790(2a), where Lord Durham's *Report* was quoted.
88. Ibid., 672(1a).
89. Ibid., 381(lc).
90. Ibid., 913(1a).
91. Ibid., 128.
92. Lee and Henry are, of course, revered for their outstanding contribution to the Revolution, but few Americans are aware of their opposition to the Constitution.
93. Herbert J. Storing, ed., *The Complete Anti-Federalist*, 7 vols. (Chicago: University of Chicago Press, 1981). See also Jackson Turner Main, *The Anti-Federalists: Critics of the Constitution 1781–1788* (New York: Norton, 1961).
94. *Debates*, 83(1c–2a).
95. If there is any merit in my suggestion, the first practical step toward implementing it might well be to bring the Confederation debates back into print. At present, it is very difficult to purchase a copy of the complete text either in English or in French.
96. Vipond, 20.

Article Two

The Nationalism of the National Policy

Craig Brown

Debating nationalism is the great Canadian national pastime. Since Confederation it has been the preeminent preoccupation of politicians, journalists, scholars, and plain ordinary citizens. All have wrestled diligently with the problem that Canadian nationalism — if such there be — does not fit any of the classic definitions of nationalism. Common language, religion, and ethnic origin must obviously be rejected. Except for the disciples of Harold Adams Innis, geography provided few satisfactory clues to the Canadian identity. And a common historical tradition, in the words of Mill, "the possession of a national history and consequent community of recollections, collective pride and humiliation, pleasure and regret, connected with the same incidents in the past," raises more questions about a Canadian "nationality" than it answers. There is no great national hero who cut down a maple tree, threw a silver dollar across the St. Lawrence, and then proceeded to lead a revolution and govern the victorious nation wisely and judiciously. There are no great Canadian charters of freedom or independence expressing the collective will of the people. But the search goes on. Historians and retired Governors General laboriously attempt to define "the Canadian identity" or "being Canadian." Many nations have manifested their nationalism through great public acts; Canada has asserted its nationalism by looking for it.

Yet there is abundant evidence that Canadians have both thought and acted like contemporary nationalists in other countries. Much, though by no means all, of the evidence is provided by the politicians.[1] The evidence is mundane, for seldom have Canadian politicians been political theorists or philosophers. Rather, their concerns have been with everyday problems of government. But within this framework their thoughts and acts have been decidedly nationalist in character. A brief look at the men who implemented and carried out the National Policy may serve to illustrate the point.

Writing to a Conservative editor in 1872, Sir John A. Macdonald noted in a postscript that "the paper must go in for a National policy in Tariff matters, and while avoiding the word 'protection' must advocate a readjustment of the tariff in such a manner as incidentally to aid our manufacturing and industrial interest."[2] In this obvious afterthought at the conclusion of a letter devoted to the necessity for finding an appropriate label for Macdonald's party is the origin of the National Policy. The context is significant. Macdonald was looking for a policy that would attract, at one and the same time, voters and dollars to his party, and the National Policy would do both. The manufacturers would contribute to the party war chest and the simplicity of the title and concept of the National Policy would appeal to an electorate looking to fulfill the promise of Confederation. Moreover, as a transcontinental railway, immigration, and opening of the Northwest were added to the tariff as items in the National Policy, it took on a strikingly familiar complexion that added to its political attractiveness. It was in most respects a duplication of a similar "national policy" designed for continental expansion in the United States. It was "a materialistic policy of Bigness"[3] in an age when expansionism appealed to nationalist sentiment. Canadians could take pride in their ability to compete with their neighbours in the conquest of the continent.

Source: *Nationalism in Canada*, ed. Peter Russell (Toronto: McGraw-Hill Ryerson, 1966), pp. 155–163. Reprinted by permission of the University League for Social Reform.

The National Policy was equally attractive because a policy of tariff protection meant another step in the long path from colony to nation within the Empire. As early as 1859, Galt argued for protection less on its economic merits than on the grounds that tariff autonomy was implicit in responsible government. Referring to Imperial objections to the Cayley-Galt tariff of that year, the crux of Galt's argument was that "self-government would be utterly annihilated if the views of the Imperial Government were to be preferred to those of the people of Canada."[4] With tariff autonomy not only achieved but emphasized by protection, in 1911 the ardent nationalist John S. Ewart proudly summed up the elements of "Canadian Independence" by pointing first to the fact that "we are fiscally independent." "By that I mean that we make our own tariffs; that we frame them as we wish; that we tax British and other goods as we please; and that neither the Colonial Office nor the British Parliament has any right whatever to interfere."[5]

That the National Policy was politically attractive, is, then, evident. By 1886 the Liberal party had been driven so far into a "me too" position that Blake in essence declared his party's policy to be, to borrow a phrase, the National Policy if necessary, but not necessarily the National Policy. It is true that in 1891, with a new leader and the new policy of Unrestricted Reciprocity with the United States, the Liberals came closer to victory than they had at any time since 1874. But within two years the Liberals had again revised their policy to "freer trade," and in 1897 the Liberal government admitted the futility of attempting to destroy Macdonald's brainchild. "I not only would not retire from the Government because they refused to eliminate the principle of protection from the tariff, but I would not remain in the Government if they did eliminate the principle of protection entirely from the tariff," wrote Clifford Sifton. He added that "the introduction of a tariff from which the principle of protection would be entirely eliminated would be fraught with results that would be most disastrous to the whole Canadian people."[6] In 1911, Sifton and 17 other "revolting" Liberals issued their manifesto against reciprocity, "believing as we do that Canadian nationality is now threatened with a more serious blow than any it has heretofore met with."[7] Robert Borden simply added that "we must decide whether the spirit of Canadianism or of Continentalism shall prevail on the northern half of this continent."[8]

In short, the idea of protection embodied in the tariff became equated with the Canadian nation itself. The National Policy, by stressing that Canadians should no longer be "hewers of wood and drawers of water" for the United States, as Tilley put it, recalled and reinforced that basic impulse of survival as a separate entity on this continent that had been born of the American Revolution, made explicit in Confederation, and remained the primary objective of Canadian nationalists. Protection and the National Policy, then, took on a much larger meaning than mere tinkering with customs schedules.

The same idea was evident in the building of the Canadian Pacific Railway and the opening of the Northwest. The Northwest was the key to the future of both the National Policy and the nation, and an expensive and partially unproductive railway through Canadian territory was the price Canada had to pay to "protect" it from American penetration and absorption. It was to be the great market for Canadian industry and the foundation of a "Canadian economy." Emphasizing that building the railway was "a great national question," Sir Charles Tupper remarked that "under the National Policy that Canada has adopted we must look forward not only to building up thriving centres of industry and enterprises all over this portion of the country, but to obtaining a market for these industries after they have been established; and I say where is there a greater market than that magnificent granary of the North-west?"[9] He added that upon the success of the venture "the rapid progress and prosperity of our common country depends."

The United States played an interesting role in the National Policy that emphasized its nationalistic assumptions. Fundamental to the thinking of the framers of the policy was the idea that the United States was much less a friendly neighbour than an aggressive competitor power waiting for a suitable opportunity to fulfill its destiny of the complete conquest of North America. The National Policy was intended to be the first line of defence against American ambitions. And this, I think, is the reason any Canadian alternative to it was unsuccessful. It was the "national" implications of the National Policy that hindered the Liberals in their attempt to formulate an opposition policy before 1896. They could not accept Commercial Union because it meant the total surrender of tariff autonomy. Unrestricted Reciprocity was adopted as a compromise that retained autonomy. But its distinction from Commercial Union was too subtle for much of the electorate to grasp and left the party open to skillful exploitation by Macdonald's "loyalty" cry. More important, the very indefiniteness of what the Liberals meant by Unrestricted Reciprocity caused confusion and disruption in party ranks and eventually led to the revelation that Unrestricted Reciprocity did not mean the complete free interchange of all Canadian and American products after all. Rather, most Liberals simply wanted a more extensive reciprocity agreement with the United States than the Conservatives. Or, to put it another way, the Liberals were interested in somewhat less protection from American competition than their opponents. W.S. Fielding's budget speech in 1897 had a very familiar ring to Canadian ears: "If our American friends wish to make a treaty with us, we are willing to meet them and treat on fair and equitable terms. If it shall not please them to do that, we shall in one way regret the fact but shall nevertheless go on our way rejoicing, and find other markets to build up the prosperity of Canada independent of the American people."[10]

Other problems in Canadian–American relations in the latter part of the nineteenth century were related to the nationalism of the National Policy. With the abrogation of the fishery articles of the Treaty of Washington by the United States, Canada was forced to adopt what can properly be called a "protectionist" policy for her inshore fisheries. The fisheries and the commercial privileges extended to Americans by the treaty were considered a national asset by Canadians. The object of their government was to use that asset for the benefit of the whole of Canada, not simply the Maritime provinces. It was for this reason that from 1871 on the fishery question was always related to reciprocity. On each occasion when Canada participated in negotiations the policy was always the same: Canada's exclusive and undoubted rights in the inshore fisheries would be bargained for the free exchange of natural products.

A different and more complex problem was presented by the Bering Sea dispute arising out of the seizure of Canadian pelagic sealers by United States revenue cruisers. The central problem was one of international law involving the doctrines of freedom of the seas and *mare clausum*. And because the Canadian vessels were of British registry, the British government assumed a much more active negotiating role than was the case in some other disputes. But Canadian participation was far from negligible, and Sir Charles Hibbert Tupper and Sir Louis Davies made a point of protecting Canadian interests. Significantly, they argued that despite the legal technicalities, it was a Canadian industry that was threatened with destruction by the illegal acts of the United States government and that the Mother Country had a clear duty to protect that industry.

The Alaska Boundary question also illustrated the relationship between the National Policy and Canada's relations with the United States. All of the evidence available suggests that the Canadian case was hopelessly weak and members of the Canadian government (Laurier and Sifton) as much as admitted it both privately and in public. Why, then, was the case pressed with such vigour? Part of the answer, it seems to me, is that when the Alaska Boundary question became important for Canadians after the Yukon gold rush began, those responsible for Canadian policy, led by Clifford Sifton, regarded the question less as one of boundary definition than of commercial competition with the United States. Definition of the boundary was important because it was related to control of the growing Yukon trade.

The intricate legal details of the boundary dispute were generally ignored by the Canadian government. Writing during the meetings of the joint High Commission in 1898, Lord Herschell complained to Lord Salisbury that "I found that the question had not been thoroughly studied or thought out by any Canadian official."[11] The urgent and ill-considered introduction of the Yukon Railway Bill of 1898 providing for a "Canadian" route to Yukon — a route which was dependent upon trans-shipment privileges at the American customs port at Fort Wrangel and on navigation rights on the American portion of the Stikine River — illustrates the same point. The "imperative reason for immediate action" was that the Yukon trade was at stake, as the Minister of Railways and Canals explained to the House of Commons: "The importance of securing that trade and preserving it to Canada becomes a national question of the greatest interest. . . . It is ours, it is within our own borders and of right belongs to us, if, by any legitimate or proper means, we can secure it for the people of our own country."[12]

Again, in the negotiations at the joint High Commission of 1898–99 the Canadians insisted that if the boundary question went to arbitration, Pyramid Harbour should be reserved for Canada to match American insistence that Dyea and Skagway be reserved for the United States. While both sides thus rejected an unqualified and impartial arbitration, it must be admitted that Dyea and Skagway were established and settled communities under American control; Canada could make no such claim regarding Pyramid Harbour. Pyramid Harbour, as a Canadian outlet to the sea with a corresponding Canadian land corridor to the interior, had not arisen in negotiations until the meetings of the joint High Commission and, as before, the Canadian claim was based primarily on the desire to secure control of the Yukon trade.

Ultimately, of course, Canadian indignation knew no bounds when Lord Alverstone reportedly suddenly changed his mind and awarded Pearse and Wales Islands to the United States in 1903. The settlement of 1903 was unquestionably diplomatic rather than "judicial." Theodore Roosevelt's pressure tactics before and during the meeting of the so-called "judicial tribunal" were certainly deplorable, and these factors, combined with the apparent sacrifice of Canadian interests by Great Britain, have supplied grist for the mills of Canadian nationalists ever since. But too often the emphasis in Canadian historiography on this point has been misplaced by concentrating solely on the alleged British sellout. The more interesting point in all the clamour surrounding the Alaska Boundary decision is that, once again, National Policy interests were considered to be threatened by the decision. Alverstone's agreement with Lodge and Root, that Pearse and Wales Islands belonged to the United States, threatened the Laurier government's first venture in transcontinental railway building. The projected terminus of the Grand Trunk Pacific, chartered just a few short months before, was Port Simpson on Observatory Inlet; Pearse and Wales Islands, which the Canadians believed could be armed by the United States, commanded the shipping lanes into Port Simpson. Thus, though the Yukon trade had drastically declined in value by 1903, from first serious consideration of the problem to final settlement, the National Policy — an "all Canadian" trade route to Yukon or a secure terminus for a new Pacific railway — dominated Canadian consideration of the Alaska Boundary dispute.

I have tried to suggest that the National Policy was a manifestation of Canadian national sentiment. Its basic assumptions — protection against the United States, the need for a "Canadian economy" with a strong industrial base and secure markets, and the implicit assumption of achieving greater autonomy within the Empire — all crystallized that ill-defined, but deeply felt, sense of difference that set Canadians apart from both their neighbours to the south and the mother country. But why did this desire to proclaim a national identity take its form in economic terms?

Perhaps a part of the answer rests in the dilemma posed at the beginning of this paper. Appeals to a common language, a common cultural tradition, or a common religion were simply impossible for Canadians, and when they were attempted they were rightly regarded by French Canadians as a violation of their understanding of Confederation. Most Canadians, especially those who built or paid for the building of the transcontinental railways, argued that the Canadian nation would have to be built in spite of its geography and regarded their efforts as "the price of being Canadian." Appeals to national history could also be a divisive rather than a unifying factor for, as often as not, the two ethnic groups disagreed as to what, in their historical tradition, was a matter of pride or of humiliation. What was necessary, then, as Cartier put it in the Confederation debates, was to "form a political nationality." And it is not at all surprising that the political nationalism of the early decades of Confederation was expressed in terms of railways and tariffs.

It is commonplace to equate the politics of North America in the latter part of the nineteenth century with self-seeking capitalism. But we might remind ourselves that the age of Darwinism and of industrialism was also a great age of nationalism. The nationalism of the large assertive states of the age — the United States, Germany, and Great Britain — was assuredly economic in its emphasis. In the United States, in particular, nationalism was equated with the problems of industrialism and industrial expansion. In keeping with Darwinian assumptions, bigness was a virtue for a nation state, and industrialism was the key to bigness. At the very time their own nation was being born, Canadians reasoned that industrialism was the determining factor in the victory of the North in the Civil War and in the apparent reunification of the United States. Industrialism meant power; power to withstand the pressures from the south and power to expand and consolidate the Canadian nation. And a political program that emphasized expansion and industrialism had the added advantage of ignoring the potentially divisive issues that would disrupt a "political nationality."

In sum, then, the National Policy, a policy for a "Canadian economy" and a "Big Canada," a materialistic policy for a materialistic age, was the obvious policy to give expression to Canadian national sentiment. That policy was adopted in 1878 and accepted by the Liberal party in 1896. Three years later J.I. Tarte urged Laurier to do more than simply accept the National Policy, to expand upon it with more railways, canals, and harbour improvements (and presumably with higher tariffs). "Voilà," he observed, "le programme le plus national et le plus populaire que nous puissons offrir au pays."[13]

NOTES

1. Carl Berger, "The True North Strong and Free," in *Nationalism in Canada* (Toronto, 1966), 3ff.
2. *Macdonald Papers* (P.A.C.), Macdonald to T.C. Patteson, February 27, 1872.
3. John Dales, "Protection, Immigration and Canadian Nationalism," in *Nationalism in Canada*, 167–170.
4. A.B. Keith, *Selected Speeches and Documents on British Colonial Policy, 1763–1917* (London, 1953), 60.
5. J.S. Ewart, *The Kingdom Papers*, vol. 1 (Ottawa, 1912), 3.
6. *Sifton Papers* (P.A.C.), Sifton to James Fleming, March 13, 1897.
7. *Manifesto of Eighteen Toronto Liberals on Reciprocity*, February 20, 1911; cited, *Canadian Annual Review* (Toronto, 1911), 49.
8. Henry Borden, ed., *Robert Laird Borden: His Memoirs*, vol. 1 (Toronto, 1938), 327.
9. *House of Commons Debates*, April 15, 1880, pp. 1424–25.
10. *House of Commons Debates*, April 22, 1897.
11. Cited in R.C. Brown, *Canada's National Policy, 1883–1900* (Princeton, 1964), 379.
12. *House of Commons Debates*, February 8, 1898, pp. 191–92.
13. *Laurier Papers* (P.A.C.), Tarte to Laurier, April 3, 1899.

Article Three

The Philosophy of Railways: Conclusions and Conjectures

A.A. den Otter

We have lost population; we have lost shipping; there has been a great depreciation in the value of our real estate; we have lost representation in parliament; we have not at all kept pace with . . . [central Canada] in manufacturing.

Saint John *Telegraph*[1]

I say the interests of this country demand that the Canadian Pacific Railway should be made a success . . . But somebody may ask what about the interests of Manitoba? Are the interests of Manitoba and the North-West to be sacrificed to the policy of Canada? I say, if it is necessary — yes.

Charles Tupper[2]

On 7 November 1885 at Craigellachie, British Columbia, Donald A. Smith, one of the Canadian Pacific Railway directors, hammered in the transcontinental's last spike. The scene symbolized the realization of the national dream, that is, the creation and consolidation of a northern transcontinental nation.[3] That vision, dominated by a desire for economic progress, always stressed the notion that the transcontinental railway was needed to build the nation of Canada. As the Toronto *Mail* noted succinctly: 'We desired to preserve our autonomy and national integrity; we desired, following the example of our bustling cousins to the south of us, to give impetus to the colonization of our vast and fertile Western territory by making the progress of the railway and settlement contemporaneous; we desired to connect the two oceans by the shortest line of railway which was possible; we desired to make the Dominion the great arterial highway between the Asiatic and the European continents; we desired to cultivate, encourage and make strong a true national sentiment in the northern half of the American continent.'[4]

The *Mail*'s cogent expression of the nationalistic purpose of the CPR — the desire to colonize the western plains, to establish Canada's independence from the United States, and to create a national identity — masked the actual, complex, and sometimes negative results of the philosophy of railways. To be sure, the CPR assisted in establishing effective communications between central and western Canada, thus expediting western settlement; it facilitated the transcontinental movement of goods and people, thus strengthening the economic bonds between the young nation's separate regions; and it located Canada strategically between Europe and Asia, thus enhancing its position in the British Empire. But did it preserve Canadian autonomy and 'national integrity'? Did it cultivate 'a true national sentiment'? Could Canada build a firm national identity on a transportation technology, artificially induced and then supported by an isolationist economic policy?

Source: A.A. den Otter, "The Philosophy of Railways: Conclusions and Conjectures" from *The Philosophy of Railways: The Transcontinental Railway Idea in British North America*, A.A. Den Otter, University of Toronto Press Inc., 1997. © University of Toronto Press Incorporated 1997. Reprinted with permission of the publisher.

As Harold A. Innis's studies of the fur trade, the CPR, and the character of communications have documented so thoroughly, transportation technologies were powerful factors in the national and cultural divisions of the American continent.[5] By its inherent integrative nature, Innis claimed, railway technology encouraged the rise of nationalism in Canada, inspired and facilitated its territorial expansion, and spurred its centralization and bureaucratic growth. The railway aided the development of metropolitan centres and their monopolies.[6] In sum, Innis believed that communications media were not marginal but strong influences on the institutions and the social characteristics of society.

Expanding on Innis's theme, J.M.S. Careless, in *Frontier and Metropolis*, has suggested that the interrelationship of the city and its hinterland profoundly affected national as well as regional identities.[7] According to Careless, metropolitan centres employed trade, transport, and finance to control their surrounding territories. These factors worked, to various degrees and through infinite combinations, in concert with political, social, and attitudinal elements to establish the city as the leading catalyst in the formation of nations and regions. Although a region may define its identity in terms of its own unique structures and attitudes, it is, according to Careless, part of a larger environment. The 'continued interactions across actual or envisioned space are copiously displayed in the exchanges between town and country, between city and region, between metropolis and hinterland,' Careless wrote. 'Their interplay builds historical experience which pervasively influences all sorts of communal identities, above all those of region and nation.'[8] Careless thus interpreted Canada's history in the context of the relationship between urban centres and their surrounding hinterlands. Each city controlled its hinterland economically, politically, and financially, but also culturally, because it sent settlers, labourers, businessmen, and professionals to the frontier where they shared their religious beliefs, their political ideas, and their ethical values. Set in a new place and time, these ambassadors helped create a unique regional identity.

Careless's 'metropolitan' thesis is useful because it draws attention to the role of transportation in the conveyance of concepts and goods between cities and hinterlands. Careless noted that 'major transport services, which tapped or filled hinterlands and fed urban places, were all but primary in Canadian metropolitan growth that had virtually to start from scratch. Moreover, transportation readily related to the needs of communication, to moving information and opinion as well as goods and people over wide distances.'[9] Transportation networks, by facilitating the transfer of ideas, goods, and people, aided in determining the personalities of cities and their hinterlands.

The observation that transportation or communication techniques bias what they transmit and therefore influence the identities of past and present cultures can be observed in western Canada during the last half of the nineteenth century. This period witnessed a revolutionary change in transportation modes from human- or animal-driven techniques to steam-powered river boats and railways.

The arrival of the steam locomotives to the Canadian prairies in 1878 was followed quickly by the completion of the CPR in 1885 and a decade and a half later by two competing transcontinental railways. By 1902, Toronto entrepreneurs Donald Mann and William Mackenzie had expanded several minor Manitoba railways to Port Arthur, providing a second access to the Great Lakes; by the end of the decade, their Canadian Northern operated a 4800-km network across the plains and was advancing westward through the Rockies and eastward across the Shield.[10] Meanwhile, the Canadian government encouraged the Grand Trunk Railway to expand into a third, 5600-km transcontinental system, a project completed just before the First World War.[11] By 1914 the North-West possessed a magnificent network of railways that established hundreds of communities across the prairies and opened them to the factories, newspapers, mail, and people of North America, Europe, and the Pacific rim. Within several decades, the technology of railways had cemented the western region to the central heartland.

The completion of the transcontinentals made the intensive agricultural settlement of the prairies and immediately adjacent boreal forests feasible.[12] While the sweeping vastness of the interior plain, with its harsh climate, short growing season, and intense cold, still tested the skills and endurance of the newcomers and shaped them into a stubborn, persisting people, it was steam technology — manifested in railways and in lake and ocean vessels — that permitted the export of a vast and bulky surplus crop to overseas markets and supplied farmers with their daily necessities — clothes, tools, fuel, food, and machinery. Railways and steamboats indirectly ameliorated severe geophysical conditions and encouraged thousands of grain growers from Ontario, the United States, Great Britain, and Continental Europe to establish farms on the prairies. Between 1881 and 1911, western Canada's population exploded from 62,260 to 461,394, occupied farms multiplied from 10,091 to 199,203, while national wheat exports soared from 2.3 million bushels in 1885 to 114.9 million in 1914.[13] The national dream, first articulated in the late 1840s, had come true.

The integration of prairie culture into that of eastern North America began several decades before the completion of the CPR and occurred so quickly that it caused serious hardship and alienation among local populations. Using a combination of American railways, river steamers, and carts, Chicago and St. Paul merchants penetrated a region previously preserved for the Hudson's Bay Company.[14] By the winter of 1857, free traders operated across the North-West, leaving only the far northern York and Mackenzie districts for the London-based company. The corporate charter was 'almost a nullity,' the firms' governor complained, 'set at nought by the Americans and their Half-breed allies.'[15] Meanwhile, the Hudson's Bay Company itself began to use Canadian and American railways to ship goods to and from Fort Garry.[16] Within a decade, the railway had ended the splendid isolation of the British American North-West and eroded the strong bond to the British empire that the company and Canadian traders had built.

Hudson's Bay Company officials were keenly aware of the implications of shipping goods through a foreign country under the supervision of foreign agents. They also wondered how the new transport route might affect the traditional cultural link between London and Rupert's Land and how the encroaching eastern North American railway empire would have an impact upon their fur preserve. 'As regards the trade with the United States,' F.G. Johnson, governor of Assiniboia, confessed, 'I feel a very strong and sad conviction that relations are being irrevocably formed between the two countries which in the peculiar conditions of both frontiers will not be conducive to British interests, and under the circumstance are detrimental both to the company's local commerce and the interests of the settlers.'[17]

Johnson's concern that changing transportation modes might erode Britain's cultural influence on the North-West reflected his awareness that the railway would revolutionize western Canada's society and economy. It would, of course, be erroneous to assume that in the pre-railway era life was static. Indeed, the fur trade had increasingly diverted native people from traditional occupations to the search for fur and provisions. It also employed mixed bloods as packers, suppliers, Red River cart drivers, York boatmen, and general labourers.[18] But the railway changed north-western life more quickly and completely than any previous alteration in transportation. In the pre-railway era, most native people migrated seasonally, subsisting on the natural products of the country. Tribal boundaries were flexible and land was held in common, with access open to all who possessed the skills to use its resources.[19] Meanwhile, the mixed-blood Metis lived in small settlements in Red River, subsisting on agriculture and seasonal work with the Hudson's Bay Company. The introduction of steam transportation unlocked the resources of the North-West to numerous American entrepreneurs, along with their capital and goods. The buffalo robe was but one commodity that assumed great value and for a time provided employment to the Metis, who settled in villages across the plains.[20] But, within decades, the bison was wiped out, leaving the prairie people destitute. By the late 1870s, the country could no longer support them; private property had replaced the commons. And, as steamers and railways displaced York boats and Red River carts, unemployment among the Metis soared. There was little left for them but poverty. The era of the 'private adventurers' was ended and most of the mixed-blood entrepreneurs, who had created wealth through their own ambition, initiative, energy, and knowledge of the plains, surrendered control over its resources to strangers armed with new skills and abundant capital.[21]

The 1885 Indian and Metis rebellion, which occurred only two years after the completion of the prairie section of the Canadian Pacific Railway, can therefore be viewed as a desperate attempt to protect the commons against the encroachment of a technological, urban society. To be sure, the virtual extinction of the bison and the resultant near starvation utterly demoralized the natives, so that a few hot-blooded young men could overrule traditional elders and lead the natives into violent rebellion.[22] That revolt coincided with the disenchantment of many Metis whose attempts to find security in traditional river-lot properties rather than township landholding patterns were dismissed by paternalistic, often arbitrary, government officials. Alone, the Metis may have endured their deteriorating economic conditions, but widespread complaints from disillusioned white settlers, the messianic leadership of Louis Riel, and the coincidental native uprising spurred them into precipitous action.

In 1885, however, conditions were very different from 1869/70. This time, the Canadian government could act speedily and, using the nearly completed CPR, it rushed troops to Saskatchewan. Within a few months, the rebellions were crushed. Little wonder that to both the native and mixed-blood rebels, the CPR represented not the consummation of Canada's grand transcontinental vision but the extension of eastern metropolitan empires to their traditional hunting and farming grounds. The insurgence expressed the deep alienation of the original prairie people.[23]

The 1885 Metis and Indian rebellion clearly illustrated that the new metropolitan-hinterland relationship, enabled by the railway, represented not an equal partnership but, in most cases, a disparate association marked by dominance and dependence. At best, that affiliation satisfied complementary needs: the metropolis, lacking the resources and markets that the frontier provided, supplied the capital, technology, and labour that the hinterland required.[24] Nevertheless, as Innis has suggested, the city, which embodied such large corporations as the Hudson's Bay Company, the Canadian Pacific Railway, and the Bank of Montreal, used the nation-state to control the region in order to protect the massive investment in transportation needed before it could exploit the resources of the frontier.[25] Western Canada had little voice in these boardroom and cabinet decisions and thus it felt estranged, perceiving an inequality that profoundly affected its identity.

The CPR, on its part, faced the problem of earning sufficient revenues to pay for the expensive, money-losing section north of Lake Superior and encountered stiff competition in central Canada from the St Lawrence seaway as well as Canadian and American railways. Logically, the company sought and obtained monopoly status in western Canada and permission to charge higher-than-average freight rates west of Thunder Bay. The latter were designed to offset losses on its eastern lines. Ontario and Québec rationalized the high rates, euphemistically called 'fair discrimination,' as necessary for national unity; western Canada, however, resented them deeply because it believed they retarded regional development.[26] Railway historian T.D. Regehr concurs and has suggested that excessive freight rates and the monopoly clause were significant factors in the slow settlement of western Canada in the last decades of the nineteenth century.[27]

The railway, in fact, affected the pace of economic development in myriad ways. The promised construction of the CPR, for example, sparked an interest in western Canada's extensive coal deposits; but it was the railway and not the prospectors who dictated the timing and location of their development. When the CPR's directors relocated the projected main line to the southern prairies, all northern exploration ceased and attention focused on Kicking Horse Pass and the southern prairies. The richer northern deposits had to await the arrival of the Canadian Northern and the Grand Trunk Pacific some two decades later. Similarly, the enormous deposits in Crowsnest Pass were not utilized until the CPR was induced to complete the first segment of this southern bypass. More significantly, as the industry's chief consumer, the railway's fuel demands determined each colliery's production cycle, resulting in highly volatile, unpredictable operations with attendant labour unrest. To break out of their cyclonic economy, western mine operators repeatedly asked the railways to lower their rates on eastward coal shipments and asked the central government to either subsidize coal movements to industrial Ontario and Québec or increase the tariff on steam coal from the United States. Both the railways and the federal government refused to grant any combination of these options and thus the western Canadian coal-mining industry never escaped the railway market.[28] To westerners, the failure to achieve a transportation subsidy or protective tariffs for its coal mines illustrated once again that railway rates and customs duties were biased favourably towards the industrialized East and adversely against the agrarian West.

Westerners clearly understood the direct relationship between the railway's prejudicial freight rates and the National Policy. Primarily intended to encourage the industrial development of the young nation, the policy was also designed to provide business for the projected transcontinental railway and shield it from the competition of the northern railways of the United States. On the one hand, the legislation restricted American and British access to the resources and markets of the North-West; on the other, it encouraged all eastern businessmen to use the CPR rather than American railways to reach western markets. The National Policy, therefore, protected the CPR and permitted the railway to create a stronger link between central and western Canada than would have been the case had trade been entirely free.

The National Policy gave a decided advantage to central Canadian businessmen. It contained measures that encouraged American factories and wholesalers to sell to Canadian wholesalers rather than directly to the country's retailers or consumers.[29] Central Canadian businessmen, therefore, competed in the North-West on more favourable terms than their American or British counterparts; they easily increased their share of the western Canadian market from virtually nothing in the early 1870s to two-thirds of the total by the mid-1880s.[30] While this increase coincided with the completion of the CPR, it owed its disproportionate growth largely to the National Policy, which in the case of farm machinery stood at 35 per cent. The tariff, coupled to personal contacts, national loyalties, and corporate purchasing policies, permitted central Canadians to capture the lion's share of the western Canadian market.

The National Policy, which the central government deemed necessary to support the CPR, therefore, became an important instrument in the dramatic shift in western Canada's suppliers, a transformation westerners resented deeply. Why, they asked, could they not purchase goods freely in the least expensive city, be that Canadian, American, or British? Why must they sell their production without any protection in a highly competitive international market, when eastern manufacturers were sheltered by tariffs?

Added to political frustrations, the tariff became a powerful symbol of central Canadian domination. Why, westerners questioned, did the Dominion government surrender political power so slowly and reluctantly to the territorial legislature? Why did it give the new provinces of Alberta and Saskatchewan what they did not want — sectarian schools — and withhold what they desired — control over resources and land? These questions, which betrayed the feeling that westerners were unable to control their own destiny, inspired several vigorous protest movements that eventually became a central part of their regional character. The territories and later the provinces shared 'a peripheral mentality' that viewed central Canada as indifferent, if not hostile, to western interests.[31]

Of all the issues that angered westerners, none was more aggravating than the indispensable railway. Unable to establish economically efficient river transportation, the North-West came to depend upon the railway as the only feasible means of transporting goods into and bulky grain out of the region. Consequently, the CPR and subsequent railways became the most obvious target for prairie discontent. Beginning with Manitoba's successful campaign against the CPR's monopoly clause, western Canadians fought numerous actions to gain rate concessions, one of which culminated in the highly favourable Crowsnest Pass rates.[32] But the West never escaped the power of the railway, and time and again its attempts to develop regional resources to their fullest were frustrated.

Not surprisingly, in 1910, western farmers constituted the largest group among the angry protesters who marched on Ottawa in an unprecedented statement against the tariff. Less than a year later, after the Liberal government lost the Reciprocity election, Westerners began to talk more earnestly about a third force to break the perceived alliance between the traditional political parties and powerful central Canadian corporations, particularly the CPR.[33] These developments represented their rebellion against the darker, imperialistic face of railway technology, a stark counterpoint to the nation-building mythology in the philosophy of railways. For western Canadians, central Canada's enthusiasm for the CPR as a nation builder appeared shallow.

Westerners' disenchantment with the CPR nation-building mythology was also caused by the rapidity with which the railway transported pioneers onto the plains. The CPR carried the majority of settlers directly from their homelands to the frontier. Moreover, as David Bercuson has explained, Canada had no continuous westward-moving frontier and the prairies absorbed the colonists raw and unassimilated.[34] Their only experience with Canada was the blur of lakes, trees, and occasional cities outside the westward-speeding train window. As a result, the newcomers' perception of Canada was an abstraction of an insecure identity buried in a fading British imperialism, a conception made real only by the commercial ties of the grain market, the bank, and the railway company. Formed by their regional rather than national environment, immigrants became westerners. The predominant influences on settlers' lives were close and near: assimilation took place in fields and barns, at the local general store or barbershop, at the elevator co-op. In other words, regionalism was more than a political struggle over control of resources. It involved a firm sense of place and community: the bonds and allegiances formed during the assimilation process were essentially local and western.

Consequently, the new prairie dwellers were more likely to perceive the railway as a highly visible symbol of domination and imperialism rather than as a creator of a transcontinental nation. Moreover, this widespread dislike of the railway became an experience that created a feeling of solidarity, a sense of unity against a common opponent. In sum, while the technology of railways achieved its intended purpose of welding together the disparate regions of Canada, the philosophy that supported its construction — and subsequently its management — established state and corporate policies that in turn created alienation and anger among western Canadians.

The policies of government and railway, which relegated prairie Canada to being a resource-extracting economy, appeared to have a similar effect on the Pacific coast. In a convincing exploratory essay, economic historian John Lutz used the boiler and marine-engine industry to demonstrate that the arrival of the CPR in Vancouver led to the erosion of manufacturing in the province.[35] In 1890, British Columbia's per capita manufacturing output was higher than in any other province, Victoria ranked tenth in industrial output among Canadian cities, and its Albion Iron Works was the largest plant north of San Francisco. Twenty-five years later, the province's overall industrial output had declined and Ontario, American, and British factories had replaced local producers of ship boilers and marine engines. Even though British Columbia's high wages were a contributing factor to the loss of the industry's competitive advantage, the railway link and discriminatory rates — that is, significantly lower rates for westward- than for eastward-moving traffic — confined coastal factories to a relatively small market while they opened its territory to continental competition and capital. Also important was the CPR's practice, as a large consumer of boilers and marine engines, of purchasing machinery abroad and in central Canada and shipping it at virtually no cost to its western mines and Pacific fleet. Other large non-local industries also avoided British Columbia products. 'The physical location of the ownership of British Columbia's resource, transportation, and manufacturing industries,' Lutz concluded, 'directed where interindustry linkages would be located.'[36] At the same time, however, Lutz also observed that by 1900 American and Scottish factories were able to displace central Canadian plants, so that Ontario itself was integrated into a larger system. 'The deindustrialization of British Columbia was a regional manifestation of the process by which Canadian manufacturing production became *centralized* in southern Ontario, itself part of a global centralization of manufacturing in a few locations such as the north-eastern United States and Britain.'[37]

The establishment of a new imperialistic-type relationship between central and western Canada, and the alienation that it produced, was not a unique experience. In the United States, sectional strife between East and West was common and railway politics had also assumed a prominent role in clashes in that country. In his study of American railway rhetoric, historian James Ward observed that in the United States railway promoters featured national unity as a central theme in their discourse, a concept they based on the notion that technology would spread the knowledge and ideas essential to the preservation of American civilization.[38] By the early 1850s, however, the American unity theme was faltering as some newspaper editors were beginning to realize that giant railway companies were creating extensive imperial systems that competed amongst themselves. Gigantic corporate structures, with no soul and a ruthless obsession with profit and survival, appeared to betray the earlier awestruck, idealist vision. The American public was awakening to the fact that these powerful railway enterprises were pitting region against region, city against city, people against people.

The themes of regional conflict and alienation, which arose out of the railway history of western Canada and of the United States also became part of eastern Canada's heritage. The advent of railways had stimulated an industrial revolution in central Canada and by the time confederation was completed in 1873, the region possessed a crucial advantage over the Maritimes. The Grand Trunk and Great Western railways were large, vertically integrated corporations with sizeable repair shops at Montréal, Hamilton, Stratford, and London. Able to build their own rolling stock, including locomotives, they were 'among the largest manufacturing firms in Canada in the period.'[39] The Great Western's expenditures on manufacturing, for example, rose from $250,000 in 1859 to $750,000 in 1874, while the Grand Trunk's disbursement grew from $600,000 per year in the 1860s to $1.5 million in the 1870s. By the mid-1850s, the Grand Trunk Railway was Canada's largest employer, with a $110,000 payroll for 2600 workers.[40] As Tom Traves and Paul Craven have argued, railways became 'Canada's first large-scale integrated industrial corporations,' and instigators of industrialization.[41] By 1867, Canada had entered the first stages of an industrial economy considerably larger in size than the economies of the Maritimes.

At the time of federation, moreover, the mainland Maritime provinces had not completed a network of railways that would allow its factories immediate access to central Canada and the United States. By the time the Intercolonial (the eastern section of the transcontinental) Railway was completed, it did not bring the rapid economic growth to the region that Charles Tupper and Leonard Tilley had envisioned. Economic historians, in their attempts to explain the problem, have focused their attention on a whole range of factors, including the region's isolation, its dearth of resources and population, government policies, and the lack of an entrepreneurial spirit.[42] Not featured prominently in this discussion is the absence of a modern and efficient inland transportation system, which was, in fact, a crucial factor in the area's subsequent marginalization. Both Tupper and Tilley had accepted the philosophy of railways as a catalyst for the economic development of their provinces, but both had failed to follow the advice of Joseph Howe, who always insisted that the Intercolonial must be completed before confederation was implemented.[43] It can be argued that, as a consequence, neither Halifax nor Saint John was given adequate opportunity to exploit its advantageous position as an Atlantic terminus on the transcontinental railway, nor were they able to develop their own hinterlands before being integrated into the national political economy and relegated to peripheral status.

In a recent study, Rick Szostak compared the speed of industrialization in England and France and posited the idea that 'a modern system of transportation was necessary for the Industrial Revolution to occur [earlier] in England.'[44] Although he acknowledged that many complex factors spurred the Industrial Revolution, Szostak argued that modern transportation, which he defined as an 'extensive and reliable system which could move bulk goods at low cost or high-value goods at high speed,'[45] created the opportunity for industrial expansion based on continuous technological change. Although he admitted that no special type of transport was necessary, Szostak argued that England's efficient land-based transportation system, particularly its railway network, had a profoundly positive effect upon the country's economy. Especially useful to an understanding of Atlantic Canada's place in Canada is his contention that modern transportation increased market size and production, causing some regions to specialize in certain products and dominate the national market. This argument fits Atlantic Canada, which in the first half-century after confederation lost its economic primacy and became a peripheral and underdeveloped region in the Canadian federation.

In two useful articles, T.W. Acheson has established the point that under the terms of federation, the imperial ties that had bound the Maritimes to Britain switched to Canada.[46] In the first decades after the union, Acheson suggested, Maritime entrepreneurs created a diversified local manufacturing sector that competed successfully on the international market in cotton, glass, sugar, confectionaries, and secondary iron and steel. Unfortunately, Acheson observed, the Canadian market could not absorb the entire domestic production and in the 1880s central Canadian producers purchased controlling interests in Maritime industries and rationalized their production by consolidating operations in their region; they also gained political control over the Intercolonial and bought connecting railways. 'Aided greatly by the reorganization of the vehicles of regional commerce,' Acheson commented, 'the Intercolonial and [CPR] Short Line railroads firmly fastened the region to Montreal and gradually eroded the traditional seaborne import trade of the Maritimes.'[47] In fact, the region became a branch-plant economy.

In his conclusions, Acheson noted that railway technology played an important role in the Maritimes' deteriorating economic status in the Canadian economic union. 'The tragedy of the industrial experiment in the Maritimes was that the transportation lines which linked the region to its new metropolis altered the communal arrangement of the entire area; they did not merely establish a new external frame of reference, they re-cast the entire internal structure.'[48] When they entered the Canadian union, the Maritimes were not a coherent region, he wrote, but separate colonies on the fringe of an empire, each with its own lines of communication and several metropolitan centres. Its waterborne transportation system was flexible and dynamic. 'In this sense the railroad with its implications of organic unity, its inflexibility, and its assumption that there was a metropolitan point at which it could end, provided an experience entirely alien to the maritime tradition,' Acheson concluded, and asserts that there is no evidence to suggest that maritime businessmen were any less efficient than those in Ontario and Québec, 'nor, given advantageous freight rates, that they could not compete for most central Canadian markets.'[49]

New Brunswick historian E.R. Forbes seconded Acheson's thesis by noting that sharply increasing freight rates in the first decades of the twentieth century were a factor in the comparative economic decline of the mainland maritime provinces.[50] Though the Intercolonial was built as part of the confederation agreement of 1867 for the economic development of Nova Scotia and New Brunswick, its managers, under the direction of their political masters, established relatively low and flexible freight rates. Wishing to remain competitive within the region, the CPR responded with similar tariffs. At the turn of the century, the rise of western Canada and its regional protest movements caused a westward shift in political power. In 1913, a Nova Scotia-born prime minister, Robert Borden, held in office by a central and western Canadian-based party, appointed a new cost-conscious management for the Intercolonial, and freight rates shot up dramatically, rapidly eroding the critical advantage that maritime industrial centres had enjoyed. With the absorption of the Intercolonial into Canadian National Railways, the central government steeply increased freight rates, effectively ending the competitiveness of Maritime factories in Canadian markets. Having acquired the extensive Grand Trunk harbour properties in Portland when it nationalized the railway, Ottawa abandoned its policy of developing the ports of Halifax and Saint John.[51] Feeling shut out of central Canada's economic prosperity, Maritimers rallied for a while under the dissident Maritime Rights movement, but when that failed to achieve the desired result, their disillusionment was profound and lasting.[52] In the end, the Maritime provinces fell into the trap described by Daniel R. Headrick in *Tentacles of Progress*.[53] Having voluntarily accepted the transfer of an encompassing technology, they became part of its imperial embrace. Tupper and Tilley's visions of the Intercolonial as an artery moving manufactured goods from the region to central Canada had lost to Galt's call for a new Canadian mercantilism.

Another dramatic victim of the philosophy of railways was Prince Edward Island. Driven by a strong sense of community, that province had consciously and explicitly scorned confederation. The island's decades-long struggle to wrest its lands from absentee landlords, its strong attachment to the soil, its fight to retain an independent government, its rural conservatism, and especially its insular isolationist mentality had created a distinct communal identity that was fiercely independent, profoundly patriotic, and sublimely optimistic. Prince Edward Islanders adamantly refused to be absorbed into a larger nation.[54]

In 1871, however, the island caught railway fever and its politicians and editors displayed all the symptoms so common two decades earlier in mainland North America. Included in the exuberant promises of infinite progress and wealth was the expectation of the industrialization of the island economy; excluded was any regard for mounting costs and unsustainable debt charges. And, as elsewhere, the opposition tended to focus on the pace and place of construction rather than on its principle and value; the legislature thus committed the island to a publicly financed trunk line and several branches.

Begun in the fall of 1871, the project was immediately ensnared in patronage and corruption, causing a considerable expansion in length and cost and eventually forcing a general election. After a rancorous, divisive campaign, in which the railway issue was complicated by quarrels about sectarian schools, Robert Poore Haythorne's Liberal party won a resounding victory. Although they had roundly criticized the Conservatives' expensive railway program, patronage considerations forced them to expand the project still further into a full-fledged trans-island railway. The new government committed the island to spend $3.8 million or

$41 per capita on railway construction, creating annual interest charges that amounted to half of its revenues, an impossible burden for a small population faced with an economic recession. Early in 1873, the anti-confederation Haythorne government sent a mission to Ottawa to discuss terms of union.[55]

The initial union package answered most of Prince Edward Island's needs. Canada promised to assume the island's debt, including that of the railway, to loan money to buy out the remaining absentee landlords, and to provide adequate representation in parliament. Late in May, the legislature accepted the conditions but called for an election. Although the Haythorne government was defeated—largely on the sectarian-schools issue—J.C. Pope's Conservative government was committed to a better-terms confederation and subsequently negotiated a financially more rewarding package.[56] The Canadian government justified the more generous treatment of Prince Edward Island on the grounds that the province needed special concessions because it had no Crown lands and because it would not profit from the construction of the Intercolonial or the CPR.[57] Although most islanders were disappointed in the loss of their independence, they took comfort in the favourable terms. By 1873, in fact, they had little choice: economic necessity forced their decision to join Canada. The impetuous adoption of the philosophy of railways, followed by hasty planning, contracting, and constructing, accompanied by bribery and patronage, had resulted in an unbearable financial burden that wore down the island's independent spirit. A deep sense of loss, exacerbated by a stagnating economy and fed by nostalgia for a lost golden age, demoralized generations of islanders. 'Thus,' lamented David Weale and Harry Baglole, the island's nationalist historians, 'although the eventual entry of the Island into Confederation was part of the unfolding of the great Canadian National Dream, it also in many ways represented the disintegration of the Island Dream.'[58]

Further to the east, in Newfoundland, the philosophy of railways had a lesser impact on the province's loss of sovereignty than in Prince Edward Island. Straddled on the far eastern fringe of Britain's North American empire, Newfoundland through most of the nineteenth century ignored the rhetoric of railways and its transcontinental dream. Although an isolated editor occasionally broached the subject, most newspapers and politicians did not embrace the expansionist boosterism of mainland railway promoters.[59] Instead, their economic and cultural inspiration remained steadfastly North Atlantic. Not surprisingly, the island spurned all union overtures from the other colonies and in 1869 an election formally ratified its oceanic orientation.[60]

Railway politics came to play an important role in the island's repeated refusals to join the continent but also in its final surrender to continentalist pressures. In the late 1860s and again in the mid-1870s, Newfoundlanders discussed the construction of a trans-island railway, but no action resulted until 1881 when William Whiteway's Conservative government signed an ambitious agreement with an American company. By then the island was fully immersed in railway mania, with proponents arguing that the technology was necessary to encourage economic development outside the traditional fishery—in mining, lumbering, and agriculture. It was time, they asserted, that Newfoundland entered the modern age and developed the full range of its natural resources. Meanwhile, their opponents, concentrated in St John's, countered that a Canadian economic policy could not be applied to Newfoundland, that the scheme constituted an unnecessary and unbearable tax burden, and that the road would expose the province's merchants to unfair external competition.[61] Despite their objections, the syndicate, incorporated as the Newfoundland Railway Company, sputtered along for the next three years and by 1884 completed a 64-kilometre rail line to Harbour Grace on Conception Bay. By then, the company was also bankrupt. Consequently, the government assumed control over construction, and four years later a Reform administration finished a branch to Argentia on

Placentia Bay. Finally, in the 1890s, a Liberal government reorganized the company and chartered Robert G. Reid of Montréal to extend the line to Port aux Basques on the south-west corner of the island. Although Reid's company completed the formidable task by 1897, the cost of construction contributed to the province's massive public debt and the financial crisis of that year. At the same time, however, Reid's success had bolstered the province's independent spirit and his lobbying among Montréal financiers helped restore its fiscal health. Once again, the province rejected a Canadian bid for union.[62]

By the turn of the century, the Newfoundland railway had become a recurrent, hot political issue. It had realigned traditional alliances and aided the fall of several administrations. In 1901, for instance, when the Robert Bond government reduced the generous land and resource concessions that a previous cabinet had granted, the Reids became actively involved in the 1909 election and contributed to Bond's defeat. The succeeding government improved the deal again, but finally, in 1923, Newfoundland bought out the company. Although railway construction had created temporary employment, it did not stop the chronic emigration of the island's young people to the mainland. It did permit, however, the settlement of some parts of the interior, the establishment of a strong pulp-and-paper industry, and the consolidation of several trading centres along the cost. Meanwhile, despite their initial fears, the railway helped St John's merchants to expand their hold over the island's trade and commerce.[63] In the end, the trans-island railway had created a disproportionally large financial debt that contributed to the province's bankruptcy in the early 1930s, the establishment of commission government, and ultimately union with Canada in 1949.

While, in the 1860s, neither Newfoundland nor Prince Edward Island had shared with Canadians the transcontinental vision of technological nationalism and instead chose to retain a distinct local culture, eventually they were fully incorporated into the transcontinental economy. As underdeveloped fringe regions in the national economy, they boarded their surplus populations on trains that carried them westward to jobs in central Canada, the western prairies, and the Pacific coast. The bonds of common language and history, essential to defining a people's identity, assisted their fusion into the nation, while the railway and the mails it carried permitted them to keep in touch with their home provinces.

The two components, the English tongue and British heritage, that allowed Anglophone Canadians to mix easily into a new culture, were not features of a large and populous region — French-speaking Québec. A unique historical tradition and distinct language prevented that province's full integration into the national psyche despite the transcontinental railway. Few French Canadians were exposed to or excited by the philosophy of railways and its western settlement and nation-building components.

Although the French language and the Québec heritage prevented the full assimilation of rural francophones into Canadian culture, their strong sense of place also militated against migration to the North-West. French Canadians identified the St Lawrence valley as their homeland — la patrie. Resident in that geographical region was a distinct people bound by their peculiar institutions of law, customs, social organizations, and church.[64]

'Notre religion, notre langue et nos lois,' La Minerve asserted. 'Ne craignons pas de répéter ce cri national, qui n'est pas plus banal qu'aucun autre motto, aucune autre devise, et aucun chant national. N'ayons pas honte de notre drapeau.'[65] To be sure, the Québécois developed a vision of economic development, a program that emphasized agriculture and forestry but also included industrialization and the construction of roads and railways.[66] They confined these schemes to their province, however, and clearly recognized that such objectives were only the materialistic aspect of several nation-building blocks. Significantly, they sought to reinforce their nationalism with cultural traits, especially their religious beliefs. 'Pour les canadiens, le catholicisme c'est la nationalité,' La Minerve concluded and implicitly explained why French

Canada considered the right to preserve their distinct identity — rooted within the confines of their national homeland — as the necessary condition for confederation.[67]

Inspired by their patriotic love for Québec, French Canadians had little interest in the settlement of the North-West. In fact, frequent appeals from the pulpit for aid to starving Metis and destitute natives, as well as bleak accounts from returning fur traders about inhospitable expanses, had created among the Québécois an image of the plains as desolate wastelands, unfit for agriculture and habitation. 'Le territoire du Nord-Ouest, quoi qu'on en dise, est une région désolée, impracticable durant une grande partie de l'année, et où rien n'attirera l'émigrant," Le Pays scoffed. 'Lorsque tout le continent américain sera peuple, qu'il n'y aura plus un pouce carré de terre disponible, peut-être alors se dirigera-t-on vers la Baie d'Hudson. Jusqu'alors on ne peut espérer des émigrants.'[68] In contrast to their Ontario and Maritime compatriots, French Canadians found little appeal in the vast lands of the western prairies. They did not share the transcontinental nation-building dream and its myths — not its pioneering aura, its agrarian radicalism, or, for that matter, the CPR.

Nevertheless, it was a French Canadian who conducted the negotiations that transferred Rupert's Land from the Hudson's Bay Company to Canada and promised a railway to British Columbia. But that diplomat, George-Etienne Cartier, was not a rural seigneur but an urban lawyer, who, as solicitor for the Grand Trunk, was fully immersed in Montréal's business world and its expansionist ethic.[69] Cartier's view of the North-West was a commercial perspective. He was not particularly interested in the North-West as a place for French Canadians, but saw it as a region that would use his city, its river and its railways, as a channel to and from Europe. 'Nous exporterons les produits de la Colombie et de Manitobe [sic] sur les marchés européens et nous importerons pour elles les produits manufactures dont elles auront besoin,' Le Courrier noted. 'Notre marine et nos importateurs en auront tout le bénéfice.'[70] As the paper observed, colonization was profitable: it meant traffic for Québec's railways, business for its merchants, and land sales for its speculators. Western Canadian trade would create jobs in Québec and keep its people home.[71] In other words, the completion of the Pacific railway became an important objective to Québec merchants and other businessmen; it represented another phase in the empire of the St Lawrence.

For Québec, therefore, a transcontinental railway, routed through the Ottawa valley to Montréal and Québec City, was 'la seule politique provinciale, vraie et nationale dans les circonstances.'[72] To achieve that objective, the province sold to the CPR its rights to the Montréal-Ottawa portion of the Québec, Montréal, Ottawa et Occidental. In this way, the province ensured that the St Lawrence port would become a major terminal on the transcontinental. Subsequently, Québec politicians forced the federal government to coerce the Grand Trunk Railway to surrender its control over the eastern section of the Québec, Montréal, Ottawa et Occidental (also known as the North Shore Line) to the CPR. Provincial and federal politicians thus ensured that Québec's capital enjoyed the services of two competing rail lines, both of which fed into major American and Canadian rail systems.[73] For Québecers, however, the Grand Trunk and Canadian Pacific railways were vehicles for promoting the economic welfare of their province and for strengthening the French-Canadian nationality, rather than tools for building a transcontinental country.[74]

Despite its inward vision, therefore, Québec participated in the establishment of the mercantile relationship between central Canada and the outlying regions. Strengthened by the commercial spirit of Anglophone Montréal, the province helped frame the national railway and tariff policies that at once consolidated the new northern empire and created its regional disparities and established major metropolitan centres and their hinterlands.

The relationship between the large cities and the countryside, which the railway cemented into place, was a complex association duplicated in miniature metropolitan empires within the nation's regions. These minor metropolitan structures, tied together by railway and telegraph communications, helped to alleviate the sense of frustration and alienation that the feelings of regionalism produced.

On the prairies, for example, rapidly growing Winnipeg took advantage of its geographical location to establish itself as a subordinate metropolitan system. Already ensconced as the territory's most important warehouse and wholesale centre, Winnipeg had the experience and access to credit to take advantage of the transportation revolution; the construction of the CPR across the plains accelerated the growth of traffic through the city and the prosperity of its business community.[75] By 1886, Winnipeg had nineteen major establishments that specialized in exploiting the commerce of the western hinterland. Its merchants formed a powerful group that persuaded the CPR to build the main line south through Winnipeg rather than Selkirk, wrested control over the grain trade from Toronto, and later demolished the CPR monopoly. More significantly, its board of trade successfully lobbied the railway and government for a 15 per cent reduction of freight rates on goods shipped west of Winnipeg, including manufactured items. In 1890, it also pressured the CPR to lower rates on items hauled from central Canada to Winnipeg.[76]

The discriminatory rate policy contributed substantially to Winnipeg's dominant position as the gateway to the Canadian prairies. The CPR's policy of charging higher rates on manufactured goods than on raw materials transported from central Canada to Winnipeg aided the city's manufacturing industry, while lower rates on westbound freight assisted its wholesale trade. Some city merchants founded subsidiaries in towns built along the main line: J.H. Ashdown, hardware wholesaler and retailer, for instance, established a hardware store in Calgary. His and other firms replenished their stock from Winnipeg suppliers, which in turn ordered from central Canada, Great Britain, or the United States depending upon price and quality. Dixon Brothers of Medicine Hat bought almost half its supplies from Winnipeg wholesalers, and most of the remainder from Montréal and Toronto.[77] Winnipeg merchants, therefore, represented a dual consolidating force: they established strong ties with central Canada, the eastern United States, and the United Kingdom and at the same time planted tight connections with the cities, towns, and villages spread across the expansive plain. That middleman position created an equivocal attitude among Winnipegers to western Canada's position in confederation.

One individual who represented Winnipeg's ambiguous metropolitan-hinterland relationship was Manitoba's Clifford Sifton.[78] Young, energetic, and pragmatic, Ontario-born Sifton believed that the exploitation of the resources of the North-West was central to the economic development of Canada. As minister of the interior in Sir Wilfrid Laurier's administration, Sifton adopted a business-like approach to the settlement process, treating the vast unsettled lands as commodities on a glutted market, to be sold cheaply through extensive advertising among experienced farmers in Britain, the United States, and Continental Euroope.[79] Although he defended the extensive cattle preserves of southern Alberta, he admired scientific and technological farming methods, and became the first minister to support large-scale irrigation projects in the North-West.[80] When Ottawa granted provincial status to Saskatchewan and Alberta in 1905, Sifton agreed that jurisdiction over their natural resources should remain with the federal government, but when Laurier appeared to set up independent Catholic school systems in the new provinces, he angrily resigned. At worst, Sifton's stand on the school question may be interpreted as a manifestation of Ontario's anti-Roman Catholic, anti-French Canadian bigotry: at best, it may be seen as an indication of the North-West's belief that all newcomers should be taught British democratic ideals in a common English language. In any case, he wanted to establish on the prairies the social structures of his native Ontario.

Instructive of Clifford Sifton's close association with central Canada is his position in the 1911 election. Although a Liberal, he did not share the enthusiasm of his colleagues when the American government suggested a reciprocal free-trade agreement. Sifton strongly opposed the trade pact and actively campaigned against his party, receiving the grateful support of Canada's manufacturing and railway interests. Central to his opposition was the belief that free trade would disrupt the east-west trade patterns that the transcontinental railway system and the National Policy had so painfully wrought. Although Sifton's stand definitely ran contrary to the views of many western Canadians, it must be noted that the Brandon constituency that had consistently returned him to office voted Tory in the 1911 election.

The defeat of free trade obviously angered many western Canadians, but their alienation did not turn into separatist feelings partly because of the dual role that Winnipeg and other western cities played in the metropolitan-hinterland relationship. On the one hand, Winnipeg was the transportation gateway into the region and the largest wholesale distribution centre in western Canada. Its vote in the 1911 election clearly exposed the political alliance that the city's business elite had made with Canada's railway interests.[81] With the city serving as the region's primary grain market, Winnipeg's merchants continuously blocked the efforts of western farm organizations to gain control over the grain trade. Western farmers, therefore, denounced the city as an ally of the nation-state and its corporate backers. On the other hand, Winnipeg provided the political power to destroy the CPR's monopoly and gain important rate differentials, popular actions that won the approval of western farmers. At times, then, the city joined common cause with the countryside in the battle against Montréal and Toronto. The city's newspapers, particularly the *Free Press*, identified and fortified the concerns of prairie farmers, opinions echoed in the towns and cities of the North-West.[82] In this love-hate relationship, Winnipeg and other emerging prairie cities were at once opponents and champions of western causes. In either case, the city strengthened the region's sense of communal uniqueness. By controlling the means of communication along with its imports and exports, the city became a regional voice for the prairies and helped to establish the region's identity.

As the example of Winnipeg has illustrated, the metropolitan-hinterland relationship was complex and intricate. The feelings of alienation, which that association so often generated, were tempered by the close common cultural ties shared among the regions. Despite western Canada's quickness to protest, the region retained a strong identification with eastern Canada because the railway, which had transported settlers and their belongings from Atlantic and St Lawrence harbours, from the Maritimes, Québec, and Ontario, and from the United States, permitted the newcomers to maintain ties with their homelands as well as with eastern cities and institutions. As a fast and efficient means of communication, the railway ensured that the western identity, which the newcomers eventually created, was derived in part from contemporary attitudes in the United States and Great Britain, as well as eastern Canada.

While the newcomers spoke of creating a new society in an empty land and laced their rhetoric with pastoral ideals and agrarian myths, with egalitarian democratic concepts, and with talk of individualism and cooperation, virility and opportunity, they quietly put in place familiar customs. Although westerners spoke of a clean slate, their community presented no spontaneous new world but an obvious derivation from western Europe; they welcomed the police, the church, legislative assemblies, national schools — or, simply put, law, order, and good government. The prophets of the new society were typically the editors of local newspapers, who never strayed far from the telegraph office or train station, and copied freely from eastern dailies. Like Patrick Gammie Laurie, the editor of the *Saskatchewan Herald*, they either looked to Great Britain for inspiration or, like J.W. Dafoe, editor of the Manitoba *Free Press*, they admired the United States.[83] They eventually created a distinctive western regional identity, but that character remained fully exposed to the latest metropolitan political, social, and economic debates. The West's radical agrarian tradition, for instance, owes an enormous debt to concepts tried on the Great Plains of the United States, while its labour radicalism found inspiration in the coal mines of Pennsylvania and the factories of Great Britain.[84]

Despite their loud claims of distinctiveness, therefore, westerners attempted to imitate many features of metropolitan life. A clear illustration of this phenomenon was the ranching community in southern Alberta. The completion of the prairie section of the CPR in 1883 made large-scale ranching economically feasible, particularly after the Canadian government awarded several large grazing leases to a number of prominent Canadian and British investors. Even though the ranching industry borrowed many of its techniques from previous frontiers, particularly those of the United States, its cultural and political inspiration came from central Canada and the United Kingdom.[85] The tennis courts and grand pianos that graced the luxurious ranges provided more than recreation in an isolated community; they served as symbols of gracious living on a crude frontier. The ranching elite, which was closely associated with the officers of the North West Mounted Police, carefully maintained lines of communication with the eastern establishment and attempted, with some success, to institute on the south-western fringe of the prairies a Victorian way of life.[86]

The shopkeepers in the small towns along the railway were no different from the ranchers; their social activities and political alliances expressed a similar conservatism. Their votes at election time demonstrated that they appreciated the strong centralization tendencies emanating from the eastern establishment, while their social activities reflected their desire to establish an orderly and peaceful society.[87] Supporting their local press and social institutions, the town's businessmen and professionals profoundly influenced the character of western Canadian society.

Since the railway provided the link between the metropolis and the hinterland, the timing of its appearance was important. The prairies were settled when the primary characteristic of its founders, the Montréal-Toronto metropolitan axis, was a Victorian industrial expansionism. The age celebrated the triumph of a laissez-faire liberalism, whose priorities included confederation, western expansion, and the construction of a transcontinental railway. Whereas the region's link with the metropolis during the fur-trade era had been slow, inefficient, and circuitous, by 1900 it was fast, efficient, and immediate. Assisted by the telegraph and postal service, the railway placed the North-West in immediate touch with central Canada. Consequently, the values of the city were transmitted directly and quickly to the frontier.

In fact, the value of progress that dominated nineteenth-century Canadian thought was accentuated in western Canada. Technology, science, and the machine promised to subdue the rigour and capriciousness of nature. After it deliberately routed the main line through the semi-arid southern prairies, the CPR established model farms throughout the West to experiment with improved hybrids and dogmatically propagate dry-land farming techniques. Its large irrigation project in southern Alberta, with its impressive dam at Bassano and massive concrete aqueduct at Brooks, demonstrated to the world that modern scientific farmers could grow crops where they pleased.[88]

Bolstered by its buoyant optimism in science and technology and its ebullient belief in moral and social progress, the prairie West possessed a utopian streak. Despite their basic political conservatism, westerners believed they were building a new and improved society on the plains. They wanted to share their vision with a perceived effete eastern Canada. Western visionaries and prophets, often disguised as politicians, travelled by train to Ottawa to participate in the councils of the nation and lay before its people the idealism of a young and vigorous region.

Despite its strong regional identity, western Canada, therefore, participated in national institutions and joined in national debates; it fitted itself into the national identity. Despite vocal protests about its regional uniqueness, the West possessed a sense of nationalism expressed at federal elections and in national organizations. A regional transportation network knitted villages, towns, and cities into a vital and dynamic entity; simultaneously, the railway blunted the sharp division between region and nation. In this integration the railway played a major part.

The prairie provinces, therefore, linked by rail and telegraph to the East, in many ways shared central Canadian values, but because they also felt threatened by that largely urban, industrializing society, they formed a unique culture. The CPR had opened the region to farmers, shopkeepers, and investors from eastern Canada; it had fulfilled — even if imperfectly — one of the hopes expressed by the Toronto *Mail*, cited at the beginning of this chapter; it had assisted in settling western Canada and in attaching the region to the Montréal-Toronto axis.[89] When the *Mail* expressed the hope, however, that the CPR would 'make strong a true national sentiment,' it articulated a central Canadian economic vision, which the railway helped to spread across the land. That aspiration met with considerable resistance in some regions and with studied rebuffs in others. It was a simplistic wish that hid the multifaceted nature of the metropolitan-frontier connection.

Similarly, to what extent was the *Mail's* wish for an independent northern nation a naïve assertion? Did the completion of the CPR 'preserve' the young nation's 'autonomy and national integrity'? Did it ensure that Canada would not be absorbed into the United States? Had the editor skimmed lightly over the intricate, constantly mutating relationships of Canada with Great Britain and the United States? Did he understand to what extent the railway was assisting the country's orientation from a transatlantic to a continental alignment?

The completion of the transcontinental at Craigellachie in November 1885 represented the culmination of a vision expressed nearly four decades earlier in the Guarantee Act of 1849. Set in a turbulent decade, that legislation embodied a scheme for a distinct northern economy, competitive with that of the United States but never completely independent from it. It incorporated an almost universal optimism in railway technology as a response to a new economic order. It implied that this revolutionary means of transportation would permit the province's businessmen to expand their commercial activities across the continent into American as well as British territory.

In 1849, when Canada's affiliation was still primarily with the United Kingdom, it used the Guarantee Act to lure British technical knowledge, financial resources, and managerial skills to the province in order to build the Grand Trunk and other railways. At mid-century, Britain was one of the few countries that possessed the vast resources of capital, equipment, labour, engineering, and management skills required to build and operate railways abroad. As Daniel R. Headrick has demonstrated so cogently, Great Britain was a mass exporter of railway technology, sending its engineers, equipment, and capital to all parts of the globe.[90] Canada, a major recipient of this technology transfer, was drawn ever more deeply into and influenced by British culture and economics.

Headrick's observation amplified Gallagher and Robinson's 'imperialism of free trade' thesis, which argued that Britain expanded its empire significantly during the mid-nineteenth century despite the predominant free-trade ideology. 'The exports of capital and manufactures, the migration of citizens, the dissemination of the English language, ideas and constitutional forms,' the authors wrote, 'were all of them radiations of the social energies of the British peoples.'[91] By defining imperialism as the 'process of integrating new regions into the expanding economy,' Gallagher and Robinson argued that the growth of British industry forced Britain to employ both formal and informal methods to link undeveloped areas into its orbit.[92] Many regions became satellite economies, providing raw materials for Great Britain, wider markets for its manufacturers, and investment opportunities for its capitalists. In Canada, the Grand Trunk Railway reinforced imperial connections and imperial objectives. Subsequently, the Canadian Pacific Railway incorporated imperial ends as an important part of its mission.[93]

In the case of British North America, however, provincial governments and businessmen used the philosophy of railways to enhance their political power and control. The growing but transformed imperial influence, represented by bankers like the Barings and the Glyns, must be considered in light of the fact that in the 1850s both Nova Scotia and New Brunswick rejected British contractors in favour of government-directed construction and that Canada insisted that domestic businessmen receive a large portion of Grand Trunk construction work. Canada's precarious financial situation throughout the 1850s, caused primarily by faltering railways, increased its political self-determination. Ruling relatively large territories and enjoying a fair measure of self-government, colonial legislatures insisted on setting their railway agendas and simultaneously developed their own fiscal policies and expanded bureaucracies. That growing self-awareness was reflected in the public-works programs in New Brunswick and Nova Scotia, in the expanded size of the Grand Trunk Railway and complex state financial-assistance techniques, in Canada's 1859 tariff, and eventually in confederation.

Although British North America's mid-century railway boom strengthened informal ties with Great Britain, it also increased the colonies' orientation to the United States. This was a logical consequence of the philosophy of railways because virtually all colonial railways were designed to provide access to American markets or ports. While some were to serve as portages between the continent's interior and New England railways, others were to siphon trade from the American West through British American harbours to the Atlantic Ocean.

The Guarantee Act, which authorized government subsidies to rival portage-railways across Canadian soil, clearly revealed that the philosophy of railways did not contain the technological nationalism that is a part of the CPR mythology. The harsh realities of economic practicality as well as the predominance of economic considerations lying beneath the idealistic rhetoric informed government policies. Throughout the pre-confederation years, Canadians sporadically considered proposals for an intercolonial railway from Québec through New Brunswick to the ice-free port of Halifax. Its circuitous route, however, lessened the practical economic value of the plan. As far as Montréal's merchants were concerned, the primary purpose of any railway was to retain for their city the trade of Upper Canada and capture that of the American Midwest; therefore, they wanted the most direct, economically efficient rail route to the Atlantic. They also intended to compete head-on with American railways that had similar objectives. In the same way, Saint John and Halifax businessmen hoped to see their cities become major seaports for both Canadian and American trade routes and they planned their railway policies accordingly.

Even though the visionary pre-confederation schemes for a transcontinental railway had British imperial goals, all proposed routing the line south of the Great Lakes through the United States. Edward Watkin's plan, which was similar to many other outlines, illustrated this international perspective. An ardent believer in free trade between Canada and the United States, Watkin clearly recognized that railway technology was not limited by political boundaries. On one level, his transcontinental railway scheme represented the extension of Britain's informal empire of finance and commerce into North America.[94] On a different level, his proposal meant the creation of a Canadian empire westward to the Pacific and the settlement of the prairies. On yet another plane, Watkin proposed to build south of the Great Lakes and thus envisioned closer integration with the United States and the creation of a continental economy.[95] At these several levels, therefore, his proposed railway symbolized the expansionist and universalizing features of technology. It embodied all the outlines of the schemes that remained in vogue until the Pacific Scandal.

British North America's railway champions certainly understood the principle that this new transportation technology fostered, extended, and strengthened the power of international commercial empires. Even though they promoted the railway as a means of building a distinct northern nation within the British Empire, they also saw it as a method for attaching themselves to the dynamic economy of the United States. Railways like the Grand Trunk, Great Western, and European and North American facilitated the union of British North America, but they could not survive if they isolated themselves from the United States. Thus, the railway builders linked their projects into the American network and increasingly adopted American principles and technologies. When their isolationist broad-gauge policy proved to be economically unsound, Canada's railway managers undertook an expensive conversion to the American standard gauge.[96] By 1873, American and Canadian rolling stock moved unhampered across the international border.[97] On the one hand, railway technology at first informally and subtly strengthened the financial and social influence exerted by the British Empire; on the other hand, subsequently it casually and inconspicuously intensified commercial and cultural relations with the United States.

The new international reality, articulated in the philosophy of railways, was ostensibly rejected during the Pacific Scandal. The political and regional rivalries that rose to the surface during the crisis accentuated Ottawa's impotence at the repeated American rejections of reciprocity overtures and the degradation during the Treaty of Washington negotiations. Prime Minister John A. Macdonald was determined that the new Pacific railway would be all-Canadian in routing and management. He resolved to use the railway as a tool of nationalism.

Despite Macdonald's intentions, the international, universalizing character of the technology of railways was still very evident in the Canadian Pacific Railway. The syndicate that eventually built the western portion of the transcontinental railway arose out of the defunct St. Paul, Minneapolis and Manitoba Railway, revitalized by a partnership of Canadian and American promoters and financiers. Following the instructions of the federal government, the CPR constructed an all-Canadian railroad from central Canada along the north shore of Lake Superior and across the prairies to the Rocky Mountains, permitting Montréal merchants to reinstitute the trade route their ancestors had lost and to re-establish their city's dominance in the North-West. But the board of directors quickly set aside the government's explicit nationalist purpose and leased, bought, or constructed several branch lines in the United States, including the Short Line from Montréal through Maine to Saint John and the Soo Line westward from Sault Ste Marie through Minnesota to St Paul and Minneapolis. On 3 June 1889, a through train ran the exact route that Hugh Allan and Jay Cooke had planned but the Pacific Scandal had scuttled, while a year later, the CPR launched operations on a direct line from Québec through Montréal and Toronto to Windsor, where it ferried cars across the river to be forwarded on the Wabash Railroad to Chicago.[98] The CPR's corporate objectives, therefore, were not defined by an exclusivist technological nationalism but by the broad internationalism of the railway and its search for profits.

The international integrative character of railway technology is muted in Canadian historiography because writers prefer to adulate the Canadian Pacific Railway as the great unifier of the northern transcontinental nation. Almost forgotten is William J. Wilgus's *The Railway Interrelations of the United States and Canada*, which studied about fifty gateways at the international boundary and concluded that the railways of Canada and the United States must be seen as an integrated network. In practice, Wilgus observed, railways operated 'as if there were no border to separate them politically,'[99] an observation that many nineteenth-century Canadians could have made and, with some reservations, applauded.

In like manner, the National Policy was never intended to completely bar American and British businessmen from Canada. In western Canada, for example, T.C. Power and Company, a trading firm based in Fort Benton, Montana, with a long history of activities on the southwestern prairies, neutralized the effect of Canada's highly protective tariff by shifting some of its purchasing to suppliers in Montréal and shipping them to the North-West on the CPR. If prices warranted, however, Power also bought goods in New York, Chicago, or St Paul and imported them by way of Winnipeg.[100] Similarly, the Hudson's Bay Company adopted a mixed policy of buying some goods in Canada and importing others from Great Britain. It also adapted its operations to the agricultural economy; it diversified its operations, expanded its selection of wares, and established sales shops wherever populations warranted.[101]

Despite the protectionism inherent in the National Policy, the CPR, as an effective means of communication, created opportunities for shrewd entrepreneurs from New York, Chicago, and London, as well as Montréal and Toronto, to conduct business in the North-West. The railway permitted hundreds of shopkeepers to establish small stores in towns along its main and branch lines and to fill their shelves with an array of products manufactured in central Canada, the United States, or Great Britain. Travelling salesmen alighted daily from inbound trains to take orders for Winnipeg and Montréal wholesalers. In fact, the CPR allowed factories, such as Harris and John Deere, to set up farm-implement dealerships in most sizeable towns on the prairies. Large flour millers, like A.W. Ogilvie, erected mills in the North-West or gathered wheat for central Canadian or European plants.

The Toronto *Mail's* claim, therefore, that the CPR would establish the national integrity of Canada has validity to the extent that, undergirded by the National Policy, the railway permitted central Canada to lay claim to the North-West and to establish its economic hegemony in the Atlantic region. It also facilitated the establishment of intercontinental trade and commerce. The assertion that the CPR would make Canada independent from the United States proved excessively sanguine when the railway connected itself to North America's railway system. In other words, British North America's philosophy of railways, first enunciated in the 1840s, helped create the Dominion but unintentionally introduced regional disparities and discontents into its mercantilistic federal structure; at the same time, while it envisioned a relatively independent Canada, it increased the nation's dependence on the United States.

The national dream, born in the heady expressionism of the mid-nineteenth century, arose out of the conviction that the railway would permit mankind to conquer the environment. This vision was especially strong in British North America, whose citizens, surrounded by an immense and seemingly hostile wilderness, eagerly embraced the new transportation technique as a potent means of freeing men and women from the harsh bonds of nature. The railway, which smoothed rough geological obstacles and softened harsh winters, promised economic growth and provincial prosperity. More intangibly, it supposedly ennobled people and promoted moral as well as economic progress. The new transportation technology promised to liberate them from the bonds of the environment and the frailties of humanity. Emboldened by such a great prospect, British North Americans ardently and totally embraced railway technology and thus set the stage for an unparalleled railway boom.

Although technology's 'moral imperative' assumed a prominent place in promotional literature, it was primarily the hope for economic growth that energized conservative and reform-minded colonists and drove them into powerful alliances. While conservatives rejected the political ideas of their liberal opponents because they feared a threat to established order, they readily accepted the formula for economic progress and colonial prosperity as the best means of preserving their favoured way of life. This consensus on economic development created the fertile ground for British North America's railway extravaganza. Despite disagreements on details, most urban British North Americans embraced the technological nationalist dream, a vision of a transcontinental country eventually realized in the completion of the Grand Trunk, the Great Western, the European and North American, the Nova Scotia, and finally the Intercolonial and the Canadian Pacific railways. Collectively, these railways revolutionized transportation in the colonies and radically altered their political, social, and economic cultures in ways their advocates never envisioned.

Few of the railway philosophers, for example, would have foreseen the interventionist role the state came to play in private business. As Peter Baskerville has observed, with colonies investing so heavily in the railways in the late 1850s, 'private and public finances were, if not indistinguishable, well on the way to being so.'[102] Confronted by massive railway debts, more-over, governments reformed, solidified, and centralized their administrative structures, placing them under expert civil servants. At the same time, they assumed considerable control over faltering railway companies and encouraged them to adopt modern, decentralized managerial strategies. The state also initiated systematic inspections and public inquiries into accidents; it demanded the publication of detailed rules and regulations; and it certified the training of supervisors.[103] This process of growing state intervention in the management of private enter-prise, theoretically abhorred by both liberal and conservative politicians, continued into the post-confederation period with the establishment of regulatory bodies and, after the First World War, with the nationalization of several bankrupt railways into a giant Crown corporation — Canadian National Railways.[104]

Simultaneously, the state increasingly used fiscal policies to direct the national economy. Ministers of finance increased customs duties to underwrite state commitments to railway construction and to protect domestic industries. But they also raised them to shield internal railways from competing American lines. This strategy, first enunciated in the Galt tariffs and fully articulated in the National Policy, became an integral part of Canada's philosophy of railways.

In the 1840s, then, British North Americans developed a comprehensive philosophy of railways, based on the perception that science and technology could help them conquer the vast wilderness in which they found themselves. For half a century they put into place the various policies that would permit them to realize their dream of a transcontinental railway. Finally accomplished in 1885, the CPR, the western segment of the transcontinental, represented the culmination of a technological nationalist vision — that of a nation tied together by bonds of steel. That belief, enunciated most strongly in the burgeoning cities of the Maritimes and the Canadas, began with the colonists relying heavily on the technological and financial wealth of Great Britain, but over the years they increasingly turned to North American resources. They drafted policies to enable them to implement their new strategy, the dream of a northern transcontinental nation. While their program implied a continental orientation, including closer economic intercourse with the United States, it also embraced strong centralist designs such as confederation and the National Policy. As an integral part of the philosophy of railways, these centralizing, nationalist approaches bestowed advantages on central Canada to the detriment of the eastern and western peripheries. The latter did not share equally in the growing prosperity of Canada and consequently expressed their alienation in regional protest movements. These remonstrations, however, were not attacks on the technology that had tied their region to the nation's heartland but opposed the policies that supported the railway. They clearly recognized that it was not the Grand Trunk, or the Intercolonial, or the Canadian Pacific Railway that determined the nature of the Canadian federation but the philosophy of railways.

NOTES

1. *Telegraph* (Saint John), 9 Jan. 1893
2. Canada, House of Commons, *Debates*, 4 May 1883
3. Pierre Berton, *The Last Spike: The Great Railway, 1881–1885* (Toronto 1971), 410–16
4. *Mail* (Toronto), 12 Jan. 1874
5. Harold A. Innis, *A History of the Canadian Pacific Railway*, foreword by Peter George (Toronto 1971); *The Fur Trade in Canada: An Introduction to Canadian Economic History* (Toronto 1962); *Essays in Canadian Economic History*, ed. Mary Q. Innis (Toronto 1956)
6. H.A. Innis, *Empire and Communications* (Toronto 1950); *The Bias of Communication* (Toronto 1951); Arthur Kroker, *Technology and the Canadian Mind: Innis/McLuhan/Grant* (Montréal 1984)
7. J.M.S. Careless, *Frontier and Metropolis: Regions, Cities, and Identities in Canada before 1914* (Toronto 1989)

8. Ibid., 74

9. Ibid., 60

10. T.D. Regehr, *The Canadian Northern Railway: Pioneer Road of the Northern Prairies, 1895–1918* (Toronto 1976)

11. G.R. Stevens, *Canadian National Railways: Towards the Inevitable, 1896–1922* (Toronto 1962), 2: 121–228

12. As noted in the previous chapter, Albert Fishlow (*American Railroads and the Transformation of the Ante-Bellum Economy* [Cambridge, Mass., 1965]), Robert William Fogel *The Union Pacific Railroad: A Case in Premature Enterprise* [Baltimore 1960] and *Railroads and American Economic Growth: Essays in Econometric History* [Baltimore 1964], and Peter George (foreword to Innis, *Canadian Pacific*) have questioned whether railways were really needed at the time for western settlement.

13. M.C. Urquhart and K.A.H. Buckley, *Historical Statistics of Canada* (Toronto 1965), 14, 351, 363–4

14. Oscar Osburn Winther, *The Transportation Frontier: Trans-Mississippi West, 1865–1890* (New York 1964), 7–11; Arthur J. Larsen, 'Early Transportation,' *Minnesota History* 14 (June 1933), 149–55

15. NAC/HBC A7/2, Simpson to Shepherd, 2 Aug. 1856

16. NAC/HBC A12/10, Simpson to Fraser, 29 June 1860; Alvin C. Gluek, *Minnesota and the Manifest Destiny of the Canadian Northwest: A Study in Canadian-American Relations* (Toronto 1965), 115–16; Theodore Barris, *Fire Canoe: Prairie Steamboat Days Revisited* (Toronto 1977), 25–30; Alvin C. Gluek, 'Minnesota Route,' *The Beaver*, Outfit 286 (Spring 1956), 44–50; A.A. den Otter, 'The Hudson's Bay Company's' Transportation Problem, 1870–85,' in John E. Foster, ed., *The Developing West: Essays on Canadian History in Honor of Lewis H. Thomas* (Edmonton 1982), 25–47.

17. NAC/HBC, A11/96, Johnson to Smith, 29 June 1857

18. Carol Judd, '"Mixt Bands of Many Nations": 1821–70,' in Carol M. Judd and Arthur J. Ray, eds, *Old Trails and New Directions: Papers of the Third North American Fur Trade Conference* (Toronto 1980)

19. Irene Spry, 'The Great Transformation: The Disappearance of the Commons in Western Canada,' in Richard Allen, ed., *Man and Nature on the Prairies* (Regina 1976), 21–45

20. Gerhard Ens, 'Dispossession or Adaptation? Migration and Persistence of the Red River Metis, 1835–1980,' Canadian Historical Association *Historical Papers*, 1988, 122

21. Irene M. Spry, 'The 'Private Adventurers" of Rupert's Land,' in John E. Foster, ed., *The Developing West: Essays on Canadian History in Honor of Lewis H. Thomas* (Edmonton 1983), 49–70

22. John L. Tobias, 'Canada's Subjection of the Plains Cree, 1879–1885' *CHR* (December 1983), 519–48

23. The historiography of the 1885 Saskatchewan rebellion is formidable and highly charged. The latest scholarly entry is the remarkably balanced but still pro-government booklet by Thomas Flanagan, *Louis Riel* (Ottawa 1992). Another excellent survey is contained in Gerald Friesen, *The Canadian Prairies: A History* (Toronto 1984), 149–56, 224–36. The classic study by George F.G. Stanley, *The Birth of Western Canada: A History of the Riel Rebellions* (Toronto 1963), still has great value because he observed that the two Metis uprisings represented a defence of a local against an invading culture. W.L. Morton's introduction to his edited version of *Alexander Begg's Red River Journal and Other Papers Relative to the Red River Resistance of 1869–1870* (Toronto 1956) provided a necessary corrective to Stanley's contention that the mixed bloods were a primitive, as opposed to a civilized, people. Bob Beal and Rod Macleod, *Prairie Fire: The 1995 North-West Rebellion* (Edmonton 1984) is still the best account of the Saskatchewan uprising.

24. Careless, *Frontier and Metropolis*, 131

25. Innis, *Fur Trade*, 397

26. T.D. Regehr, 'Western Canada and the Burden of National Transportation Policies,' in David Jay Bercuson, ed., *Canada and the Burden of Unity* (Toronto 1977), 115–17

27. Regehr, *Canadian Northern*, 20

28. A.A. den Otter, 'Bondage of Steam: The CPR and Western Canadian Coal,' in Hugh A. Dempsey, ed., *The CPR West: The Iron Road and the Making of a Nation* (Vancouver 1984), 191–208

29. Ben Forster, *A Conjunction of Interests: Business, Politics, and Tariffs, 1825–1879* (Toronto 1986), 196–7

30. Gerald Friesen, 'Imports and Exports in the Manitoba Economy, 1870–1890,' *Manitoba History* 16 (1988), 31–41

31. David Breen, 'A Peripheral Mentality: The Case of Alberta,' *Zeitschrift der Gesellschaft für Kanada-Stüdien* 9 (no. 1, vol. 15, 1989), 9–10

32. John A. Eagle, *The Canadian Pacific Railway and the Development of Western Canada, 1896–1914* (Kingston and Montréal 1989), 38–49; Regehr, *Canadian Northern*, 62–5

33. Robert Craig Brown and Ramsay Cook, *Canada 1896–1921: A Nation Transformed* (Toronto 1974), 158–63

34. David Jay Bercuson, 'Regionalism and "Unlimited Identity" in Western Canada,' *JCS* 15 (Summer 1980), 121–6

35. John Lutz, 'Losing Steam: The Boiler and Engine Industry as an Index of British Columbia's Deindustrialization, 1880–1915,' Canadian Historical Association Historical Papers, 1988, 168–208

36. Ibid., 202

37. Ibid., 201

38. James A. Ward, Railroads and the Character of America, 1820–1887 (Knoxville 1986)

39. Paul Craven and Tom Traves, 'Canadian Railways as Manufacturers, 1850–1880,' Canadian Historical Association Historical Papers, 1983, 264. For a detailed history of the Grand Trunk's Stratford shops, see Dean Robinson, Railway Stratford (Erin 1989).

40. Craven and Traves, 'Railways as Manufacturers,' 261; Paul Craven and Tom Traves, 'Dimensions of Paternalism: Discipline and Culture in Canadian Railway Operations in the 1850s,' in Craig Heron and Robert Storey, eds, On the Job: Confronting the Labour Process in Canada (Kingston and Montréal 1986), 47. Although labour played a crucial role in the construction and operation of the railway and thus contributed to its culture, workers had no voice in the creation of the philosophy of railways.

41. Craven and Traves, 'Railways as Manufacturers,' 254

42. See chapter 3, note 4, for a discussion of the historiography of underdevelopment in the Maritimes.

43. Morning Chronicle (Halifax), 14 Jan. 1865

44. Rick Szostak, The Role of Transportation in the Industrial Revolution: A Comparison of England and France (Montréal and Kingston 1991), 3

45. Ibid., 6

46. T.W. Acheson, 'The National Policy and the Industrialization of the Maritime, 1880–1910,' Acadiensis 1 (Spring 1972), 3–28; 'The Maritimes and "Empire Canada,' in Bercuson, Burden of Unity, 87–114

47. Acheson, 'Empire Canada,' 94

48. Acheson, 'National Policy,' 27

49. Ibid.; Acheson, 'Empire Canada,' 96

50. E.R. Forbes, 'The Intercolonial Railway and the Decline of the Maritime Provinces Revisited,' Acadiensis 24 (Autumn 1994), 2–26. Forbes's article is the last instalment in a running debate with Ken Cruikshank. In his latest rejoinder, Cruikshank ('With Apologies to James: A Response to E.R. Forbes,' Acadiensis 24 [Autumn 1994], 27–34) minimizes rate differentials and argues that traffic on the Intercolonial was relatively light and mainly local. In sum, Cruikshank asserts that there is insufficient data to prove that freight rates had an impact on sales of Maritime industrial goods west of Montréal.

51. Ernest R. Forbes, Aspects of Maritime Regionalism, 1867–1927 (Ottawa 1983), 13

52. Ibid., 21–2. For an elaboration of this theme, see Ernest R. Forbes, The Maritime Rights Movement, 1919–1927: A Study in Canadian Regionalism (Montréal 1979).

53. Daniel R. Headrick, The Tentacles of Progress: Technology Transfer in the Age of Imperialism, 1850–1940 (Oxford 1988)

54. David Weale and Harry Baglole, The Island and Confederation: The End of an Era (np 1973)

55. Francis W.P. Bolger, Prince Edward Island and Confederation 1863–1873 (Charlottetown 1964), 216–31, 235–42

56. Ibid., 243–80

57. Ibid., 286–8

58. Weale and Baglole, The Island and Confederation, 144

59. In the late 1840s St. John's Morning Courier ran a series of editorials that advocated that St. John's be made an entrepôt between Europe and British North America. The suggestion included a trans-island railway. See 12 June, 14 and 21 July, 14 Aug., and 1, 4, and 8 Sept. 1948. My thanks to Sean Cadigan for bringing these items to my attention. An extensive survey of Newfoundland's press during the 1850s and 1860s discovered only scant attention paid to British North America's philosophy of railways.

60. H.B. Mayo, 'Newfoundland and Confederation in the Eighteen-Sixties,' CHR 29 (June 1948), 125–42

61. James K. Hiller, The Newfoundland Railway, 1881–1949 (St John's 1981), 3–8

62. Ibid., 9–15; Harvey Mitchell, 'Canada's Negotiations with Newfoundland, 1887–1895,' CHR 40 (December 1959), 277–93

63. Hiller, Newfoundland Railway, 15–23

64. A.I. Silver, The French-Canadian Idea of Confederation 1864–1900 (Toronto 1982), 14–34

65. La Minerve (Montréal), 3 July 1880

66. Silver, French-Canadian Idea of Confederation, 48–8

67. La Minerve, 2 July 1867, considered that French Canada had attained that objective. 'Comme nationalité distincte et séparée, nous formons un état dans l'état.'

68. Le Pays (Montréal), 1 June 1869

69. Brian Young, *George Etienne Cartier: Montreal Bourgeois* (Montréal and Kingston 981)

70. *Le Courrier* (St-Hyacinthe), 14 March 1872. Copied from a *Négociant Canadien* article that forecast that the Pacific railway would unite the country.

71. Silver, *French-Canadian Idea of Confederation*, 114

72. Louis Georges Desjardins, *Discours . . . sur la résolution relative à la vente de la partie oust du chemin de fer Québec, Montréal, Ottawa et occidental* (Québec 1882), 28

73. W. Kaye Lamb, *History of the Canadian Pacific Railway* (New York 1977), 90, 101, 111, 133

74. Silver, *French-Canadian Idea of Confederation*, 115–16

75. Donald Kerr, 'Wholesale Trade on the Canadian Plains in the Late Nineteenth Century: Winnipeg and Its Competition,' in Howard Palmer, ed., *The Settlement of the West* (Calgary 1977), 130–5. Kerr estimated that before 1878, 70 per cent of goods unloaded in Winnipeg had their origin in the United States or Great Britain. See also Alan F.J. Artibise, *Winnipeg: A Social History of Urban Growth, 1874–1914* (Montréal 1975).

76. Ruben Bellan, *Winnipeg First Century: An Economic History* (Winnipeg 1978), 49–53; Eagle, *Canadian Pacific Railway*, 218–19

77. Kerr, 'Wholesale Trade,' 139–52. In 1880, Winnipeg merchants captured almost 75 per cent of the Indian department's regular treaty supplies for Treaty Four, more than 50 per cent in Treaty Six, and less than 10 per cent in Treaty Seven. Canada, Parliament, *Sessional Papers*, 1880, 4: 272–6

78. D.J. Hall, *Clifford Sifton: The Young Napoleon, 1861–1900* and *A Lonely Eminence, 1901–1929* (Vancouver 1981 and 1985), esp. 2: 221–35

79. D.J. Hall, 'Clifford Sifton: Immigration and Settlement Policy: 1896–1905,' in Palmer, *Settlement of the West*, 60–85

80. A.A. den Otter, *Irrigation in Southern Alberta, 1882–1901* (Lethbridge 1975)

81. J. Murray Beck, *Pendulum of Power: Canada's Federal Elections* (Scarborough 1968), 127–8

82. Careless, *Frontier and Metropolis*, 86–7

83. Gerald Friesen, 'The Western Canadian Identity,' Canadian Historical Association *Historical Papers*, 1973, 14

84. Paul F. Sharp, *The Agrarian Revolt in Western Canada: A Survey Showing American Parallels* (Minneapolis 1948)

85. Lewis G. Thomas, 'Associations and Communications,' Canadian Historical Association *Historical Papers*, 1973, 1–12. A more detailed explication of this theme is found in David H. Breen, *The Canadian Prairie West and the Ranching Frontier, 1874–1924* (Toronto 1983). See also Simon M. Evans, 'The Origins of Ranching in Western Canada: American Diffusion or Victorian Transplant,' in L.A. Rosenvall and S.M. Evans, eds, *Essays on the Historical Geography of the Canadian West: Regional Perspectives on the Settlement Process* (Calgary 1987), 70–94, and 'Spatial Aspects of the Cattle Kingdom: The First Decade, 1882–1892,' in Anthony W. Rasporich and Henry Klassen, eds, *Frontier Calgary, 1875–1914* (Calgary 1975), 41–56; and Sheilagh S. Jameson, 'Partners and Opponents: The CPR and the Ranching Industry of the West,' in Dempsey, *CPR West*, 71–86.

86. Macleod, *The NWMP and Law Enforcement*, 36–7, 74–88

87. A.A. den Otter, *Civilizing the West: The Galts and the Development of Western Canada* (Edmonton 1982), 161–96

88. W.A. Waiser, 'A Willing Scapegoat: John Macoun and the Route of the CPR,' *Prairie Forum* 10 (Spring 1985), 65–81; A.A. den Otter, 'Irrigation and Flood Control,' in Norman R. Ball, ed., *Building Canada: A History of Public Works* (Toronto 1988), 143–68. David C. Jones (*Empire of Dust: Settling and Abandoning the Prairie Dry Belt* [Edmonton 1987] recounts the disastrous consequences of the attempts to settle the semi-arid southern prairies.

89. *Mail*, 12 Jan. 1874

90. Headrick, *Tentacles of Progress*

91. John Gallagher and Ronald Robinson, 'The Imperialism of Free Trade,' *Economic History Review*, 2nd ser., 6, no. 1 (1953), 5

92. Ibid.

93. With steamers on the Atlantic and Pacific, the CPR provided Britain with a fast route to the Far East.

94. Gallagher and Robinson, 'Imperialism of Free Trade,' 1–15

95. Edward William Watkin, *Canada and the States: Recollections, 1851 to 1886* (London 1887), 145, 196, 232; see also chapter 18 on the Reciprocity Treaty.

96. A.W. Currie, *The Grand Trunk Railway of Canada* (Toronto 1957); Bruce Sinclair, 'Canadian Technology: British Traditions and American Influences,' *Technology and Culture* 20 (1979), 108–23

97. Currie, *Grand Trunk*, 118–21

98. Lamb, Canadian Pacific Railway, 165–75

99. William J. Wilgus, *The Railway Interrelations of the United States and Canada* (New Haven 1937), 144. Pierre Berton's monumental *The Great Railway*, which is the most extreme nationalist interpretation, does not list

Wilgus in its bibliography. Ken Cruikshank ('Managing a Fragile North American Industry: The Canadian Railway Problem Revisited,' paper, Second Business History Conference, Victoria, 1988) used Wilgus as a springboard to examine the operations of Canadian railways in their continental setting.

100. Montana Historical Society, Power Papers, vol. 13A, file 8, J. Rattray & Co. to Power, 26 Sept. 1879; vol. 4, file 2, invoices, 29 July, 3 Sept. 1880; vol. 155, file 73, invoice, 3 June 1882; vol. 120, file 6, Kavanagh Brothers to Power, 1 Feb., 11 April 1885

101. HBC/PAM, A12/27, Grahame to Wrigley, 2 May 1884, fol. 134, 22 July 1884, fol. 241; A12/27, Wrigley to Armit, 6 July 1884, fol. 376. A.A. den Otter, 'Transportation and Transformation: The Hudson's Bay Company, 1857–1885,' *Great Plains Quarterly* 3 (Summer 1983), 171–85; Arthur J. Ray, *The Canadian Fur Trade in the Industrial Age* (Toronto 1990)

102. Peter Baskerville, 'Railways in Upper Canada/Ontario: The State, Entrepreneurship and the Transition from a Commercial to an Industrial Economy,' *Zeitschrift der Gesellschaft für Kanada-Stüdien* 7m (1987), 25

103. Peter Baskerville, 'Transportation, Social Change, and State Formation, Upper Canada, 1841–1864,' in Allen Greer and Ian Radforth, eds, *Colonial Leviathan: State Formation in Mid-Nineteenth-Century Canada* (Toronto 1992), 230–56

104. Ken Cruikshank, *Close Ties: Railways, Government, and the Board of Railway Commissioners, 1851–1933* (Montréal and Kingston 1991); John A. Eagle, 'Sir Robert Borden, Union Government and Railway Nationalization,' *JCS* 10, no. 4 (1975), 59–66

Topic Two

Regional and National Conflict in the Late 19th Century

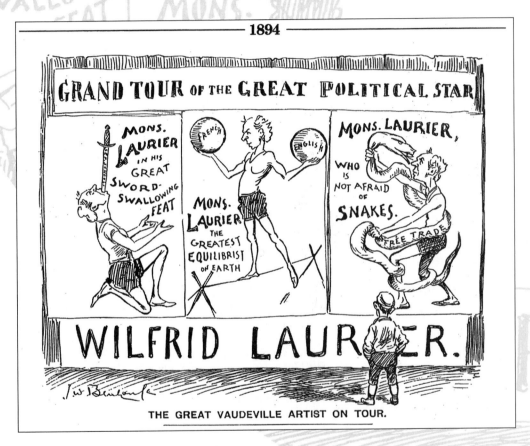

This 1894 political cartoon by J. W. Bengough demonstrates the issues that Wilfrid Laurier had to address on his way to becoming prime minister in 1896. The sword Laurier is swallowing is labelled as "Sep. Schools," the weights he is balancing are labelled "French" and "English," and he is wrestling with a snake named "free trade."

Two contentious issues dominated the late 19th century in Canada: provincial rights and English–French relations. Politically, provincial governments questioned and attacked John A. Macdonald's version of a strong central government and weak provincial governments. Culturally, a militant English-Canadian nationalism clashed with an equally powerful French-Canadian nationalism, mainly over language rights and separate schools for French-speaking Canadians outside the province of Quebec.

English-Canadian historians writing within the National School of Canadian historiography looked upon the provincial rights movement as an aberration, the result of contentious, partisan provincial premiers intent on undermining the vision of a strong federal government put forward by the Fathers of Confederation in the British North America (BNA) Act. Beginning in the 1960s, however, revisionist historians and political scientists have questioned this interpretation. Rather than denounce and underplay the provincial rights movement, they have attempted to understand its success and to judge its impact on Canada's political evolution. Political scientist Peter H. Russell explains why the provincial rights movement arose first in Ontario in terms of the pattern of Canadian politics and the nature of the Canadian system of parliamentary government. The Ontario government's success at challenging the federal government's view of the role of the provincial lieutenant governor and on the federal power of reservation and disallowance of provincial legislation, through the Judicial Committee of the Privy Council, the highest court in the British Empire, resulted in a new form of Dominion–provincial relations, what political scientists refer to as "classical federalism." The belief that Confederation was a compact entered into by sovereign provincial communities that retained the right to alter the terms of the original union reinforced this new perspective at the time. As well, an alternative compact theory emerged in the late 19th and early 20th centuries. It maintained that Confederation owed its origins to a moral compact between the two founding peoples, the French Canadians and English Canadians. These differing perspectives, Russell points out, reflected different visions of Canada in the late 19th century. He argues that they have had as much impact on Canada's political evolution as the contrary vision of Confederation, which contends that the original agreement favoured a strong central government and weak provincial governments.

Tension between French-speaking and English-speaking Canadians continued after Confederation. But both sides appeared to set aside their difference in a *modus vivendi* in order to bring about Confederation in 1867. The Confederation agreement apparently assumed that the "new nationality" that underlay the new nation of Canada was a political nationalism only, based on political union, and not a cultural nationalism based on cultural conformity. According to historian J. R. Miller, the concept of "unity in diversity" best captured this idea. Miller goes on to point out, however, that "three corrosive influences" in the 1880s undermined this vision: political opportunism, economic stagnation, and new racial theories. It resulted in a shift in perspective from "unity in diversity" to "diversity into unity."

What were the factors that contributed to the rise of the provincial rights movement and the rise of cultural nationalism in the late 19th century? In what ways do the views of the provincial rightists and those of the cultural nationalists complement and/or contradict one another? How did the ideas of the provincial rightists and those of the cultural nationalists have an impact on specific political and cultural events in the late 19th century?

For a good overview of Dominion–provincial relations, see Peter H. Russell, *Constitutional Odyssey: Can Canadians Become a Sovereign People?* (Toronto: University of Toronto Press, 1993). For an overview of Dominion–provincial relations in the late 19th century, see P.B. Waite, *Canada, 1874–1896: Arduous Destiny* (Toronto: McClelland & Stewart, 1971).

On the provincial-rights movement in Ontario, see Margaret Evans's biography, *Sir Oliver Mowat* (Toronto: University of Toronto Press, 1992); J.C. Morrison, "Oliver Mowat and the Development of Provincial Rights in Ontario: A Study in Dominion–Provincial Relations, 1867–1896," in *Three History Theses* (Toronto: Ontario Department of Public Records and Archives, 1961); and Garth Stevenson, *Ex Uno Plures: Federal–Provincial Relations in Canada, 1867–1896* (Montreal/Kingston: McGill-Queen's University Press, 1993). Christopher Armstrong discusses the evolution of relations between Ontario and the federal government in *The Politics of Federalism: Ontario's Relations with the Federal Government, 1867–1942* (Toronto: University of Toronto Press, 1981). See as well Paul Romney, *Getting It Wrong: How Canadians Forgot Their Past and Imperilled Confederation* (Toronto: University of Toronto Press, 1999).

The literature on the question of Canadian duality is extensive. Perhaps the most complete overview of relations between French and English Canadians in the late 19th century is to be found in Volume 1 of Mason Wade's *The French Canadians*, 2 vols. (Toronto: Macmillan, 1977). A short, lively summary of the issue is presented in Susan Mann's *The Dream of Nation: A Social and Intellectual History of Quebec* (Montreal/Kingston: McGill-Queen's University Press, 2002 [1983]), and a more detailed account can be found in P.B. Waite's *Canada, 1874–1896: Arduous Destiny* (cited above). The rise of a militant Anglo-Canadian Protestant movement agitating to make Canada a unilingual country, and the French Canadian response to it, is described in J.R. Miller, *Equal Rights: The Jesuits' Estate Act Controversy* (Montreal/ Kingston: McGill-Queen's University Press, 1979). Miller reviews the ideas and the activities of D'Alton McCarthy, regarded as the leading advocate for the assimilation of the French Canadians, in "D'Alton McCarthy, Equal Rights, and the Origins of the Manitoba School Question," *Canadian Historical Review* 54 (December 1973): 369–392, and "'As a Politician He Is a Great Enigma': The Social and Political Ideas of D'Alton McCarthy," *Canadian Historical Review* 58 (December 1977): 399–422. The French Canadians' changing attitude toward Confederation is explored by A.I. Silver in *The French-Canadian Idea of Confederation, 1864–1900*, 2nd ed. (Toronto: University of Toronto Press, 1997). Ramsay Cook reviews the idea of Confederation as a compact of provinces or cultures in *Provincial Autonomy: Minority Rights and the Compact Theory, 1867–1921* (Ottawa: Queen's Printer, 1969). Ronald Rudin's *The Forgotten Quebecers* (Québec: Institut québécois de recherche sur la culture, 1985) provides a history of the English-speaking population of Quebec from 1759 to 1980.

WEBLINKS

Encyclical of Pope Leo XIII
http://www.avalon.nf.ca/rcadln/leo13.htm
Pope Leo XIII's 1897 encyclical regarding the Manitoba Schools Question.

1872 Immigration Handbook for Ontario
http://www.dcs.uwaterloo.ca/~marj/genealogy/emont1872.html
A handbook published in 1872 to encourage immigrants to choose Ontario as their destination.

Territorial Evolution of Canada
http://atlas.gc.ca/site/english/maps/historical/territorialevolution
A collection of maps of Canada provided by the Atlas of Canada, detailing the changes in Canada's territorial makeup from Confederation to the present.

Manitoba Act, 1870
http://www.solon.org/Constitutions/Canada/English/ma_1870.html
The complete text of the Manitoba Act of 1870. Manitoba was brought into Confederation as the first new province through this Act.

Judicial Committee of the Privy Council
http://www.canadiana.org/citm/specifique/jcpc_e.html
A history of the British Judicial Committee of the Privy Council, and an examination of its role in Canadian law and the Canadian Constitution.

Article Four

Provincial Rights

Peter H. Russell

The great conceit of constitution makers is to believe that the words they put in the constitution can with certainty and precision control a country's future. The great conceit of those who apply a written constitution is to believe that their interpretation captures perfectly the founders' intentions. Those who write constitutions are rarely single-minded in their long-term aspirations. They harbour conflicting hopes and fears about the constitution's evolution. The language of the constitution is inescapably general and latent with ambiguous possibilities. Written constitutions can establish the broad grooves in which a nation-state develops. But what happens within those grooves — the constitutional tilt favoured by history — is determined not by the constitutional text but by the political forces and events that shape the country's subsequent history.

Canada's constitutional development in the decades immediately following Confederation is a monument to the truth of these propositions. Although a majority of the Fathers of Confederation favoured a highly centralized federation, it soon became apparent that their aspirations would not be fulfilled. Instead, the most effective constitutional force in the new federation was the provincial rights movement. Far from moving toward a unitary state, Canada, by the end of the nineteenth century, had become a thoroughly federal country.

One might have expected the stiffest challenge to Macdonald's centralism to have come from Nova Scotia or Quebec. Nova Scotians voted against Confederation in the provincial and federal elections of 1867. Immediately following Confederation a significant secessionist movement was developing in the province.[1] In 1868 Joseph Howe led a delegation to London seeking a repeal of the union. Nova Scotian opposition to Confederation, however, was not based on a desire for stronger provincial powers. In the end, Nova Scotian separatism was quelled by persuading Howe to join the federal cabinet and by offering Nova Scotia better terms, not through a constitutional amendment but by bringing its debt allowance into line with New Brunswick's.

From the very beginning, the province of Quebec, in the words of A.I. Silver, "was seen as the geographical and political expression of the French-Canadian homeland."[2] It was not just

Source: Peter H. Russell, "Provincial Rights" from *Constitutional Odyssey: Can Canadians Become a Sovereign People?* Peter H. Russell (University of Toronto Press, 1993). University of Toronto Press Incorporated 1993. Reprinted by permission of the publisher.

the *rouge* opponents of Confederation who championed the cause of provincial autonomy and resisted federal interference in provincial affairs. The *Bleus* had promoted Confederation in Quebec largely on the grounds that it would give the French majority in Quebec exclusive control over matters basic to their culture. A *bleu* paper in 1872, for example, claimed that "as Conservatives we must be in favour of provincial rights and against centralization."[3]

It was not Quebec but Ontario that spearheaded the provincial rights movement. Ontario would seem the least likely province to play this role. After all, support for Confederation had been stronger in Ontario than in any other province. With the largest and fastest-growing population, Ontario was expected to be able to dominate national politics. Why at this formative stage in the federation's history should its provincial government be in the vanguard of the provincial rights movement?

The answer is to be found in the pattern of partisan politics that developed soon after Confederation and has endured ever since. Even before Confederation, the Great Coalition of Conservatives and Reformers had broken up. The first federal government after Confederation was headed by the Conservative leader John A. Macdonald. As Ontario Reformers and Quebec Liberals began to organize a competing national party, they naturally took up the provincial cause. In the words of Christopher Armstrong, "If Macdonald's Conservatives were the party of centralism, then its opponents would become the party of localism and provincialism, recruiting the anti-Confederates of the Maritimes to the Reform cause."[4]

The Conservatives dominated the first 30 years of federal politics, holding office in Ottawa for all but four of those years. During that same period the Liberals were having their greatest success at the provincial level. Nowhere was this more true than in Ontario, where Oliver Mowat's Liberals won six successive elections between 1875 and 1896. While Mowat found Liberal allies in other provincial capitals, notably Quebec's Honoré Mercier, he was in office the longest and built the strongest record of provincial rights advocacy. Mowat's championing of this cause is remarkable in that he began his professional career as a junior in John A. Macdonald's law office, was a Father of Confederation, and had moved the Quebec Resolutions setting forth the division of powers between the two levels of government.[5]

The pattern of politics in which one party dominates at the federal level while its main opposition gathers strength in the provincial capitals has been repeated several times in Canadian history. For a long stretch of the twentieth century the Liberals dominated the federal scene while the Conservatives and other opposition parties won in the provinces. The reverse has been developing since the Mulroney Conservatives came to power in Ottawa in 1984. The fact that the largest national parties have gone through long periods in which their experience in government has been concentrated at the provincial level has done much to make provincial rights a cause that transcends partisan politics.

Although this phenomenon is one that stems from the fluctuating fortunes of partisan politics, it is closely tied to the Canadian system of parliamentary government. Responsible government tends to concentrate power in the hands of the prime minister and the Cabinet. After Confederation it soon became apparent that this concentration of power would occur in the provincial capitals as well as in Ottawa. In Canada, provincial premiers emerged as the strongest political opponents to the federal prime minister. State governors in the United States, hemmed in by an elaborate system of checks and balances, are political pygmies compared with provincial premiers who perform as political giants on the national stage. Canadians, without any conscious design, found their liberal check and balance not *within* the national or provincial capitals but in the rivalry and tensions *between* those capitals.

The success of the provincial rights movement cannot be attributed to weak governments at the national level in Canada's formative years. Quite to the contrary, federal administrations presided over by John A. Macdonald, who was prime minister of Canada for nineteen of the country's first 24 years, were strong nation-building governments not at all shy about asserting federal power. Under Macdonald's leadership, Canada's "manifest destiny" of becoming a continental nation-state was quickly fulfilled. In 1869 the Hudson's Bay Company's territories covering the prairies and the far north were purchased and added to Canada. A year later, following military suppression of the Métis led by Louis Riel, the Province of Manitoba was carved out of the Northwest Territories. In 1871 Canada was extended to the Pacific, when British Columbia became a province on terms agreeable to its colonial government. Prince Edward Island became the seventh province, agreeing to join Confederation in 1873. To this expanding national territory Macdonald's Conservatives applied a National Policy, completing the transcontinental rail link, erecting tariff walls to protect manufacturing, and stimulating immigration to populate the west and provide a market for the protected industries.[6]

Important as the achievements of Macdonald's governments were in building the material conditions of nationhood, they contributed little to a Canadian sense of political community. Nor did they translate into constitutional gains for the federal government. The Conservatives' economic nationalism, as Reg Whitaker has observed, relied "on elites and on their exclusively economic motives."[7] It did not have much emotional appeal at the mass level. Government in far-away Ottawa had difficulty competing with provincial governments for the allegiance of citizens in the new provinces. During these years it was the provinces, not Ottawa, that seized and held the initiative in constitutional politics.

The first objective of the provincial rights movement was to resist and overcome a hierarchical version of Canadian federalism in which the provinces were to be treated as a subordinate or junior level of government. An early focal point of resistance was the office of provincial lieutenant-governor. From a Macdonald centralist perspective, the lieutenant-governors were essentially agents of the federal government in provincial capitals. In the 1870s, however, Ontario, under Mowat's leadership, began to insist that lieutenant-governors had full Crown powers in matters of provincial jurisdiction and that they exercised these powers on the advice of provincial ministers. Not surprisingly, the issue first arose over a question of patronage — the power to make lawyers queen's counsels.[8] Implicit in the provincial claim was an assertion of the provinces' constitutional equality with the federal government.

No element of the Constitution was potentially more threatening to provincial autonomy than the federal powers of reservation and disallowance. These powers derived from an imperial rather than a federal structure. Under the reservation power, the lieutenant-governor of a province could refuse to sign a bill that had passed through the provincial legislature and could reserve it for consideration by the federal Cabinet. If, within a year, the lieutenant-governor was not instructed to give royal assent, the bill would die. Disallowance was simply a veto power under which the federal government could render null and void any provincial law within a year of its passage by the provincial legislature. These federal powers mirrored powers of reservation and disallowance over federal legislation that the imperial government retained and that were also written into the BNA Act.[9] The only difference was that the British government had two years rather than one to decide whether to block Canadian legislation.

The powers of reservation and disallowance are classic examples of how a shift in political sentiment and principle can render formal legal powers unusable. Well before Confederation, the British government had greatly reduced the use of its imperial powers of control over the British North American legislatures. Soon after Confederation these powers fell into desuetude. In the first decade a few Canadian bills were reserved, but royal assent was always granted and there were no reservations after 1878. Only one Canadian act was disallowed, in 1873, and the act in question was clearly unconstitutional.[10] At imperial conferences in the late 1920s declarations were made that these imperial powers would never be used and that steps would be taken to remove them from Canada's Constitution. Although the latter step was never taken, no one really cares that the powers remain formally in the Constitution because there is a clear political understanding — a constitutional convention — on both the British and Canadian sides that the powers are completely inoperative.[11] This convention of desuetude was established because use of the imperial powers was incompatible with the principle of Canadian self-government, a principle which, at least in matters of domestic policy, was so firmly in place by the 1870s that breach of it would have had the gravest political consequences.

A similar process occurred with respect to the federal government's powers of reservation and disallowance. Over time, the principle of provincial autonomy — self-government in those areas constitutionally assigned to the provincial legislatures — became so strongly held in the Canadian political system that the federal powers of reservation and disallowance, though remaining in the Constitution, became politically unusable. This did not happen all at once. It occurred only because the idea that the provinces are not subordinate to but coordinate with the federal government became the politically dominant conception of Canadian federalism.

At first federal governments — not only Macdonald's but the Liberals too when they were in power in the 1870s — made extensive use of the powers of reservation and disallowance.[12] Macdonald's first administration withheld assent on 16 of 24 provincial bills reserved by lieutenant-governors. Between 1867 and 1896, 65 provincial acts were disallowed by the federal government. Although the powers continued to be used, they came under increasing attack from the provinces, and from no province more than Ontario. Even when, as was most often the case, the rationale for using these powers was the federal government's view that the legislation was outside the province's jurisdiction, provincial rights advocates were inclined to argue that questions concerning the division of powers should be settled in the courts, not by the federal cabinet. When the Macdonald government in 1881 disallowed Ontario's Rivers and Streams Act primarily to protect the interests of a prominent Conservative, Mowat decided to fight back. He promptly had the legislation reenacted. After being disallowed and reenacted three more times, the legislation was allowed to stand. The courts had the final say when the Judicial Committee of the Privy Council upheld the provincial law in 1884.[13]

Abolition of the federal disallowance power topped the list of constitutional proposals emanating from the Interprovincial Conference in 1887. The conference was called by Honoré Mercier, premier of Quebec, who had come to power largely on the strength of Quebec's resentment of the use of federal power in the hanging of Louis Riel. Macdonald and the Conservative premiers of British Columbia and Prince Edward Island declined Mercier's invitation. Delegates from the Liberal governments of the four original provinces and from Manitoba's Conservative administration, "angered by repeated disallowances of their railway legislation,"[14] met for a week under Mowat's chairmanship behind closed doors. The 22 resolutions that they unanimously endorsed amounted to a frontal attack on the centralist conception of Confederation. Besides calling for the abolition of federal disallowance and an increase in federal subsidies, the conference proposed that half of the federal Senate be chosen by the provinces. Once these proposals had been approved by the provincial legislatures, they were to be submitted to London for enactment as constitutional amendments by the imperial Parliament.

In the end, nothing concrete came of these proposals. Only the lower houses of New Brunswick and Nova Scotia sent them on to London. The imperial authorities refused to act without having heard from the federal government or the other provinces.[15] Nonetheless, the 1887 conference is a significant landmark in Canada's constitutional politics, for it clearly demonstrated that the constitutional initiative had passed to the provinces. Strong centralist voices could still be heard, not least John A. Macdonald's, but the centralist view was losing its ascendancy in both French and English Canada.

During the first 30 years of Confederation, the provinces made their most tangible constitutional gains not through the process of formal constitutional amendment but through litigation in the courts. Their judicial victories were achieved in London before the Judicial Committee of the Privy Council. The Supreme Court of Canada had been created by the federal Parliament in 1875, but it was supreme in name only. Although the Liberal government which had sponsored the Supreme Court Act aimed at making the court Canada's highest tribunal, the Conservative opposition and the Colonial Office were able to thwart this objective.[16] The right of appeal to the highest court in the British Empire, the Judicial Committee of the Privy Council, was retained in Canada until 1949.

Retaining the Judicial Committee as Canada's highest court had significant consequences for the development of the Canadian Constitution. In the 1870s when the practice of bringing constitutional challenges against legislation in the courts was just beginning, the newly created Supreme Court of Canada decided a few cases very much in the federal government's favour. In *Severn v. The Queen*, decided in 1878, the Supreme Court found an Ontario law licensing brewers unconstitutional or *ultra vires*, outside the powers of the provincial legislature.[17] The Supreme Court judges gave the widest possible interpretation of the federal Parliament's exclusive power to make laws in relation to "the Regulation of Trade and Commerce," and supported this judgement by arguing that the Constitution's framers wished to avoid the "evils" of states rights that had plagued the American federation. A year later in *Lenoir v. Ritchie*, the Supreme Court firmly rejected provincial pretensions to Crown prerogative by denying provincial governments the power to appoint queen's counsel.[18]

It did not take long for the English law lords who manned the Judicial Committee of the Privy Council to reverse the Supreme Court's approach to the Constitution. By the 1880s a steady stream of constitutional cases was being taken on appeal to London. The fact that so many constitutional questions were coming before the courts gives the lie to the pretension of the Fathers of Confederation to have settled all questions of jurisdiction.

One of the Judicial Committee's earliest decision, *Citizens Insurance Co. v. Parsons*,[19] is a good example of the kind of issue that arose and the kind of outcome that obtained in the Judicial Committee. Section 91(2) of the BNA Act gave the federal Parliament exclusive jurisdiction over "the Regulation of Trade and Commerce." Section 92(13) gave the provincial legislatures exclusive jurisdiction over "Property and Civil Rights in the Province." At issue in the *Parsons* case was whether an Ontario statute regulating fire insurance contracts was within provincial powers. Such a law would seem clearly to be a regulation of trade and commerce and a regulation affecting property and civil rights in Ontario. Under which power did the Ontario legislation fall? The Judicial Committee reasoned that unless some limits were attached to trade and commerce and to property and civil rights, such broadly phrased powers would contradict each other. In this case they chose to put limits on the federal trade and commerce power, ruling that it applied to interprovincial and international commerce and to trade "affecting the whole Dominion," but not to the regulation of an industry within a province. Thus the Ontario act was upheld as a law relating to property and civil rights.

Between 1880 and 1896 the Judicial Committee decided eighteen cases involving twenty issues relating to the division of powers. Fifteen of these issues (75 percent) it decided in favour of the provinces. What is even more important, as Murray Greenwood has observed, is that in these decisions the committee reversed "every major centralist doctrine of the [Supreme] Court."[20] No area of policymaking was as hotly contested as the consumption of alcohol. At first, the Judicial Committee appeared to favour federal power by upholding the Canada Temperance Act, a federal law providing a nationwide system whereby towns and cities could opt for local prohibition.[21] However, in subsequent decisions it ruled that only the provinces could provide for the licensing of taverns and retail liquor outlets in areas that did not opt for prohibition.[22] Finally, in 1896, the Judicial Committee upheld an Ontario local prohibition scheme. It was in this case that the imperial court called for a restrained interpretation of the federal Parliament's general or residual power to make laws for the "Peace, Order, and good Government of Canada." That power should be confined "to such matters as are unquestionably of Canadian interest and importance," and must not encroach on any of the subjects assigned exclusively to the provinces. "To attach any other construction of the general power which, in supplement of its enumerated powers, is conferred upon the Parliament of Canada, would," wrote Lord Watson, "not only be contrary to the intendment of the Act, but would practically destroy the autonomy of the provinces."[23]

The Judicial Committee went beyond the details of the division of powers to articulate a conception of federalism which would have been anathema to John A. Macdonald. The key judgement came in 1892 in the *Maritime Bank* case and involved that touchiest of constitutional questions — sovereign Crown powers.[24] At issue was New Brunswick's use of the Crown's prerogative to claim priority over other creditors seeking to recover funds from the liquidators of an insolvent bank. In upholding the province's right to use this power, Lord Watson set down the following thesis about the purpose of the BNA Act:

> The object of the Act was neither to weld the provinces into one, nor to subordinate provincial governments to a central authority, but to create a federal government in which they should all be represented, entrusted with the exclusive administration of affairs in which they had a common interest, each province retaining its independence and autonomy.

So much for John A. Macdonald's view that "the true principle of a Confederation lay in giving to the General Government all the principles and powers of sovereignty."[25] For the tribunal which had the final say in interpreting the Canadian Constitution, the provinces were not a subordinate level of government. The federal and provincial governments were coordinate levels of government, each autonomous within the spheres allotted to them by the Constitution.

The theory espoused by the Judicial Committee of the Privy Council is often called the theory of "classical federalism."[26] There can be no doubt that Macdonald and many of Canada's constitutional founders did not think of the country they were building as a classic federation. Some of the Fathers of Confederation, however, especially Quebec leaders like Cartier and Taché, were apprehensive of the centralist view and hoped that the provinces would be autonomous in the areas of law making reserved for them. The Quebec supporters of Confederation realized they could not retain their political support if they portrayed Confederation publicly in centralist terms. The political coalition that put Confederation together never came to a clear and explicit accord on federal theory.[27] What the Judicial Committee did was to give official legal sanction to a theory of federalism congenial to those who, at the time of Confederation and afterwards, could not accept centralism.

The impact of the Judicial Committee's constitutional decisions demonstrates a fundamental feature of constitutional development which is still, at most, only dimly understood by the Canadian public. In countries with written constitutions stipulating the powers of government and the rights of citizens, and in which the constitution is taken seriously, judges will play an important role in enforcing the constitution. The process through which judges play that role is called "judicial review." In performing the function of judicial review, judges review the acts of the executive and legislature and rule null and void those that do not conform with the constitution. Through these determinations, especially those of the highest court, the meaning of the constitution's general terms is fleshed out. This process of judicial review has been so important in the United States that it is said that "the constitution is what the judges say it is."[28]

The Fathers of Confederation did not discuss judicial review. Although some of them were aware of the important role the Supreme Court was playing in the United States, they did not see that there would be an immediate need for a Canadian Supreme Court.[29] Their constitutionalism was much more British than American, and hence more attuned to an unwritten constitution. They were accustomed to having the Judicial Committee of the Privy Council, as the highest imperial court, review colonial laws for their conformity with imperial law. Since the Canadian Constitution took the form of an act of the imperial Parliament, it was logical that this mechanism of imperial judicial control would apply to the BNA Act. For enforcing the rules of federalism internally, within Canada, it is evident that the Fathers of Confederation looked more to the federal executive using its powers of reservation and disallowance than to the judiciary. Also, it was to the federal executive, not the judiciary, that the BNA Act directed minorities to appeal if they believed a province had infringed their constitutional right to denominational schools.[30]

Federal government enforcement of the Constitution made sense, of course, so long as Canadian federalism was viewed primarily as a hierarchical, quasi-imperial structure in which the provinces were a junior level of government. From this perspective, the objective of constitutional enforcement was to keep the provinces from exceeding their powers. John A. Macdonald never contemplated that Canadian courts would find federal laws unconstitutional.[31] Once, however, the hierarchical view of federalism began to be eclipsed by the theory of classical federalism and dual sovereignty, it was much more logical for a judicial tribunal independent of both levels of government to exercise the primary responsibility for applying the Constitution.

Judicial review in Canada could not be justified in the same way as it was in the United States. There it was possible to justify judicial review on the grounds that in vetoing laws passed by popular majorities, the judiciary was giving effect to the enduring will of the American people as expressed in the Constitution.[32] Given the imperial and undemocratic foundations of the Canadian Constitution, this justification could hardly be advanced in Canada. Nonetheless, the Judicial Committee's constitutional interpretation could not have made the impact it did had it not coincided with powerful political forces in Canada. By the late nineteenth century, Canada had moved too far away from colonialism toward self-government to have complied with the rulings of an imperial tribunal that were out of line with political opinion in the country. The federal election of 1896 demonstrated that in Canada's national politics, the tide was running in favour of provincial rights and a balanced view of Canadian federalism.

The 1896 election was won by the Liberals led by Wilfrid Laurier. The Liberals and Laurier were to remain in power for the next fifteen years. Laurier's political success stemmed in part from his championing of provincial rights. This support occurred in a most ironic setting — the Manitoba Schools crisis.[33] In the 1896 election, Laurier, a French Catholic from Quebec, opposed the Conservative government's threat to force Manitoba to restore the denominational schools of that province's Roman Catholic minority.

In 1890, Manitoba, which by that time had developed into a largely English Protestant province, passed legislation reducing the rights of the French Catholic minority.[34] One law made English Manitoba's official language, ignoring the clause in Manitoba's terms of union guaranteeing the use of English and French in the province's courts and legislature.[35] Nearly a century would pass before this statute would be effectively challenged in the courts.[36] The other statute replaced a dual system of Roman Catholic and Protestant schools in existence since 1871 with a system of secular public schools to be supported by all taxpayers, including parents of children attending the Roman Catholic schools. This legislation was immediately challenged on the grounds that it violated another clause in Manitoba's terms of union guaranteeing denominational school rights held "by law or practice" at the time of union.[37] Although the challenge was initially successful in the Supreme Court of Canada, it failed in the Judicial Committee of the Privy Council.[38] Nevertheless, in a subsequent decision, the Judicial Committee ruled that Manitoba's Catholics could, under another section of the constitutional guarantee, appeal to the federal cabinet to introduce remedial legislation forcing Manitoba to restore their school rights.[39] A few months before the 1896 election, the Conservatives, now led by Charles Tupper, agreed to submit a remedial bill to Parliament. This was the bill that Laurier successfully opposed in the ensuing election campaign.

It was not the substance of that bill which Laurier and the Liberals opposed. They were strongly committed to the restoration of Catholic school rights in Manitoba. In national politics the Laurier Liberals provided the main resistance to a growing movement within English Canada led by D'Alton McCarthy, president of the Ontario Conservative Association, calling for a Canada free of papism and rejecting "the *nationaliste* thesis that the French were a permanent and equal element in Canada."[40] Still, Laurier, who drew his strongest political support from Quebec, remained as committed to provincial rights as to minority cultural rights. Instead of federal coercion of a province, Laurier proposed the "sunnier ways" of negotiating an accommodation with the provincial government. In the end, it was Laurier's "sunnier ways" and his respect for provincial rights that prevailed politically.[41]

The success of the provincial rights movement did not mean that in terms either of governmental power or of citizens' allegiance the provincial political realm had come to surpass the federal. Laurier, after all, was a national leader whose government would pursue important initiatives in domestic and international politics. Indeed, Laurier and other Quebec leaders, by supporting the rights of French Catholics outside Quebec, were encouraging Quebeckers, in the words of A.I. Silver, to look beyond "the still-special home of Quebec" and see that "all Canada should yet be a country for French-Canadians."[42] Since the 1890s there have been shifts back and forth in the balance of power between the two levels of government, but there has always been a balance; neither level has been able to dominate the other. Canada's citizens have been thoroughly schizophrenic in their loyalties, maintaining strong associations with their provincial governments as well as the federal government. In this sense Canada, despite the ambiguities and contradictions in its Constitution, became, as Donald Smiley put it, "in the most elemental way a federal country."[43]

One measure of how ingrained the balanced view of federalism has become is the fate of those imperial powers of reservation and disallowance which the federal government held over the provinces. They are still in the Constitution, but they are simply not used any more. Disallowance has not been used since 1943. The last time a lieutenant-governor reserved a provincial bill was 1961, and then his action was totally repudiated by the federal prime minister, John Diefenbaker, as violating the basic principles of Canadian federalism.[44] When the Parti Québecois came to power in Quebec in the 1970s and enacted Bill 101, the Charter of the French Language, the Trudeau government in Ottawa, which bitterly opposed this legislation, did not ever indicate that it would disallow it. And again in 1988, when Quebec adopted Bill 178 to overcome a Supreme Court ruling and restore a unilingual French sign policy, although Prime Minister Mulroney and opinion leaders throughout English Canada denounced the legislation, neither government nor opposition leaders called for disallowance of the legislation. By the 1980s political parties and leaders of all persuasions, like Laurier and the Liberals a century earlier, would not protect minority rights at the cost of violating provincial rights.

The sovereignty at issue in the struggle for provincial rights was not the sovereignty of the people but the sovereignty of governments and legislatures. The sovereignty claimed and won for provincial legislatures and governments within their allotted sphere of jurisdiction was primarily a top-down kind of sovereignty.[45] Canadian constitutional politics continued to be highly elitist, with federal and provincial leaders contending against each other in intergovernmental meetings and the courts. Still, traces of a more democratic constitutionalism were beginning to appear in the rhetoric, if not the reality, of the constitutional process.

Robert Vipond has shown how exponents of provincial rights defended the sovereignty of provincial "parliaments" against federal intrusions by emphasizing the right to self-government of local electorates. Provincial leaders attacking federal intervention in provincial affairs appealed to the same principles of self-government as earlier colonial politicians had invoked in objecting to imperial intervention in internal colonial affairs. The exercise of the federal powers of disallowance and reservation was portrayed as "autocratic and tyrannical" whereas, according to Liberal leader Edward Blake, to support provincial autonomy was to sustain "the educating and glorious attributes which belong to self-government, to a government of the people, by the people, for the people."[46] Although the provincial leaders were still too British, too wedded to the notion of parliamentary sovereignty, to talk about the people as sovereign in the constituent American sense, they were edging closer to this conception of popular sovereignty when they referred to the rights of provincial legislatures as powers entrusted to them by the people.[47]

Out of this rhetoric and the political success of its authors was born the myth of Confederation as a compact entered into by sovereign provincial communities. According to the compact theory, the provinces as the founding, constituent units of the federation retained the right to alter the terms of their original union.[48] This was the theory promulgated by Honoré Mercier and the other provincial premiers who attended the 1887 Interprovincial Conference: "the conference represented all of the original parties to the compact of 1864, and the partners should now assess the state of their joint enterprise."[49] Not surprisingly, the theory found its most articulate spokesmen in Quebec, where the notion of the province as a founding community could be infused with a sense of ethnic nationalism.

What is meant in referring to the compact theory as a "myth" is that its validity depends not on its historical accuracy but on its capacity to serve as a set of "beliefs and notions that men hold, that they live by or live for."[50] Confederation, as we have seen, did involve a two-stage agreement, first between English- and French-Canadian politicians and then between Canadian and Maritime politicians. Leading participants in the agreement, including John A. Macdonald and George-Étienne Cartier, as well as some of the imperial authorities, frequently referred to the Quebec Resolutions as a treaty or pact. But it is not clear that when they used this terminology they had the same thing in mind. It is most unlikely that when John A. Macdonald talked of a treaty he meant that the parties to the agreement exercised and retained sovereign political authority.

From a strictly legal point of view, the founding colonies in 1867, as colonies, did not have sovereign powers to retain. They did not formally sign or give legal authority to the Constitution. Further, given the elitist quality of the process and the failure, indeed the disinclination, to seek a clear popular mandate for the Confederation deal, it is a total fabrication to maintain that the peoples of the founding provinces had covenanted together to produce the Canadian federal union. This fabrication flies in the face of the top-down process whereby new provinces were added — especially the two provinces carved out of the Northwest Territories in 1905. As Arthur Lower observed, "there was not the slightest vestige of a 'compact' in the Acts of Parliament that created the provinces of Alberta and Saskatchewan in 1905."[51]

Nor was the compact theory strictly followed in constitutional practice. If the Canadian Constitution was a compact or treaty among the provinces, then no changes should have been made to it without the consent of all the provinces. Formally constitutional changes, as amendments to the BNA Act, were enacted by the British Parliament, but that body would act only on a request from Canada. During the period that the compact theory was gathering force, however, several amendments were made to the BNA Act at the request of the federal government and Parliament without consulting the provinces or seeking their consent. While none of these amendments directly affected the powers of the provinces, two of them related to the structure of the federation: one empowered the federal Parliament to create new provinces and the other provided for the representation of territories in the federal Parliament.[52] Prior to the 1907 amendment,[53] which revised the subsidies paid to the provinces, Laurier did hold a federal–provincial conference and eight of the nine provinces (British Columbia held out for better terms) agreed to the federal proposal. But the provinces were not consulted on the 1915 amendment that redefined the divisions of the Senate, forming a new section out of the four western provinces.[54]

Even though the compact theory was not consistently observed in the constitutional amendment process, it had become a powerful constitutional ideal by the turn of the century. Provincial rights and the compact theory had, as Ramsay Cook put it, "attained a position close to motherhood in the scale of Canadian political values. It would be difficult to find a prominent politician who was not willing to pay lip-service to the principle of provincial rights and its theoretical underpinning, the compact theory."[55] As a constitutional doctrine, the compact theory may have contained ambiguities and lacked precision, but its strength as a political value in Canada meant that the Canadian political community that was forming would be complex and deeply pluralist. Canada would take its place in the world as an interventionist state and its nationwide activities would take on increasing significance in the lives of its citizens, but the provinces would nonetheless endure as strong constituent elements of the Canadian community.

The ambiguities of the compact theory were intensified by the coexistence of two competing versions of the compact: a compact of founding provinces and a compact of founding peoples.[56] The latter contended that Canada was founded on the basis of a covenant between English Canadians and French Canadians. In the final analysis, the making of Canada in 1867 was "the free association of two peoples, enjoying equal rights in all matters."[57] These were the words of Henri Bourassa, the theory's most eloquent spokesman and founder of the great Montreal newspaper *Le Devoir* in 1910. Again, the significance of this theory in Canada's constitutional politics rests not on its historical accuracy but on its potency as a political myth. It is easy to show that neither in law nor in politics was the BNA Act a formal agreement between the French and English people of British North America. Nonetheless, that constitutional settlement depended, as we have seen, on English- and French-Canadian leaders agreeing to a federal structure with a province in which the French Canadians would remain a majority. For many English Canadians, assent to this agreement was only grudgingly given; for French Canadians it represented liberation from Lord Durham's scheme to assimilate them into a unicultural English political community, the triumph of their cultural survival — and, indeed for many, of national survival. The expectations on the French side flowing from that agreement gave rise to the theory that Confederation was based on a compact between two founding peoples.[58]

As originally espoused by Bourassa and other French Canadians, the two founding peoples theory was applied to all of Canada. Indeed, it was advanced as the theoretical underpinning for a pan-Canadian nationalism that viewed all Canada in dualist terms. Its exponents defended the rights of the French minorities outside Quebec and of the English minority in Quebec. In this sense, it may have provided "moral support for minimizing the consequences of the compact of provinces" and of provincial rights.[59] At the same time, this dualist view of Canada always retained a special place for the province of Quebec. As the homeland of one of the founding peoples, it had the right to be secure against intrusions into its culture by the general government answerable to an English-speaking majority.

Lurking within these rival compact theories were deep-seated differences on the nature of Canada as a political community. The idea that Quebec has a special place in Confederation as the only province in which one of the founding peoples forms the majority would collide with the doctrine of provincial equality. More fundamentally, the idea of a Canada based on the English and the French as its two founding peoples would be challenged at the end of the twentieth century by Canadians who were neither British nor French in their cultural background, and by the Aboriginal peoples.

So long as Canadians were not interested in taking custody of their Constitution into their own hands, this conflict over the nature of Canada as a political community was of no great political importance. It was bound, however, to become salient once that condition changed. The time arrived in 1926, when the Balfour Declaration declared Canada and the other self-governing dominions to be "autonomous Communities" within the British Commonwealth.[60] Canada's political leaders then faced the challenge of arranging for Canada to become constitutionally self-governing.

NOTES

1. For an account see W.P.M. Kennedy, *The Constitution of Canada, 1534–1937: An Introduction to Its Development, Law and Custom*, 2nd ed. (London: Oxford University Press, 1938), 318–20.
2. A.I. Silver, *The French-Canadian Idea of Confederation, 1864–1900* (Toronto: University of Toronto Press, 1982), 111.
3. Ibid., 121.
4. Christopher Armstrong, *The Politics of Federalism: Ontario's Relations with the Federal Government, 1867–1942* (Toronto: University of Toronto Press, 1981), 14.
5. A. Margaret Evans, *Sir Oliver Mowat* (Toronto: University of Toronto Press for The Ontario Historical Studies Series, 1992).
6. For a succinct account of the National Policy see Craig Brown, "The Nationalism of the National Policy," in *Nationalism in Canada*, ed. Peter H. Russell (Toronto: McGraw-Hill, 1966), 155–63.
7. Reginald Whitaker, "Democracy and the Canadian Constitution," in Keith Banting and Richard Simeon, eds., *And No One Cheered: Federalism, Democracy and the Constitution Act* (Toronto: Methuen, 1983), 250.
8. For a full account see Paul Romney, *Mr. Attorney: The Attorney General for Ontario in Court, Cabinet and Legislature, 1791–1899* (Toronto: University of Toronto Press, 1986), chap. 6.
9. Sections 55–7.
10. R. MacGregor Dawson, *The Government of Canada*, 4th ed., revised by Norman Ward (Toronto: University of Toronto Press, 1966), 142.
11. For a contemporary statement on this point see Peter W. Hogg, *Constitutional Law of Canada*, 2nd ed. (Toronto: Carswell, 1985), 38.
12. For a full account of the use of these powers see Gerard V. LaForest, *Disallowance and Reservation of Provincial Legislation* (Ottawa: Department of Justice, 1965).
13. For a detailed account see Romney, *Mr. Attorney*, 255–56.
14. Armstrong, *Politics of Federalism*, 29.
15. See Paul Gérin-Lajoie, *Constitutional Amendment in Canada* (Toronto: University of Toronto Press, 1950), 142–43.
16. For a full account see Frank MacKinnon, "The Establishment of the Supreme Court of Canada," *Canadian Historical Review* 27 (1946): 258–74.
17. [1878] 2 s.c.r. 70. For a compendium of Supreme Court and Judicial Committee decisions on the constitution see Peter H. Russell, Rainer Knopff, and Ted Morton, *Federalism and the Charter: Leading Constitutional Decisions* (Ottawa: Carleton University Press, 1989).
18. [1979] 3 s.c.r. 575.
19. [1881] 7 App. Cas. 96.
20. F. Murray Greenwood, "Lord Watson, Institutional Self-Interest and the Decentralization of Canadian Federalism in the 1890's," *University of British Columbia Law Review* 9 (1974): 267.
21. *Russell v. The Queen* (1882), 7 App. Cas. 829.
22. *Hodge v. The Queen* (1883), 9 App. Cas. 177 (upholding provincial power), and the *McCarthy Act Reference* (not reported). For a discussion see Russell et al., *Federalism and the Charter*, 53.
23. *Attorney General for Ontario v. Attorney General for Canada*, [1896] a.c. 348.

24. *Liquidators of the Maritime Bank of Canada v. Receiver General of New Brunswick*, [1992] a.c. 437.

25. P.B. Waite, ed., *The Confederation Debates in the Province of Canada, 1865* (Toronto: McClelland and Stewart, 1963), 156.

26. For a classical statement of the theory see K.C. Wheare, *Federal Government*, 4th ed. (London: Oxford University Press, 1963). On the basis of the centralizing elements in the constitutional text, Wheare concluded that Canada was not a true federation but a "quasi-federation."

27. On the absence of a theoretical understanding or agreement on federalism at the time of Confederation see P.B. Waite, *The Life and Times of Confederation, 1864–1867: Politics, Newspapers, and the Union of British North America*, 2nd ed. (Toronto: University of Toronto Press, 1962), chap. 8.

28. The saying is attributed to Charles Evans Hughes, later chief justice of the United States. See A.T. Mason and W.M. Beaney, *American Constitutional Law* (Englewood Cliffs, NJ: Prentice-Hall, 1959), 3.

29. For a discussion of the views of the Fathers of Confederation on this subject see Jennifer Smith, "The Origins of Judicial Review in Canada," *Canadian Journal of Political Science* 16 (1983): 115–34.

30. Section 93(4).

31. For the evidence see Peter H. Russell, *The Supreme Court of Canada as a Bilingual and Bicultural Institution* (Ottawa: Queen's Printer, 1969), chap. 1.

32. See Alexander Hamilton, "The Federalist No. 78," *The Federalist Papers* (New York: Modern Library, 1937).

33. For an account see W.L. Morton, *The Kingdom of Canada: A General History from Earliest Times*, 2nd ed. (Toronto: McClelland and Stewart, 1969), chap. 19.

34. On the demographic changes see Janice Staples, "Consociationalism at Provincial Level: The Erosion of Dualism in Manitoba, 1870–1890," in Kenneth McRae, ed., *Consociational Democracy: Political Accomodation in Segmented Societies* (Toronto: McClelland and Stewart, 1974), 288–99.

35. Section 23 of the *Manitoba Act, 1870*.

36. *Attorney General for Manitoba v. Forest*, [1979] 2 s.c.r. 1032. Earlier challenges that were successful in the local courts were simply ignored.

37. Section 22 of the *Manitoba Act, 1870*.

38. *City of Winnipeg v. Barrett*, [1892] a.c. 445.

39. *Brophy v. Attorney General for Manitoba*, [1895] a.c. 445.

40. Morton, *Kingdom of Canada*, 379.

41. After the election, Laurier worked out a compromise with Manitoba premier Greenway that allowed periods of minority language and religious instruction where numbers warranted.

42. Silver, *French-Canadian Idea of Confederation*, 243.

43. D.V. Smiley, *Canada in Question: Federalism in the Eighties*, 3rd ed. (Toronto: McGraw-Hill Ryerson, 1980), 1.

44. See Edwin Black, *Divided Loyalties: Canadian Concepts of Federalism* (Montreal and London: McGill-Queen's University Press, 1975), 132–35.

45. For a fuller elaboration see Whittaker, "Democracy and the Canadian Constitution."

46. Quoted in Robert Vipond, *Liberty and Community: Canadian Federalism and the Failure of the Constitution* (Albany: State University of New York Press, 1991), 79.

47. Ibid., especially chap. 3.

48. For a full account of the theory see Ramsay Cook, *Provincial Autonomy, Minority Rights and the Compact Theory, 1867–1921* (Ottawa: Queen's Printer, 1969).

49. Black, *Divided Loyalties*, 154.

50. This is the definition of myth given by R.M. MacIver in *The Web of Government* (New York: Macmillan, 1947), 4. For the application of this sense of myth to the compact theory see Donald V. Smiley, *The Canadian Political Nationality* (Toronto: Methuen, 1967), 30.

51. Arthur R.M. Lower, *Colony to Nation: A History of Canada*, 4th ed. (Toronto: Longmans, 1964), 32.

52. The *British North America Act* of 1871 and the *British North America Act* of 1886. The third, the *Parliament of Canada Act, 1875*, concerned the privileges and immunities of the House of Commons. For a brief account of all constitutional amendments up until 1964 and how they were obtained see the Honourable Guy Favreau, *The Amendment of the Constitution of Canada* (Ottawa: Queen's Printer, 1965).

53. The *British North America Act* of 1907.

54. The *British North America Act* of 1915.

55. Cook, *Provincial Autonomy*, 44.

56. For an analysis of the relationship between the two compact theories see Filippo Sabetti, "The Historical Context of Constitutional Change in Canada," *Law and Contemporary Problems* 45 (1982): 11–32.

57. Quoted ibid., 21.

58. For an analysis of this tendency for French-speaking Canadians to view the Constitution as a compact between two peoples while the English-speaking population view the Constitution as an organic development see Daniel J. Elazar, "Constitution-Making: The Pre-eminently Political Act," in Keith G. Banting and Richard Sineon, eds., *Redesigning the State: The Politics of Constitutional Change in Industrial Nations* (Toronto: University of Toronto Press, 1985), 245–46.
59. Sabetti, "Historical Context of Constitutional Changes in Canada," 20.
60. Dawson, *Government of Canada*, 63.

Article Five

Unity/Diversity: The Canadian Experience; From Confederation to the First World War

J.R. Miller

I

While everyone conceded in the 1860s that the object of the Fathers of Confederation was to produce the bases of one political entity, no one anticipated that this task would be performed by imposing uniformity on the diverse peoples and regions of British North America. Indeed, had such a goal been sought, it would have proved impossible of attainment. The various colonies, with their unique historical development, their different religious denominations, and their distinct nationalities, could not have been homogenized culturally as they were joined politically. The peculiarities of language, creed, and regional identity had to be maintained, for several good and compelling reasons.

Diversity was both desirable and unavoidable, first, because the existing differences were simply too strong to be dismissed. This was true not just in the case of the French Canadians, but even with the local autonomists of Ontario, the Grits, and, most especially, in the Maritimes. The *Acadian Recorder* lamented: "We don't know each other. We have no trade with each other. We have no facilities or resources or incentives to mingle with each other. We are shut off from each other by a wilderness, geographically, commercially, politically and socially. We always cross the United States to shake hands." Joseph Howe, as usual, put it more pungently: "Take a Nova Scotian to Ottawa, away above tidewater, freeze him up for five months, where he cannot view the Atlantic, smell salt water, or see the sail of a ship, and the man will pine and die."[1] Diversity was a force too powerful to be exorcised.

Even were it possible to assimilate all British North Americans, to what would you assimilate them? Unlike the United States, a community created by revolution and compact, the proposed Canada was to be produced as the result of an evolutionary process by an act of an external authority, the United Kingdom. Rather than a society of revolution and consensus, Canada was to be a community of evolution and allegiance. The society of allegiance did not require conformity to any one model; the Canadians had no object of assimilation.[2] If they copied anything at all, it was the British pattern, which, since the days of imperial expansion

Source: "Unity/Diversity: The Canadian Experience; From Confederation to the First World War," *Dalhousie Review* 55, 1 (Spring 1975): 63–82. Reprinted by permission.

and Catholic Emancipation, meant not something monolithic, Protestant, and Anglo-Saxon, but a number of things more diversified. Canadians could not, at Quebec and Charlottetown, have sought unity at the expense of diversity because there was nothing to which they could conform, and no imperative of revolution to force them to make such a compact.

Finally, Canadian unity was not purchased at the price of homogenization because the colonial politicians who produced it had no intention of creating problems for themselves by debating something as abstract and theoretical as the cultural basis of the new state. These were practical politicians with painfully real problems. Their attention was devoted to solving the difficulties created by deadlock, acquisition of the Northwest, inadequate defences, and promotion of intercolonial commerce, not to searching for new ones. They were, as Donald Creighton has observed, "as far away from the dogmas of the eighteenth-century Enlightenment as they were from twentieth-century obsession with race, and with racial and cultural separatism." These men "saw no merit in setting out on a highly unreal voyage of discovery for first principles."[3] In short, the delegates at Quebec were not about to open a new can of worms by debating the place of various cultural and religious groups in Canada. Such a discussion was as undesirable as it was unnecessary.

These were the reasons why the British North American colonies, as Arthur Lower pointed out, "were carpentered together, not smelted."[4] Or, as G.F.G. Stanley observed: "The Canadian Confederation came into being not to crush but to reconcile regional diversities. . . . Union, not unity, was the result."[5] As one might expect, it was the French-Canadian leader, George-Étienne Cartier, who expressed the idea of unity in diversity most clearly:

> In our own Federation we should have Catholic and Protestant, English, French, Irish and Scotch, and each by his efforts and his success would increase the prosperity and glory of the new Confederacy. . . . They were placed like great families beside each other, and their contact produced a healthy spirit of emulation. It was a benefit rather than otherwise that we had a diversity of races. . . .
>
> Now, when we were united together, . . . we would form a political nationality with which neither the national origin, nor the religion of any individual, would interfere. It was lamented by some that we had this diversity of races, and hopes were expressed that this distinctive feature would cease. The idea of unity of races was utopian — it was impossible. Distinctions of this kind would always exist. Dissimilarity, in fact, appeared to be the order of the physical world and of the moral world, as well as of the political world.[6]

The key words were "a political nationality": the unity that Confederation was to produce was union at the political level, not cultural. While "carpentering" political unity, British North Americans would retain regional, religious, and cultural diversity; Canada was founded on unity in diversity. And, in passing, one might note the type of diversity intended — "Catholic and Protestant, English, French, Irish and Scotch." This was a very Britannic mosaic.

II

Of course, the formula "Unity in diversity" raised as many questions as it answered. What did the concept mean? How did you hold a diverse country together? Specifically, what were the rights and privileges of the most distinctive minority, the French Canadians? More specifically still, what was to become of the principle of cultural and political *duality* that had evolved in the Province of Canada (the future Ontario and Quebec) between 1841 and 1867? It would take a decade and more to work out the first set of answers to these riddles; and, then, the first essay at a resolution of them would come under attack and be modified substantially.

The first question dealt with was the fate of the duality of the Canadian union. Here the answer was starkly simple: duality would be eliminated. This did not mean any tampering with the official status of the French language that was protected by Section 133 of the British North America Act in the courts and Parliament of Canada, as well as in the courts and Legislature of Quebec. However, in succeeding years it was evident that Canadians were not prepared to foster the expansion of this limited, pragmatic recognition of French into a great principle of *duality* throughout the land. Although French was officially countenanced in Manitoba and the Northwest Territories, under special and pressing circumstances, it was not enshrined in the other new provinces of British Columbia and Prince Edward Island. Indeed, in New Brunswick, the Acadian minority suffered the loss of an important cultural bulwark in the 1870s, when their legislature deprived them of public support for their denominational schools. In short, the first generation of Canadian politicians was prepared to grant French culture official status where temporary exigencies and local pressures made it politically expedient to do so, and nowhere else. They certainly were not about to erect linguistic duality into a great principle of the federation.

Moreover, other aspects of dualism, the double political and administrative institutions that had developed in the United Province, were deliberately removed. Governor General Monck's invitation to John A. Macdonald to form the first Dominion Cabinet explicitly forbade the continuation of the dual premiership. Sectional equality in the Cabinet was replaced by a careful balancing of regional, economic, religious, and cultural interests in Macdonald's first ministry, and in almost all that have succeeded. Duality of administrative posts was also abolished, essentially because the unsatisfactory quasi-federalism of the Union was replaced by a real federation and division of powers between levels of government. There were, for example, no longer two Superintendents of Education because the schools were now the responsibility of the provinces. Similarly, two attorneys-general were not needed because French Canada's peculiar civil law was to be controlled by Quebec. And so it went. Institutional duality, whether at the political or civil service level, was eradicated because it was unnecessary and unwanted.

Whatever else the first decade demonstrated, it proved that unity in diversity did not mean the retention of any more duality than was essential. There still remained the more difficult question: if unity in diversity did not mean duality, what did it mean? How was it to be formalized, embodied, made concrete? How did you tack together "a political nationality" out of diverse elements?

The first indication of the means that would be used to hold the country together came in 1868, in Minister of Justice Macdonald's memorandum on the federal power of disallowance. Macdonald laid down guidelines for the federal veto of provincial legislation that were sweeping. They were so general as almost to be unqualified, as was suggested by the provision that provincial statutes "as affecting the interests of the Dominion generally" could be struck down if Ottawa wished.[7] This was Macdonald's instinctive reversion to the eighteenth-century Tory tradition of centralized governmental power. Under his leadership, the first government after Confederation followed a highly centralist policy, one suspects because he regarded such centralization as being as essential to the well-being of the fragile union as it was congenial to his Conservative temperament.

Gradually during the 1870s the rest of the apparatus for ensuring the unity of the state was put into place. The policy of pushing the Indians out of the arable lands of the prairie West and replacing them with white, agricultural settlers was one such project. The gargantuan task of binding the newly acquired and sparsely populated West to the rest of the country with a transcontinental railroad was another. And the policy of forcing economic diversification and regional specialization of economic function through the imposition of the protective tariff was the final means chosen to produce enduring unity out of diversity and distance. The objective of these national policies of expansion and development was to provide an economic *raison d'être* for the political state; or, if you prefer, it was the means of putting the flesh of economic self-interest on the bare bones of the constitutional skeleton. The West, once filled, would produce agricultural products for export and would serve as a captive market for Canadian manufacturers. Central Canada would manufacture goods, protected and encouraged by the tariff; would fuel her industries with Nova Scotian coal; and would sell her products to Maritimers and Westerners alike. The whole scheme would be facilitated by the network of railways that was so essential to the Canadian federation: the Grand Trunk, Intercolonial, and Canadian Pacific. And, finally, the scheme of economic nationalism — the encouragement of a transcontinental economy of diverse, but integrated economic regions — would be supervised and protected by a powerful central government.

Now, the formulation of these policies was undoubtedly much more accidental than the foregoing sketch suggests. The steps toward adoption of the various pieces were often hesitant, taken out of a sense of constitutional obligation (the promise of a railway to BC), and motivated more by partisan political calculations than nation-building ambitions. And, yet, what seems striking is the fact that the pieces fit, that they made up a coherent, compelling, and politically appealing program of national self-defence through economic expansion and integration. Furthermore, when the pieces are put together, they provide an answer to the question of how unity could be maintained amidst diversity. The answer was that diverse regions, religious groups, and nationalities could stay united politically while remaining different culturally because they had a program of economic development from which they could all benefit. And, moreover, these policies meant that the focus of political life at the federal level would not be on sensitive issues of religion and nationality, but on economic issues that cut across regional, religious, and cultural lines. Macdonald's nationalism would make unity in diversity possible by concentrating on those things that united Canadians, or, at least, did not divide them according to religion and language. The recipe was: diversity locally, but political unity in pursuit of common economic objectives.

Not the least significant feature of this concoction is the fact that, to a large extent, it succeeded. The French Canadians participated in the scheme as enthusiastically as anyone else. There were no more fervent protectionists than Quebec's leaders, who saw the industrialization of the Townships as the alternative to the continuing hemorrhage of French-Canadian youth to the detested United States. Ontario was satisfied, for the key to Macdonald's scheme was the realization of Ontario's traditional dream of opening and developing the West in Ontario's image and for Toronto's pecuniary benefit. The national policies embodied Ontario imperialism. And the Maritimes benefited too, although the advantages were offset by the general deterioration of the Atlantic economy in the waning years of wind and wood transportation. There was substantial growth in the Nova Scotian coal industry, as the industrialization encouraged by the tariff created markets for the fuel in urban Quebec.[8] The only region that did not benefit very much from the scheme was the West. There the response to centralization and the national policies was protest: formation of the Manitoba and Northwest Farmers' Union, Riel's second Rebellion, the provincial autonomy campaign in Manitoba, and the steady intonation of the litany of grievances (freight rates, elevators, and tariffs) that was to become so familiar. But, frankly, no one worried much about western complaints, for colonies were only supposed to produce wealth, not be happy. Western grievances aside, however, the Tory scheme of unity through economic expansion was quite successful.

III

This unity based on pursuit of common economic goals under the direction of a strong central government began to erode in the 1880s as the result of three corrosive influences. Political opportunism inspired an attack on centralization by the Liberal parties at the federal and provincial levels. The economic stagnation that returned after 1883 destroyed the rosy dreams of prosperity and unity. As is normally the case in difficult times, economic discontent led to internal bickering: the provinces versus Ottawa; and Ontario against the rest, especially Quebec, when the provinces succeeded in extorting "better terms" from the Conservative federal government. Finally, the desired unity within the country was eroded by the influence in Canada of radically new theories of national unity that focused upon language and culture, rather than economic cooperation, as essential criteria for unification.

The new theories which sought unity at the expense of cultural diversity were represented in the 1880s and 1890s by such men as D'Alton McCarthy and Goldwin Smith. McCarthy, an Anglo-Saxon supremacist, imperialist, and tariff reformer, was worried about the lack of cohesion in Canada and anxious about the declining power of the central government. To him the villain of the piece seemed to be the French Canadian who insisted on having his own way, thereby preventing fusion:

> My own conviction is that it is not religion which is at the bottom of the matter but that it is a race feeling. There is no feeling so strong — no feeling which all history proves so strong — as the feeling of race. Don't we find the French today in the province of Quebec more French than when they were conquered by Wolfe upon the plains of Abraham? Do they mix with us, assimilate with us, intermarry with us? Do they read our literature or learn our laws? No, everything with them is conducted on a French model; and while we may admire members of that race as individuals, yet as members of the body politic I say that they are the great danger to the Confederacy.[9]

In McCarthy's view, "It was the language of a people that moulded its nationality."[10] The "science of language" demonstrated "that there is no factor equal to language to band people together, and . . . as is demonstrated in our own case, that nothing is more calculated to keep people asunder."[11] If McCarthy's analysis was correct, then it followed that Canadian unity could be achieved only through the imposition on Canada of one language: unity was to be achieved, not through diversity, but through cultural uniformity brought about by assimilation. His program for national unity was summarized in his resolution calling for the abolition of the official use of French in the Northwest Territories: that it was "expedient in the interest of national unity that there should be community of language among the people of Canada."[12]

Goldwin Smith, free trader, continentalist, and Anglo-Saxon racist, advocated a slightly different program to achieve the same end. He believed that French Canada was an obstacle to unity not just because of its language, but also because of its obscurantism and economic backwardness, both of which were the results of clerical domination:

> Quebec is a theocracy. While Rome has been losing her hold on Old France and on all the European nations, she has retained, nay tightened, it here. The people are the sheep of the priest. He is their political as well as their spiritual chief and nominates the politician, who serves the interest of the Church at Quebec or at Ottawa. . . . Not only have the clergy been the spiritual guides and masters of the French Canadians, they have been the preservers and champions of his nationality, and they have thus combined the influence of the tribune with that of the priest.[13]
>
> The French province, the people of which live on the produce of their own farms and clothe themselves with the produce of their spinning, is uncommercial, and lies a non-conductor between the more commercial members of the Confederation.[14]

Unlike McCarthy, Smith did not seek a solution to this problem in Canada, because he believed the political parties were totally and irrevocably the tools of the Quebec clergy. To Smith it was "perfectly clear that the forces of Canada alone are not sufficient to assimilate the French element or even to prevent the indefinite consolidation and growth of a French nation."[15] The answer, then, was obvious: "French Canada may be ultimately absorbed in the English-speaking population of a vast Continent; amalgamate with British Canada so as to form a united nation it apparently never can."[16] Canada should join the Americans to form an Anglo-Saxon republic of North America in which the French Canadians would drown.

There is a two-fold significance in the emergence of such advocates of Anglo-Saxon cultural uniformity as McCarthy and Smith. The first is that they are evidence that in English Canada, for a variety of reasons, many people had by the 1890s rejected the pursuit of unity in diversity. The second is that the country as a whole rejected the extreme prescriptions put forward by continentalists and cultural assimilationists alike for coercive uniformity. Parliament's response to McCarthy's call for linguistic uniformity was a compromise resolution that said that nothing had happened since Confederation to justify taking from the French Canadians the guarantees they received at the time of union, while allowing the populace of the Northwest Territories itself to decide the fate of the official use of French on the prairies.[17] And in the 1890s such annexationist schemes as Smith's Continental Union Association were rejected by the electorate.

Though McCarthy and Smith failed, they were not without lingering influence. French Canadians, seeing assimilationist movements such as the Equal Rights Association, Equal Rights League, Protestant Protective Association, and Continental Union Association, found renewed cause for anxiety about their future as a distinct cultural entity within the Canadian "political nationality." This disquiet was aggravated by a new phenomenon of the late 1890s and early 1900s, massive European immigration to the Canadian West. As French-Canadian leaders quickly perceived, this demographic change made Cartier's doctrine of diversity a source of danger.

IV

The problem arose because of English-Canadian reaction to the immigration of the Laurier period. As thousands of Poles, Russians, Germans, Italians, Scandinavians, and Ukrainians flooded the West, middle-class, Anglo-Saxon Canadians began to join working-class critics of extensive immigration. Whereas the old trade union criticism of immigration was essentially economic in character,[18] the new critique was fundamentally concerned with the cultural effects of immigration. Stephen Leacock observed disapprovingly that the new immigration was "from the Slavonic and Mediterranean peoples of a lower industrial and moral status," and consisted of "herds of the proletariat of Europe, the lowest class of industrial society."[19] Principal Sparling of Wesley College, Winnipeg, warned that Canadians "must see to it that the civilization and ideals of Southeastern Europe are not transplanted to and perpetuated on our virgin soil."[20] While Ralph Connor fictionalized Sparling's injunction in *The Foreigner*,[21] a poet, of sorts, expressed similar ideas in verse:

> They are haggard, huddled, homeless, frightened at — they know not what:
> With a few unique exceptions they're a disappointing lot;
> But I take 'em as I get 'em, soldier, sailor, saint and clown
> And I turn 'em out Canadians — all but the yellow and brown.[22]

In the era of the Laurier Boom many Canadians recoiled from the tidal wave of immigration, sorrowfully concluding that they could "not make a nation by holding a basket at the hopper of an immigration chute."[23]

The English-Canadian answer to these cultural dangers was a drive to assimilate the "foreigner" by inculcating in him the values of British-Canadian civilization. What precisely that meant, and the danger it portended, manifested itself in the prescriptions critics of immigration put forward for the solution of the problem. "One of the best ways of Canadianizing, nationalizing, and turning all into intelligent citizens," said one Protestant clergyman in 1913, "is by means of a good English education."[24] When J.S. Woodsworth asked himself how "are we to break down the walls which separate these foreigners from us?" his conclusion was that first and foremost was "the Public School. Too great emphasis cannot be placed upon the work that has been accomplished and may — yes, must — be accomplished by our National Schools."[25] Linguistic uniformity imposed by the schools was the answer:

> If Canada is to become in any real sense a nation, if our people are to become one, we must have one language.... Hence the necessity of national schools where the teaching of English — our national language — is compulsory.

The public school system was "the most important factor in transforming the foreigners into Canadians."[26]

French Canada, not unnaturally, took alarm at such programs, which drew no distinction between the worthy French Canadian and the despised "Galician." The emerging champion of French-Canadian nationalism, Henri Bourassa, protested that the Fathers of Confederation had never intended "to change a providential condition of our partly French and partly English country to make it a land of refuge for the scum of all nations."[27] Bourassa's complaint was that diversity, by which Canadians had meant a mixture of English, French, and Scot, now seemed to mean Ukrainian, German, and Italian; and that English Canadians, in reacting to this new form of diversity, attacked French-Canadian rights as well as the pretensions of the European "scum." Bourassa knew whereof he spoke, for, in the early years of the twentieth century, Woodsworth's prescription (and Bourassa's nightmare) was realized. In 1901 and 1905 on the prairies, and in 1912 in Ontario, unilingual education was imposed in an effort to assimilate all minorities, including the French Canadians. In the era of massive European immigration, Cartier's "multicultural argument could only accelerate, not retard the unilingual process."[28]

Bourassa's, and French Canada's, response to this danger was to work out a new theory of Canadian unity that protected rather than jeopardized French-Canadian cultural rights. The new spokesman of French Canada found his justification of his culture in Providence and History. God, he argued, had placed the Latin culture of French Canada in North America as a spiritual beacon in the materialistic, Anglo-Saxon darkness. And what God planted, not even the Canadian Parliament ought to root out. Furthermore, he insisted, Canadian history was the record of the preservation of cultural duality. The Royal Proclamation of 1763 and Quebec Act of 1774 had ensured the survival of the primary agency of French Canada, the Roman Catholic Church. A political process stretching from the Constitutional Act of 1791 to the struggle over responsible government of the 1840s had expanded the limited eighteenth-century guarantees into semi-official recognition of duality. Confederation, in Bourassa's historical recitation, became the adoption by the new Dominion of Canada of biculturalism and bilingualism. Hence, French Canada should be respected because it was a coordinate partner with a special providential mission to perform. Not even the infringements of the Confederation compact in the West and Ontario between 1890 and 1912 could alter that fact. "The Canadian nation," Bourassa argued, "will attain its ultimate destiny, indeed it will exist, only on the condition of being biethnic and bilingual, and by remaining faithful to the concept of the Fathers of Confederation: the free and voluntary association of two peoples, enjoying equal rights in all matters."[29] In other words, in flight from the vulnerability of diversity, Bourassa had erected duality as a new line of defence. Bourassa and biculturalism had replaced Cartier and diversity as the theoretical justification of French Canada's right to exist.

In the first half-century of Confederation, then, Canadians' concept of their political community as a unity in diversity had come under attack on two fronts. English assimilationists had argued for cultural homogenization as an answer to disunity, and French-Canadian nationalists had responded with a messianic and historical defence of cultural duality. The two conflicting viewpoints were the subject of much public discussion in the early years of the twentieth century, as each struggled for mastery. As it turned out, with the coming of the Great War the English-Canadian assimilationist model triumphed. Several provinces terminated the official use of French; Ontario refused to soften the assimilationist thrust of its 1912 policy; and Quebec, as a result of the language issue and the conscription crisis, was politically isolated and alienated.

NOTES

1. *Acadian Recorder*, quoted in John Ricker, John Saywell, and Ramsay Cook, *Canada: A Modern Study* (Toronto, 1963), 101; J. Howe, quoted in J.M. Beck, *Joseph Howe: Anti-Confederate* (Ottawa, 1956), 15.
2. W.L. Morton, *The Canadian Identity* (Madison and Toronto, 1961), 100–107, 110–12.
3. D.G. Creighton, *The Road to Confederation* (Toronto, 1964), 141–42.
4. A.R.M. Lower, *Canadians in the Making* (Don Mills, 1958), 289.
5. G.F.G. Stanley, "Regionalism in Canadian History," *Ontario History* 51 (1959): 167.
6. P.B. Waite, ed., *Confederation Debates in the Province of Canada/1865* (Carleton Library edition, Toronto, 1963), 51 and 50.
7. Quoted in J.M. Beck, ed., *The Shaping of Canadian Federalism* (Toronto, 1971), 159.
8. P.B. Waite, *Canada, 1874–1896: Arduous Destiny* (Toronto, 1971), 184.
9. Quoted in F. Landon, "D'Alton McCarthy and the Politics of the Later Eighties," Canadian Historical Association, *Report of the Annual Meeting, 1932*, 46.
10. Stayner Speech, 12 July 1889, *Toronto Daily Mail*, 13 July 1889.
11. *Speech of Mr. D'Alton McCarthy delivered on Thursday, 12 December 1889 at Ottawa* (n.p., n.d.).
12. *Debates of the House of Commons*, Fourth Session, Sixth Parliament, vol. 29 (1890), columns 674–75.
13. G. Smith, *Canada and the Canadian Question* (Toronto, 1891), 5–6.
14. Smith, *Canada and the Canadian Question*, 206–207.
15. Smith, *Canada and the Canadian Question*, 275.
16. Smith, *Canada and the Canadian Question*, 215.
17. *Debates of the House of Commons* (1890), columns 881–82 and 1017–18.
18. With the exception, of course, of British Columbia, where the objections had been based on both economic and racial arguments. See J.A. Munro, "British Columbia and the 'Chinese Evil': Canada's First Anti-Asiatic Immigration Law," *Journal of Canadian Studies* 6 (1971): 42–49.
19. S. Leacock, "Canada and the Immigration Problem," *The National Review* 52 (1911): 317 and 323.
20. Principal Sparling, "Introduction" to J.S. Woodsworth, *Strangers within Our Gates, or Coming Canadians* (Toronto, 1909).
21. R. Connor [C.W. Gordon], *The Foreigner: A Tale of Saskatchewan* (Toronto, 1909), especially 23–25 and 37–41. This theme in Connor's work has been analyzed carefully in J.L. Thompson and J.H. Thompson, "Ralph Connor and the Canadian Identity," *Queen's Quarterly* 79 (1972): 166–69.
22. R.J.C. Stead, "The Mixer" (1905), quoted in R.C. Brown and R. Cook, *Canada, 1896–1921: A Nation Transformed* (Toronto, 1974), 73.
23. Leacock, "Canada and the Immigration Problem," 318.
24. Rev. W.D. Reid, in R.C. Brown and M.E. Prang, eds., *Confederation to 1949* (Scarborough, 1966), 84.

25. J.S. Woodsworth, *Strangers within Our Gates*, 281.
26. J.S. Woodsworth (1905), quoted in Brown and Cook, *Canada, 1896–1921*, 73.
27. H. Bourassa (1904), quoted in Brown and Cook, *Canada, 1896–1921*, 74.
28. A. Smith, "Metaphor and Nationality in North America," *Canadian Historical Review* 51 (1970): 268. This paper owes far more than this isolated quotation to Professor Smith's stimulating analysis, as students of the topic will realize.
29. H. Bourassa (1917), quoted in R. Cook, *Canada and the French-Canadian Question* (Toronto, 1966), 51.

Topic Three

The North-West Rebellion of 1885

Louis Riel addresses the jury during his trial in Regina in July 1885.

Few issues in Canadian history have generated more heated debate than the North-West Rebellion of 1885. For a long time, the debate centred on the main protagonist, Louis Riel, the ill-fated leader of both the Métis resistance of 1869/70 and the rebellion of 1885. To what extent was he alone responsible for the North-West Rebellion of 1885? Should he be seen as a rebel leader or as a mere victim of circumstances? Did he represent cultural, linguistic, or regional interests?

More recently, Canadian historians have shifted their focus from Riel to his followers. Moving away from the "Great Man Theory of History," these historians have been more interested in ascertaining why certain Métis and a small number of First Nations individuals followed Riel while others did not than in explaining why Riel led them into rebellion. They also try to discover whether Riel's followers represented particular interest groups in their respective communities.

The following two articles reflect this new historiographical trend. In "The Métis Militant Rebels of 1885," David Lee examines the cultural background of the most radical of the Métis participants in the rebellion. He shows that a correlation existed between the militancy of these individuals and their livelihood, language, age, and social outlook. A. Blair Stonechild presents a First Nations' view of the rebellion in "The Indian View of the 1885 Uprising." He emphasizes the difficulty in reconstructing a First Nations' perspective on account of the lack of traditional written sources. What Stonechild uses instead are oral histories and stories to present a refreshingly new, Native-oriented explanation for why some First Nations communities joined the rebellion while the majority did not. He maintains that to a large extent the First Nations were forced into the conflict as a result of misunderstanding on the part of Métis leaders in the region, prejudice on the part of the white settlers and military leaders, and the sinister intent of the Canadian government.

The literature on Riel and the Métis is extensive. For a concise overview of the history and culture of the Métis, see D.B. Sealey and A.S. Lussier's *The Métis: Canada's Forgotten People* (Winnipeg: Métis Federation Press, 1975). A growing literature exists on Louis Riel and the Métis in 1869–70 and 1885. The five-volume *Collected Writings of Louis Riel/Les Écrits complets de Louis Riel* (Edmonton: University of Alberta Press, 1985), under the general editorship of George F.G. Stanley, is currently available. Secondary studies include G.F.G. Stanley's *The Birth of Western Canada: A History of the Riel Rebellion* (Toronto: University of Toronto Press, 1961 [1936]); Thomas Flanagan's *Louis "David" Riel: "Prophet of the New World,"* rev. ed. (Toronto: University of Toronto Press, 1996); H. Bowsfield's *Louis Riel: The Rebel and the Hero* (Toronto: Oxford University Press, 1971) and his edited collection, *Louis Riel: Selected Readings* (Toronto: Copp Clark, 1987); Joseph Kinsey Howard's *Strange Empire* (New York: William Morrow, 1952); and B. Beal and R. Macleod's *Prairie Fire: A History of the 1885 Rebellion* (Edmonton: Hurtig, 1984). Hugh Dempsey presents one First Nations leader's response in *Big Bear* (Vancouver: Douglas and McIntyre, 1984). For a critical view of the Métis position, see T. Flanagan, *Riel and the Rebellion: 1885 Reconsidered* (Saskatoon: Western Producer Books, 1983). An opposite viewpoint is presented in D.N. Sprague, *Canada and the Métis, 1869–1885* (Waterloo: Wilfrid Laurier University Press, 1988).

George F.G. Stanley reviews the various interpretations of Riel in "The Last Word on Louis Riel — The Man of Several Faces," in *1885 and After*, eds. F. Laurie Barron and James B. Waldram (Regina: Canadian Plains Research Centre, 1986), pp. 3–22. A good historiographical article is J.R. Miller's "From Riel to the Métis," *Canadian Historical Review* 69 (March 1988): 1–20. Diane Payment's *"The Free People — Otipemiswak": Batoche, Saskatchewan, 1870–1930* (Ottawa: Canadian Parks Service/National Historic Parks and Sites, 1990) is an in-depth study of the important Métis community of Batoche. In *Views from Fort Battleford: Constructed Visions of an Anglo-Canadian West* (Regina: Canadian Plains Research Centre,

University of Regina, 1994), Walter Hildebrandt discusses aspects of the conflict between the First Nations and the Anglo-Canadians on the Prairies. His *The Battle of Batoche: British Small Warfare and the Entrenched Métis* (Ottawa: National Historic Parks and Sites, Parks Canada, 1985) discusses the military engagement at Batoche. Ramon Hathorn and Patrick Holland have compiled an interesting anthology entitled *Images of Louis Riel in Canadian Culture* (Lewiston, NY: E. Mellen Press, 1992). George Melnyk's *Radical Regionalism* (Edmonton: NeWest Press, 1981) and his edited collection *Riel to Reform: A History of Protest in Western Canada* (Saskatoon: Fifth House Publishers, 1992) examine the roots of Western protest, and its relationship to regional identity.

An important study of the Native involvement in the North-West Rebellion is Blair Stonechild and Bill Waiser, *Loyal till Death: Indians and the North-West Rebellion* (Calgary: Fifth House, 1997). For a discussion of the role that women played in the rebellion and in mythologizing white women in the context of the North-West Rebellion, see Sarah Carter, *Capturing Women: The Manipulation of Cultural Imagery in Canada's Prairie West* (Montreal/Kingston: McGill-Queen's University Press, 1997). Hugh Dempsey explains the participation of Big Bear's band in the North-West Rebellion in *Big Bear: The End of Freedom* (Vancouver: Douglas and McIntyre, 1984), as does J.R. Miller in *Big Bear (Mistahimusqua)* (Toronto: ECW Press, 1996).

WEBLINKS

North West Canada Medal
http://www.vac-acc.gc.ca/remembers/sub.cfm?source=collections/cmdp/mainmenu/group03/nwc
The North West Canada Medal was awarded to participants on the side of the Government of Canada in the suppression of the North-West Rebellion.

Virtual Museum of Métis History and Culture
http://www.metismuseum.ca/main.php
This site contains a large number of resources and documents relating to the culture and history of the Métis, including at the time of the North West Rebellion.

La Presse
http://www.histori.ca/peace/page.do?subclassName=Document&pageID=295
The response of the Montreal newspaper *La Presse* in 1885 upon the news of the hanging of Louis Riel. Debates in the House of Commons regarding Riel and the rebellion are also available at this site.

Rethinking Louis Riel
http://archives.cbc.ca/IDD-1-73-1482/politics_economy/louis_riel/
A collection of CBC radio and video footage regarding the controversial status of Louis Riel in contemporary times.

Battle of Fish Creek
http://www.collectionscanada.ca/canadian-west/052920/05292030_e.html
A letter by Thomas Bull, participant in the Battle of Fish Creek, to his father regarding the battle. This document is the first in a series regarding the North-West Rebellion.

Department of Indian Affairs Annual Reports
http://www.collectionscanada.ca/indianaffairs/020010-101.01-e.php
A database of annual reports of the Department of Indian Affairs, covering the years 1864 to 1990.

Article Six

The Métis Militant Rebels of 1885

David Lee

A great avalanche of writing on the North-West Rebellion or "resistance" of 1885 appeared in the decade preceding the centenary of that dramatic event.[1] These studies pursue a variety of themes, theories, and preoccupations, some conflicting with others. Still, the writers generally agreed on the larger picture. They viewed the rebellion of 1885 as a response by the Métis of the Northwest Territories to the trauma of an abrupt and perceivedly baneful change in circumstances. These people, of mixed Indian and French ancestry, futilely attempted (with the assistance of a few Indians) to resist the notion of change by taking up arms. The indicators of change were numerous and inescapable: the disappearance of the buffalo; decline of the fur trade; the supplanting of cart and canoe freighting by rail and steamboat; the prospect of having to live a sedentary, agricultural life; an increasingly interventionist yet dilatory government bureaucracy, slow to act on land entitlements and surveys; and the influx of aggressive immigrants who knew how to use government authority to serve their own interest. Feeling that they were about to lose control over their destiny, the Métis reacted by establishing their own provisional government on the South Saskatchewan River and by taking violent action against agents of the Canadian government.

However, despite the depth and breadth of the avalanche, some parts of the story still remain relatively unexamined. Little has been done, for example, to examine the range of opinion in the Métis community regarding the notion of rebellion, to gauge the degree of support for that course of action, to identify those Métis most militantly committed to taking up arms, or to inquire into their backgrounds.

Thomas Flanagan has written that "probably a strong majority" of the community "accepted" the notion of insurrection.[2] Walter Hildebrandt lists Gabriel Dumont and ten others as the "hardcore" of Louis Riel's followers.[3] However, Louis Schmidt, a Métis who was present during the uprising but did not fight, put the number of highly committed combatants much higher. In his memoirs, he estimated that one-quarter to one-third of the Métis fought "vaillamment" (ardently); the remainder, he recalled, participated only "mollement" (lukewarmly) or not at all, either due to a lack of ammunition or because the idea of "révolte . . . les rend timides."[4] George Woodcock has opined that it was "the wilder" of the Métis who were the most "discontented" and committed to armed insurrection; he estimated the militants to number "at most a few dozen men."[5] Discussion of commitment among the rebels, then, has been rather limited.

The study which follows will examine the people of mixed Indian and European ancestry living on the South Saskatchewan River in 1885 and, more specifically, the men who fought in the battles of Duck Lake, Fish Creek, and Batoche in the spring of that year. The study will show that there was a fairly wide spectrum of both political opinion and cultural background within the Métis community. More significantly, it will be seen that the two spectra were almost congruent with one another. It will also show that, while the most militant men in the community were chiefly older and less acculturated, the insurrectionary movement was quite deeply based.

Source: "The Métis Militant Rebels of 1885," *Canadian Ethnic Studies* 21, 3 (1989): 1–19. Reprinted by permission.

MÉTIS COMMUNITY

As might be expected, the South Saskatchewan Métis were not a fully homogeneous group but rather a community with a variety of internal divisions and tensions, both political and cultural. At one end of the cultural spectrum were a small number of Métis who, through education or perhaps solely ambition, were well on their way to acculturation; that is, they were adjusting their lifestyles to meet the demands of an increasingly intrusive Euro-Canadian society. Some of these people were active in commerce while a few held salaried, government positions. At the other end of this spectrum were Métis who (though they considered themselves distinct from, and sometimes even superior to, Indians) were, in many ways, close to the Plains Cree and Saulteaux in culture; these people were not receptive to the ways of the powerful newcomers. They were unable or unwilling to abruptly take up such new endeavours as agriculture, animal husbandry, technical crafts, or retail trade, for example. The reasons could have been lack of confidence, incentive, capital, aptitude, or education, but may also have included satisfaction and pride in their traditional lifeways. These more conservative, or "more Indian," Métis would, for example, have been far more at ease in a tent on the Plains than in a house at Prince Albert or Saskatoon. As will be seen, they were often not much different from many so-called "Treaty Indians" living on nearby reserves. With regard to the community's political attitudes, i.e., its feelings regarding the notion of insurrection, the spectrum ranged from militancy through moderation to opposition. More significantly, it will be seen that the most militant proponents of rebellion can be largely characterized as conservatives while opponents were among the most acculturated in the community.

The evidence presented in this study involves a consideration of the background, age, livelihood, religion, social structure, and language of the South Saskatchewan River Métis. The evidence is scattered, fragmented, and usually nonquantifiable, but it is nevertheless revealing in the aggregate. Before proceeding any further, two questions, both of definition, must be resolved.

The most obvious question is, if the Métis exhibited such a wide diversity of culture, how can they be identified? The problem is readily resolved, however, if (as Joe Sawchuk has suggested) one employs a concept of ethnicity (rather than of culture or biology), especially the ascriptive approach advanced by the anthropologist Fredrik Barth.[6] By ascription, anyone could be a member of the Métis ethnic group who identified himself as such and who was considered as such by others, both inside and outside the group. By this means, then, the word "Métis" can encompass wide variations in culture, such as language, degree of acculturation, and expectations for the future. It even allows for "ethnic boundaries" (as Barth calls them) to be crossed; as will be seen, in the 1880s it was not uncommon on the South Saskatchewan for people to move back and forth between Indian and Métis groups (though there was little or no interchange with the European group). Indeed, there were people in each group who were culturally quite similar, sharing, for example, the same language, the same territorial claims, historical experiences, expectations for the future, and often even religion and a common, mixed ancestry. Marcel Giraud has observed that some Métis felt inferior in the presence of whites,[7] but, nevertheless, there is no doubt that they took pride in their ethnic identification. They were especially proud of their record of individualism, self-regulating independence, equestrianism, and survival as a group. Developing in the relative isolation of the northwest, this ethnic pride had grown into a feeling of separate nationhood.

A second question which must be answered involves the meaning of the word "Indian." As will be seen later, many residents of the northwest who were considered Métis spoke only native languages while, on the other hand, many who were considered Indian were themselves of mixed ancestry and had already undergone some acculturation, for example, conversion to Christianity. For the purposes of this study, an Indian will be anyone who in the 1870s and

1880s sought official Indian status and was granted that status by the Canadian government. This is an artificial, administrative identification but it was consciously taken. These people chose to "take treaty," an act which entitled them to an annuity and other benefits from the Department of Indian Affairs; most of them lived on reserves set aside for their bands.

The territory under consideration in this study embraced two distinct Métis settlements on the South Saskatchewan River, one small, one larger. The first was the tiny community of Prairie-Ronde, located near Dundurn, a little south of Saskatoon. Initially used as a wintering camp for buffalo hunters in the 1850s, Prairie-Ronde had become a year-round Métis settlement by 1885. The population was probably less than 100, most of them members of one extended family — the Trottiers. The people of Prairie-Ronde had recently established links with White Cap's band of Sioux Indians, who had recently moved onto a reserve nearby. The community had no church or resident priest but missionaries visited frequently from Batoche, 100 kilometres to the north (downstream).[8]

The second, larger settlement consisted of a triangle of land, encompassing both sides of the South Saskatchewan River, stretching from St-Louis-de-Langevin in the north to Duck Lake on the west and Fish Creek on the south; the missions of St-Laurent-de-Grandin, Sacré-Coeur (Duck Lake), and St-Antoine-de-Padoue (Batoche) lay within this ambit. In the 1880s this triangle, 50 kilometres long at most, was often generally referred to as the South Branch settlement. Some observers have viewed the triangle as the home territory and even the final refuge of the Northwest Métis.[9] However, even this circumscribed area was not exclusively theirs; by 1885 a number of Europeans had moved in and more were expected. Living within the area were at least fifteen Anglo-Canadian families, a half-dozen or so French-Canadian households, as well as three or four French Oblate Catholic priests.[10] Just outside the triangle lay several Cree Indian reserves, including those of Beardy and Okemasis near Duck Lake, and that of One Arrow, which abutted the village of Batoche. And only 30 kilometres north of St-Louis was the fast-growing town of Prince Albert. The majority of the inhabitants in this area were Anglo-Canadian but it also included a strong component of people of mixed British and Indian ancestry, usually identified as "Halfbreeds" rather than Métis; most of this group was English-speaking and Protestant.

It was in the early 1870s that a number of Métis first decided to build permanent homes on the South Branch; many of these original settlers were people who had lived most of their lives on the Plains. Although they intended to plant gardens, good soil was not a major consideration in their choice of land; they were more interested in a spot close to productive hay-lands, good wood lots, and reliable supplies of water. In succeeding years, the area attracted two further migrations of Métis (1877–78 and 1882–83). Most of these later migrants came from Manitoba, where their most recent experience was in small-scale farming and stock raising, practices which they hoped to continue on the South Branch.[11]

For those who were serious about pursuing an agricultural life, the early years on the Saskatchewan were disappointing. Seed and equipment were expensive, local demand for their produce was weak, and, in the two years before the rebellion, unseasonable weather curtailed production. A few Métis (such as the Tourond family) did enjoy some success in agriculture, but they were not numerous. More than one outside observer felt that the Métis were not fully committed to farming as a livelihood. In 1884 Lawrence Clarke, Chief Factor for the Hudson's Bay Co. at Prince Albert, claimed that "these men are not farmers [but] merely cultivating small patches of land little larger than kitchen gardens. They live by hunting and freighting." These pursuits, he said, were in decline, so the Métis were "getting poorer by the year."[12] The Dominion Lands Agent at Prince Albert felt similarly; he concluded that most of the Métis who were pressing land claims before him were more interested in hunting than farming.[13] Many of those who applied for land in 1884 called themselves farmers but, as Diane Payment has noted: "Poussés à se déclarer agriculteurs, il est probable que plusieurs hesitent, ou négligent de dire qu'il font encore la chasse."[14] At Prairie-Ronde the population was even less involved in agriculture, as the story of Charles Trottier indicates. Although the settlement was dispersed after the rebellion, the people returned to the area in the early years of the twentieth century; Trottier, leader of the settlement (almost an Indian band chief, in fact) applied for land there on his return in 1903. In his application, he swore that "I took up this land as far back as 1855 when I was with my parents hunting the buffaloes in the plains." He said that on the eve of the rebellion he had a house and stable there and had broken fifteen acres of soil; but he admitted that he had not got around to sowing it before fleeing to the United States "on account of the rebellion."[15]

In effect most Métis on the South Saskatchewan in the mid-1880s sought their livelihood as hunters, gatherers, freighters, trappers, and farmers in varying degrees of precedence. Hunting remained important. For example, when applying for land in the years following the rebellion, some men who had taken part in that conflict still listed their occupation as "Hunter, freighter & farmer"— in that order.[16] The days of the great buffalo hunts were over, however. The last organized hunt from the Saskatchewan, led by Gabriel Dumont in 1880, had ridden as far south as the Cypress Hills and even into the United States in search of buffalo.[17] With the disappearance of the buffalo there was hunger on the Plains, it is true. But there was still other game around, even in later decades. One of the people whose family later returned to Prairie-Ronde has recalled that, while the Métis who resettled there "weren't no farmers," they were still able to hunt deer (and this was the twentieth century).[18] Augustin Laframboise, one of the fighters killed at the Battle of Duck Lake, is known to have been in the Cypress Hills — undoubtedly hunting — as late as 1882,[19] and there must have been others from the South Branch also hunting there in the years immediately preceding the rebellion. Small game, such as prairie chickens and ducks, were also still fairly plentiful on the Plains. Gathering, as a pursuit, included the traditional Métis and Cree practices of collecting duck eggs, picking berries, and digging roots — particularly Indian turnips (*Psoralea lanceolata*) — as dietary supplements. Wood was also cut and hauled for sale in Prince Albert and Saskatoon.[20]

Freighting had long been important, especially as payment was made in cash and as it provided the Métis the chance to satisfy their love of travelling the Plains. The use of Red River carts to transport freight declined with the arrival of regular steamboat service on the Saskatchewan River and the building of the Canadian Pacific Railway across the southern Plains in the 1880s. Demand for freighters rose again for awhile, however, when Fort Carlton was made a distribution point for the Hudson's Bay Co. in 1884.[21] Lastly, some Métis found they were able to shift from hunting buffalo to trapping fur-bearing animals in the parklands and woodlands north of the Saskatchewan River. Again, in addition to the economic inducement, it may have been their traditional love of travel which drew the Métis to trapping. In any case, there seems no doubt that, because they pursued other means of livelihood — hunting, gathering, freighting, and trapping — the Métis were absent for long periods from whatever crops or livestock they may have been trying to raise, and their agricultural effectiveness suffered significantly.

By mid-1884 the Métis population of the South Branch was estimated to be 1300 people. Adding the 100 or so at Prairie-Ronde, the South Saskatchewan Métis numbered no more than 1400 men, women, and children. About 1100 were originally from Manitoba.[22] The remaining 300 had been born in what, in 1870, had become the Northwest Territories. As will be seen, it was from this small group, combined with a number of men who had been born in Manitoba but had lived most of their lives on the Plains, that most of the militantly committed rebels of 1885 came.

In their fight with the Canadian authorities, the Métis had to rely almost exclusively on this small population base. Few outsiders came to join the fighting. Messages were sent to solicit assistance from Prince Albert, as well as from Métis communities at Qu'Appelle and Battleford, but the response was disappointing. A Militia Roll, drawn up after the Battle of Duck Lake, shows a fighting force of 18.5 companies, each consisting of a captain and ten soldiers — over 200 names in all.[23] This number is incomplete, however. A list provided by Philippe Garnot to Bishop Taché after the rebellion notes the names of about 280 men who were present (though not necessarily active combatants) at the Battle of Batoche.[24] The Militia Roll and the Garnot list cover the adult male population of the two South Saskatchewan communities involved and, as such, include a handful of people of mixed British and Indian ancestry who lived in the area. (A significant number of reserve Indians also joined in the fighting; their participation will be examined later.) The number of men who could take an active part in the actual fighting was limited by the supply of arms available. One report notes an initial stock of 253 guns, of which 48 were inoperative.[25] By the end of the hostilities this stock had been reduced — through loss, damage, and lack of ammunition — to only 60 or 70 guns.[26] The best estimate of the number of Métis who had any involvement in the hostilities of March, April, and May 1885 would be about 250. Not all were combatants; many served auxiliary roles — guarding prisoners, carrying messages, caring for livestock and horses, scrounging for supplies, performing reconnaissance.

MILITANT MÉTIS

An estimate of those Métis who could be considered the most militantly committed to the notion of rebellion is also difficult to compute. Upon first consideration one might think that membership in the "Exovedate" would help identify the militants. This body was the council or provisional government which Louis Riel set up to handle the administrative and military (and even theological) affairs of the community during the insurrection. Over twenty men were appointed to the council but two — J-B. Boyer and C. Nolin — were unsympathetic to the rebellion and left town. The council also included three non-Métis — White Cap, the Sioux chief from Saskatoon, and two French Canadians, conscripted for their literacy, who served for short periods as secretary. A second indicator of militancy might be appointment as captain of one of the nineteen militia companies.[27] Among these men, however, was one — W. Boyer — who refused to take up arms and quietly left town. The exceptions show that mere appointment to these two bodies is not necessarily an accurate guide to insurrectionary ardour; some men were evidently appointed in ignorance of their opinions. A third consideration in determining militancy might be the secret oath drawn up by Louis Riel on 5 March 1885, to which ten Métis affixed their marks; in it, the men swore to take up arms, if necessary, to save their country from a wicked government.[28] As will be seen, however, it would be too restrictive to limit militancy to only ten men.

Instead, this study will use two other criteria to identify the most ardent rebels. First, it will include all those who fled to the United States after the Battle of Batoche. In effect, these men identified themselves as highly implicated in rebellion. After all, removing themselves from the heartland of the Métis nation and (often) their families was a serious step; their flight will be taken as evidence that their involvement in the insurrection was so deep that they expected particularly severe treatment from the victorious Canadian authorities. Flight cannot be considered mere cowardice, for the fugitives included many men of undoubted courage. Most of the participants chose not to flee, however, and these included some of the most ardent proponents of rebellion. Canadian authorities charged many of them with the crime of treason felony. Eighteen were found guilty and sentenced to prison terms of one, three, or seven years. The second indicator of militancy, then, will be those whose involvement in rebellion was judged by the courts to deserve the severest sentence.[29] As Table 6.1 shows, at least 28 Métis rebels

Table 6.1   Fugitive and Imprisoned Militants

Name	Age	Fug./Sentence	Years in NWT	Remarks
J-Bte. Boucher Sr.	47	fugitive	since 1882	Exovede
Josué Breland		fugitive		
Ambroise Champagne		fugitive	Plains Métis*	militia captain
Norbert Delorme	48	fugitive	since 1874	Exovede
Maxime Dubois	36	7 years		
Michel Dumas	36	fugitive	since 1880	Public Servant
Edouard Dumont	45	fugitive	born in NWT	militia captain
Elie Dumont	39	fugitive	Plains Métis*	
Gabriel Dumont	47	fugitive	Plains Métis*	Exovede/took oath
Jean Dumont	52	fugitive	Plains Métis*	cousin of above three
Philippe Gariépy	48	7 years	since 1872	militia captain/oath
Pierre Henry	40	7 years	since 1882	Exovede
Antoine Lafontaine	36	fugitive		militia captain
Calixte Lafontaine	39	fugitive		militia captain/oath
Louis Lafontaine		fugitive	by at least 1876	
Pierre Laverdure	66	fugitive	by at least 1870	
Maxime Lépine	49	7 years	since 1882	Exovede/took oath
William Letendre		fugitive	Plains Métis*	
Albert Monkman	29	7 years		Protestant Halfbreed
Abraham Montour Sr.	53	fugitive	born in NWT	took secret oath
Jonas Moreau		fugitive		militia captain
Napoléon Nault	27	fugitive	since 1878	took secret oath
Julien Ouellette	36	fugitive	since 1868	
J-Bte. Parenteau	55	fugitive	since 1858	
Pierre Parenteau	72	7 years	since 1882	Exovedate Pres./oath/ famed buffalo hunter
John Ross Jr.	28	fugitive	born in NWT	took secret oath
Pierre Sansregret	44	fugitive	by at least 1866	
James Short	50	7 years	born in NWT	
André Trottier	25	fugitive	Plains Métis*	nephew of Charles Sr.
Charles Trottier Sr.	49	fugitive	Plains Métis*	Exovede
Isidore Trottier	22	fugitive	Plains Métis*	son of Charles Sr.
J-Bte. Trottier	20	fugitive	Plains Métis*	son of Charles Sr.
Johny Trottier	22	fugitive	Plains Métis*	nephew of Charles Sr.
Rémi Trottier	24	fugitive	Plains Métis*	son of Charles Sr.
J-Bte. Vandal	54	7 years	born in NWT	militia captain
Pierre Vandal	39	7 years	since 1872	sent to seek Big Bear's support
James Ward	34	fugitive	born in NWT	

*   Plains Métis: Permanent, long-time resident of what became the Northwest Territories (1870), even though perhaps born in what became the province of Manitoba (1870) and occasionally trading there.

Sources: Census, Prince Albert, Wood Mountain, and Cypress Hills, 1881, NAC, MG31, Microfilm C 13285. (Unfortunately, the pages are often illegible so the census data are not fully available.) Clarence Kipling Collection, NAC, MG 25, G 62. Dumont family genealogy in NAC, MG 17, A 17, no. 88, pp. 724–29. G.F.G. Stanley et al. (eds.), *The Collected Writings of Louis Riel* (Edmonton, 1985), vol. 5, Biographical Index. Affidavit of Père André, Canada, Parlement, *Documents de la Session, 1886*, no. 52, pp. 389–94. William Pearce Report, Canada, Parlement, *Documents de la Session, 1886*, no. 86, pp. 1–18. Diane Payment, "Monsieur Batoche," *Saskatchewan History* (Autumn 1979): 81–103. For references regarding fugitives, see note 29.

are known to have fled to the United States and nine more were sentenced to seven-year prison terms. The table includes most, but not all, of those who signed the secret oath and of those appointed to the Exovedate and as militia captains. Louis Riel is covered by none of the criteria, nor was he a member of the Exovedate or a combatant; in some ways he was an outsider and not part of the South Branch community. For these reasons, he and men such as William H. Jackson will be excluded from those considered in this study as militants.

Some weaknesses are apparent in employing the above criteria to identify the most militantly committed rebels. First, there quite possibly may have been more than 28 men who fled the country in May 1885; this figure is simply the total so far uncovered in various documentary sources. Second, there were doubtless some Métis among the nineteen killed at Duck Lake, Fish Creek, and Batoche who were as deeply committed to the uprising as those noted in Table 6.1. Death in battle is no certain indication of ardour but, undoubtedly, a number of the men, had they lived, would either have felt compelled to flee the country or have received long prison sentences for their activities during the rebellion. For example, three of the dead had signed the secret oath to take up arms if necessary. For this reason, Table 6.2, noting the men who died in the fighting, has been drawn up. Inclusion on this list can be considered as at least a secondary indicator of militancy.

Table 6.2   Men Killed in Battle

Name	Age	Battle	Years in NWT	Remarks
François Boyer	28	Fish Cr.		
Isidore Boyer	60	Batoche		
Damase Carrière	34	Batoche		Exovede
Michel Desjarlais	30	Fish Cr.		
Isidore Dumont Jr.	55	Duck L.	born in NWT	militia captain; took secret oath
Ambroise Jobin	35		born in NWT	Exovede; died of wounds, 23 May
Augustin Laframboise	46	Duck L.	Plains Métis	militia captain; took secret oath
André Letendre	48	Batoche	Plains Métis	bro. of F-X. Letendre
J-Bte. Montour		Duck L.	Plains Métis	
Joseph Montour		Duck L.		
Joseph Ouellette Sr.	93	Batoche	Plains Métis	took secret oath
St. Pierre Parenteau	25	Fish Cr.	since 1882	
Donald Ross	63	Batoche		Exovede
John Swan (Swain)	56	Batoche		
Calixte Tourond		Batoche	since 1882	
Elzéar Tourond		Batoche	since 1882	
Michel Trottier Sr.	64	Batoche	Plains Métis	uncle of Charles Trottier Sr.
Joseph Vandal	75	Batoche		
Joseph Vermette	56	Fish Cr.		

Sources: Census, Prince Albert, Wood Mountain, and Cypress Hills, 1881, NAC, MG 31. Stanley et al., *Collected Writings*, vol. 5, Biographical Index. Registre de la paroisse St-Antoine-de-Padoue (Batoche, Sask.), sépultures.
A. Ouimet, B.A.T. de Montigny (eds.), *La vérité sur la question Métisse au Nord-Ouest* (Montréal, 1889), p. 138. William Pearce Report, Canada, Parlement, *Documents de la Session*, 1886, no. 8, pp. 1–18. Payment, "Monsieur Batoche." NAC, RG 15, D II, 1, Commission on Rebellion Losses, vol. 914, f. 892,789, no. 21.

A third weakness of the criteria is that the courts may have erred in determining which men were the most deeply implicated rebels. Albert Monkman, for example, was undoubtedly one of the most militant rebels throughout most of the uprising (he was accused of forcing others to fight) and received a seven-year court sentence. By the end, however, he had aroused Riel's suspicions (perhaps for not delivering the support of the Protestant Halfbreeds of Prince Albert) and Riel had him arrested before the Battle of Batoche.[30] Sixteen trials were held at Battleford and Regina in the summer of 1885 for crimes arising out of the rebellion. The accused were generally grouped by ethnicity and locality. The largest group was the 30 residents of the South Saskatchewan who, after pleading guilty to treason felony, received their sentences at Regina on 14 August. One witness complained that, through negligence, some important rebels had never been arrested but he gave no names. All members of the Exovedate who were not dead or had not fled were charged; one received a suspended sentence, two were given three years in prison, while five received seven-year terms. Appointment as a militia captain was not considered important — seven captains were not even charged, though the three who were, received seven-year sentences. Still, the court's conclusions were not manifestly capricious. The deciding factors by which it assessed the degree of involvement in rebellion was the testimony given in affidavits by anglophone settlers whom the rebels had held as prisoners, by local priests, and by a few Métis who had taken no part in the uprising. Thus, although not foolproof, a seven-year sentence is, on the whole, not an unreasonable guide to the degree of insurrectionary involvement.[31]

At the other end of the political spectrum from the most militant rebels were a smaller number of men who opposed taking up arms. Their feelings may not have been known at the beginning of the uprising and, as a result, some of them were named to positions in the militia or the Exovedate. For several reasons, the support of these men would have brought important benefits to the insurrectionary cause. They were generally younger than the militants. Some were educated and had useful skills to offer; others were merchants with valuable stocks of provisions and ammunition. Their nomination may also have been made in a (vain) hope of uniting all sectors of the community. Table 6.3 lists ten Métis now known to have opposed the notion of rebellion and who made sure they were absent from the scene of action. When hostilities began, the merchants F-X. Letendre (also known as Batoche), for whom the village was named, and Salomon Venne were away and refused to return; Letendre's store was looted for its supplies. The other eight men fled the South Branch, taking refuge at either Prince Albert or Qu'Appelle. Louis Marion was threatened with death for treason before escaping. Charles Nolin initially supported the insurrection but, for reasons which remain unclear, reversed his position; arrested by the rebels, he feigned submission and then fled. Of course, besides these known examples, there may have been other men who left quietly to avoid enlistment into the cause.[32]

The vast majority of Métis on the South Saskatchewan can probably be said to have occupied neither end of the political spectrum — they were neither militantly committed to rebellion nor opposed to it. Some of them, initially indifferent or undecided, were undoubtedly coerced into participating. At the treason felony trial of August 1885, a number of witnesses testified that some Métis had been threatened with destruction of property and even death if they did not show proper devotion to the insurrectionary cause. The enforcers singled out were, of course, the militants; care was taken, however, to implicate only those who could not be hurt further — men such as Joseph Vandal and Damase Carrière (both killed at Batoche), or Napoléon Nault, Norbert Delorme, and Gabriel and Jean Dumont (all safely in the United States).[33] Despite the intimidation, however, morale was not a problem among the less committed, even after the first men were killed in action at Duck Lake. When Mrs. Louis Marion arrived in Prince Albert to join her husband, who had fled there, she reported

Table 6.3   Métis Who Opposed Rebellion

Name	Age	Occupation	Remarks
C-E. Boucher	20	store clerk	father a fugitive in the U.S.
J-Bte. Boucher	23	store clerk	father a fugitive in the U.S.; initially named a militia captain
J-Bte. Boyer	40	merchant	initially named to Exovedate
William Boyer	34		initially named a militia captain
Georges Fisher		merchant	
Roger Goulet		farmer	initially named a militia soldier
F-X. Letendre	44	merchant	wealthiest Métis on South Branch
Louis Marion		Pub. Servant	instructor at Beardy Indian reserve
Charles Nolin	48	entrepreneur	member of Manitoba Assembly, 1874/79; initially named to Exovedate
Salomon Venne	48	merchant	

Sources: RG 15, D II, 1, Commission on Rebellion Losses, claim of J-Bte. Boucher, vol. 915, f. 892,789, no. 64.
D. Payment, "Monsieur Batoche." D. Payment, *Batoche, 1870–1910*, p. 103. MG 26, G, (Laurier Papers), vol. 2,
A. Fisher to Laurier, 14 Mar. 1888, pp. 676–91. Stanley et al., *Collected Writings*, vol. 5, Biographical Index. Walter Hildebrandt,
The Battle of Batoche (Ottawa, 1985), p. 20.

on the situation at Batoche; though obviously not sympathetic to the rebel cause, she insisted that there had been no tears shed at the funerals and that the people were as determined as ever to resist.[34]

It is evident that the Métis who were on the end of the political spectrum which opposed rebellion (Table 6.3) were those who had found some success in adapting to the new circumstances of life in the Northwest Territories. They all seem to have had some formal education; seven of them were involved in trade while one held a government position. Most were related to one another.[35] These men comprised nearly all the incipient acculturates among the South Saskatchewan Métis. The only known exceptions — the only men with similar backgrounds who supported the notion of rebellion — were Emmanuel Champagne, Michel Dumas, and Maxime Lépine. The first was a successful farmer and fur trader who was charged with treason felony but received a suspended sentence (probably for age and health reasons). Dumas, although a farm instructor at the One Arrow Indian reserve, was a militant proponent of rebellion who fled to the United States. Lépine, a small-scale businessman and farmer, was also a militant rebel; he received a seven-year prison sentence.

The militants, for their part, were almost entirely made up of long-time freighters and buffalo hunters; they were middle-aged men who had found it difficult to adjust to a sedentary, agricultural life. Thus, it can be seen that the political and cultural spectra of the community closely corresponded. As Table 6.1 shows, seventeen were what will be referred to hereafter as Plains Métis (Marcel Giraud called them "métis de l'Ouest");[36] that is, they were men who had spent much of their lives in what, in 1870, had become the Northwest Territories, or had been born there. Some, it is true, had been born in American territory or in what had become the province of Manitoba; many traded in Manitoba regularly and a few had even received the land or scrip to which they were entitled by the Manitoba Act. Many of the Dumonts and Trottiers had this background, but there can be no doubt that they were Métis of the Plains. Another example is Jean-Baptiste Parenteau, rebel and fugitive in 1885, who was born at

Red River about 1830; in 1900, in an affidavit supporting his son's application for land, he swore that

> I was married at Winnipeg 42 years ago (1858) to Pélagie Dumont [sister of Gabriel] and since that time I have always lived in the North-west Territories & until about twenty five years ago I was a Buffalo hunter and at the time of the Red River Rebellion [1869] I was living . . . near Fish Creek where the Traders & Hunters used to winter. I never had a house in . . . Manitoba since I was married and I only went there in the Spring of each year to sell furs, returning in the fall. When I was out hunting the whole family used to follow me. My son Alexandre was born on the third day after we arrived in Winnipeg in the spring twenty five years ago and about fifteen days after his birth we started out on our journey back.[37]

Most of the militants seem to have been among the original Métis settlers of the South Saskatchewan, i.e., those who had arrived in the early 1870s; few were among the more agriculture-oriented settlers who had come after 1877. Of the militants whose age is known (Table 6.1), the average was 41 years old. A few of the militants were young, but it is revealing to learn that at least four children of fugitive militants, though living in the area and old enough to fight, took no part at all in the insurrection.[38] The evidence in Table 6.2 listing the Métis killed in action also supports a conclusion that the militants were largely made up of older (average age 51) Plains Métis, representatives of the Plains buffalo-hunting tradition. And, as will be seen, many of these men were, in various ways, close to the Plains Indians in culture.

Many Métis undoubtedly considered themselves distinct from, and superior to, Indians. Others, however, though they called themselves Métis, were not reluctant to point out the similarities between the two groups, especially the Plains Métis, who had long followed lifeways similar to their kin the Plains Cree and Saulteaux — a migratory life based on the hunt. In 1877 a number of Plains Métis petitioned the government for relaxation of the game laws and for assistance in establishing themselves on farms. They described themselves as leading "an entirely nomadic life, as the Indians on the plains."[39] Among the petitioners were at least three Métis who participated in the rebellion on the South Saskatchewan, and one, James Ward, is classified as a militant in Table 6.1. Another interesting document is a recently discovered petition forwarded by Inspector James Walsh of the North-West Mounted Police from the Cypress Hills in 1876.[40] The petitioners describe themselves as "half-breeds of the Cree and Saulteaux Tribes" who "have lived from childhood upon the prairies and adopted the customs of the Indians." They ask to be admitted into Treaty No. 4 as a group and elect their own chief. Again, among those affixing their marks to the petition were two or three Métis who later participated in the South Saskatchewan conflict. Two years later, another petition was circulated in the Cypress Hills among Métis who described themselves as having been long "in the habit of roaming over the prairies of the North-West for the purposes of hunting." They asked for a "special reserve" of land "to the exclusion of all whites" except government officials. Signing the petition were fourteen men who are listed among the militants or the dead in Tables 6.1 and 6.2.[41]

While some of those petitioners who, in the 1870s, called themselves Métis or Halfbreeds continued to identify with that group, many others ended up on reserves as Treaty Indians. Government officials early recognized that it was difficult to determine an Indian by ancestry alone;[42] people of mixed Indian and European ancestry who wished to identify themselves as Indians were permitted to "take Treaty." Many did so to take advantage of Treaty benefits — an annuity, land on a reserve, agricultural assistance and instruction, and so forth. By the mid-1880s, however, many Treaty Indians had become dissatisfied with reserve life and some of those with mixed ancestry then decided to withdraw from Treaty. Withdrawals accelerated when the government finally acted on the demand of the Northwest Métis that they, like their kin in Manitoba, should be compensated for the extinguishment of their territorial claims. The land question had long rankled the Métis, and government inaction culminated in rebellion in March 1885. The North-West Half Breed Commission established later offered the Métis compensation in the form of land or scrip.[43] This concession prompted a large number of people, who for a decade had identified themselves as Indians, to leave the reserves. In 1886 over half the Métis who were granted scrip by the Commission were mixed bloods who had withdrawn from Treaty.[44] Within a few years, some, however, were asking to be readmitted to Treaty.[45]

Thus, in the 1870s and 1880s, many people moved back and forth across the ethnic boundaries between Indian and Métis groups, for not only did the Métis retain many elements of their Indian heritage, but Indians were assimilating European traits at the same time as well. To cross the Métis ethnic boundary, it appears one had only to have mixed ancestry, profess Christianity, and identify oneself as Métis. With these characteristics, it seems that one was readily accepted as Métis and, as well, was acknowledged by outsiders as such. Mixed ancestry was essential, however; no whites are known to have been considered as Métis. One Indian, Kitwayo or Alexandre Cadieux —"une sauvage pur sang," as he was described — did live among the South Branch Métis; but, despite the French name, he was always identified as an Indian because of his unmixed parentage.[46]

Inter-ethnic movements were particularly easy on the South Saskatchewan River. In the Duck Lake area, for example, even those people who had chosen to live on reserves as Indians were almost entirely of mixed ancestry.[47] In addition, a large number of the reserve Indians had been baptized and regarded themselves Christian.[48] Indeed, the first person killed in the 1885 uprising was a Christian Cree (from the Beardy reserve) shot at the Battle of Duck Lake.[49] The Métis group may have been more orthodoxly and homogeneously Christian but still the Christianity which some of them practised included elements of Indian origin such as healing rituals, precognition, and seeing at a distance.[50]

While the Plains Métis retained traces of Indian religion, their social structures also remained remarkably similar to those of the Cree. Following the individualistic traditions of their Indian ancestors, each Métis was a generalist; that is, there was little specialization of work beyond age or sex — although there was considerable sharing within the community, each family made its own cart, dwelling, clothing and so on. On the South Saskatchewan the only exceptions were a few Métis merchants and traders. (The handful of priests and teachers living in the area were all outsiders.) Also, like the Cree, the Métis had no strong social or political hierarchy; strict obedience to leaders was common only in the buffalo hunt and in war.[51] Indeed, the organization of the Métis militia in 1885 strongly resembled Indian custom. Commanding the militia was Gabriel Dumont, whose authority was, in many ways, similar to that of a Plains Indian chief. Louis Riel wrote Sir John A. Macdonald, pointing out that, while the government had recognized even the "most insignificant" chiefs in treaties, "Gabriel Dumont was altogether ignored." This indignity, Riel claimed, "has always been rankling in his mind."[52]

When the time came for armed action, Dumont naturally expected assistance from Indians throughout the northwest. He was only partly successful. Big Bear, Poundmaker, and other Cree chiefs living up the North Saskatchewan River also rose in rebellion in the spring of 1885; Dumont sent messengers requesting their help on the South Branch but none arrived before the final defeat at Batoche on 12 May.[53] Aid was also requested from reserves to the south but the only Indians who came from that direction were White Cap and about twenty of his men from Moose Woods near Saskatoon. Surprisingly, these were Sioux with whom the Métis traditionally had few ties; there is some reason to believe that the aggressive Trottier family of nearby Prairie-Ronde coerced them to travel to Batoche. Four Sioux died in the fighting. The most important support came from Indians in the South Branch area. Scores of men arrived from the One Arrow, Beardy, Okemasis, Chakastapaysin, and Petaquakey reserves; only one was killed in the fighting, but a chief, One Arrow, was subsequently sentenced to three years in prison.[54]

Dumont and the other militants had every reason to count on support from neighbouring reserves because of the strong ties between the Métis and those Indians. Indeed, at least six Métis who participated in the rebellion had themselves been on the paylists (i.e., for annuities) of neighbouring reserves as recently as 1884.[55] Another combatant, Charles Trottier Jr., was still a Treaty Indian (Beardy's reserve) at the time of the uprising. A nephew of Charles Trottier Sr., leader of the Prairie-Ronde clan, he was married to the daughter of Okemasis, chief of a South Branch band. He fought at Duck Lake and seems to have fled the country; but, as he was a Treaty Indian, he is excluded from Table 6.1.[56]

It is not surprising that there was frequent inter-marriage between South Branch Métis and reserve Indians; Diane Payment affirms that there are numerous cases mentioned in local church registers.[57] Although the couples may not have resided full-time on the reserves, the spouse was able to collect an annuity. Several combatants of 1885 had Treaty Indian wives. One was Augustin Laframboise, Métis militia captain killed at Duck Lake; his wife was on the paylist of Petaquakey reserve.[58] Another was Michel Trottier, a Métis killed at Batoche; married to an Indian of Duck Lake Agency, he was the brother of Charles Trottier Sr.[59]

Gabriel Dumont himself had close kin on reserves, including that of One Arrow, which was only a short distance from his residence. There, his first cousin, Vital Dumont (also known as Cayol), son of his uncle Jean-Baptiste, had chosen to live as a Treaty Indian (even though both his parents were of mixed ancestry). In 1885 Vital Dumont and his two adult sons, Louis and Francis, answered Gabriel's call to arms. The three of them subsequently felt so deeply implicated in the rebellion that they fled to the United States.[60] As Treaty Indians, however, they too will be excluded from Table 6.1.

Language was another cultural trait which many Métis shared with the Plains Indians. Because most Métis had French ancestors and bore French names, they were labelled as French. Many, however, also had Indian names and, perhaps not surprisingly (given their strong kinship ties with local Indians), many of them were, in fact, unilingual Cree-speakers. This linguistic persistence was particularly evident among the Plains Métis and, indeed, among the militant supporters of the 1885 rebellion. For years Roman Catholic missionaries on the South Saskatchewan had lamented their parishioners' preference for Cree. It is known that, at religious services in the 1880s, hymns were sometimes sung in Cree. In education, however, the policy of the Church was to try to downgrade native language and encourage the use of European languages, especially French. The efforts were not always successful. As late as 1897 it was reported that most Métis school children at Batoche could understand neither French nor English![61] For many years the use of Cree remained vigorous among people of mixed ancestry living in scattered parts of the northwest. By the twentieth century, certainly, some groups had incorporated elements of European languages into their speech, thus developing a tongue known popularly as "Michif." Linguists studying Michif have discovered that, while its noun phrases are usually French in origin, syntax and verb structures are mainly Cree. As one linguist has said, "Michif is best viewed as a dialect of Cree."[62]

In August 1885 the 30 South Saskatchewan Métis charged with the crime of treason felony went on trial at Regina. At the outset, all but one requested that the court proceedings be translated into Cree and the judge complied with their wish. Even so, the lawyer for the accused remarked that his clients were still not clear about the meaning of their charge, "the interpreter not being able to translate into their language the words of the law."[63] In the end, the only Métis who did not understand Cree was given a conditional discharge while, of those who preferred Cree, eighteen were sentenced to prison, including, of course, the eleven militants listed in Table 6.1 who received seven-year terms. It can be said, then, that of all the Métis whose linguistic preference is known, the most militant proponents of insurrection in 1885 were men who were most at ease speaking the language of the Plains Indians.

Less is known of the language spoken by the other Métis listed in Tables 6.1 and 6.2. However, some impression can be gained by examining the preferences of their children. In the months after the rebellion, the Half Breed Commission visited the South Branch area offering scrip to the Métis. Few people accepted the offer in 1885, though many did in ensuing years. Naturally, those who had participated in the uprising were reluctant to apply, but two adult children whose fathers were fugitives and two whose fathers had been killed in the fighting did dare to request scrip. The Commission's procedure that year provided for an explanation of one's rights in a choice of languages. Of the four, all of whose fathers appear in Tables 6.1 and 6.2, one requested an explanation in French, two in Cree, and one in both languages.[64] This number, though small, would again suggest that, in the houses of the most militant rebels, it was the language of the Plains Cree which was spoken.

It is quite possible that the language spoken by the Métis accused of treason felony and those whose children applied for scrip after the rebellion included a degree of French in addition to Cree; that is, they probably spoke a form of incipient Michif. Even so, however, their stated preference for Cree once again indicates that most of the militant supporters of insurrection in 1885 were culturally close to Plains Indians.

From the foregoing examination of their background, age, livelihood, religion, social structure, and language, it can be seen that the Métis who were the most militantly involved in the 1885 rebellion were the most conservative, most Indian-like in the community. The militants were, with only a few exceptions, men of an older generation, former buffalo hunters and freighters only marginally involved in agriculture; they were Métis of the Plains tradition who were unable or unwilling to adjust their lives to the rapidly changing conditions of the new northwest. In contrast, the Métis who opposed taking up arms were, with no apparent exceptions, younger men who had enjoyed some success in fields which held promise in the new order of things. While there was a fair measure of diversity in both the political spectrum and the cultural spectrum of the South Saskatchewan community, the two spectra were almost congruent.

CONCLUSION

A number of implications may be seen to arise from these conclusions. For example, although both contemporaries and more recent observers commonly speak of French Métis, Scottish mixed bloods, and English Halfbreeds, this is a labelling often based only on their names. However, it is evident that in the 1880s (and even later) there was a substantial group of people of mixed ancestry outside Manitoba who spoke only native languages or whose best facility was in a native language. (Not only Cree was used; Métis beyond the Saskatchewan even today speak a number of Dene tongues.) For these people, a linguistic characterization is meaningless. Thus, insofar as one is concerned with their European traits, it may be more useful to categorize them as either Roman Catholic or Protestant mixed bloods, for they were virtually all one or the other.

The persistence of Plains hunting traditions among many Métis can have other implications — for example, in their decision in 1885 to take up arms. It should not be surprising that these people should have reacted violently when confronted with a faceless, seemingly immovable government bureaucracy which appeared to be totally indifferent to their customs, anxieties, and needs. Numerous petitions had been sent to the government, whose response was usually long in coming, if it came at all. The complicated statutes and regulations of the Department of the Interior were unfathomable to this non-literate people, and the length of time it took to obtain a decision from Ottawa became intolerable.

The Plains Métis were men of action, unaccustomed to standing passively by as their situation deteriorated. They had much honour to lose if they did not take action; and, also, as the least acculturated in the community, generally had the least property to lose if they did. The missionaries tried to talk them out of insurrection but, again as the least acculturated, their respect for the authority of the Church was perhaps not as strong as, for example, that of the men listed in Table 6.3. And when it came to military planning, the leading insurrectionists totally miscalculated the power behind the government's authority. Accustomed only to fighting Indians, the Plains Métis did not expect the soldiers to come in such great numbers; nor were they aware that, unlike Indians, the new enemy, after suffering losses at Duck Lake and Fish Creek, would be more determined to fight, not less.

The sizable number of militants which has been identified above indicates that, apart from the few, more acculturated people in the community, the insurrectionary movement on the South Saskatchewan was quite deeply based. This finding would contradict the views of some contemporary observers as well as more recent commentators. At the treason felony trial of August 1885 the missionary fathers, André and Fourmond, testified that the militant proponents of rebellion were very few — essentially just Riel and three others: Gabriel Dumont and Napoléon Nault (both fugitives in the United States) and Damase Carrière (killed at Batoche). Using tricks, threats, and lies, this handful of men were said to have seduced a large but weakly committed group of gullible Métis into taking up arms.[65] However, by resting the blame entirely on Riel and those who were conveniently beyond reach of the law, it is likely that the priests were seeking to minimize their parishioners' role in the uprising and thus mitigate the court's punishment. Similarly, the arguments of two recent historians have also diminished the importance of free will in the actions of the rebels: Thomas Flanagan and Donald McLean contend that the Métis were manipulated into rebellion either by Louis Riel, or by Sir John A. Macdonald and Lawrence Clarke, each for his own purpose.[66] By the findings of this study, however, it would appear that the rebellion was a popular movement. The militants may have tricked or coerced some Métis into participating, but those militants were a sizable group in themselves.

NOTES

1. See, for example, F.L. Barron, J.B. Waldram (eds.), *1885 and After: Native Society in Transition* (Regina, 1986); Bob Beal, Roderick Macleod, *Prairie Fire: The 1885 North-West Rebellion* (Edmonton, 1984); Thomas Flanagan, *Louis "David" Riel: "Prophet of the New World"* (Toronto, 1979); Thomas Flanagan, *Riel and the Rebellion: 1885 Reconsidered* (Saskatoon, 1983); Julia Harrison, *Métis: People between Two Worlds* (Vancouver, Toronto, 1985); Walter Hildebrandt, *The Battle of Batoche: British Small Warfare and the Entrenched Métis* (Ottawa, 1985); A.S. Lussier (ed.), *Riel and the Métis: Riel Mini-Conference Papers* (Winnipeg, 1979); Gilles Martel, *Le messianisme de Louis Riel* (Waterloo, 1984); Donald McLean, *1885: Métis Rebellion or Government Conspiracy?* (Winnipeg, 1985); Diane Payment, *Batoche (1870–1910)* (St-Boniface, 1983); J. Peterson, J.S.H. Brown (eds.), *The New Peoples: Being and Becoming Métis in North America* (Winnipeg, 1985); G.F.G. Stanley et al. (eds.), *The Collected Writings of Louis Riel*, 5 vols. (Edmonton, 1985); George Woodcock, *Gabriel Dumont: The Métis Chief and His Lost World* (Edmonton, 1975).
2. Flanagan, *Louis "David" Riel*, p. 148.
3. Hildebrandt, *Battle of Batoche*, p. 21. The ten men were D. Carrière, I. Dumont, D. Ross, N. Delorme, N. Nault, M. Dumas, M. Lépine, Ph. Cariépy, P. Garnot, and J-B. Boucher.
4. Journal of Louis Schmidt, National Archives of Canada (NAC), MG 17, A 17, no. 37.
5. Woodcock, *Gabriel Dumont*, pp. 120, 156.

6. Fredrik Barth, *Ethnic Groups and Boundaries* (Boston, 1969), pp. 9–15. See also Joe Sawchuk, The *Métis of Manitoba* (Toronto, 1978), pp. 8–10, 39.

7. Marcel Giraud, *Le Métis Canadien* (Paris, 1945; St-Boniface, 1984), p. 1190.

8. Rita Schilling, *Gabriel's Children* (Saskatoon, 1983). Norbert Walsh, *The Last Buffalo Hunter* (Mary Weekes, ed.), (Toronto, 1945), passim.

9. Beal, Macleod, *Prairie Fire*, p. 228. Diane Payment, "The Métis Homeland: Batoche in 1885," *NeWest Review* 10 (May 1985): 11, 12.

10. Report of William Pearce on South Branch land claimants, Canada, Parlement, *Documents de la Session*, 1886, no. 8b, pp. 10–18.

11. Diane Payment, "Batoche after 1885: A Society in Transition," in Barron, Waldram, *1885 and After*, pp. 174, 182. P.R. Mailhot, D.N. Sprague, "Persistent Settlers: The Dispersal and Resettlement of the Red River Métis, 1870–1885," *Canadian Ethnic Studies* 17, 2 (1985): 8.

12. NAC, MG 26A, Sir John A. Macdonald Papers, Clarke to J.A. Grahame, 20 May 1884, vol. 105, pp. 42244–50.

13. E.A. Mitchener, "The North Saskatchewan River Settlement Claims, 1883–84," in Lewis Thomas (ed.), *Essays in Western History* (Edmonton, 1976), pp. 134–35.

14. Payment, *Batoche (1870–1910)*, pp. 14–15, 34 (n. 24).

15. Saskatchewan Archives Board, homestead records, Charles Trottier affidavit, 17 December 1903.

16. NAC, RG 15, D II, 8(b), North West Half Breed land applications, A. Letendre, vol. 1329, no. 1301, and J-B. Parenteau fils, vol. 1362, no. 953.

17. Giraud, *Le Métis Canadien*, p. 1164.

18. Schilling, *Gabriel's Children*, p. 115.

19. NAC, RG 15, D II, 8(c), land applications, vol. 1353, no. 319.

20. Diane Payment, "Structural and Settlement History of Batoche Village," Parks Canada, *Manuscript Report Series*, no. 248 (1977), pp. 73–75. D.M. Loveridge, B. Potyondi, "From Wood Mountain to the Whitemud," ibid., no. 237 (1977), p. 95.

21. G.F.G. Stanley, *The Birth of Western Canada* (Toronto, 1936), p. 185. Mailhot, Sprague, "Persistent Settlers," p. 8. Giraud, *Le Métis Canadien*, p. 1171.

22. Mailhot, Sprague, "Persistent Settlers," p. 12.

23. Canada, Parliament, *Sessional Papers*, 1886, no. 43h, pp. 16–18.

24. Archives de l'Archévêché de St-Boniface (Manitoba), T, fonds Taché, lettres reçues, Garnot to Taché, 28 juillet 1885.

25. NAC, MG 17, A 17, no. 38, Cloutier report, "Effectifs."

26. Hildebrandt, *Battle of Batoche*, p. 74. NAC, MG 17, A 17, journal of Père Végreville, 16 mai 1885.

27. Listed in Canada, Parliament, *Sessional Papers*, 1886, no. 43h, pp. 16–18.

28. See text in Stanley, *Birth of Western Canada*, pp. 442–43 (n. 67).

29. For sentencing, see Canada, Parlement, *Documents de la Session*, 1886, no. 52, p. 308. References to fugitives are numerous; all are at NAC. RG 10, Dept. of Indian Affairs, Report of Sgt. Paterson, NWMP, 3 Oct. 1885, vol. 3722, file 24, 125; Insp. A.R. Cuthbert to Supt. A.B. Perry, 20 Jan. 1886, vol. 3585, file 1130-8. MG 27, I C4, Edgar Dewdney Papers, Report of J. Anderson, 29 Nov. 1885, 8 Dec. and 18 Dec. 1885, pp. 1524–26, 1531, 1536: McKay Report, 8 Jan. 1886, p. 1263; Report of O. Pichette, 1 Feb. 1886, pp. 1274–79; Report on half-breeds, 30 Mar. 1886, pp. 611–12; Nichol Report, May 1886, pp. 1290–97; Report of Cpl. Bossange, 22 April 1888, pp. 1337–39. RG 13, Dept. of Justice, B2, North-West Rebellion records, vol. 816, pp. 2398–2404, 2409–12; vol. 818, pp. 2780–86; vol. 821, pp. 3474–3518.

30. Jackson and Sanderson affidavits, Canada, Parlement, *Documents de la Session*, 1886, no. 52, pp. 399, 416. William Pearce Report, ibid., 1886, no. 8b, p. 12.

31. Affidavits and proceedings of the trial published in Canada, Parlement, *Documents de la Session*, 1886, no. 52, pp. 375–416.

32. Diane Payment, "Monsieur Batoche," *Saskatchewan History* (Autumn 1979): 95–96, 102 (n. 60). NAC, RG 13, Dept. of Justice, vol. 817, Marion testimony, pp. 2787–90. Hildebrandt, Battle of Batoche, p. 20.

33. Canada, Parlement, *Documents de la Session*, 1886, no. 52, pp. 389–416. NAC, RG 15, Dept. of the Interior, vol. 914, file 892,789, rebellion losses claim of Josephte Tourond, no. 21. NAC, RG 13, Dept. of Justice, B2, vol. 817, C. Nolin statement, pp. 2780–86.

34. NAC, MG 17, A 17, no. 37, André to Grandin, 31 mars 1885.

35. Payment, "The Métis Homeland," pp. 11, 12.

36. Giraud, *Le Métis Canadien*, p. 1148 *et passim*.

37. NAC, RG 15, vol. 1362, no. 667.

38. In addition to J-B. Boucher's sons cited in Table 6.3, the sons of Ambroise Champagne and Pierre Sansregret also avoided any involvement in the uprising. NAC, RG 15, Dept. of the Interior, vol. 1326, scrip claim no. 1555, and vol. 1331, claim no. 1504; vol. 915, rebellion losses claim, file 892,789, no. 64.

39. Canada, Parliament, *Sessional Papers*, 1886, no. 45a, pp. 4–5.

40. NAC, RG 10, vol. 3637, file 7089, petition 6 Sept. 1876.

41. N. Delorme, A. Lafontaine, L. Lafontaine, P. Laverdure, Jul. Ouellette, A. Trottier, C. Trottier, I. Trottier, J-B.Trottier, J. Trottier, I. Dumont, A. Laframboise, Jos. Ouellette, M. Trottier in Canada, Parliament, *Sessional Papers*, 1886, no. 45, pp. 10–16.

42. Alexander Morris, *The Indian Treaties of Canada* (Toronto, 1880), pp. 293–95. John L. Taylor, "The Development of an Indian Policy for the Canadian North-West, 1869–1879," Ph.D. thesis, Queen's University, 1975, pp. 228–31.

43. Ken Hatt, "The North-West Rebellion Scrip Commissions, 1885–1889," in Barron, Waldram, *1885 and After*, pp. 189–204.

44. Dept. of Interior, Annual Report, 1886, in Canada, Parliament, *Sessional Papers*, 1887, no. 7, Part I, p. 76.

45. Giraud, *Le Métis Canadien*, pp. 1217–18.

46. Canada, Parlement, *Documents de la Session*, 1886, no. 52a, p. 393.

47. David Mandelbaum, *The Plains Cree* (Regina, 1979), p. 10.

48. Canada, Indian Affairs Branch, *Annual Report*, 1892, pp. 318–19.

49. NAC, MG 17, A 17, no. 37, André to Grandin, 31 mars 1885.

50. Payment, "The Métis Homeland," p. 12. Guillaume Charette, *Vanishing Spaces: Memoirs of Louis Goulet* (Winnipeg, 1980), p. 146.

51. Mandelbaum, *Plains Cree*, p. 115.

52. NAC, MG 26, A, p. 42529, Riel to Macdonald, 17 July 1885.

53. Adolphe Ouimet, B-A-T. de Montigny (eds.), *La Vérité sur la question Métisse au Nord-Ouest* (Montréal, 1889), p. 130.

54. Canada, Parliament, *Sessional Papers*, 1886, no. 52, pp. 22, 49–50. NAC, RG 10, vol. 3584, file 1130, list of reserves, 1885.

55. RC 10, Paylists, vol. 9417, pp. 70, 85: J. Parisien, B. Deschamps, J. Vandal; vol. 9419, p. 137: J. Trottier, J. Flammant. RG 15, vol. 1369, scrip no. 1124: A. Trottier. Canada, Parliament, Sessional Papers, 1886, no. 43h, pp. 16–18, 44.

56. RG 10, Paylists, vol. 9421, p. 155. RG 15, vol. 1369, no. 1722 & no. 2108.

57. Payment, *Batoche (1870–1910)*, p. 121.

58. RG 10, vol. 9419, pp. 115–18.

59. RG 15, vol. 1369, no. 73.

60. RG 10, Paylists, vol. 9423, p. 304. RG 15, vol. 1345, no. 1251; vol. 1346, no. 148. Dumont genealogy in MG 17, A 17, no. 88, p. 727.

61. J. Brian Dawson, "The Relationship of the Catholic Clergy to Métis Society in the Canadian North-West, 1845–1885, With Particular Reference to the South Saskatchewan District," Parks Canada, *Manuscript Report Series*, no. 376 (1979), p. 255. Payment, *Batoche (1870–1910)*, pp. 44, 55, 63 (n. 6). Giraud, *Le Métis Canadien*, p. 1042. J.E. Foster, "The Métis: The People and the Term," in Lussier, *Riel and the Métis*, p. 90. Among the militants known to have Indian names were N. Delorme, C. Lafontaine, and C. Trottier Sr.

62. John C. Crawford, "What Is Michif?" in Peterson, Brown, *The New Peoples*, p. 238.

63. Canada, Parlement, *Documents de la Session*, 1886, no. 52, pp. 374, 377–78.

64. RG 15, vol. 1326, no. 1555: N. Champagne; vol. 1327, no. 1292: J. Dumont; vol. 1329, no. 1301: A. Letendre; vol. 1331, no. 1504: P. Sansregret.

65. Canada, Parlement, *Documents de la Session*, 1886, no. 52, pp. 389–94, 403–05.

66. Flanagan, *Riel and the Rebellion*; McLean, *1885: Métis Rebellion or Government Conspiracy?*

Article Seven

The Indian View of the 1885 Uprising

A. Blair Stonechild

THE INDIAN VERSION OF THE REBELLION: AN UNTOLD STORY

Although there is no shortage of written material on the North-West Rebellion of 1885, Indian Elders have said that the full story of the Indian involvement has yet to be told.

As one Elder put it, "This story was told only at night and at bedtime. And not the whole story. No way. They did not want to tell on anyone who were [sic] involved. It is like when something is covered with a blanket and held down on the ground on all four sides. They talked about it in parts only. And they got nervous telling it. They were afraid of another uprising and more trouble. And they were also afraid of getting the young people into trouble."[1]

Some Elders did not like to tell the stories simply because it made them sad. Other Elders did not tell their stories to any white person, even priests, as they were afraid that these stories would be used for the profit of others.

Most historians have used only written documents and official interpretations in their research. After the rebellion the Indian people did not have the freedom or luxury of doing their own research and putting forward their own views. As a result, contemporary interpretations of the Indian role have remained very biased.

HOW THE REBELLION STARTED

The first Indian involvement in the rebellion is said to have been at the Duck Lake fight on 26 March 1885. A few Indians were among Gabriel Dumont's group of about 30 men; but then, considering that the fight itself occurred on Beardy's Reserve, it should not be so surprising that Indians were present at all. One of the least understood aspects of the Duck Lake fight is why one of Chief Beardy's Headmen (Assiyiwin) was shot during the purported parley preceding the fight. How did an old, half-blind, unarmed Headman of the Band become involved in the fracas?

What does Indian oral history have to say about this? The following story is told by Harry Michael of Beardy's Reserve. Harry Michael's grandfather was the nephew of Assiyiwin:

> Assiyiwin had gone to town, to Duck Lake to visit a friend, a half-breed by the name of Wolfe. Over there he heard that there was going to be some trouble. Something very bad was going to happen. He had gone to town on horseback and he bought some goods from the store in Duck Lake which he tied on his saddle. He then started walking home. The town of Duck Lake was not too far from the camp.
>
> The old man had very poor eyesight — he was almost blind. And as he was approaching the reserve and the camp he noticed something. He heard a lot of voices, a lot of talking. But he could not see anything until he came near the people.
>
> It was then a half-breed spoke to him — called in Cree and said, "Stop! Don't you know what is going to happen?"

Source: "The Indian View of the 1885 Uprising," in *1885 and After: Native Society in Transition*, ed. F. Laurie Barron and James B. Waldram (Regina: University of Regina, 1986), pp. 155–70. Reprinted by permission of the author.

Assiyiwin said, "I am blind. Exactly what is it?"

The half-breed answered, "There is going to be a battle. Didn't you hear about it?"

Assiyiwin answered, "Yes, I heard about it."

The half-breed replied, "You have walked right into it. Turn back where you came from."

Assiyiwin answered, "Ha! I cannot turn back. I'm going home. This is my reserve land. If you are going to have a battle, if you are going to spill blood, you cannot do it on our reserve land." And he remained standing there with his horse.

The half-breed said, "Go back where you came from."

Assiyiwin replied, "No, I am going home."

This half-breed threw his coat to Assiyiwin. His name was Joe McKay. He said, "Step over my coat . . . I'll shoot you."

That was the time when Assiyiwin heard someone saying while he was standing there, "Don't shoot each other. Don't shoot." It was said in Cree. It was a half-breed. He must have been very brave, coming into the centre of the two sides of the people on horseback, half-breeds and Indians on one side and the Northwest [sic] Mounted Police on the other side. He was trying to tell the people not to shoot each other. He came running from the half-breed side. He did not know the name of this man. He was waving his hands shouting, "Don't shoot each other! People are trying to find a way on how they can get along better. Don't try and kill each other." He got as far as their location.

It was then Assiyiwin stepped over and passed the coat of McKay and said, "I am going home."

Assiyiwin witnessed the days of intertribal [sic] battles with the Blackfeet. Assiyiwin performed some brave acts when he had the strength and power in his legs. He had some scalps in a wooden box. He had fought and killed in battles and scalped. This was a brave man. That is why he did not back out from Joe McKay's orders. He refused Joe McKay and stepped over past the coat and said he was going to go on home. He was not about to get frightened. His bravery must have returned to him in spite [of the fact] that he was an old man.

The gun went off and fired. McKay shot the old man Assiyiwin down, hitting him in the stomach. Then there were blasts of gunfire coming from all directions.

They came later after the old man. He didn't die right away that night. He died at sunrise the following morning. He was the first Cree Indian killed. That's how my grandfather told this story.[2]

The official interpretation of the event at Duck Lake was that Beardy's Band had joined the rebellion. The story of Assiyiwin, however, presents an entirely different view. An older man, with poor eyesight, Assiyiwin was hardly likely to be associating with young fighters. Moreover, as one of Beardy's Headmen, he probably shared Beardy's disassociation from Riel's activities, and Beardy's dislike of intruders on their Indian reserve land.

It appears that Assiyiwin's mistake was being in the wrong place at the wrong time, and being too bold in asserting his indignation at what was occurring. Gabriel Dumont did not see his brother Isidore or Assiyiwin approach Crozier and McKay. What was probably not so much a parley as an effort to defuse a tense situation turned into a senseless slaughter when Joe McKay pulled his trigger.

It later became clear that Chief Beardy had not ordered his men to support the rebellion, yet through the incident at Duck Lake the Indian people were fully implicated.

INDIAN TREATIES WERE A COMMITMENT TO PEACE

In order to more clearly understand the Indian attitude at the time of the rebellion, one has to look back to the period prior to the signing of the treaties. Indian Nations waged tremendous battles against each other as a result of inter-tribal conflicts created by the expansion of the fur trade. In some battles between the Cree and the Blackfoot, such as that on the Oldman River in 1870, several hundred warriors were killed. An even greater killer — the epidemics — wiped out over half of the tribes in some outbreaks. The result of all this was the drastic depopulation of the Indian Nations, and an increasing awareness among Indian leaders that their Nations had to come to grips with a very fundamental and real issue — that of survival.

Because of these experiences a strong peace movement began to develop among the Indian Nations. One famous peacemaker was the Cree Chief Maskipitoon, who strove to mend relations between the Cree and the Blackfoot during the 1860s. He eventually fell victim to a misguided warrior's bullet. The adoption of the Cree Poundmaker by the Blackfoot Chief Crowfoot was another important development in the cementing of peaceful relations between the two Nations.

It was because of this sentiment for peace that Indian leaders were receptive to the signing of treaties in the 1870s. Not only had Indians never been at war with whites in the northwest, but they also sought to prevent such a thing from ever happening. Treaty Six stated, "they will maintain peace and good order between each other, and also between themselves and others of Her Majesty's subjects."[3] To Indian Nations, that was one of the most important principles of the treaty.

For Indians, the signing of treaties was far more than a political act — it was also a sacred act. By the ceremony of smoking the Sacred Pipe, the Indian people pledged before the Creator that they would uphold the treaties. As Senator John Tootoosis puts it, "We signed an agreement with the Crown, with the Queen not to fight any more. We were to live in peace. We had to live up to this Treaty. We promised in the name of the Creator to keep the Treaty. The Indian people feared offending the Creator."[4] If the treaty was ever broken, it would not be the Indian people who broke it first.

Around the time of the rebellion, white people did not fully appreciate the commitment of the Indian people. They had the perception that Indian people were no more than hunters and warriors. When the Marquis of Lorne, Queen Victoria's son-in-law, met Poundmaker in 1881, he expected to hear many war stories, and was surprised that instead he heard mainly about the spiritual and political ideas of the Indian people.

THE SOLUTIONS TO TREATY PROBLEMS WOULD BE POLITICAL

The Indian leadership was aware that there were serious shortcomings in the implementation of the treaties. In the councils of the political leaders the focus of attention was on the dissatisfaction being experienced by those Indians settling on reserves. During those days of "The Time of the Great Hunger," Indians were seeing few of the benefits promised them under the treaty. The meager rations provided to them did little to stop the loss of life. Between 1880 and 1885 the Indian population dropped from 32 549 to 20 170 — a death rate of nearly 10 percent per year.[5]

At the Duck Lake Council, held in early August of 1884, Indian leaders presented a list of eighteen specific treaty grievances including complaints about untamed horses and cows, inadequate rations, poor implements, lack of schools and medical assistance and general dissatisfaction with government measures. The report on their presentation stated "that requests for redress of their grievances have been again and again made without effect. They are glad that the young men have not resorted to violent measures to gain it. That it is almost too hard for them to bear the treatment received at the hands of the government after its 'sweet promises' made in order to get their country from them. They now fear that they are going to be cheated.

They will wait until next summer to see if this council has the desired effect, failing which they will take measures to get what they desire. (The proposed 'measures' could not be elicited, but a suggestion of the idea of war was repudiated.)"[6]

One measure being proposed by the Chiefs was a meeting of the Grand Council to be held on Little Pine's Reserve in 1885. The Blackfoot would be invited to attend. Once a united position was agreed upon, a delegation of Chiefs would travel to Ottawa where it was believed someone with sufficient authority could make some changes.

Thus, the Indian people were charting their own course of action to deal with Indian problems. It was a plan which called for concerted political action, and under it any outbreak of violence would be viewed as an undesirable course of events.

THE SPREAD OF THE REBELLION TESTS INDIAN LOYALTIES

Following the outbreak of hostilities at Duck Lake, Riel, attempting to spark a Territory-wide insurrection, sent messengers to many reserves urging the Indians to join him. The response of most Indian leaders was to send messages to government authorities reaffirming their loyalty.

On 28 March 1885, a delegation of Touchwood Chiefs sent a message expressing "to his Excellency the Lieutenant-Governor and through him to the Governor-General, their loyalty to their Great Mother the Queen, and further wish to express their disapproval of the course of action pursued by those at the head of the present struggle."[7]

At a meeting called by Riel's messengers at the Crooked Lakes Reserves, the Indians decided to remain loyal. Chief Kahkewistahaw made the following statement: "Agent, you remember the time I promised I would go to my reserve. I also said that I and my young men's fighting days were over. I stick to those words no matter what may be done up north, we will remain on our reserves and attend to our work."[8]

Chief Piapot, the main Cree leader in the South, wrote: "It is eleven years since I gave up fighting. When I took the government Treaty I touched the pen not to interfere with the whiteman and the whiteman not to interfere with me."[9]

Also on 28 March, Indian Agent Rae visited old Chief Mosquito on his reserve a few miles south of Battleford and received the Chief's assurances that the band would remain loyal. At about the same time, Riel's messengers were visiting both Mosquito's and Red Pheasant's Reserves.

On Mosquito's Reserve a band member named Itka had been grieving over the death of his daughter, which he blamed on Farm Instructor Payne. A few days before her death, Payne had physically thrown the frail girl out of his house. Itka decided the time was opportune for revenge, went to the Farm Instructor's home and shot him dead. Relatives of Itka, convinced that Canadian authorities would conduct an American-style retaliation against them, decided that their best alternative would be to seek refuge. They went to the house of Barney Tremont, a local farmer, demanding horses. When Tremont refused, he was shot and killed.

While these events were occurring on the Mosquito Reserve, Chiefs Poundmaker and Little Pine, concerned about the outbreak at Duck Lake, decided to travel to Battleford to express their loyalty to the Queen. Poundmaker also decided that at the same time he would take the opportunity to attempt to gain government concessions for food and other treaty provisions. Hearing this, most of the band members decided to accompany their Chiefs in the hope that they would be present for the distributions.

The two Chiefs and their followers met with Chief Young Sweetgrass on 28 March at the Sweetgrass Reserve, about ten miles west of Battleford. Farm Instructors Jefferson and Craig debated whether or not they should accompany the Indians to Battleford, but decided against it for fear of disapproval by their superiors, who wanted Indians to remain on their reserves.

Also present was Peter Ballantyne, who was operating as a spy for Edgar Dewdney. He checked on the Indians' plans and came to the conclusion that their intentions were peaceful.

Meanwhile in Battleford, rumours were rampant that Poundmaker was approaching to attack the town.

BATTLEFORD—THE SIEGE THAT NEVER OCCURRED

When Poundmaker and his followers reached Battleford on the morning of 30 March, they were surprised to find the town deserted. The residents had taken refuge in the North-West Mounted Police Barracks on the other side of the river.

Poundmaker sent a message to the fort stating his peaceful intentions and requesting a meeting with Indian Agent Rae. Rae refused to leave the fort, but Peter Ballantyne and Hudson's Bay Company Factor McKay came out to meet Poundmaker. McKay agreed to release food to the Indians from the Hudson's Bay Company store.

Governor Dewdney was sent a telegram stating, "Indians willing to go back to reserves tomorrow if their demands for clothing are met. Strongly urge you to deal with them as we are not in a position at present to begin an Indian war."[10] Dewdney later replied, although too late, that he would meet with Poundmaker.

There were other groups who had arrived at Battleford — some of the Stoneys from Mosquito's Reserve, and Riel's agitators from Duck Lake. As Ballantyne and McKay were returning to the fort after failing to arrange talks with Rae, some of the Métis took shots at them. Later that day, some of the Stoneys began to break into stores and loot. Poundmaker and Little Pine tried to restrain their followers from looting, but with only limited success.

By the next morning, Poundmaker and most of his followers were on their way home. The strain of the troubles was too great for Little Pine, who had been suffering from temporary blindness and other symptoms of starvation. He died on 31 March 1885, a few miles before reaching his reserve. Little Pine's death, and that of old Chief Red Pheasant a few days earlier, meant that Poundmaker had become the main Indian leader in the Battleford area.

Accounts of the siege were blown well out of proportion. The telegraph line had not been tampered with, allowing the Battleford residents to send out daily messages of alarm. During the 25 days before relief troops arrived, the 500 settlers barricaded in the fort were even able to obtain water safely from their only source a mile outside of the barracks. According to one observer, "one solitary individual — the cook — had the temerity to continue in residence at the old government house. He had many visitors that day, gave them to eat, when they departed without harming him."[11]

Interestingly enough, another observer reported, "They [the Indians] had been too hurried to take much; the principal looting was the work of white men. As soon as the coast was clear in the morning they came over in detachments and finished what the Indians had begun. They made a clean sweep."[12]

Not the least of these raiders was Farm Instructor Craig, who "devoted his time and attention to looting the stores and houses that had been broken into by the Indians, but his enterprise was frustrated by persistent robbing of his tent whenever he left it."[13]

Several observers were of the opinion that looting would never have taken place had the townspeople not deserted their houses and stores. By and large, the "siege" was a fabricated event.

BIG BEAR'S MISFORTUNE PEAKS AT FROG LAKE

Big Bear had become the principal leader of the northern Plains Cree in 1877, following the death of Chief Sweetgrass. Unfortunately, he had a poor relationship with the government. One of the tactics used by the government during treaty negotiations had been to fail to send notification of the meetings to Indian leaders who were considered difficult to deal with. Such was the reason for Big Bear's arrival at Fort Pitt a day after Treaty Six had been signed.

During a speech objecting to the lack of consultation with the several bands he was representing, Big Bear said:

> I have come off to speak for the different bands that are out on the Plains. It is no small matter we were to consult about. I expected the Chiefs here would have waited until I arrived. . . . I heard the Governor was to come and I said I shall see him; when I see him I will request that he will save me from that which I most dread, that is: the rope to be about my neck, it was not given to us by the Great Spirit that the red man or the white man should shed each other's blood.[14]

The official treaty interpreter had already left and Reverend McKay, whose mastery of Cree was far from perfect, misinterpreted Big Bear's words to mean a fear of hanging (*ayhahkotit*). Big Bear was actually saying that he did not wish to lose his freedom, like an animal with a rope around its neck (*aysakapaykinit*).[15] Nevertheless, the impression created of Big Bear was that he was evil and cowardly, an image which would haunt him up to his final days.

Steadfast in his belief that he could get a revision of Treaty Six, similar to those of Treaties One and Two, Big Bear held out from signing Treaty Six longer than any other Chief. He was forced to sign six years later, when it became clear that his Band members would starve unless they obtained government rations.

In 1884, after years of urging, Big Bear agreed to choose a reserve next to Poundmaker's. Deputy Superintendent-General of Indian Affairs Lawrence Vankoughnet, a man who disliked Big Bear, vetoed the plan, suggesting that it would not be a good idea to have too many "idle Indians" in one area. Instead, Vankoughnet warned Big Bear to take a reserve already set aside near Fort Pitt — a location which Big Bear had already rejected — or face a cut-off of rations during the winter of 1884–85. Big Bear refused to comply.

An unhealthy blend of ingredients was being mixed. Many members of Big Bear's band, including his son Imases and the War Chief Wandering Spirit, were becoming frustrated with the state of affairs. Compounding the problem was the presence of Indian Agent Quinn, a man known to have been abusive to Indians, and Farm Instructor Delaney, who had been accused of violating Indian women. The government was aware of the unpopularity of these men with the Indians, and had been planning to relocate them.

News of the Duck Lake fight did not reach Agent Quinn until late on 31 March 1885. The next day, 1 April or "Big Lie Day," as the Indians called it, Quinn summoned Big Bear's band members to inform them of the incident. Imases, speaking on behalf of Big Bear, who was out hunting for food for the band, replied:

> They have already risen; we knew about it before you. They have beaten the soldiers in the first fight, killing many. We do not wish to join the half-breeds, but we are afraid. We wish to stay here and prove ourselves the friends of the white man.[16]

Imases then asked Quinn to provide rations to the band. Quinn refused, saying he would have to speak to Big Bear first.

Later that day Big Bear returned empty-handed from hunting and led a delegation to request rations from Quinn. Big Bear was upset at his refusal. Imases, hoping to win a compromise, suggested that Quinn give the Indians food for a feast as a gift to the band, and he would not then have to call it rations. Quinn, however, had decided to give them nothing.

That night, unknown to Big Bear, Wandering Spirit and several members of the Rattler's Warrior Society held a dance in secret. As dawn broke some twenty armed warriors came to the Frog Lake community, waking up the residents and herding them to Quinn's house.

That morning, when asked for food and other supplies, Quinn was willing to comply, and various Indians were allowed to have goods from the stores.

That day was Holy Thursday, and two priests who had come for the occasion asked permission to hold church services. The hostages were all allowed to attend church. By this time Big Bear had learned of the trouble and had joined the whites in the church to ensure that nothing worse occurred.

As the church service progressed, the noise outside increased. The warriors had broken into the stores and had found wine, spirits, and painkillers. As these were consumed the shouting and yelling of the warriors grew louder, and they eventually began to enter the church and disrupt the service.[17]

Big Bear decided to leave the church and begin warning the other residents of the community, who were in their houses, to leave in case trouble broke out. He was at Mrs. Simpson's house when he heard shots. The church service had been cut short.

Wandering Spirit, the War Chief, ordered the whites to go to the Indian camp, a short distance away. Quinn refused to move, and after repeated warnings Wandering Spirit shot him dead.

Big Bear ran outside, yelling at the warriors to stop it, but it was too late. Urged on by the prompting of Wandering Spirit, the warriors soon killed eight white men.

Perhaps the violence would have been averted had Quinn simply given food to the starving band the day before. It did not appear that the band was thinking seriously of any sort of insurrection at that time. Even on the following day, had Quinn been liberal with Indian requests for food and simply complied with the warriors' orders, it is possible that bloodshed could have been averted entirely. The presence of alcohol and painkillers can be the only explanation for the gruesomeness of the murders. In Indian thinking, it was considered dishonourable and cowardly to kill an unarmed man for no reason at all.

Big Bear's hopes of peaceful dealings with government had all but vanished, yet he distinguished himself by protecting the lives of the remaining white captives, and by preventing greater bloodshed at Fort Pitt.

The warriors moved to seize the provisions at Fort Pitt on 14 April. Big Bear, no longer in control of the band, argued for an attempt to arrange a peaceful surrender of the Fort. He held the warriors back for one night, and the next day persuaded 44 civilians to surrender to the band. With this achieved, the North West Mounted Police detachment had little reason to stay, and was allowed to escape down the river by boat. Big Bear's vigilance was an important factor in preventing any deaths among them.

THE UNPROVOKED ATTACK ON CUTKNIFE HILL

Although Poundmaker had been forced to relinquish power to the warrior society, he was influential in maintaining calm among the Indians camped at Cutknife Hill following the so-called siege of Battleford.

Lieutenant-Colonel Otter arrived at Battleford on 24 April 1885 with close to 550 troops. Also, part of his arsenal was a Gatling gun sent for demonstration by the United States Army.

Otter's troops were sorely disappointed at not seeing action on arrival at Battleford. Otter had been ordered by Middleton to stay at Battleford and guard the townspeople. Sensing the unrest of his troops, and seeing the opportunity to gain personal glory, Otter wired Dewdney, "I proposed taking part of my force at once to punish Poundmaker leaving 100 men to garrison Battleford. Great depredations committed. Immediate decisive action necessary. Do you approve?"[18]

Dewdney, probably after consulting the Prime Minister, wired Otter with approval.

Otter planned to surprise Poundmaker and force him to surrender. On the evening of 28 April, he left Battleford for Cutknife Hill. Otter's timing was good, and he arrived at the foot of Cutknife Hill at 5:15 the following morning. Fortunately for Poundmaker's camp, an old man, Jacob With the Long Hair, was awake and heard the sounds of the approaching soldiers. He ran through the camp shouting warnings.

At that point Otter ordered his guns to open fire on the sleeping camp. The barrage knocked over some tipis, but all of the occupants managed to scramble to safety.

Some of the Indian warriors ran out to confront the troops while others began shooting from nearby coulees. According to Robert Jefferson, an eyewitness, "Not more than 50 [Indians] altogether, had taken part in the battle. This was excusable since few were armed."[19] As the battle continued throughout the morning, Otter realized that his troops were in a vulnerable position and were slowly being surrounded. Just before noon, he ordered his men to retreat.

The warriors wanted to pursue Otter. Knowing the land like the backs of their hands and gaining the advantage of nightfall, the warriors could have inflicted heavy casualties on the tiring soldiers. Poundmaker refused to agree, maintaining that while the Indians were right in defending themselves on their land, it would be wrong to go on the offensive.

There had been a split among the people at Cutknife Hill. On the one side was the pro-Riel faction consisting of the Métis agitators and the Stoney warriors. On the other side were those led by Poundmaker who wanted to have as little as possible to do with the rebellion. Poundmaker had tried to lead his followers west toward the hilly country around Devil's Lake, with plans to eventually take refuge near Crowfoot, but the warriors and Métis prevented them from leaving.

Poundmaker was essentially being used as a spokesman by the belligerent faction. An example of this was a letter to Riel dictated by Riel's sympathizers but bearing the "signatures" of Poundmaker and several other Indians. Poundmaker's lack of verbal or written knowledge of either French or English put him at a great disadvantage. The fact was that Poundmaker was not in control, and the insinuation of support for Riel contained in the letter was out of character with his actions. That letter later became the main piece of evidence used in convicting Poundmaker.

Following the Battle of Cutknife Hill, it was decided that it was no longer safe to remain on the reserve. When the pro-Riel faction decided to join Riel at Batoche, Poundmaker attempted to lead his followers west, away from trouble. The dispute nearly led to bloodshed, but Poundmaker's poorly armed followers relented. Poundmaker's lack of cooperation and additional efforts to break away from the camp slowed the Indians' progress to Batoche by several days.

Poundmaker's stalling tactics saved many Indian lives, for as they neared Batoche on 14 May, they received news that Middleton's army had just defeated the Métis. After some discussion, Poundmaker sought terms of surrender from Middleton; when refused, he surrendered unconditionally at Battleford on 26 May 1885.

Poundmaker's plan to abandon his reserve and seek refuge by moving to an isolated area was not unique. A significant number of band members, from reserves such as Mosquito's, Red Pheasant's, One Arrow's and Thunderchild's, went north to avoid any involvement in the troubles.

During this period, Sir John A. Macdonald was attempting to exploit tribal differences by inquiring about sending Indian patrols against Poundmaker and Big Bear. He wrote Dewdney on 29 March 1885, "I understand that the Crees dread the Blackfeet like the devil. Now a corps of scouts under Crowfoot might be formed."[20] Because of the relationship between Crowfoot and Poundmaker this plan never succeeded, despite repeated requests from the Prime Minister.

AT BATOCHE AGAINST THEIR WILL

Part of the strategy of Riel's provisional government was based on the belief that they held influence over the Indians. In a note to the English half-breeds on 22 March 1885, they wrote, "We are sure that if the English and French half-breeds unite well in this time of crisis, not only can we control the Indians, but we will also have their weight on our side."[21] With Indians out-numbering both Métis and whites in the northwest, their support in a conflict could be critical, but the presumption of Indian involvement was made without consultation with any of the Indian leaders.

On 18 March 1885, one day before Riel's proclamation of his provisional government, that process of "controlling" Indians began. About 40 Riel supporters arrived at One Arrow's Reserve, approximately two miles east of Batoche, taking the Indian agent and farm instructor prisoner. The next day, One Arrow and fifteen of his men came to Batoche. As One Arrow testified at his trial,

> I am an old man now. . . . I was taken to the place, Batoche's, to join Riel by Gabriel. I did not take myself to the place. They took me there. I could not say how many there were of them that took me there, but there was quite a number of them. . . . so when I went there and got there I was taken prisoner.[22]

Witnesses testified that One Arrow was seen in the area during both the Duck Lake fight and the Battle of Batoche. In his defence, One Arrow testified that,

> All that was said against me was thrown upon me falsely. I did not take up my gun with the intention to shoot at any man. I was on the brink of the hill the whole day, and I had my gun there, but, of course, not with the intention to use the gun against any man, and when I saw the whitemen coming down, I ran down the hill too, and ran off.[23]

On 10 April 1885, around twenty Riel supporters arrived at Whitecap's Reserve, a few miles south of Saskatoon. Whitecap, the Chief of a band of refugee American Dakota, had resisted Riel's overtures two weeks previous. Before the Métis began forcing Whitecap and twenty of his men toward Batoche, Whitecap managed to send a message to a white friend in Saskatoon, Gerald Willoughby, asking him for assistance. When the group reached Saskatoon, a group of nine citizens tried to persuade the Métis to allow Whitecap to return to his reserve. Outnumbered, they were unsuccessful.

When Whitecap arrived at Batoche, he was appointed the only Indian member of Riel's council on internal matters, but because he understood neither French nor Cree, he attended only one meeting.

Whitecap's men were seen at the battles of Fish Creek and Batoche. Testimony provided by the main prosecution witnesses showed that Whitecap could not be positively identified as having been among the several old Indian men at Batoche, but it was mainly because of the evidence showing that Whitecap had been coerced to fight that all charges against him were dropped.[24]

THE INDIAN TRIALS: UNWARRANTED PUNISHMENT

Poundmaker, despite evidence of his efforts to maintain peace, was convicted of treason-felony on the basis of the letter to Riel bearing his name. Speaking after hearing the guilty verdict, Poundmaker categorically denied any wrongdoing, saying, "Everything that is bad has been laid against me this summer, there is nothing of it true."[25] On hearing that he was sentenced to three years at Stony Mountain, Poundmaker declared, "I would prefer to be hung at once than to be in that place."[26] Poundmaker was released in the spring of 1886, largely because of public sympathy, but he died in June after making a trek on foot to visit his adoptive father, Crowfoot.

Although the evidence was strongly in favour of Big Bear, it appeared that the outcome of his trial was predetermined, and he was sentenced to the same three-year term as Poundmaker. There was less public sympathy for Big Bear, and he was not released until 3 February 1887, after a medical report confirmed his badly deteriorating health. He had no band to return to, as it had been dispersed by the government. Most of his family he would never see, as they were fugitives in the United States. With his heart broken and no cause to live for, he died on 18 January 1888.

When Chief One Arrow heard the charges of treason-felony translated to him, it came out in Cree as "knocking off the Queen's bonnet and stabbing her in the behind with a sword."[27] This moved One Arrow to ask the interpreter if he was drunk. The conviction of One Arrow was based on his presence at the battle sites, and his account of how he came to be there was ignored.

One Arrow was not so fortunate as to make it back to his own reserve. He was released from Stony Mountain Prison on 21 April 1886, and died four days later at Archbishop Taché's residence in St. Boniface. He was baptized just before his death and lies in St. Boniface cemetery in an unmarked grave.

In order to save money, a decision was made not to hold all of the rebellion trials at Regina. Several of them were held in Battleford instead. The atmosphere in Battleford was not hospitable toward Indians, as an editorial in the *Saskatchewan Herald* on 23 April 1885 shows:

> The petted Indians are the bad ones. The Stonies have been treated as being of a superior race, and are the first to shed the blood of their benefactors. Poundmaker has been petted and feted, and stands in the front rank as a raider. Little Pine, bribed to come north and kept in comfort, hastens to the carnage. Big Bear, who has for years enjoyed the privilege of eating of the bread of idleness, shows his gratitude by killing his priests and his best friends in cold blood. Little Poplar, a non-treaty Indian, has been liberally supplied with provisions and other necessaries and thus enabled to spend all his time in travelling up and down the land plotting mischief and preparing for this season's carnival of ruin. The petted Indians have proved the bad ones, and this gives weight to the old adage that the only good Indians are the dead ones.[28]

Judge Rouleau, who would pass the judgements, had narrowly missed being murdered along with Farm Instructor Payne, and was also bitter about the burning of his mansion at Battleford. He was known before the trials to advocate harsh punishment as a deterrent to future rebellious acts by Indians.

The eight Indians eventually hanged were at a disadvantage. They knew nothing of the legal system and had no legal counsel or other advice. No effective defence of any sort was mounted which might have created sympathy for the defendants — for example, the reality of their starvation under Indian Affairs administration, or the excesses brought on by alcohol and drugs at the Frog Lake massacre.

Several Indian Elders are certain that at least one of the Indians, Man-Without-Blood, was wrongly hanged for the shooting of Farm Instructor Payne. They claim it was done by the other Stoney, Man-With-a-Black-Blanket. According to one story,

> The two of the Stoney young men were arrested also. They were accused of killing the farm instructor and they were both arrested. And at that time people were very respectable. There was a lot of respect for the older people. Now the one who did not kill the Indian Agent, he was the one who was accused by his partner. So the one who was accused of killing the farm instructor, when he went to trial, the officer asked him, "Is it true what you did? Or is it not true?" He replied, "Maybe it is true, and maybe it is not." And he really had nothing to do with it, he didn't shoot the Indian Agent. So when he said, "Maybe they are telling the truth," that was accepted as his plea, as telling the truth. So he got the blame for the death of the farm instructor. So he was one of them that got hanged. They weren't going to sympathize with him or feel sorry for him.[29]

According to another story, "It's him who killed the ration feeder. And the one who followed him shot the dog. He was the one who got hung instead, said my father, the one who shot the dog. He did not want to report his partner."[30]

No clear evidence of committing murder was shown against Iron Body and Little Bear, two of the six Indians tried for their role in the Frog Lake massacre. They were hanged on the basis that, by aiding and abetting the others, they were equally guilty.

Four Sky Thunder received a sentence of fourteen years for burning down the Frog Lake church. Another Indian, whose only wrongdoing was having been seen with Big Bear, was sentenced to six years in prison.[31]

Several Indians were never brought to justice. Among them was Man-Who-Speaks-Our-Language, who nearly caused the outbreak of fighting with the North West Mounted Police on Poundmaker's Reserve in 1884, and was responsible for some of the killings at Frog Lake.

The hangings at Battleford took place on 27 November 1885. Indians from several reserves were there to witness the event.

A new section was built at Stony Mountain Penitentiary to accommodate the 25 Indians and eighteen Métis sentenced to prison. Several of the Indians never returned to their reserves, and are buried in the St. Boniface cemetery.

THE AFTERMATH: SUPPRESSION OF INDIANS

The government saw the rebellion as an opportunity to achieve a goal which had eluded it since 1870, that of gaining total control over Indians. In July of 1885, Assistant Commissioner Hayter Reed drew up a list of fifteen recommendations on actions to be taken following the rebellion. Among these were the following:

> The leaders of the Teton Sioux who fought against the troops should be hanged and the rest be sent out of the country;

> Big Bear's band should either be broken up and scattered among other bands or be given a reserve adjacent to that at Onion Lake;

> One Arrow's band should be joined with that of Beardy and Okemasis and their reserve surrendered;

> No annuity money should be now paid any bands that rebelled, or to any individuals that joined the insurgents;

> The tribal system should be abolished in so far as is compatible with the Treaty;

All half-breeds, members of rebel bands, although not shown to have taken any active part in the rebellion, should have their names erased from the paysheets;

No rebel Indians should be allowed off the Reserves without a pass signed by an Indian Department official; and

All Indians who have not during the late troubles been disloyal or troublesome should be treated as heretofore.[32]

Reed had also prepared a list of every Indian band in the northwest and had identified 28 disloyal bands. In his enthusiasm he erroneously included several reserves, such as Sweetgrass and Thunderchild, which had been very loyal. Most of the others had actually been loyal, with only the odd individual implicated in the rebellion. Of all the bands identified as disloyal in the rebellion, it is clear that none of the Chiefs, whether Big Bear, Poundmaker, Mosquito, Red Pheasant, Little Pine, Beardy, One Arrow or Whitecap, politically supported the rebellion. All were drawn into the conflict by circumstances beyond their personal control. In all, less than five percent of the Indian population of the northwest was involved.

The original proposal to disallow rebel Indians from leaving their reserves without a pass soon became a measure to be applied to all Indians. In approving this plan, Sir John A. Macdonald was aware that he was contravening the treaties. He noted:

> Mr. Dewdney thinks that the pass system can be generally introduced in July. If so, it is in the highest degree desirable. As to the disloyal Bands, this should be carried out as the consequence of their disloyalty. The system should be introduced in the loyal Bands as well and the advantage of the change pressed upon them. But no punishment for breaking bounds could be inflicted and in the case of resistance on the grounds of Treaty rights should not be insisted on.[33]

The measures taken against Indians, in particular those restricting them to reserves, were measures which would have a profound effect on subsequent Indian developments. What little influence Indian people had over their own lives was removed, and Indian people became vulnerable to government whim, manipulation and mismanagement.

It was regrettable that Sir John A. Macdonald, who was Superintendent General of Indian Affairs and Prime Minister, never once bothered to visit the people over whom he had charge during the eight critical years he held office, from 1879 to 1887.

Had the Indian people been able to retain their freedom of movement, things might have turned out much differently. Big Bear and other Indian leaders might have met Sir John A. Macdonald in 1885. Nationally, efforts to form the League of Indians of Canada in the 1920s and the North American Indian Brotherhood in the 1940s would have been more successful and probably would have received the bulk of their strength from the prairies. Indian political development in Canada was probably put back by two generations.

The rebellion has left a legacy of a century of suspicions about Indian political abilities and loyalties, and misconceptions about the validity of Indian treaties.

In concluding, I would say that a clear understanding of the Indian view of the 1885 Uprising is the least that can be done to right the blunders of the past.

NOTES

1. Florence Paul, interview by Wilfred Tootoosis, One Arrow Indian Reserve, 15 March 1985.
2. Harry Michael, interview by Wilfred Tootoosis, Beardy's Indian Reserve, 14 March 1985.
3. Canada, *Treaty Number Six Between Her Majesty the Queen and the Plain and Wood Cree Indians and other Tribes of Indians* (Ottawa: Queen's Printer, 1964), 5.
4. John B. Tootoosis, interview by Wilfred Tootoosis, Poundmaker Indian Reserve, 30 November 1984.

5. Canada, *Sessional Papers*, 1886, No. 36, 2.
6. Public Archives of Canada (hereafter PAC), RG 10, Vol. 3697, File 15,423, MacRae to Dewdney, 25 August 1884.
7. PAC, RG 10, Vol. 3584, File 1130, Pt. 3A, McBeath to Macdonald, 28 March 1885.
8. PAC, RG 10, Vol. 3584, File 1130, Pt. 3A, Macdonald to Indian Commissioner, 8 April 1885.
9. PAC, RG 10, Vol. 3584, File 1130, Pt. 3A, Piapot to Macdonald, 30 April 1885.
10. Dewdney Papers, Vol. 5, 1879–1880, Rae to Dewdney, 30 March 1885.
11. Robert Jefferson, *Fifty Years on the Saskatchewan* (Battleford: Canadian Northwest Historical Society, 1929), 127.
12. Ibid., 128.
13. Ibid., 126.
14. Alexander Morris, *Treaties of Canada With the Indians of Manitoba and the North-West Territories* (Toronto: Coles Publishing Limited, 1971), 239.
15. Hugh Dempsey, *Big Bear — The End of Freedom* (Vancouver: Douglas and McIntyre, 1984), 74.
16. W.B. Cameron, *Blood Red the Sun* (Edmonton: Hurtig Publishers, 1977), 33.
17. Dempsey, *Big Bear*, 155.
18. Dewdney Papers, Vol. 5, p. 1806, Otter to Dewdney, 26 April 1885.
19. Jefferson, *Fifty Years*, 146.
20. PAC, MG 26A, Vol. 526, p. 1404, Macdonald to Dewdney, 29 March 1885.
21. Bob Beal and Rod Macleod, *Prairie Fire: The 1885 North-West Rebellion* (Edmonton: Hurtig Publishers, 1984), 148.
22. Canada, *Sessional Papers*, 1886, No. 52, 33.
23. Ibid., 32.
24. Ibid., 13.
25. Ibid., 336.
26. Ibid., 337.
27. Beal and Macleod, *Prairie Fire*, 309.
28. *Saskatchewan Herald* (Battleford), 23 April 1885.
29. Lawrence Lonesinger, interview by Wilfred Tootoosis, Sweetgrass Indian Reserve, 13 March 1985.
30. Alex Sapp, interview by Wilfred Tootoosis, Little Pine Indian Reserve, date not available.
31. S.E. Bingaman, "The North-West Rebellion Trials, 1885" (Master's thesis, University of Regina, 1971), 133.
32. PAC, RG 10, Vol. 3710, File 19, 550–3, Reed to Dewdney, 20 July 1885.
33. PAC, RG 10, Vol. 3710, File 19, 550–3, Vankoughnet to Superintendent General, 17 August 1885.

Topic Four

Imperialism, Continentalism, and Nationalism

A parade proceeds through Edmonton to hear Governor General Earl Grey officially proclaim Alberta a province on September 1, 1905.

In the late 19th and early 20th centuries, Canadians debated the future of the Dominion: Should they seek greater unity with Britain through an imperial federation? Closer union with the United States in a form of continental union? Or independence? All three possibilities were, in their own ways, forms of Canadian nationalism, debated in the light of the advancement of Canadian interests.

The idea of an imperial federation or closer union of Britain and Canada became popular among English Canadians in the economically depressed and ethnically divided Canada of the late 19th century. Some 20 years after Confederation, many Canadians saw their country as a dismal failure. The National Policy had not stimulated economic growth; the anticipated population explosion had not occurred; and the nation seemed cursed by political, social, and regional dissent. At the same time, the rival German Empire and an expanding American nation challenged Britain's world supremacy. A group of imperial enthusiasts in both Canada and Britain dreamed of a consolidated British Empire that would bring glory to Britain and a "sense of power" to Canada. Carl Berger outlines the ideas of Canadian imperialists in his introduction to *Imperialism and Nationalism, 1884–1914: A Conflict in Canadian Thought*, reprinted here.

While the majority of English-speaking Canadians favoured some form of imperial federation or continental union, a significant group of French-speaking Canadians advocated greater Canadian independence. Henri Bourassa, the grandson of Louis-Joseph Papineau (the leader of the Parti Patriote before the Lower Canadian Rebellions of 1837/38), spoke for those French Canadians who felt Canada should lessen its commitments to the British Empire, although not necessarily break its ties to Britain. From the outbreak of the Boer War in 1899 to the end of the World War I in 1918, Bourassa advanced the cause of greater Canadian independence. Joseph Levitt analyzes Bourassa's ideas on Canadian nationhood, imperial defence, and the British connection. Bourassa was also an advocate of French-Canadian rights within Canada, especially with regards to the French language and separate schools outside Quebec. Levitt presents Bourassa's ideas on these important topics. He discusses as well Bourassa's views on French-Canadian cultural rights, biculturalism, and conscription.

The debate between English-Canadian and French-Canadian nationalists reached a new level of intensity at the turn of the century. Historian Phillip Buckner re-examines the Royal Tour of George, Duke of Cornwall and York, the future King George V, and his wife Mary, in 1901. They came at the height of the English-Canadian imperialist movement. Buckner shows how the imperialists used the event to try to persuade the majority of Canadians that the British monarchy embodied "an historical tradition which was part of their heritage and which continued to have relevance to them." The Tour resulted in strengthening the tie between Canada and Britain through the Empire. Buckner suggests that the enthusiasm for the Royal Tour, and the British Empire that the royal couple represented, paid off 13 years later when, in World War I, so many British Canadians "flocked to enlist to fight for a homeland many of them had never seen and others only distantly remembered."

What were the differing assumptions that English-Canadian imperialists and French-Canadian nationalists held about Britain, British imperialism, Canadian nationalism, and the nature of Canada? In what ways did the opposing visions of these two groups have an impact on specific events of the time, such as Dominion–Provincial relations and English–French cultural conflicts discussed in the readings in Topic Two? In what ways did the Royal Tour of 1901 reinforce the ideas of the English-Canadian imperialists and undermine the ideas of French-Canadian nationalists?

Carl Berger analyzes English-Canadian imperial thought in greater detail in *The Sense of Power: Studies in the Idea of Canadian Imperialism, 1867–1914* (Toronto: University of Toronto Press, 1970). For a different perspective on Canadian imperial thought, see Robert Page, "Canada and the Imperial Idea in the Boer War," *Journal of Canadian Studies* 5 (February 1970): 33–49, and his book *Imperialism and Canada, 1895–1903* (Toronto: Holt, Rinehart and Winston, 1972). A more recent study is Carman Miller, *Painting the Map Red: Canada and the South African War, 1899–1902* (Montreal/Kingston: Canadian War Museum, McGill-Queen's University Press, 1992). For British views of Canada in this period, see R.G. Moyles and D. Owram, *Imperial Dreams and Colonial Realities: British Views of Canada, 1880–1914* (Toronto: University of Toronto Press, 1988). Useful collections of essays are Colin M. Coates, ed., *Imperial Canada 1867–1917* (Edinburgh: Centre of Canadian Studies, University of Edinburgh, 1997); and Carl Berger, ed., *Imperial Relations in the Age of Laurier* (Toronto: University of Toronto Press, 1969), as well as Frank H. Underhill's collection of interpretative lectures, *The Image of Confederation* (Toronto: Canadian Broadcasting Corporation, 1964). On literature and the empire, see Barrie Davies, "'We Hold a Vaster Empire Than Has Been': Canadian Literature and the Canadian Empire," *Studies in Canadian Literature* 14, 1 (1989): 18–29. On the role that the image of white women played in promoting imperialism in the Canadian west, see Sarah Carter, *Capturing Women: The Manipulation of Cultural Imagery in Canada's Prairie West* (Montreal/Kingston: McGill-Queen's University Press, 1997).

Goldwin Smith's continentalist tract, *Canada and the Canadian Question*, first published in 1891, is a valuable primary source on the topic. Elisabeth Wallace's *Goldwin Smith: Victorian Liberal* (Toronto: University of Toronto Press, 1957) is a full-scale study of the life and ideas of this articulate advocate of Canadian and American union.

Henri Bourassa's ideas on national questions are analyzed in M.P. O'Connell's "The Ideas of Henri Bourassa," *Canadian Journal of Economics and Political Science* 19 (1953): 361–76; Susan Mann's, *The Dream of Nation: A Social and Intellectual History of Quebec* (Montreal/Kingston: McGill-Queen's University Press, 2002 [1983]), pp. 167–83; and Mason Wade's *The French Canadians, 1760–1945* (Toronto: Macmillan, 1955), pp. 447–539. See as well Joseph Levitt's brief account in *Henri Bourasssa: Catholic Critic*, Canadian Historical Association, Historical Booklet no. 20 (Ottawa: CHA, 1976).

On the role of celebrations in formulating a Canadian identity, see H.V. Nelles, *The Art of Nation Building: Pageantry and Spectacle at Quebec's Tercentenary* (Toronto: University of Toronto Press, 1999); and Ronald Rudin, *Founding Fathers: Champlain and Laval in the Streets of Quebec, 1878–1908* (Toronto: University of Toronto Press, 2003). On the role of First Nations in the Royal Tour of 1860, see Ian Radforth, "Performance, Politics and Representation: Aboriginal People and the 1860 Royal Tour of Canada," *Canadian Historical Review*, 84, 1 (March 2003): 1–32. A discussion of First Nations' perspective of the British monarchy is available in Sarah Carter, "'Your Great Mother Across the Salt Sea': Prairie First Nations, the British Monarchy and the Vice Regal Connection to 1900," *Manitoba History*, (Autumn/Winter, 2004–5): 34–48. For a review of Royal visits to Canada, consult Robert M. Stamp, *Kings, Queens and Canadians* (Markham, ON: Fitzhenry & Whiteside, 1987).

WEBLINKS

Regulation 17
http://www.uottawa.ca/academic/crccf/passeport/IV/IVD1a/IVD1a01-1.html
A digitized copy of the Government of Ontario's Regulation 17 of 1912.

Atlas of Canada: 1915
http://atlas.gc.ca/site/english/maps/archives/#2ndedition
Several maps circa 1915 regarding the economic and environmental characteristics of Canada at the time.

Yukon Territory Act, 1898
http://www.solon.org/Constitutions/Canada/English/yta_1898.html
Text of the Yukon Territory Act, which established the region as a separate territory.

Boer War
http://www.saintjohn.nbcc.nb.ca/~Heritage/boerwar/SectionIndex.htm
First-hand accounts of Canadians who participated in the Boer War.

Naval Aid Bill
http://www.gwpda.org/naval/pwr02000.htm
Text of Sir Robert Borden's proposed Naval Aid Bill.

Klondike Gold Rush
http://www.arcticwebsite.com/goldrushlist.html
A collection of photos and transcribed documents relating to the Klondike Gold Rush in Yukon.
Sample documents include a suggested 1898 supply list intended to last one year per miner.

Article Eight

Imperialism and Nationalism, 1884–1914: A Conflict in Canadian Thought

Carl Berger

INTRODUCTION

Imperialism in Canada presented many faces and its story has been told from various perspectives. Its aim was to consolidate the British Empire through military, economic, and constitutional devices. Those Canadians who supported imperial unity, or imperial federation, believed that Canada could attain national status only by maintaining the connection with the Empire and by acquiring an influence within its councils. Their opponents were convinced that imperialism was incompatible with Canada's national interests, internal unity, and self-government. The conflict between these two forces was a major theme in Canadian life in the 30 years before the First World War, and the struggle was bitter and divisive. It was fought out in many arenas, in Parliament, at Colonial and Imperial Conferences, and in polemical literature, and it centred upon several issues — commercial policy, participation in the Boer War, and military and naval preparedness. But it was above all fought out in the minds of Canadians, and it is from this point of view, as a problem in Canadian intellectual history, that it is presented in this book. The questions raised here do not concern, at least not primarily, elections, the formulation of tariff policy, or the problems of military cooperation. These readings are intended rather to bring into sharper focus the guiding ideas and divergent conceptions of the Canadian future that underlay the clash between imperialism and nationalism.

Source: *Imperialism and Nationalism, 1884–1914: A Conflict in Canadian Thought*, ed. Carl Berger (Toronto: Copp Clark, 1969), pp. 1–5. Reprinted by permission of the author.

Imperialism and nationalism are vague words which must be defined in terms of their historical context. The organized movement for imperial unity originated in the later 1880s. The cumulative impact of the long depression, the failure of Macdonald's National Policy to generate prosperity and economic integration, and the cultural crisis that followed the execution of Louis Riel produced a widespread feeling of pessimism about Canada's future. The commitment of the Liberal party to unrestricted reciprocity, or free trade with the United States, climaxed the fears of those who, rightly or wrongly, identified such a policy with continentalism. It was at this point — in 1887 and 1888 — that branches of the Imperial Federation League, an organization founded in England in 1884, were set up in Canada, and they quickly became the centres of a perfervid British Canadian patriotism. As a countermeasure to reciprocity, the supporters of imperial unity advocated the idea of an economic union of the Empire to be secured through preferential tariffs. Imperial preference remained the central plank in the agenda of Canadian imperialism long after unrestricted reciprocity was defeated in the election of 1891, and long after the Liberal party rejected it in 1893. Canadian imperialists were far more emphatic on the commercial aspects of imperial unity than were their counterparts in England. In fact the difference of opinion between those who stressed imperial preference and those who placed their faith in military and naval cooperation was one of the chief reasons why the Imperial Federation League disintegrated in 1893. Its branches in Canada, however, were simply reconstituted as organs of the British Empire League. When in 1897 the new Liberal government of Wilfrid Laurier extended a preference on British manufactured commodities entering Canada, the action was widely hailed as a practical implementation of the imperial ideal.

Imperial unity was as much a state of mind as a political platform, and the appeals of those who underlined the necessity for Canada to maintain and strengthen the British connection customarily transcended commercial and economic arguments. The leading spokesmen of imperial unity — Colonel George T. Denison of Toronto, a police magistrate and military thinker, George R. Parkin, a New Brunswick–born teacher and writer, and Rev. George M. Grant, Principal of Queen's University — all believed that Canada could grow and survive only if it held fast to the imperial connection. They were convinced, or they convinced themselves, partly through their reading of Goldwin Smith's plea for continental union, *Canada and the Canadian Question* (1891), that though unrestricted reciprocity might bring prosperity it would also ultimately end in political extinction. As a consequence, their arguments against a particular trade policy moved away from a discussion of the comparative prices of eggs in Toronto and Pittsburgh to an attempt to awaken an appreciation for, and an attachment to, those traditions and institutions which in their minds made the Canadian nationality worthy of preservation. In this sense imperial unity began as a defence of Canada.

In the later eighties and early nineties imperial unity found its main support in the older section of English Canada and particularly among the descendants of the United Empire Loyalists. Both Denison and Parkin traced their roots back to the Loyalists, who were described, in the mythology of the day, as "Canada's Pilgrim Fathers." Though the Imperial Federation League in 1889 counted one quarter of the members of the Dominion Parliament in its ranks, its most vocal and devoted supporters were drawn from a narrow group of politicians, lawyers, teachers, and Protestant ministers. It received no support from labour or the farming population, and in French Canada its progress was viewed firstly with indifference, then alarm, and finally with massive hostility. This is hardly surprising. Members of the Orange Order, who interpreted imperial federation to mean Protestant supremacy, were often members of the League, and D'Alton McCarthy, the leader of the Equal Rights Movement, which endeavoured to limit French language rights and separate schools to Quebec alone, was prominent among the adherents of imperialism. Not all imperialists, of course, were supporters of Orangeism and Equal Rights. One of the most sympathetic defences of the state-supported separate schools of Manitoba was penned by G.M. Grant, who had been instrumental in deposing McCarthy from his position in the League because he had jeopardized the cause of imperial unity. Yet in general, the obvious racial overtones of the imperial sentiment, and the strange allies with whom the imperialists consorted, were enough to alienate French Canada.

Born in a period of doubt and despair, imperialism by the late 1890s had become more impatient, assertive, and bellicose. The appointment of Joseph Chamberlain to the Colonial Office in 1895 signalized the increasing seriousness of purpose of British imperialism. In 1899, in spite of his own personal predisposition to remain uninvolved, Laurier was forced by public pressure in English Canada to dispatch Canadian soldiers to fight in the Boer War. This action was in itself a testimony to the growing strength of the imperial cause. Fourteen years before, Macdonald had shrugged off similar suggestions that Canada aid Britain in the Soudan and his reaction was endorsed by Denison, one of the most militant of Canadian imperialists, who was never one to miss a war if he could help it. The Boer War was the decisive event in the history of Canadian imperialism. To many English Canadians it was not a matter of aiding England. For them that experience was invested with all the enthusiasm of nationalism. Canada's participation, niggardly though some thought it was, marked the entry of the Dominion into world politics. She had become a force within the Empire and her path forward was straight and clear. Now that Canadians had demonstrated their willingness to support the Empire with more than emotional speeches, was it not only fair that they be accorded some influence over the direction of imperial foreign policy? French Canadians saw the matter very differently. The spectacle of Canadians fighting in so remote a war, one waged against a non-British minority with which they so easily identified themselves, generated an imperialist reaction which grew and gained momentum. Some time before, the nationalist Premier of Quebec, Honoré Mercier, had warned that the imperial federationists wanted "us to assume, in spite of ourselves, the responsibilities and dangers of a sovereign state which will not be ours. They seek to expose us to vicissitudes of peace and war . . .; to wrest from our arms our sons, . . . and send them off to bloody and distant wars, which we shall not be able to stop or prevent."[1] And the prophecy had come true. In 1899 Henri Bourassa left the Liberal party charging that Laurier had capitulated to pressure from the Colonial Office and had thereby established a precedent, fatal to Canadian self-government, that Canada must fight in all imperial wars. In 1903, in conjunction with a group of young French-Canadian nationalists, Bourassa founded the Ligue Nationaliste to combat the imperial menace. The zest with which imperialists had supported the South African war was proof to them of the essentially colonial-minded character of English Canada.

These two extremes, the one demanding that Canada take up imperial obligations and be accorded a voice in Empire affairs, the other insisting on Canadian neutrality and freedom from such burdens, were not easily reconciled, and for some time Laurier did not try to reconcile them. He turned aside Chamberlain's suggestions at the Colonial Conference of 1902 that cooperation be institutionalized. Though he declared in the same year that Canada must take some steps to ensure her security, and though in 1903, after the unpopular Alaska Boundary decision, he also urged that the Dominion make her own foreign policy, Laurier made no fundamental decisions in either direction, except for taking over the management of the naval bases at Halifax and Esquimalt. The imperial question lay quiescent until the "naval scare" of 1909 made postponement impossible. The threat that the German ship-building program would undermine the supremacy of British seapower set off a wide-ranging and acrimonious debate over what stand Canada should take. The imperialists contended that Canada, now strong and prosperous, should help sustain the force upon which her own security depended; to the anti-imperialists this appeared as the payment of tribute to the motherland whose interests were very different from Canada's. In reality the debate was more complex than this, for even imperialists were in disagreement about the exact extent and nature of Canada's contribution to imperial defence. But Laurier's proposal for the creation of a Canadian navy which in times of crisis would become part of the British fleet angered both extremes and in part accounted for his defeat in 1911. Long before this time Bourassa had come to think of Laurier as the main instrument of the imperialist conspiracy. On July 13, 1911, he wrote in *Le Devoir:* "English and African soldiers fell on the veldt for the glory of Chamberlain; women and children died of shame and misery for the grandeur of Laurier; children's entrails were cut out in the Concentration camps for the honour of the Empire." From the imperialist Stephen Leacock, on the other hand, came this greeting at the news of Laurier's defeat:

> Sir Wilfrid, it may be said, with all the gentleness of speech which is becoming in speaking of such a man on such an occasion, touched in this election upon the one point on which he never fully enjoyed the confidence of the Canadian people — our relations to the British Empire. It has been his fortunate lot to represent us on great occasions. He has ridden for us in coaches of State, to the plaudits of a London multitude. He has coined phrases for us, of summoning us to Imperial councils and the like, grandiloquent in the utterance, but meaning less and less as they recede into retrospect. That he never really understood the feelings of his English-speaking fellow citizens of Canada towards their Mother Country, that he never really designed to advance the cause of permanent Imperial unity — these things may well be doubted. . . . We are . . . groping for something which we desire but still seek in vain. The great problem of our common future is to find an organic basis of lasting union.[2]

Such was the burden of the two extremes which tore apart the man who searched for the fragile consensus.

In the 30 years before 1914, the difference between nationalism and imperialism was much more complicated than the desire for Canadian autonomy on the one hand and a willingness to live under Downing Street rule on the other. Not even the anti-imperialists thought it was that simple. John Ewart, for example, who defined nationalism as the end of subordination of one state to another, remarked that those Canadian imperialists with whom he was acquainted were really Canadian nationalists. And within the terms of his own definition he was right. What divided those who called themselves nationalists from those who preferred to be known as imperialists was not the question of whether Canada should manage her own affairs and have the power to formulate a foreign policy expressive of her interests; what divided them was disagreement over how these powers were to be acquired and for what purposes they were to be employed. The imperialists saw the British Empire as the vehicle in which Canada would attain national status; the anti-imperialists were so convinced of the incompatibility of imperial and Canadian interests that they saw all schemes for cooperation as reactionary and anti-national. In a fundamental sense, therefore, the differences between, say, Stephen Leacock and Henri Bourassa stemmed from their very different ideas about Canada, her history, and place in the world. The only way to understand the conflict between the positions these two men embodied is to understand the divergent conceptions which underlay them.

There are some limitations to the purpose of this volume as well as some particular problems that are raised by such an approach. It is not intended as a self-contained presentation of every facet and ramification of the nationalist–imperialist conflict. Such a project would require several more volumes. Nor does the approach suggest that intellectual history offers some magical key that will unlock all the puzzles and problems raised by the theme. And certainly it is not intended to supersede all other approaches. Someone has said that the practice of intellectual history is like trying to nail jelly to the wall, and indeed the entities that are subject to examination are nebulous and intangible. Any exact and scientific way of measuring the force and impact of ideas, furthermore, has yet to be devised, and the question must always arise as to the connection between ideas and the motives of those active men of power who made the crucial decisions. Yet when all this is said our understanding of Canadian history would be narrow indeed if we left out of account the climate of opinion in which the battle between imperialism and anti-imperialism took place. In the accounts of the Boer War crisis or the naval debate, for example, one invariably encounters allusions to the "imperialist pressure from English Canada" for this or that policy; yet one often comes away with the impression that we are told a good deal more about how extreme positions were accommodated or compromised at the centre than we learn about the extremes themselves. If we want to understand what imperialism and nationalism meant we must look to those who were the exponents and interpreters of these beliefs and try to grasp what these convictions meant to them. Only by doing so can we appreciate why their opposition was so fundamental and why Canadian historians are still divided as to the meaning of imperialism as a factor in Canadian history.

NOTES

1. Quoted in George R. Parkin, *Imperial Federation: The Problem of National Unity* (London, 1892), 85–86.
2. Stephen Leacock, *The Great Victory in Canada* (reprint from *The National Review,* London, 1911), 12.

Article Nine

Henri Bourassa on Imperialism and Biculturalism, 1900–1918

Joseph Levitt

Henri Bourassa had a clear vision of how to bring about Canadian nationhood, and with unbelievable stubbornness he struggled to persuade both French and English Canadians to accept his ideas. Although not an original thinker, he was well read, highly intelligent, and had absorbed the principles of three of the most important ideologies of late-nineteenth-century Western Europe: Catholicism, nationalism, and liberalism. These he integrated into the coherent world outlook which underlay his conception of a Canadian nation.

Bourassa's ideas penetrated the consciousness of his contemporaries because they dealt with the fundamental difficulties that confronted the builders of a Canadian nation: the relations between Canada and Great Britain, the relations between French and English Canadians, and the economic and social relations between rich and poor in an industrial and capitalist society.

The reception that Bourassa's contemporaries gave his ideas was enhanced by Bourassa's formidable forensic talent and massive personality. Many saw Bourassa as a great orator who skillfully articulated the aspirations of his French-Canadian audiences. Bourassa's power as

Source: *Henri Bourassa on Imperialism and Bi-culturalism, 1900–1918* (Toronto: Copp Clark, 1970). Reprinted by permission of the author.

a writer is striking even today. On the one hand, with very few exceptions, he used meticulously documented facts to appeal to reason (see his pamphlets *Great Britain and Canada* and *Que Devons-Nous à l'Angleterre?*); on the other, by always giving his ideas an ethical basis, he aroused moral passion. To Bourassa a policy was always either morally *right* or morally *wrong*.

Bourassa had unusual political gifts: forceful personality, keen intellect, eloquence. When he first entered Parliament, some believed that he would succeed Laurier as the most prominent French Canadian in the Liberal party. But Bourassa possessed characteristics fatal to any politician. In him were combined a dread of forcing a decision on his reluctant supporters and a positive distaste for exercising power. "I am of such a temperament that I never feel like being a whip," he commented. "I have enough trouble in keeping myself in line: I have no desire to keep others in line."[1] He had little or no tolerance for other people's opinions. He was totally unable to compromise. This made him hopeless as a politician but superb as a critic. Because he had no need to cope with political realities, his proposals were straightforward, clear, consistent with one another, and suffused with moral rectitude.

Although Bourassa accepted the parliamentary system, he believed that party leaders, corrupted by their love of power, too often sacrificed principle to keep themselves in office; party policy was dictated by political advantage rather than concern for the good of the country. The only way to offset this weakness in parties was to arouse public opinion to the point where it would compel politicians anxious to win elections to take up patriotic policies. It was as such an educator of public opinion that Bourassa saw himself and indeed acted. Working outside Parliament and through his newspaper, *Le Devoir*, he won the following of enough French Canadians to make the policies he advocated of pivotal importance in the elections of 1911 and 1917. As the feat of an individual, this accomplishment is unmatched in twentieth-century Canadian politics.

BOURASSA AND CANADIAN NATIONHOOD

Nationalist, Catholic, and liberal values all went into Bourassa's conception of Canadian nationhood. Accepting the nationalist nineteenth-century idea that each nation had been given a specific task by God, he believed that French Canada's mission was to build the ideal society on Catholic principles and by its example win back to the Church millions of Protestants and free-thinkers in North America. The situation of French Canadians was complicated: not only were they under British rule, but they also lived with Anglo-Canadians, more numerous than they, in the same confederation. But Bourassa was able to reconcile his patriotism to French Canada with a genuine loyalty to Canada, a British Dominion, because he was a cultural nationalist. He wished French Canada to have a culture separate from that of English Canada, but not to be a sovereign state of its own. Thus he was both a French-Canadian nationalist and a Canadian nationalist at the same time.

Bourassa desired amity between English and French Canadians. He wished to see an Anglo–French Canadian nation, one in which each group would keep its own culture but would be united with the other "in a sentiment of brotherhood in a common attachment to a common country."[2] The necessary legal framework for such a bicultural country was possible only on the basis of liberal principles: Canada must be free to choose her foreign policies on the sole basis of her own interests, not those of the British Empire, and French Canada must be free to develop her culture everywhere in the Dominion. But Bourassa's aspirations were frustrated by the majority of Canadians who believed that Canada ought to cooperate with Great Britain in imperial defence and by an English Canada that refused to accept cultural duality.

IMPERIAL DEFENCE

The turn of the century saw the heyday of the imperialist movement in England. Of the many causes of this complex phenomenon, we are concerned with only one: the growing vulnerability of the Empire to powerful rivals. Faced with potential threats, imperial defence planners turned to the Dominions for help. They wished the Dominions to contribute to a system of imperial defence controlled centrally in London. But colonial politicians saw things differently. Previously, a colony had been responsible only for its own defence while Great Britain protected the rest of the Empire. Now a centralized defence would mean that the colonies were contributing large amounts of money to further policies over which they had no control.

Canadian politicians stood firm in defence of their military autonomy. At the imperial conference of 1902 Laurier rejected any proposals for defence centralization, "not so much from the expense involved," but because it represented "an important departure from the principles of colonial self-government."[3] In 1904 his government placed all Canadian military affairs under the command of a Militia Council which itself was under the direct control of the Canadian Minister of Militia. Then in 1907, Canada helped to persuade the British General Staff to agree that Dominion officers whom it trained would be responsible to their own Cabinet ministers and not to British officials; this implied that the principle in defence relations was to be cooperation and not automatic commitment. Two years later the Laurier government was an important influence in the admiralty's decision to concede the principle of naval decentralization for the Empire. Yet while insisting on defence cooperation, Laurier did not neglect military reform. New training schemes for officers were begun and military institutions in the country were made more efficient. Such was the progress that the government accepted a plan for the dispatch of a Canadian contingent overseas if necessary.

The government's defence policy, however, aroused passionate controversy on two occasions: once in 1899 over the sending of troops to South Africa, and then again in 1910 over its decision to found a Canadian navy. At first Laurier did not believe that Canada should participate in the Boer War. He stated publicly that soldiers could not be legally sent to South Africa because the Boers did not present a threat to Canadian security. Many Anglo-Canadians, including members of his own cabinet, would not accept his decision and compelled him to change his mind; the Cabinet authorized the dispatch of troops to South Africa but emphasized that this action was not to be taken as a precedent. Bourassa, however, because he believed that the government's action was a serious step toward Canada's being automatically committed to take part in every British war, resigned from his seat in the Commons. Laurier, on the other hand, was criticized for not fully supporting the imperial cause since Canadian troops once in South Africa were to be paid by Great Britain.

As a response to the "dreadnought" crisis which had blown up in 1909 over the possibility of the German fleet catching up to the British, Laurier proposed forming a small navy which the Cabinet could turn over to the Admiralty if it thought necessary. Bourassa and his supporters opposed the Naval Bill, arguing that it would commit Canada to every British war. Many Anglo-Canadians, however, objected to Laurier's proposal for exactly the opposite reasons; it gave the Cabinet the alternative of not sending the navy and thus undermined the principle of "One King, One Fleet, One Flag." But in Quebec Bourassa's attack on Laurier's federal naval policy was so popular that candidates whom he supported in the 1911 federal election won sixteen seats from the Liberals. This loss of Quebec support contributed to the defeat of the Laurier government and the election of a Conservative administration headed by Robert Borden.

Although Canada was automatically committed to war in 1914, there was almost unanimous sentiment for participation. This did not, however, end the speculation over imperial relations. It was clear that as a consequence of their taking part in the War, the Dominions would demand a voice in imperial foreign policy; and denial of this claim would result in the shattering of the Empire. This was the thesis of a book by Lionel Curtis, the leader of a group of thoughtful imperialist-minded people devoted to building imperial unity through the exchange of information and propaganda. But it was not only these intellectuals of the Round Table (the name of a quarterly founded by Curtis in which he expounded his ideas) who were concerned with the fate of the Empire. Even while leading the Canadian war effort, Prime Minister Borden found the question important enough to help set up in London an Imperial War Conference, composed of overseas prime ministers and British cabinet ministers, to chart the future of the Empire.

BOURASSA AND THE BRITISH CONNECTION

The roots of Bourassa's disagreement with Laurier over imperial defence lay in their differing concepts of the British Empire. To Laurier, the British Empire represented liberty and justice;[4] to Bourassa, all empires, including the British, were "hateful," and stood in the way of "liberty and intellectual and moral progress." Bourassa believed that the Empire imposed serious constraints on the life of nationalities, preventing them from achieving the destiny that God had planned for them; thus it was necessary to choose between "British ideals and British domination."[5]

Bourassa was convinced that the aim of British imperialists was to assure the military, commercial, and intellectual supremacy of the Anglo-Saxon race. Since this could be achieved only by force, the British were led to demand military aid from the Dominions. To ensure that this help was forthcoming, imperialists like Joseph Chamberlain, the British Colonial Secretary, and Lord Grey, the Governor General of Canada, were plotting to revolutionize imperial defence relations so that Great Britain would continue to control foreign policy but would be able to commit the colonies, including Canada, to her wars — hence the danger of Laurier accepting the premise that when Great Britain was at war Canada was at war.[6] Canada, Bourassa insisted, could go to war only by its own consent and not by some imperial act. This reaction was anti-imperialist, not pacifist. He was ready to agree to Canada's going to war, but only if she were directly attacked or if her vital interests were in jeopardy.

Laurier's decision to send troops to South Africa had raised in Bourassa's mind the question of Canadian responsibilities in British wars. What made Laurier's action even more reprehensible to Bourassa was that Laurier had knowingly violated the existing law. Under pressure from London, Laurier had set a precedent which, if followed, would mean that Canadian forces would be automatically put at the disposal of the British in all their future wars. The consequences would be very grave for Canada: "If we send 2000 and spend $2,000,000 to fight two nations, aggregating a population of 250,000 souls, how many men shall we send and how many millions shall we expend to fight a first class power, a coalition of powers?"[7]

Bourassa was going too far to claim that a precedent had been set, even though he offered as proof the fact that Chamberlain regarded the Canadian action as such. Influential Anglo-Canadians believed that although Canada had sent troops to fight the Boers, she had not given up the right to choose whether she would engage in British wars or not. They supported Laurier when he rejected Chamberlain's plea to Canada to accept the principle of centralized defence at the Imperial Conference of 1902.

Laurier's intention to develop a Canadian navy posed the same issue. He believed that British naval supremacy was necessary to protect the Empire and all the values it stood for;

if it were threatened, Canada must aid Great Britain with all her force. But he wished the Canadian Cabinet to decide whether or not the navy should be turned over to the Admiralty. Bourassa, though, viewed the question from an entirely different perspective. The fact that the proposed fleet was to include cruisers and destroyers suggested to him that its purpose was not to defend Canadian coastal waters but to form part of the British fleet in time of war. Laurier claimed he would put the Canadian fleet under British control only if he believed the danger to Britain great enough, but Bourassa maintained that he would in fact do this for all wars in which Great Britain became involved. Bourassa did not trust Laurier: the prime minister was bound to cave in under imperial pressure in an emergency, even as he had done in 1899 over the Boer War. To emphasize his point Bourassa implied that at the Imperial Conference of 1909 Laurier had agreed that in time of war the fleet would automatically come under British control and that this commitment had been given the force of law by the Naval Bill of 1910. This was an unfair presentation of Laurier's position.

It was natural that Bourassa would be interested in the discussion on postwar imperial relations. He believed that by their contribution to the imperial war effort the Dominions had left behind their colonial status. They should not put up with less say on British foreign policy than a "single cab driver in London";[8] if the Canadian people insisted on taking part in British wars they ought to have some control over the way in which their men and money were used.

Still, for Bourassa such imperial partnership was even at best a poor alternative to complete Canadian independence. Independence would mean that Anglo-Canadians would acknowledge for once and for all that Canada and not Great Britain was their homeland. This would eliminate the major reason for quarrels between the two Canadian peoples. In foreign affairs Canada's position would be safer, for she would not be exposed to attacks from British enemies. She would have a national personality of her own and would make her decisions about war and peace for her own interests.

Such practical advantage reinforced Bourassa's ideological conviction that it was right for Canada to become independent. He believed that the natural evolution of human societies was toward nationhood. A centralized Empire was ultimately impossible because each part separated from the other by the ocean would develop in its own way according to its geographical situation, its economic needs, and its temperament. Canada, like the other communities in the Empire, was progressing toward nationhood, the achievement of which would be marked by independence — the only status that could satisfy the aspirations of a free people.

In becoming independent, Canada would be also fulfilling God's design. Bourassa believed that God had wished Canada to separate herself from the old world by breaking the imperial tie to fulfill her destiny chosen by Him in North America. That Canada, by taking part in European wars because of imperial membership, was not carrying out this mission was no small reason for Bourassa's ardent desire for her independence.

Bourassa's desire to see Canada a nation was similar to that of English-speaking Liberals like John Dafoe, the editor of the Winnipeg Free Press, or of French-speaking ones like Wilfrid Laurier. But Dafoe believed that it was possible for the Empire to be based on the principle of autonomy and that Canada could be a greater nation for being part of it; Bourassa considered Canadian autonomy or freedom and her membership in the Empire to be mutually exclusive. Laurier, too, differed from Bourassa in his conviction that autonomy was not necessarily incompatible with retaining the British connection. To Laurier, imperial sentiment in Canada, whether reasonable or not, was a force which responsible leaders must accommodate. To Bourassa it was precisely this loyalty to the Motherland that was the main barrier to Anglo-Canadians and French Canadians cooperating to build a nation and therefore this loyalty must be opposed.

FRENCH CULTURAL RIGHTS

In the decade before the war, French cultural rights outside of Quebec became a burning issue: non–French-speaking immigration to the West and French-Canadian immigration to Ontario provoked a great public debate on whether one of the functions of the schools in these areas was to further French-Canadian culture.

Responding to the demands of settlers, the Laurier government decided to form two new Western provinces. Written into the Autonomy Bill of 1905 was the legal framework for a school system that many people, including Clifford Sifton, the Minister of the Interior, believed substituted denominational for what should have been public schools. A public uproar arose; some regarded it as an attack on the autonomy of the new provinces; militant Protestants objected to turning over the direction of any schools to the Church; many Westerners favoured the idea of the melting pot and opposed a school system which would further divide a population already fragmented by ethnic origin. To satisfy these critics, Laurier rewrote the offending clause: the schools would be run by the provincial government, not by religious institutions. Catholics were free to set up a separate school in districts where they were a *minority*; however, since they clustered together, they were usually the majority in their district and thus were compelled to attend public schools. In 1905 there were only nine Catholic "separate" schools in the Northwest. French Canadians were granted two other concessions in the new provinces. They were allowed religious instruction for a half-hour after half-past-three, and could have a primary course in the French language if they desired it.

In 1912 the separate school question was briefly revived in the West when the territory of Keewatin was joined to Manitoba. A demand arose that one of the conditions of annexation would be the guarantee of the territory's right to separate schools. But Robert Borden, then prime minister, made no provision for such rights in his annexation bill and public interest soon petered out.

French cultural rights became a burning issue when the movement of French Canadians into eastern Ontario changed the relative positions of French and English in the schools. Although still the legal language of instruction, English became just another subject on the curriculum; French became the real means of communication. Toward the end of 1910 opposition to this arrangement arose in Ontario: Canadian nationalists were convinced that a common Canadian consciousness could not be created unless English were the common language.[9] Orangemen feared that the spread of French would undermine the Anglo-Saxon character of the province and so injure the Empire; Irish Catholics believed that the identification of separate schools with French would prejudice their schools receiving public grants. What these three groups had in common was a conviction that everybody must learn English and a determination to reject any legal status for French. This point of view was accepted by the two major provincial parties, the Conservatives and the Liberals.

In September 1910 at the Eucharistic Congress in Montreal, Archbishop Bourne of Westminister sparked public debate by declaring that if the Catholic Church wished to make progress in Canada, it ought to be English-speaking. Bourassa's rebuttal came in his most celebrated speech, *Religion, Langue, Nationalité*. The excitement aroused by this clash led the French-Canadian press to reveal the details of a well-kept secret: that Bishop Michael Francis Fallon, the Bishop of London, had undertaken to eliminate French in the Catholic schools of his diocese on the grounds that students were learning neither English nor French. The subsequent public furor caused the government to assign Dr. F.W. Merchant, an official of the Ontario Department of Education, to investigate the schools where French was the language of instruction. After the Merchant report found that much was lacking in the teaching of English in these schools, the Conservative provincial government issued Regulation 17 late in 1912.

Regulation 17 was to apply only to certain schools, designated each year as English–French schools. In these schools French was permitted as a language of instruction only for the first two years of school. Where French had "hitherto" been a subject of study, instruction in the French language for no more than one hour each day might be provided. (Many French Canadians, including Laurier, took this to mean that French would be prohibited in all future schools.) Any school which did not comply with Regulation 17 would no longer be entitled to public funds.

Although the government claimed to be interested only in improving the quality of the English spoken by Franco-Ontarians, the majority of French Canadians saw Regulation 17 as a prelude to the complete removal of French from Ontario schools. Franco-Ontarian teachers in the Ottawa Valley refused to comply with the Regulation and their students walked out of schools. In 1915 some 150 schools outside of Ottawa refused to accept the Regulation and gave up the provincial grant. In Ottawa itself the majority of the Separate School Board defied the Department of Education. The government responded by appointing a commission to take over its duties. Meanwhile important Quebec personalities, including Church dignitaries, led a campaign to raise funds for "les blessés d'Ontario." The Quebec legislature, asserting that the Ontario government did not understand British principles, authorized local Catholic commissions to contribute officially to the fund.

Outside intervention helped to ease the crisis. In October 1916 Pope Benedict XV issued an encyclical which most Catholics interpreted as supporting the position of Bishop Fallon: the study of French was not to be pushed to the point where it endangered Catholic schools in Ontario. Significantly, Bourassa was silent on the encyclical. A month later, the Privy Council in London established the basis for a compromise by ruling that Regulation 17 was legal, but the commission which had taken over the duties of the Separate School Board was not.

For four years the controversy had raged, becoming especially violent after the Great War began. Many French Canadians believed the majority of Ontarians hypocritical in supporting a war for freedom while repressing French at home. Armand Lavergne, a colleague of Bourassa's, spoke for many of his compatriots when he cried out in the Quebec legislature, "I ask myself if the German regime might not be favourably compared with the Boches of Ontario."[10] On their side, Anglo-Ontarians continued to support Regulation 17 because they wished Ontario to be exclusively English. Many of them believed that the French Canadians were using the question of French in Ontario schools as an excuse for not giving full support to the war and they resented what they regarded as an attempt of French Canada to compel them to change the Regulation by threatening to slow down the war effort. Either Regulation 17 or the war would have strained relations between the English and French; the conjunction of the two exacerbated hostility to a level of bitterness hitherto unknown between the two peoples.

BOURASSA AND BICULTURALISM

Bourassa became the most prominent spokesman of French-Canadian resentment. Deeply convinced that Catholics should control the schools their children attended to ensure the teaching of religious values, he also believed God had bestowed on French Canadians a particular genius, character, and temperament which could be fully expressed only through the French language. They were something more than British subjects who happened to speak French. Bourassa exhorted his compatriots to fight for French-Canadian culture. If they meekly accepted that it had no legal rights in English Canada, on what basis would they oppose the application of this false principle to Quebec itself?

For Bourassa, faith and language were inextricably united. He vehemently rejected the contention of English-speaking Catholics that it would be better for the Church to present an

English image: it was the natural right of everyone to speak his maternal tongue; to use the Church as an instrument of assimilation would be "odious." There were other practical reasons for the Church to reject the argument: English-speaking Catholics themselves were open to the social influences of Protestant and free-thinking North Americans, while apostasy was rare among French Canadians, whose language served as a barrier to heretical influences.

But such Catholic and racial values, although acceptable to significant segments of French-Canadian opinion, made little impression in English Canada where the majority was Protestant. Yet French-Canadian culture could only survive outside Quebec if Anglo-Canadians accepted cultural duality. To persuade them, Bourassa advanced two main propositions: the Constitution was based on the principle of cultural duality and the Canadian confederation could not survive unless such biculturalism was accepted by English Canada. These arguments were not mere debating tricks with Bourassa; he believed them with total sincerity.

Bourassa viewed Confederation as the result of an agreement between English and French to accept the equal rights of each culture throughout the Dominion. The Fathers of Confederation had envisaged Canada as a bicultural country. If their behests had been followed, then the West, acquired "in the name of and with the money of the whole Canadian people,"[11] would have been French as well as English, Catholic as well as Protestant. It would have been made clear to all immigrants that the West was Anglo-French.

In the first years after Confederation, maintained Bourassa, the federal government affirmed the bicultural nature of the country by the Manitoba Act of 1870 and the North West Territories Bill of 1875, each of which accepted French as one of the official languages and established a denominational school system. But in 1890, Ottawa had permitted the territorial government of the northwest to extinguish the legal status of French. Two years later, the school system began to be modified until in 1901 it was, in fact, a state school system.[12] Because the ordinances of the Territorial Government which had changed the school system violated the spirit and text of the 1875 law passed by the federal government, a government superior in authority to that of the Northwest Territories, Bourassa considered them illegal. By accepting the Sifton amendment in 1905, the government legitimized these illegal school ordinances and ratified the limitations of the rights of Western French Canadians to schools of their own.

The bicultural compact implied the right not only to separate schools but also to instruction in French. By giving both French and English official status in Parliament, the Fathers had made it clear that they wished both languages to coexist everywhere in public life: in church, in court, and in government. These rights would be meaningless if the English provinces prevented French-Canadian children from acquiring a perfect knowledge of their own language.

Bourassa also insisted that cultural duality was necessary if Confederation were to last. The materialist ethos of the United States was penetrating Canada; the unchecked consequence of the invasion of such values would lead to the slow absorption of Canada into the United States. The greatest barrier to "l'américanisme"[13] was French Canada, because being Catholic, it rejected materialism and the American way of life. But if French Canadians continued to be humiliated, they would no longer resist Americanization, for they could see no advantage to remaining British.

Refusal to accept cultural duality threatened Confederation in yet another way. French Canadians would never feel that Canada was their homeland unless their culture was free to develop. Thus national unity was conditioned on cultural duality. The alternative was constant instability and crisis. Confederation, Bourassa maintained, would not survive without the reciprocal respect of the rights of the two races.

Such was Bourassa's general attitude toward cultural duality. He also had a number of specific points to make about each issue. The Autonomy Bill specifically forbade Catholics from organizing separate schools where they were a majority in the district. Yet they would recon-cile themselves more easily to sending their children to a government school if it were called "separate" and not "public"; Catholic school boards would hire Catholic teachers and thus all lessons would be infused with a Church spirit. The new bill compelled most Catholic children to attend public schools where they could not be protected should the Minister of Education decide to suppress religious or French teaching. The advantages to Catholics of attending schools that could be called separate even though they were essentially controlled by the gov-ernment were so important to Bourassa that he declared that if the Catholics were allowed to set up such "separate" schools he would withdraw his opposition to the new bill.

Bourassa denied that instruction in French in Ontario schools would harm national unity. Even if proficient in French, French Canadians had no more intention of becoming attached to France than Americans had of becoming British colonists again. Nor did it mean, if French were granted official status in English Canada that the languages of the immigrants ought to receive similar recognition: the French claim, after all, was based on the bicultural compact. Bourassa also denied that a bilingual people could not form a homogeneous nation, arguing that discord would stem only from the attempts of the majority to force their language on the minority.

Then too there were some practical advantages to French.

Outside the English-speaking world French was useful in commerce and diplomacy. More important, it was the language of cultivated minds. When Canada had developed sufficiently to appreciate art and literature, claimed Bourassa, it would turn to French as an instrument of communication with the best of European civilization.

Bourassa's claim that Confederation was based on a bicultural pact is debatable. True, the Fathers had recognized the separateness of the French Canadians of Lower Canada: the pre-dominately French-Canadian province would still control its French Catholic schools, and French would be an official language in the federal Parliament and courts. Such measures would enable French Canadians in Quebec both to develop their own culture and take part in the public life of the new Dominion. But on the other hand, the Fathers made no provision for the legal status of French in provinces other than Quebec; the Constitution furnished no pro-tection for the Acadians. Professor Donald Creighton has shown that the Manitoba Act of 1870 and the Territorial Act of 1875 were not conscious steps in a plan to extend biculturalism to the West; instead, they were passed because of fortuitous circumstances and indeed were then quickly reversed.[14] Thus the Fathers did not object to cultural duality but neither did they determine to make Canada a bicultural country.

However, Bourassa's proposition that Confederation would not survive without cultural duality has been accepted by a large number of English-speaking Canadians. Many feel guilty about the shabby treatment given to French outside of Quebec. More important, many believe such cultural equality necessary if Quebec is to remain in Confederation.

CONSCRIPTION

As the war went on, it became clear that there was a great difference of opinion between French and English over Canada's responsibility to the Allied side. Great numbers of Anglo-Canadians believed that Canada should be ready to fight to the end of her resources in both men and money. French Canadians, however, indicated by their markedly low rate of enlistment that they thought Canada should play a relatively minor role. This issue came to the fore over the proposal of the Borden government in the spring of 1917 to conscript men for overseas service. Voluntary enlistments, which were falling due to war-weariness, could not fill the gaps left by the high casualty rate suffered by Canadian troops on the Western front since the first of the year.

Borden asked Laurier to join him in a coalition government on a program of introducing conscription. The latter refused for a number of reasons: conscription was repugnant to him personally; if he took part in a coalition he would become responsible for a policy that he had no share in making; he suspected that it was a trick to split the Liberal party. But equally important, as he emphasized to friends, if he accepted conscription, he would be breaking his promise to Quebec and thus would virtually be handing over the province to Bourassa and his friends. Borden, however, succeeded in inducing a number of Liberals to join him in a "union" government which defeated Laurier in the federal election of December 1917. In contrast to the election of 1911, Bourassa now threw his support behind Laurier.

Bourassa had no objection to conscription as such. His attitude to it was conditioned by what he thought about the war. Although in 1914 he had supported Canadian participation, by 1916 he had come to modify his opinion: the war was supposedly being fought for the right of small nations to live, but in fact the great powers were smashing up the small nationalities. He followed the lead of Pope Benedict XV in calling for an end to the war, for a negotiated peace in which neither side would emerge solely victorious. Since he believed that there was no real Canadian interest involved in the war, he was logically consistent to claim that those who opposed conscription were the most patriotic Canadians; and that if French Canadians adopted this stand, it was because they were very clear in their minds that they owed their patriotism to Canada and Canada alone, unlike Anglo-Canadians whose focus of loyalty shifted between Canada and Great Britain.

BOURASSA'S ACHIEVEMENTS

Many Canadian historians have been critical of Bourassa, presenting him as the spokesman for narrow French-Canadian clerical and racial elements that had refused to do their part in building Canadian unity. Yet it would be difficult to find any statement of his in support of Canadian autonomy within the Empire or of French-Canadian rights outside of Quebec that was not logically consistent with his program of achieving Canadian nationhood.

What his critics object to, however, is not Bourassa's program but the consequence of his determination to promote it. In 1911, by attacking Laurier, he helped bring the "more Imperialist of the two national parties"[15] to power. And since many of the Quebec members who had been elected because they had been endorsed by Bourassa gave their support to the Conservative naval program, French Canadians in Borden's Cabinet soon lost popularity in French Canada. Without influence in Quebec, their voices in Ottawa became feeble. Thus the manpower crisis was met by a government that was to all intents and purposes Anglo-Canadian.

Again Bourassa used rhetoric that was so strong about the French language issue during the war that he substantially embittered French–English relations and thereby contributed to the emotional climate out of which came the storm around conscription. In sum, the charge against Bourassa is that he went too far, that he was an extremist.

Yet from his own point of view, Bourassa's tactics made good sense. What he was trying to do in 1911, he said, was to send to Ottawa a block of members (whom he called Nationalists) who would hold the balance of power between the two parties and thus force the new government to revise the Naval Bill. What is more, he would have achieved his purpose if Borden had won a few seats less in Ontario and the Nationalists a few more in Quebec.[16] Even with the number of seats the Nationalists did win, they would have formed an important force within the Conservative government had Bourassa accepted a Cabinet position. But he was not prepared to undertake the tough responsibility of political leadership.

It was only natural for Bourassa to take advantage of the Anglo-Canadians' claim that they were fighting for freedom abroad to demand that they show good faith by granting equal rights to Franco-Ontarians at home. If as a consequence Canada's war effort were to slacken, it would not be too serious since Canada's role was a minor one and the Allies ought to be aiming at negotiating a just peace and not at winning the war.

Bourassa then had some grounds for believing that his tactics would be successful. But even without such hopes he would have acted the same way. He was not pragmatic: that he might not succeed in persuading Anglo-Canadians to do the right thing was no reason for not trying. It was on this point that Laurier differed profoundly from him. Although Laurier agreed with a great deal of Bourassa's program of Canadian nationalism, he did not defy Anglo-Canadian opinion because he wished the Liberal party to be the instrument of building unity between French and English. As an independent critic, Bourassa proclaimed what Anglo-Canadians ought to do; as a politician with responsibilities, Laurier proposed only what they would agree to do.

Many who are sympathetic with Laurier fail to see that even if he was right to contend that satisfactory relations between English and French must be founded on the possible rather than the ideal, it does not mean that left to himself he would have found the right point of compromise. Laurier's most significant action for Canadian unity was to reject conscription and refuse to join the Union coalition. This left the way open for the preservation of the Liberal party as an effective forum for the reconciliation of English and French in the postwar decade in Canada. But, as Professor Ramsay Cook has argued, Laurier's primary motive for these actions was his fear of handing Quebec over to Bourassa.[17] Because Bourassa would not compromise, Laurier was unable to compromise; it was the tension between the critic and the politician that determined the fate of the Liberal party.

Bourassa did a great deal to turn Canadian public opinion against any form of centralization of imperial foreign policy and defence. His greatest accomplishment, however, was to convince succeeding generations of French Canadians that their language ought to have the same rights as the English language. Thus he, more than any other individual, was responsible for making his dictum that Canada could only survive as a bicultural country much truer now than when he first enunciated it at the turn of the century.

NOTES

1. H. Bourassa, *Canada: House of Commons Debates*, Feb. 19, 1900, p. 500.
2. H. Bourassa, "Réponse amicale à la vérité," *La Nationaliste*, April 3, 1904.
3. Quoted in R. Preston, *Canada and Imperial Defense* (Toronto, 1976), 305.
4. H.B. Neatby, "Laurier and Imperialism," Canadian Historical Association, *Report* (1955), 25.
5. H. Bourassa, *Canadian Nationalism and the War* (Montreal, 1916), 14.
6. Bourassa usually ignored Laurier's qualifications. What Laurier said was this: "If England is at war, we are at war and liable to attack. I do not say that we shall always be attacked, neither do I say that we would take part in all the wars of England. That is a matter that we must be guided by the circumstance upon which the Canadian Parliament will have to pronounce, and will have to decide in its own best judgement." O.D. Skelton, *Life and Letters of Sir Wilfrid Laurier* (Toronto, 1965), 11: 125.
7. H. Bourassa, *Canada House of Commons Debates*, March 13, 1900, p. 1802.
8. H. Bourassa, *Independence or Imperial Partnership* (Montreal, 1916), 47.
9. C.B. Sissons quotes a small English boy to a French teacher: "This country does not belong to France and you must all learn English; my grandpa says so." C.B. Sissons, *Bilingual Schools in Canada* (London, 1917), 66.
10. *Canadian Annual Review*, 1916 (Toronto, 1917), 34.
11. H. Bourassa, *Canada, House of Commons*, July 5, 1905, p. 8848.

12. In the same speech Bourassa did not refer to the abolition of the rights of French culture in Manitoba, probably because he had supported Laurier's position on the Manitoba School question in 1896.

13. H. Bourassa, *La langue française et l'avenir de notre race* (Quebec, 1913), 17.

14. D.G. Creighton, "John A. Macdonald, Confederation, and the Canadian West," in C. Brown, *Minorities, Schools and Politics* (Toronto, 1969), 8.

15. H.B. Neatby, *Laurier and a Liberal Quebec: A Study in Political Management* (unpublished Ph.D. thesis, University of Toronto, 1956), 350.

16. J.M. Beck, *Pendulum of Power* (Scarborough, 1968), 133.

17. Ramsay Cook, "Dafoe, Laurier, and the Formation of Union Government," *Canadian Historical Review* 42, 3 (September 1961): 197.

Article Ten

Casting Daylight upon Magic: Deconstructing the Royal Tour of 1901 to Canada

Phillip Buckner

On 16 September 1901 George, Duke of Cornwall and York and heir apparent to the throne of Great Britain, arrived in Canada to begin a 35-day royal progress, which would involve crossing the country twice, from Quebec City to Victoria and back again to Halifax. For a whole generation of Canadians this was one of the most memorable public events to take place during their lifetimes. Certainly this was the view of contemporary Canadians, who turned out in unprecedented numbers to view their future King and Queen. The streets of Toronto, reported the *Telegram*, were 'aglow with happy boys and girls who will ever remember the visit of the Duke of Cornwall, as their parents remember the visit of his father to Toronto 41 years ago'.[1] The Toronto *News* described the Duke's arrival as 'one of the biggest days in Toronto's history'.[2] Similar comments were made in newspapers across the country, which carried lengthy daily reports about every aspect of the tour. Five British and 71 Canadian journalists as well as four photographers were carried on board the royal train at government expense and hundreds more tracked the tour across Canada.[3] No fewer than three books about the tour were published by British journalists, another by Sir Donald Mackenzie Wallace, who had accompanied the tour as its official chronicler, and a fifth by Sir Joseph Pope, the chief Canadian civil servant involved in organising the tour.[4] The Edison Company even produced the first (albeit rather short) moving picture of a royal tour to Canada.[5] Hector Charlesworth, one of Canada's best known journalists, described the tour in his reminiscences as 'One of the most interesting of all the assignments I covered while a reporter'.[6] John Castell Hopkins, author of a range of popular histories and a member of the organising committee when the Duke visited Toronto, included a lengthy description of the tour in his biography of Edward VII.[7] Stephen Leacock, a member of the welcoming committee in Orillia, always remembered the day he had met the future George V.[8] Thousands of Canadian homes once contained memorabilia of the tour and scrapbooks lovingly collected to be handed on to the next generation. The importance of the tour seemed self-evident to all who had been there.

Source: Phillip Buckner, "Casting Daylight upon Magic: Deconstructing the Royal Tour of 1901 in Canada," *The Journal of Imperial and Commonwealth History*, 31, 2 (2003): 158–189. Reproduced with permission of Taylor & Francis Ltd., http://www.tandf.co.uk/journals.

Its importance has not appeared equally self-evident to later Canadian historians and one looks largely in vain for even a brief mention of the tour in recently published studies of Canada at the turn of the century.[9] In part this scholarly void simply reflects the general lack of interest among Canadian scholars in the monarchy and its significance in Canadian history, despite the fact that during the second half of the nineteenth century popular enthusiasm for monarchy grew steadily stronger in Canada. Queen Victoria's birthday (24 May) became one of the most significant public holidays, and the celebrations of Queen Victoria's Golden Jubilee in 1887 and her Diamond Jubilee in 1897 were marked by widespread ceremonies across the country. Victoria became the most popular place name in Canada and virtually every Canadian urban centre acquired a Victoria Street and usually an Albert, Edward and George as well. The Jubilees and Victoria's death led to a host of public buildings and public monuments being dedicated to her memory.[10] If one is to believe the newspapers, Canadians were overcome with grief at the death of Victoria in 1901 and equally overcome with joy at the coronation of her son as Edward VII in 1902.[11] Yet all this public enthusiasm for the monarchy is generally dismissed as essentially meaningless — indeed, almost irrational. The classic example of this attitude can be seen in Robert Stamp's *Kings, Queens and Canadians* — one of the few historical studies to recognise the significance of popular royalism in Canada. Yet Stamp's subtitle — 'A Celebration of Canada's Infatuation with the British Royal Family' — tells it all.[12] Canadian enthusiasm for what was essentially a foreign institution — the 'British' monarchy — could only have been an 'infatuation'.

A more sophisticated approach argues that the popularity of the monarchy was essentially the product of indoctrination by the Canadian social elite, who had their own reasons for collaborating with the imperial authorities, a classic example of what Marxist historians would call the creation of a 'false consciousness', in the interests of maintaining hegemonic control. Most Canadian historians (and the same could be said of their Australian and New Zealand counterparts) would prefer simply to ignore the whole issue and to focus on the gradual evolution of a distinct and separate Canadian national identity with its own separate and distinct national symbols. They are deeply embarrassed by the fact that Canadians have for so long been committed to the preservation of the monarchy and that this enthusiasm was shared by men and women of virtually every class and ethnic group in Canada. But if forced to confront the appeal of popular royalism, as Jane Connors has argued about Australian historians, Canadian historians would prefer to interpret this enthusiasm 'in terms of conscious manipulation on high and an audience of "cultural dopes" down below'.[13]

Ironically, until recently, even in Britain there were few serious studies of the nineteenth-century monarchy. This pattern began to change with the publication of Eric Hobsbawm and Terence Ranger's *The Invention of Tradition*, which included David Cannadine's stimulating study of 'The Context, Performance and Meaning of Ritual: The British Monarchy and the "Invention of Tradition", 1820–1977'.[14] Cannadine may have downplayed the historical roots of some of the traditions that were 'invented' or perhaps one should say re-invented or renovated during the late nineteenth century.[15] But his argument that much of the modern pageantry surrounding the monarchy is a late nineteenth-century 'invention' designed to strengthen the monarch's popularity and its usefulness as a symbol of national unity and national identity is irrefutable. Yet for all of its strengths the 'invention of tradition' approach has some severe weaknesses, particularly in the hands of less sophisticated scholars than Cannadine.[16] Obviously all traditions have to be invented by someone at some time for some purpose, but it is not always easy to say with precision when a particular cultural tradition or symbol was manufactured, by whom and for what purpose. Even if one can establish the precise roots of an historical tradition, this 'does not explain the imaginative appeal of a symbol nor its subsequent mutations over time'.[17] Moreover, it is easy to assume that the public plays little part in the evolution of successful traditions and can be manipulated more or less at will by elites. One arrives at this conclusion teleologically, by emphasising the traditions that are successfully 'invented' while ignoring those efforts at the conscious invention of tradition that fail. The 'invention of tradition' approach also glosses over the ways in which different groups may support the same tradition for different — indeed, diametrically opposed — purposes. In fact, the 'invention of tradition' approach cannot really answer the question of why certain traditions can be invented (or re-invented) while others cannot. This is why Terence Ranger, one of the inventors of the 'invention of tradition' concept, now prefers to talk about 'imagining' (rather than 'inventing') traditions.[18] If in 1901 the majority of Canadians had not been able for logical reasons of their own to 'imagine' the British monarchy as an institution which belonged to them, no amount of propaganda and pressure, external or internal, could have persuaded them to embrace the monarchy as embodying an historical tradition which was part of their heritage and which continued to have relevance to them.

I

This is not to deny that in 1901 there was an attempt at conscious manipulation of royal symbolism. But in the case of a complex cultural event like a royal tour, there are always a variety of agendas, frequently conflicting agendas, at work. In 1901 Canadian monarchists liked to claim that it was Queen Victoria herself who 'devised and designed' her grandson's tour.'[19] In reality the Queen only unenthusiastically and under considerable duress agreed to allow the Duke of Cornwall to embark on a lengthy trip around the globe. In the 1860s there had been official tours by members of the royal family to both Canada and Australia, and for years Canada and some of the Australasian colonies had requested another formal tour by the Queen or by the heir to the throne. Queen Victoria had consistently rejected their appeals. The decisive pressure that changed her mind came from the Secretary of State for the Colonies, Joseph Chamberlain, the one-time republican mayor of Birmingham who had been transformed into a committed imperialist and monarchist. Julian Amery has argued that the 1901 tour was 'his idea from the start'.[20] This too is a partial truth. During 1900 Chamberlain was involved in negotiating the terms of union with delegates from the Australian colonies and it was the Australians who expressed the wish for a tour to open the first Australian Parliament in 1901. Chamberlain was easily persuaded since he saw the formation of the Australian Commonwealth as an important opportunity for promoting imperial solidarity and for thanking the Australian colonies for their support in the war in South Africa.[21] When New Zealand, Canada and the South African colonies asked for the tour to be extended to include them, Chamberlain supported their requests, hoping to turn the tour into a triumphal march around the British Dominions and a ringing endorsement of his policy in South Africa. The Queen was less easily convinced to part with her grandson. Reluctantly, under pressure from the Prime Minister, Lord Salisbury, the Queen agreed that the Duke of Cornwall might go to Australia and New Zealand but initially she refused to allow the tour to include Canada. In December 1900 Victoria was persuaded by Chamberlain to allow a 'short visit' to Canada to show her gratitude to the Canadians for the sacrifices 'made in her cause in South Africa, where the bravery of her Canadian soldiers had been so conspicuous'.[22]

Early in 1901 the arrangements for the tour ground to a halt with Victoria's death. Edward VII had undertaken the first official royal tour by a member of the royal family to a colony — to Canada in 1860 — and he remembered the tour affectionately since it was one of the few times in his life that he had earned even grudging respect from his royal parents. But although he had previously supported Chamberlain's request to the Queen to allow George to undertake the tour, after her death he was reluctant to see his only surviving son leave England for such an extended period of time and he only agreed to allow the tour to go ahead under pressure from the cabinet. Arthur Balfour, soon to replace his uncle as Prime Minister, was delegated to read the King a lesson in the responsibilities of being an Imperial monarch. The King, he pointed out, 'is no longer merely the King of Great Britain and Ireland and of a few dependencies whose whole value consisted in ministering to the wealth and security of Great Britain and Ireland. He is now the greatest constitutional bond uniting together in a single Empire communities of free men separated by half the circumference of the Globe.' The citizens of this empire, Balfour perceptively noted, 'know little and care little for British Ministries and British party politics. But they know, and care for, the Empire of which they are members and for the Sovereign who rules it.'[23] Faced with the determination of the cabinet, Edward agreed that the tour should take place.

The Duke of Cornwall and York — the future George V — had already agreed to go. Like his father and elder brother he had made a number of visits to the colonies (including two brief visits to Canada) but prior to 1901 he had never shown any great interest in colonial affairs. The real love of his life was the Royal Navy and he had been perfectly happy as a serving naval officer when the unexpected death of his elder brother suddenly transformed him from just another prince into the potential heir to the throne and he was compelled to retire from active service in the navy. But after retiring he had little to command his attention except his passions for hunting and for stamp collecting, although he did take seriously his responsibilities to represent the crown as a patron of worthy causes. When approached by Chamberlain, George agreed to undertake the long tour, which became even longer as more countries were added, but there was considerable truth in the comment of the London *Daily Express*: 'That the whole thing will be a bore to the Duke goes without saying; that the Duchess will cordially enjoy it, it is also unnecessary to remark'.[24] This judgement is a bit unfair to George. He did take 'keen and continuous' interest in the elaborate outfitting of the HMS *Ophir,* the ship that was selected to carry the royal party around the globe.[25] It was also his idea to carry out to the colonies the medals to be given to the colonial veterans of the South African War and to present them himself. But in many respects George was temperamentally unsuited for his new career; he did not enjoy meeting people, disliked the popular press, was a reluctant public speaker and had a limited interest in royal ceremonials, though he was a stickler in matters of protocol. When consulted what he might like to do in Canada he is reputed to have replied: 'I want a day's duck shooting, and I want to see a lacrosse match.'[26] Both the royal wishes were granted. He attended a lacrosse match during his visit to Ottawa. The Montreal committee also arranged for him to see a baseball game but the programme was too crowded and it was dropped from the itinerary. The Governor-General, Lord Minto, justified this decision on the grounds that baseball 'is looked upon as an American game and is not at all popular in Canada — moreover it has fallen entirely out of the hands of amateurs and has been taken over by the very low American professional element'.[27] The shooting party — George actually insisted on at least two day's shooting — proved somewhat more difficult to arrange. The Duke was determined to keep the number of official ceremonies to a minimum and the Canadian government was very concerned that if the Duke were to go hunting in Ontario when he had declared that he did not have time to visit a number of important communities, there would be a public outcry.[28] In the end Lord Minto arranged to hold the shooting party at a remote spot in Manitoba, where the Duke spent two happy days killing Canadian wildlife.[29] On the first day in five hours he bagged 52 ducks and expressed 'great pleasure' at the excursion.[30] The two day total for the royal hunting party was estimated at 742 ducks and 70 snipe.[31] He also added considerably to his growing stamp collection, since he was presented with complete sets of stamps of the various colonies he visited and the duties of one of his aides-des-camps was to make selective purchases for his collection. Much of the long voyage from Australia to Canada he spent pasting into albums the stamps collected in Australia.

Much of the rest of the time George was bored, especially during the repetitious welcoming ceremonies which he had to endure at each stop in the tour. Even the scenery did not normally interest him, although during the trip across the Rockies he noted in his diary that the scenery was 'so grand & so magnificent that it baffles description'.[32] George did not mind the various military ceremonies. Massive military parades were organised in Quebec city, Toronto and Halifax and smaller ones arranged at other stops. One of the most common photographs of the tour was of the Duke reviewing colonial troops or handing out to South African veterans the medals from the Imperial government which he had arranged to bring with him. On such occasions he usually wore the uniform of the Royal Fusiliers, one suspects because it included an enormous busby which helped to disguise the fact that he was only 5 feet 4 inches tall. The public image of George promoted in the press and by the books published after the tour was an extremely flattering one, emphasising his sense of duty, his dedication to meeting his subjects, and his tact and lack of pretence. In private many of the officials surrounding the Duke were less flattering. In his personal journal (but not in the book he published about the tour) Sir Joseph Pope noted that:

> The Duke of York improves on acquaintance. He is somewhat slow of thought, destitute of wit, humour or sarcasm, blunt to rudeness, says just what he thinks without much regard for anyone's feelings — in short, he is a spoiled boy. At the same time, he has, I would judge, a great sense of duty, and is disposed to be kindhearted if he can be so without inconvenience to himself. I dare say he possesses a fair share of common sense, but he knows very little. Is really meagrely educated — would never learn, I am told. Is wholly without tact.[33]

These sentiments were echoed by Lord Wenlock, the member of the royal household responsible for acting as the liaison between George and the various colonial governments. At one point he wrote to his wife that, 'The Duke and Duchess are getting terribly weary of these constant functions — and I can well understand it, but they are, so to speak, paid for the job.'[34] Fortunately for George, his lack of tact in dealing with subordinates could be hidden and his lack of interest in royal ceremonial and rather gruff personality could be portrayed by the press as endearing characteristics of a simple and straightforward man who did not like to put on airs.

Nonetheless, the real star of the 1901 tour was the Duchess of Cornwall. Mary — or May as she was commonly referred to — genuinely loved the attention showered upon her. The long sea voyage was for her a real hardship as she suffered from severe seasickness. Initially she had also to overcome her natural shyness, but over the duration of the tour her self-confidence grew steadily. This was the first royal tour to the self-governing colonies on which a prince was accompanied by his consort, and Mary's presence enabled colonial women to be far more involved in the tour than in any previous one. At every major stop the Duchess was presented with addresses, bouquets and frequently with expensive gifts from the women who formed part of the local elite and from various groups, including branches of the Imperial Order Daughters of the Empire, the National Council of Women, and the Young Women's Christian Association. The women's columns in the newspapers discussed at great length what the Duchess was wearing and, while George was the focal point at military reviews and at formal ceremonies, Mary took centre stage when visiting hospitals, exhibitions, schools and art galleries. She was not widely read but she was more widely read than George and had considerably more interest in the arts. In Britain one of the ways in which the monarchy increasingly earned its popularity was by becoming patron for a host of worthy causes.[35] Indeed, while in Canada George raised $250,000 ($200,000 of it donated by Lord Strathcona) for a British hospital fund.[36] In Canada a host of charitable and philanthropic organisations eagerly sought to acquire a royal patron and the Duke and Duchess lent their names to a variety of good causes, although their generosity rarely extended to donating any of their private income. Mary took a particular interest in women's and children's hospitals, frequently visiting them without the Duke, chatting with individual patients and donating photographs of herself and her children. Press reports made a good deal of the ease with which she moved among ordinary people. They did not focus on the fact that she was extremely class-conscious and socially very conservative. She had nothing but scorn for the women's suffrage movement. The press stressed that she was 'a womanly woman'.[37] The Kingston Daily *British Whig* noted that, 'It is said she does not admire the mannish woman. Who does?'[38] Indeed, for all her supposed sympathy for the poor, Mary was not interested in the problems of working women nor unduly sensitive to the life of toil that was the lot of most working people. In Melbourne when workers marched past with signs supporting the eight-hour day, she proclaimed how lucky they were and wished that she and George had such an easy life.

Certainly while on tour the Duke and Duchess were compelled to put in long hours. The tour included lengthy visits to Australia, New Zealand, South Africa and Canada, as well as brief stops in Aden, Malta, Ceylon and Mauritius. There was some discussion of visiting the United States, but fears that American security might be inadequate and a desire to promote imperial unity meant that the Duke went round the globe without ever leaving British soil. The royal progress —'the like of which Caesar had never dreamed'— would last from 25 March until 2 November, making it the longest in history.[39] The Duke would travel over 50,000 miles, receive 544 addresses, deliver 86 speeches, lay 21 foundation stones, inspect 62,000 troops, and award 4,329 South African medals and 142 investitures and knighthoods. It was estimated that he shook 35,000 colonial hands.[40] The cost of the tour was enormous. The colonies being visited were expected to absorb the bulk of the costs but the British Government spent £126,000 in hiring and another £56,000 in refurbishing the *Ophir*. Even this was only the tip of the iceberg since the Duke travelled with an enormous entourage, with special carriages and horses to pull them, and with a substantial naval escort. Minto estimated that the tour was costing the British Government £70,000 per month.[41] When it was asked in the House of Commons why the Duke could not afford to contribute to the costs of the tour out of the substantial revenues he received from the Duchy of Cornwall and from the civil list, the member was told by the Chancellor of the Exchequer that all the costs were to be 'provided by the nation' because of the immense advantages of the tour in consolidating the empire and 'in instructing the future ruler as to the greatness of his responsibilities'.[42]

II

One of the results of the 1901 tour was, as Chamberlain had hoped, to increase public interest in Britain in the 'little Britains' overseas and to strengthen the monarchy's identification with the unity of the empire. Both the Duke's departure and his return to Britain were turned into elaborate public ceremonies, extensively covered in the British press. Five British journalists accompanied him around the globe, and for most of the summer and autumn of 1901 British newspapers carried stories about the tour and numerous photographs. In the aftermath of the tour the Imperial Institute held a special exhibit of the various addresses and gifts the royal couple had collected during their trip.[43] Chamberlain certainly viewed the tour as 'an unqualified success'.[44] The reception that the Duke and Duchess received, especially in Canada and Australia, strengthened Chamberlain's belief in imperial federation; indeed, it led him to overestimate the degree of support for closer imperial union in the self-governing colonies. The tour also reinforced the image that the empire was solidly behind the war in South Africa, strengthening Chamberlain's position at home. George did return with a far greater sense of his Imperial responsibilities. Upon his return a special dinner was held by the city of London to honour the Duke, and in his speech he called upon Britons at home to 'Wake up' to the importance of the empire.[45] Edward VII also thought the tour a great success and used it as the justification for making his son Prince of Wales. When he inherited the throne as George V he emphasised his imperial responsibilities and encouraged frequent trips to the colonies by his sons, Edward and Albert (the future George VI), a practice continued by his granddaughter, Queen Elizabeth II, whose commitment to the Commonwealth is indisputable.[46] The tour also had a profound impact upon Mary, who saw her role as ensuring that the members of her family lived up to 'what she considered the proper royal attitude'.[47]

Yet it is important to remember that the real pressure for the tour to Canada came not from the British government nor from the crown but from the colonial politicians. Canada was added to the Duke's itinerary because of lobbying from the Canadian government. In December 1900 Lord Minto sent an official invitation declaring that the proposed visit to Australia 'has stirred the hearts of your loyal subjects in Canada' and asking that the tour be extended to Canada, where 'their visit will tend to strengthen, if possible, those ties of union that bond a loyal and patriotic people to their much loved sovereign'.[48] Minto was a strong imperialist who was concerned to promote imperial federation, but as Minto's letter made clear he was offering the invitation on the advice of his Canadian ministers. Indeed, the decision to invite the Duke could not have been taken without the consent of the Prime Minister of Canada, Sir Wilfrid Laurier, and the government's financial support. Laurier's motivation was undoubtedly political. In initially opposing the pressure to send a Canadian force to South Africa Laurier had misread English Canada's increasing determination to participate more actively in the empire and he had paid a heavy price in the election of 1900.[49] Although he had won the election, his party had lost considerable popular support in Ontario and the west, the areas of the country where the Duke would spend most of his time in 1901. At every public function Laurier and his ministers would be seen standing side by side with the royals. Newspapers described Laurier as 'the pilot of the Duke and Duchess' and the 'master of ceremonies', who 'could hobnob with Royalty on easy terms'.[50] Liberal papers in the West took special pains to note that this was Laurier's first official visit to the region in seven years, while Conservative papers complained that Liberal papers 'placed Sir Wilfrid Laurier into [their] royal pictures much more prominently than the duke'.[51] For Laurier there was a price to pay in associating himself so clearly with the royal visitors.[52] Several of the published accounts of the tour mention Laurier's enthusiasm in singing 'God Save the King'. They do not recount what Laurier must have felt on hearing for the hundredth time 'Rule Britannia' or 'The Maple Leaf Forever', which was sung with gusto by massed choruses of children at virtually every whistle stop in English Canada. During the Duke's visit 'The Maple Leaf Forever', which emphasised the permanency of the imperial connection, was 'sung by millions of Canadians scattered from Quebec to Victoria' and became, in effect, English Canada's national song.[53] The author of 'The Maple Leaf Forever', Alexander Muir, was honoured at a special ceremony in Toronto at which 'a young maple tree gaily decorated with Union Jacks' was planted by the Duke with Muir's 'assistance'.[54] Nor is it clear how enthusiastically Laurier cheered the veterans from South Africa who were presented with medals at each stage of the tour, a ceremony inevitably accompanied by speeches praising Canada's generous contribution of troops to assist Britain in its hour of need and calling for greater imperial unity in future.

Perhaps this is being too cynical. By 1901 Sir Wilfrid had moved a long way from his *rouge* roots and there is no reason not to accept his enthusiasm for the monarchy at face value. But there is also no question that the tour was designed to bring political benefits to the Liberals and to undermine attempts to impugn Laurier's loyalty to the monarchy and the empire. Although Laurier seems to have been a restraining influence on some of his Liberal followers who sought to turn the Duke's visit into a partisan event, he was not above paying off a few political debts. In a private letter Pope wrote to Laurier suggesting that some recognition should be given to the veteran Quebec Conservative politician Sir Hector Langevin, who as Mayor of Montreal had received the Duke's father during the Prince of Wales's 1860 tour. 'He is old and broken now', Pope wrote, 'and not likely to have many opportunities of a like nature.' Laurier bluntly wrote back: 'I do not at all share your views. My opinion is to leave him severely alone.'[55] Clearly the Liberals did attempt to manipulate the tour in order to shore up their political support in English Canada but surely this is a very strange kind of 'conscious manipulation from on high', since Laurier (though this was not true of some of his English-Canadian colleagues) was leading Canadians in a direction in which he did not really want to go. As Minto repeatedly stressed in his private letters home, Laurier did not share the English-Canadian enthusiasm to play a greater role in the empire; Laurier, Minto reported to the Queen, was 'a broad-minded and extremely able' man, but 'his dream is not an Imperial one'.[56] During the period of mourning after Queen Victoria's death, Minto declared to Chamberlain: 'The feeling of sorrow amongst the Canadian people has been very deep, but I can not help feeling that Sir Wilfrid Laurier does not feel as we feel.'[57] Ironically, in the aftermath of the tour, Laurier would spend much of his energies trying to hold back the enthusiasm for closer imperial integration to which the tour had contributed both in Canada and in Britain.

Lord Minto undoubtedly also hoped the tour would enhance the prestige and influence of the office of governor-general. Indeed, he was offended when it was indicated that the Duke would take precedence over him in Canada, even though Minto as governor-general was the direct representative of the King. Minto appealed to the Colonial Office but his complaint was referred to Edward VII, who personally approved the decision for his son to take precedence.[58] Partly to avoid embarrassing issues of precedence Minto decided not to accompany the tour across the country (although Lady Minto did). He was, however, determined to be the primary channel of communication with the Duke and the latter's staff in organising the tour. In late February Chamberlain confirmed that the tour would go ahead and the dates when the Duke and Duchess would visit. Other than a visit to Niagara Falls and a day's shooting the itinerary was left to the Canadian government to plan.[59] But disputes immediately arose over the point of arrival since the Canadian ministers wished the Duke to sail from Australia to Vancouver and begin the tour there. When it became clear that the Duke would land at Quebec city and would spend only 32 days in Canada, much less than he had spent in Australia, several members of the cabinet thought the tour should be cancelled since it was not possible to see all of Canada in such a short time and 'a hurried attempt . . . would do more harm than good'.[60] But Laurier was not prepared to withdraw the invitation and he appointed a cabinet committee chaired by the Minister of Finance, W.S. Fielding, to prepare the itinerary for the royal tour and to work out the arrangements for accommodation and hospitality with the governor-general. The committee seems to have met only once.[61] Although Minto had not objected to the idea of a committee so long as he chaired it, he wrote to Laurier to insist that, while 'in a bigger sense the visit must be regulated by the wishes of my Ministers', there must be 'some central authority to whom reception Committees can refer for information and to whom they can submit their proposals', and he suggested to Laurier that he and the Prime Minister constitute the central committee.[62] In fact, it was agreed that all invitations would be submitted to the Department of Secretary of State and all the programme arrangements to Minto.[63] In practice, this division of labour was impracticable and all of the details were worked out in the governor-general's office. Minto's Military Secretary, F.S. Maude, occasionally went to see the Secretary of State, R.W. Scott, 'as I thought it would please him, if he were told something from time to time'.[64] But Minto was aware of the need to submit all of the key decisions to Laurier for his approval and several changes and additions were made at the latter's request. On only one issue did Laurier and Minto seriously disagree — on the awarding of honours. Minto had hoped to use the Duke's visit as the excuse to bestow knighthoods on Frederick Borden and William Mulock, the staunchest imperialists in the cabinet who had strongly supported the decision to send Canadian volunteers to South Africa, but he was forced to defer to Laurier and withdraw the recommendations.[65] Minto was, however, able to overrule Laurier and make Thomas Shaughnessey, the head of the Canadian Pacific Railway, a Knight Bachelor, ostensibly because of the assistance he had given to the royal tour. Laurier appealed to Chamberlain against the recommendation because of the unpopularity of the CPR in western Canada and argued that 'purely social considerations ought not to prevail against political issues', but was informed by Chamberlain that the award had already been announced and that in any event it was being given on entirely non-political grounds.[66] Ironically it was not Laurier but Minto who suffered the political consequences of this decision since Liberal papers across the country made clear that the decision had been taken over Laurier's objections.

After the arrangements had been approved by Laurier, they had then to be submitted to the Duke for his approval. In the previous royal tour to Canada by the Prince of Wales in 1860 the ultimate control over the itinerary had been determined by the Secretary of State for the Colonies, the Duke of Newcastle, who had accompanied the Prince as his political adviser. By 1901, however, real control had passed from the imperial to the colonial officials. The Duke of Cornwall was accompanied by an official from the Colonial Office, John Anderson, but he was a civil servant, not a minister representing the British government. Although Anderson's salary was paid by the British government, he was considered as one of the Duke's private staff and could not therefore correspond, publicly or privately, with Chamberlain or the Colonial Office on official matters during the tour unless directed to do so by the Duke.[67] By 1901 the monarchy's own staff had become increasingly adept at organising royal events and the Duke was also accompanied by Arthur Bigge, his private secretary, and by Lord Wenlock, the head of the household staff. Bigge, Wenlock and Anderson met with the Duke to examine the proposals submitted by Lord Minto and went over every detail,[68] but their role was largely a negative one. Their primary concern (other than ensuring a hunting expedition for the Duke) was to limit the Duke's commitments and to ensure that the rigid rules of court procedure were followed to the letter. There was little more they could do since the royal party had limited knowledge about Canada and Canadian politics. When supplied with the itinerary for Quebec city, which included a visit to Canada's pre-eminent French-Canadian university, Wenlock cabled back to ask: 'What is Laval?'[69]

The burden of organising the tour fell upon Minto, who — subject to Laurier's consent — decided where the Duke would go and how long he would spend in each place. The decision about what the Duke would do within each province was primarily the responsibility of the lieutenant-governors, who organised the provincial programme in consultation with the premiers of the provinces and the municipal governments of the cities and towns fortunate to be graced with a royal visit. All the provincial plans had to be approved by Minto, who had to make the arrangements for transporting and housing the royal party. Most of the real burden fell upon Minto's military secretary, Major F.S. Maude. Maude had been involved in organising the 1897 jubilee celebrations in London, and at Minto's request he was detached from Kitchener's staff in South Africa in the spring of 1901 and sent to Canada. Maude handled most of the negotiations with the provincial and municipal authorities and he came under considerable criticism for being too rigid in his application of the rules of precedence and for overruling local committees.[70] The *Brantford Courier* complained that Maude was 'about to issue a brochure on the proper way to part with the Canadian sneeze'.[71] But Joseph Pope, the

Canadian civil servant who worked closely with Maude, denied that Maude was responsible for these decisions, declaring that in 33 years of government service in Ottawa he had never met an imperial official 'more capable, hardworking, modest and adaptable to his environment than Major Maude'. Pope pointed out that even if they sought to alter any of the rules of procedure they would be prevented from doing so by the Duke's advisers, who would 'insist on the correct ceremonial being adhered to'.[72] As the volume of criticism grew, Pope asked the editor of the Toronto *Globe*, John Willison, to set the record straight and in an editorial Willison, while complaining that there was 'too much red tape and too much "precedence" to suit a democratic country', pointed out that the rules were not invented by the governor-general and his secretary but simply reflected 'ancient usages, which they have no power to vary'.[73] How ancient many of these rules were and how inalterable are both issues open to doubt, but it is clear that Minto and Maude were only obeying guidelines laid down by the Duke and his advisers when they insisted that the rather rigid rules of court dress and court procedure be followed.

Joseph Pope was the other important behind-the-scenes official involved in organising the tour. Pope's grandfather, his father and his uncle had all been active politicians on pre-Confederation Prince Edward Island and had played a key part in bringing Prince Edward Island into Confederation. All the Popes were active and devout monarchists and imperialists, and one of Joseph Pope's earliest memories of his childhood was the visit of the Prince of Wales in 1860.[74] Pope left Prince Edward Island after Confederation and became John A. Macdonald's secretary and eventual biographer, and upon Macdonald's death he became under-secretary at the Department of Secretary of State with special charge of imperial and foreign affairs. Though extremely conservative and a strong imperialist — so strong that he wrote a pamphlet condemning those Canadians who flew the Red Ensign instead of the Union Jack[75] — he admired Laurier. Indeed, it was at Laurier's request that Pope was seconded from the Department of State to work with Maude. Pope's special responsibility was to handle the logistics, particularly the negotiations with the various railway companies, and to oversee federal expenditures. Unofficially his duties were to keep a watchful eye over what was being done in the governor-general's office.

Maude and Pope liked each other and worked well together. They were agreed that the primary function of the tour was to ensure that as many Canadians as possible should have a chance to see their future King and Queen. A train was especially constructed by the Canadian Pacific Railway to take the Duke and his party across Canada. Actually four trains were needed: one for the royal party; one for Lord and Lady Minto and their staff; a third for Laurier, various members of the Canadian government, the press and security officers; and a fourth to carry the royal carriage and horses which had been shipped out from London. Initially the Canadian government set aside $120,000 for the tour, but even though the CPR built the royal train at its own expense the final bill came to $462,881.82[76] But this did not include all the expenses, some of which were partly hidden within various departmental budgets. The military review in Toronto alone cost $228,000, mainly for the pay and transport of the troops.[77] Moreover, all of the local expenses were absorbed by the municipal or provincial governments, supplemented by private corporations or even individuals. Although the royal tour ended up costing more than the annual budget of some of the smaller provinces, there were remarkably few complaints about the expense of the Duke's visit. In Toronto there was a debate in the City Council in July 1901 over whether to reduce the city's projected expenditure from $10,000 to $5,000, but not only was the vote for $10,000 carried by 18 to 4 but in October, after the tour was over, a vote appropriating an additional $4,000 was carried by 23 to 0, indicating that the dissidents had been persuaded of the tour's value.[78] But the Toronto visit cost far more than $14,000, for the city did not pay for the arches erected by the Foresters and Manufacturers — the latter alone cost $6,500.[79] The city of Ottawa also raised its initial grant for the reception from $2,500 to

$10,000, despite the fact that the municipal government was already deeply in debt.[80] Montreal voted $15,000 for the ceremonies but another $17,000 was raised by public subscription. Winnipeg spent $4,687.[81] In Vancouver the city council gave $5,000 and another $1,300 was raised by public subscription.[82] London, Ontario, which had initially been left off the itinerary, spent $2,000 on a one-hour visit.[83] In Hamilton a three-hour visit cost the city $10,000, an amount which did lead to critical letters to the editor of the *Hamilton* Spectator.[84] The Province of New Brunswick spent $22,785 dressing up the exhibition building and the vice-regal residence in Saint John and on a military display, while the city of Saint John spent another $5,000 on the reception.[85] In fact, municipalities and provinces vied with each other to put on impressive displays of fireworks, to erect enormous arches under which the Duke would pass, and to present the Duke and Duchess with elaborate addresses and expensive gifts. It was this latter practice that raised the most criticism. *The Voice*, a weekly newspaper endorsed by the Winnipeg Trades and Labor Council, questioned why the ladies of Ottawa were giving a 'costly gift of furs' to the Duchess, who 'does not need them', when women in Ottawa were 'making pants at 60 cents a dozen, and the combined labor of three women, who work early and late, does not amount to more than four dollars a week'. The resentment against such expenditures, *The Voice* insisted, 'does not arise from any disloyalty, but the demand of the ultra imperialists that something "worthy of the occasion" shall be done is very perplexing to the average civic mind'.[86]

Many more complaints were heard about the itinerary of the tour. The Canadian organisers had to act as arbiters between two conflicting pressures. On the one hand, there was the desire of every community to be included on the route and for the royal visitors to stop for as long as possible. When it was initially announced that the royal tour was not going to include western Ontario there was a wave of protest from all the communities including Guelph, which the Attorney General of Ontario insisted would 'feel slighted' if it did not at least get a 15 or 20 minute visit.[87] In the end, one newspaper reported, 'Guelph got five minutes of the Duke, and is as proud as a dog with seven tails'.[88] Of course, much of this merely reflected civic or regional pride. London was annoyed when it was announced that the Duke was to visit Hamilton but not London. Sherbrooke claimed it merited a stop because it was the unofficial capital of the Eastern Townships. Frederictonians were livid that Fredericton was to be bypassed and that the only major stop in New Brunswick would be in Saint John. Manitobans bitterly complained that the Duke would only spend a few hours in the province. Prince Edward Islanders bitterly noted that theirs was the only province not included on the tour. Much of this anger was directed — unfairly — against the governor-general's office (which perhaps was why Laurier was quite content to let Minto take the primary role in organising the tour). In fact, the real problem was that the organisers were under pressure from the Duke to limit the number of stops and to keep them as brief as possible. By the time he arrived in Canada he had been travelling for nearly six months and he was determined not to extend the time set aside for Canada, even for a day. He wrote to his mother from Canada: 'our tour is most interesting, but it is very tiring and there is no place like dear old England for me'.[89] Minto, who carried the ultimate responsibility, was annoyed with the determination of the Duke to limit his public duties. 'I can't say how strongly I feel', he wrote to Sir George Parkin, 'that the more hail-fellow-well-met he is the better — but I tell you quite privately that I am instructed to cut things down far below what I think advisable.'[90]

When he became King, it was claimed that George had 'in a unique degree personal knowledge of all parts of his dominions',[91] but it is difficult to see how the tour could have given him much insight into Canadian life. There was an incredible sameness about the duties to be performed at each stop on the tour. In the smaller communities where the stop usually lasted for 10–15 minutes there would be a series of presentations, a song or two from a massed choir of children, the rewarding of a few medals, and the royal show was on the road again. In the larger urban centres where the Duke's visit might last from a few hours to three days there was more variety in the programme, but it would still begin with the same formal ceremony at which addresses of welcome would be presented and appropriate responses given, after which the Duke would process around the town in the carriage especially imported from Britain for this purpose. A longer visit might include a stop at the local university, where he would be given yet another honorary degree, or it might involve laying cornerstones or unveiling memorials (usually to the late Queen or to the colonial troops who had died in the South African War). He attended a number of sporting events and made a brief appearance at several industrial or agricultural exhibitions. The Duke had no great interest in art or music. In Toronto the festivities were to include the performance of an opera and some very expensive stars were imported from New York for the occasion, but at the last minute the organisers were told that the Duke would not attend, ostensibly because he was still in mourning for Queen Victoria. In the end the opera was replaced by a concert performance and the Duke — reluctantly — agreed to make a brief appearance. Most evenings there was a private dinner party to attend, usually a display of fireworks, and sometimes a public reception (public dinners and balls were forbidden while the court was still in mourning). It is hardly surprising that the Duke appeared to be bored much of the time. And there were physical limits to the endurance of the Duke and Duchess. At the public reception in Toronto they shook hands with over 2,000 people.

III

Yet there can be no doubt of the enthusiasm of Canadians to meet the royal couple. This enthusiasm was undoubtedly greatest among the social and political elites, and at every stop the list of the party on the official platform reads like a who's who of the community. For a few there was an opportunity to have lunch or dinner with the Duke and for an even smaller number more substantial rewards, since the Duke had been given special authority to confer knighthoods and invest members in various imperial orders. But at the very least an invitation to the formal reception to welcome the Duke was essential to establish one's social credentials. In every community there were volunteers who devoted hours of unpaid labour preparing for the royal visit. In Saint John, New Brunswick, for example, in addition to the General Committee which consisted of the mayor, four aldermen and 12 men, there was an 11-man Firemen and Salvage Corps Committee, a seven-man sub-committee to distribute funds, a seven-man Committee for Decorating Fire Stations and Streets and to Procure Fireworks, a ten-man committee in charge of street decorations, an 11-man civic reception committee (consisting of the mayor and the ten aldermen) and a 14-man Executive of the Citizens Committee (which one assumes had a number of sub-committees of its own).[92] Similar committees — some larger, some smaller, some more and some less representative of the community — existed in every town which the Duke visited, and an examination of their composition tells us a great deal about the structure of political and social power and about who was considered important in these communities. But the enthusiasm was not confined to the elites and occasionally social tensions surfaced. At the major reception in Toronto, where it was decided to have a large public reception, there was a huge crowd and a 'horrible crush, in which many ladies had their gowns torn to pieces'. But when an Ottawa newspaper blamed the problem on the failure to restrict access, the Toronto Mail-Empire retorted that, 'If there was any unseemly crush it must have been among the privileged set, and goes to show what an unseemly thing it is to attempt to divide the people into classes at a public event.'[93] Indeed, when it was proposed to charge an entrance fee for the military review in Toronto, there was a public outcry against the charge for barring 'many of the poorer classes from this spectacle'.[94] A number of Canadian newspapers pointed out that in the presence of the monarch all men are equal and demanded that receptions should be 'open to all, regardless of rank and clothing'.[95] Some newspapers also gleefully pointed out that the Duke did not speak with an upper-class English accent like those Canadians who sought to put on airs. In fact, George spoke 'like an educated Canadian'![96] (If true, this was probably because George had never attended a private school or Oxbridge.) If there was resentment against the local arrangements it was usually because they were too exclusive, and it was directed against the local elite for trying to limit access to the monarch, but never against the royal visitors themselves.

In addition to the formal events there were the informal. Pope, who accompanied the tour across the country, was struck by the number of people who hung ribbons or flags beside the track or who stood at a station in the middle of the night to wave at the train as it went by. In Ontario the tour was dogged by bad weather, but in Toronto the 'wind and rain had no appreciable effect upon the throngs that turned out to-day in the welcome and show of loyalty. Wrapped in water-proofs or sheltered under umbrellas the people waited for hours in the sodden streets and warmed themselves with cheers when the prince and princess finally came.'[97] It is the extent of this popular enthusiasm which casts doubt upon those who would interpret the tour as merely an excuse for a holiday. Quite obviously some of the enthusiasm was inspired by the fact that many (but not all) stores and businesses shut for a day in the Duke's honour. Equally obvious there were commercial incentives for some of the enthusiasm. For the newspapers special editions meant extra profits. For the railways large crowds travelling to the events meant more income. There was also an opportunity to promote tourism, even if it meant downplaying some of Canada's less attractive features: 'To a native of Great Britain', a pamphlet issued by the Grand Trunk railway proclaimed, 'a Canadian winter presents many interesting features.' And lest the native of Great Britain associate these interesting features with bitterly cold weather, the pamphlet declared that, 'It is no uncommon thing for the weather to be so warm around Christmas time that even a light overcoat may be dispensed with.'[98] Companies making flags and fireworks were undoubtedly overjoyed by the tour and a host of special commemorative items were produced for the occasion (including something described as 'royal wallpaper'). Pickpockets made windfall profits at the crowded events. Yet all of this activity is also a sign of popular enthusiasm for the tour. The special editions did sell out, the railways were jammed with people determined to see the royal visitors, private homes as well as government buildings and department stores were covered with decorations, and people bought the flags and waved them enthusiastically.

Quite obviously there were degrees of enthusiasm. Mackenzie Wallace noted that the crowds in Quebec were 'not such adepts in the art of vigorous cheering as our Australian and New Zealand cousins', but attributed this coolness to the fact that the French Canadians 'are by nature a more reserved and less demonstrative people'.[99] The *Toronto Daily Star* had a different explanation. It suggested that people in Quebec did not cheer because they did not realise that they were supposed to: 'the whole reception was so entirely in the hands of officials and military authorities, so fixed and formal in all its particulars, that the people felt themselves not to be participants'.[100] Neither explanation rings entirely true. Yet even in Quebec there was no overt opposition to the tour. Although some criticism initially was made of the Duke for his failure to use more French (which George spoke but not fluently), he was applauded by the French-Canadian press when he did make a short speech in French.[101] Virtually every important French-Canadian association, including the Saint Jean Baptiste Society, prepared an address warmly welcoming the Duke, and the major French-Canadian papers carried articles about the Duke and Duchess virtually identical to those found in the English-language press. French-language papers, like their English-language counterparts, printed special editions focusing on the tour and offered for sale portraits of the visitors. And French Canadians did turn out in large numbers to see their future King and Queen. Over 30,000 people — virtually the whole population of Quebec city — watched the military parade on the Plains of Abraham. *'Toute la journée Net; toute la nuit, et depuis le petit jocer ce matin, la population de la Vieille Capitale est dans l'attente de Leurs Altesses Royales.— La ville regorge d'é- trartgers.— Les rues et les places publiques sont lettéralement encombrées'*, reported *La Presse*.[102] 'Latent French-Canadian enthusiasm', the *Toronto Star* proclaimed, 'so long in germinating, sprouted and blossomed vigorously'.[103] All along the route from Quebec city to Montreal *'le people massait aux différentes gares pour voir les visiteurs royaux et pour les acclamer'*.[104] In Montreal 250,000 people turned out to see the Duke and Duchess, and 'Miles and miles of French Streets were splendidly bedecked'.[105] This showed, according to *La Presse*, that 'ici a *Montreal, les deux éléments, qui vivent dans une mutuelle estime, et sous l'empire d'une généeuse rec- iprocité de sentiments, sont égaux par l'attachment qu'ils portent aux même institutions'*.[106] Similarly, *L'Evénement* declared that the reception given to the Duke proved that *'si l'élément français de ce pays s'est toujours montré réfractaire d toute assimilation anglaise, s'il a gardé envers et contre tous et s'il gardera toujours adèlement ses traditions nationales, sa langue et sa religion, il n'en reste pas moins attaché d la Couronne et aux institutions britanniques'*.[107]

There were a few voices of dissent. *La Nation*, a nationalist journal, showed a marked ambivalence about the tour. It insisted that the ceremonies in Quebec and Montreal had been marked *'par une raideur excessive chez le Prince et par une froideur, une tenue a distance des plus visibles, chez le peuple'*.[108] Several papers suggested that the reason why French-Canadian enthusiasm was muted was the fear that loyalty to the crown might be interpreted as enthu- siasm for the policies of Joseph Chamberlain.[109] But most French Canadians in 1901 seem to have had little difficulty in reconciling loyalty to the crown and British institutions with a commitment to the preservation of their own national culture. Most houses in Quebec flew both 'a Union Jack and a tricolor'.[110] And French Canadians sang 'O Canada' with the same gusto with which English Canadians sang 'The Maple Leaf Forever'.[111]

In English Canada the crowds were large and enthusiastic everywhere. In Toronto the crowds of 'Cheering Britishers' were estimated at between 200,000 and a quarter of a million. Since the total population of the city was only around 200,000, a substantial number of the observers — perhaps as many as half — must have come from the surrounding townships and villages.[112] Nearly 8–10,000 gathered at Belleville at 9:15 in the morning for a ten minute stop.[113] In Cornwall 4,000 people waited at the station where the train made a brief stop.[114] In Kingston an estimated 50,000 visitors poured into the city.[115] Over a thousand people gathered at the railway station in Whitby, Ontario, simply to see the train go through. The train left Brockville at 7:45 pm and did not reach Belleville until 12:30 in the morning but at every little switchhouse on the line there was 'a crowd of people, cheering and waving whatever piece of cotton linen or bunting they could lay their hands on'. Even the third train, which only car- ried the mounted escort and did not arrive until 1:30 in the morning, was cheered since the crowds did not know which train was carrying 'the objects of their affection'.[116] In Vancouver and Victoria and throughout the west the size of crowds exceeded all expectations. In Winnipeg the highlight of the visit was a chorus of over 2,000 schoolchildren: 'When they sang "God Save the King" it was with emphasis. When they sang "Rule Britannia" it was with elec- trifying emphasis on the word "Britannia" that gave meaning to the song.'[117] But the Maritimes was not to be outdone. The biggest crowd in Saint John's history gathered to see the Duke, and in Halifax as many as 10,000 people poured in from the surrounding countryside, the streets were lined with 5,000 soldiers, and a crowd of 25,000 watched as the Duke laid the cornerstone of a memorial to the Nova Scotian volunteers who had fallen in the Boer War.[118] Loyalty to the institution of the monarchy was a national phenomenon, overriding the regional differences that divided Canadians.

The obvious places to look for overt resistance to the tour are in the fledgling labour movement and among Catholics, particularly those of Irish origin. Yet if there were substantial numbers of either group opposed to the tour they largely kept their opinions to themselves. Most of the (relatively few) labour papers did not spend much time on the tour but their coverage was generally positive. The organ of the Winnipeg labour movement, *The Voice,* was the most outspokenly anti-imperial newspaper in Canada. It was critical of British actions in South Africa and believed that, 'British India is worked mainly for the money there is in it for bloodsuckers, to provide a field for the swarms of parasitical officials, and to gratify the mere love of conquest'.[119] Yet it concluded that, 'As a holiday and a spectacle Winnipeg enjoyed the day [of the royal visit] to the full (those at work excepted), nothing occurred to mar the pleasantness of the visit, and though there is naturally some criticism of the arrangements and money expended, this will be largely condoned by the success of the visit.'[120] Winnipeg, it declared, had greeted the heir to the throne 'with heartiness and sincerity'. This may have been insincere. But since the labour movement in Canada was very small and its leadership was overwhelmingly British-born, indeed formed of the same kind of men who would lead the Labour Party in Britain, it is more likely that most labour supporters were as royalist as other British Canadians. During the Duke's visit the Trades and Labour Council of Brantford, Ontario, carried a resolution mourning the death of Queen Victoria and expressing their sympathy to Edward VII. Of course, labour saw the Duke's visit as an opportunity not only to parade their loyalty but also to put forward their own political agenda. A number of newspapers carried 'Labour's Loyal Petition', a lengthy poem written by a Marie Joussaye, a labour activist, which declared:

> We know that only the statesman, the soldier, the scribe, the priest,
> The high and rich and mighty may sit at the royal feast,
> But we claim this right for Labour, the right to grasp your hand,
> To look in your eyes and speak to you as man should speak to man.
> The right to tell of the struggle in the land of the Northern Zone,
> Where honest Labour is ground in the dust and Greed usurps the throne.[121]

To the great embarrassment of the Laurier government, the labour movement in British Columbia sought to present an address to the Duke which was 'in reality a petition against the Chinese, and an arraignment of the Govt for having disallowed anti-Mongolian legislation'.[122] Upon Laurier's recommendation, though the blame was generally placed on Minto and Maude, the Duke declined to accept the petition.

The issue of the tour becoming a source of controversy between Catholics and Protestants was a more serious possibility. That was precisely what had happened in 1860 when the Orange Lodge had used the visit of the Prince of Wales as an occasion for widespread anti-Catholic demonstrations. The Laurier government was determined to prevent similar demonstrations in 1901 and to incorporate Catholics fully into the celebrations. So too was Minto, who warned against the introduction into the programme of any feature 'which might tend to mar the unanimity and heartiness of the welcome' given to the Duke.[123] Thus in Quebec city, in order to balance a visit to a meeting of the synod of the Church of England, a visit to Laval was added to the programme at Laurier's request (over the initial objections of the Duke's advisers who felt the programme was already too heavy).[124] Across the country sincere efforts were made to involve Catholics. In a number of Ontario communities the massed choir of children was expanded to incorporate children from the separate schools. Indeed, in Belleville children from all the city schools gathered to sing the national anthem and 'Rule Britannia', including the pupils from the school for the deaf and dumb who used sign language.[125] In Toronto the editor of the *Catholic Register* reported that the citizens' committee of 500 was 'representative in reality of all classes and creeds' and included 'perhaps half hundred of our leading Catholic citizens'. He correctly predicted that this would ensure 'a loyal and hearty, *and united* welcome'.[126] Even among Irish Catholics there was no opposition to the tour. By 1901, Irish Catholics in Canada had been effectively integrated into the British majority and there was no serious republican movement (certainly no vocal one).[127] Yet though Irish Catholics were as 'emphatic in their declarations of loyalty' as other Canadians, they did point out in their address of welcome 'how much the Empire would be strengthened if those principles of self-government existing in New Zealand, Australia and Canada were applied to Ireland'.[128] The *Catholic Register* felt that it is 'a truth that can never be too often repeated, viz. that Irishmen, in common with all Canadians, are loyal because they have Home Rule'.[129]

Not all cultural minorities were so effectively integrated into the celebrations. In Vancouver, the *World* proclaimed that the Duke will receive a 'cosmopolitan reception . . .— Whitemen, Red Indians, Brown Japanese and Yellow Chinese Join in Acclaiming Britain's Heir'.[130] In Halifax Black Canadians and in Vancouver Chinese Canadians were encouraged to present addresses to the Duke and they eagerly sought to show their loyalty. Yet the participation of non-whites in the ceremonies was at best nominal. This was particularly the case with the native peoples. In a number of communities native people were involved in the welcoming ceremonies but they had little control over the nature of that involvement. The image of native peoples carefully cultivated by the Canadian government was of a savage and uncivilised people who had excelled only in one area of activity — warfare. Thus native peoples were encouraged to put on war dances in Ottawa and Calgary and to arrive in war canoes in Victoria and to try to appear as 'savage' as possible. The other image which the Canadian government also cultivated was its success in bringing civilisation and prosperity to the native peoples, and so there were visits to industrial schools for native peoples. The limits placed upon the involvement of native people were most clearly illustrated in the large native pow-wow arranged to entertain the King in Calgary. The Department of Indian Affairs organised the event, the North West Mounted Police (renamed the Royal North West Mounted Police) provided security, and the access of the native leaders to the Duke was carefully controlled. The official address from the more than 2,000 Indians who had gathered to welcome the Duke was read by David Wolf Carrier, a young Sarcee, but it had been written by the Canadian government's Indian Commissioner and more reflected the views of the Indian Department than the Indians themselves. When the head chiefs met individually with the Duke, they did attempt to make clear that they were far from contented with the status quo.[131] There is no evidence that the Duke was particularly moved by their grievances. Indeed, he probably shared the views of his aide-de-camp and friend, Bryan Godfrey-Faussett, who noted in his diary that although many of the chiefs seemed contented, 'others were full of growls and dissatisfaction with their lot' and complained not only that they had been disposed of the vast lands which they had once owned but that 'white men' continued to encroach upon what was left. Godfrey-Fausselt doubted that these stories were true. Altogether he found the Indians 'a very contented people' and, while they could not be blamed for being unhappy with the changes that had taken place in the west, he predicted that 'The coming generation not having known these good things will perhaps be more satisfied with its lot; they are I understand slowly but surely dieing [sic] out — a departing race & perhaps will be a good thing when they are gone.'[132]

IV

Enthusiasm for the tour was inevitably greatest among English-speaking Canadians of British ethnic origin. 'Time can weaken the strongest ties', declared the London *Morning Post*, 'but it has not yet weakened the blood tie that makes white hands throughout the British Empire clasp each other as with the knowledge of a hidden secret that will outlive life.'[133] In 1901, the vast majority of English-speaking Canadians were emigrants from Great Britain or descendants of British emigrants. In referring to themselves the term 'English Canadian' was never used; consistently the majority of Canadians of British origin referred to themselves as Britishers or British Canadians, though those of Scottish and Irish origin also referred to themselves as Scottish or Irish Canadians. In his speech given at the London Guildhall upon his return to England, the Prince of Wales (as he now was) noted how 'touching' it had been to 'hear the invariable references to home, even from the lips of those who never had been or were ever likely to be in these islands'.[134] There has been a continuing debate both in Britain and in Canada over whether there has ever existed a sense of British as opposed to an English, Irish, Scottish, Welsh or even Canadian identity. The problem with this debate is that it tends to see ethnic identities as static and as mutually exclusive. When a sense of being British emerged and how long it survived may be questions open to debate but that it existed both in Britain and in the colonies of Britons overseas in 1901 is clear. Indeed, the monarchy was one of the key institutions promoting a sense of Britishness. In Britain the monarchy had already begun to play down its English roots and to emphasise its British ones by touring Scotland (wearing a tartan, of course) and Ireland. This programme was more successful in Scotland than in Ireland, but in 1901 many Catholics in Ireland (not to mention the majority of Protestants) still had a sense of being British as well as Irish. In the 'little Britains' overseas, which were formed of immigrants from different parts of the British Isles, it was even easier to reconcile the original ethnic identities of the immigrants with a sense of Britishness. When the Duke came to the colonies he consistently stressed his British rather than his English roots. To an extent this was easy to do, since the Hanoverian dynasty had been imported from Germany and for six generations had chosen their spouses from a pool of European — predominantly German — royal families. They had hardly intermarried at all with the local English aristocracy. As the Canadian press was fond of pointing out, the Duchess of Cornwall was the first British-born princess (although even her father had been an impecunious German prince); 'the British people', the Halifax *Herald* noted, 'are now in a fair way to escape fully from a reproachful criticism which used to be made that the British Royal Family was very far from being entirely British'.[135]

The reality that Hanoverians were a bunch of German *parvenus* did not stop Canadian royalists from referring to them as part of a royal house whose roots went back 'for more than a thousand years'.[136] The implication, of course, was that their roots lay in ancient Britain when the whole country had been unified under the mystical King Arthur. In Quebec this emphasis was altered to stress the Norman (i.e., French) roots of the monarchy. In Scottish areas it was the Stuart connection which was stressed. While the Duke was giving a speech in Glengarry, Ontario, where the population was composed largely of descendants of Highland Scots, a piper struck up 'a pronounced Jacobite air', and in his speech the Duke referred to 'his Stuart ancestors', glossing over the fact that the Protestant Hanoverians had been imported to replace the Catholic Stuarts and had only succeeded after crushing the Jacobite rebellion at Culloden.[137] But what was important was that the monarchy was attempting to define itself as a British, not a purely English, institution. This effort struck a responsive chord in the colonies where the Scottish and Irish formed a much larger proportion of the population than they did in the mother country. The Victoria *Daily Times,* for example, noted as evidence of the commitment of the Heir Apparent to imperial unity that he named his eldest son George Andrew Patrick David—'those of the patron saints of our four nationalities'.[138] In Kingston a special song of welcome proclaimed that the Normans, Saxons and Celts were 'yet Britons'.[139] In 'the representatives of the royal line of the Guelphs', the *Vancouver Province* asserted, 'we have the lineal descendants of three sovereign races whose union into one people have made Britain what she is to-day, the greatest progressive force and the greatest power for good in the known world'.[140]

As Judith Bassett notes, in New Zealand the royal tour of 1901 'drew the whole country together in a celebration of New Zealand as New Zealanders wished it to be seen at that time'.[141] The same might be said of Canadians — certainly of English-speaking Canadians in 1901 — and clearly what they wanted to celebrate was, as Balfour had recognised, their membership in a global empire and their loyalty to the monarchy. Neither distance nor birth in foreign fields made the English-speaking majority feel any less British. Yet this sense of being British did not preclude an equally strong sense of being Canadian. In 1901 Canadians consciously copied British models in organising the royal tour to Canada. They copied what had been done during the 1887 and 1897 jubilee celebrations in Britain, even importing some of the same fireworks specialists. But they also sought to add a distinctively Canadian flavour to the ceremonies. They arranged for the Duke to view Canadian loggers and cattlemen and farmers at work. They organised concerts at which Canadian singers would sing songs about Canada composed by Canadians. They wanted the royal party to view Canadian wildlife (even if George was more interested in shooting it) and to learn about Canadian history, or at least a version of Canadian history which emphasised the sacrifices made by the Loyalists and the efforts of Canadians to preserve the imperial connection during the War of 1812–14. They presented the Duke and Duchess with gifts which were uniquely Canadian or at least embossed with Canadian symbolism. In all these ways they asserted their own identity within the empire as Canadians. 'We are proud to be Canadians[;] God Bless the British Empire' was the wording on one banner welcoming the Duke.[142] There was also a conscious effort to create the sense of a Canadian monarchical tradition by linking the 1901 tour with the previous 1860 tour. If a university had given the Prince of Wales an honorary degree, it sought to confer one on his son in 1901. At Brantford, Ontario, the Duke signed a bible given in 1712 to the Mohawk Church, the same bible signed by his father in 1860. In Montreal a pause was made at the Victoria Jubilee Bridge, into which the Prince of Wales had driven the last rivet in 1860. In Ottawa George viewed a lacrosse game sitting on a chair built for his father in 1860. Anyone who had been on a public platform to meet Edward in 1860 was invited back in 1901. In 1860 Laura Secord, heroine of the War of 1812, had been presented to Edward; in 1901 her daughter was presented to George. In these and in other ways Canadians — for the initiative came from them — sought to stress the continuity of the monarchical tradition in Canada.

The various ceremonies were designed to emphasise that the residents of Canada were still British and that the monarchy was not an alien institution but one which belonged as much to those who lived in the 'little Britains' overseas as to those who lived in the mother country. 'The besetting sin of the Englishmen of the present generation', noted the Toronto *Globe* (a paper consistently hostile to any idea of imperial federation), 'is that he has not come to realize that the British community includes the Britons of Greater Britain.'[143] But the rituals associated with the royal visit not only enabled the majority of British Canadians to reaffirm their commitment to the empire and their sense of being British, they also assisted Canadians in the construction of their own identity within the empire. The tour was seen as a symbol of Canada's status as a self-governing nation, taking its place alongside the other self-governing nations united by loyalty to a common crown. Supporters of imperial federation hoped that the tour would lead toward greater integration of the empire, but they represented only a minority. As the *Manitoba Free Press* pointed out, 'it would be a great mistake to suppose because of our enthusiastic greeting of Royalty and our ready acceptance to assist the mother country in South Africa that there is any disposition to undervalue the constitutional rights of the Canadian people'.[144] Whatever ambiguity this dual identity of being both British and Canadian might hold for future generations of Canadians, it clearly held no such difficulties for most English-speaking Canadians — even native-born English-speaking Canadians — in 1901. 'Far removed though Vancouver is from the seat of the empire', noted the Vancouver *World*, 'yet its citizens feel that they are as true sons of Britain as they among whom royalty dwells.'[145] The Collingwood *Bulletin* noted that the crowds in Toronto

> cheered as men and women have never cheered in Toronto before; [yet] not one in six was born in the old land beyond the seas; not one in six had heard the lark's mating song and the music of the nightingale, or had scented the hawthorn in the May morning. Yet here they were greeting with passionate acclaim a Prince, who, until that day had been to them but a name.[146]

And when the children broke out in 'Rule Britannia', the paper continued, 'it was with the flutter of several thousand Union Jacks'.[147] At the other end of Canada the Victoria *Daily Times* echoed this feeling: 'Sentiment is one of the most puissant of the forces in human nature. We are bound to the royal family by sentiment; we are joined together as Britishers in England, Scotland and Ireland, in Australia, in India, in the possessions too numerous to mention, and in Canada by sentiment.'[148] There was, of course, another reason for emphasising Canada's commitment to the monarchy. The royal tour, an Ontario paper noted, has been well covered in the United States and 'it has brought home to the minds of the American people the intense loyalty of the Canadians to the British Crown and their invincible attachment to [the] British connection'.[149]

The strength of this sentiment — the desire to build up 'a Canadian nation, yet one thoroughly loyal to the British Throne and devoted to the maintenance of those principles on which British institutions are based'[150] — would be shown in the First World War, when so many Canadians flocked to enlist to fight for a homeland many of them had never seen and others only distantly remembered. One observer noted during a remembrance ceremony in 1935 that many of the youth who sang 'God Save the King' to welcome the Duke to Toronto in 1901 'are now remembered in the cenotaph which now stands [on the spot] where in 1901 the people of Toronto heard the royal duke take pride in the fact that the first title "conferred upon me by my dear grandmother" was that of this city before it became Toronto'.[151] This sense of being British as well as Canadian, and of the royal family as belonging to those who lived in the British Dominions overseas as well as to the British at home, did not quickly dissipate after 1918, a casualty of the First World War. It had not disappeared when George's son, Edward, toured Canada as the Prince of Wales in 1919, or when his other son George VI became the first reigning monarch to visit Canada in 1939. And among many Canadians it had not disappeared in 1951 and 1959 when Elizabeth first as princess and then as queen toured Canada. Royal tours like that of 1901 did not — indeed could not — create this sentiment. It was the product of a peculiar pattern of migration, which meant that (contrary to what is usually believed) Canada was composed of two ethnic cores. In Quebec a substantial majority of the Canadian population defined its roots as French, while outside of Quebec the population of Canada was still overwhelmingly of British origin and most of those who were not were eager to be accepted as part of the British majority. 'Canada is British', proclaimed the Toronto *Globe*, 'because of the desire of its inhabitants to remain British.'[152] For these British Canadians and for several generations of their descendants, the British monarchy was not an alien institution;

it was something they could and did imagine as belonging to them, as part of their birthright and as part of their sense of national identity. It would take a major crisis of identity in the period after the Second World War — what José Igartua has called English Canada's 'Quiet Revolution'— to challenge this vision of the monarchy.[153]

NOTES

1. Toronto *Telegram*, 11 Oct. 1901.
2. Toronto *News*, 9 Oct. 1901.
3. See Memorandum of Journalists and Photographers accompanying the Royal Train, Governor General's papers, RG 7 G23, vol. 3, no.44, National Archives of Canada [hereafter NAC].
4. E.F. Knight, *With the Royal Tour* (Toronto, 1902); William Maxwell, *With the 'Ophir' Round the Empire* (London, 1902); Joseph Watson, *The Queen's Wish: How it was fulfilled by the Imperial Tour of T.R.H. The Duke and Duchess of Cornwall and York* (Toronto, 1902); Sir Donald Mackenzie Wallace, *The Web of Empire: A Diary of the Imperial Tour of their Royal Highnesses the Duke and Duchess of Cornwall and York in 1901* (London, 1902); Joseph Pope, *The Tour of Their Royal Highnesses the Duke and Duchess of Cornwall and York Through the Dominion of Canada in the Year 1901* (Ottawa, 1903). R.A. Loughnan also produced *Royalty in New Zealand* (Wellington, 1902), covering the New Zealand part of the tour.
5. Government of Canada, *Beyond the Printed Word: Newsreel and Broadcasting Reporting in Canada* (Ottawa, 1988), 118.
6. Hector Charlesworth, *Candid Chronicles: Leaves from the Note Book of a Canadian Journalist* (Toronto, 1925), 253.
7. J. Castell Hopkins, *The Life of King Edward VII* (Toronto, 1910), ch. 19.
8. Stephen Leacock, *My Discovery of England* (London, 1952), 49.
9. There is a brief discussion of the tour in Carman Miller, *The Canadian Career of the Fourth Earl of Minto: The Education of a Viceroy* (Waterloo, 1980), 183–6.
10. Victoria R. Smith, 'Constructing Victoria: The Representation of Queen Victoria in England, India and Canada, 1879–1914', Ph.D thesis, Rutgers University, 1998, esp. ch. 6; Wade A. Henry, 'Royal Representation, Ceremony and Cultural Identity in the Building of the Canadian Nation, 1860–1911', Ph.D thesis, University of British Columbia, 2001.
11. See *Morang's Annual Register for 1901* (Ottawa, 1902), section vi — Canada and the Crown.
12. Robert M. Stamp, *Kings, Queens & Canadians: A Celebration of Canada's Infatuation with the British Royal Family* (Markham, ON, 1987).
13. June Connors, 'The 1954 Royal Tour to Australia', *Australian Historical Studies*, 25 (1993), 382.
14. David Cannadine, 'The Context, Performance and Meaning of Ritual: The British Monarchy and the "Invention of Tradition" c. 1820–1977', in Eric Hobsbawm and Terence Ranger (eds.), *The Invention of Tradition* (Cambridge, 1983), 101–64; idem, 'The Last Hanoverian Sovereign: The Victorian Monarchy in Historical Perspective, 1688–1988', in A.I., Beier, David Cannadine and James M. Rosenheim (eds.), *The First Modern Society* (Cambridge, 1988), 127–65.
15. Walter L. Arnstein, 'Queen Victoria Opens Parliament: The Disinvention of Tradition', *Historical Research*, 63 (1990), 178–94; J.M. Golby and A.W. Purdue, *The Monarchy and the British People, 1760 to the Present* (London, 1988), 81.
16. See, for example, Edgar Williams, *The Myth of the British Monarch*, (London, 1989), 45, where he declares that 'the myth of the popularity of the monarchy is straightforwardly the result of incessant, universal and insidious monarchist propaganda'.
17. Ralphael Samuel, 'Introduction: The Figures of National Myth', in *Patriotism: The Making and Unmaking of British National Identity*, vol. 3 *National Fictions* (London, 1989), xxix.
18. See Terence Ranger, 'The Invention of Tradition Revisited: The Case of Colonial Africa', in T. Ranger and O. Vaughan (eds.). *Legitimacy and the State in Twentieth-Century Africa* (Oxford, 1993), 62–111.
19. *The Royal Tour: Official Programme and Souvenir 1901* (Toronto, 1901), unpaginated. See also *The Mail-Empire* (Toronto), 12 Sept. 1901.
20. Julian Amery, *Life of Joseph Chamberlain*, vol. 4 (London, 1951), 10.
21. There is a lengthier discussion of Chamberlain's motives in Phillip Buekner, 'The Royal Tour of 1901 and the Construction of an Imperial Identity in South Africa', *South African Historical Journal*, 41 (1999), 326–29.

22. Chamberlain to Minto, 22 Dec. 1900, Sir Joseph Pope papers, MG 30 E86, vol. 77, folder 54(I). NAC.

23. Balfour to Edward VII, Quoted in Kenneth Rose, *King George V* (London, 1983), 44.

24. Quoted in the *Tasmanian Mail* (Hobart), 19 Jun. 1901.

25. *HMS Ophir* (London, n.d.), 2.

26. Vancouver *World*, 28 Sept. 1901.

27. Minto to Lord Wenlock, 6 Sept. 1901, RG 7 G23, vol. 4, folder 5, NAC.

28. Minto to Laurier, 29 and 31 July 1901, papers of the Fourth Earl of Minto, MS 12557, 337–39 and 343-46, National Library of Scotland [hereafter NLS]; Minto to the King, 25 Oct. 1901, MS 12561, 97–100, NLS.

29. Minto to Laurier, private, 21 July 1901, Minto papers, MS 12557, 343–46, NLS.

30. Toronto *World*, 8 Oct. 1901.

31. Montreal *Star*, 9 Oct. 1901.

32. King George V's diary, 29 Sept. 1901, Royal Archives. Windsor Castle [hereafter RA]. I would like to acknowledge the gracious permission of Her Majesty Queen Elizabeth II for permission to make use of material in the Royal Archives.

33. Entry in Pope's diary, 21 Oct. 1901, Pope papers, MG 30 E86, vol. 48, folder 21, NAC.

34. Lord Wenlock to Lady Wenlock, 20 July 1901, papers of Lord Wenlock, DDFA (9)/5/l, Brynmor Jones Library, University of Hull.

35. Frank Prochaska, *Royal Bounty: The Making of a Welfare Monarchy* (London, 1995).

36. Journal of Captain Sir Bryan Godfrey Godfrey-Faussett, 21 Sept. 1901, BGGF 1/50, Churchill Archives Centre, Cambridge University [hereafter CAC].

37. *Courier* (Brampton), 9 Oct. 1901.

38. *Daily British Whig* (Kingston), 14 Oct. 1901.

39. Pope. *Tour*, 2.

40. 'H.M.S. Ophir: Some statistics during her visit to the colonies . . .', GV, F&V Ophir Tour, folder 2, RA.

41. Minto to Laurier, private, 2 April 1901, Minto papers, MS 12556, 249–56. NLS.

42. Great Britain, H.C. Deb., 92 (29 March 1901), 257–59; ibid., 93 (9 May 1901), 1210–11, 1245; ibid. 91 (25 March 1901), 1207.

43. *The Imperial Institute Catalogue of the Gifts and Addresses Received by Their Royal Highnesses the Duke and Duchess of Cornwall* (London, 1902).

44. Chamberlain to the Duke of Cornwall, 11 July 1901, GV/AA51/21, RA.

45. *The City of London, the Prince and Princess of Wales, and the Colonies* (London, 1902).

46. Rose, *George V*, 43–44.

47. Anne Edwards, *Matriarch: Queen Mary and the House of Windsor* (Bury St Edmonds, 1984), 118.

48. Minto to Chamberlain, 11 Dec. 1900. Pope papers. MG 30 ESG, vol. 75, folder 52(2), NAC.

49. On Canada and the war in South Africa, see Phillip Buckner, 'Canada', in David Omissi and Andrew Thompson (eds.), *The Impact of the South African War* (Basingstoke, 2002), 235–50.

50. Vancouver *World*, 18 Sept. 1901; *Daily Telegraph* (Berlin, ON), 17 Sept. 1901.

51. *Hamilton Spectator*, 24 Sept. 1901.

52. *Manitoba Free Press* (Winnipeg), 26 Sept. 1901.

53. *Toronto Daily Star*, 14 Oct. 1901.

54. Toronto *Globe*, 10 Oct. 1901.

55. Pope to Laurier, private, 4 Sept. 1901 and Laurier to Pope, 6 Sept. 1901, Pope papers, MG 30 E86, vol. 75, NAC.

56. Minto to Queen Victoria, 14 May 1899, Minto papers, MS 12561, 20–25, NLS.

57. Minto to Chamberlain, private, 15 Feb. 1901, Joseph Chamberlain papers, JC 14/13/38, University of Birmingham Archives [hereafter UBA].

58. Chamberlain to Minto, 13 Aug. 1901, which incorporates a number of questions submitted to the King and the latter's replies, Pope papers, MG 30 E86, vol. 75, folder 2, NAC.

59. Chamberlain to Minto, 21 Feb. 1901, Colonial Office papers, CO 42/881, f. 812, Public Record Office, London.

60. Minto to Chamberlain, 5 March 1901, Minto papers, MS 12557, 233–34, NLS.

61. Report of the Committee of the Privy Council, 20 April 1901, Pope papers, MG 30 E86, vol. 75, folder 52(2), NAC.

62. Minto to Sir Francis Knollys, private, 8 April 1901, and Minto to Laurier, private, 1 May and 30 May 1901, Minto papers, MS 12557, 233–34, 274–75, NLS.

63. Draft of Minto to Lieutenant Governors, confidential, 5 June 1901, RG 7 G23, folder 5, no. 4, NAC.

64. Maude to Minto, 21 July 1901, Minto papers, MS 12570, 72–76, NLS.

65. Minto to Chamberlain, private, 2 Sept. 1901, Chamberlain papers, JC 14/1/3/28, UBA.

66. Laurier to Chamberlain, private, 17 Sept. 1901, with Chamberlain's comments, JC 14/1/3/2. ibid.

67. Sir Arthur Bigge to Edward VII, 28 July 1901, VIC/W6/3A, RA.

68. King George V's diary, 17 Aug. 1901. RA.

69. Wenlock to Minto, 21 Aug. 1901, RG 7 G23, vol. 4, folder 5, NAC.

70. See, for example, the *Lindsay Weekly Post*, 18 Oct. 1901.

71. *Courier* (Brantford), 18 Oct. 1901.

72. Pope to Willison, private and confidential, 14 Aug. 1901, RG 7 G23, vol. 3, folder 7, NAC.

73. Toronto *Globe*, 17 Aug. 1901.

74. Maurice Pope (ed.), *Public Servant: The Memoirs of Sir Joseph Pope* (Toronto, 1960), 15.

75. Sir Joseph Pope, *The Flag of Canada* (n.p., 1912).

76. 'Auditor General's Account of Expenses of Reception of Duke of York', Pope papers, MG 30 E86, vol. 76, folder 53(1), NAC.

77. Deputy Minister of Militia and Defence to Pope, 19 Feb. 1902, ibid.

78. *City Council Minutes Toronto* 1901, 15 July and 28 Oct. 1901.

79. *Morang's Annual Register for 1901*, 264.

80. Toronto *World*, 26 July 1901.

81. *Morang's Annual Register for 1901*, 264.

82. *Vancouver Province*, 18 Sept. 1901.

83. *Toronto Daily Star*, 17 Sept. 1901.

84. Hamilton *Spectator*, 27 July 1901.

85. John R. Hamilton, *Our Royal Guests* (St John, 1902), 55.

86. *The Voice* (Winnipeg), 23 Aug. 1901.

87. Attorney-General of Ontario to Sir Oliver Mowat, 11 Sept. 1901, RG 7 G23, vol. 5, folder 9, NAC.

88. *Hamilton Spectator*, 14 Oct. 1901.

89. Quoted in Rose, *George V*, 52.

90. Minto to Parkin, private, 23 Aug. 1901, Minto papers, MS 12557, 379–82, NLS.

91. Sir Charles Lucas, *Greater Rome and Greater Britain* (Oxford, 1912), 143.

92. A list of the committees and their membership is found in a paper marked simply 'St John' in the Pope papers, MG 30 E86, vol. 77, folder 54(I), NAC. A list of members of the committees in the other urban centres can be found in *Morang's Annual Register for 1902*, 264–68.

93. Toronto *Mail-Empire*, 19 Oct. 1901.

94. Manitoba *Free Press*, 10 Sept. 1901.

95. Vancouver *World*, 16 Aug. 1901.

96. Toronto *World*, 12 Oct. 1901.

97. Halifax *Herald*, 11 Oct. 1901.

98. *Through the Provinces of Ontario and Quebec, Canada*, an annotated time table of the tour published by the Grand Trunk Railway system (n.p., 1901), unpaginated. A copy made can be found in the Pope papers, MG 30 E86, vol. 84, NAC.

99. Wallace, *The Web of Empire*, 362.

100. *Toronto Daily Star*, 17 Sept. 1901.

101. *L'Evénement* (Québec), 21 Sept. 1901.

102. *La Presse* (Montréal), 16 Sept. 1901.

103. Toronto *Globe*, 18 Sept. 1901, and *Toronto Daily Star*, 18 Sept. 1901.

104. *Le Journal* (Montreal), 19 Sept. 1901.

105. Toronto *World*, 19 Sept. 1901.

106. *La Presse*, 19 Sept. 1901.

107. *L'Evénement*, 17 Sept. 1901.

108. *La Nation* (Montréal), 3 Oct. 1901.

109. See, for example, *L'Avenir du Nord*, 23 Sept. 1901.

110. Wallace, *The Web of Empire*, 367.

111. So far as I have been able co discover, 'O Canada' was sung only in Quebec and in French in 1901.

112. Toronto *Telegram*, 9 Oct. 1901; Collingwood *Bulletin*, 17 Oct. 1901.

113. Montreal *Gazette*, 16 Oct. 1901.

114. Ottawa *Citizen*, 17 Oct. 1901.

115. Montreal *Star,* 17 Oct. 1901.
116. Toronto *Globe,* 16 Oct. 1901.
117. *Manitoba Free Press,* 4 Oct. 1901.
118. Unidentified newspaper clipping', dated 21 Oct. 1901, Pope papers, MG 30 E86, vol. 83, folder 60(l), NAC.
119. *The Voice,* 38 June and 9 Aug. 1901.
120. Ibid., 37 Sept. 1901.
121. A copy of the poem, published in the Toronto *Telegram,* 11 Oct. 1901, can be found in the Pope papers. MG 30 E86, vol.83, NAC.
122. Pope to Laurier, 31 Aug. 1901, Sir Wilfrid Laurier papers, MG 26 G, microfilm reel 2714, 58477–8, NAC.
123. Maude to P.T. Cronin, 17 July 1901, RG 7 G23, vol. 4, folder 5, NAC.
124. Minto to Laurier, 21 Aug. 1901, Minto papers, MS 12557, 371–74, NLS.
125. Montreal *Gazette,* 16 Oct. 1901.
126. Cronin to Minto, 13 July 1901, RG 7 G23, vol. 4, folder 5, NAC.
127. Mark G. McGowan, 'The De-greening of the Irish: Toronto's Irish-Catholic Press, imperialism and the Forging of a New Identity, 1887–1914', *Historical Papers* (1989), 118–45.
128. Quoted in Wallace, *Web of Empire,* 376. The same point was made by the *Catholic Record* (London), 27 July 1901.
129. Toronto *Catholic Register,* 26 Sept. 1901.
130. Vancouver *World,* 28 Sept. 1901.
131. Wade A. Henry, 'Imagining the Great White Mother and the Great King: Aboriginal Tradition and Royal Representation at the "Great Pow-wow" of 1901', *Journal of the Canadian Historical Association,* new series, 11 (2000), 87–108.
132. Godfrey-Faussett's journal, 28 Sept. 1901, BGGF 1/50, CAC.
133. London *Morning Post,* 1 Nov. 1901.
134. Knight, *With the Royal Tour,* 407.
135. Halifax *Herald,* 19 Oct. 1901.
136. The Reverend F.G. Scott quoted in Pope, *The Royal Tour in Canada,* 22.
137. Ibid., 43.
138. Victoria *Daily Times,* 1 Oct. 1901.
139. *Daily British Whig,* 15 Oct. 1901.
140. Vancouver *Province,* 30 Sept. 1901.
141. Judith Bassett, '"A Thousand Miles of Loyalty": The Royal Tour of 1901', *New Zealand Journal of History,* 21 (1987), 139.
142. Printed Ephemera from the Metropolitan Public Library, Canadian Institute for Historical Microreproductions, microfiche no. 4329.
143. Toronto *Globe,* 25 Sept. 1901.
144. *Manitoba Free Press,* 9 Oct. 1901.
145. Vancouver *World,* 30 Sept. 1901.
146. Collingwood *Bulletin,* 17 Oct. 1901.
147. Ibid.
148. Victoria *Daily Times,* 30 Sept. 1901.
149. *Daily Sentinel Review* (Woodstock, ON), 16 Oct. 1901.
150. *Daily News-Advertiser* (Vancouver), 3 Oct. 1901.
151. 'Our King's Visits to Canada By Fred Williams', *Mail and Empire* (Toronto), 6 May 1935, MU 2146, Miscellaneous 1901, Provincial Archives of Ontario, Toronto.
152. Toronto *Globe,* 25 Sept. 1901.
153. See José E. Igartua, 'L'Autre Revolution Tranquille. L'Evolution des Répresentations de l'Identité Canadienne-Anglaise depuis la Deuxième Guerre Mondiale', in Gérard Bouchard and Yvan Lamonde, *La Notion Dans Tous Ses Dots: Le Québec in Comparaison* (Montréal, 1997), 271–96.

Topic Five

Racism and Nationalism

The priests, nuns, and teachers of the Fort Qu'Appelle Industrial School stand behind the school's Native students in this 1899 photo.

In the past, Canadian historians were reluctant to admit to racism in their history, believing that it would detract from an image of Canada as a united and harmonious nation. If reference to ethnic groups arose, it was usually in terms of their positive contribution to the settlement of the West. If a negative perspective arose, it was in reference to ethnic radicals and insurrections, especially with regards to the Winnipeg General Strike. But shortly after the Second World War, ethnic history emerged as a sub-field of Canadian social history. Ethnic historians were interested in looking beyond the history of ethnic immigration to study their experiences as minority groups within the country. What obstacles stood in the way of their being accepted and integrated into Canadian society? What were the attitudes of the host society towards these newcomers? Although First Nations' people were not recent immigrants, they too experienced racism.

The following three articles deal with racism in the late 19th and the early 20th centuries. This proved to be a period of transition for First Nations under the federal government's aggressive policy of assimilation into Canadian society. In "Taming Aboriginal Sexuality: Gender, Power, and Race in British Columbia, 1850–1900," historian Jean Barman examines attitudes toward First Nations peoples in British Columbia. She argues that the dominant male society viewed First Nations women as sexually independent, and hence "wild" and "untamed." Such attitudes fitted into the prevailing Social Darwinist views of racial hierarchy. Social Darwinist attitudes, Barman shows, were also evident on issues of housing, the potlatch, and child care.

Historian Howard Palmer examines attitudes of assimilation toward non-British and non-French immigrants in the late 19th to the middle of the 20th centuries. He identifies three assimilation theories. The first he describes as anglo-conformity, which predominated from the 1880s to 1945. This was followed in the post-World War II period by the "melting pot" theory. Then beginning in the 1960s, a theory of "cultural pluralism" took hold, reflected in the federal government's policy of "multiculturalism." All three policies, he argues, ultimately shared an acceptance of the need for assimilation. Such attitudes, Palmer points out, challenged two Canadian myths: first, that Canadians have throughout their history been tolerant of minority groups, and, second, that Canadians have adopted a "mosaic" approach to ethnic groups that encourages ethnic differences, unlike the American "melting-pot" approach that demands conformity.

Racism reached new levels in Canada during times of war. Historian James W. St.G. Walker examines the factor of racism in the recruiting of visible minorities for the Canadian Expeditionary Force during World War I. He emphasizes that Canada was not alone in applying racist attitudes, that the other Dominions as well as the European countries in the Western world shared the same ideology of "race." They held to a common belief that this was "a white man's war." In the early years of the war when the supply of volunteers exceeded demand, "race" was a factor for rejecting certain volunteers. Only when casualties at the front eroded the number of soldiers available, and as recruitment died off, did the army recruit visible minorities; even then, they were often given lesser duties or allowed to belong to "special" segregated units only. These actions discouraged minorities from enlisting. Those who did enlist did so on the belief that if they fought for their country, their country would grant them the rights of Canadian citizenship. For many, these hopes remained unfulfilled after the war's end.

What were the common assumptions about "race" that lay behind discrimination against First Nations women in British Columbia in the settlement period, ethnic groups on the Prairies during a similar settlement period, and visible minorities in World War I? How was racism linked to nationalism, including the expressions of nationalism discussed in Topic Four? Has racism lessened over time, or simply taken a new form and been expressed in a different way today?

Brian Titley reviews the policy of the Canadian government toward First Nations in *A Narrow Vision: Duncan Campbell Scott and the Administration of Indian Affairs in Canada* (Vancouver: University of British Columbia Press, 1987). On First Nations–newcomer relations, see J.R. Miller, *Skyscrapers Hide the Heavens: A History of Indian-White Relations in*

Canada, 3rd ed. (Toronto: University of Toronto Press, 2000). A valuable article is John L. Tobias, "Canada's Subjugation of the Plains Cree, 1879–1885," *Canadian Historical Review*, 64, 4 (December 1983): 519–548. On the role of residential schools as seedbeds of racism, see J.R. Miller, *Shingwauk's Vision: A History of Native Residential Schools* (Toronto: University of Toronto Press, 1996); and John S. Milloy, *A National Crime: The Canadian Government and the Residential School System 1879–1986* (Winnipeg: The University of Manitoba Press, 1999). With regards to the Canadian government's prejudicial attitudes toward Natives in the context of farming on the reserves, see Sarah Carter, *Lost Harvests: Prairie Indian Reserve Farmers and Government Policy* (Montreal/Kingston: McGill-Queen's University Press, 1990); and Helen Buckley, *From Wooden Ploughs to Welfare: Why Indian Policy Failed in the Prairie Provinces* (Montreal/Kingston: McGill-Queen's University Press, 1992).

Howard Palmer explores racism in Alberta's history in greater depth in *Patterns of Prejudice: A History of Nativism in Alberta* (Toronto: McClelland & Stewart, 1982). On racism and European immigrants, see Donald Avery, *Reluctant Host: Canada's Response to Immigrant Workers, 1896–1994* (Toronto: McClelland and Stewart, 1979). Prejudice from the immigrant experience can be examined in R.F. Harney and H. Troper, *Immigrants: A Portrait of the Urban Experience, 1890–1930* (Toronto: Van Nostrand Reinhold, 1975); Arnold Itwaru, *The Invention of Canada* (Toronto: Tsar Publications, 1990); and from John Marlyn's novel, *Under the Ribs of Death* (Toronto: McClelland & Stewart, 1957).

On discrimination against Asians in British Columbia, see W. Peter Ward, *White Canada Forever: Popular Attitudes and Public Policies towards Orientals in British Columbia* (Montreal/Kingston: McGill-Queen's University Press, 1978). For an alternative view, see Patricia Roy's "British Columbia's Fear of Asians, 1900–1950," *Histoire sociale/Social History* 13 (May 1980): 161–72, and her book, *A White Man's Province: British Columbia Politicians and Chinese and Japanese Immigrants, 1858–1914* (Vancouver: University of British Columbia Press, 1989). See as well, Patricia Roy, "'The wholesome sea is at her gates/Her gates both east and west': Canada's Selective and Restrictive Immigration Policies in the First Half of the Twentieth Century," in *Canada, 1900–1950: A Country Comes of Age*, eds. Serge Bernier and John MacFarlane (Ottawa: Organization for the History of Canada, 2003), pp. 33–49.

On ethnic relations during wartime, see John Herd Thompson, *Ethnic Minorities During Two World Wars* (Ottawa: Canadian Historical Association, 1991). On the only African-Canadian battalion see John G. Armstrong, "The Unwelcome Sacrifice: A Black Unit in the Canadian Expeditionary Force," in *Ethnic Armies: Polyethnic Armed Forces from the Time of the Hapsburg to the Age of the Superpowers*, ed. N.F. Dreisziger (Waterloo, ON: Wilfrid Laurier University Press, 1990), pp. 178–97; and Calvin Ruck, *The Black Battalion, 1916–1920: Canada's Best Kept Military Secret* (Halifax: Nimbus, 1987). On First Nations soldiers see Fred Gaffen, *Forgotten Soldiers* (Penticton, BC: Theytus Books, 1985); and James Dempsey, *Warriors of the King: Prairie Indians in World War I* (Regina: Canadian Plains Research Center, 1999).

For a discussion of discrimination toward Japanese Canadians during World War II, see W. Peter Ward, "British Columbia and the Japanese Evacuation," *Canadian Historical Review*, 57, 3 (September 1976): 289–309, and the relevant section of *White Canada Forever* (cited earlier). See as well, Patricia Roy et al., *Mutual Hostages: Canadians and Japanese during the Second World War* (Toronto: University of Toronto Press, 1990), and J.L. Granatstein and Gregory Johnson, "The Evacuation of the Japanese Canadians, 1942: A Realist Critique of the Received Version," in *On Guard for Thee: War, Ethnicity, and the Canadian State, 1939–1945*, eds. N. Hillmer et al. (Ottawa: Canadian Committee for the History of the Second World War, 1988) pp. 101–129. Ann Gomer Sunahara's *The Politics of Racism: The Uprooting of Japanese Canadians during the Second World War* (Toronto: Lorimer, 1981) is a carefully documented study of this same issue; it should be read in conjunction with Ward's study.

WEBLINKS

Open Hearts, Closed Doors
http://www.virtualmuseum.ca/Exhibitions/orphans/english/themes/immigration/page1.html
Documents regarding Canada's immigration policies from the late 19th century to today.

Immigration Report of 1887
http://www.dcs.uwaterloo.ca/~marj/genealogy/reports/report1887west.html
Extracts from a federal immigration report from 1887.

Chinese Immigration Act
http://www.canadiana.org/ECO/PageView/9_02345/0019
Complete text of the 1885 Chinese Immigration Act, which includes among other requirements the initial "head tax" of $50 per Chinese immigrant.

Residential Schools
http://www.ainc-inac.gc.ca/ch/rcap/sg/sgm10_e.html
A chapter from the Royal Commission on Aboriginal Peoples regarding residential schools.

For more information on residential schools see
http://archives.cbc.ca/IDD-1-70-692/disasters_tragedies/residential_schools.

Wartime Elections Act
http://www.canadiana.org/ECO/ItemRecord/9_07190
A digitized copy of the 1917 Wartime Elections Act. The act allowed some Canadian women to vote, but also denied the right to vote to some naturalized Canadians from overseas.

Aboriginal Soldiers
http://www.vac-acc.gc.ca/general/sub.cfm?source=history/other/native
Detailed descriptions of the contributions made to the Canadian military by aboriginal soldiers from World War I to the present.

Article Eleven

Taming Aboriginal Sexuality: Gender, Power, and Race in British Columbia, 1850–1900[1]

Jean Barman

In July 1996 I listened in a Vancouver court room as Catholic Bishop Hubert O'Conner defended himself against charges of having raped or indecently assaulted four young Aboriginal women three decades earlier. His assertion of ignorance when asked what one of the complainants had been wearing on the grounds that, "as you know, I'm a celibate man"

Source: Jean Barman, "Taming Aboriginal Sexuality: Gender, Power, and Race in British Columbia, 1850–1950," *BC Studies*, No. 115/116 (Autumn/Winter 1997/98): 237–66. Reprinted by permission of BC Studies.

encapsulated his certainty that he had done nothing wrong.[2] He admitted to sexual relations with two of the women, but the inference was clear: they had made him do it. They had dragged him down and led him astray. The temptation exercised by their sexuality was too great for any mere man, even a priest and residential school principal, to resist.

I returned home from that day, and subsequent days in the court room, deeply troubled. I might have been reading any of hundreds of similar accounts written over the past century and more about Aboriginal women in British Columbia. This essay represents my first attempt to come to terms with Bishop O'Conner and his predecessors, made more necessary on reading the National Parole Board's decision of March 1997. The Board denied Bishop O'Conner parole, subsequent to his conviction on two of the charges, because "your recent psychological assessment indicates that you hold your victims in contempt," and "at your hearing today . . . you maintain that . . . you in fact were seduced."[3] If I earlier considered that my response to my days in the courtroom might have been exaggerated, I no longer did so. My interest is not in Bishop O'Conner's guilt or innocence in a court of law, but, rather, in tracing the lineage of his attitudes in the history of British Columbia.

The more I have thought about Bishop O'Conner, the more I realize that those of us who dabble at the edges of Aboriginal history have ourselves been seduced. However much we pretend to read our sources "against the grain," to borrow from the cultural theorist Walter Benjamin, we have become entrapped in a partial world that represents itself as the whole world. Records almost wholly male in impetus have been used by mostly male scholars to write about Aboriginal men as if they make up the entirety of Aboriginal people.[4] The assumption that men and male perspectives equate with all persons and perspectives is so accepted that it does even not have to be declared.[5] Thus, an American researcher wanting to find out about her Aboriginal counterparts discovered that "indigenous communities had been described and dissected by white men — explorers, traders, missionaries, and scholars — whose observations sometimes revealed more about their own cultural biases than about Native people. Misperceptions of Indian women were rampant because they were held up to the patriarchal model."[6]

So what happens when we turn the past on its head and make our reference point Aboriginal women instead of Aboriginal men? We come face to face with Aboriginal sexuality or, more accurately, with male perceptions of Aboriginal sexuality. The term 'sexuality' is used here in its sociological sense as "the personal and interpersonal expression of those socially constructed qualities, desires, roles and identities which have to do with sexual behaviour and activity," the underlying contention being "the social and cultural relativity of norms surrounding sexual behaviour and the sociohistorical construction of sexual identities and roles."[7] In a useful summary of recent scholarship, English sociologist Gail Hawkes tells us that the word sexuality "appeared first in the nineteenth century," reflecting "the focus of concerns about the social consequences of sexual desire in the context of modernity." Christian dogma defined sexual desire "as an unreasoned force differentially possessed by women, which threatened the reason of man" and the "inherent moral supremacy of men." According to Hawkes, "the backbone of Victorian sexuality was the successful promotion of a version of women's sexuality, an ideal of purity and sexual innocence well fitted to the separation of spheres that underpinned the patriarchal power of the new ruling class."[8] Sexuality, as Hawkes contextualizes the term, helps us better to understand the critical years in British Columbia, 1850–1900, when newcomers and Aboriginal peoples came into sustained contact.

Everywhere around the world Indigenous women presented an enormous dilemma to colonizers, at the heart of which lay their sexuality.[9] Initially solutions were simple and straightforward. During conquest local women were used for sexual gratification as a matter of course, just as had been (and still are) female victims of war across the centuries. If unspoken and for the most part unwritten, it was generally accepted that, so long as colonial women were absent, Indigenous women could be used to satisfy what were perceived to be natural needs.[10] No scruples existed over what the pioneering scholar on race Philip Mason has termed "the casual use of a social inferior for sexual pleasure."[11] The growth of settler colonies changed the 'rules of the game.' As anthropologist and historian Ann Laura Stoler astutely observes, drawing from her research on colonial Asia, "while the colonies were marketed by colonial elites as a domain where colonizing men could indulge their sexual fantasies, these same elites were intent to mark the boundaries of a colonizing population, to prevent these men from 'going native,' to curb a proliferating mixed-race population that compromised their claims to superiority and thus the legitimacy of white rule."[12]

In British Columbia gender, power, and race came together in a manner that made it possible for men in power to condemn Aboriginal sexuality and at the same time, if they so chose, to use for their own gratification the very women they had turned into sexual objects. While much of what occurred mirrored events elsewhere, some aspects were distinctive.[13] Colonizers never viewed Aboriginal men as sexual threats,[14] whereas attitudes toward women acquired a particular self-righteousness and fervor. The assumptions newcomers brought with them shaped attitudes, which then informed actions. By the mid-nineteenth century Europeans perceived all female sexual autonomy to be illicit, especially if it occurred in the public sphere, considered exclusively male. Aboriginal women in British Columbia not only dared to exercise agency but often did so publicly, convincing men in power that their sexuality was out of control. To the extent that women persisted in managing their own sexual behaviour, they were wilded into the 'savages' that many newcomers, in any case, considered all Indigenous peoples to be.[15] That is, until Aboriginal women acceded to men in power by having their sexuality tamed according to their precepts, they were for the taking, an equation of agency with sexuality that encourages Aboriginal women's portrayal, even today, as the keepers of tradition. As noted about American anthropological writing, "Native women are pictured as unchanging — clinging to a traditional way of life that exists outside the vicissitudes of history."[16] To avoid the image that men like Bishop O'Conner continue to project on them, Aboriginal women have had to be stripped of their agency past and present.

PROSTITUTION

Indigenous sexuality struck at the very heart of the colonial project. British historian Catherine Hall has noted, in reference to Victorian England, that "sex was a necessary obligation owed to men and not one which women were permitted to talk or think about as owed to themselves."[17] Sexual independence, or circumstances where that possibility existed, was the ultimate threat to the patriarchal family. Children were considered to belong to their father, who had to have the assurance that they were indeed his biological heirs. As succinctly summed up by George Stocking in his history of Victorian anthropology, "if the ideal wife and mother was 'so pure-hearted as to be utterly ignorant of and averse to any sensual indulgence,' the alternate cultural image of the 'fallen woman' coveys a hint of an underlying preoccupation with the threat of uncontrolled female sexuality." By the time Victoria came to the throne in 1837, "the basic structure of taboos was already defined: the renunciation of all sexual activity save the procreative intercourse of Christian marriage; the education of both sexes in chastity and continence; the secrecy and cultivated ignorance surrounding sex; the bowdlerization of literature and euphemistic degradation of language; the general suppression of bodily functions and all the 'coarser' aspects of life — in short, the whole repressive pattern of purity, prudery, and propriety that was to condition sexual behavior for decades to come." Counterpoised to this stereotype were "savages," who were by definition "unrestrained by any sense of delicacy from a copartnery in sexual enjoyments."[18]

Any interpretation of events in British Columbia must adopt the language of colonialism as it was applied to Indigenous women's sexual independence. Around the colonized world the charge of prostitution, engaging in a sexual act for remuneration, was used by those who sought to meddle in Indigenous lives. Sexuality was not to be talked about openly, but prostitution and all that it implied could be publicly condemned. In other words, sexuality had to be wilded into prostitution or possibly concubinage, cohabitation outside of marriage, in order for it to be tamable. Hawkes traces the fervor over prostitution back to Christianity, which both gave it prominence and held out promise for "the redemption of the prostitute, the personification of polluting and uncontrolled women's sexuality." Moving to the nineteenth century, "Victorian sexual morality was focused on, and expressed through, the 'social evil' of prostitution. Prostitution was discussed in such diverse venues as popular journalism, serious weekly reviews, medical tracts and publications from evangelical organizations devoted to the rescue of fallen women . . . prostitution provided a forum within which to express, covertly, anxieties about, and fascination with, the characteristics of women's sexuality."[19]

No question exists but that Aboriginal people in British Columbia viewed their sexuality differently than did colonizers. It is difficult, if not impossible, to reconstruct gender relations prior to newcomers' arrival, nor is it necessary to do so in order to appreciate the enormity of contact. The scholarship is virtually unanimous in concluding that, traditionally, marriages were arranged, with goods passing to the woman's family.[20] Intrusions of European disease, work patterns, and economic relations unbalanced Aboriginal societies and tended to atomize gender relations. Women possessed opportunities for adaptation not available to their male counterparts.[21] Many of the taboos normalized and universalized by Europeans simply did not exist in Aboriginal societies. If for Europeans sexuality had to be strictly controlled in the interests of assuring paternity, the link may have been less critical for Aboriginal people in that the group, rather than the immediate biological family, was the principal social unit.

To grasp the rapidity with which Aboriginal women became sexualized as prostitutes in colonial British Columbia, it is instructive to go back in time to another bishop, George Hills, first Anglican bishop of Vancouver Island. Arriving in Victoria in January 1860, he encountered a figurative tinder box, a fur-trade village which in just twenty months had been turned upside-down by the gold rush, bringing with it thousands of newcomers from around the world, almost all of them men. Bishop Hills was almost immediately condemning "the profligate condition of the population." "The Road to Esquimalt on Sunday is lined with the poor Indian women offering to sell themselves to the white men passing by —& instances are to be seen of open bargaining."[22] Bishop Hills's Methodist counterpart Thomas Crosby, who arrived in the spring of 1862, was similarly struck by "the awful condition of the Indian women in the streets and lanes of Victoria."[23]

What newcomers constructed as prostitution did become widespread during the gold rush, just as it had existed to some extent during the fur trade. The evidence may be largely anecdotal, but it is consistent and, for some times and places, overwhelming.[24] Virtually all of the descriptions come from a colonial male perspective, but they are so graphic and diverse as to leave little doubt as to the circumstances. The most visible sites were seasonal dance halls where for a price miners could while away "the long winter evenings" by interacting socially with Aboriginal women.[25] A New Westminster resident evoked its "Squaw Dance-House" frequented by miners "hastening to throw away their hardly earned gold." Her description is graphic: "As soon as eight or half-past struck, the music of a fiddle or two and the tramp of many feet began. Later on the shouts of drunken men and the screams of squaws in like condition made night hideous. Each man paid fifty cents for a dance, and had to 'stand drinks' at the bar for himself and his dusky partner after each."[26] Bishop Hills described "houses where girls of no more than 12 are taken in at night & turned out in the morning — like cattle."[27] Even while acknowledging dance halls' contribution to urban economies, the press repeatedly denounced the Aboriginal women whose presence made them possible, as in an 1861 editorial charging that "prostitution and kindred vices, in all their hideous deformity, and disease in every form, lurk there." In their San Francisco counterparts "the females were at least civilized," but "here we have all the savagery of the ancient Ojibbeways [sic], with all the vice of a reckless civilization."[28] If the decline of the gold rush from the mid-1860s put an end to dance halls' excesses and dampened down excitement over prostitution,[29] the wildness associated with Aboriginal sexuality had permeated settler consciousness.

FEMALE AGENCY

Turned on their head, contemporary portrayals of Aboriginal women during the gold rush affirm their agency. Agency is by its very nature relational and interactive. Just as occurred during the fur trade[30] and in traditional societies,[31] Aboriginal women both initiated and responded to change. They scooted around, they dared, they were uppity in ways that were completely at odds with Victorian views of gender, power, and race. Some likely soon realized that, however much they tried to mimic newcomers' ways, they would never be accepted and so might as well act as they pleased.[32] An Aboriginal woman "dragged" the friend of a man who had assaulted her to a nearby police station "to be locked up as a witness," only to have him seek "the protection of the police, which was granted" until she left.[33] The jury in a court case against a Victoria policeman accused of "having attempted to ravish the person of an Indian squaw" was told that the verdict hinged on whether "you believe the simple evidence of the three Indian women" and, "after consulting together about one moment, [the jury] returned a verdict of 'Not guilty.'"[34] In some cases Aboriginal women were encouraged or forced by the men in their lives. References abound to fathers selling their daughters "for a few blankets or a little gold, into a slavery which was worse than death,"[35] exchanges likely viewed by some as only continuing traditional marital practices. Yet even missionary accounts hint at female agency, as with Bishop Hills's comment after unsuccessfully remonstrating with "a woman making up a dress" for the dance house that night: "Poor creatures they know these things are wrong — but the temptations are too strong."[36]

Perhaps the most telling evidence of Aboriginal women's management of their sexual behaviour are the numbers who chose to live, at least for a time, with non-Aboriginal men. The nature of some decisions is suggested by Crosby's account of a twelve-year-old girl who, having "refused at first to follow a life of sin," "was visited by a great rough fellow who, with his hand full of money and with promises of fine clothes and trinkets and sweets, coaxed her and finally prevailed upon her to come and live with him."[37] Although referring to a later point in time, Emily Carr's observations in her fictionalized memoirs are particularly evocative, as in a conversation between two Aboriginal women whom she almost certainly knew personally. "'We got a house with three looms, and a sink and kitchen tap. Jacob and Paul go to school with white children. Too bad you not got white man for husband, Susan.'"[38] Aboriginal women caught in the tumultuous world that was the gold rush sometimes had to make hard decisions, whether for material goods or personal safety. In such circumstances a lonely miner's entreaties could be persuasive.

Non-Aboriginal men had their own reasons for entering into relationships. During the heady years of the gold rush, at least 30,000 White men and several thousand Chinese and

Blacks sought their fortunes in British Columbia. Most soon departed, for the difficulties of getting to the gold fields were horrendous, but however long they stayed, their utter loneliness in a sea of men cannot be discounted. The most fundamental characteristic of non-Aboriginal women in gold-rush British Columbia was their paucity.[39] A Welsh miner reported back to his local cleric how "considerable value is placed on a good woman in this country"[40] An Englishman who had already tried his hand in Australia lamented: "The great curse of the colony so far, as it must always be the curse of any colony in which such a want exists, is the absence of women . . . there must be at least two hundred men to every woman . . . I never saw diggers so desirous of marrying as those of British Columbia." "If it is one thing more than another a miner sighs for after a hard day's work, it is to see either his tent, or his log hut, brightened up by the smiles of a woman, and tidied up by a woman's hand . . . The miner is not very particular —'plain, fat, and 50' even would not be objected to, while good-looking girls would be the nuggets, and prized accordingly."[41] When a non-Aboriginal man saw an Aboriginal woman, what he may have perceived was not so much her Aboriginality as her gender and, certainly, her sexuality.

Structural factors specific to British Columbia encouraged couplings. At the level of everyday life Aboriginal people were not nearly so alien as sometimes portrayed, or as they became in the American Pacific Northwest.[42] Relations were generally peaceful, and many miners and settlers survived only because of local largesse. A German visiting the gold fields in 1858 reported that "many Indians lived in the neighborhood, who on the whole are on friendly footing with the Whites."[43] A guide to prospective settlers published a quarter of a century later asserted: "The intending settler may depend on finding the Indians peaceable, intelligent, eager to learn and industrious, to a degree unknown elsewhere among the aborigines of America."[44] Another factor was ease of communication through common knowledge of the Chinook trading jargon. Containing about 600 words and a large variety of non-verbal additions, Chinook facilitated conversations across the races. People could talk to each other on an ongoing basis, and sometimes they did more than just talk.

Although some of the relationships spawned by the gold rush extended through the couple's lifetime, many were fairly transient, two persons cohabiting for a time until one or the other decided to move on.[45] In most cases it was the man who did so, and, as one Aboriginal woman recalled,

> Oh, it was hard on Indian wives, I guess,
> But they always managed
> To raise their children
> Even if their husbands finished with them.[46]

Women might end relationships, as in the gold-rush town of Lytton in 1868 where a man "lately left by his Indian wife who had had two children by him . . . confesses having sown the seed he has reaped."[47] Other women simply ensured that their husbands knew that they could leave if they wished to do so. An early novel depicted a saloon keeper with a "squaw wife" named Desdemona whose independent character drew on the author's many years in British Columbia.

> All who know the habits of the squaws married to white men, especially if they lived in one of the towns, will remember the overmastering desire they occasionally developed for a return to their tribe, and a resumption of their old life for at least a time. To fish all night from a light cedar canoe, with no thoughts of the white man's scorn, to pick berries, cut and dry fish till their garments were saturated with the odour of salmon, gather roots, herbs, and the bark of trees for baskets, the rushes also for klis-klis or mats. To extract the beautiful and durable reds and blues from certain plants and berries, and generally to revel in God's great temple of nature.

So it was with Desdemona. "One of these calls from the wild had taken Desdemona, and when her tenase tecoup man (small white man) came in one night, the house was dark, and she and the children gone." She had "stepped into a canoe, paddled across the wide [Fraser] river, and up the salmon stream," and only when it suited her fancy did she return home to her husband.[48]

The various data from personal accounts, church records, and the manuscript censuses suggest that, in those areas of British Columbia opened up to Europeans during the gold-rush years, about one in ten Aboriginal women cohabited at some point in her life with a non-Aboriginal man.[49] The prevalence of such unions even caused the first session of the new provincial legislature, following entry into Confederation in 1871, to pass a bill, subsequently disallowed by the federal government, to legitimize children of unions between Aboriginal women and non-Aboriginal men whose parents wed subsequent to their birth.[50]

TAMING ABORIGINAL SEXUALITY

By the time British Columbia became a Canadian province in 1871 Aboriginal women had been almost wholly sexualized.[51] The perception of widespread prostitution, and if not prostitution then concubinage, gave men in power the freedom to speak openly about matters that otherwise would have been only whispered.[52] Newcomers took for granted the fall as depicted in the Bible. Human nature was weak, and the biological man could easily be tempted to evil by his female counterpart, just as Bishop O'Conner considers himself to have been a century later. It was woman's place to be docile and subservient so as not to provoke man. For all those seeking to control Aboriginal peoples, women who exercised sexual autonomy had to be subdued. Conversion to Christianity held the key, for "woman was always the slave or burden-bearer until the Gospel came and lifted her into her true social position," which was essentially as man's handmaiden.[53] Whether missionaries, government officials, or Aboriginal men, the common perception was that the only good Aboriginal woman was the woman who stayed home within the bosom of her family. So an informal alliance developed between these three groups to refashion Aboriginal women.

This tripartite alliance, wherein men in power buttressed and comforted each other, was grounded in mutual expediency and, to some extent, in mutual male admiration. With entry into Confederation, responsibility for Aboriginal people shifted to the federal government under the terms of the British North America Act, and it did not take long for newly appointed officials to realize the enormous benefit to be had from establishing cordial relations with missionaries, who were already at work across much of the sprawling province. Officially, missionaries had no status, but unofficially they became the government's foot soldiers, and its eyes and ears. Aboriginal policy, as it developed in British Columbia, was to minimize official involvement in everyday affairs, which effectively meant letting missionaries have a free hand.[54] If disagreeing in many areas, including Aboriginal people's right to an adequate land base, government officials repeatedly commended missionaries for having "taught, above all, the female portion of the community to behave themselves in a modest and virtuous manner."[55] The other prong of the alliance crossed racial boundaries in the interests of gender solidarity and mutual self-interest. Members of the Indian Reserve Commission active across British Columbia in the mid-1870s left an extensive paper trail and repeatedly expressed approval of Aboriginal "manliness" and of "the industry of the men."[56] Similarly, in missionary accounts it is almost wholly Aboriginal men who are given individuality and personality.[57] Men, particularly those who emulated colonial ways, needed to have suitable spouses, and for this reason too Aboriginal women had to have their sexuality tamed.

As for Aboriginal men, they were likely motivated by a shortage of women and also, some of them, by a desire to please their colonial mentors. Reports of a shortage are sufficiently widespread to be convincing. As early as 1866 Bishop Hills observed "a scarcity of wives" among the northern Tsimshian, many of whose members camped in Victoria on a seasonal basis.[58] The Indian Reserve Commission's census of a decade later counted 1,919 Aboriginal persons in the area extending from Burrard Inlet north to Jervis Inlet, across to Comox, and down through the Saanich peninsula, including the Gulf Islands; of these, 979 were adult males compared with 919 adult females, and 94 male youth compared with 84 female youth.[59] The enumerator of the Southern Interior, extending from Lytton through the Nicola Valley, counted 884 adult males compared with 803 adult females and lamented "the absence of females both adults and youths — those who should have been the future mothers of the tribe."[60] Some Aboriginal men, in effect, made deals to behave in accordance with missionary aspirations for them in exchange for getting wives.[61] Crosby described a visit to a Queen Charlottes village in about 1885, where local men promised him: "Sir, if you will come and give us a teacher, we will stop going to Victoria. Victoria has been the place of death and destruction to our people, as you see we have no children left to us. All our young women are gone; some of our young men can't find wives any more; and we wish that you could help them to get wives among the Tsimpshean people."[62]

The tripartite campaign to tame the wild represented by Aboriginal sexuality had two principal goals. The first was to return Aboriginal women home. The second was to desexualize Aboriginal everyday life, in effect to cleanse it so that the home to which women returned would emulate its colonial counterpart.

RETURNING ABORIGINAL WOMEN HOME

Marriage lay at the heart of newcomers' morality and, as anthropologist George Stocking concludes, "it is perfectly clear that 'marriage proper' meant proper Victorian marriage" whose "purpose was to control human (and especially female) sexuality, so that there might be 'certainty of male parentage.'"[63] As summed up by historians Leonore Davidoff and Catherine Hall for England between the late eighteenth and mid-nineteenth centuries, "marriage was the economic and social building block for the middle class." "Marriage became both symbol and institution of women's containment. It was marriage which would safely domesticate the burgeoning garden flower into an indoor pot plant; the beautiful object potentially open to all men's gaze became the possession of one man when kept within the house like a picture fixed to the wall."[64]

In theory, two marital strategies could have tamed Aboriginal sexuality. One was to encourage non-Aboriginal men to wed their Aboriginal partners, the other to return Aboriginal women home to wed Aboriginal men. Either would have satisfied Victorian notions of marriage, but the alliance of interests that existed among men in power combined with growing racism to ensure that the second option would be favoured. As early as 1873 an agitated provincial official pointed to the federal government's responsibility for "the care and protection of the native race in this Province, [and] so long as this shameful condition of things is suffered to continue unchecked, the character of that race in the social scale is practically a delusion."[65] Reserve commissioners reported on conversations with chiefs at Nanaimo, where "the evil of concubinage of their young women with the white men around were specially pointed out."[66] By 1884 an Indian agent with an Aboriginal wife and grown daughters felt able to argue, perhaps with a touch of self-interest, that "with the present state of civilization in the country and the abundance of white and educated half breed women — such a practice should be put a stop to in future."[67] Aboriginal women were needed at home to service their menfolk.

For men in power, gender and race neatly dovetailed. Within the mix of pseudo-scientific ideas associated with Social Darwinism, newcomers accepted, as seemingly demonstrated by the triumph of colonialism and technological advances, that mankind had evolved into a hierarchy with Whites on the top and Aboriginal people near the bottom.[68] Persons of mixed race ranked even lower, for, to quote a colonial visitor, "half-breeds, as a rule, inherit, I am afraid, the vices of both races."[69] Concerns grew over "a class of half-breed children . . . who, under the bond of illegitimacy, and deprived of all incentives in every respect, will in course of time become dangerous members of the community."[70] During the late 1870s such fears were exacerbated by a murderous rampage by the young sons of a Hudson's Bay trader and Aboriginal woman,[71] and given a sexual edge by female-mixed race students at a public boarding school becoming pregnant by their male counterparts.[72] While some encouragement was given to non-Aboriginal men to marry Aboriginal women with whom they were cohabiting, this was, for the most part, done somewhat grudgingly.[73] Petitions became a favoured means to compel Aboriginal women back home. The tripartite alliance developed a dynamic whereby Aboriginal men signed petitions orchestrated by missionaries who then dispatched them to government officials to justify their taking action.[74] Both Catholic and Protestant missionaries participated, as did Aboriginal men across much of the province and numerous officials at various levels of government.

In 1885 Oblates missionaries stage-managed two identical petitions to the Governor General that were affirmed with their marks by 962 Aboriginal men, including at least eighteen chiefs, from across the Cariboo and south through the Lower Fraser Valley. In the best English prose the petitions "beg[ed] to lay before your Excellency" that a "great evil is springing up amongst our people" whereas "on a dispute between a married couple, the wife leaves her husband and goes off the Reservation, and takes up with a bad white man, China man, or other Indian, and [they] live together in an unlawful state." The men sought permission to "bring back the erring ones by force if necessary."[75] Caught up in the rhetoric to tame Aboriginal sexuality, the Ministry of Justice drafted an even broader regulation for consideration by the chiefs, one which made it possible to "bring back to the reserve any Indian woman who has left the reserve and is living immorally with any person off the reserve." The proposal was only derailed by the Ministry of Justice's suggestion, made almost in passing, that the Department of Indian Affairs should "consider before it is passed whether or not the putting of it in force will lead to riots and difficulties between the Indians and the white people and others with whom the Indian women are said to be living immorally."[76] Three of the four Indian agents consulted considered that this might well happen were chiefs given such authority. One of them acknowledged female agency in his observation that, "while in some cases the Indian woman might be brought back without trouble, it would be impossible to keep her on a reserve against her will."[77] The project was shelved, even though the Catholic Bishop at New Westminster intervened directly at the federal ministerial level in an attempt to bypass the bureaucrats.[78]

The campaign to tame Aboriginal sexuality was not to be thwarted, and the Oblates were almost certainly behind a bolder petition dispatched in 1890 to the Governor General. The chiefs of fifty-eight bands, again extending from the Cariboo through the Fraser Valley, indicated by their marks that they were "much aggrieved and annoyed at the fact that our wives, sisters and daughters are frequently decoyed away from our Reserves by ill designing persons." No means existed to return "these erring women," but, even were this possible, "in most cases these women are induced to return again to their seducers." Fearing that "some of our young men who are sufferers will certainly take the law into their own hands and revenge themselves on the offending parties," the petition sought "a law authorising the infliction of corporal punishment by the lash."[79] The advisability of "legislation, making it an offence for a white man to have sexual intercourse with an Indian woman or girl without Christian marriage," was referred to the Ministry of Justice,[80] which in this case pulled the plug. The Ministry considered the legislation unnecessary, since "the laws relating to the protection of females and for the punishment of persons who seduce or abduct them, apply to Indian women as well as to white women."[81] Yet the campaign persisted, and later in 1890 the Indian agent at Lillooet urged, on behalf of "the Chiefs of the numerous Bands around here," that "a severe penalty should be imposed upon any person, not an Indian, who, harbouring an Indian woman, does not deliver her up to the Chief of the Reserve."[82]

At this point the enthusiasts may have stumbled. Acting largely independently of civil authority, the Oblates had allied themselves across much of the Interior with local Aboriginal men in order to effect control over everyday life.[83] As one Indian agent noted in the early 1890s, although the "flogging habit has been abandoned for some years past" and fines are not so common as they once were, "considerable sums of money are annually collected by the chiefs and their watchmen for the benefit of the churches whose functionaries attend to their spiritual welfare."[84] In the spring of 1892 the Oblate missionary at Lillooet, the chief, and four other Aboriginal men were brought before the local magistrate, convicted, and given jail sentences for "flogging a young girl . . . on the report only of a fourth party" for some unspecified sexual activity. "Without investigation he [priest] ordered 15 lashes. His plea was 1st ancient customs of the Indians & 2nd necessity for such punishment in order to suppress immorality." The Indian agent who made the report considered both that the "ancient customs" were not as portrayed by the missionary and that the local men should not have been punished so severely, since they "believed the Priest to be their Commander in all Church matters — and that consequently they were obliged to obey him."[85] The incident appears to have cooled the alliance between the Oblates and local men, who "were astonished at the extent of the jurisdiction of the Courts of law, when even the dictates of a Priest should be upset and the Priest himself held accountable."[86]

The Protestants could be just as enthusiastic as the Catholics in allying themselves with local men to keep women at home and then calling on federal officials to enforce what they could not effect by their own devices. In 1889 the Indian agent at Alert Bay, acting in concert with the local Anglican missionary, stopped a group of women from boarding a steamer to Victoria. His justification was that they "went with the avowed purpose of prostituting themselves" and he "had previously been requested by numbers of young men to prevent if possible their wives and sisters from going to Victoria."[87] Reflecting the tripartite alliance's perspective, the Indian agent considered that "nearly all the young women, whenever they leave their homes, whether ostensibly for working at the canneries or at the Hop Fields, do so with the ultimate idea of making more money by prostitution."[88] The steamboat company vigorously protested and the provincial Indian superintendent was lukewarm to the action, astutely observing that "the Indian women and their friends come to Victoria, and other places, in their canoes," making their restriction practically impossible.[89] Nonetheless, the Indian agent and Anglican missionary did such a successful end run to federal officials as to persuade them to propose legislation to keep at home, by force if necessary, "Indian women from the West Coast of British Columbia, who are in the habit of leaving their Villages and Reserves by steamers and by other mode of transport with the object of visiting the Cities and Towns of that Province for immoral purposes."[90]

The proposed legislation hit a snag only after the federal Minister of Justice indicated "that there is not at present sufficient material on hand to permit of the drawing up of a Bill fully dealing with the question."[91] The Minister requested the provincial superintendent to circularize Indian agents around the province. Even though the agents would likely have found it far easier to acquiesce to expectations than to dispute them, they were all, apart from those at Alert Bay and Babine in the Northern Interior, remarkably sanguine. On the west of Vancouver Island, "I do not know of a single instance on this Coast where a young girl has been taken to Victoria or elsewhere for the purposes of prostitution."[92] His neighbour was "not aware of any Indian women belonging to the Cowichan Agency who leave their Reservations for immoral purposes."[93] In the Fraser Valley and Lower Mainland, "there are very few immoral women."[94] As for the Central Interior, "the practice of Indian women leaving their Reserves for the purpose of leading immoral lives is not common in this Agency."[95] The Southern Interior agent offered a general observation: "Indians are in their nature, in consequence of their training, habits and surroundings, far less virtuous than the average whites. Their morality should not therefore be judged by the standards of the white people. The Indian woman, although, as above stated, inclined to be worse in her morals, is naturally modest."[96] The North Coast agent considered that the "Indians have learned from sad experience the effects of immorality in the cities and are rapidly improving their conduct."[97] Summarizing the responses, the provincial superintendent concluded that "the few Indian women who may be found living an immoral life in our towns and Cities are less in number as a rule than of their white sisters."[98]

Nonetheless, the depiction of Aboriginal sexuality as out of control was too attractive an explanation for missionary and government failings to be abandoned. Just three years later, in 1895, a petition signed by thirty-four men from central Vancouver Island, all but one with their marks, demanded legislation to prevent "our wives and daughters and sisters" from being "carried to Victoria for illegitimate purposes."[99] The British Columbia senator to whom the petition was addressed took its claims at face value and demanded that steps be taken to "prevent the deportation of Indian women," seeing that "Indians are wards of the government under tutelage and not qualified to manage their own affairs wisely." The senator, who simply assumed that Aboriginal women's sole role was to service their menfolk, emphasized that an "increase, instead of a decrease, is much to be desired" in the Aboriginal population.[100] The federal response is interesting because, rather than quoting from the Indian agents' reports in their files, officials emphasized the difficulties of securing legislation. In doing so, they revealed, perhaps inadvertently, that women were de facto having their travel restricted by local Indian agents "when requested by the husband or brother or anyone having proper authority, to stop a woman from going away, and so the men have the prevention of that of which they complain almost entirely in their own hands."[101] The sexualization of Aboriginal women had far less to do with reality than with the needs, and desires, of men in power. So long as settler society perceived a need to tame Aboriginal sexuality, men in power could reorder Aboriginal society with impunity.

REORDERING ABORIGINAL SOCIETY

Over time virtually every aspect of Aboriginal everyday life acquired a sexual dimension, thereby justifying its reordering. Aboriginal sexuality, or perhaps more accurately the fear of Aboriginal women's agency, became a lens through which traditional preferences in housing, social institutions, and child care were critiqued and found wanting.

The rhetoric condemning the 'big houses' inhabited by Coastal peoples made explicit Victorian fears of the body and of human sexuality. It also reflected Social Darwinian notions of the hierarchy of species, at the top of which lay Western societies premised on the monogamous conjugal family. The very existence of sites where more than a single family lived together was equated with immorality. No doubt existed but that, given the opportunity, men and women would act on their impulses. Davidoff and Hall have linked the subordination of women to the private home: "Woman had been created for man, indeed for one man, and there was a necessary inference from this that *home* was 'the proper scene of woman's action and influence.' . . . The idea of a privatized home, separated from the world, had a powerful moral force and if women, with their special aptitude for faith, could be contained within that home, then a space would be created for true family religion."[102] So also in British Columbia, the single family home came to be seen as a necessary prelude to Christian conversion.

Men in power repeatedly lauded the single-family house, as in side notes on the Reserve commission's census of Aboriginal people. At Burrard Inlet: "The houses at this place have a pleasing appearance when viewed from the sea. They are mostly of the cottage style, white washed and kept cleaner in this than is usual with most Indians." In contrast, along the Fraser River: "Most of the houses of this tribe are of the primitive style. There are however several cottages kept and fitted up in a neat manner." At Cowichan on Vancouver Island: "There are a few tidy cottages—what they require is a desire and encouragement.[103] Missionaries like Crosby were even more fervent and repeatedly linked housing to sexuality. "The old heathen house, from its very character, was the hot-bed of vice. Fancy a great barn-like building, . . . occupied by as many as a dozen families, only separated from each other by low partitions." The interior seemed made for naughty deeds. "Picture such a building, with no floor other than the ground, no entrance for light except the door, when open, and the cracks in the walls and the roof. Around the inside of such a building were ranged the beds, built up on rude platforms." "Is it any wonder that disease and vice flourished under such favorable surroundings?"[104] In sharp contrast stood "the Christian home." Crosby considered that "the only way to win the savage from his lazy habits, sin and misery" was to "be able and willing to show how to build a nice little home, from the foundation to the last shingle on the roof."[105]

Fear of Aboriginal sexuality became frenzied in the rhetoric around the institution of the potlatch. Missionaries led the campaign against this social activity practiced across most of the province, garnering support from government officials and over time from some converted Aboriginal men. Initially arguments focused on the event itself as being "demoralizing," leading to "debauchery."[106] Federal legislation banning the potlatch took effect at the beginning of 1885, but did not bring about wholesale conversion to Christianity. Missionaries soon sought both allies in Aboriginal men in search of wives and reasons, apart from themselves, to explain their failure to live up to their expectations for themselves.[107] The ethnographer Marius Barbeau concluded in 1921, after examining federal files on the potlatch, that, "as the Church has not succeeded in making converts to any material extent . . . there must be found a scapegoat, and as the potlatch already had a bad name, it was blamed."[108]

The sexualization of the potlatch had a number of components, but centred on the supposed sale of Aboriginal women as wives or prostitutes to get the money to potlatch.[109] In 1893 a Toronto newspaper reported that a group of missionaries had witnessed "blankets for potlatch procured at the expense of the virtue of women," an event which the local Indian agent determined was sensationalized. [110] By the end of the century the press was convinced that "the potlatch is the inciting cause of three-fourths of the immorality that exists among Indian women."[111] Writing shortly thereafter, the Indian agent at Alert Bay asserted the that younger generation of Aboriginal men supported his attempt to persuade his superiors in Ottawa to act against potlatching: "It looks cruel to me to see a child 13 or 14 years of age put up & sold just like sheep or a nanny goat, to a bleary eyed siwash old enough to be her grand-father, for a pile of dirty blankets, which will in turn be Potlatched to the rest of the band, and all to make the proud Father, a big Injun," rather than "let her marry a young man whom I am sure she wanted."[112] The Indian agent quoted a longtime missionary to make his point that "the girls die off and the young men for the most part cannot get wives because as a rule they have no blankets or money unless they are sons of chiefs and the others cannot get wives until they are able to command a certain sum which is so difficult as they have to compete with the older men who hold the property."[113]

The unwillingness to tolerate Aboriginal women's agency was a major factor in the determination to replace familial child care with residential schools operated by missionaries under loose government oversight. As attested by the scholarship, schools sought total control over pupils' sexuality, particularly that of girls.[114] The twinned concepts of Christian marriage and the Christian home depended on young women remaining sufficiently unblemished so that they could become good wives according to Victorian standards of behaviour. The attitudes and actions of Thomas Crosby and his wife Emma are instructive. Crosby considered that parents, "though kind and indulgent to their children, are not capable of teaching and controlling them properly" and "something must be done to save and protect the young girls . . . from being sold into the vilest of slavery."[115] "On account of the prevalence of this traffic in Indian girls, many of the early missionaries were led to establish 'Girls' Homes' for the rescue and further protection of these poor victims of this awful system."[116] The taming that went on in the Crosbys' girls' home, as in residential schools across the province, left no doubt as to Aboriginal agency. As remembered by a Crosby school matron in the early 1880s, the girls required "a great deal of Grace, Patience and determination, they were so obstinate and disobedient."[117]

The wildness associated with Aboriginal sexuality explains attitudes toward a girl's transition from pupil to wife. Reflecting the assumptions of the day, the superintendent of the Children's Aid Society in Vancouver expressed relief that "the savage was so thin and washed out" of two young women of mixed race, that they were able to find happiness with their White lovers. Yet this represented "only a glimmer of light in the darkness."[118] According to Crosby's biographer, "girls stayed at the Home until they were married, at which time a new girl would be admitted."[119] The full extent of missionaries' distrust of their charges is evident in the musings of another Crosby matron regarding the potential marriage of a fourteen-year-old student: "It would seem sinful to allow such things to be mentioned if they were white girls, but here they are safer when married young."[120]

Again, the informal alliance operated. Schools measured their success by numbers of girls who "have married Christian Indians, have helped to build up Christian homes, to civilize the people generally and to aid in developing their own neighborhood." "Instead of a young man with his friends going with property and buying a wife, as was done formerly, many of our brightest young men tried to make the acquaintance of the girls in the Home." Women might no longer be sold by their fathers, but they were no less commodities when it came to marriage. The Crosbys, like other missionaries, put a romantic spin around what was, in effect, a good being made available to a handful of men considered suitably Christian. "There was no doubt in our minds that real, true love again and again developed between the young people who thus became acquainted. This acquaintance finally resulted in their marriage and the happy life that followed."[121]

CONSEQUENCES

By the end of the nineteenth century settler society took for granted the interpretation that men in power put on Aboriginal women's agency. The ongoing frenzy over the potlatch is indicative. The press became ever more determined to expose its supposed basis in Aboriginal sexuality. "Indian girl sold for 1,000 blankets" hit Vancouver streets in 1906.[122] The story makes clear that the supposed revelation about "the awful Indian practice of potlatch" originated with an Anglican missionary who was disgruntled because a pupil had married someone other than the man she had selected for her. Later in the year both Vancouver and Ottawa newspapers trumpeted "Five Indian Girls Sold,"[123] a report that, on investigation, proved to be groundless.[124] A Vancouver paper headlined a year later, "Squaw sold for $400.00 at Alert Bay to a grizzled Chief from Queen Charlottes."[125] It turned out that, while two marriages had occurred, neither involved "a grizzled chief," and the local Indian agent considered the article to be "very misleading."[126] The press coverage prompted a host of women's voluntary associations across the country to demand legislation to "put an end to this great blot on the Civilization and Christianity of Canada."[127] Writing in 1921, a barrister who was the son of the former Indian agent at Alert Bay, and who represented Aboriginal people opposed to the potlatch ban, considered that "the strongest reason for enforcing the law against the Potlatch is the question of Indian marriages. . . . It is also contended that women are bought and sold, [but] this is not true."[128] Had the potlatch not been so successfully sexualized, it is doubtful that opponents could have maintained its illegality into the mid-twentieth century. The taming of Aboriginal sexuality had become a means to an end, as well of course as an end in itself, but the effects were no less detrimental to Aboriginal women.

For Aboriginal women, the consequences of the ceaseless rhetoric of scorn heaped on them in the interests of men in power were enormous. Some women acquiesced and returned or remained at home,[129] and the Crosbys delighted "in visiting around among the villages, to pick out these Christian mothers who had the privilege of the 'Home' life and training."[130] In a broad sense, Aboriginal societies did come to mimic their colonial counterparts, which is not unexpected given federal policies and the material advantages to be got from doing so. An Aboriginal informant explained in 1950 how "converts were sometimes termed 'made white men', as they used different types of houses and they dressed in white men's clothes, while their heathen brothers . . . indulged in all of the old rituals."[131] Some women had the decision taken out of their hands. As more marriageable White women became available and attitudes hardened, numerous non-Aboriginal men shed their Aboriginal partners. The manuscript censuses for the late nineteenth century indicate that, while some of these women did return home and enter into new unions with Aboriginal men, others scraped along at the edges of settler society.

Other women continued to dare.[132] Many inter-racial unions survived the campaign to tame Aboriginal sexuality, in some cases by the partners legally marrying or retreating outward into the frontier, or by simply standing their ground.[133] The encouragement that missionaries and government officials gave to Aboriginal men may have caused some women to disengage from their home communities in search of more satisfying life opportunities. To the extent that traditional patterns of gender relations gave way to male mimicry of European practices, so the social distance between the sexes may have widened. Women still married out, as indicated by the 1901 manuscript census[134] and evoked in a Carr vignette about a woman who had "married white" and "both loved her husband and gloried in his name," for "it was infinitely finer to be 'Mrs Jenny Smith' than to have her name hitched to an Indian man's and be 'Jenny Joe' or 'Jenny Tom.'"[135]

Most important, the campaign to tame Aboriginal sexuality so profoundly sexualized Aboriginal women that they were rarely permitted any other form of identity. Not just Aboriginal women but Aboriginal women's agency was sexualized. In the extreme case their every act became perceived as a sexual act and, because of the unceasing portrayal of their sexuality as wild and out of control, as an act of provocation. By default, Aboriginal women were prostitutes or, at best, potential concubines. Their actions were imbued with the intent that men in power had so assiduously ascribed to them, thus vitiating any responsibility for their or other men's actions toward them. Sexualization of Aboriginal women's agency occurred within a context in which they were already doubly inferior by virtue of their gender and race, thus virtually ensuring that any Aboriginal woman who dared would become colonialism's plaything. Again, the stories are legion, be it the Okanagan Valley in the 1880s, Vancouver Island in the 1920s, the North Coast in the 1960s, or Bishop O'Conner. Sometimes the accounts embody a strong element of bravado, in other cases the wish fulfillment of lonely men, but in yet others a strong dose of action, as with O'Conner.

A young Englishman who arrived in the Okanagan Valley shortly after the completion of the transcontinental railroad in 1886 exemplified a generation of newcomers who took for granted Aboriginal women's sexualization. "Most of these girls were graceful, some even pretty; clear, light bronze skins with just a touch of color in the cheeks, even teeth and glossy jet black hair, that had almost a tinge of blue in it; their black eyes would be modestly cast down in the presence of white men. And sometimes a shy upward glance of coquetry — but not if there were any bucks in sight." He recalled a contemporary who, "fed up with batching, had disturbed the monastic peace of the community by taking unto himself a dusky mistress." The sexualization of Aboriginal women's agency removed any sense of responsibility. Even as his friends were deciding whether to be jealous, "he and his lady had a bad row, and realizing that his little romance was ended he fired her out, and as none of the rest of the old boys were gallant enough to take a chance on her, the lady returned to the bosom of her tribe, and once more there was peace on earth in the little community."[136]

Even persons who supported Aboriginal people, as did the lawyer representing them in the 1920s against the potlatch ban, persisted in seeing women in sexual terms, considering that "contact between Indians and loggers has always been fraught with dire results — particularly to the Indian women." This assessment was in sharp contrast to his view of Aboriginal men: "The Indian man in his own environment is a man of dignity, big and venerable."[137]

In a generally sympathetic account of a summer sojourn in 1966 at Telegraph Creek on the North Coast, a young American made clear that Aboriginal women's agency remained sexualized. "More than they would have in the old days, I'm sure, they make fun of the Indians to me . . . [for] their limber-limbed promiscuity." A friend "eats supper with me, chatting about the morals of the Indian girls ('No morals at all if you scratch their stomachs a minute')." Their every action became a sexual action, thus his vignette relating how "earlier in the spring a girl appeared in the store, sent by her parents, and took up the broom' and began to sweep, after the historical fashion of a squaw proposing to a white man." For this young man, the wild which was Aboriginal sexuality remained mythic. Noting that "in New York to dream of woman is an unremarkable event" but "here it invests the whole night with sexual urgency," he repeatedly found himself tempted, as after "I've had a day hearing stories of . . . Indian women being mounted and screwed." He resisted, but precisely because he did accept the equation of Aboriginal female agency with sexuality: "Of course these Indian girls are too vulnerable to fool with, so I have only the past to keep me company in bed."[138]

Hence we come full circle to Bishop O'Conner who at virtually the same time that this young American was fantasizing acted on his impulses. Like so many men before him, he still considers himself to have been "seduced" and, a full generation later, remains in his heart "a celibate man." I have no doubt that O'Conner feels himself to be sincere, just as I now have no doubt of the importance of newcomers' construction of Aboriginal women's sexuality for understanding events during that critical half century, 1850–1900, when your, my, and Bishop O'Conner's British Columbia came into being.

NOTES

1. Earlier versions of this essay were presented at the BC Studies Conference in May 1997 and, thanks to Elizabeth Jameson and Susan Armitage, at the Western Historical Association in October 1997. I am grateful to everyone who has commented on the essay, especially to Robin Fisher at BCS, Elizabeth Jameson at WHA, and the two anonymous reviewers for *BC Studies*. The Social Sciences and Humanities Research Council generously funded the research from which the essay draws.

2. This statement by Bishop O'Conner was taken up forcefully in Reasons for Judgment, Vancouver Registry, no. CC9 206 17, 25 July 1996.

3. National Parole Board, Decision Registry, file 905044C, 21 March 1997.

4. The three best books for understanding Aboriginal people in British Columbia are, in my view, Robin Fisher, *Contact and Conflict: Indian-European Relations in British Columbia, 1774–1890* (Vancouver: UBC Press, 1970 and 1992); Paul Tennant, *Aboriginal Peoples and Politics: The Indian Land Question in British Columbia, 1849–1989* (Vancouver: UBC Press, 1990); and Cole Harris, *The Resettlement of British Columbia: Essays on Colonialism and Geographical Change* (Vancouver: UBC Press, 1997), each of which is driven by a male perspective as to sources, authorship, subjects, and interpretation. Much the same observation might be made about the bulk of the ethnographic literature; a recent summary of the historiography (Wayne Suttles and Aldona Jonaitis, "History of Research in Ethnology," in Wayne Suttles, ed., *Northwest Coast*, vol. 7 of William C. Sturtevant, ed., *Handbook of North American Indians* [Washington, DC: Smithsonian Institution, 1990], 84–86) does not even include private life or women, much less sexuality, as topics.

5. This general point is made by, among other authors, Sandra Harding in *The Science Question in Feminism* (Milton Keynes: Open University Press, 1986); Catherine Hall in *White, Male, and Middle-Class: Explorations in Feminism and History* (New York: Routledge, 1988); and Vron Ware in *Beyond the Pale: White Women, Racism and History* (London: Verso, 1992). A handful of exceptions by Canadian scholars are principally concerned with an earlier time period, as with Karen Anderson, *Chain Her By One Foot: The Subjugation of Native Women in Seventeenth-Century New France* (New York: Routledge, 1991); Sylvia Van Kirk, *"Many Tender Ties": Women in Fur Trade Society, 1670–1870* (Norman: University of Oklahoma press, 1980); and Ron Bourgeault, "Race, Class and Gender: Colonial Domination of Indian Women," *Socialist Studies* 5 (1989), 87–115. The two principal analyses of perceptions of Aboriginal people consider women, if at all, as extensions of their menfolk; see Robert F. Berkhofer, Jr., *The White Man's Indian: Images of the American Indian from Columbus to the Present* (New York: Vintage, 1979), and Daniel Francis, *The Imaginary Indian: The Image of the Indian in Canadian Culture* (Vancouver: Arsenal Pulp Press, 1992).

6. Jane Katz, ed., *Messengers of the Wind: Native American Women Tell Their Life Stories* (New York: Ballentine Books, 1995), 5.

7. David Jary and Julia Jary, *Collins Dictionary of Sociology*, 2nd ed. (Glasgow: HarperCollins, 1995), 590–1. It was 1914 before the Oxford English Dictionary got to the letter 's.' All of its quotes were from the nineteenth century and, while the first definition of sexuality was "the quality of being sexual or having sex," the second and third were the "possession of sexual powers or capability of sexual feelings" and "recognition of or preoccupation with what is sexual." See Sir James A.H. Murray, ed., *A New English Dictionary on Historical Principles*, vol. 8 (Oxford: Clarendon Press, 1914), 582. Interest in the concept of sexuality, and more generally in regulation of the body, mushroomed with the publication of Michel Foucault's *History of Sexuality* in 1978 (Harmondsworth: Penguin, esp. vol. 1) and Peter Gay's *The Bourgeois Experience* in 1986 (Oxford: Oxford University Press, 2 vols.). Particularly helpful for interpreting Foucault is Ann Laura Stoler's *Race and the Education of Desire: Foucault's History of Sexuality and the Colonial Order of Things* (Durham: Duke University Press, 1995).

8. Gail Hawkes, *A Sociology of Sex and Sexuality* (Buckingham and Philadelphia: Open University Press, 1996), 8, 14, 42.

9. This point underlies Ronald Hyam, *Empire and Sexuality: The British Experience* (Manchester: University of Manchester Press, 1990); and Margaret Strobel, *Gender, Sex, and Empire* (Washington: American Historical Association, 1993), which critiques Hyam's contention that empire enhanced men's sexual opportunities.

10. Among the more perceptive recent examinations of aspects of this topic are Margaret Jolly and Martha MacIntyre, ed., *Family and Gender in the Pacific: Domestic contradictions and the colonial impact* (Cambridge: Cambridge University Press, 1989); Strobel, *Gender, Sex, and Empire*; Robert Young, *Colonial Desire: Hybridity in Theory, Culture and Race* (London: Routledge, 1995); Stoler, *Race and the Education of Desire*; and Frederick Cooper and Ann Laura Stoler, ed., *Tensions of Empire: Colonial Cultures in a Bourgeois World* (Berkeley: University of California Press, 1997).

11. Philip Mason, *Patterns of Dominance* (London: Oxford University Press for the Institute of Race Relations, 1970), 88.

12. Ann Laura Stoler and Frederick Cooper, "Between Metropole and Colony: Rethinking a Research Agenda," in Cooper and Stoler, ed., *Tensions of Empire,* 5. Although Stoler and Cooper co-wrote this introductory essay, the insight is clearly Stoler's, since it is her research on colonial Asia that is cited.

13. As diverse examples of a similar sequence, if not necessarily interpretation, of events, see Albert L. Hurtado, *Indian Survival on the California Frontier* (New Haven: Yale University Press, 1988), 169–92; and Caroline Ralston, "Changes in the Lives of Ordinary Women in Early Post-Contact Hawaii," in Jolly and MacIntyre, ed., *Family and Gender,* 45–82. In *Capturing Women: The Manipulation of Cultural Imagery in Canada's Prairie West* (Montreal and Kingston: McGill-Queen's University Press, 1997), Sarah Carter links the sexualization of Aboriginal women on the Canadian prairies to their participation in the 1885 uprising (esp. 8–10, 161, 183, 187, 189).

14. In *Allegories of Empire: The Figure of the Woman in the Colonial Text* (Minneapolis: University of Minnesota Press, *1993*), Jenny Sharpe argues that, after rebellions in India in the 1850s, raped colonial women provided the basis for racializing Indigenous peoples as inferior.

15. The concept of wildness is examined in Sharon "Tiffany and Kathleen Adams, *The Myth of the Wild Woman* (Cambridge: Schenken, 1985).

16. Patricia C. Albers, "From Illusion to Illumination: Anthropological Studies of American Indian Women," in Sandra Morgan, ed., *Gender and Anthropology: Critical Reviews for Research and Teaching* (Washington: American Anthropological Association, 1989), 132. Carol Devens appears to accept this perspective in "Separate Confrontations: Gender as a Factor in Indian Adaptation to European Colonization in New France," *American Quarterly* 38, 3 (1986), 461–80; and in her *Countering Colonization: Native American Women and Great Lakes Missions, 1630–1900* (Berkeley: University of California Press, 1992). The identification of Aboriginal women's conversion to Christianity with their desire to maintain traditional values underlies much of the special *Ethnohistory* issue (43. 4, Fall 1996), "Native American Women's Responses to Christianity, edited by Michael Harkin and Sergei Kan, esp. 563–66, 574–75. 614, 629–30, 655, 675–76. Others authors sidestep issues of sexuality altogether, as with most of the essays in Laura F. Klein and Lillian A. Ackerman, ed., *Women and Power in Native North America* (Norman: University of Oklahoma Press, 1995); and Nancy Shoemaker, ed., *Negotiators of Change: Historical Perspectives on Native American Women* (New York: Routledge, 1995).

17. Hall in *White, Male, and Middle-Class,* 61–62.

18. George W. Stocking, Jr., *Victorian Anthropology* (New York: Free Press, 1987), 199–200, 202.

19. Hawkes, *Sociology of Sex,* 14–15, 42.

20. Despite its male perspective, a good basic source, although limited to Coastal peoples, remains Suttles, ed., *Northwest Coast.*

21. Especially useful is Carol Cooper, "Native Women of the Northern Pacific Coast: An Historical Perspective, 1830–1900," *Journal of Canadian Studies* 27, 4 (Winter 1992–93), 44–75, which points out that what newcomers labeled prostitution sometimes simply continued traditional social structures wherein some persons were deprived of their autonomy as "slaves" (58) and traces the seasonal migrations of North Coast women to Victoria with their families.

22. 24 September 1860 entry, Bishop George Hills, Diary, in Anglican Church, Ecclesiastical Province of British Columbia, Archives; also letter to the editor from C.T.W. in *Victoria Gazette,* 22 September 1860; and Matthew MacFie, *Vancouver Island and British Columbia* (London: Longman, Green, Longman, Roberts, & Green, 1865), 471.

23. Thomas Crosby, *Up and Down the North Pacific Coast by Canoe and Mission Ship* (Toronto: Missionary Society of the Methodist Church, 1904), 17. On the relevance of missionary accounts, see Jean and John Comaroff, *Of Revelation and Revolution: Christianity, Colonialism and Consciousness in South Africa* (Chicago: University of Chicago Press, 1991).

24. This contention is supported by Chris Hanna's extensive research on colonial Victoria, and I thank him for sharing his findings with me.

25. "Can such things be?" *Victoria Daily Chronicle,* 16 November 1862.

26. Francis E. Herring, *In the Pathless West With Soldiers, Pioneers, Miners, and Savages* (London: T. Fisher Unwin, 1904), 173–75.

27. 21 April 1860 entry, Hills, Diary; also 12 August and 24 September 1860, 31 January 1862 entries.

28. "The Dance Houses," *British Colonist,* 20 December 1861. For events in California, see Alfred Hurtado, "When Strangers Meet: Sex and Gender on Three Frontiers," in Elizabeth Jameson and Susan Armitage, ed., *Writing the Range: Race, Class, and Culture in the Women's West* (Norman: University of Oklahoma Press, 1997), 134–7.

29. In *During My Time: Florence Edenshaw Davidson, a Haida Woman* (Vancouver and Seattle: Douglas & McIntyre and University of Washington Press, 1982), 44–45, Margaret Blackman links the decline to the smallpox epidemic of 1862–63, but newspaper coverage suggests that the principal cause was fewer lone men.

30. On the maritime fur trade, see Lorraine Littlefield, "Women Traders in the Maritime Fur Trade," in Bruce Alden Cox, ed., *Native People, Native Lands: Canadian Indians, Inuit and Metis* (Ottawa: Carleton University Press, 1991), 173–85; and on the land-based trade Van Kirk, *"Many Tender Ties."* Devens probes "native women as autonomous, sexual active females" in seventeenth-century New France in *Countering Colonization*, 25 and passim.

31. For a case study, see Jo-Anne Fiske, "Fishing is Women's Business: Changing Economic Roles of Carrier Women and Men," in Cox, cd., *Native People, Native Lands*, 186–98.

32. On the concept of mimicry, sec Homi Bhabha, "Of Mimicry and Man: The Ambivalence of Colonial Discourse," in Cooper and Stoler, ed., *Tensions of Empire*, 152–60.

33. "A Squaw Arrests a White Man," British *Colonist*, 17 January 1862.

34. "Attempted rape," *British Colonist*, 17 August 1860.

35. Thomas Crosby, *Among the An-ko-me-nums, Or Flathead Tribes of Indians of the Pacific Coast* (Toronto: William Briggs, 1907), 62.

36. 1 February 1862 entry, Hills, Diary.

37. Crosby, *Among the An-ko-me-nums*, 63.

38. Emily Carr, *The Heart of a Peacock* (Toronto: Irwin, 1986), 96.

39. Adele Perry admirably tackles this and related topics in "'Oh I'm just sick of the faces of men': Gender Imbalance, Race, Sexuality and Sociability in Nineteenth-Century British Columbia," *BC Studies* 105–06 (Spring/Summer 1995), 27–43.

40. Letter of Morgan Lewis to Rev. D.R. Lewis, New Westminster, 29 October 1862, printed in *Seren Cymru*, 23 January 1863, quoted in Alan Conway, "Welsh Gold Miners in British Columbia During the 1860's," *Cylchgrawn I Iyfrgell Genedlaethol Cymru: The National Library of Wales Journal* 10, 4 (Winter 1958), 383–84.

41. *Cariboo, the Newly Discovered Gold Fields of British Columbia* (Fairfield, WA: Ye Galleon Press, 1975), 7–8, 19–20.

42. See Jean Barman, "What a Difference a Border Makes: Aboriginal Racial Intermixture in the Pacific Northwest," *Journal of the West*, forthcoming.

43. Carl Friesach, *Ein Ausflug nach Britisch-Columbien in Jahre 1858* (Gratz: Philosophical Society, 1875), reprinted in *British Columbia Historical Quarterly* 5 (1941), 227.

44. *The West Shore*, September 1884, 275, cited in Patricia E. Roy, "*The West Shore's* View of British Columbia, 1884," *Journal of the West* 22, 4 (October 1984), 28.

45. For a case study, see Jean Barman, "Lost Okanagan: In Search of the First Settler Families," *Okanagan History* 60 (1996), 8–20.

46. Mary Augusta Tappage, "Changes," in Jeane E. Speare, *The Days of Augusta* (Vancouver: J.J. Douglas, 1973), 71.

47. 27 May 1868 entry, Hills, Diary.

48. Francis E. I Herring, "Pretty Mrs. Weldon" in her *Nan And Other Pioneer Women of the West* (London: Francis Griffiths, 1913), 122, 1 24–25.

49. The base used is the greatly diminished Aboriginal population of about 25–30,000 following the devastating smallpox epidemic of the early 1860s. Another measure is the number of children resulting from the relationships, as indicated in the "Supplementary Report" to British Columbia, Department of Education, *First Annual Report on the Public Schools in the Province of British Columbia*, 1872, 38.

50. David R. Williams, . . . *The Man for a New Country: Sir Matthew Baillie Begbie* (Sidney: Gray's Publishing, 1977), 106–07.

51. The age-linked, equally essentializing counterpart was, of course, an absence of sexuality. Aboriginal woman as drudge is discussed in, among other sources, Elizabeth Vibert, *Traders' Tales: Narratives of Cultural Encounters in the Columbia Plateau, 1807–1846* (Norman: University of Oklahoma Press, 1997), 127–31, 136, and 233–39.

52. In referring to men in power, I do not mean to suggest that non-Aboriginal women were completely absent from the discourse but I do contend that, at least in British Columbia, their voices were muted compared to those of men; for a brief introduction to this literature, see Strobel, *Gender, Sex, and Empire*. Myra Rutherdale, "Revisiting Colonization to Gender: Anglican Missionary Women in the Pacific Northwest and Arctic, 1860–1945," *BC Studies* 104 (Winter 1994–95), 3–23, discusses the priorities of female missionaries but without reference to sexuality.

53. Crosby, *Among the An-ko-me-nums*, 96.

54. See, for example, private memorandum of Gilbert Malcolm Sproat, Indian Reserve Commissioner, Okanagan Lake, 27 October 1877, in DIA, RG 10, vol. 3656, file 90063, C-10115.

55. Remarks enclosed with George Blenkinsop, secretary and census taker to Indian Reserve Commission, to Sproat, Douglas Lake, 20 September 1878, in DIA, RG 10, vol. 3667, file 10,330.

56. Private memorandum of Sproat, 27 October 1877; and Alex C Anderson and Archibald McKinlay, Report of the proceedings of the Joint Commission for the settlement of the Indian Reserves in the Province of British Columbia, Victoria, 21 March 1877, in DIA, RG 10, vol. 3645, file 7936, C-10113.

57. Crosby, *Among the An-ko-me-nums*, esp. 206–32 and passim; and Crosby, *Up and Down*, passim.

58. 24 May 1866 entry, Hills, Diary.

59. Census data included with Anderson and McKinlay, Report, 21 March 1877.

60. Remarks enclosed with Blenkinsop to Sproat, 20 September 1878.

61. Such a contention is not inconsistent with Devens's view that Aboriginal men in the Great Lakes region more easily accommodated to missionaries' aspirations for them than did women; see her *Countering Colonization*.

62. Crosby, *Up and Down*, 270–71.

63. Stocking, *Victorian Anthropolopy*, 202.

64. Leonore Davidoff and Catherine Hall. *Family Fortunes: Men and women of the English middle class, 1780–1850* (London: Hutchinson, 1987), 322, 451.

65. Alex C. Anderson, J.P, to Sir Francis Hincks, MP for Vancouver District, Victoria, 26 August 1873, excerpted in undated memorandum of Anderson in DIA, RG 10, vol. 3658, file 9404, C-10115.

66. Anderson and McKinlay, Report, 21 March 1877.

67. William Laing Meason, Indian Agent of Williams Lake Agency, to I.W. Powell, Superintendent of Indian Affairs, Lillooet, 25 March 1884, in DIA, RG 10, vol. 3658, file 9404, C-10115.

68. This topic is examined in Berkhofer, Jr., *White Man's Indian*, esp. 50–61; Brian W. Dippie, *The Vanishing American: White Attitudes & U.S. Indian Policy* (Lawrence: University Press of Kansas, 1982), *passim*; Robert E. Bieder, "Scientific Attitudes Toward Indian Mixed-Bloods in Early Nineteenth Century America," *Journal of Ethnic Studies* 8 (1980), 17–30; and Robert Miles, *Racism* (London: Routledge, 1989).

69. R.C. Mayne, *Four Years in British Columbia and Vancouver Island* (London: John Murray, 1862), 277.

70. Anderson to John Ash, Provincial Secretary, of British Columbia, 16 April 1873, excerpted in undated memorandum of Anderson, in DIA, RG 10, vol. 3658, file 9404, C-10115

71. The fullest account of the events occurring in 1879 is by a descendent: Mel Rothenburger, *The Wild McLeans* (Victoria: Orca, 1993).

72. The sequence of events at Cache Creek School in 1877 was followed closely in the Victoria press.

73. Drawing on Stoler, Carter suggests that, on the prairies, opposition grew out of fears of mixed-race children becoming heirs; see *Capturing Women*, xvi, 14–15, 191–92.

74. The constructed nature of all Aboriginal petitions is indicated by the alacrity with which missionaries and others warned federal officials about upcoming petitions "purporting to come from the Indians," but which were in fact being organized by an opposing religious group or others not to their liking, as with Alfred Hall, Anglican missionary, to Superintendent of Indian Affairs, Alert Bay, 5 October 1889, in RG 10, vol. 38 16, file 57,045-1, C-10193.

75. Petitions of the Lillooet tribe of Indians and from Lower Fraser Indians, s.d. [summer and late fall 1885], and s.d. [summer 1885] in RG 10, vol. 3842, file 71,799, C-10148. On the Oblates' role see memo from Bishop Louis d'Herbomez, OMI, to the Governor General, s.d. [1887], in same.

76. George N. Burbidge, Deputy Minister of Justice, to L. Vankoughnet, Deputy Superintendent General of Indian Affairs, Ottawa, 3 February 1886, and enclosure, in RG to, vol. 3842, file 71-799, C-10148.

77. W.H. Lomas, Indian Agent of Cowichan Agency, to Powell, Quamichan, 20 May 1886; also draft of Vankoughnet to Powell, 13 February 1886; P McTiernan, Indian Agent at New Westminster, to Powell, New Westminster, 9 April 1886; Meason to Powell, Little Dog Creek, 25 March 1886; J.W. Mackay, Indian Agent of Kamloops-Okanagan Agency, to Powell, Sooyoos [Osoyoos], 2 May 1886; and Powell to Superintendent of Indian Affairs, Victoria, 21 June 1886, in RG 10, vol. 3842, file 71,799, C-10148.

78. Memo from d'Herbomez, [1887]; and Hector Langevin, Minister of Public Works, to John Macdonald, Superintendent of Indian Affairs, Ottawa, 25 April 1887, in RG 10, vol. 3842, file 71,799, C-10148.

79. Petition, New Westminster, 1 September 1890, in RG 10, vol. 3842, file 71,799, C-10148

80. Draft from Department of Indian Affairs to Deputy Minister of Justice, 17 December 1890, in RG 10, vol. 3842, file 71-799, C-10148.

81. Draft of letter from Department of Indian Affairs to A. W. Vowell, Indian Superintendent, Ottawa, 26 December 1890, in RG 10, vol. 3842, file 71,799, C-10148.

82. Meason to Vowell, Lillooet, 4 August 1890, in RG 10, vol. 3816, file 57,045-1, C-10193.

83. For the Cariboo, see Margaret Whitehead, *The Cariboo Mission: A History of the Oblates* (Victoria: Sono Nis, 1981).

84. Mackay to Vowell, Kamloops, 24 May 1892, in RG 10, vol. 3875, file 90,667-2 C-10193.

85. Meason to Vowell, Lillooet, 14 May 189 2, in RG 10, vol. 3875, file 90,667-2, C-10193. The incident, its impetus in Oblate policy, and its aftermath are summarized in Whitehead, *Cariboo Mission*, 96–7. At the behest of Catholic authorities, the Governor General remitted the sentences.

86. Mackay to Vowell, 24 May 1892.

87. R.H. Pidcock, Indian Agent of Kwawkwelth Agency, to Powell, Alert Bay 3 April 1889, in DIA, RG 10, vol. 3816, file 57045, C-10193.

88. Pidcock to Vowell, n.d., in RG 10, vol. 38 16, file 57,045-1, C-10193.

89. Vowell to Deputy Superintendent of Indian Affairs, Victoria, 25 March 1890, in RG 10, vol. 3816, file 57,045-1, C-10193.

90. Memorandum of Superintendent General of Indian Affairs to Privy Council of Canada, Ottawa, 20 February 1890, in DIA, RG 10, vol. 3816, file 57045-1, C-10193.

91. John S.D. Thompson, Minister of Justice, to Governor General in Council, 1890, in RG 10, vol. 3816, file 57,045-1, C-10193.

92. Henry Guillod, Indian Agent of West Coast Agency, to Vowell, Ucluelet, 22 August 1890, in RG 10, vol. 3816, file 57,045-1, C-10193.

93. Lomas to Vowell, Quamichan, 22 November 1890, in RG 10, vol. 3816, file 57,045-1, C-10193.

94. McTiernan to Vowell, New Westminster, 23 June 1890, in RG 10, vol. 3816, file 57,045-1, C-10193.

95. Meason to Vowell, Lillooet, 4 August 1890, in RG 10, vol. 3816, file 57,045-1, C-10193.

96. Mackay to Vowell, Kamloops, 4 July 1890, in RG 10, vol. 3816, file 57,045-1, C-10193.

97. C. Todd, Acting Indian Agent of North West Coast Agency, to Vowell, Metlakatla, 8 October 1890, in RG 10, vol. 3816, file 57,045-1, C-10193.

98. Vowell to Vankoughnet, Victoria, 25 February 1891, in RG 10, vol. 3816, file 57,045-1, C-10193.

99. Petition to Pidcock, Fort Rupert, 8 March 1895, in RG 10, vol. 38 16, file 57,045-1, C-10193.

100. Senator W.J. Macdonald to Minister of the Interior, Ottawa, 6 May 1895, in RG 10, vol. 3816, file 57,045-1, C-10193.

101. Deputy Superintendent General of Indian Affairs to Vowell, Ottawa, 20 May 1895, in RG 10, vol. 3816, file 57,045-1, C-10193.

102. Davidoff and Hall, *Family Fortunes*, 115.

103. Census data included with Anderson and McKinlay, Report, 21 March 1877.

104. Crosby, *Among the An-ko-me-nums*, 49–50. On the related issue of domestic hygiene, see Michael Harkin, "Engendering Discipline: Discourse and Counterdiscourse in the Methodist-Heiltsuk Dialogue," *Ethnohistory* 43, 4 (Fall 1996), 647–48.

105. Crosby, *Up and Down*, 74.

106. For example, Cornelius Bryant, Methodist missionary, to Lomas, Nanaimo, 30 January 1884; G. Donckel, Catholic missionary, to Lomas, Maple Bay, 2 February 1884; Lomas to Powell, Maple Bay, 5 February 1884; and Powell to Superintendent General of Indian Affairs, Victoria, 27 February 1884, in DIA, RG 10, vol. 3628, file 6244-1, C-10110.

107. This point is supported by DIA to Powell, 6 June 1884, in DIA, RG 10, vol. 3628, file 6244-1, C-10110; and stated explicitly in E.K. DeBeck, "The Potlatch and Section 149 of the Indian Act," Ottawa, 11 May 1921, in DIA, RG 10, vol. 3628, file 6244-X, C-10110; and in C.M. Barbeau, "The Potlatch among the B.C. Indians and Section 149 of the Indian Act," 1921, in DIA, RG 10, vol. 3628, file 6244-X C-10111.

108. Confidential memo to C.M.B., 17 February 1921, in Barbeau, "The Potlatch."

109. Douglas Cole and Ira Chaikin, *An Iron Hand Upon the People: The Law Against the Potlatch on the Northwest Coast* (Vancouver and Seattle: Douglas & McIntyre and University of Washington Press, 1990), 75–83; and Douglas Cole, "The History of the Kwakiutl Potlatch," in Aldona Jonaitis, ed., *Chiefly Feasts: The Enduring Kwakiutl Potlatch* (Vancouver and New York: Douglas & McIntyre and American Museum of Natural History, 1991), 150–52, discuss sexual and marriage practices of the Kwakiutl as linked to the potlatch from a perspective which, while very informative and reliable, more or less accepts at face value the critiques of men in power. In *Severing the Ties that Bind: Government Repression of Indigenous Religious Ceremonies on the Prairies* (Winnipeg: University of Manitoba Press, 1994), Katherine Pettipas essentially equates the perspective of males with the entirety of perspectives in reference both to the potlatch (90–6) and to the sundance. With a single exception noted only in passing (62), Joseph Masco does much the same in "'It Is a Strict Law That Bids Us Dance': Cosmologies, Colonialism, Death, and Ritual Authority in the Kwakwa'wakw Potlatch, 1849 to 1922," *Comparative Studies in Society and History* 37, 1 (January 1995), 41–75.

110. *Empire* (Toronto), received 9 February 1893, and letter from Pidcock, 16 March 1893, in Barbeau, "The Potlatch."

111. Crosby, *Up and Down*, 316.
112. G.W. DeBeck, Indian Agent of Kwawkwelth Agency, to Vowell, Alert Bay, 29 December 1902, and E.A. Bird, teacher at Gwayasdurus, to DeBeck, Alert Bay, 23 June 1902, in DIA, RG 10, vol. 6816, file 486-2-5, C-8538. The meaning of "child marriage" is explored in Harkin, "Engendering Discipline," 646–47.
113. Bird to DeBeck, 23 June 1902.
114. Most recently, J.R. Miller, *Shingwauk's Vision: A History of Native Residential Schools* (Toronto: University of Toronto Press, 1996).
115. Letter from Thomas Crosby, *Missionary Outlook* 9 (1989), 100, cited in Bolt, *Thomas Crosby*, 64; and Crosby, *Up and Down*, 85.
116. Crosby, *Among the An-ko-me-nums,* 63.
117. Kate Hendry to sister Maggie, 26 December 1882, Kate Hendry Letterbook, British Columbia Archives, EC/H38.
118. C.J. South, Superintendent, Children's Protection Act, to Secretary, Department of Indian Affairs, Vancouver, 20 September 1905, in RG 10, vol. 3816, file 57,045-1, C-10193.
119. Bolt, *Thomas Crosby*, 64.
120. October 1886 entry in Agnes Knight, Journal, 1885–87, British Columbia Archives, F7/W 15.
121. Crosby, *Up and Down*, 89, 92–3.
122. "Indian girl sold for 1,000 blankets,' *World* (Vancouver), 2 January 1906.
123. "Five Little Girls Sold at Alert Bay Potlatch," *World*, 4 April 1906; and "Five Indian Girls Sold, Vancouver, B.C., April 6," *Journal* (Ottawa), 9 April 1906.
124. Letter of Vowell, 16 April 1906, in Barbeau, "The Potlatch."
125. "Squaw sold for $400.00 at Alert Bay to a grizzled Chief from Queen Charlottes," *Daily News Advertiser* (Vancouver), 6 April 1907.
126. Letter of William Halliday, 9 July 1907, in Barbeau, "The Potlatch."
127. The quotes are from Emily Cummings, Corresponding Secretary, National Council of Women, to Minister of Indian Affairs, Toronto, 19 February 1910, in RG 10, vol. 38 16, file 57,045-1, C-10193, which contains the many letters, often virtually identical in language, from the different associations.
128. DeBeck, "The Potlatch and Section 149."
129. Margaret Whitehead emphasizes this point in "'A Useful Christian Woman': First Nations' Women and Protestant Missionary Work in British Columbia," *Atlantis* 18, 1–2 (1992–93), 142–66.
130. Crosby, *Up and Down*, 92.
131. John Tate (Salaben), Gispaxloats, informant, recorded by William Beynon in 1950, in George F. MacDonald and John J. Cove, ed., *Tsimshian Narratives,* collected by Marius Barbeau and William Beynon. Vol. 2: *Trade and Warfare* (Ottawa: Canadian Museum of Civilization, 1987), 207.
132. A fascinating question beyond the scope of this essay, which grows out of Foucault's work on power, concerns the extent to which some Aboriginal women internalized the assertions being made about them and considered that, yes, they must be prostitutes simply because they had been so informed so many times.
133. This topic is explored in Jean Barman, "Invisible Women: Aboriginal Mothers and Mixed-Race Daughters in Rural Pioneer British Columbia," in R.W. Sandwell, ed., *Negotiating Rural: Essays from British Columbia* (Vancouver: UBC Press, 1998).
134. The 1901 manuscript census indicates persons' "colour" and mixed-race origins, making it possible to determine the character of individual households.
135. Carr, *Heart of a Peacock,* 110–1.
136. C.W. Holliday, *The Valley of Youth* (Caldwell, ID: Caxton, 1948), 155, 226.
137. DeBeck, "The Potlatch and Section 149."
138. 16, 17, and 25 June and 11 and 26 July 1966 entries in Edward Ho agland, *Notes From the Century Before: A Journal from British Columbia* (New York: Ballantine, 1969), 92, 96, 101, 141, 186, 250.

Article Twelve

Reluctant Hosts: Anglo-Canadian Views of Multiculturalism in the Twentieth Century

Howard Palmer

INTRODUCTION

The way in which Anglo-Canadians have reacted to immigration during the twentieth century has not simply been a function of the numbers of immigrants or the state of the nation's economy. The immigration of significant numbers of non-British and non-French people raised fundamental questions about the type of society which would emerge in English-speaking Canada; hence, considerable public debate has always surrounded the issue of immigration in Canada. The questions which have repeatedly been raised include the following: Were the values and institutions of Anglo-Canadian society modelled exclusively on a British mould and should immigrants be compelled to conform to that mould? Or, would a distinctive identity emerge from the biological and cultural mingling of Anglo-Canadians with new immigrant groups? Would cultural pluralism itself give English-speaking Canada a distinctive identity? These three questions reflect the three theories of assimilation which have dominated the twentieth-century debate over immigrant adjustment.

The assimilation theory which achieved early public acceptance was anglo-conformity. This view demanded that immigrants renounce their ancestral culture and traditions in favor of the behaviour and values of Anglo-Canadians. Although predominant prior to World War II, anglo-conformity fell into disrepute and was replaced in the popular mind by the "melting pot" theory of assimilation. This view envisaged a biological merging of settled communities with new immigrant groups and a blending of their cultures into a new Canadian type. Currently, a third theory of assimilation —"cultural pluralism" or "multiculturalism" — is vying for public acceptance. This view postulates the preservation of some aspects of immigrant culture and communal life within the context of Canadian citizenship and political and economic integration into Canadian society.[1]

There has been a recent burgeoning of historical and sociological research on Anglo-Canadian attitudes toward ethnic minorities. Much of this research contradicts the view which has been advanced by some Anglo-Canadian historians[2] and politicians that Anglo-Canadians have always adopted the "mosaic" as opposed to the American "melting pot" approach. Much of this rhetoric has simply been wishful thinking. Perhaps immigrant groups did not "melt" as much in Canada as in the United States, but this is not because Anglo-Canadians were more anxious to encourage the cultural survival of ethnic minorities. There has been a long history of racism and discrimination against ethnic minorities in English-speaking Canada, along with strong pressures for conformity to Anglo-Canadian ways.

Source: Howard Palmer, "Reluctant Hosts: Anglo-Canadian Views of Multiculturalism in the Twentieth Century," adapted from *Multiculturalism as State Policy*, 1976 Canadian Consultative Council of Multiculturalism, Department of Canadian Heritage. Reproduced with the permission of Public Works and Government Services Canada, 2005.

THE "SETTLEMENT" PERIOD AND THE PREDOMINANCE OF ANGLO-CONFORMITY: 1867–1920

Among the several objectives of the architects of the Canadian confederation in 1867, none was more important than the effort to accommodate the needs of the two main cultural communities. There was virtually no recognition of ethnic diversity aside from the British–French duality. This is, of course, somewhat understandable since at the time of Confederation, only 8 percent of the population of 3.5 million were of non-British[3] or non-French ethnic origin. There were, however, significant numbers of people of German and Dutch origin, well-established black and Jewish communities, as well as a few adventurers and entrepreneurs from most European ethnic groups now in Canada.

The proportion of people of other than British, French, or Native origin in Canada remained small until nearly the turn of the twentieth century; the United States proved more attractive for most European emigrants. In fact it was attractive for many Canadians as well, and the Dominion barely maintained its population. But with the closing of the American frontier, which coincided with improving economic conditions in Canada and an active immigration promotion campaign by Wilfrid Laurier's Liberal government, many immigrants began to come to the newly opened land of western Canada in the late 1890s.[4] Immigration policy gave preference to farmers, and most non-British immigrants came to farm in western Canada. However, some immigrants ended up working in mines, laying railway track, or drifting into the urban working class.[5] During this first main wave of immigration between 1896 and 1914, three million immigrants, including large numbers of British labourers, American farmers, and eastern European peasants, came to Canada. Within the period of 1901 to 1911, Canada's population rocketed by 43 percent and the percentage of immigrants in the country as a whole topped 22 percent. In 1911, people of non-British and non-French origin formed 34 percent of the population of Manitoba, 40 percent of the population of Saskatchewan, and 33 percent of the population of Alberta.

Throughout the period of this first large influx of non-British, non-French immigrants (indeed up until World War II), anglo-conformity was the predominant ideology of assimilation in English-speaking Canada.[6] For better or for worse, there were few proponents of either the melting pot or cultural pluralism. Proponents of anglo-conformity argued that it was the obligation of new arrivals to conform to the values and institutions of Canadian society — which were already fixed. During this period when scarcely anyone questioned the verities of God, King, and country, there was virtually no thought given to the possibility that "WASP" values might not be the apex of civilization which all men should strive for.

Since at this time the British Empire was at its height, and the belief in "progress" and Anglo-Saxon and white superiority was taken for granted throughout the English-speaking world, a group's desirability as potential immigrants varied almost directly with its members' physical and cultural distance from London (England), and the degree to which their skin pigmentation conformed to Anglo-Saxon white. Anglo-Canadians regarded British and American immigrants as the most desirable.[7] Next came northern and western Europeans who were regarded as culturally similar and hence assimilable. They were followed by central and eastern Europeans, who in the eyes of Clifford Sifton and immigration agents, had a slight edge on Jews and southern Europeans, because they were more inclined to go to and remain on the land. These groups were followed in the ethnic pecking order by the "strange" religious sects, the Hutterites, Mennonites, and Doukhobors, who were invariably lumped together by public officials and the general public despite significant religious and cultural differences between them. Last, but not least (certainly not least in the eyes of those British Columbians and their sympathizers elsewhere in the country who worried about the "Asiatic" hordes), were the Asian immigrants — the

Chinese, Japanese, and East Indians (the latter of whom were dubbed "Hindoos," despite the fact that most were Sikhs). Running somewhere close to last were black immigrants, who did not really arise as an issue because of the lack of aspiring candidates, except in 1911, when American blacks were turned back at the border by immigration officials because they allegedly could not adapt to the cold winters in Canada — a curious about-face for a department which was reassuring other American immigrants that Canadian winters were relatively mild.[8]

As might be expected, prevailing assumptions about the relative assimilability of these different groups were quickly transformed into public debate over whether immigrants whose assimilability was problematic should be allowed into the country. During this first wave of immigration, considerable opposition developed to the entry of central, southern, and eastern European immigrants, Orientals, and to the three pacifist sects. Opposition to these groups came from a variety of sources, for a variety of reasons. But one of the most pervasive fears of opinion leaders was that central, southern, and eastern Europeans, and Orientals would wash away Anglo-Saxon traditions of self-government in a sea of illiteracy and inexperience with "free institutions."[9] Many English-Canadian intellectuals, like many American writers at the time, thought that North America's greatness was ensured so long as its Anglo-Saxon character was preserved. Writers emphasized an Anglo-Saxon tradition of political freedom and self-government and the "white man's" mission to spread Anglo-Saxon blessings.[10] Many intellectuals and some politicians viewed Orientals and central, southern, and eastern European immigrants as a threat to this tradition and concluded that since they could not be assimilated they would have to be excluded. The introduction in Canada of a head tax on Chinese immigrants, a "gentlemen's agreement" with Japan which restricted the number of Japanese immigrants, the passing of orders-in-council which restricted immigration from India, the gradual introduction of restrictive immigration laws in 1906, 1910, and 1919 relative to European immigration, and the tightening of naturalization laws were based in considerable part on the assumptions of anglo-conformity — immigrants who were culturally or racially inferior and incapable of being assimilated either culturally or biologically would have to be excluded.[11] Those who rose to the immigrants' defence argued almost entirely from economic grounds: immigration from non-British sources was needed to aid in economic development, not because it might add anything to Canada's social or cultural life.

Although the trend toward restrictionism during the early 1900s seemed to indicate a government trend toward anglo-conformity in response to public pressure, for the most part between 1867 and 1945, there was no explicit federal government policy with regard to the role of non-British and non-French ethnic groups in Canadian society. It was generally assumed, however, that immigrants would eventually be assimilated into either English-Canadian or French-Canadian society. A recent careful study of Clifford Sifton's attitudes toward immigrant groups in Canadian society concludes Sifton assumed that central and eastern Europeans "would be 'nationalized' in the long run through their experience on the land."[12] The federal government's concern was tied to the economic consequences of immigration, while schools, the primary agents of assimilation, were under provincial jurisdiction. The federal government had encouraged Mennonites and Icelanders to settle in blocks in Manitoba during the 1870s and had given them special concessions (including local autonomy for both and military exemptions for the Mennonites) to entice them to stay in Canada rather than move to the United States.[13] But this was not because of any conscious desire to make Canada a cultural mosaic, nor was it out of any belief in the value of cultural diversity. Block settlements, by providing social and economic stability, were simply a way of getting immigrants to settle in the west and remain there.[14] The government policy was pragmatic and concerned primarily with economic growth and "nation building"; there was little rhetoric in immigration propaganda picturing Canada as a home for oppressed minorities who would be able to pursue their identities in Canada.

Provincial governments were faced with the problems of assimilation more directly than the federal government since the provinces maintained jurisdiction over the educational systems. The whole question of the varying attitudes of provincial authorities toward assimilation is much too complex to outline in this article; suffice it to say that with some notable exceptions (like the bilingual school system in Manitoba between 1896 and 1916, and the school system which was established for Hutterites in Alberta), anglo-conformity was the predominant aim of the public school system and was an underlying theme in the textbooks.

Anglo-conformity was most pronounced during World War I as nationalism precipitated insistent hostility to "hyphenated Canadianism" and demanded an unswerving loyalty. For many Anglo-Canadians during the war, loyalty and cultural and linguistic uniformity were synonymous. During the war, western provincial governments acted to abolish the bilingual schools which had previously been allowed.[15] The formation of the Union government of Conservatives and Liberals during the First World War was an attempt to create an Anglo-Saxon party, dedicated to "unhyphenated Canadianism" and the winning of the war; even if this meant trampling on the rights of immigrants through press censorship and the imposition of the War Time Elections Act, which disfranchised "enemy aliens" who had become Canadian citizens after March 21, 1902.[16] Various voluntary associations like the YMCA, IODE, National Council of Women, Canadian Girls in Training, Girl Guides, Big Brothers and Big Sisters Organizations, and Frontier College, as well as the major Protestant denominations, also intensified their efforts to "Canadianize" the immigrants, particularly at the close of the war when immigrant support for radical organizations brought on anti-radical nativist fears of the "menace of the alien."[17] The pressures for conformity were certainly real, even if English-Canadians could not always agree completely on the exact nature of the norm to which immigrants were to be assimilated.

All the major books on immigration prior to 1920, including J.S. Woodsworth's *Strangers within Our Gates*, J.T.M. Anderson's *The Education of the New Canadian*, Ralph Connor's *The Foreigner*, Alfred Fitzpatrick's *Handbook for New Canadians*, C.A. Magrath's *Canada's Growth and Some Problems Affecting It*, C.B. Sissons' *Bilingual Schools in Canada*, and W.G. Smith's *A Study in Canadian Immigration*, were based on the assumptions of anglo-conformity. To lump all these books together is of course to oversimplify since they approached the question of immigration with varying degrees of nativism (or anti-foreign sentiment) and humanitarianism. Nor were all of the voluntary organizations' attempted "Canadianization" work among immigrants motivated solely by the fear that immigrants would undermine the cultural homogeneity of English-speaking Canada. Many of these writers and organizations saw their work with the immigrants as a means of fighting social problems and helping immigrants achieve a basic level of political, social, and economic integration into Canadian society. But it cannot be denied that their basic assumption was that of anglo-conformity. Cultural diversity was either positively dangerous, or was something that would and should disappear with time, and with the help of Anglo-Canadians.

Perhaps it should be emphasized that the individuals advocating anglo-conformity were not just the reactionaries of their day. Protestant Social Gospellers (including J.S. Woodsworth, later one of the founders of the CCF), who played such a prominent role in virtually all the reform movements of the pre–World War I period (including women's rights, temperance, and labour, farm, and penal reform), believed that immigrants needed to be assimilated to Anglo-Canadian Protestant values as part of the effort to establish a truly Christian society in English-speaking Canada.[18] Women's groups pushing for the franchise argued that certainly they deserved the vote if "ignorant foreigners" had it, and joined in the campaign to Canadianize the immigrants who "must be educated to high standards or our whole national life will be lowered by their presence among us."[19]

But there was a central contradiction in Anglo-Canadian attitudes toward ethnic minorities. Non–Anglo-Saxon immigrants were needed to open the west and to do the heavy jobs of industry. This meant not only the introduction of culturally distinctive groups, but groups which would occupy the lower rungs of the socioeconomic system. The pre-1920 period was the period of the formation of, and the most acute expression of, what was later called the "vertical mosaic." Anglo-Canadians were not used to the idea of cultural diversity, nor the degree of class stratification which developed during this period of rapid settlement and industrialization. The answer to all the problems of social diversity which the immigrants posed was assimilation. The difficulty, however, with achieving this goal of assimilation was not only the large numbers of immigrants, or the fact that not all (or even a majority) of them wanted to be assimilated. One of the major factors preventing assimilation was discrimination by the Anglo-Canadian majority.

The basic contradiction, then, of Anglo-Canadian attitudes as expressed through the "Canadianization" drives was the tension between the twin motives of humanitarianism and nativism — between the desire to include non-British immigrants within a community and eliminate cultural differences and the desire to stay as far away from them as possible because of their presumed "undesirability." This contradiction was graphically revealed at the national conference of the IODE in 1919. The women passed one resolution advocating a "Canadianization campaign" to "propagate British ideals and institutions," to "banish old world points of view, old world prejudices, old world rivalries and suspicion" and to make new Canadians "100 percent British in language, thought, feeling, and impulse." Yet they also passed another resolution protesting "foreigners" taking British names.[20]

It does not appear that this was simply a case of the Anglo-Canadian majority being divided between those who wanted to pursue a strategy of assimilation and those who wanted to pursue a strategy of subordination and segregation. Certainly there was some division along these lines, but as suggested by the IODE resolutions, discrimination and anglo-conformity were often simply two different sides of the same coin — the coin being the assumption of the inferiority of non–Anglo-Saxons.

What developed throughout English-speaking Canada during this period was a vicious circle of discrimination. Non–Anglo-Saxons were discriminated against because they were not assimilated, either culturally or socially, but one of the reasons they were not assimilated was because of discrimination against them. As one researcher noted in a 1917 report on "Social Conditions in Rural Communities in the Prairie Provinces," the group "clannishness" of immigrants which was so widely deplored by the public was caused as much by the prejudice of the "English" as it was by the groups' desire to remain different.[21]

There is no need to catalogue here the extensive patterns of social, economic, and political discrimination which developed against non–Anglo-Saxons.[22] Patterns of discrimination paralleled preferences of immigrant sources, with northern and western Europeans encountering relatively little discrimination, central and southern Europeans and Jews encountering more discrimination, and non-whites encountering an all-pervasive pattern of discrimination which extended to almost all aspects of their lives. Discrimination was one of the main factors which led to the transference (with only a few exceptions) of the same ethnic "pecking order" which existed in immigration policy to the place each group occupied in the "vertical mosaic," with the British (especially the Scots) on top, and so on down to the Chinese and blacks who occupied the most menial jobs.[23] Non-British and non-French groups not only had very little economic power; they also would not even significantly occupy the middle echelons of politics, education, or the civil service until after World War II.

The ethnic stereotypes which developed for eastern European and Oriental groups emphasized their peasant origins. These stereotypes played a role in determining the job opportunities for new immigrants and functioned to disparage those who would climb out of their place.

Opprobrious names such as "Wops," "Bohunks," and especially "foreigner" indicated class as well as ethnic origin and these terms were used as weapons in the struggle for status. The very word "ethnic" carried, for many people, such an aura of opprobrium that even recently there have been attempts to expurgate the use of the word. Ethnic food and folklore were regarded by most Anglo-Canadians as not only "foreign," but "backward" and lower class. Folklorist Carole Henderson has aptly described the views of Anglo-Canadians toward folklore (views which continue to the present day): "Except for members of some delimited regional, and usually ethnic, subcultures such as Newfoundlanders or Nova Scotian Scots, most Anglo-Canadians simply fail to identify folklore with themselves, and tend to consider such materials to be the . . . unimportant possessions of the strange, foreign, or 'backward people in their midst.'"[24]

THE 1920s AND THE EMERGENCE OF "MELTING POT" IDEAS

The 1920s brought the second main wave of non-British and non-French immigrants to Canada and saw the emergence of the second ideology of assimilation, the "melting pot." During the early 1920s both Canada and the United States had acted to further restrict immigration from southern, central, and eastern Europe and from the Orient. Chinese were virtually excluded from Canada, and central, southern, and eastern Europeans were classified among the "non-preferred" and restricted category of immigrants. But by the mid-1920s several powerful sectors of Canadian society, including transportation companies, boards of trade, newspapers, and politicians of various political persuasions, as well as ethnic groups, applied pressure on the King government to open the immigration doors.[25] These groups believed that only a limited immigration could be expected from the "preferred" countries and that probably only central and eastern Europeans would do the rugged work of clearing marginal land. The railways continued to seek immigrants to guarantee revenue for their steamship lines, traffic for their railways, and settlers for their land. With improving economic conditions in the mid-twenties, the federal government responded to this pressure and changed its policy with respect to immigrants from central and eastern Europe.

While continuing to emphasize its efforts to secure British immigrants, in September 1925 the Liberal government of Mackenzie King entered into the "Railways Agreement" with the CPR and CNR, which brought an increased number of central and eastern Europeans. The government authorized the railways to encourage potential immigrants of the "non-preferred" countries to emigrate to Canada and to settle as "agriculturalists, agricultural workers, and domestic servants."[26]

Through this agreement, the railways brought to Canada 165 000 central and eastern Europeans and 20 000 Mennonites. They represented a variety of ethnic groups and a diversity of reasons for emigrating. Most of the Ukrainian immigrants were political refugees. Poles, Slovaks, and Hungarians were escaping poor economic conditions. German-Russians and Mennonites were fleeing civil war, economic disaster, and the spectre of cultural annihilation in Russia.[27] Often they chose Canada since they could no longer get into the United States because of its quota system and the Canadian route was the only way they could get to North America. With this new wave of immigration, the proportion of the Canadian population that was not of British, French, or native origin rose to more than 18 percent by 1931.

In responding to this new wave of immigration, many opinion leaders held to an earlier belief that Canada should be patterned exclusively on the British model, and continued to advocate anglo-conformity. In national periodicals and newspapers during the 1920s, the emphasis which was placed on the need to attract British immigrants was related to this assumption that anglo-conformity was essential to the successful development of Canadian society. "Foreign" immigrants had to be assimilated and there needed to be enough Britishers to maintain "Anglo-Saxon" traditions.[28] R.B. Bennett, later to become the Conservative prime minister during the early 1930s, attacked melting pot ideas in the House of Commons and argued "These people [continental Europeans] have made excellent settlers: . . . but it cannot be that we must draw upon them to shape our civilization. We must still maintain that measure of British civilization which will enable us to assimilate these people to British institutions, rather than assimilate our civilization to theirs."[29]

The influx of new immigrants from central and eastern Europe during the mid- and late twenties also aroused protests from a number of nativist organizations, such as the Ku Klux Klan, The Native Sons of Canada, and The Orange Order, who were convinced that Canada should "remain Anglo-Saxon."[30] Nativist sentiment in western Canada was most pronounced in Saskatchewan, where one of its leading spokesmen was George Exton Lloyd, an Anglican bishop and one of the founders of the Barr colony at Lloydminster.

In a torrent of newspaper articles and speeches, Lloyd repeated the warning that Canada was in danger of becoming a "mongrel" nation: "The essential question before Canadians today is this: Shall Canada develop as a British nation within the empire, or will she drift apart by the introduction of so much alien blood that her British instincts will be paralyzed?"[31] According to Lloyd, Canada had but two alternatives: it could either be a homogeneous nation or a heterogeneous one. The heterogeneous or "melting pot" idea had not worked in the United States (as evidenced by large numbers of unassimilated immigrants at the outbreak of World War I), and could not, he argued, work in Canada. With Lloyd, as with other individuals and organizations promoting anglo-conformity at this time, one gets the distinctive feeling that they were on the defensive. Like other English-speaking Canadians who had a strong attachment to Britain and the Empire, Lloyd saw a threat to Canada's "British" identity, not only in the increasing numbers of "continental" immigrants, but also in the declining status of things British as Canadians moved toward a North-American–based nationalism which did not include loyalty to the British Empire as its primary article of faith.[32]

During the late 1920s, a new view of assimilation, the melting pot, developed greater prominence. This view of assimilation, which arose partly as a means of defending immigrants against nativist attacks from people like Lloyd, envisioned a biological merging of Anglo-Canadians with immigrants and a blending of their cultures into a new Canadian type. Whereas Lloyd and other nativists argued that since immigrants could not conform to Anglo-Canadian ideals they should be excluded, a new generation of writers argued that assimilation was indeed occurring, but to a new Canadian type.[33] Since assimilation was occurring, nativist fears were unwarranted. Indeed, immigrants would make some valuable cultural contributions to Canada during the process of assimilation. Although these writers did not all use the "melting pot" symbol when discussing their view of assimilation, one can lump their ideas together under the rubric of the "melting pot" because they did envisage the emergence of a new society which would contain "contributions" from the various immigrant groups.

Most of these writers who defended "continental" European immigration did not seriously question the desirability of assimilation. Robert England, a writer and educator who worked for the CNR, had read widely enough in anthropological sources to be influenced by the cultural relativism of Franz Boas and other anthropologists and did in his writing question the desirability of assimilation.[34] But most of these writers were concerned primarily with attempting to promote tolerance toward ethnic minorities by encouraging their assimilation, and many became involved in programs to facilitate this assimilation.

Advocates of anglo-conformity and the melting pot both believed that uniformity was ultimately necessary for unity, but they differed on what should provide the basis of that uniformity. Advocates of the melting pot, unlike the promoters of anglo-conformity, saw assimilation as a relatively slow process, and saw some cultural advantages in the mixing that would occur.

There was not, however, always a clear distinction between anglo-conformity and the melting pot. Rhetoric indicating that immigrants might have something more to offer Canada than their physical labour was sometimes only a thinly veiled version of anglo-conformity; the melting pot often turned out to be an Anglo-Saxon melting pot. For example, John Blue, a prominent Edmonton promoter and historian, wrote in his history of Alberta in 1924 that the fears about foreign immigration destroying Canadian laws and institutions had proved groundless. "There is enough Anglo-Saxon blood in Alberta to dilute the foreign blood and complete the process of assimilation to the mutual advantage of both elements."[35]

There were a variety of reasons for the development of melting pot ideas during the 1920s.[36] The growth during the 1920s of an autonomous Canadian nationalism helped the spread of melting pot ideas. Some English-Canadian opinion leaders began to discuss the need for conformity to an exclusively Canadian norm rather than a "British" norm. One of the arguments that John W. Dafoe, the influential editor of the *Winnipeg Free Press*, and J.S. Ewart, a constitutional lawyer, used in support of their view of Canadian nationalism was that non-British immigrants could not be expected to feel loyalty to the British Empire.[37]

Melting pot advocates tended to be people who had some personal experience with immigrants, and recognized both the intense pride that immigrants had in their cultural backgrounds as well as the rich cultural sources of those traditions. But they also lived in a time when recognition of ethnicity meant mostly Anglo-Canadian use of ethnicity as a basis of discrimination or exploitation. It was also a time when some ethnic groups were still close enough to their rural peasant roots that ethnic solidarity was often not conducive to upward mobility. The view of most melting pot advocates that the disappearance of ethnicity as a basis of social organization would increase the mobility opportunities of the second generation was based on a sound grasp of the realities of the day. The lifelong campaign of John Diefenbaker for "unhyphenated Canadianism" and "one Canada" grew out of this experience with ethnicity as something that could be used to hinder opportunities, and was consistent with his emphasis on human rights, rather than group rights.[38]

THE 1930s

Although immigration was severely cut back during the depression of the 1930s, the role of ethnic minorities in English-speaking Canada continued to be a major public concern. Paradoxically, although the depression witnessed the high point of discrimination against non–Anglo-Saxons, it was also during the 1930s that the first major advocates of cultural pluralism in English-speaking Canada began to be heard.

The depression affected non–Anglo-Saxon immigrants more than most other groups in the society. These immigrants, because of their language problems and lack of specialized skills, were concentrated in the most insecure and therefore most vulnerable segments of the economy. Since immigrants were the last hired and the first fired, a large proportion were forced onto relief. Government officials were gravely concerned about the way immigrants seemed to complicate the relief problem. Calls by some officials for deportation as the solution to the relief problem were heeded by the federal government; sections 40 and 41 of the Immigration Act (still essentially the same act as the one which existed in 1919) provided for deportation of non-Canadian citizens on relief, and government officials took advantage of the law to reduce their relief rolls.

While there was some continuing concern over the assimilation of non-British and non-French immigrants during the 1930s, most Anglo-Canadians were more concerned about protecting their jobs.[39]

Prior to the depression, most Anglo-Saxons were content to have the "foreigners" do all the heavy work of construction, and the dirty work of the janitors and street sweepers. But as the economy slowed down, these jobs became attractive. Whereas the pre-depression attitude was "let the foreigners do the dirty work," the depression attitude became "how come these foreigners have all of our jobs?" The 1930s also saw the high point of anti-Semitism in English-speaking Canada as the patterns of discrimination which had hindered the desires of second generation Jews for entry into the professions were extended into a vicious and virulent anti-Semitism by fascist groups.[40]

Barry Broadfoot's book *Ten Lost Years* also makes it very clear that discrimination and prejudice flourished during the depression. In the transcripts of his interviews with the "survivors" of the depression, one is struck by the all-pervasiveness of derogatory ethnic epithets in interviewees' recollections of their contact with immigrants. One does not read of Italians, Chinese, or Poles. One reads of "Dagos," "Wops," "Chinks," "Polacks," "Hunyaks."[41] One "survivor" of the depression, waxing philosophical, gives explicit expression to the prevailing attitudes of the time. He compares how the depression affected people from R.B. Bennett down to "the lowest of the low," "some bohunk smelling of garlic and not knowing a word of English."[42] Another "survivor" recalls that her boy had great difficulty finding work during the depression, and went berserk because of the blow to his self-esteem when the only job he could find was "working with a bunch of Chinks."[43]

The vicious circle of discrimination became perhaps even more vicious during the 1930s as non–Anglo-Saxons' political response to the depression further poisoned attitudes toward them. The discrimination and unemployment which non–Anglo-Saxons faced was an important factor in promoting the support of many for radical political solutions to the depression, in either communist or fascist movements. Indeed the vast majority of the support for the communists throughout Canada, and for the fascists in western Canada, came from non–Anglo-Saxons.[44] Ethnic support for these two movements, and the conflict between left and right within most central and eastern European groups and the Finns was seen as further evidence of the undesirability of non–Anglo-Saxons. The existence of fascist and communist movements in Canada was not of course due simply to the presence of immigrants bringing "old world" ideas. The leaders in both movements were predominantly of British origin,[45] and their "ethnic" support came more from immigrants reacting to depression conditions than from immigrants bringing to Canada "old world" ideas. But the depression gave further support to the notion of non–Anglo-Saxons being unstable politically; one more proof along with immigrant drinking, garlic eating, and the legendary violence at Slavic weddings, that non–Anglo-Saxons were in dire need of baptism by assimilation. Deporting immigrant radicals was seen as one alternative to assimilation and the federal government did not hesitate to use this weapon.[46]

The relationship in the public mind between ethnicity, lower social class origins, and political "unsoundness" explains why during the late 1920s so many second generation non–Anglo-Saxons who were anxious to improve their lot economically made deliberate attempts to hide their ethnic background, such as changing their names. Ethnic ties were clearly disadvantageous for those non–Anglo-Saxons seeking economic security or social acceptance. The experience of the second generation in English-speaking Canada was similar to the second-generation experience as described by a historian writing about ethnic groups in the United States. "Culturally estranged from their parents by their American education, and wanting nothing so much as to become and to be accepted as Americans, many second generation immigrants made deliberate efforts to rid themselves of their heritage. The adoption of American clothes, speech, and interests, often accompanied by the shedding of an exotic surname, were all part of a process whereby antecedents were repudiated as a means of improving status."[47]

Despite the continuing dominance of the old stereotypes concerning non–Anglo-Saxons and the continuing dominance of assimilationist assumptions, the 1930s also saw the emergence of the first full-blown pluralist ideas in somewhat ambiguous form in John Murray Gibbon's book, *The Canadian Mosaic,* and in the writings of Watson Kirkconnell, then an English professor at the University of Manitoba. These writers were much more familiar than earlier writers with the historical backgrounds of the ethnic groups coming to Canada, and they were influenced by a liberalism which rejected the assumptions of Anglo-Saxon superiority. Gibbon, a publicity agent for the Canadian Pacific Railway, wrote his book as an expansion of a series of CBC radio talks on the different ethnic groups of Canada. He traced the history of each group and related their "contributions" to Canadian society. Although he was concerned with the preservation of folk arts and music, he also went out of his way to alleviate fears of unassimilability by discussing individuals' assimilation as well as the "cement" of common institutions which bound the Canadian mosaic together. Although Gibbon was not the first writer to use the mosaic symbol, he was the first to attempt to explore its meaning in any significant way.

Kirkconnell was an essayist, poet, and prolific translator of European verse from a number of European languages. His writing on ethnic groups was based on a different approach than Gibbon's. He tried to promote tolerance toward "European Canadians" by sympathetically portraying the cultural background of the countries where the immigrants originated and by demonstrating the cultural creativity of European immigrants in Canada through translating and publishing their creative writing.[48] In his writing he attacked the assumptions of anglo-conformity, and advocated a multicultural society which would allow immigrants to maintain pride in their past:

> It would be tragic if there should be a clumsy stripping-away of all those spiritual associations with the past that help to give depth and beauty to life. . . . If . . . we accept with Wilhelm von Humboldt "the absolute and essential importance of human development in its richest diversity," then we shall welcome every opportunity to save for our country every previous element of individuality that is available.[49]

Kirkconnell was not advocating complete separation of ethnic groups so that they might be preserved. He believed that assimilation needed to occur in the realm of political and economic values and institutions but he hoped that some of the conservative values and folk culture of immigrants could be preserved.

Kirkconnell did not ignore the political differences within ethnic groups. Indeed, with the outbreak of World War II he wrote a book in which he attempted to expose and combat both fascist and communist elements in different ethnic groups.[50] But he was also active in attempts to bring various other factions of eastern European groups together in order to alleviate public criticism of divisions within ethnic groups.[51]

These advocates of pluralism believed that ethnic diversity was not incompatible with national unity. Unity need not mean uniformity. They believed that recognition of the cultural contributions of non–Anglo-Saxon groups would heighten the groups' feeling that they belonged to Canada and thus strengthen Canadian unity. But Gibbon and Kirkconnell were voices crying in the wilderness — a wilderness of discrimination and racism.

AFTER WORLD WAR II: THE EMERGENCE OF MULTICULTURALISM

The war period and early postwar period was a transitional time with respect to attitudes toward immigration and ethnicity. Although the war brought renewed hostility toward enemy aliens, a number of developments during the war eventually worked to undermine ethnic prejudice.

During the arrival of the third wave of immigration in the late 1940s and 1950s, many pre-war prejudices lingered, and ethnic minorities encountered considerable pressures for conformity. But for a variety of intellectual, social, and demographic reasons, the ideology of cultural pluralism has been increasingly accepted in the post–World War II period. The postwar decline of racism and the growing influence of theories about cultural relativism opened the way for the emergence of pluralist ideas. The arrival of many intellectuals among the postwar political refugees from eastern Europe and the growth in the number of upwardly mobile second- and third-generation non–Anglo-Canadians, some of whom felt that they were not being fully accepted into Canadian society, increased the political pressures at both federal and provincial levels for greater recognition of Canada's ethnic diversity. Some suggested that this could be achieved through the appointment of senators of a particular ethnic origin, or through the introduction into the school curriculum of ethnic content and of ethnic languages as courses (and sometimes as languages of instruction).[52]

These demands for greater government recognition of "other ethnic groups" increased during the 1960s in response to the French-Canadian assertion of equal rights and the Pearson government's measures to assess and ensure the status of the French language and culture. In 1963 the Royal Commission on Bilingualism and Biculturalism was appointed to "inquire into and report upon the existing state of bilingualism and biculturalism in Canada and to recommend what steps should be taken to develop the Canadian Confederation on the basis of an equal partnership between the two founding races, taking into account the contribution made by the other ethnic groups to the cultural enrichment of Canada." Many non-British, non-French groups, but particularly Ukrainians, opposed the view that Canada was bicultural. By 1961, 26 percent of the Canadian population was of other than British or French ethnic origin; over two hundred newspapers were being published in languages other than French and English; there were fairly well-defined Italian, Jewish, Slavic, and Chinese neighbourhoods in large Canadian cities, and there were visible rural concentrations of Ukrainians, Doukhobors, Hutterites, and Mennonites scattered across the western provinces: thus, how was it possible for a royal commission to speak of Canada as a *bi*cultural country?

This feeling that biculturalism relegated all ethnic groups who were other than British or French to the status of second-class citizens helps explain the resistance some of these groups expressed to the policies and programs that were introduced to secure the status of the French language in Canada. The place of the so-called "other" ethnic groups in a bicultural society became a vexing question for federal politicians, who had originally hoped that steps to ensure French-Canadian rights would go a long way toward improving inter-ethnic relations in Canada. The partial resolution of this dilemma was the assertion in October 1971 by Prime Minister Trudeau that, in fact, Canada is a *multi*cultural country and that steps would be taken by the federal government to give public recognition to ethnic diversity through the introduction of a policy of multiculturalism. Several provinces with large numbers of non–Anglo-Canadians have also initiated their own policies of multiculturalism.

Although most political leaders in English-speaking Canada have accepted and proclaimed the desirability of Canada's ethnic diversity, the Canadian public has not given unanimous support to pluralism. The debate over the place of ethnic groups in Canadian life continues, focusing on such questions as: Does the encouragement of pluralism only serve to perpetuate the vertical mosaic, in which class lines coincide with ethnic lines, or does it help break down class barriers by promoting acceptance of the legitimacy of cultural differences? Are the goals of current government policy — cultural pluralism and equality of opportunity — mutually compatible? Does the encouragement of ethnic group solidarity threaten the freedom of individuals in these groups, or can ethnic groups provide a liberating, rather than a restricting, context for identity? Does the encouragement of cultural diversity serve to perpetuate old-world rivalries, or will the recognition of the contributions of Canada's ethnic groups heighten their feeling that they belong in Canada and thus strengthen Canadian unity? Is government talk of multiculturalism just a way to attract the "ethnic vote," or is positive action necessary to preserve cultural pluralism when cultural diversity throughout the world is being eroded by the impact of industrial technology, mass communication, and urbanization? Does the encouragement of multiculturalism simply heighten the visibility of the growing numbers of non-whites in the country and hinder their chances of full acceptance as individuals into Canadian life, or is a public policy of multiculturalism essential to an effective campaign against racism? The nature of these arguments suggests that the prevailing assumptions about immigration and ethnicity have changed over time in English-speaking Canada. They also suggest that the discussion about the role of immigration and ethnic groups in Canadian life is still an important, and unfinished, debate.

NOTES

1. For a discussion of these three ideologies of assimilation in the United States, see Milton Gordon, *Assimilation in American Life* (New York, 1964).
2. L.G. Thomas, "The Umbrella and the Mosaic: The French–English Presence and the Settlement of the Canadian Prairie West," in J.A. Carroll, ed., *Reflections of Western Historians* (Tucson, Arizona, 1969), 135–52; Allan Smith, "Metaphor and Nationality in North America," *Canadian Historical Review* 51, 3 (September 1970).
3. The Canadian census has consistently classed the Irish as part of the "British" group.
4. Howard Palmer, *Land of the Second Chance: A History of Ethnic Groups in Southern Alberta* (Lethbridge, 1972); Norman Macdonald, *Canada Immigration and Colonization, 1841–1903* (Toronto, 1967); Harold Troper, *Only Farmers Need Apply* (Toronto, 1972).
5. Donald Avery, "Canadian Immigration Policy and the Foreign Navy," Canadian Historical Association, *Report* (1972); Edmund Bradwin, *Bunkhouse Man* (New York, 1928); H. Troper and R. Harney, *Immigrants* (Toronto, 1975).
6. Donald Avery, "Canadian Immigration Policy, 1896–1919: The Anglo-Canadian Perspective" (unpublished Ph.D. thesis, University of Western Ontario, 1973); Cornelius Jaenen, "Federal Policy Vis-à-Vis Ethnic Groups" (unpublished paper, Ottawa, 1971); Howard Palmer, "Nativism and Ethnic Tolerance in Alberta, 1880–1920" (unpublished M.A. thesis, University of Alberta, 1971); Palmer, "Nativism and Ethnic Tolerance in Alberta, 1920–1972" (unpublished Ph.D. thesis, York University, 1973).
7. H. Palmer, "Nativism and Ethnic Tolerance in Alberta, 1880–1920" (unpublished M.A. thesis, University of Alberta, 1971), ch. 1 and 2; H. Troper, *Only Farmers Need Apply* (Toronto, 1972); D.J. Hall, "Clifford Sifton: Immigration and Settlement Policy, 1896–1905," in H. Palmer, ed., *The Settlement of the West* (Calgary, 1977), 60–85.
8. H. Troper, "The Creek Negroes of Oklahoma and Canadian Immigration, 1909–11," *Canadian Historical Review* (September 1972), 272–88.
9. Rev. George Bruce, "Past and Future of Our Race," *Proceedings*, Canadian Club of Toronto, 1911, pp. 6–7; C.A. Magrath, *Canada's Growth and Problems Affecting It* (Ottawa, 1910); Goldwin Smith in *Weekly Sun*, Feb. 1, 1899, Sept. 17, 1902, Sept. 23, 1903, May 18, 1904, Aug. 16, 1905; W.A. Griesbach, *I Remember* (Toronto, 1946), 214–17, 220–21.
10. Carl Berger, *Sense of Power* (Toronto, 1970), 117–88.
11. Morton, *In a Sea of Sterile Mountains* (Vancouver, 1974); W.P. Ward, "The Oriental Immigrant and Canada's Protestant Clergy, 1858–1925," *B.C. Studies* (Summer 1974), 40–55; Ted Ferguson, *A White Man's Country* (Toronto, 1975).
12. D.J. Hall, "Clifford Sifton: Immigration and Settlement Policy: 1896–1905," in H. Palmer, ed., *The Settlement of the West* (Calgary, 1977), 79–80.
13. W.L. Morton, *Manitoba: A History* (Toronto, 1957), 161, 162.
14. J.B. Hedges, *Building the Canadian West* (New York, 1939); Frank Epp, *Mennonites in Canada, 1786–1920* (Toronto, 1974).
15. Cornelius J. Jaenen, "Ruthenian Schools in Western Canada, 1897–1919," *Paedagogica Historica: International Journal of the History of Education* 10, 3 (1970): 517–41. Donald Avery, "Canadian Immigration Policy," 374–420.

16. Avery, "Canadian Immigration Policy," 408.

17. Kate Foster, *Our Canadian Mosaic* (Toronto, 1926); J.T.M. Anderson, *The Education of the New Canadian* (Toronto, 1918); C.B. Sissons, *Bi-Lingual Schools in Canada* (Toronto, 1917); W.G. Smith, *Building the Nation* (Toronto, 1922). For a discussion of some of the concrete activities involved in these "Canadianization" programs, see R. Harney and H. Troper, *Immigrants*, ch. 4.

18. J.S. Woodsworth, *Strangers within Our Gates* (Winnipeg, 1909); Marilyn Barber, "Nationalism, Nativism and the Social Gospel: The Protestant Church Response to Foreign Immigrants in Western Canada, 1897–1914," in Richard Allen, ed., *The Social Gospel in Canada* (Ottawa, 1975), 186–226.

19. Quoted in Barbara Nicholson, "Feminism in the Prairie Provinces to 1916" (unpublished M.A. thesis, University of Calgary, 1974), 71. For the views of womens' groups on immigration and the role of immigrants in Canadian society, see pp. 83–85, 86, 114, 121, 133, 165–69, 186–87.

20. Reported in *Lethbridge Herald*, May 29, 1919.

21. J.S. Woodsworth, "Social Conditions in Rural Communities in the Prairie Provinces" (Winnipeg, 1917), 38.

22. For a fairly extensive chronicling of patterns of discrimination against a number of minority groups, see Morris Davis and J.F. Krauter, *The Other Canadians* (Toronto, 1971).

23. For an analysis of the various causes of ethnic stratification (settlement patterns, time of arrival, immigrant and ethnic occupations, ethnic values, language barriers, and discrimination and exploitation) see Book 4, *Report of the Royal Commission on Bilingualism and Biculturalism* (Ottawa, 1969), ch. 2.

24. Carole Henderson, "The Ethnicity Factor in Anglo-Canadian Folkloristics," *Canadian Ethnic Studies* 7, 2 (1975), 7–18.

25. *Canadian Annual Review* (1923), 264–65; (1924–25), 190–92.

26. *Canada Year Book* (1941), 733.

27. Olha Woycenko, *The Ukrainians in Canada* (Winnipeg, 1967); Victor Turek, *Poles in Manitoba* (Toronto, 1967), 43; J.M. Kirschbaum, *Slovaks in Canada* (Toronto, 1967), 101; Edmund Heier, "A Study of German Lutheran and Catholic Immigrants in Canada formerly residing in Czarist and Soviet Russia" (unpublished M.A. thesis, University of British Columbia, 1955), ch. 3.

28. R.B. Bennett, House of Commons *Debates*, June 7, 1929, pp. 3925–27.

29. Bennett, House of Commons *Debates*, 3925–27.

30. H. Palmer, "Nativism in Alberta, 1925–1930," Canadian Historical Association, *Report* (1974), 191–99.

31. G.E. Lloyd, "National Building," *Banff Crag and Canyon*, Aug. 17, 1928.

32. A.R.M. Lower, *Canadians in the Making* (Don Mills, Ontario, 1958), ch. 22, 27.

33. J.S. Woodsworth, "Nation Building," *University Magazine* (1917), 85–99. F.W. Baumgartner, "Central European Immigration," *Queen's Quarterly* (Winter 1930), 183–92; Walter Murray, "Continental Europeans in Western Canada," *Queen's Quarterly* (1931); P.M. Bryce, *The Value of the Continental Immigrant to Canada* (Ottawa, 1928); E.L. Chicanot, "Homesteading the Citizen: Canadian Festivals Promote Cultural Exchange," *Commonwealth* (May 1929), 94–95; E.K. Chicanot, "Moulding a Nation," *Dalhousie Review* (July 1929), 232–37. J.H. Haslam, "Canadianization of the Immigrant Settler," *Annals* (May 1923), 45–49; E.H. Oliver, "The Settlement of Saskatchewan to 1914," *Transactions of the Royal Society* (1926), 63–87; Agnes Laut, "Comparing the Canadian and American Melting Pots," *Current Opinion* 70 (April 1921), 458–62; Kate Foster, *Our Canadian Mosaic* (Toronto, 1926). Robert England, "Continental Europeans in Western Canada," *Queen's Quarterly* (1931).

34. Robert England, *The Central European Immigrant in Canada* (Toronto, 1929).

35. John Blue, *Alberta Past and Present* (Chicago, 1924), 210.

36. There were some advocates of the melting pot prior to 1920, but it did not gain widespread acceptance until the 1920s. See H. Palmer, "Nativism in Alberta, 1880–1920," ch. 1; Marilyn Barber, "Nationalism, Nativism, and the Social Gospel."

37. Douglas Cole, "John S. Ewart and Canadian Nationalism," Canadian Historical Association, *Report* (1969), 66.

38. John Diefenbaker, *One Canada* (Toronto, 1975), 140, 141, 218–19, 274.

39. H. Palmer, "Nativism in Alberta, 1920–1972," ch. 3.

40. James Gray, *The Roar of the Twenties* (Toronto, 1975), ch. 11; Lita-Rose Betcherman, *The Swastika and the Maple Leaf* (Don Mills, Ontario, 1975).

41. Barry Broadfoot, *Ten Lost Years*, 25, 70, 76, 132, 156–64, 186, 279.

42. Broadfoot, *Ten Lost Years*, 132.

43. Broadfoot, *Ten Lost Years*, 186.

44. Ivan Avakumovic, *The Communist Party in Canada: A History* (Toronto, 1975), 66–67; Lita-Rose Betcherman, *The Swastika and the Maple Leaf*, ch. 5.

45. See note 44 above.

46. H. Palmer, "Nativism in Alberta, 1920–1972," ch. 3.

47. M.A. Jones, *American Immigration* (Chicago, 1960), 298. For fictional treatments of the second generation's repudiation of the ethnic past in an attempt to become accepted, see John Marlyn, *Under the Ribs of Death* (Toronto, 1971) and Magdalena Eggleston, *Mountain Shadows* (New York, 1955), 122. See also *Change of Name* (Toronto: Canadian Institute of Cultural Research, 1965).

48. Watson Kirkconnell, *The European Heritage: A Synopsis of European Cultural Achievement* (London, 1930) and *Canadian Overtones* (Winnipeg, 1935). For a complete listing of Kirkconnell's work, see the list in his memoirs, *A Slice of Canada* (Toronto, 1967), 374–75. For an assessment of his work, see J.R.C. Perkin, ed., *The Undoing of Babel* (Toronto, 1975).

49. W. Kirkconnell, trans., *Canadian Overtones*, preface.

50. Watson Kirkconnell, *Canada, Europe, and Hitler* (Toronto, 1939).

51. W. Kirkconnell, *A Slice of Canada.*

52. For documentary evidence of changing ethnic attitudes in the post-war era and the emergence of multiculturalism as an idea and as a governmental policy, see H. Palmer, *Immigration and the Rise of Multiculturalism* (Toronto, 1975), ch. 3.

Article Thirteen

Race and Recruitment in World War I: Enlistment of Visible Minorities in the Canadian Expeditionary Force

James W. St.G. Walker

Contemporaries called it 'the war to end all wars' and 'the war to make the world safe for democracy.' During it, women throughout the North Atlantic world stepped forcefully into public affairs; subject populations in central Europe emerged into national self-determination; the proletariat triumphed beyond the Eastern front. But if World War I has thus been deemed 'progressive,' whatever its horrible cost, it was not intended as a liberal social instrument. For example, the relations between categories of people termed 'races' were regarded as immutable, and therefore expected to emerge from the war intact. Science and public opinion accepted that certain identifiable groups lacked the valour, discipline, and intelligence to fight a modern war. Since those same groups were also the subjects of the European overseas empires, prudence warned that a taste of killing white men might serve as an appetizer should they be listed against a European enemy. The obvious conclusion was that this must be 'a white man's war.'

This decision was reached by virtually all the protagonists, but it was modified by an admission that since the subject races would clearly benefit from the victory of their own masters, they might be allowed to do their bit for the cause as appropriate to their own perceived abilities. Early in the war, when they constituted the empire's largest reserve of trained men, British Indian troops from the 'martial races' of the subcontinent were committed to France.

Source: James W. St.G. Walker, "Race and Recruitment in World War I: Enlistment of Visible Minorities in the Canadian Expeditionary Force" *Canadian Historical Review*, 70:1 (March 1989): 1–26. © University of Toronto Press 1989. All rights reserved. Reprinted by permission of University of Toronto Press Incorporated (www.utpjournals.com).

But when the nature of the conflict became evident, and British forces available, it was dis-
covered that Indian combat troops were unsuitable for Europe. Most were diverted to the
Middle Eastern campaigns, where their targets were non-Europeans, though thousands of
Indian labourers remained in Europe. Similarly New Zealand sent a Maori labour unit to
Gallipoli, and a Maori labour unit to Belgium and France. Even sensitive South Africa agreed,
when labour shortages were most pressing in 1916, to enlist blacks for non-combat duties in
Europe. China's contribution as an ally was to provide 50,000 'coolies' to labour behind the
lines in France. Typically contrary, France itself began the war using its 'force noire' only at
Gallipoli and as garrison troops in the French colonies, but the huge losses of men on the
Western Front overcame the doubts of the high command and in 1916 African troops appeared
in the European trenches. When the Americans entered the war in 1917, black volunteers
were at first rejected. Though later recruited and conscripted in large numbers, fewer than 10
per cent ever fired a rifle in the direction of a German; the overwhelming majority were consigned to non-combat service battalions.[1]

Canada shared the Western ideology of 'race,' and Canadian wartime practice generally
was in step with the allies: until manpower needs at the front surmounted the obvious objections, killing Germans was the privilege of white troops. Even when called upon, members of
Canada's 'visible' minorities were accompanied overseas by a set of presumptions about their
abilities which dictated the role they were to play and which limited the rewards they were to
derive.[2] An examination of policy towards them and of their participation in the war offers a
temporary opening in the curtain which typically covers Canadian racism, revealing some
details from the set of stereotypes applied to certain minorities. The curtain also lifts upon the
determination and self-confidence of Canadian minorities, and their struggle to be accorded
equal responsibilities as well as equal opportunities. The struggle is further revealed, in many
instances, as a community effort: communities encouraged, organized, and financed the enlistment of their young men, and those men volunteered in order to gain group recognition and
to further the rights of whole communities.

In August 1914 a surge of patriotism, assisted by severe unemployment, prompted the
enlistment of more than the 25,000 volunteers initially required for the first CEF contingent.
For over a year, in fact, the supply of men exceeded demand: recruiting officers could afford to
be selective, and one of the selection criteria was the 'race' of the applicant. Under the terms
of the minister of militia's 'call to arms,' existing militia units enrolled volunteers directly, and
the local militia officers had complete discretion over whom to accept.[3] There was one exception, however: within days of the first shots in Europe, the Militia Council forbade the enlistment of native Indians on the reasoning that 'Germans might refuse to extend to them the
privileges of civilized warfare.' This directive was not, however, made public, and some
recruiting officers remained ignorant of it. Indian youth, like their white counterparts, were
anxious to participate and presented themselves to their local units. Many were enlisted only
to be turned away when their Indian status was discovered. Some were able to slip through
undetected, with or without the collusion of their commanders, so that the early contingents
did contain some native soldiers despite the official policy.[4]

Members of the other 'visible' groups were less successful. Individual unit discretion appears
to have kept East Indians entirely outside the Canadian forces, and in British Columbia, where
most of them lived, Japanese were rejected completely. The fate of Chinese Canadians is less
clear, but if any were accepted in the early years of the war their numbers must have been
extremely small.[5] In a memo of November 1914 responding to a query on 'coloured enlistment,'
the militia would only refer to the established policy that personnel selection was a matter for
each commanding officer, though the chief of general staff offered the prevailing opinion:
'Would Canadian Negroes make good fighting men? I do not think so.'[6] One Cape Breton black

volunteer, who decided that 'It's a job that I'll like killing germans,' was told he was ineligible to join any white unit; a group of about fifty blacks from Sydney, who went to enlist together, were advised: 'This is not for you fellows, this is a white man's war.'[7]

The Canadian volunteers rejected by this policy were not content to accept either their exclusion or the reasoning that went with it. They sought enlistment in large numbers, and insisted on knowing why their offer was not accepted. As early as November 1914 the black community of North Buxton was complaining to Ottawa and seeking corrective action; from Hamilton blacks came the charge that it was 'beneath the dignity of the Government to make racial or color distinction in an issue of this kind'; blacks in Saint John condemned recruitment discrimination and added for the record an account of the discrimination they met daily in their home city.[8] Saint John MP William Pugsley, at the request of Ontario and New Brunswick black representatives, raised the issue in the House of Commons. The government insisted that 'there is no Dominion legislation authorizing discrimination against coloured people,' and the militia was able to state that 'no regulations or restrictions' prevented 'enrollment of coloured men who possess the necessary qualifications,' but no remedies were offered or comment made upon clear evidence of exclusion for 'racial' reasons.[9] And yet the urge to enlist persisted. A group of Cape Croker Indians applied to four different recruitment centres and were rejected from each one; Japanese in British Columbia made repeated attempts to enlist; blacks in Nova Scotia travelled from one unit to another hoping to find acceptance.[10] To some extent this persistence must have been prompted by young men's sense of adventure and patriotism, but they were moved as well by a consciousness that a contribution to the war effort could help to overcome the disadvantages faced by their communities. The Japanese believed that war participation would earn them the franchise, a hope that was shared by some Indian groups. Blacks maintained that war for justice must have an impact on 'the progress of our race' in Canada.[11]

White intransigence was not overcome by these efforts, but a compromise seemed possible: if whites and non-whites could not stand shoulder to shoulder in defence of the empire, perhaps they could stand separately. 'Coloured candidates are becoming insistent,' a Vancouver recruiter complained, and his superior advised that 'as white men will not serve in the same ranks with negros or coloured persons,' the only solution was to create a separate unit.[12] Because of the numerous black applications in Nova Scotia, several similar suggestions were made, and one commanding officer, though rejecting individual blacks, agreed to accept an entire platoon if one were formed.[13] On the 'reliable information' that 10,000 blacks inhabited Edmonton region from whom 1000 could easily be recruited, Alberta district commander Cruikshank, with the support of the lieutenant governor, offered to create a black battalion since a racially integrated Alberta regiment 'would not be advisable.' On the same principle General Cruikshank proposed that a 'Half-Breed Battalion' be recruited in Alberta.[14] More insistent and widespread were suggestions to raise distinct regiments of native Indians. Every province from Ontario west produced proposals to enlist natives in segregated units where, under careful supervision of white officers, their 'natural' talents as fighters and marksmen could best be utilized.[15] Some of these suggestions were enthusiastically endorsed by the affected groups, believing that as a recognizable unit they could gain more attention for their communal cause,[16] but none were more energetic than the Japanese. In August 1915 the Canadian Japanese Association of Vancouver offered to raise an exclusively Japanese unit. Receiving a polite reply, the association began to enlist volunteers, eventually 227 of them, who were supported at Japanese community expense and practised their drill under British veteran and militia captain R.S. Colquhoun. With one company thus trained, the association made a formal offer to the government in March 1916 of a full battalion.[17]

The Japanese offer, like every other proposal to create a racially defined battalion, was rejected by Militia Headquarters. Officials doubted that enough volunteers from any group could be found to create and maintain a unit as large as a battalion, and furthermore its members could not be used as reinforcements in other battalions, as was frequently required in trench warfare, if integration should prove difficult. Privately, the combat abilities of blacks and Indians were considered questionable, and although Japanese were regarded as 'desirable soldiers,' their enlistment was feared as a step towards enfranchisement. Individual 'half-breeds,' blacks, and Japanese were theoretically admissible into all militia units. 'There is no colour line,' insisted the adjutant general, but commanding officers were free to accept or reject any volunteer for any reason.[18] One incident more than any other provoked this statement. In November 1915 twenty black volunteers from Saint John were sent to Camp Sussex, where they were told to go instead to Ontario where a 'Coloured Corps' was being formed. Protesting that this action was 'shameful and insulting to the Race,' the Saint John blacks pressed their case with the government general and militia minister Sir Sam Hughes. Apparently outraged, Hughes ordered a full investigation into the incident and promised that there would be no racial barriers and no segregated units in his army. When the Sussex commanding officer complained that it was not 'fair' to expect white troops 'to mingle with negroes,' a sentiment supported by all the commanding officers in the Maritime district, militia officials quickly explained that local commanders retained their discretionary powers: 'it is not thought desirable, either in the interests of such men themselves or of the Canadian Forces, that Commanding Officers should be forced to take them.'[19] Whatever Hughes's intentions, the statement reinforced the status quo. It remained a white man's war.

At the outbreak of the war a surplus of volunteers had afforded considerable latitude in selecting recruits. By the spring of 1915, when the second Canadian Contingent sailed, trench warfare had eroded all hopes for a short and glorious war, and casualty rates were horrifying. Domestic production competed with the armed services for manpower, just as more and more men were required for the trenches. Selectivity became less rigid, as height, medical, and marital requirements were relaxed, and the recruitment method itself came under scrutiny. In the fall of 1915 a new policy was substituted, enabling any patriotic person or group to form a battalion. This 'patriotic phase,' distinguished from the earlier 'militia phase,' led to the proliferation of new units and to rivalries among them for the available manpower. Since the fighting regiments were not being reinforced directly by new recruitment, the 'patriotic' policy also meant that the units thus raised almost inevitably had to be broken up on arrival in Europe to be used to fill the gaps caused by casualties in the existing regiments. The entire situation was compounded by Prime Minister Borden's announcement that, as of 1 January 1916, Canada would pledge 500,000 troops to Europe. With prevailing casualty rates, it would require 300,000 new recruits per year to maintain this figure in the field.[20]

All these developments — the scramble for men, the raising of special regiments, and their use as reinforcements for fighting overseas — had implications for recruiting 'visible' minorities. First to fall was the restriction against Indian enlistment. Certain regiments had been discreetly recruiting Indians since 1914, but when Ontario's new 114th Battalion was being formed in November 1915 its commander hoped to enlist four companies of Brantford and region Indians. His superior, the Toronto district commander, lent support to the plan on the understanding that all Indians recruited in his division would be transferred to the 114th. It was apparently this limited plan, consistent with the 'special units' policy, that was at first approved by the militia minister; Indians already in other regiments were invited to transfer to the 114th, and the new battalion was permitted to recruit Indians outside its own geographical territory.[21]

The memo that went out to commanding officers, however, stated that Indian enlistment was henceforth authorized 'in the various Units for Overseas Service,' and this impression was reinforced in individual letters to commanders permitting Indian enlistment. The confusion amongst recruiting officers was shared by the chief of general staff, Willoughby Gwatkin, who confessed that he did not know whether open enlistment was now the rule or whether Indian battalions were to be formed.[22] Meanwhile, the 114th was advertising itself, even in the public press, as *the* Indian unit, and at least a dozen regiments transferred their Indian recruits to the 114th.[23] In the event, pressure from other battalion commanders convinced divisional head-quarters to cease transferring Indians to the 114th, which was therefore unable to fill more than two Indian companies. The result was a concentration of Indians in the 114th, but others were scattered individually throughout the battalions willing to accept them.[24]

It was perhaps this reigning confusion over special units, coupled with the pressure to find a half million men, that led to one of the war's most discouraging episodes for black Canadians. In November 1915 J.R.B. Whitney, editor of a Toronto black newspaper, the *Canadian Observer*, wrote to Hughes asking if the minister would accept a platoon of 150 black men provided it would be maintained at that strength throughout the war. Hughes warmly replied that 'these people can form a platoon in any Battalion, now. There is nothing in the world to stop them.'[25] On this basis Whitney began to advertise through the *Observer*, and enlisted volunteers in the projected platoon. Early in January 1916 he was able to report to Hughes that he had enlisted a number of Toronto recruits, adding a request to second a black enlisted man for a recruitment tour of southwestern Ontario. Hughes passed this on to the adjutant general, W.E. Hodgins, for action, and this latter official was forced to return to Whitney for an explanation of what was meant by all this. In the process Hodgins discovered that no arrangement had been made with any battalion commander to receive a black pla-toon. In fact, advised Toronto's General Logie, it was doubtful if any commander would accept 'a coloured platoon' into 'a white man's Battalion,' Hodgins therefore decided that permission to recruit a black unit could not be granted, and he asked Toronto division so to inform Mr Whitney. On 15 March Whitney received a blunt letter from the Toronto recruiting officer stating that as no commanding officer was willing to enlist them, the plan must be abandoned.[26]

A very hurt Whitney asked for a reconsideration; he had already gathered forty volunteers and could not now tell them to disband. An embarrassed Hodgins begged Logie to find some unit prepared to admit Whitney's platoon, and Logie diligently conducted a canvas of his dis-trict. The responses from battalion commanders dramatically revealed the prevailing feelings among the military leadership in 1916. Most rejected the idea without explanation, stating simply their unwillingness to accept blacks. Several acknowledged that white recruitment would be discouraged, and dissatisfaction aroused amongst men already enlisted. Some con-firmed that they had already rejected numbers of black volunteers. The most ambiguous answer came from the 48th Highlanders, whose adjutant stated that 'we have, being a kilted regiment, always drawn the line at taking coloured men.' No one apologized or offered any positive sug-gestions. No one seemed to think his prejudices would not be understood, and shared, in head-quarters. Logie replied to Hodgins that the situation was obviously hopeless. Whitney's personal appeal to Hughes provoked sympathy and some furious cables, but the result could not be changed. Even with a half million soldiers to find, Ontario's military establishment could not 'stoop' to the recruitment of blacks.[27]

But Ottawa desks had been shaken, and General Gwatkin was ordered to write a report on 'the enlistment of negroes in the Canadian Expeditionary Force.' Besides Whitney's experi-ence, overtures from black Nova Scotians had become more difficult to ignore, since they were supported by several influential Conservative politicians.[28] Gwatkin's memorandum was scarcely complimentary, but it did offer an opportunity for blacks to join the war. 'Nothing is to be gained by blinking facts,' Gwatkin began:

> The civilized negro is vain and imitative; in Canada he is not being impelled to enlist by a high sense of duty; in the trenches he is not likely to make a good fighter; and the average white man will not associate with him on terms of equality. Not a single commanding officer in Military District No. 2 is willing to accept a coloured platoon as part of his battalion; and it would be humiliating to the coloured men themselves to serve in a battalion where they were not wanted.
>
> In France, in the firing line, there would be no place for a black battalion, CEF. It would be eyed askance; it would crowd out a white battalion; it would be difficult to reinforce.
>
> Nor could it be left in England and used as a draft-giving depot; for there would be trouble if negroes were sent to the front for the purpose of reinforcing white battalions; and, if they are good men at all, they would resent being kept in Canada for the purpose of finding guards &c.

Gwatkin concluded with the recommendation that blacks could be enlisted, as at present, in any battalion willing to accept them, and that a labour battalion could additionally be formed exclusively for them.[29] On 19 April 1916, with Prime Minister Borden presiding, the Militia Council decided to form a black labour battalion headquartered in Nova Scotia, provided the British command would agree. This approval was received three weeks later.[30]

'It is a somewhat peculiar command,' admitted Adjutant General Hodgins, after some difficulty was experienced in finding a qualified officer willing to head a black battalion. But Prime Minister Borden, himself a Halifax politician, took a personal interest in the new project and suggested the name of a potential commander, Daniel H. Sutherland. On 5 July, the day after Sutherland's acceptance, the Nova Scotia No 2 Construction Battalion (Coloured) was formally announced. Officered by whites, the unit was authorized to recruit blacks from all across Canada.[31] The black community in Nova Scotia heartily welcomed the formation of the No 2. 'Considerable joy and happiness' erupted, particularly among the young men, for the No 2 seemed to recognize that 'they were men the same as everybody else.' The African Baptist Association, at its 1916 annual meeting, expressed the view that through the No 2 'the African race was making history,' and pledged to do all in its power to encourage enlistment.[32] Although the all-white No 1 Construction Battalion complained bitterly about its name, fearing association with 'work which might be done by the negro race,'[33] no doubts seem to have been uttered by black representatives at the nature of the work or the fact of segregation.

By the summer of 1916 Canadian blacks, Indians, and Japanese were all being actively recruited into the services. Following the rejection of the Canadian Japanese Association's offer to form a full battalion, militia authorities encouraged other battalions to accept their volunteers who had already received basic training through their private efforts. The association itself promoted this policy, appealing to Alberta's General Cruikshank to permit Japanese to enlist in his district, since BC commanders remained adamantly opposed. On his return trip to Vancouver from Ottawa, where he had gone to present the case for a Japanese battalion, association president Yasuchi Yamazaki met with Cruikshank in Calgary, and the general immediately wrote to battalion commanders with the offer of up to 200 Japanese recruits.[34] The response was overwhelmingly positive. The 192nd Battalion offered to receive all 200, and the 191st asked for 250, but this was vetoed from headquarters as 'there is no objection to the enlistment of odd men, but large numbers are not to be enlisted,' Advertisements from Alberta recruiters appeared in Vancouver's Japanese language press, and temporary recruiting offices were established in British Columbia, though this latter practice was contrary to regulations. Battalions from other provinces, too, sought Japanese recruits. Eventually 185 served overseas in eleven different battalions, mainly in the 10th, 50th, and 52nd infantry battalions. It was undoubtedly at this time that individual Chinese were being enlisted by under-strength battalions.[35]

The rivalry to recruit Japanese was being reflected in the much larger campaign to enlist native Indians. The 114th began with the advantage of being identified as an Indian battalion, and confusion continued for several months over whether all Indians, recruited before or since December 1915, were to be transferred to it. Some Indians who had enlisted in other regiments applied to transfer to the 114th; others asked not to be transferred because they preferred not to serve with 'Mohawks.'[36] The Department of Indian Affairs lent its official support to the 114th recruitment drive, and seconded Charles Cooke to the regiment with the honorary rank of lieutenant. Described as 'the only male Indian employed in the Service at Ottawa,' Cooke toured the Ontario reserves on behalf of the 114th, sometimes in the company of an Indian commissioned officer, stressing the pride and the opportunity derived from serving in an identifiably Indian unit. Although by this time it had been determined that only two companies, that is half the battalion, would in fact consist of Indians, the 114th stressed its Indian connection. The regimental badge contained two crossed tomahawks, and its band, composed mostly of Brantford reserve Iroquois, gave concerts which included Indian war dances.[37]

Other battalions were not slow to enter the recruitment race. Hodgin's attempt to settle the 114th's jurisdiction, by giving it authority to recruit Indians beyond its regimental territory but not *exclusive* authority, seems merely to have stimulated rivalries. Other commanding officers sought to entice Charles Cooke into their service; one battalion allegedly was offering a $5 recruitment bonus to Indians plus a free trip to Europe in case the war ended before they went overseas; others were reportedly recruiting young boys from the residential schools. In July 1916, when Colonel Mewburn called for a report on Indians enlisted in Military District 2, headquartered in Toronto, the 114th had 348, including five officers, and 211 others were arrayed across fifteen different units. This did not include the 107th battalion, raised in Winnipeg and commanded by G.L. Campbell, a senior Indian Affairs official. At first intended as an all-Indian battalion, the 107th shared the experience of Ontario's 114th and eventually enlisted approximately one-half its membership among Indians.[38]

Although these numbers were all recruited, at least ostensibly, into infantry battalions, there were parallel efforts to enlist Indians in non-combatant labour and construction units, particularly for forestry. Duncan Campbell Scott, the senior Indian Affairs official, urged this movement through Indian agents across Canada. When white officers and recruits in forestry units, primarily on the west coast, objected to working amongst 'Indians and Half-breeds,' authority was granted to establish separate native companies and platoons.[39] One of the construction units to recruit amongst Indians was none other than the No 2, from Nova Scotia. Five Indians joined the No 2 at Windsor, Ontario, allegedly on the promise of becoming non-commissioned officers. Once enlisted they claimed to be disgusted by the fighting, gambling, and drinking going on in the No 2 camp, and they called for a transfer. When Colonel Sutherland's response was slow, Chief Thunderwater of the Great Council of the Tribes took up the Indians' case, claiming 'a natural dislike of association with negroes on the part of Indians.' The adjutant general in Ottawa and General Logie in Toronto had to become involved before this entanglement could be settled and the Indians moved to the 256th Railway Construction Battalion, which had a large Indian component. Chief Thunderwater admonished the adjutant general 'that you so arrange that Indians and negroes are kept from the same Battalion.'[40]

The reason the No 2 was in Windsor, Ontario, was that Sutherland had been given authority to recruit nationally, though this clearly meant that he could recruit blacks, for whom there was no inter-regimental competition. Information was sent to every commanding officer in the country authorizing 'any of the coloured men in Canada, now serving in units of the C.E.F., to transfer to the No 2 Construction Battalion, should they so wish.' Several black volunteers did transfer from other units, at least some with the overt encouragement of their officers.[41] Within Nova Scotia a regimental band was organized, holding recruiting concerts in churches and halls wherever a black audience might be attracted. In the larger black communities, Citizens Recruiting Committees were formed to encourage enlistment, the Rev. W.A. White of the African Baptist Church in Truro gave 'stirring' speeches, and black church elders lent moral support.[42] Early recruiting reports were satisfying, but by November 1916 Sutherland felt it necessary to undertake a more active campaign outside Nova Scotia. His request to recruit in the West Indies was turned down, but funds were authorized in January 1917 to take the band on a tour to Montreal and Toronto, and black centres in southwestern Ontario. After a decline between October and December, recruitment picked up again in January, most of it in Windsor, Ontario, where many American blacks joined the Canadian unit.[43] In western Canada Captain Gayfer established a recruiting office in Edmonton, from which he too conducted tours and spoke in black churches. He later moved his headquarters to Winnipeg, leaving a black enlisted man in charge of the Edmonton office while a lieutenant visited British Columbia. All across Canada young black men were being advised that 'the need of the day' was for pioneers and construction workers whose contribution to the movement forward to victory was vital.[44]

Two years into the war, recruitment policy towards 'visible' minorities had been reversed completely. But during those two years, the ardour to join their white brethren in the defence of Canadian democracy had been somewhat dampened among the minority youth. Japanese recruitment never remotely approached the thousand men projected by Yamazaki, perhaps because they were not allowed to serve in recognizable units as they believed was essential to win rights for their community. Native Indians did have the opportunity to enlist in concentrated units, but where such units existed they never recruited up to their authorized strength. The fact was that the invitation to serve was coming too late, and after a discouraging demonstration of majority attitudes towards their potential contribution. The Six Nations, who had offered their assistance as allies to the king in 1914, now opposed recruiters on the ground that they were an independent people and would enlist only upon the personal appeal of the governor general and recognition of their special status.[45] Other Indian groups complained that 'We are not citizens and have no votes, as free men'; anti-recruiters followed recruiters around the reserves, speaking out against Indian enlistment during 'Patriotic' meetings, reminding Indians of their grievances and the many government promises made to them which had been broken throughout history.[46] Other factors interfered as well. There was resentment against recruitment methods, including reports of intimidating tactics and the enrolment of underage boys. Indignation followed a rumour that overseas the Indians would be discussed as Italians, thus preventing any recognition for their accomplishments. Complaints from Indians already enlisted, alleging racial discrimination and inferior treatment in the forces, filtered back to the reserves. Other letters from Indians at the front described 'the awfulness of war' and 'openly advised the Indians not to think of enlisting.'[47]

Nor did black Canadians fail to register scepticism at the recruitment campaign. In Nova Scotia, where black community leadership was won over, many individuals 'were feeling keenly that their Loyal offers of service were refused in so many instances,' and were reluctant now to join the No 2. Blacks in the west told recruiters the same thing.[48] Resentment at previous insult was reinforced by continued insult: in Winnipeg black recruits were derided and called 'nigger' by medical staff assigned to examine them. When Colonel Sutherland decided to move his headquarters from Pictou to Truro, he rented a suitable building and had begun furnishing it when the owner suddenly cancelled the contract. The same thing happened to Captain Gayfer when the other of his recruiting office cancelled the contract 'on account of color of recruits.' Eventually established in Truro, black recruits met segregation in the local theatre. Rumours percolated through the black communities as well, for example that they were to be used only as trench diggers in France.[49] Although several prominent whites, notably Nova Scotian MPs Fleming McCurdy and John Stanfield and businessman H. Falconer McLean, assisted in the formation and recruitment of the No 2, the military hierarchy itself was less than enthusiastic, perhaps feeling that the black battalion had been imposed on them for political reasons. The chief of general staff regarded the unit as 'troublesome.' It took Sutherland two months to gain approval for his tour beyond Nova Scotia, and then only with the strictest admonitions to economize. Western recruiter Gayfer was denied office supplies, had his transport warrants delayed, and received no rations or barrack accommodation for his recruits.[50] And yet Sutherland received constant memos and cables asking him when his unit would be ready for overseas service. The first target was three months; after seven months, Sutherland was told to prepare the men already recruited for sailing, and new recruits could follow later; eventually it was in March 1917, nine months after recruitment began, that the No 2 embarked for England, and with only 603 men enlisted of an authorized strength of 1033 other ranks.[51] Because it arrived in Britain below battalion strength, the No 2 was converted to a labour company of 500 men, and Sutherland was reduced in rank to major.[52]

It was not only 'visible' minority youth who had developed a reluctance to volunteer. In July 1916 recruitment in general plummeted, from monthly peaks near 30,000 earlier in the year to fewer than 8000, and continued to fall to around 3000 a month. Not a single battalion raised after July 1916 reached its full strength, from any part of Canada. Employment in domestic war production, and increasing awareness of the carnage at the front, caused the virtual collapse of the voluntary system just at the time when the push was being made to enlist 'visible' minorities. In May 1917, when casualty rates in Europe were more than double new recruitment, Prime Minister Borden announced his intention to introduce conscription with the cry that 'the battle for Canadian liberty and autonomy is being fought today on the plains of France and Belgium.' The Military Service Act, when effected later that year, was less than a popular success among those liable to its call. Over 90 per cent of them applied for exemption.[53]

Canada's Indians were immediate and outspoken in denying the legality of their conscription. 'Indians refuse to report,' cabled one anxious Indian agent. More sophisticated responses referred to the fact that Indians were 'wards of the government,' legally 'minors' and treated as children: surely children were not being called to defend the empire? Since they had no vote, and no voice in the conduct of the war or of the councils of state, it was unfair to expect them to participate now in the war. 'We cannot say that we are fighting for our liberty, freedom and other privileges dear to all nations, for we have none,' stated an Ontario Indian declaration. BC Indians considered 'that the government attitude towards us in respect to our land troubles and in refusing to extend to us the position of citizens of Canada are unreasonable, and until we receive just treatment . . . we should not be subject to conscription.' Still others quoted the treaties made in the 1870s, and the negotiations surrounding those treaties, during which Indians were assured that they would never be called to war. Petitions flowed to Ottawa, and even to the king: if they were not to have the rights of citizens, they must not be forced to perform a citizen's duty.[54] Similar petitions came from BC Japanese, pointing out that although they were naturalized Canadians they lacked the franchise and other citizenship privileges, and they claimed exemption from obligatory military service.[55] In these objections to conscription there was a scarcely submerged articulation of the 'war aims' of Canadian minorities: if it was to be their war, it must result in the extension of equality to their people.

The government hesitated. Indians were first granted an extension of the time required to register; then they were advised officially to seek exemption under some existing regulation, such as agricultural employment.[56] Finally, on 17 January 1918, an order in council exempted Indians and Japanese, on the grounds of their limited citizenship rights and, for the former, the treaty promises. The order also referred to the War Time Elections Act which had deprived certain naturalized Canadians of the franchise and at the same time relieved them of military service. In March the regulations were amended so that any British subject disqualified from voting at a federal election was exempted from conscription. Despite the fact that they would already have been covered by this regulation, East Indians were granted a special exemption order three months later.[57]

This did not of course apply to black Canadians, who already enjoyed the franchise and therefore remained liable to conscription. The No 2, still smarting from its demotion to a labour company, immediately requested that all blacks conscripted across Canada be sent to it, so that it could be restored to battalion status. The No 2 proposal was promoted by Nova Scotian MP Fleming McCurdy, among others, and was received sympathetically by the new militia minister, General Mewburn, who confessed that 'The whole problem of knowing how to handle coloured troops has been a big one for some years back.' A collection depot was established in London, Ontario, where No 2 reinforcements could be made ready for overseas, and orders were sent to commanding officers to transfer all 'coloured men' to the London depot. The wording of the order did not appear to leave the commanders with any choice in keeping black conscripts in their own units.[58] In March, when it began to seem that black numbers were lower than anticipated, No 2 recruiters travelled to Detroit to attract black Canadians living there, but this was squelched by Ottawa on the grounds that 'we are not hunting for coloured recruits but merely making a place for them as they come in under the Military Service Act.' Again, when the British-Canadian Recruiting Mission in New York announced that 'about two thousand colored British subjects have registered,' some or all of whom could be sent to reinforce the No 2, Ottawa's answer was a terse 'none required.'[59] Deciding that the number of black conscripts coming in, directly or by transfer, was not worth the effort, Ottawa ordered the abandonment of the London reception centre in May. Sutherland was informed that his company would not be restored to battalion strength after all.[60]

There was one more try. The Rev. William White, chaplain to the No 2 and as an honorary captain 'the only coloured officer in our forces,' wrote an impassioned letter to the prime minister. 'The coloured people are proud that they have at least one definite Unit representing them in France,' he stated, requesting that the conscripted blacks be sent to strengthen the No 2.[61] As a consequence Major Bristol, secretary to the Canadian overseas militia minister in London, was asked to make a report. In a response labelled 'personal,' Bristol admitted that 'these Niggers do well in a Forestry Corps and other Labour units,' but since numbers were so limited 'the prospects of maintaining a battalion are not very bright.' Following a survey of district commanders, it appeared that scarcely more than 100 identified black conscripts were already enlisted, and 'on this showing it would hardly be possible to carry out the suggestion made' to use them to enhance the No 2. The plan was dropped once and for all.[62] Fifty-five black conscripts already gathered in Halifax were trained in Canada as infantrymen, together with white conscripts, but on arrival in England they were placed in a segregated labour unit. Eventually assigned to the 85th Battalion, the Armistice intervened before they could leave Britain.[63]

The ambivalence and the frankly racist confusion surrounding their recruitment was reflected in the overseas experiences of the enlisted minorities. The Japanese, it appears, were consistently used as combat troops, which was their purpose in volunteering.[64] The Indians had a mixed reception. The 114th, recruited with such pride as an Indian unit, was broken up on arrival in England and the men assigned to different battalions, many for labour duties. The 107th, also recruited with an Indian identity and as a fighting unit, was converted to a pioneer battalion in France, where the men dug trenches and built roads and muletracks under direct enemy fire, with heavy casualties. Some Indians did go to the front as combatants, but a sizeable contingent served in forestry work, chiefly within Britain itself.[65] Those blacks who served individually in combat regiments, since their admission had been entirely voluntary on the part of their officers, apparently met few problems. When the 106th Battalion was broken up, for example, its black members went to the Royal Canadian Regiment as reinforcements on the front lines, where they were welcomed. Undoubtedly there were many more where blacks served without incident.[66] But the No 2 itself, as a separate unit with its own administration and records, leaves a different trail. To avoid 'offending the susceptibility of other troops,' it was suggested that the black battalion be sent overseas in a separate transport ship, without escort. Since their sailing occurred during the war's worst period for German submarine attacks, it is fortunate that this suggestion was rejected by the Royal Navy.[67] The battalion arrived in England under strength, and the decision was made not to absorb the men into different units, where whites might object, but to keep them together as a labour company attached to the Forestry Corps in French territory. Working as loggers and in lumber mills, and performing related construction and shipping work, the men of the No 2 were established near La Joux, in the Jura region of France, with smaller detachments at Cartigny and Alençon. Although they laboured side by side with white units, the black soldiers were segregated in their non-working activities. Remote from any means of amusement, they had to await the creation of a separate 'coloured' YMCA for their evenings' entertainment. When ill, they were treated in a separate 'Coloured Wing' of the La Joux hospital. Those who strayed from military discipline were similarly confined in a segregated punishment compound. An extra Protestant chaplain had to be sent into Jura district 'as the Negro Chaplain is not acceptable to the White Units.' Always regarded as a problem and never seriously appreciated, the No 2 was disbanded with almost unseemly haste soon after the Armistice was announced, though the demand for forestry products remained high, and they were among the earliest Canadian units to leave France.[68]

The treatment received by 'visible' Canadians did not originate with the military; recruitment policy and overseas employment were entirely consistent with domestic stereotypes of 'race' characteristics and with general social practice in Canada. And Canadian attitudes themselves were merely a reflection of accepted and respected Western thought in the early twentieth century. Racial perceptions were derived, not from personal experience, but from the example of Canada's great mentors, Britain and the United States, supported by scientific explanations.[69] In these circumstances it is notable that the Canadian military, while by no means avoiding the influence of prevailing ideology, at least had the independence to be less restricting than most of the allies. For example, General Headquarters advised the Forestry Corps to reorganize the No 2 to conform to imperial standards, as were applied to South African, Chinese, and Egyptian 'coloured labour' units. This would have affected their pay and privileges, and for black non-commissioned officers it would mean a reduction to private. Colonel J.B. White, Forestry's La Joux commander rejected this directive because 'the men of this Unit are engaged in exactly the same work as the white labour with whom they are employed . . . and it is recommended that no change be made,' Headquarters withdrew the order and the men of the No 2 continued to be treated as other Canadian forestry units.[70] One reason for assigning the No 2 to French territory was to avoid contact and comparison with other British 'coloured labour' units 'who are kept in compounds, and not permitted the customary liberties of white troops.'[71] Black American troops in France were completely segregated, forbidden to leave their bases without supervision, and barred from cafés and other public places. Friendly relations with French civilians led to the strictest measures, including the arrest of blacks who conversed with white women, and to an official American request to the French military beseeching the co-operation in keeping the races separate. British East Indian troops were restricted in their off-base activities and were liable to a dozen lashes for 'seeking romance' from white women. Senior army officials objected to East Indian sick and wounded being treated by white nurses. South African black labourers were kept in guarded compounds. Throughout the ranks of the Allies, with the partial exception of the French, non-white soldiers and workers were humiliated, restricted, and exploited. It was simply not their war.[72]

Generally speaking, the efforts of 'visible' enlisted men did not gain recognition for themselves or for their communities at home. Postwar race riots in the United States generated the worst violence experienced by black Americans since slavery. Attempts by Punjabi veterans to gain moderate political reforms led to the infamous Amritsar Massacre in April 1919, where 379 peaceful demonstrators were killed and 1208 wounded while trapped in a box-like park. French use of African troops to occupy defeated Germany led to condemnation by the Allies and to international censure for subjecting white Germans to the horrors of black authority.[73] Respect, evidently, had not been won by four years in defence of Western ideals. There was even a Canadian incident to illustrate this situation: on 7 January 1919 at Kinmel Park Camp in Britain, white Canadian soldiers rioted and attacked the No 2 ranks on parade after a black sergeant arrested a white man and placed him in charge of a 'coloured' escort.[74] Far from expressing gratitude for their services, the militia minister in 1919 seemed unaware that the No 2 had even existed.[75] It is true that individual Japanese veterans were granted the franchise, belatedly and grudgingly in 1931 by a one-vote margin in the BC legislature, and native Indians actually serving in the forces were enfranchised by the War Time Elections Act and its successors, but their families and other members of their communities remained as only partial Canadian citizens.[76] Especially indicative of their failure to attain genuine acceptance was the fact that at the outset of World War II, 'visible' volunteers would again be rejected altogether or directed towards support and service functions consistent with their peacetime stereotypes.[77]

During World War I about 3500 Indians, over 1000 blacks, and several hundred Chinese and Japanese enlisted in the Canadian forces. To their number must be added the many who tried to enlist and were rejected. Though there was an understandable resistance to later attempts to recruit and conscript them, still the numbers in uniform were impressive, a demonstration of loyalty and a confidence that accepting equal responsibilities would win the advantages of Canadian citizenship. Individual exceptions occurred, but as a group they were denied that equal opportunity to defend their country and empire. Stereotypes which at first excluded them continued to restrict their military role, and even survived the war. In 1919 respect and equality remained beyond reach. Lessons which could and should have been learned in the first war had to be taught all over again in a second global conflict.

The experience of 'visible' minorities in World War I illustrates the nature of Canadian race sentiment early in this century. Most abruptly, it demonstrates that white Canadians participated in the Western ideology of racism. This was true not only in the general sense of accepting white superiority, but in the particular image assigned to certain peoples which labelled them as militarily incompetent. Canadian history itself should have suggested the contrary — blacks and Indians, for example, had a proud record of military service prior to Confederation — but the stereotypes derived from Britain and the United States were more powerful than domestic experience. Some degree of cynicism is discernable in the rejection of 'visible' volunteers, for example, the fear that military duty would enable them to demand political equality, yet it is not possible to read the entire record without concluding that most white Canadians, including the military hierarchy, were convinced by the international stereotypes and their supporting scientific explanations. This was carried to the point where Canada's war effort was impeded by prejudices for which there were no Canadian foundations.

Equally interesting is what the World War I experience reveals about the minorities themselves. Their persistence in volunteering, their insistence upon the 'right' to serve, their urgent demand to know the reasons for their rejection, all suggest that 'visible' Canadians had not been defeated by the racism of white society, had not accepted its rationalizations, and were not prepared quietly to accept inferior status. They retained a confidence in themselves, most obviously that they could achieve a glorious war record if given the opportunity. While recognizing the restrictions imposed on themselves and their communities, they were convinced that by their own efforts and the good will of white Canada they could remove those restrictions. Their appeals to parliament and the crown reveal as well that they had not lost faith in British/Canadian justice. The minority campaigns during World War I, for recruitment and later against conscription, were only possible for persons convinced that they were equal and could achieve recognition of their equality. Their loyalty to Canada and the empire included loyalty to an ideal which the dominant majority had forgotten.

This article was presented at the Canadian Ethnic Studies Conference, Halifax, in October 1987. I am grateful to the Social Sciences and Humanities Research Council for financial assistance, and to the following for their critical comments: John Armstrong, Norman Buchignani, Michael Craton, Thamis Gale, Roy Ito, Desmond Morton, Palmer Patterson, John Stubbs, Stephanie Walker, and Glenn Wright.

NOTES

1. For example, see Jeffrey Greenhut, 'The Imperial Reserve: The Indian Corps on the Western Front, 1914–15,' *Journal of Imperial and Commonwealth History* 11 (1983): 54–73, and 'Sahib and Sepoy: An Inquiry into the Relationship between the British Officers and Native Soldiers of the British Indian Army,' *Military Affairs* 48 (1984): 15–18; Keith L. Nelson, 'The Black Horror on the Rhine: Race as a Factor in Post-World War I Diplomacy,' *Journal of Modern History* 62 (1970): 606–8; Fred Gaffen, *Forgotten Soldiers* (Penticton, BC 1985), 24, 74–5; B.P. Willan, 'The South African Native Labour Contingent, 1916–1918,' *Journal of African History* 19 (1978): 61–86; C.J. Balesi, *From Adversaries to Comrades in Arms: West Africa and the French Military, 1885–1918* (Waltham, Mass. 1979), 112–13, 120–1; C.M. Andrew and A.S. Kanya-Forstner, 'France, Africa, and the First World War,' *Journal of African History* 19 (1978): 11–23; A.E. Barbeau and F. Henri, *The Unknown Soldiers: Black American Troops in World War II* (Philadelphia 1974); J.D. Foner, *Blacks and the Military in American History: A New Perspective* (New York 1974), 109–32. Black combat troops remained an American embarrassment. The all-black 93rd Division, for example, was first offered to the British army, and upon refusal was eventually attached to the French army for its combat service. The Chinese 'coolies' were shipped across Canada, en route to and from France, in sealed railway carriages. There are voluminous files on this episode in the Directorate of History, Department of National Defence (DND), Ottawa, and in RG 24 at the National Archives of Canada (NA).

2. A small but growing literature is available on the subject of minority Canadian participation in the world wars. Pioneering chapters on black Nova Scotians in M. Stuart Hunt, *Nova Scotia's Part in the Great War* (Halifax 1920), 148–53, and Ontario blacks and Indians in Barbara M. Wilson, *Ontario and the First World War, 1914–1918: A Collection of Documents* (Toronto 1977), cviii–cxiv, 166–75, are being supplemented with more detailed studies. Gaffen's *Forgotten Soldiers* is a colourful description of native Indian soldiers in both world wars, a welcome addition to James Dempsey's brief account, 'The Indians and World War I,' *Alberta History* 31 (1983): 1–8, and a useful corrective to Duncan Campbell Scott, 'The Canadian Indian and the Great World War,' in *Canada and the Great World War* (Toronto 1919), III, 285–328. Calvin W. Ruck, *Canada's Black Battalion: No. 2 Construction 1916–1920* (Halifax 1986), is anecdotal and illustrative, with portraits and quotations from several of the black veterans themselves. The first scholarly treatment of the No 2 is Major John G. Armstrong's 'The Unwelcome Sacrifice: A Black Unit in the Canadian Expeditionary Force, 1917–1919,' unpublished paper presented at RMC Military History Symposium, March 1986. Roy Ito, *We Went to War: The Story of the Japanese Canadians who Served During the First and Second World Wars* (Stittsville, Ont. 1984), is a valuable combination of scholarship and reminiscence, though most of the attention is paid to the second war. Further detail on World War II can be found in Patricia Roy, 'The Soldiers Canada Didn't Want: Her Chinese and Japanese Citizens,' *Canadian Historical Review* (CHR) 59 (1978): 341–58.

3. Robert Craig Brown and Donald Loveridge, 'Unrequited Faith: Recruiting the CEF 1914–1918,' *Revue internationale d'histoire militaire* 51 (1982): 56; Desmond Morton, *A Military History of Canada* (Edmonton 1985), 130; G.W.L. Nicholson, *Canadian Expeditionary Force, 1914–1919* (Ottawa 1962), 18, 19, 212, 213

4. NA, RG 24, vol. 1221, file 593–1–7, vol. 1, telegram, 8 Aug. 1914, Scott to Hughes, 16 June 1915, and reply, 23 June, Nethercott to Hughes, 11 Oct. 1915, Armstrong to Hughes, 10 Oct. 1915, and replies, 18 Oct., Brown to Hodgins, 9 Oct. 1915, and reply, 22 Oct. Gaffen, *Forgotten Soldiers*, 20, points out correctly that since 'race' was not recorded on recruitment documents, it is not possible to give precise numbers on Indian volunteers. The same caveat should apply to the other minority groups discussed here as well.

5. After the war, the minister of militia and defence, Hugh Guthrie, told the House of Commons that the CEF had enlisted 'something like twelve' Chinese and no East Indians; *Debates*, 29 April 1920, 1812. Several sources refer to larger numbers of Chinese veterans in postwar Canada, for example, Jin Tan and Patricia Roy, *The Chinese in Canada* (Ottawa 1985), 15, Edgar Wickberg et al., *From China to Canada: A History of the Chinese Community in Canada* (Toronto 1982), 200, and Carol F. Lee, 'The Road to Enfranchisement: Chinese and Japanese in British Columbia,' IBC *Studies* 30 (1976): 57–8. A search of the records in the National Archives of Canada and the Directorate of History, Department of National Defence, failed to identify these men. Some could have served as British 'coolies' rather than as Canadian soldiers. Guthrie's comment does suggest that a small number were enlisted as regular soldiers, an impression confirmed by Professors Graham Johnson and Edgar Wickberg who report in a personal communication, 31 Oct. 1987, having seen photographs of Chinese in the uniform of the CEF. A separate Sikh regiment had been suggested as early as 1911, apparently with favourable comment from Sam Hughes, but no action was ever taken; Norman Buchignani, personal communication, 14 Oct. 1987. On British Columbia's rejection of all Japanese volunteers see NA, RG 24, vol. 4740, file 448–14–262, vol. 1, Cruikshank, circular letter, 26 April 1916.

6. NA, RG 24, vol. 1206, file 297–1–21, memo, 13 Nov. 1914, Gwatkin to Christie, 30 Sept. 1915

7. NA, RG 24, vol. 4562, file 133–17–1, Bramah to Rutherford, 4 Oct. 1915, and reply, 6 Oct.; Ruck, *Black Battalion*, 58, quoting interview with Robert Shepard. Despite these obstacles, some Nova Scotia blacks are reported to have been in the first contingent which left Canada in October 1914. Ibid., 11

8. NA, RG 24, vol. 1206, file 297–1–21, Alexander to Hughes, 13 Nov. 1914, Morton to Hughes, 7 Sept. 1915, Richards to Duke of Connaught, 4 Oct. 1915, Hamilton to Duke of Connaught, 29 Dec. 1915

9. House of Commons, *Debates*, 24 March 1916, 2114–15; NA, RG 24, vol. 1206, file 297–1–21, Edwards to Stanton, 31 Jan. 1916, Hodgins to Stewart, 16 Oct. 1915

10. NA, RG 24, vol. 1221, file 593–1–7, Duncan to Scott, 19 Nov. 1915; RG 24, vol. 1860, file 54; RG 24, vol. 4740, file 448–14–262, vol. 1; RG 24, vol. 4562, file 133–17–1, Bramah to Rutherford, 4 Oct. 1915

11. Ito, *We Went to War* 8ff; NA, RG 10, vol. 2640, file 129690–3, Jacobs, circular letter, 17 Aug. 1917; RG 24, vol. 1206, file 297–1–21, *Canadian Observer*, 8 Jan. 1916

12. NA, RG 24, vol. 1206, file 297–1–21, Henshaw to Ogilvie, 7 Dec. 1915, Ogilvie to Hodgins, 9 Dec. 1915

13. Ibid., Tupper to Hughes, 11 Nov. 1915, Allen to Rutherford, 14 Dec.; NA, RG 24, vol. 4562, file 133–17–1, Langford to Rutherford, 23 Sept. 1915, Borden to Rutherford, 23 March 1916

14. NA, RG 24, vol. 4739, file 448–14–259, McLeod to Cruikshank, 25 Nov. 1915 and 20 Jan. 1916, Munton to Cruikshank, received 11 March 1916, Cruikshank to Hodgins, 11 March 1916, Brett to Cruikshank, 13 March 1916, Martin to Cruikshank, 17 March 1916; RG 24, vol. 4739, file 448–14–256, 'Half Breed Battalion,' 1915

15. NA, RG 24, vol. 1221, file 593–1–7, vol. 1, inspector of Indian agencies, Vancouver, to Fiset, 23 Dec. 1915, Jackson to Ruttan, 20 Dec. 1915, McKay to Hodgins, 3 Jan. 1916, Rendle to Department of Indian Affairs, 17 Feb. 1916, Henderson to Hughes, 18 March 1916

16. For example, see *Canadian Observer*, 8 and 15 Jan. 1916; NA, RG 24, vol. 1221, file 593–1–7, vol. 1, Chief Thunderwater, on behalf of the Council of the Tribes, to Hodgins, 29 May 1916; RG 24, vol. 1469, file 600–10–35, White to McCurdy, nd; RG 24, vol. 4662, file 99–256, resolution, BC Indian Peoples, 1 Feb. 1916

17. NA, RG 24, vol. 1860, file 54, 'Recruiting — Special Units and Aliens,' numerous letters and telegrams, Jan.–April 1916; Roy Ito, personal communication, 18 Nov. 1987. An overseas battalion in the CEF consisted of approximately 1000 men grouped in four companies each with two platoons.

18. NA, RG 24, vol. 1860, file 54, Gwatkin to Yamazaki, 21 April 1916; RG 24, vol. 1206, file 297–1–21, Gwatkin to Christie, 30 Sept. 1915, Hodgins to Tupper, 11 Nov. 1915, Hodgins to Armstrong, 19 Nov. 1915, Gwatkin to Hodgins, 22 Dec. 1915, Hodgins to Ogilvie, 23 Dec. 1915, Hodgins to Gwatkin, 21 March 1916, MacInnes to Hodgins, 25 March 1916; RG 24, vol. 1221, file 593–1–7, vol. 1, Fiset to inspector of Indian agencies, Vancouver, 29 Dec. 1915, Hodgins to McKay, 3 Jan. 1916, Gwatkin, memo, 12 Feb. 1916, Ogilvie to Hodgins, 23 March 1916; RG 24, vol. 4599, file 133–17–1, Hodgins to Rutherford, 29 Oct. 1915; RG 24, vol. 4739, file 448–14–256, Hodgins to Campbell, 15 July 1915, Hodgins to Cruikshank, 20 Nov. 1915; file 448–14–259, Hodgins to Cruikshank, 9 Dec. 1915 and 23 March 1916, Cruikshank to Martin, 27 March 1916; Ito, *We Went to War*, 25

19. RG 24, vol. 1206, file 297–1–21, Richards to governor general, 20 Nov. 1915, *Saint John Standard*, 20 Nov. 1915, Hughes to Richards, 25 Nov. 1915, Fowler to GOC Halifax, 25 Nov. 1915, Hodgins to GOC, Halifax, 29 Nov. 1915, reply, 10 Dec., Hodgins to GOC Halifax, 22 Dec. 1915, Gwatkin to Hodgins, 22 Dec. 1915, MacInnes to

Hodgins, 25 March 1916. Interestingly, at least one commanding officer interpreted the minister's statement as a direct instruction. Lt Col W.H. Allen of the 106th Battalion, Halifax, accepted sixteen black Nova Scotians into his unit, though he reported that it discouraged white volunteers, since 'word has come from Ottawa that there is to be no distinction of colour for enlistments,' Allen to GOC Halifax, 14 Dec. 1915

20. Brown and Loveridge, 'Unrequited Faith,' 59, 60; Morton, *History*, 135–41, 147; Nicholson, *Canadian Expeditionary Force*, 212–15, 223; J.L. Granatstein and J.M. Hitsman, *Broken Promises: A History of Conscription in Canada* (Toronto 1977), 22–59

21. NA, RG 14, vol. 1221, file 593–1–7, Logie to Hodgins, 23 Nov. 1915, and reply, 26 Nov., Logie to Hodgins, 27 Nov. 1915, and replies, 6 Dec. and 10 Dec.; RG 24, vol. 4383, file 34–7–109, transfer order, 11 Dec. 1915

22. NA, RG 24, vol. 1221, file 593–1–7, Hughes to Donaldson, 4 Dec. 1915, Hodgins to McLean, 9 Dec. 1915, Hodgins, circular letter, 10 Dec. 1915, Gwatkin to Hodgins, 6 Jan. and 4 May 1916

23. NA, RG 24, vol. 4383, file 34–7–109, 'Enlistment of Indians in CEF,' numerous reports, OC 44th Regiment to Logie, 17 Jan. 1916, Scott to Logie, 19 Jan. 1916, and reply, 21 Jan., OC 114th Battalion to Logie, 27 Jan. 1916

24. Ibid., Logie to OC 114th Battalion, 22 Jan. and 28 Jan. 1916, Hodgins to Logie, 31 Jan. 1916, Hodgins to Baxter, 8 Feb. 1916

25. NA, RG 24, vol. 1206, file 297–1–21, Whitney to Hughes, 24 Nov. 1915, and reply, 3 Dec. A platoon would contain about 125 men in a standard CEF overseas battalion.

26. Ibid., *Canadian Observer*, 8 and 15 Jan. 1916, Whitney to Hughes, 19 Jan. 1916, and reply, 26 Jan., Hodgins to Logie, 3 Feb., 8 and 13 March 1916, Logie to Hodgins, 4 and 10 March 1916, Trump to Whitney, 15 March 1916

27. Ibid., Whitney to Logie, 24 March 1916, to Kemp, 29 March 1916, Hodgins to Logie, 31 March 1916, Logie to commanding officers, 3 April 1916, Logie to Hodgins, 10 April 1916, Whitney to Hughes, 18 April 1916, Hughes to Logie, 3 May 1916, and reply, 4 May. Battalion replies to Logie's appeal of 3 April 1916 are found in NA, RG 24, vol. 4387, file 34–7–141, as are copies of much of the correspondence cited from file 297–1–21.

28. NA, RG 24, vol. 1206, file 297–1–21, Christie to Gwatkin, 29 Sept. 1915, Allen to GOC Halifax, 14 Dec. 1915; RG 24, vol. 4562, file 133–17–1, Langford to Rutherford, 23 Sept. 1915; RG 9, III, vol. 71, file 10–99–40, McCurdy to Harrington, 16 July 1919

29. NA, RG 24, vol. 1206, file 297–1–21, 'Memorandum on the enlistment of negroes in Canadian Expeditionary Force,' 13 April 1916

30. Ibid., Militia Council minutes, 19 April 1916, cable to War Office, 19 April 1916, and reply, 11 May

31. Ibid., Militia Council, memo, 2 June 1916; RG 24, vol. 1469, file 600–10–35, Hodgins to Gwatkin, 5 June 1916, and reply, 11 June, Hodgins to Sutherland, 13 June 1916, and reply, 4 July

32. Ruck, *Canada's Black Battalion*, 27, quoting interview with Mrs. Mabel Saunders; African Baptist Association, annual meeting, minutes, 1916

33. NA, RG 24, vol. 1469, file 600–10–35, Ripley to Hodgins, 7 and 15 July 1916, Hodgins to Ripley, 10, 19, and 21 July 1916

34. NA, RG 24, vol. 1860, file 54, 'Recruiting — Special Units and Aliens'; RG 24, vol. 4740, file 448–14–262, Ityama to Cruikshank, 24 April 1916, Cruikshank, circular letter, 26 April 1916

35. Ibid., OC 192nd Battalion to Cruikshank, 28 April, 19 May, 4 Aug. 1916, Cruickshank to OC 192nd Battalion, 16 and 20 May and 1 Aug. 1916, Cruikshank to Hodgins, cable, 4 May 1916, and reply, same date, Cruikshank to Yamazaki, 5 May 1916; Ito, *We Went to War*, 34, 70 and App. III, and personal communication, 18 Nov 1987. RG 24, vol. 1860, file 54, gives the number of Japanese Canadians enlisted as 166, while the militia minister reported 194 Japanese enlistments; House of Commons, *Debates*, 29 April 1920, 1812. On Chinese recruits see note 5, above.

36. NA, RG 14, vol. 1221, file 593–1–7, vol. 1, Chief Thunderwater to Hodgins, 29 May and 20 June 1916; RG 24, vol. 4383, file 34–7–109, Mewburn to OC 119th Battalion, 26 April 1916, OC 227th Battalion to Mewburn, 4 May 1916. Although the adjutant general directed in February that Indian transfers should thereafter be carried out only when 'special circumstances exist, as in the case of brothers,' Colonel Mewburn was still writing in April demanding the transfer of Indians to the 114th. See Hodgins to Baxter, 8 Feb. 1916.

37. NA, RG 24, vol. 1221, file 597–1–7, vol. 1, Cooke to minister of militia, 15 Dec. 1916; RG 24, vol. 4383, file 34–7–109, Hodgins to Logie, 31 Jan. 1916, Baxter to Hodgins, 2 Feb. 1916, Scott to Logie, 22 Jan. 1916, Logie to Hodgins, 22 Feb. 1916, Thompson to Mewburn, 13 April 1916; Gaffen, *Forgotten Soldiers*, 23

38. NA, RG 24, vol. 4383, file 34–7–109, Hodgins to Logie, 22 Feb. 1916, Thompson to OIC Divisional Recruiting, 1 March 1916, Thompson to Mewburn, 20 April 1916, Mewburn to OC 227th Battalion, 10 April 1916, and reply, 26 April, various regimental reports to Mewburn, July 1916; Gaffen, *Forgotten Soldiers*, 23

39. NA, RG 10, vol. 6766, file 452–13, Scott to Renison, 15 Jan. 1917, cables to Indian agents, 15 Jan. 1917, Militia Department to Tyson, 5 April 1917; RG 24, vol. 1221, file 597–1–7, vol. 1, Scott to Fiset, 15 Jan. 1917,

vol. 2, Ogilvie to Hodgins, cable, 22 March 1917; RG 24, vol. 4662, file 99–256, Ogilvie to Hodgins, 23 March 1916, Reynolds to Ogilvie, 20 March 1917, Tyson to Scott, 21 March 1917, Ogilvie to Hodgins, 22 March 1917

40. NA, RG 24, vol. 1221, file 593–1–7, vol. 1, Chief Thunderwater to Hodgins, 30 Dec. 1916, 2 Jan. 1917, Hodgins to Logie, 8 Jan. 1917, vol. 2, John to Thunderwater, 19 Feb. 1917, Mrs. Maracle to Thunderwater, 17 Feb. 1917, Thunderwater to Hodgins, 23 Feb. 1917, Hodgins to Logie, 9 and 22 March 1917, Logie to Hodgins, 15 and 24 March 1917. Colonel Thompson of the 114th Battalion had rejected the offer of Whitney's Toronto black volunteers by explaining 'The introduction of a coloured platoon into our Battalion would undoubtedly cause serious friction and discontent.' RG 24, vol. 4387, file 34–7–141, Thompson to Logie, 4 April 1916

41. Ibid., Wright to Logie, 4 April 1916; RG 24, vol. 4680, file 18–25–2. Adjutant General's Office to district commanding officers, circular letter, 16 August 1916; RG 24, vol. 4486, file 47–8–1, transfer order, 28 Aug. 1916

42. NA, RG 24, vol. 1469, file 600–10–35, Sutherland to McCurdy, 7 August 1916, Hodgins to Sutherland, 8 Aug. 1916; RG 24, vol. 1550, file 683–124–2, Sutherland to Hodgins, 27 Nov. 1916, to McCurdy, same date

43. NA, RG 24, vol. 1469, file 600–10–35, Sutherland to Hodgins, 25 Aug. 1916, Elliott to Hodgins, 19 Oct. 1916, Hodgins to Sutherland, 1 Dec. 1916; RG 24, vol. 1550, file 683–124–2, Sutherland to Hodgins, 27 Nov. 1916 and 4 Jan. 1917, memorandum, Minister's Office, 5 Jan. 1917, adjutant general to GOC Halifax, 23 Jan. 1917; RG 24, vol. 4486, file 47–8–1, Morrison, memo, 31 Aug. 1916. The Sailing List of the No 2 Construction Battalion, 28 March 1917, contains information on the birth place, recruitment place and date for each man, so that monthly and regional totals can be compiled.

44. NA, RG 24, vol. 4739, file 448–14–259, Duclos to Cruikshank, 8 Sept. 1916, Gayfer to Cruikshank, 6 and 18 Sept. 1916, 9 and 15 Oct. 1916; No 2 Recruitment Poster, Ruck, *Canada's Black Battalion*, Appendix, 126

45. NA, RG 10, vol. 6765, file 452–7, Cooke to Scott, 12 Feb. and 4 March 1916; minutes of the Six Nations Council, 15 Sept. 1914, in Wilson, *Ontario and the First World War*, 174

46. NA, RG 24, vol. 1221, file 593–1–7, vol. 1, Chief George Fisher to Gray, 19 Feb. 1916; RG 24, vol. 4383, file 34–7–109, Baxter to Williams, 18 Dec. 1915, Whitelaw to Baxter, 31 Dec. 1915; RG 10, vol. 6765, file 452–7, Cooke to Scott, 4 April 1916

47. NA, RG 24, vol. 1221, file 593–1–7, vol. 1, Chief Thunderwater to Hodgins, 20 June and 29 Nov. 1916, Indian Mothers from Saugeen Reserve to Sir Robert Borden, 12 Oct. 1916, Smith to Scott, 1 Oct. 1916; RG 10, vol. 6765, file 452–7, Cooke to Scott, 28 Feb. 1916

48. NA, RG 24, vol. 1469, file 600–10–35, Sutherland to Hodgins, 18 Dec. 1916; RG 24, vol. 4599, file 20–10–52, Gayfer to Gray, 22 Nov. 1916; RG 9 III, vol. 81, file 10–9–40, Sutherland to Perley, 27 April 1917

49. NA, RG 24, vol. 4599, file 20–10–52, Gayfer to GOC Winnipeg, 23 Oct. 1916, to Gray, 22 Nov. 1916; RG 24, vol. 1469, file 600–10–35. Stackford to McCurdy, 7 Sept. 1916, Sutherland to Hodgins, 17 Jan. 1917, to Kemp, 18 Jan. 1917; RG 24, vol. 4558, file 132–11–1, GOC Halifax to Sutherland, 5, 8, and 10 Sept. 1916; Ruck, *Canada's Black Battalion*, 24, and Appendix interviews

50. NA, RG 24, vol. 1469, file 600–10–35, Gwatkin to Hodgins, 18 Sept. 1916; RG 24, vol. 1550, file 683–124–2, Militia Ottawa to GOC Halifax, 23 Jan. 1917; RG 24, vol. 4739, file 448–14–259, Gayfer to Cruikshank, 6 Sept., 18 Sept., 4 Oct., and 7 Nov. 1916, and replies, 9 Sept., 19 Sept., 10 Oct., Cruikshank to Grant, 6 Nov. 1916, Aitken to Cruikshank, 9 Nov. 1916

51. NA, RG24, vol. 4558, file 132–11–1, Hodgins to GC Halifax, 31 July 1916, to Sutherland, 22 Dec. 1916. Sailing List, No 2 Construction Battalion, 28 March 1917. Of the 603 enlisted men and non-commissioned officers (not including white officers), 342 were Canadian-born, 72 were West Indian, 169 American, and 20 of various other nationalities. Nova Scotia supplied 296, Ontario 207, and the west 33.

52. NA, RG 9 III, vol. 81, file 10–9–40, Sutherland to Perley, 27 April 1917, McCurdy to Perley, 1 Oct. 1917, and reply, 1 Nov., White to Stanfield, 18 Oct. 1917

53. Brown and Loveridge, 'Unrequited Faith,' 55–6, 60–4, 67, App. D, 76; Nicholson, *Canadian Expeditionary Force*, 344, 347, 350, App. C, 546; Morton, *History*, 153, 156–8; Granatstein and Hitsman, *Broken Promises*, 60–104; A.M. Williams, 'Conscription 1917: A Brief for the Defence,' CHR 37 (1956): 338–51

54. NA, RG 10, vol. 6768, file 452–20, Mississauga of New Credit to Scott, 22 Oct. 1917, Nishga to prime minister, Nov. 1917, Chief Peter Angus to the King, 13 Nov. 1917, Committee of Allied Tribes to prime minister, 17 Nov. 1917, BC Indian agent to department, 26 Nov. 1917, Chief John Prince to Scott, 27 Nov. 1917, Garden River Reserve to governor general, 4 Dec. 1917, Katzelash band to Department of Indian Affairs, 4 Dec. 1917, Kitzumkalwee band to department, 4 Dec. 1917, Michipocoten band to department, 5 Dec. 1917, Edmundston, NB, Reserve to department, 15 Dec. 1917, Manitoba Rapids Reserve to department, 24 Dec. 1917, Hurons of Lorette to government general, 10 Jan. 1918; RG 24, vol. 11221, file 593–1–7, vol. 2, Military Sub-committee to Chisholm, 28 Nov. 1917, and reply, 29 Nov.

55. DND, DHist, minister of justice to Governor General in Council, 31 Dec. 1917

56. NA, RG 10, vol. 6788, file 452–20, Scott to Ditchburn, 1 Dec. 1917, to Anaham Reserve, 14 Dec. 1917.

57. PC III, 17 Jan. 1918; Military Service Regulations, Sections 12 and 16 as amended, 2 March 1918; PC 1459, 12 June 1918

58. NA, RG 24, vol. 1469, file 600–10–35, McLean to McCurdy, 10 Oct. 1917, McCurdy to Perley, 14 Nov. 1917, White to McCurdy, nd, Gwatkin to adjutant general, 21 Oct. 1917, Shannon to adjutant general, 16 Jan. 1918, McCurdy to Mewburn, 17 Jan. 1918, and reply, 21 Jan., adjutant general to Shannon, 5 Feb. 1918, Shannon to adjutant general, 13 and 21 Feb. 1918, adjutant general, circular letter to commanding officers, Feb. 1918, White to Sir Robert Borden, 11 Aug. 1918

59. Ibid., Young to Milligan, 13 March 1918, Shannon to adjutant general, 19 April 1918, adjutant general to Shannon, 24 and 30 April 1918, British-Canadian Recruiting Mission, New York, to adjutant general, 1 May 1918, and reply, 2 May

60. Ibid., adjutant general to Brown, 8 May 1918, to Sutherland, 22 May 1918

61. Ibid., White to Sir Robert Borden, 11 Aug. 1918

62. Ibid., Bristol to Creighton, personal, 26 Aug. 1918, Creighton to AG Mobilization, 14 Sept. 1918, cable to commanding officers, 17 Sept. 1918, and replies, Creighton to Bristol, personal, 28 Sept. 1918. The record of black conscripts provided by commanding officers showed London, Ont. 23, Toronto 10, Kingston 4, Halifax 55, Saint John 13. The Military Service Council asserted, however, that it had 'no record of coloured men who are liable to draft, as all men are shown according to Nationality regardless of colour,' Ibid., Captain Newcombe, memo, 25 Sept. 1918.

63. Ruck, *Canada's Black Battalion*, 37–9, and interview with Isaac Phills, 57

64. Ito, *We Went to War*, 70 and App. III. Of 185 volunteers, 54 were killed and 119 wounded.

65. NA, RG 9 III, vol. 5010, War Diaries, 107th Pioneer Battalion. In 1918 the 107th was disbanded and the men absorbed into an engineering brigade. See also Gaffen, *Forgotten Soldiers*, passim.

66. Ruck, *Canada's Black Battalion*, 65, interview with Sydney Jones of the 106th. At a black veterans' reunion in 1982, reference was made to eight different units, besides the No 2, in which the survivors had enlisted; ibid., chap. 6, Reunion and Recognition Banquet. Mr. Thamis Gale of Montreal, himself a World War II veteran and whose father was in the No 2, has been assiduously tracking down every black to serve in the CEF. From his as-yet unpublished results it appears that there may have been more than 1200 blacks in the CEF, which would mean over 600 distributed in various units outside the No 2; personal communications, 16 and 24 June 1986 and 14 Feb. 1988

67. NA, RG 24, vol. 1469, file 600–10–35, Mobilization to Gwatkin, 19 Feb. 1917, and reply, nd, memo to naval secretary, 21 Feb. 1917 and reply, 23 Feb.; Hunt, *Nova Scotia's Part*, 149–50

68. NA, RG 24, vol. 1469, file 600–10–35, Morrison to Bristol, 20 Dec. 1917; RG 9 III, vol. 1608, file E–186–9, director of forestry to YMCA, 9 June 1917, OC No 12 District to Timber Operations, 17 Jan. 1918, OC No 9 District to Timber Operations, 19 Aug. 1918, director of timber operations to General Headquarters, 28 Nov. 1918, and signal, 30 Nov. 1918; RG 9 III, vol. 4616, file c-B–8, assistant director to director, Chaplain Services, 20 Feb. 1918; RG 9 III, vol. 4645, folder 747, War Diaries, 2nd Canadian Construction Coy (Colored), vol. 11–10, 13, and 22 March 1918, vol. 12–14 and 17 April 1918, vol. 13–8 and 12 May 1918

69. There is of course a huge literature on the nature and extent of Western racist thought, and it is not considered necessary to recount its features here. Studies which explicitly set Canadian developments within a broader context, usually imperial or continental, include Carol Bacchi, 'Race Regeneration and Social Purity: A Study of the Social Attitudes of Canada's English-Speaking Suffragists,' *Histoire Sociale/Social History* 11 (1978): 460–74; Carl Berger, *The Sense of Power: Studies in the Ideas of Canadian Imperialism, 1867–1914* (Toronto 1970), and *Science, God, and Nature in Victorian Canada* (Toronto 1983); Douglas Cole, 'The Origins of Canadian Anthropology, 1850–1910,' *Journal of Canadian Studies* 8 (1973): 33–45; Terry Cook, 'George R. Parkin and the Concept of Britannic Idealism,' *Journal of Canadian Studies* 10 (1975): 15–31; Robert A. Huttenback, *Racism and Empire: White Settlers and Colored Immigrants in the British Self-Governing Colonies, 1830–1910* (Ithaca and London 1976); and Howard Palmer, 'Mosaic Versus Melting Pot? Immigration and Ethnicity in Canada and the United States,' *International Journal* 31 (1976): 488–528.

70. NA, RG 9 III, vol. 1608, file E–186–9, Provisional Mobilization Store Table for a Labour Company, White to GHQ, 10 Jan. 1918, and reply, 14 Jan.

71. NA, RG 9 III, vol. 81, file 10–9–40, Morrison to Bristol, 20 Dec. 1917

72. DND, DHist, 'Secret Information Concerning Black American Troops'; Foner, *Blacks and the Military*, 121–2; Balesi, 'From Adversaries to Comrades,' 112–13; Jeffrey Greenhut, 'Race, Sex and War: The Impact of Race and Sex on Morale and Health Services for the Indian Corps on the Western Front, 1914,' *Military Affairs* 45 (1981): 72–3; Willan, 'South African,' 71–3.

73. Nelson, 'Black Horror,' passim; Robert C. Reinders, 'Radicalism on the Left. E.D. Morel and the Black Horror on the Rhine,' *International Review of Social History* 13 (1968): 1–28; John C. Cairns, 'A Nation of Shopkeepers

in Search of a Suitable France,' *American Historical Review* 79 (1974): 718; Bernard Shaw, *What I Really Wrote About the War* (New York 1932), 32–3; Robert A. Huttenback, *The British Imperial Experience* (New York, 1966), 175–89

74. NA, RG 9, III, vol. 1709, file D–3–13, Collier to OC Canadian Troops, 10 Jan. 1919; Ruck, *Canada's Black Battalion*, 58–60, interviews with Robert Shepard and A. Benjamin Elms. See also Desmond Morton, 'Kicking and Complaining: Demobilization Riots in the Canadian Expeditionary Force, 1918–19,' CHR 61 (1980): 341, 343, 356

75. House of Commons, *Debates*, 20 June 1919, 3741

76. Ito, *We Went to War*, 73; Roy, 'Soldiers,' 343; Provincial Elections Act Amendment Act, *Statutes of British Columbia*, 1931, C 21; War Time Elections Act, *Statutes Canada*, 1917, C 39

77. See, for example, NA, RG 24, vol. 2765, file 6615–4-A, vol. 6, secret memorandum no 1, to all chairmen and divisional registrars, 20 Nov. 1941, and order from adjutant general to all district commanders, 12 July 1943; RG 27, vol. 130, file 601-3-4, 'Conscription of East Indians for Canadian Army'; DND DHist, 'Sorting out Coloured Soldiers' and 'Organization and Administration: Enlistment of Chinese'; *The Kings Regulations and Orders for the Royal Canadian Air Force*, 1924, amended 1943; *Regulations and Instructions for the Royal Canadian Navy*, amended by PC 4950, 30 June 1944. Ito and Roy give considerable detail on Chinese- and Japanese-Canadian efforts to enlist during World War II.

Topic Six

The Impact of Industrialization

Workers in a textile factory around 1908.

The emergence of Canadian social history shifted the focus of Canadian history from political events and economic trends to social change. Social historians have been especially interested in the transformation of Canada from an agricultural and commercial to an industrial economy. A number of them have examined the impact of the shift from rural to urban living on the "average" Canadians living in industrial cities — the working class and the urban poor. Many Canadian families had to adjust to living in slum areas of a city, and to having at least one parent, and, in many cases, both parents, as well as older children, working outside the home. Such changes affected the composition, social dynamics, and even decision-making process within the family. For working-class males, industrial life meant insecurity of work with the constant threat of layoffs for extended periods of time, low wages, and monotonous jobs that afforded them little or no sense of self worth or pride in their work. They sought out places where they could meet other workers and develop a sense of camaraderie.

The following two readings examine the impact of industrialization on family life and on working-class males in Montreal in the late nineteenth century — the period when the transition to industrialization first occurred. In her article, "Gender at Work at Home: Family Decisions, the Labour Market, and Girls' Contributions to the Family Economy," historian Bettina Bradbury examines how a division of labour along sexual lines in the workplace had already been shaped by decisions in the family based on gender as to who should work outside the home. Such family decisions were based as much on the family economy as on the economy of the workplace. Using predominantly census data for two working-class wards in Montreal, Bradbury shows that there was a trend as to whether sons or daughters went out to work based on family structure, attitudes of patriarchy, and the dynamics of a capitalist economy.

Historian Peter DeLottinville explains how Joe Beef's Canteen, a tavern in downtown Montreal, assisted sailors and longshoremen, and cultivated a working-class culture in the late nineteenth century, through a sketch of the owner, Charles McKieran, a re-creation of the atmosphere of the pub, and an examination of a cross-section of the patrons. He then goes on to explain the demise of the tavern in the 1880s as a result of changing work patterns, the rise of the Knights of Labor, and new attitudes toward leisure and urban conditions.

What were the factors that affected the decision in working-class families as to whether to send sons or daughters out to work? What were the cultural dynamics in working-class Montreal in the period from 1869 to 1889 that Joe Beef's Canteen both contributed to and benefited from? Both Bradbury and DeLottinville study working-class culture in Montreal in the same time period, but from different perspectives. In what ways are their perspectives and conclusions similar and different?

On the subject of women who work outside the home, see the relevant sections in Alison Prentice et al., *Canadian Women: A History*, 2nd ed. (Toronto: Harcourt Brace, 1996); Marjorie Griffin Cohen, *Women's Work, Markets, and Economic Development in Nineteenth-Century Ontario* (Toronto: University of Toronto Press, 1988); and Graham S. Lowe, *Women in the Administrative Revolution: The Feminization of Clerical Work* (Toronto: University of Toronto Press, 1987). Mary Kinnear, ed., *First Days, Fighting Days: Women in Manitoba History* (Regina: Canadian Plains Research Centre, 1987) contains several essays on women workers. See also *Women at Work: Ontario, 1850–1930*, eds. Janice Acton et al. (Toronto: Women's Educational Press, 1974), and Wayne Roberts, *Honest Womanhood: Feminism, Femininity and Class Consciousness among Toronto Working Women, 1893 to 1914* (Toronto: New Hogtown Press, 1976). A comparative study of men and women workers in the Ontario towns of Paris and Hanover is provided by Joy Parr in *The Gender of Breadwinners: Women, Men, and Change in Two Industrial Towns, 1880–1950* (Toronto: University of Toronto Press, 1990). For an interpretative article, see Ruth A. Frager, "Labour History and the Interlocking Hierarchies of Class, Ethnicity, and Gender: A Canadian Perspective," *International Review of Social History*, 44

(1999): 197–215. On the impact of industrialization on women and/or the family, see Bettina Bradbury's *Working Families: Age, Gender and Daily Survival in Industrializing Montreal* (Toronto: McClelland and Stewart, 1993) and the essays in Section 4 of her *Canadian Family History: Selected Readings* (Toronto: Copp Clark Pitman, 1992), as well as Peter Gossage, *Families in Transition: Industry and Population in Nineteenth-Century Saint-Hyacinthe* (Montreal/Kingston: McGill-Queen's University Press, 1999), and R. Marvin McInnis's "Women, Work and Childbearing: Ontario in the Second Half of the Nineteenth Century," *Histoire sociale/Social History* 24, 48 (November 1991): 237–62.

Three excellent primary sources on the impact of industrial growth in Canada at the turn of the century are *The Royal Commission on the Relations of Labour and Capital, 1889.* An abridged version has been published under the title *Canada Investigates Industrialism*, edited and with an introduction by Greg Kealey (Toronto: University of Toronto Press, 1973); and the two collections, *The Workingman in the Nineteenth Century*, ed. M.S. Cross (Toronto: Oxford University Press, 1974), and *The Canadian Worker in the Twentieth Century*, eds. I. Abella and D. Millar (Toronto: Oxford University Press, 1978). Three worthwhile collections are *Canadian Working Class History: Selected Readings*, eds. Laurel Sefton MacDowell and Ian Radforth (Toronto: McClelland and Stewart, 1992); *Essays on Canadian Working Class History*, eds. G. Kealey and P. Warrian (Toronto: McClelland and Stewart, 1976); and *Canadian Labour History: Selected Readings*, eds. D.J. Bercuson and David Bright (Toronto: Copp Clark, 1994). Terry Copp provides an in-depth study of working-class life in Montreal in his *The Anatomy of Poverty: The Conditions of the Working Class in Montreal, 1897–1929* (Toronto: McClelland and Stewart, 1974). A similar study for Toronto is Greg Kealey's *Toronto Workers Respond to Industrial Capitalism, 1867–1892* (Toronto: University of Toronto Press, 1980). A second valuable study on Toronto is Michael Piva's *The Conditions of the Working Class in Toronto, 1900–1921* (Ottawa: University of Ottawa Press, 1979). For Ontario in general, see Paul Craven, ed., *Labouring Lives: Work and Workers in Nineteenth-Century Ontario* (Toronto: University of Toronto Press, 1995). On Atlantic Canada, see Daniel Samson, ed., *Contested Countryside: Rural Workers and Modern Society in Atlantic Canada, 1800–1950* (Fredericton: Acadiensis Press, 1994). David Bright looks at the history of the labour movement in Calgary in his *The Limits of Labour: Class Formation and the Labour Movement in Calgary, 1883–1929* (Vancouver: University of British Columbia Press, 1998).

For a discussion of working-class culture, see Bryan Palmer's *A Culture in Conflict: Skilled Workers and Industrial Capitalism in Hamilton, Ontario, 1860–1914* (Montreal/Kingston: McGill-Queen's University Press, 1979), and his *Working-Class Experience: The Rise and Reconstitution of Canadian Labour, 1800–1991*, 2nd ed. (Toronto: McClelland and Stewart, 1993). On the importance of Labour Day parades as a cultural phenomenon, see Craig Heron and Steve Penfold, "The Craftmen's Spectacle: Labour Day Parades, The Early Years," *Social History/Histoire sociale*, 29, 58 (November 1996): 357–389.

WEBLINKS

Canadian Labour History
http://www.civilization.ca/hist/labour/lab02e.html
An account of early unions in Canada, with historical interviews from workers.

Industrialization in Newfoundland and Labrador
http://www.heritage.nf.ca/society/industry.html
A detailed description of the changes that industrialization and diversification brought to the economies of Newfoundland and Labrador.

Industrial Architecture of Montreal
http://digital.library.mcgill.ca/industrial/showbuilding.php?id=IN139
Interior illustrations of a Montreal factory in 1891. This site is part of a larger database of
images relating to Montreal's industrial architecture.

Article Fourteen

Gender at Work at Home: Family Decisions, the Labour Market, and Girls' Contributions to the Family Economy

Bettina Bradbury

INTRODUCTION

"Gender at work" can be read in two ways. In the first, work is a noun, and the central question is "How do definitions of skill, of appropriate work for men and women, get negotiated within the workplace by men and women, workers and capital?" Recent discussions of the sexual division of labour in diverse industries, of "gender at work," of the social construction of skill, and of the role of unions in perpetuating women's unequal position in the workforce have made major contributions to our understanding of the complexities of the relationships between gender and class, between patriarchy and capitalism. Historical research in this field is rich and fascinating, and is reshaping both women's history and working-class history in Canada as elsewhere.[1]

"Gender at work" can also be read, if my grammar is correct, as a verb. Here the question posed would be "How does gender work as a process in society which means that men and women end up with different work and life experiences?" To answer this question involves consideration of factors other than those found in the workplace. In this paper I would like to argue that while workplace-centred approaches go a long way toward explaining sex segregation within specific trades, they ignore different levels of decision making and other institutions that have already gendered the workforce before it arrives at the factory gate.[2] Equally, while approaches stressing the strength of patriarchal ideology or the importance of domestic labour help explain why married women remained out of the workplace, they fail to grasp the complex interactions between patriarchy and capitalism. Furthermore they are more difficult to apply when dealing with the work of daughters rather than their mothers.

Within families, decisions were made about who should stay home to look after children and do housework and who should earn wages which had wide-reaching impact on the composition of the workforce. Such decisions were never made in an ideological or economic vacuum; they represented a complex and often unconscious balance between basic

Source: *Canadian and Australian Labour History*, ed. Gregory S. Kealey and Greg Patmore (Sydney: Australian Society for the Study of Labour History and the Committee on Canadian Labour History, 1990), pp. 119–40. Reprinted by permission.

need, existing ideology and practice regarding gender roles, the structure of the economy, and the particular economic conjuncture. Schools taught specific skills and implanted tenacious ideas about future roles. At its broadest level this paper represents a simple plea to those looking at divisions of labour in the workplace to also consider the work done by historians of the family and education. In Canada such work offers some clues about this broader process, although little research systematically examines the question.[3] To the extent that historians interested in how gender is worked out within the workplace and in the unions ignore what happens prior to men's and women's arrival at work, their explanations will fail to consider the wider and deeper sexual division of labour, which not only relegated women to jobs defined as less skilled in workplaces shared with men and to feminine ghettos, but also determined that large numbers would simply not enter the workforce or would do so only sporadically.

More specifically, the paper focuses on one aspect of the question, namely, how family decisions in interaction with the nature of local labour markets influenced sons' and, in particular, daughters' contributions to the family economy.[4] The paper concentrates on the micro-level, examining what I have been able to deduce about family decision-making processes regarding which family members should seek wage labour in two Montreal working-class wards between the 1860s and 1890s. A brief description of the major sectors employing males in Montreal is followed by an assessment of the importance of additional wage earners to working-class families. The respective work of sons and daughters within the family economy is evaluated.

I argue that the sexual division of labour within the family, and the need for additional domestic workers as well as extra wage labourers, meant that the context, timing, and contours of boys' and girls' participation in wage labour were different. By looking at the role of girls in the family economy and not just in the labour market,[5] we can better see how the major changes accompanying the emergence of industrial capitalism in Montreal did not modify the dominant sexual division of labour.

MONTREAL FAMILIES AND WAGE LABOUR, 1860–1890

The years 1860 to 1890 were characterized by the growing dominance of industrial capital in the economic structure of Montreal and the increasing dependence on wage labour of a major proportion of its population. Canada's first and largest industrial city, "the workshop" of Canada, had a wide and complex array of industries. Most important were those relating to rail and water transportation, shoemaking, clothing, and food and beverages. The metallurgy sector, dominated by production for the railroads, provided jobs for skilled immigrants from Great Britain, and some French Canadians with a long tradition of working in metal. In shoe-making and dressmaking, as in numerous other smaller trades, artisanal production was rapidly, if unevenly, giving way to production in large factories. Minute divisions of labour accompanied the utilization of new types of machinery throughout the period, drawing immigrants and French Canadians new to the city into the myriad of largely unskilled jobs that were being created. Broadly speaking, the male workforce was divided into four groups. Best paid and most secure were the relatively skilled workers involved in the new trades that emerged with the industrial revolution — the engineers, machinists, moulders, and others who worked in the foundries and new factories. More subject to seasonal and conjunctural unemployment were skilled workers in the construction trades. A third group comprised those workers in trades undergoing rapid deskilling and reorganization; most important among these were the shoe-makers. General unskilled labourers made up the other major subgroup within the working class.

About 25 cents a day separated the average wage of each of these groups, setting the stage for potential differences in their standard of living and their family economy.[6] Women and girls worked largely in separate sectors of the economy, particularly as domestic servants and dressmakers and in specific kinds of factory work. In virtually every sector, their wages were half those of males or less.[7]

THE IMPORTANCE OF ADDITIONAL EARNERS IN THE FAMILY WAGE ECONOMY

These disparities of approximately 25 cents a day had the potential to separate the working class into identifiable fractions, each capable of achieving a different standard of living in good times, and each vulnerable in diverse ways to the impact of winter, cyclical depressions, and job restructuring. Throughout most of the period, the most skilled had more flexibility in their budget and a greater chance of affording to eat and live at a level that may also have helped to ward off the diseases that spread only too quickly through the poorly constructed sewers and houses of the city. This greater margin of manoeuvre which higher daily wages, greater job security, and the possession of skills that were scarce and usually in demand gave to the skilled was not constant. It was particularly likely to be eroded in times of economic depression or of rapid transformations in the organization of work.

While some skilled workers organized successfully during this period, the major element of flexibility in the family income, for skilled and unskilled alike, lay not so much in the gains that organization could offer, but in the ability to call on additional family members to earn wages, to gain or save money in other ways, or to limit the necessity of spending cash. Decisions about who additional family workers would be were therefore crucial in determining the contours of the family economy and of the labour force. An examination of the importance of secondary wage earners and of who they were in terms of their age and sex allows a better grasp of the interaction between family labour deployment decisions, the "gendering" of the workforce, and the structure of the economy. This section therefore assesses the importance of additional wage earners in families headed by men in different types of occupations.[8] The following section then attempts to determine who such workers were.

The average number of workers reported by the families of the two working-class areas studied here, Ste. Anne and St. Jacques wards, fluctuated over the family life cycle. Among young couples who had not yet borne children, the wife would occasionally report an occupation, and sometimes another relative lived with the couple, contributing to the number of workers in the household, so that until 1881 families averaged just over one worker at this first stage of a couple's married life. Most families then passed through a long period of relative deprivation as children were born, grew, and required more food, clothing, and larger living premises. Between the time when the first baby was born and some children reached twelve or thirteen, the families of Ste. Anne and St. Jacques continued to have only slightly more than one worker. Then children's contribution began to make up for the difficult years. In 1861, families where half the children were still under fifteen averaged 1.34 workers; once half were fifteen or more they averaged 1.97. In subsequent decades the expansion of wage labour made children's contribution even more important. Whereas in 1861 the average family with children over the age of eleven had only 0.48 of them at work, in 1881 it had 1.16. By 1871 the average family with offspring aged fifteen or more had nearly as many children living at home and working as there had been total number of workers a decade earlier. From 0.85 children at work, the number reported increased to 1.85. The total number of family workers increased from an average of under two at this stage in 1861 to nearly three a decade later. Children's wages became more and more important as children came to constitute a wage-earning family's major source of security.

The prosperity that this number of workers could have secured was temporary. It depended largely on the ability of parents to keep their wage-earning children in the household. As older sons or daughters began to leave home to work or marry, the average dropped down again. If both members of a couple survived they would find themselves struggling again in their old age on a single wage, or no wage at all. For aged working-class widows and widowers, the situation was particularly bleak if there were no children able to help.[9]

Over these years the patterns of the working-class and non-working-class families diverged. In 1861 the non-working class, particularly in St. Jacques, included a high proportion of artisans and shopkeepers, men whose family economy required not the wages, but the work of wives and children. As a result, the average number of workers and of children at work in their families was higher than in all other groups except the unskilled. Over the next two decades, artisans became less and less common. Family labour was increasingly limited to enterprises like small corner groceries. Professionals and some white-collar workers became more important among the non-working-class populations. After 1871, the reporting of jobs by children was least likely among this group.

It was within the working-class family economy that the most dramatic changes occurred over this period, although there were significant and changing differences between the skilled, the unskilled, and those in the indentured trades. The inadequacy of the $1.00 a day or less that a labourer could earn remained a constant throughout this period. As a result, unskilled families consistently relied on additional workers when they were able to. In 1861 they averaged 1.45 workers, compared to 1.27 among the skilled. Over the next two decades the growing number of jobs available allowed them to increase the average number of family workers to 1.62, then 1.66. Among those with working-age offspring, the average number at work increased by 123 percent, from 0.60 in 1861 to 1.34 two decades later.

For these unskilled workers, the period before children were old enough to work was the most difficult. It is worth examining how some such families managed at the critical stage of the family life cycle and later, as children matured. Olive Godaire, wife of labourer Pierre, worked, probably at home as a dressmaker, in 1861, to help support their three children, aged two to eight. Ten years later, it was her eighteen-year-old daughter who was taking in sewing, while a ten-year-old boy was apprenticed to be a tinsmith.[10] In the case of labourer John Harrington's family, the period when the father was the only earner within the nuclear family lasted for at least eighteen years. When John and Sarah's children were under ten, they took in boarders and had John's 50-year-old father, also a labourer, living in the household. Whatever money these extra family and household members contributed would have helped compensate for John's low wages or irregular work, and they continued to take in boarders over the next ten years. Their oldest son, Timothy, was still going to school in 1871, and the family was cramped in a rear dwelling where rent was minimal. Somewhere between 1871 and 1881, the boys joined their father in seeking general labouring jobs. For the first time, the family lived alone, without additional household members. With three wage earners — indeed, three labourers — they must have enjoyed a standard of living that was relatively high compared to the previous year.

The degradation of work conditions and lower wages that typified trades like shoemaking appear to have been counteracted by families' sending growing numbers of their members to seek steady work. In 1861, families in such trades had only 1.08 workers — fewer than any other group. By 1881, they averaged 1.62 workers. Most dramatic was the increased importance of the contribution of children resident at home. Among families with children of working age, the average number of children reporting a job nearly tripled over the two decades, from 0.55 to 1.51. At that date, a few families, like that of Angeline and Alexis Larivière, had four workers. Their two daughters, 22-year-old Josephine and sixteen-year-old Marie-Louise, worked as general labourers. The twenty-year-old son, Charles, was a stone-cutter.[11]

The relative superiority of the wages of skilled workers seems clear in 1861, when they appear to have been able to manage with fewer workers than other groups — averaging only 1.27. A decade later, with 1.5 workers, they still needed fewer than the rest of the working class. The depression that hit in 1874, however, appears to have eroded much of the superiority of the skilled workers. In 1881, after seven years of major depression, which was only just lifting and which must have left many a family heavily indebted, the pattern of family labour deployment was similar to that of the unskilled and those in the indentured trades.

This convergence of experiences within the working class over this period is not surprising, given the impact of the depression, combined with the degeneration of work conditions in some skilled trades. In the metal-working trades, for example, trade was said to be dead in the winter of 1878. Half the local unionized workers were said to be "working at any kind of labouring work." Two years earlier, a moulder drew attention to the desperate condition of Montreal mechanics, "working on a canal at 60 cents per day, men who have served years in securing a trade, the wages they receive being only a mockery of their misery."[12]

Families clearly attempted to shape their own economies by adjusting the numbers of wage earners to fit their expenses when they were able to do so. Additional wage earners were not only needed, but were used by all fractions of the working class, with differences stemming from the economic conjuncture, the nature of the labour market, and their own life cycle and earning power. In this way, working-class families influenced the city's labour pool and enhanced their own survival. The increasing availability of wage labour in the factories, workshops, and construction sites of Montreal meant that even in times of depression more and more sons and daughters could and did find work. The reliance of employers in certain sectors on women and youths resident at home depressed male wages generally, while offering families the opportunity to counter a father's low earnings.

Economic transformation thus interacted dialectically with family needs, reshaping the labour market, the family economy, and the life course of children. This interaction is clearest in the case of workers in those sectors undergoing the most dramatic transformation. The continued reorganization of production in trades like shoemaking was reflected not only in the greater increase in the number of their children seeking waged work over the period, but also in a tendency to delay marriage and reduce family size. In the labour market in general, children living at home became a much more significant proportion of workers.[13] In the sewing trades, for example, one-quarter of the workers had been co-resident children in 1861; by 1881, 55 percent were.

AGE, GENDER, AND ADDITIONAL FAMILY EARNERS

To try to grasp the decision-making processes behind these patterns of change in the average numbers of family members reporting work over this period, it is necessary to determine who the family workers were in terms of age and gender, and to examine the families from which they came.

Older sons still living at home were the most usual second earners in a family. The number of really young children or married women reporting a job was insignificant beside the importance of children in their late teens or twenties, despite the attention focused on such young workers by contemporaries.[14] Once sons, in particular, reached fifteen or sixteen, they were expected to work. "In our culture," reported Alice Lacasse, the daughter of a French-Canadian immigrant to New Hampshire, "the oldest children always went to work."[15] Wage labour for boys over fifteen became the norm in this period, as more and more were drawn into the labour force. Growing numbers of girls did report a job, but the proportion of boys at work remained consistently higher than that for girls in all age groups. And the pattern of involvement over a girl's life course continued to be completely different from a boy's.

By the age of fifteen or sixteen, 30 percent of the boys who lived at home in these two wards were reporting a job in 1861. Others no doubt sought casual labour on the streets, working from time to time, at other times roaming together in the gangs of youths that dismayed middle-class contemporaries, and filled up the local police courts. In 1871, when times were good, and industrial capitalism more entrenched, nearly 46 percent of boys this age could find a job, while in the depression of the 1870s and early 1880s, the percentage dropped back to 37 percent. After the age of sixteen, and increasingly over the period, boys' involvement with wage labour or other work would grow steadily as they aged. At ages seventeen to eighteen, 50 percent reported a job in 1861, nearly 68 percent two decades later. By age 21 nearly 90 percent of boys listed a job at the end of the period.

Among the girls of Ste. Anne and St. Jacques wards, the work found and the pattern of job reporting over their lives was very different from that of the boys. Once boys passed their early teens, they found work in a wide variety of jobs in all sectors and workplaces of Montreal. Girls, in contrast, remained concentrated within specific jobs and sectors. For girls as for boys, the chances of finding work clearly expanded with the growth of Montreal industry. At ages fifteen to sixteen, for instance, only 13 percent reported a job in 1861, compared to 30 percent in 1881. At the peak age at which girls reported working, nineteen to twenty, 25 percent worked in 1861, nearly 38 percent in 1871, and 35 percent in 1881. Even then, however, the visible participation rate of girls was only half that of boys.[16] After age twenty, the experiences of boys and girls diverged quickly and dramatically, as most, but never all, women withdrew from the formal labour market while most men found themselves obliged to seek work for the rest of their lives.

For those girls who did earn wages, then, paid labour was apparently undertaken for a brief period of their lives prior to marriage. At any one time, most girls aged fifteen or more who remained at home with their parents in these wards reported no job at all. Joan Scott and Louise Tilly have suggested that within the "industrial mode of production" "single women are best able to work, since they have few other claims on their time."[17] The discrepancy in the formal wage labour participation rates for boys and girls in these two Montreal wards suggests to me that single women did, in fact, have other claims on their time. In particular, the heavy and time-consuming nature of nineteenth-century housework, the prevalence of disease, the wide age spread among children in most families, and the myriad of other largely invisible pursuits and strategies necessary to survival for the working-class family meant that many of these girls were needed by their mothers to help with work at home. Their role in the division of labour within the family is highlighted on one census return where members' roles were explicitly described. Louis Coutur, a carter who was 50 in 1861, reported that his 21-year-old son was a shoemaker and that his wife's job was "housework."[18] It seems fair to assume, making allowance for the under-enumeration of steady labour and casual work among daughters, that most of the girls who listed no job or school attendance worked periodically, if not continually, at domestic labour as mother's helpers in and around the home. It is thus in the light of family decisions about the allocation of labour power at home, as well as in the structure of jobs available in the marketplace, that the patterns of children's wage labour as well as of their schooling must be interpreted.

At home, girls served an apprenticeship in the reproduction of labour power — in babysitting, cleaning, mending, sewing, cooking, and shopping and, by the end of the century, in nursing and hygiene.[19] Religious leaders were explicit about the need for mothers to educate their daughters in their future roles. "Apply yourselves especially to the task of training your daughters in the functions they will have to perform for a husband and family, without neglecting your other children," wrote Père Mailloux in a manual for Christian parents that was republished several times between the middle and end of the nineteenth century.[20] When girls attended school, the subjects learned were not very different. Education for females, except in a few expensive academies out of reach of the working class, taught only the most basic and general of subjects and housekeeping-type skills. Whereas boys' schools offered book-keeping and geography, girls' schools offered music, needlework, and sewing.[21] Curriculums aimed to prepare girls for their future role as housekeeper, wife, and mother.[22] The minister of education was explicit. He feared that too many young women were being educated above their station in life, and suggested that bookkeeping and domestic economy constituted the best basis of female education.[23]

Girls, then, were increasingly likely to become secondary wage earners within the working-class family economy during this period, but remained less likely to report a job than were boys. The importance of their contribution to domestic labour, the lower wages they could make in the formal labour market, or an ideological repulsion to girls' labour either within the working class or among capitalists constitute partial explanations for their lower rate of participation. In the absence of interviews or written memoirs, it is important to examine the work patterns of specific families more closely to see what reasons can be deduced from the evidence.[24]

Even among the families apparently in greatest need, sons seem to have been sent out to work in preference to daughters. If any families needed to draw on as many workers as possible, it should have been those headed by the labourers or shoemakers of these wards. In such families, food costs alone for a family with several growing children rapidly outstripped a man's incoming wages. Yet even these families appear to have avoided sending girls out to work, if possible. Among labourers' families in Ste. Anne in 1881, for example, 66 percent of those who had boys over ten reported having a son at work, while only 28 percent of those with girls the same age did so. If older brothers were working, girls generally did not. Girls of age twenty or more would stay at home while a teenage son worked. Their respective roles seem clearly defined. Twenty-six-year-old Ellen Mullin, for example, reported no occupation. Two brothers, aged nineteen and 23, worked as carters. Ellen's role was to help her mother with the domestic labour for the three wage earners and her fourteen-year-old younger brother.[25]

In Ste. Anne, even families without sons, or with young sons only, seem to have been either unwilling to send girls to work or unable to find work that was seen as suitable in the neighbourhood. Forty-two-year-old Octave Ethier must surely have had trouble supporting his four daughters, aged one to seventeen, and his wife on his labourer's wages. Yet neither seventeen-year-old Philomène nor fifteen-year-old Emma reported having a job.[26]

The girls in labourers' families who did report an occupation fell into two categories. Half were the oldest child, either with no brothers or only brothers who were much younger than they were. Nineteen-year-old Sarah Anne Labor, for instance, was the oldest in a family of six children. The closest brother was only seven. She worked as a soap maker. Her wages, and the fact that the family shared the household with several other families, must have helped make ends meet.[27]

The second group of girl workers in Ste. Anne and St. Jacques came from labourers' families that sent almost all their children to work regardless of gender. Catherine Harrigan, for instance, was fourteen. She worked as a servant. Her two brothers, aged fifteen and twenty, were labourers like their father. In the family of St. Jacques labourer Damase Racette, four girls, aged seventeen to 25, were all dressmakers, as was his wife, Rachel. A 27-year-old son was a cigar maker.[28] This latter group of families appears the most desperate, perhaps because of recurrent illness or the habitual drunkenness of a parent. When Commissioners Lukas and Blackeby were examining the work of children in Canadian mills and factories in 1882, they reported finding too many cases in the cities and factory districts where parents with "idle habits" lived "on the earnings of the children, this being confirmed" in their eyes by one instance where three children were at work, having a father as above described.[29] Yet, such a family could simply have been taking advantage of the fact of having more children of working age to make up for years of deprivation on the inadequate wages most family heads could make. Two years later, reports made to the Ontario Bureau of Industries stressed the inadequate wages of family heads as the major cause of children's working, while mentioning that dissipation of the husband or father was less often a cause.[30] When a father was chronically ill or a habitual drunkard, the wages of several children would indeed have been necessary to support a family. The use of daughters and of children aged ten to twelve to earn wages in this minority of labourers' families contrasts with the absence of such workers in other labourers' families, highlighting the relative infrequency of a daughter's work, even among those in greatest need.

Was it in part working-class ideology that kept girls at home if at all possible, seeing the workplace as unfit for them, or was it rather a pragmatic response to the fact that boys' wages rapidly outstripped those of girls? Pragmatism, made necessary by the exigencies of daily life, must certainly have played an important part. It made good sense to have boys earn wages rather than girls, for while young children of each sex might earn a similar wage, once they reached fifteen or sixteen, girls' wages were generally half those of young men. On the other hand, when there was work available that girls could do, more were likely to report a job. Thus, the labourers of St. Jacques were more likely to have daughters at work than those of Ste. Anne. St. Jacques labourers' families with children aged eleven or over had an equal percentage of girls and boys at work. The fact that nearly 80 percent of these girls worked in some branch of the sewing industry shows how families took advantage of the availability of this kind of work in the neighbourhood.

Family labour deployment decisions, then, were forged in the context of their own needs, invariably arising partly from the size, age, and gender configurations of the family, as well as from the kind of work the family head could find. They were realized in relationship with the structure of the local labour market, of job possibilities, and of local wage rates for men and women, boys and girls. And they were influenced by perceptions, ideologies, and gut reactions about what was appropriate for sons and daughters. Thus, it was not just the fact that sewing was available in St. Jacques ward that made this such a popular choice for daughters living in that ward, for putting out could theoretically operate anywhere in the city or the surrounding countryside. It was, I suspect, the very fact that it could be done at home that was crucial. For, while domestic service no doubt took some young women from families in these wards away from their own families and into the homes of others, sewing usually kept daughters working at home.[31]

Home-work offered parents, and mothers in particular, several advantages. First, they could oversee their daughters' work and behaviour, avoiding the individualism that working in a factory might encourage and skirting the dangers and moral pitfalls that at least some contemporaries associated with factory work for young, unmarried women.[32] More important, girls sewing at home, like their mothers, could combine stitching and housework, take care of younger children, run odd errands, or carry water as needed, because they were right there and were always paid by the piece.

The clustering of two to five family members, all seamstresses, commonly found in the census returns for St. Jacques ward suggests very strongly that here was a centre of the home-work that was crucial to Montreal's sewing and shoemaking industries during this period. It was not uncommon to find three to four sisters, ranging in age from eleven to 28, all working, presumably together, as sewing girls. In the Mosian family of St. Jacques ward, for instance, four daughters worked as seamstresses in 1871. The father was a labourer, and although the wife reported no occupation, she probably also did some sewing at home at times.[33] In 1881, the family of Marie and Michel Guigère had reached a relatively secure stage in their family life cycle. With nine children at home, aged two to 23, this joiner's family reported seven workers. Four of the girls, aged thirteen to 23, were seamstresses; one son worked as a labourer; and the thirteen-year-old son was an apprentice. The girls could combine sewing with helping their mother keep house for other workers, care for the younger children, shop, cook, clean, and also look after her husband's 70-year-old father, who lived with them. Marie too probably helped sporadically with sewing.[34]

Some parents with the liberty to choose must have been reluctant to expose their daughters to the long hours, continual supervision, exhausting work, and brutal forms of discipline that existed in some of Montreal's workshops and factories. Work at home could counteract such factors of "repulsion"[35] in some of the sectors employing girls. Cigar-making factories provided jobs for girls and boys in Ste. Anne and St. Jacques alike. While some manufacturers appear to have been decent men, neither fining nor beating their employees, others, in an apparently desperate attempt to control their youthful workforce, resorted to physical violence, heavy fines, even locking up children, as they strove to mould this young generation of workers to industrial work. Children, like adults, in these factories worked from six or seven in the morning until six at night, and sometimes later.[36] Unlike adult males, they were subject to a vast array of disciplinary measures aimed at making them more productive and more responsible as workers. One child reported:

> If a child did anything, that is, if he looked on one side or other, or spoke, he would say: I'm going to make you pay 10 cents fine, and if the same were repeated three or four times, he would seize a stick or a plank, and beat him with it.[37]

Mr. Fortier's cigar-making factory was described as a "theatre of lewdness." There was said to be "no such infamous factory as M. Fortier's . . . nowhere else as bad in Montreal." There, one cigar maker described apprentices as being "treated more or less as slaves."[38] It was the evidence of the treatment of one eighteen-year-old girl that really shocked both the public and the commissioners examining the relations between labour and capital in 1888. Georgina Loiselle described how Mr. Fortier beat her with a mould cover because she would not make the 100 cigars as he demanded.

> I was sitting, and he took hold of me by the arm, and tried to throw me on the ground. He did throw me on the ground and beat me with the mould cover.
>
> Q. Did he beat you when you were down?
>
> A. Yes, I tried to rise and he kept me down on the floor.[39]

The case of Mr. Fortier's cigar factory was not typical. It created a sensation when the evidence was heard. At least some of the mothers of girls working there got together, perhaps encouraged by Mr. Fortier, to give evidence to counteract the impact of such bad publicity. "I am the mother of a family and if I had seen anything improper I would not have stayed there," explained a Mrs. Levoise. "I have my girl working there."[40]

While conditions in other Montreal factories were not as extreme, there was sufficient evidence of beatings, other draconian forms of discipline, and heavy fines to explain why many girls and their parents may have wished to avoid factory labour. In cotton factories there was some evidence of boys and girls being beaten. Furthermore, fines in at least one Montreal cotton factory could reduce pay packages by between $1.00 and $12.00 in two weeks. Work there began at 6:25 a.m. and finished at 6:15 p.m. When extra work was required, employees had to stay until 9 p.m., often without time off for supper.[41] There were some perks to working in the textile industry. Nineteen-year-old Adèle Lavoie explained that the girls were accustomed to "take cotton to make our aprons." Apparently this was usually allowed, but on at least one occasion she was accused by the foreman of having taken 40 to 50 yards. When a search of her house produced no results, she reported that the foreman returned to the factory to insult and harass her sister. When she did not produce the cotton, "he stooped at this time and raising the skirt of my sister's dress, he said she had it under her skirt."[42]

Airless, hot, dusty factories, such sexual abuse by foremen, work conditions, and the long hours were all factors that may have discouraged parents from sending girls into factory work. More significant were the wages they earned. For children under fourteen or so, wages varied little by sex. After that, male and female differentials hardened. Girl apprentices in dressmaking, mantlemaking, and millinery sometimes earned nothing for several years until they learned the trade; then they received around $4.00 a week only. "Girls" in shoe manufactories received $3.00 to $4.00, compared to the $7.00 or $8.00 earned by men. A girl bookbinder made between $1.50 and $6.00 weekly, compared to an average of $11.00 for male journeymen. Even on piece-work, girls and women generally received less than men. In general, wage rates for women were approximately half those of men.[43]

Over this period, more and more working-class boys would have reached manhood accustomed to wage labour. Because of duties at home and low wages, however, their sisters, whether they worked in or outside the home, were much more likely to move backwards and forwards between paid work and housework in response to the family's economic needs and their position in the household. Once boys, and particularly those who had been fortunate enough to acquire a skill in demand in the marketplace, reached their late teens, their earning power might rival that of their father. Wage labour offered such children potential freedom from their family in a way that had not been possible in family economies based on shared work and the inheritance of property. Such freedom was seldom possible for girls, unless they were willing to complement wage labour with prostitution.

AGE, GENDER, AND CHANGING PATTERNS OF RESIDENCE, SCHOOLING, AND DOMESTIC LABOUR

Yet, boys in general do not appear to have taken dramatic advantage of such potential freedom. Nor did girls.[44] In 1861, living with others was still an important stage in the lives of some young people of both sexes. Among the seventeen-year-old girls residing in Ste. Anne and St. Jacques, 35 percent were boarding with other families, living with relatives, or working and living in as a servant. Twenty years later, only 12 percent of girls that age were not living with their parents, and half of these were already married. Among boys aged eighteen, 34 percent were not living with their parents in 1861, compared to only 17 percent two decades later. Living longer at home with their parents was a fundamental change in the life cycle of boys and girls alike during this period of industrial expansion.[45]

Behind the percentages of children living with their parents or elsewhere lies a complex history of tension between family needs and individual desires, of children balancing off the advantages of the services offered at home against the relative independence that living with strangers, or even relatives, might offer.[46] For all families who had passed through at least fifteen years of budget stretching, house sharing, and debt building while their children were young, the relative prosperity that several workers could offer was to be jealously guarded. It was precisely "because young adults could find jobs" that it "was in the interest of parents to keep their children at home as long as possible."[47] The patterns of residence of children suggest that, whatever conflicts there were overall, in these two wards of Montreal between 1861 and 1881, it was increasingly the parents who were the winners.

The motives behind individual decisions, the weight of traditions of family work, are difficult to grasp in the absence of written records. The factors constraining or encouraging one choice or another are clearer. Most children would have left home once they had a job only if their wages were adequate to pay for lodgings and they felt no commitment to contributing to the family income.[48] Clearly, more older boys earned enough to pay for room and board than did girls. Thus, in 1871, when work was readily available, 29 percent of the 23-year-old males living in these wards were boarding or with relatives, 39 percent were living with their parents, and 32 percent had married. Among girls the same age, the low wages they could make severely limited their options. Only 15 percent were boarding, 41 percent were still with their parents, and 44 percent were already married. The contraction of work and the lower wages that accompanied the depression that hit in 1874 limited the possibility of leaving home to lodge with others or to marry. In 1881, the percentage of 23-year-old boys married had dropped to 25 percent; only 10 percent were boarding or living with relatives. Sixty-five percent remained at home with their parents, presumably pooling resources to survive the difficult times. The depression appears to have hastened the decline of this stage of semi-autonomy. What occurred in subsequent years remains to be determined.

The different roles of boys and girls in the family economy are confirmed in the different patterns of school attendance by age and sex. In general, school and work appear to have been complementary rather than in competition. Some children began school at four years old. By age seven, approximately 60 percent of boys and girls were receiving some education. In 1881, this percentage rose to a peak of 78 percent for eight- and nine-year-old boys, and around 80 percent for girls aged nine to twelve, then fell off rapidly once both sexes reached thirteen. The proportion of children receiving some schooling increased, but not dramatically, between 1861 and 1881. Age, gender, and the economic conjuncture created variations within this overall trend. Most important was the more erratic pattern in the attendance of boys that hints at relationships between age, gender, schooling, and wage labour that require further investigation. Overall, the percentage of ten- to fourteen-year-old girls at school increased slowly but steadily, from 57 percent in 1861 to 68 percent in 1881.[49] The increase was greater in St. Jacques than Ste. Anne, but the pattern was similar. Among boys in each ward, in contrast, the proportion at school was lower in 1871 than any other year, and the proportion of ten- to nineteen-year-olds at work increased. In Ste. Anne, in particular, the factories, workshops, and general labouring jobs attracted growing numbers of these youths. The percentage of fifteen- to nineteen-year-old boys reporting working in that ward increased from 38 in 1861 to 64 a decade later. While a certain number of families appear to have taken advantage of boom periods to draw their sons, in particular, out of school, the majority of families appear to have got the best of both worlds. Most working-class boys went to school for varying lengths of time before they reached thirteen or so, and then sought wage labour.

These figures confirm the greater importance of a son's wage contribution to the family economy. Girls' role is clear in the high proportion that continued to report neither a job nor school attendance. Transformations of the economy and the passage of time were slow to modify this gender difference in the relationship between girls' and boys' schooling and their roles in the family economy. A study conducted in Quebec in 1942, just before school was finally made compulsory in that province, found that among children quitting school before the age of sixteen, 61 percent of girls gave as their reason, "Maman avait besoin de moi," while 50 percent of boys stated, "Ma famille avait besoin d'argent." Only 10 percent of girls gave that reason.[50] The centrality of girls' domestic labour in a different Canadian city, Toronto, is corroborated by evidence showing that potential foster parents in that city at the turn of the century were four times more likely to seek girls than boys, specifically for their usefulness as domestics and nursemaids.[51]

CONCLUSION

Filial Piety

Gender was clearly at work in both senses of the word in nineteenth-century Montreal. On the one hand, the labour market was characterized by a sexual division of labour which, despite the rapid and dramatic changes occurring in the period, limited the numbers of jobs where capitalists considered employing women. This was not immutable, as the cases where "girls" were used as strikebreakers made clear. Montreal's labour market included major sectors, particularly sewing and shoemaking, that employed large numbers of girls and women. Yet, the figures of labour-force participation rates for the two wards studied here suggest strongly that girls and women seldom entered the workforce in proportions equivalent to their brothers or boys the same age, and that over their life courses their participation was totally different.

The reasons why lie at least partially within the workings of the family-wage economy. Working-class families in Montreal clearly both needed and used additional family workers to counteract low wages, and to improve their standard of living. The number of extra workers varied with the skill of the family head and the worth of that skill in the labour market. Thus, while skilled workers managed, in good times, with fewer family workers than the unskilled or those in indentured trades, economic depression eroded such superiority. Yet in whatever complex and probably tension-loaded decisions were made about who would seek what kind of work, boys were much more likely to be the auxiliary wage earners than girls.

To explain why brings us, in a sense, to the heart of the debate about the relative importance of patriarchy and capitalism in explaining women's oppression.[52] That the domestic labour of wives has been crucial both to family survival and to women's inequality has long been recognized both empirically and theoretically. But where do daughters fit in? Fathers, one could argue, by keeping girls at home along with their mothers to serve their daily need for replenishment, ensured that the work of all women was viewed as intermittent and secondary to that of the major wage earners.[53] Alternatively, the accent can be put on the nature of specific industries, or more generally on the capitalist labour market, which, by setting women's wage rates at half those of men, made it logical to send boys to work rather than girls.[54] Unequal access to work on the same terms as men thus not only perpetuated women's position in the home, but tragically disadvantaged those single women and widows who alone, or supporting children or elderly parents, had to live on such wages.

Clearly a dialectic is at work here. Neither empirically nor theoretically can the workings of patriarchy or capitalism be neatly separated from each other.[55] The nature of the interaction between the two and the weight of one over the other will vary historically and geographically. Among Montreal families, decisions were made in part in relation to existing jobs and wage rates, and such decisions perpetuated and reified the idea that women's work was temporary, performed before marriage or in moments of family crisis.[56] Admitting the dialectic adds complexity to the explanation but remains, I suspect, insufficient, because the emphasis remains on the formal, wage-earning labour market. Domestic labour in the nineteenth century was fundamental to family survival, to the transformation of wages into a reasonable standard of living, and to the reproduction of the working class. Historians have recognized the importance of this job for the working-class wife and mother; the role of daughters has been examined less explicitly.[57] Yet, for nineteenth-century mothers whose children were widely spaced in age and in whose homes technology had made virtually no inroads to lighten their labour, the help of daughters was invaluable. Housewives had no control over the amount of wages the husband earned, and little over how much was turned over to them. Housework was labour intensive and time consuming. One of the only ways in which wives could control the content and intensity of their work was to get children to help. Wherever possible, once girls reached an age where they could be of use to the mother, they were used to babysit, to run errands, to clean, sew, and cook. If this could be combined with wage-earning activities, as in the case of homework in the sewing industry, then such girls did work more formally. If there were no brothers of an age to earn, daughters might work in factories, offices, or shops, or as domestics. But the need of mothers for at least one helper at home would mean that the rate of formal labour-force participation for girls would generally be lower than that for boys.[58] Patriarchal ideas within the working class, elements of male pride and self-interest, economic pragmatism, and the daily needs of mothers and housewives thus interacted, creating a situation in which most girls served an apprenticeship in domestic labour prior to, or in conjunction with, entering the workforce.[59] In cities and towns where the labour market was completely different, where whole families or women were explicitly sought by employers, this division of labour, indeed, the very institutions of marriage and the family, could be modified. The question of how to ensure that the necessary domestic labour was performed, however, would remain fundamental.[60] The working out of roles by gender at home would continue to influence the configurations of gender at work.

NOTES

1. Heidi Hartmann, "Capitalism, Patriarchy, and Job Segregation by Sex," *Signs* 1 (Spring 1976): 137–69; Judy Lown, "Not So Much a Factory, More a Form of Patriarchy: Gender and Class during Industrialisation," in E. Garmarnikow et al., *Gender, Class, and Work* (London, 1983); Sonya O. Rose, "Gender at Work: Sex, Class, and Industrial Capitalism," *History Workshop Journal* 21 (Spring 1986): 113–31; Nancy Grey Osterud, "Gender Divisions and the Organization of Work in the Leicester Hosiery Industry," in Angela V. John, *Unequal Opportunities: Women's Employment in England, 1800–1918* (Oxford: Basil Blackwell, 1986), 45–70; Sylvia Walby, *Patriarchy at Work: Patriarchal and Capitalist Relations in Employment* (Minneapolis: University of Minnesota Press, 1986); Ruth Milkman, *Gender at Work: The Dynamics of Job Segregation by Sex during World War II* (Urbana: University of Illinois Press, 1987). For Canadian articles touching on the question, see Gail Cuthbert Brandt, "The Transformation of Women's Work in the Quebec Cotton Industry, 1920–1950," in *The Character of Class Struggle: Essays in Canadian Working Class History, 1840–1985*, ed. Bryan D. Palmer (Toronto: McClelland and Stewart, 1986) pp. 115–134; Mercedes Steedman, "Skill and Gender in the Canadian Clothing Industry, 1890–1940," in *On the Job: Confronting the Labour Process in Canada*, ed. Craig Heron and Robert Storey (Montreal: McGill-Queen's University Press, 1986), 152–76; Marta Danylewycz and Alison Prentice, "The Evolution of the Sexual Division of Labour in Teaching: A Nineteenth-Century Ontario and Quebec Case Study," *Histoire sociale/Social History* 6 (1983): 81–109; Marta Danylewycz and Alison Prentice, "Teachers, Gender, and Bureaucratising School Systems in Nineteenth-Century Montreal and Toronto," *History of Education Quarterly* 24 (1984): 75–100; Jacques Ferland, "Syndicalisme parcellaire et syndicalisme collectif: Une interprétation socio-technique des conflits ouvriers dans deux industries québécoises, 1880–1914," *Labour/Le Travail* 19 (Spring 1987): 49–88.

2. This argument is obviously not mine alone. It is fundamental to much of the discussion of the workings of patriarchy and to the domestic labour debate, where too often it remains at an abstract theoretical level or based on cursory historical data. It is worth making here because much theoretical work places too much emphasis on either capitalist relations or reproduction and patriarchy, simplifying the complexity of relations between the two, while historical literature on the workplace or the family tends to treat the relation between the two simplistically.

3. Joy Parr's recent articles offer the first major sustained analysis in which decisions and conditions in the home and in the workplace and the relationship between the two are constantly and systematically examined.

See especially "Rethinking Work and Kinship in a Canadian Hosiery Town, 1910–1950," *Feminist Studies* 13, 1 (Spring 1987): 137–62; and also "The Skilled Emigrant and Her Kin: Gender, Culture, and Labour Recruitment," *Canadian Historical Review* 68, 4 (Dec. 1987): 520–57, reprinted in *Rethinking Canada: The Promise of Women's History,* 2nd ed., ed. Veronica Strong-Boag and Anita Clair Fellman (Toronto: Copp Clark Pitman, 1991), 33–55. Gail Cuthbert-Brandt does so in a different sense in "Weaving It Together: Life Cycle and the Industrial Experience of Female Cotton Workers in Quebec, 1910–1950," *Labour/Le Travailleur* 7 (Spring 1981). Mark Rosenfeld's recent article "'It Was a Hard Life': Class and Gender in the Work and Family Rhythms of a Railway Town, 1920–1950," *Historical Papers* (1988), and reprinted in this volume [i.e., *Canadian and Australian Labour History*], carefully unravels how the rhythms of work in the running trades structured the family economy and gender roles in Barrie, Ontario, a railway town.

4. No Canadian work directly confronts this question either in the econometric sense in which Claudia Goldin poses it in "Family Strategies and the Family Economy in the Late Nineteenth Century: The Role of Secondary Workers," in *Philadelphia: Work, Space, Family and Group Experience in the Nineteenth Century,* ed. Theodore Hershberg (New York: Oxford University Press, 1981), 277–310, or in the more feminist and qualitative way that Lynn Jamieson poses it in "Limited Resources and Limiting Conventions: Working-Class Mothers and Daughters in Urban Scotland c. 1890–1925," in *Labour and Love: Women's Experience of Home and Family, 1850–1940,* ed. Jane Lewis (Oxford: Basil Blackwell, 1986), 49–69.

5. Marjorie Cohen makes a similar argument without elaborating on its implications for daughters in stating that "the supply of female labour was limited by the labour requirements of the home." *Women's Work, Markets, and Economic Development in Nineteenth-Century Ontario* (Toronto: University of Toronto Press, 1988), 139. Her insistence on the importance of domestic production and women's work in the home for rural and urban families alike and for an understanding of the wider economy represents an important contribution to economic history as well as to the history of women and the family in Canada.

6. On the average, in the early 1880s, for example, a labourer earned around $1.00 a day, a shoemaker $1.25, a carpenter $1.50, and various more highly skilled workers anything from $1.75 (blacksmith) up. See Bettina Bradbury, "The Working-Class Family Economy, Montreal, 1861–1881" (Ph.D. diss., Concordia University, 1984), 18; Canada, Parliament, *Sessional Papers,* 1882, Paper No. 4, Appendix 3, Annual Report of the Immigration Agent, 110–11, lists wages in a variety of trades.

7. In this, Montreal and Canada were little different from other cities and countries, nor has much of the discrepancy been eliminated today.

8. The figures used in this paper are derived from research done for my Ph.D. thesis, currently under revision for publication. A 10 percent random sample was taken of households enumerated by the census takers in Ste. Anne and St. Jacques in 1861, 1871, and 1881. This resulted in a total sample of 10 967 people over the three decades. They resided in 1851 households and 2278 families as defined by the census takers.

9. For a brief and preliminary examination of how widows of all ages survived, see my "Surviving as a Widow in Nineteenth-Century Montreal," *Urban History Review* 17, 3 (1989): 148–60, reprinted in *Rethinking Canada,* 2nd ed., ed. Strong-Boag and Fellman.

10. These life histories were re-created by tracing families between the censuses of 1861, 1871, and 1881.

11. Mss. Census, St. Jacques, 1881, 17, p. 110.

12. *Iron Moulders Journal,* Jan. and June, 1878, Report of Local 21; *Iron Moulders Journal,* Jan. 1876, Report of Local 21 and open letter from Local 21 to the editor, cited in Peter Bischoff, "La formation des traditions de solidarité ouvrière chez les mouleurs Montréalais: la longue marche vers le syndicalisme, 1859–1881," *Labour/Le Travail* 21 (Spring 1988): 22. Bischoff suggests, sensibly, that among moulders the homogenizing experience of these years of depression left them more open to the idea of including less skilled workers in their union in the 1880s. The widespread appeal of the Knights of Labour could be seen in the same light.

13. In 1861, for example, only 16 percent of those reporting jobs in these two wards were children residing at home; twenty years later nearly one-third of all reported workers were offspring living with their parents. Peter Bischoff found a similar trend among moulders. The percentage of moulders for the entire city of Montreal that were sons living with their parents rose from 25 percent in 1861 to nearly 40 percent in 1881. Peter Bischoff, "Les ouvriers mouleurs à Montréal, 1859–1881" (M.A. thesis, Université de Québec à Montréal, 1986), 108.

14. There is no doubt that the wage labour both of young children and married women was under-enumerated. However, as no labour laws existed in Quebec until 1885, and education was not compulsory until 1943, it is unlikely that fear of repercussions would have inhibited parents from responding as it might have elsewhere. It seems fair to assume that the under-reporting of children's jobs, and probably married women's, would have been no greater in Montreal than in other cities of Canada, England, or America, and probably less.

15. Tamara K. Hareven and Randolph Langenbach, *Amoskeag: Life and Work in an American Factory City* (New York: Pantheon Books, 1978), 262.

16. Caution has to be exercised when using reported jobs for women and children. There is a tendency now in some of the literature on the subject to suggest that gender differentials in workforce participation are largely a result of women's work not being adequately enumerated. While I am sure that some under-enumeration of women's work occurred in Montreal, as elsewhere, I don't think that under-enumeration can explain away the differential. Nor is the phenomenon easy to measure. More important, I think, was the nature of women's work, which, because of its lack of regularity, its more informal nature, was less likely to be reported. On the problem of under-reporting, see, in particular, Sally Alexander, "Women's Work in Nineteenth-Century London: A Study of the Years 1820–1850," in *The Rights and Wrongs of Women*, ed. Juliett Mitchell and Ann Oakley (London: Penguin Books, 1976), 63–66; Karen Oppenheim Mason, Maris Vinovskis, and Tamara K. Hareven, "Women's Work and the Life Course in Essex County, Massachusetts, 1880," in Tamara K. Hareven, *Transitions: The Family and the Life Course in Historical Perspective* (New York: Academic Press, 1979), 191; Margo A. Conk, "Accuracy, Efficiency and Bias: The Interpretation of Women's Work in the U.S. Census of Occupations, 1890–1940," *Historical Methods* 14, 2 (Spring 1981): 65–72; Edward Higgs, "Women, Occupations, and Work in the Nineteenth-Century Censuses," *History Workshop* 23 (Spring 1987).

17. Joan Scott and Louise Tilly, *Women, Work, and Family* (New York: Holt, Rinehart and Winston, 1979), 231.

18. Mss. Census, 1861, St. Jacques, 11, p. 7750.

19. By the end of the century the need for this kind of education of daughters was being explicitly preached by Montreal doctors and by church representatives, and was formalized in Quebec with the creation of *écoles ménagères* after the 1880s. Carole Dion, "La femme et la santé de la famille au Québec, 1890–1940" (M.A. thesis, Université de Montréal, 1984).

20. A. (Père) Mailloux, *Le manuel des parents Chrétiens* (Quebec, 1851, 1910), cited in Carole Dion, "La femme et la santé de la famille," 60–65.

21. L.A. Huguet-Latour, *L'Annuaire de Ville Marie: Origine, utilité, et progrès des institutions catholiques de Montréal* (Montreal, 1877), 165–70.

22. Marie-Paule Malouin, "Les rapports entre l'école privée et l'école publique: L'Académie Marie-Rose au 19e siècle," in *Maîtresses de maison, maîtresses d'école*, ed. Nadia Fahmy-Eid and Micheline Dumont (Montreal: Boreal Express, 1983), 90.

23. Québec, *Documents de la Session*, 1874, "Rapport du Ministre de l'instruction publique," vii.

24. In Lynn Jamieson's study of working-class mothers and daughters in Scotland, which is based on interviews, she makes it clear that mothers made different demands upon boys and girls in terms of the contributions they should make to the family economy. Mothers "pre-occupied with their housekeeping responsibilities" were much more likely to keep girls home from school to help with housework than to encourage boys to go out and earn. If a father died, for example, daughters or sons might enter full-time paid employment, but if a mother died "only daughters left school early to become full-time housekeepers." "Working-Class Mothers and Daughters in Scotland," in *Labour and Love*, 54, 65.

25. Mss. Census, Ste. Anne, 1881, 5, p. 1.

26. Mss. Census, Ste. Anne, 1881, 5, p. 1.

27. Mss. Census, Ste. Anne, 1881, 9, p. 208.

28. Mss. Census, St. Jacques, 1881, 17, p. 340.

29. "Report of the Commissioners Appointed to Enquire into the Working of the Mills and Factories of the Dominion and the Labour Employed Therein," Canada, Parliament, *Sessional Papers*, 1882, Paper No. 42, p. 2.

30. Annual Report of the Ontario Bureau of Industries, 1884, cited in Cohen, *Women's Work*, 128.

31. The fact that domestic service was Montreal's leading employment for girls, and that it usually involved living in, complicates this analysis of the work of children. Girls could work away from home as domestics and contribute their pay to their parents; they would not, however, figure among the average number of workers found in census families, nor would their experience be captured in the proportion of girls having a job. On the other hand, neither is that of any boys who left to find work in construction shanties, lumbering camps, railroad work, etc. The figures given in the text are always the percentages of those living in the ward, and with their parents, who reported a job. Those who lived and worked elsewhere are thus always removed from both the numerator and the denominator.

32. On the commissioners' concerns about this, see Susan Mann Trofimenkoff, "One Hundred and One Muffled Voices," in *The Neglected Majority: Essays in Canadian Women's History*, ed. Susan Mann Trofimenkoff and Alison Prentice (Toronto: McClelland and Stewart, 1977). How the working class viewed these morality issues requires examination.

33. Mss. Census, St. Jacques, 1871, 6, p. 137.

34. Mss. Census, St. Jacques, 1881, 12, p. 101.

35. Sydney Pollard, *The Genesis of Modern Management: A Study of the Industrial Revolution* (London: Edward Arnold, 1965), 162.

36. Royal Commission on the Relations of Capital and Labour (RCRCL), *Quebec Evidence*, evidence of Wm. C. McDonald, tobacco manufacturer, p. 529.

37. RCRCL, *Quebec Evidence*, anonymous evidence, p. 42.

38. RCRCL, *Quebec Evidence*, pp. 44–47.

39. RCRCL, *Quebec Evidence*, p. 91.

40. RCRCL, *Quebec Evidence*, evidence of Mrs. Levoise.

41. RCRCL, *Quebec Evidence*, evidence of a machinist, Hudon factory, Hochelaga, pp. 273–74.

42. RCRCL, *Quebec Evidence*, evidence of Adèle Lavoie, pp. 280–82.

43. RCRCL, *Quebec Evidence*, evidence of Patrick Ryan, cigar maker, p. 37; machinist, Hudon Mills, p. 271; Samuel Carsley, dry goods merchant, p. 15; Oliver Benoit, boot and shoemaker, p. 365; Henry Morton, printer, p. 297; F. Stanley, foreman at the Star, p. 331.

44. Here I am referring to the percentage of children at home as opposed to boarding, living with relatives, or living in someone else's house as a servant. The samples taken in each census do not allow me to follow children over time and identify those who actually left home.

45. The same process occurred in Hamilton, and in other cities that have been studied. See Michael Katz, *The People of Hamilton*, 257, 261; Mary P. Ryan, *The Cradle of the Middle Class: The Family in Oneida County*, New York, 1790–1865 (New York: Cambridge University Press, 1981), 168–69; Richard Wall, "The Age at Leaving Home," *Journal of Family History* 8 (Fall 1983): 238.

46. For a careful analysis of the relationship between women's wages, costs of board, and decisions about where to live, see Gary Cross and Peter Shergold, "The Family Economy and the Market: Wages and Residence of Pennsylvania Women in the 1890s," *Journal of Family History* 11, 3 (1986): 245–66.

47. Paul Spagnoli, "Industrialization, Proletarianization and Marriage," *Journal of Family History* 8 (Fall 1983): 238.

48. Michael Anderson's careful analysis of which children left home shows that boys in Preston, Lancashire, were more likely to do so than girls. He believes children made "a conscious calculation of the advantages and disadvantages, in terms of the standard of living which they could enjoy," based on the wages they could make, their father's wage, and the amount they were required to hand over to their parents. *Family Structure*, 67, 127–29.

49. A similar, but greater, increase in girls' school attendance is described for Hamilton by Michael B. Katz and Ian E. Davey in "Youth and Early Industrialization," in *Turning Points: Historical and Sociological Essays on the Family*, ed. John Demos and Sarane Spence Boocock, pp. 81–119.

50. "Le problème des jeunes qui ne fréquent plus l'école," *École Sociale Populaire* 351 (April 1941), 26, cited by Dominique Jean, "Les familles québécois et trois politiques sociales touchant les enfants, de 1940 à 1960: Obligation scolaire, allocations familiales et loi controlant le travail juvenile" (Ph.D. diss., Université de Montréal, 1988).

51. "First Report of Work Under the Children's Protection Act," p. 26; "Third Report of Work Under the Children's Protection Act," p. 10, cited in John Bullen, "J.J. Kelso and the 'New' Child-Savers: The Genesis of the Children's Aid Movement in Ontario" (Paper presented to the CHA Annual Meeting, Windsor, Ont., June 1988), 35–38.

52. The usefulness of taking a category of women other than wives and mothers to test the soundness of contemporary feminist theory on this question is clear in the article of Danielle Juteau and Nicole Frenette, who start with an examination of the role of nuns in late-nineteenth- and early-twentieth-century Quebec, and use their insights to critique much contemporary feminist theory. "L'évolution des formes de l'appropriation des femmes: Des religieuses aux 'mères porteuses,'" *Canadian Review of Sociology and Anthropology* 25, 2 (1988).

53. One of the great advantages of the domestic labour debate was its recognition of the importance of housework and reproduction of labour power to capitalism. Less clear in much of the writing was the failure of most writers to acknowledge the interest of men in the perpetuation of domestic labour. For an elaboration of this critique, see Walby, *Patriarchy at Work*, 18–19.

54. Ruth Milkman criticizes labour-segmentation theory, early Marxist-feminist writing, and Hartmann's description of patriarchy for paying insufficient attention to the effect of industrial structure on the sexual division of labour and struggles over "woman's place" in the labour market. Looking much more concretely than theorists have done at specific industries, she argues that "an industry's pattern of employment by sex reflects the economic, political, and social constraints that are operative when that industry's labour market initially forms." *Gender at Work*, 7.

55. Herein lies the problem of the "dual systems" approach of Hartmann and others. Heidi Hartmann, "Capitalism, Patriarchy and Job Segregation by Sex," *Signs* (1977); Varda Burstyn, "Masculine Dominance and the State," in

Varda Burstyn and Dorothy Smith, *Women, Class, Family, and the State* (Toronto: Garamond Press, 1985), pp. 45–89; Sylvia Walby succeeds better than others in drawing out the links between the two, but insists on their relative autonomy in *Patriarchy at Work*.

56. Canadian historians, whether in women's history or working-class history, are only just beginning to unravel this complex, dialectical relationship between the structure of the economy and the needs of the family, in interaction with both capital's and labour's definitions of gender roles. It is an unravelling that must continue if we are to understand how gender was at work and continues to work outside the workplace as well as within it.

57. Some of the problems faced by feminist theoreticians grappling with the relationship between women's oppression by males within marriage, their subordination in the labour market, and the wider forces of patriarchy stem from the assumption that only wives perform domestic labour. This seems to me a profoundly ahistorical view, and one that downplays the importance of the family as a place of socialization and training.

58. Here would be an example of mothers making choices that made their lives easier, but that in the long run perpetuated, even exaggerated, men's more privileged position in the marketplace. On this, see Gerder Lerner, *The Creation of Patriarchy* (Oxford: Oxford University Press, 1986), cited in Bonnie Fox, "Conceptualizing Patriarchy," *Canadian Review of Sociology and Anthropology* 25, 2 (1988): 165.

59. Psychological, Freudian theories about gender identity seem less important here than the practical day-to-day experience in the home and the role model of the mother. Nancy Chodorow, *The Reproduction of Mothering* (Berkeley: University of California Press, 1978).

60. For a superb description of the complex ways in which women in Paris, Ontario — a knitting town where job opportunities for women were much greater than for men — dealt with domestic labour, see Joy Parr, "Rethinking Work and Kinship in a Canadian Hosiery Town, 1910–1950," *Feminist Studies* 13, 1 (Spring 1987): 137–62.

Article Fifteen

Joe Beef of Montreal: Working-Class Culture and the Tavern, 1869–1889

Peter DeLottinville

Montreal was a city of contrasts. The casual tourist, following the advice of his *Strangers' Guide to Montreal*,[1] would spend days viewing florid Gothic and ornate Italian church architecture, the engineering marvel of Robert Stevenson's Victoria Bridge, and the various monuments to commercial power. This faithful *cicerone*, however, would not give the tourist the total picture of a nineteenth-century urban landscape. The official face of Canada's first city consisted of monuments to individual industry, public morality, and social harmony. Absent from the official guide were the inhabitants of the narrower streets — the factory workers, the frequenters of taverns, the waterfront street gangs, or the crowds of longshoremen outside the Allen Line office waiting for work. What the tourist needed to see was a monument to Montreal's working class. Had he accidentally wandered into Joe Beef's Canteen, the tourist might have found it, where the rules and procedures of official Montreal had little value.

During the late nineteenth century, Joe Beef's Canteen was a notorious part of that underworld which existed in the Victorian city.[2] Located in the centre of the waterfront district, the Canteen was the haunt of sailors and longshoremen, unemployed men and petty thieves.

Source: "Joe Beef of Montreal: Working-Class Culture and the Tavern, 1869–1889," *Labour/Le Travailleur* 8/9 (1981/1982): 9–40. © Canadian Committee on Labour History.

Middle-class Montreal saw this tavern as a moral hazard to all who entered and a threat to social peace. Yet if critics called the Canteen's owner, Charles McKiernan, the "wickedest man" of the city, working-class residents along the waterfront claimed McKiernan as their champion. His tavern was a popular drinking spot, but also a source of aid in times of unemployment, sickness, and hunger. For its patrons, Joe Beef's Canteen was a stronghold for working-class values and a culture which protected them from harsh economic times.

Primarily, this essay describes the working-class culture which grew around Joe Beef's Canteen and analyzes that culture in terms of the community which supported it. The efforts of middle-class organizations to improve the conditions of the waterfront labourers are examined in the light of this culture. Finally, by placing this culture within the major developments influencing Montreal during the 1880s, the decline of Joe Beef's Canteen can be understood. Through this process a clearer understanding of the relationship between cultural change and historic development can be reached.

As the recent lively debate bears witness,[3] the concept of working-class culture in historical analysis is both fruitful and problematic, and before entering into a detailed discussion of the working-class tavern, it is necessary to define this concept and establish the limitations of its application. Working-class culture covers a wide range of recreational, social, and job-related activities from labour day parades and trade union picnics to charivaris and the secret ceremonies of the Knights of Labor. While each form of culture can only be understood within its specific time and place, there was a common thread which made particular cultures working-class cultures. As Raymond Williams has stated, working-class culture embodies "a basic collective idea and the institutions, manners, habits of thought and intentions which proceed from this."[4] By assuming an "active mutual responsibility"[5] between workingmen, working-class culture offered an alternative to the individualist, competitive philosophy of the nineteenth-century middle class. Nothing was as common as a tavern in nineteenth-century Montreal, and because of this, working-class taverns probably represented one of the most basic forums of public discussion. Drawing their customers from the neighbouring streets, such meeting places were the first to sense a change in mood, or experience the return of economic prosperity. Joe Beef's Canteen, while attracting a wider clientele than most taverns, was essentially the same type of focal point for the dockyard workers. The uncommon aspect of the Canteen was the remarkable ability of Charles McKiernan, the tavern's owner, to transform this rather commonplace forum into a dynamic force for the working class of Montreal.

The depression which accompanied the 1870s had a great impact on those who, like the patrons of Joe Beef's Canteen, were at the bottom end of the economic scale. Gareth Stedman Jones, in his study of casual labour and unemployment, *Outcast London*, demonstrated that middle-class London saw the casual labourers of East London as unregenerated workers who had yet to accept the industrious habits of their fellow workingmen of the factories.[6] These "dangerous classes," much like the patrons of the Canteen, were perceived as a threat to social order. While Montreal's waterfront could not compare to the horrors of East London, Montreal's middle classes were concerned about a "dangerous class" united by a forceful, if eccentric, spokesman who articulated labourers' frustrations and demands. Joe Beef would have been taken much less seriously had his success not coincided with the increasing number of factory workers, both skilled and unskilled, who appeared on the streets of Montreal. Municipal authorities, encouraged by middle-class reformers, paid more attention to questions of public order and morality in the face of such a mass of new residents. Drunkenness, blood sports, and street brawls associated with the waterfront taverns could not be permitted to flourish if all workers were to adopt the disciplined virtues of the new industrial society.

Charles McKiernan was born on 4 December 1835, into a Catholic family in Cavan County, Ireland. At a young age, he entered the British Army and, after training at the

Woolwich gunnery school, was assigned to the 10th Brigade of the Royal Artillery. In the Crimean War, McKiernan's talent for providing food and shelter earned him the nickname of "Joe Beef," which would stay with him for the rest of his life. In 1864, McKiernan's Brigade was sent to Canada to reinforce the British forces at Quebec. By then a sergeant, McKiernan was put in charge of the military canteens at the Quebec barracks and later on St. Helen's Island. If army life had seemed an alternative to his Irish future, then McKiernan saw better opportunities in North America. In 1868, McKiernan bought his discharge from the Army and with his wife and children settled in Montreal, opening the Crown and Sceptre Tavern on St. Claude Street.[7]

By settling in Montreal, McKiernan joined an established Irish community which accounted for 20 percent of the total population. Centred in Griffintown, the largely working-class Irish had their own churches, national and charitable societies, political leaders, and businessmen.[8] And as a tavern owner, McKiernan entered a popular profession in a city with a liquor licence for every 150 inhabitants.[9] The increasing number of taverns caused one temperance advocate to lament that if trends continued Montreal was destined to become "the most drunken city on the continent."[10] The Crown and Sceptre, commonly known as "Joe Beef's Canteen," had a central location, with Griffintown and the Lachine Canal to the east and the extensive dockyards stretching out on either side. Business was good for Charles McKiernan.

In spite of the large numbers of taverns, Joe Beef's Canteen had an atmosphere, and a reputation, which was unique. Located in the waterfront warehouse district and at night identified only by a dim light outside the door, the Canteen housed a fantastic assortment of the exotic and the commonplace. One visitor described it as "a museum, a saw mill and a gin mill jumbled together by an earthquake; all was in confusion."[11] The barroom was crudely furnished with wooden tables and chairs, sawdust covering the floor to make cleaning easier. At one end of the bar, great piles of bread, cheese, and beef supplied the customers with a simple meal. Behind the bar a large mirror reflected a general assortment of bottles, cigar boxes, and curios. One bottle preserved for public display a bit of beef which lodged — fatally — in the windpipe of an unfortunate diner. The quick-witted McKiernan served his patrons with an easy manner. An imposing figure with a military bearing and fierce temper, the owner had few problems with rowdyism.[12]

Joe Beef's Canteen had a special type of patron, and McKiernan aptly referred to his establishment as the "Great House of Vulgar People." His clientele was mostly working class. Canal labourers, longshoremen, sailors, and ex-army men like McKiernan himself were the mainstays of the business. Along with these waterfront workers, Joe Beef's Canteen attracted the floating population along the Atlantic coast. W.H. Davies, in his *Autobiography of a Super-Tramp*, remarked that, "not a tramp throughout the length and breadth of the North American continent . . . had not heard of [Joe Beef's Canteen] and a goodly number had at one time or another patronized his establishment."[13] McKiernan's tavern was also a well-known rendezvous for the "sun-fish" or "wharf-rats" of the harbour who lived a life of casual employment and poverty. Newspaper reporters often dropped into the tavern to check on petty criminals who mingled with the crowd. Unemployed labourers visited the Canteen in the early morning to look for a day's labour and often remained there throughout the day in the hope of something turning up. In all it was not a respectable crowd[14] and, no doubt, was shunned by the more self-respecting artisans of the neighbourhood.

For working-class Montreal, the tavern held attractions beyond the simple comforts of food and drink. With no public parks in the immediate area, and only occasional celebrations by national societies and church groups, their daily recreational activities were centred around places like Joe Beef's Canteen. McKiernan's tavern was exceptionally rich in popular recreations. A menagerie of monkeys, parrots, and wild cats of various kinds were from time to time exhibited in the Canteen, but it was McKiernan's bears which brought in the crowds. Joe Beef's first bear, named Jenny and billed as the "sole captive" of the "courageous" 1869 expedition to the North West, never retired sober during the last three years of her life. One of her cubs inherited the family weakness. Tom, who had a daily consumption of twenty pints of beer, was often as "drunk as a coal heaver" by closing. Indeed, Tom was one of the regulars, usually sitting on his hind quarters and taking his pint between his paws, downing it without spilling a drop. Local temperance men had always pointed out that drink turned men into animals, but in observing Tom's habits Joe Beef could point out this curious reversal of behaviour which the Canteen produced.[15] Other bears were kept in the tavern's cellar and viewed by customers through a trap door in the barroom floor. Occasionally, McKiernan brought up the bears to fight with some of his dogs or play a game of billiards with the proprietor.

The tavern was not an ideal place for animals and one observer remarked on the mangy, dirty, and listless character of the bears.[16] Beatings were often used to rouse the animals into their "naturally" ferocious state. Sometimes McKiernan was mauled during these demonstrations and once a buffalo on exhibit sent him to hospital for a number of days.[17] A Deputy Clerk of the Peace, inspecting the tavern to renew its licence, was bitten by one of Joe Beef's dogs.[18] There was little public outcry over these conditions. Montreal's Royal Society for the Prevention of Cruelty to Animals was still a fledgling organization in the 1870s which spent its time regulating butchers' practices and prosecuting carters for mistreatment of their horses. As long as they presented no public danger, McKiernan's menagerie was left undisturbed.

Although lacking formal education, Charles McKiernan considered himself a man of learning and regularly read the *New York Journal*, the *Irish American*, the *Irish World*, and local newspapers. He employed a musician (which was illegal under the terms of his licence) to entertain his customers. Regular patrons played the piano in the tavern. McKiernan, however, led much of the entertainment. Drawing on personal experience and varied readings, McKiernan eagerly debated topics of the day, or amused patrons with humorous poems of his own composition. He had a remarkable ability to ramble on for hours in rhyming couplets. Sometimes to achieve this end, he distorted the accepted English pronunciation beyond recognition. This disgusted some middle-class visitors to the Canteen, but regular customers clearly enjoyed these feats of rhetoric.[19] Behind the bar, two skeletons were hung from the wall and served as props for McKiernan's tales. From time to time, the skeletons represented the mortal remains of McKiernan's first wife, his relatives in Ireland, or the last of an unfortunate temperance lecturer who mistakenly strayed into Joe Beef's Canteen one night.

From the occasional poetry which McKiernan printed in the newspapers, the style and subjects of these evenings can be seen. Concentrating on the figures of authority in the workingman's life, the employer, the Recorder, the landlord, or the local minister, McKiernan's humour allowed his patrons a temporary mastery over the forces which dominated their lives outside the Canteen doors. Inside the Canteen, the rights of the common man always triumphed. On local issues, McKiernan complained about the lack of municipal services for the waterfront community. He demanded,

> Fair play for Sammy, Johnny and Pat as
> well as the Beaver Hall Bogus Aristocrat![20]

Legal authority, most familiar to his patrons through the Recorder's Court, was also denounced, but feared. An engraving of the Recorder looked down on the patrons from above the bar, and wedged into the frame were a number of dollar bills and notes which served as a reserve fund. McKiernan used this fund to pay fines imposed upon his regular customers.[21] Since most depended upon day labour, even a short jail term could spell disaster for the labourers' families. Imprisonment in lieu of fines was a very contentious issue, as the vehemence of the following poem illustrates.

> They have taken me from my father,
> They have taken me from my mother,
> They have taken me from my sister,
> They have taken me from my brothers,
> In this wintry season of woe
> And for the sake of *one* paltry, lousy *Dollar,*
> Down to jail, for to die, like a Dog, amongst *Bugs* and *Vermin,* I had to go.
> I died amongst howling and laughter,
> I died howling for a drink of water
> But you living *Tyrants,* and *Two Legged Monsters* take warning and remember that cold, cold Saturday Morning!!!
> For man's vengeance is swift, though God's vengeance is with some, rather slow.[22]

McKiernan himself was no stranger to the Recorder's Court. In July 1867, the tavern keeper faced charges from a disgruntled patron who had been roughly thrown into the street for rowdyism. On different occasions, McKiernan's musician and a former servant complained of beatings they had received for drunkenness on the job.[23] Along with the violations of his liquor licence, such incidents illustrated that Joe Beef's legal opinions were grounded in experience.

Another prominent subject in Joe Beef's Canteen was the economic depression which hovered over Montreal for much of the 1870s. As casual labourers, the Canteen's patrons were severely affected by commercial slumps. In "Joe Beef's Advice to Biddy, the Washerwoman," McKiernan wrote,

> I must tell you that Kingston is dead, Quebec is
> Dying and out of Montreal, Ottawa and Toronto hundreds are flying
> In the country parts unless you can
> Parlez-vous, There is nothing for you to do
> And in John's office it is all the cry
> No Union printers for work need apply
> And if the landlord his rent you cannot
> Pay your sewing machine he will take
> Away. So in the fall God help the
> Poor of Montreal.[24]

The unwillingness of the private and public authorities to provide adequate relief systems also attracted Joe Beef's notice. In a parody of the economic theories of industrialists, McKiernan professed,

> Joe Beef of Montreal, the Son of the People,
> He cares not for the Pope, Priest, Parson or King
> William of the Boyne; all Joe wants is the Coin.
> He trusts in God in the summer time to keep him
> from all harm; when he sees the first frost and
> snow poor old Joe trusts to the Almighty Dollar
> and good maple wood to keep his belly warm.[25]

These were problems which his patrons had little difficulty in understanding.

Central to all of McKiernan's pronouncements was the belief that the common problems of casual labourers and the poor of Montreal should overcome the religious and national differences which separated them. Joe Beef did "not give a damn Whether he is an Indian a Nigger a Cripple a Billy or a Mich"[26] when attempting to help the unemployed. What the unemployed and casual labourer lacked, in McKiernan's opinion, was a common voice. Since no one else was likely to assume that role, Joe Beef became the self-appointed champion of the waterfront workers. His success was remarkable as he gained the confidence of his neighbours and attracted the attention of many residents who were unaware of the poor conditions on their doorstep. He made friends with both English and French journalists, and Joe Beef's Canteen and the waterfront community appeared regularly in the press. While such publicity was good for the Canteen, few accused McKiernan of self-interest. "Joe Beef" became so well known that few knew precisely who Charles McKiernan was. And despite his Irish background, Joe Beef had considerable appeal to French-Canadian workers as well, if one can judge popularity from the coverage Joe Beef received in the French-language press.

The recreational aspects of Joe Beef's Canteen covered only a narrow spectrum of the interaction between the tavern owner and his patrons. As the focal point of social activities, Joe Beef's Canteen also provided the initiative for a number of social services which were a logical outgrowth of the close relationship between McKiernan and his neighbourhood. His role in alleviating problems of housing, job hunting, health care, and labour unrest indicated the possibility of a collective response to the common problems among casual labourers of Montreal's waterfront.

The most visible service which Joe Beef's Canteen offered was a cheap place to stay for transient and single workers. In the Crown and Sceptre, the barroom was situated next to a dining room and sleeping quarters. The sleeping area contained about 40 wooden sofas which served as beds. At eleven o'clock, boarders deposited ten cents at the bar and were handed a blanket. The men then spread a mattress over the wooden sofa, stripped off all their clothes, and went to sleep. McKiernan insisted that all his boarders sleep naked as a matter of cleanliness. Those found dirty were ordered upstairs to use one of the wash tubs. Each boarder also had to have his hair cut short, and those failing to meet the standards were sent to Joe Beef's "inspector of health," or barber, to comply. No conversation was permitted after eleven o'clock and everyone was roused out of bed at seven sharp. These rules were enforced personally by McKiernan in his best British Army sergeant's manner. Three-quarters of the tavern's boarders were boys between the ages of twelve and fourteen who earned their living selling newspapers. For twenty cents a day, they received their food and lodging and, although the conditions set down by Joe Beef might be draconian, they were clearly preferred to similar facilities offered by church organizations. Indeed, the Crown and Sceptre proved such a popular place that one of the prime reasons for moving to Common Street in 1876 was the lack of space. His waterfront location had room for 200 men.[27]

Fees for room and board were often waived for those without the means to pay such modest sums. McKiernan's tavern was also close to the sources of casual employment, which was an important consideration when a day's work might depend on arriving early on the job site. McKiernan often loaned shovels to men engaged in snow shovelling and other jobs. And as the natural resting place for all types of labourers on the docks, Joe Beef's Canteen was an ideal location to learn who might be hiring in the future. In this way, the tavern allowed transient workers to familiarize themselves with the local labour market and to make a decision whether to stay in Montreal or move on.[28]

Other social services grew informally as local residents turned to McKiernan for assistance in times of trouble. When a Lachine Canal labourer was injured during a blasting operation, fellow workers brought him to Joe Beef's to recuperate. After two men got into a drunken brawl and the loser stripped naked in the street, the crowd brought the man to Joe Beef's for care. A young immigrant who collapsed on the docks also ended up in the tavern for convalescence. While Joe Beef's served as a neighbourhood clinic, McKiernan's folk cures left much to be desired. The young immigrant was treated with a vinegar-soaked towel bound tightly around his head. McKiernan also professed faith in cayenne pepper and whiskey to cure cramps and Canadian cholera. All this in twenty minutes.[29] Still, many people in the nineteenth century attributed medicinal powers to alcohol, and McKiernan did state an intention to take courses at the Montreal General Hospital to improve his knowledge of basic medicine.

These experiences led the tavern owner to lobby established medical institutions to improve health care services for waterfront residents. In December 1879, he set up a collection box in his tavern for the Montreal General Hospital and invited his customers to contribute. Donating one-tenth of his receipts from all his dinners and a similar share of his boarding house income, McKiernan hoped to raise $500 a year. In the following years, McKiernan offered $100 to the Montreal General if they would provide a doctor to attend the poor in their homes. The hospital declined the offer. Unsuccessful in a more formal improvement of health care services, McKiernan continued to provide emergency relief. When the body of a suicide was buried in August 1883, the tavern keeper provided a tombstone.[30]

The question of class allegiance was most clearly defined by the incidents of labour unrest which periodically disrupted the city. In December 1877, over 1000 labourers working on the enlargement of the Lachine Canal abandoned their picks and shovels after a reduction in wages. The Irish and French workers paraded behind a tricolour flag along the canal banks and drove off those who refused to participate in the strike. Following a riot at the offices of canal contractor William Davis, during which the strike leader was shot, the Prince of Wales Rifles were called out to protect the canal and those workers who continued to work at reduced wages.[31] The strikers demanded a wage increase to a dollar a day, a nine-hour day, regular fort-nightly payments, and an end to the "truck system" of payment.[32] Among the Montreal citizens, there appeared to be some sympathy with the poor working conditions of the labourers, notably from the *Montreal Witness* and local MP Bernard Devlin,[33] but the militant behaviour of the strikers was generally condemned.

Strongest support for the strikers came from the waterfront community. Practical in all things, McKiernan realized that strikers, like the army, travel on their stomachs. On the morning of 20 December, he sent 300 loaves of bread, 36 gallons of tea, and a similar quantity of soup. These supplies required two wagons to be delivered. In addition to feeding the strikers, McKiernan took in as many as the Canteen could hold. One night 300 people found shelter under his roof. Throughout the strike McKiernan was observed "carting loaves and making good, rich soup in mammoth boilers, as if he were a commissary-general with the resources of an army at his back."[34] No doubt his military training was put to the test in maintaining order in his kitchen. That background also made the tavern keeper aware of the awkward position of the Prince of Wales Rifles who had been hastily summoned to guard the canal. To ensure that the soldier ate as well as a striker, McKiernan despatched a wagon of bread to the men on duty. The soldiers saw the humour in Joe Beef's assistance and gave most of the bread away to the crowd.[35] Some of the tension between striker and soldier was successfully released.

McKiernan, of course, was not popular with the canal contractors for his whole-hearted support of the labourers. William Davis, pointing suspiciously to the fourteen taverns in the immediate area, wrote that the strike was caused by outside trouble makers. Another contractor was more direct in his accusations. "All of the trouble which we have had on the canal this winter has been caused mostly by men that never worked a day on the canal and have been started in a low Brothel kept by one *Joe Beef* who seems to be at the head of it all."[36] Despite this claim, McKiernan had only a supporting role in the labourers' actions, but such comments indicated the success of McKiernan's efforts to aid the strike.

Besides using his Canteen to take care of the strikers' physical needs, McKiernan also used his skills as an orator to attract public attention to the strikers' demands. By 1877, Joe Beef was a figure of some notoriety in Montreal and the local press found that his exploits made good copy. His support of the strike was reported extensively in Montreal and even in one Ottawa newspaper. The strikers' first meeting took place outside Joe Beef's Canteen and the tavern owner was asked to say a few words. Those nightly discussions in the tavern had given McKiernan a remarkable ease with language, and his talent for speaking in rhyming couplets was not wasted. Most of his speech to the crowd was in rhyming form, which so impressed the *Montreal Witness* reporter that he apologized for only reporting the substance of the speech and not its form as well. McKiernan explained his actions in the following terms.

> I have been brought up among you as one of yourselves since I was a boy running about barefooted. When I heard of the strike on the Lachine Canal, I thought I would try to help you, for I knew that men employed there had much to put up with. So I sent you bread to help you hold out. I could not send you whiskey, because you might get drunk, and commit yourselves. In this way you might have injured your cause, and perhaps made the volunteers fire on you. (Laughter) . . . The greatest philanthropists in the world are in Montreal, and the public here will sympathize with you. They will not see you tyrannized over. But if you are riotous, depend upon it, as sure as you are men before me, the law will take it in hand and crush you. I have nothing against the contractors and you will succeed by speaking rightly to them. You will get your $1 a day for nine hours, or perhaps for eight hours (cheers) or perhaps more (loud cheers). But keep orderly; mind your committee.[37]

The speech was received with "deafening" cheers.

These mass meetings organized by the strike committee were an important part of their efforts to secure better working conditions. Since the canal enlargement was a federal project, Alexander Mackenzie's government was anxious to have it completed before the next election. Failure to live up to this previous election promise would cost the Liberals votes in Montreal.[38] By rallying public support for their cause, the strikers hoped that Ottawa would intervene on their behalf and compel the contractors to make concessions. As the strike continued, the size of the mass meetings grew. In Chaboillez Square 2000 people assembled to hear McKiernan and other speakers. Joe Beef lectured on the theme of the "Almighty Dollar."

> My friends, I have come here tonight to address you on "the Almighty Dollar." The very door bells of Montreal ring with the "Almighty Dollar." The wooden-headed bobbies nail you, and you have to sleep on the hard floor provided by the City Fathers, and the next morning the fat Recorder tells you: "Give me the 'Almighty Dollar,' or down you go for eight days." The big-bugs all have their eyes on the "Almighty Dollar," from the Bishop down, and if you die in the hospital, they want the almighty dollar to shave you and keep you from the students. No one can blame you for demanding the "Almighty Dollar" a day. The man who promises 90¢ a day and pays only 80¢ is no man at all. The labourer has his rights.[39]

Public support for the strikers did not alter the fact that the labourers were without income, and after eight days on strike, they returned to the canal at the old wages.[40]

The canal labourers, however, refused to admit defeat. In mid-January, a strike committee went to Ottawa with funds raised by McKiernan and others in order to plead their cause before Alexander Mackenzie. They reduced their demands to the single request that the contractors pay them every fortnight in cash.[41] Mackenzie was sympathetic but non-committal. When the committee returned to Montreal, the mass meetings became overtly political and the problems of the canal labourers were attributed to the inaction of the Liberal government.[42] Meanwhile,

Mackenzie had ordered an investigation into the Lachine situation which revealed the widespread use of store payment which considerably reduced the real wages of the labourers. Sensing a political disaster in the making, the government ordered the contractors to end store payments.[43] All contractors complied immediately and the labourers won a modest victory. McKiernan's efforts, while not the only factor in this outcome, did help the strikers publicize their demands and eased their physical hardships. In doing so, he demonstrated the potential strength of a waterfront community united in a common cause.

The canal labourers' strike was McKiernan's most extensive effort in aiding strikers, but not his only involvement. During a strike against the Allen line, ship labourers used the Canteen as a rallying point and the flag they used in their parades came from the tavern. In April 1880, when the Hochelaga cotton mill workers struck, Joe Beef again assumed his role as people's commissary-general by supplying the strikers with bread.[44] Such incidents illustrated how the working-class culture which centred around the tavern could be mobilized to produce benefits for the Canteen's patrons. But in doing so, McKiernan also attracted the criticism of middle-class reformers who felt that such a culture encouraged workers in a dangerous behaviour which threatened the social stability of Montreal.

During the 1870s, middle-class reformers began to enter into the waterfront community to assist the workingman in overcoming his social and economic poverty. The YMCA, the Salvation Army, as well as local employers and clergy, all found themselves confronted by an existing culture and community services centred around Joe Beef's Canteen. Their response to McKiernan's activities illustrated the immense social differences between the middle and working class of Montreal. One visitor to the city described Joe Beef's Canteen as a "den of robbers and wild beasts" over which McKiernan presided, "serving his infernal majesty in loyal style." The patrons were "unkempt, unshaven, fierce-looking specimens of humanity," and "roughs of various appearances, ready apparently, either to fight, drink, or steal, if the opportunity offered." In conclusion, this visitor wrote, "As we came away from his canteen where we felt that dirt, bestiality, and devilment held high carnival, my friend said, 'I believe Joe is worse than his bears and lower down in the scale of being than his monkeys. No monkey could ever be Joe's ancestor, though he is the father of wild beasts that prey on society.'"[45] While Montreal's middle class did not engage in the "slumming parties" which were popular in London, portrait painter Robert Harris and his companion William Brymmer visited the Canteen to satisfy their curiosity.[46] The actions of middle-class men on the waterfront revealed a fundamental misunderstanding of the nature of the working-class behaviour which they observed.

The common middle-class picture of the waterfront community was one of drunkenness, immorality, and lawlessness. Waterfront taverns like the Canteen, or French Marie's, were described by the Montreal Police Chief as "hot beds of all that is vicious" whose patrons were "always on the look out for mischief, and whose chief and most relished pastime seems to consist in attacking the police, rescuing prisoners, and spreading terror."[47] Sub-Chief Lancy reported that the only reason why police did not close down Joe Beef's Canteen was that "it is better to have all these characters kept in one place so that they might be dropped upon by the detectives."[48] Indeed, there was much truth to police complaints about public order on the waterfront, but they were less than candid in public statements about the role which men like Charles McKiernan played in the maintenance of order. The Black Horse Gang, composed of working-class youths, roamed the waterfront for years, extorting drinking money from lone pedestrians and robbing drunken sailors. Implicated in at least one death, the Black Horse Gang rarely faced prosecution because their violent reputation intimidated many witnesses from pressing charges. And the Black Horse Gang did frequent Joe Beef's Canteen, or at least until October 1876, when McKiernan threw four of its members out into the street for rowdiness. Ironically, one of the gang members attempted to lay charges against the tavern owner for injuries resulting from the incident.[49] The waterfront also harboured "Joe Beef's Gang," which in November 1878 was involved in a market square battle with local butchers.[50]

Violations of public order, however, must be distinguished from acts of criminality. Indeed, McKiernan was known to assist the police in their efforts to capture criminals. Police arrested ten men on charges of highway robbery in September 1880 following a tip from McKiernan. In minor cases, the tavern owner was called upon to give character references for waterfront residents. McKiernan's censure was enough to send a local street gang leader to two months' hard labour. When the prisoner tried to retaliate by charging Joe Beef's Canteen with violations of its liquor licence, the judge, grateful for the favour to the court, refused to admit the evidence.[51] McKiernan, like many working-class people, did not consider occasional drunkenness or acts of rowdyism sufficient cause to send men to jail, especially if imprisonment meant certain ruin for a labourer's family. The informal, if sometimes rough, justice which McKiernan enforced upon his patrons was obviously preferable to the legal penalties of the court. While not publicly admitting such an accommodation, the Montreal police found that such informal cooperation worked in their favour.

The difference between the middle-class attitude toward the police and that of the waterfront residents was illustrated by the experience of the YMCA's first venture into the area. As an alternative to the saloon, the YMCA established a reading room on Craig Street. In January 1877, eight men were arrested there for creating a disturbance, and the *Montreal Witness* accused McKiernan of offering a reward to the men who closed down the operation. The tavern owner refuted these charges by pointing out that the incident had occurred only because of the YMCA's mishandling of the situation. As McKiernan explained, "Joe Beef never called on one policeman to arrest any of those men who frequent *his* place. If those eight had only been sent to him he would have given them work and food and sent them back better behaved."[52] By using the police to settle their problems, the YMCA violated one of the unwritten rules of behaviour on the waterfront.

The influence of waterfront taverns upon sailors visiting Montreal was a constant concern among ship owners. Searches for deserting sailors often started with a visit to Joe Beef's Canteen and a quick check of its customers. As an alterative to the tavern, the Montreal Sailors Institute was established in 1869 "a stone's throw" from nine taverns. Open from May to November, the Institute had a reading room, writing desks, stationery, and sabbath services. Food, for a price, could be bought but not alcohol. In 1879, the Institute sold 4885 cups of coffee and confidently concluded that "Every cup lessen[ed] much the demand for whiskey." Encouraging sailors to sign abstinence pledges, the Institute recognized that sober sailors were dependable sailors.[53] But like the YMCA, the Institute had little understanding or sympathy for the working-class culture of the neighbourhood. The Institute manager, Robert R. Bell, described tavern patrons as "the lowest and most depraved human beings."[54] Dock workers, in particular, he found "a class much given to alcoholic liquors."[55] Bell lamented the inability to enforce the Sunday liquor laws and suggested the local policemen were in league with the tavern keepers. In his attempts to save the waterfront workers from their own culture as well as from economic hardship, Bell was typical of the middle-class professionals who came into the area. With 60 percent of the Institute's budget earmarked for the salary of Bell and his two assistants, and liberal contributions from local ship owners,[56] the motives behind such projects were viewed suspiciously by the waterfront workers.

The most ardent attempts to reform the moral and social habits of the waterfront workers came from Montreal's clergy. The importance of the church in nineteenth-century social welfare services need not be recounted here,[57] but the resources of Montreal's various churches dwarfed anything which the waterfront community could organize on its own. McKiernan's public attitude toward all denominations of clergy was openly hostile. He wrote that "Churches, Chapels, Ranters, Preachers, Beechers and such stuff Montreal has already got enough."[58] The cartoon from *Le Canard* illustrated quite clearly that Joe Beef would look almost anywhere for salvation before turning to the church. Respectable Montreal was shocked in 1871 when McKiernan buried his first wife. On leaving the cemetery, he ordered the band to play the military tune, "The Girl I Left Behind Me." This so outraged the *Montreal Witness* that its editor only described the funeral as a "ludicrous circumstance" without going into details.[59] And, probably to his great delight, McKiernan actually convinced the census taker in 1881 that he was a practising *Baptist!*[60]

Clergy who ventured onto the waterfront, however, were sometimes pleasantly surprised at McKiernan's behaviour. John Currie, a Presbyterian minister, ventured into Joe Beef's Canteen to preach to its patrons as an "act of Faith." After some initial heckling from the tavern owner, Currie was allowed to finish his sermon. On its conclusion, McKiernan offered any man who went to Currie's services a dinner and night's lodging for free.[61] The YMCA and a "Hot Gospeller" at different times held religious services in the dining room attached to Joe Beef's Canteen. The apparent contradiction in McKiernan's public and private behaviour originated with his general distrust of a clergy which was essentially middle class. Once he viewed individual ministers at close range and found them willing to treat his patrons as their equals — at least before the eyes of God — then the tavern keeper had no objection to their work. As Joe Beef reported to the press,

> A Preacher may make as many proselytes as he chooses in my canteen, at the rate of ten cents a head. That's my price . . . for if I choose to give myself the trouble I could make them embrace any faith or none at all or become free thinkers.[62]

Not all preachers received a welcome into Joe Beef's Canteen. Mr. Hammond, a travelling revivalist whose views on tobacco and drink were at odds with McKiernan's, was invited to the Canteen for a debate. Before the evening was out, Mr. Hammond had been chased around the Canteen by a pack of Joe Beef's bears and dogs to the general amusement of the tavern's patrons.[63] When the Salvation Army first appeared in Montreal, McKiernan supported them. With their military bearing and brass-band approach to salvation, they were a natural to play outside the Canteen, and McKiernan paid them to do so. This harmonious relationship abruptly ended when an Army officer called the Canteen "a notorious *rendez-vous* of the vicious and depraved."[64] Shortly afterwards the band was arrested for disturbing the peace and McKiernan was suspected of being behind the complaint.

These clashes between the local clergy, reform groups, the police, and Joe Beef were carefully chronicled by the editor of the *Montreal Witness,* John Dougall. Dougall founded the *Witness* to instruct the general public in the Christian way of life and frequently drew upon Joe Beef for examples of modern depravity. Dougall was not unsympathetic to the economic hardships of Montreal's working class. He gave extensive coverage to the 1877 canal labourers' strike and attacked industrialists for their lack of concern over the moral implications of modern industry upon employees. But Dougall was convinced that the working-class culture which centred around taverns was a dangerous influence for all workingmen. As one contemporary described Dougall, he was "a fighter in the cause of temperance, of political purity, of public morals, of municipal righteousness, of Free Trade and of aggressive Christianity."[65] The unyielding earnestness of Dougall's public statements made him a frequent target for Joe Beef's satires. A typical verse stated,

> Bitter beer I will always drink,
> and Bitter Beer I will always draw
> and for John and his song singing
> Ranters never care a straw.[66]

When the *Witness* dismissed six of its printers for belonging to the International Typographers Union, McKiernan naturally sided with the union's efforts to have the men reinstated.[67]

Dougall characterized Joe Beef as the "hunter for the souls of men"[68] and, instead of seeing the social services which surrounded the Canteen as a positive contribution to the community, believed that these were merely clever ways of entrapping unsuspecting workers into a world of drink and sin. The death of John Kerr in April 1879 confirmed Dougall's conviction. Kerr was a regular at the Canteen who made his living doing odd jobs around the docks. One day in April, Kerr did not go out to work and by nightfall had drank himself to death. During the Coroner's inquest, McKiernan explained his policy of never calling in the police. When men got rowdy, he simply put them in a room under the bar to sleep it off. Customers, McKiernan went on, were never treated roughly and they were "all in good health. We never club them; you know you can squeeze a man to make him do what you want, without beating him."[69] Kerr, a well-behaved man and often sick, was never treated in this manner. Yet the existence of the "Black Hole" (as the jury foreman described it) caught Dougall's attention. In a scathing editorial, the *Witness* charged that McKiernan preyed on the unemployed in a merciless way.

> What an empire within an empire is this, where law is administered and Her Majesty's peace kept without expense to Her Majesty. How joyfully should Government renew the licence of this carer of the poor, who can squeeze a man even to the last cent he wants, even to go uncomplainingly to prison, or to working for him all day with the snow shovel he provides, and bringing home his earning daily and nightly to hand over the counter for the poison which is his real pay.[70]

Dougall demanded the Canteen's licence be revoked. The coroner's jury, however, did not see anything illegal in the unconventional practices of Joe Beef.

"Into Africa" was the phrase that one visitor to the waterfront used to describe his experience, and the social isolation of the middle and working classes of Montreal in the 1870s was quite remarkable. Yet these initial failures for the reformers did not stop their efforts, and throughout the coming decades they continued to establish links between the waterfront and the rest of the city. McKiernan, though suspicious, was not entirely hostile to these men addressing themselves to the obvious problems of the casual labourers. Their working-class culture was still strong enough to ensure that social assistance did not mean social control. Forces beyond the control of the waterfront community, however, were already weakening that culture.

The world of Joe Beef, which developed during the 1870s, continued to function throughout the 1880s, but its dynamic qualities appeared to be on the wane. Joe Beef's public profile certainly declined in the 1880s. The eventual disintegration of this culture cannot be attributed to any single factor either within the working-class community or from some of the larger developments of the decade. A combination of factors, including a decasualization of dockwork, the rise of the Knights of Labor, plus new attitudes toward leisure and urban conditions, made the survival of Joe Beef's Canteen beyond the death of its owner unlikely.

As a waterfront tavern, Joe Beef's Canteen depended upon the patronage of the longshoremen who unloaded and loaded the ships in the Montreal harbour. Longshoremen worked irregular hours, sometimes as long as 36 hours at a stretch. Crews were hired by stevedores who contracted with a ship's captain to unload the vessel for a fixed price and provided the necessary equipment. Longshoremen, therefore, spent long periods of time on the docks either working, or contacting stevedores about the prospects for employment. With between 1700 and 2500 men competing for work, individuals had to spend much of their time ensuring that they earned the average wage of $200 per season.[71] Given these job conditions, the attraction of a waterfront tavern where one could eat, sleep, drink, and scout around for employment cannot be underestimated.

The nature of employment on the docks began to change in the mid-1880s. H. & A. Allen Company, one of the larger shipping firms in the port, introduced a system of contract labour. Over 100 longshoremen signed contracts directly with the shipping company, which guaranteed steady employment for the season. The contract specified that each contract employee would have to pay 1 percent of his wages toward an accident insurance plan, as well as agree to have 10 percent of his total wages held back until the end of the season. Any man who left before the term of his contract forfeited claim to these wages. With a rate of 25 cents per hour, the pay of the Allen contract employees was slightly better than that of regular longshoremen, but these relinquished their traditional rights to refuse work which did not suit them.[72] Longshoremen testifying before the 1889 Royal Commission on the Relations of Capital and Labour were certainly critical of the contract system, which most felt gave the company a guaranteed labour supply without contributing greatly to the welfare of the longshoremen.[73] While the contract system accounted for only a fraction of the total labour force on the docks, the Allen Company's desire to "decasualize" their labour force was an indication of the future. Such a system made a convenient tavern unnecessary.

It was no coincidence that the Allen Company attempted to introduce the contract system among longshoremen at the same time that labour organizations appeared on the waterfront. Edmund Tart told the Royal Commission that he belonged to a "secret trades organization" which existed on the docks.[74] Possibly a local of the Knights of Labor, the union had its own benefit plan to offset the Allen Company insurance scheme. Patrick Dalton, a longshoreman for the Allen Company, testified against the contract system. Pointing to the organization of the Quebec City longshoremen, Dalton stressed that only the organization of all longshoremen could guarantee higher wages. Dalton concluded by saying that labour unions were not fundamentally concerned with wages, but with bettering "the condition of the men, socially and morally."[75]

The rise of the Knights of Labor in the mid-1880s produced profound changes in the dynamics of working-class development, and the culture surrounding Joe Beef's Canteen was shaken up by their emergence. Along with lawyers, bankers, and capitalists, the Knights of Labor banned tavern owners from their ranks. Testifying before the Royal Commission on the Liquor Traffic, Louis Z. Boudreau, president of the Montreal Trades and Labour Council, reflected this attitude toward drink when he stated that "people we meet in the Trades and Labor Council are not drinking men as a whole. They are a good class of men."[76] As skilled workers accepted the need for temperance, the unskilled waterfront labourers might also reexamine the benefits of tavern life. This did not signal an alliance between organized labour and the temperance advocates who attacked Joe Beef in the 1870s. Spokesmen for organized labour criticized most of these temperance workers for failing to realize that much of the drunkenness among workingmen resulted from economic hardship. Clearly, William Darlington, a prominent Montreal Knight of Labor, shared McKiernan's distrust of the clergy's attempt to reform the workingman. Darlington told the Liquor Commission that "the workingmen feel that the church is a religious institution without Christianity, and that the clergy is simply a profession, got up for the purpose of making money in some instances, and in others, for preaching in the interest of capital against labour. . . . They find out in reality that the Knights of Labor preach more Christianity than the churches."[77] Despite such similarities, there was no room for Joe Beef in the Knights of Labor.

Outside of the working-class neighbourhoods, other forces were emerging which shaped public attitudes toward Joe Beef's Canteen. Throughout the 1880s, Montreal's middle-class residents grew more critical of the police force's inability to enforce the liquor laws. This new mood was captured by the Law and Order League (also known as the Citizens League of Montreal) which was formed in 1886. The League's purpose was to pressure police to enforce the liquor and public morality laws by publicizing open violations. Operating in cooperation with the Royal Society for the Prevention of Cruelty to Animals, the League was able to effect a dramatic increase in the number of prosecutions against tavern owners.[78] Under such pressure, the police were less likely to work informally with Joe Beef on matters of public order.

New attitudes toward leisure activities were also coming to the fore during the 1880s. With the growth of the YMCA and the Amateur Athletic Associations, urban youths were encouraged to spend their time in organized sport and develop the socially useful traits of "teamwork, perseverance, honesty and discipline — true muscular Christianity."[79] As one YMCA lecturer told his audience, recreation had to "invigorate the mind and body, and have nothing to do with questionable company, being regulated by Christian standards."[80] While such campaigns were not designed to recruit former members of street gangs, but rather the middle-class youth and clerks from the new industrial factories, these new approaches to recreation did have an impact on general tolerance of the waterfront culture. Prize fighting, probably a favoured sport of Joe Beef's patrons, was publicly denounced as a barbaric and dangerous sport.[81] With the growing alliance between the RSPCA and the Law and Order League, the Canteen's menagerie could not have survived a public outcry. New recreational opportunities for working-class Montreal, such as the opening of Sohmer Park in the early 1890s,[82] indicated that the necessity to centre all recreational life around the tavern was diminishing.

There was also a perceptible shift in public attitudes toward poverty and the city slums. With the reformers' concentration on the physical aspects of their city — clean water, paved streets, public parks, and adequate fire protection — urban slums were no longer seen only as places for poor people to live, but as potential threats to public health. Herbert Ames, a pioneer in efforts to clean up Montreal, stated that in matters of public health a simple rule existed — "the nearer people live to each other, the shorter they live."[83] Such programs as the Fresh Air Fund, which sent mothers and children of the slums to a country retreat for temporary escape from the noise and smoke of the city, testified to the concern among middle-class reformers about the dangerous effects of an industrial city.[84] The *Montreal Star* carried a series of reports on the terrible living conditions in Montreal's slums.[85] In 1885 during a smallpox epidemic, riots broke out when health authorities tried to vaccinate working-class people against the disease.[86] The great physical dangers which the slums created for the city, let alone the social danger, forced local authorities to take a closer look at the waterfront neighbourhoods.

Many of these fears and developments seem to have been familiar to the reporter who visited the Canteen in 1887. While the bears received the familiar treatment, the reporter was quite disturbed at the new attitude among the patrons. He wrote, "Nothing is more striking than the demeanor of the poor folk who fill the room. No oaths are uttered, no coarse jests, no loud talking, and never a laugh is heard. A very quiet, not to say sombre, lot of men. One would like to see a little more animation and liveliness, to hear now and then a good hearty laugh."[87] Nor was this brooding silence unique to Joe Beef's Canteen, as the reporter found several other taverns similarly devoid of their regular good cheer. These dull vacant looks, the reporter went on, "are the kind of faces one meets in the east end of London and other similar districts; but we should hardly expect to find them here. They are here, though, you see."[88] The reporter's reference to East London was repeated a few years later by the author of *Montreal by Gaslight*, a muckraking study of the city's "underworld." For the local observer, the most frightening prospect for his city was to duplicate the urban miseries of the East End of London. In *Montreal by Gaslight*, the author warned against the social consequences of drink and crushing poverty. "Last and greatest of all, think you that the modern plague of London is not known to us? Are we not infected?"[89] Along the waterfront, the silence of the labourers was feared to be the incubation period of this great urban disease. Of its eventual outbreak, one author wrote, "It may be that some day labor will raise and demand that for which it now pleads. That demand will mean riot, strike, and even civil war."[90] *Montreal by Gaslight* was written as a warning that a solution must be found before it was too late. The general outcome of such fears was that middle-class Montreal began to pay more attention to its waterfront area just as the social and economic circumstances which gave rise to Joe Beef's Canteen were changing.

The rough life along the waterfront had its own hazards and on 15 January 1889 Charles McKiernan died of heart failure in his Canteen while only 54 years of age. His death was received with great sadness in many quarters of the city and the funeral attracted large crowds. As the *Gazette* reporter commented, "Every grade in the social scale was represented in those assembled in front of the 'Canteen.' There were well known merchants, wide awake brokers, hard working mechanics and a big contingent of the genus bum, all jostling one another for a glimpse of the coffin containing what remained of one, whatever may have been his faults, who was always the poor man's friend."[91] After a short Anglican service, McKiernan's body was carried out of the tavern and the procession started for Mount Royal Cemetery. Among those in the procession were representatives from 50 labour societies who acknowledged for the last time Joe Beef's support of the trade union movement. The exception to this general sympathy was the *Montreal Witness,* which published its own death notice.

> Joe Beef is dead. For twenty five years he has enjoyed in his own way the reputation of being for Montreal what was in former days known under the pet sobriquet of the wickedest man. His saloon, where men consorted with unclean beasts was probably the most disgustingly dirty in the country. It has been the bottom of the sink of which the Windsor bar and others like it are the receivers. The only step further was to be found murdered on the wharf or dragged out of the gutter or the river, as might happen. It was the resort of the most degraded of men. It was the bottom of the pit, a sort of *cul de sac,* in which thieves could be corralled. The police declared it valuable to them as a place where these latter could be run down. It has been actively at work over all that time for the brutalizing of youth — a work which was carried on with the utmost diligence by its, in that sense, talented proprietor.[92]

Perhaps more than any of Joe Beef's lampoons, this editorial showed the limits of the *Witness's* Christian charity.

With McKiernan's death, Joe Beef's Canteen declined. The transient customers were the first to suffer. Thomas Irwin, a "protege" of the Canteen, was arrested a few days after McKiernan's death for stealing a piece of flannel. In explaining his crime, Irwin stated "There is no use for me trying to make my living now that poor old Joe is dead and gone. I must get a home somewhere in winter; won't you admit that? Well, I stole to get a lodging."[93] For the wharf-rats and sun-fish, Joe Beef's was closed. His bears met an ignoble end as well. In April police officers shot Joe Beef's bears on the request of McKiernan's widow. She planned to have them stuffed.[94] By 1893 the Canteen was gone. The Salvation Army bought the tavern and under the banner of "Joe Beef's Converted" continued many of the services to transient workers which McKiernan had pioneered. Masters at adapting popular culture to their religious beliefs, the Salvation Army transformed one of their most troublesome enemies into a prophet for bread and salvation.[95]

In assessing the significance of Charles McKiernan to the Montreal working class in the 1870s and 1880s, one must remember that when McKiernan arrived in 1868 he did not create the working-class culture associated with Joe Beef's Canteen. That culture, which had grown out of the daily routines of the casual labourers on the docks, already existed. What Joe Beef accomplished was to give that culture a public face and voice, a figure upon which the local press and reformers could focus. In doing so, Joe Beef saved that culture from the obscurity which generally surrounds work cultures. The material necessary for that culture was amply demonstrated by the numerous community services which grew up around the tavern.

This waterfront culture possessed its own values of mutual assistance, hard work, good cheer, and a sense of manly dignity. The necessity to "act like men," which McKiernan urged upon striking canal labourers, was an important code of ethics which the tavern owner used as a measure of all things. Clergy who treated his patrons "as men" were allowed into the Canteen, but organizations which resorted to the police to settle problems deserved condemnation for such unmanly behaviour. Even McKiernan's denunciations of Montreal industrialists, the "Big Bugs," or John Dougall were denunciations of individuals and not social classes. Indeed, the tendency to personalize every problem facing the waterfront community pointed out the necessity for longshoremen to find some larger institutional framework through which they could preserve the values that their work culture generated. The Knights of Labor provided this opportunity, but the Knights built upon the traditional values preserved and strengthened by Joe Beef.

While Joe Beef's controversies with the middle-class reformers who entered into his neighbourhood were genuine, the lasting influence of such incidents appeared small. For all his bluster, Joe Beef was a limited threat to the social order of Montreal. As a spokesman for rough culture, Joe Beef satirized only the pretensions and hypocrisy which he saw in the smooth behaviour of middle-class men. He did not advocate class antagonism, but a fair deal. For a short time, Joe Beef's influence was able to reach a fair deal with municipal authorities. What frightened some observers was the possibility that the growing numbers of unskilled factory workers, that unknown quantity of industrial transformation, would adopt the working-class culture of Joe Beef, with its violence and disregard for legal and moral authority. No doubt these observers were pleased that the new factory hands followed the lead of respectable skilled workers within the Knights of Labor.

The culture represented by Joe Beef was certainly different than that of the skilled tradesmen of Montreal. Only with difficulty can one imagine an experienced typographer making regular trips to the Canteen to see the bears. Though rough and respectable cultures interacted, they were clearly separate.[96] The culture surrounding the casual labourers grew out of a physically demanding life of marginal economic benefit, obtained through the common exertion of labour. In these respects, Joe Beef's world was closer to the world of Peter Aylen and the Shiners of the Ottawa Valley than to that of the typographers in the offices of the *Montreal Witness* or of the cotton mill workers of Hochelaga.[97] The waterfront world had its own internal hierarchy as Joe Beef vigorously defended his patrons against middle-class charges of drunken violence, but then threw them into the street when they got rowdy. While McKiernan's background, as his Irish verses confirm,[98] was rural, he lived in an industrial city and had to contend with the economic and social restrictions which this implied. Realizing the growing power of the police and social reformers to define the limits of acceptable behaviour, Joe Beef attempted to convince these men of the validity of working-class culture. He was not very successful. To the very end, McKiernan was rooted in the culture of his tavern and neighbourhood. For him, the liquor business was not a means of upward mobility and the tavern owner's sons remained working class.

Joe Beef's Canteen illustrated the complex nature of working-class culture. In the narrow, traditional sense of culture as artistic creation, the satiric verses, engravings, or cartoons by McKiernan and others about Joe Beef contributed in a minor way to the nineteenth-century radical literature in Canada. Local historians of Montreal were well aware of this tradition left behind by Joe Beef.[99] In the broader sense of culture as popular culture, the tavern life of bears, debates, and songs acknowledged a recreational culture created by the working class and not for them. The coming of rational recreation would weaken this tradition, but McKiernan's death had little long-term effect on this level. Finally, Joe Beef's Canteen represented a material culture of community services relating to the employment, housing, and health of the working-class neighbourhood. This culture was the most important manifestation of the Canteen in terms of class conflict.[100] All aspects of culture surrounding Joe Beef's Canteen demonstrated the integral nature of the life of the labouring men along the waterfront who would probably not have recognized distinctions between recreation and work, between a popular and material culture.

To label Joe Beef's Canteen a "pre-industrial" fragment in an industrial world obscures the fact that working-class culture was a fluid culture borrowing from its own past and from contemporary middle-class culture. Middle-class disgust at Joe Beef's antics grew largely out of his ability to parody their most pious thoughts. While Joe Beef rejected these new industrial virtues, this hardly distinguished him from thousands of other Montreal labourers and skilled workers. In many ways, the culture of Joe Beef had reached its own limits. Successful in bargaining social questions of public conduct and order, McKiernan played only a supporting role in the economic struggles in the factories and on the docks. The attempt to form new alliances between skilled and unskilled, men and women, tradesman with tradesman, would be made not by the Joe Beefs of the nineteenth century but by the Knights of Labor.

NOTES

1. Montreal Illustrated; or The Strangers' Guide to Montreal (Montreal, 1875). For a more thematic guide to the city in the 1880s, see S.E. Dawson, Hand-Book for the City of Montreal and Its Environs (Montreal, 1883). Lovell's Historic Report of the Census of Montreal (Montreal, 1891) is a good example of how the material progress of Montreal was equated with social and moral improvements. As Lovell stated, "Peace, happiness and prosperity abound, and brotherly love forms a link that might be prized in any city. The policeman is seldom needed. Intemperance is becoming a thing of the past." (45) Lovell's private census should not be confused with the Dominion census conducted that same year. The Montreal Star, in its 16 September 1886 issue, carried special stories on the city's capitalists and their contribution to social development.

2. This underground Montreal is given a muckraker's treatment in Montreal by Gaslight (Montreal, 1889), which contains a chapter on Joe Beef's Canteen. Charles McKiernan's landlord, F.X. Beaudry, was closely connected with the local prostitution trade, as his obituary (Montreal Witness, 25 March 1885) details. On gambling dens, see Montreal Witness, 14 September 1876, and Montreal Star, 30 October 1889. The Star, 23 January 1872, carries an article on a local cockfight.

3. The most recent contributions to this debate are Kenneth McNaught, "E.P. Thompson vs. Harold Logan," Canadian Historical Review 62 (1981): 141–68; Gregory S. Kealey's "Labour and Working-Class History in Canada: Prospects in the 1980s," and David J. Bercuson's "Through the Looking Glass of Culture," both from Labour/Le Travailleur 7 (1981): 67–94, 95–112. The history of Joe Beef hopefully shows some of the merits of a cultural approach to working-class history.

4. Raymond Williams, Culture and Society (London, 1960), 327.

5. Williams, Culture and Society, 330.

6. Gareth Stedman Jones, Outcast London (Oxford, 1971). Comparisons between Montreal and London, at least on general terms, are not as tenuous as might first appear. Contemporary observers of the waterfront often compared these slums to those of East London. Herbert Ames's attempt to introduce model housing for the workingman was modelled on the efforts of Octavia Hill's plan to help the London poor (The City Below the Hill [Toronto, 1972], 114). McKiernan received his training at Woolwich, which William Booth studied before founding his Salvation Army. The Salvation Army was one of the more successful groups in the waterfront neighbourhood.

7. Montreal Star, 16 January 1889. See also Edgar A. Collard's Montreal Yesterdays (Toronto, 1962) for a good general assessment of Charles McKiernan, and the Montreal City Archives clipping file R. 3654.2 "Rues, Commune, Rue de la," for general press coverage of McKiernan by Collard and other Montreal historians.

8. Dorothy Suzanne Cross, "The Irish in Montreal, 1867–1896," (M.A. thesis, McGill University, 1969) gives a general account of the Montreal Irish community. For contemporary descriptions, see John Francis Maguire's The Irish in America (Montreal, 1868), and Nicholas Flood Davin, The Irishman in Canada (Toronto, 1877).

9. Montreal by Gaslight, 10. Other well-known taverns were Tommy Boyle's The Horseshoe, which catered to those who followed prize fighting, and the Suburban, which had a reputation for giving the poor man a helping hand (94–105).

10. *Montreal Star*, 14 February 1888. Liquor licences, which included hotels, restaurants, saloons, and groceries, increased from 723 in 1879 to 1273 in 1887. Joe Beef's Canteen had a hotel licence.

11. *Montreal Witness*, 4 April 1881.

12. *Toronto Globe*, 14 April 1876; *Halifax Herald*, 28 June 1880; *Montreal Star*, 3 October 1887.

13. W.H. Davies, The Autobiography of a Super-Tramp (London, 1964), 131, cited in Clayton Gray, *Le Vieux Montreal* (Montreal, 1964), 16.

14. *Montreal Witness*, 4 April 1881. In an account of Joe Beef's encounter with the census taker, the problems of tracing the transient population were made clear. Of all the one-night guests which the Canteen provided for, only ten men were found by the census taker. Two of these, an Irish musician and a Spanish cook, were probably employees of the tavern. Also listed were an English coachmaker, an Irish blacksmith, an American barber, a Scottish commercial agent, an English (Quaker) leather merchant, an Irish accountant, an English labourer, and an Irish tanner. McKiernan's fifteen-year-old son was listed as a rivet maker and was likely serving an apprenticeship. See Public Archives of Canada (hereafter PAC), RG 31, *Census of Canada*, 1881, Manuscript, Montreal, West Ward, Division 3, p. 1.

15. *Toronto Globe*, 14 April 1876.

16. *Montreal by Gaslight*, 115.

17. *Montreal Star*, 10 September 1883; 11 September 1883; 3 October 1883.

18. *Montreal Witness*, 17 March 1881; 22 March 1881.

19. *Montreal Herald*, 21 April 1880; *Montreal Witness*, 6 August 1875. Jon M. Kingsdale, "The Poor Man's Club: Social Functions of the Urban Working Class Saloon," *American Quarterly* 25 (1973): 472–89, provides an excellent background to the discussion which follows and demonstrates that many of the Canteen's services were common to nineteenth-century taverns.

20. *La Minerve*, 2 August 1873.

21. *Toronto Globe*, 14 April 1876; *Halifax Herald*, 28 June 1880; *Montreal Star*, 3 October 1887.

22. *La Minerve*, 20 January 1874.

23. *Montreal Star*, 14 July 1876; *Montreal Witness*, 22 October 1873; 12 November 1877.

24. *La Minerve*, 7 November 1873. John was John Dougall of the Montreal Witness who had recently dismissed some union employees. Although the Canteen was a male bastion, McKiernan was not unaware of the growing number of women workers in the Montreal labour force. For the employment of women, see Dorothy Suzanne Cross's "The Neglected Majority: The Changing Role of Women in Nineteenth Century Montreal," *Social History* 12 (1973): 202–203.

25. *Montreal Yesterdays*, 273–74.

26. *La Minerve*, 28 December 1878.

27. *Toronto Globe*, 14 April 1876.

28. The integration of transient labour into urban centres was very important and a failure to do so is described in Sydney L. Harring's "Class Conflict and the Suppression of Tramps in Buffalo, 1892–1894," *Law and Society Review* 11 (1977): 873–911. See also James M. Pitsula's "The Treatment of Tramps in Late Nineteenth-Century Toronto," *Historical Papers* (1980), 116–32.

29. *Montreal Star*, 5 February 1877; *Witness*, 2 August 1876; *Star*, 3 October 1879.

30. *Star*, 15 January 1878; 29 December 1879; 27 February 1880; 25 March 1880; 1 April 1880. H.E. MacDermot in his History of the Montreal General Hospital (Montreal, 1950) wrote that Joe Beef's Canteen was "a particularly staunch supporter, and entries of donations from 'Proceeds of iron box, barroom, of Joe Beef' are frequent, or from 'his own skating Rink,' as well as contributions for the care of special patients" (55). MacDermot's work was cited in Edgar Collard's "All Our Yesterdays," *Montreal Gazette*, 9 January 1960. William Fox Beakbane, who drowned at Allan's wharf on 29 July 1883, was buried in the McKiernan family plot in Mount Royal Cemetery (*Star*, 10 August 1883).

31. *Witness*, 17 December 1877; 19 December 1877. Strike leader Lucien Pacquette spent several days in hospital recovering from his wound. For contractor William Davis, this was not the first time his workers reacted violently to his labour practices. A year earlier someone tried to blow up the contractor's house and severely damaged the building (*Witness*, 20 December 1877).

32. *Witness*, 17 December 1877.

33. *Witness*, 19 December 1877, 20 December 1877. Bernard Devlin (1824–80) came to Quebec in 1844 and published the *Freeman's Journal and Commercial Advertiser*. He ran unsuccessfully for the 1867 Parliament against Thomas D'Arcy McGee, who accused Devlin of being secretly in support of the Fenians. Devlin served as a Liberal MP for Montreal West from 1875 to 1878 (DCB 10: 250).

34. *Star*, 20 December 1877; *Witness*, 24 December 1877.

35. *Star*, 19 December 1877.

36. PAC, Dept. of Public Works, RG11, B1(a), vol. 474, p. 2534, Whitney & Daly to F. Braun, 22 January 1878.

37. *Witness*, 21 December 1877.

38. *Witness*, 22 December 1877.

39. *Witness*, 21 December 1877.

40. *Witness*, 26 December 1877.

41. Ottawa Citizen, 18 January 1878. The Citizen carried a copy of a strikers' petition to Mackenzie which was signed by 122 people including McKiernan. Most of the signers were untraceable in local business directories, but some local grocers and dry goods merchants did support the strikers' demands and this suggests some degree of neighbourhood support. Original petition in PAC, RG11, B1(a), vol. 473, pp. 2514–20.

42. *Ottawa Citizen*, 24 January 1878. An admitted weakness of this study is the failure to document the political connections which McKiernan had with municipal politicians. Federally, McKiernan was a Conservative and this no doubt played some part in his attack on Mackenzie. During the 1872 election, McKiernan led a group of sailors into a Liberal polling station and began serenading them with a concertina. When surrounded by an angry crowd, McKiernan pulled out a pistol and fired into the air. In the tumult which followed McKiernan and his companions were beaten and had to be rescued by the police. *Montreal Witness*, 28 August 1872.

43. PAC, RG11, B1(a), vol. 473, pp. 2514–69. Not all contractors paid their workers in truck, and those who did argued that the workers benefited from the arrangement. Davis argued that monthly pay periods increased productivity. "On Public Works as a Rule, a large number of men lose time after pay day, and, thereby disarrange and retard the progress of the Works." (Davis to Braun, 21 January 1878, p. 2532). John Dougall of the *Montreal Witness*, however, published an account of the supplies given to a labourer instead of cash. For $1.75 owing in wages, the worker received whiskey, sugar, tobacco, cheese, and bread valued at $1.05. The goods were on display throughout the strike at Joe Beef's Canteen (*Witness*, 22 January 1878).

44. *Star*, 17 April 1880; *Witness*, 21 April 1880.

45. *Halifax Herald*, 28 June 1880.

46. PAC, MG28, I 126, vol. 15, *Royal Canadian Academy of Art scrapbook*; *Montreal Gazette*, 7 February 1916, cited in Montreal Yesterdays, 271.

47. "Third Report of the Select Committee of the House of Commons respecting a Prohibitory Liquor Law," *House of Commons Journals*, 1874, Testimony of F.W. Penton, 9.

48. *Montreal Gazette*, 22 April 1880. The importance of battles between the police and working-class people is illustrated by Robert D. Storch in "The Policeman as Domestic Missionary: Urban Discipline and Popular Culture in Northern England," *Journal of Social History* 9 (1976): 481–509.

49. Star, 30 October 1876. The Black Horse Gang's activities are reported in the *Witness*, 26 May 1875; 27 May 1875; *Star*, 1 February 1876; *Witness*, 24 July 1880; 10 May 1882. Street gangs in general are discussed in the *Witness*, 31 May 1875.

50. *Witness*, 19 November 1878; 18 November 1878. The *Witness* story on the incident was protested by "Joe Beef's Gang" who turned up in the editor's office and claimed that they were "respectable mechanics and that the butchers are on the contrary not noted for their respectable behaviour."

51. *Witness*, 28 September 1880; 24 July 1879.

52. *Witness*, 8 February 1877.

53. *Annual Report of the Montreal Sailors Institute for the Year Ending January, 1870* (Montreal, 1870), 5; *Annual Report of the Montreal Sailors Institute of 1870* (Montreal, 1871), 8.

54. Royal Commission on the Liquor Traffic, *House of Commons Sessional Paper*, no. 21, 1894, 584.

55. *House of Commons Sessional Paper*, no. 21, 1894, 589.

56. *House of Commons Sessional Paper*, no. 21, 1894, 586.

57. The difference of religious sentiment was reflected in the organization of benevolent associations. Roman Catholic Montreal had its own hospitals and dispensaries, thirteen benevolent institutions caring for the aged, orphaned, and widowed. Nine Catholic charitable societies also contributed to the welfare of the impoverished citizens. Protestant Montreal, besides having its hospitals, had sixteen benevolent institutions for the same clientele as the Catholic institutions as well as homes for female immigrants and sick servant girls. Religious differences were further complicated by the national origins of Montreal residents. To aid fellow countrymen there were several national societies including the St. George, St. Andrew, St. Patrick, St. Jean Baptiste, Irish Protestant, Italian, Welsh, Scandinavian, and Swiss benevolent organizations. See Lovell's *Historic Report of the Census of Montreal* (Montreal, 1891), 62–63, 72–73. See also Janice A. Harvey's "Upper Class Reaction to Poverty in Mid-Nineteenth Century Montreal: A Protestant Example," (M.A. thesis, McGill University, 1978) for descriptions of Protestant charities.

58. *Montreal Yesterdays*, 273–74.

59. *Montreal Star*, 29 September 1871; *Montreal Yesterdays*, 272–73. McKiernan's 25-year-old wife Mary McRae and her baby died on 26 September 1871, and it is uncertain whether the contemporary accounts correctly interpreted McKiernan's actions. Interestingly enough, McKiernan's republican sentiments exhibited themselves on his wife's gravestone. Her inscription read in part,

> I leave a husband and four orphan babes
> To mouth their mother's loss
> Who will never return.
> But let that tree, which you see
> Be the tree of Liberty
> And in its stead never let the tree of [Bigotry]
> Be planted between them and me.

60. *Montreal Witness*, 4 April 1881; PAC, RG31, *Census of Canada*, 1881 Manuscript, Montreal, West Ward, Division no. 3, p. 1.
61. *Montreal Yesterdays*, 279–80.
62. *Toronto Globe*, 14 April 1876; *Montreal Star*, 31 July 1876.
63. *Halifax Herald*, 28 June 1880. For Mr. Hammond's preaching style see *Montreal Star*, 18 March 1880.
64. Edgar Collard, "Of Many Things," *Montreal Gazette*, 28 February 1976. For the legal problems of the Salvation Army, see the *Montreal Star*, 19 August 1886; 3 September 1886; 14 September 1886.
65. *Montreal Star*, 9 January 1911. See J.I. Cooper's "The Early Editorial Policy of the Montreal Witness," Canadian Historical Association, *Report* (1947), 53–62, and Dougall's obituary in the *Montreal Star*, 19 August 1886.
66. *La Minerve*, 13 March 1873.
67. *Montreal Star*, 26 November 1872; 27 November 1872; 28 November 1872.
68. *Montreal Witness*, 8 February 1877.
69. *Montreal Witness*, 4 April 1878.
70. *Montreal Witness*, 5 April 1879.
71. Royal Commission on the Relations of Capital and Labour, 1889, *Quebec Evidence*, vol. 1, pp. 150–86.
72. Royal Commission on the Relations of Capital and Labour, Testimony of R.A. Smith, 156–60; James Urquhart, 173–75.
73. Royal Commission on the Relations of Capital and Labour, Testimony of Patrick Dalton, 183–85.
74. Royal Commission on the Relations of Capital and Labour, Testimony of Edmund Tart, 175–81.
75. Royal Commission on the Relations of Capital and Labour, Testimony of Patrick Dalton, 186.
76. Royal Commission on the Liquor Traffic, 512.
77. Royal Commission on the Liquor Traffic, 583.
78. *Montreal Star*, 28 January 1886. On the Law and Order League, see *Star*, 16 August 1887; 24 January 1889; 16 February 1889, 10 March 1887.
79. Alan Metcalfe, "The Evolution of Organized Physical Recreation in Montreal, 1840–1895," *Social History* 21 (1978): 153. For the role of the YMCA in the new attitude toward leisure activities, see David Macleod, "A Live Vaccine: The YMCA and Male Adolescence in the United States and Canada, 1870–1920," *Social History* 21 (1978): 5–25. An excellent study of recreation in England is Peter Bailey, *Leisure and Class in Victorian England* (Toronto, 1978).
80. *Montreal Star*, 15 November 1873.
81. For denunciations of prize fighting see *Star*, 4 January 1887; 9 May 1887; 20 May 1887; 23 May 1887; 15 September 1887.
82. *Montreal Star*, 6 June 1893; 13 July 1893. Richard Bell of the Montreal Sailors Institute preferred that sailors drink at Sohmer Park rather than in the waterfront taverns. Royal Commission on the Liquor Traffic, 584–89.
83. Herbert B. Ames, "Why We Should Study the Municipal System of Our City," *Abstract of a Course of Ten Lectures on Municipal Administration* (Montreal, 1896), 7.
84. *Montreal Star* contains several articles promoting the Fresh Air Fund: see 11 June 1887; 18 June 1887; 25 June 1887; 6 July 1887. On the Fresh Air Home, see *Star*, 23 June 1888.
85. *Star*, 24 December 1883; 29 December 1883.
86. *Star*, 29 September 1885.
87. *Star*, 3 October 1887.
88. *Star*, 3 October 1887.
89. *Montreal by Gaslight*, 10.
90. *Montreal by Gaslight*, 35.

91. *Montreal Gazette,* 19 January 1889.
92. *Montreal by Gaslight,* 119.
93. *Star,* 24 January 1889.
94. *Star,* 29 April 1889.
95. *Star,* 26 May 1893; 27 May 1893. R.G. Moyles, in The Blood and Fire in Canada (Toronto, 1977), remarked that this was a new venture for the Salvation Army. "Whereas other men's hostels had been designed as rescue centres for ex-prisoners and for total derelicts, Joe Beef's was a hostel for transients, providing a cheap bed for the unemployed man with little money and a cheap meal for the poor city labourer" (69).
96. Peter Bailey's "Will the Real Bill Banks Please Stand Up? Towards a Role Analysis of Mid-Victorian Working-Class Respectability," *Journal of Social History* 12 (1979), offers some interesting insights into the differences between rough and respectable workingmen.
97. Michael S. Cross, "The Shiners' War: Social Violence in the Ottawa Valley in the 1830's," *Canadian Historical Review* 54 (1973): 1–26. For a description of an early Ottawa tavern see W.P. Lett, "Corkstown," Recollections of Old Bytown (Ottawa, 1979), 81–86.
98. See the attitudes reflected in "Spurn Not the Poor Man," *La Minerve,* 7 January 1874; "I am Long Past Wailing and Whining," *La Minerve,* 27 January 1874; and "The Big Beggarman," *La Minerve,* 13 January 1874. Poetic style makes it unlikely that these verses are from McKiernan's pen, but by printing them with his advertisements he demonstrated a sympathy with their author.
99. Frank W. Watt, "Radicalism in English Canadian Literature since Confederation" (Ph.D. thesis, University of Toronto, 1957). Watt does not mention McKiernan but Watt's description of a literature disillusioned with nation building and inclined to associate patriotic feelings with the motives and methods of capitalist exploitation could accommodate much of McKiernan's verse.
100. Bryan D. Palmer's A *Culture in Conflict* (Montreal, 1979) contains the fullest discussion of the importance of culture in Canadian class conflict. See also Gareth Stedman Jones, "Working-Class Culture and Working-Class Politics in London, 1870–1900," *Journal of Social History* 7 (1974): 460–508.

Topic Seven

Late-19th-Century Cultural Values in English-Speaking Canada

The touring Chicago Blackstockings baseball team in New Brunswick, 1891.

The cultural history of both the Victorian and Edwardian eras has received a great deal of study in Britain but much less in English-speaking Canada. What work has been done has tended to focus on what we call high culture — music, art, and literature. Only recently have historians turned to popular culture — attitudes reflected in the issues, events, and icons that affect "ordinary people."

The following three articles reflect this new trend in cultural studies with a particular emphasis on gender studies. In "Idealized Middle-Class Sport for a Young Nation: Lacrosse in Nineteenth-Century Ontario Towns, 1871–1891," Nancy B. Bouchier reconstructs the values of the emerging dominant middle-class male population through a study of amateur lacrosse in the southwestern Ontario towns of Ingersoll and Woodstock. She shows how the leading male members of the emerging middle class drew on the support of church leaders to help inculcate the masculine qualities of strength, endurance, and manliness along with middle-class values of respectability, teamwork, self-sacrifice, and moral purity, so as to establish a middle-class cultural hegemony. In the end, however, their efforts were undermined by professional competitive sports that upheld opposing values.

In "Gendered Baselines: The Tour of the Chicago Blackstockings," Colin Howell studies the impact of an American women's baseball team's tour of the Maritimes in 1891 on attitudes towards "the relationship of the sexes, the prevailing notions of respectable behaviour, and the ways in which baseball served to delineate and shape existing definitions of masculinity and femininity." He argues that baseball relegated women to the rule of spectator, reinforced differentiating roles for men and women based on "ideologically constructed images of both the body natural and the body politic," and, in the case of the Blackstockings' tour, led to "the commercialization and marketing of women as spectacle."

In "Femininity First: Sport and Physical Education for Ontario Girls, 1890–1930," Helen Lenskyj shows how the establishment of physical education for girls in the Ontario school curriculum upheld the prevailing attitudes toward women, and restricted women's participation in competitive sports. She maintains that women's roles as wives and mothers — and thus their reproductive role — governed the types of physical education and sports deemed to be appropriate.

In what ways does a study of popular culture offer a different perspective on Victorian society than one of "high culture"? What common attitudes towards the role of physical activity and sports on acceptable male and female characteristics are evident in the three readings? What do these studies tell us about cultural values in the Victorian era, and in what ways do they advance our understanding of the age?

A useful collection of essays dealing with cultural attitudes in the context of gender is *Gender and History in Canada*, eds. Joy Parr and Mark Rosenfeld (Toronto: Copp Clark, 1996). Wendy Mitchinson studies the attitude of Victorian doctors to women and childbirth in *The Nature of Their Bodies: Women and Their Doctors in Victorian Canada* (Toronto: University of Toronto Press, 1991). Also useful are the essays in *Caring and Curing: Historical Perspectives on Women and Healing in Canada*, eds. Diana Dodd and Deborah Gorham (Ottawa: Carleton University Press, 1994), and Angus McLaren, *Our Own Master Race: Eugenics in Canada, 1885–1945* (Toronto: McClelland and Stewart, 1990).

On the larger issue of gender relations from a female perspective, see the essays in Franca Iacovetta and Mariana Valverde, eds., *Gender Conflicts: New Essays in Women's History* (Toronto: University of Toronto Press, 1992), and in Veronica Strong-Boag and Anita Clair Fellman, eds., *Rethinking Canada: The Promise of Women's History*, 2nd ed. (Toronto: Copp Clark, 1991). For the Maritimes, see Janet Guilford and Suzanne Morton, eds., *Separate Spheres: Women's Worlds in the 19th Century Maritimes* (Fredericton: Acadiensis Press, 1994), and Colin Howell and Richard J. Toney, eds., *Jack Tar in History: Essays in the History of Maritime Life and Labour* (Fredericton: Acadiensis Press, 1991). For British Columbia, see the special issue on gender history of *BC Studies* (November 1995). The Dionne quintuplets as cultural icons are examined in a special issue of the *Journal of Canadian Studies* (Winter 1994–95); see, as well, Pierre Berton's *The Dionne Years* (Toronto: McClelland and Stewart, 1977).

Although male gender studies are less numerous, students should consult Michael Kaufman, *Cracking the Armour: Power, Pain and the Lives of Men* (Toronto: Viking, 1993), and the essays in his edited collection, *Beyond Patriarchy: Essays by Men on Pleasure, Power and Change* (Toronto: Oxford University Press, 1987).

A number of good regional studies have been written in gender-related history. For the Maritimes, see Judith Fingard, *The Dark Side of Life in Victorian Halifax* (Halifax: Potters Field, 1989); Colin Howell, *Northern Sandlots: A Social History of Maritime Baseball* (Toronto: University of Toronto Press, 1995); Suzanne Morton, *Ideal Surroundings: Domestic Life in a Working-Class Suburb in the 1920s* (Toronto: University of Toronto Press, 1995); Eric Saeger, *Ships and Memories* (Vancouver: University of British Columbia Press, 1993), especially the chapters on masculinity and family, pp. 106–17 and 97–105, respectively. For Ontario, see Karen Dubinsky, *Improper Advances: Rape and Heterosexual Conflict in Ontario, 1880–1929* (Chicago: University of Chicago Press, 1993); Thomas Dunk, *It's a Working Man's Town: Male Working-Class Culture in Northwestern Ontario* (Montreal/Kingston: McGill-Queen's University Press, 1991); Ruth Frager, *Sweatshop Strife: Class, Ethnicity and Gender in the Jewish Labour Movement of Toronto, 1900–1939* (Toronto: University of Toronto Press, 1992); Franca Iacovetta, *Such Hard-Working People: Women, Men and the Italian Immigrant Experience in Postwar Toronto* (Montreal/Kingston: McGill-Queen's University Press, 1992); Joy Parr, *The Gender of Breadwinners: Women, Men and Change in Two Industrial Towns, 1880–1950* (Toronto: University of Toronto Press, 1990), a study of Hanover and Paris, Ontario; Joan Sangster, *Earning Respect: The Lives of Working Women in Small-Town Ontario, 1920–1960* (Toronto: University of Toronto Press, 1995), a study of Peterborough, Ontario; and Carolyn Strange, *Toronto's Girl Problem: The Perils and Pleasures of the City, 1880–1930* (Toronto: University of Toronto Press, 1995). For British Columbia, see Jean Barman, *Growing Up British in British Columbia: Boys in Private School* (Vancouver: University of British Columbia Press, 1984).

On sports and masculinity, see Alan Metcalfe, *Canada Learns to Play: The Emergence of Organized Sport, 1897–1914* (Toronto: McClelland & Stewart, 1987); and the relevant essays in Morris Mott, ed., *Sports in Canada: Historical Readings* (Mississauga, ON: Copp Clark Pitman, 1989). For a discussion of an emerging middle-class culture in English-speaking Canada, see Andrew C. Holman, *A Sense of Their Duty: Middle-Class Formation in Victorian Ontario Towns* (Montreal/Kingston: McGill-Queen's University Press, 1999); and Lynne Marks, *Revivals and Roller Rinks: Religion, Leisure, and Identity in Late Nineteenth Century Small-Town Ontario* (Toronto: University of Toronto Press, 1996); and on cultural hegemony, Keith Walden, "Speaking Modern: Language, Culture, and Hegemony in Grocery Window Displays, 1887–1920," *Canadian Historical Review*, 70, 3 (1989): 285–310.

WEBLINKS

Multimedia History of Lacrosse
http://archives.cbc.ca/300c.asp?id=1-41-824
A history of lacrosse in Canada utilizing the radio and television archives of the CBC.

Morality and Medicine

http://individual.utoronto.ca/twix/anatomy/nineteenth.htm
A description of the relationship between morality and medicine as practised in the 1800s.

Alberta Rural Life

http://www.abheritage.ca/pasttopresent/rural_life/beaver_lake_good_year.html
First-hand accounts of the rural life of farmers growing grain in Alberta, beginning in the late 19th century.

Canadian Illustrated News: 1869–1883

http://www.collectionscanada.ca/cin/index-e.html
Includes fully transcribed copies of the *Canadian Illustrated News*, a popular magazine in Canada of the 19th century.

Sheet Music from Canada's Past

http://www.collectionscanada.ca/sheetmusic/index-e.html
A database of sheet music from the 1800s and early 1900s, demonstrating the musical trends and preferences of the time.

Four Alberta Diaries

http://folklore.library.ualberta.ca/dspCitation.cfm?ID=499
Diaries of four Alberta women at the turn of the century.

Article Sixteen

Idealized Middle-Class Sport for a Young Nation: Lacrosse in Nineteenth-Century Ontario Towns, 1871–1891

Nancy B. Bouchier

During the late nineteenth century, social groups attempting to establish a cultural hegemony used sport as a site for their struggles over culture.[1] Although the coalition of interests best denoted as the respectable Victorian middle class won this battle, the victory was neither complete nor truly coherent. Thus, a study of the local adoption of amateur lacrosse in Ingersoll, and its nearby arch-rival Woodstock, Ontario,[2] provides a way of exploring how social groups in small localities used sport to experience, and contribute to, the formulation of a hegemonic culture.[3]

One outcome of this late-nineteenth-century process is a most enduring legacy. It is the notion that games somehow build character, and, by extension, that sport is a potent vehicle for achieving and reinforcing certain social goals, and rectifying the physical and moral ills of society. Perhaps best known through the phrase "muscular Christianity,"[4] this notion deeply

Source: *Journal of Canadian Studies*, 29, 2 (Summer 1994): 89–110. Reprinted with permission.

pervaded the amateur sport movement that created the institutional framework necessary for sport competition to thrive during the last century, and for the acceptance of sport as an integral aspect of our education system today.[5]

In their quest to project their world view of respectability through team sport, sport reformers approached it from a rational, utilitarian perspective.[6] Their claims about sport's character-building qualities and the sporting performances choreographed to buttress these claims constitute the stories that Canadian sport reformers were telling about themselves and their world.[7] By doing so, they rendered sport an arena for the acting out of the hegemonic process. Since in the process the voices of those who they deemed to be their opponents have been muted, not recorded, or suppressed through time, detractors remain a hazy group. Thus, we are left mainly with the legacy of those who held the dominant agenda for sport. However, we do have some clues to the identity, actions, and perhaps belief of those who resisted their efforts.

Amateur lacrosse is a particularly ripe sport in which to study the phenomenon of sport as a site for an emerging hegemony. It advanced the popular, late-nineteenth-century notion that games build character, and it bore a particular "Canadian" stamp. It provides a fascinating example of the larger sport-reform phenomenon during the era of Canada's birth as a nation and a particular vision of how sport could cultivate "Canadian character." Although lacrosse had origins in Indian religion, tradition, and society, white urban men with a specific social agenda devised its organized form.[8] These men took the Indian game and "reinvented" it in the effort to create a version of a Canadian sporting culture that projected their particular vision of reality and belief system (that was class-bound, racist, and gender-specific).[9] Lacrosse was conceived by them as a vehicle for cultivating Canadian nationalism, manliness, and respectability in male youth, and to keep the leisure activities of males in check. Projecting lacrosse as a quintessentially Canadian sport, lacrosse propagandists, like propagandists for other popular sports of the day, received support from social reformers, religious leaders, and educators.[10] They maintained that such sports cultivated and contributed to the emerging urban-industrial Canadian nation.

This research addresses several interrelated issues in the use of sport in hegemonic struggles over culture through an examination of the development of lacrosse in the two towns during the sport's heyday, between 1871 and 1891. It first identifies certain social themes embraced both locally and nationally by the organized lacrosse movement, particularly nationalism, manliness, and youth reform through rational recreation. These themes mark lacrosse as a sport with a social agenda based upon a particular vision. Then, using demographic data on the Ingersoll and Woodstock clubs, it identifies the organizers and players who masterminded and carried out this process of reforming local sport. The research also shows that middle-class reformers were keenly aware of harmful diversions (such as swearing, drinking, gambling, immorality) that surrounded sport, and were concerned about the acceptability of certain sports themselves (such as horseracing, dog and cockfighting, bull and bear baits, and pugilism).[11] The reformers sought to monopolize the forms and meanings that local sport was to take. By the late 1880s, town councils allowed these men, who were connected to an evolving cult of respectability, to organize annual community civic holidays through their local Amateur Athletic Associations (AAAs), which regulated community sport. Finally, the research shows the ways in which sport reformers infused urban boosterism into their social agenda for lacrosse.

AAA efforts to define legitimate activities for others, like similar efforts to sublimate and marginalize unacceptable traditions, remained ongoing in the hegemonic process. While they did manage to systematize and rationalize some familiar sports and to remove others from the athletic grounds while promoting utilitarian, respectable, and representative team sports such as lacrosse, the social agenda of sport reformers met with resistance.[12] Ironically, boosterism fuelled playing field violence during intense competition as well as rowdiness in the stands. Such responses caused problems for idealistic visions of sport, prompting middle-class sport reformers to make concessions in order to maintain their hegemony.

Like other social thinkers concerned with physical health, youth, and Canadian society, the headmaster of Woodstock College, J.E. Wells, believed that physical development played an essential role in the shaping of a national character in Canadian youth. Some seven years after Confederation, he wrote in the *Canadian Monthly and National Review* that physically well-developed youth were needed for young Canada to assume "the attitudes and tones, and to some extent the responsibilities of, nationality." Wells believed that Canadians possessed certain inheritable qualities, which, tempered by climatic conditions, would "prove most favourable to mental as well as physical development." The latter was viewed as the key to national development: "bone and muscle and nerve fibre must be necessary antecedents of brain power."[13] This, in turn, undergirded nation building. Like other educational institutions, Wells's Woodstock College, which later became McMaster University, sought to stimulate the mental and physical development of youth through "a rational program of gymnasium work and outdoor sports featuring lacrosse."[14]

Wells was not alone in his concerns and efforts. Proselytizers for lacrosse throughout Canada shared this nationalist orientation and, through it, hoped to create a culture of purposeful sport.[15] For example, Dr. William George Beers, the Montreal dentist credited with facilitating the early development of the Canadian Dental Association, spearheaded the creation of the National Lacrosse Association in 1867, advocating that lacrosse could shape boys into manly Canadian nationalists.[16] With an almost evangelical fervour his *Lacrosse: The National Game of Canada* (1869) proposes a nationalist agenda for his vision of sport.[17] Beers pushed his point as far as he could:

> It may seem frivolous, at first consideration, to associate this feeling of nationality with a field game, but history proves it to be a strong and important influence. If the Republic of Greece was indebted to Olympian games; if England has cause to bless the name of cricket, so may Canada be proud of Lacrosse. It has raised a young manhood throughout the Dominion to active, healthy exercise; it has originated a popular feeling in favour of physical exercise and has, perhaps, done more than anything else to invoke the sentiment of patriotism among young men in Canada; and if this sentiment is desirable abroad, surely it is at home.[18]

Despite such claims, lacrosse is not our national sport: we simply do not have one. Still, the myth persists. It was initiated in the nineteenth century by men such as Beers, and W.K. McNaught, author of *Lacrosse and How to Play It* (1873), who commended lacrosse as having "a nationalizing influence upon all who come in contact with it, and, for this reason alone, if for no other, it ought to be encouraged." More recently, Canadian sport historian Don Morrow has argued that the notion that lacrosse is our national sport continues to be supported through "a kind of consensual validity: if something is claimed to be true enough times, it is often accepted as truth — then and now."[19]

Part of the lacrosse myth's success can be attributed to late-nineteenth-century efforts to point to the Aboriginal origins of the game in order to vindicate and justify the sport as a national symbol. In his writings Beers made all of the necessary connections. For example, he romanticized Indians as noble savages, themselves a feature of the rugged Canadian northern landscape, which white men were successfully conquering through their nation-building pursuits.[20] By extension, he believed that the Indian game could be used toward nationalist ends.

Beers was certainly not alone in this effort. In "The Northern Character: Theme and Sport in Nineteenth Century Canada," Canadian sport historian David Brown traces the blending of the northern theme with Victorian beliefs in muscular Christianity.[21] He points out that Beers developed and fused the themes of northern character and national sport in *Lacrosse: The National Game*, at the same time that R.G. Haliburton published *The Men of the North and Their Place in History*. Beers's approach, Brown argues, "provided Canadian nationalists with another medium through which they could promote their country and its benefits vigorously on both a national and international scale."[22]

Lacrosse promoters credited the physical robustness that they believed Indians had (but which white urban males, who were doomed to sedentary occupations, lacked) to the vigorous demands that lacrosse made on their physiques. They linked this attribute to their ability to conquer the Canadian wilderness by reshaping it to suit middle-class, white-male, urban culture. It would produce "the greatest combination of physical and mental activity white man can sustain." They believed that they significantly elevated the moral tone of lacrosse. Beers bluntly claimed his version of lacrosse was "much superior to the original as civilization is to barbarism."[23]

Repeated themes —"nation building," "boyish sport," and "young manhood"— were central to the promotion of lacrosse as a rational recreation aimed primarily at Canadian male youth. The concern of social and sport reformers with the "problem" of urban youth helped to fuel lacrosse's reform agenda. As high school enrolments increased (nearly doubling in Ontario between 1875 and 1895), and as the apprenticeship system declined, middle-class males were dependent on their families for longer periods of time than had previously been the case.[24] With children and adolescents increasingly under female scrutiny — in schools and in the home — some social observers feared that boys were becoming increasingly feminized and were lacking in male role models.[25] Many argued that, unchecked, this situation would result in males becoming physically weak and, therefore, powerless. Keenly concerned about this, parents and social reformers sought appropriate spare-time activities to occupy young males. Through these activities they hoped to expose them to masculine role models and to teach them the importance of manly physical activity in an increasingly sedentary world.

In both Ingersoll and Woodstock clergymen repeatedly stressed the relationship between manliness and the leisure habits of male youth. Sermon titles reveal their preoccupations: "How Does Physical Welfare Affect Moral Conduct?"; "Young Man's Leisure"; "Where Do You Spend Your Time?"; "True Manhood"; and "A Manly Man."[26] As Ingersoll's Rev. P. Wright asserted in 1872, the lack of a conception of true manhood was a "fruitful source of failures in young men." He determined that, with a grasp of this concept, "evil has no chances for young men." Simply cultivating brute strength and courage in youth was not sufficient for the pursuit of manliness: each element had to be "suitably controlled."[27]

To Canadian social and sport reformers lacrosse was one solution to the problem of urban male youth. Lacrosse was a means to the end of cultivating manliness in youth and developing character so that young men would remain on the path of righteousness. Its newness appealed to the reform-minded since it was socially insulated from taverns and other unsavoury institutions where illegal and publicly castigated sports, such as pugilism and cockfighting, thrived in an environment of alcohol and gambling. As George Beers put it, lacrosse did not have "debasing accompaniments such as the bar room association" that plagued other sports.[28] When responding to the Commission Appointed to Enquire into the Prison and Reformatory System about potential cures for youth idleness, Woodstock's gaoler offered: "I would keep children employed at something or other," for example, "good honest play, a game of lacrosse or similar amusement."[29] Presumably, similar efforts to keep boys on the right path led to the granting of the title "Tzar" of the Beavers Lacrosse Club to Woodstock's Chief Constable T.W. McKee.[30]

Lacrosse superbly embodied the notion that games build character, a key ingredient in nineteenth-century conceptions of muscular Christianity.[31] Historians J.A. Mangan, David Brown, and other scholars have shown how this powerful ideology of sport was a class-bound phenomenon rooted in British mid-nineteenth-century public school reform.[32] Public school sports played under the watchful eye of men such as Dr. Thomas Arnold at the Rugby school aimed to instill valued character traits such as team work, self-sacrifice, courage, manliness, and achievement. School masters believed that these traits were transferable to other real-life situations. Popular novels by English authors Charles Kingsley and Thomas Hughes, and writings by American Thomas Wentworth Higginson, among others, brought these beliefs to life.[33] They projected sport as a means of character building and not an end in itself.

Such arguments undercut prevailing ascetic-pietist objections to sports as useless, immoral, and socially improper.[34] Protestant clergymen, educators, and social observers had, until this time, encouraged moderate forms of physical activity simply to keep people's bodies and minds refreshed and fit for work, but they still held deep suspicions of the fun and frivolity surrounding sporting activities.[35] Higher motives for sport were thus needed to transform rowdy, idle diversion to a morally uplifting, socially sanctioned activity appropriate to the social and physical changes of an increasingly industrialized society. According to Canadian sport historian Gerald Redmond, muscular Christianity's social construction attempted "to reconcile the centuries-old Christian faith with the new realities of the modern world to the apparent satisfaction of Victorian and Edwardian consciences."[36] It met with a considerable degree of success: its rise marked the evolution from a tradition of ascetic Protestantism to one of a moral athleticism. Church leaders and religious institutions emerged as patrons, rather than critics, of sport.[37] After the turn of the century, such support lent credibility to incorporating sport into the public school curriculum as a means of providing for the social and moral education of students, while at the same time physically educating their bodies.

Amateur lacrosse upheld muscular Christian principles. In fact, the National Lacrosse Association received its most prestigious award, the Claxton Flags, from a charter member and sometime president of North America's first Young Men's Christian Association.[38] The deed of gift records Montreal millionaire, philanthropist, and social reformer James T. Claxton's desire to "promote by every means in his power the fostering of clean, amateur athletics amongst the youth of Canada."[39] This occurred long before the YMCA embraced sport as a means of cultivating the spiritual, social, and physical dimensions of man.[40]

The muscular Christian influence on lacrosse resulted in demands that players develop a rational, educated strength: speed and agility were to be carefully circumscribed by an idea of right action.[41] To this end, the rules of lacrosse restricted what players were to do, both physically and socially.[42] Bruises, cuts, scrapes, and broken bones were likely to occur if 24 players on the field, sticks in hand, were simply to charge after a single ball. A "scientific" approach aimed to eliminate violence and injury by de-emphasizing physical contact for the presumed higher social skills believed to be obtained through the activity.[43] This system of beliefs relegated brute force to the status of being inherently unmanly. Organized clubs aimed to reinforce learning experiences through the creation of a sporting "freemasonry" of those similarly indoctrinated.[44]

Expressions of manly camaraderie were commonplace: lacrosse club members shared grief in their losses and celebrated their accomplishments.[45] For example, local merchant Edward W. Nesbitt, secretary of Woodstock's Beavers, received an exquisite silver tea service from the club at a testimonial to him honouring his forthcoming marriage in 1879. A beautiful parchment scroll, elaborately detailed in gold, accompanied the gift. Its inscription with its echoes of the Sermon on the Mount speaks volumes about the club's social and moral goals:

> We feel it is no empty boast when we say that it is an honour to belong to the Beaver Lacrosse Club of Woodstock. The Young men who organized this Club nine years ago have retired and now occupy positions of trust and honour in our community leaving their places in the Club to be filled by other and younger men who bid fair to follow in the footsteps of their predecessors. At home and abroad the name of the Beaver Lacrosse Club has been and is now a synonym of honesty, uprightness, and fair dealing. Taking defeat in the same good natured and gentlemanly manner that they have scored victories, and on all occasion, recognizing the golden rule *To do to others as they wished to be done by*.[46]

In 1871, some four years after the creation of the National Lacrosse Association, Ingersoll and Woodstock sportsmen turned their attentions to cultivating this stylized approach to sport. Their involvement in lacrosse coincided with local baseball clubs losing their single-handed dominance of the towns' interurban, amateur team competition.[47] Not surprisingly they had turned first to baseball, a likely candidate for their reform efforts, since it was a highly familiar and popular activity among children and youth.

In 1864 Woodstock's first known sports club for young men, the Young Canadian baseball club, created the Silver Ball award (which came to be popularly known as the emblem of the Canadian Baseball Championship), to stimulate interurban, challenge-match competition.[48] Over the next five years Woodstock's home team defended its Canadian championship title, with a home field advantage, against rivals from Ingersoll, Guelph, and other Ontario towns. The *New York Clipper*, the premier sporting journal of the day, kept North American readers abreast of Woodstock and Ingersoll team activities.[49]

By the late 1860s and early 1870s, however, a growing emphasis on winning had begun to undercut organized baseball's early social orientation and to tarnish its clean image. With rowdyism, gambling, and professionalism on the rise in amateur baseball, local reformers began to promote lacrosse as *the* organized sport of the day. It was precisely at the point when intense competition and pressure to win resulted in the Woodstock Young Canadians losing their Canadian championship to their arch-rival, the Guelph Maple Leafs, that matters worsened. Associations between baseball and rowdyism surfaced among players and fans, illustrating the difficulties reformers faced in eradicating alternate traditions. At an 1868 Silver Ball match between the Young Canadians and the Maple Leafs, fights broke out as toughs roamed the stands, "no one" daring "to interfere with them in their nefarious work."[50]

According to sport reformers, baseball's respectability wavered because teams paid players under the table and heated competition sparked lively betting.[51] Baseball reformers repeatedly sought new solutions to these dilemmas — creating new leagues to reaffirm their intention, requiring amateur documentation from players to limit the involvement of itinerant professional athletes, having amateur sponsoring agencies fund team expenses through gate receipts to lessen the impact of money on the game. Yet the behaviour of players, fans, and others ensured that the plague persisted. In 1884, the Woodstock amateur club presented their strongly worded view of the matter: "we have no sympathy whatever with 'professional sport,' as it is now carried on in the interests of speculators and gamblers . . . the result of a professional baseball match has no more interest for us than the result of a fight between two ownerless street curs."[52]

In the midst of such controversy, local sport reformers turned their focus on lacrosse, packaging it as a purer, and a particularly Canadian, team sport. They were confident in the ability of the existing national-level regulatory agency (the NLA) to oversee the sport locally. Demographic data on Ingersoll and Woodstock club organizers and players reveal the identities of the people who masterminded and carried out this reforming of local sport. The organizers of Ingersoll and Woodstock lacrosse clubs are readily found in local historical records. The names of the men who ran local lacrosse clubs between 1871 and 1890 read like a local social register; indeed, their names are still present on local buildings, street signs, and memorials.[53]

Seventy-two Ingersoll and Woodstock men who organized local lacrosse between 1871 and 1890 show striking demographic similarities, and while the data includes a considerable range of affluence and power (especially regarding occupation), some important conclusions can be drawn. For example, they operated within an exclusively male network. Presumably they never officially prohibited females from involvement because existing social and cultural constraints had already done this work.[54] And, with only three exceptions, for almost twenty years group members were exclusively Protestants.[55] Beyond this, their shared social background united the reformers and differentiated them from other local males. If one applies a taxonomy to census data and uses it as a proxy for class, those data reveal that, as a group, these men had a very different occupational pattern than the overall local workforce.[56] (See Table 16.1.)

Only a very small group of manual workers, drawn from labour's small aristocracy of skilled artisans, were lacrosse organizers. Middle-class men (holding non-manual occupations in banks, law offices, mercantile establishments, and publishing offices) dominated lacrosse organizations. As such, they vastly overrepresented their segment of the local workforce hierarchy.

Their local voluntary association and political involvement also afford highly suggestive glimpses into the social similarities and shared values of these sport reformers. To summarize the data in Table 16.2, lacrosse organizers engaged in remarkably similar voluntary activities.

Table 16.1   Occupational Characteristics of Ingersoll and Woodstock Lacrosse Executives Compared to Local Male Workforces, 1871–1890*

Occupational Categories	Lacrosse Organizers	Male Workforce[+]
Non-manual	94%	26%
Manual skilled	6%	48%
Manual unskilled	0%	26%
Total number	72	2883

*   In rounded figures.
[+]   Combined, Ingersoll and Woodstock male workforces over 16 years derived from 1881 manuscript censuses.

Table 16.2   Voluntary Organization Profiles of Ingersoll and Woodstock Lacrosse Club Executives, 1871–1890*

Type of Organization	% Involved One Organization	More than Two
Sports clubs	100%	66%
Social/fraternal orders	44%	24%
Town council	32%[+]	—
Board of trade	15%	—
Total number	72	

*   In rounded figures.
[+]   Six held the office of mayor or reeve.

At least two-thirds of them were officers in more than one sports club, and slightly less than one-half of them held offices in reform-based societies and other fraternities. Beyond this, one in three sat on the local town council, while roughly one in six sat on the board of trade.

Though exclusively male sport clubs, reform societies (for example, Royal Templars of Temperance), and fraternal lodges (for example, the Independent Order of Odd Fellows), these men created environments in which notions of respectability could be formulated and then promoted. The ritual, literature, and social practices of their various organizations emphasized certain key ingredients that they deemed to be essential to their cause: responsibility, sobriety, honesty, thrift, support for the dominant religion, and personal and sexual morality. Christopher Anstead has shown how, with their policing of individual members' behaviour, these groups spread the ideology of respectability to a wider audience.[57] Other voluntary activities, such as membership in the board of trade and election to the town council, provided avenues for other commitments, such as boosting their town's economic development through supporting aspects of industrial growth.

Because lacrosse clubs drew members from different social backgrounds than club organizers, there was a need for cooperation, presumably based in consent, from certain members of the subordinated classes. Between 1880 and 1889, three-quarters of club members were between 15 and 21 years of age — a small cohort drawn from what was only 14 percent of the local male population. Their membership was touted by the press as a matter of social prestige and envy for other boys.[58] As seen in Table 16.3, the youth in these clubs came from more socially diverse backgrounds than club organizers. Proportionately more lacrosse players came from a home where the household head worked with his hands than did lacrosse organizers. Still, no players came from homes of unskilled workers.

In short, amateur lacrosse in Ingersoll and Woodstock was a class-based phenomenon like the amateur movement itself. Lacrosse reformers, like reformers for other sports, wished to restructure local sport along carefully circumscribed social lines, and they appear to have elicited support through working-class youth involvement. Just as sport organizers in both towns adopted lacrosse as a vehicle for their reform agenda, they also envisioned creating a local institution to carry out their agenda for sport on a grander scale. One way to achieve this agenda was through the creation of a multi-sport amateur agency which aimed to regulate all local sport.

In April 1884, Woodstock's Beaver lacrosse club, together with the local amateur baseball and bicycle clubs, organized a local multi-sport regulatory agency, the Woodstock Amateur Athletic Association (WAAA). Two years later Ingersoll sports reformers, including leaders of the Dufferin lacrosse club, followed suit and created the Ingersoll Amateur Athletic

Table 16.3 Occupational Characteristics of Ingersoll and Woodstock Lacrosse Players Compared to Male Workforces, 1880–1889*

Occupational Categories	Lacrosse Players	Male Workforce+
Non-manual	46%	26%
Manual skilled	54%	50%
Manual unskilled	0%	24%
Total number	147	2883

* In rounded figures for occupation of household head.

+ Combined, Ingersoll and Woodstock male workforces over 16 years estimated for 1885, derived from 1881 and 1891 manuscript censuses.

Association (IAAA), which was incorporated in 1889.[59] In both cases these umbrella organizations for sports clubs (notably for lacrosse, baseball, cycling, and tennis) were designed to encourage and regulate amateur sports. The respective town councils also authorized their AAAs to be responsible for creating community sporting and social entertainments for the Queen's Birthday and Dominion Day civic holidays.[60] This "stamp" of approval from local government ensured sport reformers important opportunities to display and disseminate their version of sport.

Under AAA governance local sport was structured in ways that middle-class sport reformers preferred; these preferences were institutionalized and their underlying rationales were articulated through exclusive gentleman's clubs.[61] AAA constitutions asserted their reform orientation through the mandate, "the encouragement of athletic sports, the promotion of physical and mental culture among, and the providing of rational amusements for members."[62] Like other middle-class voluntary associations, the AAAs had strict rules carefully circumscribing the conduct of members. Club rooms prohibited all drink, gambling, betting, lotteries, and profane language. Those defying the rules of "gentlemanly conduct," were expelled.[63]

Modelling their own associations on the exclusive and powerful Montreal Amateur Athletic Association (1881), IAAA and WAAA organizers sought to suppress all but carefully restricted amateur sports which bore the mark of muscular Christianity.[64] Stressing what they called morality and justice in sport, they emphasized efficiency and organization, and denigrated any alternative in order to elevate their own vision for sport. Determined to establish amateur sport as *the* natural and only legitimate version of sport, they strove to marginalize other practices. To this end, local AAA officials attempted to suppress certain sports by eliminating them from the landscape of community sport, especially holiday competitions, and by limiting which sports were granted AAA club affiliation. Amateur regulations demanding that athletes be "carded" in order to compete, while limiting club membership, also worked toward this goal.

Local AAA sport reformers and town councillors alike believed that socially exclusive amateur sports would enhance their town's physical and moral greatness. Yet the AAAs were joint-stock ventures capitalized through membership fees — and one had to first pass a black-balling to enter AAA ranks. Socially exclusive, they were nevertheless designated by town councils to represent the town. Thus the AAAs upheld the façade, though not the substance, of democracy.[65]

The social fabric of a group of 103 Ingersoll and Woodstock AAA executives similarly belies any notion of democracy. The AAA officials, while individually possessing a considerable range of affluence and power, exhibited certain social traits as a group that sharply set them apart from the local populace. Like the lacrosse executives, they almost all held non-manual occupations of a professional, commercial, or administrative nature. (See Table 16.4.)

Like sport reformers generally, IAAA and WAAA organizers tended to be engaged in other voluntary and fraternal activities by which they shaped and reflected their world-view of respectability and capitalism. (See Table 16.5.)

The intricate ties between the amateur clubs and the agendas of social reform and boosterism promoted by their organizers can also be seen in interurban lacrosse competition and in the ways in which it was supported locally.[66] By infusing sporting events with their vision, they aimed to reinforce their appearance as natural social and political leaders.

From the early 1870s club organizers and town councillors had featured lacrosse matches on Dominion Day holidays.[67] Thousands flocked into town to view these events. After noon-time parades, speeches from local dignitaries, and picnics, the afternoon sport performance began.

Table 16.4 Occupational Characteristics of IAAA and WAAA Executives and Local Male Workforces, 1884–1896*

Occupational Category	AAA Executives	Male Workforces[+] 1891
Non-Manual	95%	26%
Manual skilled	5%	51%
Manual unskilled	0%	23%
Total number	103	4400

* In rounded figures.

[+] For occupation of household head in the workforce of males over 16. Combined and averaged between 1891 Ingersoll and Woodstock manuscript censuses.

Table 16.5 Voluntary Profiles of IAAA and WAAA Executives, 1884–1896*

Type of Organization	Organization Executives % Involved
Amateur sport clubs Executives	100%
Fraternal order Executives[+]	63%
Town Council	23%[+]
Board of Trade	16%
Total number	103

* In rounded figures.

[+] Data on social and fraternal order membership kindly supplied by Christopher Anstead.

The profits derived from ten cent admission fees to holiday matches alone could support a club's expenses for the entire season. To ensure successful holiday-sport events, Woodstock clubs, like clubs from Montreal and Toronto, arranged exhibition matches against Indian teams from nearby reserves.[68] The war-painted Indians also performed war dances and concerts after the matches. Appropriately costumed, they played their tightly choreographed role, though whatever they themselves thought of that role remains unknown. There is no doubt, however, that the lacrosse propagandists created the extravaganzas to symbolize and celebrate what Canada as a young nation had become. The productions aimed to fortify and celebrate one version of pride in locality and Canadian nation, while evoking images of the sport's distant origins in Aboriginal culture.[69]

One sketch published in the 1893 Dominion Day edition of the *Sentinel* gave the desired effect of reinforcing what lacrosse propagandists saw as the intimate connection between lacrosse and the Canadian nation. The sketch consisted of a crest with symbols for each province surrounded by scenes of Canadian wilderness. A well-placed lacrosse stick in the diagram gave the illusion that lacrosse, geography, and climate worked together to unite the Canadian nation.[70]

To sport reformers lacrosse offered all sorts of possibilities for creating and maintaining a cultural hegemony. Lacrosse teams, seen by local government to be legitimate agents of local boosterism, were projected to represent the town's merit, and were themselves considered capable of cultivating high civic standards. Throughout the year citizens followed Ingersoll and Woodstock teams through NLA divisional competition. Club victories often prompted community-wide celebrations; for example, in 1888 Ingersoll citizens petitioned the mayor to declare a half-holiday so they could celebrate the advancement of the Dufferins to the southern district championship. In 1901, on the occasion of Woodstock's birth as a city, the *Sentinel* proclaimed that the Beavers had given Woodstock "an enviable reputation in the realm of sport."[71] This reputation, it implied, was both a symptom and an emblem of the type of drive and determination that had nurtured the town's rise to city status. Team uniforms, themselves symbols of order and respectability, and team names reinforced ties to the home town, providing myth-makers with opportunities to tell stories about themselves and their reality; in such narratives sports fields became symbolic battlegrounds.[72]

Community organizations, mayors, local professional men, and merchants strongly supported club efforts. As early as 1871 even Woodstock's Ladies Benevolent Society publicly offered their support. They graced the Beavers with a $15 donation and embroidered goal flags, "worked in gold [and] surmounted by a Beaver." Like the Claxton Flags, which were the emblem of the Canadian championship, they were a treasure to behold. Individuals also handed out rewards to club players for their social and sporting skills.[73] In keeping with the thrust of amateurism, the awards were symbolic rather than monetary. In 1874 Dr. Turquand, sometime executive of the Royal Arcanum, ten-year town council veteran, and sometime mayor, donated a silver cup for Woodstock's best all-round player. In 1880 Samuel Woodroofe, local jeweller, sometime WAAA executive, and executive of the local bicycle and football clubs, donated a silver medal for a club running competition. He shrewdly placed it in his store window for a week, thus calling attention to the team and drawing in curious customers. In 1888, sometime president of the WAAA and newly elected president of the Canadian Lacrosse Association, local grocer E.W. Nesbitt donated a diamond pin for the best all-round player who showed punctual attendance.[74]

Yet the residual element of a displaced rowdiness could be found within the connection between team and town that was fostered by capitalist boosterism, and shaped by the hand of middle-class businessmen. With its growing popularity in the late 1870s and 1880s and with the increasing associations between lacrosse teams and the corporate community, the gap between what sport reformers hoped to achieve through lacrosse, and what actually happened, widened significantly.[75] Pressures for victory, coupled with intense fan and player identifications with the home team, undermined reformers' efforts.[76] So, too, did greater player commitment to winning for the glory of the team and the honour of the town. Of course, rewards for proper conduct and punctual attendance would have been needless if individual players had been behaving in desired ways.

Despite prohibitions, frequent newspaper reports of money won and lost showed that fans still bet on sport competition, especially when their home team was involved. In 1879 Simcoe's team and their backers arrived for a match in Woodstock "supplied with heaps of wealth," which Beaver supporters "readily took up."[77] It was only a short step from betting to game fixing and under-the-table payments to amateur players. In July 1887 the Brantford Brants had courted Beaver players Kennedy, Kelly, and Laird with offers of jobs that guaranteed a sizable $20 per week salary during season play. One week later certain Brantford fans reportedly offered Beaver player (and Patterson Factory worker) Ed Kennedy $20 to throw a game. The local press decried the action and praised Kennedy's refusal to take part in the schemes. The *Sentinel* claimed: "this is the sort of thing that is ruining lacrosse, it is the betting spirit that leads to such attempts at fraud. Unless betting and the influence of betting men is stamped out, amateur lacrosse is dead — in fact it don't deserve to live."[78]

Efforts to eradicate betting and other prohibited behaviours at local playing grounds were to no avail. Obviously, many resisted. Some flatly refused to behave in prescribed ways while at games. Others simply refused to participate in the community event. They found nearby spots — the cemetery hill overlooking the WAAA grounds, for example — where they could sit on tombstones and watch the performances *gratis*. Resisting the WAAA social agenda, such hill-sitters garnered the best of both worlds. They had the pleasure of watching an afternoon's sport on their own terms: segregated from those who would presume to tell them how to behave, they could enjoy a good drink, a cuss, and a bet among like-minded people while watching a game of lacrosse. Better yet, they were physically distanced from, but quite visible to, frustrated WAAA executives. Abhorred by the recalcitrants "flaunting" their disdain for the WAAA agenda and its visions of what was appropriate personal behaviour, the frustrated WAAA officials appeared flabbergasted that their appeals to honour and decency fell on deaf ears: the hill-sitters were unmoved by WAAA threats to publish the names of "sneaks" and to photograph them in the act.[79]

Lacrosse organizers also had difficulty constraining other forms of resistance, like violent behaviour on the field. Tremendous player commitment to winning stretched the limits of rules on the playing field. The emphasis of lacrosse increasingly shifted from the process of character building to the goal of mere victory. Lacrosse play also shifted from cultivating and displaying an educated strength toward exhibiting unrestrained brutality. Like hockey today, the sport bred player violence during emotion-packed competition. This, of course, ironically enhanced the sport's appeal to those inclined toward unsavoury, or brutal sport.

During one visit to Ingersoll in 1888, for example, Woodstock players found themselves under attack in the heavily charged environment of lacrosse competition.[80] During the match (refereed by what the Woodstock press referred to as "daisy" umpires), one Woodstonian player checked his opponent. Hundreds of Ingersoll fans responded by mobbing him and his team-mates. The melee lasted fifteen minutes. After the field cleared and play recommenced, one obscenity-screaming spectator (who just happened to be the local police chief), chased down a rough Woodstock player and, catching him by the throat, thrashed him.

Lovers of the sport throughout southwestern Ontario knew well the antipathy between the two towns that was prompted by playing-field battles. Commenting on this state of affairs, an Embro *Courier* editorial pointed a harsh finger at overzealous fans: "if the spectators of these two towns would keep quiet and not interfere so, much of the bad feeling between the boys would die out." The Tillsonburg *Liberal* similarly blamed the spectators who, it maintained, should "keep their mouths shut and not interfere with the players disputes which occur on the field." The *Chronicle* responded to the indictment, acknowledging the displaced rowdiness inherent in intense interurban competition: "if you expect the spectators in rival towns to keep quiet you make a great big mistake." Fan behaviour at lacrosse competition, encouraged by boosterism, thus undercut images of respectability, especially with fans howling "like maniacs."[81] And while this rowdiness was mostly in the stands, rather than at the centre of public display, it was still problematic for sport reformers since it was far from invisible.

Often the local press, an instrument of persuasion in the hegemonic process, stepped into the battle, admonishing locals to be "gentlemanly." But even the papers exhibited elements of displaced rowdyism when, for example, after the Woodstock match in question, the *Chronicle* suggested that "had the spectators stepped in and hammered some of them and maimed them for life the punishment would be no less than they deserve."[82]

This situation, although testifying to lacrosse's immense popularity as a form of action-packed competition and entertainment, undercut attempts to reform the sport. With its rising popularity, by the 1890s lacrosse increasingly became an antithesis to the vision of Canadian youth and sport first expounded by middle-class sport reformers. As the gap between ideation and behaviour widened, lacrosse clearly did not live up to expectations of it as a truly national game that united social groupings under the leadership of a small, select group of men.

The social reform agenda for sport, and the search for sport forms that appeared to solve the social, physical, and moral ills of society, are resilient legacies from the sports-conscious decades of the last century. So, too, is the manipulation of sport to buttress a certain vision of reality. In the case of lacrosse, middle-class reformers aimed to make their (racist, class- and gender-bound) reality credible, and, in so doing, to legitimize their role as the natural leaders of society. With working-class youth filling lacrosse clubs, they appear to have enlisted some cooperation and support from subordinated groups. Even so, their hegemony was never complete, nor truly coherent. The notions of building character through wholesomely Canadian amateur team sport and of playing for the honour of the town, institution, or country one represented just did not comfortably fit, and residual elements — violence, and rowdyism in particular — remained. Yet, at the same time the notions upon which the amateur lacrosse movement was built laid a general foundation for organized sport to assume its prominent role in Canadian culture today. The contradictions in the belief that games build character while, at the same time, that sport competition says something about the competitors and, more importantly, the places or institutions that they represent, thrives today in Canadian sporting culture.

NOTES

1. For a discussion of a hegemonic struggle, see Keith Walden, "Speaking Modern: Language, Culture, and Hegemony in Grocery Window Displays, 1887–1920," *Canadian Historical Review* 70, 3 (1989): 285–310. A now dated discussion of the trend of Gramscian-influence historical research is found in T.J. Jackson Lears, "The Concept of Cultural Hegemony: Problems and Possibilities," *American Historical Review* 90, 3 (June 1985): 567–93.

2. Both communities are located in Oxford County in southwestern Ontario. Between 1871 and 1891 Ingersoll, the smaller of the two, had a population that hovered between 4000 and 4200 people. Woodstock, the County Seat, though initially smaller than Ingersoll, experienced a doubling of its population size, from nearly 4000 to over 8600 people. By 1901 Woodstock achieved city status. For the history of both towns see Brian Dawe, *Old Oxford is Wide Awake! Pioneer Settlers and Politics in Oxford County 1793–1855* (Woodstock: John Deyell Co., 1980); and Colin Read, *The Rising in Western Upper Canada 1837–1838* (Toronto: University of Toronto Press, 1982). On Ingersoll see James Sinclair, *A History of the Town of Ingersoll* (Ingersoll, c.1924); George N. Emery, "Adam Oliver, Ingersoll and Thunder Bay District," *Ontario History* 68, 1 (1976): 25–44; Ronald Adair Shier, "Some Aspects of the Historical Geography of the Town of Ingersoll" (B.A. thesis, University of Western Ontario, 1967). On Woodstock see Marjorie Cropp, "Beachville the Birthplace of Oxford" (reprint Beachville Centennial Committee, 1967); and John Ireland (pseud.), "Andrew Drew and the Founding of Woodstock," *Ontario History* 60 (1968): 231–33.

3. See Mark Dyreson, "America's Athletic Missionaries: Political Performance, Olympic Spectacle, and the Quest for an American National Culture, 1896–1912," *Olympika* 1 (1992): 70–90 for a good analysis of America's professionalizing middle class's attempts to engineer a cultural hegemony through sport and the making of an American national culture in the context of progressive-era modernity.

4. On muscular Christianity see Peter McIntosh, *Sport and Society* (London: C.A. Watts, 1963), 69–79; Gerald Redmond, "The First Tom Brown's Schooldays and Others: Origins of Muscular Christianity in Children's Literature," *Quest* 30 (Summer 1978): 4–18; Guy Lewis, "The Muscular Christianity Movement," *Journal of Health, Physical Education and Recreation* (May 1966): 27–30; J.A. Mangan, *Athleticism in the Victorian and Edwardian Public School: The Emergence and Consolidation of an Educational Ideology* (Cambridge: Cambridge University Press, 1981); Idem. *The Games Ethic and Imperialism: Aspects of the Diffusion of an Ideal* (Markham: Viking Press, 1986); David Brown, "Athleticism in Selected Canadian Private Schools for Boys to 1918" (Ph.D. dissertation, University of Alberta, 1984).

5. For a survey of the rise of organized sport in Canada, see Don Morrow, et al., *A Concise History of Sport in Canada* (Toronto: Oxford University Press, 1989) and Idem., "Canadian Sport History: A Critical Essay," *Journal of Sport History* 10,1 (September 1983) 67–79. Other related works include: Alan Metcalfe, *Canada Learns to Play. The Emergence of Organized Sport 1807–1914* (Toronto: McClelland & Stewart, 1987); Richard Gruneau, *Class, Sports and Social Development* (Amherst: University of Massachusetts Press, 1983); Morris Mott, *Sports in Canada. Historical Readings* (Toronto: Copp-Clark, 1989); Sid Wise, "Sport and Class Values in Old Ontario and Quebec," *His Own Man. Essays in Honour of A.R.M. Lower*, eds. W.H. Heick and Roger Graham (Montreal/Kingston: McGill-Queen's University Press, 1974) 93–117.

6. Peter Bailey, *Leisure and Class in Victorian England. Rational Recreation and the Quest for Control, 1830–1885* (Toronto: University of Toronto Press, 1966); and Chris Waters, "'All Sorts and Any Quantity of Outlandish Recreations': History, Sociology, and the Study of Leisure in England, 1820–1870," *Canadian Historical Association Historical Papers* (1981): 8–33.

7. Clifford Geertz, "Notes on the Balinese Cockfight," *The Interpretation of Cultures* (New York: Basic Books, 1973) 417.

8. I use the term Indian because the lacrosse writers of the era used this term. Their ethnocentrism limited their ability to see Aboriginal peoples as having any "culture." For a view of the game from the Indian oral tradition, see *Tewaarathon (Lacrosse): Akwesasne's Story of Our National Game* (North American Indian Travelling College, 1978). On European interpretations of lacrosse in Indian cultures see Stewart Culin, "Games of the North American Indians," *Twenty-fourth Annual Report of the Bureau of American Ethnology* (Washington: Government Printing Office, 1907); George Catlin, *Letters and Notes on the Manners, Customs and Condition of the North American Indians*, vol. 2 (London: The Egyptian Hall, 1871); and Michael A. Salter, "The Effect of Acculturation on the Game of Lacrosse and on Its Role as an Agent of Indian Survival," *Canadian Journal of the History of Sport and Physical Education* 3, 1 (May 1972): 28–43.

9. On organized lacrosse, see Don Morrow, "The Institutionalization of Sport: A Case Study of Canadian Lacrosse," *International Journal of History of Sport* 9, 2 (August 1992): 361–51. See also, Robert W. Henderson, *Ball, Bat and Bishop* (New York: Rockport Press, 1947); Alexander M. Weyand and M.R. Roberts, *The Story of Lacrosse* (Baltimore: H & A Herman, 1965); T.G. Vellathottam and Kevin G. Jones, "Highlights in the Development of Canadian Lacrosse to 1931," *Canadian Journal of the History of Sport and Physical Education* 5, 2 (December 1974): 37; Christina A. Burr, "The Process of Evolution of a Competitive Sport: A Study of Lacrosse in Canada, 1844 to 1914" (M.A. Thesis, University of Western Ontario, 1986); and Metcalfe 181–218.

10. The motto of the National Lacrosse Association, "Our Country, Our Game," and the title of William George Beer's great treatise, *Lacrosse the National Game of Canada*, give the impression that lacrosse is Canada's national sport. See Kevin G. Jones and T. George Vellathottam, "The Myth of Canada's National Sport," *CAPHER Journal* (September–October 1974): 33–36; *Globe and Mail*, 20 December 1868; Morrow 53–54.

11. For example, the activities found in Edwin C. Guillet, *Pioneer Days in Upper Canada* (Toronto: University of Toronto Press, 1979), especially chapters IX and X. For a good social analysis of a particularly castigated sport, see Elliott J. Gorn, "'Gouge and Bite, Pull Hair and Scratch': The Social Significance of Fighting in the Southern Backcountry," *American Historical Review* 90, 1 (February 1985): 18–43.

12. For an extended discussion, see Christopher J. Anstead and Nancy B. Bouchier, "From Greased Pigs to Sheepskin Aprons: Rowdiness and Respectability in Victorian Ingersoll's Civic Holidays," unpublished manuscript, 1993.

13. J.E. Wells, "Canadian Culture," *Canadian Monthly and National Review* (1875): 459–67. This item was brought to my attention in David Brown, "Prevailing Attitudes Towards Sports, Physical Exercise and Society in the 1870's: Impressions from Canadian Periodicals," *Canadian Journal of History of Sport* 17, 2 (December 1986): 58–70.

14. See *Sentinel-Review Express Industrial Edition* February 1906; *Woodstock College Memorial Book* (Woodstock: Woodstock College Alumni Association, 1951). On physical education and sports programs in Canadian schools: Frank Cosentino and Maxwell L. Howell, *A History of Physical Education in Canada* (Toronto: General Publishing Co., 1971); M.L. Van Vliet, *Physical Education in Canada* (Scarborough: Prentice-Hall, 1965); Brown, "Athleticism in Selected Canadian Private Schools"; Jean Barman, *Growing Up in British Columbia: Boys in Private School* (Vancouver: University of British Columbia Press, 1984), chap. 4; G.G. Watson, "Sports and Games in Ontario Private Schools: 1830–1930" (M.A. thesis, University of Alberta, 1970).

15. Nationalism through sport thrived elsewhere, too. See Donald Mrozek, *Sport and American Mentality, 1880–1910* (Knoxville: University of Tennessee Press, 1983); Peter Levine, *A.G. Spalding and the Rise of Baseball* (New York: Oxford University Press, 1985). On cultural motifs and nationalism see Eric Hobsbawm, *Nations and Nationalism since 1780: Programme, Myth, Reality* (New York: Cambridge University Press, 1990).

16. Peter Lindsay, "George Beers and the National Game Concept. A Behavioral Approach," *Proceedings of the 2nd Canadian Symposium on the History of Sport and Physical Education* (Windsor: University of Windsor, 1972), 27–44. On the Canadian nationalist theme in sport see: Morrow, "Lacrosse as the National Game," in

A Concise History of Sport, 45–68; Alan Metcalfe, "Towards an Understanding of Nationalism in Mid-Nineteenth Century Canada — A Marxian Interpretation," *Proceedings of the 2nd Canadian Symposium on the History of Sport and Physical Education*, 7–14; R. Gerald Glassford, "Sport and Emerging Nationalism in Mid-Nineteenth Century Canada," in ibid. 15–26.

17. George Beers, *Lacrosse: The National Game of Canada*. His other lacrosse-related publications include: "Canadian Sports," *Century Magazine* 14 (May–October 1879): 506–27; Goal Keeper (pseud.) *The Game of Lacrosse* (Montreal: The Montreal Gazette Steam Press, 1860); "The Ocean Travels of Lacrosse," *Athletic Leaves* (September 1888): 42, "A Rival to Cricket," *Chambers Journal* 18 (December 1862): 366–68.

18. Beers, *Lacrosse: The National Game* 59.

19. W.K. McNaught, *Lacrosse and How to Play It* (Toronto: Robert Marshall, 1873) 21. Morrow, *A Concise History of Sport*, 54.

20. Beers, "Canadian Sports," 506–27; "Canada in Winter," *British American Magazine* 2 (1864): 166–71; "Cheek," *Canadian Monthly* 11 (1872): 256–62; "Canada as a Winter Resort," *Century* (1854–55): 514–29.

21. David Brown, "The Northern Character Theme and Sport in Nineteenth Century Canada," *Canadian Journal of History of Sport* 20, 1 (May 1989): 52. See also Carl Berger, "True North Strong and Free," *Nationalism in Canada*, ed. Peter Russell (Toronto: McGraw-Hill, 1966), 3–26; Idem., *The Sense of Power. Studies in the Ideas of Canadian Imperialism 1867–1914* (Toronto: University of Toronto Press, 1970), 128–53.

22. Brown, 47–48, 52.

23. Beers, *Lacrosse: The National Game*, 32, 33. The comparison continues: "or [as] a pretty Canadian girl to any uncultivated squaw."

24. M.C. Urquhart and K.A.H. Buckley, *Historical Statistics of Canada* (Toronto: Macmillan, 1965), 591. On schools and reform: Susan E. Houston, "Politics, Schools, and Social Change in Upper Canada," *Canadian Historical Review* 53 (September 1972): 249–71; Idem, "Victorian Origins of Juvenile Delinquency: A Canadian Experience," *History of Education Quarterly* 20 (Fall 1972): 254–80; Houston and Alison L. Prentice, *Schools and Scholars in Nineteenth Century Ontario* (Toronto: University of Toronto Press, 1988); and Alison L. Prentice, *The School Promoters. Education and Social Class in Mid-Nineteenth Century Upper Canada* (Toronto: McClelland and Stewart, 1977).

25. This point has recently been a focus of sport history scholarship. See Steven A. Riess, "Sport and the Redefinition of Middle Class Masculinity," *International Journal of the History of Sport* 8, 1 (May 1991): 5–27; J.A. Mangan and James Walvin, eds., *Manliness and Morality. Middle Class Masculinity in Britain and Americas, 1800–1940* (Manchester: Manchester University Press, 1987). See also: E. Anthony Rotundo, "Body and Soul: Changing Ideals of Middle Class Manhood," *Journal of Social History* 14 (1983): 23–38; Joseph Maguire, "Images of Manliness and Competing Ways of Living in Late Victorian and Edwardian Britain," *British Journal of Sports History* 3, 3 (December 1986): 265–87; David Howell and Peter Lindsay, "Social Gospel and the Young Boy Problem, 1895–1925," *Canadian Journal of History of Sport* 17, 1 (May 1986): 79–87; David I. MacLeod, "A Live Vaccine. The Y.M.C.A. and Male Adolescence in the United States and Canada," *Social History/Histoire Sociale* 11, 21 (1978): 55–64.

26. Reprints of Sermons, in whole or part, found in *Woodstock Sentinel*, 20 November 1887; *Woodstock Herald*, 14 March 1845; *Ingersoll Chronicle*, 25 October 1888, 30 January 1868.

27. *Chronicle*, 7 November 1872. In 1867 Ingersoll male youths were exhorted not to "make a great bluster and be rough and hard, thinking to be manly. Be a little quiet in the house, gentle with your little sisters, and not tiring mother with a great deal of noise. . . . When your work is over and it's the right time for sport kick up your heels and have lots of fun outdoors" (*Chronicle*, 20 June 1867). One Mr. Harstone from nearby St. Mary's evoked similar arguments. In his appeal to the town council for the establishment of a public park, he clearly connected the issues of youth, social reform, and sport: "boys who grow up fond of sports make the best citizens. Cultivate the spirit of good manly sport and they will avoid many vices. Where towns do not give support to athletic sports, the greatest numbers are found going into the wrong paths" (*St. Marys Journal-Argus*, 8 September 1871). On 29 January 1889 the *Sentinel* reported on a lecture given in nearby Brantford by the Rev. Dr. Nichol who spoke at the YMCA rooms on vices peculiar to young men. He "warned his hearers very strongly against practices that were destroying the manhood of thousands and supplying our insane asylums with occupants." Presumably playing fields "suitably controlled," in cathartic fashion, sexual urges and the dreaded "secret vice" of masturbation.

28. Beers, *Lacrosse: The National Game*, 35.

29. Ontario, *Report of the Commissioners Appointed to enquire into the Prison and Reformatory System Sessional Papers* XXIII Part III (No. 7), 1891, 529. Thanks to Susan Houston for bringing this item to my attention.

30. *Sentinel*, 19 April 1880.

31. McIntosh, *Sport and Society*, 69–79; Lewis, "The Muscular Christianity Movement"; Redmond, "The First Tom Brown's Schooldays and Others."

32. Mangan, *Athleticism in the Victorian and Edwardian Public School*; Idem, *The Games Ethic and Imperialism*; Brown, "Athleticism in Selected Canadian Private Schools"; Watson, "Sports and Games in Ontario Private Schools"; Gruneau, *Class, Sports and Social Development* 101–3; Eric Dunning, "Industrialization and the Incipient Modernization of Football," *Stadion* 1, 1 (1975): 103–39.

33. This is best exemplified in Thomas Hughes's widely read classic *Tom Brown's Schooldays* (1857), in the fiction of Charles Kingsley, and in Thomas Wentworth Higginson's "Saints and their Bodies." The writings of Canadian novelist Ralph Connor are also reminiscent of this approach. See Bruce Haley, "Sport and the Victorian World," *Western Humanities Review* 22 (Spring 1968): 115–25; Idem, *The Healthy Body and Victorian Culture* (Cambridge: Cambridge University Press, 1978).

34. On the ascetic-pietist legacy and sport, see Barbara Schrodt, "Sabbatarianism and Sport in Canadian Society," *Journal of Sport History* 4, 1 (Spring 1977): 22–23; Dennis Brailsford, "Puritanism and Sport in Seventeenth Century England," *Stadion* 1, 2 (1975): 316–30; Peter Wagner, "Puritan Attitudes Towards Physical Recreation in 17th Century New England," *Journal of Sport History* 3 (Summer 1976): 139–51; Nancy Struna, "Puritans and Sports: The Irretrievable Tide of Change," *Journal of Sport History* 4 (Spring 1977) 1–21.

35. Gerald Redmond, "Some Aspects of Organized Sport and Leisure in Nineteenth Century Canada," *Sports in Canada. Historical Readings,* ed. Morris Mott (Toronto: Copp Clark Pitman, 1989), 97–98.

36. Ibid., 98.

37. Howell and Lindsay, "The Social Gospel and the Young Boy Problem, 1895–1925"; C.H. Hopkins, *History of the YMCA in North America* (New York: Associated Press, 1951). Also see Diane Pederson, "Keeping Our Good Girls Good," *Canadian Women Studies* 7, 4 (1986): 20–24.

38. On early formation of the National Lacrosse Association see Peter Lindsay, "A History of Sport in Canada, 1807–1867" (Ph.D. dissertation, University of Alberta, 1969), 114–32.

39. Claxton's obituary from *Sunday World,* 1908, as cited in Harold Clark Cross, *One Hundred Years of Service with Youth: The Story of the Montreal YMCA* (Montreal: Southam Press, 1951), 144. The flags, donated by the Montreal millionaire wholesaler in November 1867, were valued at $250.

40. These dimensions were to become symbolized through the association's hallmark, the triangle. See Cross, *One Hundred Years of Service with Youth.* Local connections between lacrosse and the YMCA in Woodstock also pre-dated the association's full-scale involvement in sport. At its outset in 1871 the Woodstock YMCA's aim, "the improvement of the religious, mental, and social conditions of young men in Woodstock," overlooked sport. Yet within two years the Beavers and the YMCA contemplated combining their energies to form a gymnasium. By 1874 the Beavers were using YMCA club rooms for lacrosse meetings. (*Sentinel*, 24 October 1873, 29 May 1874). On Woodstock's YMCA: W. Stewart Lavell, *All This Was Yesterday The Story of the YMCA in Woodstock, Ontario, 1868–1972* (Woodstock: Talbot Communications, 1972).

41. This point is taken from John Weiler, "The Idea of Sport in Late Victorian Canada," *The Workingman in the Nineteenth Century,* ed. Michael Cross (Toronto: University of Toronto Press, 1974), 228–31.

42. On rational recreation see Bailey, *Leisure and Class in Victorian England*; Idem., "'A Mingled Mass of Perfectly Legitimate Pleasures': The Victorian Middle Class and the Problem of Leisure," *Victorian Studies* 21, 2 (Winter 1978): 7–28.

43. Beers, *Lacrosse: The National Game of Canada*, 51–56. Burr analyzes the evolution of the *science* of the game in "The Process of Evolution of a Competitive Sport."

44. Beers, *Lacrosse: The National Game,* 50. Beers's use of the term "freemasonry" is apt and intended to appeal to his middle-class male audience. Lacrosse and nineteenth-century freemasonry shared a number of key elements: secret bonding; a sub-community within a corporate community which also exists within a national and provincial network; an esoteric body of knowledge; and a particular style of dress. On fraternal societies see Christopher J. Anstead, "Fraternalism in Victorian Ontario: Secret Societies and Cultural Hegemony" (Ph.D. dissertation, University of Western Ontario, 1992); J.S. Gilkeson, *Middle Class Providence, 1820–1940* (Princeton: Princeton University Press, 1986).

45. The Beavers, for example, paid for the funeral of their mascot, little Jimmy Kinsella, who died in an accident at Karn's Organ Factory, *Sentinel,* 22 January 1887. On club celebrations for individuals, *Chronicle,* 7 July 1887, *Sentinel,* 30 June 1887.

46. "Testimonial to Edward W. Nesbitt. Woodstock 26 November 1879." Woodstock Museum (my italics).

47. On June 16, 1871 the *Sentinel* reports, "with the loss of the late lamented Silver Ball lacrosse seems to be the favoured game this season." Journalist Henry Roxborough argues that because of baseball's immense popularity in the area, the adoption of lacrosse generally lagged in southwestern Ontario. Henry Roxborough, *One*

Hundred Not Out: The Story of Nineteenth Century Canadian Sport (Toronto: Ryerson Press, 1966), 40. On the Guelph–Woodstock rivalry that led to the Woodstonians' dethroning see *Guelph Evening Mercury*, 5 August 1868; *Guelph Evening Telegram*, 27 September 1923; and William Humber, *Cheering for the Home Team: The Story of Baseball in Canada* (Erin: The Boston Mills Press, 1983).

48. *Hamilton Spectator*, 11 August 1864; *Chronicle*, 13 and 20 July; 21 and 26 August 1869. The Silver Ball, long lost, is pictured in *Star Weekly*, 19 July 1924. This earliest attempt to create a Canadian "national" baseball association in 1864, led by Woodstock's Young Canadian Club, relied almost completely on the American model of the national Association of Baseball Players (NABBP). The Canadian association, like most baseball ventures throughout the period between 1860 and 1885, structured competition on a challenge match, or exhibition basis. See Hamilton *Times*, 24 August 1864 and *Spectator*, 11 and 24 August 1864; Ingersoll *Chronicle*, 26 August, 7 October 1864; *The New York Clipper*, 14 September 1864.

49. *The New York Clipper*, 14 September 1864; 1 October 1864; 27 June 1868; 19 and 26 June, 17 July 1869; 28 May 1871.

50. *Guelph Evening Mercury*, 5 August 1868. Apparently "stragglers" from Guelph, who did not make the costly $1 trip to Woodstock, but who reportedly "had staked small piles on the game," congregated at Guelph's telegraph office to keep abreast of match developments. In the ensuing weeks after the near-riot, Woodstock and Guelph newspapers continued the rivalry: Guelph's *Evening Mercury* likened Woodstock to "a huge snake after getting a nock [sic] on the head, [which] writhes about in a fearful mental agony" (see 6, 8, 15 August 1868). Also see *Guelph Evening Telegram*, 27 September 1923; Humber, *Cheering for the Home Team*, 29, refers to this incident as well.

51. See Humber, *Cheering for the Home Team* 27–37; Metcalfe, *Canada Learns to Play*, 85–98 and 164–66. Metcalfe rightly notes that baseball was alienated from the mainstream of the amateur sport movement and that it was "significantly different from the other [amateur] sports in that its movement toward league competition came at a slower rate" (88). Baseball lacked well-rooted protectionist agencies (a sporting press; a "national" baseball association; or an institutional tradition) in the face of the American professional model, especially after 1871.

52. On the 1876 Canadian League see *The New York Clipper*, 22 April, 6 May 1876; *Bryce's 1876 Canadian Baseball Guide* (London, Ontario, 1876); *Canadian Gentleman's Journal of Sporting Times*, 28 April 1876; George Sleeman Collection, Regional Collections; File 4065, D.B. Weldon Library, University of Western Ontario; *Star Weekly* 19 July 1924. Other short-lived ventures, in 1880, 1884, and 1890 were centred in southwestern Ontario. *Sentinel*, 24 May, 30 July 1880; *Empire*, 24 May 1880; *Globe*, 22 May 1880; *Globe*, 17 May 1884; *Sentinel*, 14 May 1889; *Chronicle*, 11 and 17 April 1890; *Sentinel*, 18 April 1884.

53. The names of sport players and executives were extracted from reports in local newspapers and Canadian and American sport periodicals, team photographs, various local history sources, and sport-related collections. They were hand-linked to corresponding manuscript census rolls for the urban populations of Ingersoll and Woodstock. Demographic data (age, place of birth, religion, marital status, occupation, and the name and occupation of household head) were derived from the record linkage. Occupation information was corroborated, supplemented, and verified through town directories, tax assessment rolls, local histories, and local genealogies. Data on social and fraternal orders kindly supplied by Christopher Anstead.

54. On the sporting activities of females and social constraints impinging on them see Patricia Vertinsky, *The Eternally Wounded Woman: Women, Exercise and Doctors in the Late Nineteenth Century* (Manchester, England: Manchester University Press, 1990); Helen Lenskyj, *Out of Bounds. Women, Sport, and Sexuality* (Toronto: The Women's Press, 1986); and Michael Smith, "Graceful Athleticism or Robust Womanhood: The Sporting Culture of Women in Victorian Nova Scotia, 1870–1914," *Journal of Canadian Studies* 23, 1/2 (Spring/Summer 1988): 120–37.

55. Religion itself played a significant role in community social-class formation. A systematic relationship exists between the religious and social-class background distributions in the populations. For a statistical analysis of this phenomenon, see Nancy B. Bouchier, "'For the Love of the Game and the Honour of the Town': Organized Sport, Local Culture and Middle Class Hegemony in Two Ontario Towns, 1838–1895" (Ph.D. dissertation, University of Western Ontario, 1990), 90–92.

56. The occupational classification is based on Gerard Bouchard and Christian Pouyez, "Les Catégories Socio-Professionelles: Une Nouveau Grille de Classement," *Labour/Le Travail* 15 (Spring 1985): 145–63.

57. This understanding of fraternal orders is the central argument of Anstead, "Fraternalism in Victorian Ontario." See also Mary Ann Clawson, *Constructing Brotherhood: Class, Gender and Fraternalism* (Princeton, 1989); Brian Greenberg, "Workers and Community: Fraternal Orders in Albany, New York, 1845–1885," *The Maryland Historian* (1977).

58. *Sentinel*, 20 June 1887.

59. *Sentinel*, 4, 11, 18 April 1884; *Chronicle*, 3 and 10 June 1886; *Woodstock Amateur Athletic Association Constitution and Bylaws* (Woodstock: Sentinel-Review Co. Printers, 1908). This followed resolution of difficulties over obtaining acceptable playing field space. *Sentinel*, 4, 11, 18 April 1884; *Chronicle*, 3 and 10 June 1886, 29 March 1889, 1 April, 30 May 1890; *Ingersoll Amateur Athletic Association Constitution and Bylaws* (Ingersoll, 1889).

60. Nancy B. Bouchier, "'The 24th of May is the Queen's Birthday': Civic Holidays and the Rise of Amateurism in Nineteenth Century Canadian Towns," *International Journal of the History of Sport* 10, 2 (August 1993): 159–92. Sport clubs often hosted some form of sports events during the Queen's Birthday and Dominion Day holidays. For example, the Montreal Lacrosse Club organized matches against teams from the St. Regis and Caugnawaga Reserves (*Gazette*, 23 May 1884, 22 May 1885).

61. On gentlemen's clubs see Gilkeson, *Middle Class Providence* especially chap. 4, "The Club Idea." On clubs, sport, and Toronto's interlocking social elite, see R. Wayne Simpson, "The Elite and Sport Club Membership, Toronto, 1827–1881" (Ph.D. dissertation University of Alberta, 1987). On the social-class background of other sports clubs see Bouchier, "'For the Love of the Game and the Honour of the Town,'" especially chap. 4.

62. WAAA, *Constitution and Consolidated Bylaws* (Woodstock: Sentinel-Review Co. Printers, 1908), Article II; *IAAA Constitution and Bylaws* (Ingersoll, 1889), Article II.

63. In *Canada Learns to Play* Metcalfe argues that amateurism, with its requisites for gentlemanly behaviour, was a form of social reproduction squarely rooted in the English social-class system, and that the philosophical basis of amateurism originated in the patterns of eighteenth-century English aristocratic social reproduction. Many scholars concur with this line of thought. Mangan and Brown show that the emphasis placed on muscular Christian sports in the reformed British public school system replaced the anti-utilitarian approach to sport heretofore taken by England's elite. Dunning and Gruneau suggest further that the muscular Christian precepts of the "games-build-character" approach to sport popularized by the public schools indicated a mutual accommodation between declining aristocratic interests and a rising industrial bourgeoisie. See Metcalfe, 120–21; Mangan, *Athleticism in the Victorian and Edwardian Public School*; Brown, "Athleticism in Selected Canadian Private Schools"; Gruneau, 101–3; Dunning, "Industrialization and the Incipient Modernization of Football." WAAA, *Constitution and Consolidated Bylaws*, Article IX; *IAAA Constitution and Bylaws*, Article IX.

64. See Don Morrow, "The Powerhouse of Canadian Sport: The Montreal Amateur Athletic Association, Inception to 1909," *Journal of Sport History* 8, 3 (Winter 1981): 20–39; Idem, *A Sporting Evolution*; Alan Metcalfe, *Canada Learns to Play*; Charles Ballem, *Abegweit Dynasty, 1899–1954. The Story of the Abegweit Amateur Athletic Association* (Charlottetown, 1986); Gerald Redmond, "Some Aspects of Organized Sport and Leisure in Nineteenth Century Canada," *Sport in Canada. Historical Readings*, ed. Morris Mott (Toronto: Copp Clark Ltd., 1979), 81–106; Wise, "Sport and Class Values."

65. WAAA, *Constitution and Consolidated Bylaws*, Article VI; *IAAA Constitution and Bylaws*, Article VI. On the socially exclusive nature of amateurism see Alan Metcalfe, "The Growth of Organized Sport and the Development of Amateurism in Canada, 1807–1914," *Not Just a Game. Essays in Canadian Sport Sociology*, ed. Jean Harvey and Hart Cantelon (Ottawa, 1988), 33–50.

66. Anstead and Bouchier, "From Greased Pigs to Sheepskin Aprons."

67. Between 1871 and 1890, Ingersoll featured lacrosse on eight Dominion Day holidays, while Woodstock did so on eleven holidays.

68. In 1871 the Beavers paid the Grand River Indians $60 to compete against them in the 24 May match. Ten cent admissions covered this outlay and brought a $159 profit to the club (*Sentinel*, 7 July 1871). Other Indian teams were the Tuscaroras, Onondagas, Muncitown, Sioux, and Six Nations. *Sentinel*, 7 July 1871, 31 May, 23 August 1872, 26 June 1874, 23 May, 4 July 1879, 30 April 1880, 23 June 1882, 25 May 1887. *Chronicle*, 9 May 1877. George Gray, a Woodstonian, recorded his observations about two such matches in his diary 3 July 1871 and 24 May 1872. Woodstock Museum, George A. Gray Diaries, 1857–1878.

69. This is very much in keeping with the dominant theme of the 1876 and 1883 Canadian lacrosse tours to Britain. Don Morrow, "The Canadian Image Abroad: The Great Lacrosse Tours of 1876 and 1883," *Proceedings of the 5th Canadian Symposium on the History of Sport and Physical Education* (Toronto: University of Toronto Press, 1982), 17. On sporting tours and empire see David W. Brown, "Canadian Imperialism and Sporting Exchanges: The Nineteenth Century Cultural Experience of Cricket and Lacrosse," *Canadian Journal of History of Sport* 18, 1 (May 1987): 55–66.

70. *Sentinel-Review*, 1 July 1893.

71. *Chronicle*, 14 September 1888. *Sentinel*, "Birth of the Industrial City," 9 July 1901.

72. On the relationship between team and town, see Morris Mott, "One Town's Team: Souris and its Lacrosse Club, 1887–1906," *Manitoba History* 1, 1 (1980): 10–16; Carl Betke, "Sports Promotion in the Western Canadian City: The Example of Early Edmonton," *Urban History Review* 12, 2 (1983): 47–56.

73. *Sentinel*, 7 July 1871. *Chronicle*, 13 July 1871, 30 June 1885, 19 May 1887, 10 May 1888.

74. *Sentinel*, 1 April 1874. *Sentinel*, 21 May 1880. Also 21 November 1884. *Sentinel* 16 May 1888.

75. On escalating violence and rowdyism in lacrosse see Metcalfe, 181–218; Idem, "Sport and Athletics: A Case Study of Lacrosse in Canada, 1840–1889," *Journal of Sport History* 3, 1 (Spring 1976): 1–19; Burr, "The Process of the Evolution of Lacrosse."

76. Barbara S. Pinto, "'Ain't Misbehavin': The Montreal Shamrock Lacrosse Club Fans 1868 to 1884." Paper presented to the North American Society for Sport History (Banff, Alberta, 1990).

77. *Sentinel*, 22 and 29 August 1879, 25 August 1882, 15 September 1886, 28 and 30 June 1887; *Chronicle*, 23 June 1887; *Sentinel*, 22 August 1879.

78. *Sentinel*, 20 July 1887. *Chronicle*, 23 June 1887. *Sentinel*, 30 July 1887.

79. *Sentinel*, 3 July 1885.

80. *Sentinel*, 6 September 1888.

81. Reported in *Sentinel*, 7 August 1885. Related to the incident *Sentinel*, 7 and 14 August 1885; *Chronicle*, 6 August 1885. *Sentinel*, 30 July 1887. *Tillsonburg Liberal* editorial reprinted with comments *Chronicle*, 28 June 1888. *Chronicle*, 28 June 1888.

82. *Sentinel*, 30 July 1887.

Article Seventeen

Gendered Baselines: The Tour of the Chicago Blackstockings

Colin D. Howell

Early in August 1891 two baseball promoters, M.J. Raymond and William Burtnett, arrived in Saint John from Boston and registered at the Hotel Stanley. What made their visit different from that of the advanced agents of most barnstorming baseball clubs was that they represented a female nine, the Chicago Young Ladies' Baseball Club, known as the Blackstockings, and were interested in arranging a tour of the Maritime provinces. Their hope was to have the club, which was at that time playing a series of games in Portland, Old Orchard, and Bangor, Maine, spend a month in the Maritimes, appearing in Fredericton, Saint John, Sussex, Moncton, Amherst, Truro, Halifax, and Yarmouth, and any other towns along the way that might be interested in hosting them. The thought of young women intruding on what was regarded traditionally as male leisure terrain caused great excitement and considerable consternation throughout the Maritimes. The ensuring tour brought into sharp relief the question of the relationship of the sexes, the prevailing notions of respectable behaviour, and the ways in which baseball served to delineate and shape existing definitions of masculinity and femininity.[1]

It is hardly a novel insight to point out that the development of baseball, like other forms of organized team sport, was a gendered process. Yet most accounts of baseball have taken its masculine character for granted, seemingly satisfied that the game had little to do with the female sex. In fact, the general exclusion of women from organized sporting activity — except

Source: Colin D. Howell, "Gendered Baselines: The Tour of the Chicago Blackstockings," from *Northern Sandlots: A Social History of Maritime Baseball*, Colin D. Howell, University of Toronto Press, 1995. © University of Toronto Press Incorporated 1995. Reprinted with permission of the publisher.

as spectators who were thought of as a civilizing force, restraining rowdyism and thereby consolidating notions of respectable masculinity — should alert us to the centrality of the gender question to the making of the nineteenth-century leisure world. It also invites inquiry into the relationship between leisure activity and work. Sonya Rose has demonstrated the many ways in which gender differentiation was connected to the production and reproduction of the emerging industrial-capitalist order, noting at the same time that the engendering of the labour process was only one aspect, albeit a vital one, of the 'cultural process distinguishing females and males in all social relations.'[2] Indeed, although the separation of leisure and work accelerated with the emergence of modern industrial capitalism, the relationship between work, leisure, and capitalism was a symbiotic one in which common class and gender issues can be perceived. This symbiosis deepened, moreover, as leisure itself increasingly fell under the disciplining influence of the capitalist market-place, where play was reconstituted as work, and games were presented as commodities to be purchased and consumed.

This chapter addresses three separate yet related issues pertaining to the laying down of baseball's gendered baselines. In the first place, it deals with the relegation of women to the role of the spectator — to that of a consumer rather than producer of sporting entertainment — and the concomitant use of an idealized image of the 'lady' spectator, an ideological construct that served at once to constrain class rowdiness and promote a conformist definition of respectable behaviour that transcended class lines. Related to this is the way in which the differentiated gender roles in baseball, and in other sports, were part of the broader social construction of masculinity and femininity, at once shaping and shaped by a set of discursive relations involving human biology and psychology, which drew upon ideologically constructed images of both the body natural and body politic. And finally, by concentrating upon the Blackstockings' tour — and that of other women's teams at the end of the nineteenth century — it is possible to show how the development of baseball as a marketable product resulted in the commercialization and marketing of women as spectacle. This process contributed in turn to the consolidation of gender and class hierarchies, the exploitation of women baseball 'workers,' and a reaffirmation of notions of male hardiness and female frailty.

Although women had been playing baseball in the United States since the early 1860s, their involvement in the sport was largely confined to spectatorism. Despite the interest of both moral reformers and sport entrepreneurs in attracting women to baseball in order to enhance its respectability and profitability, however, women made up only a minor part of the nineteenth-century baseball audience. Ironically, during the 1850s and 1860s, when baseball was still a fraternal, club-based, recreational sport for young men of the advancing middle class, women often attended the matches, dinners, dances, and other social functions that were associated with the game. But female patronage declined as baseball became increasingly popular with workingmen. 'When photographs of the crowd showed men in caps more numerous than men in hats,' Allen Guttmann observes, 'few women are to be seen.'[3] Middle-class women apparently feared damage to their reputations if they patronized a sport associated with gambling, alcoholism, tobacco-chewing, and other disreputable forms of behaviour.

One might have expected young working-class women to respond to the growing interest in the game evinced by their brothers, boyfriends, and fathers, but they did not flood the parks either. Not only did many young girls have domestic responsibilities that left them little time for leisure, but as Kathy Peiss has pointed out, leisure was experienced in different ways by men and women of working-class backgrounds. For workingmen, who asserted their independence from their employers in the public space of the saloon, lodge, or ball diamond, control over their own leisure time involved not only resistance against capitalist control, 'but a system of male privilege in which workers' self-determination, solidarity, and mutual assistance were understood as "manliness".' The leisure activities of nineteenth-century women, by contrast, tended to be segregated from the public realm and remained 'sinuously intertwined with the rhythms of household labor and the relations of kinship.' As the nineteenth century drew to a close, however, women's leisure patterns were beginning to change. Employed more frequently as wage-earners outside the home, young women came to regard organized leisure as a distinct realm of activity to which they could demand access. Yet young women's pursuit of pleasure led them not to the traditional leisure domain of workingmen, but to the new commercialized forms of recreation, such as dancehalls, amusement parks, excursion boats, and vaudeville theatres.[4]

Baseball promoters none the less took pains to encourage female attendance in order to counteract baseball's reputation for attracting 'drunken rowdies, unwashed loafers, and arrant blacklegs.'[5] Women in the stands, it was hoped, would have a civilizing effect. The 'presence of an assemblage of ladies purifies the moral atmosphere of a baseball gathering,' said an article in the *Baseball Chronicle*, 'repressing as it does, all the outburst of intemperate language which the excitement of a contest so frequently induces.'[6] Warren Goldstein has pointed out that there was always a tension in baseball between the notion of manly self-control and the excitement that the game produced, and because rules-makers and promoters of the game alike recognized that the players and audiences might lose control in the heat of the fray, women were regarded as 'agents of control' whose presence restrained 'potentially unregulated passion.'

Baseball clubs tried to attract women in a number of different ways. The provision of grandstand seating separated women from the unruliness of the crowds that stood along the foul lines, where a rope barrier was often the only thing restraining the crowd from spilling onto the field. Most clubs admitted women to the grandstand free of charge, so long as they had a male escort. The cost of purchasing a grandstand ticket also meant that those in close proximity to women spectators would likely be less inclined to offensive behaviour than the general ticket holder. The press also encouraged the attendance of women, and often criticized the foul language and smoking habits of male patrons as offensive to women spectators. Indeed, the impulse towards genteel behaviour that had led to the disciplining of theatrical audiences was evident at the ballpark, where promoters, reformers, and journalists found the idealized notion of the 'lady-like' spectator a useful ideological construct in their struggle against 'rowdyism.'

One of the most successful inducements to female attendance was ladies' day; not only were women admitted to the park free, but also in coming to the park a woman would likely find a number of her sisters in attendance. Most semi-pro teams routinely admitted women without charge. At the professional level, where a number of games were played weekly, ladies' days were usually restricted to one or two days per week. Club owners often came up with additional incentives to ensure a good turn-out on ladies' day. In Minneapolis, women were not only admitted to the grounds free, but had the privilege of being included in a group photograph of the patrons of the grandstand, and subsequently receiving a copy from the management.[7] By the end of the century, in fact, regularly scheduled ladies' days had become so effective in attracting female spectators that they had begun to outlive their usefulness. In Pittsburgh, where for years Tuesdays and Fridays had been ladies' days at the park, male patrons complained bitterly that women were crowding the grandstands and taking the best seats even though they paid no admission. 'There is no doubt but that the ladies have abused our kindness at the park in years past,' said President Kerr of the Pittsburgh club at the beginning of the 1896 baseball season. 'There were almost a thousand of them in the grand stand every Tuesday and Friday last season, and they, of course, took the best seats . . . When a man pays 75 cents . . . he wants a good seat.'[8]

Whatever the merits of this case, by the time of the Chicago women's team tour of the Maritimes during the summer of 1891 the role of women within baseball had been firmly established. Women were spectators rather than players, and as such were expected to serve as agents of respectability and control. When women played the game, they contradicted the image of feminine decorum that promoters and social reformers employed for their own purposes. Even worse was playing the game for money, which placed women baseballists on the same level as bawdy theatrical performers, or even prostitutes, willing to barter their femininity for filthy lucre. As women barnstorming teams toured the country, the press routinely referred to women ballplayers as 'Amazons,' 'freaks,' or 'frauds,' while at the ballpark women players had to put up with verbal and physical assaults that belittled and degraded them.

The Chicago team, known as the Blackstockings, was the brainchild of W.S. Franklin, a rather unsavoury New York speculator and dramatic agent who had been involved in women's baseball since 1879 and considered himself—in something of an exaggeration—to be 'the father, founder and originator of baseball playing by young ladies in America.'[9] In August 1980 Franklin had advertised in the New York *Clipper* for fifty girls, 'young, not over 20, good looking and good figure,' to stock a female baseball league of four to six clubs. Applicants from outside of New York who were unable to appear in person were asked to send a photograph with their application. The successful girls were promised a salary of five to fifteen dollars a week plus expenses, plus an extended engagement to travel. Franklin's Dramatic Agency at 1162 Broadway was immediately besieged with interested candidates, and scores of letters flowed in from across the country. Five clubs were organized for the 1891 season, representing Chicago, Cincinnati, Boston, New York, and Philadelphia, but by the end of that summer only three remained. One of those was on tour in Massachusetts, another headed west to California, and the third came north to Maine and the Maritimes.[10]

In establishing his teams, Franklin was keenly aware of the objections that were usually raised against women on the sporting diamond, and he took steps to assure the public that the exhibitions were 'free from all objectionable features.'[11] Club rules strictly regulated conduct, and provided hefty fines for breaches of etiquette. Any quarrelling or demonstrative complaints while travelling, or about the quality of hotel rooms, would resulting a twenty-five-cent fine for each offence. No team member would be allowed to enter, either day or night, any saloon or bar where intoxicating drinks were sold, or face a fifty-cent to one-dollar fine. 'Flirting,' 'mashing,' or making the acquaintance of men on trains or steamboats, in depots or hotels, 'or permitting the least familiarity,' carried a fine of twenty-five cents to a dollar depending on the seriousness of the incident, and hotel clerks were instructed not to forward notes to the girls from 'dudes' or would-be seducers.

If Franklin had had his way, the girls would have had little time for 'mashing,' lounging around bar-rooms, or loafing in hotel offices. Franklin wanted his girls to learn lacrosse, polo, bicycle riding, and fencing, how to play the cornet and trombone, beat a snare drum, and play the fife, so that they could parade before the game and attract more paying customers. In fact the procession to the ballpark was often as entertaining as the game itself. Outfitted in red and black striped jockey caps, light-coloured flannel blouses, red and black striped dresses reaching to the knees, and black stockings, the Chicago girls would march to the park, often accompanied by the town band. In Halifax, for example, the girls drove through the city in open carriages, attired in their uniforms, carrying banners and flags, and headed by a brass band.[12] Playing for a club such as this, the Saint John *Progress* concluded, was 'a grand opening for girls who are "quick to learn", and have mastered the art of never getting past twenty years of age.'[13]

Although women's baseball was relatively new to the Maritimes,[14] women had been playing the game for some time in the United States, where their participation usually met with formidable opposition. Moralistic denunciations from the clergy, prevailing notions of biology that emphasized woman's nurturing character and physical frailty, genteel assumptions about the feminine personality, and an idealized notion of the family that identified the young girl as 'the quintessential angel in the house,' all combined to discourage participation in competitive sports.[15] When women did play, they usually did so 'only within limited behavioural boundaries which confirmed the separate spheres of the sexes and the superiority of men.'[16]

The medical profession provided a powerful biological rationale for restricting women's activity in sport. Contemporary medical wisdom suggested that women's bodies were fundamentally unhealthy, placing them at a distinct disadvantage when compared to or competing against men. Wendy Mitchinson has argued that medical doctors regarded men's bodies as the biological norm; in those areas where women's bodies deviated from men's they were considered problematic. Fascinated by a woman's gynaecology, most practitioners saw women as prisoners of their reproductive systems, predisposed to weakness, ill health, and nervous disorders of various sorts.[17] Dr Andrew Halliday, of Stewiacke, Nova Scotia, for example, noted the importance of understanding 'the more weakly organized physical constitution of the female sex, and . . . the important series of phenomena which occur at the period of puberty, when extra demands are being made on what is perhaps an already weak constitution and while . . . a nerve storm is raging both in the cerebro-spinal and sympathetic systems.'[18] Given women's physiological weakness and nervous instability, it followed that neither their bodies nor their minds should be placed under too great a strain. 'A woman who lived 'unphysiologically'— and she could do so by reading or studying in excess, by wearing improper clothing, by long hours of factory work, or by a sedentary, luxurious life,' threatened her own future well-being and that of her offspring.[19] Doctors thus counselled moderate forms of exercise for women, while popular magazines such as *Good Housekeeping, Ladies Home Journal, Woman's Home Companion*, and *Godey's Ladies Book* extolled the virtues of physical culture. Competitive sports such as baseball, however, were believed to be 'unnatural' activities that could have debilitating consequences.

The rhetorical emphasis on the declining health of nineteenth-century women was connected to notions of degeneracy and nervous depletion and to anxieties about the development of a highly industrialized and urban society. Although fears about declining vigour involved people of either sex, women were considered especially prone to debility. Worried that women were becoming less hardy than their grandmothers, especially those who had academic or intellectual aspirations, newspapers, magazines, and health manuals warned of the deleterious consequences of maternal weakness. Those who aspired to higher education were considered susceptible to all sorts of maladies, and in their desire to emulate men lost their sexual attractiveness and femininity. 'Very intellectual women,' the *Christian Guardian* suggested in 1872, 'are seldom beautiful; their features and particularly their foreheads, are more or less masculine.'[20] At the same time, hereditarians warned that because women had a special influence over heredity and the reproduction of the race, they were more likely than men to pass on any constitutional weakness, or diathesis, to their offspring. As a result, women's physical well-being became of increasing concern to those interested in combating degeneracy.[21]

Although most Victorians regarded competitive sport as inappropriate activity for those of the so-called weaker sex, women had begun to play baseball as early as the 1860s. In taking to the diamond, women challenged the prevailing myth of female weakness, an ubiquitous assumption in a society characterized by notions of male superiority. At the same time, however, new conceptions of female beauty that encouraged a growing attention to physical exercise were emerging in the context of national expansion and rapid industrialization. As Lois Banner has suggested, 'the post-Civil War years were a confusing period, when varying types of beauty vied with each other.' Although most nineteenth-century fashion magazines portrayed the ideal woman as thin and pale, a more buxom ideal emerged in the third quarter of the century, followed by a more athletic look in the 1890s and after 1900.[22]

The changing conception of the ideal body type was also related to the medical profession's struggle to assert its legitimacy and maintain professional influence in the face of challenges from its competitors. During the 1860s and early 1870s orthodox practitioners had begun to lose confidence in an earlier 'heroic' therapy, which depended upon brisk purgatives, the regulation of secretions through leeching or venesection, and counter-irritant therapy such as blistering to reduce inflammation in engorged bodily organs. Increasingly sceptical of traditional drug therapy — the dosing of patients with cathartics (that is, purgatives, laxatives, or 'drastics'), expectorants such as iodine or the carbonate of ammonia, and anodynes or stimulants such as opium, codeia, chloral hydrate, and alcohol — the profession increasingly came to rely on the healing power of nature. The result was a new emphasis on a strong and healthy female form, suited to child-bearing. The vogue among medical men for supporting the ideal of plump and voluptuous women after the Civil Wars was, in part, an effort to regain control of women by devaluing their minds and re-emphasizing their bodies,' Patricia Vertinsky has argued. 'Large bosoms and swelling hips were extolled as a visual manifestation of woman's only purposeful role — maternity.'[23]

During the last quarter of the nineteenth century the emphasis on physical regeneration through appropriate exercise became a standard element in the therapeutic orientation of the orthodox medical profession. As doctors increasingly preached the virtues of physical culture they began to bridge the gap between medical orthodoxy and a larger health-reform movement that urged people to engage actively in their physical purification through regular exercise and good eating habits. Like their counterparts in the Maritimes, American physicians prominent in the physical culture movement, such as Dan Sergeant, Edward Hitchcock, Dioclesian Lewis, Charles McIntyre, and William Anderson, stressed the need for exercise programs in the public schools to reduce mental strain, counteract the evils of sedentary work, and correct physical imperfections resulting from poor posture. To do nothing to counteract the physical weakness of many young schoolgirls, argued Dr Clara Olding of Saint John, was to place stress upon the bright young mind 'with a body physically incapable of sustaining it.' At the same time, however, most doctors remained committed to a dualistic vision of the sexual relation. Stressing the fundamental biological differences between women and men, doctors believed that physical training for women should be undertaken in such as way as to enhance the essential characteristics of womanhood — her domesticity, passivity, moral refinement, and nurturing nature.

Employers of female domestic and factory labour also began to question the virtue of feminine weakness. On the one hand, the belief in female frailty served to legitimize patriarchal dominance and promoted notions of passivity and feminine subservience; on the other, it impeded the employer in his desire for more efficient production. It was hard to idealize the weak and frail female, when her weakness meant absenteeism and unproductive work. Employers wanted healthy, yet docile, workers. 'Public opinion,' said the editor of the *Acadian Recorder* in August 1875, 'seems to be setting in favor of strong and healthy girls. Pale faces are not thought to be as interesting now-a-days as they used to be. A sneer goes round at the inefficiency of the women who work for a living and ask for good wages.'[24]

Attitudes towards women's involvement in competitive sports such as baseball met with a similar ambivalence. Reflecting the growing acceptance of a more physically active womanhood in the post-bellum period, a newspaper editor from western New York in 1867 urged women to play ball, contending that baseball was 'worth twice as much as this insipid, Amanda-Arabella game called "Crow-K", which is nothing but a mighty poor kind of billiards on grass.'[25] More commonplace, however, were suggestions that baseball was a man's game, and that women were not suited to playing such a physical sport. 'A woman may be able to throw a rolling pin at the object of her undying affections with grace and accuracy, but she never can learn to throw a ball,' said one misogynistic student from Columbia University. 'Up shoots the arm, back bends the body; her toes dig convulsively in the ground, and then suddenly she shuts up like a jack-knife; while her arm, without bending a joint, flies over like the paddle-wheel of a mud-scow; and away the ball goes — about six or seven feet — in just the direction she had the least idea of throwing it.'

Women none the less threw baseballs, swung bats, and ran the bases. At Vassar College in Poughskeepie, New York, founded in 1861 by wealthy brewer Matthew Vassar, women were playing baseball as early as 1866, just seven years after the first men's intercollegiate match between Amherst and Williams in June 1859.[26] Although he rejected the notion that female weakness was inherent in women, Vassar felt that the flower of feminine beauty 'too often blooms but palely for a languid or a suffering life, if not for an early tomb,' and advocated vigorous physical exercise for young women.[27] Women also played baseball at Smith College in Northampton and at Mount Holyoke in South Hadley, Massachusetts. That women's colleges provided a setting in which young women could play baseball is understandable, given the controversial nature of women's involvement in higher education, and the likelihood that those women who enrolled in these colleges were more willing than most of their sex to confront the prevailing assumptions of a patriarchal society. Female colleges were important aspects of the women's rights movement, concerned not only with developing the intellectual capacities of women, but also with their right to develop and control their own bodies. As Kate McCrone has argued in her excellent study of sport at the Oxbridge women's colleges, early women athletes spearheaded a movement towards greater female autonomy and provided extremely valuable role models for other women. 'Every sphere of university life women penetrated, whether it was the lecture hall, the honours examination or the sports field,' she writes, 'told in favour of opening up new spheres and conceding to women rights to personal and public liberty.'[28]

Yet, while women's colleges encouraged changing beliefs about appropriate activity for women, the importance of physical exercise, and the unhealthy character of restrictive dress, they did not mount a fundamental challenge against the sexual division of labour. Nor did they subvert conventional concepts of femininity and well-entrenched notions of ladylike behaviour. Instead, most of these colleges attempted to turn out '"refined" ladies of leisure.'[29] At Mount Allison University in Sackville, New Brunswick, the first institution to grant a bachelor's degree to a woman in the entire British Empire, tension between the academic and 'ornamental' traditions in women's education remained largely unresolved before the First World War.[30] Although the college continued to emphasize the need for a rigorous academic education for women, many of those well-to-do Maritimers who sent their daughters to Mount Allison regarded it as a finishing school. Most would have agreed with David Allison, an early president of the college, that 'any woman's best and highest sphere [was in] . . . aiding some good, honest, faithful man in discharging the duties of life.'[31]

The involvement of women in physical education on campus, which touched upon deeper uncertainties about the relationship between the sexes, also took place amidst a debate about the impact of higher education on the nervous systems of men and women alike. It was commonly understood that the individual's vital life force, both physical and intellectual, was limited, and that excessive indulgence in either physical — including sexual — or intellectual activity would result in enfeeblement of the body or mind.[32] In a speech in Saint John in 1882, for example, the Hon. John Boyd (MP) criticized the competitive, high-pressure educational system that 'shattered or partially destroyed the health of so many young men and women.'[33] Advocates of the theory of vitalism attacked the overstimulation of the intellectual capacities of young children, of working people whose 'dull' minds supposedly limited their capacity to think deeply, and, of course, of women, who were regarded to have a fragile nervous system that could not withstand the demands of intellectual development. In these cases, said one turn-of-the-century alienist, the attempt to broaden the mind beyond its limits of expansion was 'far too often, a direct offence to physiological law.'[34]

Edward R. Clarke's *Sex in Education or a Fair Chance for the Girls* (1873) drew heavily upon vitalism in its attack on higher education for women. Clarke was convinced that an educational system that treated men and women equally was responsible for the 'grievous maladies' of womanhood, sapping her vitality, taxing her delicate nervous system, and creating 'crowds of pale, bloodless female faces, that suggest consumption, scrofula, anemeia, and neuralgia,' The 'female organization,' Clarke argued, predisposed women to the bearing and raising of children. An overemphasis on education placed a great physiological burden on the constitution of the female, whose natural role was that of procreation. Women were endowed with a set of reproductive organs 'whose complexity, delicacy, sympathies, and force are among the marvels of creation,' If those organs were properly cared for, they would be the source of strength, but if neglected would 'retaliate upon their possessor with weakness and disease, as well of the mind as of the body.' The contemporary fascination with women's education, Clarke believed, meant neglect of 'the temple God built for her,' and explained why in the nineteenth century each succeeding generation had become feebler than its predecessor.[35]

In order to clinch his point, Clarke drew upon a comparison between New England and Nova Scotian girls offered by a recent traveller to the Maritime provinces. Clark's anonymous female commentator provided a highly romanticized account of an idyllic Nova Scotian world, whose people lived close to nature and remained unspoiled by the demands of excessive education. In the town of Wolfville, 'just beyond the meadows of the Grand Pré, where lived Gabriel Lajeunesse, and Benedict Bellefontaine, and the rest of the "simple Acadian farmers,"' she came upon a Sunday School whose services had just ended. Thirty or forty boys and girls emerged, all with 'fair skins, red cheeks, and clear eyes; . . . all broad-shouldered, straight and sturdy.' She was struck not only by the robust healthiness of the children but of their parents, who 'were broad-shouldered, tall, and straight, *especially the women*.' In Halifax, during the celebration of the anniversary of the Province, Clark's traveller saw a similar sight: hundreds of children marched in the day's parades, but she counted 'just eleven sickly children.' She attributed the difference between the blooming youth of Nova Scotia and the unnatural weakness and premature decay of young girls in New England to the fact that until recently 'there have been in Nova Scotia no public schools, comparatively few private ones; and in these there is no severe pressure brought to bear on the pupils.'[36]

Ironically, women's college administrators and students were able to use Clarke's arguments to their advantage, emphasizing the necessity for physical recreation and sport as an antidote to mental strain and female weakness. Everywhere, advocates of physical education used the critique of women's mental frailty to legitimize entry into a sporting terrain that was regarded as a male preserve. For example, Dr Grace Ritchie, a well-known Halifax feminist, spoke at the annual conference of the National Women of Canada in 1895, and made an earnest plea for physical training for young women. Ritchie noted the increased strain that accompanied the cultivation of the female intellect. 'Their nervous systems are apt to be overworked,' she said, 'and we must counteract this. The best way . . . is by giving them healthy exercise in some form or another.'[37]

These arguments were directed more to young college students, however, than to the young women who played for the Chicago Blackstockings, most of whom were working-class girls still in their teens who had left home to find employment. Unlike college women, who played in the protected preserve of the campus and outside of the derisive gaze of male spectators, the lady barnstormers challenged the gender apartheid of nineteenth-century sporting culture without any elaborate intellectual defence. As would be the case with black barnstorming teams in the twentieth century, these women's teams were tolerated because of their 'novelty' or 'entertainment' value rather than from a sense of legitimacy of their involvement in a more egalitarian social order. They were also subject to ridicule and abuse. Nevertheless, by pressing into a field of activity that had been closed to them, even if they could not escape the indignities, exploitation, and stereotyping that accompanied their involvement, women and black baseball players — like others of their race and gender in the emerging entertainment industry — resisted those who would deny their full humanity.

The earliest barnstorming teams were organized in June 1879 as a money-making speculation by theatrical agents W.F. Franklin of New York and William J. Gilmore of Philadelphia. The Reds, who hailed from and represented New York, and the Blues from Philadelphia first played in public on 4 July in Oakdale Park, Pennsylvania. After that they left on an eastern tour through Maryland, Massachusetts, and New Hampshire. The tour started out splendidly, to the delight of both the promoters and the players. On 7 and 8 July they played a two-game series in Baltimore and amassed gate receipts of $1450. Games followed in Boston, Lowell, and Manchester, New Hampshire, and the New York *Clipper* reported that the women 'conducted themselves in an unexceptional manner on and off the ball-field.'[38] Then things went awry. On 5 August, after an exhibition game in Worcester, one of the managers absconded with the team's funds, leaving the players penniless.

Within two weeks the teams were reorganized, and the women began a western road trip through Ohio and Kentucky. This tour was even more disastrous than the previous one. At Louisville, on 25 August, they played before a noisy and boisterous crowd that insulted and pelted them with stones when they tried to leave the ground. A couple of days later a number of the girls were arrested in Cincinnati. As a result, when the women arrived in Springfield, Ohio, there were only eleven players available to play. Trouble soon arose between a group that the *Clipper* described as 'hoodlums' and 'some negroes,' apparently because the black spectators had yelled insults at the women, a privilege presumably restricted to whites. 'Hot words led to blows, and the upshot was that one of the negroes was fatally wounded by being hit on the head with a piece of board.' After the game, the team manager took the gate receipts of $250, and left for Columbus for the ostensible purpose of arranging a game there. The girls, who were already ticketed, followed by train, but upon reaching the city they found that the manager had once again left them high and dry.[39] They would not play again that season, nor in the following year.

After another brief and unsuccessful effort in 1881, Franklin tried to resuscitate the experiment during the 1883 season. The Reds and the Blues, now also known as the Blondes and the Brunettes, were revived, with Harry H. Freeman and W.F. Phillips as team managers. (Phillips would later manage the Chicago Blackstockings and accompany them on their tour of the Maritimes.) Once more the teams faced frequent insults and legal difficulties. After a game in Pittsburgh against the Alleghany club, Freeman and Phillips were arrested and subsequently released on payment of a licence and costs. Freeman, it would appear, was frequently in trouble with the law. Reports circulated that he recruited his women not only as ballplayers, but also as prostitutes. After several complaints that he had convinced young girls to run away from home against their parents' wishes, Freeman was eventually arraigned in May 1886 as a 'dangerous and suspicious character.'[40] Similar claims were made about Sylvester F. Wilson, a one-time backer of the Reds, described in the press as 'female baseball manager, ticket scalper, all-around swindler, and professional debaucher of female morals.' In October 1891 Wilson was convicted, sentenced to a five-year term at Sing Sing prison, and fined $1000 for having abducted Libbie Sutherland, who played on one of his female clubs.[41]

Part of the problem that the women faced while on tour was that they were amateurish players, assembled merely as a speculative venture that would attract fans because of the novelty of their participation. In addition to the insults that came their way as a result of their 'unladylike' behaviour, they were ridiculed for their inept play. After a game at the grounds of the Manhattan Athletic Club that attracted about a thousand spectators, the New York

Clipper observed that 'there were just four of the eighteen who would handle the ball at all, and but one of these four was even approaching expertness.' Newspaper reports from city after city echoed these sentiments. Finally, the reputation of their poor — some might even say fraudulent — performances caught up with the clubs in the middle of a southern tour. At the end of November they were stranded and out of money in St Louis. The experiment 'deserved no better fate,' said the *Clipper*. 'It was from the first nothing but a sensation.'

In early December thirteen of the girls, the oldest of whom was only seventeen, had made it to Chicago, where they hoped to raise enough money to be sent home, but a benefit on their behalf raised only thirty-five dollars. At this point the *Clipper* interviewed Miss Temple, the pitcher of the 'Reds.' She was asked:

> Are any of them tired of the fun?
> Yes, I guess they are; I know I am.
> You don't mind it, do you, in warm weather, when you are in good luck?
> On, no. It's all right then, but we made a mistake in starting out on this last trip. It was too late in the season.
> Do any of the girls ever get their teeth knocked out or anything during the progress of a game?
> No, we don't throw as hard as the men do, and if a ball comes too fast for us we look out for No. 1 and dodge it you know.
> Where did the girls of the company come from? Were any of them ever on the stage?
> They're mostly from Philadelphia. Only two of them have ever been on the stage — one as Topsy and the other as Eva in a juvenile 'Uncle Tom' party a year or two ago. The rest are working-girls and school-girls who like the fun and the travel.

Harold Seymour believed that the girls were mostly normal-school or Sunday-school graduates, seeking to emulate their Ivy League counterparts, but this benign characterization hardly conforms with Miss Temple's description of her teammates.[42]

The 1891 tour of the Chicago Blackstockings was much better organized than those of earlier years, and perhaps because of this the players avoided some of the violence, theft, and exploitation that had surrounded the previous ventures. Better equipped than before, the team carried with it a 300-foot canvas fence that could be erected on any suitable field if they were denied access to regular club grounds. In addition, though they were by no means adroit players, the women were athletic and enthusiastic, and unlike earlier tours when they played mainly against a rival women's team, they now competed against community men's teams. William Burtnett, the team's advance agent, described the women as excellent players, with a 'fast pitcher, dandy batters and quick fielders and baserunners,' and suggested that they were the equal of the best amateur teams in the country.[43]

The reality was somewhat different. After the first game in Fredericton, a reporter noted that 'while the girls were more agile than might have been expected,' they were really not proficient players. Most people were disappointed with what they saw, especially after Burtnett's pre-game hype. When May Howard, the team's catcher and captain, came to the plate, the *Daily Gleaner* reported, the crowd was 'breathless' with anticipation. The Fredericton pitcher opened the game with a couple of swift curveballs, but immediately 'the truth flashed across every mind when she offered faintly at two or three and finally struck out . . . [The girls] could not bat, catch, throw or pitch.' In particular, their pitcher had great difficulty finding the plate, and the centre fielder 'had to make two or three throws in order to get the ball to second base.'[44]

This was a common refrain as the tour continued. The Saint John *Progress* called the Blackstockings team a 'grand fake,' adding sarcastically that 'there were two frisky members . . . that could actually pick up a ball from the ground.'[45] After a game in Moncton, played in a downpour, the local *Transcript* found them 'quite active, and with fine weather their attempts to bat, field and throw balls and run bases, in all of which they show amusing awkwardness, would be interesting.' A report of a game in Amherst between the Amherstians and the Amazons, in the Halifax *Morning Herald,* observed that the locals 'treated them gallantly and took no undue advantages either by a large display of science or in indulging in the usual wordy rows that generally characterize baseball matches.' Still, the town had been excited by their visit. After the game, the jovial crowd, including a 'large number of ladies' who 'were bound to have a look at the departing girls base ball players,' accompanied the girls to the Amherst railway station. It was generally felt, said one newspaper report, 'that a large number of our citizens would go to see them play again, and there was just a whisper that they will probably come again.'[46]

As the Blackstockings' tour continued, considerable opposition to their visit developed. The Truro *Daily News* reported that a clergyman in New Glasgow had spoken strongly against the tour at a local prayer meeting, while in Truro a delegation of citizens unsuccessfully lobbied the mayor to prevent the team from playing.[47] On the day of the game, the Truro newspaper noted that 'many people, doubtless, will be there to witness the antics of the girls, but if all reports be true, the propriety of attending is very questionable.'[48] After the games in Truro and New Glasgow, the local press criticized the women as frauds who could not compete on equal terms with men although they presumed to do so.[49] 'They are nothing better than a lot of hoodlums from a crowded city,' said the New Glasgow *Eastern Chronicle,* 'and any boys from 10–14 years of age could knock them out, throw them out, or catch them out every day of the week. They are frauds of the first water.'[50]

The Blackstockings received mixed reviews in the three largest cities in the Maritimes. In both Moncton and Saint John the women were refused access to the local amateur athletic association grounds. As a result, no game was played in Saint John; in Moncton the girls had to erect their portable canvas fence for the game. After the match in Moncton, however, the local *Transcript* announced the intention of local officials to invite the women to play another match in the city on their return trip from Nova Scotia. In Halifax there was considerable support for the girls. The game was such a topic of conversation in the week or so before their arrival that an overflow crowd was expected, and when Herbert Harris of the Law and Order League petitioned the mayor of Halifax to prevent the girls from playing on moral grounds, James Pender, manager of the Socials, denounced this as an attack on the respectability of all 'gentlemanly' baseball players in the city. He observed that the managers and players 'have reputations to sustain and they look upon the petition as an insult.' Pender and the manager of the Mutuals had made the arrangements to bring the Blackstockings to Halifax, and they did so believing baseball to be "just as modest and pretty a recreation or sport as lawn tennis, or cricket; all of which are played by respectable ladies.' They also felt that 'nobody has either right or reason to object to those young ladies playing here until they have seen or heard something detrimental to their character.'[51]

Before the game in Halifax, the *Acadian Recorder* predicted that the novelty of seeing the young women play baseball would attract an immense crowd.[52] On game day over three thousand people jammed the Wanderers' Grounds in Halifax. Outside the park young boys scaled electric-light poles and trees to get a look at the game, and a large crowd of men and women congregated on Citadel Hill overlooking the grounds as well. A full half-hour before the match, the entire 550-seat grandstand, including 'more than the usual number of ladies present for an outdoor event,' had been completely sold out. The *Morning Herald* noted that many in attendance were witnessing baseball for the first time, having heard of the 'technicalities of the great American game' without ever attending a match. 'Old and young, rich and poor, bald heads and well-covered craniums — all were represented.' In addition, many women in the audience seem to have considered this a perfect opportunity to introduce themselves to the sport.

'The game is spoken of as being too exciting and accompanied with some rough play and a little danger. When one of the teams was composed of ladies there could be no fear of those disagreeable episodes.'[53]

As usual, the game itself was disappointing. The Halifax team had great trouble to keep from scoring runs and had to give what assistance they could to their opponents in order to keep the score close. 'The girls are not baseball players,' said the *Morning Herald*. 'Their battery was "girlish", and their fielding was just good enough to stop the balls which the gentle batting of the men treated them to; running was the best of their play.'[54] The *Acadian Recorder* observed that the spectators were not long in becoming tired, and were disappointed when they observed that many of the girls were young and small, an appearance that was emphasized by their short skirts. At the same time, 'there was nothing indecorous in their conduct, and the crowd contented themselves with loudly applauding the few long hits by members of the visiting team, and two catches of foul flies by the backstop.' The game was called after two hours, with the score 18 to 15 in favour of the women, although under the circumstances the result had little meaning.[55]

In retrospect, the Blackstockings' tour revealed the serious constraints that women laboured under in trying to legitimize their involvement in what was considered a 'manly' sport. Many of the young women who signed on to play were no doubt attracted by the prospect of seeing the country and having fun, while some may have taken the opportunity to escape unfortunate circumstances at home. Nevertheless, the conditions that they worked under were both difficult and demeaning, and the price they paid for their involvement was high. At the mercy of employers who demanded their obedience and docility, and of unscrupulous managers who sometimes preyed upon them, touring women's teams were always one step away from abandonment and even imprisonment. If the advance agents reneged on paying field rent or licence fees, the women might find their belongings seized, leaving them with only the clothes they had on their backs.[56] If their managers ordered them to play on Sundays in violation of the local by-laws, they faced the prospect of legal action.

On the field the women had to contend with the hoots of derision from male spectators and the prospect of violence and physical assault or being accosted by unwanted 'admirers' at the end of the match. Just defending themselves from such advances risked further abuse. The *Acadian Recorder* reported an incident of this sort in Halifax. When the women returned to their hotel after attending a performance at the Lyceum theatre, a number of 'young lads' were waiting for them on the street and blocked their way. Apparently they were angry about an incident at the theatre, in which a young man about eighteen had caught hold of one of the girls by the hair. She had advised him to stop, but when he refused, she struck him on the face and he fell to the floor. Their masculine pride seemingly injured, the group proceeded to make known their feelings about the 'unladylike' character of the girls.[57]

The assumption that women who played baseball could not be 'ladies' dogged the girls throughout their travels. President Byrne of the Brooklyn baseball club, for example, called the women's teams 'a disgrace to baseball.' Byrne refused to lease his grounds for 'such a disgusting exhibition,' and called upon all other managers to follow his example.[58] Just as often it was other women who objected to the female baseballists. In Freeport, New York, for example, the women of the town, upon hearing of a proposed match, 'rallied in righteous wrath and let their husbands know that attendance at the game would constitute grounds for divorce.'[59]

Critics of women in sport argued that involvement in 'manly' pursuits undermined femininity and created a more masculine womanhood. Helen Lenskyj has observed recently that over the past century of women's participation in organized sport, 'femininity and heterosexuality have been seen as incompatible with sporting excellence: either sport made women masculine, or sportswomen were masculine at the outset.'[60] Nineteenth-century degeneracy theorists such as R. von Krafft-Ebing believed that involvement in competitive sporting activity revealed the atavistic character of those women who participated and, furthermore, that the preference for playing masculine sports was a symptom of lesbianism. Opposition to women's involvement in competitive sport on these grounds suggested a fear of the potential anarchy of uncontrolled female sexuality.[61] Indeed, for women to attack the bastions of male sport was to bring into question all of the assumptions of women's passivity and sexual passionlessness that Victorian moralists had erected into the 'archetype of human morality.'[62] If women were to compete as men, what impact would this have on the 'natural' evolution of 'true womanhood?' Cesare Lombroso had distinguished modern women from 'savage peoples' by their attention to those maternal functions that 'neutralize her moral and physical inferiority.' In modern society, he believed, lofty sentiments accompanied motherhood, pity replaced cruelty, and maternal love counteracted sexual passionlessness. Would women competing with men not mean an end to womankind's nurturing sensibilities and 'a desire for license, idleness, and indecency?' Would not a rejection of her traditional maternal role lead to the degeneration of the race?[63]

The fact that the women who toured the Maritimes, like other barnstorming female clubs, could not compete on equal terms with competitive men's teams meant that the challenge to masculine authority was not as threatening to men as it might have been. Had they been more proficient athletes it is likely that they would have been regarded as women who were traitors to their sex, aggressive, unfeminine, obtrusive, and dangerous radicals thrusting themselves into activity that they had no right to enter. However, their inability to play well — understandable as it may have been considering their young age and their limited experience in the game — made them appear as frauds and subjected them to uncommon abuse. When the American Female Baseball Club visited Cuba in the spring of 1893 a crowd of Alamendares became so upset at having paid to see women who could not play ball that they attempted to attack the players. 'Horrible confusion ensued,' said the *Sporting News*,' and the shrieks of the frightened young women could be heard mingled with the execrations of the mob.' The players, including the men of the Cuban club, took refuge in a house, but the mob pursued them, obtained entrance, and pillaged the residence. Only the valiant efforts of the Cuban players and the quick arrival of the police saved the girls from being more seriously hurt.[64]

Notwithstanding their limitations as ballplayers, and the controversy surrounding their involvement in such a 'manly' sport, the Chicago team's tour of the Maritimes provided an important impetus to the organization of women's baseball teams throughout the region. Women played baseball in several urban communities in the Maritimes and New England before 1900, and even in smaller communities such as Bocabec, Chatham, and Newcastle in New Brunswick and Oxford, Nova Scotia, teams of women baseballists risked the wrath of the churches as they pushed into a formerly male sporting domain. In addition to baseball, the 1890s witnessed the involvement of women in several new forms of leisure activity, from competitive swimming to cycling and even ice hockey. In Prince Edward Island married women took the ice against single women in 1893. The Alpha hockey club of Charlottetown, formed in 1895, was perhaps the finest women's team of the day. The Alphas also organized a baseball club in 1905.[65] After the turn of the century, women's ice hockey gained a foothold in the colleges, and teams like the Kanenites of New Glasgow gained a reputation for aggressive and skilful play.

Nothing contributed more to the growing physical emancipation of women than the cycling craze of the mid-nineties. The development of a bicycle safe enough for female use was an important catalyst of social change. Middle- and working-class women alike turned to the bicycle as a form of physical exercise, but also as an instrument of liberation from the constraints of Victorianism. Cycling affected courtship patterns, dress and fashion, and attitudes towards women's physical development, and contributed to new systems of credit, advertising, and consumption.[66] Some critics worried that the bicycle offered young girls too much freedom in their courtship practices, and others that riding created sexual excitement and 'a distinct orgasm in women.'[67] Cycling was also believed to be the source of a number of maladies, including bicycle 'hump,' 'arm' and 'knee,' and some believed that it could lead to insanity.[68]

All of these fears reflected the concern that by proceeding beyond her 'proper sphere' a woman faced a number of disabling consequences to her femininity.[69] In his study of women and sport in the Maritimes, Michael Smith has argued that the development of more aggressive feminine sporting activity at the turn of the century raised fears that competitive sports and strenuous exercise programs were exerting a masculinizing effect on those women who participated in them. Advocates of sport and exercise for women cautioned against immoderation in physical activity, and feminized rules in sports such as basketball and ice hockey in order to curb destructive competition. 'Fearful of the "masculinizing" tendencies of the manly sports and concerned that the "new women" threatened the stability of the existing order,' Smith writes, 'male and female reformers worked to develop a feminine sporting tradition distinct from that of male athletics.'[70]

Those occasions on which women and men competed against each other were infrequent, and often popular because of their novelty. In 1905, the Boston Bloomer Girls, a barnstorming baseball team that had begun operations in 1897 and had toured all across the United States from Maine to California, took a swing through the Maritimes. The star of the club was Maud Nelson, a twenty-four-year pitcher and third baseman, and fine all-around ball-player, who was a dominant figure in women's baseball and softball until the Second World War. As with many of the touring teams after the turn of the century, the Bloomer Girls' roster, though made up mostly of women, was supplemented by two or three men known as 'toppers' who occasionally wore wigs and skirts in order to pass as women. Most often the teams carried a male catcher, infielder, and outfielder. Sometimes playing under assumed names, the male players were usually first-rate athletes: indeed, eventually Hall of Famers Rogers Hornsby and Smokey Joe Wood both toured with Bloomer Girls teams at the beginning of their careers.

As the First World War approached, women were becoming increasingly active in team sports such as baseball, but they were none the less urged to compete amongst themselves and in such a way as to keep their athletic prowess within the bounds of feminine propriety. Accordingly, in June 1910, when the Halifax *Morning Herald* encouraged girls to play ball and not allow their brothers to monopolize the game, it could not help but note that 'bloomers and gym jackets make dandy suits for the diamond — and the boys may be requested to remain away.'[71] As women took a prominent role in organizing the home front during the First World War, however, criticism of their involvement diminished and prevailing notions of female frailty came under assault. 'For tens of centuries man had pictured woman as a lovely, but inferior being whose glory was merely the reflection of his own superior light,' wrote F.M. Bell in *A Romance of the Halifax Disaster,* published in 1918. 'And then came the war, and . . . she rose to her full height . . . In the brighter light . . . she towered above him, a new idol, a new ideal, the woman who could work as well as play, who could fight as well as love, who could be silent under sorrow and cheerful in the face of tragedy.' Yet if this realization made it less difficult for women to engage in athletic endeavours, women would continue to face considerable opposition in their struggle for physical emancipation.

As more women played the game after the war, some became proficient enough to compete with and now and then play for competitive men's teams, while others joined various Bloomer Girls aggregations. One of these was Edna Lockhart, from Avonport, Nova Scotia, a fine all-around athlete who starred in basketball, softball, swimming, and bowling, and played for two years with Margaret R. Nabel's New York Bloomer Girls as a pitcher and third baseman in the mid-1930s.[72] Another was Elizabeth 'Lizzie' Murphy, a Rhode Island native who was 'known as the "Queen of Baseball" throughout New England and eastern Canada' during the interwar years.[73] A slick-fielding and hard-hitting first baseman who once played for a New England All Star team in a match with the Boston Red Sox, Murphy toured the postwar Maritimes as a member of Ed Carr's Auburn All-Stars, a team made up mostly of college and semi-pro players from the Boston area.

What is most striking, however, is that despite the attempts of women to breach the male monopoly over competitive baseball, the game remained essentially a masculine sport. Although it became increasingly acceptable for women to play the game as the force of Victoria moralism weakened during the twenties and thirties, it was assumed that only the unusual woman would be able to do so with proficiency. Indeed, this was one of the ironies of teams such as the Chicago Blackstockings that challenged baseball's gender divide. In their attempt to penetrate what was regarded as a male leisure space, these women also helped confirm and reinforce notions of masculine superiority. Subject to exploitation by their employers who sought to extract a profit from their performances, off the field they submitted to a series of regulations that required them to behave like 'ladies.' In addition, because the early promoters were more interested in profit than in quality of performance, stereotypes of the physically untalented and awkward female athlete continued to abound. Even in the postwar years, as a new and more physically athletic feminine ideal began to emerge, women were regarded as inferior to their male counterparts. Cast in the role of spectator or cheerleader, where they could offer support to the more 'productive' male, women at the ballpark were expected to replicate their role at home, providing sustenance and support to the male provider. At the same time, young boys participated freely in a game that most people believed moulded masculine character and turned youth into men.

NOTES

1. *Acadian Recorder*, 4 August 1891
2. Sonya Rose, *Limited Livelihoods: Gender and Class in Nineteenth Century England* (Berkeley: University of California Press 1992), 191
3. Allen Guttmann, *Sports Spectators* (New York: Columbia University Press 1986), 114
4. Kathy Peiss, *Cheap Amusements* (Philadelphia: Temple University Press 1986), 4–5
5. Quoted in Harold Seymour, *Baseball: The Early Years* (New York: Oxford University Press 1960), 91
6. Quoted in Melvin Adelman, *A Sporting Time* (Urbana and Chicago: University of Illinois Press 1986), 158
7. *Sporting News*, 8 August 1895
8. *Sporting News*, 7 April 1896
9. *Clipper*, 1 August 1890
10. *Progress*, 6 September 1890. Franklin had chosen only twelve girls at first, and put a barnstorming team together to compete in New York state. The club scheduled games at Glen Falls, Schenectady, Albany, Troy, Ballston, Saratoga, Whitehall, and Cohoes in August, and in New York City and the surrounding area between 1 and 10 September (*Clipper,* 16 August 1890). Franklin had earlier issued a circular in which he stated that the Young Ladies Base Ball Club of Cincinnati would like to visit Montreal, but there is no indication that any such game was played (*Daily Gleaner,* 18 July 1890).
11. *Clipper*, 6 September 1890
12. Halifax *Morning Herald*, 22 August 1891
13. *Progress*, 6 September 1890
14. The *Globe*, 11 July 1890, reported a game between the ladies of Chatham and Newcastle, in which Chatham prevailed by a score of 51–50.
15. Deborah Gorham, *The Victorian Girl and the Feminine Ideal* (Bloomington: Indiana University Press 1982), 7
16. Kathleen E. McCrone, *Playing the Game: Sport and the Physical Emancipation of English Women 1870–1914* (Lexington: University Press of Kentucky 1988), 13

17. This is a similar position taken by Edward Shorter, *A History of Women's Bodies* (New York: Basic Books 1982). Shorter argues that until recently women were prisoners of their bodies, and that before the turn of the century real liberation for women was impossible. Shorter sees that liberation emerging from advances in medical knowledge and therapeutic efficiency. In this he is at odds with much of the recent work on the relationship of doctors and women in the nineteenth century. Wendy Mitchinson, *The Nature of Their Bodies: Women and Their Doctors in Victorian Canada* (Toronto: University of Toronto Press 1991); Patricia Vertinsky, *The Eternally Wounded Woman: Women, Exercise and Doctors in the Late Nineteenth Century* (Manchester: Manchester University Press 1990)

18. A. Halliday, 'Hysterical Conditions, with Clinical History of a Case,' *Maritime Medical News*, January 1894: 211

19. Carroll Smith-Rosenberg and Charles Rosenberg, 'The Female Animal: Medical and Biological Views of Woman and Her Role in Nineteenth Century America,' in Judith Walzer Levitt, ed., *Women and Health in America* (Madison: University of Wisconsin Press 1984): 14. The Rosenbergs note the nineteenth-century fear that American women were weaker than their European counterparts, owing to excessive education. Health reformers emphasized physical education and the salutary impact it would have on maternal competence and upon the future development of the race (p. 16).

20. Quoted in Alison Prentice et al., *Canadian Women: A History* (Toronto: Harcourt Brace Jovanovich Canada 1988), 158.

21. Gregory Kent Stanley, 'Redefining Health: The Rise and Fall of the Sportswoman. A Survey of Health and Fitness Advice for Women, 1860–1940,' unpublished Ph.D. dissertation, University of Kentucky, 1991

22. Lois Banner, *American Beauty* (New York: Knopf 1983), chap. 7

23. Patricia Vertinsky, 'Body Shapes: The Role of the Medical Establishment in Informing Female Exercise and Physical Education in Nineteenth-Century North America,' in J.A. Mangan and Roberta Park, eds, *From 'Fair Sex' to Feminism: Sport and the Socialization of Women in the Industrial and Post-Industrial Eras* (London: Frank Cass and Co. 1987), 259.

24. *Acadian Recorder*, 16 August 1875

25. Quoted in *Morning Chronicle*, 28 September 1867

26. Debra A. Shattuck, 'Bats, Balls and Books: Baseball and Higher Education for Women at Three Eastern Women's Colleges, 1866–1891,' *Journal of Sport History* 19, 2 (Summer 1992): 91; Gai I. Berlage, 'Sociocultural History of the Origin of Women's Baseball at the Eastern Women's Colleges during the Victorian Period,' in Alvin L. Hall, ed., *Cooperstown Symposium on Baseball and the American Culture* (1989) (Oneonta, NY, and Bridgeport, Conn.: Meckler Publishing, in association with the State University of New York College at Oneonta, 1991), 100, 109.

27. Quoted in Betty Spears, 'The Emergence of Women in Sport,' in Barbara J. Hoepner, ed., Women's Athletics: Coping with Controversy (Oakland, Calif.: DGWS Publishers 1974), 27. See also Matthew Vassar, 'Matthew Vassar and the Vassar Female College,' *American Journal of Education* 7 (1862): 52–6.

28. McCrone, *Playing the Game,* 53

29. Carole Dyehouse, *Girls Growing up in Late Victorian and Edwardian England* (London, Boston, and Henley: Routledge & Kegan Paul 1981), 58. 'The new institutions were certainly not characterized by any attempt to challenge the sexual division of labour any more than they were by any other kind of social radicalism,' Dyehouse argues. 'The reformers rejected the idea that it was "feminine" to be ignorant and waste one's time in trivial pursuits, and emphasized the desirability of educating women to be cultivated wives and mothers . . . The reformers *redefined* the Victorian concept of femininity: they did not (in the main) *reject* it' (58–9).

30. John Reid, 'The Education of Women at Mount Allison, 1854–1914,' *Acadiensis* 12, 2 (Spring 1983): 3–33

31. Quoted in ibid., 15

32. Michael Bliss, '"Pure Books on Avoided Subjects": Pre-Freudian Sexual Ideas in Canada,' in S.E.D. Shortt, ed., *Medicine in Canadian Society: Historical Perspectives* (Montreal and Kingston: McGill-Queen's University Press 1981): 266–71

33. Saint John *Daily Sun*, 6 May 1882

34. W.H. Hattie, 'The Role of Education in the Development of Self Control,' *Maritime Medical News* 14, 8 (April 1902): 281

35. Edward H. Clarke, MD, *Sex in Education; or, A Fair Chance for Girls* (Boston: James R. Osgood and Co. 1873), 22, 27–8

36. Ibid., 162–7. Clarke also quoted as follows from Harriet Beecher Stowe. 'The race of strong, hardy, cheerful girls, that used to grow up in country places, and made the bright, neat New-England kitchens of olden times,— the girls that could wash, iron, brew, bake, harness a horse and drive him, no less than braid straw, embroider, draw, paint, and read innumerable books,— this race of women, pride of olden time, is daily lessening; and, in their

stead, come the fragile, easy-fatigued, languid girls of a modern age, drilled in book-learning, ignorant of common things.' (168).

37. Quoted in Michael Joan Smith, 'Graceful Athleticism or Robust Womanhood: The Sporting Culture of Women in Victoria Nova Scotia, 1870–1914,' *Journal of Canadian Studies* 23, 1 (Spring 1988): 127

38. *Clipper*, 9 August 1879

39. Ibid., 13 September 1879

40. Howard Seymour, *Baseball: The People's Game* (New York: Oxford University Press 1990), 456

41. *Bridgetown Monitor*, 28 October 1891. See also *Clipper*, 7 January 1893.

42. Seymour, *People's Game*, 455

43. *Daily Gleaner*, 6 August 1891. Burnett's assistant, M.J. Raymond, reported that the club was about twelve years old, and some of its players had been connected with the game for half a dozen years. They had a 'remarkably fast' pitcher, Nellie Williams, but she was not able to play to her potential because their catcher, May Howard, who captained the team, was not able to hold her fastball. The rest of the line-up included Kitty Grant 1b, Angie Parker 2b, Edith Mayves 3b, Edna Mayves SS, Alice Lee lf, Annie Grant cf, and Lottie Livingstone rf. Ibid., 6, 14 August 1891

44. *Daily Gleaner*, 17 August 1891

45. Quoted in *Truro Daily News*, 19 August 1891

46. *Acadian Recorder*, 21 August 1891

47. *Daily News*, 18 August 1891

48. Ibid., 19 August 1891

49. Ibid., 21 August 1891. Over 400 people, 'many of whom were women,' attended the game in Truro. 'The girls can't play ball,' said one reporter, 'but the boys gave them every opportunity to score as many runs as would be consistent without continuing the game too long.'

50. *Eastern Chronicle*, 21 August 1891

51. *Morning Herald*, 14 August 1891

52. *Acadian Recorder*, 14 August 1891

53. *Morning Herald*, 24 August 1891

54. Ibid., 24 August 1891

55. *Acadian Recorder*, 24 August 1891

56. *Clipper*, 19 July 1890. Such an incident occurred in Akron, Ohio, where a constable attached the trunks containing all the girls' clothes. The women were obliged to wear their ball suits around the hotel until the matter was settled.

57. *Acadian Recorder*, 25 August 1891

58. *Progress*, 6 September 1890

59. *Clipper*, 7 July 1890

60. Helen Lenskyj, *Out of Bounds: Women, Sport and Sexuality* (Toronto: Women's Press 1986), 95

61. G.J. Barker-Benfield, *The Horrors of the Half-Known Life: Male Attitudes toward Women and Sexuality in Nineteenth-Century America* (New York: Harper & Roy 1976)

62. Nancy F. Cott, 'Passionlessness: An Interpretation of Victorian Sexual Ideology, 1790–85,' in N.F. Cott and Elizabeth Pleck, eds, *A Heritage of Her Own: Towards a New Social History of American Women* (New York: Simon and Schuster 1979), 162–81

63. B.S. Talmey (*Genesis: A Manual for the Instruction of Children in Matters Sexual* [New York: Practitioners Publishing Co. 1910]) was concerned that feminism would lead to uncontrolled sexuality in those who supported it. Talmey believed that women, particularly those who aspired to a college education, had to be 'warned against the danger in the sex overevaluation of the most unhealthy sensualists of indulgence, found in the modern literature of the so-called feminists.' The passion there is 'perverted, unsatisfied, masturbatic.' Talmey condemned feminists for 'their intoxication of sensuality as a new religion of the personality' (160). Cesare Lombroso, *The Female Offender* (New York: Appleton 1898); see also Gina Lombroso-Ferrero, *Criminal Man, According to the Classification of Cesare Lombroso* (Montclair, NJ: Patterson Smith 1972).

64. 'The Female Twirlers: Women Players Warmly Met in Cuba,' *Sporting News*, 11 March 1893

65. *Daily Post* (Sydney), 30 May 1905

66. Richard Hammond, 'Progress and Flight: An Interpretation of the American Cycle Craze of the 1890s,' *Journal of Social History* 5 (Winter 1971): 235–57; Heather Watts, *Silent Steeds: Cycling in Nova Scotia to 1900* (Halifax: Nova Scotia Museum 1985)

67. *Canadian Practitioner* 21 (November 1896): 848. See also *Dominion Medical Monthly and Ontario Medical Journal* 7 (September 1896): 256. Mitchinson, *The Nature of Their Bodies*, 114

68. See Michael J.E. Smith, 'Female Reformers in Victoria Nova Scotia,' M.A. thesis, Saint Mary's University, Halifax, 1988: esp. chap. 4.

69. The most striking indictment of demanding physical activity for women was that of Dr Arabella Kenealy, 'Woman as an Athlete,' *Living Age* 221 (May 1899): 367. Kenealy thought it inappropriate for women to cultivate muscularity, believing that women lost their charm when they entered into too-active exercise. The bicycle created movements that were 'muscular and less womanly' than were appropriate, and undermined the graceful and quiet bearing of the ideal woman.

70. Smith, 'Graceful Athleticism or Robust Womanhood,' 130, 133

71. *Morning Herald*, 4 June 1910

72. *The Advertiser* (Kentville), 6 December 1988

73. Debra Shattuck, 'Women in Baseball,' in John Thorn and Peter Palmer, eds, *Total Baseball*, 2d ed. (New York: Warmer Books 1989), 617

Article Eighteen

Femininity First: Sport and Physical Education for Ontario Girls, 1890–1930

Helen Lenskyj

Physical education was formally established in the school curriculum in Ontario at a time when educators, social reformers and medical professionals were growing increasingly concerned at the effects of rapid social change upon the next generation. Many women, they believed, had abandoned their "proper sphere", thus abdicating the responsibility to teach their daughters appropriate "feminine" behaviour. The formalization of physical education instruction, and the parallel developments in domestic science instruction at the turn of the century, were two official responses to the perceived problem, signifying the public takeover of aspects of gender-role socialization formerly entrusted to the private family, and the entrenchment of a sex-differentiated curriculum.

Developments in physical education for girls in the period 1890–1930 need to be examined in the context of prevailing attitudes towards women's health, and societal forces which restricted women's participation in sporting and recreational activities. The tendency to define physical activity in exclusively male terms was widespread at the turn of the century. Inspectors' reports in the 1890's, for example, consistently cited "manliness" as an important outcome of physical education, but corresponding references to its value for girls' character training were conspicuously absent.[1] The definition of a "feminine woman" did not encompass competence in sports and physical activities beyond a level necessary for health, or more specifically, for reproductive health.[2] Medical and pseudomedical opinion provided fuel for the debate over girls' sport, as medical "experts" assumed the role of "moral physiologists".[3] By the turn of the century, doctors were warning against excessive *inactivity* on the part of females, since a moderate amount

Source: Helen Lenskyj, "Femininity First: Sport and Physical Education for Ontario Girls: 1890–1930" from *Canadian Journal of the History of Sport*, XIII, 2 (December 1982): 4–17. Reprinted with permission of the author.

of exercise was believed to be conducive to health and fertility. Changing views of human sexuality were partly responsible for the new position, as Vertinsky has pointed out in her study of parallel trends in the U.S.A. behind the drive to promote organized sport, physical education and guided recreation for children and youth was "masturbation phobia": educators and social workers, campaigning to produce strong and healthy (hence, "pure" mothers of the next generation) realized that the methods which served "as a means of refrigerating the passions and creating Spartan habits" among boys must surely be of value to girls, too.[4] This view of the value of sport and recreation was emerging in Canadian educational circles by the turn of the century.

With this basis in medical opinion shaped by social convention, it is not surprising that contemporary researchers find it difficult to identify all the criteria on which authorities of this period based their judgements. Gerber identified certain common features of "acceptable" sports and activities: they could be performed gracefully, without sweating, and were primarily the domain of upper-class women with leisure time and access to private facilities.[5] A more sophisticated schema was developed by Metheny, who identified principles which determined the acceptability of certain activities for women. Those considered inappropriate included activities requiring women to overcome the resistance of the opponent by bodily contact, or the resistance of a heavy object by direct application of bodily force. Activities requiring movement over a long distance or for a long period of time were also viewed as undesirable. Modified versions were sometimes acceptable: for example, the use of objects of light or moderate weight, races of moderate length or duration, activities producing aesthetically pleasing movement, those using a manufactured device to increase speed (such as in skating), and games where a spatial barrier, such as a net, prevents bodily contact.[6] It will be seen that developments in physical education for girls in Ontario generally conformed to these standards.

The school experiences of girls in Ontario prior to 1900 did little to promote physical fitness or athletic competence. Despite various department of education regulations alloting class time for drill, gymnastics and calisthenics, only 57% of all students engaged in these activities in 1894.[7] An instructional manual written in 1866 was used in normal schools until 1893, but, like other publications of this time, it appears to have concentrated on the instruction of boys. An 1893 textbook, *Public School Physiology and Temperance*, included a twenty-page chapter on exercise. It stated that beneficial exercise depended upon the age, health, sex and occupation of the individual, and proceeded to warn against an excess of competitiveness: "the satisfaction of defeating an opponent at lawn tennis . . . may goad a young girl or an ambitious youth to physical harm."[8] Thirty-two exercises in a program of light gymnastics, based on the German and Swedish systems, were included in the chapter; these were obviously intended for girls, since all the illustrations depicted a female figure, wearing a dress reaching her ankles and a tight-fitting jacket and belt.[9] This kind of attire perhaps necessitated the direction to stop exercising if dizziness or discomfort resulted. Using bending, stepping, and arm-swinging motions, these exercises involved the use of dumb-bells (which, the reader was advised, should be "too light" rather than "too heavy"), wands and small rings. Other manuals added bean bags and Indian clubs to this list of light objects which were to be held, or waved, but never thrown. The development of "grace and freedom of movement", and the correction of "false positions and habits of sitting, standing and walking" were the stated aims of this "physical culture" program. There was, perhaps advisedly, no suggestion in the text that girls would find this program enjoyable, or that competence in such activities would bring any extrinsic rewards. It did point out, however, that physical culture constituted mental as well as physical exercise, by requiring quick responses to commands or signals.

Organizations like the Young Women's Christian Association (Y.W.C.A.) viewed physical culture as a way of promoting the spiritual and social welfare of "working girls". The London Y.W.C.A., for example, organized two clubs in factories in 1902, holding lunch-hour meetings with singing and physical culture. An article in the 1900 Y.W.C.A. *Gazette*, despite its tone of amazement that young women were capable of performing "very difficult" exercises, stressed the fact that the participants were capable of both serious effort and actual enjoyment during physical training.[10] Two prominent American educators, Gertrude Dudley and Frances Kellor, made more sweeping claims for the value of athletic training in a 1909 publication:

> . . . aside from this health value . . . (athletics) develop on the mental side keen perceptions and complex thought processes; on the esthetic side, good personal habits and improved appearance; and on the social side, group consciousness, with its many varying expressions of graciousness and power.[11]

Prescriptive literature of the "health and beauty" variety was beginning to stress the association between mental health, physical well-being, and the maintenance of harmonious marital relationship. A 1904 publication, *My Lady Beautiful,* presenting exercises for developing "a beautiful, wellrounded bust", reminded the reader. "It is essential to refrain from indulgence in anger, grief, worry, jealousy, etc. if you desire the best results from this or any other exercise."[12] A comparison of these exercises with those in the physiology textbook suggests that "bust development" was one of the goals of the physical culture program, too.

Warnings against tight clothing and uncomfortable shoes were given in several health manuals of this period, including the textbook, *Public School Hygiene,* first published in 1910. Loose and light clothing was recommended, especially in the area of the chest and abdomen, and the "narrowed waist" was cited as "the forerunner of indigestion, weakness, nervous debility and consumption."[13] It is not coincidental that medical authorities predicted these same consequences, and others more dire, for those who engaged in "the secret indulgence". A chapter on masturbation in *The Science of a New Life,* a book aimed at adult, married, readers, carried this warning:

> The wearing of corsets — whether worn tight or not — or constrictions of any kind around the body, prevent a free circulation of the blood, and also operate against its purification, confining it in abnormal quantities in the pelvic portion of the body, and so irritating and creating a desire in the sexual department of the woman. . . .[14]

So pervasive was the "masturbation phobia" of this author, John Cowan, M.D., that even hairstyles "covering that part of the brain in which amativeness is located" were condemned for their part in promoting "sexual excess" in women.[15]

It is clear that a warning against masturbation was implicit in the Ontario hygiene textbook, but, like the earlier physiology text, it avoided explicit treatment of topics related to human sexuality. In view of the delicate manner in which books for adult readers addressed these topics, this tendency is hardly surprising. In contrast, a topic which had little immediate relevance for public school age children — temperance — was treated in considerable detail: five chapters on alcohol in the hygiene text, and a section on the effects of alcohol and tobacco in each of eleven chapters of the physiology text.[16]

Physical culture clearly met the requirements of graceful movement involving light objects and requiring little exertion. Decorum was ensured by the conduct of such classes out of public view. In 1895, however, there was a report of a performance of "calisthenic entertainment" by female students from the department of physical education at McGill University. Praising the student's marching, the reporter, using the usual methods of comparison with male performance, claimed that their precision "would have done credit to a veteran infantry corps". Predictably, too, the performers were commended for their gracefulness:

> the grace with which the gayly beribboned hoops were manipulated, now making a frame for the face, now slowly circling around . . . as the body swayed to one side or the other, was simply charming.[17]

Opportunities for university women, and for the more privileged sector of society, were expanding by the turn of the century. Tennis, basketball, croquet, golf, fencing, field and ice hockey, and the ubiquitous physical culture, were among the activities for female students at the University of Toronto and at McGill, both of which had diploma courses in physical education for women by 1908. Private clubs, some of which were established by and for women, facilitated the participation of middle class women in activities such as bicycling, tennis and swimming. More often, women had to share the facilities with men, using them on designated "Ladies' days". Although the Y.W.C.A. was offering swimming as an important part of its physical culture program by about 1914, the women's facilities at this time rarely included pools, and some even lacked gymnasiums. Women, consequently, used the facilities of the Young Men's Christian Association (Y.M.C.A.).[18]

Women's participation in sports like basketball and ice hockey appears incompatible with prevailing notions of a "feminine woman". An examination of the "feminine version" of these sports, however, reveals that, in most cases, the usual criteria were met. A very effective method of keeping the nature and pace of women's sport "ladylike" was to require participants to wear voluminous and constrictive clothing; corsets, stockings, long skirts, tight bodices and belts, and, for outdoor activities like bicycling, hat and gloves. Despite Amelia Bloomer's innovation of the 1850's — "bifurcated" skirts which permitted greater freedom of movement — it was not until the introduction of the bicycle to Canada in 1885 that women adopted this "unconventional" mode of dress in large numbers. A more common solution to the problem of restrictive female clothing, and the one usually advocated by men, was the introduction of a "foreshortened version" of the sport for women.[19] Examples of this trend are numerous: the 1899 Spalding official basketball rules for girls and women, lighter stones in curling, shorter courses for golf. Even when no formal modifications were made, women's dress often compelled a minimum of movement: tennis, for example, was played "standing still", according to Gerber's account, and a male swimming instructor in 1899 claimed that "a swim of one hundred yards (in a woman's bathing suit) proved as difficult as a mile in my own suit."[20]

Early events in women's ice hockey illustrate how standards of "feminine" behaviour were incorporated into activities generally viewed as "masculine". Ice hockey was well established at the University of Toronto by 1902, and intercollege (later, inter-faculty) competition was common; as well, Jarvis and Harbord Collegiate teams played Victoria College. The university teams initially adopted the men's inter-college rules, but this soon developed into a major issue. At a 1910 meeting, a motion was passed "to eliminate bodychecking, which means that no shoving of a person into the boards by using bodily strength would be permitted." A 1961 publication of the women's athletic association of the university observed that "a similar meeting has been called almost every year, and fifty years later this problem is still with us."[21] The element of body contact in hockey had to be controlled, if it were to remain an "approved" activity for high school and university women. Predictably, it did not achieve the popularity of basketball, which, when played under the rules for women, was a relatively slow-paced "non-interference game."

The introduction of lines, and the rules against snatching the ball and close guarding ensured a minimum of body contact or rough play. Women's attire for these and most other physical activities remained bulky, but "ladylike": skirts or bloomers were worn, and the legs were concealed by black stockings. Dudley and Kellor drew attention to players' clothing in their discussion of teaching methods for basketball: "It is difficult to avoid holding and catching clothing because of the loose, baggy suits, and *special training is needed to avoid such plays*" (my emphasis).[22] It is significant that they did not recommend more practical attire for players, but instead required that girls and women adapt to the clothing.

Improvements in facilities came about gradually. A department of education regulation in 1909 required a gymnasium to be built in all collegiates within two years, or collegiate status would be forfeited. By 1920, all collegiates and half the high schools had gymnasiums. Segregation of boys' and girls' facilities was common. For example, there was often a large "boys' gym" and a small "girls' gym", a schoolyard divided by a line to separate the sexes, even a "boys' entrance" and a "girls' entrance". At Jarvis collegiate, one tennis court was provided for girls, three for boys.[23]

In 1911, physical education programs across Canada received impetus through the Strathcona Trust Fund. The relatively small amounts of financial support were used to purchase equipment and texts, but, more importantly, in order to qualify, schools were required to conform to a system of physical education set forth by the fund's administrators. Since 50% of the amount had to be used for military drill and rifle shooting, the benefits to girls' physical education were halved at the outset.[24] Patriotic fervour during the war years contributed to the tendency to equate physical education to military drill, and the resulting approach to teaching was of limited value to either girls or boys. Another stipulation of the fund was that the British system (which in turn was based on the Swedish, Swiss and other European methods) be adopted. Commonly referred to as Swedish exercises or Swedish gymnastics, this system stressed precision and uniformity of movement, in response to commands. Thus, for girls' physical education, the Strathcona System served merely to entrench sex-differentiated programs and a militaristic approach to physical training. It is doubtful that the component which has been shown to have an impact on adult involvement in sport — enjoyment of school physical education — was ever present while this system held sway. Some educators, however, were opposed to the militarism of this approach, and their numbers grew as attitudes changed in the post-war period, with the result that the physical education curriculum was extended in 1921 to include games. By the end of the 1920's, the "Swedish system" had been replaced by the "Danish system."[25] The speed with which this new system was adopted, following North American tours by Danish gymnasts demonstrating these exercises in the 1920's, suggests that girls' physical education curriculum was subject to *ad hoc* changes rather than rational planning to meet educational priorities and goals. There was, however, one aspect of female involvement in sport about which teachers, doctors, philosophers, and even the pope felt compelled to voice their concern — competition.

By the 1920's, women were participating in increasing numbers in competitive sports, despite the conservative approach of many physical educators at the public and high school levels. Most Ontario high schools, by this time, had girls' athletic associations which played a key role in the organization of intramural competition; in addition, interschool competition in basketball, track and field, and softball, which began in 1918, continued to expand until 1931.[26] Competition was well established at universities: McGill, for example, had intramural and/or intercollegiate tournaments in archery, badminton, basketball, ice hockey, swimming and tennis by the early 1930's.[27] Although university education was only accessible to a limited number of middle class women, the proportion of female students was increasing significantly at this time, from 13.9%, in 1919–20, to 23.9% in 1929–30; over 25% of graduate students were female.[28] Several, but not all, of the successful athletes in the twenties and thirties benefited from the opportunities which university offered. There were, however, other avenues for female athletes to train competitively, as the number of sports clubs and organizations for women increased, especially in the Toronto area. Corporate and individual sponsors contributed to the development of women's athletic clubs at this time, removing some of the financial constraints which, until this time, had restricted working class women's participation. A prominent example was Bobbie Rosenfeld, 1928 Olympic silver medallist in the 100 m sprint and member of the women's relay team which won a gold medal. Rosenfeld worked at a chocolate factory in Toronto, and competed for a club funded by the company, the Patterson Athletic Club. Another gold medallist, in the high jump, Ethel Catherwood, was sponsored by the mining millionaire, Teddy Oke, who was also responsible for founding the Parkdale Ladies' Athletic Club.[29]

Women's participation in track and field events in the 1928 Olympics was an issue which mobilized the opposition in the continuing debate over women's "proper place" in sport. It was this kind of competition, particularly the proposed 800 metre run, that prompted Pope Pius XI to condemn women's participation in track events. (The 800 m run was dropped until 1960, leaving the longest race for women the 200 m, an "appropriate" distance for females.)[30]

In the U.S.A., the argument over competition had been partly resolved six years earlier, when the national athletic union, a male organization, took control over women's athletics and virtually abolished competitive sport for young women.[31] In Canada, a similar fate seemed imminent in 1924, when the amateur athletic union of Canada (A.A.U.) formed a standing "women's committee", with a male chair and female secretary. By 1926, however, this had become the women's amateur athletic federation, with a female executive, affiliated with the A.A.U. but virtually autonomous.[32] Unfortunately, physical educators in Ontario tended to follow the American example, discontinuing almost all interschool competition by the mid-1930's, but, outside of the school system, opportunities for participation through clubs, leagues, Y.W.C.A.'s, etc. continued to grow at this time, and Canadian women's remarkable progress in sport was reflected in their numerous successes in international competition, a high level of spectator interest, and extensive newspaper reporting of women's sport.[33] The authorities, however, continued to agonize over the dangers of physical activity for women's health; specifically, their participation in competitive sporting events during menstruation was considered to be a serious threat to their physical and mental well-being. Although earlier attitudes towards menstruation had been somewhat modified by the 1920's, with compulsory rest no longer viewed as either necessary or beneficial, doctors continued to warn against "excessive exercise" and activities requiring jumping or tumbling. Physical education textbooks (for teacher-training) at this time dealt with this issue in remarkable detail, some giving arguments pro and con, and other selectively citing the research which supported the restrictive position. Agnes Wayman's book, *Education through Physical Education*, is typical of the latter kind. The conclusions of a Dr. E. Arnold, following "experiments" at his normal school, cited by Wayman, deserve to be reproduced here to do justice to the "logic" of the argument:

> Whenever economic efficiency is the deciding factor, restriction of menstruation is profitable; whenever fertility is of importance, it is undesirable. This would seem to interdict a regimen of exercise which will diminish the menstrual function for that period in a woman's life when she should be fertile . . . What is needed is a restriction in quantity of competition in any form. What is further needed is to diminish the quality of competition by taking the intensiveness of competition out of women's athletic efforts. The exploitation of oncoming womanhood by national or international competition is a menace to womanhood, the magnitude of which one can only contemplate with a shudder.[34]

This type of argument was used as a rationale for the elimination of interschool competition for adolescent girls. It is significant that a physical education professor of Wayman's stature, and many of her female colleagues throughout the U.S.A., accepted this kind of alarmist pseudo-medical pronouncement so uncritically. Wayman even added her own unsupported generalizations to the debate: "physicians state that the hospitals and sanitaria are increasingly full of girls and women who will never be able to become mothers — girls with misplaced organs, "nervous diseases and other ailments" caused by participation in "the wrong kind of sports".[35] Clearly, interschool competition fell in this category, but intramural was permissible, when conducted "under the leadership of properly trained women instructors, who have the educational value of the game in mind rather than winning." Among the alleged dangers of interschool competition were the out-of-town travel and cheering audiences which threatened the already "unstable" emotional makeup of the adolescent girl.[36] The notion of the "dictatorship of the ovaries" which had dominated medical thinking before the turn of the century continued to colour the thinking of doctors and educators.[37] The comments of a Dr. Lindsley, cited by another prominent figure in women's athletics, Florence Somers in *Principles of Women's Athletics*, typify the view that the various systems in the adolescent girl's body are competing for a finite supply of available resources, with the developing reproductive system obviously first in its demands:

> The entire endocrine balance is being established and the adolescent girl who is subjected to highly emotional situations is but sowing the seed for a nervous breakdown later on by putting undue stress on these glands themselves to the physiological changes taking place at that time, and are really having all they can do.[38]

The pre-occupation with the reproductive health of adolescent girls is evident in Somers' bibliography, where she listed 60 references to journal articles related to the topic of menstruation and physical activity. At a time when the predominantly male medical profession had assumed responsibility for the "normal" functioning of women's reproductive cycles, it is perhaps not surprising that they viewed any *variation* as an *abnormality* which they must correct. Canadian doctors were strongly influenced by the views of their American colleagues: medical textbooks and journals originated, for the most part, in the U.S.A., and American "experts" were invited to Canadian athletic and medical conferences and cited at length in Canadian literature.[39] Dr. A. S. Lamb, head of McGill's Physical Education department, led the attack on women's competitive athletics during the Olympic debate, employing the arguments by which his American counterparts had successfully swayed public opinion several years earlier. Even then, the questions remained unchanged: did sport jeopardize women's reproductive health? Did physical activity enhance women's health and, therefore, make them better wives and mothers? Did female athletes experience less difficulty in child-bearing? No one asked: Did sport promote confidence and self-esteem in women? Did women enjoy the challenge of competition, the joy of movement and the satisfaction of personal progress in athletic activities? These questions were not asked because the answers were not considered important; the "wife and mother" issue was paramount. Not all of the official pronouncements, however, stemmed from concern for the next generation of mothers. The actions of the medical profession, in particular, were motivated by self-interest: the goal was to maintain the predominantly male monopoly over women's reproductive health which had been achieved through the promotion of hospital births and the outlawing of midwifery.[40] In addition to the financial benefits of maintaining the status quo, the male-dominated medical profession enjoyed its role as an authority on moral issues, especially those related to female mortality. Like other conservative sectors of the male business community, it had a vested interest in maintaining a social system in which women's position remained subordinate. Thus, it was undesirable, purely in economic terms, to promote a spirit of competition in women, in the field of sport, which might have implications for their participation in fields like education and business — and threaten the comfortable status quo. A physical education instructor cited by Dudley and Kellor expressed this fear regarding interschool competition: "There is a great danger of sacrificing some of the finer traits (of girls) for the peculiar boldness which outside contests bring out."[41] Similarly, Wayman claimed:

> There is . . . no real reason why girls should participate in the same games and sports as boys. The girl does not need to have her combatic instincts developed. She is not or should not be interested primarily in making or breaking records. She should be interested in events and types of activities which make for grace, poise, suppleness, quickness, agility, dexterity, beauty, general strength and endurance . . . events where form and skill is emphasized, rather than in events requiring great strength and speed.[42]

In other words, sport for girls should enhance what were viewed as their "natural" physical traits — grace and beauty. [G]irls do not need to compete, to fight, to achieve, to excel because such behaviour lies in the male domain.

It must be recognized, at this point, that the rationale for these restrictive attitudes did not stem solely from the prevailing ideology of woman's frailty and her subordinate position in society. From the medical perspective, contemporary sports medicine research has substantiated some of the claims related to menstrual variations. A recent study found delayed menarche among female athletes of up to two years.[43] Menstrual irregularity and amenorrhea (cessation of menstrual periods) has been found to occur among athletes more than in the general population, but the primary cause is loss of weight or body fat, not exercise per se. Similarly, in the case of delayed menarche, there is no clear causal relationship: body fat, again, is an important factor, and it has been suggested that the thin, late-maturing athletes are the ones who continue to train strenuously, thus maintaining the conditions which delay menarche. The "myth of the misplaced uterus" has been debunked, although it is acknowledged that women who already have prolapse of the uterus may experience more symptoms during vigorous exercise. The role of exercise in either reducing or increasing menstrual cramps remains undetermined, but it is encouraging to note that contemporary medical attitudes towards this and other issues in sports gynecology appear to be more positive towards female athletes than in the past. Popular literature on this topic frequently makes the observation that fear for the safety of the female's reproductive organs, and not the male's, is somewhat curious, in the light of their respective locations in the human body.[44]

From the ideological perspective, the "separate but equal" philosophy of some of the pioneers in women's sports would find support among some contemporary feminists, but it is generally agreed that boys and girls should play and compete together until puberty, when the different growth spurts give an unfair advantage, first to girls and ultimately to boys, in terms of weight and height. Pedagogically, the claim that competition serves only the talented, and deprives less competent students of the opportunity to improve, was valid, but the fact that its early proponents viewed the inter/intramural debate as an either/or situation resulted in talented girls being deprived of the opportunity to excel, merely because excellence in sport was not considered necessary or desirable for a girl —"she is not, or should not be interested in making or breaking records". Significantly, there seems to have been little agonizing over the plight of boys who lacked the talent for interschool competition, perhaps because the budget for boys' sport was sufficient to provide facilities and instruction for both levels.

The historical materials presented here illustrate the significance of socialization determinants for women's involvement in physical activity at the beginning of the century. There was clearly a conflict between the notion of "feminine woman" and "athletic woman", particularly after the reproductive health of active girls came under scrutiny; the pseudo-medical claims that sport jeopardized girls' child-bearing capability were virtual proof of the ancient fear that sport masculinizes females. Traditionalists were alarmed to observe, too, that situations such as sporting contests brought out "masculine" traits in girls, hence, those who preferred to deny that girls enjoyed physical challenge, excitement, the struggle to win and to achieve excellence, took the necessary steps to repress such traits, by abolishing competition.

Sport was viewed as a means of developing feminine beauty and grace, only for boys was the goal to build physical and mental endurance, and control of one's body. For boys, this kind of learning was functional in the "world of men", as was illustrated by the old saying that wars were fought on the playing fields of Eton. The so-called male bonding which took place on the field could be observed by women, as spectators, but never emulated by them.

NOTES

1. See, for example, *Ontario Department of Education Report, 1895* (Toronto, Warwick, 1896). As part of their 1895 reports, inspectors were required to respond to questions about the physical health of staff and pupils, and sanitary conditions in the schools under their jurisdiction.
2. The definition, of course, was class-bound. There was little concern that working class women could lose their "femininity" by engaging in the kind of strenuous physical activity — labour, not leisure — which was necessary for their survival.
3. The term "moral physiologists" was used by Barbara Vertinsky in "The Effect of Changing Attitudes Towards Sexual Morality Upon the Promotion of Physical Education for Women in 19th Century America," *Canadian Journal of History of Sport and Physical Education*, vii, 2 (1976), pp. 26–38.
4. *Ibid.*
5. Ellen Gerber, "The Changing Female Image," *Journal of Health, Physical Education and Recreation*, (Oct. 1971), p. 59.
6. Eleanor Metheny, *Connotations of Movement in Sport and Dance* (Dubuque, Iowa: Brown, 1965), pp. 48–52.
7. Department of education inspectors' reports, cited by Helen Bryans, "Secondary School Curriculum for Girls," in M. Van Vliet, Ed., *Physical Education in Canada* (Toronto: Prentice-Hall, 1965), p. 126.
8. William Nattress, *Public School Physiology and Temperance* (Toronto: Briggs, 1893), p. 178.
9. *Ibid.*, pp. 100–101.
10. Cited by Josephine Shaw, *When Women Work Together* (Toronto: Y.W.C.A., 1966), pp. 130–131.
11. Gertrude Dudley and Frances Kellor, *Athletic Games in the Education of Women* (New York: Holt, 1909), pp. 26–7.
12. Alice Long, *My Lady Beautiful* (Chicago: Progress, 1908), p. 167.
13. A.P. Knight, *The Ontario Public School Hygiene* (Toronto: Copp Clark, 1919), p. 106.
14. John Cowan, *The Science of a New Life* (New York: Ogilvie, 1919), p. 366.
15. *Ibid.*
16. *Public School Hygiene*
17. A Montreal newspaper report cited by Jesse Herriott in "The Department of Physical Education for Women," *McGill News* (Autumn, 1935), p. 36.
18. Herriott, pp. 37–38; Jean Cochrane *et al*, *Women in Canadian Life: Sports* (Toronto: Fitzhenry & Whiteside, 1977), pp. 24–33; Shaw, p. 131.
19. The view that women are "truncated males" who can only engage in "foreshortened versions" of men's sports, was presented as recently as 1969, by Paul Weiss in *Sport, A Philosophic Inquiry* (Urbana, Illinois: Southern Illinois University Press). His "philosophy" was popular with some physical educators, but has been attacked by feminist scholars, including Thomas Boslooper and Marcia Hayes in *The Femininity Game* (New York: Stein & Day, 1973), and Jan Felshin in *The American Woman in Sport*, Ellen Gerber *et al*, eds. (Reading, Mass: Addison-Wesley, 1974).
20. Gerber, "The Changing Female Image," p. 59; Edwin Sandys, Swimming Instructor, 1899, cited by Marjorie Loggia, "On the Playing Fields of History," *MS Magazine* (July, 1973), p. 63; Canadian developments at this time are described by Lindsay, "Women's Place in 19th Century Canadian Sport," *Canadian Women's Studies* 1:4 (Summer 1979), pp. 22–4, and by Alison Griffiths, "They Who Risked Their Delicate Organs," *Branching Out*, V. 4 (1978), pp. 10–13.
21. A.E. Parkes, *The Development of Women's Athletics at the University of Toronto* (Toronto: University of Toronto Press, 1961), pp. 5–6.
22. Dudley and Kellor, pp. 179–180, p. 194.
23. *Girls' Sport, A Century of Progress* (Ontario: OFSAA, 1979), pp. 23–24.

24. Frank Cosentino and Maxwell Howell, *A History of Physical Education in Canada* (Toronto: General Publishing, 1971), pp. 27–9.
25. *Ibid.*, p. 44.
26. *Girls' Sport*, p. 10.
27. Herriott, pp. 37–8.
28. DBS Statistics cited by Mary Vipond, "The Image of Women in Mass Circulation Magazines," in Susan Trofimenkoff and Alison Prentice, Eds., *The Neglected Majority* (Toronto: McClelland & Stewart, 1977), p. 118.
29. Donald McDonald, "Twenties and Thirties were the Golden Age," *Champion* (March, 1981), pp. 4–6.
30. Frank Cosentino and Glenn Leyshon, *Olympic Gold* (Toronto: Holt, Rinehart & Winston, 1975), pp. 81–82; McDonald, p. 5.
31. Boslooper and Hayes, p. 98.
32. Nancy Howell and Maxwell Howell, *Sport and Games in Canadian Education* (Philadelphia: Lee & Febiger, 1934), p. 200.
33. Cochrane, pp. 37–43.
34. E. Arnold, cited by Agnes Wayman, *Education Through Physical Education* (Philadelphia: Lee & Febiger, 1934), p. 200.
35. *Ibid.*, p. 127.
36. Florence Somers, *Principles of Women's Athletics* (New York: Barnes, 1930), pp. 37–42.
37. Barbara Ehrenreich and Diedre English used the term "Dictatorship of the Ovaries" in their discussion of medical attitudes of female health, in *For Her Own Good* (Garden City, N.Y.: Anchor), 1979.
38. Dr. Lindsley, cited by Somers, p. 44.
39. See Wendy Mitchinson, "Historical Attitudes Towards Women and Childbirth," *Atlantis* 4:2; Part II (Spring, 1979).
40. Susan Buckley, "Ladies or Midwives," in Linda Kealey, Ed., *A Not Unreasonable Claim* (Toronto: Women's Press, 1979), pp. 131–149.
41. Cited by Dudley and Kellor, p. 1551.
42. Wayman, pp. 128–9.
43. W.D. Ross and R. Ward, "Growth Patterns, Menarche and Maturation in Physically Active Girls," Proceedings of the Conference on the Female Athlete, Institute of Human Performance, Simon Fraser University, 1980, pp. 63–71.
44. *Ibid.*, p. 69; Mona Shangold, "Sports Gynecology," *The Runner* (June, 1981), pp. 35–8; Gary Selden, "Frailty, Thy Name's Been Changed," *MS Magazine* (July, 1981), pp. 51–53, p. 95.

Topic Eight

Urbanization in Canada

Pollution on the Toronto harbourfront, 1912.

In 1867, Canada was an overwhelmingly rural society, with more than 80 percent of the population living in small villages and hamlets or on farms. By 1921, more than 50 percent of the Canadian population was urban. Industrialization best explains the rapid shift from a rural to an urban society; increased industrialization accelerated urbanization. But the shift from rural to urban living involved more than a shift in locale. It affected all aspects of life for those who made the transition from farms or hamlets to cities. Urban historians have studied the multiple ways that cities shaped Canada with different values; in doing so, they often borrow from work done by social historians in other areas that overlap with that of urban history.

The following two studies reveal urban attitudes through, in one case, a study of the development of urban parks, and, in the other, through the advent of the motor car. In "'Holy Retreat' or 'Practical Breathing Spot,'? Class Perceptions of Vancouver's Stanley Park, 1910–1913," historian Robert A. J. McDonald looks at three groups who had opposing views of the role of Vancouver's Stanley Park in the formative prewar debate on the subject. These three groups included an élite group who upheld a romantic view of parks; organized workers who had a more utilitarian perspective; and the Park Board, representing middle-class reformers, who wanted to "incorporate some of the latest reform notions about the value of athletic activity for adults and of structured play for children." The three groups clashed on three proposals for the Park: the construction of a tramway across Stanley Park; the beautification of Coal Harbour; and the creation of a huge Coal Harbour Stadium. McDonald examines the external and local influences that lay behind the opposing views of the development of Stanley Park.

In "'Reckless Walking Must Be Discouraged': The Automobile Revolution and the Shaping of Modern Urban Canada to 1930," historian Stephen Davies argues that the automobile revolutionized all aspects of Canadian life in the first three decades of the 20th century. He focuses less on the obvious physical changes and instead on the cultural and social reorientation of cities and rural areas.

What were the views of the élite, middle class, and working class towards the utilization of Stanley Park as a major recreational site in the years 1910–1913? In what ways did the advent of the automobile revolutionize Canadian society? What do McDonald's and Davies's articles tell us about the scope and nature of urban history?

On urbanization in general, see J.M.S. Careless's *The Rise of Cities: Canada before 1914*, Canadian Historical Association, Historical Booklet no. 32 (Ottawa: CHA, 1978) and his collection of essays, *Frontier and Metropolis in Canada: Regions, Cities, and Identities in Canada before 1914* (Toronto: University of Toronto Press, 1989). Students should also consult Richard Preston, "The Evolution of Urban Canada: The Post-1867 Period," in *Readings in Canadian Geography*, 3rd ed., ed. R.M. Irving (Toronto: Holt, Rinehart and Winston, 1978), pp. 19–46, and the collection of articles in *The Canadian City: Essays in Urban and Social History*, rev. ed., eds. G.A. Stelter and A.F.J. Artibise (Ottawa: Carleton University Press, 1984 [Toronto: McClelland and Stewart, 1977]). The Canadian Museum of Civilization (formerly the National Museum of Man) has sponsored eight volumes in its series of illustrated histories of Canadian cities: J.M.S. Careless, *Toronto to 1918* (1984); James Lemon, *Toronto since 1918* (1985); Patricia Roy, *Vancouver* (1980); Max Foran, *Calgary* (1978); Alan Artibise, *Winnipeg* (1977); John Weaver, *Hamilton* (1982); John Taylor, *Ottawa* (1986); and J. William Brennan, *Regina* (1989). Bob Hesketh and Frances Swyripa have edited a collection of essays on Alberta's capital, *Edmonton: The Life of a City* (Edmonton: NeWest Press, 1995).

A detailed study of urbanization in the Maritimes is J.M.S. Careless's, "Aspects of Metropolitanism in Atlantic Canada," in *Regionalism in the Canadian Community, 1867–1967*, ed. M. Wade (Toronto: University of Toronto Press, 1969), pp. 117–29. On Nova Scotia, see also Del Muise, "'The Great Transformation': Changing the Urban Face of Nova Scotia,

1871–1921," *Nova Scotia Historical Review* 11, 2 (1991): 1–42. On British Columbia and the Prairies, consult Paul Voisey, "The Urbanization of the Canadian Prairies, 1871–1916," *Histoire Sociale/Social History* 8 (May 1975): 77–101; A.F.J. Artibise, "The Urban West: The Evolution of Prairie Towns and Cities to 1930," *Prairie Forum* 4 (Fall 1979): 237–62; and A.F.J. Artibise, ed., *Town and City: Aspects of Western Canadian Urban Development* (Regina: Canadian Plains Research Centre, 1981). Donald B. Smith's *Calgary's Grand Story* (Calgary: University of Calgary Press, 2005) looks at the history of 20th-century Canada from the vantage point of two adjacent heritage buildings, both completed in 1912: the Grand Theatre, and the Lougheed office building. On the topic of leisure and cities, see Michèle Dagenais, "Political Dimensions to Leisure and Cultural Activities in Canadian Cities, 1880–1940," *Urban History*, 26, 1 (1999): 55–70.

Little has been written about the impact of urbanization on Canadian society. The most useful sources on the topic are papers published in the *Urban History Review/Revue d'histoire urbaine (UHR/RHU)*, and the major reference work in the field, A.F.J. Artibise and G. Stelter, *Canada's Urban Past: A Bibliography to 1980 and Guides to Canadian Urban Studies* (Vancouver: University of British Columbia Press, 1981).

WEBLINKS

Vancouver Historical Photographs
http://www3.vpl.vancouver.bc.ca/spe/histphotos/
A searchable database of historical photographs of Vancouver. Suggested search terms include "Stanley Park" and "Lions Gate Bridge."

Canadian Motorist
http://www.gov.ns.ca/nsarm/virtual/dennis/exhibit.asp?ID=82
A copy of a 1929 edition of the *Canadian Motorist* magazine, including an article by Clara Dennis, "Into the North of Cape Breton by Motor."

Early Automobile Use in Nova Scotia
http://www.littletechshoppe.com/ns1625/automobiles.html
Pictures, documents, and newspaper excerpts regarding the initial use of automobiles in Nova Scotia.

Ontario Highway History
http://www.thekingshighway.ca/
Detailed overview of major highway construction in Ontario, with many accompanying photographs.

History of the Bus in Montreal
http://www.stcum.qc.ca/English/en-bref/a-autobus.htm
A photographic history of early public transit and "Chars à bancs" (bus) use in Montreal.

Article Nineteen

"Holy Retreat" or "Practical Breathing Spot"?: Class Perceptions of Vancouver's Stanley Park, 1910–1913

Robert A. J. McDonald

Stanley Park is one of North America's largest city-centre parks.* Like Toronto's High Park, Montreal's Mount Royal, and Winnipeg's Assiniboine Park, it was created as part of the urban parks movement that spread through Britain, the United States, and Canada during the last half of the nineteenth century. The 960-acre peninsula, originally set aside in 1863 for military purposes, was granted to Vancouver by the Dominion government in 1887 for use as a public recreation spot.[1] Almost entirely covered by primeval forest, it formed, according to one English visitor, 'surely one of the finest natural parks in the world, with monster trees of the Pacific slope rising to dizzy heights and boasting extraordinary diameter measurement[s].'[2] Initially, limited alterations made Stanley Park accessible while preserving its wilderness character. But as attitudes toward parks and athletics changed and as pressure on existing recreational facilities mounted, Vancouverites demanded a park that more accurately reflected their newer perceptions of urban green space and more fully served their increasingly varied recreational needs. Starting in 1910, conflicting views of how best to utilize this major recreational grounds crystallized into a four-year debate about Stanley Park's future. New ideas clashed with traditional assumptions about the character and role of urban parks. The discussion provides a rare glimpse of Canadian attitudes toward public green space during a period of transition in urban park history.

Canadian historians have displayed little interest in urban parks. Asking traditional questions, existing literature examines Frederick Law Olmsted's landscape design for Mount Royal in Montreal; the chronology of park creation in several nineteenth-century cities; the emergence of Canada's playground movement; real estate promotion and reform as factors in the development of Winnipeg's public park system; and the overwhelming influence of businessmen in Vancouver.[3] This work is most easily categorized by reference to the principal approaches in British and American park historiography, which it follows. The first explores the principles and underlying cultural assumptions of landscape architecture. Typically, authors trace the ideas and ongoing influence of outstanding landscape designers such as Capability Brown, Humphrey Reton, and John Claudius Loudon in Britain and Olmsted in the United States.[4] But British and American writers also emphasize the middle-class origins of urban parks.[5] They find that, from the inception of the park movement in the mid-nineteenth century to the introduction of more bureaucratic and service-oriented motives for expansion in the inter-war years of the twentieth, public parks were urged by members of the middle class for reform or civic booster purposes. Especially popular is the thesis that middle-class advocates of rational reform planned public parks as an antidote to urban society's moral and physical decay,

*I would like to thank Sharon Meen, Jill Wade, Maria Tippett, Norbert McDonald, Ken Coates, Peter Ward, and Allan Smith for their helpful assistance in the preparation of this article.

Source: Robert A. J. McDonald, "Holy Retreat" or "Practical Breathing Spot"?: Class Perceptions of Vancouver's Stanley Park, 1910–1913" *Canadian Historical Review*, 65:2 (June 1984): 127–153. © University of Toronto Press 1984. All rights reserved. Reprinted by permission of University of Toronto Press Incorporated (www.utpjournals.com).

and thus as a mechanism for social control.[6] Studies of design and promotion both look at park history from the top down, stressing the role of landscape planners, recreational reformers, and businessmen at the creative forefront of the movement.

But recently several historians have questioned these approaches, arguing that they obscure broader social influences on the design and use of public parks. Peter Bailey and Hugh Cunningham see the early history of Britain's parks as but one aspect of the history of leisure.[7] They suggest that the working as well as the middle and upper classes played a positive role in shaping Victorian leisure patterns, including the creation and control of recreational space. In a similar manner, Roy Rosenzweig and Stephen Hardie argue that workers in late nineteenth-century Worcester and Boston, Massachusetts, refused to accept passively the imposition of middle-class romantic parks.[8] Workers asserted their own more utilitarian views of how and where recreational space should be laid out, successfully influencing policy in both centres. According to this third approach, popular attitudes toward parks and recreation cannot be ignored, nor can the possibility that in certain instances the lower portions of society participated actively in urban park development. Missing from Canadian literature is work that places parks within this broader social framework, linking changes in leisure patterns with social competition for open space.[9]

This article, which examines the issues, background, and significance of Vancouver's pre-war debate about Stanley Park, well illustrates the complexity of urban park history. In particular, it portrays the growing confusion in early twentieth-century Canada about the purpose and design of urban parks. At one extreme, the Vancouver discussion featured élite spokesmen advocating the purest form of traditional park, based on romantic principles, while at the other organized workers urged an entirely utilitarian and practical play space. In the centre was the Park Board representing the several strands of middle-class thought about parks: respect for traditional principles, interest in beautification, and a desire to incorporate some of the latest reform notions about the value of athletic activity for adults and of structured play for children. Attitudinal differences were rooted in the divergent cultural backgrounds, economic conditions, and social needs of the contending groups. This article concludes that urban park history must be examined within the social context that shaped it.

Throughout the article the terms 'class' and 'élite' are employed to convey an impressionistic rather than scientific meaning. Limited social evidence about the participants and their supporters in the Stanley Park debate necessitates the use of broad analytical categories. Vancouver society is conceived to have been divided into two broad classes, 'working' and 'middle.' Each is defined by occupation: the 'working class' by blue-collar wage labour and the 'middle class' by business, professional, and white-collar occupations. 'Élite' defines a small subgroup within the middle class distinguished by its coherent set of distinctive views about Stanley Park and by its privileged economic and social position at the summit of Vancouver's class structure. 'Popular culture' is used as Hugh Cunningham employs it, to mean 'of the people,' rather than 'the culture of those in positions of power and authority.'[10] The concept transcends blue collar/white collar boundaries.

First of all, what issues were being contended between 1910 and 1913? Discussion centred on three proposals: the construction of a tramway across Stanley Park; the beautification of Coal Harbour; and the creation of a huge Coal Harbour stadium. Stemming directly from the growing problem of overcrowding, the first question centred on whether to allow an electric railway into the forest. The Hundred Thousand Club, a booster organization, initiated discussion of a tramline in mid-1906 by urging Commissioners to consider the need for cheaper transportation. Though strongly opposing a railway, the Park Board responded by allowing a public plebiscite on the issue. Little public discussion ensued, but a solid majority of the small number of property holders and tenants who voted rejected the tramline.[11] In August 1910 concern surfaced again when a private organization, The Electric Railway Construction Co. Ltd., offered to run electric trolleys around the peninsula's circumference on concrete piers built over the foreshore. The problem of the park's inaccessibility had become more acute since 1906 and debate on the issue was correspondingly more intense. In the face of sharp opposition from the majority of Park Commissioners and from certain middle-class groups, the company simplified its plans from a circumference line to a straight track through Stanley Park linking Coal Harbour with Siwash Rock (see map).[12] Enthusiastic support by the Trades and Labour Council forced another plebiscite, this time in January 1912, on the question of a municipally owned park railway, but voters rejected the tramway idea and in effect killed the issue.[13]

The controversy surrounding suggested improvements for Stanley Park's Coal Harbour entrance stemmed from two basic problems: the 1888 bridge leading into the park was old and collapsing; and the tidal flats above the bridge were foul-smelling and unsightly. In January 1908 ratepayers approved the necessary monies to carry out long-held Park Board plans to build a causeway and beautify the area. The first improvement plan, submitted in 1909, proposed a

Figure 19.1 Map of Stanley Park

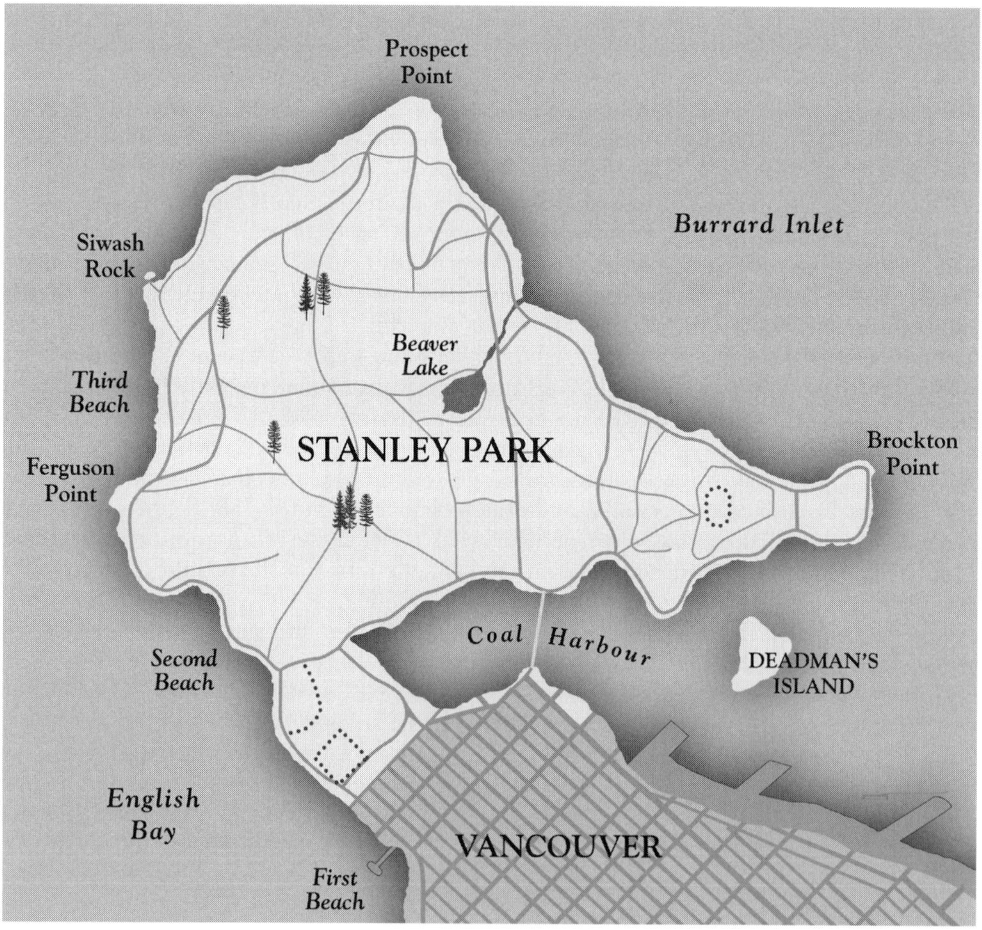

Source: Map Collection, Vancouver City Archives, No. 368

causeway and lagoon landscaped in a simple rustic manner. When the Board finally decided two years later that a professional architect should be hired, City Beautiful thought had become highly popular in Vancouver and one of Britain's most successful park designers, Thomas Mawson, had announced his availability for consultation.[14] Hired by the Vancouver Park Board as an adviser, Mawson presented preliminary plans for Coal Harbour in April 1912 and more detailed suggestions for the tidal flats and parts of Stanley Park in October.

Mawson's ideas about Coal Harbour reflected much of the recent thinking in Britain about landscape architecture. Mawson was sensitive to demands for active, organized leisure in parks; he had high regard for the Gardenesque landscape style of manicured and logically organized gardens; he was fond of mixing formal and informal elements in the same design; and, influenced by America's City Beautiful movement, he advocated parks embellished with grandiose architectural features.[15] He incorporated these views into three separate plans for Coal Harbour.[16] The first, called the 'landscape plan,' would retain the natural tree-fringed waterline on the north side of a lagoon created by the proposed causeway into Stanley Park. The second plan proposed that the whole upper end of Coal Harbour be filled and made into children's playgrounds and adults' playing fields. The third plan, clearly Mawson's favourite, suggested a design in the 'Grand Manner.' Emphasizing 'ordered balance and symmetry,' it urged that the upper end of Coal Harbour be developed around a circular pond centred by a statue atop a 'great shaft.' Encircling the pond at right angles from this focal point would be three neo-classical buildings: a huge stadium on the south side; a natural history museum on the west; and a restaurant on the north at the park entrance. Stanley Park itself was not to be spared Mawson's improving touch. Seeing the peninsula as a 'wild and impenetrable jungle,' he proposed the addition of a rock garden centring on a chain of manmade pools and streams, the enlargement and relocation of the zoo, and the establishment of a botanical garden.

Though suggested again by Mawson in 1912, the notion of a Coal Harbour stadium had first been introduced in October 1911 by Frederic Heath, president of Tacoma, Washington's park board and its leading architect. He had offered to build a 45,000-seat sports and recreation amphitheatre, a concrete structure designed to imitate Rome's Colosseum and his own recently completed stadium in Tacoma. Four of Vancouver's five Park Board members journeyed to the American city at the end of October to examine Heath's work and returned enthusiastic about the stadium proposal. To serve as a centre for games, amusements, rallies, and military parades, the facility would, according to Park Commissioner A.E. Lees, 'foster civic spirit' and serve as an 'invaluable commercial and advertising asset.' Discussion of the issue languished until Mawson's plans were introduced, after which Heath and his associates resubmitted their proposal, this time calling for a 50,000-seat outdoor arena.

Showing little concern for the scheme's impact on Stanley Park, Vancouver City Council quickly endorsed the stadium concept, hoping to receive a majestic civic asset for nothing.[17] But others in the city were less enthusiastic, and for the next several months the stadium proposal fuelled an already heated debate over Mawson's recommended improvements for Vancouver's forest playground. In 1913 the controversy ended as the Mawson and stadium plans fell victim to their own impracticality, public opposition, and a severe economic depression.

Opinions about Stanley Park ranging from defence of its natural character to demands for a multi-use recreational park were advanced during the pre-war period by three Vancouver groups: an élite of business and social leaders; organized labour; and the Park Board. At one extreme were twenty-one economically and socially prominent Vancouverites who rejected Mawson's beautification plans and presented an uncompromising defence of the area's wilderness qualities. No more trees were to be cut or underbrush removed. Employing a term central to the romantic conception of nature, élite spokesmen argued that the magnificent natural cathedral was more than beautiful: it was 'sublime.'[18] The forest's charm, fascination, and almost mystical qualities resulted from the fact that its green depths were difficult to penetrate. Stanley Park did not give all to everyone but held back its most delicious pleasures for those who were willing to take pains to explore it. A tramline would destroy the peninsula's unique solitude by carrying 'thousands of people with lunch baskets and bottled beer into the park's recesses.'[19] Demands for playgrounds, golf courses, and other attractions would soon follow, turning the forest into little more than a 'commonplace city park.'[20] In addition, a tram's 'clattering noise and unsightly appearance' symbolized the mechanized, bustling world of commerce;[21] yet natural parks were intended to serve as sanctuaries against these very influences. Finally, since the park was truly beautiful 'as God made it,' adornments such as those proposed by Thomas Mawson were not required.[22] Attempts to make Stanley Park 'pretty' had to be resisted as forcefully as efforts to make it more accessible. 'For God's sake,' cried anti-development leader F.C. Wade, 'hands off Stanley Park.'[23]

Similar arguments were advanced against the proposed stadium. 'The size of the complex would require the removal of several acres of trees. The building's monumental scale and essential artificiality would clash with the lines and form of the nearby forest. Particularly intrusive would be the noise. Thousands of 'people, fans, rooters and all' would crowd into the stadium, 'chewing gum and howling with leather lungs.'[24] In the words of bank manager J.P. Roberts, peacefulness, rest, and quiet, the people's 'greatest recreation' in Stanley Park, would be lost to 'the raucous shouting of a frenzied baseball multitude rending the quiet air.'[25]

Expressing views diametrically opposed to those of the élite were organized working men, who of the three groups were the least sympathetic to Stanley Park's traditional scenic character. In keeping with their view that the park should be made as functional as possible to serve the varied recreational needs of the largest number of people, labour union spokesmen strongly endorsed the tramway scheme, approved a stadium, and supported Mawson's suggestion that the entire upper end of Coal Harbour be made into playing fields.[26] The vast majority of pedestrians entering Stanley Park were workers and their families, the Trades and Labour Council argued, but without a tramline 'all portions of the park' could not be 'made accessible to all sections of the community.'[27] Mawson's second plan, calling for Coal Harbour to become a vast playground, would help to rectify Vancouver's shortage of free athletic space. Local workingmen supported a stadium because it would facilitate spectator sports and offer a much-needed place where large meetings could be held and visiting orators heard. For trade union spokesmen, tramways, stadiums, and cleared playing grounds were acceptable additions to the forest landscape because they provided recreational facilities desired by the popular majority. Summarizing labour's attitude to parks, Trades Council secretary J.H. McVety concluded that Stanley Park 'should not be treasured as a holy retreat, but should be a practical breathing spot, and should be considered at its used value.'[28]

This view allowed little room for romantic sentiment about greenery. While working men did not argue that the peninsula be cleared of its natural cover, they were quite willing to remove trees when necessary. A transportation corridor through the forest was an essential precondition to its more democratic use. Heavy timber on the northwest side, the point farthest from the park entrances, would have to be removed if people, once transported there, were to enjoy the area. The Trades and Labour Council proposed that land between Prospect Point (at the First Narrows) and Siwash Rock in the northwest corner be cleared, the steep banks terraced, and 'an extensive promenade' added to the foreshore.[29] Artfully contrived landscape forms were particularly distasteful to workingmen. Once the novelty had worn off, argued a sawmill worker, local people would pass statuary 'without looking at it.'[30] Similarly, schemes for park beautification might attract tourists, 'but what of the men who live in this city?'[31] Vancouverites possessed so much glorious natural scenery they grew tired of it. Vancouver was already surrounded by 'water space,' concluded a local bricklayer; what it needed was more 'playing space,' not a Coal Harbour lagoon or ornamental pool.[32]

The Vancouver Board of Park Commissioners articulated a middle range of opinion. Controlled by city entrepreneurs and to a lesser extent by professional men since its inception in 1888, the Board in 1910–13 included six modestly successful members of the middle class and one leading businessman, Jonathan Rogers.[33] Recent trends in park planning strongly influenced Board members. Enthusiastic about new planning ideas advanced by the City Beautiful movement, the majority supported Mawson's grandiose third option for Coal Harbour and the proposed stadium.[34] The lack of unanimity in support for the two projects merely reflected the sometimes contradictory nature of reform ideas about playgrounds and beautification. But the Commissioners expressed no such confusion in rejecting the élite's purely romantic notion of parks: Stanley Park had to be made more usable. Commissioner A.E. Lees opposed the tramway but strongly endorsed other improvements, especially the addition of children's playgrounds. Likewise Jonathan Rogers, while standing apart from his colleagues in rejecting the stadium and Mawson proposals, defended the Board's plan to clear twenty-five acres west of Pipeline Road for a military parade ground. 'The time has come,' he said, 'when public opinion is not averse to clearing some of the park for playgrounds. The park is for the many, not for the few, and the clearing of 25 acres would only be further evidence of this.'[35] Yet, while urging a more practical park, middle-class Board members were not willing to accept the uncompromising utilitarianism of workers. Stanley Park should remain natural but might have to be modified to accommodate modern needs. The trade unionists' Coal Harbour-to-Siwash Rock railway, which the Commissioners quickly rejected, clearly went beyond the limits of this accommodation.

Electoral evidence only hints at the extent to which élite lobbyists, trade unionists, and Park Commissioners represented public opinion in Vancouver. Voting statistics outline the socio-economic contours separating voters on park questions less sharply than do literary sources the boundaries dividing leading spokesmen. But one issue, the tramway proposal, does appear to have split the community. Approximately 800 white- and blue-collar wage earners, including many clerks, skilled workers, and labourers, signed mid-1911 petitions urging the reluctant Park Board to put the tramway proposal to a plebiscite vote.[36] In the subsequent January 1912 plebiscite, for which both property owners and tenants were eligible to participate, the proposal was rejected by a difference of 782 votes (4,606 to 3,824), or nine per cent of the total ballot. Vancouver's lower middle and working class east and southeast wards marginally approved a municipally owned park tramway, but the downtown and middle-class west-side wards strongly opposed the idea. Ward 1 in the West End, home of prominent business and professional families and in 1909 residence of three-quarters of all leading Vancouver businessmen, voted massively against the park railway, thus ensuring the plebiscite's defeat.[37] At least on the issue of park transportation, the upper levels of society, committed to preserving Stanley Park's natural beauty, appear to have held markedly different views from lower levels urging functional use of the forest playground.

Park entrance development plans generated a different cleavage, separating the vast majority of electors from supporters of the élite dedicated to forest preservation. In the hotly contested Park Board election of January 1913, which centred on the Mawson and stadium proposals, voters endorsed the Board's plans to add more features to the park and to make it more practical. The two victorious candidates advocated more functional use of Vancouver's major park, and one of them, W.R. Owen, favoured turning Coal Harbour into a large playground that would include a stadium. Owen swept six of eight wards, including the city's east side. By contrast, two candidates who opposed all development in Stanley Park were soundly defeated. The City Beautiful Association's anti-development candidate received the largest plurality in Ward 1 but fared badly in all other wards.[38] In summary, electoral evidence supports the contention that opinion about Stanley Park development ranged from demands for forest preservation by a privileged minority within the middle class to pleas for more utilitarian play space by a vocal minority within society's less favoured strata. The Park Board represented the centre ground of majority opinion, combining defence of natural park principles with a need to modernize. Clearly, support for this view crossed class lines. The exact contours of each constituency, and especially the views of ethnic minorities and unskilled wage labourers, remain unspecified.

The opinions expressed during Vancouver's Stanley Park debate are to be explained by a variety of influences both external and local. The former locate Stanley Park's history within the mainstream of park experience in Canada, Britain, and the United States and make Vancouver's discussion a valuable indicator of the general drift of thinking about recreational space in Canada as a whole. But the peculiarities of local place also mediated this general pattern, determining the timing of discussion and the intensity of commitment by Vancouverites to preserve Stanley Park from excessive development. Ultimately, whether originating from inside or outside the community, attitudes about Stanley Park were rooted in the divergent social conditions and cultural backgrounds of the three contending groups: middle-class Park Board, anti-development élite, and labour.

From the formation of Vancouver's Park Board in September 1888 until new parks were added to the system starting in 1902, one principle premised all other Board policies: parks should be left 'in a state of nature.'[39] This policy stemmed primarily from imported ideas about public parks. Whether in the form of hunting estates or formal gardens, parks traditionally had been the private preserves of the aristocracy. But increasingly, middle-class reformers demanded that green space be set aside for public use to alleviate urban congestion. Preceded by rural cemeteries,[40] the public parks movement was given full expression at mid-century with construction of London's Victoria Park (1845), Liverpool's Birkenhead Park (1847), and New York's Central Park (1858).[41] They were conceived as unified works of art,[42] with natural vegetation and landscape forms, artfully controlled by man, their central features. The eighteenth-century English landscape tradition underlay their assumptions about the control of nature. Drawing on an essentially romantic view of nature, which rejected the firm ordering of the Renaissance garden into precisely defined geometric forms, the English landscape tradition featured the unsymmetrical scattering of vegetation, the clustering of trees and shrubs, and the creation of serpentine lakes with unkempt and irregular shorelines. Though modified after mid-century by the 'Gardenesque' tradition of displaying trees and other plants individually, by the introduction of flowers, and later by renewed interest in more axial and geometric design elements, romantic assumptions remained the guiding principles of naturalistic parks. Such parks would serve as 'breathing spaces where citizens might stroll, drive or sit to enjoy the open air'[43] and beautiful scenery. Natural parks were to be used principally for passive rather than active recreation.

Local conditions reinforced external influences in determining the Vancouver board's policy to maintain Stanley Park's natural state. First was the fact that as a wilderness area retaining much of its original forest cover, Stanley Park did not have to be created; it merely required some modification to improve access. This was especially important given that the city, having only 13,000 inhabitants in 1891 and being surrounded by forest, experienced no immediate need for recreational green space. During Vancouver's early years, then, inertia as much as deliberate design served to preserve the peninsula's wilderness character.

Stanley Park's economic function had a similar effect. The inspiration to create Stanley Park was primarily economic. Leadership in organizing the May 1886 petition to Ottawa, asking it to set aside the Burrard Inlet military reserve as a park, came from three businessmen actively involved in promoting local land sales. Two of them, Canadian Pacific Railway Land Commissioner L.A. Hamilton and Mayor David Oppenheimer, were among the early city's most powerful entrepreneurs.[44] Park promoters were clearly enthusiastic about the forest reserve's possible contribution to civic boosterism, claiming that as 'an attraction for tourists and visitors to the city,' it had 'what might be termed a commercial value . . .'[45] The growing recognition of Stanley Park as a Vancouver symbol merely enhanced its tourist potential in the new century and reaffirmed the need to preserve its natural qualities. This was so even after the Board had accepted the need for manicured gardens, utilitarian athletic fields, and children's playgrounds elsewhere in the city.

The geographic proximity of Vancouver's most prominent middle-class neighbourhood to Stanley Park served to solidify the Park Board's traditional view of how the forest should be managed. In the city's first decade of growth prominent business and professional families, led by CPR managers, built homes along the bluff overlooking Coal Harbour and Stanley Park, and after 1900 they spread throughout the west end. The residents' desire to protect their neighbourhood from excessive noise or pollution led them to oppose industrialization of the waterfront near Stanley Park or commercialization of the park itself. Thus, in the mid-1890s leading businessmen spoke out strongly against a marine railway scheme for Deadman's Island, located near Stanley Park's shoreline in Coal Harbour. Said Board of Trade president H.O. Bell-Irving, eastside sites 'in the vicinity of shipping, the iron works[,] the mills and employers' dwellings, would seem more fitted' for the purpose of locating noisy repair facilities than would land near the westside 'residential portion of the City.'[46] Furthermore, a marine railway would depreciate west end property by 'many thousands of dollars.'[47] Concern by Vancouver's more prosperous elements to preserve the quality of residential life offered by a west end location thus encouraged their support for a Stanley Park that was quiet and natural. Smoking industries, commercial recreational attractions, and noisy sports stadiums were incompatible with this goal.

As a consequence of these various inducements to leave Stanley Park in its natural state, the forest was altered little in the pre-World War I period. In 1913 the Board could proudly claim that since 1888 only 48 of 960 acres had either been cleared or underbrushed.'[48] It had also severely limited commercial activity, closely regulating the sale of refreshments and thwarting proposals for a merry-go-round, a miniature railway, motion pictures, and an electric tramway. The Board had allowed some alterations that seemed to contradict romantic park principles: space for animal 'attractions,' including a buffalo paddock, an elk grounds, a deer run, and a zoo; a children's play area; picnic grounds; and a sports field for active athletic games. But large parks in other cities were also being modified, especially along their outer margins, in the face of growing demands for more entertainment features and more practical recreational space.[49] In this sense, Stanley Park's slight deviation from romantic principles was entirely compatible with trends elsewhere and was probably affected by them.

By 1910, new influences originating both outside and inside the city were bringing into question the principles of nineteenth-century parks, forcing the Vancouver Board to re-evaluate its previous reluctance to alter Stanley Park. Foremost among the external sources of change was the playground movement. Begun in the 1880s in Boston, the movement had soon expanded in the United States into a widespread demand for children's play space. Interest then spread to Canada.[50] One of a number of late nineteenth-century reform movements centring on children, it reflected middle-class concern about the social impact of urbanization. The playground movement was founded on the conviction that properly directed play was essential for the best moral and physical development of youngsters.[51] While it stemmed in part from the desire to protect children from physical danger in the streets, more important was the reformers' underlying desire to prevent future disorder by reinforcing traditional values.

Playgrounds became linked in the public imagination with parks. In her history of urban parks in America, Galen Cranz argues that the characteristic urban park of the nineteenth century was displaced by something quite different, the 'reform park,' in the first third of the twentieth.[52] Strongly influenced by the social control assumptions of the playground movement, the new reform parks were small rather than large, flat and ordered rather than undulating and irregular, and designed for active rather than passive recreation. The new park was intended for specific groups, especially young children but also working-class adults, rather than for whole families. Through supervised instruction parks were to reform human character. As August Heckscher has noted, the twentieth-century parks philosophy emphasized 'the raising of men and women rather than grass or trees.'[53]

Even though the impulse for reform stemming from local conditions was much weaker in Vancouver than in the older and larger cities of eastern North America, by 1910 reform ideas had permeated the thinking of middle-class Vancouverites. Between 1906 and 1912 the School Board set up four unsupervised playgrounds and the Park Board created Vancouver's first fully equipped children's recreation area, at McLean Park in the east-central part of the city.[54] The reform-minded Vancouver Council of Women, concerned that 'boys and girls were falling victims to the lure of the streets,' advanced as a solution the 'wholesome moral effect' on youths of gardens and scenery.[55] At the same time an Assistant Physical Director of the YMCA urged that supervised children's playgrounds be employed to decrease 'petty crimes.'[56] The 'Y' and several churches sponsored numerous sports teams both for children and adults.[57] Pre-war support by Park Commissioners Owen and Rogers for additional open space and more children's playgrounds in Stanley Park merely demonstrated this increasingly reformist view of parks and recreation within Vancouver's middle class.

The City Beautiful movement, popular in the early twentieth century throughout North America and, to a lesser extent, in Britain, also influenced middle-class thinking about public green space. Dating from the Chicago World's Fair of 1893, it spread to Canada, peaking there between 1910 and 1913. While conceptually ill defined, City Beautiful focused on the need to improve cities' aesthetic qualities. Improvement would result from the removal of visually disruptive elements such as billboards and smoke, the introduction of gardens and greenery, and the addition of monumental architectural features. Grand buildings designed in the neo-classical style would enhance civic pride and add visual variety. Emphasizing the 'improvement' and 'adornment' of public green space, City Beautiful thought affected popular perceptions of recreation grounds by challenging the conceptual integrity and naturalness of romantic parks.[58]

Scholars have interpreted City Beautiful supporters variously as unselfish and public-spirited philanthropists, boosters concerned mainly with economic growth, and reformers intent on restoring to society social cohesion and the dominance of middle-class values.[59] The two strands of Vancouver's City Beautiful movement exhibited both booster and reform motives. The commercial thrust for beautification was advanced for more than a decade by the Vancouver Tourist Association, formed in 1902 to represent the booster interests of middle-level businessmen in advertising, real estate, and tourist-related enterprises. The Vancouver Beautification Association, formed in 1912 primarily upon the initiative of the reform-minded Council of Women, drew more support from social and economic leaders than did the Tourist Association and was motivated more by the plight of urban children.[60] The City Beautiful features of Thomas Mawson's Coal Harbour plans evoked an enthusiastic response from most Park Board members and many middle-class Vancouverites but sharp opposition from élite defenders of the wilderness forest.

A decade of rapid economic growth in Vancouver added local pressure to these external stimuli for park alterations. Between 1901 and 1911 Vancouver's population jumped from 27,000 to 121,000, reaching a level almost four times that of its nearest rival, Victoria.'[61] The Burrard Inlet community now served as the regional transportation entrepôt, the provincial headquarters for resource companies and banks, the centre of active speculation in hinterland resources and urban land, and the home of major British Columbia commercial houses.[62]

Clerical workers and professionals swelled the middle class as Vancouver consolidated its metropolitan status. Augmented by immigration, the city's blue-collar labour force grew swiftly as well. British-born newcomers were especially prominent, advancing from sixteen to thirty-four per cent of the total population and reinforcing the city's already sharply defined Anglo-Saxon character.[63] Newly arrived clerks, labourers, businessmen, and professionals joined long-settled inhabitants in pushing back residential boundaries well beyond the limits of the old central core. By 1910 Vancouver was a more economically advanced and more spatially dispersed community than it had been a decade earlier.

Starting in 1902 the Vancouver Park Board responded to increased demand for parks by successfully presenting to city ratepayers a number of by-laws for the purchase and improvement of local green space. The first to be acquired was the Cambie Street sports field in Vancouver's centre. Since 1886 the city had rented the poorly prepared but functional grounds from the CPR for $5 per year, thus providing the only park open to use by all citizens for games, circuses, carnivals, and military parades. Other small parks purchased throughout the city were urged by neighbourhood landholding groups and citizens for both booster and recreational purposes. Designed as decorative gardens, utilitarian games fields, and in one case a structured children's playground, they too reflected current eclectic notions about parks and provided a sharp contrast to the conceptual unity and romantic principles of Vancouver's forest playground.[64]

In pre-war Vancouver, however, no recreational attraction could match the latter's appeal. Construction of a streetcar line to Stanley Park's Coal Harbour entrance in 1897 had provided inexpensive access to almost all citizens,[65] making possible the increased attendance that accompanied rapid city growth. During the summer months from 1905 to 1911 both larger numbers and a growing percentage of Vancouverites came to Stanley Park (Table 19.1), where they engaged in such essentially passive recreational activities as sitting, strolling, bathing, picnicking, or watching sports matches at the one centre of competitive activity, the Brockton

Table 19.1 Stanley Park Census of Users[(a)] for a One-Week Period in July[(b)] 1905, 1907, 1909, 1911

Year	People[(c)]	Autos	Hacks	Buggies	Saddle	Bicycles	Total City Population[(d)]	Stanley Park Users as % of Population
1905	14,664	38	155	711	81	821	45,000	32.6
1907	23,251	227	160	715	136	609	60,000	38.8
1909	32,840	383	291	1,144	387	625	78,900	41.6
1911	53,255	1,114	295	1,171	459	660	111,240	47.9

(a) In 1905 only those arriving at the two main entrances were surveyed; by 1911 all entrances were manned for the census.

(b) The census was taken in 1905 from 23–9 July; 1907, 22–8 July; 1909, 26 July–1 Aug.; and 1911, 10–16 July.

(c) The word 'pedestrians' was used in 1905, 1907, and 1911, but 'people' in 1909. By 1913 the census was referring to 'No. of Persons Entering the Park.' I have assumed that in each census the words 'pedestrians' and 'people' refer to all who walked or rode into Stanley Park.

(d) These figures are drawn from Vancouver's 'Annual Report,' which provides yearly population statistics. The 1911 total of 111,240 is 10,000 higher than the Canadian census count for Vancouver only but 10,000 lower than the number for Vancouver plus its two principal suburbs, South Vancouver and Point Grey.

Source: Vancouver City Archives (VCA), 48-A-2, Vancouver Parks Board (VPBP), Vol. II. Minute Book, 1907; VCA 48-A-3, VPBP, Vol. III, Minute Book, 11 Aug. 1909 and 26 July 1911; and Vancouver, BC [Comptroller], *Financial Statements and Annual Reports* (Vancouver, BC), 'Annual Report, 1913,' 68–9.

Point grounds. Maintaining that Stanley Park's popularity transcended class boundaries, socialist R. Parm Pettipiece described it as 'the one spot in the city' where Vancouverites could 'enjoy life irrespective of social standing.'[66] By 1912 citizens complained that 'it was a hard proposition to get to Stanley Park on a streetcar, owing to the crowd.'[67] Sundays were especially busy, the one day when the 'plain every-day people'[68] from Vancouver's east side could find time in their work-filled schedules for family recreation.

Confronted by an evolving parks philosophy and local pressures to make Stanley Park more practical, the Vancouver Park Board in 1910–13 adopted a middle course for developing the peninsula. Unlike east side Vancouver's once-scenic Hastings Park, which after 1910 became a commercial exhibition, amusement, and sports centre,[69] the forested Stanley Park was too fixed in the public imagination and too important to the local tourist economy to be altered fundamentally into a utilitarian, multi-purpose recreational centre. Yet the Board had also come to accept the view that to make or maintain beautiful parks was no longer sufficient. Consequently, after gaining broad support for its new policies in the 1913 election, the Board added tennis courts, putting and bowling greens, children's play apparatus, and other play facilities.[70] Commercial enterprises, whether amusement spectacles or electric tramways, remained forbidden. The product of these alterations was a compromise consistent with middle-class attitudes: by the 1920s a modified Stanley Park combined 'within itself something of the majesty and magic of the primaeval forest' as well as modern recreative advantages.[71]

The Park Board's middle course did not go unchallenged. Just as élite groups in Montreal, Boston, and New York had been formed to protect the conceptual integrity of nineteenth-century romantic parks,[72] so too in Vancouver an élite emerged to defend Stanley Park against beautification and modernization. Urging that the peninsula's wilderness landscape be left untouched by man, it harkened back to romantic principles more idealistic than those that had guided designers of the great nineteenth-century landscaped parks. Why, then, the emergence of a small élite vigorously protecting Stanley Park's natural features almost a quarter century after the park's formation?

The élite's most obvious characteristic was its advantaged economic and social status.[73] The twenty-one who most openly supported leaving Stanley Park alone were a privileged group, numbering among them four bankers, a dentist, a physician, an architect, two engineers, and two other university graduates. Members included two of Vancouver's first CPR officials, engineer H.J. Cambie and treasurer W.F. Salsbury; Vancouver's leading intellectual figure of the period, newspaperman Francis Carter-Cotton; the city's most active supporter of amateur sports, banker Campbell Sweeny; and the head of Vancouver's most prominent society family after 1898, Sir Charles Hibbert Tupper. They were led by F.C. Wade, a university-educated lawyer and writer 'well-read in legal lore, history, and the English classics.'[74] Serving as president of the *Vancouver Sun*,[75] a daily newspaper that during the debate articulated élite opinion about Stanley Park, Wade was an intellectual fully conversant with a wide range of public issues. Superior education and extensive travelling undoubtedly had familiarized the group with the romantic tradition in art and literature and sharpened its emotional attachment to the peninsula's natural forest.

But the existence in Vancouver of a minority educated to appreciate nature was not new to the period before World War I. Even some of Vancouver's pioneer businessmen had viewed the recreation spot as more than a source of profit. Board of Trade president H.O. Bell-Irving, born in Scotland, educated in Germany, and himself a landscape painter, had specifically identified Stanley Park's 'picturesque' features as valuable when arguing in 1896 against the industrial development of nearby Coal Harbour.[76] Similarly, upon arrival in Vancouver in 1884 L.A. Hamilton, CPR Land Commissioner and Stanley Park promoter, had begun to paint scenes of Stanley Park and the surrounding area, hoping to preserve the image for posterity.[77] In addition, his designs for the first footbridges in Stanley Park were clearly intended to be 'picturesque.'[78]

Consequently, the late development of a cultural rationale for Stanley Park must be explained by another factor, the park's history. The circumstances of Stanley Park's formation in the 1880s had not required a full articulation of park principles. The forest already existed, and the original promoters were committed to maintaining it for practical economic reasons. If some early supporters had been moved by an idealism that transcended economic pragmatism, the city's laissez-faire attitude to the recreation spot had not required that they publicly defend the park's wilderness features. Such was not the case by 1910. The élite's emergence as an outspoken public lobby coincided with the confluence of forces that for the first time brought into question Stanley Park's fundamental character. By then, the élite was well entrenched within Vancouver society. More than sixty per cent had arrived within five years of the city's incorporation and over eighty per cent within fifteen. As Vancouver's founders they were committed to retaining Stanley Park as they had known it, and as educated men of the nineteenth century they embraced an earlier, elitist parks philosophy than that emerging in the twentieth.

Less easily assessed is the influence on this timing of North America's wilderness movement. Originating in the United States with a small group of 'Romantic and patriotic literati,' wilderness appreciation had by the early twentieth century grown into a national cult in the United States and a substantial movement in Canada.[79] Inspired by the enthusiasm of romantic painters and writers for things strange and remote and by the transcendentalism of Thoreau and Emerson, the wilderness ethic rejected the artificiality and materialism of modern society. Wilderness parks, camping, canoeing, mountain climbing, and boy scouts were the movement's characteristic manifestations, but under its influence some urban park designers and supporters also expressed an increasing appreciation for the natural features of city parks.[80] The extent to which Vancouver's anti-development élite had embraced the wilderness ethic is unclear, but the influential F.C. Wade, who constantly referred to recent work by American silviculture experts, must have been aware of it.[81]

High socio-economic status and age, both important in explaining the élite's reaction to Coal Harbour beautification, also account for its passionate opposition to the proposed park entrance stadium. Initially sports teams in Vancouver had belonged to the Brockton Point Athletic Association,[82] a distinctly middle-class organization formed in 1888 with the support of virtually every prominent businessman in early Vancouver. Reflecting the class bias of Park Board policy, the Association had been allowed to clear and manage a ten-acre Brockton Point site at the eastern end of Stanley Park for use by athletic teams. The Association was to have 'absolute control' of the grounds, and any sporting club using the facilities had to become a fee-paying member. The lease arrangement and the Association's underlying sports philosophy discriminated against the less well organized and less wealthy lower classes.

Professionalism especially was anathema to the Brockton Point Athletic Association, whose sports philosophy stemmed from the upper-middle-class British ideal of amateurism. According to this view, sports was a social, not a competitive, pastime. What mattered was the way the game was played, not its outcome. Embracing an idea central to the British public school ethos, amateur sports enthusiasts believed that lessons learned on the playing field would guide one through life. Manly sports could teach one self-control, honesty, compassion, personal courage tempered by a willingness to put 'the common cause before selfish interests,' and respect for discipline and authority.[83]

Elite opponents of a Coal Harbour stadium embraced this class-based view of sport. Yet, the increasing democratization of organized sporting activity and the spread of professionalism challenged the middle-class ethic of 'good, clean, amateur sports,' in Vancouver as elsewhere in Canada.[84] The separation of work from leisure and the increased availability of leisure time had resulted in a blossoming of teams playing organized games. Whereas in the 1880s Vancouver sportsmen had been mainly businessmen, professionals, and clerks, by 1905 blue collar workers were also well represented on sports teams.[85] Organizations sponsoring teams ranged from solidly middle-class corporations, churches, and the YMCA to the more popular fraternal societies, trade unions, and neighbourhood groups.[86] Professional sports, including baseball in 1905, lacrosse in 1909, and hockey in 1912, also arrived in Vancouver during the pre-war decade. By contrast, the Brockton Point Athletic Association, crippled by public indifference to its financial plight and handicapped by aging leadership, was forced to relinquish control of the Brockton Point grounds in 1913, seventeen years before the termination of its lease.[87] Thus, élite opposition to a stadium that could host professional sports must be seen as more than a neighbourhood's defence of its peace and serenity; it also represented the reaction of a group whose cherished values and ideals were then increasingly under popular attack.

Sharply at odds with élite arguments were those of trade unionists. Demanding that Stanley Park be valued for its utility rather than its beauty, labour spokesmen laid bare the class bias of the élite's idealism and the Park Board's mixture of tradition, boosterism, and reform. As with the other two groups, the arguments of workingmen emerged from the past as well as the present, and from the outside world as well as the local community.

Roy Rosenzweig has argued that the 'most fundamental constraint on working class recreation . . . was work itself.'[88] The statement applies to both recreational time and space and points to one of the principal determinants of working class attitudes to parks: economic condition. Long hours of work and limited financial resources necessitated space that was local and accessible.[89] Starting in the 1890s, Vancouver workingmen urged that neighbourhood parks be established throughout the city. But the local parks created in Vancouver from 1902 often did not satisfy workers' demands for neighbourhood grounds with flat, playable surfaces. Ratepayers who viewed parks as economic assets opposed turning new open spaces into sports grounds, arguing that beauty spots laid out as flower gardens would enhance the value of nearby property, while social reformers intent on transforming neighbourhood parks into children's playgrounds coveted scarce space otherwise available for adult athletic fields.[90] When caught between groups advocating fundamentally different types of urban recreation areas, the middle-class Park Board usually resolved the issue in a manner contrary to working-class demands. Faced with the ongoing shortage of play space throughout the city, the Trades and Labour Council looked to Stanley Park, in 1910 still accessible by streetcar from most city locations, as a resource capable of satisfying workers' expanding athletic needs.

A bitter political conflict in Vancouver's early history exposed the essential utilitarianism of popular environmental attitudes and pointed to labour's later rejection of Thomas Mawson's grandiose plans for Coal Harbour beautification. The issue erupted in 1899 when the federal government leased the seven-acre Deadman's Island, then thought by many to be part of Stanley Park, to industrialist Theodore Ludgate for a sawmill.[91] The dispute divided leading entrepreneurs from small businessmen and labourers and separated the middle-class west side of town from the lower-middle and working-class east.[92] Westside residents saw the lease as a theft of Vancouver's legal right to control and tax the island. In addition, many businessmen and professionals feared the effect of a mill on 'one of the prettiest spots on the Inlet.'[93] Working people still suffering from the effects of a long economic depression wanted 'work, not scenery.'[94] In the words of the Reverend George Maxwell, eastside spokesman and federal MP, 'Vancouver had enough scenery and too few industries and manufactures.'[95]

Economic circumstance within the local community did not alone condition popular attitudes to parks and recreation. Vancouver's English-speaking immigrant workers shared with other workers of the era a cultural heritage of leisure. Emerging out of the pre-industrial past, this pattern of attitudes and practices had been shaped and altered by nineteenth-century industrial experience. Hugh Cunningham argues that the basic elements of popular culture in mid-nineteenth-century Britain were drink, spontaneity, emotional involvement, and physical contact. In contrast, the middle class preferred ordered, disciplined, improving educational leisure that was rational.[96] J.B. Jackson notes a similar distinction between upper- and lower-class definitions of parks in the nineteenth-century United States: the former emphasized 'cultural enlightenment and greater refinement of manners,' the latter 'fun and games.'[97] Elsewhere, Robert Snow and David Wright examine the success of another important manifestation of popular culture, turn-of-the-century amusement parks. They find that the 'extroverted, fast-paced, time-structured, sensuous and sensual experience' produced by Coney Island's 'mechanized leisure' appealed most to the 'working classes.'[98] Missing from popular culture was the middle-class's educated appreciation of environment and its reticence about commercialized leisure. By contrast, to fulfil their quest for entertainment and escape within severely limited periods of leisure time, working people easily accepted commercial pubs, music halls, amusement parks, and professional sports.

With the emergence of mass culture in the late nineteenth and early twentieth centuries, the sharp cultural distinctions of the mid-nineteenth century were breaking down.[99] Yet, echoes of a once distinctive popular culture of leisure could still be heard in pre-war Vancouver. The Cambie Street grounds had always been truly a 'people's park,' catering to 'celebrations, ceremonies, carnivals, circuses,' and games for common folk.[100] And the Vancouver Exhibition at Hastings Park provided a midway of commercial entertainment that quickly gained popular acceptance, along with scorn from some respectable observers. One can speculate that labour's enthusiasm for a stadium and sports grounds at Coal Harbour also emerged from the rich cultural past of Vancouver workers.

Another part of the workingman's heritage, the radical secular tradition of British skilled workers, influenced Vancouver labour spokesmen in a more explicit way. Emphasizing the values of collectivism, self-help, respectability, and egalitarianism, labour radicalism had flourished in early Victorian Britain but remained an enduring part of artisanal culture.[101] Its influence persisted in the consciousness of Vancouver's skilled workers, the vast majority of whom were British in origin. The egalitarian principle in particular determined their view that recreational facilities be plentiful, free, and easily accessible to the majority. Two examples illustrate the point. Starting in 1891 the Trades-and Labour Council, comprised mainly of skilled workers, demanded that English Bay (or First Beach), at the Beach Street entrance to Stanley Park, be improved and maintained as a public facility. Labour argued that private swimming clubs should not be allowed to monopolize the beach; the people, not private interests, should own all such 'public rights.' In 1898, responding to Trades and Labour Council pressure, City Council initiated the public reclamation of English Bay.[102] Basing its views on the same egalitarian principle, labour also persisted in criticizing the Brockton Point Athletic Association's monopoly of Stanley Park's only sports grounds, at Brockton Point. The fees charged by this exclusive organization, they asserted, made the grounds unavailable to the masses.[103]

Labour's demand that a tramway be built into Stanley Park was founded on the same principle. Vancouver's social classes may have mingled at the park gates, but they did not share equal access to the entire forest interior. During a one-week period in July 1911, no more than 6,752 park users had reached the peninsula's northwest corner between Prospect Point and Siwash Rock. Of this group 5,321 were conveyed in various kinds of vehicles while only 1,431 walked.[104] Yet the vast majority attracted to the pleasure ground (at least 47,000 of the 53,255 total) had entered on foot (see Table 19.1). Varying levels of family economic resources, aided by the Park Board's biased policy of allowing privately owned automobiles and horse-drawn vehicles into Stanley Park but not inexpensive public transportation, had produced sharply different park-use patterns. The class wealthy enough either to maintain or hire suitable vehicles enjoyed access to the park's farthest reaches. By contrast, white- and blue-collar workers arriving by tram with families and picnic baskets in hand seldom ventured far beyond the points of entry. Severe congestion at the entrances resulted. On a Sunday afternoon, the Trades and Labour Council complained, the Coal Harbour side of the Park presented 'the appearance of an open air mass meeting, with large numbers of people walking around unable to find seats, even on the grass, owing to the density.'[105] The resolution of this park congestion problem would have to await wider social distribution of automobile ownership in the following decades.

The issue of access underlines for historians the importance of recognizing that working people held their own views of how recreational space should be managed. At one level Vancouver's forest playground before 1913 served as a social unifier, drawing disparate groups into a single leisure-time community. Stanley Park attracted large numbers of citizens from all levels of society. But as the pre-war controversy reveals, beneath the surface consensus lay a persistent pattern of class differences. The park had been created according to mid-Victorian middle-class aesthetic and recreational values. A small group, distinguished by its high status and long association with Stanley Park, continued to maintain a rigid commitment to romantic park principles. But for the middle class as a whole, the spreading ethos of athleticism and reform had brought into question the essentially passive and contemplative purposes of traditional parks, producing instead a more eclectic notion of city recreational space. By 1913 its view of Stanley Park had come to combine both modern and traditional assumptions. By contrast, workingmen's attitudes, at least as revealed by trade union spokesmen, remained relatively constant throughout Vancouver's early history. Fundamentally different from that of the middle class and the élite, the parks and recreational philosophy advanced by working men was devoid of the former's commercialism and interest in reform and the latter's romantic sentimentalism. Reflecting their limited material resources, circumscribed leisure time, and distinctive cultural heritage, wage-earners argued for parks that were free, readily accessible, and suitable for active play. The Stanley Park controversy illustrates graphically the importance of understanding the function of class in shaping perceptions of, and social competition for, recreational space in early twentieth-century Canada.

NOTES

1. For the early history of Stanley Park see William C. McKee, 'The History of the Vancouver Park System 1886–1929' (MA thesis, University of Victoria 1976), chap. 4

2. Vancouver Board of Park Commissioners, *First Annual Report* (Vancouver 1911), 53.

3. A.L. Murray, 'Frederic Law Olmsted and the Design of Mount Royal Park,' *Journal of the Society of Architectural Historians,* XXVI (1967), 163–71; Elsie M. McFarland, *The Development of Public Recreation in Canada* (Vanier, Ont. 1970); Mary Ellen Cavet, H. John Selwood, and John C. Lehr, 'Social Philosophy and the Early Development of Winnipeg's Parks,' *Urban History Review,* IX (June 1982), 27–39; McKee, MA thesis and 'The Vancouver Park System, 1886–1929: A Product of Local Businessmen,' *Urban History Review,* 3–78, 33–49. Also see Diane Beverly Hinds, 'The Evolution of Urban Public Design in Europe and America: Vancouver Adaptation to 1913' (MA thesis, University of British Columbia 1979).

4. George F. Chadwick, *The Park and the Town: Public Landscape in the 19th and 20th Centuries* (London 1966); G.B. Tobey, *A History of Landscape Architecture. The Relationship of People to Environment* (New York 1973); and Laura Wood Roper, *FLO: A Biography of Frederick Law Olmsted* (Baltimore 1973).

5. In *The Politics of Park Design: A History of Urban Parks in America* (Cambridge, MA 1982), Galen Cranz goes beyond the two themes emphasized here to examine the relationship between design, origins, and management.

6. Geoffrey Blodgett, 'Frederick Law Olmsted: Landscape Architect as Conservative Reformer,' *Journal of American History,* LXII (1975–6), 869–89; Michael P. McCarthy, 'Politics and Parks: Chicago Businessmen and the State Recreation Movement,' *Journal of the Illinois State Historical Society,* LXV (1972), 158–72; and Cranz, *Urban Parks in America,* chap. 2

7. Peter Bailey, *Leisure and Class in Victorian England: Rational Recreation and the Contest for Control, 1830–1885* (London 1978) and Hugh Cunningham, *Leisure in the Industrial Revolution c. 1780–c. 1880* (London 1980)

8. Stephen Hardy, "'Parks for the People": Reforming the Boston Park System, 1870–1915,' *Journal of Sport History*, VII (1980), 5–24 and Roy Rosenzweig, 'Middle-Class Parks and Working-Class Play: The Struggle over Recreational Space in Worcester, Massachusetts, 1870–1910,' *Radical History Review*, XXI (Fall 1979), 31–46

9. An exception is Alan Metcalfe's 'The Evolution of Organized Physical Recreation in Montreal, 1840-1895,' *Histoire Sociale/Social History*, XI (May 1978), 144–66, which, while discussing only briefly the development of parks, does emphasize the socially divisive nature of sport and the social competition for recreational space in nineteenth-century Montreal.

10. Cunningham, *Leisure*, 38

11. Vancouver City Archives (VCA), 48-A-1, Vancouver Park Board Papers (VPBP), vol. 11. Minute Book, 11 July and 12 Dec. 1906; *Vancouver Daily News-Advertiser (N-A)*, 13 Dec. 1906 and to Jan. 1907; VCA, MCR-4, Vancouver City Clerk's Dept, *Nominations and Elections*, 1 (1886–1924), 1907 Election Returns, 211

12. VCA, 48-c-3, file 1, 'Description of Proposed Foreshore Railway, Stanley Park, Vancouver, B.C.' [Aug. 1910] and G.J. Ashworth to Board of Park Commissioners, 27 Sept. 1910, 4 May 1911, and 10 June 1911

13. VCA, MCR-4, Vancouver City Clerk's Dept, *Nominations and Elections*, 1 (1886–1924), 1912 Election Returns, 294

14. *Ibid.*, 1908 Election Returns, 215; N-A, 21 Oct. 1909; VCA, Add. Mss. 54, Major Matthews Collection, Stanley Park Correspondence, 'Proposed Plan for the Improvement of Coal Harbour . . . suggested by Jonathan Rogers and Geo. H. Webster, C.E.,' 8 Sept. 1909; VCA, 48-A-3, VPBP, vol. VIII, Minute Book, 9 Nov. 1910; and VCA, 48-E-1, VPBP, file 10, R.A. Pope to Mayor of Vancouver, 4 Oct. 1911

15. Chadwick, *The Park and the Town*, 221–5

16. VCA, 48-E-1, VPBP, file 7, Thomas H. Mawson to Chairman and Members, Vancouver Board of Park Commissioners, 17 Apr. and 20 June 1912 and file to, *ibid.*, 16 Oct. 1912. Mawson's October submission actually presented four improvement proposals, with the fourth slightly modifying the third. I have classified both of these latter two plans as his 'third' proposal.

17. VCA, 51-B-5, VPBP (hereafter cited as PB), *Vancouver World*, 27, 28, and 31 Oct. 1911; *Vancouver Province*, 3 and 17 Dec. 1912; PB, N-A, 12 Dec. 1912; and VCA, 48-E-1, VPBP, file 11, Wm McQueen to W.S. Rawlings, 17 Dec. 1912

18. *Province*, 17 Dec. 1912, 3

19. PB, *Saturday Sunset*, 13 Jan. 1912

20. *Loc. cit.*

21. VCA, 48-c-3, VPBP, file 1, J.W. Campion to Jonathan Rogers, 22 Aug. 1911

22. PB, *Province*, 10 Jan. 1912 and PB, *World*, 7 Jan. 1913

23. PB, *Sun*, 17 Dec. 1912

24. *Ibid.*, 18 Dec. 1912

25. PB, *Sun*, 4 Jan. 1913

26. PB, *Province, Sun*, and *N-A*, 15 Oct. 1912; *Province*, 3 Dec. 1912; VCA, 48-c-3, VPBP, file 1, J.W. Wilkinson and Jas. H. McVety to Sec., Vancouver Board of Park Commissioners, 16 Aug. 1911; and VCA, 48-E-1, VPBP, file 8, VTLC to Board of Park Commissioners, 6 June 1912

27. VCA, 48-e-3, VPBP, file 1, J.W. Wilkinson and Jas. H. McVety to Sec., Vancouver Board of Park Commissioners, 16 Aug.1911

28. N-A, 17 Aug. 1911

29. PB, *World*, 17 Aug. 1911

30. PB *Sun*, 15 Oct. 1912

31. PB, *Province*, 15 Oct. 1912

32. *Loc. cit.*

33. Park Commissioners' occupations are listed in McKee, NIA thesis, Appendix 2, 146-9. For Rogers' status, see R.A.J. McDonald, 'Business Leaders in Early Vancouver, 1886–1914' (PH.D. thesis, University of British Columbia 1977), 151, 496

34. PB, *Province*, 31 January 1912 and N-A, 24 Oct. and 12 Dec. 1912. For discussion over whether to make Coal Harbour a lagoon or playground see N-A, 19 Oct. 1911.

35. PB, *Province*, 21 Mar, 1912 and 7 Jan. 1913

36. VCA, 48-c-3, VPBP, file 1, Petitions to the Board of Park Commissioners, n.d.

37. See note 12 above and N-A, 21 Dec. 1911. Some prominent middle-class Vancouverites did support the tramway, however. See VCA, 48-c-3, VPBP, file 1, Petition to the Board of Park Commissioners, 15 Oct. 1911

38. PB, *Province*, 7 Jan. 1913 and PB, *Sun*, 7 and 10 Jan. 1913

39. N-A, 16 Nov. 1897

40. David R. Goldfield and Blaine A. Brownell, *Urban America: From Downtown to No Town* (Boston 1979), 185–6

41. For the origins of the park movement in Britain and the United States, see Chadwick, *The Park and the Town*, 50; August Heckscher, *Open Spaces: The Life of American Cities* (New York 1977), chap. 7; and McFarland, *Public Recreation*, 8. Some open spaces in Canada had been set aside before Confederation, including the Halifax Common (1763), squares in Montreal (1821) and Hamilton (1862), and the Garrison Reserve in Toronto (1848). One of the first public parks was laid out in Kingston, Ontario, in the 1850s (suggested by J.R. Wright in a presentation to the Guelph Urban History Conference, Aug. 1982). The public parks movements in both Canada and the United States, while beginning earlier, gained widespread acceptance in the latter part of the century.

42. Romantic park characteristics and nineteenth-century alterations to the concept are discussed in Chadwick, *The Park and the Town*, chaps. 1–10 and Tobey, *History of Landscape Architecture*, chaps. 14–17.

43. McFarland, *Public Recreation*, 14

44. *N-A*, 19 May 1886, 31 Jan. 1888, 30 Aug. 1888, and 23 Sept. 1908; and VCA, Add. Mss. 54, Major Matthews Collection, 'Stanley Park Acquisition' file, L.A. Hamilton to Major J.S. Matthews, 11 Apr. 1932

45. VCA, 48-A-1, VPBP, Minute Book, vol. 1, 1 June 1891

46. *N-A*, 22 Jan. 1896

47. *Ibid.*, 23 Jan. 1896

48. VCA, 48-E- 1, VPBP, file 8, W.S. Rawlings to Major A.B. Carey, 4 Jan. 1913

49. Stephen Hardy, *How Boston Played: Sport, Recreation, and Community 1865–1915* (Boston 1982), chap. 4 and Cranz, *Politics of Park Design*, 40

50. For the United States see Mark Kadzielski, '"As a Flower Needs Sunshine": The Origins of Organized Children's Recreation in Philadelphia, 1886–1911,' *Journal of Sport History*, IV (1977), 1–19 and Hardy, *How Boston Played*, chap. 5; for Canada see McFarland, *Public Recreation*, chap. 2.

51. Jacob A. Riis, 'The Value of Playgrounds to the Community,' Canadian Club of Toronto, *Proceedings*, x (1912–13), 271–9

52. Cranz, *Politics of Park Design*, chap. 2 and 236–9. The social control thesis is also emphasized in McFarland, *Public Recreation*; 38; Kadzielski, '"As a Flower Needs Sunshine,"' 177–9; and Don S. Kirschner, 'The Ambiguous Legacy: Social Justice and Social Control in the Progressive Era,' *Historical Reflections*, II (1975), 69–88.

53. Heckscher, *Open Spaces*, chap. 7, quotation from 177

54. McFarland, *Public Recreation*, chap. 2; McKee, MA thesis, 87; VCA, 48-c-1, VPBP, file 2, Geo. H. Healey to Chairman, Vancouver Board of Park Commissioners, 31 July 1908; and PB, *Province*,19 Oct. 1911 and 12 July 1912

55. *N-A*, 23 Feb., 9 May, and 16 May 1912

56. PB, *Saturday Sunset*, 16 Nov. 1912

57. VCA, 48-C-2, VPBP, vol. II, Minute Book, 26 Apr. 1905 and 9 May 1906

58. For the City Beautiful movement see Hinds, 'Urban Public Park Design,' chap. 4; Walter Van Nus, 'The Fate of City Beautiful Thought in Canada, 1893–1930,' Canadian Historical Association, *Historical Papers* (1975), 191–210; and Paul Boyer, *Urban Masses and Moral Order in America, 1820–1920* (Cambridge, MA and London 1978), chap. 8.

59. Boyer, *Urban Mosses*, 263–4 and 272–6 and William H. Wilson, J. Horace McFarland and the City Beautiful Movement,' *Journal of Urban History*; VII (May 1981), 320–30

60. For the Vancouver Tourist Assn see McDonald, 'Business Leaders in Early Vancouver,' 320–30 and *N-A*, 26 and 28 June 1902. For the City Beautiful Assn see *N-A*, 21 Jan., 23 Feb., 9 May, and 16 May 1912.

61. The Vancouver total includes the city, South Vancouver, and Point Grey. Drawn from the *Fifth Census of Canada 1911*, 1, 554 and Patricia E. Roy, *Vancouver: An Illustrated History* (Toronto 1980), Table 2, 168, it differs slightly from the city government figures employed in Table [19.] 1 of this article.

62. Vancouver's economic development is discussed in McDonald, 'Business Leaders in Early Vancouver' and 'Victoria, Vancouver and the Evolution of British Columbia's Economic System, 1886–1914,' in *Town and City: Aspects of Western Canadian Urban Development*, ed. Alan F.J. Artibise (Regina 1981), 31–55; and L.D. McCann, 'Urban Growth in a Staple Economy: The Emergence of Vancouver as a Regional Metropolis, 1886–1914,' in L.J. Evenden, ed., *Vanouver: Western Metropolis* (Victoria 1978), 17–41.

63. Norbert McDonald, 'Population Growth and Change in Seattle and Vancouver, 1880–1960,' in *Historical Essays on British Columbia*, ed. J. Friesen and H.K. Ralston (Toronto 1976), 201–27

64. University of British Columbia, Special Collections, Pamphlet Collection, Major J.S. Matthews, The Historic Cambie Street Grounds: Our Pioneer Park,' unpub. pamphlet, n.d., and McKee, MA thesis, chap. 6

65. A streetcar line was built along Robson St to Denman St near the park in 1895 and a Pender St line was completed to the Coal Harbour entrance in 1897.

66. PB, *Province*, 15 Oct. 1912

67. *Ibid.*, 15 Nov. 1912

68. PB, *N-A*, 7 Jan. 1913

69. David Breen and Kenneth Coates, *Vancouver's Fair: A Political and Administrative History of the Pacific National Exhibition* (Vancouver 1982)

70. VCA, PD-S-12, Vancouver Board of Park Commissioners, 'Annual Report,' 1913–20, 1923–4, and 1929

71. W.S. Rawlings, comp., *Vancouver, British Columbia: Its Parks and Resorts* (Vancouver 1919?), 35

72. McFarland, *Public Recreation*, 11; Hardy, *How Boston Played*, 83; and Cranz, *Politics of Park Design*, 244

73. The anti-development élite of 21 men was chosen from those most vocal in arguing against changes in Stanley Park. The list was compiled from the following newspaper stories: *N-A*, 12 Aug. 1910; *Province*, 20 Dec. 1912, p 32; and PB, *Sun*, 17 and 20 Dec. 1912 and 1–4 Jan. 1913. The 21 formed a clearly definable élite: 7 of the 21 (33.3 per cent) numbered among Vancouver's 90 most powerful entrepreneurs; 13 (61.9 per cent) were part of a larger 1886–1914 group of 322 leading city businessmen; and 14 (66.7 per cent) were members of Vancouver's 370-family social élite. Pre-war Vancouver's business élite and second-level business leaders are identified, and the methods used to select them are described, in McDonald, 'Business Leaders in Early Vancouver,' chaps. 1 and 6 and 'The Business Elite and Municipal Politics in Vancouver 1886–1914,' *Urban History Review*, XI (Feb. 1983), note 11. The 370-family pre-war social élite has been identified in an as-yet-incomplete study. The methodology employed to define all socially prominent Vancouverites from 1910–14 is the same as that outlined in 'Business Leaders in Early Vancouver,' 219–26, where socially prominent leaders among top businessmen are examined.

74. D.A. McGregor, 'Adventures of Vancouver Newspapers: 1892–1926,' *British Columbia Historical Quarterly*, x (1946), 120–7

75. VCA, Add. Mss. 44, F.C. Wade Papers, file 1, unassigned letter from F.C. Wade, n.d., 1912? and *N-A*, 23 Feb. 1912

76. C. W. Parker, ed., *Who's Who in Western Canada*, 1 (Vancouver 1911), 106; Bill McKee, 'Images along the Line,' *Glenbow*, July/Aug. 1983, 4; and *N A*, 22 Jan. 1896

77. VCA Add. Mss. 54, Major Matthews Collection, file 44, J. Lonsdale Doupe, 'Lauchlan A. Hamilton' and vol. IV, bound typescript (comp. 1944), Matthews, 'Early Vancouver: Narratives of Pioneers of Vancouver, B.C.,' L.A. Hamilton to J.S. Matthews, 15 Aug. 1935

78. *Vancouver News*, 1 Sept. 1886

79. See Roderick Nash, *Wilderness and the American Mind* (New Haven and London 1967); George Altmeyer, 'Three Ideas of Nature in Canada, 1893–1914,' *Journal of Canadian Studies*, XI (Aug. 1976), 21–36; and Douglas Cole, 'Artists, Patrons and Public: An Enquiry into the Success of the Group of Seven,' *Journal of Canadian Studies*, XIII (Summer 1978), 69–78.

80. Murray, 'Frederic Law Olmsted,' *passim*

81. VCA, Add. Mss. 44, F.C. Wade Papers, vol. v, file 1, F.C. Wade to ?, n.d.

82. For the organizational history of the grounds see *N-A*, 8 May 1888, 10 May 1888, 15 May 1888, 3 June 1888, 17 Sept. 1889, 12 Oct. 1889, and 31 Dec. 1889.

83. *Ibid.*, 10 May 1895; *Province*, 20 Apr. 1907; and Bailey, *Leisure and Class*, 127–9

84. *Province*, 20 Apr. 1907; Cunningham, *Leisure in the Industrial Revolution*, chaps. 4 and 5; Gunther Barth, *City People* (New York 1980), chap. 5; and Frank Cosentino, 'A History of the Rise of Professionalism in Canadian Sport' (Ph. D. thesis, University of Alberta 1973), 22, 64, 119, 128–46, and 175–7

85. For example, it appears that the city's principal lacrosse club, composed of white-collar workers in 1890–1, had become blue-collar by 1906 (see VCA, Add. Mss· 54, Major Matthews Collection, 'Lacrosse' file; VCA, Pamphlet 1 906–19, 'Championship Lacrosse'; and *Province*, 3 and 12 April 1905)

86. VCA, 48-A-2, VPBP, Minute Book, vol. 11, 26 Apr. 1905 and 9 May 1906

87. *Province*, 20 Apr. 1907, 10 May 191 1, and 12 Mar. 1913; and *N-A*, 23 May 1912 and 21 June 1912

88. Rosenzweig, 'Middle-Class Parks and Working-Class Play,' 43

89. Shortage of playing space was a chronic problem in the late nineteenth century that retarded working-class participation in team sports. See H.E. Meller, *Leisure and the Changing City, 1870–1914* (London 1976), 234–6 and Metcalfe, 'Organized Physical Recreation in Montreal,' 145, 166.

90. PB, *Province*, 11 Aug. 1911; McKee, MA thesis, 84; VCA, 48-a-3, VPBP, Minute Book, vol. III, 1 Apr. 1910–1 June 1910; VCA, 48-c-1, VPBP, file 1, Albert L. Rodway to Board of Park Commissioners; and PB, *World*, 10 May 1911

91. *N-A*, 31 May 1892, 5 June 1894, 1 and 15 Oct. 1895

92. *Ibid.*, 27 Apr. 1899

93. *Ibid.*, 21 Feb. and 21 Apr. 1899

94. *World*, 28 Apr. 1899

95. PB, *Sun*, 1 Jan. 1913 and *N-A*, 17 and 19 Feb. 1899

96. Cunningham, *Leisure in the Industrial Revolution*, 91

97. John Brinckerhoff Jackson, *American Space: The Centennial Years 1865–1876* (New York 1972), 214–15

98. Robert E. Snow and David E. Wright, 'Coney Island: A Case Study in Popular Culture and Technical Change,' *Journal of Popular Culture*, IX (Spring 1976), 960–75

99. John F. Kasson, *Amusing the Millions: Coney Island at the Turn of the Century* (New York 1978), 3–9 and Metcalfe, 'Organized Physical Recreation in Montreal,' 160–1

100. See above, note 63

101. Bryan D. Palmer, 'Most Uncommon Common Men: Craft and Culture in Historical Perspective,' *Labour/Le Travailleur*, 1 (1976), 5–31

102. *N-A*, 4 Aug. 1891, 6 Aug. 1895, 3 Sept. 1898

103. *Ibid.*, 31 Aug. 1895, 19 Apr. 1898

104. VCA, 48-c-3, VPBP, file 1, J.W. Wilkinson and Jas. H. McVety to Sec., Board of Park Commissioners, 16 Aug. 1911

105. *Loc. cit.*

Article Twenty

"Reckless Walking Must Be Discouraged": The Automobile Revolution and the Shaping of Modern Urban Canada to 1930

Stephen Davies

"Civilization," wrote Dr. Frank Crane in 1918, "is a matter of transportation. The true symbol of the twentieth century, the sign of its soul, the indicator of its spirit, is the wheel." And, as Crane went on to argue, the greatest adaptation of the wheel was the automobile.[1]

In the three decades that followed its introduction into Canada at the turn of the century, the automobile revolutionized all aspects of Canadian life. However, in a society in which the presence of the automobile has become an inseparable part of daily life, the nature and magnitude of change created by its rapid proliferation are readily overlooked. The following is an exploration of the automobile's impact on Canadian society during the first three decades of the twentieth century.[2] One can easily comprehend the physical alterations: road-building, traffic signs, and the ever-growing problem of congestion. But there is another aspect to be considered, one which must be balanced against the unbridled enthusiasm and optimism of individuals such as Crane. Change cannot always be directed or controlled, and the automobile, like other major innovations, also brought unanticipated and, in many instances, undesired consequences.

Not all change was as physically apparent as, for example, the automatic traffic signals that began to appear in Canadian cities during the 1920s. There was also a crucial, though less obvious, cultural and social reorientation. What must not be overlooked is an element of irony

Source: Adapted from "'Reckless Walking Must Be Discouraged': The Automobile Revolution and the Shaping of Modern Urban Canada to 1930," *Urban History Review* 18, 2 (October 1989): 123–38. Used by permission.

connected with the automobile's proliferation, in that many of the changes were the opposite of what the auto's introduction had promised. One of the unforeseen by-products of the automobile's appeal was the increasing number of restrictions and regulations imposed upon the Canadian public. The growing array of regulatory detail created one of the great paradoxes of the automobile: a vehicle ostensibly designed to increase freedom and personal mobility could become a means for the increased restriction of society. Rather than creating freedom, the automobile created the myth of carefree motoring. As Edward Sapir noted in 1924, although man may have harnessed machines to his use, he had also harnessed himself to the machine.[3] Mobility must not be confused with, nor mistaken for, freedom.

The diffusion of the automobile in Canada prior to 1930 was phenomenal. Ontario enjoyed the distinction of having the highest number of passenger vehicles of any province. Thus, it was often in Ontario that changes, generally on a scale greater than in the other provinces, were first observable. The 535 automobiles registered in Ontario in 1904 increased to 31 724 by 1914, 155 861 by 1920, 303 736 by 1925, and 490 906 by 1930.[4]

The number of autos remained considerably lower in the other provinces, but at the outbreak of World War I, Ontario ranked only fifth in automobiles per capita, with Saskatchewan a surprising first.[5] However, Ontario's rank altered rapidly, and by 1928 it ranked first (one motor vehicle per 7.3 individuals), while Saskatchewan had dropped to third (one motor vehicle per 7.8 persons).[6] The degree to which Canada readily embraced the automobile is apparent if one considers that in 1929 Canada ranked third behind the United States and the Hawaiian Islands in the world in per capita automobile registrations.[7]

The last years of World War I, and the several years immediately following it, represented the crucial period of expansion for automobile ownership in Canada. This growth can be attributed to a combination of both intellectual and economic factors. At one level, the automobile's rapid spread reflected an alteration of perceptions regarding its role in Canadian society. By the 1920s it was no longer simply a rich man's toy but had been transformed, as the *Canadian Motorist* argued in 1915, into a necessity rather than a luxury.[8]

An important economic consideration was the effect the war had on the automobile's rise in numbers. Wartime inflation and demand had increased automobile prices in Canada, but that rise was more than offset by higher wages. By 1920, automobile prices had begun to drop. This decline, and the introduction of new financing plans such as those first extended by GMAC in 1919, stimulated automobile purchases. In the four years following 1920, the selling price of the average automobile dropped by approximately 38 percent.[9] In fact automobile prices dropped continuously throughout the 1920s. The average selling price for an automobile in 1921 was $906, a figure which declined to $695 by 1926.[10]

The attendant expansion in ownership meant a physical alteration of the urban landscape in one manner or another. The most obvious change was the increased number of vehicles visible on the streets of Canada's cities. As registrations rose, so too did traffic congestion. While the growth of the former was generally lauded as concrete proof of the country's progress, the latter was accepted as an unfortunate by-product of that progress. A comparison of traffic on Dundas Street ten miles west of Toronto in 1908 and 1912 graphically illustrates the changes in traffic patterns wrought by the automobile. In a ten-hour period in mid-August 1908, one site on Dundas witnessed the passing of six automobiles. By 1912, 382 automobiles passed that same spot within the ten-hour period, leading the president of the Ontario Good Roads Association to remark how the automobile had "revolutionized traffic conditions everywhere."[11]

Yet the true revolution was yet to come, as comprehensive traffic surveys conducted in 1914 and 1922 demonstrate. In these studies more than 200 stations were monitored on various roads throughout southern Ontario during the summer months. Two examples suffice to convey a sense of how dramatically traffic had increased in only eight years. On the

Toronto–Hamilton Highway at Long Branch Park, an average of 268.8 automobiles a day passed in 1914, with the maximum for one day reaching 382. That same spot in 1922 witnessed an average of 8236.4 automobiles a day, with a maximum of 12 296 on Labour Day. A survey conducted at Fruitland, on the Hamilton–Niagara Road, arrived at similar figures. In 1914 that road bore an average of 189 vehicles a day, with a one-day high of 253. By 1922 the traffic passing the same spot had risen to a daily average of 2849.8 with a one-day maximum of 5030.[12] Taken together, traffic surveys and registration figures create some understanding of the physical implications of the automobile. Undoubtedly it heralded an age of personal mobility, but it also introduced a new range of problems, of which increased traffic flow and congestion were only a part.

One overlooked alteration to the urban environment, and indeed to the country as a whole, was the decline of the automobile's nearest competitor, the horse. The traffic censuses of Ontario conducted in 1914, 1922, and 1925 give some notion of the shift under way. At Port Credit on the Toronto–Hamilton Highway, the daily average of horse-drawn vehicles in 1914 was 158.7, which by 1922 had declined to 25.3.[13] In Toronto the change was even more startling. A survey of traffic on Dundas Street at Bloor in 1914 showed 349 automobiles and 248 horse-drawn vehicles passing in a day. By 1925 the daily total of automobiles had risen to 7943, while horse-drawn vehicles had declined to a mere 15. "One noticeable feature of this tabulation," noted the Toronto and York Road Commission, which had undertaken the Dundas and Bloor survey, "is the constant dwindling, almost to the vanishing point, of horse-drawn traffic on the main roads, pointing to the conclusion that the main roads of the future must be designed primarily for motor traffic."[14]

Even roads removed from the larger urban centres witnessed a decline of horse-drawn vehicles. For instance, a survey on the Guelph–Owen Sound Road saw the number of horse-drawn vehicles decline to 30.2 per day in 1922 from a level of 39.0 in 1914.[15] The declines varied from area to area and were sometimes only slight, particularly in predominantly agricultural areas. At best the number of horse-drawn vehicles in use remained static in the face of a rising population.[16]

The decline of horse-drawn vehicles was indicative of fundamental changes taking place in cities, towns, and villages. The movement from horse to horseless carriage meant that urban life acquired a quicker pace in the first decades of the twentieth century. Along with this faster pace of life, the dominance of the automobile meant a distinct change in urban sights, sounds, and smells. Taken together, such changes had created by 1930 a greatly altered urban environment.

Traffic congestion by the automobile was not a significant problem in Canada prior to 1910. The chief constable of Toronto reported in 1907 no problems with congestion, though he was perturbed about automobile speeding. A 1910 report on transit in Toronto could still conclude that, as for ordinary vehicular traffic, there existed no "extraordinary congestion."[17]

By the end of the first decade of the century, however, indications were already present that increasing automobile traffic was to have a serious impact on Canadian cities. As the Civic Improvement Committee for Toronto reported in 1911, problems engendered by the automobile's proliferation were becoming increasingly clear. The report noted that a "courageous endeavor" was required if the transportation problem was not to prove detrimental to the interests of the city.[18] Apparently this growing apprehension had some effect for, in 1913, members of the Toronto police force were sent to New York City and London, England, to learn how to handle traffic more effectively.[19] Though concern was not limited to Toronto, it had the greatest concentration of automobiles in Canada and generally experienced problems of congestion first and to a greater degree. Even Ottawa, which had fewer than 1900 automobiles at the end of World War I, was reporting serious traffic problems by 1920.[20]

Growing automobile congestion meant that two new concerns had to be addressed in urban planning. One was where to park vehicles, and the other was how to keep them moving quickly and efficiently. By 1916, the *Canadian Motorist*, a publication representing motorists across Canada, was noting how parking was a problem for all urban centres. "The automobile," the *Canadian Motorist* editorial pointed out, "is a latecomer in the general scheme of things and the best must be made of inadequate parking facilities. Cities of the future no doubt will be planned in such a way as to provide for the parking of cars in convenient and accessible parts of the business district."[21]

Yet even as the *Canadian Motorist* was putting forward its case, the Toronto City Council, equally aware of the problem, had already designated streets where parking was permissible. On all other streets, in an effort to reduce traffic slowdown, drivers could be given a summons by the police for leaving their automobiles unattended for more than a few minutes.[22] This approach, however, offered little more than a temporary solution. Toronto's chief constable lamented in 1926 that the city's streets were "just an open air garage."[23] By the following year the problem had intensified, prompting the chief constable to call for a strict enforcement of parking bylaws:

> Vehicles should be prohibited from standing unattended in that district [downtown] or for a period longer than necessary to take on or discharge passengers, or load or unload merchandise.[24]

Automobile parking was only part of the larger crisis imposed on urban planning by the automobile's presence. Civic bureaucracies became increasingly preoccupied, from World War I onwards, with the problems created by automobile traffic.[25] As Blaine Brownell has argued in the case of the United States, and it is a point equally applicable to the Canadian situation, one by-product of the automobile's rapid spread was a significant evolution in urban planning.[26] Planning for the automobile was, according to Brownell, an evolutionary process, whereby "most planners perceived at least the broad outlines of the motor vehicle's impact, and even the necessity of redesigning the city to accommodate the innovation."[27] In this context the automobile exerted yet another unexpected influence. The growing necessity for traffic planning helped advance the status — not to mention the business — of urban planning and consulting.[28]

In 1926 Toronto's chief constable, still concerned with regulating traffic in the city, introduced recommendations that would quickly and permanently alter the urban landscape. Noting that traffic problems were common in most cities, he suggested using "Mechanical Automatic Controls" for all street intersections in the downtown Toronto area.[29] Acting on that recommendation, in 1928 Toronto installed automatic traffic signals at 71 intersections.[30] In addition, given the realization that, as the chief constable expressed it, "our present streets were not laid out with any idea of the amount of traffic they would be called upon to carry," recommendations were put forward to improve traffic flow by revising existing street patterns. This trend had been under way in many cities since the early 1920s. Ottawa's planning commission, for example, had been busy throughout the decade "rounding corners" to facilitate a faster movement of traffic.[31] Toronto's planning commission responded in a similar fashion to the new problems of the automobile, noting that the primary need of the city was the development of a series of through and paved streets for modern vehicular traffic.[32] Such alterations provided the city of 1930 with a look that unmistakably distinguished it in appearance from the city that had existed only two decades previously.

One of the rarely considered legacies of the automobile has been its impact on the form of urban residential structures. "As an architectural unit," the *Canadian Motorist* argued in 1915, "the garage is rapidly coming into its own."[33] The automobile garage was not merely a useful accessory but, by 1915, was touted as an essential component of housing design. Thus, garages were no longer an afterthought, but were being integrated into new housing structures whenever possible. According to the *Canadian Motorist*, this integration had gained favourable acceptance. As the journal noted:

> The merits of such an arrangement have gained wide popularity for this style of a garage. In the new residential districts of our Canadian cities thousands of such are to be seen. Sometimes they are located under verandas and porches, frequently under conservatories, sun rooms, dens, breakfast rooms, etc. When so located, they are, of course, part of the architectural scheme of the house — indeed part of the house itself.[34]

Thus, along with the more obvious changes in street appearance and structure, the automobile ushered in a new era of housing design whereby residential structures were altered or entirely redesigned to accommodate the new technology.

However, the automobile's introduction had far more serious implications than just the transformation of housing styles. Automobiles also introduced a new element of risk and destruction to Canadian streets, for as their number grew, so too did the number of related deaths and injuries. By the late 1920s, Ontario, with the largest automobile population in the country, was experiencing the highest number of such fatalities. In 1927, for example, Ontario had 387 motor fatalities, a figure that represented more than 40 percent of Canada's automobile-related deaths. With a significantly smaller population than Ontario, British Columbia had only 77 such fatalities.[35] In terms of fatal motor accidents per 100 000 persons, Ontario, with 12.1, ranked second behind British Columbia (with 13.4).

The cities had the most lethal concentration of motor vehicles. Although Toronto experienced only one motor fatality in 1907, the number had reached 17 by 1912, 48 by 1922, and 87 by 1927.[36] Thus, in 1927, Toronto accounted for more than 10 percent of the country's total number of deaths related to motor vehicles. And yet Toronto did not have the highest number of urban automobile fatalities. Montreal held that dubious distinction with 126 deaths. Nearly one-quarter of all Canadian automobile fatalities occurred in the two cities.[37] Such was the paradoxical nature of the automobile that a vehicle which promised increased freedom and mobility also meant death and injury for thousands.

The new element of danger did not pass unnoticed. When, in 1913, advertisements for the Hupmobile pointed out that the countryside was "better, cleaner and safer than city streets," it was not merely rhetoric.[38] City streets had become dangerous places, particularly for children. Inspired partly by the presence of the automobile, and partly as an attempt to instill a degree of moral and social guidance in the young, local playground movements developed in the early twentieth century. In an editorial that commented on the opening of a new playground in 1918, a Hamilton newspaper underscored the role which the automobile had played:

> Playgrounds are becoming more a necessity than ever. The automobile and the motor truck have driven the children off the streets.[39]

Hamilton had established its first playground in 1909, but as advertisers pointed out, the streets remained a dangerous place for children. Even with the establishment of playgrounds throughout the city, Hamilton children, and the children of all urban centres, continued to fall victim to the automobile. From January to September 1922, 789 street accidents occurred in Hamilton. Of those, 162 involved children under the age of 14, of whom 41 were injured while playing on the streets. Influenced by the growing number of fatalities, an editorial queried:

> Should we encourage properly supervised playgrounds, or, by neglect, make the streets unhealthy "plague" grounds, a menace to the safety and sanity of child life?[40]

Playgrounds, like the addition of automatic traffic signals, or the newly designed traffic routes, contributed to a new look for the urban environment of the post-1920 period. Many of the physical changes caused by the automobile were minor or of a subtle nature, but their cumulative effect was to substantially alter the face of the Canadian city by 1930.

The overt physical alteration of the urban environment was only part of a much wider social transformation created by the automobile's presence. The automobile, or more specifically the new mobility provided by the automobile, caused a reassessment and reorientation of established spatial norms. This alteration of established spatial relationships, particularly the relationship between rural and urban society, perhaps held the greatest consequences. Within a relatively short period of time the automobile became synonymous with a new freedom of space, distance, and speed.

However, because of the inherently restrictive nature of the urban environment, the countryside became the logical location to experience the new boundaries of mobility as defined by the automobile. The rural environment, with its open spaces and unchecked speeds, became the ideal location to experience the full potential of the automobile's ability for spatial reorientation.

The attraction of the rural environment for the urban dweller was not based solely on the possibilities of speed. While the countryside represented the appeal of the outdoors with all the associated virtues (independence, open space, and a slower pace of life), the automobile remained the key to enjoying those virtues. A 1908 article in the Toronto *Globe* asked its readers,

> Who is the owner of an automobile who has not many a time used it to hurry far away from the madding crowd to the quiet spots of nature, where he can breathe freely and receive the endless inspirations of fine scenery?[41]

Moreover, the opportunities opened by the automobile were themes reinforced by advertising. Automobile advertising placed an emphasis on the virtues of rural space. Automobiles were portrayed as the means of escape from the urban maelstrom — they held out the hope of tranquility in a hurried world.

Copywriters often waxed eloquent about the joys to be found in the nonurban environment. One Chevrolet advertisement in 1929 reminded the reader:

> There's a shady woodland nook awaiting you. Beside the blue waters of a placid lake are rest and relaxation. A laughing, leaping brook is calling you to come! Break down the barriers of everyday. There's happiness ahead.[42]

A Ford advertisement nine years earlier had enticed the reader "out beyond the pavement" to "the unexplored woodlands and remote farmlands." The automobile became a necessity to explore such areas, for as Ford pointed out:

> Nature's loveliest beauty spots, her choicest hunting grounds are far removed from the railroads, away from the much travelled highways.[43]

Advertisements with an outdoor theme did more than comment on the superiority of the outdoors: by implication, if the rural environment was healthy, the urban environment must be unhealthy. A Chevrolet advertisement in 1924 urged readers to escape "from the dust of the city" to where one could "drive through the fresh air to some inviting spot amid the beauties of nature."[44] Some advertisements were more forceful in denouncing the city, juxtaposing the benefits of the country with the liabilities of the city, and making the choice between the two appear obvious. That year Ford asked potential customers, "which shall it be this summer?" and then went on to lay out two choices:

> City streets for a playground, or the open country where the air is perfumed with the scent of growing things and the butterflies dance in the sunshine? The Ford car is the friend of childhood — the modern Magic Carpet that will transport them and you from the baking asphalt to the shady country lanes whenever you wish to go.[45]

Thus, the assessment that the countryside represented an environment that was, according to Hupmobile, "better, cleaner and safer than city streets" was not simple advertising rhetoric, particularly in the light of the death toll previously discussed.[46]

Advertisers did not so much create the contrast between urban and rural environments as they exploited themes already prevalent in society and adopted them as marketing techniques. And, as the ease of travel from one locale to another by the automobile created a greater interaction between the two environments, comparisons were made increasingly easy. By contrasting the two environments, advertisers reinforced the differences, real and imagined, between the two. The irony was that just as urban families came to experience the countryside, they changed it.

Until the 1920s in Ontario, when the provincial government assumed responsibility for highway traffic and locational signs, private organizations such as the Ontario Motor League undertook the task of erecting signs throughout the province. Road signing to aid touring motorists often unintentionally altered the character of rural society. Sign campaigns threatened a sense of identity which, for many small rural communities, had remained unchanged for years before the coming of the automobile. One possible consequence of the motor league's sign efforts was illustrated in the case of Green River, Ontario:

> The unwary traveller might pass through and go for miles beyond still looking for it, did he not know that the church set among the trees on one side of the stream and the small general store on the opposite side of the stream, each hidden from the other, were two positive evidences that it was a village.[47]

Since the post office at Green River displayed no sign, the members of the motor league arbitrarily decided where to place a name sign announcing the village, a necessary step "so that the travelling tourist might know when he came to certain villages."[48]

The local population, however, displayed little enthusiasm for the process. When a nearby farmer was asked whether it was an appropriate place for a Green River sign, he replied, "Well, boys, I guess it is as good as any, as the store and post office are across the crick."[49] The apparent indifference of local inhabitants was understandable, given that in their minds there already existed a clearly defined local identity of place and circumstance, even if it went unsigned. If signs did not create an identity for such communities, they did so for outside interests such as touring motorists. Signs, and the motorists they served, meant that communities such as Green River were slowly integrated into the wider fabric of provincial life with their "new" identity. In turn such communities were forced to sacrifice some of the local identity that relative isolation and anonymity had provided.

In any consideration of the mobility and freedom provided by the automobile, the question of speed is crucial. Speed, and the fascination with it, were integral parts of the early-twentieth-century consciousness. And the automobile was, as *Maclean's* noted in 1914, "the sign of a quicker-moving age."[50] Speed naturally became an important selling feature (for some manufacturers the prime selling point) in automobile advertising. The Auburn billed itself as "America's Fastest Stock Car," while the Willys-Knight pointed out that its six-cylinder model "Accelerates like a Flash — 5 to 40 miles in $14\frac{1}{2}$ seconds."[51]

Judging from police reports and newspaper accounts, owners certainly were partaking of the sensations a speeding auto provided. It soon became apparent that regulation was necessary to check the appetite for speed. By 1911 Hamilton employed plainclothes policemen on the city's thoroughfares to time the speed of, and to apprehend, offending "buzz wagons." Shortly thereafter the Hamilton police resorted to using officers disguised as tramps in order to time suspected speeders, an early instance of unmarked speed traps.[52] Despite official checks and traps, the public's thirst for speed appeared unquenched. The difficulty lay in controlling the belief that, as it was expressed in *Maclean's*, "the automobile has been invented in vain if it is to be forbidden to travel quickly."[53]

Ontario's actions to deal with motorists in general, and not just speeding drivers, were typical of the regulatory revolution that the country as a whole underwent. In 1903 the province introduced its first motor vehicles act (3 Edw. VII c. 27), which formed the nucleus of all subsequent motor vehicle legislation. The 1903 act consisted of 12 sections; 7 were concerned with administrative details and the remaining 5 dealt with such items as speed limits. By 1912 the Motor Vehicles Act of Ontario had expanded to 55 sections, and by 1923 to 227 sections, subsections, and clauses; this expansion highlighted the province's growing concern for all aspects of automobile use. Driving was no longer a matter of paying a registration fee and taking the vehicle directly onto the road.

The substance of these regulations, and, as importantly, their form, would alter early-twentieth-century Canadian society. The *Canadian Motorist* pointed out in 1914:

> Regulations governing the use of motor vehicles in Canada at the present time vary in each Province of the Dominion, and motorists who have occasion to drive from one province to another are frequently perplexed and sometimes greatly inconvenienced by the divergent laws as to speed, display of numbers and lights, and other less important features of motoring.[54]

In February 1915, the same journal noted with approval the plan undertaken by the Association of Police Chiefs of America to develop a standard set of rules and regulations with respect to the automobile.[55] The following year it endorsed the compilation of a standard code of traffic regulations by the street traffic committee of the Safety First Federation of America, which would "be welcomed by everyone conversant with the present chaotic conditions caused primarily by the varying traffic ordinances in force in our municipalities."[56] The committee was hopeful that such regulation would be enforced in every city in North America with 5000 or more residents.[57] Thus, the automobile had, by the time of World War I, set in motion a process that would revolutionize the character of the urban environment. Local characteristics would never be entirely eliminated, but more and more cities came to resemble one another under the influence of a commonly shared technology. Ironically, it was the very technology which purported to be an expression of individualism that contributed significantly toward a more homogeneous urban environment.

Automobile legislation was unique in an important respect, in that it often meant the regulation of Canadian society as a whole, nonmotorists as well as motorists. A case in point was the reduced status of the urban pedestrian. Animosity quickly developed between the motorist and the pedestrian after the turn of the century, each claiming priority over the other. In the struggle to assert their claims, pedestrians gained an early sympathy in some quarters. The pedestrian, as the premier of Ontario made clear in 1910,

> has the first right of the road. The chauffeur who thinks that, because he gives warning of his approach, he is entitled to the road, is utterly and entirely wrong. He comes after the pedestrian and even after the man on the bicycle. It is not the pedestrian who must get out of the way of the automobile, but the automobile that must get out of the road of the pedestrian, even if he is standing still.[58]

Yet within a decade, as the number of motor vehicles grew at an unprecedented rate, a reversal of positions was under way. Initially, calls were made for the "re-education" of the pedestrian. One contributor to the *Canadian Motorist* in 1916 argued that the automobile's presence required a change of attitude among pedestrians, but unfortunately a large number of pedestrians had

> not yet graduated from the parochial, or colonial, or wayback attitude, whatever one may call it, in spite of the enormous increase in all kinds of vehicular traffic.[59]

Education alone did not appear to have a significant effect on reducing the conflict between the two, particularly in view of the rising number of pedestrian-related automobile accidents. Many arguments in support of automobiles were built upon accident statistics to demonstrate that, if automobiles were indeed dangerous, pedestrians brought that danger upon themselves. By 1925, the *Canadian Motorist* argued that "reckless walking" must be discouraged and "pedestrian traffic, like all other traffic, regulated."[60] It was not surprising, therefore, that the journal should smile upon legislation passed in Connecticut that made "reckless walking" an indictable offence.[61] The logical extension of this attitude regarding pedestrian education, and one increasingly favoured by many, was the regulation of the pedestrian.

By 1920 changes were under way to redefine the relationship between pedestrian and motor vehicle in Canada's cities. F.C. Biggs, the Minister of Public Works for Ontario, stated in 1921:

> The sooner this House or the cities wake up and ask pedestrians to cross the street at street intersections and not anywhere they have a mind to hop off the sidewalk, the sooner we are going to get away from 90 per cent of the accidents in the Province.[62]

Biggs, a boisterous good-roads advocate and auto enthusiast, was a biased witness to events. Nevertheless, his statement signalled an official recognition of a change of attitude due to the automobile. Moreover, Biggs was not alone in demanding the regulation of the nonmotorist. What provided freedom and mobility for one segment of the urban population brought regulation and loss of freedom for another. Claims of prior rights by pedestrians were dismissed by an editorial in the *Canadian Motorist* in 1923 as "so much idle prattle."[63] By that time it had become evident that pedestrians had lost the primacy of consideration to motorists on the nation's streets.

By the onset of the Great Depression, Canada had experienced major alterations brought about by the automobile's presence. It was a transition filled with conflicts and decisions, the long-term consequences of which had been unforeseen. Given the pattern of concentration, it was to be expected that the urban environment would exhibit striking examples of that change. In everything from sound and smell, to housing design, to street patterns and congestion, the automobile profoundly affected urban life. Although the potential for increased mobility was immediately recognized, the degree to which it ultimately would alter established patterns of temporal and spatial reality (patterns based on nineteenth-century transportation technology) went unappreciated.

The automobile also irreversibly altered stable established forms of interaction between the rural and urban environments. Similarly, the presence of the automobile required a greater level of societal control than had previously existed. The effects of regulation spread beyond the motoring public, and all city dwellers were subject to restriction forced by the automobile. The automobile was fraught with irony, particularly evident in the paradox of freedom versus regulation — a technology that traded heavily on the possibilities of personal liberation simultaneously introduced an escalating level of restriction on personal conduct. The introduction of the automobile into Canadian society not only demonstrated how unpredictable a technology's ultimate effects might be, but also underscored how technological innovations affect the public in ever-widening and increasingly complex circles.

NOTES

1. *Canadian Motorist* (hereafter CM) (June 1918): 387.
2. The termination date of 1930 has been chosen because most of the changes precipitated by the automobile were either already in place or at least under way by that date. As well, the exceptional social and economic conditions of the Great Depression and their impact on the spread of the automobile in Canada would in themselves require a separate study.
3. Edward Sapir, "Culture, Genuine and Spurious," *American Journal of Sociology* 29 (Jan. 1924): 408.
4. Ontario, *Sessional Papers*, 1942. Annual Report of the Department of Highways, Report of Motor Vehicle Registrations, 1941.
5. CM (April 1914): 168.
6. *Preliminary Report: Registration of Motor Vehicles, 1922–24, 1926–56* (Ottawa, 1956).
7. Ibid.
8. Don Kerr and Stan Hanson, *Saskatoon: The First Half-Century* (Edmonton, 1982), 258; CM (Feb. 1915): 35.
9. *The Automobile Industry in Canada, 1924* (Ottawa, 1925).
10. *The Automobile Industry in Canada, 1921* (Ottawa, 1922); *Automobile Statistics for Canada, 1926* (Ottawa, 1927).
11. Ontario, *Sessional Papers*, 1923. President's Address, Eleventh Annual Convention, Ontario Good Roads Association.
12. Ontario, *Sessional Papers*, 1915. Annual Report on Highway Improvement, 1915, appendix D; 1923. Annual Report on Highway Improvement, 1922, appendix G. The 1914 census was conducted for a twelve-hour period, from 7 a.m. to 7 p.m. However, because of the prevalence of night traffic, the 1922 census was conducted from 6 a.m. to 10 p.m.
13. Ontario, *Sessional Papers*, 1915. Annual Report on Highway Improvement, 1915, appendix D; 1923. Annual Report on Highway Improvement, 1922, appendix G. In this comparison I have considered only one-horse carriages, which most closely correspond to the passenger automobile. However, even two-horse vehicles, which would be used in hauling or for light industry, also declined at approximately the same rate, according to census figures.
14. *Report of the Toronto and York Roads Commission* (Toronto, 1926), 33.
15. Ontario, *Sessional Papers*, 1915. Annual Report on Highway Improvements, 1915, appendix D; 1923. Annual Report on Highway Improvement, 1922, appendix G.
16. The rise of the automobile at the expense of the horse is readily apparent in the decline of the carriage and wagon industry. In Ontario in 1920 there were 217 manufacturers of carriages and wagons, which by 1930 had declined to only 80 such producers. Other forms of transportation also experienced a decline with the growing popularity of the automobile. The automobile meant the eventual decline of the steamboats that served the resort areas of Lake Simcoe and Georgian Bay. Even Ontario's inter-urban railways, built expressly for the efficient movement of passengers, suffered a decline in passenger levels during the 1920s because of the automobile. *Preliminary Report of the Carriage and Wagon Industry in Canada, 1920* (Ottawa, 1922); *Preliminary Report on the Carriage and Wagon Industry in Canada, 1929 and 1930* (Ottawa, 1932); John Craig, *Simcoe County: The Recent Past* (The Corporation of the County of Simcoe, 1977); *Report of the Commission Appointed to Inquire into Hydro-Electric Railways* (Ontario, Sessional Papers, 1922), 53; John F. Due, *The Intercity Electric Railway Industry in Canada* (Toronto, 1966), 25, 33–36, 53, 61–95.
17. *Annual Report of the Chief Constable of the City of Toronto*, 1907, 1910.
18. Ibid., 1911.
19. Ibid., 1913.
20. CM (Feb. 1918): 71; J.H. Taylor, *Ottawa: An Illustrated History* (Toronto, 1986), 146.
21. CM (July 1918): 445.
22. CM (Dec. 1916): 496.
23. *Annual Report of the Chief Constable of the City of Toronto*, 1926.
24. Ibid., 1927.
25. James Lemon, "Tracey Deavin Lemay: Toronto's First Planning Commissioner, 1930–1954," *City Planning* (Winter 1984): 4–5.
26. Blaine Brownell, "Urban Planning, the Planning Profession, and the Motor Vehicle in Early Twentieth Century America," in *Shaping an Urban World*, ed. G.E. Cherry (London, 1980), 60.
27. Ibid., 69.
28. Ibid., 67.
29. *Annual Report of the Chief Constable of the City of Toronto*, 1926.
30. Ibid., 1928.

31. Taylor, *Ottawa*, 48.
32. *Report of the Advisory City Planning Commission* (Toronto, 1929), 11.
33. CM (Oct. 1915): 345.
34. CM (Sept. 1915): 306. The *Canadian Motorist* also added a note of warning to owners of houses with garages joined by conservatories. Noting the danger to plants when the doors are thrown open in winter, the journal advised that there would be no problem "so long as the chauffeur sees to it that the communicating door between the conservatory and the garage is kept shut."
35. *Deaths Due to Motor Vehicle Accidents* (Ottawa, 1934).
36. Ibid.; *Annual Report of the Chief Constable of the City of Toronto*, 1907; CM (Feb. 1923): 76.
37. *Deaths Due to Motor Vehicle Accidents* (Ottawa, 1934).
38. *Maclean's* (July 1913).
39. *Hamilton Times*, 6 July 1918.
40. *Hamilton Spectator*, 6 May 1924.
41. *Globe*, 21 March 1908.
42. *Maclean's* (1 May 1929).
43. *Maclean's* (15 Oct. 1920).
44. *Canadian Magazine* (May 1924).
45. *Maclean's* (July 1924).
46. *Maclean's* (July 1913).
47. P.E. Doolittle, "The Pleasure of Erecting Road Signs," CM (April 1914): 146–47.
48. Ibid., 182.
49. Ibid.
50. James Grantham, "The Law and the Motor," *Maclean's* (May 1914): 29.
51. *Maclean's* (1 May 1927); *Canadian Magazine* (April 1927).
52. *Hamilton Herald*, 14 June 1911; *Hamilton Herald*, 19 Aug. 1912.
53. Grantham, "The Law and the Motor," 30.
54. CM (Aug. 1914): 319.
55. CM (Feb. 1915): 40.
56. CM (Feb. 1916): 38.
57. CM (May 1916): 163.
58. *Toronto Daily Star*, 10 March 1910.
59. CM (Aug. 1916): 292.
60. CM (Jan. 1925): 19.
61. CM (Jan. 1923): 31.
62. Ontario, Legislative Assembly, *Debates*, 8 March 1921.
63. CM (Feb. 1923): 89.

Topic Nine

World War I

Members of the 29th (Vancouver) Batallion advance across "No Man's Land" at Vimy Ridge in April 1917.

In 1914, Canada participated in its first large-scale war. Over the next four years, the nation of fewer than 10 million people provided more than half a million men as soldiers, sailors, and fliers, as well as several thousand women as nursing sisters, to the Allied war effort. More than 60 000 Canadians died fighting in the struggle. English-Canadian historians have used this tremendous war effort as evidence of Canada coming of age as a nation, arguing that Canadian nationalism was born on the battlefields of Europe. But not all groups contributed equally to the war effort, and certainly not all Canadian soldiers experienced fighting as a glorious feat. Many returned maimed in both body and mind, scarred forever by their experience.

The following three articles take a more critical look at the war. The Talbot Papineau–Henri Bourassa correspondence reminds us that many French Canadians opposed Canada's involvement in the war in Europe, and especially conscription, for a war that they believed was of no interest or benefit to them. But equally, the Papineau–Bourassa correspondence reminds us that many French Canadians *did* fight in World War I despite the obstacles they faced. Canadian historians have tended to focus on the opposition among French Canadians at the expense of recognizing those who did fight. The correspondence shows that both sides had compelling reasons for the positions taken.

Today it is difficult for students to visualize the conditions of trench warfare in World War I. The horrendous experience that soldiers endured serves as a reminder of the magnitude and horrifying nature of that war. The following excerpt from Will R. Bird's war memoirs, *Ghosts Have Warm Hands*, published in 1930 but based on extensive diary entries written during the war years, gives a vivid account of life in the trenches and at the front in general. Bird's account adds the personal feelings and human tragedies of war absent from the "official" military accounts. This particular excerpt describes his experience during the battle of Vimy.

Voluntary recruitment of soldiers for the war effort passed through various phases between 1914, the advent of war, and 1917, the implementation of conscription. Historian Ronald G. Haycock examines the role that Sam Hughes, the Minister of Militia, played in the recruitment effort. Haycock maintains that Hughes failed to appreciate the difficulties of recruiting soldiers in a geographically enormous country, and one divided by the war effort. Haycock is also critical of Hughes's archaic views that winning the war required more and more soldiers, and not necessarily better-trained soldiers.

What are the arguments for and against French-Canadian enlistment put forward in both the Papineau–Bourassa correspondence and in Haycock's article? How does Will Bird's account of fighting at the front tie in with Haycock's study of Sam Hughes's views on recruitment? Primary sources are essential for good historical writing. What are the strengths (and weaknesses) of using the Papineau–Bourassa correspondence and Will Bird's memoirs as sources for World War I?

For a compelling account of the war years from the perspective of social history, see Desmond Morton and Jack Granatstein, *Marching to Armageddon: Canadians and the Great War, 1914–1919* (Toronto: Lester and Orpen Dennys, 1989); Daniel Dancocks, *Spearhead to Victory: Canada and the Great War* (Edmonton: Hurtig, 1987); and Desmond Morton, *When Your Number's Up* (Toronto: Random House, 1994). For an overview of the war years, see the relevant chapters in R.C. Brown and R. Cook's *Canada, 1896–1921: A Nation Transformed* (Toronto: McClelland and Stewart, 1974). A quick overview is found in Roger Sarty and Brereton Greenhous, "The Great War," *Horizon Canada* 85 (1986): 2017–23. A valuable collection of essays is B.D. Hunt and R.G. Haycock, eds., *Canada's Defence: Perspectives on Policy in the Twentieth Century* (Toronto: Copp Clark Pitman Ltd., 1993). A number of biographies of key politicians during World War I contain useful discussions of the war years. The most important are: R.C. Brown's *Robert Laird Borden: A Biography*, vol. 3, *1914–1937* (Toronto: Macmillan, 1980); J. Schull's *Laurier: The First Canadian* (Toronto: Macmillan, 1965); Robert Rumilly's *Henri Bourassa* (Montreal: Chantecler, 1953); and R. Graham's *Arthur Meighen*, vol. 1, *The Door of Opportunity* (Toronto: Clarke, Irwin, 1960). On Canada's most important military commander in World War I, see A.M.J. Hyatt, *General Sir Arthur Currie: A Military Biography* (Toronto: University of Toronto Press, 1987). A new collection of essays on the war years is David MacKenzie, ed., *Canada and the First World War: Essays in Honour of Robert Craig Brown* (Toronto: University of Toronto Press, 2005).

John Swettenham's *To Seize the Victory* (Toronto: Ryerson, 1965) and Robert James Steel's *The Men Who Marched Away: Canada's Infantry in the First World War, 1914–1918* (St. Catharines: Vanwell, 1989) describe Canadian participation at the front, as does Sandra Gwyn's *Tapestry of War: A Private View of Canadians in the Great War* (Toronto: HarperCollins, 1992). On Canada's involvement in the Ypres Salient, see Daniel Dancocks, *Welcome to Flanders Fields: The First Canadian Battle of the Great War, Ypres, 1915* (Toronto: McClelland and Stewart, 1988). Pierre Berton tells the story of Canada's greatest battle in *Vimy* (Toronto: McClelland and Stewart, 1986). On the nature of trench warfare, see Bill Rawling, *Surviving Trench Warfare: Technology and the Canadian Corps, 1914–1918* (Toronto: University of Toronto Press, 1992); and Tim Cook, *No Place to Run: The Canadian Corps and Gas Warfare in the First World War* (Vancouver: University of British Columbia Press, 1999).

On the issue of conscription, see Elizabeth Armstrong's *The Crisis of Quebec, 1914–1918* (New York: Columbia University Press, 1937); J.L. Granatstein and J.M. Hitsman's *Broken Promises: A History of Conscription in Canada* (Toronto: Oxford University Press, 1977; new edition, 1984); Desmond Morton's "French Canada and War, 1868–1917: The Military Background to the Conscription Crisis of 1917," in *War and Society in North America*, eds. J.L. Granatstein and R. Cuff (Toronto: Nelson, 1970), pp. 84–103; Brian Cameron's "The Bonne Entente Movement, 1916–17: From Cooperation to Conscription," *Journal of Canadian Studies* 13 (Summer 1978): 1942–55; the relevant chapters in John English, *The Decline of Politics: The Conservatives and the Party System, 1901–1920* (Toronto: University of Toronto Press, 1977); and Jean Pariseau, "La participation des Canadiens français à l'effort des deux guerres mondiales: Démarche de ré-interprétation," *Canadian Defence Quarterly/Revue canadienne de défense* 13, 2 (Autumn 1983): 43–48. Henri Bourassa's views are presented in Joseph Levitt, ed., *Henri Bourassa on Imperialism and Bi-culturalism, 1900–1918* (Toronto: Copp Clark, 1970). The Papineau–Bourassa debate over conscription is reviewed in Sandra Gwyn, *Tapestry of War: A Private View of Canadians in the Great War* (Toronto: HarperCollins, 1992).

Two novels help to re-create the atmosphere of Canada during World War I: Philip Child's *God's Sparrows*, published in 1937 and reprinted in 1978 with an introduction by Dennis Duffy (Toronto: McClelland and Stewart), and Timothy Findley's award-winning *The Wars* (Toronto: Clarke, Irwin, 1977). Grace Morris Craig's *But This Is Our War* (Toronto: University of Toronto Press, 1981) is both her own recollection of the war years at home in Ontario and a collection of letters from her two brothers at the front.

Modris Ekstein's *Rites of Spring: The Great War and the Birth of the Modern Age* (Boston: Houghton Mifflin, 1989) looks at the Great War from a broader perspective. Jonathon F. Vance's *Death So Noble: Memory, Meaning and the First World War* (Vancouver: UBC Press, 1997) is an excellent study of the image of the Great War in the popular culture of the interwar years.

WEBLINKS

Canada and World War I

http://www.collectionscanada.ca/firstworldwar/index-e.html
War diaries, letters, and other documents detailing the experiences of Canadian soldiers in World War I.

Propaganda Posters

http://www.firstworldwar.com/posters/canada.htm
A series of propaganda posters used in Canada during the time of World War I to boost recruitment and support for the Canadian forces.

Canadian Expeditionary Force Photographs

http://gateway.uvic.ca/spcoll/Digit/WOD/index.htm
A collection of photographs of the Canadian Expeditionary Force recruiting and training in Quebec prior to their departure for Britain in 1914. Photographs were taken by J.A. Miller of the *Montreal Daily Star*.

National Film Board of Canada: World War I

http://www.nfb.ca/enclasse/ww1/en/frame_index.php
Films of training and conflict in World War I documented by the National Film Board of Canada.

Canvas of War

http://www.civilization.ca/cwm/canvas/1/cwd1e.html
A series of paintings depicting events in World War I from the Canadian War Museum.

Vimy Ridge

http://www.cbc.ca/news/background/vimy/
A detailed description of the battle for Vimy Ridge, with links to related websites.

Echo in My Heart

http://ca.geocities.com/echoinmyheart@rogers.com
A series of letters between Canadians Fred Albright and Evelyn Albright spanning their marriage in 1914, Fred's enlistment in 1916, and his participation in the war until 1917.

Article Twenty-One

An Open Letter from Capt. Talbot Papineau to Mr. Henri Bourassa

(A copy of this letter was sent to Mr. Bourassa by Mr. Andrew-R. McMaster, K.C., on July 18, 1916. It was published, on July 28, in most Montreal, Quebec, Ottawa, and Toronto papers, both English and French.)

In the Field,
France, March 21, 1916.

To Monsieur Henri Bourassa,
Editor of *Le Devoir*,
Montreal.

My dear Cousin Henri,
I was sorry before leaving Quebec in 1914 not to have had an opportunity of discussing with you the momentous issues which were raised in Canada by the outbreak of this war.

Source: *Canadian Nationalism and the War.* Published in Montreal, 1916.

You and I have had some discussions in the past, and although we have not agreed upon all points, yet I am happy to think that our pleasant friendship, which indeed dates from the time of my birth, has hitherto continued uninjured by our differences of opinion. Nor would I be the first to make it otherwise, for however I may deplore the character of your views, I have always considered that you held them honestly and sincerely and that you were singularly free from purely selfish or personal ambitions.

Very possibly nothing that I could have said in August 1914 would have caused you to change your opinions, but I did hope that as events developed and as the great national opportunity of Canada became clearer to all her citizens, you would have been influenced to modify your views and to adopt a different attitude. In that hope I have been disappointed. Deeply involved as the honour and the very national existence of Canada has become, beautiful but terrible as her sacrifices have been, you and you alone of the leaders of Canadian thought appear to have remained unmoved, and your unhappy views unchanged.

Too occupied by immediate events in this country to formulate a protest or to frame a reasoned argument, I have nevertheless followed with intense feeling and deep regret the course of action which you have pursued. Consolation of course I have had in the fact that far from sharing in your views, the vast majority of Canadians, and even many of those who had formerly agreed with you, were now strongly and bitterly opposed to you. With this fact in mind, I would not take the time from my duties here to write you this letter did I not fear that the influence to which your talent, energy, and sincerity of purpose formerly entitled you, might still be exercised upon a small minority of your fellow countrymen, and that your attitude might still be considered by some as representative of the race to which we belong.

Nor can I altogether abandon the hope — presumptuous no doubt but friendly and well-intentioned — that I may so express myself here as to give you a new outlook and a different purpose, and perhaps even win you to the support of a principle which has been proved to be dearer to many Canadians than life itself.

I shall not consider the grounds upon which you base your opposition to Canadian participation in this more than European — in this World War. Rather I wish to begin by pointing out some reasons why on the contrary your whole-hearted support might have been expected.

And the first reason is this. By the declaration of war by Great Britain upon Germany, Canada became "ipso facto" a belligerent, subject to invasion and conquest, her property at sea subject to capture, her coasts subject to bombardment or attack, her citizens in enemy territory subject to imprisonment or detention. This is not a matter of opinion — it is a matter of fact — a question of international law. No arguments of yours at least could have persuaded the Kaiser to the contrary. Whatever your views or theories may be as to future constitutional development of Canada, and in those views I believe I coincide to a large extent, the fact remains that at the time of the outbreak of war Canada was a possession of the British Empire, and as such as much involved in the war as any country in England, and from the German point of view and the point of view of International Law equally subject to all its pains and penalties. Indeed proof may no doubt be made that one of the very purposes of Germany's aggression and German military preparedness was the ambition to secure a part if not the whole of the English possessions in North America.

That being so, surely it was idle and pernicious to continue an academic discussion as to whether the situation was a just one or not, as to whether Canada should or should not have had a voice in ante bellum English diplomacy or in the actual declaration of war. Such a discussion may very properly arise upon a successful conclusion of the war, but so long as national issues are being decided in Prussian fashion, that is, by an appeal to the Power of Might, the liberties of discussion which you enjoyed by virtue of British citizenship were necessarily curtailed and any resulting decisions utterly valueless. If ever there was a time for action and not for theories it was to be found in Canada upon the outbreak of war.

Let us presume for the sake of argument that your attitude had also been adopted by the Government and people of Canada and that we had declared our intention to abstain from active participation in the war until Canada herself was actually attacked. What would have resulted? One of two things. Either the Allies would have been defeated or they would not have been defeated. In the former case Canada would have been called upon either to surrender unconditionally to German domination or to have attempted a resistance against German arms.

You, I feel sure, would have preferred resistance, but as a proper corrective to such a preference I would prescribe a moderate dose of trench bombardment. I have known my own dogmas to be seriously disturbed in the midst of a German artillery concentration. I can assure you that the further you travel from Canada and the nearer you approach the great military power of Germany, the less do you value the unaided strength of Canada. By the time you are within fifteen yards of a German army and know yourself to be holding about one yard out of a line of five hundred miles or more, you are liable to be enquiring very anxiously about the presence and power of British and French forces. Your ideas about charging to Berlin or of ending the war would also have undergone some slight moderation.

No, my dear Cousin, I think you would shortly after the defeat of the Allies have been more worried over the mastery of the German consonants than you are even now over a conflict with the Ontario Anti-bilinguists. Or I can imagine you an unhappy exile in Terra del Fuego eloquently comparing the wrongs of Quebec and Alsace.

But you will doubtless say we would have had the assistance of the Great American Republic! It is quite possible. I will admit that by the time the American fleet had been sunk and the principal buildings in New York destroyed the United States would have declared war upon Europe, but in the meantime Canada might very well have been paying tribute and learning to decline German verbs, probably the only thing German she *could* have declined.

I am, as you know, by descent even more American than I am French, and I am a sincere believer in the future of that magnificent Republic. I cannot forget that more than any other nation in the world's history — England not excepted — she has suffered war solely for the sake of some fine principle of nationality. In 1776 for the principle of national existence. In 1812 for the principle of the inviolability of American citizenship. In 1860 for the preservation of National unity and the suppression of slavery. In 1896 for the protection of her National pride and in sympathy for the wrongs of a neighbouring people.

Nor disappointed as I am at the present inactivity of the States will I ever waiver in my loyal belief that in time to come, perhaps less distant than we realize, her actions will correspond with the lofty expression of her national and international ideals.

I shall continue to anticipate the day when with a clear understanding and a mutual trust we shall by virtue of our united strength and our common purposes be prepared to defend the rights of humanity not only upon the American Continent but throughout the civilized world.

Nevertheless we are not dealing with what may occur in the future but with the actual facts of yesterday and today, and I would feign know if you still think that a power which without protest witnesses the ruthless spoliation of Belgium and Serbia, and without effective action the murder of her own citizens, would have interfered to protect the property or the liberties of Canadians. Surely you must at least admit an element of doubt, and even if such interference had been attempted, have we not the admission of the Americans themselves that it could not have been successful against the great naval and military organizations of the Central Powers?

May I be permitted to conclude that had the Allies been defeated Canada must afterwards necessarily have suffered a similar fate.

But there was the other alternative, namely, that the Allies even without the assistance of Canada would *not* have been defeated. What then? Presumably French and English would still have been the official languages of Canada. You might still have edited untrammeled your version of Duty, and Colonel Lavergne might still, publicly and without the restraining fear of death or imprisonment, have spoken seditiously (I mean from the Prussian point of view of course). In fact Canada might still have retained her liberties and might with the same freedom from external influences have continued her progress to material and political strength.

But would you have been satisfied — you who have arrogated to yourself the high term of Nationalist? What of the Soul of Canada? Can a nation's pride or patriotism be built upon the blood and suffering of others or upon the wealth garnered from the coffers of those who in anguish and with blood-sweat are fighting the battles of freedom? If we accept our liberties, our national life, from the hands of the English soldiers, if without sacrifices of our own we profit by the sacrifices of the English citizen, can we hope to ever become a nation ourselves? How could we ever acquire that Soul or create that Pride without which a nation is a dead thing and doomed to speedy decay and disappearance?

If you were truly a Nationalist — if you loved our great country and without smallness longed to see her become the home of a good and united people — surely you would have recognized this as her moment of travail and tribulation. You would have felt that in the agony of her losses in Belgium and France, Canada was suffering the birth pains of her national life. There even more than in Canada herself, her citizens are being knit together into a new existence because when men stand side by side and endure a soldier's life and face together a soldier's death, they are united in bonds almost as strong as the closest of blood-ties.

There was the great opportunity for the true Nationalist! There was the great issue, the great sacrifice, which should have appealed equally to all true citizens of Canada, and should have served to cement them with indissoluble strength — Canada was at war! Canada was attacked! What mattered then internal dissentions and questions of home importance? What mattered the why and wherefore of the war, whether we owed anything to England or not, whether we were Imperialists or not, or whether we were French or English? The one simple commending fact to govern our conduct was that Canada was at war, and Canada and Canadian liberties had to be protected.

To you as a "Nationalist" this fact should have appealed more than to any others. Englishmen, as was natural, returned to fight for England, just as Germans and Austrians and Belgians and Italians returned to fight for their native lands.

But we, Canadians, had we no call just as insistent, just as compelling to fight for Canada? Did not the *Leipzig* and the *Gneisnau* possibly menace Victoria and Vancouver, and did you not feel the patriotism to make sacrifices for the protection of British Columbia? How could you otherwise call yourself Canadian? It is true that Canada did not hear the roar of German guns nor were we visited at night by the murderous Zeppelins, but every shot that was fired in Belgium or France was aimed as much at the heart of Canada as at the bodies of our brave Allies. Could we then wait within the temporary safety of our distant shores until either the Central Powers flushed with victory should come to settle their account or until by the glorious death of millions of our fellowmen in Europe, Canada should remain in inglorious security and a shameful liberty?

I give thanks that that question has been answered not as you would have had it answered but as those Canadians who have already died or are about to die here in this gallant motherland of France have answered it.

It may have been difficult for you at first to have realized the full significance of the situation. You were steeped in your belief that Canada owed no debt to England, was merely a vassal state and entitled to protection without payment. You were deeply imbued with the principle that we should not partake in a war in the declaration of which we had had no say. You believed very sincerely that Canadian soldiers should not be called upon to fight beyond the frontier of Canada itself, and your vision was further obscured by your indignation at the apparent injustice to a French minority in Ontario.

It is conceivable that at first on account of this long-held attitude of mind and because it seemed that Canadian aid was hardly necessary, for even we feared that the war would be over before the first Canadian regiment should land in France, you should have failed to adapt your mind to the new situation and should for a while have continued in your former views;— but now — now that Canada has pledged herself body and soul to the successful prosecution of this war — now that we know that only by the exercise of our full and united strength can we achieve a speedy and lasting victory — now that thousands of your fellow citizens have died, and alas! many more must yet be killed — how in the name of all that you hold most sacred can you still maintain your opposition? How can you refrain from using all your influence and your personal magnetism and eloquence to swell the great army of Canada and make it as representative of all classes of our citizens as possible?

Could you have been here yourself to witness in its horrible detail the cruelty of war — to have seen your comrades suddenly struck down in death and lie mangled at your side, even you could not have failed to wish to visit punishment upon those responsible. You too would now wish to see every ounce of our united strength instantly and relentlessly directed to that end. Afterwards, when that end has been accomplished, then and then only can there be honour or profit in the discussion of our domestic or imperial disputes.

And so my first reason for your support would be that you should assist in the defence of Canadian territory and Canadian liberties.

And my second would be this:—

Whatever criticism may today be properly directed against the Constitutional structure of the British Empire, we are compelled to admit that the *spiritual* union of the self-governing portions of the Empire is a most necessary and desirable thing. Surely you will concede that the degree of civilization which they represent and the standards of individual and national liberty for which they stand are the highest and noblest to which the human race has yet attained and jealously to be protected against destruction by less developed powers. All may not be perfection — grave and serious faults no doubt exist — vast progress must still be made — nevertheless that which has been achieved is good and must not be allowed to disappear. The bonds which unite us for certain great purposes and which have proved so powerful in this common struggle must not be loosened. They may indeed be readjusted, but the great communities which the British Empire has joined together must not be broken asunder. If I thought that the development of a national spirit in Canada meant antagonism to the "spirit" which unites the Empire today, I would utterly repudiate the idea of a Canadian nation and would gladly accept the most exacting of imperial organic unions.

Hitherto I have welcomed your nationalism because I thought it would only mean that you wished Canada to assume national responsibilities as well as to enjoy its privileges.

But your attitude in the present crisis will alienate and antagonize the support which you might otherwise have received. Can you not realize that if any worthy nationality is possible for Canada it must be sympathetic to and must cooperate with the fine spirit of imperial unity? That spirit was endangered by the outbreak of European war. It could only be preserved by loyal assistance from all those in whom that spirit dwelt.

And so I would also have had you support Canadian participation in the war, *not* in order to maintain a certain political organism of Empire, but to preserve and perpetuate that invaluable *spirit* which alone makes our union possible.

The third reason is this: You and I are so called French Canadians. We belong to a race that began the conquest of this country long before the days of Wolfe. That race was in its turn conquered, but their personal liberties were not restricted. They were in fact increased. Ultimately as a minority in a great English-speaking community we have preserved our racial identity, and we have had freedom to speak or to worship as we wished. I may not be, like yourself, "un pur sang," for I am by birth even more English than French, but I am proud of my French ancestors, I love the French language, and I am as determined as you are that we shall have full liberty to remain French as long as we like. But if we are to preserve this liberty we must recognize that we do not belong entirely to ourselves, but to a mixed population, we must rather seek to find points of contact and of common interest than points of friction and separation. We must make concessions and certain sacrifices of our distinct individuality if we mean to live on amicable terms with our fellow citizens or if we are to expect them to make similar concessions to us. There, in this moment of crisis, was the greatest opportunity which could ever have presented itself for us to show unity of purpose and to prove to our English fellow citizens that, whatever our respective histories may have been, we were actuated by a common love for our country and a mutual wish that in the future we should unite our distinctive talents and energies to create a proud and happy nation.

That was an opportunity which you, my cousin, have failed to grasp, and unfortunately, despite the heroic and able manner in which French-Canadian battalions have distinguished themselves here, and despite the whole-hearted support which so many leaders of French-Canadian thought have given to the cause, yet the fact remains that the French in Canada have not responded in the same proportion as have other Canadian citizens, and the unhappy impression has been created that French Canadians are not bearing their full share in this great Canadian enterprise. For this fact and this impression you will be held largely responsible. Do you fully realize what such a responsibility will mean, not so much to you personally — for that I believe you would care little — but to the principles which you have advocated, and for many of which I have but the deepest regard? You will have brought them into a disrepute from which they may never recover. Already you have made the fine term of "Nationalist" to stink in the nostrils of our English fellow citizens. Have you caused them to respect your national views? Have you won their admiration or led them to consider with esteem, and toleration your ambitions for the French language? Have you shown yourself worthy of concessions or consideration?

After this war what influence will you enjoy — what good to your country will you be able to accomplish? Wherever you go you will stir up strife and enmity — you will bring disfavour and dishonour upon our race, so that whoever bears a French name in Canada will be an object of suspicion and possibly of hatred.

And so, in the third place, for the honour of French Canada and for the unity of our country, I would have had you favourable to our cause.

I have only two more reasons, and they but need to be mentioned, I think, to be appreciated.

Here in this little French town I hear all about me the language I love so well and which recalls so vividly my happy childhood days in Montebello. I see types and faces that are like old friends. I see farm houses like those at home. I notice that our French-Canadian soldiers have easy friendships wherever they go.

Can you make me believe that there must not always be a bond of blood relationship between the Old France and the New?

And France — more glorious than in all her history — is now in agony straining fearlessly and proudly in a struggle for life or death.

For Old France and French civilization I would have had your support.

And in the last place, all other considerations aside and even supposing Canada had been a neutral country, I would have had you decide that she should enter the struggle for no other reason than that it is a fight for the freedom of the world — a fight in the result of which like every other country she is herself vitally interested. I will not further speak of the causes of this war, but I should like to think that even if Canada had been an independent and neutral nation she of her own accord would have chosen to follow the same path of glory that she is following today.

Perhaps, my cousin, I have been overlong and tedious with my reasons, but I shall be shorter with my warning — and in closing I wish to say this to you.

Those of us in this great army, who may be so fortunate as to return to our Canada, will have faced the grimmest and sincerest issues of life and death — we will have experienced the unhappy strength of brute force — we will have seen our loved comrades die in blood and suffering. Beware lest we return with revengeful feelings, for I say to you that for those who, while we fought and suffered here, remained in safety and comfort in Canada and failed to give us encouragement and support, as well as for those who grew fat with the wealth dishonourably gained by political graft and by dishonest business methods at our expense — we shall demand a heavy day of reckoning. We shall inflict upon them the punishment they deserve — not by physical violence — for we shall have had enough of that — nor by unconstitutional or illegal means — for we are fighting to protect not to destroy justice and freedom — but by the invincible power of our moral influence.

Can you ask us then for sympathy or concession? Will any listen when you speak of pride and patriotism? I think not.

Remember too that if Canada has become a nation respected and self-respecting she owes it to her citizens who have fought and died in this distant land and not to those self-styled Nationalists who have remained at home.

Can I hope that anything I have said here may influence you to consider the situation in a different light and that it is not yet too late for me to be made proud of our relationship?

At this moment, as I write, French and English Canadians are fighting and dying side by side. Is their sacrifice to go for nothing or will it not cement a foundation for a true Canadian nation, a Canadian nation independent in thought, independent in action, independent even in its political organization — but in spirit united for high international and humane purposes to the two Motherlands of England and France?

I think that is an ideal in which we shall all equally share. Can we not all play an equal part in its realization?

I am, as long as may be possible,

Your affectionate Cousin,
TALBOT M. PAPINEAU.

MR. BOURASSA'S REPLY TO CAPT. TALBOT PAPINEAU'S LETTER

Montreal, August 2nd, 1916.

Andrew-R. McMaster, Esq., K.C.,
189 St. James St.,
City.

Dear Sir,

On my return from an absence of several weeks, I found your letter of the 18th ult., and the copy of a letter apparently written to me by your partner, Capt. Talbot Papineau, on the 21st of March.

Capt. Papineau's letter, I am informed, appeared simultaneously, Friday last, in a number of papers, in Montreal, Quebec, Ottawa, and elsewhere. You have thus turned it into a kind of political manifesto and constituted yourself its publisher. Allow me therefore to send you my reply, requesting you to have it transmitted to Capt. Papineau, granting that he is the real author of that document. I can hardly believe it. A brave and active officer as he is has seldom the time to prepare and write such long pieces of political eloquence. Then, why should Capt. Papineau, who writes and speaks French elegantly, who claims so highly his French origin and professes with such ardour his love of France, have written in English to his "*dear cousin Henri*"? How is it that a letter written on the 21st of March has reached me but four months later, through your medium? For what purpose did you keep it so long in portfolio? and why do you send me a copy, instead of the letter itself?

It is, you say, an "open letter." It was, nevertheless, meant to reach me. It opens and ends with forms of language bearing the touch of intimate relationship — more so even than could be expected from the rare intercourse which, in spite of our blood connection, had so far existed between your partner and myself. The whole thing has the appearance of a political manoeuvre executed under the name of a young and gallant officer, who has the advantage or inconvenience of being my cousin. That Capt. Papineau has put his signature at the foot of that document, it is possible; but he would certainly not have written it in cool thought, after due reflection. It not only expresses opinions radically opposed to those I heard from him before the war; it also contains inaccuracies of fact of which I believe him honourably incapable.

He mentions "some discussions in the past," "differences of opinion," which have left "uninjured" a "pleasant friendship," dating, he says, "from the time of [his] birth." From his childhood to his return from Oxford, I do not think we had ever met, and certainly never to exchange the slightest glimpse of thought or opinion. Of matters of national concern we talked but once in all my life. From that one conversation I gathered the impression that he was still more opposed than myself to any kind of imperial solidarity. He even seemed much disposed to hasten the day of the Independence of Canada. Since, I met him on two or three occasions. We talked of matters indifferent, totally foreign to the numerous questions treated with such eloquent profuseness and so little reasoning in his letter of the 21st of March.

How can he charge me with having expressed "unhappy views" "at the outstart of the war," in August 1914, and held them stubbornly "unchanged" till this day? In August 1914, I was abroad. My first pronouncement on the intervention of Canada in the war is dated September 8th, 1914. In that editorial, while repelling the principles of Imperial solidarity and their consequences, and maintaining the nationalist doctrine in which Capt. Papineau — and you as well — pretends to be still a believer, I pronounced myself in favour of the intervention of Canada, *as a nation,* for the defence of the superior interests uniting Canada with France and Britain. My "unhappy views" were thus analogous to those of your partner. It is but later, long after Capt. Papineau was gone, that my attitude was changed and brought me to condemn the participation of Canada in the war,— or rather the political inspiration of that participation and the many abuses which have resulted therefrom. The reasons of that change are well known to those who have read or heard with attention and good faith all my statements on the matter. To sum them up is now sufficient.

The free and independent participation of Canada — free for the nation and free for the individuals — I had accepted, provided it remained within reasonable bounds, in conformity with the conditions of the country. But the Government, the whole of Parliament, the press, and politicians of both parties all applied themselves systematically to obliterate the free character of Canada's intervention. "Free" enlistment is now carried on by means of blackmailing, intimidation, and threats of all sorts. Advantage has been taken of the emotion caused by the war to assert, with the utmost intensity and intolerance, the doctrine of Imperial solidarity, triumphantly opposed in the past by our statesmen and the whole Canadian people, up to the days of the infamous South African War, concocted by Chamberlain, Rhodes, and the British imperialists with the clear object of drawing the self-governing colonies into "the vortex of European militarism." That phrase of your political leader, Sir Wilfrid Laurier, is undoubtedly fresh in your mind. After having given way to the imperialistic current of 1899, Sir Wilfrid Laurier and the liberal party had come back to the nationalist doctrine. The naval scare of 1909 threw them again under the yoke of imperialism; the war has achieved their enslavement: they united with the tory-jingo-imperialists of all shades to make of the participation of Canada in the war an immense political manoeuvre and thus assure the triumph of British imperialism. You and your partner, like many others, have followed your party through its various evolutions. I have remained firmly attached to the principles I laid down at the time of the South African war and maintained unswervingly ever since.

As early as the month of March 1900, I pointed out the possibility of a conflict between Great Britain and Germany and the danger of laying down in South Africa a precedent, the fatal consequence of which would be to draw Canada into all the wars undertaken by the United Kingdom. Sir Wilfrid Laurier and the liberal leaders laughed at my apprehensions; against my warnings they quoted the childish safeguard of the "no precedent clause" inserted in the Order in Council of the 14th of October 1899. For many years after, till 1912, and 1913, they kept singing the praises of the Kaiser and extolling the peaceful virtues of Germany. They now try to regain time by denouncing vociferously the "barbarity" of the "Huns." Today, as in 1900, in 1911, and always, I believe that all the nations of Europe are the victims of their own mistakes, of the complacent servility with which they submitted to the dominance of all Imperialists and traders in human flesh, who, in England as in Germany, in France as in Russia, have brought the peoples to slaughter in order to increase their reapings of cursed gold. German Imperialism and British Imperialism, French Militarism and Russian Tsarism, I hate with equal detestation; and I believe as firmly today as in 1899 that Canada, a nation of America, has a nobler mission to fulfill than to bind herself to the fate of the nations of Europe or to any spoliating Empire — whether it be the spoliators of Belgium, Alsace, or Poland, or those of Ireland or the Transvaal, of Greece or the Balkans.

Politicians of both parties, your liberal friends as well as their conservative opponents, feign to be much scandalized at my "treasonable disloyalty." I could well afford to look upon them as a pack of knaves and hypocrites. In 1896, your liberal leaders and friends stumped the whole province of Quebec with the cry "WHY SHOULD WE FIGHT FOR ENGLAND?" From 1902 to 1911, Sir Wilfrid Laurier was acclaimed by them as the indomitable champion of Canada's autonomy against British Imperialism. His resisting attitude at the Imperial Conferences of 1902 and 1907 was praised to the skies. His famous phrase on the "vortex of European militarism," and his determination to keep Canada far from it, became the party's byword — always in the Province of Quebec, of course. His Canadian Navy scheme was presented as a step toward the independence of Canada.

Then came the turn of the Conservatives to tread in the footsteps of the Nationalists; they soon outstripped us. A future member of the conservative Cabinet, Mr. Blondin, brought back to life an old saying of Sir Adolphe Chapleau, and suggested to pierce the Union jack with bullets in order to let pass the breeze of liberty. The tory leaders, Sir Robert Borden, Sir George Foster, the virtuous Bob Rogers, and even our national superKitchener, Sir Sam Hughes, while trumpeting the purity of their Imperialism, greeted with undisguised joy the anti-imperialist victory of Drummond-Arthabaska, and used it for all it was worth to win the general elections in 1911.

By what right should those people hold me as a "traitor," because I remain consequent with the principles that I have never ceased to uphold and which both parties have exploited alternately, as long as it suited their purpose and kept them in power or brought them to office?

Let it not be pretended that those principles are out of place, pending the war. To prevent Canada from participating in the war, then foreseen and predicted, was their very object and *raison d'être*. To throw them aside and deny them when the time of test came, would have required a lack of courage and sincerity, of which I feel totally incapable. If this is what they mean by "British loyalty" and "superior civilization," they had better hang me at once. I will never obey such dictates and will ever hold in deepest contempt the acrobats who lend themselves to all currents of blind popular passion in order to serve their personal or political ends.

This, let it be well understood, does not apply to your partner. His deeds have shown the sincerity of his political turn. Without agreeing with his new opinions, I admired his silent courage in running to the front at the first call. His verbose political manifesto — supposing he is really responsible for it — adds nothing to his merits. Still less does it enhance the dignity and moral worth of the politicians and pressmen of all kinds, who, after having denounced war and imperialism, and while taking great care not to risk their precious body, have become the apostles of war and the upholders of imperialism.

I will not undertake to answer every point of the dithyrambic plea of my gallant cousin. When he says that I am too far away from the trenches to judge of the real meaning of this war, he may be right. On the other hand, his long and diffuse piece of eloquence proves that the excitement of warfare and the distance from home have obliterated in his mind the fundamental realities of his native country. I content myself with touching upon one point, on which he unhappily lends credit to the most mischievous of the many anti-national opinions circulated by the jingo press. He takes the French Canadians to task and challenges their patriotism, because they enlist in lesser number than the other elements of the population of Canada. Much could be said upon that. It is sufficient to signalize one patent fact: the number of recruits for the European war, in the various Provinces of Canada and from each component element of the population, is in inverse ratio of the enrootment in the soil and the traditional patriotism arising therefrom. The newcomers from the British Isles have enlisted in much larger proportion than English-speaking Canadians born in this country, while these have enlisted more than the French Canadians. The Western Provinces have given more recruits than Ontario, and Ontario more than Quebec. In each Province, the floating population of the cities, the students, the labourers and clerks, either unemployed or threatened with dismissal, have supplied more soldiers than the farmers. Does it mean that the city dwellers are more patriotic than the country people? or that the newcomers from England are better Canadians than their fellow citizens of British origin, born in Canada? No; it simply means that in Canada, as in every other country, at all times, the citizens of the oldest origin are the least disposed to be stampeded into distant ventures of no direct concern to their native land. It proves also that military service is more repugnant to the rural than the urban populations.

There is among the French Canadians a larger proportion of farmers, fathers of large families, than among any other ethnical element in Canada. Above all, the French Canadians are the only group exclusively Canadian, in its whole and by each of the individuals of which it is composed. They look upon the perturbations of Europe, even those of England or France, as foreign events. Their sympathies naturally go to France against Germany; but they do not think they have an obligation to fight for France, no more than the French of Europe would hold themselves bound to fight for Canada against the United States or Japan, or even against Germany, in case Germany should attack Canada without threatening France.

English Canada, not counting the *blokes*, contains a considerable proportion of people still in the first period of national incubation. Under the sway of imperialism, a fair number have not yet decided whether their allegiance is to Canada or to the Empire, whether the United Kingdom or the Canadian Confederacy is their country.

As to the newcomers from the United Kingdom, they are not Canadian in any sense. England or Scotland is their sole fatherland. They have enlisted for the European war as naturally as Canadians, either French or English, would take arms to defend Canada against an aggression on the American continent.

Thus it is rigorously correct to say that recruiting has gone in inverse ratio of the development of Canadian patriotism. If English-speaking Canadians have a right to blame the French Canadians for the small number of their recruits, the newcomers from the United Kingdom, who have supplied a much larger proportion of recruits than any other element of the population, would be equally justified in branding the Anglo-Canadians with disloyalty and treason. Enlistment for the European war is supposed to be absolutely free and voluntary. This has been stated right and left from beginning to end. If that statement is honest and sincere, all provocations from one part of the population against the other, and exclusive attacks against the French Canadians, should cease. Instead of reviling unjustly one-third of the Canadian people — a population so remarkably characterized by its constant loyalty to national institutions and its respect for public order,— those men who claim a right to enlighten and lead public opinion should have enough good faith and intelligence to see facts as they are and to respect the motives of those who persist in their determination to remain more Canadian than English or French.

In short, English-speaking Canadians enlist in much smaller number than the newcomers from England, because they are more Canadian; French Canadians enlist less than English Canadians because they are totally and exclusively Canadian. To claim that their abstention is due to the "baneful" influence of the Nationalists is a pure nonsense. Should I give way to the suggestion of my gallant cousin, I would be just as powerless as Sir Wilfrid Laurier to induce the French Canadians to enlist. This is implicitly acknowledged in Capt. Papineau's letter: on the one hand, he asserts that my views on the participation of Canada in the war are denied by my own friends; on the other he charges the mass of the French-Canadian population with a refusal to answer the call of duty. The simple truth is, that the abstention of the French Canadians is no more the result of the present attitude of the Nationalists than the consequence of the liberal campaign of 1896, or of the conservative appeals of 1911. It relates to deeper causes: hereditary instincts, social and economic conditions, a national tradition of three centuries. It is equally true, however, that those deep and far distant causes have been strengthened by the constant teaching of all our political and social leaders, from Lafontaine, Cartier, Macdonald, Mackenzie, to Laurier inclusively. The only virtue, or crime, of the Nationalists is to persist in believing and practising what they were taught by the men of the past, and even those of today. This is precisely what infuriates the politicians, either *blue* or *red*. To please the Imperialists, they have renounced all their traditions and undertaken to bring the French Canadians under imperial command. Unable to succeed, they try to conceal their fruitless apostasy by denouncing to the hatred of the jingos the obtrusive witnesses of their past professions of faith.

The jingo press and politicians have also undertaken to persuade their gullible followers that the Nationalists hinder the work of recruiters *because* of the persecution meted out to the French minorities in Ontario and Manitoba. This is but another nonsense. My excellent cousin, I am sorry to say,— or his inspirer — has picked it up.

The two questions are essentially distinct; this we have never ceased to assert. One is purely internal; the other affects the international status of Canada and her relations with Great Britain. To the problem of the teaching of languages we ask for a solution in conformity with the spirit of the Federal agreement, the best interests of Confederation, and the principles of pedagogy as applied in civilized countries. Our attitude on the participation of Canada in the war is inspired exclusively by the constant tradition of the country and the agreements concluded half a century ago between Canada and Great Britain. Even if the irritating bilingual question was non-existent, our views on the war would be what they are. The most that can be said is, that the backward and essentially Prussian policy of the rulers of Ontario and Manitoba gives us an additional argument against the intervention of Canada in the European conflict. To speak of fighting for the preservation of French civilization in Europe while endeavouring to destroy it in America, appears to us as an absurd piece of inconsistency. To preach Holy War for the liberties of the peoples overseas, and to oppress the national minorities in Canada, is, in our opinion, nothing but odious hypocrisy.

Is it necessary to add that, in spite of his name, Capt. Papineau is utterly unqualified to judge of the feelings of the French Canadians? For most part American, he has inherited, with a few drops of French blood, the most *denationalized* instincts of his French origin. From those he calls his compatriots he is separated by his religious belief and his maternal language. Of their traditions, he knows but what he has read in a few books. He was brought up far away from close contact with French Canadians. His higher studies he pursued in England. His elements of French culture he acquired in France. The complexity of his origin and the diversity of his training would be sufficient to explain his mental hesitations and the contradictions which appear in his letter. Under the sway of his American origin, he glories in the Revolution of 1776; he calls it a war "for the principle of national existence." In good logic, he should approve highly of the tentative rebellion of the Sinn Feiners, and suggest that Canada should rise in arms to break the yoke of Great Britain. His American forefathers, whom he admires so much, fought against England and called upon France and Spain to help them against their mother-country, for lighter motives than those of the Dublin rebels. The Imperial burden they refused to bear was infinitely less ponderous than that which weighs today upon the people of Canada.

With the threat contained in the conclusion of his letter, I need not be concerned. Supposing always that he is truly responsible for that document, I make broad allowance for the excitement and perturbation resulting from his strenuous life. He and many of his comrades will have enough to do in order to help Canada to counteract the disastrous consequences of the war venture in which she has thrown herself headlong. To propagate systematically national discord by quarrelling with all Canadians, either French or English, who hold different views as to the theory and practice of their national duty, would be a misuse of time. Moreover, it would be a singular denial of their professions of faith in favour of liberty and civilization.

As to the scoundrels and bloodsuckers "who have grown fat with the wealth dishonourably gained" in war contracts, I give them up quite willingly to their just indignation. But those worthies are not to be found in nationalist ranks: they are all recruited among the noisiest preachers of the Holy War waged for "civilization" against "barbarity," for the "protection of small nations," for the "honour" of England and the "salvation" of France.

Yours truly,
HENRI BOURASSA

P.S.— I hope this will reach you before you leave for the front: no doubt, you have been the first to respond to the pressing call of your partner.   H.B.

Article Twenty-Two

Ghosts Have Warm Hands

Will R. Bird

He led us down a long trench, and at last we were really at the front. We had become used to the slamming roar of gunfire and now we also heard the barking of machine-guns. Bullets came singing overhead, to go swishing into the darkness. Some struck on wire and we heard the sibilant whine of ricochets. We had sandbags to fill. One man held them and the other shovelled

Source: Excerpt from Will R. Bird, *Ghosts Have Warm Hands: A Memoir of the Great War, 1916–1919.* Reprinted with permission.

in gruel-like mud. When twenty were filled a man jumped on top and emptied the bags as they were handed up to him. It was ticklish work, as the one emptying had to jump down when machine-guns opened on that section.

We got soaked to the skin. The cold slime ran down our wrists as we lifted the bags, and our boots sunk in the mire until our feet were numbed, sodden things. All the next day we growled at Tommy for causing us such a night. Then, at dusk, Stevenson found us. Three of us were to go at once to an emplacement used by a big mortar they called a "flying pig."

When we got there we noticed a peculiar odour. All the shapeless ruin of Neuville St. Vaast stank of decay and slime, but this new smell halted us. "Here's bags," said Stevenson. "Go in there and gather up all you can find, then we'll bury it back of the trench. Get a move on."

A "flying pig" had exploded as it left the gun and three men had been shredded to fragments. We were to pick up legs and bits of flesh from underfoot, place all in the bags and then bury them. It was a harsh breaking-in. We did not speak a word as we worked. When we were done Stevenson told us we could go, but Tommy and I lingered in a trench bay and stared over the dark, flickering, silhouetted landscape.

Over the tangle of wire in front lay the no man's land about which we had heard. Not two hundred yards away were the Germans in their trenches. A thin stalk of silver shot up as we looked, curved over in a graceful parabola and flowered into a luminous glow, pulsating and wavering, flooding the earth below with a weird, whiteness. It was a Verey light. We craned our necks and stared. Jumbled earth and debris, jagged wreckage: it looked as if a gigantic upheaval had destroyed all the surface and left only a festering wound. Everything was shapeless, ugly and distorted.

We went on doing working parties and gradually got acquainted with the rest of the company. There were only a few "originals," the rest were reinforcements like ourselves, mostly from the 92nd of Toronto. Back we went to Mont St. Eloi and were billeted in huts on the hillside. It was wet and freezing cold at night. After the first day of sleeping and resting the men grew garrulous, and we listened to all they said about different craters such as Patricia, Birken, Common and Vernon. Across from where we slept was a Scot who was always singing "Maggie frae Dundee" or quarrelling with Stevenson, who had charge of the hut. Next to him was a tall, clean-built man, Roy MacMillan, from the 92nd. He and I became friends and he told me his experiences on the Somme.

When we went back for a second trip in the line, the wind was raw with driving rain. Once more we were on working parties. All this time we had not got to know an officer, and when we asked who commanded the company all they grunted was "Dugout Ray." One night Tommy and I were detained by Stevenson, who had us repair a place that had caved in. We were wet and cold and hungry. Rations were very slim, six men to one loaf of bread, and only bully and hardtack to help out. The hot tea kept up the morale. We got our messtins from our bunks and went over to a corner, where a sullen-faced man dished out the dinner. We stayed in the dugout and heated tea and mulligan and though we avoided shell fire we did not envy him his lot. There was no tea for us, he announced, but at that moment Stevenson came and got his messtin full.

We stepped forward and looked in the Dixie. There was plenty more and I said so. The cook snarled back that we had better be in France more than five minutes before trying to run things. Tommy took charge. He was well built and fast with his hands. He gave the fellow one short minute to fill his tin or else. The tin was filled. Later, when we were supposed to be sleeping, I heard the "old-timers" discussing us. They agreed it would be bad policy to try to run us, and the cook received no sympathy.

It was another six-day trip, but when we went back to Mont St. Eloi we felt old soldiers, and "Maggie frae Dundee" rang out merrily. This time there was a parade. Our company commander was a genial-looking gentleman. Our platoon officer was a MacDonald and seemed a good sort. We were taken to the "baths." In an old building through which the winter wind whistled, we undressed on a floor covered with slime and in turn crouched under an icy trickle from overhead pipes, the water always failing when one had soaped himself. When we went to get dressed we found our shirts were gone and a bleary-eyed character tossed over any size garment he happened to pick up, with unmatched socks.

When we went back to the line, Stevenson told me I would be one for Vernon Crater, and from the way he said it I judged it would be something unusual. Roy MacMillan joined me and said that he was to team up with me, that Vernon was a three-sentry post, had not been held in daytime before, and was not more than sixty yards from German posts. We were to hold the place for four days.

The weather turned the coldest France had known in thirty years. All the ground was frozen like iron. We wore leather jerkins over our greatcoats, had Balaclavas under our steel helmets, and socks on our hands. The supply of gloves was only enough for the oldtimers. It was very clear weather and every sound carried, so that we moved with utmost caution and very slowly. The main trench was a long, black-shrouded ditch full of dark figures muttering to each other, and there were hissed curses when a steel helmet clanged against a rifle barrel.

We turned from the main trench and went up a low-walled reach to the post, a wide affair in three sections. The right-hand corner was like an enlarged well with a fire step. Two men were placed there. On the left was a similar post and in it were Laurie and old Dundee. MacMillan and I were in the centre, a cup-like hollow. Behind us was a roofed space about six feet square in which Corporal Sellars, in charge, stayed. He had a seat there, a flare pistol and flares, and extra bombs. A blanket was hung over the rear entrance.

MacMillan explained everything about sentry duty, and I did not duck when the first flares went up. We could hear the Germans walking in their trenches, hear them coughing, hear them turning a creaking windlass that would be hauling up chalk from a dugout under construction. At daylight we put up small periscopes on slivers stuck in the sandbagged parapet and watched through them until dark.

The next night I saw my first uncaptured German. He was only a boy, as young-looking as Mickey, and he was standing waist-high above his trench wall as one of our flares burst directly above him and placed him in dazzling light.

He did not move at first — both sides had strict orders against any movement when a flare burst — but I knew he had seen me because I was as high on our side. He waved, and some wild impulse caused me to wave back to him as I jumped down. MacMillan cursed me soundly. After midnight I stepped back to talk with Sellars and, as it was bright moonlight, pushed aside the blanket at the rear and looked toward our trench. Ping! A bullet embedded itself in the wooden post beside me. I ducked back, very frightened. There were hurried steps outside and a corporal from the trench wanted to know if anyone was hit. A new draft of men, the 132nd from New Brunswick, had come into the line and one of them had watched our post all the time, thinking it was the German front.

A light snow fell the next day and whitened the jagged wilderness between the lines. There was a wrecked cart near the German wire, and as I peered at it, it blotted out, then appeared again. A whisper alerted MacMillan, and we detected two of the enemy crawling outside their post. "If we can catch them it's leave for us," hissed MacMillan. "Strip off your gear."

We shed jerkins and greatcoats and steel helmets, and examined our rifles. Unluckily mine stood at the back of the post and water from melted snow had frozen over the muzzle. MacMillan's had the breech uncovered and it was a lump of mud and ice. We jumped for our bombs and found them blocks of frozen mud, then looked over and saw the Germans re-entering their post. With first light we cleaned our rifles and bombs and made sure they would remain in good order.

Each morning a sergeant brought a rum issue just before light. I did not take mine and Laurie did not take his. A dozen or more of us in the draft never drank or smoked. This morning an officer was with the sergeant. He came in and stood beside me as MacMillan had his turn off and asked many questions while the sergeant was at the post on the right. He told me his name was Larson, that he was from Bear River, Nova Scotia, and thrilled with the front line. He wanted to know how near the Germans were.

I told him and he said it sounded unreal to him. It had become light as he talked, and when I put up the periscope it was shot away by a German sniper. "That fellow must be very near," said Larson.

"I'll take a quick look."

"Don't!" I yelled and grabbed at his coat. He stretched up in spite of my protest. The bullet entered his forehead and went out the back, breaking the strap of his helmet and carrying it to the rear of the post. I lowered the body to the trench floor and covered the face with a clean sandbag.

MacMillan was shocked. "Too much rum!" he said. The sergeant came from the other post and he was stunned. He said he would report what had happened and was hardly away when we heard a shot on the left post. The sergeant had given old Dundee two extra rum rations, mine and Laurie's, and the Scot had seized his rifle and started to clean it, saying he was going to get the sniper. The weapon went off in his hands and the bullet stuck the frozen side of the post, chipping bits from it. One struck Laurie on the foot and stung badly.

MacMillan tried to calm Dundee but he refused to listen. The rum had him wild. He raised up to aim his rifle, and the German shot. Dundee's head was turned so that the bullet took both eyes out. He tumbled down, clawing at his face and groaning.

Something had to be done and quickly. Sellars would not go for help. So I shed my equipment and crouched low as the sergeant had done. It was hard to keep that way, but when I raised ever so little a bullet burned the back of my neck like a hot iron. I reached the trench and got a stretcher bearer and stretcher. We were careful going in and arrived safely. But Dundee was in a bad state. We had to tie him on the stretcher, as he would not listen to anyone. Getting the stretcher and its load to the trench took almost half an hour. The stretcher bearer was ahead, pulling the stretcher, and I pushed from the rear. Finally it was done. Then I crawled back and sat all day beside the dead officer.

At dark we were relieved by the Princess Patricias. We went to Neuville St. Vaast again and into the cellars. Before morning a few of us were called out to form a ration party and we saw how easily a man could get a "blighty." We passed an old ruin with a long wall extending beyond it, light flickering through a small opening as flares went up. As we passed by there was a snapping of machine bullets overhead but they were disregarded, since the wall protected us. Then a man behind us yelled. A chance bullet had come through that brick-sized opening and hit him in the leg. He was bandaged and went cheerfully down the line.

When we returned with the rations I slept several hours, then was wakened and told to put on my pack and go with three other men to Mont St. Eloi. There we would meet a sergeant who would take us to a bombing school. The three of us met, had no conversation, but trudged out of the line and in due course arrived at long huts, where we found ourselves with men of the other battalions of the brigade. We were to be instructed in shooting rifle grenades and throwing Mills bombs. Our practice would be with live ones.

It was very pleasant. The hours were short and the rations plentiful. The next day at noon as we lolled in our bunks, there was a sudden shrill tearing sound and a terrific explosion just outside. Pieces of shrapnel came through the side of the hut. We leaped to the floor and raced from the building. A second shell came and there were loud cries for stretcher bearers. Four men were killed and seven wounded, but there was not a third shell.

To my delight I quickly learned the proper elevation for shooting rifle grenades, made top marks and also did well with the throwing. The battalion came to the huts at Mont St. Eloi and had it easy. When our six-day course was over I reported back to the platoon and was told I had been transferred to the battalion bombers. Tommy declared I had pulled strings to get such a shift. The weather became colder than ever, and we went into the line again and relieved the Pats.

The bombers were a grand lot, and I teamed with Sammy Sedgewick, a real gentleman. Chiefly we had to patrol the trenches. We had a good dugout and plenty of rations, and our hours were much easier than in the company, where a man did six hours on and six hours off with monotonous regularity all the time he was in the line. There you came down from your post, chilled through, dazed from lack of sleep, and pushed your way into the crowded underground to your chicken-wire bunk. You could lie and eat your rations, and consider yourself lucky if there was any lukewarm tea. The warmth of the men thawed the earth and chalk walls enough to make them ooze dampness. Rats were everywhere, podgy brutes with ghoulish eyes. They crawled over you as you lay under a blanket and tried to shiver yourself warm.

Twice in one night Sammy and I had a bomb target. A sentry stopped us and whispered as he pointed to dark blurs working at the German wire. We sent two grenades among them and a Lewis gun helped to complete the job. Later another sentry said the Germans were working at something opposite his post; he could hear thumping sounds, as if they were driving posts. We listened and heard the noise, set our rifles carefully and fired. There was the red flash of explosion and then a long drawn yell that ended in a screaming heard all along the line. The enemy sent over "darts" in reply, but none fell near us.

It was cold as ever the next night and no working parties were about. The ground was like rock. Sammy and I found a Lewis gun crew asleep, every man, and removed the gun, threw chalk and wakened them. They had a bad minute and didn't likely doze again that night. Sometimes I stopped with Mel Baillie or Mickey or Jenkins and talked with them of the home town.

The war changed men mightily. Down in dugouts where there was hardly room to breathe, men who had come from comfortable homes moved without complaint. All grousing was reserved for the "brass hats," who were supposed to be responsible for all that went wrong. The men were unselfish, each with a balance and discipline of his own. We endured much. Dugouts reeked with odours of stale perspiration and the sour, alkaline smell of clothing. There was never enough water to permit frequent washing and when we could get warm the lice tormented us. The vermin were in every dugout, millions of descendents of the originals of 1915. We seared the seams of our shirts with candles, fought them constantly but never conquered them.

The third afternoon the sergeant sent me on an errand up La Salle Avenue, a trench often strafed. Another man was walking ahead of me, and as we hurried along I heard the familiar *phew-phew-phew* in the air and yelled. The fellow sprinted like mad and I tried to follow suit, but my world crashed in a bang. A million bells rang in my ears. Lights danced and sparkled and I could not get my breath. Hands tugged at me. Eventually I got up, to stare at a smoking crater not ten feet from where I had fallen. The big "rum jar" had fallen between us, though the other man was twice as far from it. He was shell-shocked and taken from the line. I was sick for an hour and my head throbbed half the night but I stayed in the trenches.

The next night I stopped to talk with Fernley, a quiet fellow of the 42nd who was a real friend. He stood his rifle against the side of the trench and was pacing up and down and beating his chest with his arms in an effort to get warm. We chatted a time and then I moved on and was about ten yards from him when a German "dart" burst on the parapet several feet from where Fernley was walking. He sank to the duckboards like a wet sack. I hurried to him and spoke but he did not answer. He was dead.

There was not a mark on him. I got the sergeant and he examined Fernley, but he was mystified too. We carried him to the dressing station and they stripped him and could not find a mark of injury. I went back to the trench and looked around. Suddenly I noticed Fernley's rifle still standing there — and the top part of the bayonet gone! The mystery was soon solved. The piece had entered an armpit and pierced his heart. Not a drop of blood had issued from the wound.

We were in supports again, then back in the front trench. Seven men went out with sickness, two with foot trouble, and I found myself on a crater post doing a regular turn of six hours on. It was very cold and I was about fifteen yards from the main trench. One night I saw someone coming up the sap with no rifle. That meant he was an officer, and when he stood with me in the post and asked questions I was careful, for a time, about what I said. He asked me where I was from, what I had done before the war. I told him of taking up a homestead in Alberta, the big money I had made for a time working for an eccentric American who used the name Smith. Smith had imported four wolf hounds from Russia and purchased a pair of half-broken broncos and a buckboard. He built a large box on the back of the buckboard and put the hounds in it. The box had a door attached to a wire. When be saw a coyote we drove past it, and at the second of passing the door was flipped up and out shot the hounds, who would run the coyote down. There was a bounty of fifty cents per coyote snout. I told the officer about our hunts, about the hard work on the harvest field, and about the sugar maple trees in the hills where I was born. He stayed and stayed and brought the talk around to the battalion. How did I like the infantry? I was careful, and he knew it. He laughed at some of my answers and finally asked me if I knew who he was. I said I had no idea. He asked who commanded the 3rd Division.

"Major-General Lipsett," I said.

"Does he ever come to the front line?" was the next question. I said I did not know. We were standing shoulder to shoulder in the narrow post and he nudged me. "You're an interesting fellow, Bird," he said. "I am Lipsett!"

The information was so surprising I became tongue-tied and he nudged me again. "I don't blame you in the least if you don't believe me," he said, "so I'm going to give you a snapshot I had taken in 1913. All I ask is that you will not tell your mates I did so."

He tugged the postcard-size snapshot from an inner pocket and gave it to me, shook my hand warmly and left. I still have that picture.

The sergeant came and said I was for a reconnaissance with him. We crawled out under our wire at a place where it had been raised, and moved away by inches as we wormed between Durrand and Duffield Craters. After each yard we listened, so that it was an hour before we were in a position to examine the enemy wire. When we got back to our trench we were nearly frozen. The other bombers said a raid was to be made from both our craters and from the Patricia posts. The next day the Stokes mortars pounded the German line.

The raid was on February 13 and zero hour was 9:15 a.m. The German trench was to be given a baptism of rifle grenades, so each bomber was given ten grenades. We had exactly two minutes to shoot them. It was easy to make a mistake and cause a premature burst, but no accident occurred and we got our barrage away on time. Then we went into a tunnel entrance and awaited the raiders' return. Two officers and six men were wounded. Two prisoners were taken.

That night we relieved the "Van Doos" and it was my job to guide their bombers to our dugout. There were only six of them and they had me nervous before my chore ended. They had had too much rum, they lagged all the way, talked loudly, and one man played a mouth organ.

The 42nd bombers took a chance overland and we got out ahead of the company. Shortly after they took over, the Germans gave the Van Doos a housewarming in the shape of a "Minnie" bombardment. We were told they had thirty casualties in the hour.

The next day we marched and marched and marched, going through several towns, and at last arrived at Divion. After the long session in the crater line with little exercise, it was a hard grind. Three fellows dropped out. My legs were very tired but I lasted the route. We moved into a billet and a runner arrived to tell us the bombers were no more. A re-organization was taking place and we were to return to our respective platoons.

When I woke in the morning I was very stiff and sore. Someone reported me, and the battalion medical sergeant, a prince of a fellow, came and asked me about my experience with the "rum jar." He said I had undoubtedly suffered a concussion, that I was to remain in billets and go on sick parade in the morning. Our billet was a French cottage, a miner's home. Downstairs was a fair-sized room with a tall, pot-bellied stove, table and chairs. Two small bedrooms opened from it. Upstairs was one large space. There was no window and we slept on the first floor, four of us.

Article Twenty-Three

Recruiting, 1914–1916

Ronald G. Haycock

Military records show that by the end of the Great War 619 636 Canadian men and women had served with the army. It took four years to raise such a number, and well over half enlisted while Sam Hughes was war minister. By late 1916 when he was fired from the cabinet, the army overseas had four divisions and another ready for organization. But Canadians at home had lost much of their enthusiasm for volunteering to feed the field force. However, two years earlier the opposite had been true when the majority of Canadians seemed determined to do their duty. After the first contingent left Valcartier, the prime minister authorized a second one in mid-October. The next month militia headquarters decided to maintain 30 000 men under arms in Canada. By July 1915 the overall total was 150 000 and three months later 250 000. On New Year's Day 1916, the prime minister announced that the national establishment of the Canadian Expeditionary Force (CEF) would be a half million men. It all looked so easy. But by mid-1916, the volunteer system began to falter all over the country. As the war effort stepped up, the demands of the other equally vital forces of industry and agriculture competed for the men. Enlistments slowed down. In English Canada pessimistic conscription rumours turned into open demands; and as enlistments dried up before the mounting casualties in Europe, French Canadians recoiled at the prospect of being drafted for a foreign war, which by 1916 they no longer considered much of their concern.

To avoid a national schism — perhaps even an open rebellion — the government desperately tried other solutions. By the fall of 1916 national registration to co-ordinate the wealth of the nation had come and gone. In early 1917, amid the crescendo of English-Canadian

Source: From *Sam Hughes: The Public Career of a Controversial Canadian, 1885–1916*, Ronald G. Haycock, Wilfrid Laurier University Press in collaboration with the Canadian War Museum, the Canadian Museum of Civilization, and the National Museums of Canada, 1986, pp. 198–224. Used with permission.

voices demanding conscription, the harried Borden administration attempted to free volunteers for the front by establishing the Canadian Defence Force for domestic duty, but it too failed. That spring, after the British authorities predicted the need for more and more troops, the prime minister finally resigned himself to military conscription. In May 1917 he announced his intention and padded the blow by promising to bring in conscription through a union government. In the next six months, the declaration split the country along French and English lines, irrespective of party, and by the general election in December 1917, Canada had both coalition government and conscripts[1] The story of these events involves Sam Hughes, and to a large degree he, like his prime minister, must bear both praise and blame.

Sam Hughes' one-man mobilization effort in 1914 set the tone for recruiting in the next two years. Hughes gave to the recruitment effort nerve-end leadership — spirit, enthusiasm, vigour, hope, and confidence — but little order and less administration. He conceived of Canada's war contributions mainly in terms of fighting troops in a national army. But he never appeared to understand fully the modern needs of such a force. He could not see, first, that national war must have at least a semblance of consensus of the nation's people — both French and English — and second, that limits on the size of the force and the method of keeping it at established strength were problems which eventually would have to be faced. Force size was a political problem that belonged to the government as a whole but one for which Sam Hughes as militia minister must give sound and realistic advice to the cabinet. Maintenance of strength, however, was an administrative question that for the most part belonged to Sam Hughes. Instead of understanding these dimensions, he seemed governed solely by a desire to show Canada's martial prowess on the battlefield in a huge patriotic and volunteer army without regard for the effects of unrestrained recruiting on industry, agriculture, or the combat efficiency of the force.[2] But in 1914 and 1915 the faults of Sam Hughes's recruiting system were not immediately obvious because the demands of war were not known; and in all fairness to Hughes, few of his fellow ministers in the beginning had any more of an accurate conception of how best to respond to the crisis. For months all of them worked in the dark using dilapidated tools of state. Some found both light and better utensils; Hughes never did.

When the first contingent had sailed in October 1914, Hughes had been thankful that Borden had allowed all the volunteers to go, a sure sign that both men agreed in the limited and archaic view that the best way to pursue the war effort was with soldiers in large numbers. When Hughes returned from England early the next month he immediately plunged into the organization of the second contingent, recently announced by the prime minister. In terms of manpower, he swung back to the old decentralized recruiting arrangements that had been with the militia since Confederation. In the scheme, authority rested with the officers commanding the divisions, who in turn gave quotas to each of the militia units of their areas. The quotas were supplied by headquarters, but beyond that there was little help from Ottawa in personnel, funds, or organization. In the first three years of the war, Ottawa spent only $27 000 on recruitment, most of it in 1917. But then little help was expected.[3]

The months from August 1914 to July 1915 are best described as ones of the enlisting rather than recruiting. Nearly 60 000 had joined in 1914 alone. By February 1915 Hughes announced that a third contingent would be sent and optimistically told the Commons that "I could raise three more contingents in three weeks if necessary." As yet there was no perceived shortage of manpower in industry or agriculture. But it was the off-season for agriculture, and others presumed that the recession-induced unemployed were being conveniently siphoned off into CEF units. By June 1915 the overseas force had 100 247 officers and men. During the special session of Parliament the year before, Hughes had made it clear that as far as he was concerned this war would be one of volunteers, not conscripts. The prime minister had agreed when he told a Halifax audience in December that "there has not been, there will not be compulsion or conscription." The only technique Hughes applied during this period was to keep close watch on who got the commands of each new battalion.[4] Sometimes the divisional commanders asked that units be allowed to organize in their districts; other times — and increasingly so — Hughes made arrangements himself with specific individuals, then informed the divisional organization to expect a new unit in the area. True to his romantic view of war, the minister was convinced that in a crisis a citizen's patriotic sense of duty would be sufficient to supply all the volunteers necessary. All he had to do was constantly remind them of it. As soon as he recovered sufficiently from the illness that had put him in the hospital in late December, Hughes took to his private rail car late in January to encourage volunteering. He had to get back to Ottawa by the opening of the new session on 5 February but before that he covered seven thousand miles in two weeks and delivered over twenty-five recruiting speeches across the country.[5]

Hughes gave out the stuff that many wanted to hear: the Empire was threatened; Canada had to do its duty. Canadians could do it and would do it; it was the moment of national greatness; Canada was a principal in the war, not a colony. Hughes's battle message, mixing national pride and imperial obligation, was contagious. No wonder Castell Hopkins considered him during those early days to be the single most visible and enthusiastic recruiting agent in the country.[6] The minister's confidence, pride, and cajoling also added to the impression that manpower resources were infinite and no other government facilities except Sam Hughes's sermons were necessary in raising the country to war.

The illusion was substantially aided by patriotic citizens themselves. The fervour seemed so great that the problem was not in stirring it up but in controlling it. The various gifts of money and food sent to the Belgian Relief Fund and to the British government in the early days were ample evidence of that spirit; so were the campaigns in many communities to contribute to the well-being of the soldiers. Local councils quickly arranged for gifts of money, clothing, and the small amenities like cigarettes and socks. Many churches and women's organizations across the country did their bit as well. The Ontario government donated a half million dollars to the Imperial War Fund in Great Britain. The same special session of Parliament that brought the ominous War Measures Act into being in August 1914 also created the Canadian Patriotic Fund, of which Hughes was one of the honorary vice-presidents. This group was dedicated to raising and distributing money to soldiers' families and it expanded and carried out this function throughout the war. In fact, the general shortage of equipment produced such a spontaneous public response of private donations, like "the machine gun movement," that militia officials and Borden were so embarrassed by the summer of 1915, they refused to accept such gifts. Hughes, however, had no such pangs. His role, he knew, was to encourage the people on to new heights of patriotic effort. In fact, Robert Borden's biographer claims that this sort of decentralized war responsibility was a calculated "policy decision at the beginning of the war." Hughes's activities in recruiting, therefore, were not out of tune with the rest of the government's general view of its role in promoting active citizen participation in the war effort.[7]

However, by the spring of 1915 there were signs that these time-honoured concepts were not adequate. There were thirty-six thousand Canadians already overseas, with an entire division in the trenches after February 1915. The war had lasted longer than the predicted six months; Christmas had come and gone and there were yet no victories. Then in mid-March, the British reported thirteen thousand casualties, including one hundred Canadians, at Neuve Chapelle, and bungled the opportunity for the elusive "breakthrough" on the western front to regain the magic mobility every general sought. Even though few Canadian were victims, the twenty-five thousand lost on both sides was a terrible omen for Canadians. The CEF did not have long to wait: a few weeks later the Canadians held a bulging section of the line near Ypres in Belgium. Late in the day of 22 April, the Germans smashed into the French colonial troops to the left of the Canadians with artillery and the dreaded chlorine gas. In a ferocious defensive battle lasting nearly a week, Canada's tenacious amateurs restored the line at the terrible price of nearly six thousand men. They won the admiration of all. Their effort was quickly followed by smaller but similarly expensive defences at Festubert in May and Givenchy in June. The Germans torpedoed the supposedly unarmed British liner *Lusitania* off the coast of Ireland on 8 May. It took twelve hundred lives, one hundred of them from Ontario. This was indeed war; Canadians were stunned.[8]

Back home the successes of the CEF in these battles stirred the Canadian soul; but they also were a rude awakening to the true sacrifices. The Canadian Ross rifle, it was reported, had not worked well. Some said gunners had not had enough artillery shells to give adequate support to the Canadian infantry. But the most shocking revelations were the casualty lists. An increasing number of Canadian homes mourned the loss of loved ones; and it was not likely to stop. At the end of May the British government announced, largely as a result of the jolt to its own complacency caused by the German spring offensive, that "His Majesty's Government would accept with deep gratitude" any number of troops the Canadians could send.[9] Hughes took it as a personal signal.

But would Hughes's non-system of recruiting provide the reinforcements? Even before Ypres there were signs that the rural militia units were having trouble filling their enlistment quotas. *Globe* columnist Peter McArthur demanded that it was time the militia minister co-ordinate his actions with the Agriculture Department in some definite recruiting policy. Part of the flash of enthusiasm which had given nearly sixty thousand volunteers in 1914 was that most of the ranks — over 70 percent in the first contingent — were not Canadians, but British-born immigrants. Initially native Canadians had little enthusiasm to fight for king and Empire in Europe. This fact made no impression on Hughes, at least not one that he nor anyone else admitted publicly. Yet suspicions indicated something extra was needed. Other citizens began stepping into the breach with or without Sam Hughes. The same month as Neuve Chapelle, the Speakers Patriotic League, the joint brainchild of H.A. Ames, a Quebec Conservative MP, and N.F. Davidson, an Ontario Tory organizer, was created in Toronto. It was the first of many private civilian associations designed to promote all facets of the patriotic response to the war, including a more systematic recruiting organization. From this point, private recruiting leagues appeared all over English Canada. Their proliferation in Ontario was so rapid that by November 1915 they combined into a central organization — the Ontario Recruiting Association with branches throughout the province working hand in hand with local militia authorities.[10]

Hughes was all for the local organizations and a personal approach to the war effort, as he had been since he had sent out his famous 226 night telegrams mobilizing the first contingent shortly after the war started. After that he had used the existing local militia structure to funnel into the CEF whole battalions closely associated with particular areas. But he did not do it without opposition. Since September 1914, the chief of the general staff had warned Hughes that he could not keep adding such units to the overseas force. What should be done, Gwatkin had then protested, was to establish modern centrally located depots providing basic training for the unbrigaded troops before they were syphoned off as reinforcements for the veteran line units. Before the war Sir Ian Hamilton had also warned Hughes about this lack of depots. Their reasons were solid. More efficient training and use of manpower and a smaller casualty rate were three important ones. As well, authorities would have some accurate idea of available resources on hand, a fact not always present in the anachronistic and decentralized method which Hughes had followed since the outbreak of hostilities. The American Civil War, of which Hughes claimed to be a student, had pointed out the perils of constantly raising new battalions, then sending these fresh but green troops into battle. But the minister did not believe it was so; the Boer war needed no such elaborate and soulless depots to produce good fighting men, so he ignored his staff.[11]

After the spring battles of 1915, the shocking casualties and increased demands reaffirmed Hughes's resolve to secure more men. The second contingent had lingered long in Canada awaiting transport and billets in England. Hughes was anxious to get it overseas. By the middle of June it sailed, but the recruiting news at home, while gratifying, was not as spectacular as it had been. It seemed that just as the manpower demands were rising remarkably, the will to supply them was faltering. The possibilities of a substantial short-fall were obvious after it became clear at the end of June that Hughes wanted to form a Canadian corps of two divisions. The thought horrified Connaught; he secretly confided to Kitchener that the move was a ruinous one contrived by Hughes for no other reason than to satisfy his ego for a Canadian national force "possibly with a view of obtaining the command . . . himself." The Duke also suffered from his own form of exaggeration: he was afraid of an invasion by German-Americans from the still neutral United States, and even more of a revolt in the west by recent immigrants from enemy countries. Troops should therefore be kept in Canada. More accurately, Connaught worried about the disastrous effect on vital agricultural and industrial production caused by Hughes's wholesale recruiting. Connaught protested to Lord Kitchener that it was "extremely doubtful" if the Dominion could "keep an Army Corps in the field up to its proper establishment."[12]

It was not probable that Hughes had duped Borden into supporting the formation of a Canadian corps, as the governor general also imagined. The prime minister was himself determined to send more troops. Nevertheless, the governor general had put his finger on the exact point that caused the regular soldiers so much anxiety. An army corps meant at least fifty thousand troops in France. A corps was also the natural precursor of an army. Gwatkin and Deputy Minister Fiset had been greatly alarmed at the wastage of the CEF in the spring of 1915. At that time, Canada had to contend only with one division. The possibility of twice as many casualties came with the formation of a corps. An army, if it came out of that, would be impossible to maintain. Gwatkin wanted no more than a corps, and certainly not an army. In June when he told Borden that Hughes's grandiose plans were a "mistake;" it had made no impression. A few days later, in responding to an enthusiastic militia colonel, who like many of the patriots wanted many more men sent, Gwatkin bluntly stated that it was wrong "to go on adding to the number of regiments, batteries, and battalions at the front." Better, he thought, to train reinforcements and produce war material rather than to be drawn into an intolerable and exhausting war effort because of a commitment to an unrealistic combat force.[13] The true import of his and the Duke's message was that Sam Hughes's vision of a massive field effort was courting ruin, and that there were different ways to make war other than by sending warriors. Also implicit was that Hughes should advise Borden that a realistic establishment had to be determined and then adopt an efficient method of maintaining it that was in tune with national capabilities.

It was not to happen. On 8 July 1915, Robert Borden increased the CEF force to 150 000.[14] The new figure meant more recruits. While the monthly enlistments had gone up in June, they were not sufficient to allow for even normal wastage in the new national goal.

In response Hughes remained largely on the old personal course. But a few weeks earlier, he had made some small concessions in applying direct government aid for recruiting when he decided that central rather than regimental recruiting offices would be set up and that recruiting would be continuous. In August, as a further inducement for volunteers, he approved from afar a national recruiting poster campaign; one hundred thousand of them were distributed from coast to coast. After that no other national advertising went on out of the militia headquarters for over a year, and even then the minister rejected the Canadian Press Association's offer to cooperate in a national newspaper campaign to stimulate recruiting.[15]

In the summer of 1915, Hughes spent two months in England. Like the prime minister who was also there, Hughes went to the front where he saw the magnitude, the horror, and the deadlock of the war situation. When he got back to Canada in early September, what he had seen and heard only cemented his determination to step up the national effort. Canada now had a corps, but victory was not close; the British had not handled the first year at all well. What was needed was more and more troops. At the end of September, enlistment figures dipped threateningly. Hughes told reporters about his new local battalion and billeting plans. Modelled in part on Lord Derby's battalions in England, Hughes promised to house and train troops in any centre that could raise twenty-five or more district recruits. Surely, he reasoned, it would help the citizens realize the importance of the war as well as comfort men anxious about doing initial duty in a strange place. But the other aspect of the scheme had its roots in the traditional local unit structure of the non-permanent militia. Indeed, that was its very essence and the sum of Sam Hughes's forty-one years of experience in the Canadian volunteers. Hughes believed in the time-honoured technique of raising citizen-soldiers by appointing prominent politicians and businessmen as lieutenant-colonels to enlist battalions in their own local areas.[16] Sometimes these men were the minister's personal and political friends who had no particular military knowledge. Over the next year, because recruiting "was continuous" and the men were penny-packeted across the country, the training was a hit and miss affair. The first man to enlist trained most, the last man hardly at all. Often those early volunteers, in effect, immediately became recruiters themselves in the desperate rush to get other men. The local billeting made the plan costly. In some cases supervision was nearly impossible and consequently discipline was often poor. Evidently the plan also deviated from the central recruiting centres set down earlier in the summer. Implicit in Hughes's scheme was the suggestion that recruits raised from the same locality would go overseas and fight together. As it turned out, the units were broken up in England to maintain the strength of the corps in France. A.M.J. Hyatt and Desmond Morton have called Hughes's scheme variously a "confidence trick" or a hoax. Since the labels both imply deliberate intent to defraud, such charges are not fair to Hughes any more than they are to Borden who supported the methods. Yet continuous recruiting until the moment of departure made retraining in England almost a certainty. Nevertheless, these problems were not Hughes's concern; and even though they should have been, his mind could not handle those sorts of details, if he saw the flaws at all. He wanted men, and at October's end, Borden followed Hughes's lead, again raising the national commitment to 250 000.[17]

Why Borden did this is not clear. His biographer suggests the cause was rising casualties, more and more demands, poor leadership in London and Ottawa, and the lack of decisive victory. The papers of Captain Harold Daly, Hughes's assistant, explain more:

> Once toward the end of 1915, he [Hughes] decided to raise another 100 000 men. He went over to see Sir Robert Borden, got authority for it, and told me to send over and get an atlas showing the different [political] constituencies. He then dictated about a hundred telegrams to different people, one in each constituency and out of that I think we got 60 000–70 000 men. He knew everybody all over the country who was popular and who could raise men.[18]

If Daly's memory is correct, the comment epitomizes the personal improvised nature of Hughes's recruiting ideas. But more than that, Daly's observations point out the scope of political party organization; with its emphasis on patronage as the means, the party system had traditionally performed many of the social duties that, in later days, Canadians expected the state to undertake. When war was declared this party machinery geared up to help solve the country's recruitment problem.

Hughes was one of the chief supporters and users of this traditional party system. In 1914 it was at the root of his 226 night telegrams; it was present in his retention of control over military offices and later recruiting. As represented by Sam Hughes, the government provided the impulses to the party structure to secure volunteers. What was in the interest of the party was good for the country. On that October day in 1915, when he told Daly to get out the constituent map, he was really calling for a stepped-up effort by the old party system as one of the normal pieces of machinery running that portion of the war effort. The episode also illuminates the relationship and similarity of ideas between Hughes and Borden. For a short time at least, it appeared that Hughes's recruiting rationale was paying off. With the new establishment set that October, enlistments jumped by five thousand in November, and again in December.[19]

While men like Daly may have thought the minister's recruiting accomplishments "wonderful," the other powerful reasons for the success remained the loyal and hard work of the volunteer citizens, recruiting leagues, and sufficient men who were willing to join. Yet Hughes remained, with his continuous touring, speeches, and inspections, the most visible single national recruiting figure in the entire improvised scheme. The apparent success of the combination, which he believed was mostly due to his own efforts, stirred the minister to make bigger promises and more boastful claims. Already on record the previous February as claiming that he could raise three more contingents in three weeks, a little later he told a Montreal audience that he could "send a fifth [division] a sixth, a tenth or a twentieth." In Toronto in October, he declared to an enthusiastic recruiting rally: "We are coming General Kitchener, 500 000 strong." By the end of the year, Borden had translated that optimism into a half-million-man establishment for the CEF.[20]

On 30 December, when Hughes and two other cabinet colleagues, White and Reid, met with Borden, the prime minister proposed that the overseas forces' establishment should be raised to five hundred thousand. The move, Borden was convinced, would be welcomed by English Canadians who were beginning to think that the Conservative administration, except for Hughes's activities no doubt, was not fighting the war vigorously enough. He also believed that the larger the physical contribution the greater would be Canada's influence over British war policy. With the way events were going at the front, the prime minister went on to reason, surely such a force would be needed. If all three visitors were surprised by the proposal, Hughes at least expected and wanted the new commitment; and he supported it fully. By 12 January, the establishment of the CEF was put at five hundred thousand men. The question was: Could it be done?[21]

By now there were even Canadians who felt that it was too dangerous and too difficult a task; and as for others, maybe because they were Englishmen or professional soldiers or both, no one had bothered to consult General Gwatkin, the governor general, or the people at the War Office; all of them were opposed. Borden also ignored R.B. Bennett, his parliamentary secretary, who had complained earlier that December that the new figure was impossible. Evidently few other ministers were consulted before Borden's decision was made. The new goal had been an impulse supported by Hughes, by White and Reid, and indirectly endorsed by Sir George Foster in the trade department, who naively thought that if 40 percent of the population of about eight million was of military age then a five hundred thousand man CEF was not unrealistic. Ironically, Foster also thought that Hughes's recruiting methods were unrealistic and chaotic.[22]

But there was no doubt in the militia minister's mind that they could get the half million. Neither a challenge to the prime minister's judgment nor a doubt of its subsequent effect on other vital sectors of the war effort came from Hughes. Privately he told Borden, "we can easily live up to your offer, if right systems are pursued." Immediately he plunged into the new challenge by commissioning more local battalions and more local prominent citizens, friends, and businessmen. In 1915 alone, beyond the elements of the second contingent, Hughes had already approved of 141 CEF units; in 1916 the same method added 79 more; and as the local sources were no longer as fruitful, Hughes encouraged special interests, which encouraged the proliferation of Highland battalions, "Pals" and "Bantams" formations, and Irish regiments.

Early in 1916 Hughes also promised that he would bring the best of the overseas officers home from the front to raise new units, a proposal which must have alarmed CEF commanders already suffering from serious shortages of reinforcements and experienced officers. As before, the minister rejected using only the regular military structure; what he sought, he said, was "strong men who have successful business or professional training . . . the best soldiers are such men as engineers, barristers, contractors, large businessmen with military training . . . They far surpass the professional soldier."[23]

Ministerial optimism knew no bounds. In January 1916 Hughes easily convinced Borden to approve the establishment of a fourth Canadian division; the announcement sparked Max Aitken, the minister's chief overseas agent, to wire flatteringly: "Your exertions may save the Empire." Certainly the accolade spurred the militia minister on; in February he told a New York *Times* reporter that he could raise one and three-quarter million men without compulsion in a matter of a few months. In Ottawa he laid out an elaborate plan to raise nearly twenty more divisions. It was unrealistic. Toronto was to give five, Ontario four; Manitoba and Saskatchewan, Quebec, British Columbia, and the Maritimes each gave two.[24]

By then the magnitude of Hughes's plans started to frighten his cabinet colleagues. Frequently council meetings, already stormy, became even more bitter. Thomas White was now alarmed. Hughes, he complained, "wants to press recruiting regardless of other considerations." It was true. Even the prime minister was finally having doubts about his own national pledge in the hands of Sam Hughes. He asked the militia minister not to recruit so that it dislocated other national priorities or denuded some localities of their manpower. Hughes paid little heed, but continued to cajole the country into sending more of its sons. From January to March 1916 over ninety thousand Canadians joined up.[25]

But in the spring of 1916 there were pressing public arguments against unrestrained enlistments. Ironically much of the discontent came from those groups which had often been the minister's most fervent recruiting aids — the civilian recruiting leagues. Dissatisfied for some time, they all agreed that the government could no longer count on volunteering to provide the resources. Now that Canadian industry, agriculture, timber, and mining resources were beginning to feel the strains of full wartime employment, the government had to impose a centralized and integrated recruiting policy to avoid harming the effort of the home-front. Moreover, the burden had to be distributed so that all parts of the Dominion were sharing it equally; and many identified Quebec as delinquent in doing its share. To some, what was needed was a national registration of the manpower, to others, an inventory of all wealth of the nation including human, and to even others, compulsion if necessary. But they all agreed that the Borden government could no longer avoid direct involvement in recruiting and national mobilization.

Two of the most prominent critics were Lord Shaughnessy, president of the CPR, and Senator James Mason, the seventy-three-year-old former commanding officer of the 10th Royal Grenadiers. Both men had been great supporters of the war effort. But by March they were sceptical about meeting the new national pledge of half a million men. When Shaughnessy spoke out in Montreal about the goal's harmful effect on national production, Hughes scornfully dismissed the warning as a "piffle," and publicly told Shaughnessy to mind his own business. Privately Borden agreed, choosing to believe that Shaughnessy's statement was nothing more than a political conspiracy against his administration. But then James Mason laid bare for his senate colleagues the hard realities of Borden's goals and the weaknesses of Hughes's improvised recruiting. "This large number [500 000]," he told a hushed chamber, "means that we shall have to provide each month . . . at least 25 000 new men — or 300 000 a year. There can be no question that the additional 250 000 to bring our quota up to 500 000 and the 300 000 if required annually to keep it at that figure will not be obtained under the present system of enlistment."[26] To Hughes it was still "piffle."

But it was not so to others. Many of the provincial governments had organized their war effort far better than Hughes had his own department. The Canadian Manufacturers' Association followed up Shaughnessy's predictions in a memorandum critical of Hughes's unlimited and unorganized recruiting. Various patriotic and recruiting leagues called for conscription or at least creation of a national register of wealth. So did Sir John Eaton, and executives of the Nova Scotia Steel Company, Consumers Gas, and the Dominion Steel Corporation. In April the New Brunswick Legislature passed a resolution asking Borden to employ "scientific means" in recruiting to protect industry and agriculture; and many national newspaper editorials carried similar messages. The old Tory, Castell Hopkins, sadly reported to readers of his *Canadian Annual Review* that during these months "the arbitrary policy and personality of Sam Hughes sometimes worked against recruiting as his enthusiasm and efforts worked for it." There was more alarming evidence long before the year was through. By April the monthly recruiting figures started to plummet from over thirty-four thousand in March to a low of about six thousand by September 1916, where they remained for some time. However, the previous spring while the protest was rising and the enlistments falling, Borden had done little publicly to change Hughes's improvised methods. In April the prime minister refused to hear a delegation of recruiting league members who had come to him hoping that he would do something in terms of registration and compulsion. When he refused to act, as Sir George Foster confessed to the delegates the next day, it was because the cabinet was afraid of riots in Quebec. In the same month, the frustrated recruiters formed the Canadian National Service League and openly lobbied for the draft.[27]

While Hughes remained in effective control of his department through 1915 and 1916, he continued to ignore the criticisms that his method of recruiting did not work. But many of his newly minted colonels who were raising local battalions were increasingly aware that there were serious problems. Frequently Hughes had authorized several units in the same area, and the battalion commanders ended up in cutthroat competition for men. Many used any method they could to secure the quotas; and it varied from bribing to shaming the individual into enlisting. None of it encouraged the hesitant volunteer. Two examples seem typical of those who had problems. Late in 1915 the militia minister let his old friend, William Price, raise a unit, the 204th, in Quebec's Eastern Townships. After spending three months and a great deal of his time and money, and still never forming much of a battalion, Price lost his enthusiasm. His complaints to Hughes's aide in February 1916 sum up many unit commanders' frustrations and the minister's inability to give recruiting some structure:

> I can now see that there will be difficulty in raising many men in this province. The organization is rotten and there is a complete misunderstanding of how to get French-Canadians to recruit. Each battalion should be given a certain district and should be forced to recruit from there and not allowed outside. This would force the battalions to recruit their localities thoroughly; at present, they do as they like and steal from each other. The way things go I am going to have a hard time to raise my men. . . . You might tell Sir Sam after what I have, it is impossible with the present organization to raise twenty thousand men from the district. To do so requires a complete new system and some slave driver at the head with the power of sacking.[28]

This unit never completed its establishment. Further west, where recruiters did not have to contend with reluctant French Canadians, Lieutenant-Colonel W.A. Griesbach, commanding officer of the 49th (Edmonton Regiment), had much more success. But he still complained of the lack of organization and the disastrous effects of interbattalion competition.[29] One of the problems was that Hughes would not establish a centrally controlled system. The "slave driver," as Price said, also needed to be one who was willing to delegate authority and to pay close attention to routine detail.

But it was not only the home-front that suffered under Hughes's recruiting improvisations. Once in England the supposedly trained Hughes battalions were mercifully broken up and retrained by the British, then transferred to France as drafts. Consequently, now unemployed, bitter, and increasingly vocal officers were an embarrassment to the Canadian government. Hughes ignored, then denied their existence as a problem, but the complaints continued to embarrass all. So too did the slowly emerging realization that Hughes's labyrinth of an overseas organization was starving the front of desperately needed reinforcements. One side-effect was to encourage Hughes to try to add more divisions to the Canadian corps as a simple solution. Yet the corps commander, General Alderson, knew that this was not the answer; steady and adequate reinforcement of his existing divisions was. By mid-February 1916, he actually returned to England to try to solve the reinforcement bottleneck. But with little help from Hughes's appointees there, and desperate in the expectation of huge casualties in the spring and summer fighting, the frustrated Alderson circumvented Hughes by placing his grievances directly before his old army friend, the Duke of Connaught. The facts, he told the governor general, spoke for themselves: of the 1476 officers and 25 087 men in the Canadian camp at Shorncliffe, only 75 and 2385, respectively, were trained to go to France. The problem, according to Alderson, was due not only to Hughes's multi-headed overseas administration, but also to the poor state of the recruits coming from Canada.[30]

By then Hughes was not insensitive to the reinforcement problem, but he would not let anyone else try to resolve it. In March, when Parliament was halfway through its 1916 session — and at a time when rumours of Militia Department scandals were growing steadily — Hughes decided to rush over to England to straighten out personally the problems in reinforcement and administration. In the meantime, Gwatkin, who had likely been alerted by Connaught, informed Hughes's temporary replacement, A.E. Kemp, of the dangerous reinforcement situation due to the minister's snafu in training. If Kemp had hoped to improve things during Hughes's absence, a severe political storm focusing directly on Hughes prevented it. Before he could solve anything in England, the attacks on his administration became so acute that Borden had to order him back to Canada in April. It left the situation in England and at the front unresolved. On his return Hughes commissioned General Lessard to make a confidential inspection of training depots in England. After touring the camps for several weeks in April and May, Lessard confirmed Aldersons's and Gwatkin's charges. But Hughes never made public Lessard's damning report. To do so would have been to admit the failure of the minister's local recruiting and training program. If the prime minister knew about it, there [were] also certain benefits for the government in keeping silent on Lessard's findings. Opposition attacks during the parliamentary session, which had ended in mid-May, were very heavy. Most of them were focused on the militia minister and, thereby, the entire Conservative administration. Two royal commissions also were still pending; and both were concerned with Sam Hughes's office. With the recent high casualties coming from the Battle of St. Eloi in March and April, Lessard's news would not be welcomed by the public. But whatever the motives for suppressing the report, the problems of the surplus officers and the quality and training of the troops continued for more months — the months of Mount Sorrel and the Somme.[31]

If Sam Hughes's recruiting policy caused problems in English Canada where the majority viewed the war as a national crusade, then it proved calamitous in French Canada where there was no such passion. As the war progressed, the difference in attitudes between French and English Canada became more and more obvious; and with the imposition of conscription in 1918, it led to near open rebellion that spring. During the previous three years, with a population of about two million, French Canada had given far fewer soldier to the overseas battalions than had English Canada. Soon there were charges that Quebec was not doing its duty.

In response, the province became increasingly more sullen: it was a foreign war; Canada was not threatened; there were more pressing problems at home, especially when English Ontario was trying to take away the French-language school rights of her French-speaking citizens. There was also little attraction for most Quebecois in giving their lives for either Great Britain or France. Of the fourteen thousand or so French Canadians who actually joined during Hughes's tenure, many did so not because of patriotism, but for economic and other practical reasons. Yet in the end, the Quebecois in particular — for French Canadians in other parts of the Dominion had enlisted in about the same proportion as their English-speaking confrères — were more seriously divided from the rest of the nation than they had ever been since Confederation. Whose fault was it? As Desmond Morton has pointed out, since Confederation the militia had become increasingly anglicized in men, manners, and equipment. Consequently fewer French Canadians joined its ranks.[32]

Sam Hughes was an important part of the process that led to that alienation. It did not matter much in peacetime, but it did in war. The minister had always been remarkably insensitive to French Canadians. For a long time Hughes foolishly believed that his remote Huguenot ancestry and his friendship with nationalists like Armand Lavergne made him acceptable to Quebec. He was peculiarly unaware that his previous campaigns against separate schools, French priests, Canadian Papal Zouaves, French-Canadian military representation in Catholic ceremonies, and his Orange Lodge activities had overpowered the limited attractions of ancestry or friendship. Nor was he aware that his image as an imperialist, however nationalistic, was not attractive to many French Canadians, who were not at all concerned about defending the Empire outside of Canada.[33]

None of it augered well for a war in 1914. It was not that Sam Hughes did not want to recruit French Canadians. He did. But he did not realize that by scrapping the Gwatkin mobilization scheme, which gave a balanced national representation to French Canada in the form of their own units, he scuppered separate French-Canadian battalions in the first contingent. Still he wanted Quebec's numbers. One of the first things he did was visit Cardinal Begin of Quebec in September 1914 in an attempt to secure priests for the initial force, but the Cardinal gave him little hope of obtaining any number for overseas service.[34] With this warning, the minister should have seen that Quebec was going to need special care if recruiting for a foreign war was to succeed in the province.

Yet the outbreak of the war did produce some initial sympathy in Quebec for participation; and Hughes wanted a national effort. That had been part of the rationale behind his nationalistic "fiery-cross" call to arms in August. But as the response to it poured into Valcartier he allowed for no separate identity by giving privileges as well as responsibilities to members of the various French-Canadian regiments who turned out. Instead units like the Carabiniers Mont-Royal, the Chasseurs Canadiens, the Voltigeurs de Quebec, and the Carabiniers de Sherbrooke were absorbed into the 12th and 14th Battalions, both of which were English-speaking. Only the 14th went to France where it was reinforced by French Canadians from the 12th Battalion. When Liberal MP and former cabinet minister Rodolphe Lemieux requested the creation of a separate French-Canadian unit with its own officers in the first contingent, Hughes refused. Even the attestation documents were worded in such a fashion that no French-Canadian volunteer could record his racial origin. There were over twelve hundred French Canadians at Valcartier in 1914, sufficient to assemble one complete battalion including officers.[35]

At the beginning of the war, the militia minister had two ready-made native sons of Quebec and generals at his disposal to rally the Canadiens: François Lessard and Oscar Pelletier. Both were regular soldiers of substantial experience. But while Hughes was in office, no meaningful role was ever given them, in spite of pleas by prominent English-Canadian Tories, like Toronto MP and patronage co-ordinator Edmund Bristol, who wanted Lessard to command the second contingent. All Hughes gave him was public abuse over his Toronto mobilization trials and a bitter ministerial squabble over inspection services. As late as 1916, Hughes again refused to make him an overseas brigadier, or even use him in the disastrous Quebec recruiting drives of that year. Only after Hughes was fired did Lessard get a Quebec battalion to recruit. But by then it was too late; he secured only ninety-two men, and he had no battle experience, so was unsuitable for overseas command. As for Pelletier — the son of a Liberal senator and the man whom Hutton had chosen as commander of one of his Boer war infantry columns — in 1919 the minister could only give the major-general command of a half dozen troops guarding a wireless station on Anticosti Island — and that was all.[36]

If Sam Hughes made little use of individual French Canadians, he had not much greater concern for their units. Once the first division got into the fighting, it was this bloody experience that trained many of the future officers of the subsequent divisions. Because the first contingent had few middle and senior level French-Canadian officers beyond the company level, there never would be enough of them to lead other units of their own culture, even if Hughes had wanted to send them. He seemed to think of Quebec with its two-million population only as a place to get numbers, not French Canadians. But the Canadiens themselves had been concerned in September 1914. Then Rodolphe Lemieux and Dr. Arthur Mignault, a wealthy Quebec pharmaceutical manufacturer, led a delegation of fifty-eight influential Liberal and Conservative Quebecois to Ottawa to make sure that at least the second contingent had an identifiable battalion. They warned Borden that if care was not taken to give Quebec representation on the national fighting force, there was a strong risk of losing its active support. Apparently with hardly more sympathy than Hughes, Borden only consented after the militia minister had sailed for England. The result was the formation of the 22nd Battalion commanded by F.M. Gaudet, which went to France with the second contingent the next spring. By then even it was having trouble: 10 percent of the number were English-speaking, and French-Canadian troops had to be transferred from two other battalions recruiting in Quebec before it could sail. In the first two contingents, then, French Canadians were represented only by one battalion and it was to remain the only official one in the Canadian Corps during the entire war.[37]

There was hardly any doubt about the potential enthusiasm for enlistment in French Canada just before and after the 22nd was announced. However, Hughes appeared unappreciative of it. In February 1915 he could only give vague answers about establishing a French-Canadian brigade when questioned in the Commons, and he even seemed unsure of the number of French Canadians who by then had enlisted. Just before the second division sailed for France in mid-1915, a French-Canadian lawyer and militia soldier, Colonel J.P. Landry, who had been given command of one of its brigades as a small conciliation to Quebec, was removed. To replace him came a Tory journalist friend of the minister, Brigadier David Watson, fresh from the First Division. It was inevitable that Landry should lose out. His fate was one of the earliest consequences of Hughes's not including French Canadians of middle and high command in the first contingent the previous year. Landry had no battle experience, and no one willingly was going to jeopardize lives and efficiency with an untested brigadier. Watson had nearly a year under his belt. Back in Canada, however, no one in Quebec would question Landry's competence. To them there was another obvious reason for his removal. The deposed brigadier's father, Conservative Senator Philippe Landry, had been a major spokesman in the defence of the Franco-Ontario's fight against their Tory government's infamous Regulation 17 denying them French-language rights; to many French Canadians Hughes, the vengeful Orangeman, had simply retaliated.[38]

After mid-1915 when Hughes was trying to recruit the Third and Fourth Divisions, to encourage Quebec enlistments he brought home some of the few French Canadians who had served with the corps overseas. But there were never enough veterans even to begin the job.

Mostly he had to use the same method employed in the rest of Canada — prominent citizens and promises of local battalions.[39] From October until the summer of 1916, twelve such groups canvassed in various areas of the province. Most of them had little success. By then an unmoved or lukewarm clergy, stories of the horrors waiting on Flanders' battlefields, and the general shortcomings of the militia minister's recruiting system, all made the Canadiens stubbornly resist any foreign military service. The new munitions industries with their steady and lucrative employment represented a far safer calling. The sneers and accusations of English Canada and the relentless antiwar campaign of Henri Bourassa and his nationaliste allies were strong inducements for many Quebecois to stay away from the colours. Nevertheless Hughes pressed for the numbers.

Wealthy French Canadians were not so willing to become some of Sam Hughes's recruiting colonels as were many in English Canada. As a result, many whom Hughes chose were less than worthy and their units were often doomed. One such example was the 41st Battalion. After a scandalous record both in Canada and England, which included desertion, two murders, and many court-martials, the unit was finally broken up to feed the 22nd in France.[40] Others were little more successful. In the fall of 1915, Hughes asked Armand Lavergne to raise a unit in Montreal. The year before he might have done it, but now his response was an embarrassing public letter in the columns of Bourassa's *Le Devoir* in which he refused to accept what he said was nothing more than an interesting adventure in a foreign country. Unexpectedly, the offer was then accepted by Olivar Asselin — an ardent nationaliste. Whatever his real motives for doing it, Asselin had a little more success than many others. His energy, popularity, and discipline got recruits and better officers, but not full ranks. Only too quickly Asselin discovered that Hughes had authorized a Conservative lawyer, Tancrède Paquelo, to raise the 206th Battalion in the same area. Paquelo was a former commanding officer of the 85th militia regiment and was representative of the declining quality of French-Canadian officers brought about by increasing anglicization in the militia. While Asselin brought men into his unit by hard work and discipline, Paquelo seduced his by appealing to baser values and promises of being "le dernier regiment à parter, le premier à profiter de la victoire." Asselin was so frustrated at the cutthroat competition between the two rivals, he demanded that Hughes get rid of Paquelo's battalion. Asselin's unit was transferred to Bermuda, not France; and Paquelo's was disbanded, with the bulk of them being transferred to the distraught Asselin. When the furious Paquelo heard what was to happen, he paraded his men and told those few who had not already disappeared to desert. For this he was court-martialled, and during the trial it was found that he and some of his officers had also defrauded the unit of funds. Paquelo went to jail.[41]

On other occasions, when Hughes could not get suitable French-Canadian colonels, he chose English-Canadian ones to recruit in Quebec. William Price was one. In spite of the general popularity the Price family had had in Quebec for years, there was little attraction to serve an imperialist "English" colonel in a foreign war; and Price, already encumbered by Hughes's bad system, added his own insensitivities, and so failed. According to Price: "I tell them what no politician dare tell them, that they are away behind all the other provinces and that though they have a double duty, one to the Empire and one to France, yet they are laggards and that they should as a matter of fact furnish more than any other province."[42]

In the summer of 1916, the half dozen battalions still trying to reach their quotas were really only fragments of military units. With a lack of discipline and equipment and ranks thinned by desertion and drafts to other battalions, few were sent to England. Of those who got there, they were broken up to reinforce the 22nd in France. In all, by 1916 the possibility of having a French-Canadian brigade, native sons in senior command, or any serious encouragement for national war participation had all but disappeared under Sam Hughes. Instead the spectacle of most of those French-Canadian battalions stumbling incompetently and often dishonestly through a vain quest for full establishments caused the Quebecois to withdraw further into demoralized and sullen inaction in the province; outside of it, the show reaffirmed the belief that French Canadians were incompetent and unpatriotic.

If Hughes was a major cause of the situation, others must also share the guilt with him. During the first two years, Borden in particular had little more appreciation of cultural politics than did Sam Hughes. Since the prime minister had scant support in the province even after the 1911 election, he should have realized that Quebec would be a special case in a national crisis. Just before the war, he and Monk had parted. The prime minister's failure to respond to the Quebec delegation that wanted a French unit in the first force, his failure to find any post for Lessard, his securing the resignation of two of his three French-Canadian cabinet ministers in the fall of 1914 — all these actions held little evidence of an understanding of French Canada. His position on the imperialist side in the naval debate in 1910, and in 1913 the question of cash contributions to the Admiralty only confirmed the nationalists' charges after 1914 that French Canada was being tossed into a foreign war. So did Borden's quick acceptance of sending more and more troops thereafter. Even after the reshuffle in 1914, his cabinet had no French Canadians with any credibility to defend war participation. Nearly all of them had campaigned for votes in the 1911 election by attacking Laurier's naval bill as conscriptionist. After 1914, how could these same men persuade their confrères that they must participate in a British war? Similarly, Borden and his cabinet seemed to be incapable of or unwilling to support the Franco-Ontarians against the English-speaking "Boches" in the Ontario schools question.[43]

Like Hughes, Borden tried to enthuse Quebec. Early in 1916 he told Hughes that he should be sure that French Canadians who had distinguished themselves at the front were rewarded with decorations that the French government had put at his disposal. The prime minister also suggested that, if Hughes would authorize a Quebec unit for service in the French army, recruiting would be greatly encouraged. But General Gwatkin knew better and so advised against it; he recognized that French Canadians had no particular loyalty to France and that pay difference between the two forces would discourage any chance of success. No one seemed to listen to Gwatkin. Overseas Max Aitken, the government "Eye-Witness" in France, offered Hughes and Borden "a French mission . . . sent to Canada by the Jesuits or other religious orders for religious purposes but really to assist recruiting in Quebec." In all, these schemes represented the bankruptcy of Hughes's and Borden's attitudes to French Canadians. To them France was never an attraction; Canada was. But in order to gain French Canada's support of an external policy, national leaders first would have to give the minority a definite, identifiable, and responsible role and to ensure its well-being at home. Neither Hughes nor his prime minister seemed aware of this. What came from them came too little and too late.[44]

But one of the most objectionable things about Borden for French Canadians was that he would not or could not control Sam Hughes. Most of the time Hughes continued to proclaim his belief that French Canada would measure up to his expectations, or, as Mason Wade puts it, Hughes kept his honest opinion about French Canada to himself. That may be true, but from time to time he made some stupid public moves, often in themselves small but collectively lethal, concerning recruiting in Quebec. When again unsuccessful in obtaining support from Cardinal Begin in mid-1916, the minister uttered his infamous statement in Lindsay that Quebec had not done its duty. Earlier he had countered questions from an opposition MP, asking why western French Canadians were not organized into a battalion, by saying that their numbers were too small, that they would be better off in English-speaking battalions, and that the local French-Canadian officer of the proposed unit was incompetent. When the same member confronted Hughes with the 1911 census figures indicating that there were over forty thousand French Canadians in the west, Hughes replied that he would order two French-Canadian "half-breed" battalions to be raised. Perhaps the most celebrated and distorted case of Hughes's neglect of sympathetic organization in French Canada occurred in August 1916 when the minister was again out of the country. Military authorities wanted a new enlistment drive in the Montreal area to be jointly headed by two clergymen as representatives of both cultures and faiths. By that time, however, no French Canadian priest would accept the post. But the campaign proceeded anyway, headed by a Methodist clergyman, Reverend C.A. Williams. Williams was hardworking and far more tolerant of French Canada than many have given him credit for. But predictably his efforts ended in failure. The Williams affair was not as it was portrayed by extreme nationalists — an example of Hughes's anti-Catholicism. Nor was Williams a bigoted Orangeman sent by the minster to ride herd on French Canada. The entire episode represented what was tragic about the minister's methods. He could not understand that French Canada required a different approach than the rest of the population. Quebec, because it provided the basis of Laurier's power, was suspect to an old party politician like Hughes. In the past two years he had given Quebec nothing except discrimination to be enthusiastic about. Soon the province was not interested and soon Hughes and his local military officers had run out of prominent French Canadians for such duties; authorities had to use whomever they could get. So they got men like Williams. Common sense, however, should have dictated that it not be a Methodist clergyman. But by then it was a vicious circle.[45]

The militia minister showed more creative imagination in recruiting foreigners for military duty than he did French Canadians. For example, there was the minister's "American Legion" scheme. Soon after the war began, Hughes offered and had accepted for overseas service a battalion of American citizens living in Canada; the offer was a substantial mental somersault for Hughes's usual anti-Americanism. A few weeks later, he extended the project to three "corps of splendid fighters," numbering "sixty thousand," which now included Russians and Serbs.[46]

The British authorities could not co-ordinate their reaction. The Colonial Office authorities were hesitant because they said that such a force would violate the US Foreign Enlistment Act of 1818, and that they did want to keep relations as cordial as possible with the neutral republic. By the same token they did not want to tread on Canadian sensitivities, especially those in the hands of the prickly Sam Hughes. Consequently, the British referred the question back to the governor general, whom they said was free to act as he saw fit. Connaught, who had never seen the first communications between Hughes and Kitchener, and did not like being left out, was puzzled. So he enquired at militia headquarters. The deputy minister said he knew nothing about the scheme either; nor did the Militia Council, but if such a proposal had been made by Hughes, they recommended it be quickly dropped. Meanwhile Kitchener, supported by the king, Churchill, Sir Richard McBride, and Acting High Commissioner Perley gave Hughes permission to send at least one American unit, providing no recruiting went on outside of Canada.[47]

Hughes did not move on the issue until domestic volunteering started to slow down in the fall of 1915. Then he allowed the limited acceptance of American citizens resident in Canada to mushroom ultimately into plans for a full-fledged American brigade of five overseas battalions. The minister had created a special cap badge with an American flag surrounded by clusters of maple leaves. As the first of these units, designated the 97th Overseas Battalion, quickly filled up its ranks during the winter of 1915–1916, Hughes got the idea that he could recruit unlimited numbers. As a result he authorized four more by the late spring (the 211th, 212th, 213th, and the 237th) and labelled them the "American Legion." Their cap badge was a variation of the 97th and all of them wore American Legion shoulder flashes. As was the case elsewhere, none of these units had much success. The minister created each new battalion long before the others finished recruiting, and so they competed, often viciously, with each other for volunteers and none of them ever reached establishment — most of them reached less than half of it. During June 1916, 20 percent of the legion deserted. Hughes also used the typical special agent to organize the entire scheme. C.W. Bullock, who had suggested the brigade idea to the minister, was an American citizen and a Unitarian minister whose military career, as General Gwatkin scornfully commented, "is remarkable. Appointed chaplain with the honorary rank of captain in October last [1915], he is now a lieutenant-colonel commanding an overseas battalion." Whether Hughes ordered it or not is not known, but recruiting took place on American soil. Certainly the minister aided it by making a personal arrangement with customs officials to turn a blind eye to these recruits when they were brought across the border.[48]

These frequent abuses of American neutrality aggravated and embarrassed the Washington and London authorities equally. Every time Connaught confronted Hughes about the foreign recruiting, the minister denied it and then blatantly let it continue. American authorities increasingly objected to the continued use of the US flag displayed at various Canadian recruiting offices; and so there were several stiff diplomatic notes exchanged with British diplomats over Hughes's scheme. In Ottawa, Gwatkin, Fiset, and the governor general had no more success in stopping the plan. For their part, the British would not let the legion come to England until all outward connections with the United States were cut.[49]

By the mid-spring 1916, tired of the long wait, endless changes in officers, and constant haggling, the legionnaires were frustrated. Desertions and resignations mounted while enlistments nearly stopped. Like some of the other battalions Hughes had authorized, the legion had its share of scandal. The Toronto chief of police described the 97th as the "worst behaved battalion in the city." Drunkenness, fraud, embezzlement (including the decamping of the 97th's first commanding officer with all the unit funds), and incompetence plagued the force. In May Fiset said he would be pleased to send the legion overseas before "they all desert," but not until they got rid of American insignia. Connaught's constant complaints and Hughes's lack of response finally brought the prime minister into the picture.[50]

Like many others, Borden was totally surprised at what had so far taken place. Hughes had not told him much in the previous two years and precious time was now wasted while he tried to sort through the minister's mess. In the process, it involved Borden in a first-class row with the governor general, whom the prime minster felt was exerting far too much pressure in a domestic Canadian matter. By late July, when Hughes was out of the country, Borden ended the affair by consolidating the legion's five battalions into one, the 97th, and sending it overseas, shorn of all its insignia. The process only added to its further demoralization. With financial and leadership problems still festering in its ranks, in the end it was broken up to feed the corps' battalions in France.[51]

The prime minister's decision on the American Legion was part of a larger judgment on Hughes's entire domestic administration. In August 1916 he took recruiting out of Sir Sam's hands. First Borden tried a director general of recruiting to give order to the chaos and to secure the vital enlistments; then in the autumn he tried the National Service Board which was responsible to the cabinet and dedicated to the same causes. Both had little success. By the spring of 1917, large numbers of casualties and the conviction that it was essential to have a Canadian voice in imperial councils made a reluctant prime minister believe that only conscription could do it. By year's end compulsory service had arrived at the hands of the newly elected union government. The war would be pursued to bitter victory. But over a year before, Borden had got rid of Hughes, a major cause of his bad luck; and before Hughes had gone in 1916, he too had come out hotly for conscription — typically without consulting anyone and apparently oblivious to its party or national cost.[52]

By the end of 1916 there were over 250 overseas battalions. Hughes had authorized most of them while he was minister. But earlier that summer, the Canadian Corps was complete at 48 battalions. Except for some reinforcements, it remained at that level in spite of Hughes's attempts to add two more divisions before he left office. The remaining battalions either suffered collapse before they left Canada or were doomed to be broken up in England. Over the previous two years, Sam Hughes had taken the declaration of war as a personal challenge to lead a national crusade to raise as many men as possible. In doing so, he had little regard for dislocation, or for the advice of his professional staff, or for responsibility to his government. He showed no more awareness of the cultural politics of French Canada. While trying to heighten patriotism and enlistment by throwing responsibility to the citizens, he left them confused and adrift when the war demands transcended the ability of individuals, of the party structure, and of local groups to handle them on a national scale. Yet he constantly interfered even in this process because he could neither delegate the necessary authority nor apply himself to the daily routine of coordinating a national effort. Moreover, the local battalions ended up being destroyed by the same spontaneity that created them and that helped sour and alienate the two cultures, both from the government and one from the country. Certainly Hughes's prime minister must bear some of the blame. In part Borden put up with Hughes's recruiting ways because in those early years the militia minister gave the most vitality to a pale and hesitant war administration. But neither man checked each other with sound advice or firm control. That Sam Hughes demonstrated initiative, confidence, and an unrelenting energy, which helped rally many Canadians to the early war effort, cannot be doubted. But there was also overwhelming evidence that he lacked the skills of sound administration which the larger war — the one of 1916 and after — demanded. Ironically he was a major force in creating the particular size of the Canadian war effort but he could not cope with its demands. He was a spirited improviser, intolerant of criticism, jealous of power, and imbued with the philosophy of the citizen-solider in a conflict which no longer belonged to the individual citizens. He did not see that Canada had created, with the masses of his recruits, professional demands and a professional modern army. As long as the spirit and manpower were in abundance, and the sophisticated needs few, Sam Hughes's local talents remained unchallenged. When these lagged, Hughes's regime collapsed.

NOTES

1. Desmond Morton, *Canada and War: A Military and Political History* (Toronto: Butterworth's, 1981), chap. 3.
2. *Hansard*, 1917, pp. 261, 269–70 for Hughes's own description of his recruiting methods.
3. R.C. Brown, *Robert Laird Borden, a Biography*, vol. 2, 1914–1937 (Toronto: Macmillan, 1979), 27–28; and Barbara M. Wilson, *Ontario and the First World War 1914–1918: A Collection of Documents* (Toronto: Champlain Society, 1977), xxxi.
4. *Canadian Annual Review of Public Affairs* (hereafter *CAR*), 1915, p. 188; J.L. Granatstein and J.M. Hitsman, *Broken Promises: A History of Conscription in Canada* (Toronto: Oxford University Press, 1977), 34; *Hansard*, special session, 1914, pp. 17, 95; Col. A.F. Duguid, *The Official History of the Canadian Forces in the Great War 1914–1919* (Ottawa: King's Printer, 1938), app. 55; and Address, 18 Dec. 1914, Sir Robert Laird Borden Papers, Public Archives of Canada (hereafter PAC), MG26, p. 34672.
5. *CAR*, 1915, pp. 187–88.
6. Murray Donnelly, *Dafoe of the Free Press* (Toronto: Macmillan, 1968), 76.
7. Wilson, *Ontario and the First World War*, xxi, xxix–xlii; G.N. Tucker, *The Naval Service of Canada* (Ottawa: King's Printer, 1952), chap. 13; note on Canadian Expeditionary Force, Edmund Bristol Papers, Public Archives of Ontario (hereafter PAO), 283, Armour file; *CAR*, 1915, pp. 213–14; and Brown, *Borden*, 2:68–69.
8. John Swettenham, *To Seize Victory: The Canadian Corps in World War One* (Toronto: Ryerson Press, 1965), 71–95; Wilson, *Ontario and the First World War*, xxx.
9. Perley to Borden, 29 May 1915, in Canada, Department of External Affairs, *Documents on Canada's External Relations 1909–1918*, vol. 1 (Ottawa: Queens Printer, 1967), 73–74.
10. *Globe* (Toronto), 22 Jan. 1915, 6; Wilson, *Ontario and the First World War*, xxxv–1, 6–8, B4; Duguid, *The Official History of the Canadian Forces*, app. 86; Canada, Senate, *Debates*, 1916, p. 406; Granatstein and Hitsman, *Broken Promises*, 23–24; and R. Mathew Bray, "Fighting as an Ally: The English-Canadian Patriotic Response to the Great War," *The Canadian Historical Review* 61 (2 Nov. 1980), 147–49.

11. Gwatkin to Hughes, 21 Sept. 1914, W.G. Gwatkin Papers, PAC, MG30; G13, F4; PAC, Pamphlet, no. 4039, p. 8; Gen. Charles F. Winter, *Lieutenant General the Hon. Sir Sam Hughes, K.C.B., M.P., Canada's War Minister 1911–1916* (Toronto: Macmillan, 1931), 88–89.

12. Connaught to Kitchener, 1 July 1915, Lord Kitchener Papers, Public Records Office, London, 30/57/56, FNG 43A and B.

13. Gwatkin to Mason, 3 July 1915, Gwatkin Papers, f2; and Gwatkin to Christie, 24 May 1915, Borden Papers, p. 709601.

14. Brown, *Borden*, 2:28.

15. Wilson, *Ontario and the First World War*, xxxii, 8, B5, Militia Order no. 340, 12 July 1915; Basset to Winter, 19 Aug. 1915, John Basset Papers, PAC, MG 30, E 302; *CAR*, 1915, p. 190; and P.D. Ross, *Retrospects of a Newspaper Person* (Toronto: Oxford, 1931), 206–11.

16. "Memorandum on Recruiting in England Prior to the Derby Recruiting Scheme," Borden Papers, OC313, claims Hughes's method was similar to that in Britain; an improvised, local volunteer response with little government planning. Also see G.W.L. Nicholson, *Official History of the Canadian Army in the First World War: The Canadian Expeditionary Force, 1914–1919* (Ottawa: Queen's Printer, 1962), 109; and PAC, RG 24, vol. 6999, 593-1-40.

17. *Hansard*, 1916, pp. 3288–89; "Report on the work of the Department of Militia and Defence to Feb. 1, 1915," Memorandum no. 1, Gwatkin to the Prime Minister, 1 Feb. 1915, PAC, RG 24, vol. 413; Memorandum no. 3, Gwatkin to the Prime Minister, 1 Dec. 1916, PAC, RG 24, vol. 413; McCurdy to Borden, 7 Oct. 1916, Borden Papers, OC313; *Hansard*, 1917, p. 263; Canada, National Defence Headquarters, Ottawa, Directorate of History, Historical Section, *Canadian War Records*, vol. 1, *A Narrative of the Formation and Operations of the First Canadian Division, to the End of the Second Battle of Ypres*, May 4, 1915 (Ottawa: Historical Section, General Staff, King's Printer, 1920), 3; and Desmond Morton, *A Peculiar Kind of Politics: Canada's Overseas Ministry in the First World War* (Toronto: University of Toronto Press, 1982), 44.

18. "Memoire notes," Harold Mayne Daly Papers, PAC, MG 27, 111, f9, D.

19. Nicholson, *Official History of the Canadian Army in the First World War*, 213–14, 546; and John English, *The Decline of Politics: The Conservatives and the Party System, 1901–1920* (Toronto: University of Toronto Press, 1977), 95–105.

20. *CAR*, 1915, pp. 187–93, 222–27; and *Hansard*, 1915, p. 438.

21. Canada, Department of the Secretary of State, *Copies of Proclamations, Orders-in-Council and Documents relating to the European War* (King's Printer, 1915 and 1917), no. 556; PC 36, 12 Jan. 1916; and Brown, *Borden*, 2:32–34.

22. Bennett to Borden, 7 Dec. 1915, Sir George Perley Papers, PAC, MG27, II, D12, vol. 5; Stanton to Blount, 31 Dec. 1915, in Sir Robert Laird Borden, *Robert Laird Borden: His Memoirs*, ed. Henry Borden, vol. 1 (Toronto: Macmillan, 1938), 529; 10 Aug. 1915, Sir George Foster Diaries, PAC; Memorandum no. 3, PAC, RG 24, vol. 413; and Brown, *Borden*, 2:33–35.

23. *Hansard*, 1917, pp. 269–71; Sir Robert Laird Borden, *Private Diaries*, 18 Jan. 1916, PAC; Desmond Morton, *Canada and War* (Toronto: Butterworth's, 1981), 60; Wilson, *Ontario and the First World War*, xxxvi, xlv; *Free Press* (Winnipeg), 29 May 1916; and *CAR*, 1916, p. 256.

24. *Times* (New York), 27 Feb. 1916, 3; *CAR*, 1916, p. 303; and General Hughes, no. 2, Lord Beaverbrook Papers (BBK), The House of Lords Record Office, Westminster, Great Britain; Hughes to Aitken, 15 Jan. 1916, IP; and Aitken to Hughes, 19 Jan. 1916, IP.

25. Borden, *Private Diaries*, 18 Jan. 1916 and 5 Feb. 1916, PAC; Flavelle to W.E. Rundle, 14 June 1916, Joseph Wesley Flavelle Papers, Queen's University, Douglas Library, C25, B2, pp. 1,500–502; and *Hansard*, 1917, pp. 269–70.

26. Senate, *Debates*, 7916, pp. 127–32; Borden to Perley, 14 March 1916, Perley Papers, vol. 5; *CAR*, 1916, p. 319; *Hansard*, 1917, pp. 269–71; and *Daily Herald* (Calgary), 11 March 1916, 6.

27. For instance, in Ontario see Wilson, *Ontario and the First World War*, li–Iii. Also see *Hansard*, 1916, pp. 145, 440, 498–500, 3550; Nicholson, *Official History of the Canadian Army in the First World War*, 219; *CAR*, 1916, pp. 310–24; *Citizen* (Ottawa), 14 April 1916, 1; *Globe* (Toronto), 28 June 1916, 6; *Daily Herald* (Calgary), 29 March 1916, 6.

28. Price to Bassett, 25 Feb. 1916, Bassett Papers, vol. 5. On the recruiting methods in Ontario, see Wilson, *Ontario and the First World War*, xlii–Iiii.

29. Griesbach to Hughes, 13 May 1915, Major-General W.A. Griesbach Papers, PAC, MG30, E15, vol. 1.

30. Report of IG (Imperial) on Canadian Troops, no. 47/560/MT2, 16 June 1915, app. A, in Lessard to Hughes, May 1916, F.L. Lessard Papers, PAC, MG 30, G 47; Hughes to Lessard, 16 April 1916, F.L. Lessard Papers; Nicholson, *Official History of the Canadian Army in the First World War*, 202, 225; Duguid, *Official History of the Canadian Forces in the Great War*, app. 8; Alderson to Governor General, 17 Feb. 1916, Sir Edward Kemp Papers,

PAC, MG27, II, D9, vol. 110; McCurdy to Hughes, 21 July 1916, and Hughes to Borden, 2 Aug. 1916, Borden Papers, OC318. When Hughes was fired, Perley resolved the problem of surplus officers by sending them home or letting them go to France with a lesser rank. Nicholson, *Official History of the Canadian Army in the First World War*, 223–24.

31. Gwatkin to Kemp, 1916, Kemp Papers; Hughes to Lessard, 16 April 1916, and Lessard to Hughes, May 1916, Lessard Papers; Borden to Hughes, 19 Aug. 1916, Borden Papers, OC318; and Gwatkin to Christie, 27 June 1916, Borden Papers, OC322.

32. For an overview, see Granatstein and Hitsman, *Broken Promises*, 22–34; Desmond Morton, "French Canada and the War, 1868–1917: The Military Background to the Conscription Crisis of 1917," in *War and Society in North America*, ed. J.L. Granatstein and R.D. Cuff (Toronto: Nelson, 1971), 84–103.

33. Mason Wade, *The French Canadians, 1760–1967*, vol. 2 (Toronto: Macmillan, 1968), 640–41. See ibid., 640–726 for the trials of French Canadians during the war. Also Elizabeth A. Armstrong, *The Crisis of Quebec, 1914–1918* (Toronto: McClelland and Stewart, 1974), 35–160.

34. Winter, *Lieutenant-General the Hon. Sir Sam Hughes*, 140.

35. Duguid, *Official History of the Canadian Forces in the Great War*, app. 85, "Composition of Provisional Infantry Brigades and Battalions, Valcartier Camp, Sept. 3, 1914," app. 88, "Questions to be put before attestation," and app. 86; Morton, "French Canada and the War, 1868–1917," 96; *Hansard*, 1916, p. 3283; Gwatkin to Sladen, 27 Aug. 1915, Gwatkin Papers, F2.

36. Bristol to Borden, 17 Oct. 1914, and Bristol to Hazen, 17 Oct. 1914, Bristol Papers, PAO, 285, political 1914; *Hansard*, 1916, p. 3281; Morton, "French Canada and the War, 1868–1917," 102; and Wade, *The French Canadians, 1760–1967*, 2:668, 708, 709; and Oscar Pelletier, *Memoires, Souveniers de Famille et Récits* (Quebec, 1940), 382–90.

37. Duguid, *Official History of the Canadian Forces in the Great War*, apps. 74, 711, 843; and Armstrong, *The Crisis of Quebec*, 70, 83–84.

38. Department of Militia and Defence, *The Militia Lists of the Dominion of Canada, 1875–1920*, Sept. 1914, p. 204; Henry James Morgan, ed. *The Canadian Men and Women of the Time: A Handbook of Living Characters* (Toronto: Briggs, 1912), 436, 447; Morton, "French Canada and the War, 1868–1917," 97.

39. Desmond Morton, "The Limits of Loyalty: French Canadian Officers and the First World War," in *Limits of Loyalty*, ed. Edgar Denton (Waterloo: Wilfrid Laurier University Press, 1980), 92–93.

40. Gwatkin to Sladen, 27 Aug. 1915, Gwatkin Papers, 172; and Desmond Morton, "The Short, Unhappy Life of the 41st Battalion CEF," in *Queens Quarterly* 81, 1 (1974), 70–80.

41. CAR, 1916, p. 194; *Hansard*, 1916, p. 3283; Oliver Asselin, *Pourquoi Je m'enrole* (Montreal, 1916), esp. 32; and Morton, "The Limits of Loyalty," 92–94.

42. Price to Bassett, 24 Feb. 191:6, Bassett Papers, vol. 5.

43. Granatstein and Hitsman, *Broken Promises*, 30.

44. Aitken to Borden, 17 May 1916, Beaverbrook Papers, E, 7–8; Borden to Hughes, 25 Jan. 1916, Borden Papers, OC68; Gwatkin to Kemp, spring 1916, Gwatkin Papers, Fl; and CAR, 1916, p. 258.

45. Wade, *The French Canadians, 1760–1967*, 2:727; E.M. MacDonald, *Recollections: Political and Personal* (Toronto: Ryerson Press, 1939), 335; *Current Opinion* (Sept. 1917),158; *Free Press* (London), 12 June 1916, 4; *Daily Herald* (Calgary), 18 July 1916, 6.; *Hansard*, 1916, pp. 1373–74; Mason Wade, *The French Canadian Outlook* (Toronto: McClelland and Stewart, 1964), 52; Nicholson, *Official History of the Canadian Army in the First World War*, 221; and Morton, "French Canada and the War, 1868–1917," 98–99.

46. Law to Governor General, 30 Aug. 1914, and Kitchener to Hughes, 7 Sept. 1914, Borden Papers; and Duguid, *Official History of the Canadian Forces in the Great War, app.* 87, Hughes to Kitchener, 29 Aug. 1914.

47. Fiset to Sec. External Affairs, 24 Oct. 1914, and McBride to R.L. Borden, 25 Nov. 1914, Borden Papers, OC322, vol. 70. Also see W.S. Churchill memo, 5 Sept. 1914, Edwin Pye Papers, Directorate of History, National Defence Headquarters, Ottawa (hereafter DHist), F1, f5; and Perley to Borden, 2 Dec. 1914, First Viscount Harcourt Papers, Oxford University, Box 465, p. 49.

48. Minute of Militia Council, 13 Jan. 1916, PAC, RG 24, vol. 1542, 689-1174-1; Gwatkin to Sladen, 31 July 1916, PAC, RG 24, vol. 14071, vol. 461; Gwatkin to Cliristie (HQC 1562), 18 June 1916, Connaught to Borden, 25 June 1916, and DMD memo, 4 July 1916, Borden Papers, OC322, vol. 70; J.G. Mitchell, Department of Interior to Sam Hughes, 3 Nov. 1915, Pye Papers, DHist, Fl, f5; and PAC, RG 24, vol. 1383, 593-6-1-93.

49. F? to Spring-Rice, 17 July 1916, Beaverbrook Papers, E/18, 97th Battalion; Spring-Rice to Connaught, 2 May 1916, US Department of justice to US Secretary of State, 17 Jan. 1916, Beaverbrook Papers, RG 7, 14071, vol. 452; Spring-Rice to Governor General, 1 July 1916, Beaverbrook Papers, RG 7, 14071, vol. 455; and *Free Press* (Detroit), 19 Dec. 1915, 24 Dec. 1915, and 6 Jan. 1916, editorial.

50. "Notes by Pye," CGS to AG, 3 March 1916, Pye Papers; and Fiset to Christie, 27 March 1916, Borden Papers, OC322, vol. 70.

51. R.G. Haycock, "The American Legion in the Canadian Expeditionary Force, 1914–1917: A Study in Failure," in *Military Affairs* 43, 3 (Oct. 1979), 115–19.

52. Morton, "The Limits of Loyalty," 91; Hughes to Borden, 23 Oct. 1916, Borden Papers, OC318; and CAR, 1916, pp. 265–66. For a review of Borden's course after 1916, see Brown, *Borden, vol.* 2, chaps. 8–10. As early as August 1914, Sir Charles Ross had protested the loss of his skilled machinists in Hughes's "fiery cross" mobilization. See Ross to Hughes, 6 Aug. 1914, Sir Charles Ross Papers, PAC, MG30, A95, vol. 5.

Topic Ten

Unemployment and the Welfare State in the Interwar Years

A labour march in Drumheller, Alberta, 1940s.

The subject of social welfare received little attention from Canadian historians prior to the 1960s due to an emphasis on Canadian political and economic history in this earlier period. But with the rise of the "new social history," historians began to explore issues related to the evolution of an industrial society, particularly issues of health and social welfare legislation. Social historians, anxious to do history "from the bottom up," focused on the working class and the poor. Indeed, class analysis became an important component of this new approach to history. Beginning in the 1980s, historians interested in the history of social welfare found support, and insights into their topic, from other subfields of Canadian history, such as women's history, the history of the family, labour and working class history, and the history of social reform.

The following three articles examine the rise of the welfare state in the interwar years. Historians have tended to see the advent of social welfare as a post–World War II phenomenon when measures such as Unemployment Insurance and the Mothers' Allowance were implemented. But these articles show that World War I, labour unrest in the 1920s, and the catastrophic effect of the Great Depression contributed to a changed attitude to social assistance that made possible the implementation of the social welfare state in the post–World War II era.

In "The Great War, the State, and Working-Class Canada," Craig Heron and Myer Siemiatycki examine the role of World War I in the rise of working-class organizations, their resistance, and their radicalization that spilled over into the postwar era, evident in a series of strikes across the country and culminating in the Winnipeg General Strike of 1919. The authors show that the federal government's draconian measures to control labour unrest left workers embittered, forcing them to look to alternative means to achieve their demands.

In "'We Who Have Wallowed in the Mud of Flanders': First World War Veterans, Unemployment and the Development of Social Welfare in Canada, 1929–1939," historian Lara Campbell examines the role that the political protests of the veterans during the 1930s played in the acceptance of the idea of social welfare. She argues that veterans saw social welfare as a right that should be associated with the benefits of full citizenship rather than based on charitable aid. Their views, Campbell shows, had the effect of restricting the number of people entitled to social welfare.

The attitude toward social assistance put forward by veterans and outlined by Lara Campbell helps to explain the anti-welfare sentiments of government officials that historian James Struthers analyzes in "Canadian Unemployment Policy in the 1930s." Struthers argues that the nature of the Canadian economy, and the prevailing attitudes toward work, explain why the Canadian government failed to respond adequately to the massive unemployment problem of the 1930s. Only during World War II and into the postwar era did politicians enact a social welfare program that provided a safety net for the less advantaged in Canadian society.

All three articles deal with attitudes toward unemployment and relief in the interwar years. What were the attitudes that both undermined the formation of a social welfare program in the interwar years and led, ultimately, to the formation of the welfare state in the post–World War II period? To what extent were the demands of the workers in the post–World War I era and those of the veterans in the 1930s similar and different? Struthers argues that attitudes toward employment and unemployment in the 1930s were not all that different than today. To what extent have attitudes changed or stayed the same over the last half century or so?

For an overview of the interwar years, see John Herd Thompson with Allen Seager, *Canada, 1922–1939: Decades of Discord* (Toronto: McClelland & Stewart, 1985); and Robert Bothwell, Ian Drummond, and John English, *Canada, 1900–1945* (Toronto: University of Toronto Press, 1987). On labour unrest in World War I and in the postwar era, see Craig Heron, ed., *The Workers' Revolt in Canada, 1917–1925* (Toronto: University of Toronto Press, 1998); and Greg S. Kealey, "State Repression of Labour and the Left in Canada, 1914–1920: The Impact of the First World War," in Franca Iacovetta et al., eds., *A Nation of Immigrants: Women,*

Workers, and Communities in Canadian History, 1840s–1960s (Toronto: University of Toronto Press, 1998), pp. 384–412. David Bright looks at labour in Calgary in *The Limits of Labour: Class Formation and the Labour Movement in Calgary, 1883–1929* (Vancouver: UBC Press, 1998). On labour in Quebec in the 1930s, see Evelyn Dumas, *The Bitter Thirties in Quebec* (Montreal: Black Rose Books, 1975). Bryan Palmer provides a history of the working class in *Working-Class Experience: The Rise and Reconstitution of Canadian Labour 1880–1991*, 2nd ed. (Toronto: Butterworths, 1993). On the Winnipeg General Strike, see D.C. Masters, *The Winnipeg General Strike* (Toronto: University of Toronto Press, 1950); Kenneth McNaught and David Bercuson, *The Winnipeg Strike: 1919* (Toronto: Longman, 1974); David Bercuson, *Confrontation at Winnipeg: Labour, Industrial Relations, and the General Strike*, rev. ed. (Montreal/Kingston: McGill-Queen's University Press, 1990); Norman Penner, ed., *Winnipeg 1919: The Strikers' Own History of the Winnipeg General Strike*, 2nd ed. (Toronto: James Lorimer, 1975); and with regards to the One Big Union, David Bercuson, *Fools and Wise Men: The Rise and Fall of the One Big Union* (Toronto: McGraw-Hill Ryerson, 1978).

James Struthers's work on unemployment relief in the 1930s is presented in greater detail in *No Fault of Their Own: Unemployment and the Canadian Welfare State, 1914–1941* (Toronto: University of Toronto Press, 1983). For developments in Ontario, see his *Limits of Affluence: Welfare in Ontario, 1920–1970* (Toronto: University of Toronto Press, 1994). Also useful is Dennis Guest's *The Emergence of Social Security in Canada* (Vancouver: University of British Columbia Press, 1980); and the collection of essays in Raymond B. Blake and Jeff Keshen, eds., *Social Welfare Policy in Canada: Historical Readings* (Toronto: Copp Clark, 1995). John Graham examines the transition of a Toronto charity from a religious to a professional organization in "The Haven, 1878–1930: A Toronto Charity's Transition from a Religious to a Professional Ethos," *Social History/Histoire sociale*, 25, 50 (November 1992): 283–306. In "A Profession in Crisis: Charlotte Whitton and Canadian Social Work in the 1930s," *Canadian Historical Review* 62 (1981): 169–85, Struthers looks at Canada's best-known social worker of the period; see also P.T. Rooke and R.L. Schnell, *No Bleeding Heart: Charlotte Whitton, A Feminist on the Right* (Vancouver: University of British Columbia Press, 1987). For an examination of gender and the welfare state, see Nancy Christie, *Engendering the State: Family, Work, and Welfare in Canada* (Toronto: University of Toronto Press, 2000). On the impact of the Great Depression on women and families in Montreal, see Denyse Baillargeon, *Making Do: Women, Family and Home in Montreal during the Great Depression* (Waterloo: Wilfrid Laurier University Press, 1999); for Ontario, see Cynthia R. Comacchio, *"Nations Are Built of Babies": Saving Ontario's Mothers and Children, 1900–1940* (Montreal/Kingston: McGill-Queen's University Press, 1993); and Margaret Jane Hillyard Little, *"No Car, No Radio, No Liquor Permit": The Moral Regulation of Single Mothers in Ontario, 1920–1977* (Toronto: University of Toronto Press, 1998).

WEBLINKS

Historical Statistics of Canada
http://www.statcan.ca/english/freepub/11-516-XIE/sectiona/toc.htm
A detailed collection of economic and demographic statistics that compare trends in Canada over the 20th Century.

Winnipeg General Strike
http://www.histori.ca/peace/page.do?pageID=347
Newspaper accounts and photographs of the Winnipeg General Strike of 1919.

Birth of Medicare
http://archives.cbc.ca/300c.asp?id=1-73-90
A history of medicare in Canada as shown through television and radio archives.

"On to Ottawa"
http://www.histori.ca/peace/page.do?pageID=348
A summary of the "On to Ottawa" labour protest of 1935, and excerpts from House of Commons debates regarding the march.

Canada's Public Pensions
http://www.civilization.ca/hist/pensions/cpp1sp_e.html
A history of public pensions in Canada and information regarding their role in the modern welfare state

Alberta InWord
http://asalive.archivesalberta.org:8080/access/asa/documents/
A searchable database of textual records held in the archives of Alberta. Suggested search terms include "William Aberhart" and "residential schools."

Veterans and Veterans' Programs
http://www.civilization.ca/cwm/newspapers/canadawar/veterans_e.html
Newspaper articles highlighting the concerns of veterans returning to Canada from World War II.

Cabinet Conclusions: 1944–1973
http://www.collectionscanada.ca/archivianet/020150_e.html
A searchable database of digitized documents from federal cabinet meetings in the time period of 1944 to 1973. Suggested search terms include "medicare" and "bilingualism."

Article Twenty-Four

The Great War, the State, and Working-Class Canada

Craig Heron and Myer Siemiatycki

Wars in the modern world are never merely military campaigns. They are rare moments that allow national states to mobilize the resources and collective will of their citizenry to a degree seldom, if ever, attempted during peacetime. The self-interest that drives the capitalist economy and the social relations within in it are challenged by new ideologies of self-sacrifice and national service. At the same time, longstanding social antagonisms can be inflamed by the unusual economic, social, and political conditions of wartime society. In some countries revolutions have erupted. In Canada the First World War eventually disrupted the dynamics of pre-war working-class life and provided new pressures and opportunities that would fuel large-scale working-class organization, resistance, and radicalization across the country. It turned out to be quite a 'Great War' of class forces on the home front.[1]

Source: From "The Great War, the State, and Working-Class Canada" from Craig Heron, ed., *The Workers' Revolt in Canada, 1917–1925*, University of Toronto Press Inc., 1998. © University of Toronto Press Incorporated 1998. Reprinted with permission of the publisher.

THE GREAT WAR IN CANADA

The European war that erupted in the late summer of 1914 never extended to Canadian soil, but Canadians nonetheless found it a profoundly disruptive event. Although it galvanized the country into a single national purpose and revitalized a sagging economy, it also transformed the role of the state and unleashed a new flood of protest from many sectors of Canadian society.

For Canadian industrialists, their employees, and thousands of primary producers, war would eventually become an economic godsend. Initially, however, it deepened the depression that had hung over the country since 1913 by restricting access to foreign capital and by disrupting some vital trade and commerce. Economic recovery was slow and uneven across the country. British officials delayed placing orders for military supplies in Canada because of worries about the ability of the Dominion's manufacturers to produce to the exacting specifications required. The cost and complications of retooling for uncertain war production gave many industrialists pause before they took war contracts. Not until mid-1915 did the increasing orders for food, lumber, munitions (mostly shells), uniforms, and other supplies for British and French troops bring fuller employment for factory workers in central Canadian cities, where the bulk of these contracts were filled. Eventually Canada supplied a huge proportion of the ammunition that the Allies fired at the enemy.

Other sectors of the economy got a similar boost. Miners began to feel the heavier demand for their labour power by early 1916. On the east and west coasts and on the Great Lakes, new shipbuilding operations drew together large new workforces. Prairie farmers quickly expanded their acreage in response to the voracious European demand for Canadian wheat. Certainly by the end of 1916, although construction and a few other sectors were still stagnant, unemployment had dried up virtually everywhere in the country. As more people found jobs, consumer spending at home also took off. The wartime boom nonetheless reinforced longer-term patterns of uneven development in the Canadian capitalist economy. The Maritime provinces shared least in the prosperity, while Ontario and Quebec probably enjoyed the most benefits. Manufacturing and agriculture got a far greater boost than most resource industries. On the whole, though, the massive death and destruction under way in Europe allowed the Canadian economy to surge to unprecedented heights of production and profit.[2]

First and foremost, of course, the war was a military event. Before the war, the dominant strain of English-Canadian nationalism had been 'imperialism'— a passionate identification with the Empire — and the previous half-decade had seen a flurry of military preparedness (militia reforms, cadet training, and the like) under the frenetic Minister of Militia, Colonel Sam Hughes. As the loyal administration of a colonial state within the British Empire, Robert Borden's Conservative government responded to Britain's declaration of war by organizing a contingent within the British armed forces known as the Canadian Expeditionary Force. What began as a jaunty little adventure that was expected to end by Christmas became more than four agonizing years of carnage and destruction. More than six hundred thousand Canadians would eventually don the khaki uniform of the Canadian Armed Forces during World War I, while fifty thousand more served in other allied armies. In all, roughly a third of the male population at military age enlisted. Nearly one in ten did not return from the battlefields. Thousands more limped back with physical and psychological wounds.[3]

Initially, the federal government tried to carry out its responsibilities for the war effort overseas and at home with as much voluntary and philanthropic organization as possible. Private individuals and organizations took on responsibilities for recruitment (and, to some extent, equipping) of individual battalions, pro-war propaganda, munitions production, resource coordination, and assistance for soldiers' families and returned veterans.[4] Newspaper editors, Protestant clergymen, and school teachers whipped up jingoistic fervour. Local voluntary recruiting leagues organized parades and nabbed men for the army. Branches of the Canadian Patriotic Fund solicited donations to support soldiers' families. Women's organizations knitted socks for the men in the trenches. Schoolchildren collected scrap metal. Women volunteered to replace men in traditionally male jobs. At every turn in their daily lives, Canadians were exhorted to buy war bonds.[5] The passions aroused occasionally boiled over into violent attacks on German-Canadians and other 'aliens,'[6] but, on the whole, this was an orderly national moral crusade. Pacifists and others opposed to the war, especially radical labour leaders, were overwhelmed and isolated. The pre-war resolutions of the Trades and Labor Congress calling for a general strike in the event of war were quietly shelved. Even such traditionally cautious French-Canadian leaders as Sir Wilfrid Laurier and Henri Bourassa pledged their support for the cause. Few noticed the quiet indifference to all this hoopla in the Maritimes, Quebec, and much of the rural countryside generally.[7]

Wartime propaganda initially emphasized Canadian obligations to the British Empire, but calls for private sacrifice and public service increasingly highlighted a fight against 'Prussianism' or 'Kaiserism,' and the 'great war for democracy.' Paradoxically, by the end of 1916 such rhetoric stood in increasingly sharp contrast to life on the home front. Voluntarism was giving way to state compulsion and authoritarian restriction of civil liberties. The sweeping War Measures Act had made such moves possible since 1914, and some measures dated that far back. A press censor monitored and hectored the country's newspaper editors to avoid revealing such evidence of social discontent as strikes. (A press blackout became one of the more effective devices for undermining the first major wartime munitions strike.) Within the country's eastern-European immigrant communities, many men were loosely and often inaccurately branded 'enemy aliens' and interned or ordered to register each week with local police departments. Despite their lack of love for the Austro-Hungarian Empire, Ukrainians probably felt the fullest weight of these measures. The Dominion Police and Royal North-West Mounted Police also recruited spies to report on labour activities that looked threatening to the war effort. In 1916 strikes in war-related industries were brought under the regulatory mechanisms of the Industrial Disputes Investigation Act (IDIA), the pre-war federal labour legislation that required workers and their bosses in resource, transportation, and utilities industries to submit their demands to compulsory conciliation before initiating strikes or lockouts.[8]

In the first two years of the war, the state moved cautiously in expanding its traditionally limited role. In 1917, however, it became sharply more interventionist. The Director of Public Information took over coordination of propaganda activities. Most shocking for French Canadians, farmers facing labour shortages, and socialist labour leaders — all of whom were decidedly cool to this imperialist war — was the government announcement in 1916 that registration of all manpower would be necessary to deal with labour shortages at home and in the trenches. The National Service Board was put to work registering and classifying the country's workforce. Amid the steady pressure of rising casualty rates and imperial demands for more soldiers in the trenches, full-scale military conscription followed the next year. The state even invaded Canadians' leisure time. Beer drinkers found their supply cut off by provincial prohibition legislation in 1916 and 1917 and eventually by federal action in March 1918 — all in the name of a more efficient war effort. Everyone had to adjust their clocks in an unpopular new scheme, known as 'Daylight Saving,' aimed at more efficient use of light. Early in 1918 the federal government even went so far as to pass the 'Anti-Loafing Act,' which required adult males to make themselves available for wage-earning work or face criminal prosecution. A series of orders-in-council in September and October 1918 brought the heaviest repressive legislation, which outlawed several radical labour organizations (and their newspapers) and banned strikes. By this point the cabinet had become accustomed to ruling by order-in-council.[9]

The state had also entered into unprecedented economic regulation, though never on the scale that it would in World War II. As much as possible it recruited help from the private sector, rather than expanding the civil service. The Imperial Munitions Board, established late in 1915 to replace the much-maligned Shell Committee in administering war contracts, was like its predecessor a committee of industrialists and experts. The board set new standards for coordination of production across the country's metalworking plants, with centrally controlled inspection and factory-administration guidelines in some six hundred firms by 1917. The board also set up its own production facilities, known as National Factories, to manufacture shells, explosives, aircraft, and ships. In 1917 the federal government moved much more decisively into the economy: it established a Board of Grain Supervisors, a Coal Controller, a Canadian Wool Commission, and a Natural Resources Commission, and made its first moves to take over the floundering railways that would become the Canadian National Railways in 1919.

Meanwhile, public outrage over wartime 'profiteering' had not been placated by orders-in-council denouncing hoarding and price gouging or by the introduction of direct taxation in the form of a business war-profit tax in 1916 and a 'temporary' income tax the next year. The government therefore appointed a Cost-of-Living Commissioner in 1917 to investigate and report on price inflation (though not to prosecute). The food controller also undertook to investigate food prices; in 1918 his work was transferred to a Food Board with powers to fix prices and control supplies. Concerns about labour shortages brought campaigns to recruit more farm labour and eventually the creation of a nationally coordinated Employment Service of Canada. A new federal ministry was charged with the reintegration of returned soldiers into Canadian life. The War Trade Board created in February 1918 had sweeping powers to effect centralized coordination of the private-enterprise economy.[10]

As Canadian capitalists took on administrative roles in many of these new bodies, traditional liberal conceptions about the separation of capital and the state were eclipsed by a growing fascination with some kind of corporatist state (denounced on the left in Britain as the 'servile state'). State institutions would more directly sustain the capitalist economy, and the principles of efficiency and managerial expertise — the hallmarks of what is often called pre-war 'progressivism'— would prevail over narrow party spirit. The recently established National Research Council seemed a promising example of this new notion of capitalist collaboration within the state. The Board of Commerce, appointed in 1919 to deal with soaring price inflation, was another.[11]

It was the Conservative Party that presided over this more activist state apparatus at the national level and in five provinces at the beginning of the war (Nova Scotia, Quebec, Saskatchewan, and Alberta were the exceptions). The war did not eliminate the easy morals that had so often characterized Tory administrations. Sam Hughes and the 'minister of elections,' Robert Rogers, made sure that Tory supporters were well rewarded with jobs, commissions, and contracts, turning the war into what historian John English has called 'a massive Conservative rally.' By the end of 1915 newspapers were regularly publishing stories about the misuse of patronage and the serious flaws in military training and equipment. Abandoning the party truce, the Liberal opposition repeatedly attacked the government's apparent favouritism, corruption, and general mismanagement, especially in the distribution of war contracts through the hastily improvised Shell Committee, which was dissolved in November 1915. From press, pulpit, and Canadian Club auditoriums, the public outcry against narrow party allegiances grew louder.

The Conservatives eventually responded by creating the coalition Union government in October 1917. In the emotion-charged re-election campaign that followed, the Unionists rallied the country to the war effort, the Empire, and the Anglo-Saxon 'race,' and denounced their opponents with unprecedented rhetorical venom. The cynical, flagrantly corrupt procedures of that election — which included giving the vote to all soldiers and (for the first time) all their female relatives and taking it away from all those who had arrived from enemy countries since 1902, regardless of naturalization — were probably the most blatant example of the Tory willingness to give democracy short shrift. In December the Unionist forces won a smashing victory (outside Quebec) that consolidated the Tory hegemony and marginalized official Liberalism within national politics until after the war was over.[12]

Many other traditional threads of Canadian Toryism — elitism, imperialist jingoism, and bigotry, in particular — found their fullest expression in this context of single-minded national commitment. Official intolerance of ethnic minorities flourished. Anti-French sentiment once again broke through into Ontario politics, as the English-Canadian majority in the federal Parliament endorsed the provincial government's move to curb francophone schooling in 1916. Manitoba followed Ontario's example the same year. In the 1917 federal election French Canadians faced vicious attacks from Unionist candidates for their resistance to military conscription.[13] The government's campaign also fanned the growing resentment against European immigrants. Not surprisingly, 97 per cent of the 152 Unionists elected were white Anglo-Canadian Protestant males from prosperous business or professional backgrounds.[14]

By 1917 workers were not alone in raising questions about the longer-term implications of wartime developments. The combination of war-induced moral fervour, strong inducements to subordinate private to public concerns, and popular outrage at the unsavoury practices of business and the state tore loose many groups of Canadians from their traditional social and ideological moorings and opened wide-ranging, intense debate about 'reconstruction' in post-war society. Numerous social movements presented their own agendas and competing visions, most of them projecting little confidence in the existing political and economic institutions. The moral energies of the Protestant churches' 'social gospel,' which had spilled over into patriotic passion for the war effort, were now focused as never before on the social and moral purification of Canadian society. Prohibition was the moral reformers' great wartime triumph, but they looked for more. In 1918 the Methodist Church of Canada went so far as to announce its commitment to production based on 'co-operation and service' rather than 'competition and profits.'[15] Many of the women involved in these campaigns were delighted that politicians were finally won over to the justice of giving them the right to vote in most provinces and at the federal level in 1918.[16] Intellectuals from many backgrounds looked for new solutions to the moral crisis; indeed, seldom had Canada seen such an outpouring of books prescribing remedies for all that ailed industrial capitalist society in Canada.[17] The farmers gave a far angrier edge to this ferment. Throughout rural Canada they were organizing against the erosion of their incomes and way of life, once again placing Canadian tariff policies at the centre of their demonology.[18] Veterans soon joined the chorus of angry voices. Returning from the trenches with their various scars and resentments, they became another volatile new force in Canadian society and politics — a force that found expression in spontaneous crowd action in the streets and, more persistently, through new organizations such as the Great War Veterans' Association.[19] All of this political turmoil spilled over into the months after the Armistice, when the restraints set by cries of support for the military effort had lifted. For many Canadians, much was at stake in 1919–20.

The third year of the war, then, proved a turning point, with the shift from voluntarism to more authoritarian state intervention, the growing popular uneasiness about private enterprise, the divisive political crisis over conscription, the take-off of retail price inflation, the increasing demoralization and disaffection of a war-weary population. It was in this broad context that the workers' revolt began to take shape in Canada.

FUELLING A REVOLT

In the first two years of the war, working-class Canada showed considerable support for the war effort — sending sons to war, buying war bonds, holding back 'selfish' demands. But by 1917 workers' cynicism about the Great War was growing. A spirit of revolt was in the air, primarily as a result of the war's impact on working-class life.

The war economy had certainly shifted the balance of class forces in Canadian labour markets. At the outbreak of hostilities in 1914, Canadian workers had already suffered through more than a year of prolonged lay-offs, short time, and wage cuts in the deepest economic slump yet seen in the twentieth century. 'There have been other periods of depression in times gone by,' the executive of the British Columbia Federation of Labor noted that summer, 'but there has never been one so extensive and so entirely devoid of promise of improvement for years to come, as the present one.' Similarly gloomy comments were heard across the country. Many city councils had to face large demonstrations of jobless workers demanding 'work or bread.' It is not surprising, then, that the first military recruits were often the unemployed, particularly recent British immigrants. Indeed, during the early stages of the war few sections of Canadian society provided more soldiers than the labour movement. By the end of 1915 incomplete returns from unions in Canada showed that some thirteen thousand union members — one in twelve — had already enlisted. In many cases there was clearly more than patriotism motivating the decision to go to war. The sting of widespread unemployment and hunger 'conscripted' many. Since enlistment entitled the families of the recruits to support from the Canadian Patriotic Fund, and held the possibility of improving their eligibility for relief payments, many unemployed workers regarded overseas service as a means of providing for loved ones. As James McVety, president of the Vancouver Trades and Labor Council, reported in November 1914, 'Many of the families of the men who enlisted were so hard up that relief had to be given almost before the names were hardly dry on the enlistment roll.'[20]

Unemployment soon disappeared, however, as a result of both military recruitment and opportunities in the quickening industrial economy, especially munitions. The closing of immigration prevented the replenishment of pools of labour in the traditional way, and employers taxed their ingenuity to find workers and hold on to them. By the end of 1916 the Imperial Munitions Board was pushing employers to hire women workers for the shell plants. Perhaps thirty-five thousand ultimately worked in munitions. During the next year male labour shortages also brought women into such traditionally male jobs as bank teller and streetcar conductor. Far more of these female wage earners were married than ever before, though single women still predominated.[21] Youngsters were similarly pulled out of school and retired workers from old-age homes in the search for more wage earners.[22] 'Enemy aliens' were also shipped from internment camps to industrial centres where their labour was needed. European immigrants in general found their way into much better jobs than had been available to them in the ethnically stratified pre-war labour markets, which had typically left them on the lowest rungs of the occupational ladder.[23]

Free from the haunting fear of unemployment and bottomless poverty, Canadian workers showed a new confidence by 1916 that was in sharp contrast to their desperation in the pre-war slump. At home, working-class families in Canada began to feel the relief from economic insecurity that the bigger wage packets brought into their households. Families that had been doubled up in rented accommodation could now afford to rent their own places. They ate more meat. Player pianos and victrolas appeared in more working-class parlours. Some savings went into war bonds.[24] This was a familiar pattern from pre-war years — families taking advantage of economic upturns to clear away debts and take a few steps towards improving their living standards before another depression forced them back into a much more pinched existence.[25]

On the job, wage earners also revived time-worn means of using the tighter labour market to their advantage. They could risk a cockier manner and thumb their noses at their foremen's efforts to get them to work harder. They could take an afternoon off work to enjoy a ball game or a movie, or even a move to another job, where the boss was probably willing to pay still higher wages to get help. They could even discuss unions more openly. 'Employment is so easily obtained that workmen change from one occupation to another for no apparent reason,' Nova Scotia's factory inspector reported in 1917, 'and employers complain that it is impossible to enforce discipline in their factories.' The same year, a Cominco official wrote from the other end of the country, 'Workers have been absolutely independent, knowing that if they were fired from one job they could get another immediately.' Toronto's John Inglis Company complained that it was '[a]lmost impossible to co-operate with present class of help as they appear to be getting too much money and don't want to work,' while Hamilton's National Steel Car plant bemoaned the difficulty 'to get our men to average 9 hours a day. It is not a question of too little money with them, but the trouble is they have too much. The surplus amount allows them to take a great deal more time off than they ordinarily would.' Another manufacturer later complained, 'Taking a day off was a frequent occurrence for many men who were receiving double, possibly treble, what they had ever done before.' By the end of the war, according to a government study, 'Turnover was universally high, many employers stating that 30 per cent of their staff was floating. Absence was also abnormal, amounting to 5 per cent per day and often running as high as 10 per cent.'[26]

These would hardly seem to be the conditions to promote a revolt. In fact, during 1915–16 most wage earners seemed more interested in making hay while the sun shone. Although union membership increased gradually and workers staged some significant confrontations (notably the 1916 strikes in the Thetford asbestos mines, Montreal shipyards, Hamilton munitions plants, Cobalt silver mines, and Alberta coalfields),[27] two features of working-class activity in the period predominated: the mobilization of as many able-bodied members of the household as possible to bring in wages; and the remarkable labour turnover, as workers jumped from job to job in search of better wages and less oppressive working conditions.

Yet the wartime boom was unsettling for workers at home and on the job. First, the new-found prosperity was soon threatened in many working-class households by the retail price inflation that began a dizzying four-year ascent in 1917. Canadian workers had already faced sharp price increases before the war, especially in the 1912–13 period, but no one could remember prices rising as fast or as high as they did in this new inflationary burst. An average weekly food basket for a family of five that had cost $10.11 at Christmas 1916 was fetching $12.25 the next Christmas (a jump of 20 per cent), and the addition of fuel, lighting, and rent brought the total increase to 31 per cent. By December 1918 the cost of this family budget had leaped by 46 per cent over the 1916 level and, at the peak of the inflationary spiral in July 1920, by 82 per cent. At that point the food basket cost a whopping 128 per cent more than it had on the eve of the war in 1914. (The European belligerents had much higher inflation rates, though Britain's was only moderately higher at 158 per cent; the United States was slightly lower at 115 per cent, and Australia and New Zealand fell well behind at 94 and 67 per cent respectively.)[28] Almost every day, Canadian newspapers splashed stories across their front pages about the high cost of living, or 'H.C.L.' At a conference of international unionists held in 1917, delegates worried that Canadian workers were confronting a 'serious depression of their standard of living occasioned by the increase in the price of necessities of life.'[29] The problem was that wages were not keeping pace. All recent attempts to determine working-class income in Canada in this period have pointed to serious erosion of real wages after 1917 (although all these studies are marred by the use of the only available data, namely, the hourly wage rates of relatively skilled men, rather than their actual take-home pay or the earnings of the less skilled).[30]

Here was a family-based issue that irked the working-class housewife as much as her wage-earning husband.[31] Searching angrily for explanations for this injustice, workers invariably suspected that shady, unscrupulous profiteers were at work — in the words of the Regina trades council, 'feasting on the nation's suffering' and 'fattening on our soldiers' blood.'[32] Such highly publicized scandals as the revelations about the super-profits of pork-packer Sir Joseph Flavelle generated a deepening hostility towards the leading figures of Canada's business establishment. 'Having been engaged in recording Canadian political events for the past quarter century,' one veteran Conservative politician cautioned Prime Minister Borden in the wake of the Flavelle controversy, 'I can truly say that I never before met with such wide spread [sic] *rage* over any other scandal.[33] In households and workplaces across Canada, deference to captains of finance and industry came unhinged as news of alleged corporate profiteering spread. As the federal government's numerous initiatives failed to curb the continuing price inflation through 1920, resentment at unknown profiteers who threatened rising working-class income raged across working-class dinner tables throughout the country. 'The authorities have had enquiry after enquiry made but they only show more clearly the gravity of the evil,' a Montreal commissioner reported in 1919. 'The masses understand nothing, they are driven mad for no remedy comes from anywhere.'[34] This 'madness' had prompted the Trades and Labor Congress, in 1917, to call for an end to 'gambling in foodstuffs by speculators' and to propose controls on (even the nationalization of) food-processing plants, coal mines, and railways.[35] From all parts of the country came demands for the 'conscription of wealth' as well as, or in preference to, the conscription of people (the new income tax was the government's reluctant and extremely limited response).[36] Workers also confronted the rising cost of living with a measure of self-help. Cooperative stores blossomed across the country — at least nineteen in British Columbia, more than one hundred on the Prairies, twenty in Ontario, and thirteen in the Maritimes — many of them in working-class communities.[37]

Workers became even more fearful about their household finances after the Armistice, when many lost their jobs in munitions work and unemployment rose steeply across the economy in the early months of 1919. In March unions reported levels of joblessness among their members that had not been seen since the end of 1915. Somewhat fuller employment returned during the next year and a half, broken by some slackness in the winter of 1919–20. Uncertainty hung over most industries, however, until the great crash in the winter of 1920–21, when enterprises closed or curtailed production drastically and thousands of wage earners were thrown out of work.[38] These could be the conditions that would allow employers to get the upper hand again, as they always had in previous economic downturns. So, through the lurching uncertainties and instability of the post-war era, wage earners and their families looked anxiously into the future and grasped at ways to build more collective economic security into their lives.

The wartime boom also had a disruptive effect on the capitalist workplace. In most industries employers accelerated production in order to meet the pressing demands for goods. Particularly in manufacturing, the high-volume production and the general labour shortage encouraged employers to cut costs and reorganize work to a degree unimaginable in the more limited pre-war markets. Workers in the busy clothing industry felt these pressures.[39] In munitions thousands of untrained workers were recruited to run narrowly specialized machines on piecework — a process soon known as 'dilution' of the crafts. The trend towards mass production that had begun at the turn of the century — the Second Industrial Revolution — was accelerating.[40] Craftsmen, especially in the metalworking plants, recognized that the prolonged attack on their crafts had intensified.[41] They resented losing more of the control they had long exercised over the labour process. Their craft pride was also offended by the erosion of the status hierarchy in their workplaces. The skilled workers who had so far survived the Second

Industrial Revolution, such as the machinists, and those who had emerged within new work processes, such as the steelworkers, were disgruntled to see untrained, transient men (and sometimes women) taking home previously unimaginable wages earned on high-volume piecework, while their more skilled, longer-service workmates who set up and maintained the machinery enjoyed far smaller increases. The gap between skilled and unskilled was narrowing to the apparent detriment of the craft worker. 'It is true that young girls, with no experience . . . [got] higher wages for doing soft snaps than skilled mechanics whose labor was indispensible to the proper carrying on of the work received,' one workman blustered in 1917.[42] 'The majority of the men on the plant did not share in these high wages, because they were kept in their old positions of skill and responsibility in order that the whole plant might continue to operate successfully,' Nova Scotia steelworkers complained three years later.[43]

The concern about disruptions in established workplace hierarchies extended to more workers as Europeans and Asians gained access to labour markets previously closed to them. To meet the chronic shortage of labour, many employers intensified the recruitment of non-Anglo-Canadian labour that they had begun before the war.[44] Now they drew in more European peasant-labourers from the resource industries of the north and west into the heavy secondary manufacturing of central and eastern Canada. The federal government even obliged by shipping interned enemy aliens, mostly non-Austrian citizens of the Austro-Hungarian Empire, to some large corporations short of less skilled labour, including railways, coal mines, and steel mills. In 1917 the *Canadian Annual Review* noted that 'the labour shortage everywhere [has] resulted in the employ of Austrian and German aliens in works of all kinds — the Imperial Munitions Board, the Lindsay Arsenal and many munitions and other industrial plants.'[45] Many Anglo-Canadian wage earners were outraged. The press heaped fuel on the fires of resentment with regular reports of high wages among these workers. White, English-speaking commentators also resuscitated pre-war fears of cultural degeneration they believed they saw in the immigrants' crowded-boardinghouse lifestyle, ignoring the reality that many of these men were simply biding their time until the re-opening of immigration allowed them to return to Europe or Asia.

By the end of 1917 returning soldiers had become the loudest and most belligerent critics of the employment of 'interlopers' and 'enemy aliens,' terms applied loosely to Europeans of many different backgrounds. Over the next two years the veterans often took to the streets to attack the men they alleged were stealing their jobs and to demand that the government intern or deport them. Early in 1919 there were violent assaults on eastern European immigrants in Calgary, Drumheller, Winnipeg, Port Arthur, Sudbury and Halifax. Employers also felt the wrath of their workers, who demanded that the 'enemy aliens' be fired. Many companies complied to varying degrees. By 1919 this nativistic backlash was simmering in every part of the country where southern and eastern Europeans or Asians were working in large numbers.[46]

The huge strike wave that swept over all parts of the country after 1916 was also fed by the unflinching refusal of employers to deal with their workers collectively. In strike after strike, workers ended up on the picket lines because their bosses would not discuss the demands presented to them by workers' representatives. Capitalists dug in their heels to prevent wartime conditions from introducing any permanent changes in power relations in their enterprises. Workers who saw their employers profiting handsomely from big war contracts found their intransigence unfair and unacceptable: this was the issue that would ignite some of the biggest strikes in 1919, including the Winnipeg General Strike.

Part of what made these issues of shop-floor politics so unusually intense and widespread was the way in which the state was implicated, particularly the Borden government. Here was an administration that seemed to have lost its right to rule. For the thousands of families whose menfolk were dying in the trenches, grief mingled with bitterness at the apparent ineptitude and corruption in the prosecution of the war. Those working on the home front were no less outraged. The government had imposed rigid, authoritarian controls, from prohibition to national registration to restraints on strikes. It seemed to be protecting profiteers (the best known, Flavelle, was head of the Imperial Munitions Board). It offered no sympathy to workers who locked horns with their employers (indeed, in restraining strikes by means of the Industrial Disputes Investigation Act, it seemed to be tying the hands of unionists). And it refused to involve labour representatives in its wartime deliberations, in contrast to well-publicized initiatives in Britain and the United States.[47]

The creation of the Union government late in 1917 temporarily shored up the state's crumbling legitimacy, but the apparent insensitivity to working-class concerns continued into the post-war period. Many workers in Quebec and in the West were horrified by the heavy-handed use of the Military Service Act to impose conscription. Huge demonstrations and bloody riots broke out in the streets of Quebec.[48] In British Columbia draft dodgers were harassed and chased through the woods. Thousands of Vancouver unionists stopped work on 2 August 1918 to protest the fatal shooting of the fugitive draft dodger and radical unionist Albert 'Ginger' Goodwin.[49] The orders-in-council introduced in September and October 1918 to repress radical organizations and ban strikes were the final straw. Protest meetings against such attacks on civil liberties helped to radicalize the labour movement still further in cities as politically diverse as Toronto, Winnipeg, and Vancouver.[50]

The problem for this government was that the war had created new expectations of public morality among the mass of the population. Since 1914 workers had been urged to remember the men in the trenches and the cause they were allegedly fighting for and to hold their personal desires in check for the great crusade against 'Kaiserism.' From pulpits and street corners, on billboards and slips in their pay packets, workers had been asked to follow the banner of public service and self-sacrifice, ideals not often proclaimed in a capitalist society organized fundamentally on the basis of self-interest. By 1917 it appeared that many capitalists, especially their employers, were not showing the right spirit of self-denial. Nor were politicians and state officials themselves. In 1917 the constraining power of patriotic pro-war rhetoric began to fade and a deepening cynicism about the war effort spread. The last time patriotism was used to effect was in the 1917 federal election, but the elitism of the Union government and the flagrant electoral abuses left a foul odour.

A few months later the Imperial Munitions Board's director of labour reported a 30 per cent drop in productivity in war plants; 'all the enthusiasm and all the idea that munitions are vitally essential had gone out of the minds of the workpeople,' he noted, 'and . . . today they take the War, and the work related to it, as they take the sunrise — an incident of the day.'[51] That summer the government's own security adviser, Montreal lawyer C.H. Cahan, reported that workers' discontent stemmed from 'the weakening of the moral purpose of the people to prosecute the war to a successful end,' a deepening awareness of 'the bloody sacrifices and irritating burdens entailed by carrying on the war,' and 'the growing belief that the Union government is failing to deal effectively with the financial, industrial, and economic problems growing out of the war.'[52] The country had been saturated with the rhetoric of service and the noble goal of fighting to defend 'democracy,' and workers now bitterly threw these words back at those in power. In 1918 Sydney's labour paper stated, '[T]he people of Cape Breton have suffered too dearly on the fields of Flanders and at home to be ruled by an autocracy [in the local steel plant].'[53] Western labour leaders similarly viewed the government's draconian labour legislation in the fall of 1918 as 'Prussianism at home.'[54] Democracy had become the new touchstone of industrial relations and politics.

Workers and their leaders could take heart that other Canadians — farmers, clergymen, intellectuals, veterans, women, and more organized groups — had similar concerns. Labour activists were also increasingly aware that they were part of an international working-class ferment. In scattered parts of the globe workers were challenging established political and economic power with bold new programs, and they were winning. Almost every day, there appeared in the press stories of massive strikes in Britain, Europe, and the United States. Canadian labour papers reported favourably on the British shop stewards' movement and 'Triple Alliance' (of coal miners, railwaymen, and transport workers), as well as on the new industrial unionism in Australia, especially the One Big Union. Labour Party breakthroughs in Australia also attracted much attention, as did the decision of England's revitalized Labour Party early in 1918 to transform its program from a weak labourist project into an overtly socialist vision.[55] These international working-class challenges were further legitimized when delegates at the post-war peace conference in Paris felt compelled to issue a set of principles governing industrial relations that guaranteed workplace standards and rights to organize.[56]

The pockets of socialist activists across Canada received even more inspiration from Russia's fragile new experiment in workers' power. Some of the European immigrant communities, especially the Ukrainians, Russians, Jews, and Finns, were particularly excited about the new radicalism in Eastern Europe. The Edmonton socialists even named their new newspaper *The Soviet* early in 1919. For socialists in Canada, Russia was a shining example rather than an ideological reservoir, since Bolshevik theoretical work had scarcely touched North America at this stage. The left in Canada soon found surprisingly large audiences for its efforts to educate Canadian workers on the emerging soviet system. Montreal's Tom Cassidy spoke for many long-time socialist activists in crowing that, since the Bolshevik revolution, Canadian workers were far more interested in socialism than in 'the days when we stood out on the bald prairies howling and lonesome like a native coyote.'[57] What many Canadian workers drew from the Bolshevik experience was a boundless belief that what could be yearned and struggled for could also be achieved. For one Winnipeg labourer, the Russian example promised a resolution of all working-class problems: 'equal rights for men and women, no child labor, no poverty, misery and degradation, no prostitution, no mortgages on farms, no revolting bills for machinery to keep peasants poor till the grave, no sweatshops, no long hours of heavy toil for a meagre existence but an equal opportunity for all, a life made worth living with unlimited possibilities to all, aided by splendid machinery to make [the] earth a real paradise where nothing but happiness can prevail . . . this is Bolshevism.'[58] The Canadian government's decision to send troops to join the military invasion of the Soviet Union in 1919 brought cries of protest from the left of the Canadian workers' movements. Labour newspapers and socialist rallies regularly drew connections between all these dramatic international developments and the aspirations of Canadian workers.

The workers' revolt in Canada at the end of World War I, then, was not the desperate cry of a downtrodden and poverty-stricken proletariat. Rather it grew out of a newfound confidence in working-class power, a profound sense of injustice, and a determination that society could run differently. It was fuelled by a volatile mixture of those factors that had prompted working-class resistance in Canada for more than half a century and some special wartime conditions. Labour struggles over living standards in working-class households and wage earners' rights on the job were hardly new. But the prosecution of the war and the (mis)management of the wartime economy, which gave the national state such prominence, had unified many previously fragmented struggles around the country and given them some common focus. Wartime ideals, especially the fight for democracy, had also injected into public debate in Canada and abroad a moral fervour that piqued workers' imagination and heightened their expectations about the future. Old ways of viewing (and justifying) social relationships in capitalist society were dissolving. The wartime convergence of material and ideological forces thus facilitated the creation of the most broad-based, anticapitalist workers' movements that had ever appeared in Canada. And, as the revolt took shape, workers inspired each other; the remarkable success of working-class mobilization in the final years of the war bred a heady confidence in the potency of workers' collective action.

THE LIMITS OF A LABOUR MOVEMENT

In 1914 working-class organizations in Canada were in no shape to face the shock waves that the Great War would send through Canadian society. They included two distinct and often hostile camps on the industrial front: craft unionism and industrial unionism. At the turn of the century the craft unionists had hitched their star firmly to the new narrowly focused, bureaucratically structured 'international' unions based in the United States and affiliated with the American Federation of Labor (AFL). For the most part, the craft unionists sought from their employers nothing more than a regularized contractual relationship that would protect their craft status and workplace power, in return for labour peace and wage stability.[59] Despite an effort at revival in the pre-war boom, the craft unionists had been driven out of most of the major urban industries. Local trades and labour councils across the country nonetheless still tried to represent the collective interests of these skilled workers. Their national organization, the Trades and Labor Congress of Canada (TLC), continued to pose as the central 'House of Labour' in the country, despite its acceptance of the autonomy of the big internationals and of the right of the American Federation of Labor to mediate jurisdictional disputes, and despite its weakness in the Maritimes and the West.

In those regions in particular, many workers had turned to new industrial unions that signed up everyone in one workplace. Some leaders of these organizations hoped to rally Canadian workers for a general assault on the capitalist system. In western Canada some of them had organized for the colourful Industrial Workers of the World, which had been launched in 1905 and had made its greatest impact among more transient workers in the region between 1909 and 1912.[60] Less flamboyant versions of industrial unions put down roots among coal miners, longshoremen, textile and clothing workers, and a few other groups, and just before the war led these workers out in some of the biggest, most bitter strikes in living memory.[61] Employers attacked the new unions with the same tactics they had used against the craftsmen — strike-breakers, special police, industrial spies, and blacklists. By 1914 industrial unions had carved out a place for themselves within the various workers' movements in the country, but few of them had much numerical strength or bargaining clout. Nor had they overcome the divisions along lines of race and ethnicity and gender; both craft and industrial unionists were predominantly white, male, anglophone and francophone Canadians. In Quebec the Roman Catholic clergy were promoting a less aggressive form of unionism based on clerical supervision of the workers' movement and Franco-Catholic solidarity across class lines, but by 1914 they too had only limited success to report.[62]

There were further splits in the Canadian workers' movement by the outbreak of the war. Industrial struggles had become rigidly separated from political campaigns, and, within the realm of independent working-class politics, two ideological tendencies — labourism and socialism — confronted each other. Both groups had a tiny handful of their standard-bearers elected to provincial legislatures and municipal councils, but their overall impact on Canadian politics was extremely limited.[63]

Although the workers' movements in Canada had undergone some important changes in structure and ideology since the turn of the century, by 1914 they were still fragmented by occupation, industry, locality, race and ethnicity, gender, and ideology. Within working-class communities they represented an extremely limited force (the 166,000 unionists reported in

1914 amounted to barely 10 per cent of all wage earners in the 1911 census and were confined principally to railways, coal mining, and skilled urban trades). Their economic and political power had been shattered by employers' attacks and the devastating depression of 1913–15. Traditions of solidarity had been either seriously weakened by these assaults or not yet fully developed in communities overwhelmed with newcomers.

Some of the first stirrings of a collective working-class response to the new wartime conditions came from craft-union officials, particularly the Trades and Labor Congress of Canada. The new importance of the Canadian state put pressure on the Congress to intervene as the major working-class lobbying agency at the national level. For this task the organization had only two permanent officers: the president since 1910, former British Columbia miner and socialist James Watters, and the secretary since 1900, printer Paddy Draper, once described as a 'straight line "pure and simple" trade unionist.'[64] Rounding out the Congress executive were three additional members, elected by convention, who remained on staff with their respective unions (provincial executives also maintained relations with their respective governments). In its dealings with the state, the Congress confined itself strategically to traditional lobbying methods, eschewing any attempts at mass mobilization to advance its claims. Its officers preferred personal correspondence and private meetings, asserting the urgency of concessions by the state and capital lest rank-and-file militancy escalate beyond union officials' restraining capacities.[65] Labour's lobby, however, proved ineffectual. As Borden confided to his diary, the Congress's annual meetings with the federal cabinet took on an inert ritual of their own. After both the 1914 and 1915 meetings, the prime minister noted that the views expressed by Watters and Draper were both moderate and sensible, and his own cautious, non-committal response brought an end to their consideration for another year.[66] Labour's inability to lobby its way to redress would be part of the alchemy of the rising working-class revolt.

During the first three years of the war, the Congress's weakness was starkly exposed by its failure to make a dent in government policy in three prime areas of concern. First, the Congress pressed the Borden government repeatedly to alleviate the hardship of early wartime unemployment through more generous relief programs and an expansion of public works. It got neither.[67] Second, as the war economy took off in 1915, the Congress and its affiliates spent over a year pleading with the Borden government and the Imperial Munitions Board to impose fair wage clauses on military production in order 'to protect our people from extortion on the one hand and grinding poverty on the other.'[68] Instead, Ottawa extended the discredited Industrial Disputes Investigation Act to wartime industries, thereby imposing compulsory conciliation against strike attempts by discontented workers. Across the country labour's frustration at this outcome was vented not only at the government but also at the Congress leadership, condemned by the Toronto District Labor Council for not exercising 'the proper vigilance and care . . . when a measure of the character referred to has been allowed to become law.' At the TLC convention in September 1916, a majority of delegates voted for the act's repeal. Over the next two years, however, the federal government turned ever more frequently to IDIA boards, special royal commissions, roving labour department troubleshooters, and threats of coercion under the War Measures Act (seldom actually used) to head off strikes and maintain industrial peace.[69]

Third, the Congress failed to influence the conduct of the war itself, an issue that proved highly divisive within the house of labour. Before 1914 no representative body in Canadian society had developed a stronger anti-war position than the Congress. In 1913 it had even reaffirmed its willingness to call a general strike in the event of hostilities. Canadian labour, however, proved no more capable of preserving its pacifist principles than its European counterparts. At its September 1914 convention, the Congress reiterated its abhorrence of war but voted to support a war effort now characterized not as an internecine conflict among the capitalist classes of Europe, but as principled struggle pitting British and French democracy against German autocracy. The organization's position was not so surprising. Most unionists undoubtedly supported the Allied cause at this point; nor could there be any doubt that to persist with resistance might result in mass arrests, possibly culminating in an outright ban on unions. Besides, support for the war might enhance unions' legitimacy with both government and employers. A similar resolution in support of 'the cause of freedom and democracy' passed in 1915, though this time with a larger chorus of dissent.[70]

The creation of the National Service Board in October 1916 to undertake a compulsory national workforce registration placed the Congress leadership in a delicate position. Not only was labour characteristically excluded from board representation, but the whole procedure appeared to be at odds with the 1915 Congress resolution that emphatically declared 'unchangeable opposition to all that savours of conscription.' Many in the labour movement regarded registration as a prelude to military conscription and regimentation at work. Yet, after meeting with Borden in December and receiving his word that registration was unconnected to any specific plans for conscription, the Congress executive issued a statement recommending that all affiliated workers complete their registration forms. Labour leaders in Quebec and the West immediately denounced the statement. When conscription was introduced the following spring, Borden noted cheerfully that Canada's house of labour would mount only ritualistic opposition to the measure it had decried for years. 'They were very receptive and good natured,' he observed after meeting with the Congress executive, 'but we may have a good natured tilt with them as they said.'[71]

The Congress leaders were clearly attempting to barter their services to the state in return for recognition. Thus, immediately after signing on for registration, they urged Borden to bring a labour representative into the cabinet. (Watters had already begun quietly promoting himself for the job, to the prime minister's great exasperation.)[72] A campaign of resistance to military conscription was more important as leverage in pressing for greater recognition of organized labour by the Borden government. Accordingly, the summer of 1917 witnessed the Congress's most energetic anti-government campaign yet. In early June it convened a four-day conference to discuss problems confronting the labour movement. Delegates from across the country, representing eighty different affiliated unions, participated in wholesale condemnation of the Imperial Munitions Board, the high cost of living, and conscription itself. The Congress leadership stepped up the call for labour representation in policy development and demanded that wealth be conscripted before lives. Yet once conscription received parliamentary assent, the Congress executive faithfully fell into line, recommending to the September 1917 convention that Canadian labour not oppose the government's forced call to arms. At this point, however, they faced a large minority in opposition, which unleashed a torrent of passionate rhetoric against conscription and in favour of a general strike against the policy.[73] In this context, it is not surprising that the Congress leadership endorsed the creation of a Canadian Labor Party as a safer channel into which to direct this working-class anger over state policy.

Borden's government also sensed the dangers in continuing to ignore or deflect the labour leadership. As the December 1917 federal election approached, appointing a labour minister seemed essential to conferring greater legitimacy and workers' support on the new Union cabinet and its labour policies. Borden's choice was inspired. Gideon Robertson was Canadian vice-president of one of the country's consistently 'safe and sane' railway brotherhoods, the Order of Railroad Telegraphers. He already sat in the Senate and privately admitted to Borden to having 'done all possible since 1914 to maintain industrial peace in Canada, which is essential to efficient results in our war work.' He promised 'to support [the Borden government's] war policy, [and] to promote industrial peace in Canada.' Robertson's appointment to the cabinet as minister without portfolio was followed by a decided shift in state labour policy, no doubt inspired by the new tripartite structures recently introduced by the American government. In January 1918 four cabinet ministers held extensive discussions with fifty-six labour leaders carefully selected by Congress officials from forty different unions. For the first time, labour received representation on a host of state regulatory bodies and, most important, the Labour Sub-Committee of the cabinet's Reconstruction and Development Committee. Moreover, the Congress executive triumphantly informed its affiliates, all such labour appointees would have to be recommended by, or acceptable to, 'the recognized heads of our movement.' As a symbol of the new openness to labour, AFL President Samuel Gompers was invited to address Parliament. According to James Watters, the war showed 'the necessity of co-operation, not alone on the actual field of battle, but in every industrial activity associated with the prosecution of the war. . . . Competition has, therefore, given place to co-operation — co-operation between the State and Capital and Labor.' Here were the terms of the social contract that labour leaders hoped to establish. In exchange for their commitment to harmonious workplace relations and production, these officials expected the quid pro quo of reciprocal recognition from the state and capital.[74]

Pursuing such a course inevitably drove Canada's top union leadership towards intensified commitment to the government's industrial agenda. The Congress endorsed a second registration campaign for a further inventory of the country's labour force. More important, labour officials accepted the government's apparent commitment to conciliation of industrial disputes (including some of their proposed amendments to the IDIA) and worked assiduously to prevent strikes. Union staff and structures were mobilized to restrain working-class militancy. In two critical sectors — coal mining and shipbuilding — unions participated in tripartite forums with employers and state officials to discuss means of averting strikes and boosting production.[75] A national strike of thirty thousand railway shop workers was averted only by the threats of charter revocation from international headquarters. The use of the 'big stick,' as one labour paper termed it, brought compliance from the Canadian bargaining committee representing the rail workers and the imposition of a collective agreement patterned on a recent American rail settlement.[76] In a number of instances, such international union directives against strike action in Canada were prompted by a direct federal government appeal. Watters himself became something of a roving troubleshooter acting on government request to curb militancy, as in the Nova Scotia steel industry in the spring of 1918.[77] In the same year, on at least three occasions during 1918 Gideon Robertson called on APL President Sam Gompers and Secretary Frank Morrison to prevent strikes of Cape Breton coal miners and British Columbia shipbuilders and electrical workers.[78]

During 1918, however, it became apparent that the state was dictating the terms of its rapprochement with labour and that the new relationship produced no demonstrable advances in state labour policy. In fact, in both its legislative and employer roles, the federal government showed renewed intransigence in its dealings with labour. Although it announced a policy endorsing unionization that summer, the government provided no enforcement mechanisms and, in fact, enacted its most coercive labour legislation of the war during 1918 — first the infamous 'Anti-Loafing Act' in April and then the orders-in-council outlawing radical organizations and banning strikes in the fall. On none of these measures was labour consulted. An order-in-council in July announcing the terms of employment that workers had a right to expect, including collective bargaining, lacked any enforcement mechanism and therefore had no significant impact on labour relations in the country. The Trades and Labor Congress leadership had been incorporated into the state apparatus not to shape policy, but to enhance the legitimacy of coercive measures deemed necessary by the Borden government.

Nor did the new ties to the Congress transform the federal government's treatment of its own employees. Public-sector employees had been particularly victimized by wartime inflation. At the federal level wage restraint was the byword of a government straining to meet its wartime expenditures. Indeed, federal intransigence in the face of wage appeals from letter carriers brought western Canada to the brink of a massive general strike in the summer of 1918. When a paltry government wage offer was rejected in July, letter carriers went off the job in six centres, and within forty-eight hours widening strike action left twenty centres with no mail service. In contrast to their coverage of most other wartime strikes, the country's press was uniformly sympathetic to the aggrieved strikers. The *Calgary Herald* branded Ottawa 'utterly careless and lacking in the first principles of common decency as employers.'[79] When letter carriers in thirteen western cities rejected a new settlement negotiated by their leaders, the postmaster general instructed local postmasters to begin hiring strike-breakers and served notice that all strikers would be dismissed unless they returned to work within twenty-four hours. Several unions in the West threatened sympathy strikes, and a settlement was quickly negotiated to restore mail service by 1 August.[80]

The 1918 postal strike revealed two problems that confronted labour officialdom in its new relationship with the state — first, persistent tendencies to intransigence and coercion in state labour policies and, second, a union membership no longer willing to accept its leadership's restraining hand. The workers' movements that were taking shape across the country would not be tied down to the narrow project of corporatist accommodation among state, labour, and capital. 'The fact is they have got beyond our control,' one union official lamented in the summer of 1918.[81] . . . Despite the machinations of national labour leaders in and around Ottawa, workers wanted a labour movement that was more flexible, more militant, and often more radical: it was a challenge as much to their established leadership as to capital and the state.

THE IRON FIST AND VELVET GLOVE

The Canadian state never flinched in the face of the escalating, widely based labour revolt. However much the legitimacy of the Borden government had been undermined in the popular mind, state institutions in Canada had not crumbled as they had in Germany, Austria-Hungary, or Russia, and political leaders and officials moved quickly to fashion new tools of statecraft to curb the working-class challenge. The federal government shared business fears about the post-war economy and the need for restraint on labour demands. Borden told a national audience in September 1919 that the challenge was to foster greater production, efficiency, and cooperation in industry while avoiding measures that would 'drive away capital, restrict industry or hinder development.' But the government's concerns were also political. Now guided in its response to the revolt by the rigidly conservative Arthur Meighen, the government recoiled in horror at the size and radical overtones of the workers' movements in Canada, especially those in the West. Since September 1918, when a secret report on mushrooming radicalism in Canada crossed the cabinet's desks, politicians and state officials had been aware that more was at stake than wages and working conditions. The secret security apparatus of the Dominion Police and the Royal North-West Mounted Police was strengthened to allow the placement of spies inside labour organizations. The spectre of Bolshevik-style revolutions hung over the cabinet table as these agents' reports inflated the radical undercurrents in strike settings where workers took direction from leaders with a long-term anti-capitalist agenda. According to the labour minister, the government was also deluged with 'insistent inquiries and requests . . . that something be done immediately or that Bolshevism may prevail, property and life held lightly, and the country be destroyed.' Although it still hoped to direct workers' aspirations into safe channels until the normal market mechanisms of peacetime could tame them, the government was even more determined to show that radical options were not necessary and would not be tolerated.[82]

The infamous orders-in-council in September 1918 — the first effort to stifle the new radicalism, especially in the immigrant communities and in the West generally — had been followed by several arrests. 'Alien' internment and press censorship (now aimed at socialist, not anti-war, ideas) continued for more than a year after the Armistice. The secret security reports advised that the spirit of revolt was continuing to spread in all parts of the country. The Western Labour Conference of March 1919 seemed particularly menacing. In this context, the well-established machinery of industrial conciliation was set aside in favour of blunt coercion. Winnipeg workers became the first post-war strikers to confront the full state arsenal of weapons for strike-breaking and repressing radicalism. Troops and 'special' police were deployed to harass strikers and to take back control of public space. Arrests were made under a hastily legislated measure for deporting immigrants ('alien' or British) who were deemed seditious. (The strike leaders were ultimately tried under pre-existing criminal law against seditious conspiracy; immediately after the strike, the Criminal Code's definition of sedition was broadened through the addition of the infamous Section 98.)

Winnipeg's workers were not the last to face such measures. In a similar effort to control the streets, the military clamped down on all public working-class gatherings during the subsequent Vancouver general strike. Four years later in Sydney, steelworkers were hit with similar military and legal repression, as were the Nova Scotia miners in 1925, this time at the hand of the provincial government. After crushing the Winnipeg strike, the federal government collaborated in the anti-radical Red Scare that businessmen and conservative journalists were promoting across the country. The workers' revolt had thus pushed the state to create more powerful, centralized mechanisms for combatting radicalism than had existed in pre-war Canada.[83]

Borden's government was astute enough to realize that repression alone could have backfired had the outrage it prompted unified all labour leaders in opposition. It therefore made conciliatory gestures to the voices of caution and moderation in the labour movement. First, in the spring of 1919 a royal commission on industrial unrest — chaired by Justice T.G. Mathers and including Trades and Labor Congress President Tom Moore and another reliable union leader, John Bruce — visited twenty-eight centres across the country to allow for an airing of grievances and a show of official concern, just at the height of militancy within the workers' revolt. In September there occurred the most remarkable public dialogue ever held between capital, labour, and the state — the National Industrial Conference. Convened in the Senate Chamber in Ottawa, this tripartite domestic peace conference was modelled on a similar gathering in Britain a few months earlier: a labour representation of eighty-eight 'responsible' men and women, carefully handpicked by the TLC leadership, faced an equal number of employers (chosen by the Canadian Manufacturers' Association and assorted trade associations) and thirty-four public representatives nominated by the government.

The results of both the royal commission and the conference were inconclusive. Neither body straightforwardly endorsed the eight-hour day or the right to organize and bargain collectively. Both endorsed industrial councils but never clarified whether these were to include unions. Precisely the same stand-off on important issues developed when the government sent representatives of labour and capital to the recently established International Labour Organization. Within a year these conciliatory gestures were no longer felt to be necessary, and labour requests that the industrial conference be reconvened were politely ignored. Having beaten labour into submission on the picket lines, neither capital nor the state felt the need for concessions in the name of stability. Fifty years later John Bruce recalled his experience with the Mathers Commission as 'one of the bitterest lessons that ever I learned about political chicanery.'[84]

The Great War transformed the social relations of production in Canada. Workers gradually developed a measure of material and ideological confidence in wartime society, but also the grounds for a deep-seated sense of injustice. Their outrage was vented at shadowy profiteers, intransigent employers, and, to an unprecedented degree, an insensitive state. The national labour leadership never managed to defend workers' interests effectively and fell victim to the national government's determined efforts to derail the workers' revolt. These common features of the Great War experience in working-class Canada were played out in particular ways in each region of the country.

NOTES

1. On the impact of war on the home front, see Marwick, *War and Social Change*; Fussell, *Great War and Modern Memory*; Winter, *Great War and the British People*; Eksteins, *Rites of Spring*; Read, ed., *Great War and Canadian Society*.
2. Shortt, 'Economic Effects of War'; R.T. Naylor, 'Canadian State'; Norrie and Owram, *History of the Canadian Economy*, 411-40; Thompson, *Harvests of War*, 50–6.
3. The course of the Canadian military effort can be followed in Morton and Granatstein, *Marching to Armageddon*. The plight of the Canadian soldier in this war is sensitively treated in Morton, *When Your Number's Up*.
4. Corry, 'Growth of Government Activities.'
5. On social life in Canada during the war, see Read, ed., *Great War and Canadian Society*.
6. For example, coal miners in western Canada's District 18 of the United Mine Workers used a strike in 1915 to get 'enemy aliens' removed from the mining operations where they worked. In April 1917 the office of a German newspaper was ransacked in Regina. Avery, 'Ethnic and Class Tensions,' 80, 89. See also Wilson, *Ontario and the First World War*, lxx-lxxxiv.
7. Socknat, *Witness against War*, 43–59.
8. Steinhart, *Civil Censorship*; Cole, 'War Measures Act'; Keshen,' All the News'; Siemiatycki, 'Munitions and Labour Militancy'; Peter Melnycky, 'The Internment of Ukrainians in Canada,' in Swyripa and Thompson, eds., *Loyalties in Conflict*, 1–24; Gregory Kealey, 'State Repression.'
9. Corry, 'Growth of Government Activities'; Smith, 'Emergency Government in Canada'; Thompson, *Harvests' of War*, 27–44; Boudreau, 'Western Canada's "Enemy Aliens"'; Swyripa and Thompson, eds., *Loyalties in Conflict*; Rasporich, *For a Better Life*, 75–92; Craven, *Impartial Umpire*; Granatstein and Hitsman, *Broken Promises*, 22–104; Spence, *Prohibition in Canada*; Hallowell, *Prohibition in Ontario*, 7; Forbes, 'Prohibition and the Social Gospel'; Heron, 'Daylight Savings'; Reilly, 'General Strike in Amherst.'
10. Corry, 'Growth of Government Activities'; Smith, 'Emergency Government in Canada'; Brown and Cook, *Canada, 1896–1921*; Cuff, 'Organizing for War'; Morton and Wright, *Winning the Second Battle*.
11. Hinton, *First Shop Stewards' Movement*; Owram, *Government Generation*; Thistle, *Inner Ring*; Traves, State and Enterprise, 55–70; Struthers, No Fault of Their Own, 16–43.
12. English, *Decline of Politics*, 88–221; Brown, Robert Borden.
13. Armstrong, *Crisis of Quebec*.
14. English, *Decline of Politics*, 136–203; Brown, *Robert Borden*, 83–125; Graham, *Arthur Meighen*, 145–210; Granatstein and Hitsman, *Broken Promises*, 70–83.
15. Bliss, 'Methodist Church'; Allen, *Social Passion*, 63–103; Thompson, 'Beginning of Our Regeneration'; Gray, *Booze*; Hallowell, *Prohibition in Ontario*.
16. Cleverdon, *Woman Suffrage Movement*; Bacchi, *Liberation Deferred?*
17. See, for example, Miller, ed., The New Era in Canada; Bland, *The New Christianity*; Irvine, *Farmers in Politics*; King, *Industry and Humanity*; Leacock, *Unsolved Riddle*; MacIver, *Labor in the Changing World*. For a discussion of this intellectual ferment, see Owram, *Government Generation*, 80–106.
18. Thompson, *Harvests of War*; Morton, *Progressive Party*; Wood, *History of Farmers' Movements*; Young, 'Conscription, Rural Depopulation, and the Farmers of Ontario.'
19. Morton and Wright, *Winning the Second Battle*; Morton, *When Your Number's Up*, 253–75.
20. BC Federationist, 3 July 1914; Siemiatycki, 'Labour Contained,' 10–15; Roy, 'Vancouver: "The Mecca of the Unemployed,"' 400–2; Matters, 'Public Welfare Vancouver Style'; Schulze, 'Industrial Workers of the World'; Goeres, 'Disorder, Dependency and Fiscal Responsibility,' 39; Avery, 'Ethnic and Class Tensions,' 80; Heron, 'Working-Class Hamilton,' 206; Piva, Condition of the Working Class, 76–82; Larivière, Albert Saint-Martin, 109–18; Ewen, "Quebec: Class and Ethnicity," in *The Workers' Revolt in Canada*, 1917-1925, pp. 87–143;

Canada, Dept. of Labour, Labour Organization in Canada, 1915, 17; UBC Archives, Vancouver Trades and Labor Council Minutes, 19 November 1914; Morton and Granatstein, Marching to Armageddon, 7–8; Morton, When Your Number's Up, 278–9. According to Morton's calculations, nearly two-thirds of the Canadian Expeditionary Force counted in March 1916 had been manual workers.

21. Price, 'Changes in the Industrial Occupations of Women'; Ramkhalawansingh, 'Women during the Great War'; Lowe, Women in the Administrative Revolution; Linda Kealey, 'Women and Labour during World War I'; Naylor, New Democracy, 130–6; Piva, Condition of the Working Class, 40–3; Heron, 'Working-Class Hamilton,' 388–90.

22. Copp, Anatomy of Poverty, 56; Piva, Condition of the Working Class, 40–3; Heron, 'High School and the Household Economy'; and 'Working-Class Hamilton,' 29.

23. Bliss, Canadian Millionaire; Carnegie, History of Munitions and Supply; Avery, 'Dangerous Foreigners'; Andrij Makueh, 'Ukrainian Canadians and the Wartime Economy,' in Swyripa and Thompson, eds., Loyalties in Conflict, 69–78; Heron, 'Working-Class Hamilton,' 319–24 and Working in Steel, 140.

24. Heron, 'Working-Class Hamilton,' 237–8.

25. See Bradbury, Working Families; Synge, 'Transition from School to Work' and 'Self-Help and Neighbourliness'; Abella and Millar, eds., Canadian Worker in the Twentieth Century, 76–150; Copp, Anatomy of Poverty; Piva, Condition of the Working Class; and Heron, 'High School and the Family Economy'

26. Nova Scotia, Factories' Inspector, Report, 1917, 6; Naylor, New Democracy, 34; Siemiatycki, 'Labour Contained,' 111; NAC, MG 30, A16 (Sir Joseph Flavelle Papers), Vol. 2, File: Department of Labour, Basil Magor to J. Flavelle, 7 June 1916; 'The Industrial Slacker,' Canadian Foundryman 9, no. 5 (May 1918), 105; Piva, Condition of the Working Class, 106; Carnegie, History of Munitions and Supply, 252–3; Heron, 'Working-Class Hamilton,' 238–9 and Working in Steel, 114–16.

27. Ewen, "Quebec: Class and Ethnicity," in The Workers' Revolt, pp. 87–143; Hogan, Cobalt, 24–31; Siemiatycki, 'Munitions and Labour Militancy'; Seager, 'Proletariat in Wild Rose Country.'

28. Labour Gazette, September 1917, 736–7; January 1918, 48–9; August 1919, 1004–5; July 1921, 972. Calculations of percentages are ours.

29. Canada, Dept. of Labour, Labour Organization in Canada, 1917, 38–9.

30. Naylor, 'Canadian State,' 83–7; Piva, Condition of the Working Class, 27–59; Copp, Anatomy of Poverty, 30–43; Bartlett, 'Real Wages and the Standard of Living,' 57; Sutcliffe and Phillips, 'Real Wages and the Winnipeg General Strike'; Makahonuk, 'Class Conflict,' 98–100; Heron, Working in Steel, 139.

31. See Frank, 'Miner's Financier.'

32. Quoted in McCormack, Reformers, Rebels, and Revolutionaries, 127.

33. Bliss, Canadian Millionaire, 329–62; NAC, MG 26, H 1(a) (Sir Robert Borden Papers), Northrup to Borden, 21 July 1917.

34. Quoted in Copp, Anatomy of Poverty, 134.

35. Canada, Dept. of Labour, Labour Organization in Canada, 1917, 38–9; McCormack, Reformers, Rebels, and Revolutionaries, 121–3.

36. Robin, Radical Politics and Canadian Labour; McCormack, Reformers, Rebels, and Revolutionaries, 128–9.

37. MacPherson, Each for All, 63–66. Working-class consumer co-ops are discussed in Heron and De Zwaan, 'Industrial Unionism,' 169, 172; and Heron, 'Working-Class Hamilton.'

38. Labour Gazette, 1919–20.

39. Steedman, 'Female Participation in the Canadian Clothing Industry'; Ewen, "Quebec: Class and Ethnicity," in The Worker's Revolt, pp. 87–143; Heron, 'Working-Class Hamilton,' 422.

40. In the decade before the war many of Canada's new corporate employers, both domestic and foreign, had begun to reorganize their work processes with more centralized, authoritarian managerial structures and new labour-saving technology. The transformation of their workplaces was most evident in such central Canadian cities as Montreal, Toronto, and Hamilton, where trend-setting American managerial styles had their greatest impact, but was far from complete in most industries by the outbreak of the war. Heron, Working in Steel and 'Second Industrial Revolution'; Heron and Palmer, 'Through the Prism of the Strike'; McKay, 'Strikes in the Maritimes'; Lowe, Women in the Administrative Revolution; Armstrong, 'Quebec Asbestos Industry'; Stacey, Sockeye and Tinplate; Rajala, 'Managerial Crisis' and 'Rude Science'; Hovis, 'Technological Change and Mining Labour'; Babcock, 'Saint John Longshoremen'; Foster, 'On the Waterfront'; Steedman, 'Skill and Gender'; Tuck, 'Union Authority'; Marshall, Southard, and Taylor, Canadian-American Industry.

41. Heron, 'Crisis of the Craftsman'; Roberts, 'Toronto Metal Workers.'

42. Industrial Banner (Toronto), 7 September 1917.

43. Quoted in Heron, Working in Steel, 140.

44. Avery, 'Dangerous Foreigners'; Andrij Makuch, 'Ukrainian Canadians and the Wartime Economy' in Swyripa and Thompson, Loyalties in Conflict, 70; Wickberg, ed., From China to Canada.

45. Makuch, 'Ukrainian Canadians and the Wartime Economy,' 71; Peter Melnycky, 'The Internment of Ukrainians in Canada,' in Swyripa and Thompson, eds., *Loyalties in Conflict*, 14–15; Morton, *Canadian General*, 343; Avery, *'Dangerous Foreigners'*, 32.

46. Bradwin, *Bunkhouse Man*; Harney *Gathering Place*; Ramirez, *On the Move*; Heron, *Working in Steel*; Avery, 'Ethnic and Class Tensions,' 79–98 and *'Dangerous Foreigners'*, 73–89; McCormack, *Reformers, Rebels, and Revolutionaries*, 121; Heron, 'Working-Class Hamilton,' 320–7; Wickberg, ed., *From China to Canada*, 120–2; McKay, 'The 1910s,' 222.

47. Robin, *Radical Politics and Canadian Labour*; McCormack, *Reformers, Rebels, and Revolutionaries*, 122–3.

48. Provencher, Québec sous la loi des mesures de guerre; Armstrong, Crisis of Quebec; Ewen, "Quebec: Class and Ethnicity," in *The Worker's Revolt*, pp. 87–143.

49. Mayse, *Ginger*; Hanebury, *Ginger* Goodwin.

50. James Naylor, "Southern Ontario: Striking at the Ballot Box," in *The Workers' Revolt in Canada, 1917–1925*, pp. 144–175; Robin, Radical Politics and Canadian Labour, 163–9; McCormack, Reformers, Rebels, and Revolutionaries, 152–4.

51. NAC, MG 30 (Sir Joseph Flavelle Papers), A16, Vol. 38, File 1918–19, Mardi Irish to Flavelle, 20 June 1918.

52. Quoted in Robin, *Radical Politics and Canadian Labour*, 165.

53. Quoted in Heron, *Working in Steel*, 142

54. Quoted in Bercuson, *Fools and Wise Men*, 71.

55. Bercuson, *Fools and Wise Men*, 75–8.

56. The leadership of the Winnipeg General Strike made much of this declaration. See Penner, 1919, 40–1; and Ian McKay and Suzanne Morton, "The Maritimes: Expanding the Circle of Resistance," in *The Workers' Revolt in Canada, 1917–1925*, pp. 43–86.

57. Public Archives of Manitoba, Robert Russell Papers, Cassidy to Stephenson, 19 January 1919.

58. McCormack, *Reformers, Rebels, and Revolutionaries*, 139–43 (quote at 141); Avery, *'Dangerous Foreigners'*, 70–6; Krawchuk, *Ukrainian Socialist Movement*; Laine, 'Finnish Canadian Radicalism.'

59. Babcock, *Gompers in Canada*.

60. McCormack, *Reformers, Rebels, and Revolutionaries*; Leier, *Where the Fraser River Flows*.

61. McKay, 'Industry Work, and Community'; MacFwan, *Miners and Steelworkers*; Seager, 'Proletariat in Wild Rose Country'; Foster, 'On the Waterfront'; Rouillard, *Les travailleurs du coton*; Steedman, 'Female Participation in the Canadian Clothing Industry.'

62. Rouillard, *Les syndicats nationaux*.

63. Robin, *Radical Politics and Canadian Labour*; McCormack, *Reformers, Rebels, and Revolutionaries*; Frank and Reilly, 'Emergence of the Socialist Movement'; Krawchuk, *Ukrainian Socialist Movement*; Laine, 'Finnish Canadian Radicalism'; Fraser, 'Radical Portraits'; Heron, 'Labourism and the Canadian Working Class.'

64. Wisconsin State Historical Society, American Federation of Labor Papers, Flett to Gompers, 3 October 1916.

65. Siemiatycki, 'Labour Contained,' 51–6.

66. NAC, MG 26, H 1(a), Borden Diaries, 5 June 1974; 15 June 1915.

67. Siemiatycki, 'Labour Contained,' 25–8.

68. NAC, MG 30, A16, Watters to Borden, 22 November 1915.

69. NAC, Toronto District Trades and Labor Council, Minutes, 6 April 1916; Siemiatycki, 'Munitions and Labour Militancy'; Tucker, 'World War I and the Post-War Labour Revolt.'

70. Canada, Dept. of Labour, *Labour Organization in Canada*, 1914, 18–19; Socknat, *Witness against War*, 37; Trades and Labor Congress of Canada (TLC), *Proceedings*, 1914, 20; 1915, 14, 91.

71. TLC, *Proceedings*, 1915, 15; NAC, MG 26, H 1(a), Borden Diaries, 21 May 1917.

72. Siemiatycki, 'Labour Contained,' 153–4.

73. Ibid., 155–8.

74. NAC, MG 26, H 1(a), Robertson to Borden, 23 August 1917; Watters and Moore, 'To Organized Labor in Canada' (undated circular); TLC, *Convention Booklet*, 1918.

75. *Halifax Herald*, 26 February 1918; *Machinists' Monthly Journal*, May 1918, 455.

76. *Labor News*, 26 July 1918.

77. Heron, 'Great War and Nova Scotia Steelworkers,' 17.

78. Siemiatycki, 'Labour Contained,' 216–17.

79. *Calgary Herald*, 23 July 1918.

80. Siemiatycki, 'Labour Contained,' 203–4.

81. *Toronto Telegram*, 23 July 1918.

82. Canada, National Industrial Conference, *Report*, 6; Graham, *Arthur Meighen*, 211–44; Horrall, 'Royal North-West Mounted Police'; Gregory Kealey, 'State Repression of Labour'; Canada, Senate, *Debates*, 2 April 1919, 194.

83. Mitchell, 'To Reach the Leadership'; Bercuson, Confrontation at Winnipeg, 115–75; Macgillivray, 'Military Aid'; Frank, 'Trial of J.B. McLachlan'; Allen Seager and David Roth, "British Columbia and the Mining West: A Ghost of a Chance," in *The Workers' Revolt in Canada, 1917–1925*, pp. 231–267. On federal collaboration in the Red Scare, see Canada, Department of Labour, Information Respecting the Russian Soviet System and Its Propaganda in North America (Ottawa: King's Printer 1920). Before the war radicalism that seemed menacing was simply repressed in an ad hoc fashion. Local municipal police forces would simply lock up soapbox socialists who caused a seditious nuisance. Any combination of large-scale militancy and radicalism would generally result in the mobilization of the militia to occupy the streets. Leier, Where the Fraser River Flows; Schulze, 'Industrial Workers of the World'; Frank and Reilly, 'Emergence of the Socialist Movement,' 89–90; McCormack, Reformers, Rebels, and Revolutionaries, 105–7; Heron, 'Working-Class Hamilton,' 654–55; Morton, 'Aid to the Civil Power.'

84. Canada, Royal Commission on Industrial Relations, *Report* (Ottawa: King's Printer 1919) (the unpublished testimony is available in the Labour Canada Library in Hull); Canada, National Industrial Conference, *Report*; Siemiatycki, 'Labour Contained,' 355–67; Naylor, *New Democracy*, 188–214 and 'Workers and the State,' 28–35; Gerber, 'United States and Canadian National Industrial Conferences'; Hucul, 'Canada and the International Labour Organization'; NAC, John Bruce Papers, Interview, 30 March 1963.

Article Twenty-Five

"We Who Have Wallowed in the Mud of Flanders": First World War Veterans, Unemployment and the Development of Social Welfare in Canada, 1929–1939

Lara Campbell

The Great war was fought for Freedom and Democracy, as against control and power by Might through Wealth and Rank . . . we see little or no evidence of those principles for which we fought, our country being dominated and ruled by the power of wealth . . . the interests of money are held in higher esteem than Health, Employment or material welfare and life itself.[1]

The years of the Great Depression, from 1929 to 1939, witnessed the development of a new ideology of social welfare in Canada. While much research has been done on the consolidation of the welfare state, few historians have studied the role played by veterans and their political protests in the development of new notions of entitlement and the expansion of social welfare.[2] However, the rapid organization of veterans into a number of groups after the First World War, and their consolidation into the Royal Canadian Legion in 1925, marks them as a vocal, articulate, and politically aware constituency that developed during the post-war discontent. By the

I would like to thank Karen Dubinsky, Eric Wredenhagen, and the paper's anonymous readers for their helpful comments and encouragement. I would also like to acknowledge the funding received from Queen's University School of Graduate Studies and Research.

Source: Lara Campbell, "'We Who Have Wallowed in the Mud of Flanders': First World War Veterans, Unemployment and the Development of Social Welfare in Canada, 1929–1939," *Journal of the Canadian Historical Association* (2002): 125–149. Used with permission.

1930s, veterans were engaged in political protest against the effects of unemployment and government policy on ex-servicemen. This protest was crucial to the development of government support for broader ideas of economic and social security, and the idea that social welfare was a right associated with the benefits of full citizenship. An analysis of the response of veterans to the Depression helps, in part, to explain why discussions of welfare state entitlement were so narrowly rooted in the language of contract, service, duty, and individual responsibility. Veterans' protests also illustrate the complex tensions that emerged as the unemployed challenged and defined the limits of need and entitlement.

While the development of welfare state policy is often studied from the perspective of political or intellectual history, the impact of organized protest and unorganized resistance throughout the 1930s must also be examined in order to fully understand the shifts in government policy and the eventual shape of various social programs.[3] The 1930s were characterized by a diversity of activism, such as the successful organizing of the Workers Unity League, the development of local organizations of the unemployed, the birth of the Co-operative Commonwealth Federation, and numerous local relief protests and hunger marches, the most famous being the relief camp protests and the On-to-Ottawa Trek in 1935. Various groups sustained a critique of government inaction on unemployment, ranging from increased government intervention in the economy to provide work or unemployment insurance, to demands for adequate relief, to proposals for a radical restructuring of the social and political order.[4] Some historians have acknowledged the influence of grassroots organizing and protest on state programs and policy. As American historian Linda Gordon has demonstrated, welfare recipients have resisted and fought back against welfare agencies and officials, and continually offered new definitions of their problems. Gordon argues that popular political activism of the 1930s, such as writing letters to politicians or participating in relief or eviction protests, created a shift in public opinion that cohered around a belief in the entitlement of citizens to state-sponsored economic security.[5]

However, most citizens did not envision a universal welfare state or propose the full social entitlement of all citizens. Rather, the 1930s witnessed an uneasy co-existence between the burgeoning number of those who sought benefits on the basis of rights and entitlement, and older notions of charitable aid based on the distinction between the deserving and undeserving poor. Citizens who made claims to entitlement from the state were grappling with the tension between civil and social citizenship. In framing demands for aid in the language of civil citizenship, which used the economic discourse of "commercial exchange," and by linking demands to the classical liberal rights of freedom of exchange and private property, claimants could place their claims in the discourse of a politically powerful rhetoric.[6] However, while these demands helped to expand social welfare provision and government responsibility, they did not ultimately challenge the contract-based ideology of citizenship that based the reward of social provision on service. Arguments for entitlement were clothed in rights-based rhetoric to give them legitimacy, and this discourse was expressed in the language of citizenship and contract. To have certain rights as a citizen (and in the 1930s many of these rights revolved around access to jobs and a living wage and to a lesser extent, proper support during times of unemployment) an individual had to fulfill certain duties and expectations of citizenship. The more one could identify oneself as a true citizen of Canada, the greater the degree of entitlement to social and economic benefits.

Further, in a society where full participation in state and society was predicated on employment and economic independence, the highest form of citizenship was gendered masculine, since entitlement to jobs was firmly entrenched as a masculine right. Furthermore, since front-line action, the most prestigious form of war service, was reserved for men, the veterans' call to economic justice, with its emphasis on duty and reciprocity, was deeply entwined with gendered notions of entitlement and citizenship.[7] Citizenship itself, of course, was already gendered; formal political rights, such as the right to vote, were still relatively new for women on the eve of the Great Depression. Citizenship was therefore measured by gender, ethnicity, class, marital status, age and degree of service to the state, leading to a complicated hierarchy of who was most deserving and entitled to jobs and aid.

Though the language of reciprocity, duty and contract was limiting, entitlement could still be expanded to mean more than market-based reciprocity. At the same time as citizens made demands using the language of entitlement, they claimed social rights of citizenship, such as economic security, the right to employment and a living wage, and a comfortable standard of living for their families, including aid that was not administered in a stigmatizing way. These demands pushed the limits of a definition of entitlement based on contractual exchange by insisting on the possibility of a relationship between citizens and the state that honoured more than individualistic, market-based wage-labour relationships. Unemployed men and women argued that unemployment and the need for relief was neither inherently stigmatizing nor an inevitable sign of individual failure. Arguments for entitlement to economic security could be based on fulfilling the gendered duties of either father and protector, or mother, homemaker and wife; upon upholding Canadian citizenship and patriotism based on British ethnicity and loyalty; and on duty and sacrifice for the state. These claims were attempts to de-commodify the understanding of entitlement by placing it, at least partially, outside the realm of the labour market.

Veterans were a crucial component in the growing and dynamic public debate over the extent of government responsibility for the support of its citizens. But as this paper will show, veterans' arguments for entitlement also excluded many citizens, and the tensions and conflicts between developing ideas of entitlement and older notions of charity would become encoded in future welfare policy.[8] By looking at a variety of sources, such as letters written by veterans directly to Ontario politicians during the 1930s, the records of veterans' organizations, and welfare case files, it is possible to examine the full contours of problems facing ex-servicemen in the Depression years, and how they interacted with and attempted to influence government policy through protest, organization, and resistance.

Like most citizens who criticized government inaction during the Depression, veterans tended to emphasize traits of good character, honesty and sobriety. To be a good Canadian citizen was to be white, hardworking, respectable, married and raising a family. Good citizens, however, argued that in return for fulfilling these duties, the government had a reciprocal duty to support and maintain them, particularly in times of financial hardship. Veterans identified themselves as good citizens, but they alone had "wallowed in the mud of Flanders," and were therefore entitled to "a chance to make a few dollars and keep the Respectability of ourselves and our families."[9] In return for their wartime sacrifices, veterans believed the state had promised them "a new world of justice and goodwill" and a "future free of want," in "a country which thoroughly understood and thoroughly appreciated the magnitude of his sacrifice" made for Civilization, the Empire, Liberty, and the Home.[10] "I am a war veteran and twice wounded in action," wrote Arthur Knight, married with three children and unemployed since 1931, who was receiving what he felt was an inadequate disability pension of $7 a month. "Now Sir I had the impression when I went to defend my country in 1915 that my country would take care of me and mine in the event of my being unable to do so."[11]

As the economic crisis deepened and unemployment increased, veterans became increasingly bitter over the perceived failure of the government and the public to reward them properly. They angrily pointed out that those who had stayed home had profited from "the blood and tears of the other." Arguing for "Equality of Sacrifice," they charged that while soldiers had fought for Canada's security, those at home had benefited from higher salaries and war bond investments.[12] Those who stayed home and grew affluent were "cynical" and "smirking patriots" who "counted their own blessings in the dividends transmuted from the blood of the victims."[13] Veterans pointed to their injuries and disabilities, the years of lost wages and promotions, privation for their families, and their return home to unemployment and poverty. "I would have been better to have never come back than to go through what I am going through now," said one veteran to Premier Henry.[14] As the Great Depression wore on, veterans pointed out that men who enlisted in 1914 had "enlisted at the wage rates for labour which prevailed in 1914, a rate which was maintained for the whole period of service . . . These men had no opportunity to take advantage of the high wages paid in some of the war industries at home."[15] Soldiers saw that their incomes, frozen at $1.10 per day through the war, made their poverty "the result of conscious public policy," and not of individual failure or lack of character.[16] Careers, education and training that were sacrificed or interrupted, and the physical and psychological "strain of war" were factors that made unemployment a war-related problem to veterans.[17] In addition, Legion leaders and members, as well as government commissions, continually pointed out that most veterans were in their late 40s, so their age and physical condition made it difficult for them to work at manual labour.[18] *The Legionary* occasionally treated veterans' unemployment problems with sarcasm and humour. One cartoon in 1930 showed character Edward Jay Muggins proudly reading a job offer to his comrades: "the exceptional experience gained by you, during the great War, as an explosive expert has come to our notice, and after due deliberation, we . . . take great pleasure in offering you a position . . . you will be required to organize a special experimental department, with a view to perfecting a new explosive, for the purpose of blowing holes in doughnuts."[19]

Veterans felt a disconnection between their role as "heroes" during the war and the reality of the interwar years, when they struggled to re-integrate into society and deal with unemployment and disability.[20] Government propaganda and censorship meant that accounts of the warfront depicted men as "heroic and almost divine," and films and novels emphasized the romance, adventure and heroism of the soldiers' life on the war front.[21] At home, however, many bitterly maintained that their demands for greater recognition were inadequately recognized by the government. As one ex-serviceman lamented, "the Government as [sic] no more use for me now they got the best out of me I was one of the first to go when the country was in trouble now we are left with nothing only the relief we get."[22] Both ex-servicemen and their leaders in the Legion voiced criticisms of the failure of both the government and the general public to appreciate the moral value of their service, and to reward them adequately for the sacrifices they had made. In a 1931 poem entitled "The End of the Hero," Cecil E. Morgan of Brantford, Ontario captured the sense of disillusionment and bitterness felt by many veterans:

I heard the drums, I saw the flags, the girls they marched between,
The files of other fools like me enlisting in '14.
They gave me jam and cigarettes, and mitts to warm my hands
And shipped me off from Angleterre with hugs and cheers and bands.

"We only ask you, Tommy dear, your poor old life to risk,
To save the world for heroes and from William's mailed fist
And, if you are not killed, old chap, a hero YOU will be,"
The Country cried, "Your future you may safely leave to me."

Then Armistice — I hurried home — Oh, how I thanked the Lord.
What — ! — bother for a gangrened bone — I don't want no Board.
What if it bothers later on? — They promised they would pay
I'm worth a dozen deaduns yet and this — Armistice Day.

But now, in 1931, my race is nearly run.
They laugh —"A pension — Like your cheek. You left the war A.1."
So where are those who sent me socks and called us heroes now?
Oh, Country!— Now we're on the rocks — Home, keep your war time vow?

For I, who fought the best I could, was nothing but a fool,
When, fit and strong, I left my wife, and little kids at school.
Believing politicians' words, I truly was a sap,
I fought, I suffered, bled and now, I die — forgotten scrap.[23]

Most veterans' calls for government aid centred on entitlement to jobs and the right to earn a living on the grounds that they had earned that entitlement through their war service.[24] As with most criticisms of the unemployment crisis, veterans called for government intervention in the economy and the creation of full employment "at a living rate of wage." Veterans' arguments of sacrifice were woven together with the deeply entrenched belief in masculine entitlement to jobs. For men, the ability to be a breadwinner and to support a family was a powerful claim on the state for jobs at a living wage. "I myself am a returned man with four years of service for my country," argued an unemployed veteran. "It certainly does not make me feel very nice to think I helped to defend a country that will not help me in times when I and my family need it badly."[25] F.J. Shaw demanded a job, arguing it was "unjust and unfair that I should have to appeal to charity organizations to procure the bare necessities of life for my wife and children."[26] When wartime sacrifice was combined with the manly duties of supporting a family, assertions of the right to jobs could create a powerful sense of entitlement among veterans. As the Dominion Legion President claimed in 1930: "No enfranchised [sic] loyal British subject and Canadian citizen has a greater right to influence the prospect of this nation's future."[27] The Legion demanded enforcement of preferential hiring for ex-servicemen in the civil service, and encouraged local and provincial branches to remain vigilant over the number of veterans hired at public works projects.[28] Submissions by the Legion influenced the recommendations of the Hyndman report, initiated in the waning days of R.B. Bennett's power. Partially adopted by the King government in 1936, the report reserved jobs issuing radio licences for unemployed veterans and gave wage subsidies for veterans' job training.

By the early 1930s, the Legion had made unemployment the focus of its criticism and concern. In 1931, the Ontario Provincial Command decried the problem of veteran unemployment, calling for increased taxation of the wealthy and preferential hiring in government and industry. At the Ontario Provincial Convention in 1933, the Unemployment Committee demanded employment at fair wages, and generous social insurance for unemployment, old age and illness. At the 1934 Dominion Legion Convention, the Unemployment Committee condemned the effect of unemployment on families, and acknowledged the "branding of those compelled to accept relief as a class apart and outcast, and the perpetuation of conditions likely to create a permanent and dependent pauper class deprived of moral economic privileges and rights," as well as the "tendency of some employers to exploit the circumstances of the unemployed in offering inadequate wages for temporary employment."[29]

Legion leaders and members reflected the deeply entrenched tension between charity and entitlement as they argued for more generous pension rights, preferential hiring, and access to adequate relief. "I don't want charity I want a position," wrote J.W. Alfred Rowe of Windsor to Premier Henry, asserting that, "I feel with all my services to the Empire that I am deserving."[30] The Legion leadership was reluctant to support a "war bonus," a monetary compensation proposed for all veterans for wartime service. In November 1933, Sir Arthur Currie claimed, "the great mass of returned men in Canada never had the thought that because they fought for their country they were entitled to preferred treatment by their country, in comparison with other citizens,"[31] yet the idea of a bonus for war service was obviously popular among veterans themselves. In January 1919, when the GWVA vets called for a $2000 bonus for war service, its membership increased from twenty to two hundred thousand members.[32] Legion leaders walked a fine line, however, expanding their definition of entitlement as the Depression continued, arguing for the special rights of "pre-aging" and "burnt-out" veterans, and emphasizing the war-related reasons that veterans suffered from unemployment. While insisting that veterans were not asking for special entitlement, and condemning the "bonus indolence," Legion leaders continually expanded their definition of entitlement, coming precariously close to arguments based on compensation for war service. "Every man who experienced the hardships of war is paying some penalty," argued Sir Arthur Currie in 1929.[33] The government should grant all unemployed ex-servicemen a well-paid pension, argued the Ottawa branch president, even if "in the majority of cases this would be a life pension."[34]

Veterans' demands privileged work and economic independence. Men like Thomas Frith of Pembroke, Ontario, did not believe that unemployment was caused by an individual moral failing. Rather, he considered it unfair that he had spent over three years at war and was nevertheless unemployed, while "men that never did anything for the Government can be holding down permanent jobs and the likes of me face poverty."[35] Yet, even as relief was characterized as a "degrading" form of "pauperism," veterans increasingly portrayed adequate relief as "a right" they had earned through war service.[36] Local branches became aware that many veterans who had small disability pensions were ineligible for municipal relief, which the Legion deemed "pathetic," since "immigrants who only a few years ago were enemies of this country" were eligible for relief.[37] The Legion argued for more generous top-ups to relief given to veterans, and by 1932–33, 14,368 pensioners were in receipt of the extra "departmental relief" given by the Department of Pensions and National Health.[38] The author of the Hyndman report (commissioned in January 1935 by R.B. Bennett) listened to delegations representing ex-servicemen, and recommended that the term "relief" (which they felt was inappropriate for veterans) should be changed to "unemployment assistance." The Commission also recommended that veterans receive cash rather than vouchers, and that it be issued in an amount equal or higher to that given to the "civilian population."[39]

The intersection of the idea of masculine entitlement to employment with that of manly service and duty to the state provided a powerful argument for jobs and recognition. The idealized soldier had fulfilled his manly duty to protect his nation, home, and family by going to war. As Jeffrey Keshen points out, propaganda downplayed the atrocities of the war while celebrating male adventure, the "saintliness . . . of sacrifice," and the power and success of "Johnny Canuck's" incredible feats of valour, strength, and stoicism.[40] In wartime rhetoric, the masculine image of the boyish and youthful soldier was combined with the image of the soldier as the masculine icon of hardiness, mythic courage, and heroism; all of these images were linked further to the alleged Nordic strength of the Canadian nation. In the words of a war-era song: "Men from the mountain the rock and the river/Men from the forest the lake and the plain/strike for our flag and defend it forever."[41] Canadians and soldiers were "a hardy race of men . . . a race that is stalwart brave and free."[42]

On return from war, however, masculinity was threatened by disability and unemployment. By the 1930s, the very men previously upheld as the epitome of manhood had been neutered by age, disability, psychological stress, and unemployment. Ironically, veterans' organizations began, as the 1930s progressed to portray ex-servicemen increasingly as "burnt-out," pre-aged, and unable to compete with younger, healthier men due to age and disability. By 1930, the Legion had successfully helped convince the government to implement the War Veterans'

Allowance Act, which recognized that men who served overseas and who suffered no obvious disability on demobilization had still experienced "premature aging" or "physical and mental deterioration."[43] President General Alex Ross claimed that veterans were unable to compete with "vigorous youth" and that "a man who served overseas, even though unscathed, suffered a marked depression in physical energy."[44] The images of lost youth, boyishness and innocence, portrayed side by side with images of men fulfilling the gendered expectations of citizenship by obeying the call to manly service, created a compelling picture of wounded ex-servicemen in crisis and in need of aid.

However, these images of masculinity were contradictory and not easily reconciled. Re-establishment propaganda proclaimed "Once a soldier always a man," yet pre-aged, wounded or disabled veterans were the very antithesis of the strong, healthy "boys" who initially went off to war.[45] Legion leaders emphasized a fractured manhood, while at the same time celebrating the manliness, duty and courage of former soldiers. "When MEN were needed to save our nation," claimed the Legion in 1934, "the boys responded to the call unselfishly, upholding the best traditions of our Empire . . . Promises of Freedom and Security have been broken or Forgotten."[46]

There is evidence that veterans themselves resisted fully embracing a discourse that emphasized their weakness, illness and disability, finding such characterizations of their position humiliating and frustrating. In response to hearing a political speech by a Legion leader that claimed that all veterans had been psychologically damaged by war, an anonymous soldier took offence, claiming that such assertions were distorted and that he was a "Front Line Survivor — and still NORMAL!!"[47] Similarly, an anonymous columnist challenged perceptions that he was not "normal," arguing that war service created men of great "character," "courage," "virility" and "self-confidence," and that if veterans were unable to re-adapt to civilian life it was "by reason of the failure of many 'sub-normal' citizens to fulfill war promises." The column included the following poem:

NORMAL men, proud and strong
Rallied to the flag; marched along

Weak and old men forced to stay
With other men* of softer clay.
(*Eligibles)[48]

The discourse of wounded manhood, which was used to justify claims for increased aid, undermined the idea of a strong, healthy, and independent masculinity. Veterans saw themselves as deserving, full citizens, too proud to accept charity, but they also argued that it was not shameful to demand government aid after serving the state in war. Perhaps this is why calls for aid were so strongly clothed in the discourse of contract and entitlement, which has been long associated with independent manhood, and which helped to maintain images of masculine strength despite the untenable economic position of many veterans.[49]

Work, home and family were also closely linked to veterans' sense of masculinity and sacrifice, making it evident that they saw a close relationship between the prosperity and stability of the home and the security of the state. Osborne Dempster, an unemployed mason whose family was on relief in Toronto, sold his furniture to pay rent arrears and avoid eviction. "It will be a strong man patriotically who this winter will drown out the cries of his children for bread with the strains of the 'Maple Leaf Forever,'" he told Premier Henry. "My children are receiving less nourishment I than received while in a Soviet prison in Moscow."[50] In 1934, the

Legion's Dominion Unemployment Committee criticized the "decreasing relief benefits with increasing living costs resulting in more general malnutrition and ill-health in the home of the unemployed," and the "insecurity of tenure of homes." The Committee also pointed out "the increasing determination of the unemployed to defend their homes by any available means against the social injustice of enforcing degrading and perilous poverty upon them."[51] Unemployed veterans continually linked the economic security of their families and homes to service in the war. Their role in the Great War was a crucial part of the organic relationship between citizen and state, and re-establishment and integration into civilian life, as Morton and Wright point out, was seen by veterans as an ongoing process, a governmental responsibility that had not ended in 1919.[52]

The home itself was an important signifier of citizenship in the community. Ratepayers' organizations throughout the Depression, for example, used their status as homeowners and taxpayers to organize for aid, and veterans argued that they had gone to war to protect these very rights to private property and home-ownership. As one veteran complained to Premier Henry in 1931, house-owning men brought up families, paid taxes, and should therefore receive "our share in the relief works programmes," especially those who "have done our duties in every respect as Citizens, some seeing service in the War 1914–1918."[53] As one man reminded Premier Henry, "we thought that when two of our boys went overseas, that they went to protect our home."[54] In 1934, the Legion's Ontario Provincial Command claimed that the problem of evictions faced by veterans and their families was also linked to the war. Those in mortgage arrears, they argued, "would be in a position to pay their taxes today had they not been loyal to their country's call."[55] As veterans and their families continually pointed out, the past and future security of the Canadian nation rested on the willingness of young men and their families to send their youth to war. As one deserted woman who was arguing for a veterans' pension wrote: "at the same time after I have struggled to raise my boys up to manhood the Government would expect my boys to step out and do their do their share to protect the country should a war break out; that go [sic] to show how much respect the Government has for the citizens of the country."[56] Men and women both argued that economic security and the ability to support a home and family were expressly linked to loyalty to the state. One mother reminded Premier Henry: "If this country ever has to fight again it can call on my eight boys to protect it well you cannot expect them to protect homes they haven't got."[57]

Historians have documented the growth of a Canadian political and cultural nationalism in the interwar years, but few have looked at how national identity was formed at the popular level.[58] One of the enduring myths of the Great War, as Jonathan Vance has pointed out, is that of the birth of the independent Canadian nation in the victories of the battlefield.[59] "The freedom of the nation rests upon sacrifice," claimed the Canadian Legion; "The boys of Canada established the freedom of Canada."[60] Soldiers wrote "Canada's name high on the world's roll of honour," and won Canada "international prestige."[61] To give meaning to the losses of war, Vance argues, wartime victories were used as a tool to unify the divisions of class, region, ethnicity and race into an Anglo-Canadian national culture. As Vance claims, however, this myth of the war was not simply imposed on society as a means to preserve the status quo, but was shaped by veterans and the public out of a sense of grief and loss, as a way to ensure a loving and meaningful remembrance for those who had died as soldiers.[62]

Soldiers had served the Empire, fought for Britain, and helped to create a new Canada, and were therefore the embodiment of true Britishness, Canadian loyalty and civic patriotism. Earlier war propaganda had explicitly linked Britishness to Canadian soldiers, and emphasized the common interests of the Empire and Canada. In the words of one song, "So if you are white/You will join the fight/and rally round the/(come and enlist boys)/guns." Canadian soldiers were also "old Britain's pledge upholding/The Empire's honor true/That's why our ladies are fighting/As British boys always do."[63] The war effort was strongly associated with both Britishness and whiteness, and an Anglo-Canadian nationalism that was closely entwined with British ethnic heritage. The recruitment of visible minorities for war service was severely restricted as Black, Native, Japanese, Chinese and East Indian Canadians were generally considered unfit for war service based partly on racial stereotypes and partly on the fear that they would demand full citizenship rights after enlistment.[64] Other factors that strengthened the association of the war with Britishness were the conscription crisis, restrictions on the rights of "enemy aliens," and the demographics of the CEF, the majority of whom were not Canadian born until after the Military Services Act was implemented. The categories of whiteness and Britishness were often collapsed, so full citizenship rights and entitlement claims were associated with whiteness and an Anglo-Canadian background.[65] The code of Britishness, combined with veterans' rhetoric of sacrifice and duty, was a powerful way for veterans to set themselves apart as dedicated protectors of the country and of civilization. Claims to economic security, social insurance and full employment was, for white workers in the Depression, one way to protest against economic exploitation and government intransigence in dealing with poverty and unemployment.[66] For unemployed and poor veterans, the rhetoric of Britishness and national pride, so closely entwined with the duty of war service, was even more deeply connected to "pride of citizenship" and demands for entitlement.[67]

Veterans bolstered their arguments for preferential treatment by claiming a special link to the Canadian nation and loyalty to the traditions of the British Empire. They juxtaposed their patriotism with the threat of communism and "foreigners" allegedly stealing jobs. Wrote an unemployed veteran and Legion member from Fort Frances: "I have often wondered whether it might not be quite appropriate to emblazon a few foreign ensigns on the fly of the Union Jack, for it seems to me a foreigner has more privileges and is thought more of in our workshops than true British subjects who have fought for our good old flag."[68] Anti-alien sentiment ran high among Legion leaders and members, a tradition that extended back to the early years of the veteran movement. In 1918, for example, after several days of "anti-alien rhetoric" at the GWVA convention in Toronto, veterans and civilians led a series of attacks against the city's Greek restaurants.[69] In 1930, the Fort William branch of the Legion recommended that all non-naturalized participants in the local May Day Parade be deported, and the report of the 1931 Ontario Legion Unemployment Committee resolved that all un-naturalized aliens, or all those naturalized after July of 1931, be fired from government jobs and replaced by veterans.[70] In 1932, the Dominion Command protested the potential layoffs of nearly 600 veterans by the CNR of Winnipeg and in other locations across Canada. The Legion demanded that all un-naturalized persons be fired and that union seniority be determined by the date of naturalization. Dominion Legion chair A.E. Moore claimed that the foreign born had "stolen" seniority from veterans by securing jobs during the war years, and thereby established seniority that "rightfully belonged to men on active service." In addition, he concluded, some foreign-born workers were "avowed Communists."[71]

Connected closely with anti-immigrant sentiment and emphasis on British loyalty was a strong anti-Communism within the rank and leaders of the Legion. *The Legionary* proudly reported the work of local members in helping police "maintain law and order when threatened by subversive elements," and in upholding "British law and British institutions." Branch members could be sworn in as special constables to help suppress riots and "inflammatory demonstrations."[72] In Sudbury, in response to fear that "Reds" were trying to incite the population, especially the "alien-born," police swore in forty Legion members as a temporary police squad. By June 1932, the police had called on this squad over six times, twice engaging in "active combat . . . ending in the complete rout of the demonstrations."[73] In Windsor, the local veterans' branch unanimously endorsed a resolution that supported city council's decision to ban all "Red parades" or assemblies, claiming that such groups, "particularly if influenced by foreign quarters," were "contemptible and dangerous" and a threat to "human freedom."[74] The Oshawa branch protested against a Communist rally in a park, held in front of the war cenotaph, explaining that communists should be banned from the "Garden of the Unforgotten."[75] The Port Arthur branch, "determined to oust the Red menace from their locality," sent a sixty-man delegation to city council with a proposal to end all "sinister Red activities." The delegation convinced the council to vote unanimously to implement a by-law restraining all parades and demonstrations, and to outlaw distribution of "communistic literature."[76]

Despite such conservative, anti-immigrant and anti-communist rhetoric, the economic alternatives suggested by some veterans indicate that there was some diversity of political opinion. Most veterans did not blindly uphold patriotism, loyalty and Britishness, but did appeal to these values to make powerful claims of entitlement to economic security. As Lieutenant W.J. Osborne Dempster pointed out in a letter to Premier Henry in October of 1931:

> I am no extremist or radical but conditions as they exist in Toronto today are very similar to those that existed in Petrograd in October 1917 making the Bolshevik revolution possible . . . starvation breeds revolution . . . Would you Mr. Premier in the case of an emergency which may come expect, us, who bore the brunt in 1914 to 1918 and are now paying two fold for our loyalty today, to again man the breach [?][77]

Patriotism, loyalty and Britishness could therefore also be used to claim respectability and full citizenship, and to demand changes in the social and economic structure. For veterans, a commitment to the Canadian nation, rooted in the traditions of the Empire, was not simply a conservative means of preserving the status quo. Veterans called for an improvement of the economic conditions of loyal Canadian citizens in general, but particularly of the patriotic citizen-soldiers who had fought for their country and the Empire. Veterans denounced "Bolshevism" and expressed anti-immigrant sentiment, but they also denounced government inaction on unemployment, supported unemployment insurance, and fought for subsidized health care. Veterans embraced "British justice," and life under the "old old flag — the Union Jack," but this Britishness included the right to economic and social security.[78] In 1934, the Ontario Provincial Command went on record as "being favourable to the principle of state medicine,"[79] and the Unemployment Committee of the Dominion Legion recommended free medical treatment for all pensioners. In 1930, the East Hamilton branch petitioned both the federal and provincial governments and the Canadian Manufacturers Association for tripartite unemployment insurance. In 1938, the Dominion Command pressed the federal government for legislation for low-rent housing, and in 1939, the Legion claimed success in winning free hospital care for poor veterans.[80]

Some veterans voiced more radical solutions to the social and economic problems of the 1930s, indicating there was a range of political opinions within the veterans' movement. W.T. House from Toronto wrote to the editors of *The Legionary* condemning the profit system and suggesting "public ownership of factories, etc., and operation thereof to supply the wants of the people at cost . . . our medium of exchange — money — must also come under public ownership so that the people will have money to buy back all that is produced . . . Unemployment would be ended because everyone would become a full partner in the business of supplying his own wants."[81] In the early 1930s, delegates at the Ontario Convention made powerful demands for a more egalitarian social and economic order, linking the problems and poverty of the working class with those of ex-servicemen. "The welfare of the ex-servicemen is identical with the welfare of the civilian worker," announced a unanimous resolution of 1933. "The Legion supports any movement which has for its goal the social and economic welfare of the producing classes as opposed to the accumulation of wealth by exploitation both of Natural and Human resources."[82]

In 1931, the Unemployment Committee of the Ontario Command claimed that national wealth "was held in comparatively few hands," demanded that "monied people be asked to make the sacrifice in the present crisis that we, the war veterans were asked to make in 1914–1918," and suggested a more steeply graded tax system that would reduce the tax burden on the "wage-earning population," which included "ex-servicemen and their families."[83] The 1933 Windsor "Manifesto" lamented the forgotten promises of "a State of Society that would bring all men the blessedness of Peace, [and] security from want," and called for comprehensive employment and social insurance. Delegates strongly condemned a political and economic system based on inequality, arguing that a just state existed for "the care, the protection and the prosperity of all the citizens of our country without class distinction," and not to implement "class legislation" or uphold "a Government dominated by financial interests."[84]

The case files of the Soldiers Aid Commission, Ontario Canteen Fund (OCF), illustrate the tension between charity and entitlement in the 1930s. As a blend of public and private welfare, the OCF was established with money collected from overseas military canteens, and was attached to the Ontario Department of Public Welfare in 1931.[85] The Fund, headed by Major Lewis, was set up as a form of temporary emergency assistance for veterans in limited financial circumstances due to injury or illness, and was administered by a group of trustees who were war veterans. Case files can pose difficult questions for historians, particularly with the problem of how to find the voices of clients when the language was shaped by official rules and regulations, and by the summaries of administrators or investigators. But in taking the purpose and intent of case files into consideration, they reveal the complex web of interactions between veterans, their families and welfare bureaucracy, and illustrate how clients attempted to get financial aid for themselves and their families.[86] For example, in their applications for assistance, veterans used the language of supplicants, while in letters written directly to politicians or veterans' organizations, demands were made more often on the basis of entitlement. Yet the language of the applications does not mean that those who wrote them were passive, or saw themselves as victims rather than agents. Rather, applicants for charity had to find a number of ways to convince the Ontario Canteen Fund they were worthy of, and entitled to aid.

In addition to raising questions about the agency of charity recipients, the files also illustrate the deep social, psychological, and medical problems faced by veterans and their families. By the 1930s, struggling with the effects of shell shock, gassing, or physical injuries, veterans were no longer healthy young men. The profound physical and psychological effects of the First World War were still serious problems through the Depression.

Many veterans complained of unspecified nervous ailments or chronic breathing problems. James Fedder of Toronto suffered from chronic bronchitis and "rapidity of heart," while Jack Bryant of Toronto received two grants for stomach trouble and bronchitis caused by "hardships endured in France," and for headaches and dizzy spells suffered from a shrapnel wound to the head.[87] Jason Downey struggled to make the OCF understand his difficulty in keeping employment when he had poor nerves, shell shock and a chronic "nauseating feeling in my stomach through not being able to digest or keep a decent meal without vomitting [sic] it back."[88] Walter Acker failed to convince the board that his unemployment resulted from what his doctor called a "hyperactive nervous system," and "extreme restlessness and sleeplessness which leaves him fatigued throughout the better part of the day."[89] The shortness of breath, emphysema, bronchitis, and chronic cough and sputum suffered by James Baker resulting from gas exposure did not convince the OCF that he was ill enough to warrant aid.[90] Some veterans were too psychologically or physically damaged to do the heavy labour typical of relief works, while others, who suffered stomach and digestion disorders, needed extra money for special diets.

Veterans groups complained of unfairness in medical exams for pension purposes, particularly on the question of whether illness or injury was "attributable" to war service. Other veterans found that a fund set up to help in times of medical distress was ill equipped to meet the demand of chronic medical problems that made it difficult to hold down a job of any kind. The medical profession and the state had yet to fully understand the physical and psychological consequences of trench warfare, poison gas, and the toll of constant fear and anxiety that emerged after service on the war front.[91] The Ontario Canteen Fund was intended to give assistance only to veterans whose financial problems were related to a documented illness, so many applicants were rejected because their problems were deemed unemployment-related rather than illness related. Walter Collins, age fifty-five, was rejected twice because the board deemed his problems were due to unemployment rather than true illness. Despite a doctor's note on his behalf outlining his problem of "gastric neuroses" (which included stomach pains, vomiting after every meal, and insomnia) he was informed that he was fully capable of earning his "own living."[92]

These kinds of conflicts over access to the Fund provide evidence that veterans were not quiescent or passive, but attempted to manoeuvre around the Fund's rules and requirements. Many did not give up after being rejected, but continually wrote to ask for help, disregarding the explanations for their ineligibility.[93] Others wrote to make clear their sense of entitlement and their frustration with administrators. When Walter Collins' application in September of 1930 was rejected because his "difficulties are the result of unemployment," his wife took matters into her own hands by visiting the OCF office, where she personally asked the Fund to reconsider the application because their landlord was threatening to evict them. Several weeks later, they were given a $25 grant.[94] Emily Knight of Verona personally took her husband Arthur's application to the home of a local investigator, asking for "assistance to clothe the children, suitably for school [sic]."[95]

Those who refused to accept rejection often ultimately won small grants. Jason Downey, after being rejected for assistance despite his doctor's testimony concerning his poor health due "to shock of the nervous system as the result of active service in the world war," penned his own letter of request, resulting in a $12 grant. "Perhaps," he argued to Lewis, "you have never suffered from gastritis or neurosis caused by being blown up with a shell. That may be the reason for not considering it very serious."[96] David Cooper of Toronto, unemployed, with "cardiac hypertrophy and arterio-sclerosis," applied for assistance more than eight times; he never gave up despite being told several times that he was ineligible. Needing money for rent, gas, electricity bills and food for his wife and two children, while facing eviction in July of 1932, he managed to receive a total of eight grants before he was cut off in August of 1935.[97] Victor Platov of Toronto, a Russian-born Canadian veteran, injured at work, was given a grant of $12 after his teenaged daughter Martha wrote a letter in June of 1934 explaining that their rent was in arrears and they owed money for grocery and butcher bills. "How I tried to stand for this country with full faith," wrote Platov, who applied twelve more times between 1934 and 1939 despite five rejections that claimed he had been helped too often and that his problems were actually unemployment, rather than illness, related.[98] John Nicholson, despite two rejections, finally received four grants after repeatedly explaining that he was unable to work due to illness and that his children needed food. He finally enlisted a local sergeant to write a letter documenting his financial position and his "worthy" status as a husband and father. He continued to ask for money even after receiving a five percent pension "which does not enable me to do much for my children."[99] When Fred Granby of Ottawa was denied aid in April of 1932, after explaining that he was unemployed and his wife ill in a mental hospital, he had his lawyer, a relative, write to demand an explanation.[100]

Applicants also enlisted their doctors to convince the board that their injuries or illnesses rendered them unable to work. Doctors were overwhelmingly supportive, writing notes that claimed men could not work, either temporarily or permanently, because of various illnesses. After rejecting Geoff Blackwood, the OCF contacted Christie Street Hospital to ask if his "persistent" claims that he was too ill to work were valid. According to Dr. Clark, his neuritis made it temporarily impossible for him to work.[101] Doctors wrote of their patients' inability to work or do hard labour due to bronchitis, asthma, shortness of breath, and emphysema.[102] Many doctors supported their patients' claims that they could not work due to "nervous conditions," gastric ulcers or gastritis, the need for a special diet, nervous disability or nervousness, insomnia, and "gastric distress."[103] The case of Arthur Knight, a forty three year-old veteran with three children, provides one example of the relationship between doctor and veteran in the attempt to procure financial aid. Initially rejected for help because he was in receipt of a pension, Knight argued that $7 was not enough to support his family, particularly when he was not well enough to do heavy labour. In his second application, he emphasized his medical problems, rather than his unemployment and material debts, claiming that he had suffered gunshot wounds while in France. His doctor, M.E. Harris, included a letter explaining that in his opinion, Knight was a "badly wrecked veteran, a positive service casualty," with "nerve injuries," "tremors and shaking," and "a type of melancholy which is aggravated by privation." Similarly, his wife was ill because of a nervous breakdown which he attributed to "worry and privation" over her family's situation. They received a grant of $25.[104]

An examination of the reasons for assistance that applicants listed on their forms shows that though the fund was intended for illness-related unemployment, applicants attempted to use it as a form of emergency relief for rent or mortgage arrears, and for food, clothing and utilities bills. As Chester Black of Cookstown wrote, "I hear these funds are being used for the relief to help the return men [sic] who are in need."[105] Despite many rejections, Charles A. Duncan continually demanded help, and claimed that "this money in question belongs to return men [sic] and if was properly used should be divided equally between them."[106] Almost all the veterans who applied for aid were unemployed, and many had been out of work for months or even years. Indeed, it is difficult to decipher the basis on which the OCF determined the difference between unemployment and illness-related problems, since it often made decisions that seemed arbitrary. Sometimes, grants were given in cases where problems were clearly related to unemployment. Mrs. Lake of Toronto was ill with boils on her head and neck, due, her doctor said, to "malnourishment and undernourishment." Her husband was unemployed, owed three months' rent, $100 in grocery and bakers' bills, and they had a family of six children who needed clothes, boots, fuel and medicine. They received a grant of $20.[107] Harry Davis received six grants after complaining of burns on his hand and a stomach ulcer, and the need to pay for rent and electricity bills in arrears.[108] Herbert McKay of Toronto received a grant of $30 after he claimed that his wife was pregnant, and he needed money for medical bills and for rent, gas, and electricity arrears.[109]

Other applicants found it more difficult to convince the OCF that they were eligible for aid. John Nicholson of Hamilton was turned down a number of times because his troubles were deemed related to unemployment rather than illness. He needed rent, fuel and food money, as he was ineligible for relief because he could not meet the residence requirements.[110] Cecil Wilson of Hamilton, who suffered from a stomach problem, found his wife facing eviction while he was in the hospital. When his application was rejected, he refused to accept the verdict. "You said," he wrote, "you could not find any condition for any help from you" but he felt his need for rent and food money was more than enough reason for help. His wife later wrote, insisting that she needed rent money to avoid eviction; she was given a grant of $10.[111] Edna Barber, wife of Horace, found it difficult to convince the OCF that they, a farming family in rural Ontario, needed financial help because of her husband's chronic gastritis. On relief, with nine children, she argued after her first rejection that they deserved financial aid for their children's education and for proper food for her husband's special diet. "Our children are bright enough to do something worthwhile," she wrote. "I only wish I had known it was 'only lies' they told my husband 20 years ago —'Nothing will be too good for you'— and that's exactly what he's had so far — Nothing! . . . Neither Bill, Ginny or the other 3 girls have decent clothes right now, but they have an ailing Dad who served 26 months in France for *OUR Country* [sic]." Two months after receiving her letter, the OCF granted her family $15.[112]

Though ex-servicemen developed what was a partial and often restrictive outlook, particularly regarding gender roles, race and ethnicity, veterans in the Depression attempted to uphold the dignity of the unemployed, and demanded the right to full economic security even when on relief. Veterans lobbied for and won a number of concessions from the national government. Though the response was piecemeal and success was uneven, Ottawa gradually began to acknowledge that support for veteran re-establishment was an ongoing responsibility of the federal government. The Depression years saw a gradual loosening of eligibility requirements surrounding pensions, and the establishment of, and continual amendments to, War Veterans' Allowances. Persistent criticisms over lack of adequate relief and unemployment won "unemployment assistance" for veterans: cash-based payments that attempted to make up the difference between municipal relief and pensions. Hiring preference in government public works and the civil service, plus expanded job training were other examples of government responses to veteran unemployment.[113] But veterans, like the unemployed in general, never won a cohesive plan to fight unemployment, let alone gain more expansive social insurance. Veterans and their organizations waged constant political battles over eligibility for pensions, and over whether preference on public works and in the civil service was being honoured. The long and often tedious process of political negotiation between veterans, their leaders and the state illustrates the extent to which they were treated as political participants and not entirely as supplicants by the government. However, the more radical and progressive of the veterans' demands emerged mainly from provincial and local branches, and were eventually overtaken by the formal political process centred in Ottawa. Veterans and their families also had some hard-won local success in gaining recognition from welfare administrators and doctors. By continually applying for assistance for material needs, refusing to accept rejection, enlisting doctors to support their applications, and occasionally expressing their anger and disappointment with the OCF in person or by letter, veterans and their dependents clearly did not view themselves as passive recipients of aid. Rather, they attempted to force administrators to take their problems seriously and, at times, won recognition for their definition of problems as medically and economically intertwined.[114]

Veterans claimed the highest level of citizenship in the 1930s, arguing that they had made crucial sacrifices for Canada and the British Empire, and had acted with courage, honour and a sense of duty. In return, they believed they deserved adequate recognition and compensation by the state, in the form of access to employment, adequate relief, and the right to preferential treatment above other unemployed workers making competing claims on the state. Employing the language of contract, veterans used the ideas of reciprocity, service and duty to argue for compensation and government intervention in the economy and the provision of social welfare. These arguments were an important component in the development of welfare provision based on regulated and measurable standards of eligibility. As Canadian historians have pointed out, in the years following the Great War, veterans organized and pressed for a variety of programs and policies based not on charity but on a sense of "moral entitlement" to state support.[115] By 1917, the newly formed Great War Veterans' Association (GWVA) supported more generous pensions for the war disabled, the right to appeal pension decisions, the conscription of wealth and the nationalization of all war industries, increased taxation, free hospital care for veterans and their dependents, proper medical care for the mentally ill, and price controls.[116] Veterans challenged inadequate retraining courses, pushed for more generous pension benefits and aid to widows and the disabled, and insisted on preferential hiring in government jobs.

Although veterans won a degree of recognition and forced some changes in government policy, there is little information on what happened to veterans themselves in the years of the Great Depression.[117] Desmond Morton argues that veterans tried to forget economic hardship through commemoration, and that their history "ends in disappointment, sickness, and death."[118] However, veterans of the First World War did not mysteriously disappear with the onset of the Depression, despite a very real penchant for commemoration and memorialization.[119] Rather, veterans were a vocal, lively and articulate and political force in the 1930s who adapted to changing economic conditions, became increasingly concerned with the impact of unemployment, and whose rhetoric linked wartime service with the problems of unemployment and the inadequacy of relief.

The complex tensions within the veterans' critique of unemployment, and the rhetoric of reciprocity, duty, contract and entitlement were never fully resolved.[120]

The extent of state responsibility for veterans' welfare, the role of veterans and their families in the postwar national fabric, and the degree to which duty and sacrifice for the national community were recognized, were topics that played an important role in the gradual formation of welfare state policy. In their position as supplicants seeking charitable aid, as members of veterans' organizations, and as individual citizens protesting government policies, veterans in the Depression were active, articulate and politically involved citizens who played a crucial role in the demand for social change in welfare reform.

NOTES

1. Report of the Ontario Provincial Command, The Canadian Legion of the British Empire Service League, Annual Convention, 1933.

2. The only political history of veterans' organizations is Desmond Morton and Glenn Wright, *Winning the Second Battle: Canadian Veterans and the Return to Civilian Life, 1915–1930* (Toronto: University of Toronto Press, 1987). The authors argue that government policies for veterans "became the cradle of Canada's post-war welfare state." See pp. 222–224.

3. See Michael Gauvreau and Nancy Christie, *A Full-Orbed Christianity: The Protestant Churches and Social Welfare in Canada, 1900–1940* (Montreal: McGill-Queen's University Press, 1996); Dennis Guest, *The Emergence of Social Security in Canada* (Vancouver: University of British Columbia Press, 1985); Allan Moscovitch and J. Albert, *The Benevolent State: The Growth of Social Welfare in Canada* (Toronto: Garamond Press, 1987); Doug Owram, *The Government Generation: Canadian Intellectuals and the State* (Toronto: University of Toronto Press, 1986). For an analysis of the role of gender in welfare state development in Canada, see Margaret Jean Hillyard Little, *"No Car, No Radio, No Liquor Permit": The Moral Regulation of Single Mothers in Ontario, 1920–1997* (Toronto: Oxford University Press, 1998); Patricia M. Evans and Gerda R. Wekerle, *Women and the Canadian Welfare State: Challenges and Change* (Toronto: University of Toronto Press, 1997); Jane Ursel, *Private Lives, Public Policy: 100 Years of State Intervention in the Family* (Toronto: Women's Press, 1992); Ruth Roach Pierson, "Gender and the Unemployment Insurance Debates in Canada," *Labour/Le travail* 25 (Spring 1990): 77–103.

4. See, for example, James Struthers, *No Fault of Their Own: Unemployment and the Canadian Welfare State, 1914–1941* (Toronto: University of Toronto Press, 1983); Michiel Horn, *The League for Social Reconstruction* (Toronto: University of Toronto Press, 1980); Joan Sangster, *Dreams of Equality: Women on the Canadian Left, 1920–1950* (Toronto: McClelland and Stewart, 1989); Carmela Patrias, "Relief Strike: Immigrant Workers and the Great Depression in Crowland, Ontario, 1930–1935," in *A Nation of Immigrants: Women, Workers and Communities in Canadian History, 1840s–1960s*, eds. Franca Iacovetta and Robert Ventresca (Toronto: University of Toronto Press, 1998).

5. Linda Gordon, *Pitied But Not Entitled: Single Mothers and the History of Welfare, 1890–1935* (Cambridge: Harvard University Press, 1994): 241–245. See also Linda Gordon, *Heroes of Their Own Lives: The Politics and History of Family Violence* (New York: Penguin Books, 1988); Craig Jenkins and Barbara G. Brents, "Social Protest, Hegemonic Competition, and Social Reform: A Political Struggle Interpretation of the Origins of the American Welfare State," *American Sociological Review*, 54 (December 1989): 891–909; Ann Shola Orloff, "Gender and the Social Rights of Citizenship: The Comparative Analysis of Gender Relations and Welfare,"

American Sociological Review 58 (1993): 305; Frances Fox Piven and Richard A. Cloward, *Regulating the Poor: The Functions of Public Welfare* (New York: Random House, 1971). In Canada, see Victor Howard, *"We Were the Salt of the Earth": the On-to-Ottawa Trek and the Regina Riot* (University of Regina: Canadian Plains Research Centre, 1985); Dominique Marshall, "The Language of Children's Rights, the Formation of the Welfare State, and the Democratic Experience of Poor Families in Quebec, 1940–55," *Canadian Historical Review* 78/3 (September 1997): 409–39; Shirley Tillotson, "Citizen Participation in the Welfare State: An Experiment," *Canadian Historical Review* 78/3 (September 1997): 409–39.

6. See Nancy Fraser and Linda Gordon, "Contract versus Charity: Why is there no social citizenship in the United States?" *Socialist Review* 22/3 (July–September, 1992), who argue that American social welfare policy is framed by the oppositional categories of charity, a gift to which the recipient has no right or claim, and contract, based on principles of civil exchange and patterns of male labour force participation. See also *Democracy and the Welfare State*, ed. Amy Gutmann (Princeton: Princeton University Press, 1988): 3.

7. See Pierson, "Gender and the Unemployment Insurance Debates"; Jonathan Vance, *Death So Noble: Memory, Meaning and the First World War* (Vancouver: University of British Columbia Press, 1997).

8. Guest, *The Emergence of Social Security in Canada*; Michael Katz, *In the Shadow of the Poorhouse: A Social History of Welfare in North America* (Basic Books, 1986).

9. Archives of Ontario, (AO), RG 3-8, Office of the Premier, (OTP), Henry Papers, MS 1759, file: Department of Public Works, East Block, Mr. F. Kelly to Henry, 24 May 1933.

10. *The Legionary* 8/12 (December 1933): 7, and 8/1 (August 1937): 2. See also Vance, *Death So Noble*, 90–107.

11. AO, RG 29-65, Box 8, #8051, letter from Arthur Knight to Ontario Canteen Fund (OCF), 14 November 1934.

12. *The Legionary* 8/5 (May 1933): 8.

13. "Veterans' Position," *The Legionary* 8/1 (August 1937): 2.

14. AO, RG 3-8, OTP, MS 1752, file: general correspondence, H. Vandervelde to Henry, 16 April 1932.

15. George L. Rosser, "A Knotty Problem," *The Legionary* 12/4 (November 1936): 25, 30.

16. Morton and Wright, *Winning the Second Battle*, 223.

17. *The Legionary* 5/4 (September 1930).

18. See, for example, *The Legionary* 12/6 (January 1937): 13.

19. Ibid., 4/11 (April 1930): 21.

20. See Keshen, *Propaganda and Censorship*.

21. Ibid., 12.

22. AO, RG 3-8, OTP, Henry Papers, MS 1759, file: Department of Public Works, Thomas Frith to Henry, 31 August 1933.

23. Cecil A. Morgan, "The End of the Hero," *The Legionary* 6/7 (December 1931): 5.

24. Report of the Ontario Provincial Command, 8th Annual Convention, 1934: *The Legionary* 10/3 (March 1935): ; 10/6 (June 1935): 8.

25. AO, RG 3, Series 9, OTP, Hepburn Papers, #180, file: unemployment relief, William Kinsman to Henry, 17 December 1934.

26. AO, RG 3-8, OTP, Henry Papers, MS 1745, file: Returned Men, F.J. Shaw to Henry, August 1931.

27. *The Legionary* 5/2 (July 1930): 1.

28. See ibid., 9/3 (March 1934): 17–18.

29. Report of the Ontario Provincial Command, Annual Convention, 1931; Report of the Ontario Provincial Command, Annual Convention, 1933; *The Legionary* 9/4 (April 1934): 7.

30. AO, RG 3-8, OTP, Henry Papers, MS 1744, file: Positions, General, June 1931–January 1933, J.W. Alfred Rowe to Henry, 9 August 1931.

31. Sir Arthur Currie, "The Great Sacrifice — What has it served?" *The Legionary* 8/12 (December 1933): 7–8.

32. Morton, "The Canadian Veterans' Heritage," 24.

33. *The Legionary* 4/7 (December 1929): 5.

34. Ibid., 12/4 (November 1936): 30. According to the 1937 report of the Veterans' Assistance Commission, opinion divided over supplementary assistance to municipal relief. Colonel J.G. Rattray, chair of the commission, repudiated any form of extra assistance, while Commissioners Lt.-Col. H.L. de Martigny and Robert Macnicol [sic] advised, "It is well known that there is considerable unrest amongst the unemployed ex-servicemen in Canada and this is evidenced by the propaganda for a war bonus, etc." Increased government aid would therefore "improve the morale of the veterans." *The Legionary* 12/9 (April 1937): 9.

35. AO, RG 3-8, OTP, Henry Papers, MS 1759, file: Department of Public Works, T. Frith to Henry, 9 October 1933.

36. *The Legionary* 10/6 (June 1935): 8, and 10/3 (March 1935): 1.

37. Ibid., 10/4 (April 1935): 9.

38. Morton and Wright, *Winning the Second Battle*, 218, 214.

39. National Archives of Canada (NAC), RG 27-3, vol. 187, file 614.06:6, "Unemployment of Ex-Servicemen," 1935.

40. Keshen, *Propaganda and Censorship*, 17.

41. Ibid., "Canadian Battle Song, 1918."

42. "Canadians Never Budge" (1918), in "Songs of the Canadian Soldier: The Great War, 1914–1918," ed. Jean-Michel Viger (unpublished manuscript held at the library of the Dominion Command of the Royal Canadian Legion, Ottawa, Ontario).

43. *The Legionary* 4/10 (March 1930): 5. Under Prime Minister Mackenzie King, the WVA Act extended Old Age Pensions to "broken down or burned out" soldiers' usually at age 65, five years earlier than the OAP. However, the WVA Act was not administered like a pension but as an allowance. It was discretionary, administered by a three-member board, means-tested, and allowed a maximum of $40 per month for married men. See Guest, *The Emergence of Social Security in Canada*, 95.

44. "Re-establishment of Unemployed Veterans," *The Legionary* 9/6 (June 1934): 4.

45. Morton and Wright, *Winning the Second Battle*, Military Hospitals Commission, poster reproduction.

46. AO, RG 3 Series 9, #180, OTP, Hepburn Papers, file: unemployment relief, Canadian Legion Unemployment Committee to Hepburn, December 1934.

47. *The Legionary* 6/11 (April 1932): 7.

48. Ibid., 7.

49. Fraser and Gordon, "Contract versus Charity," 54–6.

50. AO, RG 3-8, OTP, Henry Papers, MS 1747, file: unemployment relief #3, Lieutenant Osborne Dempster to Henry, 8 October 1931.

51. *The Legionary* 9/4 (April 1934).

52. Morton and Wright, *Winning the Second Battle*, 141.

53. AO, RG 3-8, OTP, Henry Papers, MS 1747, file: unemployment relief #3, C. Peterson to Henry, 15 September 1931.

54. Ibid., MS 1762, file: unemployment relief, homeowners, Mr. H.V.W. to Henry, 8 September 1933.

55. 8th Provincial Convention, Ontario Command, 1934.

56. AO, RG 3 Series 9, OTP, Hepburn Papers, #180, file: unemployment relief #2, Mrs. J.W. to Hepburn, 6 September 1934.

57. AO, RG 3-8, OTP, Henry Papers, MS 1744, file: Positions, general, Mrs. A.B. to Henry, 27 June 1931.

58. See, for example, Carl Berger, *The Writing of Canadian History: Aspects of English Canadian Historical Writing since 1900* (Toronto: University of Toronto Press, 1986); John Herd Thompson and Allen Seager, *Canada: Decades of Discord, 1922–1939* (Toronto: McClelland and Stewart, 1985): 158–192; Mary Vipond, "Nationalism and Nativism: The Native Sons of Canada in the 1930s," *Canadian Review of Studies in Nationalism* 9/1 (Spring 1982); Vipond, "The Nationalist Network: English Canada's Intellectuals and Artists in the 1920s," *Canadian Review of Studies of Nationalism* 7/1 (Spring 1980).

59. See John Swettenham, *Canada and the First World War* (Toronto: Ryerson Press, 1969); Desmond Morton, *When Your Number's Up: The Canadian Soldier in the First World War* (Toronto: Random House, 1993): 169; Desmond Morton and Jack Granatstein, *Marching to Armageddon: Canadians and the Great War, 1914–19* (Toronto: Lester and Orpen Dennys, 1989). See also the criticism by Vance, *Death So Noble*, 10–11.

60. *The Legionary* 4/8 (January 1930): 6.

61. Ibid., 4/7 (December 1929): 13.

62. Vance. *Death So Noble*, 227–56.

63. "The Call" (n.d.); "British Boys" (1916), in "Songs of the Canadian Soldier," ed. Viger, 107, 49.

64. James St.-G. J. Walker, "Race and Recruitment in WWI: Enlistment of Visible Minorities in the Canadian Expeditionary Force," in *Constructing Modern Canada: Readings in Post-Confederation History*, ed. Chad Gaffield (Toronto: Copp Clark Longman Ltd., 1994): 259–283.

65. Desmond Morton, *When Your Number's Up: The Canadian Soldier in the First World War* (Toronto: Random House, 1993), 273. Canadian-born members of the CEF became a majority of 51.2% by November of 1918.

66. See David Roediger, *The Wages of Whiteness: Race and the Making of the American Working Class* (London: Verso, 1991).

67. Ibid., 11.

68. *The Legionary* 13/6 (June 1938): 12.

69. Morton and Wright, *Winning the Second Battle*, 82.

70. *Legion*, (January 1986): 17; Report of the Ontario Provincial Command, Annual Convention, 1931.

71. *The Legionary* 6/12 (May 1932): 7.

72. Ibid., 1/1 (April 1935): 20.

73. Ibid., 7/1 (June 1932): 26.

74. Ibid., 4/11 (April 1930): 26.

75. Ibid., 5/2 (August 1930): 26.

76. Ibid., 5/2 (August 1930): 29.

77. AO, RG 3-8, OTP, Henry Papers, MS 1747, file: unemployment relief #7, Lieutenant Dempster to Henry, 8 October 1931.

78. AO, RG 3-10, OTP, Hepburn Papers, #205, file: Resolutions, Progressive Veterans in Canada to Hepburn, 27 July 1936.

79. Report of the Ontario Command, 8th Provincial Convention, 1934.

80. *The Legionary* 9/4 (April 1934); *Legion* (January 1986): 17, 32, 34.

81. Ibid., 14/5 (December 1938): 19.

82. Report of the Ontario Provincial Command, Annual Convention, 1933.

83. Report of the Ontario Provincial Command, Annual Convention, 1931.

84. Report of the Ontario Provincial Command, Annual Convention, 1933.

85. William and Jeannette Raynsford, *Silent Casualties, Veterans' Families in the Aftermath of the Great War* (Madoc: Merribrae Press, 1986).

86. Franca Iacovetta and Wendy Mitchinson, *On the Case: Explorations in Social History* (Toronto: University of Toronto Press, 1998).

87. AO, RG 29-65, S.A.C., O.C.F., Box 2, #2978; Box 6, #1918.

88. AO, RG 29-65, S.A.C., O.C.F., Box 6, #7799.

89. AO, RG 29-65, S.A.C., O.C.F., Box 18, #15,756, letter of Dr. E.I. Morton, 6 December 1938.

90. AO, RG 29-65, S.A.C., O.C.F., Box 14, #12,301; letter of Dr. H.J. Edward, 7 March 1937.

91. Morton, *When Your Number's Up*, 122–131: 228–250.

92. AO, RG 29-65. Soldiers Aid Commission, Ontario Canteen Fund, Box 2, #2935. In accordance with the rules of the Freedom of Information Act agreement signed with the Archives of Ontario, identifying information and file numbers have been changed to protect privacy.

93. Some historians have argued that making claims itself is a political act. See Gordon, *Pitied But Not Entitled*, 247.

94. AO, RG 29-65, S.A.C., O.C.F., Box 2, #2935.

95. AO, RG 29-65, S.A.C., O.C.F., Box 8, #8051, letter to Major Lewis from Bella Boulder, 12 September 1933.

96. AO, RG 29-65, S.A.C., O.C.F., Box 6, #7799.

97. AO, RG 29-65, S.A.C., O.C.F., Box 4, #3540.

98. AO, RG 29-65, S.A.C., O.C.F., Box 10, #9046, letter from Victor Platov to Major Lewis, 28 April 1937.

99. AO, RG 29-65, S.A.C., O.C.F., Box 2, #2197, letter from Sgt. Trembly to Major Lewis, 6 May 1931 and letter to OCF from Nicholson, 30 November 1934.

100. AO, RG 29-65, S.A.C., O.C.F., Box 6, #5463.

101. AO, RG 29-65, S.A.C., O.C.F., Box 8, #7875, letter from OCF to Dr. Clark, 15 August 1933, and response, 18 August 1933.

102. See records of, for example, AO, RG 29-65, S.A.C., O.C.F., Box 2, #2978; Box 9, #846; Box 9, #1938; Box 6, #6814; Box 14, #12,391.

103. See records in AO, RG 29-65, S.A.C., O.C.F., Box 2, #2064; Box 9, #776; Box 6, #5799; Box 6, #5684; Box 10, #9527.

104. AO, RG 29-65, S.A.C., O.C.F., Box 8, #8051, letter of Dr. M.E. Harris to Major Lewis, 29 November 1934.

105. AO, RG 29-65, S.A.C., O.C.F., Box 6, #5148, letter from Chester Black to OCF, March 1932.

106. AO, RG 29-65, S.A.C., O.C.F., Box 14, #2341, letter from Charles A. Duncan to OCF, 2 August 1937.

107. AO, RG 29-65, S.A.C., O.C.F., Box 6, #6814.

108. AO, RG 29-65, S.A.C., O.C.F., Box 2, #2945.

109. AO, RG 29-65, S.A.C., O.C.F., Box 2, #2217.

110. AO, RG 29-65, S.A.C., O.C.F., Box 2, #2197.

111. AO, RG 29-65, S.A.C., O.C.F., Box 14, #3028.

112. AO, RG 29-65, S.A.C., O.C.F., Box 14, #2520.

113. See *The Legionary*, 1929-39, and Morton and Wright, pp. 209–220.

114. See files of the Soldiers Aid Commission. See also Gordon, *Heroes of their Own Lives*.

115. Morton, "The Canadian Veterans' Heritage from the Great War," in *The Veterans Charter and Post-World War II Canada*, eds. Peter Neary and J.L. Granatstein (Montreal: McGill-Queens' University Press, 1998): 23.

116. Morton and Wright, *Winning the Second Battle*, 71, 79–80.

117. See Morton and Wright, *Winning the Second Battle*; Jeffrey A. Keshen, *Propaganda and Censorship*; Neary and Granatstein, *The Veterans Charter*.

118. Morton, "The Canadian Veterans' Heritage," 28.

119. In particular, the massive organizing drive required for the 1936 Vimy pilgrimage. See also Jonathan Vance, "Today they were alive again": The Canadian Corps Reunion of 1934." *Ontario History*, LXXXXVII/4 (December 1995): 327–344, and Vance, *Death So Noble*.

120. See Theda Skocpol, "Delivering Young Families: The Resonance of the GI Bill," *The American Prospect 27/28* (Sept.–Oct. 1996): 66–72, who argues that the mix of conservatism, patriotism and economic critiques in the American Legion was also a powerful grassroots proponent of welfare state expansion.

Article Twenty-Six

Canadian Unemployment Policy in the 1930s

James Struthers

I

One of the problems of discussing unemployment during the Great Depression is the danger of becoming overcome by a sense of déjà vu. Today unemployment officially stands at over 12 percent of the workforce; perhaps as many as 2 000 000 Canadians are without work and according to the Economic Council of Canada the jobless total is unlikely to drop below 10 percent until 1987. Yet despite these appalling figures, our government, as in the 1930s, tells us it cannot act to create jobs because its first priority must be to reduce the deficit in order to restore business confidence.

Although the arguments behind today's economic policies are certainly different from those of the 1930s, many of the essential moral homilies remain unchanged. Canadians in the 1980s, like their parents and grandparents of the 1930s, are being told they can't expect to hope for recovery without practising severe restraint, self-discipline, hard work, and much tightening of belts. Despite these frightening parallels, however, we haven't yet been surrounded by soup kitchens, relief camps, food vouchers, bankrupt provincial governments, and trainloads of hungry single men "riding the rods" in search of work or relief. Yet all these sights and problems were characteristic of the failure of governments to respond to unemployment during the 1930s. Why this was so I will attempt to explain in this paper.

To a large extent the unemployment policies pursued by R.B. Bennett and Mackenzie King in the 1930s were continuations of approaches and attitudes toward joblessness that had been widespread in Canada before 1930. Canadians had become well acquainted with cyclical unemployment — or trade depressions as they were then called — well before the "dirty thirties." The 1870s, the early 1890s, and the years 1907–08, 1913–15, and 1920–25, were all

Source: *Windy Pine Occasional Paper no. 1*, Canadian Studies Program, Trent University, 1984. Reprinted by permission.

periods of heavy unemployment in this country. From this perspective it is best to think of the Great Depression as simply the most intense and long-lasting of a series of "waves" of unemployment which battered all western industrial economies during the last half of the nineteenth and first third of the twentieth centuries.

Because of our climate we were also quite familiar with seasonal unemployment. Canada is infamous for being an "eight months country." Each winter tens of thousands of Canadians working in the country's great outdoors industries — construction, agriculture, forestry, fishing, and transportation — routinely lost their jobs, often for up to six months of the year, due to bad weather. Even in the boom years of the so-called "roaring twenties" (1926–29), winter unemployment rates averaged well over 10 percent of the workforce. So the sight of hungry, jobless men walking the streets in search of work or relief was quite familiar to most urban-dwellers in Canada.

Why, then, did the Great Depression take us so much by surprise? Why, for example, didn't Canada follow Great Britain's lead in 1911 by devising new institutions and policies, such as a national system of unemployment insurance and a state employment service, to cope with the problem of joblessness? There were a number of reasons for our unpreparedness but three were particularly important. In the first place, seasonal unemployment was predictable. Winter was a fact of Canadian life; therefore, newspapers, politicians, businessmen, and others argued that workingmen should save up enough money during the summer to tide themselves and their families over the winter. Moreover, it was simply assumed (without any evidence) that wages for seasonal labour were high enough to allow them to do so. To provide the seasonally unemployed with relief, it was argued, would discourage habits of thrift, frugality, and self-reliance.

As for cyclical unemployment, attitudes toward this problem were shaped by two factors. First, recovery in the past had always occurred eventually. The market did correct itself. Therefore, all a country could do was to "tough it out" by practising restraint and doing nothing to discourage business confidence, especially on the part of foreign investors. Second, Canada was a New World society with a developing farm frontier. It was also a country which, in the three decades before 1930, had become increasingly preoccupied with rural depopulation. And it was a country in which farmers were still politically powerful and were continually complaining about the shortage of farm help at affordable wages. For these reasons, legislation such as unemployment insurance, which might be appropriate in more crowded, congested, and highly urbanized societies such as Great Britain, was deemed by business and farm leaders to be inappropriate for Canada. There was always work for the unemployed, even if only for room and board and little more, they argued, on the nation's farms during the winter. If life in the city was made too easy through doles and unemployment insurance for the idle, might not even more men and women be encouraged to leave the land altogether?

Finally, working-class political pressure, in the form of strong trade unions and labour parties, was extremely weak in Canada before World War II. Farmers and businessmen, on the other hand, were politically powerful. Hence governments responded to their views on the unemployment question and not to the views of those who were most likely to become unemployed.

As a result of these attitudes, Canadian governments, although well acquainted with unemployment before 1930, were hopelessly ill equipped for dealing with it. No one kept unemployment statistics; there was no efficient state employment service; no public welfare departments existed at the federal or provincial level and there were only four at the municipal level. In all of Canada before 1930 there were less than 400 trained social workers. Relief, where available, was granted by private religious charities or by nineteenth-century poor law "Houses of Industry," both of which operated at the local level. In Toronto as late as 1932, jobless men still had to line up at the local House of Industry, first built in the 1830s, to get a bag of groceries or a basket of coal and were expected to saw wood or break rocks in exchange for this miserly relief. Moreover, with the brief exception of the years 1920–21, when the threat of unemployed World War I veterans loomed large throughout Canada, provincial governments along with Ottawa denied any responsibility for coming to the aid of the jobless. Public relief where given was an exclusively local matter financed solely out of local taxes, chiefly on property. One of the sad ironies of the "dirty thirties" was that although no other country, except perhaps the United States, was more economically devastated by the Great Depression than Canada, no other country was as ill-prepared for dealing with its consequences. On the eve of 1930 we lacked even the bare bones of a permanent welfare structure for relieving those in need.

II

The origins of Canadian unemployment policy in the depression lie within the 1930 federal election. On the one hand, Mackenzie King went into the election — at a time when unemployment was about 12 percent — denying that there was a jobless problem and bragging that he would not give a "five cent piece" to any Tory provincial government for unemployment relief. King also claimed that the whole idea of an unemployment crisis was simply a Conservative pre-election plot.

Bennett, on the other hand, made what from our perspective today seem like recklessly extravagant promises. He claimed he would "end unemployment," "abolish the dole," and provide "work and wages for all who wanted it." Not surprisingly, Bennett won the election, largely on the strength of his promises to do something about the unemployment crisis.

Despite the boldness of his rhetoric, however (which reflected his egotism, arrogance, and over-confidence in his own abilities), Bennett really had very traditional ideas about how to deal with unemployment. Like King, he believed the problem in 1930 was largely a seasonal and temporary phenomenon which would quickly right itself. Unlike King, Bennett, as a good Tory, also believed that sharply boosting the protective tariff would stimulate investor confidence, create jobs by reducing reliance on imports, and ultimately force other nations to lower their trading barriers against Canadian exports. It was through these tariff hikes that Bennett hoped to "end unemployment."

But these hikes would take time to produce results. Since Bennett had promised to provide jobs immediately, he also introduced a $20 000 000 emergency relief act in the summer of 1930 to tide people over what was expected to be a difficult winter. Sixteen million dollars was to be spent on public works, and, most significantly, the projects were to be administered by local and provincial governments who together were expected to contribute 75 percent of their cost. Unemployment relief, Bennett insisted like King before him, was primarily a local responsibility. Ottawa's help was on a temporary, emergency basis only, and would last only until the effects of his tariff hike were felt.

Through providing money for relief projects such as provincial road-building, Bennett also hoped to deal with another pressing problem. Transient, unemployed single men, largely immigrants, were trapped in Canadian cities because the lumber, construction, and agricultural industries which normally drew them out of cities were closed down. Such men, cut off from family ties, coming from different cultural backgrounds, and with nothing to lose, were considered to be a serious menace to law and order. Bennett's relief projects would draw them out of the cities and put money into their pockets for the winter months ahead.

Between the fall of 1930, when he first took office, and the spring of 1932, Bennett adhered to this policy of using public works or relief works, as they were called, to fight unemployment. Indeed, throughout the fiscal year 1931–32 his government spent almost $50 000 000, or more than twice as much as it had the previous year, on this approach. Nevertheless, by the spring of 1932 unemployment stood above 20 percent of the workforce and the federal deficit was over $151 000 000, almost half of total government revenue for that year. As a result, Bennett quickly became disillusioned with public works as a means of relieving unemployment.

In the first place, he had used this approach only as a temporary stopgap expedient. Neither he nor anyone in his government were believers in Keynesian deficit-spending as a way out of depression; therefore there was no expectation that public employment could be used in itself as a recovery strategy. Moreover, by 1932 it had become obvious that the depression was more than a "temporary" problem. Second, by 1932, local and provincial governments, especially in the west, could no longer afford to pay their 75 percent share of the cost of these increasingly expensive relief works and Bennett had no intention of assuming a larger share of the cost. Finally, Bennett and Canadian businessmen were increasingly alarmed at the size of the federal deficit and the level of taxation which in themselves appeared to be a threat to investor confidence, and hence a barrier to recovery.

For all these reasons, then, Bennett reversed his unemployment policy in the spring of 1932, virtually abandoning reliance on public works, and instead depended almost solely on direct relief or the provision of a "dole" to tide the unemployed over the worst of the depression until recovery began. His chief unemployment policy, now that tariffs and public works had failed, was to attempt to eliminate the deficit and to balance the federal budget. This meant keeping expenditure on the jobless down to the lowest level consistent with their physical survival. At the same time, Bennett also refused to modify his policy that unemployment relief was primarily a provincial and local responsibility. His government would pay only one-third the cost of direct relief in any town or city and would contribute nothing to the costs of its administration.

III

Once Bennett opted for a policy of direct relief as his sole remaining means of dealing with unemployment, he entered into a nightmare of contradictions, ironies, and paradoxes which he had never anticipated and which would ultimately destroy his administration. Five such anomalies were of particular importance. The first was the paradox of residency requirements for relief. Since local governments, under Bennett's policy, had to assume anywhere from one-third to one-half the cost of relief on a rapidly diminishing and highly regressive property tax base, they attempted to limit their own relief costs in the only way possible, namely, by restricting eligibility for relief to their own municipal residents. Only those who could prove anywhere from six months' to, in some cases, three years' continuous residence in a city before applying for the dole were deemed eligible to receive it. In a country like Canada, with a geographically diverse and highly mobile labour market, many of the unemployed who had been on the road looking for work could not qualify for relief when they needed it. To get the dole they had to return to their home town, which they had left in the first place because there was no work. Bennett's policy, then, discouraged the unemployed from looking for work outside their town or city for fear of becoming ineligible for relief.

Transients also posed a contradiction. Tens of thousands of Canada's unemployed were immigrant, seasonal workers — bunkhouse men — who by the very nature of their work on the frontier could not qualify for relief in any city. Bennett's earlier public works policy had, in part, been intended once again to get them out of urban areas. Now, without public works, they had no choice but to drift back into Canadian cities where they could find neither relief nor work. As a result, transient single men "riding the rods" from town to town were quickly recognized as a serious menace to law and order. Since the cities refused to assume responsibility for them, and since Bennett refused to assume responsibility for relief, he decided on another alternative suggested to him by General Andrew McNaughton of the Canadian army — relief camps, run by the Defence Department. Here the men could be kept out of the cities, provided with room, board, and clothing and put to work on useful projects to preserve their morale. There was only one hitch. Since Bennett had already abandoned public works as a relief policy, the men couldn't be paid a wage, not without arousing serious unrest from married unemployed men on direct relief. Instead they were paid a 20¢ daily "allowance" in return for their labour in the camps.

Why would single men go into such camps for 20¢ a day? Cut off from direct relief in the cities, they had no choice except starvation, which is why the 20 000 men in the camps after 1933 quickly referred to them as "slave camps" and ultimately organized the relief camp strike and "On to Ottawa Trek" of 1935, which ended in a bloody two-hour riot with the RCMP in Regina. As one camp inhabitant cynically put it in 1933, "You come in broke, work all winter and still you are broke. It looks like they want to keep us bums all our lives."

Relief standards posed a third source of contention. By insisting on primary local and provincial responsibility for the financing of relief, and by assuming no share in the cost of administering relief, Bennett's government ensured that relief scales — that is, how much money or its equivalent in food vouchers a family would receive — varied dramatically from city to city, depending on the health of local economies and the political complexion of local city councils. A survey by the Canadian Welfare Council of relief standards in 50 Canadian cities during September 1936 showed just how far such scales of aid could differ. In London, Ontario, a family of five could receive no more than $40.39 a month for food, fuel, and shelter costs. That same family in Toronto could get $58.87; in Hamilton $34.40; in Ottawa $45.32; in Quebec City $26.66; in Calgary $60.00; and in Halifax a mere $18.86. Such gross variations in support within cities of comparable living costs was, of course, morally indefensible. Within Ontario, the Canadian Association of Social Workers discovered, in a survey of 107 municipalities, that not one provided the food allowance recommended by the Ontario Medical Association as the minimum necessary to maintain nutritional health. Food allowances in Toronto alone were 40 percent below the minimum standard which the League of Nations defined as necessary to maintain health. Since Bennett had promised, when elected in 1930, to "abolish the dole," such gross variations and substandard levels of support in a policy of direct relief which his adminis-tration had initiated was political catastrophe.

The bankruptcy of first local and then provincial governments was the fourth disastrous consequence of Bennett's relief policy. By insisting that local and provincial governments were to be held primarily responsible for the cost of relief, Bennett's unemployment policy concen-trated the fiscal cost of the depression where its impact was greatest — that is, in western Canada. By 1932, all four western provinces were technically bankrupt because of the cost of paying their two-thirds share of direct relief and were only kept solvent by continual federal loans and grants. By 1937 Ottawa would be paying 85 percent of all relief costs in Saskatchewan; 71 percent in Alberta; 69 percent in British Columbia; and 68 percent in Manitoba; while still insisting that relief was a local responsibility. In Ontario and Quebec, in contrast, Ottawa paid only 29 percent and 32 percent, respectively, of relief costs.

To give an equally paradoxical example of the contradictions of this policy, in Forest Hill, a very wealthy area of Toronto with few unemployed, per capita relief costs to taxpayers averaged only $4.00 a month in 1934. In East York, a working-class borough only a few miles away, with almost 50 percent of its population on relief, the cost of the dole averaged $2.50 a month per tax-payer. Yet the people of Forest Hill, in many cases, were the employers of those living in East York. By drawing municipal boundary lines around themselves, they could enjoy the lowest relief taxes in Canada and shove the burden of the depression onto their unfortunate employees.

The final irony of direct relief was the fact that you had to be totally destitute to receive it. Insurance policies, bank savings, home equity, automobiles, everything of value had to be liquidated, in many municipalities, before a family could become eligible for the dole. Hence, what was the point of saving for a rainy day if you knew beforehand that all your assets would be confiscated before you could become eligible for aid? Far better to spend your money while you had it, since if you lost your job you would soon be just as badly off as the man down the road who had saved nothing.

IV

Because of contradictions such as these, by 1933–34 Bennett was desperately looking for alternatives to his relief policy. There were two directions he could go. The first, urged increasingly by the provinces, the municipalities, organized labour, some social workers, and the unemployed, was to take over total responsibility for unemployment relief instead of continuing to contribute on a one-third basis. Had Bennett followed this option, residency requirements for relief could have been abolished; the provinces, particularly in the west, and the municipalities would once again have been fiscally solvent; and most importantly the levels of assistance for families on the dole across Canada could have been raised to a national minimum standard sufficient to ensure that everyone received at least enough food, shelter, and clothing to remain healthy and to enjoy reasonably decent living standards.

Bennett had absolutely no interest in taking this route, however. In the first place, it would have cost far more to the federal government, already concerned primarily in reducing, not increasing, its deficit. Second, it would have necessitated the creation of a permanent federal welfare bureaucracy at a time when Bennett was still convinced that the unemployment crisis was temporary. Finally, and most important, Bennett and his advisers believed that a national minimum standard of relief would increase the numbers of those unemployed. Why? Because wage rates for those already working in Canada, particularly unskilled labourers, had been so lowered by the depression (clothing workers in Montreal and Toronto, for example, often made only $10.00 for a 60-hour work week) that for a large segment of Canada's working class a dole which provided healthy and decent living standards would be preferable to work.

This was certainly the conclusion of Charlotte Whitton, Canada's best-known social worker, an arch social conservative, and Bennett's key adviser on relief policy in the 1930s. In a 1932 report to the government on relief in western Canada, Whitton told Bennett that 40 percent of those living off the dole on the prairies didn't really need it; that the very existence of direct relief in the west was drawing tens of thousands of farm families into the western cities during the winter, thus artificially boosting the unemployment rate; and that by contributing to local and provincial relief efforts, Bennett's government had only succeeded in making thousands of immigrant and poor rural families "permanently dependent at a scale of living which they never had and never will be able to provide for themselves."

With this kind of advice coming from the chief executive of the Canadian Welfare Council, it was small wonder that Bennett himself concluded in 1934 that the people had become "more or less relief-conscious and were determined to get out of the Government, whether it be municipal, provincial, or federal, all they could." Instead of opting to take over total responsibility for unemployment relief, Bennett decided over the winter of 1934 to move in exactly the opposite direction: to sever all of Ottawa's ties with the dole and turn the whole ugly, embarrassing business completely back to the provinces and municipalities.

From this perspective, unemployment insurance, which the British had pioneered in 1911, began to appear more and more attractive as a policy alternative for the Bennett government.

In the first place, at a time when unemployment still hovered at 20 percent of the workforce, Bennett simply could not withdraw from direct relief and abdicate all responsibility for the jobless. He had to have some political alternative to put in its place. Unemployment insurance fit the bill nicely for a number of reasons. Businessmen, particularly bankers and insurance company and real estate executives, favoured such a measure by 1934. These financial organizations now held many worthless municipal and provincial bonds and had become convinced that direct municipal relief was a highly inefficient way to finance the costs of unemployment. Far better, such businessmen argued, to build up an unemployment fund in good times through insurance premiums which could be used to aid the jobless during depressions. Better yet, unemployment insurance seemed to reinforce thrift. Since the premiums were compulsory, it forced workers to defer part of their incomes for a rainy day. Thus, unlike the dole, it didn't reduce everyone to complete and utter destitution before they could become eligible for aid. Moreover, because 80 percent of the cost of unemployment insurance could be financed by compulsory premiums paid by workers and employers, it would cost the federal government only a fraction of what was presently being spent on relief. As a result, unlike the dole, unemployment insurance would not interfere as directly with the widely shared desire among businessmen to see a balanced federal budget.

Finally, precisely because it was called unemployment "insurance," actuarial science, not nutritional standards of human need, could provide an arbitrary ceiling on benefits which in any case would always be kept to a fixed percentage of existing wage rates. In this way unemployment insurance seemed to pose no threat to the market-determined distribution of income. Under the legislation Bennett eventually introduced in the early months of 1935, Canadians had to work a minimum of 40 weeks over two years to be eligible for any benefits whatsoever, which in any case were set at a maximum of $11.40 a week for a family of five, almost 40 percent below the $17.30 a week which the Montreal Council of Social Agencies recommended as the minimum amount necessary to maintain health.

Under Bennett's unemployment insurance act, then, only those workers who were most regularly employed could qualify for benefits and the levels were set low enough to ensure that in no case would life on unemployment insurance be preferable to any form of work offered by Canadian employers anywhere in the country. In other words, unemployment insurance, as drafted by Bennett's advisers, was designed to reinforce the work ethic and to provide a perfect political cover for a federal withdrawal from relief. It was not designed to reduce poverty or to provide unemployed Canadians with a level of support adequate to maintain health and decency.

Most important, unemployment insurance offered nothing to the 1.2 million Canadians who were already on relief in 1935. Since their family breadwinners were obviously not working, they could not pay any premiums or qualify for benefits. It was a good idea for future depressions, but unemployment insurance really provided no solution to the problems of the 1930s.

Nevertheless, Bennett proceeded with his strategy. In June 1934, he told the premiers that all federal support for relief would be cut off on August 1. After tremendous political pressure, he subsequently modified this policy to a 22 percent federal cutback in relief spending. Then, in September, Bennett asked the provinces whether they would be willing to surrender their exclusive jurisdiction over unemployment insurance to Ottawa. Outraged by his high-handed pressure tactics and unilateral cutbacks, the premiers understandably refused. As a result, faced with an election and almost certain defeat in 1935, Bennett simply introduced his unemployment insurance bill in Parliament as part of his package of New Deal reforms, knowing full well that without provincial agreement the bill was probably unconstitutional and hence useless, as indeed it turned out to be.

After five years in office, Bennett went down to spectacular defeat in the 1935 election, his party losing all but 39 seats. He also left a very meagre legacy for his successor, the Liberal leader Mackenzie King. The attempt to provide work for the jobless had been abandoned after 1932; relief standards across Canada were grossly inadequate everywhere; four provincial governments were technically bankrupt; single unemployed men in the relief camps had walked out and rioted in their attempt to reach Ottawa; and unemployment insurance, the only creative piece of legislation on the jobless crisis to emerge from Bennett's administration, was clearly unconstitutional.

V

In what ways, if any, did Mackenzie King pursue different policies for the remainder of the depression? Unlike Bennett in 1930, King made no promises in the 1935 election beyond pledging to provide sober, orderly government. As a result, he had no political I.O.U.'s to redeem. In fact, the most striking aspect of King's unemployment policy is that from December 1935 until the spring of 1938 it was virtually a carbon copy of Bennett's. In the first place, he continued to insist that the jobless were primarily a local and provincial responsibility. Second, after a quick hike in federal relief contributions immediately after the election, King began systematically to cut back on Ottawa's support of the dole to such an extent that by 1937, in cities such as Winnipeg, Ottawa was paying only 20 percent of relief costs and on a national basis, only 30 percent, compared to the one-third share Bennett had paid throughout most years of his administration. Like the Tory prime minister, King's first priority was to balance the budget.

King's administration also refused to define any national minimum standard of relief, based on medical or nutritional standards. Instead, his government defined a national maximum. In October 1937 King's minister of Labour, Norman Rogers, announced that Ottawa would in no province pay more than 30 percent of the dole's cost, and in every city the standard of living on relief had to be kept below the average going rate for unskilled labour in the surrounding area, in order that "work incentives" could be enforced. This policy was adopted at a time when most provinces had no minimum wage for men.

Although King did abolish Bennett's hated relief camps for single men in 1936, the alternative he put in place was, in many ways, much worse. This was a farm placement scheme which paid about 45 000 of Canada's single unemployed $5.00 a month to work on farms across the country. This was less than the infamous 20¢ daily "allowance" the men had received in the camps, and there was no guarantee that food, clothing, shelter, and medical care provided by individual impoverished farmers across Canada would be comparable to what the army had offered in the relief camps. As one army commander pointed out when the camps were shut down in 1936 and many men refused to leave, "the men prefer to stay where they have 'regular hours' and good food, rather than leave for farms, where they have to work harder, longer hours, and for lower wages, with a possibility that they may not collect their wages in the fall." Although cynical in its conception, King's farm placement scheme nonetheless did solve the problem of chronic unrest among transients. Spread out individually across Canada rather than concentrated in the camps, single men proved almost impossible to organize politically after 1936.

King's overall unemployment strategy duplicated Bennett's in two other ways. As Bennett had done after 1932, until the severe recession of 1938, King rejected public works as an antidote to unemployment, in marked contrast to the massive works schemes pioneered by Franklin Roosevelt's New Deal south of the border. Instead, King relied totally on direct relief as a means of caring for the jobless. King also refused to enact an unemployment insurance plan, claiming that the political opposition to the measure by New Brunswick, Quebec, and Alberta made impossible the unanimous consent which he claimed was necessary for a constitutional amendment.

In only two areas did King take actions significantly different from Bennett's. In April 1936 he appointed a National Employment Commission, chaired by Montreal industrialist Arthur Purvis, to investigate the unemployment and relief situation and to come up with recommendations for reform. Second, in August 1937, he appointed a Royal Commission on Dominion–Provincial Relations, chaired by Supreme Court justice Newton Rowell, to investigate and attempt to straighten out the tangled web of federal–provincial financial relations, particularly the continuing inability of the western provinces to stay fiscally solvent without federal loans and grants.

The most significant result of both these commissions is that they ended up saying the same thing. The NEC, which reported in January 1938, and the Rowell-Sirois Commission, as it came to be called, which reported in May 1940, both argued that the first step in combating unemployment and restoring fiscal solvency to the provinces and local governments was for Ottawa to put in place immediately a national employment service and system of unemployment insurance, and to assume total financial and administrative responsibility for unemployment relief. In short, both commissions argued that Ottawa should take the route both Bennett and King had rejected throughout the entire depression, namely to accept primary responsibility for unemployment. The jobless crisis, both commissions argued, was a national problem, reflecting Canada's national economy; consequently, relief to those without work should be first and foremost a national responsibility. Only Ottawa through its unlimited taxing power, they argued further, possessed the fiscal strength to pay for these relief costs. Finally, reflecting the new Keynesian sophistication being developed within the department of finance, both commissions concluded that only Ottawa could inject enough purchasing power into the economy through insurance and relief payments and public works to push levels of demand up high enough to stimulate economic growth and thus ultimately to eliminate unemployment.

It would be pleasant to report that after receiving this sensible advice, King realized the error of his ways and reversed his economic policies. In fact, he did no such thing. When he discovered that the NEC was about to recommend federal control of relief, King pulled out every stop he could to kill the commission's final report. When that proved impossible, thanks to Arthur Purvis's integrity, King simply ignored it. Why? The reason was best expressed by Mary Sutherland, King's closest confidant on the NEC and the author of a dissenting minority report. In it, Sutherland articulated the basis for Ottawa's continued resistance throughout the 1930s to accepting primary responsibility for the jobless. "No matter which government is responsible for and administers relief," Sutherland wrote, "there will be constant pressure to increase the benefits and to enlarge the base of admittance to benefits. If responsibility is centralized in the Dominion government, the counter-pressure from local taxpayers will be eased. The irksome, unwelcome, and hard check provided by necessity, by municipal officials, harrassed by mounting demands on diminishing revenues, will be removed."

In short, Sutherland, like King and R.B. Bennett, believed that national responsibility for relief would cost too much and would erode the work ethic. If Ottawa controlled relief, it would have to define a national minimum standard of support, or in effect a national poverty line, across the country. In a country like Canada with widely diverse regional wage rates and living standards, such a national minimum would inevitably be higher than existing wage rates for many of the working poor. The result would be to attract this class out of work and onto relief, thus increasing unemployment. Sutherland's argument was, in this sense, almost identical to the one first put forward by Charlotte Whitton in her 1932 report on relief in western Canada. Only by keeping relief a local responsibility and local governments on the edge of bankruptcy could relief costs and benefit levels be kept to the barest minimum.

Ironically, putting more purchasing power directly into the hands of the jobless and their families in the form of higher relief benefits was exactly what was needed in order to push up consumption and effective demand to levels that would in turn encourage investment and employment. But as long as the Bennett and King administrations continued to approach the relief question from the angle of its effects upon the work ethic of individuals rather than upon the purchasing power of all the unemployed, they simply could not see this. As a result, in their relief policy, as in their wider economic policies of balanced budgets, a sound dollar, and regressive taxation, Bennett and King inhibited the chances of recovery.

VI

In 1940, after World War II had begun, Canadians finally did see enacted a constitutionally valid scheme of unemployment insurance. The pressures of war and the need for national unity had dissolved the political objections of the three dissenting provinces. More important, King's own fear of postwar unemployment, and of how jobless veterans would respond to relief of the 1930s variety, now galvanized him into making unemployment insurance a first priority of the government, particularly with an election looming on the horizon in 1940. Wartime mobilization and the potential labour shortage also gave the federal government a vital need for creating a national employment service, a motive which had not been present during the heavy labour surplus of the 1930s. Finally, the necessity for massive war expenditures gave Ottawa an overpowering political argument for trying out new Keynesian ideas such as deliberately incurring large deficits, a policy which would have left most Canadian businessmen aghast in the depression.

The tragedy of unemployment policy in the 1930s is that strategies for dealing with joblessness which were politically possible, indeed essential in the context of the war, were not deemed possible, given Canada's political landscape in the depression. The essential continuity and the essential failure of the policies pursued by both R.B. Bennett and Mackenzie King lay in their refusal to accept that the unemployed were a national responsibility. This refusal, in turn, was rooted in what might be termed the dilemma of "less eligibility" in a market economy. In a private enterprise system, business and the market set wage levels and living standards. During the 1930s, for many working Canadians, these standards and wages were below what was necessary to ensure a decent and healthy standard of living. As a result, both the Bennett and King governments believed they could not provide higher relief benefits for the jobless without attracting many of the working population onto the dole. Without direct state intervention or trade union pressure to improve working conditions and living standards for low-income Canadians, or in other words, without massive intervention into the marketplace, the government felt limited in the benefits it could provide for the unemployed. And in the political context of the 1930s, given the absence of a serious political threat from the left or a strong labour movement, the pressure simply was not there for either Bennett or King to move in a direction that would have been regarded by Canadian businessmen as serious meddling in their affairs.

Only war, with the full employment it would bring and the strong labour union organization it would permit, could create a political climate in which it would be possible to effect these kinds of permanent structural reforms to underpin working-class incomes. By 1945, then, Canadians were finally ready to fight the Great Depression of the 1930s.

Topic Eleven

Foreign Policy and World War II

Members of the Royal Canadian Engineers briefly pray with a chaplain immediately prior to boarding their aircraft for the D-Day invasion.

Historians of Canadian foreign policy have disagreed in their evaluation of Canada's foreign policy in the 1930s. Those historians who have looked at it from the national perspective praise Prime Minister William Lyon Mackenzie King for keeping Canada united and autonomous from Britain. Political scientist James Eayrs offers a different perspective in "'A Low Dishonest Decade': Aspects of Canadian External Policy, 1931–1939," borrowing the descriptive phrase from W.H. Auden's famous poem, "September 1st, 1939." While dated, Eayrs's article, now roughly half a century old, remains a classic in Canadian foreign policy analysis. It presents an interpretation that has yet to be challenged. Eayrs argues that Canada's isolationist policy in the 1930s resulted in the country turning its back on European problems at the very time when a strong concerted position by Britain and her allies might have prevented World War II.

In "Staring into the Abyss," historian Jack Granatstein examines Canada's shifting foreign policy in the World War II period. He argues that although Canada had already begun to distance itself from Britain and to ally itself with the United States in World War I and in the interwar years, it was Britain's military weakness during World War II that drove Canada into the arms of the United States. He sees the signing of the Ogdensburg Agreement between Canada and the United States in August 1940 as the turning point but argues that this Agreement should not be seen as a Canadian "sell out to the United States" but rather as an attempt to maintain Canadian autonomy.

In "Battle Exhaustion and the Canadian Soldier in Normandy," historian J. Terry Copp examines the impact of battle exhaustion, "the catch-all term used by the Army to describe stress-related neuro-psychiatric casualties," on the Canadian infantry during the important World War II battle in Normandy. Copp explains how psychiatrists accounted for battle exhaustion, how they assessed those believed to be suffering from the disease, and what methods of treatment they used.

What were the assumptions about the nature of Canada, of Canadian-British relations, and the nature of World War II that underlay the formulation of Canadian foreign policy in the 1930s and during World War II? Noted Canadian analyst Harold A. Innis once described Canada's foreign policy from 1914 to 1945 as going from "colony to nation to colony." How accurate was his assessment in light of Eayrs's and Granatstein's analysis? What does Terry Copp's discussion of battle exhaustion during World War II reveal about the experience of Canadian soldiers at the war front? How does the experience of soldiers in World War I as described in Will Bird's personal account in Topic Nine compare with those of World War II?

In *In Defence of Canada*, vol. 2, *Appeasement and Rearmament* (Toronto: University of Toronto Press, 1965), James Eayrs provides an exhaustive analysis of Canadian foreign policy in the late 1930s. Two alternatives to Eayrs's critical views of Canada's position of isolationism are H. Blair Neatby's "Mackenzie King and National Unity," in *Empire and Nations: Essays in Honour of Frederick H. Soward*, eds. H.L. Dyck and H.P. Krosby (Toronto: University of Toronto Press, 1969), pp. 54–70, and J.L. Granatstein and R. Bothwell's "'A Self-Evident National Duty': Canadian Foreign Policy, 1935–1939," *Journal of Imperial and Commonwealth History* 3 (1975): 212–33. A good documentary collection on the 1930s is R. Bothwell and G.N. Hillmer, *"The In-Between Time": Canadian External Policy in the 1930's* (Toronto: Copp Clark, 1975). For an overview of Canadian foreign policy in the interwar years, see: C.P. Stacey, *Canada and the Age of Conflict*, vol. 2, *1921–1948: The Mackenzie King Era* (Toronto: University of Toronto Press, 1981); Richard Veatch, *Canada and the League of Nations* (Toronto: University of Toronto Press, 1975); and Norman Hillmer and J.L. Granatstein, *Empire to Umpire: Canada and the World to the 1990s* (Toronto: Copp Clark Longman, 1994). Norman Hillmer et al., eds. present several articles on Canada on the eve of war in *A Country of Limitations: Canada and the World in 1939* (Ottawa: Canadian Committee for the History of the Second World War, 1996). For Mackenzie King's views of Hitler, see Robert H. Keyserlingk, "Mackenzie King's Spiritualism and His Views of Hitler in 1939," *Journal of Canadian Studies*, 20, 4 (Winter 1985–6): 26–44.

On Mackenzie King's foreign and domestic policies during the war years, see J.L. Granatstein, *Canada's War: The Politics of the Mackenzie King Government, 1939–1945* (Toronto: University of Toronto Press, 1975, 1990). R.D. Cuff and J.L. Granatstein review aspects of Canadian-American relations in *Ties that Bind: Canadian-American Relations in Wartime from the Great War to the Cold War*, 2nd ed. (Toronto: Samuel Stevens Hakkert, 1977). For an overview, see Robert Bothwell, Ian Drummond, and John English, *Canada, 1900–1945* (Toronto: University of Toronto Press, 1987); Desmond Morton, *Canada and War: A Military and Political History* (Toronto: Butterworths, 1981); and J.L. Granatstein and Desmond Morton, *A Nation Forged in Fire: Canadians and the Second World War, 1939–1945* (Toronto: Lester & Orpen Dennys, 1989).

WEBLINKS

Diaries of Prime Minister Mackenzie King
http://king.collectionscanada.ca/EN/
The complete digitized diaries of Prime Minister Mackenzie King. The diaries are very extensive and cover King's life from 1893 to 1950.

Declaration of War on Germany
http://www.dfait-maeci.gc.ca/department/history/keydocs/keydocs_details-en.
asp?intDocumentId=18
A transcribed copy of the Government of Canada's declaration of war against Germany. Further documents regarding Canada's international affairs in this time period are available at: http://www.dfait-maeci.gc.ca/department/history/keydocs/keydocs_views-en.asp?RefValue=1900&view=4

World War II Collections
http://web.mala.bc.ca/davies/letters.images/collection.pages/WWII.htm
A diverse collection of documents and photographs of Canadian combatants and civilians in World War II.

Canadian Newspapers and World War II
http://warmuseum.ca/cwm/newspapers/intro_e.html
A searchable database of the published content of Canadian newspapers such as *The Globe and Mail* and *Hamilton Spectator* with regard to World War II.

Japanese-Canadian Internment
http://archives.cbc.ca/IDD-1-71-568/conflict_war/internment/
Radio and video footage of the internment of Japanese Canadians during World War II. Also includes interviews with those who had been interred, and shows government action taken in modern times to compensate them for the experience.

National Film Board of Canada: D-Day
http://www.nfb.ca/enclasse/dday/dday.html
D-Day video archives of the National Film Board of Canada.

Article Twenty-Seven

"A Low Dishonest Decade": Aspects of Canadian External Policy, 1931–1939

James Eayrs

There has not yet taken place in Canada that debate on the wisdom of appeasement in which British statesmen and scholars have been engaged since the appearance of Professor Feiling's *Life of Neville Chamberlain*. If this seems a remarkable fact, it is not hard to explain. Had the Canadian government of that day urged a more sturdy resistance to the Nazi tyranny, it is doubtful that events would have taken a significantly different course. German policy was unresponsive to the action or inaction of the Dominions; and it seems unlikely that Chamberlain would have been deflected from the path of the appeaser any more by the prime minister of Canada than he was by the prime minister of New Zealand, which is to say not at all. Canada's external policy during the years 1931–1939, so far from requiring extended apology, appears to most of its historians to possess the self-evident vindication of having brought a united and determined nation to Britain's side on September 10, 1939. The evidence which might sustain a contrary interpretation is still scanty. Documents from the files of the Department of External Affairs have yet to be published; the private papers of the prime ministers of the period are withheld from the scholar's domain;[1] both R.B. Bennett and Mackenzie King retained a jealous hold upon the External Affairs portfolio and conducted foreign policy possessively, even stealthily, so that few of their colleagues and subordinates have been able to throw strong light upon shadowy though crucial episodes; and a tradition unlike that prevailing at Westminster (where politics and literature — or politics and journalism — honourably combine) assists in their concealment. These are some (but by no means all) of the circumstances accounting for the remarkable early appearance of an Authorized Version of events not yet three decades removed.

The time is now approaching when a revisionist interpretation will be possible; one or two significant steps in this direction have already been taken.[2] The present paper has a more modest purpose. It attempts to discuss some aspects of Canadian external policy during the 1930s to which insufficient attention has perhaps been paid, and to bring to more familiar themes evidence previously overlooked. Although the title[3] may suggest an excess of moral indignation, its point of view is rather that of Lord Vansittart, who, writing of Dominion policies during the period in which he laboured with such prescience and to such little avail, remarked, perhaps too generously: "One could not blame them, one could not admire them, one could not admire anybody."[4]

THE NEW WORLD AND THE OLD

In 1919 Canadians turned away from Europe, leaving behind their dead. However misguided it might appear to those of a later generation drawn as their fathers had been into "the vortex of militarism," isolationism in Canada was a natural response to the four-year ordeal on the Western front. The Great War remade the map, but left unchanged the scale and the projection.

Source: *The Growth of Canadian Policies in External Affairs*, ed. H.L. Keenleyside. Reprinted by permission of James Eayrs.

How could a conflict in which major gains were measured by hundreds of yards, and a million lives exchanged for a few desolated acres of mud, affect in any way the traditional concepts of geography? It brought half a million Canadians to Europe but Europe no closer to Canada. The world was still wide. To the Oceans and the Fleet might now be added as purveyor of security the great and friendly guardian to the South. Canada was a "fire-proof house, far from inflammable materials";[5] and its fortunate inhabitants peered indistinctly at the distant continent from which invasion seemed so improbable. "At present danger of attack upon Canada is minor in degree and second-hand in origin," Mackenzie King had insisted as late as 1938;[6] and although his military advisers were less certain of Canada's immunity,[7] their misgivings were not allowed to disturb unduly the complacency of the public or the size of the defence estimates.

Isolationism was the product of geography; it was shaped by distrust, a distrust born of the Great War and confirmed at the council tables of Paris. "It was European policy, European statesmanship, European ambition, that drenched this world with blood," N.W. Rowell told the First Assembly of the League of Nations. "Fifty thousand Canadians under the soil of France and Flanders is what Canada has paid for European statesmanship trying to settle European problems. I place responsibility on a few; I would not distribute it over many; but nevertheless it is European."[8] These bluntly accusing words, an official of the Canadian delegation wrote privately at the time, "hurt and stung many people," and in his view "marred the performance."[9] But they conveyed, however tactlessly, the sense of Canadian feeling; and the prime minister wrote to their author to express his "appreciation of the stand you took in stating to the Conference, as frankly as you did, the price the world has paid for the European diplomacy of the last hundred years."[10] Nor, as it seemed, had the trauma of the trenches changed Europe for the better. Ancient enmities and grievances arose once more, or were replaced or supplemented by new disorders; the scope for intrigue and for disaster was if anything enhanced. "Everywhere there are signs of trouble," wrote one of Canada's representatives at the Paris Peace Conference in 1919. "Egypt is now disturbed with the fever for self govt.— the vicious results of Wilson's doctrine of ill or nondefined self determination. Asia Minor and Turkey are disorganized — Roumanians threatened on three sides by Bolshevists and Hungarians — Russia poisoned and poisoning — Hungary communist and Germany in near chaos. 'Tis surely a sad mess out of which to evolve a new Europe."[11]

Distrust and disapproval of Europe's statecraft and statesmen passed easily into an assertion of North American moral superiority. In Canada as in the United States there was nourished the conviction that the New World in its national life and international behaviour exhibited standards above and beyond those of the Old. Like Mr. Herbert Hoover, Canadians

> returned in 1919 from several years abroad . . . steeped with two ideas: first, that through three hundred years [North] America had developed something new in a way of life of a people, which transcended all others of history; and second, that out of the boiling social and economic cauldron of Europe, with its hates and fears, rose miasmic infections which might greatly harm or even destroy . . . the hope of the world.[12]

Rare was the Canadian who, addressing himself at Geneva or at home to the theme of his country's place in world affairs, did not elaborate this contrast. "[W]e think in terms of peace," remarked Senator Dandurand in 1924, "while Europe, an armed camp, thinks in terms of war."[13] "After listening to and participating in the proceedings of the League," Mackenzie King declared in 1928, "I have come back to Canada with a more profound conviction than ever that there is no land on the face of the globe in which the lot of men, women and children is cast in a pleasanter place than in this Dominion."[14] In 1936 he referred to Canada's "tremendous, absorbing and paramount tasks of achieving economic development and national unity, which with us take the place of the preoccupation with the fear of attack and the dreams of glory which beset older and more crowded countries";[15] a few weeks later, at Geneva, he contrasted his country's friendly relations with the United States and Europe's "violent . . . propaganda and recriminations hurled incessantly across the frontiers, the endeavours [in Europe] to draw all countries into one or other extremist camp, the feverish race for rearmament, the hurrying to and fro of diplomats, the ceaseless weaving and unravelling of understandings and alliances, and the consequent fear and uncertainty of the peoples";[16] and in March 1939, soon after Hitler's seizure of Czechoslovakia, he referred despairingly to the "continent that cannot run itself," in implied contrast to that North American continent which could.[17]

Such comparisons were frequently joined to moral exhortation. The rostrum of the Palais des Nations became for successive Canadian spokesmen a pulpit from which Europe was urged to forswear her foolish ways, to abandon intrigue, violence, hostility, to adopt those institutions which (they claimed) had brought a century of peace to North America. Canada and the United States, Mackenzie King informed the Ninth Assembly of the League of Nations, had ceased "to rely upon force, we have looked to reason as the method of solving our differences, and reason has supplied us from time to time with conference, conciliation or arbitration in a form . . . sufficient to settle our various differences as they have arisen."[18] Let there be a European Rush-Bagot Treaty, a European International Joint Commission — tranquillity would follow for a hundred years. As a prescription for Old World ills, these New World remedies were altogether inadequate, arising as they did from a wholly different situation.

> The toad beneath the harrow knows
> Exactly where each tooth-point goes;
> The butterfly upon the road
> Preaches contentment to that toad.

Moreover, they were compounded of a series of fictions unrelated to things as they were. "Not a single soldier, not a single cannon," the Canadian delegate had told the Fifth Assembly of the League, faced the famous frontier. This was simple falsehood. The International Joint Commission had been able to function without major difficulty only because each government had refrained from submitting disputes other than those over waterways. As for the Rush-Bagot Agreement, "the truth is," Mackenzie King had written privately in 1922, "our American friends have been steadily evading [it], until it has become more or less of a mockery to speak of its terms in the manner in which we do."[19]

However ill-justified, Canada's moralizing at Europe led logically not to isolation but engagement. Ought not the practitioners of the New World's higher mortality try by more active participation in the affairs of the Old to lead it into the paths of righteousness? That is not what happened. More potent than the zeal of the missionary was the desire to escape contamination. The less the New World came in contact with the Old, the better; the more, the greater the chance of succumbing to those "miasmic infections" which threatened to invade and to destroy the healthy bodies politic of North America. "Bolshevism," wrote the editor of the *Canadian Annual Review* in 1918, "had a basis wherever Russians and Jews and other foreigners gathered together" in Canada's cities; if foreigners brought Bolshevism, Canadians should keep clear of foreigners. "We are told there are enormous numbers of people on the continent of Europe who want to come [here]," remarked a former Minister of Immigration in 1922. "I want to say I regard it of the dimensions of a national menace that there is any danger whatever of the bars being let down."[20] Questioned in 1920 on Canada's readiness to accept a mandate for Armenia, the leader of the opposition wrote that the proposal "would provoke general protest from one end of the Dominion to the other," for "a sort of reaction has set in . . . with respect to interference by the Governments of this Continent with European Affairs."[21] As the twenty years' crisis developed and deepened, isolationism became if anything more firmly rooted in the Canadian people and their governors. Early in 1922 the Canadian government refused to contribute funds in the form of an interest-free loan for the relief of famine in Russia, and turned down a Soviet request for credit to buy Canadian seed wheat. In 1924 it ignored an appeal to contribute to the relief of famine in Albania. In 1925 it refused the invitation to sign the Geneva Protocol, and it was largely at Canada's insistence that an article was inserted in the text of the Locarno Agreements specifically exempting the Dominions from their provisions. "I do not see," Ernest Lapointe observed some years later, "that Canada should assume obligations in connection with the boundaries between France and Germany . . . [or] guarantee any boundaries in central Europe or elsewhere."[22] And an influential member of the Canadian government wrote before sailing for the Imperial Conference in the spring of 1937:

> The conference will be interesting, and probably in some ways revealing; but the more I see of the whole thing, the more I am certain that our destiny is on the North American continent and that if Europe is going to insist on destroying itself, it is no part of our mission to destroy ourselves in attempting to prevent it.[23]

THE LEAGUE AND THE NATION

If other countries entered the League of Nations in something of the spirit expressed by Smuts' phrase —"the tents have been struck and the great caravan of humanity is once more on the march"— Canada may be said to have been mainly concerned lest she be called upon to do more than her share of the work in breaking camp or be compelled to march without the consent of her Parliament. It is usual to attribute the reserve with which Canadians watched the Geneva experiment to the coercive characteristics of the Covenant, and to suppose that so long as the League confined itself to conciliatory methods it could count upon Canadian approval. This view has the weighty support of Professor Mansergh, who writes that "from the first the League was welcomed as a means of furthering international co-operation, as a forum for debate and discussion," and that it was only "as a means for enforcing, as distinct from maintaining, peace" that it aroused the suspicion and censure of successive Canadian governments.[24] Certainly it is difficult to overestimate the agitated concern lest through Articles X and XVI of the Covenant the newly independent Dominion be placed at "the beck and call of a Council not responsible to the nation for its actions," or, even worse, become involved "in conflicts in some far-away section of Europe, or in some distant portion of South America."[25] Fears such as these lead to that policy; "remarkable," as Professor Mansergh observes, "for its consistency," by which Canada tried at first to have Article X removed entirely from the Covenant; that proving unsuccessful, introduced an interpretative resolution which, though it failed by one vote to receive the unanimous support required for adoption, had the desired effect of weakening the obligations of League membership; and finally, when the League was confronted with the two decisive tests of its procedures for collective security, did what could be done to weaken the effectiveness of sanctions.

But this interpretation may be misleading. It implies a degree of attachment to the League as a non-coercive agency for peaceful conciliation which, whatever might be said in public, no Canadian minister really felt. For Canadian suspicion of Geneva derived basically from Canadian distrust of Europe; and it was as a European institution that the League appeared from Canada. "The League was born ostensibly as a world League," commented a former official of the Department of External Affairs in 1926, "but really is a European League with the non-Europeans tacked on. The most distinctive and powerful New World people went out of it." A Canadian had no more legitimate concern "with the administration of Danzig or of the Saar Valley" than had "a Nova Scotian . . . [with] the municipal government of Vancouver."[26] "Let us . . . conciliate Quebec and Ontario," remarked a member of Parliament in 1923, "before we start conciliating Roumania and Ukrainia."[27] "The League of Nations is a preposterous and expensive farce," wrote Sir Clifford Sifton, "and amounts to nothing more than a part of a machine designed to involve us in European and Imperialistic complications. Canada ought to call a halt on this business."[28] The views of those in office were much the same. Sir Joseph Pope, the Undersecretary of State for External Affairs until 1925, dismissed the Covenant as "not worth the paper it is written on," and wrote in his diary: "Our reps are making a great stir at the League of Nations, advertizing Canada and incidentally themselves. I think it all absurd, and am convinced that Canada's true policy right now is to develop her resources and to leave European questions such as the Bessarabian frontier &c to our Imperial statesmen and the trained experts of Downing Street."[29] His successor, O.D. Skelton, while holding "the trained experts of Downing Street" in somewhat lesser regard, was no more sympathetic to the Geneva experiment. Mackenzie King, as his official biographer remarks, "was the type of uplifter who might have been expected to give the League his full and enthusiastic support," but his attitude toward the League in its formative years "was one of studied neglect."[30] In the 1930s this was to develop into an attitude of profound hostility, especially after the "Riddell incident" of November 1935. W.A. Riddell, the Canadian Permanent Delegate at Geneva, left in some perplexity as a consequence of the General Election a few days earlier, proposed on his own initiative the imposition of certain sanctions against Italy, and in the brief period until his action was repudiated by the Canadian government, set Canada's policy upon a course it had never before taken. In his published recollection of this celebrated episode, Dr. Riddell attributes his repudiation partly to the fact that the prime minister and the undersecretary of state for External Affairs were at the time out of the country, leaving the Department of External Affairs in charge of "two French Canadians," Ernest Lapointe and Laurent Beaudry. On reporting to Mackenzie King in Ottawa, Dr. Riddell writes, he found him, "as always, most gracious," while Lapointe seemed "cold, critical and overbearing."[31] But beneath a mask of practiced cordiality King was no less angered than Lapointe, probably more so, by Riddell's initiative. A Canadian newspaperman has recorded an interview with the prime minister soon after the event:

> Had a few words with Mr. King re the Italo-Ethiopian settlement and he spoke with surprising frankness. I never knew before Mr. King's general attitude towards the League and foreign affairs. King complained angrily about Dr. Riddell's gasoline [sic], steel and coal proposal. "I am certainly going to give him a good spanking," was the way he put it. . . . He said that excessive idealism in politics should be avoided. Canada's policy, he believed, should be dictated by considerations of geographical location and population. After all we are but 10 millions on the north end of a continent and we should not strive to over-play our part. . . . He is very dubious about foreign commitments, and, also, about getting into the League too deeply. He said that the only real difference of opinion he had ever had with Lapointe was with regard to Canada's acceptance of the presidency of the League Assembly [in 1925]. He had opposed it on the ground that it would stimulate League thought in Canada, tend to lead us more deeply into League affairs and, possibly, foreign commitments.[32]

"We should not strive to over-play our part." This theme was henceforth to be heard in nearly all of the prime minister's infrequent public statements on the European crisis until the outbreak of war, a refrain in praise of diffidence. "After all, . . . there is such a thing as a sense of proportion in international affairs," he said in the House of Commons in February 1936. "Do hon. members think that it is Canada's role at Geneva to attempt to regulate a European war?" If he had not disavowed Riddell's proposal, "the whole of Europe might have been aflame today."[33] A few days later he added: "Our country is being drawn into international situations to a degree that I myself think is alarming."[34] Within a fortnight Hitler was to invade the Rhineland.

THE LAW AND THE JUNGLE

If distrust of European politics contributed to isolationist sentiment in Canada in the years between the wars, it also helped to thwart understanding of what was happening to Europe during the deepening crisis of the later 1930s. With a very few exceptions, notably J.W. Dafoe,[35] Canadians did not recognize Fascist Italy and Nazi Germany for what they were. Totalitarianism was thought to be merely an aggravation of that malaise from which Europe traditionally suffered; there was little if any suspicion that it might be a distinctively twentieth-century phenomenon arising from the tensions and insecurities of twentieth-century man. The fascist apparition was no new menace for which the old responses would no longer suffice, but a rebirth of the intrigues, the rivalries, the nationalisms of prewar European diplomacy. Thus it required no special explanation; created no new problems; needed no exceptional precautions.

A significant section of the Canadian public was indeed disposed to view fascism in its Mediterranean setting not merely without alarm but with undisguised approval. The lofty sentiments of Fascist doctrine elaborated by Mussolini's publicists, with their apotheosis of order, discipline, family, nation, their pseudo-syndicalist remedies for industrial unrest, gained powerful support among the elite of French Canada. "The work of Mussolini and of the Fascist Party finds among a certain number of my compatriots admirers," remarked Mr. Paul Gouin in 1938. "They have the same attitude towards the corporative movement of Salazar. . . . We may ask ourselves if it would not be to the advantage of our Province and of Canada to borrow what is best in these different formulae, while naturally avoiding their excesses."[36] Few French-speaking Canadians saw anything for adverse comment in the description of General Franco's forces offered by the newly appointed Papal Delegate to Canada and Newfoundland as that "army of heroes, justly called Christ's militia,"[37] any more than they resented the valedictory pronounced by Maxime Raymond in the House of Commons on the occasion of the departure of the Mackenzie–Papineau Brigade: "This, I admit, does not give me any sorrow; it will rid us of these undesirable people, provided they do not return home here."[38] If there was no emulation in French Canada of General O'Duffy's Blueshirts, who went from Eire to fight in Spain for Franco, it was due not to want of sympathy for the Nationalist cause but to the even stronger hold of isolationism.

National Socialism was something else again. No religious or ideological link could bind Quebec to a regime which had so soon and so obviously singled out the Catholic Church for brutal destruction. But diagnosis of the Nazi movement was hindered in Canada by the magnitude of domestic crisis and by the isolationist tradition. Events in Germany were consistently misconstrued as a nationalist revival of the conventional type, distinguished, perhaps, by the odd fanaticism of its leaders, by the strut and swagger of its rank and file, but for all that a movement which might be comprehended in traditional terms, appeased and contained by traditional methods. When Hitler entered the Rhineland there was aroused among English-speaking Canadians little of the emotion produced by Mussolini's attack on Ethiopia. On the contrary, there was a widely held conviction that in reoccupying the demilitarized zone Hitler was only avenging the wrongs of Versailles, taking possession of what rightfully belonged to Germany. Why shouldn't a man walk into his own backyard? With the significant exception of Dafoe's *Free Press*, nearly all Canadian newspapers urged, on March 9, 1936, a sympathetic understanding of Hitler's position. "Canadians who do not allow themselves to be swayed by a personal dislike for Hitler and his unpleasant colleagues," wrote the editor of the Vancouver *Sun*, "will feel a measure of sympathy for this new attitude of the German people. . . . Canada is only a spectator. There are not enough moral principles at stake to induce her to become otherwise. . . . Whatever morality lies in the scales seems to be, this time, on Germany's side of the balance." "After eighteen years," the Edmonton *Bulletin* observed, "Europe can afford to restore Germany to full standing in the concert of nations." "Nothing can ever be gained," argued the editor of the Montreal *Gazette*, "by persistently treating Germany as though she were national enemy No. 1 in perpetuity. It would likewise be dangerous and futile to regard Adolf Hitler in no other light than as one whose designs are wilfully antagonistic to forces that hate war."

It is possible that had Canada been represented in Germany by a diplomat of insight and influence, a less reassuring image of National Socialism would have reached its government and people. As it was, the Canadian government, having no diplomatic mission at Berlin, necessarily relied on whatever Whitehall might select for its instruction from the dispatches of Sir Nevile Henderson — dispatches which conveyed a sadly erroneous interpretation of Nazi policy.[39] This unhelpful source was supplemented by the assessment of the Canadian High Commissioner at London, so closely associated with the group which moved with such great and disastrous effect between Cliveden, Printing House Square, and Downing Street that nothing he learned from its members seems likely to have provided a useful corrective to the misleading dispatches passed on by the Dominions Office. "Walked about the grounds in the forenoon with Vincent Massey, talking politics," wrote Thomas Jones in his diary on June 7, 1936. "I begged him to stress the urgency of dealing with Germany and not to wait upon France."[40]

But the most misleading impression was derived more directly. In 1937 Mackenzie King decided to go from the Imperial Conference to Germany. There he met and talked with Hitler and other leading personalities of the Third Reich. It was not a wholly useful confrontation. It is true that King did not allow so unique an opportunity to pass without stressing in Berlin what he felt unable to disclose in London, namely, that in the event of "a war of aggression, nothing in the world would keep the Canadian people from being at the side of Britain."[41] Heeded or not heeded, this message was at least delivered, and more valuable service could hardly have been rendered. But its value was diminished by the way in which the Canadian prime minister fell victim to the Führer's remarkable capacity for mesmerizing his visitors. "There is no doubt that Hitler had a power of fascinating men," Mr. Churchill wrote in his memoirs; and added the sage advice: "Unless the terms are equal, it is better to keep away."[42] And between the prime minister of Canada and the perpetrator of the Nazi *Schrecklichkeit* the terms were far from equal. The extent of Hitler's advantage may be measured by the opinions with which King returned to Canada. According to Mr. Bruce Hutchison, to whom he related them soon afterward, King found Hitler

> a simple sort of peasant, not very intelligent and no serious danger to anyone . . . obsessed with the recovery of neighboring territory inhabited by Germans, a natural feeling. When he had brought these territories into the Reich . . . he would be satisfied . . . he would not risk a large war. His ambitions were centered entirely in Germany and the narrow irredentist regions beside it. For this reason [there would be] . . . no early trouble in Europe.[43]

And to the Canadian people Mackenzie King declared, three weeks after his talks with the German leaders:

> Despite every appearance to the contrary, I believe the nations of Europe have a better understanding of each other's problems to-day than they have had for some years past. Moreover, despite all appearances, they are prepared, I believe, in an effort to work out a solution, to co-operate to a greater degree than has been the case for a long while. . . . Of this I am certain . . . that neither the governments nor the peoples of any of the countries I have visited desire war, or view the possibility of war between each other, as other than likely to end in self-destruction, and the destruction of Europe civilization itself.[44]

That the destruction of European civilization was precisely the object of the man he had so recently talked with in the Reichskanzlei was a thought unlikely to have crossed the mind of the Canadian prime minister; for, as was remarked of him in a different connection, "Mr. King never quite got it into his head during his economic studies at Toronto and Harvard that our civilization is dominated by carnivorous animals."[45]

EMPIRE AND REICH

In 1923 the prime minister of Canada had protested vigorously and decisively against the Imperial Conference "assuming the rights of a cabinet in the determination of foreign policy . . . expressing approval of the present [British] Government's foreign policy . . . , trying to shape the affairs of Europe."[46] By 1937 Mackenzie King's suspicions of "Downing Street domination" had been sufficiently allayed to allow him to do what he had never done before — to endorse at an Imperial Conference a united Commonwealth policy on international affairs. As it happened, the policy for which the Dominions offered their collective approval and support was the ill-fated policy of appeasement. "[T]he settlement of differences that may arise between nations," asserted the section of the *Proceedings* of the Conference dealing with foreign affairs, "should be sought by methods of co-operation, joint enquiry and conciliation . . . differences of political creed should be no obstacle to friendly relations between Governments and countries . . . nothing would be more damaging to the hopes of international appeasement than the division, real or apparent, of the world into opposing groups."[47] These sentiments, which, as Professor Mansergh rightly remarks, are "hardly consistent with the dignity of a great Commonwealth confronted with the shameless aggression of European tyrants unmatched for their cruelty and faithlessness since the Dark Ages,"[48] continued to be uttered by Mackenzie King during the interval between the end of the Conference and the beginning of war. For the first time since becoming prime minister in 1921, he found himself able to pay public tribute to "the unremitting care and anxiety which those responsible for the foreign policy of Britain have devoted to their task"; he spoke of "their strong and determined effort to establish peace."[49] This was followed by a series of press statements in praise of British policy. When the news of the proposed mission to Berchtesgaden reached him, Mackenzie King announced that he had "conveyed to Mr. Neville Chamberlain the deep satisfaction with which my colleagues and I have learned that his proposal for a personal conference with Herr Hitler . . . has been agreed to" and described "this far-seeing and truly noble action on the part of Mr. Chamberlain" as "emphatically the right step." A further statement issued after the British Cabinet's decision to support the principle of self-determination for Sudeten Germans referred to the "courage and vision" displayed by the government of the United Kingdom in seeking "to avert recourse to force by finding a peaceful and agreed solution of the present clash of interests in Central Europe." Following Chamberlain's radio address of September 27, 1938 ("How horrible, fantastic, incredible it is that we should be digging trenches and fitting gas-masks because of a quarrel in a far away country"), Mackenzie King proclaimed the Canadian government's "complete accord with the statement Mr. Chamberlain has made to the world today." Word of the impending visit to Munich called forth the most ecstatic endorsement of all:

> The heart of Canada is rejoicing tonight at the success which has crowned your unremitting efforts for peace. . . . My colleagues in the Government join with me in unbounded admiration at the service you have rendered mankind. . . . On the very brink of chaos, with passions flaming, and armies marching, the voice of Reason has found a way out of the conflict.

It may be safely assumed that these utterances were carefully noted and transmitted to Berlin by the German consul general at Ottawa, Herr Windels; and to the extent that the disordered diplomatic apparatus at the Wilhelmstrasse was capable of bringing them to the attention of the Führer they can only have reinforced his belief that the British Empire was too weak and too craven to oppose his plans for the subjugation of Eastern Europe as a prelude to the destruction of the West. Appeasement, the only foreign policy on which the Commonwealth has ever been in substantial agreement, thus came close to accomplishing its ruin. Offered in the hope of peace, it led it straight to war.

Yet while Mackenzie King had by 1937 become able to support Britain's appeasement of Germany, his earlier fear of centralized control persisted in the realm of defence. All attempts on the part of the United Kingdom to cooperate militarily and industrially with Canada in advance of the outbreak of war were rebuffed. "From 1936 onwards," the official history of the Royal Air Force recalls reproachfully, "Canada, which enjoyed an ideal strategic position and a convenient proximity to the vast industrial resources of the United States, was repeatedly approached [with the request to make facilities available for training of pilots and aircrew]; but the Canadians, largely for domestic reasons, felt unable to accept our proposals."[50] At the Imperial Conference of 1937 "the principal Supply Officers' Committee tried to pilot through . . . an agreement with Canada about wartime supplies of bauxite and aluminium," but failed largely because of Canadian opposition.[51] In the summer of 1938 the Board of Trade entered into negotiations with the Canadian government to make provision in advance of war for adequate supplies of certain strategic materials; but Ottawa being unwilling to assume such commitments, by September 1939 "virtually no preparations had been made for the war-time purchase of raw materials in North America."[52] Munitions fared little better; with the exception of a contract for Bren machine guns, nothing was done by the Canadian government to assist United Kingdom defence officials in their effort to stimulate the manufacture of arms in the overseas Dominions.[53]

It is thus a major irony of Commonwealth history that Canadian influence on British policy was at this stage brought to bear in the worst of all possible ways. In external policy, as Professor Mansergh observes, "what was most of all required was not a greater consensus of Commonwealth opinion but the more vigourous expression of independent and conflicting opinion";[54] in defence policy what was most of all required was a united effort to create a deterrent of imperial power. The Canadian response was to voice with unaccustomed fervor approval of British statecraft while resisting Britain's efforts to improve the Empire's defences. While "no evidence so far published suggests that doubts about the unity of the Commonwealth were a major factor in encouraging German aggression,"[55] a firmer signification of the Commonwealth's will to resist might have given Hitler pause; in any event the opportunity was both too good and too rare to be squandered. Certain it is that a fuller measure of defence preparation would have made his defeat less costly and precarious. The margin of superiority with which Britain faced the Axis in the summer of 1940 remained excruciatingly narrow. Had the RAF failed, for want of aircraft or of pilots, to deflect and defeat the Luftwaffe, would not those responsible for Canadian policy during the prewar years have to share the blame?

STATECRAFT AND UNITY

On January 20, 1937, the Canadian prime minister spoke in confidence to a meeting of his parliamentary supporters. He urged them to reject the views of Mr. Arthur Meighen, the Conservative leader in the Senate, "that the amount in the [defence] estimates was not enough, that we were concerned with the defence of the Empire as a whole; that the first line of our defence was the Empire's boundaries." Equally he urged them to reject the alternative offered by J.S. Woodsworth, the leader of the socialist group in the House of Commons, who, he said, "would do nothing at all" for defence. "The safe policy is the middle course between these two views. . . . Let us explain that policy to our people and let us above all strive at all times to keep Canada *united*."[56] This insistence upon the overriding importance of national unity appears again and again in Mackenzie King's statements on external policy during the years immediately preceding World War II. It served to explain his reluctance to participate in projects or pronouncements likely to deter potential aggressors. To do so, as he remarked in the House of Commons on May 24, 1938, "would bring out deep and in some cases fundamental differences of opinion, [and] would lead to further strain upon the unity of a country already strained by economic depression and other consequences of the last war and its aftermath."[57] Of the wisdom of this policy its architect betrayed neither doubt nor misgiving, and believed it fully vindicated by events. On September 8, 1939, he spoke as follows in the House of Commons:

> I have made it, therefore, the supreme endeavour of my leadership of my party, and my leadership of the government of this country, to let no hasty or premature threat or pronouncement create mistrust and divisions between the different elements that compose the population of our vast dominion, so that when the moment of decision came all should so see the issue itself that our national effort might be marked by unity of purpose, of heart and of endeavour.[58]

It is a matter for debate whether this "supreme endeavour" was not altogether too restricted. Politics is the art of the possible. But how much was possible during the years before the war? More, perhaps, than the prime minister of Canada allowed the nation, or himself, to believe. Never was Mackenzie King more satisfied than when enunciating the dictum that his country was difficult to govern. It was, and is, difficult to govern, in the sense that government is at all times and in all places an exacting and complicated craft. Compared to the ordeals which nearly every twentieth-century nation has undergone — destruction and occupation in war, civil conflict, malevolent and scouring tyrannies — Canadians might consider their situation extraordinarily favourable. Nor were those wearying comparisons between the continent of the undefended frontier and "the continent which cannot run itself" too easily reconciled with plaintive references to exceptional domestic difficulties invoked to justify inaction. So much harping upon the need for unity and the obstacles in its path exaggerated the degree of internal discord, just as repetition of the difficulties encountered in governing the country obscured the fact that it was a good deal less difficult to govern than most. Was it not misleading "to emphasize the precariousness of Canada's export markets, but not the value of her exports; to speak of regional and cultural tensions within but not of the growing sense of unity; of the conflicting pulls of geography and history to which indeed every 'settled' country is subject, but not of the immense strength of Canada's position in the heart of the English-speaking world"?[59] When the history of these years is set out in detail, many of the portents of disunity in the Dominion will be seen to have been greatly overdrawn. For example, it is commonly believed that had the United Kingdom gone to war over Czechoslovakia in September 1938, the CCF (Socialist) party in Canada would have demanded a policy of neutrality. But Professor McNaught has discovered that "correspondence in the Saskatchewan C.C.F. files . . . leaves no doubt that the C.C.F. leaders who defeated the Woodsworth–Farmer neutrality motion in the emergency National Council meeting in [September] 1939 had concluded at least as early as September, 1938, that 'it is already decided that if Britain declares war, Canada must accept the situation.'"[60]

A direct result of reducing Canadian policy to the lowest common denominator of public agreement was the condition of the nation's defences, "utterly inadequate," as the official historian of the Canadian Army observes, "by comparison with the scale of the coming emergency."[61] Another harmful consequence was the effect upon United Kingdom policy. Just as the Canadian government seized with alacrity upon stress and strain in the Dominion's domestic affairs as an excuse for passivity in all external policies save that of appeasement, so the British government fastened upon the difficulties of members of the overseas Commonwealth to justify its own cautious conduct. Disunity in the Dominions plays a major part in the arguments of apologists for Britain's prewar policy. "The fact remains that the Commonwealth Governments were unwilling to go to war on the issue of Czechoslovakia," a former British foreign secretary has written of that period. "Dominion opinion was at the time overwhelmingly against a world war. This opposition was continually in our minds. Time after time we were reminded of it, either by the High Commissioners in London, or by Malcolm MacDonald, the Secretary of State for the Dominions. As early as March 18, 1938, we had been told that South Africa and Canada would not join us in a war to prevent certain Germans from rejoining their fatherland."[62] While "the actual policy Mr. Chamberlain followed in September 1938 owed little or nothing to dominion inspiration,"[63] there can be no doubt that dispiriting responses from the Dominions were used by him to discourage those within the British Cabinet who urged a less cowardly posture in the face of German threats.[64] In Canada's case their effect was the more damaging for their misrepresentation of the real intention of its government. For had war broken out at the time of Munich, the prime minister "was prepared to call Parliament within two weeks and submit to it a policy of Canadian participation. . . . The Cabinet was unanimous."[65]

Over half a century ago the French historian André Siegfried had noted the timidity of Canada's political leaders. "They seem," he wrote, "to stand in fear of great movements of public opinion, and to seek to lull them rather than to encourage them and bring them to political fruition."[66] It will be observed that Canadian political leadership at the time of M. Siegfried's examination was provided by Sir Wilfrid Laurier; and that it was upon Sir Wilfrid Laurier's leadership that Mackenzie King had faithfully modelled his own. "You do Sir Wilfrid Laurier an injustice in regarding him as an opportunist," King had written a friend during the controversy over naval policy in 1909. "He is other than that. . . . We have had no man in Canada who had done as much to reconcile differences of race and creed and to make of the people one nation. If he hesitates to go to the length that some desire, it is because he does not wish disruption and believes that a united progressive Canada is a more valuable asset to the Empire, and will be so through time, than a Canada divided in opinion, or professing an obligation it is not in a position to meet."[67] But hesitation for the sake of unity was not the inevitable response of all Canadian leaders to the tensions of their plural society; there were those to whom its tensions the more insistently demanded bold and imaginative statecraft. "In our Dominion where sections abound," Mr. Arthur Meighen once declared, "a Dominion of races, of classes and of creeds, of many languages and many origins, there are times when no Prime Minister can be true to his trust to the nation he has sworn to serve, save at the temporary sacrifice of the party he is appointed to lead."[68] Faithfully practising this doctrine, Mr. Meighen was compelled to retire from public life. Mackenzie King's very different concept of political leadership, no less faithfully practised and resulting in political longevity only once surpassed in the history of the Commonwealth, must face a very different kind of criticism. It "would have been improved," his official biographer has conceded,

> had he been more venturesome and more willing to offer forthright advice to the nation. King's tactics enabled him to secure and retain office — the indispensable first step. But King, too frequently, stopped right there; and because he was reluctant to press on and try to realize some independent conception of the national interest, his policies slipped into the mire of pure expediency. King was always reluctant to venture into the unknown. He avoided taking risks, and he would postpone action, if by so doing he could ensure a greater degree of safety. He dreaded

unnecessary discussion which might lead to disagreement and even threaten the existing party solidarity on which the whole security of his position rested. He was not prepared to use his own power extensively in an effort to modify the character and scope of those common elements on which he sought to base his policy. He was too willing at times to yield his own judgment when confronted with opposing opinion. He was slow to admit that he had a duty as leader to exert a moderate pressure in the direction in which he believed the country should move.[69]

This verdict is the more severe coming as it does from "one who is in general sympathy with Mr. King and his work and career."[70] There is no part of Mackenzie King's long responsibility for Canadian affairs to which it may with more justice be applied than to his conduct of external policy during that "low dishonest decade" when the world lay "defenceless under the night" and so few free men in power dared to "show an affirming flame."

NOTES

1. The Bennett Papers have been deposited by Lord Beaverbrook, their owner, at the Library of the University of New Brunswick. The King Papers are in the Public Archives of Canada and became the property of the Crown in 1975. The present writer, having assisted in the preparation of the official biography of W.L. Mackenzie King, has had access to this immense collection; he has permission from Mr. King's Literary Executors to quote from the King correspondence to the end of 1923, the period covered by the published first volume of the official biography. [Editors' note: Eayrs was writing this in 1960.]

2. See K.W. McNaught, "Canadian Foreign Policy and the Whig Interpretation: 1936–1939," Canadian Historical Association, Report of the Annual Meeting (1957), 43–54.

3. It is taken from the poem by W.H. Auden, "September 1, 1939": "As the clever hopes expire/Of a low dishonest decade."

4. The Mist Procession: The Autobiography of Lord Vansittart (London, 1958), 529.

5. League of Nations, Official Journal, Special Supplement no. 23, Records of the Fifth Assembly (1924), 222. It is interesting that this most celebrated of Canadian utterances on foreign affairs goes unremarked in the unpublished autobiography of Senator Raoul Dandurand, its author.

6. Canada, House of Commons Debates (1938), 3: 3179.

7. See Colonel C.P. Stacey, Six Years of War: The Army in Canada, Britain and the Pacific (Ottawa, 1955), 10.

8. League of Nations, Records of the First Assembly (1920), 379.

9. Loring C. Christie to Sir Robert Borden, Dec. 12, 1920, Borden Papers (Public Archives of Canada).

10. Arthur Meighen to N.W. Rowell, Jan. 10, 1921, Rowell Papers (PAC).

11. Diary of Sir George Foster, entry for April 7, 1919 (PAC).

12. The Memoirs of Herbert Hoover: The Cabinet and the Presidency, 1920–1933 (New York, 1951), v.

13. League of Nations, Official Journal, Special Supplement no. 23, Records of the Fifth Assembly (1924), 221.

14. "Address Delivered by the Right Hon. W.L. Mackenzie King on November 9th, 1928, at a Banquet of the League of Nations Society in Canada" (Ottawa, 1928), 22.

15. Canada, H. of C. Debates (1936), 4: 3862.

16. League of Nations, Verbatim Record of the Seventeenth Ordinary Session of the Assembly, Sept. 29, 1936, p. 1.

17. Canada, H. of C. Debates (1939), 3: 2419.

18. League of Nations, Official Journal, Special Supplement no. 64, Records of the Ninth Assembly (1928), 60.

19. Mackenzie King to Wallace Nesbitt, Oct. 2, 1922, King Papers.

20. Sir Clifford Sifton, "Immigration," in Addresses Delivered before the Canadian Club of Toronto, 1921–2 (Toronto, 1923), 185–86.

21. Mackenzie King to Aneuran Williams, Feb. 18, 1920, King Papers. A portion of this letter is quoted in R. MacGregor Dawson, William Lyon Mackenzie King: A Political Biography, vol. 1, 1874–1923 (Toronto, 1958), 404.

22. Canada, H. of C. Debates (1928), 2: 1960.

23. T.A. Crerar to J.W. Dafoe, April 17, 1937, Dafoe Papers (PAC).

24. Nicholas Mansergh, Survey of British Commonwealth Affairs: Problems of External Policy, 1931–1939 (London, 1952), 112.

25. Canada, H. of C. Debates (1919, Special Session), 102, 103.

26. Loring C. Christie, "Notes on the League of Nations Meeting of March, 1926," April 14, 1926, Borden Papers.

27. Canada, H. of C. Debates (1923), 4: 4001.

28. Sir Clifford Sifton to J.W. Dafoe, Nov. 19, 1920, Dafoe Papers.

29. Entry for Dec. 11, 1920, Pope Papers (PAC).

30. Dawson, *William Lyon Mackenzie King,* 1: 403.

31. W.A. Riddell, *World Security by Conference* (Toronto, 1947), 140.

32. Grant Dexter to J.W. Dafoe, Dec. 17, 1935, Dafoe Papers.

33. Canada, *H. of C. Debates* (1936), 1: 97, 98.

34. Quoted in F.H. Soward et al., *Canada in World Affairs: The Pre-War Years* (Toronto, 1941), 23.

35. Of whose newspaper it was well remarked that "what the Free Press thinks today, Western Canada will think tomorrow and the intelligent part of Eastern Canada will think a few years hence." Frank H. Underhill, "J.W. Dafoe," *Canadian Forum* 13 (Oct. 1932): 22.

36. Quoted in Henri Saint-Denis, "Fascism in Quebec: A False Alarm," *Revue de l'université d'Ottawa* (Jan. 1939), 4. See also "S," "Embryo Fascism in Quebec," *Foreign Affairs* 16 (April 1938): 454–66.

37. *Le Devoir* (Montreal), July 14, 1938.

38. Canada, *H. of C. Debates* (1937), 1: 910.

39. During the Munich crisis in the fall of 1938, Henderson wrote of "Hitler's own love for peace, dislike of dead Germans and hesitation of risking his regime on a gambler's throw." Quoted in Felix Gilbert, "Two British Ambassadors: Perth and Henderson," in Gordon A. Craig and Felix Gilbert, *The Diplomats, 1919–1939* (Princeton, 1953), 543.

40. Thomas Jones, *A Diary with Letters, 1931–1950* (London, 1954), 218. See also Thomas Jones to Lady Grigg, March 8, 1936, Jones, *A Diary,* 179–81; *The History of "The Times": The 150th Anniversary and Beyond, 1912–1948,* part 2, *1921–1948* (London, 1952), 938; John Evelyn Wrench, *Geoffrey Dawson and Our Times* (London, 1955), 369.

41. Canada, *H. of C. Debates* (1944), 6: 6275.

42. Winston S. Churchill, *The Second World War,* vol. 1, *The Gathering Storm* (London, 1949), 250.

43. Bruce Hutchison, *The Incredible Canadian* (Toronto, 1953), 226.

44. Speech given over the National Network of the Canadian Broadcasting Corporation, July 19, 1937.

45. Frank H. Underhill, "The Close of an Era: Twenty-Five Years of Mr. Mackenzie King," *Canadian Forum* 24 (Sept. 1944): 125.

46. Quoted in Dawson, *William Lyon Mackenzie King,* 1: 474.

47. Imperial Conference, 1937, *Summary of Proceedings,* pp. 14, 16.

48. Mansergh, *Survey . . . : Problems of External Policy,* 89.

49. Canada, *H. of C. Debates* (1938), 3: 3182.

50. Denis Richards, *Royal Air Force, 1939–1945,* vol. 1, *The Fight at Odds* (London, 1953), 72–73.

51. *History of the Second World War,* United Kingdom Civil Series, M.M. Postan, *British War Production* (London, 1952), 89.

52. *History of the Second World War,* United Kingdom Civil Series, J. Hurstfield, *The Control of Raw Materials* (London, 1955), 254.

53. See *History of the Second World War,* United Kingdom Civil Series, H. Duncan Hall, *North American Supply* (London, 1954).

54. Nicholas Mansergh, *Survey of British Commonwealth Affairs: Problems of Wartime Co-operation and Post-War Change, 1939–1952* (London, 1958), 17.

55. Mansergh, *Survey . . . : Problems of External Policy,* 446.

56. Quoted in Stacey, *Six Years of War,* 14.

57. Canada, *H. of C. Debates* (1938), 3: 3184.

58. Canada, *H. of C. Debates* (1939, Special War Session), 1: 25.

59. Mansergh, *Survey . . . : Problems of External Policy,* 111.

60. McNaught, "Canadian Foreign Policy," 54 n. 40.

61. Stacey, *Six Years of War,* 35.

62. Viscount Templewood, *Nine Troubled Years* (London, 1954), 323.

63. Mansergh, *Survey . . . : Problems of External Policy,* 439.

64. See *Old Men Forget: The Autobiography of Duff Cooper* (London, 1954), 239–40.

65. "Back Stage in Ottawa," *Maclean's Magazine* 2 (Nov. 1, 1938).

66. André Siegfried, *The Race Question in Canada* (London, 1907), 142.

67. Mackenzie King to Lord Stanhope, July 23, 1909. Quoted in Dawson, *William Lyon Mackenzie King,* 1: 215.

68. Arthur Meighen, *Unrevised and Unrepented: Debating Speeches and Others* (Toronto, 1949), 319.

69. Dawson, *William Lyon Mackenzie King,* 1: 417–18.

70. Dawson, *William Lyon Mackenzie King,* 1: viii.

Article Twenty-Eight

Staring into the Abyss

Jack Granatstein

'HISTORY REPEATS ITSELF.' That is a popular view of the past, but it is not, I suspect, a view shared by most historians. The differences in personalities, in context, in subtleties and shadings usually combine to persuade historians that the crisis of one decade or century is different in class and kind from that of another. But, sometimes, history really does seem to repeat itself.

In the First World War . . . the United Kingdom's weakened financial condition led Whitehall to pressure Canada to turn to the United States to raise money. At the same time, Britain proved unable or unwilling to take all the food and munitions produced by Canada unless Ottawa picked up a greater share of the costs, and the Canadian government had little choice other than to agree. In an effort, both politically and economically inspired, to keep munitions factories working at full blast in Canada, the Imperial Munitions Board, a Canadian-operated imperial procurement and production agency, actively sought contracts from the U.S. War Department. At the same time, other arms of the Canadian government lobbied in Washington to get their share of scarce raw materials. The net effect of the First World War on Canadian-American relations was to strengthen the links across the border and to increase the number and complexity of the ties of economics, politics, and sentiment that bound the two North American nations together. The defeat of reciprocity in the 1911 election, therefore, seemed only a temporary check, one virtually nullified by the greater necessity of wartime integration and cooperation.

It should have been no surprise, then, that Canada entered the 1920s with Conservative Prime Minister Arthur Meighen urging Britain to seek an accommodation with the United States and not to renew the Angle-Japanese Alliance.[1] Nor was it a surprise that Canada welcomed more investment from the United States while, despite repeated efforts by the Liberal governments of Mackenzie King to enhance trade with the United Kingdom, its commerce with its neighbour continued to increase.[2] The Great Depression and the massive increases in the American tariff put in place by a protectionist Congress and then matched by Canadian governments, however, temporarily cut into Canadian-American trade.

While these restrictions led many Canadians to look overseas with renewed imperial fervour, some Britons nonetheless feared for Canada's survival as a British nation in the face of the power of the United States. One example of the first tendency was Harry Stevens, soon to be minister of trade and commerce in R.B. Bennett's government, who told the voters in 1930 that 'My ambition for Canada is that she may become a unit of the Empire and concerned not with a few petty tariff items, but with all the great problems confronting the Home Government.' No worse fate could have befallen Canadians! In contrast, Leo Amery, the dominions secretary in 1928, returned from a trip to Canada worried that 'the din and glare of the great American orchestra' might drown out Canada. His hopes were bolstered, however, by the conviction that there was 'no deeper fundamental instinct of the Canadian national character than dislike of the United States as belonging to an inferior political civilisation.'[3] For their part, officials of the United States government, as Peter Kasurak has noted, began 'from

Source: "Staring in the Abyss" from J.L. Granatstein, *How Britain's Weakness Forced Canada into the Arms of the United States*, University of Toronto Press Inc., 1989. © J.L. Granatstein 1989. Reprinted with permission of the publisher.

a single point of view in the area of Canadian affairs — fear that Britain was forging its Empire into an international colossus which would dominate world trade.'[4] To Washington, that fear seemed to be realized after the Ottawa Conference of 1932.[5]

But not even the Imperial Economic Conference and the imperial preferences agreed on at Ottawa could truly reverse the historic trend towards North American continentalism that had accelerated during the Great War. The two 'hermit kingdoms,' to use Charles Stacey's phrase uttered from this platform a dozen years ago,[6] had a great deal in common in an era when British trade as a percentage of world trade continued its decline and Britain's overall military power ebbed. Mackenzie King had begun the transformation of the empire into the Commonwealth during the Chanak affair of 1922 and at the Imperial Conference of 1923, where 'the decisive nature of the English defeat at Mackenzie King's hands' was nothing less than a 'surrender, which changed the course of the history of the empire.'[7] Those apocalyptic phrases were the considered judgment of Correlli Barnett, 'the Jeremiah of British historians,' or so Noel Annan has recently called him.[8] They sound very similar in tone to the words of Donald Creighton, the Jeremiah of Canadian historians, who wrote that King, 'a stocky barrel-like figure, with an audible wheeze when in full voice,' was no 'bulky St. George confronting a slavering imperial dragon.' He was 'a citizen of North America . . . determined to destroy' the Commonwealth.[9]

When Mackenzie King came back to power in the middle of the Great Depression in 1935, the Ottawa agreements had demonstrably not restored Canada's economic health. Prime Minister Bennett had seemingly recognized the failure of the imperial initiative by launching his own somewhat desultory efforts to strike a trade agreement with Washington, but his attempt at an accommodation with the United States could not come to fruition before the voters eagerly dispensed with the Tory government's services.[10] It fell to the new prime minister, choosing what he described to the United States minister in Canada as 'the American road,' to negotiate that trade agreement with the Roosevelt administration.[11] Mackenzie King reinforced it with another trade pact with the United States three years later.[12] Simultaneously, King and his advisers in the Department of External Affairs looked with dismay at the wide-ranging rivalry between London and Washington, most pronounced in the Pacific where the two English-speaking powers jostled for economic and political dominance with each other and an aggressive Japan. Conflict between Canada's mother country and its nearest neighbour held out only the prospect of terrible divisiveness in Canada.[13] Nonetheless, the prime minister gladly accepted and immediately reciprocated President Franklin Roosevelt's assurances, delivered at Queen's University in Kingston on 18 August 1939, 'that the people of the United States will not stand idly by' if Canada were ever threatened.[14] That guarantee had to be called upon just two years later.

By 1939, as the Nazis prepared to plunge Europe into the war that was to ensure America's half century of world economic hegemony, U.S. companies and investors and the American market had already established their pre-eminence in Canada. The United States provided 60 per cent of the foreign capital invested in Canada while British sources put up only 36 per cent. In 1914 the figures had been 23 and 72 per cent, respectively. In terms of Canadian exports, shipments to the United States in 1939 exceeded those to Britain by 20 per cent; in 1914 exports to Britain had been 10 per cent higher than those to the United States. Similarly, in 1914 Canada had imported three times as much from the United States as from the United Kingdom; in 1939 Canada imported four times as much.[15] The years of the Great War had provided the impetus for Canada's shift from the British to the American economic sphere.

During the Second World War, the events of the Great War were repeated with a stunning similarity. To be sure, different men from different political parties were in charge in Canada. Mackenzie King, that most unadmired of Canadian leaders, was at the helm in Ottawa, and his attitudes and prejudices were certainly far different from those of Sir Robert Borden.

Ramsay Cook predicted almost two decades ago that King was certain to become the subject of a book of readings for students under the title 'Mackenzie King: Hero or Fink?' Cook knew that the fink side of the debate would be easy to document. He suggested that King had become the central figure in the Canadian mythology, the most convenient one of all, because he was the 'cause of all our failings,' including the decline and fall of the British Empire in Canada.[16] Cook was certainly correct in assessing the little man's place, and few have yet come forward to argue that Mackenzie King was a great Canadian hero. Charles Stacey, in the last words of his Joanne Goodman lectures in 1976, however, did say — and I expect he was only half-jesting — that he would 'not be altogether surprised if he turned up, one of these days, as the patron saint of the new nationalism.'[17]

Still, King is difficult to elevate to sainthood. Even (or especially) those who observed or worked intimately with him had scant admiration for him. Tom Blacklock, a Press Gallery member in the 1920s, complained that King was 'such a pompous ass that an orang-outang that would flatter him could choose its own reward.'[18] Leonard Brockington wrote speeches for King for a time during the early years of the Second World War, and when he quit in exasperation he told a friend that he was 'sick and tired of being mid-wife to an intellectual virgin.'[19] Senator Norman Lambert ran elections for the Liberal leader, and Mackenzie King gratefully elevated him to the Upper Chamber. Nonetheless, Lambert told Grant Dexter of the *Winnipeg Fire Press* that 'he simply can't stand the worm at close quarters — bad breath, a fetid, unhealthy, sinister atmosphere like living close to some filthy object . . . But,' the senator added, 'get off a piece and he looks better and better.'[20]

That last comment on Mackenzie King I have always thought the nearly definitive one. Up close, there was little that was admirable about the Liberal leader, much that was slippery and sleazy. But acquire some distance, get off a piece, as Lambert said, and the dumpy little laird of Kingsmere — and Canada — began to look not unlike a giant. To bring us back to Earth, I might point out that the fine Canadian novelist Hugh Hood has his main character in *The Swing in the Garden* note, 'I think always of W.C. Fields when I think of Mackenzie King.'[21] That may be *the* definitive description.

I have no intention of trying to paint Mackenzie King as a superhero here, though, despite years of reading Donald Creighton and W.L. Morton, I cannot yet bring myself to see him as a filthy object or even as a fink. For me, the crucial factor in assessing the common charge that Mackenzie King sold us out to the Americans is that the prime minister during the Second World War faced similar, but greater, problems to those Sir Robert Borden had had to confront a quarter century before. But though he had more resources at his disposal than his predecessor in the Prime Minister's office, King had no greater freedom of action when British military and economic weakness forced his country into grave difficulties. When it came to directing the weak corner of the North Atlantic Triangle in its efforts to stay safe and secure in a world suddenly unstable, King, much like Borden before him, had to turn to the United States for assistance.

One major factor was different in the Second World War. In the Great War, Britain and France lost battles but they did not suffer catastrophic defeats that placed their survival as nation-states at stake. In May and June 1940, of course, Hitler's astonishingly effective armies defeated Britain and France in the Low Countries and in France, the French capitulated, and the British Army, without equipment, found its way home thanks only to a miracle at Dunkirk.

For Canada in that terrible summer of defeat and despair, the changes in the military balance of power were catastrophic. The country had gone to war with the idea that it could fight as a junior partner with 'limited liability.' The government had hoped that its war effort could be small, balanced, and relatively cheap, and Quebec and the country had been promised that there would be no conscription for overseas service. Now, the planning of late 1939 had to be scrapped. Canada, with its population of eleven million and suddenly Britain's ranking ally, was in the war to the utmost — except for conscription, which was still politically unacceptable. Moreover, a huge proportion of this country's under-equipped and partially trained air, army, and naval forces was already in the United Kingdom, and if — or when — Britain fell they were certain to be completely lost. The Royal Navy had its hands full in trying to protect home waters and block the expected Nazi invasion. The aircraft necessary to operate the centrepiece of the Canadian war effort, the British Commonwealth Air Training Plan, had been scheduled to come from Great Britain, but now would not arrive. If Britain fell and, especially, if the Royal Navy passed into German hands, Canada was likely to be subject to Nazi attack.[22] Britain's military weakness in July and August 1940 was exposed for all to see; so too was Canada's.[23]

The military weakness of the United States was also apparent, but there can be no doubt that President Franklin Roosevelt's country was the only hope of the Allies — and of Canada. Many in Canada recognized this truth in the days after Dunkirk, and they realized the new obligations this would force on the dominion. Donald Creighton, writing years later, noted that for many Canadians — and he had his despised colleague Frank Underhill in mind — the war's course 'hastened the growth' of Canada's 'new North American nationality by proving that . . . Great Britain . . . could no longer act as Canada's main defence against danger from abroad.'[24]

At the time, the bureaucratic response to the new state of affairs came from Hugh Keenleyside of the Department of External Affairs, who set out the fullest statement of the likely Canadian situation as France surrendered to Hitler. It was improbable, he wrote, that the United States would protect Canada without 'demanding a measure of active cooperation in return. It is a reasonable expectation that the United States will expect, and if necessary demand, Canadian assistance in the defence of this continent and this Hemisphere.' Canada, he noted, would feel some obligation to participate; 'thus the negotiation of a specific offensive-defensive alliance is likely to become inevitable.'[25]

President Roosevelt himself was thinking along these lines. In August, Loring Christie, the Canadian minister in Washington, reported to Mackenzie King that the president 'had been thinking of proposing to you to send to Ottawa 3 staff officers . . . to discuss defence problems . . . He had in mind their surveying [the] situation from [the] Bay of Fundy around to the Gulf of St. Lawrence. They might explore [the] question of base facilities for United States use.'[26] But on 16 August Roosevelt asked King to meet him at Ogdensburg, NY, the next day to discuss 'the matter of [the] mutual defence of our coasts on the Atlantic.'[27]

What the president wanted was the creation of a Permanent Joint Board on Defence with equal representation from each country and a mandate limited to the study of common defence problems and the making of recommendations to both governments on how to resolve them. Delighted at the prospect of forging a military alliance with the United States, King queried only Roosevelt's desire that the board be 'permanent.' 'I said I was not questioning the wisdom of it,' King noted, 'but was anxious to get what he had in mind.' According to King's diary, Roosevelt replied that he wanted 'to help secure the continent for the future.'[28] The Canadian leader sometimes suffered from 'the idea,' in the superb Australian novelist Thomas Keneally's phrase, 'that the only empire you need to suspect is the British.'[29] Mackenzie King probably ought to have asked whose empire and whose future, but in August 1940 that question was virtually impossible even to raise — when the fear was that it might be Adolf Hitler's empire and Germany's future if no action were taken.

The decision to create the PJBD was an important one. The board sprang into existence within two weeks and began surveying defences on both the Atlantic and the Pacific coasts. A Joint Canadian-United States Basic Defence Plan, produced by the board's military members, aimed to meet the situation that would arise if Britain were overrun. In that event, strategic control of Canadian forces was to pass to the United States. A second plan, produced in the spring of 1941 and called ABC-22, looked at Canadian-American cooperation in a war in which the United States was actively engaged on the side of the Allies. The Americans again sought strategic control of Canadian forces and to integrate the Canadian east and west coast regions directly into their military commands. It was one thing to agree to American military direction in a war that saw North America standing virtually alone; it was another thing entirely in a war where Britain remained unoccupied and the United States was a partner. 'The American officers,' to use Keneally again, 'listened . . . with that omnivorous American politeness . . . we poor hayseeds would come to know so well and mistrust, perhaps, not enough.'[30] Nonetheless, Canada refused to accept Washington's aims for ABC-22 and won its point, thereby demonstrating that Mackenzie King's government could and would fight for its freedom of action.[31] Whether such independence could have survived a German or Japanese invasion happily never had to be tested.

The significance of the PJBD in its context of August 1940 was that a still-neutral United States had struck an alliance with Canada, a belligerent power. 'That had to be seen as a gain for Britain — and for Canada, too. Important as that was, for the war, the true meaning of the Ogdensburg meeting was that it marked Canada's definitive move from the British military sphere to the American. The British had lost whatever capacity they might have had to defend Canada, and in August 1940 their ability even to defend the British Isles successfully was very much in doubt.[32] In the circumstances, Canada had no choice at all. Canada had to seek help where help was to be found, and that meant Washington.

Few people truly realized the significance of the Permanent Joint Board on Defence and the Ogdensburg Agreement that had created it in the summer of 1940. Some Conservatives grumbled at Mackenzie King's actions, former Prime Minister Arthur Meighen being the most caustic. He had noted that 'I lost my breakfast when I read the account this morning and gazed on the disgusting picture of these potentates'— that is, King and Roosevelt —'posing like monkeys in the very middle of the blackest crisis of this Empire.'[33] Most Tories and almost all the Canadian press showed more sense.[34]

The one critic who shook Mackenzie King, however, was Winston Churchill. The new British prime minister, in office only since 10 May 1940, had replied to King's telegram on the Ogdensburg meeting by stating 'there may be two opinions on some of the points mentioned. Supposing Mr. Hitler cannot invade us . . . all these transactions will be judged in a mood different to that prevailing while the issue still hangs in the balance.'[35] Churchill, disgustedly seeing Canada scurrying for shelter under the eagle's wing, evidently realized that a major shift had occurred. What he would have had Canada do, what he would have done differently had he been Canadian prime minister, was never stated. Certainly he failed to recognize that with its security now guaranteed by the United States, Canada could send every man and weapon possible to defend Britain, something it dutifully and willingly did.

As for me, no matter how often I try to appraise the situation, I cannot see any other option for Mackenzie King. The issue potentially was the survival of the Canadian nation in face of an apparently defeated Great Britain and a victorious Nazi Germany. King did what he had to do to secure Canada's security. The reason Mackenzie King had to strike his arrangement with Roosevelt was the military weakness of Great Britain in the summer of 1940.[36]

The immediate result of the Ogdensburg Agreement was wholly beneficial to Canada and Canadian interests. But we can see now that the long-term implications included the construction of major American installations and the presence in substantial numbers of American troops in the Canadian Northwest from 1942,[37] the 1947 military agreement with the United States that continued joint defence cooperation, the North American Air Defence Agreement of 1957–8, and eventually even Cruise missile testing and the possibility of Star Wars installations in the Canadian North.

Many Canadians may be less than happy with the way matters turned out. In his *Lament for a Nation*, George Grant wrote:

> In 1940, it was necessary for Canada to throw in her lot with continental defence. The whole of Eurasia might have fallen into the hands of Germany and Japan. The British Empire was collapsing once and for all as an international force. Canada and the United States of America had to be unequivocally united for the defence of this hemisphere. But it is surprising how little the politicians and officials seem to have realized that this new situation would have to be manipulated with great wisdom if any Canadian independence was to survive. Perhaps nothing could have been done; perhaps the collapse of nineteenth-century Europe automatically entailed the collapse of Canada. Nonetheless, it is extraordinary that King and his associates in External Affairs did not seem to recognize the perilous situation that the new circumstances entailed. In all eras, wise politicians have to play a balancing game. How little the American alliance was balanced by any defence of national independence![38]

Much of Grant's assessment is correct. Certainly, Canada had no choice in August 1940 in the situation in which it found itself. But to me, Mackenzie King's actions in August 1940 were an attempt to protect Canadian independence — and ensure Canada's survival — in a world that had been turned upside down in a few months by the defeat of Britain and France. Grant, writing a quarter century after the event, does not say what King might have done after Ogdensburg to achieve a balance to the American alliance. Nor did Churchill in 1940. In the remainder of this essay, I will try to show how King successfully struggled to preserve at least a measure of financial independence for Canada.

Those who believe, like George Grant and Donald Creighton, that the Ogdensburg Agreement and its aftermath were a virtual sell-out to the United States have an obligation to offer an alternative vision. If there was 'a forked road' in August 1940 and if Canada went in the wrong direction, where might the other road have led? What should Mackenzie King and his government have done that they did not do? I await the response.

The Ogdensburg Agreement had secured Canada's physical defences, but it had done nothing to resolve the country's economic difficulties. As in the Great War, the problem came about because Canada was caught between a strong United States and its desire to help an economically weak Great Britain. Indeed, Britain was weak. The ambassador in Washington, Lord Lothian, summed it up when he told a group of reporters: 'Boys, Britain's broke. It's your money we want.'[39] It was soon to be Canada's money that London wanted too.

Britain had begun the war in 1939 convinced that purchases had to be switched away from North America to conserve scarce dollar exchange. That laudable goal threatened Canadian tobacco, fruit, and wheat exports and provoked extraordinary outrage in Ottawa and threats that such a policy might hurt what Mackenzie King delicately called 'our ability to render assistance.' Similarly, British munitions orders in the Phoney War months were less than expected; that too angered the King government. But the same German victories that forced Canada to seek assistance to the south also obliged London to look to Canada for more — more money, more food, more munitions, more of everything.[40]

By February 1941, therefore, the Department of Finance in Ottawa estimated that the British deficit with Canada was $795 million, an amount that had been covered by transfers of gold, debt repatriation, and a large sterling accumulation in London.[41] Ottawa also predicted that war expenditures for the year would amount to $1.4 billion and that $433 million was needed for civil expenditure. A further $400 million would be required to repatriate additional Canadian securities held in Britain, in effect a way of giving Britain additional Canadian dollars with which to pay for the goods it bought in Canada. At the same time, the mandarins in Finance estimated that the provincial and municipal governments would spend

$575 million for a total governmental expenditure of almost half Canada's Gross National Income.[42] Could the country function, they asked, if half of all production were devoted to government operations?

Historically, Canada's economic position had depended on the maintenance of a 'bilateral unbalance within a balanced "North Atlantic Triangle."'[43] That meant, in effect, that our chronic trade deficit with the United States was covered by a surplus with Britain. Pounds earned in London were readily converted to American dollars, and thus the bills could be paid. But now sterling was inconvertible, and as Canada built up large balances in London, these could no longer be used to cover the trade deficit with the United States.

Compounding the problem was that as Canada strained to produce greater quantities of war material and food for Britain, more components and raw materials had to be imported from the United States. Every time, for example, that a truck, built in Canada by General Motors or Ford, went to Britain, it contained an imported engine, specialty steels, and a variety of parts brought in from south of the border. Almost a third of the value of a tank, ship, or artillery piece had to be imported. The result was a classic squeeze. Canadian goods went to Great Britain where the British could pay for them only in sterling, which was of little use to Canada outside the British Isles (though we could buy New Zealand lamb or Malayan tin, for example, with it). In effect, Canada was financing the British trade deficit. But at the same time and as a result of war production for Britain, Canadian imports from the United States were expanding rapidly, far more so than exports to the United States. The result was a huge trade deficit with the United States, one that grew worse the more Canada tried to help Britain. In April 1941 Ottawa's estimates of the deficit for that fiscal year were $478 million; by June, officials argued that imports from the United States had risen by $400 million a year while exports to the south had increased by only half that sum.[44]

Canada had been trying to grapple with this problem for some time. Efforts had been made since September 1939 to control foreign exchange, to promote Canada as a tourist mecca for Americans ('Ski in a country at war,' the advertisements could have said), and by devaluing the dollar to 90 cents U.S. to restrict imports from and encourage export sales to the United States. Each measure had some positive results, but together they amounted to very little against the flood of components pouring over the border for an expanding war industry. Soon, Ottawa slapped stringent controls on the U.S. dollars Canadian travellers could acquire, and a wide range of import prohibitions were put in place in December 1940 on unnecessary imports. Those measures, strong enough to anger the American government and American exporters, also failed completely to reverse the steady growth in the deficit with the United States.[45]

What else remained? A loan from the United States government? O.D. Skelton, the undersecretary of state for external affairs until his death in January 1941, told Pierrepont Moffat, the very able American minister in Canada, that 'it would be disastrous to face a future of making heavy interest payments to the United States year after year in perpetuity, or alternatively having a war debt controversy.'[46] Canada was physically too close to the United States to owe debt directly to Washington, or so Skelton and his colleagues in the Ottawa mandarinate believed. What then? Could Canadian investments in the United States, estimated at $275 million to $1 billion in worth, be sold off to raise American dollars? They could, but those investments cushioned Canada from the strain of her foreign indebtedness, and there were obvious political problems in forcing private investors to sell their holdings at wartime fire-sale prices.[47] That was not a feasible route for the Mackenzie King government.

At this point, the situation altered dramatically. The United States Congress accepted President Roosevelt's proposal for Lend-Lease, a scheme to permit the United States to give the Allies war materiel effectively free of monetary cost, though there were political costs of which the British were all too aware.[48] The initial appropriation accompanying the bill was

$7 billion. This was, as Churchill called it, 'the most unsordid act,' an extraordinarily generous step by the still-neutral United States. But Lend-Lease posed terrible problems for Ottawa. First, the Canadian government did not want to take charity from the United States—'the psychological risk,' two historians noted, 'of becoming a pensioner of the United States was too great.'[49] Second, if Britain could get war materiel from the United States free of charge, what was to happen to the orders it had placed in Canada and for which it had to pay, even if only with inconvertible sterling? C.D. Howe, presiding over Canada's war production as the minister of munitions and supply, told the Cabinet War Committee that he was 'gravely concerned' that those orders might be shifted to the United States.[50] If that happened, what would the impact be on Canada's war employment and wartime prosperity? It was the spring of 1917 all over again, and history repeated itself.

The British characteristically and quickly saw the advantages offered by the situation and began to press Canada. Although junior ministers in Churchill's cabinet bemoaned what they saw as Canada's accelerating drift out of the empire,[51] the hardheaded officials at the Treasury knew what they wanted. Cut purchases of non-essential goods in the United States, Ottawa was told. Accept Lend-Lease. Sell off Canadian securities held in the United States. Such a regimen meant higher taxes and inflation for the Canadians, the British knew, but as the Treasury officials said, 'It is as much in their interests as in ours to act along these lines, seeing that our only alternative, if we are unable to pay for our orders in Canada, is to place them instead in the United States in cases in which we should be able to obtain the goods under the "Lease and Lend" Act.'[52]

Thus Canada's problem. Some way had to be found to keep the British orders, so essential for wartime prosperity, without selling the country lock, stock, and barrel to the United States. Though the Liberal government faced no immediate election, as had Borden in 1917 in similar circumstances, the retention of prosperity was every bit as much a political necessity. At the same time, and again the parallel with Sir Thomas White's refusal to borrow from the U.S. government is clear, the King government was adamant in its refusal to take Lend-Lease. That was little better than a loan and, while relations with Franklin Roosevelt's Washington were very good, no one wanted to be quite so indebted to the great nation with which Canada shared the continent. The Americans, as Clifford Clark, deputy minister of finance, noted fearfully, might later drive a very hard bargain on tariffs.[53] Nonetheless, Canada's trade with the United States somehow had to be brought into balance.

The ideal solution, as Canadian officials came to realize in the spring of 1941, was an arrangement that would see the United States increase its purchases in Canada and, in addition, supply the components and raw materials Canada needed to produce munitions for the United Kingdom. Those components could be charged to Britain's Lend-Lease account, a clever device that could let Canada keep its war economy going at full blast without bankrupting itself in the process. In the meantime, desperate to ensure the continuation of orders in Canada, Ottawa agreed to finance the British deficit with Canada.[54] That was again a repetition of the events of 1917. Though there is no sign in the files that anyone realized this parallel, so too was the Canadian proposal to the United States.

The Hyde Park Declaration, signed by Mackenzie King and Franklin Roosevelt on 'a grand Sunday' in April, put the seal on the Canadian proposal. The United States agreed to spend $200–300 million more in Canada, largely for raw materials and aluminum. 'Why not buy from Canada as much as Canada is buying from the United States,' Mackenzie King said he had told the president,'—just balance the accounts. Roosevelt thought this was a swell idea.[55] In addition, the president agreed that Britain's Lend-Lease account could be charged with the materials and components Canada needed to produce munitions for export.[56] That too dealt the trade deficit a mighty blow.

The declaration signed at Hyde Park was a splendid achievement for Canada. Howe told Mackenzie King that he was 'the greatest negotiator the country had or something about being the world's best negotiator,' the prime minister recorded.[57] Howe soon created War Supplies Limited, a crown corporation with E.P. Taylor as its head, to sell Canadian-manufactured war equipment and raw materials in the United States.[58]

The Hyde Park Declaration allowed Canada to do its utmost for Britain without fear of financial collapse. Most important, King had won Roosevelt's agreement without having to give up anything tangible — in the short-run. Unlike Great Britain, Canada was not obliged to sell off its investments prior to receiving U.S. aid; nor was Canada to be required to take Lend-Lease, both measures that the government sought to avoid.[59] Knowing that the desperate plight of the British had forced him to seek assistance for Canada from the United States, Mackenzie King had secured that help on the very best terms. For his part, Roosevelt could agree to King's proposals (incidentally, entirely on his own without any consultation with Congress or the State Department) because they cost the United States almost nothing, because he was friendly to Canada, and because he considered that his country's long-term interests would be best served by having an amicable and prosperous Canada on his northern border, a nation tightly linked to the United States. Undoubtedly, Roosevelt was correct. He served his country's interests well.

In retrospect, however, we can see that the inextricable linkages created or strengthened by the Second World War were the key long-term results of the 1941 agreement. The Hyde Park Declaration effectively wiped out the border for war purposes, allowing raw materials to pour south while munitions components came north. To help the war effort, to produce the goods for a desperate Great Britain, Mackenzie King's Canada tied itself to the United States for the war's duration. There is no point in complaining about this almost a half century later. The Hyde Park Declaration was one of many actions that were necessary to win the war against Hitler, and everything done to further that end was proper and right. But neither is there any point in blinking at the facts. Canada tied itself to the United States in 1941, just as it had done in 1917, because Britain was economically weak. That weakness forced Canada to look to Washington for assistance, and the Americans provided it, freely and willingly. It served Washington's interests; it served Canada's immediate interests; above all, it served the cause of victory.

The short-term results of the Hyde Park Declaration were much as the Canadian government had hoped. American purchases in Canada rose rapidly, and Canada's dollar shortage came to an end in 1942; indeed, the next year controls had to be put in place to prevent Canada's holdings of U.S. dollars from growing too large. The wartime prosperity that Hyde Park solidified was such that in 1942 Canada could offer Great Britain a gift of $1 billion, and the next year Canada created a Mutual Aid program that eventually gave Britain an additional $2 billion in munitions and foodstuffs. The total of Canadian aid to Great Britain during the war was $3.468 billion,[60]— and a billion then was really worth a billion. That was help to a valued ally and friend, of course, just as much as it was an investment in continued high employment at home. As an official in the Dominions Office in London noted, 'Per head of population the Canadian gifts will cost Canada about five times what lend lease costs the United States. Canada's income tax is already as high as ours; it may have to go higher . . . Canada is devoting as large a proportion of her national income to defence expenditure as any other country; in no other country is the proportion of defence expenditure which is given away in the form of free supplies anywhere near so high as in Canada.'[61] The war had cost Canada about $18 billion, and almost one-fifth of that staggering total was given to Britain in the form of gifts. That Canada could offer such assistance freely was the best proof possible that Mackenzie King's policy in 1941 had been correct and successful.

Still, there can be no doubt that the Hyde Park Declaration reinforced the trends that had begun to take form during the Great War. Some of those were psychological. Two bureaucrats who dealt with the United States regularly during the War had gushed fellowship in an article they published in the *Canadian Journal of Economics and Political Science* at the end of the war. 'There has been the open exchange of confidence between the Americans and Canadians, the warm welcome, the freedom from formality, the plain speaking and the all-pervading friendship,' Sydney Pierce and A.F.W. Plumptre wrote. 'This was the result of 'our common background of language and culture, and to the close trade and industrial relationship: in part it is due to the fact that our approach to problems is similar.'[62] That was all true, too.

Other trends were financial and commercial. By 1945 American investment had risen to 70 per cent of the total foreign capital invested in Canada. Exports to the United States were more than three times what they had been in 1939 and were 25 per cent greater than war-swollen Canadian exports to Britain. Imports from the United States were now ten times those from Britain.[63] The war undoubtedly had distorted Canada's trade figures, but the direction was clear and it would be confirmed by the events of the reconstruction period.

By 1945 Canada was part and parcel of the continental economy. It was a two-way North American street now, and the North Atlantic Triangle, if it still existed at all, was a casualty of the world wars. Despite this . . . the Canadian government tried desperately, if unsuccessfully, to restore the traditional balance in the postwar years.

NOTES

1. See Philip Wigley, *Canada and the Transition to Commonwealth: British-Canadian Relations 1917–1926* (Cambridge 1977), 129ff. D.C. Watt erroneously saw 'geographical or racialist factors' responsible for 'the pro-American orientation' of Canadian foreign policy, and he argued that British actions here were taken 'for the sake of keeping Canada in the Empire.' *Succeeding John Bull: America in Britain's Place 1900–1975.* (Cambridge 1984), 50, 52

2. King expressed strong support for the effort to widen imperial preferences at the Imperial Economic Conference of 1923. See R.M. Dawson, *William Lyon Mackenzie King*, vol. 1: *A Political Biography 1874–1923* (Toronto 1958), 469ff. The 1930 Liberal budget lowered the duties on 270 British goods exported to Canada and threatened countervailing duties against the United States. See H.B. Neatby, *William Lyon Mackenzie King*, vol. II: *The Lonely Heights* (Toronto 1963), 323–4. On reaction to U.S. investment in this period and after see Peter Kresl, 'Before the Deluge: Canadians on Foreign Ownership, 1920–1955,' *American Review of Canadian Studies* 6 (spring 1976), 86ff.

3. Quoted in Norman Hillmer, 'Personalities and Problems in Anglo-Canadian Economic Relations between the Two World Wars,' *Bulletin of Canadian Studies* 3 (June 1979), 5, 8

4. Peter Kasurak, 'American Foreign Policy Officials and Canada, 1927–1941: A Look Through Bureaucratic Glasses,' *International Journal* 32 (summer 1977), 548

5. The best study of the Ottawa Conference, including its origins and aftermath, is in Ian Drummond, *Imperial Economic Policy 1917–1939* (London 1974), chap. 5ff.

6. C.P. Stacey, *Mackenzie King and the North Atlantic Triangle* (Toronto 1976), chap. 2

7. Correlli Barnett, *The Collapse of British Power* (London 1972), 195. Barnett's index reference under Mackenzie King refers to this episode as 'destroys imperial alliance.' Stacey's judgment is more sensible and accurate: King 'challenged this idea of a common foreign policy and, essentially, destroyed it.' Stacey, *Mackenzie King*, 33

8. 'Gentlemen vs Players,' *New York Review of Books* (29 Sept, 1988), 63

9. Donald Creighton, "The Decline and Fall of the Empire of the St. Lawrence,' *Historical Papers* 1969, 21

10. Within a year of giving up the Conservative party leadership, Bennett left Canada to live in England. 'It's grand to be going home,' the New Brunswick-born Bennett said as he left for the mother country. That may have been the most revealing comment ever made about Canadian Conservatism prior to the Second World War. Bennett soon violated Canadian law by accepting a peerage.

11. F.D. Roosevelt Library, Roosevelt Papers, PSF, box 33, Armour to Phillips, 22 Oct. 1935

12. On the decline in British trade see Paul Kennedy, *The Rise and Fall of the Great Powers* (Toronto 1987), 316. On the Canadian-American trade agreements see J.L. Granatstein, *A A Man of Influence* (Ottawa 1981), chap. 3, and R.N. Kottman, *Reciprocity and the North Atlantic Triangle, 1932–1938* (Ithaca 1968).

13. This is the subject of Gregory Johnson's York University doctoral dissertation in progress on the relations of Canada, the United States, and the United Kingdom in the Pacific from 1935 to 1950.

14. R.F. Swanson, *Canadian-American Summit Diplomacy, 1923–1973* (Toronto 1975), 52ff. According to D.C. Watt, Mackenzie King was 'yet another channel by which disguised isolationist ideas could be fed to the president.' *Succeeding John Bull*, 78

15. M.C. Urquhart and K.A.H. Buckley, eds., *Historical Statistics of Canada* (Toronto 1965), F345–56: F.H. Leacy, ed., *Historical Statistics of Canada* (Ottawa 1983), G188–202. I have used 1939 data, though Canada's trade with the United States was higher then than throughout the rest of the decade since that was the first year that showed the impact of the 1938 trade agreement. In other words, had the Second World War not distorted trade patterns, the 1939 trends would likely have continued.

16. *Globe Magazine*, 15 Aug. 1970, quoted in Norman Hillmer, "'The Outstanding Imperialist': Mackenzie King and the British,' Part 1 of *Britain and Canada in the Age of Mackenzie King*, Canada House Lecture Series No 4 [1979], 3–4

17. Stacey, *Mackenzie King*, 68

18. National Archives of Canada (NA), Robert Borden Papers, Note by Loring Christie, nd, f 148398

19. L.L.L. Golden interview, 3 Oct. 1965

20. NA, John W. Dafoe Papers, Grant Dexter to Dafoe, 18 April 1941

21. Hugh Hood, *The Swing in the Garden* (Toronto 1975), 165

22. The fate of the Royal Navy naturally concerned the United States and involved Mackenzie King in an excruciating role between Churchill and Roosevelt. See David Reynolds, *The Creation of the Anglo-American Alliance 1937–1941* (Chapel Hill, NC 1982), 115ff, for an American historian's view.

23. Barnett nonetheless argues that the presence of a Canadian corps in England did not make up for the dispatch of British troops to the Middle and Far East. 'The nations of the empire were true "daughters" of the Mother Country in that at no time during the war did their contributions defray the cost of their own strategic keep.' Barnett, *Collapse*, 586. In his later book, *The Audit of War* (London 1986), 3, he adds that the empire produced only 10 per cent of the munitions of war supplied to British and imperial forces. So much for Canada's unstinted contribution to the war.

24. D.G. Creighton, 'The Ogdensburg Agreement and F.H. Underhill,' in C. Berger and R. Cook, eds., *The West and the Nation* (Toronto 1976), 303

25. NA, Department of External Affairs Records (EAR), vol. 781, file 394, 'An Outline Synopsis,' 17 June 1940

26. NA, W.L.M. King Papers, Black Binders, vol. 19, Christie to King, 15 Aug. 1940. Reynolds, *Creation*, 118, describes FDR'S request for the Ogdensburg meeting as being necessary to formulate 'contingency plans in case Britain lost control of the North Atlantic.' See also Reynolds, *Creation*, 132, 183.

27. J.W. Pickersgill, ed., *The Mackenzie King Record*, vol. 1: 1939–44 (Toronto 1960), 130–1

28. Ibid., 134

29. Thomas Keneally, *The Cut-Rate Kingdom* (London 1984), 125. This novel of Australia's experience with, among other things, the United States in the Second World War has some useful and suggestive parallels for the Canadian case.

30. Ibid., 14

31. J.L. Granatstein, *Canada's War: The Politics of the Mackenzie King Government, 1939–45* (Toronto 1975), 131–2

32. Gerard S. Vano has suggested that there had been a reversal of military obligation within the empire by this period. No longer was Canada under the British military shield, but 'Britain was, to a degree, falling under a Canadian shield.' *Canada: The Strategic and Military Pawn* (New York 1988), 87. Reynolds, *Creation*, 136, notes that Australia and New Zealand, as well as Canada, were forced closer to the United States by the events of the summer of 1940.

33. NA, R.B. Hanson Papers, file S-175-M-1, Meighen to Hanson, 19 Aug. 1940

34. Professor Underhill, who spoke the truth about the changed Canadian relationships produced by the war, almost lost his job at the University of Toronto as a result. See Creighton, 'Ogdensburg Agreement,' 300ff, and Douglas Francis, *F.H. Underhill: Intellectual Provocateur* (Toronto 1986), chap. 10.

35. NA, Privy Council Office Records, Cabinet War Committee Records, Documents, Churchill to King, 22 Aug. 1940

36. Even the usually shrewd observer of Canadian-American relations, Gordon Stewart, has missed this key point. He noted that in the 1940s, Canada 'participated willingly in military and defense integration . . . it is inaccurate

to regard American policy as being imposed on an unwilling and unknowing country. If the United States is judged guilty of imperialism, then Canada must accept a ruling of contributory negligence.' "'A Special Contiguous Country Economic Regime": An Overview of America's Canada Policy,' *Diplomatic History* 6 (fall 1982), 354–5. True enough, but Britain aided and abetted the process. John Warnock in *Free Trade and the New Right Agenda* (Vancouver 1988), 255, notes similarly that 'The Mackenzie King government chose to conduct the war effort on a continental basis' and thus 'greatly undermined Canadian sovereignty.' Some choice in August 1940!

37. The King government was slow to recognize the dangers posed to Canadian sovereignty by the U.S. presence. But once it was alerted to the problem (by the British high commissioner to Canada!), it moved quickly to appoint a special commissioner in the northwest and, at war's end, Canada paid the United States in full for all facilities built in Canada — quite consciously in an effort to ensure that its rights were fully protected. See Department of External Affairs, Records [DEA], documents on files 52-B(s), 5221-40C, the records of the special commissioner (NA, RG 36–7), and Granatstein, *A Man of Influence*, 120ff.

38. George Grant, *Lament for a Nation* (Toronto 1965), 50

39. Cited in David Dilks, 'Appeasement Revisited,' *University of Leeds Review* 15 (May 1972), 51

40. Based on Hector Mackenzie, 'Sinews of War: Aspects of Canadian Decisions to Finance British Requirements in Canada during the Second World War,' Canadian Historical Association paper 1983, 3

41. King Papers, W.C. Clark to King, 9 April 1941, ff 288021ff

42. H.D. Hall, *North American Supply* (London 1955), 230. Later, more accurate assessments put war spending in 1941–42 at $1.45 billion, aid to the United Kingdom at $1.15 billion, and civil expenditures at $1 billion. With a national income of $5.95 billion, public expenditure amounted to 60.5 per cent. King Papers, 'Canada's War Effort,' 4 April 1941, ff 288088ff

43. The phrase is R.S. Sayers's in *Financial Policy, 1939–45* (London 1956), 322–3. The balance, however, was less than real for the British. They had large peacetime trade deficits with the United States and could pay Canada in U.S. dollars only because they received them from other parties in a pattern of multilateral settlement that ended with the outbreak of war. I am indebted to Professor Ian Drummond for this information.

44. King Papers, Clark to King, 9 April 1941, ff 288014ff. The actual figures were even worse than these estimates. See Urquhart and Buckley, eds., *Historical Statistics*, F334–47. But whether the situation was as bleak as government officials believed at the time is less certain. Although munitions exports to Britain did stimulate the growth of imports from the United States, still more came from the war effort itself, which stimulated imports directly (in the form of components) and indirectly (by increasing consumer demand and domestic investment in plant and equipment). I am again indebted to Professor Drummond.

45. Granatstein, *Canada's War*, 135–6; Granatstein, *A Man of Influence*, 94ff

46. EAR, vol. 35, 'United States Exchange Discussions,' 20 Nov. 1940

47. Urquhart and Buckley, eds., *Historical Statistics*, F164–92; King Papers, Clark to King, 9 April 1941, ff 288018ff; Queen's University Archives, Grant Dexter Papers, Memorandum, 11 March 1941

48. On the costs to the United Kingdom see Barnett, *Collapse*, 591ff. Churchill was asked if Britain would be able to repay the United States for its aid: 'I shall say, yes by all means let us have an account if we can get it reasonably accurate, but I shall have my account to put in too, and my account is for holding the baby alone for eighteen months, and it was a very rough brutal baby.' Quoted in David Dilks's introduction to Dilks, ed., *Retreat from Power*, vol. II: *After 1939* (London 1981), 14

49. Robert Bothwell and John English, 'Canadian Trade Policy in the Age of American Dominance and British Decline, 1943–1947,' *Canadian Review of American Studies* 8 (spring 1977), 54ff. A.F.W. Plumptre commented that 'Ottawa apparently believed that it is well to keep Canada as independent as possible and to avoid borrowing or begging as long as may be.' *Mobilizing Canada's Resources for War* (Toronto 1941), 80. Cf R.W. James, *Wartime Economic Cooperation* (Toronto 1949), 32

50. Cabinet War Committee Records, Minutes, 18, 26 Feb. 1941

51. Public Record Office (PRO), London, Prime Minister's Office Records, PREM4/43B/2, Cranborne to Churchill, 5 March 1941; ibid., Treasury Records, T160/1340, Amery to Kingsley Wood, lo May 1941

52. Ibid., T160/1054, 'Canadian Financial Assistance to this Country,' nd [14 March 1941]

53. Granatstein, *Canada's War*, 139

54. Cabinet War Committee Records, Minutes, 12, 13 March 1941; Sayers, *Financial Policy*, 338ff

55. Dexter Papers, Memo, 21 April 1941

56. The text of the Hyde Park Agreement is printed as an appendix to R.D. Cuff and J.L. Granatstein, *Canadian-American Relations in Wartime* (Toronto 1975), 165–6.

57. Pickersgill, ed., *Mackenzie King Record*, 1, 202

58. C.P. Stacey, *Arms, Men and Governments* (Ottawa 1970), 490; Richard Rohmer, *E.P. Taylor* (Toronto 1978), 106

59. This was seen as a virtual miracle. See *Financial Post*, 26 April 1941.

60. See J.L. Granatstein, 'Settling the Accounts: Anglo-Canadian War Finance, 1943–1945,' *Queen's Quarterly*, 83 (summer 1976), 246.

61. PRO, Dominions Office Records, DO35/1218, Minute by A.W. Snelling, 26 Jan. 1943; Sayers, *Financial Policy*, 350ff

62. S.D. Pierce and A.F.W. Plumptre, 'Canada's Relations with War-Time Agencies in Washington,' *Canadian Journal of Economics and Political Science* 11 (1945), 410–11

63. Urquhart and Buckley, eds., *Historical Statistics*, F345–56; Leacy, ed., *Historical Statistics*, G188–202

Article Twenty-Nine

Battle Exhaustion and the Canadian Soldier in Normandy

J. Terry Copp

The fortieth anniversary of the Normandy invasion brought forth a new flood of books, each purporting to tell the real story of the battle. Strategic questions have been reassessed, the significance of Ultra brought to light and the personalities of the leading figures re-examined. There is a good deal of new information in the recent studies of the 1944 campaign but almost all of it[1] relates to questions which are quite remote from the actual experience of the young men who fought the battle in close contact with the enemy.

The purpose of this paper is to attempt to get some measure of the experience of the Canadian infantry soldier by examining the phenomenon of Battle Exhaustion, the catch-all term used by the Army to describe stress-related neuro-psychiatric casualties. But before attempting to analyze this small part of the story it seems necessary to explain some facets of the organization of the Canadian and British forces who set out to invade Normandy on 6 June 1944 and to make some comments of the nature of the campaign in Normandy.

We must first always remind ourselves that the Allied plan for the invasion of northwest Europe was dependent upon the ability of the Red Army to continue operations which occupied the energies of three-quarters of the German army. The Allies had simply not created a force large enough to confront the bulk of the German army. Indeed British (and thus Canadian) preparations for Operation Overlord were strongly affected by the overall war policy of Great Britain which was based on the desire to defeat the enemy by means other than direct conflict with substantial elements of the German army. In the spring of 1944 the British-Canadian component of the Allied forces, available for the invasion of Normandy, included a formidable tactical air force, a naval commitment of unparalleled power, and a small army which was rich in every resource except infantry.

Twenty-one Army Group which was charged with the responsibility for the invasion was to have an establishment of some 750 000 men but there were only nine infantry divisions (including two Canadian) available. Fifteen percent of the total troops were infantry,[2] but the

Source: From *The British Army Review* 85 (April 1987), 46–54. Reprinted with permission from the author.

designation "Infantry" should not be confused with actual commitment to battle in a rifle company. A standard 1944 infantry division contained 915 officers and 17 247 men, but less than half were infantry and of those only 4500 served in the thirty-six division rifle companies.[3]

The British had long since determined, as the Germans in Normandy were soon to discover, that artillery was to be the army's principal weapon and fully 18 percent of the troops in the bridgehead were artillerymen.[4] The planners also hoped that the fourteen armoured brigades allotted to 21 Army Group would play a prominent role in cracking the German defenses. It was hoped that these two Arms, together with the 2nd Tactical Air Force, would ensure that the Battle of Normandy would not become a bloody replay of the Western Front in World War I.

Viewed in hindsight the Normandy campaign went much better than the planners hoped. Not only were the Germans unable to bring substantial reinforcements from the Eastern Front (the Russian summer offensive which began two weeks after D Day was to cost the Germans close to one million casualties) but the Allied deception scheme "Fortitude" kept large elements of their western forces away from Normandy until it was too late. The Tactical Air Force, naval guns, the heavy bombers, and the artillery struck the German defenders with such a weight of high explosives that it may reasonably be argued that the Germans were blasted out of Normandy acre by acre.

But, and it is a very large but, the skill and resilience of the German defenders meant that the Allied infantry were required to attack, occupy, and hold small parcels of ground under circumstances which fully paralleled the horrors of the fighting of the Western Front in the first World War.

Modern memory has a firm image of "suicide bombers" and long casualty lists in the First World War, but we are not accustomed to thinking of Normandy in these terms, perhaps because of the relatively short duration of the campaign (88 days) and the overwhelming victory which climaxed the battle. A single crude comparison will help to make the point. During a 105-day period in the summer and fall of 1917, British and Canadian soldiers fought the battle known as 3rd Ypres which included the struggle for Passchendaele. When it was over our forces had suffered 244 000 casualties[5] or 2324 a day. Normandy was to cost the Allies more than 200 000 casualties or 2325 a day and 70 percent of these casualties were suffered by the tiny minority of men who fought in infantry rifle companies.[6]

So far what we have been trying to establish is that the fighting in Normandy placed a burden of almost unbearable proportions on one small Arm of the Allied armies — the Infantry. British (and thus Canadian) planners had not, despite the lessons of Italy, been willing to prepare for this eventuality. Well before D Day Montgomery had been worried that reserves of infantry replacements were dangerously limited. The War Office had already calculated that "at least two infantry divisions and several separate brigades might have to be disbanded by the end of 1944 for lack of reinforcements."[7] By early July the character of the Normandy battle had brought this crisis to hand and infantry battalions were frequently operating well below strength. By early August the Canadians, for whom infantry casualties were running at 76 percent of the total,[8] were reporting a deficiency of 1900 general duty Infantry[9] or the equivalent of four battalions of riflemen. By the end of August shortages had reached the staggering figure of 4318.[10]

This situation, which was proportionally only slightly less serious among British divisions, forced Montgomery to cannibalize the 59th division. On 14 August he told Alanbrooke, "My infantry divisions are now so low in effective rifle strength they can no longer — repeat, no longer — fight effectively in major operations. The need for action has been present for some time, but the urgency of the battle operations forced me to delay a decision."[11]

Perhaps enough has been said to indicate something of the context within which the Infantry fought in Normandy. Let us turn to the impact which the battle had upon the men who fought it as measured by the phenomenon of Battle Exhaustion. Needless to say, Battle Exhaustion was largely an infantry-man's problem. More than 90 percent of the known cases were among infantry. The large majority of individuals diagnosed as suffering from Battle Exhaustion exhibited what the psychiatrists described as acute fear reactions and acute and chronic anxiety manifested through uncontrollable tremors, a pronounced startle reaction to war-related sounds, and a profound loss of self confidence. The second largest symptomatic category was depression with accompanying withdrawal. Conversion states such as amnesia, stupor, or loss of control over some physical function, which had made up a large component of those described as "shell shocked" in World War I, were rarely seen in World War II.[12]

In preparing for Operation Overlord the Canadian Army was able to draw upon its own experience with Battle Exhaustion in the Italian campaign as well as the much more extensive information available from British and American sources. The assumptions of Canadian military authorities in May of 1944 may be summarized quite briefly.

The most commonly used method of measuring exhaustion rates was the so-called NP ratio which measured neuropsychiatric casualties in relation to total non-fatal battle casualties. Experience in the Mediterranean among British, American, and Canadian units suggested that a NP ratio of 23 percent, more than 1 in 5 of non-fatal casualties, was normal for infantry divisions in combat.[13]

Neither the military planners, frightened by the shrinking pool of General Service infantry reinforcements, nor the psychiatrists, professionally committed to reducing the NP ratio, were happy with either the quantity or predictability of neuropsychiatric casualties. The military authorities could and did, on occasion, issue directives attempting to forbid soldiers from breaking down. The major impact of such orders was to make life difficult for the Regimental Medical Officer and to make it nearly impossible for historians to compile accurate battle exhaustion statistics. Shortly after General Burns assumed command of 1st Corps, RMOs were ordered to be strict and hold all NP cases until it was certain that they could not be returned to unit and regimental CO's were told that battle exhaustion was their responsibility and if it occurred in the coming action "it would be taken as a reflection upon the ability of these officers."[14] General Guy Simonds never went quite that far, but it is evident that he had little patience with the policies of First Canadian Army relating to battle exhaustion.[15]

The psychiatrists in the Canadian Army, fully supported by their Allied colleagues, took a different approach. If battle exhaustion was a psycho-neurosis, i.e.

> an emotional disorder in which feelings of anxiety, obsessional thoughts, compulsive acts and physical complaints, without objective evidence of disease, in various patterns, dominate the personality,

then their training indicated that the neurotic individual must have been predisposed to neurosis by childhood experiences. If enough attention was paid to screening combat units for predisposed individuals, then the NP ratio could be significantly reduced. Dr. Arthur Manning Doyle, the First Division psychiatrist (and the only Canadian psychiatrist, in May 1944, with direct experience of battle exhaustion) did admit that "stress of battle" as well as pre-disposition was a variable, but he could only offer advice on the desirability of "weeding" units to remove the pre-disposed.[16]

Doyle's careful investigation of the NP ratio in the various regiments of the 1st Division should have suggested that a more elaborate diagnosis was required. His own figures showed that the Loyal Edmonton Regiment had less than half the NP casualties of some other regiments and that the variation between regiments was very large. It was also evident that 3 Brigade continued to have a much higher NP ratio than other brigades,[17] but no conclusions were drawn or indeed questions raised about these striking differences.

For Overlord the emphasis was on "weeding" and Dr. Gregory, the 3 Division psychiatrist, rejected 150 men — including three officers and one senior NCO — in the weeks before D Day, even though the division's regiments had been repeatedly "weeded" in the long months of assault training.[18] Once in combat the division utilized one of its Field Dressing Stations as an exhaustion unit, treating 208 men in the first two weeks of combat.[19] Exhaustion soon became the "outstanding problem"[20] for the medicals and in early July, Colonel Watson, the division's ADMS, issued instructions asking units to keep what he called "physical exhaustion" cases with the left-out-of-battle personnel. True battle exhaustion cases should come to the attention of the medical services only after they had had a rest.[21]

Colonel Watson and the divisional psychiatrist became convinced that common sense was "the first quality required" in the control of battle exhaustion. The truly neurotic soldier was a "menace to the stability of the force, even during rest periods" and must be removed. But for the rest, common sense meant:

> planned rest periods on a company, unit, brigade or division basis with diversions in the form of movies, sport, etc. must be arranged. During battle this can only be done on a platoon or company basis.
>
> During these periods, even if bombing or shelling are only remotely possible, adequate protection in the form of solid buildings and numerous slit trenches should be readily available to the soldier. For psychological reasons, the soldier should not be in a position where he is constantly having to search for a place to duck in an emergency; if so, he becomes cowardly; plenty of obvious slit trenches makes him feel secure and he becomes brave and does not require to use them. Troops in rest areas, even where odd shells are falling, should sleep above ground.
>
> (d) The Divisional Psychologist (sic) should be possessed of a degree of common sense well above that of the average officer. It is an essential appointment for the right man. His duty is to discuss with the ADMS all measures which will raise the morale of the fighting soldier as they apply to each separate situation and to examine and classify all casualties which are referred to him. He should not have to make a professional show by having specially allotted Field Dressing Stations or Field Ambulances filled with cases on which he can base statistics and lengthy reports to Headquarters. In fact, if he has many patients and issues long reports, he should be removed at once for failing in his job.
>
> The 'G' staff should be alert to the fact that providing the medicals have done their job, a high incidence of exhaustion cases indicates deficient training, poor leadership with a low fighting ability of the force. Battles are won by causing exhaustion in the enemy's ranks!![22]

All of this was at least an improvement on the preoccupation with childhood neuroses, but it was quite remote from the actual experience of 3 Division rifle companies. In *Maple Leaf Route: Falaise*, Robert Vogel and I reproduced the only battalion casualty report we found that dealt frankly with the problem of Battle Exhaustion. This report by the Officer Commanding the Canadian Scottish Regiment noted that, on 28 July, the regiment (which had begun the campaign with 38 officers and 815 other ranks) had suffered 569 casualties and contained only 15 officers and 321 other ranks who had landed on D Day. Many of the survivors were, of course, not rifle-men. Of the 421 men who had been "wounded" to that date, 117 had been evacuated as Battle Exhaustion cases. Not included on the list were the "24 men sent down to Corps Rest Camp and a large number (approx. 36) withdrawn from the front line during periods of relative quiet who, in the opinion of the company commanders and Medical Officers, required twenty-four or forty-eight hours of rest."[23]

The Canadian Scottish Regiment was, by any standards, well led, well trained and was as effective a unit as the Allied armies possessed. Furthermore, unlike a number of its sister regiments, it had yet to experience[24] one of those single day disasters that had scarred units like the Royal Winnipeg Rifles, The North Nova Scotia Regiment or the Highland Light Infantry. The Canadian Scottish had, however, remained in the line continuously under fire and had taken part in some of the most difficult battles.

By late July the Canadian Scottish, like the rest of the division, had reached a dangerous state of nervous tension and Colonel Watson, the senior Medical Officer, "drew the attention of the GOC to the situation in a letter which he in turn discussed with the Brigade Commanders who strongly supported the request for a rest of seven to ten days ... "[25] The Third Division was finally pulled out of the line.

The experiences of British 3 Division which fought alongside the Canadians in the first phase on the Normandy campaign was similar with 253 cases in June and 736 cases in July.[26] Overall the exhaustion ratio in 2 British Army rose from 9.5 percent in June to 22 percent in late July.[27] The 2 Army psychiatrist, Major A. Watterson, described the situation in these terms:

> The high optimism of the troops who landed in the assault and early build-up phases inevitably dwindles when the campaign for a few weeks appeared to have slowed down. Almost certainly the initial hopes and optimism were too high and the gradual realization that the "walk-over" to Berlin had developed into an infantry slogging match caused an unspoken but clearly recognizable fall of morale. One sign of this was the increase in the incidence of psychiatric casualties arriving in a steady stream at the Exhaustion Centres and reinforced by waves of beaten, exhausted men from each of the major battles. For every man breaking down there were certainly three or four ineffective men remaining with their units.[28]

The pattern of battle exhaustion casualties in both 3 Canadian and 3 British Division could be understood in the terms outlined by Watson and Gregory — psychiatric casualties would increase over time if units were not relieved. What disturbed Canadian Army authorities was the sudden influx of NP casualties from 2 Division in the early weeks of combat. It must be stressed that no accurate count of NP casualties is possible. Indeed, given the attitude of 2 Canadian Corps headquarters that "there will be no evacuation of psychiatric casualties in 2 Corps"[29] and the refusal to accept a divisional psychiatrist on the staff of 2 Division,[30] estimates for the 2 Division are even more difficult to arrive at than for 3 Division.

First Canadian Exhaustion unit, which had been activated with 2 Corps, dealt with 2 Division NP casualties during mid-July before divisional recovery centres were functioning. In the period 13 July to 24 July it reported approximately 300 cases from 2 Division, including 13 officers.[31] After 24 July, 4 Canadians FDS [Field Dressing Station] was used as a divisional recovery centre and, in the first seven days, it admitted 118 cases.[32] A similar number were admitted to the Corps Exhaustion unit that terrible week.[33] For the entire period, 13 July to 15 August, First Canadian Exhaustion Unit reported 576 cases from 2 Division and as many as 200 further cases were treated at Field Dressing stations; 23 officers were evacuated to hospital.[34] This indicates a NP ratio well above 30 percent and clearly demonstrates that 2 Division's first weeks in battle were even more horrific than existing accounts of the battles of Verrières Ridge suggest.

The extent of battle exhaustion casualties in 2 Division became a subject of considerable notoriety in the Canadian Army and, after the Battle of Normandy was over, Dr. Burdett McNeel who had commanded the Corps Exhaustion Centre in July and August, was asked to investigate the situation in 2 Division.[35] By eliminating the first nine days of the division's frontline experiences from consideration, McNeel was able to show that the division's exhaustion rate was not higher than 3 Division's. This did nothing to clarify the situation. However, McNeel's own War Diary and quarterly report covering the entire period do provide some insight.

The first wave of exhaustion cases from 2 Division included truckloads, complete with NCO's, of "dirty, haggard and dejected men"[36] from a regiment whose lead companies were caught by their own artillery barrage. The next day these were joined by more than one hundred cases largely from the three regiments shattered in the dying hours of Operation Goodwood on the rain-drenched and deadly slopes of Verrières Ridge.

In conversation with Dr. McNeel some forty years later,[37] it was evident that he had known nothing of the military situation which precipitated the evacuation of so many men from the 2 Division, either on 20th July or in the aftermath.

It seems quite clear that a detailed knowledge of the events of mid-July provides an adequate explanation of the extent of Battle Exhaustion in 2 Division. The Division was ordered into the Normandy battle in the final stages of an operation (Goodwood) which had already failed. The decision to commit two "green" infantry brigades to a frontal attack on a position which the Germans were steadily reinforcing was not a wise one. The results were horrific. The division suffered 1149 casualties in its first battle since Dieppe and four of its regiments were devastated. Everything was out of control and no one's morale was in very good shape after the battle.

The renewal of offensive operations on 25th July (Operation Spring) was a replay of the disasters of the 19th–20th. The Canadian army experienced a catastrophe of almost Dieppe proportions, losing 1500 men, most of them from 2 Division, in the space of 24 hours. No division could be expected to absorb these kinds of casualties in offensive operation which were clearly failures and maintain high morale. Substantial Battle Exhaustion casualties were simply inevitable.

At the time psychiatrists, wedded to their theories on pre-disposition, could only assume that 2 Division had been less carefully screened than 3 Division. The Exhaustion Units' diagnosis of cases seen in this period suggest just how committed to personality development theory the psychiatrists were. Almost half the evacuees were labelled psychopathic personalities, i.e.:

> a disorder of behaviour towards other individuals or towards society in which reality is clearly perceived except for an individual's social and moral obligations, . . .

Even a layman can be forgiven for doubting that the two harassed psychiatrists who dealt with hundreds of cases in a matter of a few days, would have accurately diagnosed 197 psychopaths![38]

However, McNeel's report on 2 Division which was written in late September reflected his growing awareness of the nature of warfare in Northwest Europe. He spoke with both medical and line officers in 2 Division and became convinced that casualty statistics and exhaustion ratios were of doubtful value in assessing personnel or performance. He wrote:

> The source of error in the compilation of statistics and the use of such a figure as an exhaustion ratio are so numerous as to make any conclusion based on statistics alone of very doubtful value. The incidence of exhaustion in any unit is only a part of the picture of that unit's efficiency and is outweighed in a positive direction by a generally high standard of performance and in a negative direction by large numbers of AWOL, POW, and trivial illnesses. I have been told that one regiment which has a high exhaustion ratio is always reliable and has never withdrawn from an action, whereas another regiment with a low exhaustion ratio has usually withdrawn from an action whenever the stress became great . . . The exhaustion ratio will also be altered by the wholesale evacuation of trivial sick or wounded . . . For these reasons the thoughtful appraisal of a unit's overall performance by responsible officers who know all the factors is of more value than any set of statistics or ratios can ever hope to be. However the latter may be used as a lead.[39]

McNeel gave a further illustration of the problems of using battle exhaustion ratios. He had spoken with an RMO in July about the number of evacuations from his regiment and urged him to keep the men with the unit. Later he had occasion to compliment the RMO on the changed situation only to be told "Well, I don't know — we had 50 men AWOL today."[40]

McNeel's superior officer, Colonel P.H. van Nostrand, was equally dubious about the value of exhaustion ratios. The Colonel, who had been pulled out of regimental duties in 1942 when General McNaughton had become alarmed over the number of psychiatric case in the Army overseas, assumed responsibility as the Consultant Neuropsychiatrist Canadian Army overseas. "Van", as he was universally known, brought a degree of common sense and unpretentiousness to psychiatric work that was badly needed. McNeel tells the story of a discussion on NP ratios as predictive tools in which he, McNeel, was fumbling for a statement of his own doubts when Van Nostrand calmly brought the debate to a halt with these lines:

> There was a young man named Paul
> Who had a hexagonal ball
> The square of its weight
> Plus his penis times eight
> Was two-third of three-fifths of ****-all.[41]

The conclusion of the Battle of Normandy brought an end to the battle exhaustion crisis. Cases were rare during the September pursuit and, when neuropsychiatric casualties began to accumulate again in October, there was no sudden influx of large numbers. There was now time available for more careful diagnosis and treatment.

Dr. Travis Dancey, the new Corps Exhaustion psychiatrist wrote:

> The type of NP case seen . . . has been much different from that so frequently described in the literature and from that admitted this summer. Although recent reinforcements who break down tend to show gross demoralization characterized by conversion-hysteria or anxiety-hysteria, we are handling an increasing number of men who have carried on under considerable stress for long periods of time . . . We are not dealing with chronic psychoneurotics, or with men who could be called inadequate in any sense of the term.[42]

Dancey, who was not in France during the Normandy battle, was not yet prepared to challenge the literature or to suggest that the Normandy experience be reassessed. It was not until the battle of 1945, when a more elaborate system of diagnosing and treating NP casualties was developed, that new evidence began to accumulate.[43] Many "predisposed" neurotic personalities had functioned very well and many "normal" individuals had broken down. It further became evident that every infantry soldier who remained for any length of time in combat developed neurotic traits which, in civilian life, would have indicated serious personality disturbance. The question was, why some men became incapacitated by stress and why others (often with "weaker" personalities) did not.

William C. Menninger who served as Chief Consultant in Neuropsychiatry to the US Army provided this answer:

> The breakdown of the soldier in combat, whether it was during his first week or his fifteenth month, was related to the ability of his personality to maintain further the balance between stress and compensating support. Support was derived from various sources. The external situation which presented the necessity of killing in order not to be killed, was stimulus to keep the aggression mobilized for action Fear, if controlled, was a factor in maintaining … alertness. Very significant aids in the control of this aggression were the approval and command of the leader and the identification and close association with a group of men who shared the same plight.
>
> The same psychological reinforcements which made it possible for the soldier to fight were potential causes of the development of psychiatric casualty, if they suddenly disappeared. Because of great dependence on them, the ego was left without support in their absence . . .

The very occasional soldier might carry on alone . . . More often, as the tension increased, the personality tried to relieve its distress by transforming anxiety into symptoms.[44]

Canadian army psychiatrists never quite went this far, though one study of 544 cases did conclude with the following:

> Two thirds of the cases gave no apparent history of neurotic predisposition or previous instability . . . only 19% of the total could have been considered as originally unfit . . . 30% were sensitized by long service alone (average 230 days). 23% had an added factor of being previously wounded and 18% had been previously evacuated for exhaustion . . . A further finding of interest was that of the 167 cases with long front-line service . . . 42 cases or 23% had carried on in spite of the fact that they had histories of previous nervous disorders or evident traits predisposing to neurotic breakdown . . . even a neurotic can stand a long period of battle stress when he has good drive, morale and character . . . a man can be "burnt out" due to long exposure to battle conditions even when he is considered quite normal.[45]

Here we are less interested in the education of Canadian psychiatrists than we are with the solider in Normandy so I will say no more about psychiatric reports. When Canadians and other Allied veterans assemble this June to commemorate the beginning of the campaign to liberate the peoples of Western Europe all of them will be deserving of our gratitude but perhaps it would not be unfair if we kept a special place in our hearts for the rifleman who fought "without promise of reward or relief." For no one, not even a psychiatrist or an historian "however he may talk has the remotest idea of what an ordinary infantry soldier endures."

NOTES

1. See John Ellis, *The Sharp End of War* (London, 1980), which attempts to describe combat in World War II from the point of view of the ordinary soldier. Carlo D'Este, *Decision in Normandy* (London, 1983). This contains a good discussion of infantry manpower problems.
2. The figures adjusted to include Canadian personnel are from L.F. Ellis, *Victory in the West* (London, 1962), vol. 1, HMSO, app. 4.
3. M. Hitsman, *Manpower Problems of the Canadian Army*, Report #63 Historian Section, Department of National Defense, app. L, 352.
4. Ellis, *Victory in the West*, app. 4.
5. John Terraine, *The Smoke and the Fire* (London, 1980), 46.
6. C.P. Stacey, *The Victory Campaign* (Ottawa, 1960), calculates Canadian infantry casualties as 76 percent of the total. The figure of 70 percent appears to be an accepted average for all allied casualties. See Ellis, *The Sharp End of War*, 158.
7. D'Este, *Decision in Normandy*, 252.
8. Stacey, *The Victory Campaign*, 284.
9. C.P. Stacey, *Arms, Men and Government* (Ottawa, 1970), 435.
10. Ibid. 438–39.
11. D'Estem *Decision in Normandy*, 262.
12. There does not seem to be any adequate explanation for this difference.
13. A.M. Doyle, "Report of 1 Cdn. Neuropsychiatrist, period 1 April–20 June 1944," Public Archives of Canada (hereafter PAC), Record Group (hereafter RG) 24, vol. 15, G46, p. 11.
14. W.R. Feasby, *Official History of the Canadian Medical Services 1939–45*, vol. 2 (Ottawa, 1956), 58.
15. On 29 August Simonds in a letter to his divisional commanders urged greater efforts to limit straggling, absenteeism, and battle exhaustion and suggested that the latter problem should not occur under the conditions of fighting in Normandy.
16. It should be noted that by 1945 Dr. Doyle was arguing that: the following factors are those that affect the incidence of Neuropsychiatric casualties in order of importance.
    a) Quality of Personnel
    b) Degree and severity of action

c) Duration of Action

d) Quality of leadership

e) Considerations such as weather, opportunity for rest and recreation and other such items relating to the welfare of the soldier.

Doyle's emphasis on quality of personnel was reflected in his overall conclusion that "the units which have shown consistently high neuropsychiatric ratios are those units who have had in their ranks too many inadequate, neurotic or mentally defective personnel." This judgment was to be challenged by the end of the Northwest European campaign.

See Lt. Col. A.M. Doyle "Psychiatry with the Canadian Army in Action in the C.M.F." *The Journal of the Canadian Medical Services*, vol. 3 (January 1946), 93. I wish to thank Dr. Bill McAndrew (DHist, National Defence) for discussing this point with me and sharing his own research into battle exhaustion in Italy.

17. Doyle may well have been thinking about 3 Brigade in particular when he emphasized quality of personnel but the difficulties encountered by 3 Brigade from training through its first months in combat require a far more complex analysis than this.

18. Dr. Dick Gregory was an unusual individual. Energetic, gregarious and colourful, he won the confidence of the ADMS, Col. Watson, and of the Regimental Medical Officers. He was able to arrange for the officers of each divisional Field Ambulance to attend an American School of Psychiatry and did much to prepare both medical and non-medical personnel for battle exhaustion casualties to their unit after brief treatment at the Field Ambulance recovery centre. This "success rate" was so extraordinarily high that his fellow psychiatrists were frankly dubious. However it is clear that 3 Division, as a whole, was better prepared for dealing with psychiatric casualties than the other divisions and it may be early rest and reassurance did work well. R.A. Gregory "Psychiatric Report 3 Division," 18 March 1944, 11 April 1944, and 17 May 1944, PAC, RG 24, vol. 15 661. Interview with Dr. B.H. McNeel (3 Dec. 1982) "War Diary 1 Cdn. Exhaustion Unit," July 1944, PAC, RG 24, vol. 15 659.

19. "War Diary, ADMS 3 Cdn. Inf. Division," June 1944, PAC, RG 24, vol. 15 661.

20. "War Diary, ADMS 3 Cdn. Inf. Division," July 1944, PAC, RG 24, vol. 15 661.

21. Ibid.

22. Ibid.

23. Terry Copp and Robert Vogel, *Maple Leaf Route: Falaise* (Alma, Ont., 1983), 34.

24. The Canadian Scottish were to experience such a day on 15 August when the Regiment took 130 casualties in the space of a few hours at Pt. 168, north of Falaise. The royal Winnipeg Rifles lost 128 men on D Day, 256 on 8 June in the defence of Putôt-en-Bessin and 132 on 4 July in the attack on Carpiquet Airport. The North Nova Scotia Regiment lost more than 200 men on 7 June and a similar number on 25 July. The Highland Light Infantry were reduced to 50 percent of their strength in their first major battle 8 July at Buron.

25. "War Diary, ADMS 3 Cdn. Inf. Div.," July 1944, PAC, RG 24, vol. 15 661.

26. "Way Diary, ADMS 3 Division," July 1944, PRO, WO 177/344. There was an extraordinary variance in N.P. ratios among the regiments of the division but the overall ratio was under $10\frac{1}{2}$ for June and over $30\frac{1}{2}$ for July (app. C, August War Diary ADMS).

27. "Report by Psychiatrist attached 2nd Army" for Month of July 1944, app. AI, WO 1777/321.

28. Ibid.

29. Quoted from an interview with Dr. B. McNeel, 3 Dec., 1982.

30. Dr. John Burch had been assigned as 2 Division psychiatrist but he was quickly transferred out. No psychiatrist was appointed to 4 Division.

31. John Burch, "Quarterly Report 1 Cdn. Exhaustion Unit 1 July–30 Sept. 1944," PAC, RG 24, vol. 15 659.

32. "War Diary, 4 Cdn. Field Dressing Station," July 1944.

33. "War Diary, 1 Cdn. Exhaustion Unit," July 1944, PAC 24, vol. 15 659.

34. Burch, "Quarterly Report."

35. B. McNeel, "Report on Exhaustion Cases 2 Cdn. Inf. Division."

36. "War Diary, 1 Cdn. Exhaustion Unit."

37. McNeel Interview.

38. Burch, "Quarterly Report."

39. B.H. McNeel, "Re: Cases of Exhaustion — 2 Cdn. Inf. Div. War Diary," app. DDMS 2 Cdn. Corps Oct. 1944.

40. McNeel Interview.

41. Ibid.

42. "Quarterly Report, 1 Cdn. Exhaustion Unit, 30 Sept.–30 Dec. 1944," PAC, RG 24, vol. 15 569.

43. See, for example, B.H. McNeel and Travis Dancey, "The Personality of the Successful Soldier," *American Journal of Psychiatry* 102, 3 (Nov. 1945), 338.

44. William C. Menninger, *Psychiatry in a Troubled World* (New York, 1948), 145.
45. Quoted in J.C. Richardson, "Neuro-psychiatry with the Canadian Army in Western Europe, 6 June 1944–8 May 1945." Typescript 17 pages nd (loaned to the author by Dr. Richardson.)

COMMENT BY DIRECTOR OF ARMY PSYCHIATRY, BRITISH ARMY

It may seem easy for a well-informed historian to deride the follies of the military authorities who attempted "to forbid soldiers from breaking down" or medical commanders who maintained that the "specially allotted Field Dressing Stations or Field Ambulances filled with cases" were merely a "professional show."

They were, however, guilty of overlooking the clearly established lessons of World War I, a trap into which every new generation is in danger of falling.

Battle exhaustion, battleshock as we now call it, is simply an inseparable concomitant of the kind of ferocious warfare in which "lead companies were caught by their own artillery barrage" and friends are killed and injured on all sides: "1500 men, most of them from 2 Division, in the space of 24 hours."

But that is not the end of the story. It is unfortunate that Professor Copp fails to record crucially important figures which put the whole question in perspective. From the Exhaustion Centres in that same terrible battle for Normandy 70 percent returned to duty of whom no more than 7 percent relapsed. The exhaustion or shock need only be temporary and it is up to everyone from junior commanders to doctors to see that it is so. (See note 18.)

Topic Twelve

Gender and the Consumer Society

Women shop in a Woodward's department store in Vancouver.

The history of consumerism is a growing field of study, especially when linked to gender history. Social historians have revealed how advertisers projected images of the ideal woman or man, representations they believed fit the stereotype of the age, to assist in selling consumer products. One period of interest is the 1950s, because it was a time of adjustment after a period of depression and war. Gender roles in particular were re-examined and re-defined. The 1950s were also a time of economic prosperity based on consumerism. Advertisers found sophisticated and subtle ways of selling consumer goods to a Canadian society eager to purchase them and with money to do so. But advertising was as much about selling image and identity — both gender identity and Canadian identity — as selling products.

The following two articles examine consumerism in the period from 1940 to 1960 in the context of gender analysis. In "Home Dreams: Women and the Suburban Experiment in Canada, 1945–1960," historian Veronica Strong-Boag examines the role that residential suburbs played in separating the role of men and women by looking at the economic, and, more importantly, the psychological factors that reinforced the image of residential suburbs as the "woman's domain." She shows that suburban women were deeply divided as to whether the suburban experience benefited or worked against their sense of self-identity.

In "Fatherhood, Masculinity, and the Good Life During Canada's Baby Boom, 1945–1965," historian Robert Rutherdale examines the impact that the changing view of fathers in advertising, from workers to masculine domestics, had on family life. He argues that materialism and masculinity went together, because it was the ability of fathers to provide material comfort and pleasure that was projected as a positive defining role of masculinity in this period.

What role did advertising and mass media play in constructing the image of suburban Canadian women as domestics and Canadian men as fathers and masculine domestics in the period 1945 to 1965? To what extent are Strong-Boag's and Rutherdale's studies of gendered roles during the same period complementary and/or contradictory? What contribution does the history of consumerism make to our understanding of the years 1945–1960?

A general study of the post–World War II period is Robert Bothwell, Ian Drummond, and John English, *Canada since 1945: Power, Politics, and Provincialism*, rev. ed. (Toronto: University of Toronto Press, 1989). For more of an emphasis on social history, see Alvin Finkel, *Our Lives: Canada After 1945* (Toronto: James Lorimer, 1997). Doug Owram, *Born at the Right Time: A History of the Baby-Boom Generation* (Toronto: University of Toronto Press, 1996) is most informative. Joy Parr examines consumerism in *Domestic Goods: The Material, the Moral, and the Economic in the Postwar Years* (Toronto: University of Toronto Press, 1995). Paul Rutherford looks at the role of television in this period in *When Television Was Young: Primetime Canada, 1952–1962* (Toronto: University of Toronto Press, 1990). An excellent collection on gender roles in history is Kathryn McPherson et al., *Gendered Pasts: Historical Essays in Femininity and Masculinity in Canada* (Toronto: Oxford University Press, 1999).

On women in the postwar era, see the report of the Royal Commission on the Status of Women in Canada (Ottawa: Information Canada, 1970); Micheline Dumont et al., *Quebec Women: A History* (Toronto: Women's Press, 1987); and Alison Prentice et al., *Canadian Women: A History*, 2nd ed. (Toronto: Harcourt Brace, 1996). Women in Ontario are examined in Joy Parr, ed., *A Diversity of Women: Women in Ontario since 1945* (Toronto: University of Toronto Press, 1995). Valerie Korinek studies a women's magazine in *Roughing It in the Suburbs: Reading* Chatelaine Magazine *in the Fifties and the Sixties* (Toronto: University of Toronto Press, 2000); see as well her article, "'Mrs. Chatelaine' vs. 'Mrs. Slob': Contestants, Correspondents and the *Chatelaine* Community in Action, 1961–1969," *Journal of the Canadian Historical Association*, New Series, 9 (1998): 209–223. Alexandra Palmer, *Couture and Commerce: The Transatlantic Fashion Trade in the 1950s* (Vancouver: UBC Press, 2001) discusses the world of fashion.

Studies of masculinity are limited. A valuable companion piece to that of Rutherdale's is Chris Dummitt, "Finding a Place for Father: Selling the Barbecue in Postwar Canada," *Journal of the Canadian Historical Association*, New Series, 9 (1998): 209–223.

WEBLINKS

Programming for the Modern Homemaker
http://archives.cbc.ca/IDD-1-69-1192/life_society/women_programming/
A sample of CBC programming aired in the late 1940s and in the 1950s generally intended for women.

Canadian Mail Order Catalogues
http://www.collectionscanada.ca/mailorder/h33-101.02-e.php#g
Digitized mail order catalogues spanning the 20th century including the postwar period.

Canadian War Brides
http://www.canadianwarbrides.com
Statistics and stories of many British and European women who immigrated to Canada, after marrying Canadian serviceman who were stationed overseas during World War II.

Canadian Home Journal
http://www.crcstudio.arts.ualberta.ca/canadianmagazines/viewtext.php?s=browse&tid=154&route=bytitle.php&start=12
A digitized 1945 copy of the *Canadian Home Journal*, a popular magazine in Canada at the time.

Chatelaine
http://www.crcstudio.arts.ualberta.ca/canadianmagazines/viewtext.php?s=browse&tid=73&route=bytitle.php&start=36#
A digitized 1948 copy of *Chatelaine*, a popular woman's issues magazine that continues publishing to this day.

Statistics Canada: Labour Force
http://www.statcan.ca/english/freepub/11-516-XIE/sectiond/sectiond.htm
Comparative statistics regarding the labour force in Canada generally over the time period of 1946 to 1975.

Article Thirty

Home Dreams: Women and the Suburban Experiment in Canada, 1945–1960

Veronica Strong-Boag

In the years after the Second World War in Canada, residential suburbs provided symbolic female counterparts, "bedrooms" as it were, to the male-dominated, market-oriented world of modern cities.[1] Tracts of new housing embodied a separation of the sexes that held women particularly responsible for home and family, and men for economic support and community leadership. Such a gendered landscape was far from new or unusual in Canada. Women and men had long moved in somewhat different worlds, presiding over residential and public space in varying degrees as dictated by custom and, sometimes, by law.[2] After 1945, however, women's, particularly wives', rising labour-force participation might have suggested that spatial segregation on the suburban frontier was ill-timed. Why and how, then, did there occur a massive increase in residential suburbs remote from opportunities for employment, lacking many community resources, and reliant on female labour? What did female residents and contemporary observers make of this investment on the suburban frontier? This article begins to answer these questions by examining the conditions that gave rise to postwar suburbs, the character of housing initiatives, and the nature and meaning of that experience for Canadian women.

Historians of the United States have associated postwar housing development not only with technological improvements, gas and oil discoveries, and a massive increase in the number of private automobiles, but also with political conservatism, racism, and domestic roles for women.[3] While scholars studying Canadian suburbs will find much that is useful in American assessments, particularly in their exploration of suburbia's gendered terrain, Paul-André Linteau's question, "Does the border make a difference?"[4] inevitably arises. Works like Michael A. Goldberg and John Mercer's *The Myth of the North American City: Continentalism Challenged* (1986) and Caroline Andrew and Beth Moore Milroy's *Life Spaces: Gender, Household, Employment* (1988) have offered the beginnings of a reply. In particular, Andrew and Milroy point to safer and more livable cities, a long tradition of resource towns, and "the particular institutional and policy framework that exists in Canada,"[5] all of which distinguish Canadian women's lives. Although comparisons with the United States remain peripheral to the study here, my reading of the Canadian suburban "script" suggests that, for all the proliferation of American influences in the years after 1945, life north of the forty-ninth did indeed differ. In particular, Canada's cities, lacking racial divisions comparable with those in the United States, never lost their attraction for citizens of all classes. And just as flight from urban dangers does not seem as influential in Canada, suburbia does not appear as homogeneous as many American commentators have suggested. Communities composed of war veterans, industrial workers, rural emigrants, newcomers to Canada, and the middle-class native- and urban-born contribute to a picture that, as the sociologist S.D. Clark convincingly demonstrated in *The Suburban Society* (1968), seems every bit as complicated as what was happening downtown. While middle-class WASPs were a major presence, they were never alone on the outskirts of cities. Suburbia's meaning is further complicated by the influence of region. The background

Source: Veronica Strong-Boag, "Home Dreams: Women and the Suburban Experiment in Canada, 1945–1960," *Canadian Historical Review* 72: 4 (December 1991): 471–504. © University of Toronto Press 1991. Reprinted by permission of University of Toronto Press Incorporated.

Table 30.1 Age-Specific Fertility Rates for Canadian Women, 1921–1960

Year	Age Group of Women						
	15–19	20–4	25–9	30–4	35–9	40–4	45–9
1960	59.8	233.5	224.4	146.2	84.2	28.5	2.4
1940	29.3	130.3	152.6	122.8	81.7	32.7	3.7
1921	38.0	165.4	186.0	154.6	110.0	46.7	6.6

Source: John R. Miron, *Housing in Postwar Canada* (Kingston and Montreal, 1988), from table 3, p. 35.

of residents and the rate of suburbanization in these years varied from one part of the country to the other, distinguishing the experience of Montreal from Toronto and from Halifax, Winnipeg, Edmonton, and Vancouver. Facing as they did a different set of contingencies, Canadian women were not mere reflections of American suburbanites. The nature of their story is set out below.

The postwar experiment with the promise of a spatial segregation that placed Canadian women in suburban homes and men in employment located elsewhere was fuelled by high rates of fertility. During the Second World War and into the 1950s, couples married at ever younger ages. First and second babies came earlier in these marriages, and increasing numbers of women gave birth to third children (see Table 30.1). Fewer women had no children. Bigger families increased women's home-based responsibilities. Not surprisingly, women were often preoccupied with their roles as wives and mothers. Housing where children could be cared for comfortably and safely was an urgent priority in many women's lives.

Whereas their parents had often had to be crowded and uncomfortable, postwar Canadians aspired to something better. Between 1945 and 1960 nearly continuous prosperity, high employment, the extension of the welfare state, and the presumption of a limitless bank of natural resources generated income and hopes for a better life, and, if possible, the lifestyle of comfortable homes and new products advertised since the 1920s in the continent's popular media.[6] Rising car ownership offered unprecedented numbers of citizens the opportunity to search for homes well beyond areas where employment opportunities were concentrated.[7] Many male breadwinners, the most likely both to drive and to control the use of cars,[8] no longer had to rely on walking or public transit to get to work. An increase in the production of oil, gas, and hydroelectric power was available to power both new cars and the central heating characteristic of new homes.[9] Residential suburbs on the periphery were the beneficiaries of these developments.

New housing that enshrined a gendered division of labour also responded to a generation's anxiety about changes in the world about them. The threat of the Cold War and the Korean War encouraged citizens to prize the private consumption and accumulation of products in the nuclear family household as proof of capitalism's success. Stable families, full-time mothers, and the benefits they produced in sound citizenship were to provide the first defence against the "Red Menace," symbolized in Canada by the Gouzenko Affair.[10] Suburban housewives at home in ever larger houses epitomized the promise that prosperity would guarantee both individual happiness and the final triumph over communism.[11]

The inclination to concentrate on private matters and to cling to the faith in women's particular talent and responsibility for family survival was fostered further in the 1940s and 1950s by the highly publicized predicament of many of the world's citizens. The statelessness of the "Displaced Persons," or "DPs," as the 165 000 who had come to Canada by 1953 were commonly known,[12] like the plight of concentration camp survivors, captured especially poignantly what it meant to lose families and homes. The arrival of 48 000 war brides added to Canadians' consciousness of how much the future depended on the establishment of new households and the persistence of marital bonds.[13] The promise of a renewed family life, secured by all the benefits of a revived capitalist economy, became in some ways the *leitmotif* of the second Elizabethan Age. As one typical enthusiast put it, "the Duke and Duchess of Edinborough [*sic*] are young, modern parents who, like many other young people, in an anxious and insecure world, find their deepest happiness and satisfaction in the warm circle of family life."[14] In suburban homes and families, Canadians endeavoured modestly to echo the ideals embodied in the domesticated monarchy of the youthful Elizabeth II.

The popular and academic social sciences of the day sanctioned the inclination to believe that collective happiness and well-being were most likely when women concentrated their energies on the home front. Experts' secular sermons, frequently presented in the guise of a celebration of female nature, stressed women's unique qualities. With some few exceptions, assertions of inferiority were out of fashion. As one Toronto psychiatrist observed, "Today we think of marriage as a partnership of equals."[15] To this end, modern fathers were encouraged to take on some care of children.[16] Yet, while up-to-date advisers flattered their female audiences with claims for equality, even superiority, "true" women had normally to demonstrate their authenticity by pursuing roles centred on the private rather than the public sphere. Women's ability to take on a broad range of duties, so well demonstrated during the years of depression and war, was conveniently dismissed as an aberration. In advising Canadians how to live, experts returned to opinions that were reminiscent of the 1920s.[17]

Lives that were gender-specific lay at the heart of a number of influential texts that enjoyed general circulation across Canada in the years after the Second World War. Among the earliest and most influential was Dr. Benjamin Spock's best-selling *Common Sense Book of Baby and Child Care* (1947).[18] As one Canadian from the suburb of Lachine, Quebec, recalled, "Dr Spock of course was my 'Bible.'"[19] Although most women consulted the good doctor for practical advice on treating childhood ills, his answers reinforced conventions holding women primarily responsible for the emotional and practical functioning of the household. A veteran of suburbs in Cooksville and North York, Ontario, summed up the conclusions of many of her generation: "I felt quite sure in those days that women who chose to have a family should stay home and raise them! I had worked as a social worker for the Children's Aid Society and had seen the emotional devastation in children separated from mothers."[20]

Spock was far from alone in applauding women who mothered. Ashley Montague's best seller *The Natural Superiority of Women* (1953) celebrated women both for their gentler dispositions and for their biological superiority. Not coincidentally, he concluded that "the most important of women's tasks is the making of human beings . . . [and] because mothers are closer to their children than fathers, they must of necessity play a more basic role in the growth and development of their children."[21] A self-proclaimed women's champion, Montague applied his reading of modern science to "undermine the age-old belief in feminine inferiority,"[22] but in the process he reasserted the faith that biology was destiny. The capacity for motherhood was, as with both the older anti-feminist and the maternal feminist tradition, identified as the very source of superiority.

Ashley Montague's fundamentally conservative message appeared in the same year as the publication of *Sexual Behaviour in the Human Female* (1953),[23] the second volume on human sexuality by Alfred Kinsey and his colleagues. In the forefront of the "sexology" of its day, this volume documented women's possession of a powerful libido, the physiological equivalent of male sexual response.[24] Under the influence of such scientific authority, an active sexuality became increasingly accepted as the prerequisite of satisfactory personal and marital life.[25]

The result could be higher levels of intimacy and equality between the sexes, but women's erotic potential could easily be incorporated into an updated domestic ideal. Kinsey's support for the female libido and his opposition to guilt and shame about sexual acts were closely tied to marital and social stability. His early work was used to justify Canadians' youthful marriage: only then could sexuality find its proper channels.[26] Ultimately, Kinsey's pioneering studies reinforced the tendency to dedicate women to private life.

The assignment of women to roles as wives and mothers was further legitimated by the popularity of the functionalist school of sociology that dominated the discipline as it established itself throughout Canada. The work of the leading American "father" of this tradition, Talcott Parsons, drew on the "anatomy is destiny" psychiatry of Freud and his followers to argue that women and men naturally had different, albeit compatible and equal, roles within society. Women were responsible for expressive functions of mediating and nurturing; men for instrumental functions of struggle and leadership. The first responsibilities directed women to the private sphere and the second legitimated men's domination of public life. Husbands concentrated on the workplace and its values of "rationality, impersonality, self-interest," while wives guided children in the traditional family values of "love, sharing, cooperation."[27] Domestic life might no longer require long hours of hard physical labour, but the unremitting pressure of modern corporate life on men appeared to make women irreplaceable in the home as psycho-sexual managers.[28] The appropriate division of duties was summed up by Bell Telephone's company magazine, *The Bluebell*, which pointed to wives' appropriate role in a short story entitled "WE Were Promoted."[29] Both capitalist prosperity and humanized relationships were to be guaranteed by the functionalist division of labour. Such conclusions became the stock-in-trade of Canadian sociologists like J.R. Seeley, R.A. Sim, and E.W. Loosley, the authors of one of the foremost North American studies of suburban life, *Crestwood Heights* (1956).

Home-grown authorities like the popular gynecologist Dr. Marion Hilliard of Toronto's Women's College Hospital regularly voiced the conservative conclusions of the contemporary social sciences. Speaking to her own patients and countless others through articles in *Chatelaine*, she spread prevailing medical opinion:

> The burden of creating a happy marriage falls mainly on the wife. A man's life is much more difficult than a woman's, full of the groaning strain of responsibility and the lonely and often fruitless search for pride in himself. A cheerful and contented woman at home, even one who must often pretend gaiety, gives a man enough confidence to believe he can lick the universe. I'm certain that the woman who enriches her husband with her admiration and her ready response gets her reward on earth, from her husband.[30]

Hilliard and most other Canadian "experts" on home and family joined their American colleagues in arguing that women's most basic satisfactions came through service to others in the domestic sphere.

The verdict of professionals was repeatedly echoed in the dominion's mass media. Typical advertisements credited the housewife with "the recipe for good citizenship . . . for a woman's influence extends far beyond the horizons of housekeeping. She guards the family health by her buying standards; she shares in plans for the family welfare; hers is the opportunity of training her children . . . of promoting good character and good citizenship."[31] Companies readily championed a feminine ideal that offered them real benefits. Corporate profits and male careers alike depended on women's concentrated efforts in the private sphere, more especially in new suburban homes, where opportunities for purchases were unsurpassed.

Advertising in these years was only one part of a commercial onslaught hitting Canadians. Newspapers, magazines, radio, films, and, by the 1950s, television entered households with a distinct message about the meaning of the "good life." Radio soap operas such as *Road of Life*, *Big Sister*, *Lucy Linton*, *Life Can Be Beautiful*, and *Ma Perkins* offered women escape from isolation and loneliness in dreams of consumption, romance, and improved family life.[32] Television shows like *The Adventures of Ozzie and Harriet*, *I Love Lucy*, *The Honeymooners*, and *Father Knows Best* made it quite clear that good wives and mothers stayed properly at home, far from the temptations of employment. Just as important, they suggested that women reaped real advantages from this division of duties. Wives may have looked a little foolish in these sitcoms, but audiences were encouraged to join in a conspiracy of good-humoured silence about the real power that they wielded. Housewives, after all, had the freedom to construct their own routines, while spouses were tied to onerous duties as breadwinners.

What the experts and the media largely ignored after World War II was a massive increase in the labour-force participation rate of married women. This increased from 4.5 percent in 1941, to 11.2 percent in 1951, to 22.0 percent in 1961. In the same years, wives rose from 12.7 percent to 30.0 percent to 49.8 percent of all women in paid employment.[33] For all this dramatic change meant in terms of disposable family income and the nature of the labour market, it appears to have done little initially to challenge women's primary identification as labourers in the domestic workplace.[34] Many postwar wives accepted periods of employment before childbirth and, sometimes, after children were in high school, as intervals in a modern life cycle that still saw them as chiefly responsible for home and family. In particular, energetic young wives could take pride in establishing families on a sound economic footing. Such was true of a "white-collar wife" in her early twenties employed by Montreal's CIL. Vivian used her salary to purchase new housing and "other rewards: electrical kitchen appliances, bedroom and living room furniture, a small English car." Her husband, David, paid other expenses. Traditional appearances were maintained when she assumed responsibility for most housework and received an allowance from David. Vivian planned to leave CIL at about the age of 25 to have between two and four children.[35] Many women hoped to do the same. The same assumption underlay the "putting hubby through school" phenomenon that first attracted public attention with the return of war veterans to university.[36] Women's work in the labour market regularly represented an investment in a more domestic future.

Incentives for female citizens to return home as soon as possible always remained considerable. Never missing were unequal opportunity and wages. Resources in support of female workers were meagre.[37] Matters at home were hardly better. Most families could afford only one car, on which the husband had first claim, and few settlements boasted adequate public transportation. Nor was that all. Working wives had to face the "double day of labour." One refugee from a clerical office explained that she had cheerfully given up a schedule that required "twelve hours or more a day, seven days a week."[38] Another clerical worker from North Toronto added:

> As a married woman for fourteen years and a working wife for less than one year . . . the two don't go together. You can't be a success at both. So I decided to quit my job to save my marriage.
>
> You simply can't look after a home and go to the office too. I don't care who you are or how well organized you are, you can't be a good wife and mother, hostess and housekeeper and also do a good job for your employer all at the same time. When you try, someone is bound to get cheated.[39]

Working wives had no right to hope for relief at home. As one writer for the *Star Weekly* insisted: "I don't see how a job gives a woman a legitimate out on housekeeping. She still has the basic responsibility to run a home for the family . . . [and] a man whittles himself down to less of a man by consistently performing woman's work."[40] In the decades after the

Second World War, income tax law, the absence of daycare, formal and informal bars to female employment,[41] and school schedules combined with a commercially fuelled celebration of domesticity and maternity and the general reluctance of husbands to assume household responsibilities to confirm the wisdom of staying home, if you had a choice.

Such decisions were applauded by experts who feared the worst. In 1953 a counsellor for Toronto's Family Court and the United Church summed up prevailing opinion, arguing that "where the husband and wife are both working outside the home, very often a dangerous spirit of independence exists. Finally, it is quite impossible to do two jobs well."[42] Women who dismissed such arguments could look forward to being scapegoated for a host of society's problems, blamed for homosexual sons, juvenile delinquents, mental cripples, wandering and alcoholic husbands, and school truants.[43]

When authorities repeatedly insisted that women were needed at home, the corollary often was that men were too weak to have them anywhere else. As the Kinsey reports had documented in detail, sexual orientation was conditional; men were the more vulnerable sex. When men's physical weakness was further disclosed by experts like Ashley Montague,[44] female discontent or competition appeared enormously threatening. A wife's wages might endanger the very core of the fragile male personality.[45] By the same measure, houseworking men challenged the very basis of contemporary masculinity. The Montreal psychiatrist Dr. Alastair MacLeod plaintively summed up modern problems for *Chatelaine*'s readers:

> Father no longer has opportunities for pursuing aggressive competitive goals openly at work. Some of his basic masculine needs remain unmet. Mother no longer feels she has a real man for a husband and becomes openly aggressive and competitive herself, even moving out of the home into industry in her efforts to restore the biological balance.
>
> Faced with an increasingly discontented and dominating wife, father becomes even more passive and retiring. . . . Certain trends in modern industry are theoretically capable of disturbing the biological harmony of family organization. The resulting disharmony can lead to psychological and psychosomatic illnesses.[46]

The message was clear: domestic women guaranteed both their own femininity and their husbands' masculinity.

In the 1940s and 1950s Canadians had many reasons to believe that the gendered division of labour was the most appropriate response to their own and their nation's needs. While some citizens always challenged too narrowly defined roles, many were prepared to accept the fact that women and men had different duties in the family and in society at large. Residential suburbs that enshrined the notion of largely separate spheres for the two sexes proved attractive because most Canadians preferred women at home and out of the labour market.

The recurring housing crisis of the 1940s and 1950s provided the crucial opportunity to fix this preference in space.[47] The dominion entered the postwar years with "a large stock of aging and substandard housing, communities that lacked appropriate municipal services, rural areas that lacked electric power, and with a substantial number of households living in crowded conditions or paying shelter costs they could ill afford."[48] Families with youngsters were particularly hard hit. A boom in babies and immigrants raised the costs of even inferior accommodation.[49] The January 1946 occupation of the old Hotel Vancouver protesting the lack of housing for veterans and their families, like the later seizure of several government buildings in Ottawa by members of the Veterans' Housing League, were only the most visible symptoms of widespread dissatisfaction and rising unrest.[50] The *Star Weekly* summed up popular sentiments: "It must be remembered that the whole situation is charged with an intense emotional desire on the part of veterans and non-veterans alike to have homes of their own. The years of loneliness and being apart, the years of cramped, semi-private living, have created a desire as strong as the migrating instinct in birds to have a home."[51] Not surprisingly, crowded accommodation was regularly cited as contributing to family breakdown and social disarray.[52]

Prime Minister Mackenzie King's postwar government, already alerted by the report of the Advisory Committee on Reconstruction on housing and planning to the magnitude of the housing shortage[53] and fearful of the appeal of the Co-operative Commonwealth Federation, moved to fill the gap. The passage in 1944 of the second National Housing Act (NHA) and the creation of the Central Mortgage and Housing Corporation (CMHC) one year later confirmed the significance of housing for peacetime construction.[54] With some few exceptions, strong anti–public housing sentiments and official reluctance to interfere with the "free market" sharply limited the reclamation of urban residential cores.[55] Across the dominion, despite the substantial investment in urban infrastructure — sewers, schools, public transportation, sidewalks, churches, and the like — that cities represented, they did not become the focus of government housing initiatives. Attention focused instead on the construction of new houses in the suburbs.

Despite their neglect by governments, city neighbourhoods continued to attract middle- and working-class Canadians, but many tried to maximize dollars and improve family situations by turning to new residential communities. Not all benefited from state support. In British Columbia's Lower Mainland, poorer citizens made do with little better than squatters' quarters in Bridgeview, a marginal Surrey settlement, without sidewalks and sewers.[56] In Quebec the Montreal working class had to satisfy its land hunger in Ville Jacques Cartier. There the discomfort and distress of life in tarpaper and tin shacks on postage-sized lots bought on the installment plan helped embitter the future separatist Pierre Vallières.[57] In Newfoundland, the city of St. John's was surrounded by "fringe areas . . . characterized by very poor, substandard housing, complete lack of services (piped water and sewer facilities, garbage collection, street-lighting, etc.), poor roads and low family incomes."[58] Few residents in such locations used the provisions of the National Housing Act, since borrowers in the years after World War II had to earn steadily higher gross family incomes in order to pay rising down payments and interest rates.[59]

Atlantic Canadians, poorer on average than their contemporaries elsewhere, were particularly unlikely to receive federal mortgage help: between 1954 and 1966 only 23.4 percent of all new "dwelling units" in the Atlantic region were completed with CMHC assistance, compared to 51.9 percent in Ontario in the same period.[60] The variability of financing meant that housewives in different regions sometimes confronted dramatically different working conditions. In 1960 and the first five months of 1961, for example, 38.5 percent of new units located in Atlantic Canada lacked flush toilets and 41.9 percent furnace heating, compared with 8.7 percent and 8.2 percent, respectively, in Ontario.[61] Such distinctions helped ensure that accommodation on the urban periphery varied, often tremendously, from one part of the country to the other. In the Maritimes, suburbia would be neither as extensive nor as prosperous as in many other regions of the country.

In contrast to the plight of the poor, the housing predicament of a broad range of Canadians was addressed by federal enthusiasm for subsidizing the construction of single-family homes and the desire of private developers, contractors, and mortgage lenders to maximize profits. For those who could meet income requirements, mortgage money, at artificially low rates, was made available to build hundreds of thousands of three-bedroom "residential units."[62] While the foremost scholar of Canadian suburbs, S.D. Clark, has concluded that residents were frequently "middle class in terms of income . . . Canadian born, of British origin, and of Protestant religious affiliation,"[63] suburbs always attracted ambitious working-class and immigrant citizens as well. One daughter remembered that "as refugees from Hungary," her parents "could hardly wait to leave" downtown Toronto "for [what was], to them, the lavish splendour of the suburbs," where they settled without regret.[64] In a subdivision of owner-built houses in Cooksville, Ontario, in the 1950s, an English immigrant remembered friendly Italian neighbours whose comfortable homes were constructed by their labouring and small-contractor husbands.[65] The Yugoslav immigrant who began work as a carpenter and plasterer when he arrived after the war and went on to achieve his dream of a suburban bungalow, in his case in Winnipeg's West Kildonan, may not have been in the majority, but he had imitators from one end of the country to the other.[66] The eclectic nature of the suburban community was captured by the comment from a resident who insisted that her modest suburb west of Toronto, whose residents included Olga, Grand Duchess of Russia, was "neither purely WASP nor dull."[67]

Once families moved to suburbia, they often found themselves with people of similar income and in houses of similar price. Neighbours were "all in the same boat."[68] New communities often revealed a distinct class and ethnic character, one that was sometimes legally imposed. Until their overthrow by the Supreme Court in 1951, residential covenants that included race as criteria were commonplace. Drawing on Canadian property law, they were used by land developers to exclude "undesirables" and to set minimum house values.[69] Even after covenants had lost some of their power, homogeneity often survived, a testament to more informal support. In 1957 the new North York suburb of Don Mills, for example, attracted certain occupational groups: 32.1 percent of male homeowners were executives, 23.7 percent professionals, 19.9 percent skilled technicians, 11 percent salesmen, and 3.8 percent teachers and professors, with the remaining 9.5 percent listed as miscellaneous.[70] The hopes of many suburbanites were summed up by one observer in 1945: "It's not just a house, but a way of life that people are seeking . . . Most people wanted to be a part of a community which consisted of congenial people, equality of income — restricted house values."[71] Different suburbs could have distinctive characters, depending on the ability of different groups to afford the cost of houses in their community.

The availability of CMHC mortgages for new homes, relatively low land costs, and builders' incentives, such as that by Saracini Construction in NHA's Glen Park development in Etobicoke in the early 1950s, which gave purchasers the "option of taking a lower priced home and completing part of it at a later date,"[72] made a difference to many Canadians. Despite the continuing decline in the rural population, where ownership was most common, the number of owner-occupied houses in Canada increased from 57 percent in 1941 to 65 percent in 1951 to 66 percent in 1961.[73]

Immediately after the Second World War much new housing was constructed, either individually, often by "do-it-yourselfers," or as part of developments of a few to several hundred houses. Most early construction took place either within older suburbs like East Vancouver or East York in Toronto or in the first ring of surrounding townships or municipalities, such as British Columbia's Burnaby and Ontario's Etobicoke. By the early 1950s, however, high demand plus the enlarged scale of the development industry increasingly directed growth to more remote areas, many without existing municipal services. There, in sites like Halifax's Thornhill Park, Toronto's Don Mills, and Edmonton's Crestwood, appeared the suburban, automobile-dependent sprawl that came to characterize the last half of the twentieth century. Between 1951 and 1961 the population in metropolitan areas around city cores grew far more than that in city centres (see Table 30.2).

These first homes meant a great deal. Coming out of depression and war, couples struggled to become property owners. A team effort was common. As one observer noted of veteran housing: "There is hardly a single case among all these veteran-builders of a wife lounging about. They have been as active in all weathers as their husbands."[74] Such couples had good

Table 30.2   Percentage Increases in Population for the Central Cities and Remaining Parts of the 1961 Census Metropolitan Areas, Canada and the Regions, 1951–1961

Census Metropolitan Area	Central City	Remainder of Metropolitan Area
Canada	23.8	110.7
Atlantic	11.7	70.6
Quebec	27.9	117.7
Ontario	15.5	116.3
Prairies	50.2	133.0
British Columbia	10.9	90.7

Source: Peter McGahan, *Urban Sociology in Canada* (Toronto, 1986), from table 61.

reason to prize long-awaited houses. Tenants in particular, like one longtime inhabitant of Montreal's Verdun, her husband, and three children, aged five, three, and seven months, were delighted to use CMHC mortgages to move, in their case to Lachine's "Dixie" suburb.[75] Their enthusiasm was matched by the York Township resident in Ontario who remembered being "very poor in the depression — 8 people in a 4 room one storey house." She was understandably "really excited — To have a 5 room brick bungalow for the two of us! Such Luxury!!"[76] A Scottish immigrant expressed the same sense of achievement: "We came from a society where houses were scarce, renting was almost impossible unless one had the proper connections, and from a country which had spent 6 years at war. So owning a house in the suburbs was a dream for us, a dream we achieved after only 6 years in Canada."[77]

While new suburbs varied in many particulars,[78] all shared a commitment to the gendered division of labour. Purchase of a home — whether in a highly planned community like Etobicoke's Thorncrest Village with its provision of a wide range of urban services expected by upper-middle-class buyers[79] or in a mass-produced subdivision like Scarborough's Wishing Well Acres, where the one millionth new house constructed after VE-Day was officially opened[80]— was part of a child-centred strategy for many Canadians. As a study by Vancouver's Lower Mainland Regional Planning Board discovered, "to a young family without much money, faced with the alternative of a small apartment in the city . . . it is no small thing to be able to look out of the living-room window at one's children playing in relative freedom with fields and woods beyond them."[81] As a mother of two in Toronto's Iondale Heights suburb explained in 1957, "We moved to the suburbs because of the children. We wanted to give them room to romp, where they wouldn't have to worry about street cars and fiend-driven automobiles. True, we have no museums or art galleries. But the children can go outside and see nature as it is."[82] Such commentators took for granted that greater opportunities for children depended ultimately on maternal supervision.

Finally responsible for child care and house maintenance, modern suburban wives were tethered to their communities in ways that few husbands could match. In 1958 one speaker for a Toronto construction company described the suburban home: "A woman is there all the time, she lives there. A man just boards there: he gets his meals there. She is there all day long."[83] A male architect characterized his own experience of gender relations even more vividly: "I spend every day in my Mobile Room [car] going to and from the women at either end [in the office or in his suburban home]."[84] As these remarks suggest, the suburban house remained first of all a workplace for female residents. For husbands, lengthy commutes and long hours at work, not to mention individual preferences, meant that domestic responsibilities were largely subordinated to the demands of waged work.[85] Nor did the suburbs make joint efforts easy. As one husband recalled:

> Like most of my fellow male suburbanites I was the sole auto driver. I also drove a lot in my job. Rushing home to take a child to cubs or brownies, to take my wife to a class in the city, to drive to hockey practice or to a game, or to be shopping driver when required was a daily task. Work pressures made this more difficult. There were the open spaces to cut, cultivate and shovel. Social evenings required a driver to pick up the sitter, drive into town, return home and drive the sitter home. The automobile was an itching appendage needing constant scratching.[86]

To be sure, some suburban wives always joined their husbands in leaving home for employment. As the expansion of Avon's and other door-to-door sales in these years suggested, earning extra money was never far from many residents' minds.[87] So-called "working" wives shored up families' aspirations to a better standard of living; the husband of a young Bank of Commerce clerk, for instance, was reconciled to her job so she could furnish the house they were building in Saskatoon in 1952.[88] Yet women's ideal primary role remained, especially after babies arrived, in the home. As one resident of a Toronto suburb remembered, her husband "didn't want me to work, and I thought that no one could look after my children as well as I could."[89]

While they may not have remained in the labour market, wives regularly contributed to husbands' careers. Women married to professionals or businessmen often functioned as part of a marital "team," spending hours as unpaid assistants, typing, translating, or entertaining. The wife of a successful academic remembered that "in university circles a wife was expected to entertain — often upwards of 50 people."[90] Another academic spouse found her eyes giving out as she typed the manuscripts that advanced her husband in his profession.[91] Acknowledgement of such contributions forms a regular refrain in scholarly prefaces.

The great majority of wives remained crucially dependent on male wages. Women's financial vulnerability was worsened by the fact that many families purchased suburban homes only by rigorous self-denial. More than one investigator discovered that "Baby sitters were done without, food costs reduced, less spent on clothing, and a hundred and one other small ways discovered to save money. 'I'm not going dancing no more' gave expression certainly to the financial plight of more than one suburban housewife."[92] While such careful juggling of finances was not true of all suburbanites, the strains of budgeting, large or small, were likely to be borne unevenly. Not only did male wage-earners usually have prior right of access to what they commonly held to be "their money,"[93] they frequently had to maintain certain standards as conditions of employment. Women and children could dress, eat, and travel much less well without immediately endangering the family economy.[94]

Suburban houses were the stage on which women explored the meaning of separate spheres. That setting varied greatly depending on income and individual preference, but the introduction of CMHC inspections under the 1954 revision of the Housing Act encouraged the giving way of "individual, custom-built homes" to "mass, speculative development" with standardized shapes, sizes, and configurations.[95] In the late 1940s and 1950s master plans and more stringent municipal zoning by-laws across the country, which represented efforts to control errant developers, also contributed to the increasing uniformity of the emerging suburban landscape.[96] CMHC's support of Canadian Small House competitions after the Second World War,[97] like the *Star Weekly*'s sponsorship of the All Canadian Home in 1959,[98] for all their good intentions, had the same effect. In the heady days of easy sales, developers threw up one imitation after another, differing in little but colour and trim. Most models came as Cape Cods, and, increasingly, as bungalows or split levels. Like the split-level winner of the first coast-to-coast architectural contest in 1953,[99] almost all boasted three bedrooms, an L-shaped living–dining-room combination, and, in most areas of the country, a full basement. Increasingly, too, a rumpus or recreation room appeared below level, which, together with the proliferation of televisions, encouraged families to spend leisure time more privately. In these homes, more comfortable than many had ever encountered, women were to forge the moral basis for postwar Canada.

Female residents were expected and urged to bring uniqueness to uniformity through a careful attention to decoration and design. As one commentator insisted, "The bugaboo of uniformity bothers her not at all, because every woman knows she can work out her own individual design for living with colours and furnishings and personal touches."[100] Their choice of furniture, appliances, art, and even clothes was to transform the identical into the distinguishable, in the process confirming housewives' skills and status. No wonder that practically every issue of popular Canadian women's magazines like *Bride's Book, Canadian Home Journal, Canadian Homes and Gardens,* and *Chatelaine,* not to mention their American competitors, offered readers ways, thrifty and otherwise, to personalize suburbia. In a Special Issue in March 1955, for example, *Chatelaine* offered lessons on "How to Live in a Suburb," "A Spring Fashion Bazaar for Suburban Living," and "How to Furnish a New Home without Panic Buying." Subscribers consulted such experts but also prided themselves on developing styles that suited their families best.[101] The mistress of a Rexdale, Ontario, bungalow on "a corner-lot so at least it didn't match everything beside it in either direction, but of course, it matched the house on the corner across the street," spoke for a renovating sisterhood when she reflected that "I almost wrecked it trying to create something unique."[102]

Many women soon found more to concern them in the limitations of the environment at large. Conspicuous in their absence from many new developments in the 1940s and early 1950s, before local governments became more demanding, were public spaces and facilities, such as sidewalks, monuments, parks, and cemeteries. A mother of two children settled in a bungalow on Toronto's outskirts typically remembered that "there were no sidewalks and the road was not paved. The mud and dust were a real pain."[103] For many years developers also counted on the open country that surrounded many subdivisions to provide children with nearby recreational space. In time, as the process of urban sprawl accelerated, this resource disappeared, as it did around Scarborough's Wishing Well Acres subdivision in the 1960s, without any provision for its replacement. For women, the presumed mistresses of suburbia, collective provision was almost always curiously lacking. If landscape was any guide, meeting and play were not part of the female mandate.

The location of most commercial shops and services on the periphery or, more occasionally, in the centre of residential development, either in a strip pattern along major roads or in suburban plazas, showed the same lack of attention to women's needs. Patterns of consumption centred increasingly on shopping centres, which first made their appearance in Canada in 1947 in suburban Winnipeg. By 1951, with the construction of Norgate Plaza in Montreal and Park Royal Plaza in West Vancouver, about 46 shopping centres, all poorly served by public transit and demanding access to a private car,[104] drew buyers from surrounding suburbs.

One Don Mills veteran characterized shopping experiences that were not very different from those of the majority of her contemporaries, especially those whose husbands didn't have the option of commuting by train to work: "Walked and pushed baby carriage to most places. Never had a second car — poor bus service especially with 3 children! Little co-operation, wives did not own car — walked to local shops. Traffic was hazardous on highway & only route to major shopping centre (suburbs were designed for the car & most of us had only one which husband used)."[105] Once visitors got there, new plazas, lacking free public space and cultural amenities, offered them little beyond a community based on a common commitment to purchase. As a self-satisfied Canadian retailer put it, "Suburban living, by its basic structure, generates wants and brings latent desires more sharply into focus. The not-so-subtle effect of competitive living is also a potent influence in creating an environment that encourages liberal spending for better living."[106] The domestic and individualistic orientation of women, families' major purchasers, was readily reaffirmed.

While plazas were increasingly influential, door-to-door sales and deliveries were commonplace in the 1940s and 1950s. Phone orders were taken by butchers, grocers, and department stores, and trucks with milk and bakery goods made their way among suburban homes. Avon ladies, who might be members of a local church, and Hoover, Electrolux, Fuller Brush, and Watkins salesmen were also occasional visitors. The latter were described by a former client as canvassing a Montreal suburb "once or twice per year and I always kept their wonderful salve, 'Good for Man or Beast.' Very strong, didn't burn and helped heal cut knees very quickly. They also had wonderful flavourings and food colourings."[107]

In Metropolitan Toronto, another purchaser implied advantages beyond mere convenience: "We liked to see a vegetable man come along the street. Ice, milk and bread were delivered as were beer and pop. The Avon lady and the Fuller Brush man provided some new faces."[108] Such sentiments were shared by a resident of Clarkson's Corners (Mississauga) who recalled, with affection, a milk man who "always poked his head in to say good morning and took the children on his van for a ride." She observed, "Obviously these services were very important. I realize, however, that my mother had far more people calling than I. (She even had a Hellicks coffee man, Duggan's bakery, etc.)."[109] Although they grew less in time as the private automobile undermined their viability, such deliveries helped knit new communities together in ways that more modern shopping alternatives rarely did.

Suburbia's households were also connected by schools and churches. Although it often happened that housing sprawled well beyond the capacity of religious groups and municipalities to ensure even minimum services, by the 1950s their institutions were normally included in the initial planning of developments. Even then they might well be strained to their limits or inconvenient to reach, as with schools offering shift classes or located across busy intersections. For all such shortcomings, as well as their tendency to deal with female clients almost solely in their roles as mothers and wives, such institutions constituted important collective resources to a community lacking common habits of working together. Parent–teacher associations, or home and school groups, were the most effective in mobilizing women, from room mothers to fund-raisers and executive officers.[110] Auxiliaries and Sunday schools were critical for some residents who kept suburban churches expanding in these years.[111] Work with local institutions offered more activist and sociable suburbanites the chance to combine domestic duties with a manageable level of public involvement.

As they had done in other Canadian settings, women wove the fabric of day-to-day life. As one observer noted, "For most of the day while the men are away at work the women run the community. After the bulldozers have pulled out, the spadework to make a real community out of your particular collection of houses has to be done by . . . the homemakers."[112] Women commonly moved beyond their homes through contacts with children and "in turn, the fathers get to know their neighbours through their own ubiquitous wives."[113] Casual meetings, dismissed by critics as "coffee klatches," or even encounters between Avon "ladies" and their clients, might be followed by both intimate friendships and formal associations. These ties helped women cope with limited resources and new environments. Since children were rarely far from mothers' minds, much cooperative activity centred on them. After the war, women in North Burnaby's new subdivisions established "parent–teacher groups . . . in an endeavour to promote better school conditions and assist in providing hot lunches for the children."[114] In Don Mills, where young children were abundant and teenagers rare, women established baby-sitting co-operatives.

In Thornhill, Ontario, mothers formed a community kindergarten and encouraged the fathers, who, "though somewhat apathetic at first . . . to contribute some time and energy in making odds and ends of school equipment."[115] In 1955 mothers at North York's York Mills School, alarmed by sexual attacks on local children, created a Parents' Action League.[116] In Etobicoke's Rexdale development, women protested their lack of public transit to local council and to the Toronto Transit Commission. As they explained, "Nearly all of us have children and they have to be taken to the dentist or doctor occasionally. It takes a full day to make the trip and two days to rest up afterwards."[117] Also in 1955, mothers from North York's Livingstone School fought the Board of Education's transfer of pupils to another school.[118] In Clarkson's Corners a Quebecker prompted her neighbours to create French conversation groups and to fund high school scholarships.

Concerns sometimes broadened beyond children to include a variety of community issues. Thorny questions related to sewers, libraries, and garbage disposal provided lessons in collective action and political lobbying. In North York, residents created the North York Women Electors Association on the model of its Toronto counterpart in September 1954.[119] In Etobicoke, a year later, 22 mothers with children in tow from Goldwood Heights subdivision "stormed" a council meeting, demanding "action — not answers" to the problem created by their developer's failure to finish sidewalks, sodding, and ditching.[120] In effect, such women were transforming suburbs into good neighbourhoods. As volunteers they facilitated the creation of everything from schools, hospitals, and churches to libraries.

For all the evidence of activism, however, the majority of women were rarely visible on the public stage. For many, suburbia constituted a period of deep engagement in the day-to-day running of the family. Very few had assistance with household duties, particularly on weekdays, when most husbands were absent. While a few sometimes found substitutes for their own labour in cooperatives or paid help, others, like a Montreal suburbanite, remembered that "even babysitters were all but unavailable (No Teens, no Grannies)."[121] Questioned about their days as mothers of young children, both happy and unhappy veterans of suburbia remember themselves engrossed in time-consuming duties:

> I had helped my mother in bazaars, tag days, processions, etc. etc., fund-raising, church charitable organizations from the time I was knee high. However, once married, I was apolitical. I guess, basically, because I was so very busy [with nine children].[122]
>
> I guess there were clubs and political parties but I really didn't have much time or energy with four small children to get involved. I've always been aware of my own limitations in terms of time and energy.[123]
>
> Not much [leadership from women] in my age group at the time. Too busy at home . . . it was a man's world.[124]
>
> There was no energy or time to do anything about it [feminism].[125]
>
> I didn't participate in politics when my children were small, I was too too too busy. None of my neighbours with children seemed to be involved.[126]

Unless they were especially gregarious, such child-rearing women were likely to devote precious free-time moments to private rather than public pursuits.

To the present day, a baleful mythology associated with postwar suburbs and their female residents persists. Suburban women provided a focus for much contemporary debate about the merits of modern life. In particular, in the minds of critics of mass society who flourished in the years after the Second World War,[127] the suburb emerged as the residential and female expression of the moral bankruptcy they identified in society at large, more particularly in giant corporations, big governments, and the "organization men" who served them.

The most famous indictment from North American feminists was provided by Betty Friedan's *The Feminine Mystique*.[128] This soon-to-be-classic identification of "The Problem

That Has No Name" captured the imagination of a generation no longer satisfied with the restricted options of life in suburbia. As one Canadian reader explained:

> I truly considered my genes disturbed until I read Friedan's book. After all, I'd spent my life working to earn, and indeed cherishing, the one compliment that topped them all—"You think like a man."
> But I was afraid of that book. I read it in very small snatches, because it stirred me greatly, and I couldn't see any purpose to that. There I was, a relatively uneducated woman with two small children to raise.[129]

More than anyone else, Friedan helped women challenge the egalitarian claim of North American abundance. Ultimately, she argued, and many readers agreed, the gendered experience of suburbia betrayed women, consigning them to subordination and frustration within society and unhappiness within the family. Limited options for women also meant an immeasurably poorer "Free World," a critical point when winning the Cold War was all-important. In Canada, Friedan's dismissal of modern housekeeping as neither sufficiently dignified nor time-consuming to require full-time dedication by wives and mothers was matched by a barrage of popular articles in the 1950s.[130]

Whatever Friedan's insights, her work concentrated on a privileged minority. Her suburban women, pushed by the forces of a commercialized culture, appeared to have made the "great refusal" in rejecting purposeful and independent lives in the public sphere. A considerable amount of women-blaming goes on in *The Feminine Mystique*. As with many of her Canadian imitators, Friedan associated suburban women with the evils of modern society — its secularism, superficiality, and materialism. Her feminism, with its support for broader interpretations and expressions of female ability, gave her message special meaning, but the message itself, like attacks on suburbia from social critics unconcerned about sexual inequality, finally ignored the complexity of female lives.

Nonfeminist critics of modern society routinely targeted female suburbanites. Marshall McLuhan's *The Mechanical Bride: Folklore of Industrial Man* identified "millions of women who live isolated lives from 8:00 to 6:00 p.m."[131] in suburbia as part of the dilemma of modern men. In 1956 in "You Take the Suburbs, I Don't Want Them," the novelist Hugh Garner, flexing his muscles as a home-grown literary "bad boy," rejected a world in which men could not make the rules.[132] Suburbia's psychological failings were brutally diagnosed by the assistant director of Montreal's Mental Hygiene Institute. In 1958 Dr. Alastair MacLeod warned *Chatelaine*'s readers that "The suburbs give children fresh air, but take away their fathers. They give women efficient kitchens, but are hard on their femininity and gentleness. They give men pride in providing so handsomely, but drive many of them to drink to make up for their watered-down maleness."[133] This psychiatrist damned suburbs as "matriarchies, manless territories where women cannot be feminine because expediency demands that they control the finances and fix drains and where night-returning men cannot be masculine because their traditional function of ruler and protector has been usurped."[134] While Friedan located suburbia's limitations in the domestic definition of womanhood, few psychiatrists acknowledged that many women needed outlets beyond those provided by purely domestic life.

The indictments of social critics were elaborated most fully in *Crestwood Heights*, a case study of Toronto's Forest Hill, an "inner suburb" built before the Second World War. Dissecting the family lives of an upper-middle-class sample of WASP and Jewish Torontonians, the authors revealed what many critics of mass society feared. Men concentrated on making money, ignoring families' emotional and spiritual needs. Dissatisfied women wielded power in a community in which they were the dominant adults for the daylight hours. Mothers were preoccupied with their offspring, to the detriment of themselves and their children. Both sexes were overly materialistic. The contribution of men and women to the wider society was intrinsically limited. Despite the lack of comparability of this older suburb to what was happening on the periphery of Canadian cities, Crestwood Heights rapidly became the measure by which modern suburbia was judged.[135]

The Royal Architectural Institute of Canada added to the chorus of dismay. Its 1960 *Report* on the design of the residential environment summed up the views of professional architects and representatives of University Women's Clubs and the National Council of Women in its dislike for "the essential identity of houses, the denial of differentiation, built into new sub- urbs."[136] The *Report* was alert to suburbia's failure to reflect changing Canadian demography. While new buildings took for granted a father in paid employment and a mother at home with two children, many households were very different.[137] The land-eating sprawl of three- bedroom Cape Cods, bungalows, or split levels dependent on private transportation and reflec- tive of a single style of family life was not what all Canadians needed. Preoccupied with aesthetics, however, the *Report* never confronted the problem embodied in the gendered nature of suburban space.

Arguments about the merits of suburban life were not always restricted to polite discourse. Residents of Scarborough's Highland Creek, which their MPP characterized as "a normal Ontario suburban community,"[138] were outraged in 1956 when S.D. Clark, of the University of Toronto, was quoted as accusing them of sexual immorality and hard drinking. The leakage of these observations from a private report to a research group forced him to apologize publicly to Scarborough's residents. Even then there were threats of vigilante justice.[139]

Perhaps chastened by this experience, Clark produced a path-breaking study, *The Suburban Society* (1968), which rejected any simple characterization of suburbia. Dismissing *Crestwood Heights* as unrepresentative in its "culture of a particular urban social class and, in large degree, particular ethnic group,"[140] he championed suburbia's variety and vitality. It was this hetero- geneity that Friedan and other critics of modern life, with their focus on middle-class, highly organized communities, had so largely missed. And yet, ironically enough, for all his stress on suburbia's variety, Clark joined critics of mass society in readily sterotyping women. *The Suburban Society* casually dismissed the female resident as "the suburban housewife seeking amusement or instruction in light reading" and the "lone miserable suburban housewife."[141] Making easy generalizations about the "social waste" of women left behind in suburbia,[142] Clark never applied his insight about the complexity of suburban patterns to any consideration of the role of gender. To a significant degree, women continued to be both victims and authors of their own misfortune, keys to the failings of contemporary family life and thus to much of the imperfection of the modern world.

Suburban women, then and today, have their own contributions to make to this debate. In 1959 *Chatelaine's* readers responded passionately to the attack on suburban women issued by the assistant director of Montreal's Mental Hygiene Institute, Dr. Alastair MacLeod. In more than 300 letters they captured the complexity of women's lives. In all, 42 percent defended women, men, and suburbia itself, one critic bluntly summing up her rejection of the psychia- trist's misogyny as "Bunk." A further 11 percent of respondents blamed the problems of modern life on something other than suburbia, while 8 percent gave it mixed reviews. The remaining 39 percent agreed, more or less, with MacLeod's criticism of suburban women. Most readers were reluctant to limit women to domestic labour as a solution to the ills of modern society. One woman from Rexdale, Ontario, pointed out that many young wives had more than enough business experience and brains to manage the home and its finances. It didn't make sense to "restrict them to the monotonous unthinking roles of mere cooks and floor waxers."[143] Most suburban women did much more and did it well. A few readers, while admitting something was wrong, refused to blame women. A Regina contributor, for instance, argued that women were feeling frustrated and inadequate because their "opportunity for economic contribution has largely been taken from the four walls of her home."[144] The whole tenor of the published answers to MacLeod's condemnation of suburban womanhood suggested a diversity of opinion and experience.

Suburbia's veterans still remain divided about its meaning. In letters, memos, interviews, and answers to a questionnaire about their experience in the suburbs between 1945 and 1960,[145] women, whose families ranged from the well-to-do to the economically marginal, reflected on what those years had meant. Many, like one Etobicoke, Ontario, resident, offered a blunt calculation of benefits: "Suburban life was fine. We had an auto so we weren't isolated from the Toronto scene. It also enabled us immigrants to make friends. I'd do it over again. Everyone benefited . . . When you live a situation you aren't always analyzing it. The decision was economic. I wasn't buying into an image."[146] Like many others, whose satisfaction seemed grounded in happy marriages, this writer argued that suburban life was vital and fulfilling. Helpmate husbands did much to make suburbia a good place for wives.

Favourable assessments also sprang from a recognition that life in the suburbs was a step up in terms of convenience, comfort, and security. Days spent previously as tenants, in too few rooms and without domestic conveniences, could make even modest bungalows feel very good. While not without flaws, suburbs were a good deal better than the alternatives. The benefits for children were stressed repeatedly, but women, like the two speakers below, were likely to convey a strong sense of their own good fortune as well:

> It was the right choice for us . . . We did not want to raise our kids on city streets, although I realize now they did miss out on many things such as museums, libraries, etc. . . . I think all who chose the life benefited from the freer life, the men for a lot of companionship with neighbours . . . It was a happier time because we no longer worried about friends and acquaintances, schoolmates who were overseas and in danger.[147]
>
> Those were good years for us. My husband was getting ahead and I saw myself as a help-mate . . . For children suburbia really worked. They always had playmates and they had multiple parenting . . . [but] Suburbia tended to narrow our vision of the outside world. We thought we had the ideal life . . . We knew little about the world of poverty, culture, crime and ethnic variety. We were like a brand new primer, "Dick and Jane."[148]

In reflecting on their suburban lives, women who counted them successful firmly rejected any portrait of themselves as conformists and insisted that the suburbs worked best for the independent and self-motivated. An artist noted that she and her friends "were already in charge of our lives and didn't feel abused."[149] Whether they were gregarious and heavily involved in the community or took pleasure in quiet family pastimes, positive commentators revealed a strong sense of achievement. Happy children, rewarding relationships with spouses, and strong communities were their trophies.

Cheerful accounts contrasted markedly with those who remembered the suburbs as "hell." Days spent largely alone with demanding infants and lack of support from friends, relatives, and sometimes husbands were to be endured. The result could be desperation. One Ontario survivor captured her predicament, and that of others as well, when she wrote: "I began to feel as if I were slowly going out of my mind. Each day was completely filled with child and baby care and keeping the house tidy and preparing meals. I felt under constant pressure."[150] Some women recollected feeling guilty about such unhappiness: If families were more prosperous than ever and husbands doing their jobs, what right did they have to be less than content? When a desperately lonely neighbour hung her three children in the basement, however, one resident of Don Mills put self-doubts aside and set out to create mothers' groups to compensate for the shortcomings of suburban life.[151]

Critics sometimes observed that dissatisfaction extended beyond their sex. Two women explained: "Certainly didn't work for me. I would have been much happier in row housing . . . It seems to me that everyone loses — Women are isolated. Men don't know their families. Children don't know their fathers."[152] And, "I don't think anybody benefited, exactly. You could say men, but they benefited from marriage, suburbs or not . . . And I think a lot of men were miserable trying to play the part imposed upon them in the wasteland."[153] From the perspective of such veterans, women in particular and society as a whole were the poorer because of the investment on the suburban frontier.

Unlike their contemporaries who relished memories of days nurturing children and husbands, critics yearned for lives that offered them more contact with the wider world, more appreciation of their diverse skills, and more financial independence. For them the suburban landscape entailed an unacceptable restriction on options, a source of frustration, anger, and depression. This group often rejected the domestic ideal embodied in suburbia as soon as possible, ridding themselves of unsatisfactory husbands, moving to more congenial settings, and taking paid employment.

Accounts from suburban women rarely match the image presented by Friedan and the critics of mass society. Their experiences were neither homogeneous nor uncomplicated. They were much more than merely the female counterparts of "organization men." Women were both victims and beneficiaries of a nation's experiment with residential enclaves that celebrated the gendered division of labour. Suburban dreams had captured the hopes of a generation shaken by war and depression, but a domestic landscape that presumed that lives could be reduced to a single ideal inevitably failed to meet the needs of all Canadians after 1945. In the 1960s the daughters of the suburbs, examining their parents' lives, would begin to ask for more.

NOTES

1. See Susan Saegert, "Masculine Cities and Feminine Suburbs: Polarized Ideas, Contradictory Realities," *Women and the American City*, ed. C. Stimpson, E. Dixler, M. Nelson, and K. Yatrakis (Chicago, 1981), 106. The appeal of suburbs was not limited to cities. New resource towns, of which 46 appeared between 1945 and 1957, provided numerous instances of what have been termed "suburbs in search of a town," "suburbs in the wilderness," "suburbia in the bush," "transplanted suburbia," "experiments in conformity," "displaced southern suburbs," and "suburbs without a metropolis." Cited in Margaret P. Nunn Bray's useful overview, "'No Life for a Woman': An Examination and Feminist Critique of the Post–World War II Instant Town with Special Reference to Manitouwadge" (MA thesis, Queen's University, 1989), 46. While produced by many of the same forces, the gendered landscape of the resource town is, however, distinctive. This article explores the suburban experience only as it manifested itself around cities.

2. See, for example, the discussion of gendered space in the provocative studies by Joy Parr, *The Gender of Breadwinners: Women, Men, and Change in Two Industrial Towns, 1880–1950* (Toronto, 1990), and Peter DeLottinville, "Joe Beef of Montreal," *Labour/Le Travailleur* 8/9 (Autumn/Spring 1981/2): 9–40 [reprinted in this volume].

3. Among the major studies, see Kenneth Jackson, *Crabgrass Frontier: The Suburbanization of the United States* (New York, 1985); Robert Fishman, *Bourgeois Utopias: The Rise and Fall of Suburbia* (New York, 1987); Elaine Tyler May, *Homeward Bound: American Families in the Cold War Era* (New York, 1988); Margaret Marsh, *Suburban Lives* (New Brunswick and London, 1990); and Dolores Hayden, *Redesigning the American Dream: The Future of Housing, Work and Family Life* (New York and London, 1984).

4. "Canadian Suburbanization in a North American Context: Does the Border Make a Difference?" *Journal of Urban History* 13, 3 (May 1987): 252–74.

5. Caroline Andrew and Beth Moore Milroy, eds., *Life Spaces: Gender, Household, Employment* (Vancouver, 1988), 4.

6. See Veronica Strong-Boag, *The New Day Recalled: Lives of Girls and Women in English Canada, 1919–1939* (Toronto, 1988).

7. The number of passenger automobiles registered in Canada rose from 1 281 190 in 1941 to 2 105 869 in 1951 to 4 325 682 in 1961. Series T147–194, *Historical Statistics of Canada,* 2nd ed. (Ottawa, 1983).

8. See Charles L. Sanford, "'Woman's Place' in American Car Culture," *The Automobile and American Culture,* ed. David L. Lewis and Laurence Goldstein (Ann Arbor, 1983).

9. See Series Q13–18 to Q75–80, *Historical Statistics of Canada.*

10. See, for example, John Thomas, "How to Stay Married," *Canadian Home Journal* (April 1955): 2–3.

11. For a useful discussion of the impact of the Cold War on sex roles in the United States, see May, *Homeward Bound.*

12. James Lemon, *Toronto since 1918* (Toronto, 1985), 94.

13. See Joyce Hibbert, *The War Brides* (Toronto, 1978), for revealing portraits of the brides who came to Canada.

14. Alice Hooper Beck, "Royal Mother," *Chatelaine* (Jan. 1951): 63. See Hector Bolitho, "The Queen's Conflict: How Can One Woman Fulfill the Dual Role of Monarch and Mother?" ibid. (Feb. 1953): 12–13, 36, 38, 40. See also David Macdonald, "Farewell to the Fifties," *Star Weekly* (2 Jan. 1960): 10–11, 14, who saw the decade as "frantic . . . an age of anxiety," 24.

15. Dr. K.S. Bernhardt, "Happily Ever After," *Bride's Book* (Fall/Winter 1952): 75.

16. See Fred Edge, "Are Fathers Necessary?" *Canadian Home Journal* (Feb. 1953): 24, 63; John Thomas, "Are Fathers Necessary?" ibid., 24, 63–4, and "Father's a Parent, Too," *Canadian Home and Gardens* (April 1952): 29–31.

17. See Strong-Boag, *New Day.*

18. See J. Ronald Oakley, *God's Country: America in the Fifties* (New York, 1986).

19. Mildred Grade Baker, "Canadian Women and the Suburban Experience, 1945–60: Questionnaire for Residents" (henceforth "Questionnaire"), to author (1991), 8. See also note 147 below.

20. Marjorie Bacon, "Questionnaire," 16.

21. A. Montague, *The Natural Superiority of Women* (New York, 1953), 188. See the favourable assessment in Joan Morris, "The Scientific Truth about 'Male Superiority,'" *Canadian Home Journal* (July 1957): 15, 45.

22. Ibid., 25.

23. See the positive, if cautious, review of Kinsey's work by J.R. Seeley and J. Griffin in *Canadian Welfare* (15 Oct. 1948); the optimistic assessment of the utility of early marriage for women, based on Kinsey's findings, in Miriam Chapin, "Can Women Combine the B.A. and the Baby?" *Saturday Night* (21 Feb. 1948): 24; and the positive attitude to the similarity of male and female sexuality in Eleanor Rumming, "Dr. Kinsey and the Human Female," ibid. (15 Aug. 1953): 7–8. See also Gary Kinsman, *The Regulation of Desire: Sexuality in Canada* (Toronto, 1987), 113–15.

24. See Regina Markell Morantz, "The Scientist as Sex Crusader: Alfred C. Kinsey and American Culture," in *Procreation or Pleasure: Sexual Attitudes in American History,* ed. T.L. Altherr (Malabar, 1983).

25. See "Dr. Kinsey Talks about Women to Lotta Dempsey," *Chatelaine* (Aug. 1949): 10–11, 59–60; and Claire Halliday, "A New Approach to the Problem of Frigidity," *Canadian Home Journal* (June 1956): 9, 69.

26. See "The Age for Marriage," *Chatelaine* (May 1948): 2.

27. Jan E. Dizard and Howard Gadlin, "Family Life and the Marketplace: Diversity and Change in the American Family," in *Historical Social Psychology,* ed. K.J. Gergen and M.M. Gergen (Hillsdale and London, 1984), 292.

28. See, for example, Elsieliese Thorpe, "Does He Resent Your Working?" *Star Weekly* (May 1953), who emphasized the husband's right "to have a wife's undivided attentions at times when he needs to unburden himself, the right to have a companion and a friend when he needs one," 7; Charles Cerami, "Are You Jealous of Your Husband's Job?" ibid. (8 Nov. 1958): 30–41; and J.K. Thomas, "If He Lost His Job . . . ," *Canadian Home Journal* (Feb. 1957): 10–11.

29. Ken Johnstone, "How Do You Rate with Your Husband's Boss?" *Chatelaine* (March 1953): 70. See also the fierce rejection of the role of business helpmate in Mrs. John Doe, "An Open Letter to My Husband's Boss," *Canadian Home Journal* (May 1954): 10–11, 90, 93.

30. Dr. Marion Hilliard, *A Woman Doctor Looks at Love and Life* (Toronto, 1957), 72–73.

31. Full-page ad for Eaton's, *Saturday Night* (9 Aug. 1949): 19.

32. See the response of 2000 members of *Chatelaine's* Consumers' Council in Mary Juke, "It Makes Married Life Easier," *Chatelaine* (Sept. 1948): 22–23. On television, see Paul Rutherford, *When Television Was Young: Primetime Canada, 1952–1967* (Toronto, 1990), 200–1, which includes a useful discussion of the sexism of broadcasting in these years.

33. S.J. Wilson, *Women, the Family and the Economy* (Toronto, 1972), 19.

34. For discussion of this phenomenon, see Meg Luxton, Harriet Rosenberg, Sedef Arat-Koe, *Through the Kitchen Window: The Politics of Home and Family,* 2nd ed. (Toronto, 1990).

35. Zoe Bieler, "White-Collar Wife," *Chatelaine* (Aug. 1953): 22–4, 37–40.

36. See, for example, Gwyn Le Capelan, "I Worked My Husband's Way through College," *Chatelaine* (April 1949): 4–5. See also the discussion in National Archives of Canada (NA), MG 31, K8, Mattie Rotenberg Papers, vol. 1, folder 66, radio broadcast "Changing Patterns" (Jan. 1954).

37. See Ruth Roach Pierson, "Gender and the Unemployment Insurance Debates in Canada, 1934–1960," *Labour/Le Travail* 25 (Spring 1990): 77–103.

38. See Anita A. Birt, "Married Women, You're Fools to Take a Job," *Chatelaine* (Jan. 1960): 41.

39. Dorothy Manning, "I Quit My Job to Save My Marriage," ibid. (June 1955): 16.

40. Jean Libman Block, "Husbands Should Not Do Housework!" *Star Weekly* (16 Nov. 1957): 6.

41. See the complaint about discrimination against women in Francis Ecker, "Will Married Women Go to War Again?" *Saturday Night* (30 Jan. 1951): 21–3. For a more extended discussion of the policies of the federal government in this area, see Ruth Roach Pierson, *"They're Still Women after All": The Second World War and Canadian Womanhood* (Toronto, 1986), chap. 2.

42. John G. McCulloch, "How to Be Sure of a Happy Marriage," *Bride's Book* (Spring/Summer 1953): 86. See also John K. Thomas, "How to Stay Married: Can Motherhood and Career Mix?" *Canadian Home Journal* (March 1955): 4, 6. For a contemporary assessment of women's own reservations about paid work, especially for mothers with young children, see Department of Labour, "Married Women Workers: The Home Situation," in *Canadian Society: Sociological Perspectives*, ed. B.R. Blishen, F.E. Jones, K.D. Naegele, and J. Porter (New York, 1961), 176.

43. See, for example, John Nash, "It's Time Father Got Back in the Family," *Maclean's* (12 May 1956), 28; S.R. Laycock, "Homosexuality — A Mental Hygiene Problem," *Canadian Medical Association Journal* (Sept. 1950): 247, as cited in Kinsman, *Regulation*, 115; Mary Graham, "Mama's Boy," *Canadian Home Journal* (Oct. 1952): 18–19, 37–39; and Hilliard, *Woman Doctor*, passim. The most famous example of "woman-blaming" in these years was Marynia Farnham and Ferdinand Lundberg, *Modern Woman: The Lost Sex* (1947), with its classic Freudian claim that "anatomy is destiny."

44. Montague, as cited in Robert McKeown, "Women Are the Stronger Sex," *Weekend Magazine, Vancouver Sun* (22 Jan. 1955): 2. See also Dr. Ashley Montague, "Why Men Fall in Love with You," *Chatelaine* (Oct. 1958): 23, 58, 99; Joan Morris, "The Scientific Truth about 'Male Superiority,'" *Canadian Home Journal* (July 1957): 15, 45; and Florida Scott-Maxwell, "Do Men Fear Women?" *Chatelaine* (Nov. 1959): 39, 50, 54–55.

45. See the argument by the anonymous author of "Careers and Marriage Don't Mix," *Saturday Night* (1 Nov. 1949): 32, who concluded that she had been letting her husband down, despite her higher salary of $10 000 a year, by not keeping up the domestic side of their life.

46. *Chatelaine* (March 1959): 214.

47. See J.N. Harris, "One Vacancy!" *Saturday Night* (15 Nov. 1947), 20; E.L. Chicanot, "Juvenile Immigration Will Help Canada," ibid. (6 Dec. 1947): 24, 37; Benjamin Higgins, "Better Strategy and Tactics to Win the Housing War," ibid. (14 Feb. 1948): 6–7; J. Bhaidlow, "Proper Rentals to Ease Housing Predicament," ibid. (17 April 1948): 17, 32; D. Wilensky, "War's Impact on Family Life," *Canadian Welfare* (15 Oct. 1945): 8–16.

48. Canada Mortgage and Housing, *Housing in Canada, 1945–1986: An Overview and Lessons Learned* (Ottawa, 1987), 6.

49. Ibid., 10.

50. Jill Wade, "'A Palace for the Public': Housing Reform and the 1946 Occupation of the Old Hotel Vancouver," *BC Studies* (Spring/Summer 1986): 288–310; "'Squatter Fever' Spreads to Canada," *The Enterprise* (Lansing, ON), 10 Oct. 1946.

51. John Clare, "Where Are the Houses?" *Star Weekly* (8 June 1946): 5.

52. See Dorothy Livesay and Dorothy Macdonald, "Why B.C. Divorces Soar," *Star Weekly* (15 May 1948): 16; and Marjorie Earl, "Canada's Divorce Headache," ibid. (12 June 1948): Section 2, 2.

53. See Canada, Advisory Committee on Reconstruction, Housing and Community Planning, SubCommittee *Report, No. 4* (Ottawa 1944).

54. For an excellent review of policy, see Albert Rose, *Canadian Housing Policies (1935–1980)* (Toronto, 1980).

55. See John Bacher, "From Study to Reality: The Establishment of Public Housing in Halifax, 1930–1953," *Acadiensis* 18, 1 (Autumn 1988): 120–35; and Albert Rose, *Regent Park: A Study of Slum Clearance* (Toronto, 1958).

56. Graduate Students in Community and Regional Planning, *Bridgeview: A Sub/Urban Renewal Study in Surrey, B.C.* (University of British Columbia, 1965).

57. See his *White Niggers of America* (Toronto, 1971). For an equally unflattering description of Ville Jacques Cartier, see John Gray, "Why Live in the Suburbs?" *Maclean's* (1 Sept. 1954): 7–11, 50–52.

58. See Project Planning Associates Ltd., *City of St. John's Newfoundland: Urban Renewal Study* (Toronto, 1961), 6.

59. See David Bettison, *The Politics of Canadian Urban Development*, vol. 1 (Edmonton, 1975), 110.

60. CMHC mortgage assistance was tied to the earnings of the family head; if earnings were too low, then assistance was denied. In low-income areas such as the Maritimes, CMHC loans were correspondingly fewer. For a discussion of the regional implications of CMHC policy, see Atlantic Development Board, *Urban Centres in the Atlantic Provinces* (Ottawa, 1969), 74.

61. Ibid., 76.

62. For a discussion of the impact of mortgaging by government, see Lawrence B. Smith, *The Postwar Canadian Housing and Residential Mortgage Markets and the Role of Government* (Toronto, 1974), chap. 9, and also Rose, *Canadian Housing Policies*, chap. 3. In 1951 single-family construction made up 77.3 percent of all the dominion's housing starts; in 1955, 71.5 percent and in 1960, 61.7 percent. Smith, *Postwar Canadian Housing*, 22–23.

63. S.D. Clark, The Suburban Society (Toronto, 1968), 101.

64. Krisztina Bevilacqua to author, 10 May 1991.

65. Marjorie Bacon, interview with author, 7 June 1991.

66. See John Gray, "A New Life Begins in Winnipeg," *Star Weekly* (9 July 1960): 2–4, 6–7.

67. Lois Strong to author, 29 May 1991.

68. Montreal suburbanite 1, "Questionnaire," 7.

69. See John Weaver, "From Land Assembly to Social Maturity: The Suburban Way of Life of Westdale (Hamilton), Ontario, 1911–1951," *Histoire sociale/Social History* (Nov. 1978): 437.

70. "More Than Half Don Mills Home Owners Professional Men or Executives Survey Shows," *The Enterprise* (Lansing), 26 May 1957.

71. Dottie Walter, "Homes for Tomorrow," *Canadian Home Journal* (June 1945): 30, 33.

72. "Saracinis Will Build 106 Islington Homes," *Etobicoke Press*, 13 April 1950.

73. Rose, *Housing in Postwar Canada*, 168–71.

74. Ronald Hamilton, "You Need a Wife Who Can Saw," *Maclean's* (July 1950): 36.

75. Mildred Grace Baker, "Questionnaire."

76. Helen M. Boneham, "Questionnaire," 5.

77. Catherine Cunningham to author, 14 May 1991.

78. See Clark, *Suburban Society*, 16–18, for his classification of different suburban types. These included "I. The Single-Family Residential Development of the 'Pure' Suburban Type; II. The Semi-Detached Residential Development of the 'Pure' Suburban Type; III. The Single-Family Residential Development in a Built-Up Area; IV. The 'Packaged' or Semi-Packaged Residential Development; V. The Cottage-Type Residential Development; VI. The Residential Development of the 'Pure' Suburban Type, Now Five to Ten Years Old." In the context of this classification, "pure" meant lacking "form and structure" (12) and "packaged" meant growing up "as a result of careful planning and direction" (15).

79. See Collier Stevenson, "City Living in the Country," *Canadian Home Journal* (Nov. 1947): 55–56. For a Scarborough example, see "Guildwood Village on the Move," *The Enterprise* (West Hill) (25 Sept. 1958).

80. "All-Canadian Home Designed from Results of Newspaper Survey," *Canadian Builder* (Jan. 1960): 62, and "Million Mark Reached," ibid. (Oct. 1956): 41. See also "Scarborough Has Canada's Millionth New Home," *The Enterprise* (West Hill) (26 July 1956).

81. The Lower Mainland Regional Planning Board, *The Urban Frontier*, Pt. 2: Technical Report (New Westminster, BC: Oct. 1963): 37.

82. As quoted in William MacEachern, "Suburbia on Trial," *Star Weekly* (18 May 1957): 2. See also, for a continuation of this preoccupation with children, Isabel Dyck, "Integrating Home and Wage Workplace: Women's Daily Lives in a Canadian Suburb," *Canadian Geographer/Le géographie canadien* 33, 4 (1989): 329–41.

83. Mrs. Woods, Saracini Construction, "What the Experts Say about Kitchens," *Canadian Builder* (June 1958): 50.

84. Anthony Adamson, "Where Are the Rooms of Yesteryear?" *Canadian Architect* (June 1958): 74.

85. See, for example, Frank Moritsugu, "Learn How to Relax," *Canadian Homes and Gardens* (Jan. 1955): 7–9, 38–39, 41.

86. Male former resident, Oakridge Acres, London, Ontario, to author, 10 June 1991.

87. See R.D. Magladry, "Door-to-Door Salesmanship Fills the Gap," *Financial Post* 54 (5 March 1960): 13; "Beauty Aid Sales Soar," ibid. (20 Aug. 1960): 1; and J. Schreiner, "Door-to-Door Is a Booming Business," ibid. 55 (30 Dec. 1961): 24.

88. "Wife or Working Girl?" *Bride's Book* (Fall/Winter 1952): 4, 6.

89. Boneham, "Questionnaire," 14.

90. Alaine Barrett Baines, "Questionnaire," 8.

91. Scarborough suburbanite, interview with author, March 1991.

92. Clark, *Suburban Society*, 121.

93. On this male attitude, see Meg Luxton, *More Than a Labour of Love: Three Generations of Women's Work in the Home* (Toronto, 1980), 163–65.

94. On the existence of two standards of living within the family, see the bitter observation in Mrs. John Doe, "An Open Letter to My Husband's Boss."

95. Bettison, *Politics*, 110.

96. As a sign of this interest the Community Planning Association of Canada was created in 1946. See Gerald Hodge, *Planning Canadian Communities* (Toronto and New York, 1986).

97. See the bungalow winner for 1947 in *Etobicoke Press*, 17 March 1947.

98. "First All Canadian Home Completed in Etobicoke," *Star Weekly* (12 Sept. 1959): 14–18.

99. "Home '53," *Canadian Home Journal* (Aug. 1953): 19, 45, 46, 48, 50, 52–53, 58–60.

100. Mary-Ella Macpherson, "Postwar Houses," *Chatelaine* (May 1945): 96.

101. See Betty Alice Marrs Naylor, "Questionnaire."

102. Helen Wallis, "Suburban Experience" (typescript), to author, 3.

103. Boneham, "Questionnaire," 5.

104. John Leaning, "The Distribution of Shopping Centres in Canada," *Canadian Builder* (June 1956): 41–45.

105. Bacon, "Questionnaire," 12.

106. H.J. Barnun, Jr, executive vice-president, Salada-Shirriff-Horsey, Toronto, as cited in "Calls Suburbs Best Place to Develop Retail Sales," *Style Fortnightly* (15 Jan. 1958): 35.

107. Mildred Fox Baker, "Questionnaire," 12.

108. Patricia Margaret Zieman Hughes, "Questionnaire," 12.

109. Alaine Barrett Baines, "Questionnaire," 13.

110. See Eileen Morris, "Your Home-and-School Faces a Crisis," *Chatelaine* (Nov. 1955): 11–13.

111. Between 1947 and 1962, for example, the United Church established 2000 new churches. See Mary Anne MacFarlane, "A Tale of Handmaidens: Deaconesses in the United Church of Canada, 1925 to 1964" (MA thesis, OISE/University of Toronto, 1987), 80.

112. Doris McCubbin, "How to Live in a Suburb," *Chatelaine* (March 1955): 35.

113. See Frank Moritsugu, "The Amazing Don Mills," *Canadian Home and Gardens* (Dec. 1954): 13–19, 55–60, 68.

114. *Vancouver Sun*, 6 Jan. 1951.

115. "Thornhill Women Are Proud of Their Flourishing Nursery School," *The Enterprise* (Lansing), 19 April 1951.

116. "Parents Unite to Catch Man Molesting Children," ibid., 28 April 1955.

117. "1,000 Families Protest Isolation of Rexdale," *Etobicoke Guardian*, 13 Jan. 1955.

118. "Parents Protest Board Moving School Children," *The Enterprise* (Lansing), 2 June 1955.

119. D. Smith, "Don Mills Memo," ibid., 7 Oct. 1954.

120. "Subdivision Problems Cause Angry Mothers to Storm Council Meeting," *Etobicoke Press*, 19 April 1956.

121. Montreal West suburbanite 1, "Questionnaire," 6.

122. Mildred Fox Baker, "Questionnaire," 14.

123. Surrey, BC, suburbanite 1, "Questionnaire," 14.

124. Betty Marrs Naylor, "Questionnaire," 14.

125. Toronto West suburbanite 1, "Questionnaire," 15.

126. Jasper Place, Alberta, suburbanite, "Questionnaire," 14.

127. For one of the few discussions of these critics in Canada, see Rutherford, *When Television Was Young*, esp. chap. 1. For a provocative assessment of the connection between fears about mass society and the maintenance of masculinity, see Barbara Ehrenreich, *The Hearts of Men* (Garden City, NY, 1983).

128. Published in New York in 1963.

129. Wallis, "Suburban Experience," 23.

130. See Richard Roe, "I'm Sending My Wife Back to Work," *Canadian Home Journal* (April 1954): 4–5, 98; Jean Pringle, "How I Broke Out of Solitary Confinement," *Chatelaine* (May 1948): 34; Beverly Gray, "Housewives Are a Sorry Lot," *Chatelaine* (March 1950): 26–27, 37; Isabel T. Dingman, "A Widow Writes an Open Letter to Wives," *Chatelaine* (June 1954): 20–21, 34–35, 37; Dr. Marion Hilliard, "Stop Being Just a Housewife," *Chatelaine* (Sept. 1956): 11, 90; Patricia Clark, "Stop Pitying the Underworked Housewife," *Maclean's* (19 July 1958): 8, 37–38; Jane Hamilton, "Housewives Are Self-Centred Bores," *Star Weekly Magazine* (22 Aug. 1959): 38, 45.

131. Published in New York in 1951. The quote is from page 76.

132. H. Garner, "You Take the Suburbs, I Don't Want Them," *Maclean's* (10 Nov. 1956): 30.

133. Dr. A. MacLeod, "The Sickness of Our Suburbs," *Chatelaine* (Oct. 1958): 23.

134. Ibid., 94–95.

135. See Robert Olson, "What Happened to the Suburb They Called Crestwood Heights?" *Maclean's* (12 Oct. 1957): 24–25, 34–36, 38. The strength of this legacy can be seen in the incorrect identification of Crestwood Heights as Don Mills in McGahan, *Urban Sociology in Canada*, 187.

136. Committee of Inquiry into the Design of the Residential Environment, *Report* (Ottawa 1960), *Journal of the Royal Architectural Institute of Canada* (May 1960): 186.

137. Ibid.

138. "R.E. Sutton Censures Story of 'Carefree' Life at H. Creek," *The Enterprise* (West Hill), 25 Oct. 1956.

139. "There Is No Joy in Highland Creek," *Globe and Mail*, 23 Oct. 1956; "Professor's Report Creates Furor," *The Enterprise* (West Hill), 25 Oct. 1956; and "Letters to the Editor," 1 Nov. 1956.

140. Clark, *Suburban Society*, 6.

141. Ibid., 4.

142. Ibid., 224.

143. Ruth Drysdale, "What Our Readers Say about Suburbia," *Chatelaine* (Jan. 1959): 50.

144. Mrs. J.M. Telford, ibid., 53.

145. Contacts with these women, 32 as of 15 June 1991, are part of an ongoing effort to get in touch with as many women as possible from different types of suburbs in different regions of the country. These women are asked to specify how they wish to be identified, whether anonymously, by community, or by name, and their choice is reflected in the footnotes to this article. After the completion of a manuscript now entitled "Home Dreams: Women and Canadian Suburbs, 1945–60," these research materials, with certain restrictions on their use, will be deposited in a public archive.

146. Etobicoke suburbanite 1, "Questionnaire," 17.

147. Mildred Fox Baker, "Questionnaire," 17.

148. Metro Toronto suburbanite 1, "Questionnaire," 17.

149. London, Ontario, suburbanite 1, "Questionnaire," 17.

150. Niagara-on-the-Lake suburbanite 1 to author, 10 May 1991.

151. Marjorie Bacon to author, 6 April 1991.

152. Toronto West suburbanite 1, "Questionnaire," 17.

153. Wallis, "Suburban Experience," 27.

Article Thirty-One

Fatherhood, Masculinity, and the Good Life During Canada's Baby Boom, 1945–1965

Robert Rutherdale

Family historians examining the baby boom years may find it difficult to establish the relationships between how the period was represented and how it was actually experienced. Popular depictions of family life, whether in film, print, or radio or through the new medium of television, projected images usually designed to appeal to wide audiences. While actual experiences varied enormously — in rural and urban settings, among families that were poor or wealthy, newcomer or settled — commercial and popular representations of family life tended to displace reflections of reality with those of an ideal, or constructed, norm. Regardless of

Source: Robert Rutherdale, "Fatherhood, Masculinity, and the Good Life During Canada's Baby Boom, 1945–1965" from *Journal of Family History*, 24, 3 (July 1999), pp. 351–73, copyright © 1999 by Sage Publications Inc. Reprinted by Permission of Sage Publications.

local, ethnic, or class differences, mainstream depictions disseminated through the most powerful channels of communication often reflected the aims of consumerism: to create imagined familial contexts for products associated with household formation and consumption. Since the commodification of family life in mass media and advertising helped to promote a very real surge in goods and services consumed by baby boom families, we might expect some distance between images and realities in family life throughout the baby boom years. Conventional depictions of white, middle-class conjugal families served to smooth the edges of a more complex reality at a time when manufacturers and service suppliers competed for increased markets created by unprecedented levels of household formation.[1]

Given their tendency to homogenize family life, hegemonic representations during the baby boom can, nonetheless, provide evidence of shifting tastes, preferences, styles, and values within a commercial mainstream, something often quite distinct from the actual experience of subgroups in Canadian society as a whole. Notions of the ideal, what was expected in the "normal" family, can also influence how a period is remembered, a pattern I encountered frequently while gathering the life stories of men who were fathers in the 1950s and early 1960s. How were the activities of the home handyman, the father on vacation with his family, the baseball coach, or the backyard barbecuer considered masculine in the memories I collected and in samples of journalism typical for the period? The gendered norms delineated in such texts can help us assess for the baby boom generation of husbands and parents what researchers have increasingly approached as evidence of masculine domesticity in histories of fatherhood generally.[2]

The concept of masculine domesticity was first used by Margaret Marsh to describe the adoption of family- and home-centered practices among fathers responding to suburbanization and among the expanded sectors of middle-class men in the wage economy.[3] As a cultural invention, its rise coincided with urban and industrial growth that stretched back well into the nineteenth century. As preconditions, three structural factors permit the emergence of masculine domesticity: family incomes sufficient for a middle-class standard of living, daily work schedules that permit fathers of companionate marriages to return home on a regular basis, and sufficient family living spaces that permit recreational space both inside the home and in the immediate neighborhood. Masculine domesticity was not real feminism but can be best understood as the particular ways men acted within roles associated with home life, from active parenting to household maintenance. It was, as Marsh sees it,

> a model of behavior in which fathers would agree to take on increased responsibility for some of the day-to-day tasks of bringing up children and spending their time away from work in playing with their sons and daughters, teaching them, taking them on trips.

A family man would more often spend his evenings with his wife rather than with his "male cronies."

> While he might not dust the mantel or make the bed except in exceptional circumstances, he would take a significantly greater interest in the details of running the household and caring for the children than his father was expected to.[4]

In American contexts, Marsh traces shifts toward the "domestic man" between mid-century and 1915, while Robert L. Griswold, in *Fatherhood in America*, examines the more family-centered roles that mostly middle-class fathers assumed as part of the new fatherhood of the 1920s.[5]

Part of this study is based on oral histories collected from thirty-four fathers and grandfathers living in Prince George and Abbotsford in the province of British Columbia, men who fathered baby boomers during the 1950s and 1960s. Prince George is centrally located in the northern interior, a timber-rich region that remains heavily dependent on forest product industries. Pulp production began in the early 1960s, drew thousands of young families to the area, and stimulated continued growth in the city from fewer than ten thousand in the mid-1950s to more than fourteen thousand a decade later, before population levels surged in sharp crests toward eighty thousand in the mid-1990s. Growth took place in tandem with the opening of each of three pulp mills and brought with it increased demands for local services. Expanding local infrastructures, from schools and hospitals to shopping and recreational centers, were crucial for newcomers, especially for younger families establishing themselves in the city's new suburban developments. While the timing of Prince George's postwar modernization coincided with trends on both sides of the Canada–U.S. border, it was more intense than most areas and affords an attractive place to study family life on a resource-based "job frontier:" It was, simply put, a city of newcomers, especially during the baby boom.[6]

Population growth in the Abbotsford area, located in the Fraser Valley farm belt, was less dramatic, reflecting the continued importance of agriculture in the region, supplemented by new produce-processing plants and growth in agricultural suppliers.[7] An influx of newcomers throughout the baby boom was nonetheless significant there as well. The 1951 census recorded 15,108 people living in Matsqui, Sumas, and the village of Abbotsford, now amalgamated as a single municipality. By 1966, the figure had jumped to 23,398, a gain of 54.9 percent.[8] Many of the narratives I collected were, of course, concerned with some aspect of household formation, from accounts of marriage and childbirth to how new family homes were acquired or built, in either locale.

This study begins in a time when the idealization of home life can be partly explained as something that had been denied to so many for nearly an entire generation. As Doug Owram has stated in his study of Canada's baby boom, the "idea of home thus had very powerful connotations by the end of the war, ranging from material comfort to renewed relationships, to peace itself." This "romanticized and idealized vision of family," he suggests, was a natural human reaction to years of disruption.[9] Since rising economic prosperity and household formation characterized the period, representations of leisure and consumption in particular were selected as key aspects of historical shifts in masculine domesticity during the postwar era. Forms of masculine domesticity associated with consumption and leisure were intricately connected to significant changes in household demography and to changing family practices.[10]

Relationships between consumption, gender, and household formation can only be partly understood by focusing on the roles played by wives and mothers in the home and marketplace. Veronica Strong-Boag, for example, has considered the conflicts that Canadian women experienced between domestic and paid labor demands that point to part of a larger picture of the gender/power relations shaping how families divided their incomes and time and how they constructed social roles based on sexual difference.[11] Even if attention remains focused on women's domestic roles in postwar homes, the rapid rise in consumption since the late 1940s reflected a host of family practices that intersected with the gendered experiences and responses of fathers as well as of their partners. This work leads us to consider parallel segments of masculine behaviors during the postwar boom years. Widening our consideration of postwar consumerism to include fathers and domestic masculinity as a cultural response — in particular, to consider the preferences and practices of fathers as consumers of goods and services applied to family leisure — can help us gain a broader picture of changes in family life brought about by the economies and culture of postwar consumerism.

The tendency to see mothers at home and fathers at work can obscure the relevance of fatherhood as part of family life. Owram is somewhat guilty of this in suggesting that domestic leisure was dominated by stay-at-home mothers, while fathers remained on the margins, though he notes that their roles as recreational leaders expanded considerably. "The anti-authoritarian views of family life and the accentuation of the sexual division of labour," as he put it,

> meant that children could expect a full-time camp counselor, leisure coordinator, and chauffeur in Mother. Father was present only in the evening and on weekends, but he was much softened when compared to the foreboding figure of Victorian times. Fathers too were supposed to be pals, to take an active part in the world of children and leisure. Thousands of part-time hockey and baseball coaches around the nation testified to the power of this social role.[12]

Although only coaching is mentioned directly here, an important part of our understanding of fatherhood at this time needs to be broadened to consider how fathers refashioned their domestic roles during the period.

What Griswold refers to as an "ideology of breadwinning" among fathers continued to shape gender relations and define their "sense of self, manhood and gender" during the baby boom as in other periods.[13] But the objects and activities on which disposable incomes were spent increased, and new patterns of masculine domesticity emerged. How evidence of this survives as oral histories of fatherhood and family leisure and how it was represented in the print media became a focus for my fieldwork and sampling of the journalistic discourse of the period. Although breadwinning roles remained a central and defining characteristic of fatherhood, an inquiry directed at how print media depictions and self-representations of fatherhood intersect with experiences of a real past, of cultural ideals shaped by higher consumption levels, can also shed light on what forms masculine domesticity assumed in the period. Fathers too expressed themselves at home, at play, on vacation, and as spouses and parents in pursuit of family or community recreation. And these roles left their own discursive patterns, which survive in memory; in the photographs, illustrations, and advertising copy that circulated during these years; and in popular journalism concerned with family life at that time.

APPROACHES TO THE PRINT MEDIA AND TO THE LIFE STORIES OF FATHERHOOD

In 1955, as the midpoint of the baby boom approached and the dramatic upswing in postwar consumption had become well established, journalist Fred Bodsworth published a general interest piece in *Maclean's* magazine, Canada's most popular English-language weekly, called "The Best Way to Take a Holiday." While it seemed timely and appropriate as an entertaining how-to segment on family automobile camping, replete with statistics on its sudden popularity, it also presented a father's perspective on family adventure and masculinity. After championing its economy (just $2.08 per day for each family member!) and the cohesion it could bring to "team" members, Bodsworth added something, somewhat tongue in cheek, that we might take more seriously, "though I might be a fool for revealing it," as he put it.

> It's a wonderful thing for male prestige. It puts the male back in his traditional role as provider and protector. If you are one of those husbands who bungles every household job and finally stands back humiliated while your wife finishes, you need to take her camping. Setting up a camp looks tough to a woman — to her it belongs with carving-a-home out of the wilderness — but it really isn't that tough at all. In fact, it's a lot easier than mending a leaky faucet, but don't let her find out. Those primitive skills like fire lighting will impress a woman much more than coming home from the office with news that your Whatzit sales are thirty-eight percent higher than the same month last year. For it is one of life's great injustices that, while Man has become thoroughly civilized, Woman still admires him most in a thoroughly uncivilized back-to-nature role.[14]

This depiction, with its ironic portrait of the incompetent father at home or the playful gender-based rivalry between young parents, seemed partly embedded, at least with respect to the possibility of male assertiveness, in family adventure. Like the idealization of home that both wives and husbands engaged in at this time, the idealization of recreation embraced its own mythology, much of which intersected with masculinity and consumption. If not entirely part of the "father's world," family outings depended in part on fathers making that world possible. Finding the good life, on vacation, in tents, boats, cottages, on trains, and even aboard new flights to Europe or some sunny destination, was portrayed in the print media, and in the oral narratives I have recorded, as an important aspect of manful assertiveness.

The style and content of popular journalism that dealt with fatherhood at this time often harmonized with other media messages and images of ideal male parenting. This is particularly true of advertising, considered here as a useful indicator of normative or idealistic depictions designed to appeal to targeted consumers. As generic, commercial forms of representation, images of ideal consumption may have served as models of family life in particular historical contexts, but by no means should they be equated with lived experience. Like Bodsworth's anecdotal account of the family camp out, advertising images in mass-circulating magazines simply suggest how readers were expected to conceive of objects or practices not as reality but as symbols of desire.[15]

A similar point can be made for the use of oral history. As Elizabeth Tonkin has argued, oral narratives are not directed solely by the researcher and the teller but are better understood as cultural constructions embedded in the many norms and ideals that societies create. This "multivocality" of memory is arguably its most significant characteristic. Strictly speaking, as Tonkin notes, oral narratives usually develop as dialogues between researchers and subjects. Many factors shape their construction, and their structures, as she states, are "not reducible to the separate component contributions" of either researchers or their subjects.[16] As a meeting ground between the individual and society, oral histories of fatherhood offer rich sources that transcend individual experience or self-representation. Narratives of fatherhood roles tend to be rooted in languages that also uncover conventional portraits of the ideal man as father, husband, parent, worker, companion, and so on, and the origins of those very ideals need to be historicized.

Memories of fatherhood experiences, usually construed by the teller as individual and unique, tend to be situated within a normative sense of fathers' roles, something researchers should be wary of as both problematic and potentially useful. In generating stories in languages derived from values, attitudes, and beliefs that appeared to be predominant at the time, therefore, the men I interviewed drew self-portraits that can be situated within a more significant collective past. Although many fathers believed that they had led self-directed lives or had formed their opinions independently, I chose to assess memories of fatherhood for both internal and comparative consistencies that suggested societal and cultural influences.[17] From colorful colloquialisms to crisp metaphors, shared and seemingly popular tropes often suggested how certain masculinities were deployed and inscribed in the culture of a previous generation.

Such evidence could be generated at any point in the interview; however, the following questions (introduced toward the end of each session) often provided the best opportunities: "What did you think was important about being a father and why'?" "What did you like/dislike most about it?" "What made a 'good' and a 'bad' father in your day?" "How were you the same as (and different than) your father?" "Did you know other fathers well?" "Did they influence you?" "What worked out well for you as a father?" and "If you had the chance, what would you do differently?" Interviews were tape-recorded and generally required two to three hours to complete. Two fathers participated in follow-up sessions and, for comparative scrutiny, four wives/mothers and two grown children were interviewed separately. These, however, proved superfluous to my main interest in the subjective reconstruction of fatherhood through life stories. Questioning strategies were designed to educe autobiographies that placed narratives in the context of each subject's life cycle.[18] Special attention was also paid to gendered experiences. How, for example, was labor in their childhood families divided between parents? Were brothers and sisters required to do the same or different chores? Portraits of the subjects' own fathers were then developed, conveying impressions of sentiment, power, and the distribution of work in childhood homes.

Recent work in Canada and elsewhere has shed light on how gender relations within families accommodate the demands of work both inside and outside the home.[19] This was often expressed in the narratives I collected concerning sentiments fathers laid claim to, especially when the men I interviewed spoke of the love and respect they had held for their wives as homemakers or when they recalled the need to divide their productive tasks or how they came to be divided. As Raphael Samuel and Paul Thompson suggest, life stories, including those of fathers, can "become a vital document of the construction of consciousness, emphasizing both the variety of experience in any social group, and also how an individual story draws on a common culture."[20] The culture of fatherhood, like other human experiences constructed through generational transmission, both creates and relies on its own sense of the past.

MASCULINITY, FAMILY ADVENTURE, AND THE GOOD LIFE

What Bodsworth called the "best way to take a holiday" leads us to a favorite subject among the men I interviewed: family recreation. Many accounts of vacations placed fathers at the center of constructing some material part of their exercise, if not their occurrence, as a realized aspiration. The precise length of boats and trailers used, the intricacies of cottage construction, and in many cases, the sheer necessity of providing for an annual family trek ran through several narratives. "That was a must — was a holiday every year, somewhere," as Adam Edwards put it.[21] "We bought a small, fifteen-foot trailer, and I had a sixteen-foot boat," David Robson said.[22] "Well, we always . . ." Bob Crawford recalled, "we bought a trailer. Bought a twenty-five-foot Nash way back . . . around '55, '56."[23] "I had a thirty-five horse," Ed Ralston remembered. "It was big enough for the small boat that I built . . . Lotta fun building. Just as much fun as riding it!"[24] Robson's fifteen- and sixteen-footers, Crawford's twenty-five-foot Nashua, and Ralston's thirty-five horsepower outboard were part of a pattern of narrating life stories in androcentric terms.

Self-portraits of family manhood that combined prudence and foresight with the items used in carving out a stake in the good life surfaced repeatedly, both in the oral histories I recorded and in many images of masculine domesticity depicted in recreational advertising. "Here comes Summer!" announced one advertisement for Johnson outboard motors: "be ready with a new quiet Johnson Sea-horse." Featured was an illustration of a man and woman, presumably husband and wife, pulling into a dock with a neat cottage in the background, as a youngster accompanied by a dog ran down to greet them. "Superb engineering and design" in this engine were touted as something that could help make for the "happiest summer ever!"[25] However idealized recreational consumption became, memories of summer were often expressed in gendered terms that included having fun with an outboard motor. "So we'd go to Cultus Lake, and places like that," Jim Black recalled. "We had a new ten horsepower outboard, which put the boat to a very good pace."[26]

It would be a mistake, however, to place fathers at the center of vacation planning and organization in all depictions, whether in print media or in memory. The new masculine domesticity of the baby boom celebrated companionate marriage as the model. And nothing was to be more cooperative, at least as a cultural ideal, as planning the family vacation. By 1963, *Chatelaine* magazine tapped into a well-established industry when it ran a feature in its July issue titled "Family Camping," the "New 'In' Way to Holiday." Listing a plethora of products as the "basics you'll need" to take along, the article urged consumers to accumulate an astonishing array of products for extended outings.

> EXTRAS, for comfort and fun, could range from our 15-foot Fiberglass Dover outboard, with seats that flatten into beds, to the tiny Optimus kerosene stove for indoor cooking. Also handy, 128-ounce Thermos cooler; battery lantern with red flasher signal; small plaid cooler for picnics; transistor radios, one with a shoulder strap and one deluxe model with a short wave band.

Other suggestions included a seven-inch television and a windup razor. Getting away from it all, in part, seemed to mean bringing it all with you. Special recipes for mothers as "camp cooks" were included and readers were advised to "remember, outside appetites appreciate a generous cook."[27]

Yet throughout the baby boom years, many popular representations of the family vacation put fathers in the driver's seat when it came to domestic roles that extended beyond the confines of home. "My work," Joseph N. Bell explained in a *Maclean's* article that ran in August 1957, "frequently sends me on . . . trips, and we feel that, when opportunity permits, the kids should enjoy this broadening influence too." After mention was made of some half-million gas stations, fifty thousand motels, and half a trillion miles of car travel in North America each year, Bell pointed to what he saw as a "curious anomaly." The automobile, "which takes us increasingly away from home, at the same time provides an effective aid to family unity and education. For our family, the car has brought a closer association than seems possible in any other way." As a parent on vacation, Bell seemed to step into a highly involved role as a father, stating that parenting on the road is "just a matter of planning, patience, and psychology once you learn how children think on wheels."[28]

Traveling in the family car also became a central part of how vacations and even weekend outings were remembered by many of the fathers I interviewed. "Course in the summertime," Ron McGregor recalled, "we'd go down to Osoyoos" among other places. "We used to go down to Seattle, Portland, and Long Beach," he said, adding "we used to do a lot of camping."[29] "When the kids were older," Wayne Davis recounted, "we went back to the Prairies. They all went along then." Davis marked those memories with his first new car: "It was in 1965 when we had the first new vehicle we had—a '65 Dodge station wagon, one of those small ones. Took a tent along, and the boys slept in the tent and we slept in the station wagon."[30] Some narratives depicted a sense of adventure with the father in control while the children were thrilled by the scenery along highways, many of which were new or under construction. "The first time we went up the old highway, y'know, the canyon, the kids were scared as hell, 'cause it wasn't wide like it is now," Drew Jackson remembered. "They hid under a blanket on the back seat 'cause you looked right down, y' know, scared as could be."[31]

Casual weekend drives, with dad at the wheel, became a part of family leisure as well. "Sometimes," Ed Ralston noted, "just on a Saturday afternoon, we'd pack up and go for a drive, and then on the way home stop for a hamburger."[32] The car also changed how young parents went to the movies. When asked how free time with the family was spent, for instance, Wayne Davis said,

> Well, go to the movies, we used to. There used to be the drive-in at Chilliwack. You could take small kids in there. . . . You didn't have to worry about babysitting. It was usually movies that would appeal to the kids, as well as us. There used to be one movie down towards Langley, a drive-in down there we went to. And there was one over in Mission, a drive-in, so that's where we did most of our movie-going.[33]

"The exploding ownership of automobiles," as Owram has also noted,

> brought a new possibility. . . . The family could pack itself into the car and herd off to the drive-in, where peanuts, popcorn, and toys could keep the kids amused. 'Bring the Children . . . Come as You Are' was the way one drive-in chain enticed families in 1953. Double features often catered to families by showing a children's movie first; when that was finished, the kids would, parents hoped, drift off to sleep in the back seat.[34]

Masculine domesticity in its many facets included hobbies, sometimes depicted in pursuits of rising cost as well as popularity. "In the era of the forty-hour week," Shirley Mair noted in 1962,

> most workers spend another eighty hours eating, sleeping, grooming and commuting. What's left — forty-eight hours each week — is pure leisure and at a very conservative estimate Canadians are spending three billion dollars a year to outfit themselves for hobbies with which to occupy their leisure.

Although fathers were not the sole consumers in this burgeoning market, from Mair's list of pastimes it seems clear that masculine pursuits were driving most sales to unprecedented levels. "Some radio-controlled model plane hobbyists will spend $600 to get one plane air-borne. In Canada, five million dollars worth of plastic and wooden modeling kits, ranging in price from twenty-five cents to $200, were sold last year."[35]

Voluntary time spent in coaching, scouting, and other service to youth groups involved fathers in communal parenting roles that extended the time spent with one's children and peers and provided a structure for fathers to participate actively in their children's socialization.[36] On this level, fathers' involvement in community-based parenting can be approached as a set of activities that regulated masculinity for male parents and served to inculcate appropriate forms of recreation within local, community-based parameters. Memories of being in loco parentis, in particular, appeared to involve transmitting principles observed at home to groups of boys from the community.

Throughout the two decades following the war, historical and local circumstances brought an urgency, often acute, to communal parenting, which affected both fathers and mothers. The baby boom, the housing shortage, and rising service and recreational expectations all contributed to putting facilities under stress. Pressing requirements for the new families that poured into cities like Abbotsford and Prince George had to be met, and fathers, as community members, were frequently called on to help as volunteers. As Charles Thompson of Abbotsford recalled, "The community was starting to grow and they needed, y'know, a number of [Boy Scout] troops."[37] A local professional with good organizational skills, Thompson served on the planning board for Scouts in the Fraser Valley during the movement's rapid growth in the 1960s. In Prince George, Ken Wilson explained how participation in scouting skyrocketed during his years as an organizer at the local and, later, provincial levels.[38]

Coaching too combined a growing need for organized youth recreation with the desire of many fathers to take a more active part in their children's recreation. Advertising images of fathers as expedition leaders also emphasized stalwart men well equipped for masculine adventure in the new era of automobile travel and outdoor recreation. "Long time between quarts, now that I'm using Quaker State," one dad declared as he stood behind his open station wagon as his grinning son knelt in the back with fishing rod cases beside him. The father stood tall and proud, dressed in hiking boots and an outdoor hat with one hand on the open door and the other poised as if to make his point. Masculine domesticity included popular depictions of fathers consuming products that made such outings possible: "Pure Pennsylvania Grade Crude Oil, the world's finest, is super-refined in special ways to make it best for today's engines," this advertisement proclaimed. "Proved superior in every test, in the engine laboratory and on the highway. Try it!"[39]

Father-and-son relationships, especially in hobbies or in outdoor recreation, celebrated a significant aspect of masculine domesticity. Pepsi Cola ran an advertisement in May 1962 with a full-page photograph of a father and son, the boy holding a model airplane while the father held a bottle of Pepsi above copy that read, "Thinking young is a state of mind."[40] One *Maclean's* cover in February 1957 featured a boy and his dad, presumably dreaming of summer, as they examined a sailboat in a boating store, while others could be seen through the window clearing snow on the street outside.[41]

In many ways, common, everyday practices associated with fatherhood changed dramatically with the economy and with patterns of domestic consumption. Relatively high employment, rising wages, and both the demand and supply of new products associated with recreation, including big-ticket items such as boats, motors, and trailers, all changed what fathers did with their families during their free time. So did television, and so did the weekend or evening chores associated with maintaining the exterior of family properties.

While the arrival of television was an event for the whole family, fathers played a major role in purchasing and installing (or at least overseeing the installation of) the first models. Several spoke of how they managed to get clear reception, despite warnings against buying too soon before transmission stations were set up in their areas. "At the time," Bob Crawford recalled,

> we had a heck of a job getting the guy to bring it. He said, "Well there's just no way you could ever get any reception there. You're too darn low. And there's the mountain on the south of you so that . . ."— yeah. But anyway, he brought it over and they stuck up a temporary television aerial, up on top of the roof, and turned it on. And cripes it just boomed in! King [the nearest station], King was — he said, "It's coming in better than we can get in Mission." So that's how I got the first television set.[42]

For some fathers, becoming one of the first in the neighborhood to own a television set seemed a matter of pride. "We were the only ones in the neighborhood" who owned a set, Ron McGregor recalled. "And all the neighborhood kids used to gather at our place to watch TV. Yeah, I think we were one of the first ones."[43] "We were the first ones in Clayburn to have a television set," Crawford claimed.[44] Once the sight of rooftop antennas became fairly commonplace, fathers easily felt the urge to keep up with this stage of household consumption. "Probably because our friends had them, I guess,' David Robson conceded, he decided to buy one too. "One of these things you gotta keep up with." Like other family members, Robson, a devoted baseball fan, soon found himself spending part of his leisure time in front of the new box.

> Another thing, y'know, was pretty intriguing was the World Series, y'know. Like, you'd listen to the World Series on the radio for years. And then, all of a sudden, well like, when you listen to the radio you imagine what people look like. And now you could see them on TV. It was, it was a big deal to watch.[45]

Like the family car, television sets were a consumer item that fathers took an active part in using as well as in acquiring. Family living spaces that included a television could, at times, be redrawn in gender terms when it came to who watched what. While the whole family might watch a variety of shows, sports programming, including such favorites as *Hockey Night in Canada*, ensured the reconstituting of spectator sports in family homes. Fathers were the prime targets of advertisements sponsored by Canada's leading brewery and petroleum companies.[46]

To approach how household spaces were occupied and used by family members in gendered terms requires consideration both of the interior and exterior property, which in memory and in advertising images represented entirely different domains. Fathers uniformly recalled that they "took care of the yard," particularly when it came to the heavier chores of cutting the grass, raking the leaves, or maintaining the house exterior. Since a significant portion of such tasks was indeed carried out by men as home owners and as consumers, advertising was constructed to match certain products with certain images of masculine domesticity as a cultural ideal.

Masculine domesticity in this period was often portrayed and recalled as a manful assertion of material success directed toward domestic consumption and leisure. Whether in tales of family men in outdoor settings, in expatiations on the number of feet of lake frontage acquired or boat length or horsepower at their command, or in the many advertisements associated with family vacations, the appeal of home ownership, and other forms of family-centered leisure, fathers cast themselves in memory as they had been cast in the print media of their day: as central figures in the provision and enjoyment of the good life. A wide range of advertisements encouraged fathers to participate in family-based consumption, particularly in purchases associated with home maintenance and family-centered leisure. They typically portrayed fathers in active, even creative roles within domestic settings. But they continued to define gendered boundaries through manful forms of recreation and household work within the family circle. Such images supported the expectation that fathers would spend time with their families but in a consumer-based culture that celebrated manliness and postwar consumption in prescribed contexts, from the backyard grass cutter to the vacation traveler.

For the most part, memories of fatherhood during the baby boom seem profoundly influenced by the tastes and values of a comparatively acquisitive period in history. In some cases, however, fathers referred to aspects of their parenthoods in terms of unfavorable, disadvantaged childhood experiences that they strove to overcome. Some drew contrasts between what they remembered as tough, rugged, or even abused childhoods and the measures of success they managed to gain as fathers. Built around notions of self-made men, such narratives might seem in keeping with the usual stories of material advance, of gains fathers proudly recounted that they had achieved for their families in contrast to the circumstances, rooted in the depression, of their own childhoods. But their broader implications, that a contented masculine domesticity did not come easily for some or that their actual experiences of fatherhood differed markedly from fatherhood's most popular images, leads us to consider contradictions in these life stories that challenged the myths of contented domestic masculinity circulating in the print media of that time.

CONFRONTING MYTHS OF HAPPINESS AND SUCCESS

Signs of negative or ambivalent experiences were not uncommon during my fieldwork. Markers, for instance, of fixed gender regimes in marital relations, apparently rooted in male breadwinning, cropped up regularly during interviews.[47] Next to often detailed narratives of working in paid employment, for instance, stood many deprecating, androcentric references to spousal housework. "No, she didn't work," one stated. "She was just a housewife, with the kids."[48] Another maintained that his marriage partner "didn't work. When she had the two children she didn't have a job besides. . . . She just looked after the children and socialized and looked after the house."[49] Some accounts, though rarely explicit in this regard, seemed indicative of patriarchal boundaries. "A father first of all," Sam Taylor said, "has to be a leader. Somebody has to be a leader. If the woman is a leader, the other men laugh at the father, don't they? . . . 'Oh hell, you know who wears the pants in the family,' y'know.' As Taylor developed his stories, often vivid in detail, a deeply rooted yearning to overcome his own father's influence became apparent. He also presented another common theme, his life overcoming scars of the hardships of the depression, and in his case, scars his own father left.

Taylor described his father's drunkenness, how he abused him and ultimately abandoned the family altogether. One poignant memory stood out.

> I can remember running all the way home from that school up here all the way downtown to tell my father that I stood second in the class of forty kids. I never stood second, up that high. And this one girl beat me because she was the school inspector's daughter and got teaching at home and so on. But I stood second. And that big idiot stood there and said, "What the hell good is that, standing second? If you can't stand first, don't stand anything." I expected a dime, or a reward, or a kind word. And then he walks away. I never worked in school after that. He took it out of me in grade five! At eleven years of age, or ten I think it was at the time. He knocked it right out me, right there.

He also said,

> My father was very, very bigoted. And it rubbed off on me. It rubbed off on my brothers. And I had quite a struggle with it all my life. Everybody was a Chink, or a Wop, or a Kike, or a Jap, or a Jew, or y'know, or Bohunk, and y'know. You find yourself repeating those things you see. And now you've got to, oh. It's a struggle. It's a struggle, y'know. It really is. And — your impressionistic age — you repeat your elders. You don't learn from your little brother or little sister. You learn from ones above you, don't you? This is why it's so important for fathers to be a good role model for their children. And I think I've coped very well.[50]

A sense of pride accompanied his fatherhood memories of minor hockey, when he served as a coach and league organizer. Taylor praised the Canadian Amateur Hockey Association for making him a better coach. He described how he and "a few other dads" got together to reorganize minor hockey in the city and got far more boys into it, while underscoring the difficulty he had appreciating that competition could prevent kids from simply having fun. The son who recalled his father's crushing words, "If you can't stand first, don't stand anything," described a scene behind the bench when one of his young players pleaded with him to ease up on his incessant criticism. "I'm trying to do what you say, coach, but I'm only an eleven-year-old boy."[51] Taylor recalled trying to come to terms with his proper role, given the poor example set for him, and claimed that he succeeded in the end, developing in coaching a sense of fairness that applied equally to his six boys at home.

In Prince George, Roy Gibson remembered his community service as a scoutmaster. His leadership philosophy seemed influenced by a depression-scarred childhood. Gibson's father died when he was nine, leaving him, with his sister and mother, nearly destitute on a small farm in Saskatchewan. As he explained, "I . . . shouldn't say that I felt I was head of the family, but I felt a responsibility. . . . There was no asking for it — put it that way." Later he said, "Growing up in the depression — there was no room for arguing." "You had to look at the facts and take what was there and go from there." Both as a father and a scoutmaster, Gibson felt that self-reliance, more than anything, had to be instilled in boys. He remembered hoping that his hard lessons might serve as their best example. "You were in a corral," he said of his childhood,

> and within that corral certain things had to be done and that was all there was to it. Whether you liked it or not, you did it. Now that's — my years with the scouting movement — this is what I put across to the boys.

His three sons all joined Scouts. He claimed to show no favoritism, but more significantly, he suggested close parallels between the values he espoused as a parent and those he upheld as a scoutmaster. When asked in a general way what good fatherhood was all about, Gibson replied,

> teaching the kids to paddle their own canoe. . . . If you can't take care of yourself nobody else is going to. And yet, they're teaching in the schools, and this I found very difficult to counter

in scouting — I was teaching one set of values and they would see another set. And they couldn't make up their minds as to who was right. And it was the older group of boys, basically after they left my group — where they went in Venturers — where you'd see it finally, where the boy made up his mind. And he fell off the fence one way or another. And, if they fell off on my side of the fence, OK, they're still around the community. They're members of the community — some of the others are in jail![52]

David Robson remembers how little time his father was able to spend with him during the depression when he managed a large mill in Mission. "He gave his life to the damn mill," Robson remembered with some bitterness. He also recalled how he became much more involved in parenting and in communal parenting as a baseball coach. "I coached kids' softball for quite a few years," he added later.

I coached Jimmy a little bit. . . . But Frank, the youngest one, another fellow and we coached their team for about five or six years, I guess, as they went through the ranks. Took them over to Vancouver Island to a tournament one year. It was a way to be with your kids, y'know.[53]

Virtually all of the men I interviewed could draw sharp contrasts, particularly in material terms, between how they grew up and how their children did. "When I grew up, y'know," Robson also recalled,

like kids didn't have much, y'know. I mean you were lucky to have a set of clothes and a pair of gum boots and — you never had toys. Most kids eventually got around to having a bicycle, which was quite a — y'know if you could have a bicycle when you were in public school, it was quite a feat.[54]

A sense of having done far better than their own fathers could have dreamed of was commonplace. "He was a man," Ron McGregor said of his father, "that was, I think, he was very disappointed in life because of his inability to get steady employment, y'know."[55]

Contrasts between the hardships of growing up in the depression and the opportunities they enjoyed as breadwinners in the 1950s and beyond often served to structure their life stories. While most baby boom fathers struggled to get a foothold in the vastly improved economy of the 1950s, their successes as wage earners became a central part of their self-concepts and contributed to the generational perspectives they held of being self-made men. To be sure, they did "do better" than their fathers had. "I think," said Drew Jackson, "I did a lot better than I ever thought I would, y'know."[56] As Ed Ralston put it,

Right after the war things were not exactly that rosy. But we still, well actually once I moved to the Island, had a regular job, and I could budget better and certain things you could do, look after the family quite well, we didn't really suffer there — we could earn enough money to build a house and get things set and all that.[57]

The rising expectations of the period, something uniformly recalled, were generally cast in contrast to the scarcity of toys, bikes, and other recreational goods available to most children before the war. "But when I get back to my own kids," as Robson put it,

well I mean they all expected a bike at a certain age. And you might get them a little bike, and then get them a bigger bike and so on, y'know, which is an expensive way to do it. . . . I remember Judy having Barbie dolls, and some of the kids having machine guns and stuff like that, y'know, playing cowboys and Indians.[58]

And yet, what these fathers provided in material terms, as markers of their manhood and respectability, contributed to a sense of change that was not without its critics.

The panacea of television-centered home entertainment wore thin for at least one *Maclean's* contributor that same year. While new sets were still being turned on for the first time across Canada, Vivien Kimber described how she and her husband, Earl, attempted to turn back the clock, at least temporarily.

> Last October my husband and I finally worked up enough courage to try an experiment: we took the TV set out of the house for a month, just to see how (or maybe I should say "if") we and our five children would get along without it.

They were seen, Kimber suggested, as having taken a rather extreme step. "Most of our friends were aghast. You'd have thought we proposed to stop eating for a month instead of just moving a piece of furniture." The television, it seemed, had been their children's pied piper. "In spirit," Kimber related,

> they were wherever the TV set took them. Many a time Earl would come home from work, shout "Hi, kids!" and have to step over the mob watching TV to get to his chair. Only when the program was over would they turn around and look at him in astonishment and say, "Hello, Daddy! When did you come home?"

In many ways, Kimber's account offered readers an idealized portrait of her family's "vacation," their return to a place, however mythologized, of lost, home-centered leisure. Expressed in terms of a fun-seeking, provisional resistance to a television-centered present, set here in 1957, Kimber recounts her husband joining her in restoring those traditional pastimes, as they imagined them, that may have seemed outmoded by the distractions of consumerism in general and television in particular. "Earl and I," she said of their plans, "spent that first evening mapping out what promised to be an exciting vacation at home." She implied, as well, that the recentering of their family away from television helped to secure a more active and, for the children, recognizable place for Earl as their father. The rest of their adventure, predictably enough, recounted how reading, crafts, and other hobbies made their way back into their family routines until they could take back television on their own terms.[59]

By this time, however, the new leisure of the 1950s, much of which was focused on family recreation and consumption, especially weekend consumption, gave popular commentators and columnists openings for the occasional piece of satire. "But I *DON'T WANT* the new leisure," Robert Thomas Allen of *Maclean's* wrote in one of his many humorous columns of the mid-1950s. "I happened to be watching one of my neighbours the other day," Allen stated with his usual satirical lilt,

> as he bored a hole though his window for a TV lead. This took him about five minutes. Then he wandered around with his power drill; looking for something else to drill a hole through, gave up, and slowly worked his way back into the house like a kid on summer holidays trying not to step on cracks in his sidewalk.

Through comical vignettes of flustered fathers in the midst of backyard barbecues, failed workshop projects, and endless reels of home movies, Allen lampooned the new leisure from the ironic pose of a suburban father who witnessed one man sending barbecue smoke into his neighbor's backyard while his counterpart responded by blasting back Beethoven's Fifth Symphony from his new hi-fi. Backyard antics seemed to have become something a satirist could easily poke fun at, as masculine forms of domestic consumption thrust new hobbies into the hands of fathers now plagued by weekend leisure. As Allen put it facetiously,

> Sometimes I think we should all just go back to being frankly bored over the weekend in a stiff, dull, motionless way — the way we used to be on Sunday when we were kids; when we couldn't hammer, saw, shout, or get dirty.[60]

Whether at home engaged in some new hobby or behind the wheel on the annual family vacation trek, fatherhood and leisure attracted the humorist's gaze in these and other pieces with such titles as "How to Train for Your Vacation." "Want a bang-up holiday?" Stuart Trueman asked in the spring of 1955, "then start getting ready now. There's a good chance the family will get so sick of you they'll leave you home." After recounting some fanciful larks, such as deliberately slamming on the car brakes or walking barefoot in the rain to simulate the discomforts of travel, Trueman appealed to dads facing the upcoming summer to

> kindly line up on the right and for the small sum of two dollars you have my new Happy Holidays Kit, complete with informative leaflet, one phonograph record of ocean waves and seagulls (on the opposite side, truck horns honking and a New Year's Eve party in full progress) and three live mosquitoes.[61]

Popular images of the bungling dad, haggard by hobbies or by the amusing discomforts of family travel, stood alongside those of the stalwart adventurer, the proud home owner, and the generous benefactor — the family man who had secured his family's place in the consumer markets and recreational opportunities of a profoundly acquisitive period. This brings us back to connections between representations and reality that opened this discussion. As a revamped cultural ideal, masculine domesticity took shape in the first two decades following the Second World War within an expanding consumer economy that privileged fatherhood by valorizing a variety of home-centered and family-based pursuits from the backyard gardener to the Scout leader or hockey coach. Respectable manhood translated into companionate marriages and involved parenting, not something altogether new. But it also placed new emphasis on gendered aspects of consumption and recreation that moved fathers toward the center of many family- and leisure-based activities, from acquiring the first television to buying a new car or boat or taking the family on vacation. And this did reflect very real and significant shifts in disposable income and domestic buying patterns compared to those of the previous generation.

Oral histories certainly indicate the strong influence this had on shaping memories of being a father at this time. Time and again, stories associated with material accomplishment, especially acquiring objects of leisure and recreation, recalled their acquisition as central to a manful father's role in providing for a dependent family. In uncovering how family men of this era construct their memories, my fieldwork points to the prevalence of shared experiences in a culture of consumption, that fathers knew what was expected of them as prosperous parents and saw much of it as an opportunity to assert themselves as successful family men, not just conform to behaviors designed for particular target markets. The men I interviewed often structured their life stories on perceptions of manful success as home owners, automobile and recreational vehicle owners, television buyers, and cottage builders — accounts of self-made men who lived and worked to afford the ideals of family consumption. Even men's participation in community activities such as scouting and coaching came from gains in leisure time and prosperity after the war. In this way, postwar consumerism survives today as a dominant influence in the social construction of memories connected to masculine domesticity.

Certain memories of fatherhood and the occasional article or column could point to a more complex and ambiguous past or even to critiques of consumer-based family life. Some men who succeeded as fathers in material terms also cast their stories of self-made success within larger narratives that began with abused or deprived childhoods. They recalled spending their years as younger parents trying to overcome the scars of childhood or apply its hard lessons. Many questioned whether gains made in material terms had actually helped spoil the next generation. Moreover, some popular authors lampooned the new leisure, questioned the hold that television had on family recreation, or highlighted concerns that consumer fetishes had become an affront to their sense of days gone by, however pastoral or mythical that sense might have been. At times, the happy blend of masculine domesticity and consumption was challenged, though hardly overthrown. At last, after years of depression and war, able to acquire houses, cars, boats, and cottages, items often beyond the means of their own fathers, the men who shared their life stories with me equated certain forms of consumption with manful assertiveness and lay claim to it in representing themselves as breadwinners and as family men. This appears to have left a profound mark on the masculinity of family men in the generation preceding our own. Future research on fatherhood in this period might do well to consider the influence of consumerism on depictions and histories of masculine domesticity and ideal fatherhood in near-contemporary settings.

NOTES

1. As Doug Owram states in his study of the baby boom in Canada, "The decentralized medium of television perfectly matched the growing suburban needs of families with young children." See Doug Owram, *Born at the Right Time: A History of the Baby Boom in Canada* (Toronto: University of Toronto Press, 1996), 89. For a comprehensive study of the impact of television on popular culture in Canada, see Paul Rutherford, *When Television Was Young: Primetime Canada, 1952–1967* (Toronto: University of Toronto Press, 1990). On stereotypical portraits of the postwar suburb, see Joanne Meyerowitz, "Introduction: Women and Gender in Postwar America" in *Not June Cleaver: Women and Gender in Postwar America, 1945–1960*, ed. Joanne Meyerowitz (Philadelphia: Temple University Press, 1994). Meyerowitz also cites several simplistic portraits of women and family life in recent college textbooks.

2. For an extended discussion of masculine domesticity, see Ralph LaRossa, *The Modernization of Fatherhood: A Social and Political History* (Chicago: University of Chicago Press, 1997), especially 31–34. LaRossa draws distinctions between *masculine domesticity* and *domestic masculinity*, more than a matter of semantics as he sees it. Like Margaret Marsh, LaRossa sees domestic masculinity as "doing domestic activities in a masculine way." To illustrate, he points to doing child care and housework in a manly or virile manner. Fathers taking their sons hunting for the sake of instilling the masculine virtues of aggressiveness, competitiveness, and dominion over nature would be exhibiting masculine domesticity. So would fathers who did housework the macho way, or the military way, or the corporate capitalist way, since all of these imply either a manly disposition or a manly world.

    This, LaRossa argues, should be separated from domestic masculinity, since "domesticating someone who is masculine is something else." It is, but I might add, a caveat. Boundaries between masculine domesticity and domestic masculinity may be drawn for a particular context but may shift across time. Fathers may do certain things around their families that they see as appropriate for a man, such as reading their children to sleep, that their fathers would not have done. Casting masculine domesticity and domestic masculinity as separate strands for fathers, in other words, tends to essentialize masculinity in fatherhood rather than see it as historically plural and variable.

3. Margaret Marsh, "Suburban Men and Masculine Domesticity, 1870–1915," *American Quarterly* 40 (June 1988): 165–86, and "From Separation to Togetherness: The Social Construction of Domestic Space in American Suburbs, 1840–1915," *Journal of American History* 76 (September 1989): 506–27.

4. Marsh, "Suburban Men and Masculine Domesticity," 166.

5. Robert L. Griswold, *Fatherhood in America: A History* (New York: Basic Books, 1993), especially chap. 5.

6. On demographic change, modernization, and local family/community formation during the baby boom era in Prince George, see Robert Rutherdale, "Approaches to Community Formation and the Family in the Provincial North," *BC Studies*, 104 (winter 1994): 103–260. By 1961, for instance, nearly 80 percent of the city's family dwellings had been built since the end of the Second World War. Figures for the province (51.5 percent) and country (44.2 percent), while much lower, reflect significant corresponding jumps in housing starts (p. 124).

7. On the agricultural industry in the area, which embraced in this period Matsqui, Sumas, and Abbotsford, see John Warnock, "Agriculture and Food Industry," in *After Bennett: A New Politics for British Columbia*, ed. Warren Magnusson et al. (Vancouver: New Star Books, 1986), and David Demeritt, "Visions of Agriculture in British Columbia," *BC Studies* 108 (winter 1995–96): 29–59.

8. *Census of Canada*, vol. 2 (Ottawa: Statistics Canada, 1971), 112, Table 2, Population of Census Subdivisions, 1921–1971, 92–702. Figures combine Abbotsford, Matsqui, and Sumas.

9. Owram, *Born at the Right Time*, 12.

10. On the federal government's role in promoting household improvement prior to 1940, see Margaret Hobbs and Ruth Roach Pierson, "'A kitchen that wastes no steps . . . 'Gender, Class and the Home Improvement Plan, 1936–40," *Histoire Sociale/Social History* 21 (May 1988): 9–37. For the post–World War II period, see Veronica Strong-Boag, "'Their Side of the Story': Women's Voices from Ontario Suburbs, 1945–1965," and Joan Sangster, "Doing Two Jobs: The Wage-Earning Mother, 1945–1970," in *A Diversity of Women: Ontario, 1945–1980,* ed. Joy Parr (Toronto: University of Toronto Press, 1995): 46–74 and 98–134, respectively. On women and appliance shopping, see Joy Parr, "Shopping for a Good Stove: A Parable about Gender, Design and the Market," also in *A Diversity of Women.*

11. Veronica Strong-Boag, "Home Dreams: Women and the Suburban Experiment in Canada, 1945–60," *Canadian Historical Review* 72 (1991): 471–504 [see this volume], and "Canada's Wage-Earning Wives and the Construction of the Middle Class, 1945–60," *Journal of Canadian Studies/Revue d'études Canadiennes* 29 (1994): 5–25.

12. Owram, *Born at the Right Time,* 85–86.

13. Griswold, *Fatherhood in America,* 2.

14. Fred Bodsworth, "The Best Way to Take a Holiday," *Maclean's,* June 11, 1955, 34.

15. A diverse field, advertising continues to attract new research. T. J. Jackson Lear's *Fables of Abundance: A Cultural History of Advertising in America* (New York: Basic Books, 1994) provides a comprehensive and useful survey.

16. Elizabeth Tonkin, *Narrating Our Pasts: The Social Construction of Oral History* (Cambridge: Cambridge University Press, 1992), 67. For perceptive commentaries on the multifaceted nature of authoring in oral history, see Michael Frisch, *A Shared Authority: Essays on the Craft and Meaning of Oral and Public History* (Albany: State University of New York Press, 1990). See also Paul Thompson, *The Voice of the Past,* 2d ed. (Oxford: Oxford University Press, 1988), and Luisa Passerini, "Mythbiography in Oral History," in *The Myths We Live By,* ed. Raphael Samuel and Paul Thompson (London: Routledge, 1990), 52–53. Recent studies of subjectivity in oral reconstructions of the past abound. In addition to some excellent examples in Samuel and Thompson, and poignant discussion of its many aspects in Tonkin, see Ronald J. Grele, ed., *International Annual of Oral History, 1990: Subjectivity and Multiculturalism in Oral History* (New York: Greenwood, 1992). For a recent application set in British Colombia, see Alexander Freund and Laura Quilici, "Exploring Myths in Women's Narratives: Italian and German Immigrant Women in Vancouver, 1947–1967" *BC Studies,* 105/106 (spring 1995): 159–82.

17. Although the age range of this sample spans just over a generation, all reared offspring were infants, adolescents, or young adults during the mid-1940s to the end of 1960s. This variety permitted consideration of historical change during an extended period of comparatively high fertility and economic growth. Of the thirty-four men interviewed, five were professionals, fourteen were managerial, and fifteen were laborers or in semiskilled positions during their paid working careers. While all had children who grew up in the 1950s and early 1960s, the oldest was born in 1909 and the youngest in 1943.

18. This approach proved most natural in establishing a coherent flow between informants and myself. As well as establishing a useful biographical context, many developed self-portraits that connected aspects of their lives by the end of the interviews that might otherwise have seemed scattered or without foundation. Martine Burgos and J. P. Roos offer useful analysis of this tendency in "Life Stories, Narrativity, and the Search for the Self," *Life Stories/Récits de vie* 5 (1989): 27–38.

19. Canadian historians are beginning to turn their attention to family and gender studies situated in the 1950s and 1960s. In addition to recent work by Veronica Strong-Boag, cited above, see Joy Parr, *The Gender of Breadwinners: Women, Men and Change in Two Industrial Towns, 1880–1950* (Toronto: University of Toronto Press, 1990). On the experience of men, work, and family life, see Mark Rosenfeld, "'She Was a Hard Life': Work, Family, Community and Politics in the Railway Ward of Barrie, Ontario 1900–1960" (Ph.D. thesis, York University, 1990). In addition to Robert L. Griswold's work, also cited above, recent studies in the United States include Elaine Tyler May's *Homeward Bound: American Families in the Cold War Era* (New York: Basic Books, 1988). An extensive sociological literature on American fathers and family life is also available. See, for example, Mirra Komarovsky, *Blue Collar Marriage* (New York: Random House, 1962); Barbara Ehrenreich, *The Hearts of Men: American Dreams and the Flight from Commitment* (Garden City: Anchor, 1983); Scott Coltrane, *Family Man: Fatherhood, Housework, and Gender Equity* (Oxford: Oxford University Press, 1996); and Kathleen Gerson, *No Man's Land: Men's Changing Commitment to Family and Work* (New York: Basic Books, 1993). See also Thomas Dunk, *It's a Man's World: Male Working-Class Culture in Northwestern Ontario* (Montreal: McGill-Queen's University Press, 1991) for an anthropologist's interpretation of male culture in Thunder Bay, Ontario. While conceptual approaches to family and gender now constitute a diverse and growing literature, R. W. Connell's *Gender and Power: Society, the Person and Sexual Politics* (Stanford: Stanford University Press, 1987) and *Masculinities* (Cambridge: Polity, 1995) provide useful theoretical overviews.

20. Samuel and Thompson, *The Myths We Live By,* 2.

21. Interview 32, March 12, 1997 (all informants are identified by pseudonyms).
22. Interview 26, March 5, 1997.
23. Interview 25, March 4, 1997.
24. Interview 31, March 11, 1997.
25. *Maclean's*, April 30, 1955, 38.
26. Interview 22, February 26, 1997.
27. Jessie London et al., "Family Camping . . . New 'in' Way to Holiday," *Chatelaine*, July 1963, 30–34.
28. Joseph N. Bell, "We Travel with Our Kids — And Like It," *Maclean's*, August 3, 1957, 25.
29. Interview 27, March 5, 1997.
30. Interview 29, March 6, 1997.
31. Interview 30, March 11, 1997.
32. Interview 31, March 11, 1997.
33. Interview 29, March 6, 1997.
34. Owram, *Born at the Right Time*, 152.
35. Shirley Mair, "Form Chart on Hobbies: Who's Out in Front in the National Scramble to Find a Newer and Better One," *Maclean's*, January 27, 1962, 19–31.
36. On scouting and organized leisure, see Owram, *Born at the Right Time*, 100–101.
37. Interview 23, March 3, 1997.
38. Interview 5 (pt. 2), March 28, 1995.
39. *Maclean's*, April 2, 1955, 84.
40. Ibid., May 19, 1962, 49.
41. Ibid., February 2, 1957, front cover.
42. Interview 25, March 4, 1997.
43. Interview 27, March 5, 1997.
44. Interview 25, March 4, 1997.
45. Interview 26, March 5, 1997.
46. For a critical examination of the arrival of television in Canada, see Paul Rutherford, *When Television Was Young: Primetime Canada, 1952–1967* (Toronto: University of Toronto Press, 1990).
47. In her work on cultural perception and gender, Sandra Lipsitz Bem has developed an approach to the production of meaning that can be useful when interpreting interview transcripts. Self-awareness and awareness of others, formed and expressed through language, are constituted in gendered terms. In particular, Ben considers masculine consciousness as the product of gendered perception, a cultural lens that distorts, reconfigures, or even omits the presence of women in male-dominated societies. This pattern of thought, or androcentrism, has long dominated men's perceptions of who they are, how they act, and how the world of their experience has evolved. How androcentric perspectives shaped the language, concerns, topics, and assumptions of each life story proved significant in this study, whether fathers discussed parenting, breadwinning, leisure, or consumption. See Sandra Lipsitz Bern, *The Lenses of Gender: Transforming the Debate on Sexual Inequality* (New Haven: Yale University Press, 1993).
48. Interview 8, March 22, 1995.
49. Interview 3, March 6, 1995.
50. Interview 4 (pt. 1), March 9, 1995.
51. Interview 4 (pt. 2), March 15, 1995.
52. Interview 7, March 22, 1995.
53. Interview 26, March 5, 1997.
54. Ibid.
55. Interview 27, March 5, 1997.
56. Interview 30, March 11, 1997.
57. Interview 31, March 11, 1997.
58. Interview 26, March 5, 1997.
59. Vivien Kimber, "What Happened When We Threw Out Our TV Set," *Maclean's*, March 30, 1957, 17–62.
60. Robert Thomas Allen, "But I *DON'T WANT* the New Leisure," Ibid., November 27, 1957, 27–64.
61. Stuart Trueman, "How to Train for Your Vacation," Ibid., April 16, 1955, 48.

Topic Thirteen

Multiculturalism and Canadian Identity

Dr. Frank Calder, a Nisga'a, speaks with reporters in 1973. Calder's court case *Calder v. Attorney General of British Columbia* ended that year with a landmark decision that established, for the first time, that Aboriginal title exists in modern Canadian law.

In 1971, the Liberal government under Prime Minister Pierre Elliott Trudeau adopted multiculturalism as an official government policy. The policy has four aims: to support the cultural development of ethnocultural groups; to help members of ethnocultural groups overcome barriers to full participation in Canadian society; to promote creative encounters and interchange among all ethnocultural groups; and to assist new Canadians in acquiring at least one of Canada's official languages. This policy became Canadian law in 1988 in the Multiculturalism Act. Ethnic historians interested in the history of multiculturalism see its emergence as a popular concept in the post–World War II era as a reaction to the intolerance and prejudice evident in the 1930s and during World War II. Within Canada, the idea gained popularity particularly in the 1960s when the Liberal government under Lester B. Pearson established the Royal Commission on Bilingualism and Biculturalism. Its mandate was to examine French-English relations in Canada in an effort to achieve an equal partnership between the two founding races. However, many non-British and non-French groups in Canada resented their exclusion from this debate. They convinced the Canadian government to include them in a third volume of the B and B Commission as "the Others." Out of this encounter came Trudeau's decision in 1971 to adopt a policy of multiculturalism.

Since 1971, the policy and the act have been the subject of ongoing debate, with advocates and opponents disagreeing whether the policy was the right one to adopt, whether it has succeeded in achieving its objectives, and what impact it has had on the development of a Canadian identity. In "The Merits of Multiculturalism," philosopher Will Kynlicka argues that multiculturalism is the right policy for a country like Canada with so many different ethnic groups that need to be integrated into mainstream society. He claims that the policy has been a resounding success as evident in the number of immigrants who have chosen to become Canadian citizens, in the participation of ethnic Canadians in Canadian mainstream politics, in ethnic Canadians acquiring one of Canada's two official languages, and in increased intermarriage rates.

In "Multiculturalism, National Identity, and National Integration: The Canadian Case," John Harles argues that the objective of multiculturalism has been integration, which means ethnic Canadians maintaining their own distinct identity while being part of a larger Canadian identity — a sense of "unity in diversity" to borrow a phrase used by J.R. Miller in his article in Topic Two on English-Canadian and French-Canadian relations. Harles evaluates the wisdom of such a policy in terms of the creation of a Canadian identity, and concludes that "multiculturalism is an insufficient, though in the Canadian context an understandable, substitute for a strong Canadian identity."

What are the opposing perspectives on multiculturalism, including the one put forward by Howard Palmer in his article in Topic Five? Has the policy of multiculturalism helped or hindered the development of a Canadian identity? Does multiculturalism pose certain challenges for Canada as it enters the 21st century?

Two overviews of Canadian immigration policy are Ninette Kelley and Michael Trebilcock, *The Making of the Mosaic: A History of Canadian Immigration Policy* (Toronto: University of Toronto Press, 1998) and Donald H. Avery, *Reluctant Host: Canada's Response to Immigrant Workers, 1896–1994* (Toronto: McClelland & Stewart, 1995). For a critical view of Canadian immigration, see Daniel Stoffman, *Who Gets In: What's Wrong with Canada's Immigration Policy — And How to Fix It* (Toronto: Macfarlane Walter & Ross, 2002), and Reg Whitaker, *Double Standard: The Secret History of Canadian Immigration* (Toronto: Lester & Orpen Dennys, 1989).

Will Kymlicka's defence of Canada's policy of multiculturalism can be found in greater detail in *Finding Our Way: Rethinking Ethnocultural Relations in Canada* (Toronto: Oxford University Press, 1998), from which the excerpt "The Merits of Multiculturalism" is taken.

See as well, Andrew Cardozo and Louis Musto, eds., *The Battle over Multiculturalism* (Ottawa: Pearson-Shoyama Institute, 1997); Richard J.F. Day, *Multiculturalism and the History of Canadian Diversity* (Toronto: University of Toronto Press, 2000); and Augie Fleras and Jean Leonard Elliott, *Engaging Diversity: Multiculturalism in Canada*, 2nd ed. (Toronto: Nelson Thomson Learning, 2002). For criticisms of multiculturalism, consult: Reginald Bibby, *Mosaic Madness: The Poverty and Potential of Life in Canada* (Toronto: Stoddart, 1990); Neil Bissoondath, *Selling Illusions: The Cult of Multiculturalism in Canada*, rev. ed. (Toronto: Penguin Canada, 2002); and Richard Gwyn, *Nationalism without Walls: The Unbearable Lightness of Being Canadian* (Toronto: McClelland and Stewart, 1995). Vanaja Dhruvarajan's "People of Colour and National Identity in Canada," *Journal of Canadian Studies*, 35, 2 (Summer 2000): 166–175 adds to the debate on multiculturalism and Canadian identity.

Racism and discrimination are examined in Evelyn Kallen, *Ethnicity and Human Rights in Canada*, 2nd ed. (Toronto: Oxford University Press, 1995); B. Singh Bolaria and Peter S. Li, *Racial Oppression in Canada*, 2nd ed. (Toronto: Garamond Press, 1988); Frances Henry, *The Caribbean Diaspora in Toronto: Learning to Live with Racism* (Toronto: University of Toronto Press, 1994); Eleanor Laquian et al., *The Silent Debate: Asian Immigration and Racism in Canada* (Vancouver: Institute of Asian Research, 1998); Frances Henry et al., *The Colour of Democracy: Racism in Canadian Society*, 2nd ed. (Toronto: Harcourt Brace, 2000); and Leo Driedger and Shiva S. Halli, *Race and Racism: Canada's Challenge* (Montreal/Kingston: McGill-Queen's University Press, 2000). An important historiographical work is J.W. Berry and J.A. Lapointe, eds., *Ethnicity and Culture in Canada: The Research Landscape* (Toronto: University of Toronto Press, 1994). An essential work is Paul Robert Magocsi, ed., *Encyclopedia of Canada's Peoples* (Toronto: University of Toronto Press, 1999).

WEBLINKS

Kim Campbell
http://www.collectionscanada.ca/primeministers/h4-3475-e.html
A biography of Kim Campbell, Canada's first female prime minister. Includes selected speeches.

Bill C-250
http://www.parl.gc.ca/common/Bills_House_Private.asp?Language=E&Parl=37&Ses=2#C-250
A copy of Bill C-250, which added sexual orientation to the list of identifiable groups that may be criminally subject to hate propaganda.

Canadian Charter of Rights and Freedoms
http://laws.justice.gc.ca/en/charter/index.html
The Canadian Charter of Rights and Freedoms.

FirstVoices
http://www.firstvoices.com
Sound clips, alphabets, and dictionaries of the languages of the indigenous peoples of Canada.

Statistics Canada: Ethnic Diversity Survey
http://www.statcan.ca:8096/bsolc/english/bsolc?catno=89-593-X
A statistical look at ethnic diversity in Canada, based on the 2001 census.

James Bay Project and the Cree
http://archives.cbc.ca/IDD-1-69-94/life_society/james_bay/
CBC video and radio archives detailing the controversial nature of the James Bay Project between the Government of Quebec and the Cree living in the north of the province.

Road to Bilingualism
http://archives.cbc.ca/IDD-1-73-655/politics_economy/bilingualism
A series of video and radio files detailing the origins of Canada's bilingual policy and its controversial existence.

Article Thirty-Two

The Merits of Multiculturalism

Will Kymlicka

In 1971 Canada embarked on a unique experiment by declaring a policy of official "multiculturalism." According to Pierre Trudeau, the prime minister who introduced it in the House of Commons, the policy had four aims: to support the cultural development of ethnocultural groups; to help members of ethnocultural groups overcome barriers to full participation in Canadian society; to promote creative encounters and interchange among all ethnocultural groups; and to assist new Canadians in acquiring at least one of Canada's official languages.[1] This policy was officially enshrined in law in the 1988 Multiculturalism Act.

Although the multiculturalism policy was first adopted by the federal government, it was explicitly designed as a model for other levels of government, and it has been widely copied. "Multiculturalism programs" can now be found not just in the multiculturalism office in Ottawa, but also at the provincial and municipal levels of government and in a wide range of public and private institutions, including schools and businesses.

Such programs are now under attack, perhaps more so today than at any time since 1971. In particular, they are said to be undermining the historical tendency of immigrant groups to integrate, encouraging ethnic separatism, putting up "cultural walls" around ethnic groups, and thereby eroding our ability to act collectively as citizens. It is understandable that Canadians have had anxieties about multiculturalism, and it would be a mistake to ascribe all of them to xenophobia or prejudice. The process of integrating immigrants from very different backgrounds, including every conceivable race, religion, and language group, who share little in common, is never easy, and historically Canada has been fortunate in having avoided serious ethnic conflict. Canadians have naturally worried that any dramatic change in our approach to integration — such as the adoption of the multiculturalism policy — would change this dynamic, igniting ethnic separatism and conflict.

Thus it is worth having a vigorous discussion about multiculturalism. So far, though, the debate has generated much more heat than light. One reason is that it has been carried on without enough attention to the empirical evidence; as we will see, the critics of multiculturalism are simply uninformed about the consequences of the policy.

But defenders of multiculturalism, including the federal government itself, must also share part of the blame. Virtually every study of the policy in Canada has concluded that it has been "barely explained at all to the Canadian public," and that "no serious effort was made by any senior politician to define multiculturalism in a Canadian context."[2] Insofar as the policy has been defended, the usual approach has been simply to invoke "cultural diversity" and "tolerance," as if these were self-evidently or unqualifiedly good things. In fact, both diversity and tolerance have limits. Diversity is valuable, but only if it operates within the context of certain common norms and institutions; otherwise it can become destabilizing. Similarly, tolerance is a virtue, but only within certain boundaries; otherwise it can threaten principles of equality and individual rights. It is on these questions of the limits or boundaries of multiculturalism that defenders have been strangely inarticulate.

As a result, the debate over multiculturalism in the last few years has taken on an air of unreality. On the one hand, uninformed critics level unfounded charges of ethnocultural separatism, without regard for the evidence; on the other hand, defenders invoke "diversity" and "tolerance" as a mantra, without explaining the common institutions and principles that define the context within which diversity and tolerance can flourish.

To bring some order to this confusion, I will focus on the evidence regarding the impact of multiculturalism since its adoption in 1971, to show that critics of the policy are indeed misinformed.

THE DEBATE

The debate over multiculturalism has heated up recently, largely because of two best-selling critiques: Neil Bissoondath's *Selling Illusions: The Cult of Multiculturalism in Canada* (1994) and Richard Gwyn's *Nationalism without Walls: The Unbearable Lightness of Being Canadian* (1995).[3] Bissoondath and Gwyn make very similar claims about the results of the policy. In particular, both argue that multiculturalism has promoted a form of ethnic separatism among immigrants. According to Bissoondath, multiculturalism has led to "undeniable ghettoization."[4] Instead of promoting integration, it encourages immigrants to form "self-contained" ghettos "alienated from the mainstream," and this ghettoization is "not an extreme of multiculturalism but its ideal: a way of life transported whole, a little outpost of exoticism preserved and protected." He approvingly quotes Arthur Schlesinger's claim that multiculturalism reflects a "cult of ethnicity" that "exaggerates differences, intensifies resentments and antagonisms, drives even deeper the awful wedges between races and nationalities," producing patterns of "self-pity and self-ghettoization" that lead to "cultural and linguistic apartheid."[5] According to Bissoondath, multiculturalism policy does not encourage immigrants to think of themselves as Canadians; even the children of immigrants "continue to see Canada with the eyes of foreigners. Multiculturalism with its emphasis on the importance of holding on to the former or ancestral homeland, with its insistence that *There* is more important than *Here*, encourages such attitudes."

Gwyn makes the same claim, in very similar language. He argues that "official multiculturalism encourages apartheid, or to be a bit less harsh, ghettoism."[6] The longer multiculturalism policy has been in place, "the higher the cultural walls have gone up inside Canada." Multiculturalism encourages ethnic leaders to keep their members "apart from the mainstream," practising "what can best be described as mono-culturalism." In this way the Canadian state "encourages these gatekeepers to maintain what amounts, at worst, to an apartheid form of citizenship."

Bissoondath and Gwyn are hardly alone in these claims; they are repeated endlessly in the media. To take just one example, Robert Fulford recently argued in *The Globe and Mail* that the policy encourages people to maintain a "freeze-dried" identity, reducing intercultural exchange and relationships, and that time will judge it to be one of Canada's greatest "policy failures."[7]

It is important — indeed urgent — to determine whether such claims are true. Surprisingly, however, neither Bissoondath nor Gwyn provides any empirical evidence for his views. In order to assess their claims, therefore, I have collected some statistics that may bear on the question of whether multiculturalism has promoted ethnic separatism, and discouraged or impeded integration. I will start with evidence from within Canada, comparing ethnic groups before and after the adoption of the multiculturalism policy in 1971. I will then consider evidence from other countries, particularly countries that have rejected the principle of official multiculturalism, to see how Canada compares with them.

THE DOMESTIC EVIDENCE

How has the adoption of multiculturalism in 1971 affected the integration of ethnic groups in Canada? To answer this question requires some account of what "integration" involves. It is one of the puzzling features of the Gwyn and Bissoondath critiques that neither defines exactly what he means by integration. However, we can piece together some of the elements they see as crucial: adopting a Canadian identity rather than clinging exclusively to one's ancestral identity; participating in broader Canadian institutions rather than participating solely in ethnic-specific institutions; learning an official language rather than relying solely on one's mother tongue; having inter-ethnic friendships, or even mixed marriages, rather than socializing entirely within one's ethnic group. Such criteria do not form a comprehensive theory of "integration," but they seem to be at the heart of Gwyn's and Bissoondath's concerns about multiculturalism, so they are a good starting point.

Let us begin with the most basic form of integration: the decision of an immigrant to become a Canadian citizen. If the Gwyn/Bissoondath thesis were true, one would expect naturalization rates to have declined since the adoption of multiculturalism. In fact, naturalization rates have increased since 1971.[8] This is particularly relevant because the economic incentives to naturalize have lessened over the last 25 years. Canadian citizenship is not needed in order to enter the labour market in Canada, or to gain access to social benefits. There are virtually no differences between citizens and permanent residents in their civil rights or social benefits; the right to vote is the only major legal benefit gained by naturalization.[9] The primary reason for immigrants to take out citizenship, therefore, is that they identify with Canada; they want to formalize their membership in Canadian society and to participate in the political life of the country.

Moreover, if we examine which groups are most likely to naturalize, we find that it is the "multicultural groups"— immigrants from nontraditional source countries, for whom the multiculturalism policy is most relevant — that have the highest rates of naturalization. By contrast, immigrants from the United States and United Kingdom, who are not seen in popular discourse as "ethnic" or "multicultural" groups, have the lowest rates of naturalization.[10] In other words, those groups that are most directly affected by the multiculturalism policy have shown the greatest desire to become Canadian, while those that fall outside the multiculturalism rubric have shown the least desire to become Canadian.

Let's move now to political participation. If the Gwyn/Bissoondath thesis were true, one would expect the political participation of ethnocultural minorities to have declined since the adoption of multiculturalism in 1971. After all, political participation is a symbolic affirmation of citizenship, and reflects an interest in the political life of the larger society. Yet there is no evidence of decline in such participation.[11] To take one relevant indicator, between

Confederation and the 1960s, in the period prior to the adoption of multiculturalism, ethnic groups became increasingly underrepresented in Parliament, but since 1971 the trend has been reversed, so that today they have nearly as many MPs as one would expect, given their percentage of the population.[12]

It is also important to note the way ethnocultural groups participate in Canadian politics. They do not form separate ethnic-based parties, either as individual groups or as coalitions, but participate overwhelmingly within pan-Canadian parties. Indeed, the two parties in Canada that are closest to being ethnic parties were created by and for those of French or English ancestry: the Parti/Bloc Québécois, whose support comes almost entirely from Quebeckers of French ancestry, and the Confederation of Regions Party, whose support came almost entirely from New Brunswickers of English Loyalist ancestry.[13] Immigrants themselves have shown no inclination to support ethnic-based political parties, and instead vote for the traditional national parties.

This is just one indicator of a more general point: namely, that immigrants are overwhelmingly supportive of, and committed to protecting, the country's basic political structure. We know that, were it not for the "ethnic vote," the 1995 referendum on secession in Quebec would have succeeded. In that referendum, ethnic voters overwhelmingly expressed their commitment to Canada. More generally, all the indicators suggest that immigrants quickly absorb and accept Canada's basic liberal-democratic values and constitutional principles, even if their home countries are illiberal or nondemocratic.[14] As Freda Hawkins put it, "the truth is that there have been no riots, no breakaway political parties, no charismatic immigrant leaders, no real militancy in international causes, no internal political terrorism . . . immigrants recognize a good, stable political system when they see one."[15] If we look at indicators of legal and political integration, then, we see that since the adoption of multiculturalism in 1971 immigrants have been more likely to become Canadians, and more likely to participate politically. And when they participate, they do so through pan-ethnic political parties that uphold Canada's basic liberal-democratic principles.

This sort of political integration is the main aim of a democratic state. Yet from the point of view of individual Canadians, the most important forms of immigrant integration are probably not political, but societal. Immigrants who participate in politics may be good democratic citizens, but if they can't speak English or French, or are socially isolated in self-contained ethnic groups, then Canadians will perceive a failure of integration. So let us shift now to two indicators of societal integration: official language acquisition and intermarriage rates.

If the Gwyn/Bissoondath thesis were true, one would expect to find that the desire of ethnocultural minorities to acquire official language competence has declined since the adoption of multiculturalism. If immigrant groups are being "ghettoized," are "alienated from the mainstream," and are attempting to preserve their original way of life intact from their homeland, then presumably they have less reason than they did before 1971 to learn an official language.

In fact, demand for classes in English and French as second languages (ESL; FSL) has never been higher, and actually exceeds supply in many cities. According to the 1991 Census, 98.6 percent of Canadians report that they can speak one of the official languages.[16] This figure is staggering when one considers how many immigrants are elderly and/or illiterate in their mother tongue, and who therefore find it extremely difficult to learn a new language. It is especially impressive given that the number of immigrants who arrive with knowledge of an official language has declined since 1971.[17] If we set aside the elderly — who make up the majority of the Canadians who cannot speak an official language — the idea that there is a general decrease in immigrants' desire to learn an official language is absurd. The overwhelming majority do learn an official language, and insofar as such skills are lacking, the explanation is the lack of accessible and appropriate ESL/FSL classes, not lack of desire.[18]

Another indicator worth looking at is intermarriage rates. If the Gwyn/Bissoondath thesis were true, one would expect intermarriage to have declined since the adoption of a policy said to have driven "even deeper the awful wedges between races and nationalities" and to have encouraged groups to retreat into "monocultural" ghettoes and hide behind "cultural walls." In fact, intermarriage rates have consistently increased since 1971. There has been an overall decline in endogamy, both for immigrants and for their native-born children. Moreover, and equally important, we see a dramatic increase in social acceptance of mixed marriages.[19] Whereas in 1968 a majority of Canadians (52 percent) disapproved of Black–white marriages, the situation is now completely reversed, so that by 1995 an overwhelming majority (81 percent) approved of such marriages.[20]

Unlike the previous three indicators of integration, intermarriage is not a deliberate goal of government policy; it is not the business of governments either to encourage or to discourage intermarriage. But changes in intermarriage rates are useful as indicators of a broader trend that is a legitimate government concern: namely, the extent to which Canadians feel comfortable living and interacting with members of other ethnic groups. If Canadians feel comfortable living and working with members of other groups, inevitably some people will become friends with, and even lovers of, members of other ethnic groups. The fact that intermarriage rates have gone up is important, therefore, not necessarily in itself, but rather as evidence that Canadians are more accepting of diversity. And we have direct evidence for this more general trend. Canadians today are much more willing to accept members of other ethnic groups as co-workers, neighbours, or friends than they were before 1971.[21]

Other indicators point to the same trends. For example, despite Gwyn's and Bissoondath's rhetoric about the proliferation of ethnic "ghettos" and "enclaves," studies of residential concentration have shown that permanent ethnic enclaves do not exist in Canada. Indeed, "it is scarcely sensible to talk of 'ghettos' in Canadian cities."[22] What little concentration does exist is more likely to be found among older immigrant groups, like the Jews and Italians, whose arrival preceded the multiculturalism policy. Groups that have arrived primarily after 1971, such as Asians and Afro-Caribbeans, exhibit the least residential concentration.[23]

In short, whether we look at naturalization, political participation, official language competence, or intermarriage rates, we see the same story. There is no evidence to support the claim that multiculturalism has decreased the rate of integration of immigrants, or increased the separatism or mutual hostility of ethnic groups. As Orest Kruhlak puts it, "irrespective of which variables one examines, including [citizenship acquisition, ESL, mother-tongue retention, ethnic association participation, intermarriage or] political participation, the scope of economic involvement, or participation in mainstream social or service organizations, none suggest a sense of promoting ethnic separateness."[24]

THE COMPARATIVE EVIDENCE

We can make the same point another way. If the Bissoondath/Gwyn thesis were correct about the ghettoizing impact of our official multiculturalism policy, we would expect Canada to perform worse on these indicators of integration than other countries that have not adopted such a policy. Both Gwyn and Bissoondath contrast the Canadian approach with the American, which exclusively emphasizes common identities and common values, and refuses to provide public recognition or affirmation of ethnocultural differences. If Canada fared worse than the United States in terms of integrating immigrants, this would provide some indirect support for the Bissoondath/Gwyn theory.

In fact, however, Canada fares better than the United States on virtually any dimension of integration. Its naturalization rates are almost double those of the United States.[25] Canada's rates of political participation and official language acquisition are higher, and its rates of residential segregation are lower.[26] In addition Canadians show much greater approval for intermarriage. In 1988, when 72 percent of Canadians approved of interracial marriages, only 40 percent of Americans approved, and 25 percent felt they should be illegal![27] And ethnicity is less salient as a determinant of friendship in Canada than in the United States.[28]

On every indicator of integration, then, Canada with its multiculturalism policy, fares better than the United States, with its repudiation of multiculturalism. We would find the same story if we compared Canada with other immigrant countries that have rejected multiculturalism in favour of an exclusive emphasis on common identities — such as France.[29] Canada does better than these other countries not only in actual rates of integration, but also in the day-to-day experience of ethnic relations. In a 1997 survey, people in twenty countries were asked whether they agreed that "different ethnic groups get along well here." The percentage of those agreeing was far higher in Canada (75 percent) than in the United States (58 percent) or France (51 percent).[30]

This should not surprise us, since Canada does better than virtually any other country in the world in the integration of immigrants. The only comparable country is Australia, which has its own official multiculturalism policy — one largely inspired by Canada's, although of course it has been adapted to Australia's circumstances.[31] The two countries that lead the world in the integration of immigrants are countries with official multiculturalism policies. They are much more successful than any country that has rejected multiculturalism.

In short, there is no evidence to support the claim that multiculturalism is promoting ethnic separateness or impeding immigrant integration. Whether we examine the trends within Canada since 1971 or compare Canada with other countries, the conclusion is the same: the multiculturalism program is working. It is achieving what it set out to do: helping to ensure that those people who wish to express their ethnic identity are respected and accommodated, while simultaneously increasing the ability of immigrants to integrate into the larger society. Along with our fellow multiculturalists in Australia, Canadians do a better job of respecting ethnic diversity while promoting societal integration than citizens of any other country.

EXPLAINING THE DEBATE

This finding raises a genuine puzzle. Why do so many intelligent and otherwise well-informed commentators agree that multiculturalism policy is impeding integration? Part of the explanation is that many critics have simply not examined the actual policy to see what it involves. For example, both Gwyn and Bissoondath claim that, in effect, multiculturalism tells new Canadians that they should practise "monoculturalism," preserving their inherited way of life intact while avoiding interacting with or learning from the members of other groups, or the larger society.[32] If this were a plausible interpretation of the policy's aims, it would be only natural to assume that ethnocultural separatism is increasing in Canadian society.

In reality, as the government's documents make clear, the main goals of multiculturalism policy (and most of its funding) have been to promote civic participation in the larger society and to increase mutual understanding and cooperation between the members of different ethnic groups. Unfortunately, neither Gwyn nor Bissoondath quotes or cites a single document published by the multiculturalism unit of the federal government — not one of its annual reports, demographic analyses, public education brochures, or program funding guidelines.

Their critiques are thus double unreal. They describe a (nonexistent) policy of promoting "monoculturalism" among ethnocultural groups, and then blame it for a (nonexistent) trend toward "apartheid" in Canadian society. They have invented a nonexistent policy to explain a nonexistent trend.

But if the Bissoondath and Gwyn accounts are so ill-informed, why have they been so influential? Both books were generally well reviewed, and often praised for their insight into ethnocultural relations in Canada. Why were so many Canadians persuaded by their claims about growing ethnocultural separatism, even though these claims had no empirical support, and indeed are contradicted by the evidence? Why were so many Canadians persuaded by their mistaken characterization of the policy?

Part of the answer, I think, is that defenders of the policy have been strangely inarticulate. The federal government has not clearly explained the aims of the policy, nor has it provided criteria for evaluating its success. Even though the policy has been demonstrably successful, the government itself has made little attempt to demonstrate its success; so far as I can tell, it has never attempted to gather together the various findings on integration discussed in this chapter, or to monitor them systematically so as to measure changes in integration over time.

Collecting and publicizing this sort of information would provide Canadians with the tools to question and deflate the exaggerated claims and misinformed critiques we find in Gwyn and Bissoondath. Yet even if this information were more widely available, it would likely not entirely alleviate public anxiety about multiculturalism. Lack of information cannot, by itself, explain public attitudes. In the absence of information, why do so many Canadians assume that multiculturalism has had negative consequences? Why are they fearful of multiculturalism, rather than confident about it?

Part of the problem may be that Canadians have no clear sense of the limits of multiculturalism. They are not sure that certain "non-negotiable" principles or institutions will be protected and upheld, even if they conflict with the desires or traditions of some immigrant groups. Canadians are not averse to multiculturalism within limits, but they want to know that those limits exist. They value diversity, but they also want to know that this diversity will be expressed within the context of common Canadian institutions, and that it doesn't entail acceptance of ethnic separation. Similarly, Canadians are generally tolerant, but they also believe that some practices, such as clitoridectomy, are intolerable, and they want to know that they won't be asked to "tolerate" the violation of basic human rights.

So long as Canadians feel insecure about the limits of multiculturalism, publicizing statistics about the beneficial effects of multiculturalism will have only limited success in changing public attitudes. The statistics may look good today, but what about tomorrow? Perhaps the policy has worked until now to promote integration, but only because the full "logic" of multiculturalism has not yet been implemented. Perhaps the logic of multiculturalism is to undermine the very idea that there are any principles or institutions that all citizens must respect and adhere to. It is this sort of insecurity that explains, at least in part, the popularity of the Bissoondath/Gwyn account. Until defenders of multiculturalism explain its limits, these sorts of critiques will continue to strike a chord among Canadians, touching deeply felt anxieties about ethnocultural relations.

I think it is possible to address these concerns. In order to do so, however, we need to understand how multiculturalism fits into a larger set of government policies regarding ethnocultural relations in Canada. It is precisely this larger context that is typically ignored in debates about multiculturalism. Both critics and defenders of multiculturalism often talk as if the adoption of the policy in 1971 ushered in an entirely new era in ethnic relations in Canada, overturning the government policies developed over the previous 150 years of immigration.

This is a very misleading picture. In many respects, the government policies that encourage the historical integration of immigrants remain firmly in place. After all, multiculturalism is not the only — or even the primary — government policy affecting the place of ethnic groups in Canadian society; it is just one small piece of the pie. Many aspects of public policy affect these groups, including policies relating to naturalization, education, job training and professional accreditation, human rights and anti-discrimination law, civil service employment, health and safety, even national defence. It is these other policies that are the major engines of integration, for they encourage, pressure, even legally force immigrants to take steps toward integrating into Canadian society.

The idea that multiculturalism promotes ethnic separateness stems in large part, I think, from a failure to see how multiculturalism fits into this larger context of public policy. When we do situate multiculturalism within this larger context, we see that it is not a rejection of integration, but a renegotiation of the terms of integration — a renegotiation that was in general not merely justified but overdue.

NOTES

1. Trudeau in *House of Commons Debates*, 8 Oct. 1971: 8545–6.
2. Freda Hawkins, *Critical Years in Immigration: Canada and Australia Compared* (Montreal: McGill-Queen's University Press, 1989), p. 221.
3. Neil Bissoondath, *Selling Illusions: The Cult of Multiculturalism in Canada* (Toronto: Penguin, 1994); Richard Gwyn, *Nationalism without Walls: The Unbearable Lightness of Being Canadian* (Toronto: McClelland and Stewart, 1995).
4. The passages quoted in this paragraph can be found on pages 111, 110, 98, and 133 of *Selling Illusions*.
5. Schlesinger, *The Disuniting of America* (New York: Norton, 1992), p. 138. According to his analysis, the United States is witnessing the "fragmentation of the national community into a quarrelsome spatter of enclaves, ghettoes, tribes . . . encouraging and exalting cultural and linguistic apartheid" (137–38). Bissoondath argues that the same process is occurring in Canada.
6. The passages quoted in this paragraph are from pages 274, 8, and 234 of *Nationalism without Walls*.
7. Robert Fulford, "Do Canadians Want Ethnic Heritage Freeze-Dried?," *The Globe and Mail*, 17 Feb. 1997.
8. Citizenship and Immigration Canada, *Citizenship and Immigration Statistics* (Ottawa: Public Works, 1997), Table G2 and Table 1.
9. The remaining differences between citizens and permanent residents relate to (a) minority language rights; (b) protection against deportation; and (c) access to a few sensitive bureaucratic positions, none of which are relevant to most immigrants.
10. The average length of residence before naturalization is 7.61 years, with immigrants from the UK taking the longest (13.95 years); immigrants from China, Vietnam, and the Philippines all take under five years on average (Citizenship Registrar, Multiculturalism and Citizenship Canada, 1992). In 1971, only 5 percent of the Americans eligible to take out citizenship in Canada chose to do so. See Karol Krotki and Colin Reid, "Demography of Canadian Population by Ethnic Group," in *Ethnicity and Culture in Canada: The Research Landscape*, ed. J.W. Berry and Jean Laponce (Toronto: University of Toronto Press, 1994), p. 26.
11. For surveys of the political participation of ethnocultural groups in Canadian politics, see the three research studies in Kathy Megyery, ed., *Ethnocultural Groups and Visible Minorities in Canadian Politics: The Question of Access*, vol. 7 of the Research Studies of the Royal Commission on Electoral Reform and Party Financing (Ottawa: Dundurn Press, 1991); Jean Laponce, "Ethnicity and Voting Studies in Canada: Primary and Secondary Sources 1970–1991" in Berry and Laponce, eds., *Ethnicity and Culture*, pp. 179–202; and Jerome Black and Aleem Lakhani, "Ethnoracial Diversity in the House of Commons: An Analysis of Numerical Representation in the 35th Parliament," *Canadian Ethnic Studies* 29, 1 (November 1997): 13–33.
12. Daiva Stasiulus and Yasmeen Abu-Laban, "The House the Parties Built: (Re)constructing Ethnic Representation in Canadian Politics" in Megyery, ed., *Ethnocultural Groups*, p. 14; cf. Alain Pelletier, "Politics and Ethnicity: Representation of Ethnic and Visible-Minority Groups in the House of Commons," in ibid., pp. 129–30.
13. Geoffrey Martin, "The COR Party of New Brunswick as an 'Ethnic Party,'" *Canadian Review of Studies in Nationalism* 23, 1 (1996): 1–8.

14. For evidence of the quick absorption of liberal-democratic values by immigrants, see James Frideres, "Edging into the Mainstream: Immigrant Adults and their Children" in *Multiculturalism in North America and Europe: Comparative Perspectives on Interethnic Relations and Social Incorporation in Europe and North America,* ed. S. Isajiw (Toronto: Canadian Scholars' Press, 1997); Jerome Black, "The Practice of Politics in Two Settings: Political Transferability among Recent Immigrants to Canada," *Canadian Journal of Political Science* 20, 4 (1987): 731–53. Studies show that students born outside Canada, as well as students for whom English was not a first or home language, knew and valued their rights as much as their Canadian-born, English-speaking counterparts. See, for example, Charles Ungerleider, "Schooling, Identity and Democracy: Issues in the Social-Psychology of Canadian Classrooms" in *Educational Psychology: Canadian Perspectives,* ed. R. Short et al., (Toronto: Copp Clark, 1991), p. 204–5.

15. Hawkins, *Critical Years,* p. 279.

16. Some 63 percent of immigrants have neither English nor French as their mother tongue, yet only 309 000 residents in the 1991 Census couldn't speak an official language. Most of these were elderly (166 000 were over 55). See Brian Harrison, "Non Parlo né inglese, né francese" (Statistics Canada: Census of Canada Short Article Series, #5, September 1993).

17. Derrick Thomas, "The Social Integration of Immigrants," in *The Immigration Dilemma,* ed. Steven Globerman (Vancouver: Fraser Institute, 1992): 224.

18. Susan Donaldson, "Un-LINC-ing Language and Integration: Future Directions for Federal Settlement Policy" (M.A. thesis, Department of Linguistics and Applied Language Studies, Carleton University, 1995).

19. Morton Weinfeld, "Ethnic Assimilation and the Retention of Ethnic Cultures," in Berry and Laponce, eds., *Ethnicity and Culture,* pp. 244–45.

20. Jeffrey Reitz and Raymond Breton, *The Illusion of Difference: Realities of Ethnicity in Canada and the United States* (Toronto: C.D. Howe Institute, 1994), p. 80; Leo Driedger, *Multi-Ethnic Canada: Identities and Inequalities* (Toronto: Oxford University Press, 1996), p. 277.

21. Driedger, *Multi-Ethnic Canada,* p. 263.

22. John Mercer, "Asian Migrants and Residential Location in Canada," *New Community* 15, 2 (1989): 198.

23. Thomas, "Social Integration," pp. 240, 247.

24. Orest Kruhlak, "Multiculturalism: Myth versus Reality," unpublished paper prepared for the Institute for Research on Public Policy project "Making Canada Work: Towards a New Concept of Citizenship" (1991), p. 10.

25. For example, the naturalization rate of immigrants who arrived in the United States in 1977 is around 37 percent. The comparable rate in Canada is between 70 percent and 80 percent, and is much higher in some multicultural groups (e.g., 95 percent of the Vietnamese refugees have become citizens). For a comparative study of naturalization policies and trends, see Dilek Cinar, "From Aliens to Citizens: A Comparative Analysis of Rules of Transition," in *From Aliens to Citizens: Redefining the Legal Status of Immigrants,* ed. Rainer Baubock (Aldershot: Avebury, 1994), p. 65. For the case of Vietnamese "boat people" in Canada, see Frideres, "Edging into the Mainstream."

26. Krotki and Reid, "Demography", p. 40.

27. Reitz and Breton, *The Illusion of Difference,* pp. 80–81.

28. Ibid., p. 60.

29. See Cinar, "From Aliens to Citizens," p. 65; Stephen Castles and Mark Miller, *The Age of Migration: International Population Movements in the Modern World* (London: Macmillan, 1993), pp. 220–21; Sarah Wayland, "Religious Expression in Public Schools: Kirpans in Canada, Hijab in France," *Ethnic and Racial Studies* 20, 3 (1997): 545–61.

30. Angus Reid, *Canada and the World: An International Perspective on Canada and Canadians.* The polling data is available on the Angus Reid Web site at www.angusreid.com. Australia came second on this question, with 71 percent of respondents agreeing that ethnic groups get along well in Australia.

31. As Freda Hawkins notes, multiculturalism was adopted in both countries in the 1970s "for the same reasons and with the same objectives" (*Critical Years,* p. 214). And they have evolved in similar directions since the 1970s, from an emphasis on cultural maintenance to issues of public participation and institutional accommodation. For a detailed comparison of their origins, see Hawkins, "Multiculturalism in Two Countries: The Canadian and Australian Experience," *Review of Canadian Studies* 17, 1 (1982): 64–80. For a more up-to-date account, see James Jupp, *Explaining Australian Multiculturalism* (Canberra: Centre for Immigration and Multicultural Studies, Australian National University, 1996), and Stephen Castles, "Multicultural Citizenship in Australia," in *Citizenship and Exclusion,* ed. Veit Bader (London: St. Martin's Press, 1997).

32. Similarly, Fulford argues that the multiculturalism policy disapproves of inter-marriage and interethnic friendships ("Do Canadians Want Ethnic Heritage Freeze-Dried?").

Article Thirty-Three

Multiculturalism, National Identity, and National Integration: The Canadian Case

John Harles

> Integration is not synonymous with assimilation. Assimilation implies almost total absorption into another linguistic and cultural group. An assimilated individual gives up his cultural identity, and may even go so far as to change his name. Both integration and assimilation occur in Canada, and the individual must be free to choose whichever process suits him, but it seems to us that those of other than French or British origin clearly prefer integration.
>
> Canadian society, open and modern, should be able to integrate heterogeneous elements into a harmonious system, to achieve "unity in diversity."[1]

When the Royal Commission on Bilingualism and Biculturalism (RCBB) included the foregoing observations in the fourth volume (1969) of its report on the nature of the Canadian polity, it voiced a perspective that had been influential in Ottawa for more than a generation — national integration was possible, even preferable, without assimilation.[2]

Two years later, on the inauguration of multiculturalism as an official policy of government, that assumption became part of the Canadian public ethos. As an integrative strategy, multiculturalism emerged out of a concern to coalesce, socially and politically, the ethnically diverse population introduced into Canada as a consequence of twentieth-century — especially post-World War II — immigration. At its most basic level, the policy intended to make those immigrant-stock individuals of other than Anglo-Irish or French lineage feel that they, too, were an indispensable part of the Canadian political community. When Pierre Trudeau, building on the recommendations of the RCBB, introduced the official policy of multiculturalism to the Commons, his remarks reflected this unity in diversity theme:

> We believe that cultural pluralism is the very essence of Canadian identity. Every ethnic group has the right to preserve and develop its own cultures and values within the Canadian context. . . . A policy of multiculturalism within a bilingual framework commends itself to the government as the most suitable means of assuring the cultural freedom of Canadians. . . . National unity, if it is to mean anything in the deeply personal sense, must be founded on confidence in one's own individual identity; out of this can grow respect for others and a willingness to share ideas, attitudes, and assumptions. A vigorous policy of multiculturalism will help create this initial confidence. It can form the base of a society which is based on fair play for all.[3]

A principled desire to reconstitute Canadian national identity was not first among the reasons why multiculturalism was advanced by the Trudeau government. Most immediately, the policy aimed at shoring up Liberal electoral support in Western Canada and urban Ontario. In that respect, official multiculturalism was driven by an elite accommodation mode of Canadian politics, a means of mollifying the leadership of certain ethnic groups — representatives of the Ukrainian community were particularly vocal — who rejected the "two nations" view of Canada, French and English, endorsed in the RCBB report. Subsequent grants to minority

Source: John Harles, "Multiculturalism, National Identity, and National Integration: The Canadian Case" from *International Journal of Canadian Studies*, 17 (Spring 1998): 217–248. Reprinted with permission.

ethnic organizations, and the development of a bureaucratic structure designed to give ethnic groups a formal, consultative role in government policy-making, served to institutionalize cultural differences and solidify the electoral support of ethnic elites for the party in power. More controversially, Trudeau's endorsement of multiculturalism may also be interpreted as an attempt to reduce Quebec's appeal as a pole of political attraction rivalling Ottawa. On this reading, Trudeau intended the policy to counter the RCBB's emphasis on Canada as a bicultural state, thereby relegating French-Canadians to the status of simply one ethnic group in Canada among many others. Beyond such calculations, however, Trudeau's enthusiasm for multiculturalism appears tepid.[4]

No matter. Over the last twenty-seven years, multiculturalism has become an explicit strategy of national consolidation in Canada. During that period, Canada's commitment to accommodate, celebrate and promote ethnic diversity has been constitutionally entrenched in section 27 of the Canadian Charter of Rights and Freedoms (1982) and reiterated and amplified in the Canadian Multiculturalism Act of 1988. More than this, multiculturalism has been affirmed by the federal government and all provincial governments save one as a fundamental characteristic — perhaps *the* fundamental characteristic — of Canadian identity and an essential prop of the political order. The dominant view of multicultural policy has remained that it "should assist and encourage the integration (but not assimilation) of all immigrants."[5] As the federal Secretary of State for Multiculturalism and the Status of Women has warned:

> We have too many examples of what can happen when we don't promote that Canadian mosaic which fundamentally says the world is here, we are all Canadians, and that the plurality, the multicultural, the cultural communities, the mix, is fundamental to Canada, and without an understanding of the complexities that that brings, this country will not be a united country . . . One can choose how one wants to live in this country and *there is no need to be assimilated. It is a matter of integration* . . . [emphasis added].[6]

The present paper considers whether multiculturalism can bear the weight of this integrative task. The argument will be that multiculturalism is an insufficient, though in the Canadian context an understandable, substitute for a strong Canadian identity. If Canada is to find an integrative national identity, one that would fix the boundaries of a distinctly Canadian political community by specifying the common beliefs and values of its members, norms which Canadians would be expected to assimilate, a civic variety of nationalism may be the most promising alternative. On this approach, national identity is forged out of citizen participation in and commitment to the deliberative processes of democratic government. Yet even here there is reason for only the most guarded optimism. Now as ever, the disposition of Quebec hangs over any discussion of Canadian integration.

I

National integration is a fundamental task of any political system. The reason is clear: periodically the state requires its members to make sacrifices for the good of the whole. Absent a sense of collective destiny, individuals will find it difficult to subordinate private interest to public welfare. Military service is the most dramatic and the most elementary example of this general point. The decision to risk death in defense of the community turns, in part, on whether an individual believes that community sufficiently expresses his or her own identity and interests and is worthy of protection. But the issue of sacrifice applies to more mundane matters as well — taxation, for instance. Not even the most doctrinaire capitalist will readily argue that the market can provide all desired public goods and services; the state must undertake some of the required functions that the market cannot or will not do. At the very least, provision must be made for domestic security, though in the modern era, the public catalog of services will be far more extensive. And all of these services must be funded in large measure by tax revenues collected from individuals whose remittances may be quite disproportional to the personal benefits they bring. Still, if the state is to fulfil its agenda, it must have the compliance of those who do not immediately profit from its assistance. Belief in a common national identity, and consequently an acceptance of mutual civic obligations, is one reason to forego current satisfactions for diffuse benefits. Indeed, from the viewpoint of individual citizens, membership in such an "imagined community" may offer emotional satisfaction, meeting a perceived need for social solidarity in modern, impersonal, market-driven societies.[7] It is this sense of a shared political fate — Durkheim called it the "collective conscience" of a people[8]— that from the perspective of the citizenry may be termed polity, and from the perspective of the state, national integration.

It is a common place among students of the Canadian political system that Canada is not a well-integrated and unified polity. Titles in the bibliography of Canadian political studies are indicative. Over the last few years they have included: *The Roots of Disunity;*[9] *Mosaic Madness;*[10] *Deconfederation;*[11] *The Unmaking of Canada;*[12] *Canada at Risk;*[13] *Reimagining Canada;*[14] and most directly, *The Collapse of Canada?*[15]

Scholarly assessments are equally forthright. Thus, Anthony Birch asserts that "the level of national integration in Canada . . . may be lower than any other advanced democratic state."[16] Carolyn Tuohy observes that "Canadian ambivalence extends to the very legitimacy of the state itself and to the identification of the political community."[17] R. Kenneth Carty and W. Peter Ward remark that "this continuing ambivalence has perpetrated a set of conflicts about the essence of Canadianness that lies at the heart of the political system. Canadians divide between Anglophone and Francophone, old and new, immigrant and Aboriginal, partly because there is no common meeting ground, no agreement on what constitutes a Canadian."[18] And Charles Taylor maintains that, "[a] basic fact about Canada which we often have trouble accepting is that we are still far from achieving a universally agreed definition of our country as a political community. . . ."[19] Even the British news weekly, *The Economist,* weighs in with an appraisal: "It seems unlikely that Canada's future is going to be a country with a strong national purpose. The glue that holds the place together is no more adhesive than maple syrup, and there is little prospect of replacing it with something stickier."[20]

It is often observed that a root cause of such difficulties is that Canada does not possess a unifying political nationalism, or, more precisely, that it is without the common beliefs and values, the collective political commitments, that would drive such a nationalism.[21] Canada's problem in achieving a country-wide consensus on constitutional reform, despite five formal attempts to do so since 1960, may be symptomatic. In the judgment of James Tully, a "crisis of identification" is responsible, discrete cultural and regional constituencies being unable or unwilling to agree on a constitutional document that might bridge their particularisms.[22] Consequently, the question of a consolidating political identity in Canada is regularly framed in terms of the need for a "pan-Canadian" nationalism, suggesting that to the extent national sentiment exists in Canada it does not predominantly accrue to the Canadian state.[23]

If one searches in vain for comparable treatments of pan-French, pan-British, or pan-American nationalisms — indeed, in the United States, "pan-American" has continental connotations — the reason may be that these countries possess what Canada does not and perhaps cannot possess: national identities conceived largely in ethnic or ideological terms. With regard to matters of integration, the difference between these two ideal-types of nationhood is critical. On both accounts the bearers of a national identity will share geographic attachments and a common cache of historical memories. But in the instance of ideologically grounded identities, commitment to a particular system of political belief further delimits the political community. In such cases, common political values are not merely a necessary condition of a well-integrated polity but a sufficient one, membership in the political community being determined by them. Because this sort of identity is creedal, it is also essentially voluntaristic. Its acquisition is primarily a matter of individual civic commitment, though its content will extend beyond the mere assumption of citizenship. And this may be contrasted to those polities whose national identities are understood in terms of broader ethnic or cultural affinities — those based on belief in a common lineage, history, language, religious orientation or way of life. Here, the valuational and behavioral boundaries of the political community might include, but will not be limited to, shared ideological convictions. To the degree that national identity is expressed by way of ethnic and cultural homogeneity, membership in the political community will be a function of ascription as much as choice. At least, the acceptance of ethnic minorities as members of the polity in good standing will require significant cultural transformation on their part.

The United States and Great Britain illustrate the distinction. American identity is ideologically centred. In the United States a Lockean liberal political creed, granting republican and populist overtones, is widely regarded as definitive of the national community.[24] Historically, acceptance of that creed, with a few shameful exceptions, has enabled immigrant-stock individuals of varying cultural backgrounds to be fully received into the polity, in effect to become American in more than strictly a legal sense. In Britain, on the other hand, ideological conviction would not seem sufficient reason to bar one from the political community — when questioned about the legitimacy of the British Communist party, Churchill is reported to have replied that it was comprised of fellow Englishmen, people from whom there was nothing to fear — but lack of appropriate ethnic credentials might well do so. At least until late, it has been difficult to imagine that one could become British in more than a legal sense absent the relevant Anglo-Saxon or Celtic cultural characteristics (and possibly lineage).

Doubtless such distinctions are idealized. National self-conceptions are negotiated over time, and the difference between an ideological and ethnically based identity is a matter of degree. In the early years of the republic, American identity was strongly ethnic in nature — Anglo-Saxon and Protestant, or at least northern European, in character. Only under the pressure of large numbers of immigrants who did not fit that mold, as well as the centripetal force of two world wars, did the American identity turn decisively in an ideological direction.[25] Similarly, it has been pointed out that traditionally British nationhood included a commitment to the principle of constitutionalism, and that a more precise and updated statement of the distinctive political values of the British polity might help to resolve the current crisis of British identity.[26] Still, the disparate emphases of the American and British political communities is suggested by the use of the ethnic hyphen. It is common to refer to German-Americans, Mexican-Americans, Chinese-Americans and so on because, in the United States, political identity can be divorced from cultural identity. One suspects that the hyphen is conspicuous by its absence in Britain because there cultural and political identity are more of a piece.

In the case of countries with relatively well-established national identities, students of politics commonly regard assimilation as the primary vehicle of congealing an ethnically diverse citizenry into a stable political whole. Among democratic theorists, John Stuart Mill provides the prototypical discussion. In *Considerations on Representative Government*, Mill maintains that individual nationalities — groups sharing a common lineage, language, religion or history — are inclined to demand self-government, a condition to which, on democratic principle, they are entitled. If for reasons of geography the creation of distinct national governments is not possible, Mill maintains, "[e]xperience proves that it is possible for one nationality to merge and be absorbed in another. . . . Whatever really tends to the admixture of nationalities, and the blending of their attributes and peculiarities in a common union is a benefit to the human race."[27] Moreover, as "it is in general a necessary condition of free institutions that the boundaries of free governments should coincide in the main with those of nationalities,"[28] Mill warns that the alternative to assimilation (a term he does not use) is susceptibility to despotism — a government of divide and rule in which antagonistic cultural groups are played off against one another and the power of the central authorities is thereby enhanced.

Contemporary scholars, often more solicitous of the rights of cultural minorities, do not so much advise assimilation as they observe and endorse its politically coalescent effect.[29] In the settler societies of the "New World," where ethnic diversity is largely the result of voluntary migration rather than conquest or dynastic alliance, assimilation is considered an especially appropriate strategy of nation-building.[30] And as the United States is in aggregate the greatest of all immigrant receiving societies, it is not surprising that the integrative advantages of assimilation receive particular attention from students of American politics.[31]

The conventional manner of employing the term assimilation is simply to indicate conformity to the preexisting norms, political norms included, of a dominant social group. Accordingly, assimilation nears its endpoint when others come to identify most closely with the imperatives of that group, and when this contingent is willing to accept individuals who were not originally members as equal participants in group life.[32] Yet the form that assimilation takes, and its implications for ethnic out-groups, will vary depending upon which understanding of nationhood — ethnic or ideological — prevails in a given polity. In countries whose national identities are culturally centred, provided that the principal ethnic group is amenable — and it may not be if it defines itself primarily in terms of race or lineage — assimilation will demand considerable sacrifice from ethnic minorities; not simply political ideas but more extensive cultural commitments are at issue. But in countries whose national identities are ideologically centred, assimilation as apolitical process may not require the loss of minority cultural distinctives, save for potentially dissonant ethnic political values.

That said, should a country lack a clear understanding of its national identity, be it culturally or ideologically grounded, it would seem to want for the ability to incorporate ethnic minorities, to furnish them with the shared commitments and common public culture which characterize a cohesive political community. On that reading, in a sense Canada may pursue integration without recourse to assimilation because it cannot do otherwise. In light of what is commonly considered the indeterminate nature of Canadian nationhood, assimilation in Canada is an implausible integrative strategy; conceptually there is little to assimilate to and no certain focus of political incorporation. To be sure, the policy of multiculturalism — and of integration without assimilation — was not adopted *because* of the long-standing debate over Canadian national identity. Yet its subsequent prominence in defining what it means to be Canadian must be seen in the context of that debate. Integrative national identities are constructed across history, but in Canada history has worked against a single unifying and assimilative identity and ultimately in favour of multiculturalism.

II

The prospect of Canada building a national identity on culturally exclusive grounds is ruled out in the first instance by the nature of the relationship between its two founding European traditions. Originally, Canada was a culturally dualist country — one culture being Anglophone, Protestant and of British origin, the other, Francophone, Catholic and of French provenance. Notwithstanding the British government's pre-Confederation flirtations with the idea of assimilating the French, the cultural resilience of French Canada — cause and effect of early legal recognition from London, most famously via the Quebec Act of 1774 — as well as its geographic concentration in the province of Quebec has meant that, at a minimum, Canada has remained a bilingual polity — a status somewhat weakly acknowledged in the initial constitutional provisions of the British North America Act (1867), though presently entrenched through the Official Languages Act (1969) and the Charter of Rights and Freedoms.

Nevertheless, as a focus for a comprehensive integrative national identity, something to which ethnic minorities might become assimilated, the dualist reading of confederation appears to be a non-starter. Dualism suggests that from its creation Canada was not to be an integrated national whole but at best an "equal partnership between the two founding races"— an approach, of course, that leaves indeterminate the status of Canada's Aboriginal peoples and immigrant "others." Granted, as Ken McRoberts has argued, for the first hundred years of confederation, dualism may have been a viable formula for achieving a measure of political civility between the English and French Canadian solitudes. Even so, a history of conflict e.g., the Riel/Northwest rebellions, the Manitoba and Ontario Schools controversies, the conscription crises during the two World Wars — suggests that the national partnership was marked as much by rivalry as harmony. Over the last generation, English-Canadian support for the idea of Canada as a contract between communities — *provincial* as opposed to *cultural* communities, in the Anglophone perspective — has been eroded by a more individualistic, rights-based and Ottawa-centred idea of the nation, in McRoberts' analysis, a legacy of the Trudeau government's national unity strategy.[33] And whereas the language of cultural compact continues to resonate with many French-Canadians who support a united Canada,[34] among Quebec Francophones, a pan-Canadian dualist approach to the political community has progressively lost ground to the view that the French-Canadian culture is to be nurtured and protected within the administrative structures of Quebec.[35] Related measures to make Quebec officially unilingual, as well as efforts by *indépendantistes* and federalists alike to secure special concessions for the province, are typically resented elsewhere in Canada, as the failure of the Meech Lake and Charlottetown Accords may have indicated, where they are interpreted as evidence of divided political loyalty.[36]

This points to a further difficulty with a dualist understanding of Canada: the two cultural communities have not been equally yoked. Things may not always have been this way. In the era when the dualist interpretation of Canada was unrivalled, in Anglophone Canada, immigrants and their progeny were encouraged to assimilate to what were regarded as Anglo-Saxon cultural and political standards.[37] So R.B. Bennett argued that Canada must "maintain our civilization at that high standard which has made the British civilization the test by which all other civilized nations in modern times are measured. . . . We desire to assimilate those whom we bring to this country to that civilization . . . rather than assimilate our civilization to theirs."[38] Legally, too, Anglo-conformity was an implied Canadian norm. Until 1947, Canadian citizenship was defined essentially in terms of being a subject of the United Kingdom. And immigration policy, at least until the late 1940s, was designed in many respects to give precedence to immigrants with British credentials, the assumption being that individuals of other lineages were less assimilable.[39] Shortly after the end of the Second World War, Canada's director of immigration, A.L. Joliffe, presented a confidential memorandum to the Cabinet which well stated the prevailing orthodoxy:

> The claim is sometimes made that Canada's immigration laws reflect class and race discrimination: they do, and necessarily so. Some form of discrimination cannot be avoided if immigration is to be effectively controlled in order to prevent the creation in Canada of expanding non-assimilable racial groups, the prohibiting of entry to immigrants of non-assimilable races is necessary.[40]

Given a perceived post-war need for immigrant labour as well as for population growth in the interest of an expanded consumer market — an outlook advanced by leading public officials and members of the business community alike — legal considerations of immigrant ethnicity gradually relaxed.[41] Yet even of late, when asked their ethnicity, Canadians of British origin are more likely than respondents of any other ancestry to identify themselves simply as Canadian.[42]

Despite a residue of affection for things British, Canada's diminishing political and demographic connection to the United Kingdom means that English-Canada — more precisely, English-speaking Canada — can no longer be classified primarily in terms of a single cultural identity.[43] In the strictest sense, Francophone Canada is not ethnically homogeneous either. But by comparison, the French-speaking community bounded by Quebec appears far more culturally cohesive and politically confident than its Anglophone counterpart in the rest of Canada.

Nowhere is the contrast greater than with respect to the significance of language in the two communities.[44] In Canada outside Quebec, English has become a mode of communication rather than a distinct cultural symbol, a circumstance brought on in some part by immigration itself. When at the turn of the century the Canadian government began to recruit immigrants from countries other than primarily the British Isles in an effort to populate the prairies, the result was that English was increasingly employed as the most practical means of discourse between individuals of various ethnic backgrounds. That English is the *lingua franca* of the majority of Canadians does have important political implications: it makes Canada outside Quebec vulnerable to American cultural penetration and threatens to undermine any distinctive English-Canadian identity. Consequently, numerous government initiatives in the cultural industries — the Canadian Broadcasting Company, the National Film Board, the Canada Council, Canadian content laws for radio and television broadcasting, tax disincentives for split-run editions of American magazines — have been taken with a view toward nurturing and protecting English-Canadian sensibilities.

In Quebec, on the other hand, the cultivation of the French language has been seen as a matter of preserving the identity of a French-Canadian nation — especially given the waning of the nation's other historic distinctives, its Catholic and agrarian character. As Quebec has opened its doors to immigration, which it was reluctant to do until a decline in post-war French-Canadian birth rates made labour recruitment a necessity, the linguistic disposition of the foreign-born has been a major concern.[45] The province's accessibility to Lebanese, Haitian and Indochinese immigrants, individuals with a greater likelihood of knowing French in their countries of origin, is an indication of this.[46] For economic reasons both outside and inside Quebec, the great majority of immigrants have been attracted to Anglophone Canada. On balance, non-French speaking immigrants have most often been perceived as a threat to French-Canadian identity. The Quebec language legislation of the 1970s, which among other things required immigrant children to be schooled largely in French — an assimilationist emphasis of sorts — had as its primary aim ensuring the demographic stability of the French cultural community in Canada. Similarly, while the Quebec government rejects official federal multiculturalism, it affirms many of the same policies through provincial "interculturalism," albeit with the understanding that the French culture and language is normative for ethnic minorities in Quebec. On that basis, provided that "*pure laine*" Quebeckers accept these individuals, one is tempted to argue that ethnic minorities may be integrated in Quebec in a way that they cannot be integrated in the rest of Canada — assimilated to a relatively well-defined, linguistically centred political identity.

Were Canada to possess a unifying political ideology that articulated the values, purposes and aspirations of the Canadian political community and established the terms by which ethnic minorities might come to affirm a distinctly Canadian identity, its historic cultural dualism might be of lesser political consequence. But it is partly because of the relationship between French and English Canada that a consolidating ideology has been difficult to construct.[47]

Although Canadians subscribe to the essential propositions of liberal-democratic political practice — political authority based on the consent of the governed as effectuated through elected representatives, equal political rights, including the equal ability to influence political decision-making, toleration of dissent, freedom of expression, conscience and association — this is considerably less than an overarching and unifying national vision. Such procedural commitments alone cannot distinguish a distinctly Canadian identity from that of other advanced industrial democratic states, nor do they provide sufficient reason for identifying with a Canadian as opposed to, say, an American national community. Even then, it has been suggested that the gloss placed on liberal-democratic ideals in Quebec and the rest of Canada is different: a substantive and collective rights based orientation in the former instance, a procedural and individual rights based orientation in the latter.[48] By entrenching these disparate readings of what Canadian democracy requires, the Charter of Rights and Freedoms itself has become a source of considerable political conflict across Canada.[49] Contrary to the nation-building aspirations of its framers, the Charter is not widely regarded as defining shared Canadian values: a 1991 Angus Reid poll indicated that only 45 percent of Canadians were willing to describe the document in this way.[50]

It is not just that Canada is marked by diverse ideological traditions — conservatism, liberalism, socialism and populism have all made their electoral presence known — but that the leading candidates for a unifying political creed are compromised by Canadian political history. Thus, the integrative potential of toryism, often cited as a major influence on the Canadian political perspective and one distinguishing it from the United States,[51] has been hindered by its connection with loyalism. Conservatism, then, has had a fundamentally different colouring in French Canada than in English Canada. In Anglophone Canada, conservatism can be traced to the immigration of loyalists from the United States. If, in the view of some scholars, these individuals were disgruntled and anti-revolutionary American liberals as much as dyed-in-the-wool tories,[52] what seems clear is that their political allegiances and identity were directed toward the British Crown.[53] By contrast, the conservatism of pre–Quiet Revolution French Canada had both a different source — arguably the legacy of a mildly feudal and authoritarian seventeenth century French fragment of settlement — and a different point of reference. After the Conquest, a French Catholic priestly elite pursued a conservatism that may have partially cohered with that of English Canada, but which was exercised in the interest of insulating French-Canadians from what were perceived as anti-clerical and liberal English-Canadian ideas, and in which the British connection was tolerated at best and anathema at worst.[54]

Within English Canada, too, loyalism would appear to have frustrated the emergence of an ideologically based political community. Allegiance to the British Crown, which long provided the focal point of English-Canadian national identity, may have impeded the development of an indigenous Anglophone identity. As David Bell has put it, loyalist myths "encouraged (Canadians) to honour colonial symbols instead of adopting (their) own, and to substitute for nationalism a peculiar variety of coattails imperialism."[55] Early Canadian nationalists — members of the Canada First Movement and the Imperial Federation League — championed greater independence for the Dominion, but they rarely did so outside the context of a markedly British empire.[56] Granted, some of these individuals envisioned that Canada might actually supplant Great Britain as the dominant player in a federated empire, but few called for outright independence or even, as with Goldwin Smith, a Canadian-American union. Comparatively high levels of foreign investment and ownership — predominantly British until the mid-1920s, American thereafter[57]— most likely compounded the difficulty of constructing an autonomous national vision.[58] In the measure that

English-Canadian political identity was vicariously expressed, the demise of British power worldwide and the postwar attenuation of the British political connection left Anglophone Canada in the lurch. What remained was the obverse of the loyalist heritage but a staple of Canadian identity since before Confederation — the desire not to be American.[59] Indeed, Sylvia Bashevkin *defines* Canadian nationalism as "the organized pursuit of a more independent and distinctive Canadian in-group on the North American continent, primarily through the introduction by the federal government of specific cultural, trade and investment policies that are designed to limit US out-group influences."[60]

Although the sentiment is understandable, that English-Canadian nationalism should be equated with fear of Americanization may have cost the cause of Canadian integration in at least two ways. First, considering the possibility that the dominant political tradition among English Canadians is in fact liberal (if with conservative nuances), since the United States is the quintessentially liberal nation, liberalism cannot function as Canada's integrative ideology — it is guilty by association.[61] More than this, the very idea of a Canadian equivalent to Americanization — that is to say of an assimilative and consolidating ideology constructed on any basis whatsoever — is diminished by the most vigilant defenders of Canada's national integrity precisely for reason of being American.[62] In the view of critics such as Andrew Stark, the result is a Canadian nationalism that is "diffident, hesitant, and reticent,"[63] a nationalism which advances the "peculiar conception of the 'identity-less citizen',"[64] in brief, a nationalism inauspicious for the cause of Canadian integration.

III

Against this background, committed multiculturalists propose to reconfigure Canada's national character. Under the rubric of integration without assimilation, multiculturalism seeks to make a virtue of the very diversity that otherwise frustrates the search for a unifying Canadian national identity. Cultural pluralism is no longer feared for its political consequences, rather it is acclaimed — perhaps indulged — as the substance of a flexible Canadianism.

Foreshadowing the logic of integration without assimilation, a generation ago W.L. Morton observed that "there is no process in becoming Canadian akin to conversion, there is no pressure for uniformity, there is no Canadian way of life."[65] On Morton's reading, "the society of allegiance [Canada] admits of a diversity the society of compact [the United States] does not, and one of the blessings of Canadian life is that there is no Canadian way of life, much less two, but a unity under the crown admitting of a thousand diversities."[66]

Following Morton, contemporary multiculturalists judge the lack of a precise national sense as no bad thing. Single, integrative national identities are rejected as too confining and static, inappropriate to post-modern political realities.[67] What is required, instead, is constitutional provision for deep cultural diversity, official recognition that citizens can and do maintain multiple political commitments within the boundaries of a single state. Cultural communities merit a measure of autonomy on this perspective, even at the risk of asymmetry in the distribution of political power. In fact, advocates of multiculturalism sometimes argue that it may actually be easier to integrate ethnic minorities into a Canadian political community that is not already well formed, that such individuals may more readily commit to a polity if they believe they can make some contribution to its character.[68]

Hence the integrative vision of the architects of Canadian multiculturalism: an ethnically responsive and equitable procedure of political decision-making, the public approval of which is transferred to those institutions within which the procedure takes place. Through the establishment of bureaucratic agencies and public funds earmarked for the purpose, federal and provincial governments have expended considerable effort to promote the idea that ethnic minorities are of equal dignity and merit equal treatment. And by removing discriminatory barriers to, as well as expanding opportunities for, the social, economic and political inclusion of ethnic minorities in Canadian life — most prominently via employment equity programs that sanction preferential treatment for disadvantaged visible minorities — multiculturalism seeks to create the necessary conditions for national integration. At the limit, multiculturalism itself becomes an integrative ideology —*the* Canadian ideology:

> Multiculturalism is not only commensurate with Canadian social norms. More to the point, multiculturalism is the quintessential Canadian value. It constitutes a distinctive feature of our celebration (however understated) as a people, and distinguishes us from the melting pot of the United States. As the cornerstone of Canada's nation-building process, multiculturalism shapes our identity, unites us in a distinct society with a national vision, and invigorates us as a people with a destiny.[69]

If multiculturalism is destined to become the integrative strategy of choice among states increasingly confronted by global population flows and the ethnically diverse citizenries they create, it is an approach to national consolidation that would seem especially well-suited to the Canadian experience. And that is because multiculturalism addresses each of the major sociopolitical obstacles to Canadian nation-building. In Canada outside Quebec, given the diminishing strength of the imperial connection, increasing numbers of immigrants of non-British heritage, and the demise of Anglo-conformity as an integrative model, multiculturalism proffers a new national identity: immigrant and native-born Canadians are to be united by the values of multiculturalism — committed, at a minimum, to cultural pluralism and equal opportunity for ethnic, especially visible, minorities. By legitimating the devolution of disproportionate amounts of political power to distinct cultural constituencies, in theory multiculturalism can accommodate Quebec's claim to be a province *"pas comme les autres"* (as well as the territorial imperatives of Aboriginal groups), although not exclusively so. And since America can be offered as a foil — the mosaic presuming to distinguish Canada, said to revel in its cultural tolerance and ethnic diversity, from the United States, which allegedly under the assimilationist logic of the melting pot does not — multiculturalism aspires to a triply useful statement of the Canadian political character.

Yet as a vehicle of national integration, multiculturalism is compromised, both theoretically and empirically. On the former account, there is a wooliness about the way that the concept is deployed. The RCBB's observations, though antedating by two years the introduction of official multiculturalism, suggest the ambiguity of integration without assimilation. In the Commission's view, integration was largely a matter of removing barriers to the full economic and social participation of immigrants within Canada's two founding linguistic and cultural communities. Unity within diversity was thereby to be accomplished. Newcomers were expected to acculturate — that is to adapt their behavior to the lifestyle of the community of which they had become a part — but not to assimilate, which according to the RCBB suggested a more thoroughgoing cultural transformation. And yet if integration without assimilation merely indicates the functional adaptation of ethnic minorities to an open economic marketplace — that they must learn the dominant language, social conventions and commercial culture simply in order to feed their families, albeit without being required to give up the majority of their ethnic heritage — then as a matter of necessity everyone will be integrated to greater or lesser degree and integration as a political concept will have little meaning.[70]

At the most basic and uncontentious level, multiculturalism may describe the fact of an ethnically diverse Canadian society. Or more normatively, and as the RCBB presaged, multiculturalism may point to a public policy that tolerates, even encourages, expressions of cultural diversity and prohibits discrimination against ethnic minorities. In this respect, it is important to distinguish between Canada's official understanding of multiculturalism, which is limited in scope — the "thin" position on multiculturalism, one might call it — and the more expansive connotations that multiculturalism may carry in public and scholarly discourse. When official multiculturalism was inaugurated in 1971, it had four stated objectives: the removal of cultural (and by the 1980s, racial) barriers to full participation in Canadian society; cultural exchange and appreciation; official-language training for immigrants; and state funding for cultural maintenance activities (e.g., support for ethnic minority associations, for ethnic expression in the visual and performing arts, ethnic heritage festivals, and to a much smaller extent, for training in "heritage languages"— those other than English or French). If this is the sum total of multiculturalism, then among Canadians its provisions are widely endorsed.[71] Only in the instance of employment equity and, to a lesser degree, cultural maintenance programs have such propositions been at all contentious. But if multiculturalism is simply a matter of "the right of individuals to be different yet the same, from within a context of commonly shared core values,"[72] it begs the question of what these commonly shared core values are, that is to say the essence of Canadian identity and the grounds on which national integration might be achieved. At best, such norms might supplement a consolidating sense of nationhood, but they cannot replace it.

That multiculturalism often aspires to more than this is suggested by the heightened profile that the concept seems to have in Canada, in particular the way in which multiculturalism has become for its proponents "a key element in symbolic expressions of national identity."[73] One of Canada's foremost students of ethnicity, Robert Harney, delineates this "thick" version of multiculturalism as "an innovative and altruistic civic philosophy of democratic pluralism to replace loyalty to the British empire as a legitimizing principle for the Canadian state."[74] Indeed, the most aggressive formulations of multiculturalism make cultural identity the *sine qua non* of political involvement and representation. On this approach, in an ethnically pluralist state integration is achieved by organizing the political process so as to validate and empower group differences.[75] Ironically, perhaps, national cohesion becomes a function of maximizing the social and institutional autonomy of ethnic groups.

Thick multiculturalism's appraisal of the principle of nationality and assimilation is double-sided and mutually reinforcing. Given that this form of multiculturalism maintains that a primary purpose of politics is to affirm group differences, not to elide them, national identities are considered artificial and culturally exclusivist, and the process of assimilation whereby those identities are taught is discredited. Conversely, because assimilation is rejected as a means whereby the most powerful social contingents within a state seek to absorb or at least to marginalize cultural minorities so, too, the national identities which are inculcated via assimilation. In the interest of legitimizing and promoting social diversity, the most ardent advocates of the "politics of identity" condemn assimilation as a strategy of group oppression.

The argument fails to persuade on at least three counts. First, the group identities that multiculturalism champions are not any more genuine than national identities.[76] The social and political construction of ethnic and racial identity is a fundamental of modern sociological thought. It is disingenuous to suggest that in the political arena ethnic interests should be prior to and transcendent of national ones because assimilation to a national identity is coercive in a way that the assumption of an ethnic identity is not. Ethnic and racial identities equally may be the result of compulsion, both from without — e.g., via government imposition of ethnic and racial caste distinctions — and from within — most vividly, perhaps, in the way that certain religiously based cultural communities shun members who wish to leave, but more broadly in the stigma which may be imposed by minority groups on co-ethnics who refuse to embrace fully their cultural heritage, especially in a climate of enhanced ethnic consciousness.

Second, from a political perspective, the multicultural critique misreads what assimilation requires. In fact, Robert E. Park, who helped introduce assimilation into the social science lexicon, maintained that it was more properly a political than a cultural concept. In Park's opinion, assimilation did not insist that ethnic minorities sacrifice their cultural traditions in order to be accepted as fully members of the national political community, but rather that they demonstrate a commitment to "those ideas, practices and aspirations which are national . . . the generally accepted social customs and political ideas and loyalties of a community or country."[77] In terms of the distinction drawn earlier in this essay, Park appeals to an ideological as opposed to a cultural understanding of national identity and assimilation. To reiterate, ethnicity and membership in a national community are not necessarily one and the same. If constructed primarily on ideological and not cultural grounds, a national identity will leave considerable room for the expression of ethnic differences. Thus, the principle of nationhood does not invariably demand that ethnic groups betray their cultural legacy, only that they subscribe to the norms and values of a common public culture communicated through the process of assimilation. The American case, often the object of multiculturalist disapprobation, including those Canadians who contrast an ethos of integration without assimilation to an alleged American melting pot, is instructive. Under the canopy of an integrative and assimilative public creed, in the United States cultural pluralism yet flourishes in the private domain — the Amish and Hasidim are regarded as no less American for all their cultural idiosyncracies.

Third, thick multiculturalism risks reducing the polity to little more than a dispassionate forum for cultural interaction and economic exchange. As the idea of a strong and consolidating sense of nationhood is depreciated so, too, is a substantive community interest informed by the public values that comprise that national identity and which might be shared over and above discrete group interests. The diverse cultural contingents that comprise the polity may come together to discuss the issues of the day and to decide on matters of public policy — indeed they will require a settled constitutional framework to do so — but they will always do so with an eye to maintaining their individual autonomy and integrity.

In this respect, multiculturalism is politically naive. Assuming that minority groups will participate in the democratic political process so as to remedy their collective grievances by making claims on public resources, they will need to forge political coalitions.[78] Otherwise, there is no assurance that their demands will be met. In fact, in the measure that democracy relies on the vote counting device of majority rule as a procedural expedient, such groups may find themselves consistently outvoted on issues about which they most deeply care. Democratic participation may actually deepen the frustrations and mutual suspicions of opposed and self-contained minorities. To what shared values will such groups appeal so that they may attract sympathetic allies and forward their political aims? The ideals expressed in a common national identity may be one answer, but it is an answer not open to the most committed of multiculturalists.

Perhaps more important than multiculturalism's theoretical brittleness, however, is that as a cornerstone of Canadian identity and a basis for national cohesion it has modest support among the Canadian public.[79] The contemporary debate over integration without assimilation suggests that historic questions concerning the nature of Canadian identity — questions which multiculturalism seeks to address — are far from resolved.

Consider the desire for a Canadian identity separate from that of the American republic. In the judgement of many social scientists, multiculturalism does not distinguish Canada from the United States.[80] The nuances of multicultural policy in the two countries may be different — in the US multiculturalism is most strongly rooted in the race issue whereas in Canada it initially played off of the French/English divide — but its substance is effectively the same. Descriptively, the United States is as ethnically pluralist a society as Canada. Institutional indicators of the robustness of ethnicity in the US are plentiful: the diversity of the countries of origin from which sizable numbers of immigrants continue to arrive, the residential concentration of ethnic groups, ethnic clustering in certain occupations, political mobilization on an ethnic basis, the vitality of the foreign-language media, the variety and number of ethnic festivals, and so on.

But lack of official status in the United States notwithstanding, multiculturalism has a prescriptive hold on Americans as well. Precisely because ethnicity counts in the United States, myriad public and private agencies, including the Bureau of the Census, routinely classify Americans according to an "ethno-racial pentagon"— Euro-American, Asian-American, African-American, Native-American, and Hispanic.[81] Affirmative action is the way in which such distinctions have mattered dramatically for public policy, but funding for bilingual education, accommodating linguistic minorities in the publication and dissemination of election materials, and legislative redistricting in the interest of empowering ethnic and racial minorities are additional examples. Relatedly, American courts have been forced to accommodate the issues that a multicultural society raises — of preferential hiring strategies, of public funding for parochial schools, of culture used as a legal defense. Educational institutions, too, have conceded the special claims of race and ethnicity, whether through admissions offices concerned to recruit a representative student body or a curriculum that aims at sensitizing Americans to the dynamics of a multicultural society. No wonder that according to certain comparative surveys, Americans are even more likely to support the retention of ethnic cultures than are Canadians.[82] And if in the US, as in Canada, there is presently a backlash against special public benefits accruing to ethnic minorities, it is a function of the imagined seriousness of the multicultural threat. Indeed, in relating the liabilities of multiculturalism, American apologists for assimilation often cite Canada as an example to avoid.[83] If Canadian and American identities are to be distinguished, multiculturalism will not suffice.

Neither does multiculturalism resolve the different national conceptions of Anglophone and Francophone Canadians. Predictably, in Quebec multiculturalism is disparaged as an attempt to undermine the province's status as a distinct society by making French Canadians appear as merely one of any number of equal contributors to a Canadian ethnic mosaic.[84] In the opinion of many Quebecois, multiculturalism's origins are in the Trudeau government's explicit rejection of Canada as a culturally dualist state, a partnership of Anglophones and Francophones dear to the hearts of Quebecois of various political stripe. To illustrate, the Quebec public is far more likely to endorse a dualist reading of confederation than are other Canadian citizens; a 1995 *Maclean's*/CBC poll reported that 45% of Quebec respondents viewed Canada as a pact between two founding groups, French and English, as opposed to 22% of Canadians living elsewhere.[85] Moreover, to the degree that multiculturalism undermines official bilingualism in Canada by negating any necessary relationship between linguistic and cultural privilege, it may further alienate Francophones. It is not surprising, then, that "les différents gouvernements du Québec n'ont jamais accepté la notion fédérale d'une 'mosaique' multiculturelle . . . (Conseil des communautés culturelles et de l'immigration du Québec, 8 February 1988)."[86]

Immigrants, too, can be decidedly wary of multiculturalism. An irony of Canadian multiculturalism is that it is often discredited by the very immigrant constituencies it is designed to embrace. Many newcomers fear that on the official account they will be ghettoized as "everlasting immigrants," understood as members of the discrete groups constituting the Canadian polity, not respected as individuals who might be coalesced into some greater political totality. Most famously, Neil Bissoondath, he of East Indian origin by way of Trinidad, in his Canadian best-seller, *Selling Illusions: The Cult of Multiculturalism in Canada* (1994), makes the case that multiculturalism fails immigrants and the native-born alike. "In eradicating the centre," writes Bissoondath, "in evoking uncertainty as to what and who is a Canadian, (multiculturalism) has diminished all sense of Canadian values, of what is a Canadian."[87] A case study of Lao immigrants in Canada reveals much the same disenchantment.[88] In qualitative interviews, Lao respondents indicate that whereas they appreciate multiculturalism's intent to combat discrimination against visible minorities, they doubt the wisdom of retaining a separate cultural identity at the risk of social isolation and political disunity. As one interviewee relates, "(Cultural groups) all have their different beliefs and different opinions and there are too many to try and become one. It would be better if the people who all came here would just become Canadians — they would become one united country and there would not be too many groups separate from each other."[89] What newcomers may most desire from the Canadian host society is a clear statement of an integrative national identity, one establishing the criteria of social and political acceptance for discrete immigrant communities, something to which they can be assimilated. If immigrants to Canada do achieve integration without assimilation, their national loyalties may be forged more by the dynamics of migration itself, animated by the imagined deficiencies of the homeland and the promise of a new life in Canada, than by multiculturalism per se."[90]

IV

Canadians often seem to desire a more secure and precise national identity than multiculturalism allows, a set of definitive public commitments which for newcomers to Canada might afford integration *with* assimilation.[91] For example, Canadians regularly indicate concern for the disruptive potential of immigrant beliefs and attitudes. In a 1994 Decima survey, 43 percent of the individuals polled indicated that relations between immigrant and nonimmigrant communities had worsened; the primary cause of this deterioration — the choice of 25 percent of the respondents — was attributed to the different values of immigrant and non-immigrant groups.[92] A recent policy statement of the Department of Citizenship and Immigration Canada, recommending a revised Citizenship Act as a means of promoting common Canadian values, builds on a similar reading of public opinion: "Newcomers need to participate in the larger community and to respect the core values and principles upon which Canadian society and its institutions are based. . . . If newcomers are to integrate successfully into Canadian society, they need a better sense of what it means to be Canadian. They need to understand the values and principles that this society is based on."[93] Yet when it comes to specifying these national norms, Canadians often seem at a loss. In a further 1994 Decima poll, when asked what "most ties us together as a nation," the leading response was "our system of government"— the choice of only 7 percent of the sample. When prompted with specific answers to the same question, the top two replies, with 75 percent and 70 percent of the poll in Canada outside Quebec respectively, were health care and hockey.[94]

Here one confronts the conceptual conundrum of the debate over multiculturalism: if not multiculturalism, then in what does Canadian identity consist? Are there alternative grounds of nationhood on which Canada can hope to be an integrated polity? In response, several students of Canadian politics have explored the unifying potential of an active Canadian citizenship — a non-national, political identity, largely independent of fixed ideological or cultural content. Such individuals draw on a consistent strain of thought about Canadian nationality, one stretching back at least to Confederation and the desire of the Canada East/Quebec Conservative leader, Sir George-Étienne Cartier, that Canada develop a political as opposed to a cultural standard of nationhood. From this perspective, given the reality of a culturally and, one might add, an ideologically pluralist society, Canada must find its character primarily in its structures of government, its source of national unity in allegiance to and involvement in consolidating political institutions.[95]

According to some of its advocates, this civic brand of nationalism turns on what the sociologist Edward Shils has called "allocative integration,"[96] gratitude for the social benefits and economic well-being that the Canadian government provides.[97] But participatory citizenship is recommended for its emotional affect as well, promising a sense of national inclusion to those who exercise its rights and responsibilities.[98] The glue of the pluralist polity, this analysis holds, is a function of the citizenry's willingness to participate in an ongoing national "conversation" concerning the central issues of political life. That conversation will be constrained by a modicum of shared values, particularly with respect to the procedural norms of political engagement, but in terms of substantive policy ends, any national consensus achieved will be moving and provisional. Ultimately it is to the conversation itself and to the national forum in which it occurs that citizens will express their allegiance.[99] If an integrative and assimilative Canadian identity is at all to be found, on this view it will be found in process, a function of citizen involvement in shaping the future direction of the polity, its common mores and values.[100]

It is not the intention of the present paper to evaluate systematically the integrative potential of this civic variety of nationalism. There may be reason for optimism. In the sequence of nation-building, statehood has often preceded and informed the construction of nationhood.[101] Clearly, there is a connection between the public policies emerging out of the process of deliberative democracy and national identity itself. Such policies help to express the values constitutive of nationhood by indicating the priorities and commitments of the public culture. In that respect, one should not dismiss the inclination of many Canadians to cite public health care as a major component of Canadianism — a commitment, moreover, that does distinguish Canada from the United States. It is not inconceivable that a discrete national identity might emerge from the open political process which advocates of civic nationalism anticipate. In the Constitution Act (1982), and especially in its Charter of Rights and Freedoms, Canada has already taken a considerable step toward articulating the institutional framework and guiding principles of the civic conversation. Further, if the democratic process of which civic nationalists conceive requires "an open dialogue in which all points of view are represented,"[102] then to the degree that Canada is constitutionally committed to at least a thin theory of multiculturalism and to a politics of ethnic inclusion, the prospects for shaping an integrative identity are brighter.

Still, outstanding questions need to be addressed. A national identity that comes as a *quid pro quo* for perceived economic benefits appears less than secure, especially in light of global economic pressures that governments hold responsible for the need to reduce their social welfare commitments.[103] Likewise, one may doubt how emotionally satisfying a civic nationalism can be absent a clear statement of the ideals and purposes of the national community. To paraphrase Burke, to love our country, must not our country first be lovely? Moreover, given that a discrete legal definition of Canadian citizenship emerged relatively late in Canada's national history (and even then, the Citizenship Act of 1947 simultaneously preserved British subject status for Canadian citizens, a provision that was removed only in 1977), and that it entitles the bearer to few privileges that permanent residence does not — mainly the right to vote and run for office in federal and some provincial elections, priority in hiring for certain jobs, and the right to leave and reenter the country on a Canadian passport — Canadian citizenship may not be sufficiently robust to claim an individual's political allegiance.[104] In Canada, the provisional nature of civic national identity may be especially problematic, since the constitutional framework that is to guide the search for that identity was not submitted to popular ratification in 1982 when Canada's original constitution — the British North America Act (1867) — was patriated and amended, and thus, arguably, lacks a popular mandate. One also may wonder whether proponents of civic nationalism exaggerate the inclination of ordinary Canadian citizens to participate in the political process and thereby set the bar of national identity too high.

And if the events surrounding Charlottetown are any indication, Canada's efforts at a "national conversation" may aggravate underlying political differences as much as resolve them.

Most significant of all, Quebec is not firmly part of Canada's constitutional family. In 1982, the Canada Act was passed over Quebec's strident objections and successive provincial governments have never agreed to the original terms of patriation. It is not too much to say that subsequent attempts to oblige Quebec and to gain greater democratic legitimacy for the Constitution, via the Meech Lake and Charlottetown Accords, have unraveled precisely because Canada is such a culturally and regionally diverse society.

In this, advocates of civic nationalism might do well to remember the prejudice of those classical political theorists — Aristotle, Machiavelli, Rousseau, among others — to whose republican conceptions of citizenship they are indebted: the communal spirit necessary to a polity is advantaged by cultural homogeneity. Civic nationalism may be hard pressed to bridge the identity divide between Quebec and the rest of Canada, a Quebec that most often affirms a decidedly cultural conception of nationhood, one which, for reasons already cited, is largely inappropriate to the rest of Canada.[105] As David Miller has cautioned, in culturally pluralist societies, a common sense of national allegiance may in fact be a prerequisite of an integrative citizenship, not its consequence.[106] Separatist movements are not readily subject to this discipline.

There is a hard but simple truth here: as long as Canada includes Quebec, pan-Canadian questions of identity and integration may be incapable of resolution. With one exception, in Canada outside Quebec, questions of political belonging appear resolved in favour of Canada. Survey evidence indicates that only in Newfoundland — perhaps a function of it being the last province to enter confederation (in 1949, and then by a slim margin in a popular referendum), geographic isolation, and the gravity of its economic difficulties — do provincial or regional identifications rival identification as Canadian.[107] By contrast, Quebec Francophones, who comprise over eighty percent of the province's population, are persistent outliers. If there is hope in civic nationalism, Canada may yet achieve national integration, but — dare one say it — as long as Quebec remains part of the confederation, the odds do not seem favourable.

V

As this essay has argued, largely because of the tension between its two founding European communities, Canada possesses neither the ethnic and cultural homogeneity nor the ideological consensus that typically serve as foci of integration in other democratic political systems. Absent a clear sense of Canadian national identity, political assimilation, in the sense of being socialized to the defining beliefs and values of a cohesive polity, is a difficult prospect. Consequently, as a means of incorporating ethnic minorities into a unified Canadian political community, multiculturalism and the ethos of integration without assimilation with which it is twinned are understandable alternatives to a strong consolidative notion of Canadian identity.

Yet in the measure that advocates of multiculturalism wish it to function as a substitute Canadian identity, it must be found wanting. Should national identities be important to political unity, giving citizens strong reasons to undertake collective efforts in the interest of the common good, even when those efforts will not always be individually rewarded, then multiculturalism can hardly constitute an adequate basis for identity and integration. Multiculturalism may be part of a reconfigured Canadian identity (thin multiculturalism), but it cannot be the major part of it (thick multiculturalism). Multiculturalism does not in fact provide a satisfying answer to outstanding issues surrounding Canadian identity — the attempt to distinguish Canada from the United States, the desire of immigrants to affirm a common

Canadianness, the need to address Quebec's claim to be a distinct society. Nor is multiculturalism able to articulate a distinctive core of beliefs that might hold the Canadian polity together, a common public culture that would unite Canadians of diverse cultural backgrounds in relationships of mutual support and obligation. In the interest of championing the politics of difference, multiculturalism actually denudes the public sphere that makes that common life possible. What Gertrude Stein once observed of Oakland seems equally apropos of multiculturalism as a mechanism for Canadian consolidation — in the final analysis, there is no there, there.

NOTES

1. *Report of the Royal Commission on Bilingualism and Biculturalism*, Volume 1V (Ottawa: The Queen's Printer, 1969), p. 5, p. 7.
2. Leslie A. Pal, *Interests of State: The Politics of Language, Multiculturalism, and Feminism in Canada* (Montreal: McGill-Queen's University Press, 1993), pp. 74–90.
3. Canada, Parliament, House of Commons, *Debate* (Hansard). October 8, 1971, p. 545.
4. Raymond Breton, "Multiculturalism and Canadian Nation-Building," in *The Politics of Gender, Ethnicity, and Language in Canada*, eds. Alan Cairns and Cynthia Williams (Toronto: University of Toronto Press, 1986), pp. 27–66; Kenneth McRoberts, *English Canada and Quebec: Avoiding the Issue* (North York: Robarts Centre for Canadian Studies, 1991), pp. 27–30.
5. Standing Committee on Multiculturalism, *Multiculturalism: Building the Canadian Mosaic* (Ottawa: The Queen's Printer, 1987), p. 47.
6. "I Don't Enjoy Neil Bissoondath," *The Globe and Mail* (Toronto) February 7, 1995: A21.
7. See Benedict Anderson, *Imagined Communities: Reflections on the Origins and Spread of Nationalism* (London: Verso, 1983), p. 129ff.; Liah Greenfeld, *Nationalism: Five Roads to Modernity* (Cambridge: Harvard University Press, 1992), pp. 78–20; David Miller, "In Defence of Nationality," *Journal of Applied Philosophy*, 10, no. 1 (1993), pp. 3–16.
8. Emile Durkheim, *The Division of Labor in Society* (1893; rpt. New York: The Free Press, 1984), pp. 60–61.
9. David V.J. Bell, *The Roots of Disunity: A Study of Canadian Political Culture*, 2nd ed. (Toronto: Oxford University Press, 1992).
10. Reginald W. Bibby, *Mosaic Madness: The Poverty and Potential of Life in Canada* (Toronto: Stoddart, 1990).
11. David Jay Bercuson and Barry Cooper, *Deconfederation: Canada Without Quebec* (Toronto: Key Porter Books, 1991).
12. Robert Chodos, Rae Murray, and Eric Hamovitch, *The Unmaking of Canada: The Hidden Theme in Canadian History since 1945* (Toronto: J. Lorimer, 1991).
13. G. Bruce Doern and Byrne B. Purchase, eds., *Canada at Risk: Canadian Public Policy in the 1990s* (Toronto: C.D. Howe Institute, 1991).
14. Jeremy Webber, *Reimagining Canada: Language, Community and the Canadian Constitution* (Montreal and Kingston: McGill-Queen's Press, 1994).
15 R. Kent Weaver, ed. *The Collapse of Canada?* (Washington: The Brookings Institute, 1992).
16. Anthony Birch, *Nationalism and National Integration* (London: Unwin Hyman, 1989), p. 178.
17. Carolyn Tuohy, *Policy and Politics in Canada: Institutionalized Ambivalence* (Philadelphia: Temple University Press, 1992), p. 5.
18. R. Kenneth Carty and W. Peter Ward, "The Making of a Canadian Political Citizenship," in *National Politics and Community in Canada*, eds. R. Kenneth Carty and W. Peter Ward (Vancouver: University of British Columbia Press, 1986), pp. 76–77.
19. Charles Taylor, "Alternative Futures: Legitimacy, Identity and Alienation in Late Twentieth Century Canada," in *Constitutionalism, Citizenship and Society in Canada*, eds. Alan Cairns and Cynthia Williams (Toronto: University of Toronto Press, 7985), p. 221.
20. "For Want of Glue: A Survey of Canada," *Economist*, June 29, 1991, p. 19.
21. Reg Whitaker, "Images of the State in Canada," in *The Canadian State: Political Economy and Political Power*, ed. Leo Panitch (Toronto: University of Toronto Press, 1977), p. 49; also see Bell.
22. James Tully, "The Crisis of Identification: The Case of Canada, "Political Studies, XLII (1994), pp. 75–76.

23. See, for instance, Sylvia Bashevkin, *True Patriot Love: The Politics of Canadian Nationalism* (Toronto: Oxford University Press, 1991), pp. 1–28.

24. See, for instance, Louis Hartz, *The Liberal Tradition in America* (New York: Harcourt, 1955); Samuel Huntington, *American Politics: The Promise of Disharmony* (Cambridge: Harvard University Press, 1981); Stephen Dworetz, *The Unvarnished Doctrine: Locke, Liberalism and the American Revolution* (Durham: Duke University Press, 1988); Thomas L. Pangle, *The Spirit of Modern Republicanism: The Moral Vision of the American Founders and the Philosophy of Locke* (Chicago: University of Chicago Press, 1988); Seymour Martin Lipset, *Continental Divide: The Values and Institutions of the United States and Canada* (London: Routledge, 1990).

25. Philip Gleason, "Americans All: World War II and the Shaping of American Identity," *The Review of Politics*, vol. 43, no. 4 (1981), pp. 483–518; also Michael Lind, *The Next American Nation: The New Nationalism and the Fourth American Revolution* (New York: The Free Press, 1995).

26. David Miller, *On Nationality* (Oxford: Oxford University Press, 1995), pp. 165–180.

27. John Stuart Mill, *Considerations on Representative Government* (1867; rpt. London: J.M. Dent and Sons, 1972), pp. 363–64.

28. Mill, p. 362.

29. Louis Hartz, *The Founding of New Societies* (New York: Harcourt, Brace, and World, 1964), esp. p. 14; Myron Weiner, "Political Integration and Political Development," *The Annals of the American Academy of Political and Social Science*, 358, (1965), 55–57; Nathan Glazer, "Individual Rights Against Group Rights," in *Ethnic Dilemmas: 1964–1982*, ed. Nathan Glazer (Cambridge: Harvard University Press, 1983), pp. 254–73; Anthony D. Smith, *The Ethnic Origins of Nations* (Oxford: Blackwell, 1986), p. 151 ff.

30. Michael Walzer, "Pluralism in Political Perspective," in *Dimensions of Ethnicity*, ed. Stephen Thernstrom (Cambridge: Belknap Press, 1982), pp. 1–28.

31. Hartz, The Liberal Tradition; Robert A. Dahl, *Who Governs?* (New Haven: Yale University Press, 1961), p. 318; Huntington, *American Politics*, pp. 230–31; Arthur M. Schlessinger Jr., *The Disuniting of America: Reflections on a Multicultural Society* (New York: W.W. Norton, 1992).

32. Raymond H.C. Teske and Bardin H. Nelson, "Acculturation and Assimilation: A Clarification," *American Ethnologist*, vol. 1 (1974), pp. 351–67.

33. Kenneth McRoberts, *Misconceiving Canada: The Struggle far National Unity* (Toronto: Oxford University Press, 1997), pp. 184–88.

34. McRoberts, *Misconceiving Canada*, chs. 1, 2, 10.

35. Douglas V. Verney, *Three Civilizations, Two Cultures, One State: Canada's Political Traditions* (Durham: Duke University Press, 1986), p. 226ff; also McRoberts, *Misconceiving*.

36. For example, Philip Resnick, *Letters to a Quebecois Friend* (Montreal: McGill-Queen's University Press, 1990).

37. Howard Palmer, "Mosaic versus Melting Pot?: Immigration and Ethnicity in Canada and the United States," *International Journal*, summer 1976, pp. 493–502.

38. House of Commons, *Debates*, June 7, 1928, 3925–7.

39. Freda Hawkins, *Critical Years in Immigration: Canada and Australia Compared*, 2nd ed. (Montreal and Kingston: McGill-Queen's University Press, 1991), pp. 328.

40. Quoted in Irving Abella and Harold Troper, *None Is Too Many: Canada and the Jews of Europe, 1933–1948* (Toronto: Lester, 1983), p. 199.

41. Abella and Troper, p. 239ff. As the authors point out, however, at least with respect to the admission of Jewish refugees, immediate post-war Canadian policy was grudging; in this case, the establishment of the state of Israel in 1944 removed some of the pressure for Canadian immigration authorities to be more generous.

42. Leo Driedger, *The Ethnic Factor: Identity in Diversity* (Toronto: McGraw-Hill Ryerson, 1989), p. 41.

43. The percentage of Canadians who state they belong to ethnic groups of other than Anglo-Irish or French descent are: 1881—11%; 1901—12.3%; 1921—16.4%: 1941—20%; 1961—25.8%; 1981—33.1%; 1991— 42% (Census of Canada, various dates).

44. See, for example, Charles Taylor, *Reconciling the Solitudes: Essays on Canadian Federalism and Nationalism* (Montreal: McGill-Queen's Press, 1993).

45. See, for instance, the discussion in Jerome A. Black and David Hagen, "Quebec Immigration Politics and Policy: Historical and Contemporary Perspectives," in *Quebec: State and Society*, ed. Alain-G. Gagnon (Scarborough: Nelson Canada, 1993), pp. 280–303. A 1990 policy statement of the Quebec ministère des Communautés culturelles et de l'Immigration proposed that by 1995 at least 40 percent of individuals arriving in Quebec should be French-speaking. In 1989, only 28.3 percent of immigrants admitted to Quebec either spoke or had knowledge of French; by 1992, 36 percent of newcomers could claim that distinction. Employment and Immigration Canada, *Immigration Statistics 1992* (Hull: Minister of Supply and Services Canada, 1992), p. 36.

46. Every year from 1973 through 1988, Lebanon, Haiti and/or Laos, Kampuchea and Vietnam were among the top five countries sending immigrants to Quebec. In the case of Indochinese immigrants, however, only a minority are actually proficient in French. Simon Langlois et al., *Recent Social Trends in Quebec, 1960–1990* (Montreal and Kingston: McGill-Queen's University Press, 1992), p. 544.

47. Allan Smith, "National Images and National Maintenance: The Ascendancy of the Ethnic Idea in North America," *Canadian Journal of Political Science*, vol. 14, no. 2 (1981), pp. 227–57.

48. Taylor, *Reconciling*, pp. 172–79, There is, on the other hand, a good deal of survey evidence suggesting that the matter of language rights aside, residents of Quebec are among the most individualistic citizens in Canada. See, for example, Webber, p. 50.

49. See the discussion in F.L. Morton, "The Charter and Canada Outside Quebec," in *Beyond Quebec: Taking Stock of Canada*, ed. Kenneth McRoberts (Montreal and Kingston: McGill-Queen's University Press, 1995), pp. 93–114; also see Peter H. Russell, *Constitutional Odyssey: Can Canadians Become a Sovereign People?* (Toronto: University of Toronto Press, 1992).

50. Angus Reid Group, Multiculturalism *and Canadians: Attitude Study 1991 — National Survey Report* (Ottawa: Multiculturalism and Citizenship Canada, 1991), p. 13.

51. See, for instance, S.F. Wise, *God's Peculiar Peoples: Essays on Political Culture in Nineteenth Century Canada* (Ottawa: Carleton University Press, 1993), ch. 9; Lipset, esp. ch. 1; Kenneth McRae, "The Structure of Canadian History," in Hartz, *The Founding of New Societies*, pp. 234–44; Gad Horowitz, "Conservativism, Liberalism, and Socialism in Canada: An Interpretation," *Canadian Journal of Economics and Political Science*, XXXII, no. 2 (1966), pp. 141–71; Philip Resnick, *The Masks of Proteus: Canadian Reflections on the State* (Montreal and Kingston: McGill-Queen's Press, 1990), ch. Z.

52. Bell, pp. 38–40.

53. Sec W.L. Morton, *The Canadian Identity,* 2nd ed. (Toronto: University of Toronto Press, 1972), pp. 85, 100, 104; also see McRae; Verney; Lipset; Bell.

54. See McRae; Verney; Bell.

55. Bell, p. 67.

56. See Carl Berger, *The Sense of Power: Studies in the Ideas of Canadian Imperialism, 1867–1914* (Toronto: University of Toronto Press, 1970).

57. W.T. Easterbrook and Hugh G.J. Aitken, *Canadian Economic History* (Toronto: Macmillan, 1956), pp. 401–02, pp. 572–74.

58. See, for instance, Resnick, *The Masks of Proteus*, ch. 8.

59. Reg Whitaker, *A Sovereign Idea: Essays on Canada as a Democratic Community* (Montreal and Kingston: McGill-Queen's Press, 1992), p. 288.

60. Bashevkin, pp. viii–ix.

61. Bell, p. 86.

62. See, for example, Ramsay Cook, *The Maple Leaf Forever: Essays on Nationalism and Politics in Canada* (1971; rpt. Toronto: Macmillan of Canada, 1977), p. 187; H.G. Thorburn, "Canadian Pluralist Democracy in Crisis," *Canadian Journal of Political Science*, vol. X1, no. 4 (1978), p. 734; also W.L. Morton.

63. Andrew Stark, "English-Canadian Opposition to Quebec Nationalism," in *The Collapse of Canada?*, ed. R. Kent Weaver (Washington D.C.: The Brookings Institution, 1992), p. 134.

64. Stark, p. 136.

65. W.L. Morton, p. 85.

66. W.L. Morton, p. 111.

67. See, for example, Crawford Young, "The Dialectics of Cultural Pluralism: Concept and Reality," in *The Rising Tide of Cultural Pluralism: The Nation-State at Bay?*, ed. Crawford Young (Madison: University of Wisconsin Press, 1993), pp. 3–35; Iris Marion Young, "Together in Difference: Transforming the Logic of Group Political Conflict," in *The Rights of Minority Cultures*, ed. Will Kymlicka (Oxford: Oxford University Press, 1995), pp. 155–76; Janet Mclellan and Anthony H. Richmond, "Multiculturalism in Crisis: A Postmodern Perspective on Canada," *Ethnic and Racial Studies*, vol. 17, no. 4 (1994), pp. 662–83; Ian Angus, *A Border Within: National Identity, Cultural Plurality, and Wilderness* (Montreal and Kingston: McGill-Queen's University Press); Webber.

68. William Kaplan, "Who Belongs?: Changing Concepts of Citizenship and Nationality," in *Belonging: The Meaning and Future of Canadian Citizenship*, ed. William Kaplan (Montreal and Kingston: McGill-Queen's University Press, 1993), pp. 255–56.

69. Augie Fleras and Jean Leonard Elliot, *Multiculturalism in Canada: The Challenge of Diversity* (Scarborough: NelsonCanada, 1992), p. 125. Also see the analysis in Kogila Moodley, "Canadian Multiculturalism as Ideology," *Ethnic and Racial Studies*, vol. 16, no. 3 (1983), pp. 320–331.

70. For this insight the author is indebted to Byron Shafer.

71. Rudolf Kalin and J.W. Berry, "Ethnic and Multicultural Attitudes," in *Ethnicity and Culture in Canada: The Research Landscape*, eds. J.W. Berry and J.A. Laponce (Toronto: University of Toronto Press, 1994), pp. 293–321; Fleras and Elliot, ch. 5; Richard Gwyn, *Nationalism Without Walls: The Unbearable Lightness of Being Canadian* (Toronto: McClelland and Stewart, 1996), Ch. 11.

72. Fleras and Elliot, p. 141.

73. Yasmeen Abu-Laban, "The Politics of Race and Ethnicity: Multiculturalism as a Contested Arena," in *Canadian Politics*, 2nd ed., eds. James P. Bickerton and Alain-G. Gagnon (Peterborough: Broadview Press, 1994), p. 246.

74. Quoted in Gilles Paquet, "The Political Philosophy of Multiculturalism." in *Ethnicity and Culture in Canada: The Research Landscape*, eds. J.W. Berry and J.A. Laponce (Toronto: University of Toronto Press, 1994), p. 67.

75. See, for example, I. Young.

76. Miller, *On Nationality*, pp. 133–35.

77. Quoted in Philip Gleason, *Speaking of Diversity: Language and Ethnicity in Twentieth Century America* (Baltimore: Johns Hopkins University Press, 1992), p. 55.

78. See, for instance, the discussion in Miller, *On Nationality*, pp. 139–40.

79. See, for instance, the study for Canadian Heritage as reported in the *Globe and Mail* (Toronto), "Ottawa fails to sell multiculturalism," 18 October 1996, A8.

80. For instance Palmer; John Porter, "Melting Pot or Mosaic: Revolution or Reversion?," in *Perspectives on Evolution and Revolution*, ed. Richard A. Preston (Durham: Duke University Press, 1979), pp. 152–79; Howard Brotz, "Multiculturalism in Canada: A Muddle," *Canadian Public* Policy, vol. 6, no. l, pp. 41–46; Garth Stevenson, "Multiculturalism: As Canadian as Apple Pie," *Inroads*, vol. 1, no. 4 (1995), pp. 72–87.

81. See, for example, David A. Hollinger, *Postethnic America* (New York: Basic Books, 1995), ch. 2.

82. Jeffrey G. Reitz and Raymond Breton, *The Illusion of Difference: Realities of Ethnicity in Canada and the United States* (Toronto: C.D. Howe Institute, 1994), ch. 2.

83. Schlessinger, p. 13; Nathan Glazer, "Reflections on Citizenship and Diversity," in *Diversity and Citizenship: Reconsidering American Nationhood*, eds. Gary Jeffrey Jacobsohn and Susan Dunn (Lanham: Rowman and Littlefield, 1996), pp. 86–87; Peter D. Salins, *Assimilation American Style* (New York: Basic Books, 1997), p. 11.

84. McRoberts, *English Canada*, pp. 27–30.

85. "Taking the Pulse," *Maclean's*, January 1, 1996, pp. 32–33.

86. Quoted in Elliot L. Tepper, *Changing Canada: The Institutional Response to Polyethnicity* (Ottawa: Carelton University Mimeo, 1988), p. 46.

87. Neil Bissoondath, *The Cult of Multiculturalism in Canada* (Toronto: Penguin, 1994), p. 71.

88. John C. Harles, "Integration Before Assimilation: Immigration, Multiculturalism and the Canadian Polity," *Canadian Journal of Political Science*, XXX: 4 (1997), pp. 711–36.

89. Harles, p. 26.

90. Herbert Guindon, *Quebec Society: Tradition, Modernity, and Nationhood* (Toronto: University of Toronto Press, 1988), p. 139; Hawkins, p. 217; Harles.

91. See, for instance, Stevenson; also Philip Resnick, *Thinking English Canada* (Toronto: Stoddart, 1994).

92. "The Poll," *Maclean's*, January 2, 1995, pp. 30–31.

93. Citizenship and Immigration Canada, *Into the 21st Century: A Strategy for Immigration and Citizenship* (Ottawa: Minister of Supply and Services Canada, 1994), pp. 16–17.

94. "In Search of Unity," *Maclean's*, July 1, 1994, p. 17.

95. See, for example, W.L. Morton; Cook.

96. Edward Shils, *Center and Periphery: Essays in Macrosociology* (Chicago: University of Chicago Press, 1975), p. 66.

97. See, for example, Keith Banting, *The Welfare State and Canadian Federalism* (Montreal and Kingston: McGill-Queen's University Press, 1982), p. 119; Raymond Breton, "From Ethnic to Civic Nationalism: English Canada and Quebec," *Ethnic and Racial Studies*, vol. 11, no. l (1978), pp. 85–100; Bibby, p. 158ff.

98. F.L. Morton, pp. 93–114; Bissoondath, pp. 215–224.

99. Tully; Paquet; Webber, p. 188ff.

100. Thomas J. Courchene, "Staatsnation v. Kulturnation: The Future of the ROC," in *Beyond Quebec: Taking Stock of Canada*, ed. Kenneth McRoberts (Montreal and Kingston: McGill-Queen's Press, 1995), pp. 388–99.

101. See the discussion in Anthony Smith, *The Ethnic Origins of Nations*.

102. Miller, *On Nationality*, p. 150.

103. See, for example, Jane Jenson's discussion of the disintegrative effects of neoliberal political economy on Canadian national solidarity, "Fated to Live in Interesting Times: Canada's Changing Citizenship Regimes," *Canadian Journal of Political Science*, XXX: 4 (1997), pp. 627–44.

104. See the discussion in Kaplan.
105. Pursuing this distinction, Marcel Masse (1994), former Minister of Communications in the Mulroney Government and himself from Quebec, contends that because Canadians in the rest of Canada lack a strong sense of cultural identity — indeed, in Masse's experience English-Canada depreciates the political value of culture — they tend to understand what unites them in narrow public policy terms. According to Masse, "(Canada) must be the first example in history of '*J'ai un système de sécurité sociale, donc je suis* (I have a social security system, therefore I am)'." Marcel Masse, "A World Beyond Borders," *Canadian Forum*, vol. 73, no. 835 (1994), p. 12.
106. David Miller, "Citizenship and Pluralism," *Political Studies*, vol. 43, no. 3 (1995), pp. 432–50.
107. See, for instance, Ross Laver, "How We Differ," *Maclean's*, January 3, 1994, pp. 9–11; also Gibbins, pp. 188–93.

Topic Fourteen
Quebec/Canada

Prime Minister Pierre Trudeau reaches to shake hands with Quebec Premier René Lévesque. The two were at the meeting of First Ministers in Ottawa, November 2, 1981.

Since 1867, Quebec–Canada relations have been acrimonious, particularly on questions of language and culture. Although French-Canadian nationalists fought a number of battles in the late 19th and early 20th centuries to preserve the French language and separate schools in provinces outside Quebec with a sizeable French-Canadian population, they won few victories. The French language consistently lost ground, and separate schools came to have a lesser status to public schools in terms of provincial funding. Yet, despite these drawbacks, few French-speaking Quebeckers advocated the separation of Quebec from the rest of Canada prior to 1960.

From 1960 to 1966, Quebec underwent significant changes under the provincial Liberal government of Jean Lesage that were so far ranging that a journalist baptized the new era the "Quiet Revolution." Internally, the Quebec government enacted laws aimed at democratizing political life and increasing the role of the state. It took over jurisdiction of education and health, areas previously controlled by the Roman Catholic Church, and also took control in the economic and cultural spheres, with the nationalization of hydro-electricity, and the establishment of a Ministry of Cultural Affairs. In the area of education, Quebec governments since 1960 have enacted a number of language laws designed to strengthen the French language within Quebec by regulating whose children could attend English-language schools in the province.

Externally, the Quebec government worked with other provincial governments to overhaul the British North America Act so as to establish a new division of power between the federal and the provincial governments that would give more power to the provinces. As well, since 1960, successive Quebec provincial governments, even federalist administrations, have fought for greater autonomy from the federal government, and for "special status" among the other nine provinces that would in essence recognize Quebec as an autonomous political state within Canada.

The following two articles examine Quebec–Canada relations essentially since the Quiet Revolution, one in terms of internal changes in Quebec around the issue of language laws in the province, the other in respect to external changes with regards to constitutional issues. Both authors, however, begin by making reference to earlier Quebec–Canada relations going back at least to Confederation if not to the Conquest itself, as a reminder that Quebec–Canada relations since 1960 must be seen in the larger historical context. In "Politics and the Reinforcement of the French Language in Canada and Quebec, 1960–1986," historian Richard Jones examines the language debate in Quebec that led to a series of bills to promote the French language in Quebec. In "Québec–Canada's Constitutional Dossier," Alain-G. Gagnon uses a historical-institutional approach to federal–provincial relations. He divides his study into three periods: the historical foundations from 1760 to 1960; the period of transition from 1960 to 1982; and from 1982, the year of constitutional repatriation without the consent of Quebec, to the present time. He examines events from the Quebec perspective in an attempt to explain the context for Quebec referendums, the rise of "separatist" parties both within Quebec and within the Canadian Parliament, and current Quebec–Canada tension.

How do the Quebec language laws reflect and reinforce Quebec–Canada relations? Have constitutional changes since 1960 strengthened or undermined Canadian federalism? To what extent do Quebec's language laws and the province's constitutional stance reinforce each other, and reflect the ideology of the political parties in power in Quebec at the time they were enacted?

For an overview of Quebec in the last half-century, see Kenneth McRoberts, *Quebec: Social Change and Political Crisis*, 3rd ed. (Toronto: McClelland and Stewart, 1988), and for the current period, his *Misconceiving Canada: The Struggle for National Unity* (Toronto: Oxford University Press, 1997). In French, see Y. Belanger, R. Comeau, and C. Metivier, *La Revolution tranquille, 40 ans plus tard: Un bilan* (Montreal: VCB Éditeur, 2000). For the English-Canadian viewpoint, see J.L. Granatstein and K. McNaught, eds., *English Canada*

Speaks Out (Toronto: Doubleday, 1991). Other histories include Susan Mann, *The Dream of Nation: A Social and Intellectual History of Quebec* (Montreal/Kingston: McGill-Queen's University Press, 2002 [1983]), chs. 17–20, and Paul-André Linteau et al., *Quebec since 1930* (Toronto: James Lorimer, 1991). *Quebec since 1945: Selected Readings*, ed. M. Behiels (Toronto: Copp Clark Pitman, 1987) contains useful articles and documents, as does Hubert Guidon, Roberta Hamilton, and John McMullan, eds., *Tradition, Modernity, and Nationhood: Essays on Quebec Society* (Toronto: University of Toronto Press, 1988). On the important topic of Quebec nationalism, see Ramsay Cook, *Canada, Quebec and the Uses of Nationalism*, 2nd ed. (Toronto: McClelland and Stewart, 1995). Alain-G. Gagnon, ed., *Quebec, State and Society*, 3rd ed. (Peterborough, ON: Broadview Press, 2004), and Guy LaForest, *Trudeau and the End of a Canadian Dream*, trans. Paul Leduc Browne and Michelle Weinroth (Montreal/Kingston: McGill-Queen's University Press, 1995) contain valuable essays on Quebec and Canada. For one historian's view after interviewing a number of historians, politicians, and contemporary commentators, see Robert Bothwell, *Canada and Quebec: One Country, Two Histories* (Vancouver: University of British Columbia Press, 1995).

On the Duplessis era, see Conrad Black, *Duplessis* (Toronto: McClelland and Stewart, 1977), and Richard Jones's brief overview in *Duplessis and the Union Nationale Administration*, Canadian Historical Association, Historical Booklet no. 25 (Ottawa: CHA, 1983). The opposition to Premier Maurice Duplessis in the late 1940s and 1950s is analyzed in M. Behiels, *Prelude to Quebec's Quiet Revolution: Liberalism versus Neo-Nationalism, 1945–1960* (Montreal/Kingston: McGill-Queen's University Press, 1985).

For a good overview of the Quiet Revolution, see Jacques Rouillard, "The Quiet Revolution: A Turning Point in Quebec History," in *Readings in Canadian History: Post-Confederation*, 6th ed., eds. R. Douglas Francis and Donald B. Smith (Toronto: Nelson Thomson Learning, 2002), pp. 440–453. Also consult Dale C. Thomson, *Jean Lesage and the Quiet Revolution* (Toronto: Macmillan, 1984), and articles by Ramsay Cook in his collection *Canada, Quebec, and the Uses of Nationalism*, 2nd ed. (cited above). On the Parti Québécois, see Graham Fraser, *PQ: René Lévesque and the Parti Québécois in Power* (Toronto: Macmillan, 1985). Peter Desbarats's *René* (Toronto: McClelland and Stewart, 1976) reviews the life of the founder of the Parti Québécois. See also Lévesque's *Memoirs* (Toronto: McClelland and Stewart, 1986). On Pierre Elliott Trudeau, see Richard Gwyn, *The Northern Magus* (Toronto: McClelland and Stewart, 1980), and Stephen Clarkson and Christina McCall, *Trudeau and Our Times*, vol. 1, *The Magnificent Obsession* (Toronto: McClelland and Stewart, 1990), and vol. 2, *The Heroic Delusion* (Toronto: McClelland and Stewart, 1994). The October Crisis of 1970 is discussed in Francis Simard, *Talking It Out: The October Crisis from Inside*, trans. David Homel (Montreal: Guernica, 1987).

Edward McWhinney analyzes the early stages of the constitutional crisis in *Quebec and the Constitution, 1960–1978* (Toronto: University of Toronto Press, 1979), and in his *Canada and the Constitution, 1979–1982: Patriation and the Charter of Rights* (Toronto: University of Toronto Press, 1982). On the post–1982 period, see Alan Cairns, *Charter versus Federalism: The Dilemmas of Constitutional Reform* (Montreal/Kingston: McGill-Queen's University Press, 1992). The aftermath of the first Quebec referendum and the patriation of the BNA Act are discussed in *And No One Cheered: Federalism, Democracy and the Constitution Act*, eds. Keith Banting and Richard Simeon (Toronto: Methuen, 1983). Philosopher Charles Taylor proposes an original analysis of French–English relations in *Reconciling the Solitudes: Essays on Canadian Federalism and Nationalism*, ed. Guy LaForest (Montreal/Kingston: McGill-Queen's University Press, 1993).

Among the many publications bearing on Meech Lake are: Michael Behiels, ed., *The Meech Lake Primer: Conflicting Views of the 1987 Constitutional Accord* (Ottawa: University of Ottawa

Press, 1989); Andrew Cohen, *A Deal Undone: The Making and Breaking of the Meech Lake Accord* (Vancouver: Douglas and McIntyre, 1990); P. Fournier, *A Meech Lake Post-Mortem: Is Quebec Sovereignty Inevitable?* trans. S. Fischman (Montreal/Kingston: McGill-Queen's University Press, 1991); and R.L. Watts and D.M. Brown, *Options for a New Canada* (Toronto: University of Toronto Press, 1991). Susan Delcourt's *United We Fall: The Crisis of Democracy in Canada* (Toronto: Viking, 1993) looks at the aftermath of the referendum on the Charlottetown Accord in 1992. John F. Conway's *Debts to Pay: English Canada and Quebec from the Conquest to the Referendum*, 2nd ed. (Toronto: James Lorimer, 1996) includes a chapter on the second Quebec referendum of 1995. Dominique Clift has translated the memoirs of Lucien Bouchard as *Lucien Bouchard, On the Record* (Toronto: Stoddart, 1994).

Analyses of the language question include Eric Waddell, "State, Language and Society: The Vicissitudes of French in Quebec and Canada," in *The Politics of Gender, Ethnicity and Language in Canada*, eds. Alan Cairns and Cynthia Williams (Toronto: University of Toronto Press, 1986), pp. 67–110; Michel Plourde, *La politique linguistique du Québec, 1977–1987* (Québec: Éditions IQRC, 1988); Marc V. Levine, *The Reconquest of Montreal: Language Policy and Social Change in a Bilingual City* (Philadelphia: Temple University Press, 1990); and Richard Joy, *Canada's Official Languages* (Toronto: University of Toronto Press, 1992).

Two interpretative articles are Léon Dion, "The Mystery of Quebec," *Daedalus* 117, 4 (Fall 1988): 283–318, and Keith G. Banting, "If Quebec Separates: Restructuring North America," in *The Collapse of Canada?*, ed. R. Kent Weaver (Washington: Brookings Institution, 1992), pp. 159–78.

WEBLINKS

Bill 101
http://archives.cbc.ca/IDD-1-73-1297/politics_economy/bill101
A history of Bill 101 in Quebec as seen in CBC radio and television archives.

Official Languages Act
http://laws.justice.gc.ca/en/O-3.01/90080.html
Full text of the Official Languages Act as passed in 1985.

René Lévesque
http://archives.cbc.ca/IDD-1-74-870/people/rene_levesque
A multimedia biography of René Lévesque's political life.

Pierre Elliott Trudeau
http://www.collectionscanada.ca/primeministers/h4-3375-e.html
A biography of Pierre Elliott Trudeau and some of his selected speeches.

Aboriginal Peoples and the 1995 Quebec Referendum
http://www.parl.gc.ca/information/library/PRBpubs/bp412-e.htm
A paper prepared by the Parliamentary Research Branch of the Library of Parliament regarding Aboriginal peoples in Quebec and their importance regarding the 1995 Quebec referendum.

Clarity Act
http://laws.justice.gc.ca/en/C-31.8/33882.html
Complete text of the Clarity Act as passed by the Government of Canada in 2000.

Article Thirty-Four

Politics and the Reinforcement of the French Language in Canada and Quebec, 1960–1986

Richard Jones

It is commonplace to affirm that language has been a political issue in Canada ever since 1760, when the British completed their conquest of New France, and the colony's approximately 70 000 French-speaking inhabitants came under British domination. The new masters hoped that time would enable them to transform the French Canadians into good English-speaking members of the Church of England[1] or that British immigration would eventually swamp them. Although the English language rapidly assumed a privileged place in Quebec and in Canada, the French did not disappear; indeed they multiplied prolifically.[2] When Canada assumed Dominion status with a federal form of government in 1867, Quebec, the territory inhabited largely by francophones, became a separate province.[3]

Confederation did not open an era of linguistic harmony in Canada. Indeed, bitter language conflict burst forth frequently as French-speaking minorities outside Quebec saw their few linguistic rights, particularly in the area of education, curtailed or eradicated by English-speaking majorities.[4]

Until 1960, it could be said that the status of the French language in Canada was at best stagnating and that citizens who spoke French or were of French ethnic origin were clearly disadvantaged compared with those who spoke English or were of British ethnic origin.[5] This article seeks to show that, since 1960, the status of the French language in Canada, as well as the position of francophones in Canadian society, has, in many ways, improved markedly. Governments, at both the federal and provincial levels, have played a major role in this evolution; they intervened because of powerful political pressures applied by Canada's French-speaking population.[6] Yet many of the changes at the federal level and in the provinces with English-speaking majorities have been cosmetic or at least not very far-reaching. The really significant transformation has occurred in the province of Quebec.

THE FEDERAL GOVERNMENT AND THE ENGLISH-SPEAKING PROVINCES

The Royal Commission on Bilingualism and Biculturalism was established by the federal government in 1963 in response to demands for greater linguistic equality that were being formulated by French Canadians. According to its terms of reference, the Commission was expected to "recommend what steps should be taken to develop the Canadian Confederation on the basis of an equal partnership between the two founding races."[7] During the 1968 federal election campaign, linguistic equality was one of the themes developed by Liberal Prime Minister Pierre Elliott Trudeau. Trudeau was convinced that the federal government had to demonstrate to French Canadians that it was the government of all Canadians, not of English-speaking Canadians alone. Trudeau's concern was that the government of Quebec would succeed in portraying itself as the real representative of French Canadians; this situation could only

Source: *Quebec since 1945: Selected Readings,* ed. Michael Behiels (Toronto: Copp Clark Pitman, 1987), pp. 223–40. Reprinted by permission.

undermine national unity.[8] The following year, Parliament adopted the Official Languages Act, the objective of which was to increase the percentage of French-speaking civil servants, augment the use of French within the civil service, and make French-language services at the federal level available for most French-speaking Canadians.[9] Finally, in 1982, linguistic rights were enshrined in the Canadian Charter of Rights and Freedoms,[10] an integral part of the Canadian Constitution.

Fifteen years after its adoption, the Official Languages Act had, in the words of Language Commissioner d'Iberville Fortier, produced some remarkable achievements but fallen far short of creating the equality between the two official languages that, after all, was the stated objective of the legislation. In his opinion, Canada had reached a "kind of watershed between the solid accomplishments of the past and new challenges which will take us beyond mere statements of principle."[11]

Since the late 1960s, most of the nine Canadian provinces with English-speaking majorities, and particularly New Brunswick and Ontario, have taken measures to assist their French-language minorities. New Brunswick, approximately one-third of whose population is French-speaking, adopted its own largely symbolic Official Languages Act in 1969. Ontario, with nearly half a million citizens of French mother tongue,[12] has also extended French-language rights in areas such as education and the courts, though, probably to avoid a backlash, it has refused to become officially bilingual. Other provinces have also taken initiatives, although, in some important cases, they have acted only under judicial pressure.[13]

This flurry of linguistic activity in Canada has had no effect on the relatively rapid assimilation, into the English-speaking majority, of francophones living in the eight provinces that are massively anglophone. The Task Force on Canadian Unity, created in 1977 with a broad mandate to obtain and publicize the views of Canadians regarding the state of their country, waxed pessimistic in this regard. Attributing the phenomenon to, among other factors, relatively high rates of intermarriage of francophones with anglophones, the Commission concluded: "The rate of linguistic assimilation of French-speaking minorities is quite high, and appears to be accelerating in all English-speaking provinces other than New Brunswick."[14]

The 1981 census figures confirmed this sombre diagnosis, showing that 32.8 percent of Canadians of French mother tongue, living outside Quebec, had shifted to English as the main language of the home. The 1971 figure had been 29.6 percent. Thus, the French mother tongue group now represents only 5.3 percent of Canada's population outside Quebec, and the group for which French is the language spoken in the home constitutes an almost negligible 3.8 percent of the population.[15]

There can be no doubt that, without the presence of the province of Quebec, the situation of the French language in Canada would be bleak indeed.[16] Although the francophone minorities outside Quebec have long been agitating for better treatment, the pressures they could exert on their respective provincial governments as well as on the federal government have been relatively modest. In addition to lacking economic clout, the group has been simply too small, too widely dispersed geographically, and, until recently, too disorganized to wield much weight.

Quebec's presence, then, has been decisive for the French fact in Canada. Four out of five French-speaking Canadians live in that province, Canada's second largest in terms of population. Just as the rest of Canada has become relatively more English-speaking as the francophone minorities retreat, Quebec has, in recent years, become increasingly French-speaking. The 1981 census showed that 82.4 percent of Quebeckers were of French mother tongue and that virtually the same proportion generally spoke French in the home.[17] In other words, languages in Canada seem to be undergoing a territorialization whereby Quebec becomes more French while the rest of Canada registers consistent gains for the English language.[18] Ultimately, this phenomenon could strengthen division within Canada.

THE BEGINNINGS OF THE LANGUAGE DEBATE IN QUEBEC

Respecting the reinforcement of the French language in Canada since 1960, Quebec has been a theatre of dramatic activity, and state intervention has been constant and has had measurable impact. The undeniable result has been to strengthen the position of the French language in that province, though the extent of that improvement and particularly its durability remain subjects of rather acrimonious debate.

By the late 1960s, the major political parties in Quebec were all debating the language question and attempting to conceive policies that would not only satisfy their members but also ensure wide support at the polls. The context, as we shall see, favoured the most nationalistic of the three major parties, the Parti Québécois, ideologically committed to a French Quebec. Although after coming to power in 1976 it had to contend with realities that it could neither change nor ignore, it was able to accomplish its objectives in matters of language to a considerable degree.

A series of factors contributed to transforming the issue of language into an increasingly controversial subject in Quebec and finally to forcing the government to legislate. From 1944, the very conservative rural-based Union Nationale had been maintained in power under the firm and, according to his foes, dictatorial hand of Maurice Duplessis.[19] Duplessis died in 1959 and, the following year, the Liberals under Jean Lesage gained power, promising to modernize Quebec. The pace of change became so breathless that a journalist soon baptized the new era the "Quiet Revolution."[20]

The reforms of the Quiet Revolution aimed at modernizing the institutions, developing the economy, and furthering the welfare state. But they also had considerable nationalistic content since they were designed to improve the lot of francophones as well as the position of Quebec in Confederation. The nationalization of the private Anglo-Canadian and American hydroelectric power utilities,[21] Quebec's epic confrontations with the federal government over questions of money and power, and the province's ventures into the domain of international relations, notably with France, were at least partly based on nationalist considerations.

The educational system, revamped at least structurally by the reformers of the Quiet Revolution, began turning out more and more graduates seeking employment. Certainly the expansion of the provincial government during these years created many new jobs for francophones. In other fields, though, Anglo-dominated structures blocked opportunities. The federal civil service as yet offered few possibilities to francophones unwilling to do virtually all their work in English. In addition, private enterprise, particularly the upper echelons, remained an anglophone preserve that French Canadians had great difficulty penetrating. Social scientists have abundantly described the rise of this new francophone middle class.[22] For its members, tangible and intangible objectives of an individual character linked to self-interest, questions of jobs, money, and social status, were not the only motivations. Aspirations of a collective nature were also important. Many francophones were less and less disposed, after the "cultural mutation"[23] of these years, to continue to accept what they perceived as second-class citizenship. This group would be the standard-bearer of the new nationalism.

Nationalists in Quebec were highly sensitive to the nationalist currents that in the early 1960s were sweeping parts of Europe and the newly emancipated states of Africa and Asia. Some Quebeckers saw their province's status as akin to that of a colonized state and they began preaching Quebec's independence.[24] Naturally, an independent Quebec was to be a French state.[25]

The Quiet Revolution can be said to have marked the demise of the traditional Quebec, a Quebec whose identity was based on Catholicism, French language and culture, and ruralism. Of course, since the early twentieth century, the traditional society had been in decline; indeed, by 1921, Quebec's population was half urban. By the mid-1960s, Quebec was rapidly becoming a secular society as the Church withdrew from its temporal preoccupations. What remained to distinguish French Canadians from other North Americans?[26] Language and culture, no doubt, and the nationalists would give the promotion of these traits their full attention.

The preoccupation with language also stemmed from profound feelings of insecurity among francophones. For example, the decline of the birth rate could have potentially disastrous effects on the proportion of the French population in Canada as well as in Quebec. As late as 1947, some observers, like Paul Sauriol, a journalist at the nationalist daily *Le Devoir*, foresaw the day when French-speaking Canadians would form the largest linguistic group in Canada.[27] Traditionally, a high birth rate was seen as a means of counterbalancing the influx of immigrants into Canada, few of whom spoke French or learned that language. But, by the late 1950s and early 1960s, the birth rate began to decline precipitously. In 1954, the rate was still 30.4 per thousand. By 1965, it had dropped to 21.3.[28] The dream of the "revenge of the cradle" was apparently over.

Another worrisome trend was the fact that the great majority of immigrants settling in Quebec chose to send their children to English-language schools[29] and to integrate into the English-speaking minority. For them, English was simply the most "attractive" language. Should they leave Quebec, they would obviously require an excellent knowledge of English. Within Quebec, it did not appear essential for them to learn French, particularly for those living in the Montreal area. Some demographers hypothesized that Montreal would be close to having an English-speaking majority by the year 2000.[30] Not surprisingly, the increasingly vocal nationalist lobby urged that French be established, to a much greater degree, as the language of work and of education. Only the government could bring about the desired changes.

But the government, regardless of what party was in power, had to be forced to act. The nationalists suspected that, without powerful popular pressure, the parties committed to federalism, specifically the Liberals and the Union Nationale, would not dare adopt the bold pro-French measures that they deemed necessary. But there was another more attractive possibility. Perhaps the nationalists, now more and more favourable to independence for Quebec, could themselves ride to power within a party whose backbone they would form. Then they could write and apply the language legislation. This, precisely, was to come about.

Before studying the ways in which the three major political formations dealt with the language issue, a brief description of each is necessary. The Liberal party, largely urban-based, was the force behind Quebec's modernization in the early 1960s. It was quite willing to promote nationalist causes; still, there were limits beyond which a party committed to maintaining Quebec within Confederation could not go. In addition to widespread backing among francophones, the party enjoyed the support of big enterprise, mostly anglophone, and of the anglophone minority in general.

On the specific issue of language, the Liberals were disposed to taking modest steps to strengthen the position of French. They were, however, unwilling to risk alienating those groups relatively satisfied with the status quo, particularly their English-speaking supporters and the business community. Nor, in the years from 1960 to 1966, when the Liberals held power, was the nationalist lobby sufficiently strong to force it to go further. In their 1960 election program, the Liberals promised to take measures to assist the French language and culture and notably create an Office de la langue française.[31] Few could feel threatened by these proposals. In 1966, the Liberals went somewhat further, declaring themselves willing to make French "the main language of work and of communication in Quebec" in order to "guarantee the vitality of the language and at the same time enable the majority of [Quebec's] population to live in French." Reassuring the hesitant, they declared that this objective was to be accomplished "with full respect for the undeniable rights of the anglophone minority."[32]

The Union Nationale, in power from 1966 until 1970, might have been expected to produce bolder policies than the Liberals. During the Duplessis years, had it not boasted of being the vehicle of nationalism and the ardent defender of Quebec's autonomy?[33] Moreover, it was less beholden to the English-speaking minority, from which it received relatively few votes. Yet it was perhaps more the flag-bearer of an old-style nationalism in which the defence of language through government intervention was not judged necessary. Nor did it desire to rouse English-speaking Canada against it. Thus, in 1966, the party devoted just a single line in a twenty-page program to the subject, vaguely promising to give French the status of "national language."[34] Clearly, the nationalist lobby could not hope for satisfaction from this party!

The impetus for movement on the language question was to come from a new party, established in October 1968, called the Parti Québécois. This left-of-centre political formation was the vehicle of the nationalist aspirations of Quebec's new middle class, the intelligentsia that had come of age during the Quiet Revolution. Teachers, professors, professionals, students, and elements of the working class formed the backbone of the new group.[35] It proposed a modified form of independence for Quebec called "sovereignty-association," a sort of hybrid formula implying political sovereignty for the province coupled with an economic association with the rest of Canada.

The language policy of the Parti Québécois reflected both its orientation toward independence and its middle-class composition. The independentist option meant that it viewed Quebec as a separate entity. The anglophone minority in Quebec was thus not perceived as part of a Canadian majority, a position that, in the eyes of the Liberals and the Union Nationale, justified special status for that group. Rather, Quebec anglophones were simply another minority that would have to learn to participate in the life of a French Quebec. As for the party's middle-class power base, it implied that employers' views risked being given short shrift. Still, it should be noted that the Parti Québécois, mainly because of the powerful influence exerted by its charismatic leader, René Lévesque, did not propose to abolish the English-language school system. Its position on this question would provoke considerable tension within the party.

LANGUAGE LEGISLATION: FROM BILL 85 TO BILL 22

All three parties ultimately had to wrestle with the language issue, both in opposition and in power. It was during the Union Nationale's mandate from 1966 until 1970 that pressures heated up considerably. In 1968, a local school council in the town of St. Leonard on Montreal Island voted the gradual elimination of schooling in English for the large number of Italian children enrolled in the district. The Italian community protested vehemently while the nationalist camp welcomed the commission's decision. "What we need are ten, twenty, fifty St. Leonards," contended Le Devoir editorialist Jean-Marc Léger, echoing the campaign of the group that was spearheading the movement for obligatory French schooling.[36] The English-language community demanded that the government intervene to guarantee by law unimpeded access to English-language schools for any Quebec child. Obviously, anglophones were concerned that this isolated incident could snowball into a powerful and dangerous trend and that the English-language school sector would be deprived of the not inconsiderable reinforcements furnished by the "allophone" community.[37]

The Union Nationale government was thus obliged to come to grips with this very volatile issue. Many of its members in the National Assembly,[38] conservatives from rural districts, had little interest in this question that concerned mainly Montreal and they were primarily concerned with preserving social peace. Pressures from the powerful anglophone community urged legislative action to guarantee what it contended were its rights.[39] But the Union Nationale also counted a few nationalists who were convinced that action was needed to defend the French language. The premier would have to arbitrate these differences.

Daniel Johnson, Quebec's premier from 1966 until September 1968, was assuredly a nationalist. He had frequently criticized the lack of rights of the French-speaking minorities in the other provinces, demanding "Equality or Independence" as well as additional legislative powers for Quebec in the framework of a new constitution.[40] Still, he was a shrewd politician and he found the subject of St. Leonard a slippery banana peel indeed. At a press conference held a few hours before his sudden death, he responded ambiguously to English-speaking journalists who queried him repeatedly on the affair. "We will take all useful measures, not by legislation but by other means, to make non-French-speaking Quebeckers part of Quebec so that they feel at home and learn French, the dominant language of Quebec." But he went on to say that language rights had to be protected and that it was inadmissible that local school commissions have the power to define them.[41] Just like the celebrated Marquess of Plaza-Toro, Johnson seemed to want to mount his horse and ride off in all directions at once. He certainly feared the political consequences of any action his government might take.

Johnson's successor, Jean-Jacques Bertrand, desired a rapid solution. A convinced federalist, he represented a rural district one-quarter of whose population was English-speaking. Perhaps for those reasons he was less given to pushing nationalist themes. In any case, he indicated his intention to legislate "free choice" in respect to the language of instruction, hoping thus, vainly as it turned out, to gain anglophone support in a by-election held to fill a vacancy in the Assembly.[42] Nationalist groups objected strenuously, as did several Union Nationale legislators, and Bertrand decided to withdraw the proposed bill.[43] With the objective of gaining time, he also decided, in the tried and true Canadian manner, to have a study done. He thus set up the Gendron Committee, whose mandate was to "make an inquiry into and submit a report on the position of French as the language of usage in Quebec."[44]

September 1969 brought riots between opposing French and Italians in St. Leonard, where the school commission struggled to find a solution acceptable to all sides. The prime minister's office was besieged with letters and telegrams, and the English-language press urged: "Mr. Bertrand must act."[45] In the Assembly, the opposition Liberal party also applied pressure, signifying that, although the Union Nationale appeared divided on the issue, the Liberals would support Bertrand.[46] Disorders in Montreal linked to illegal strikes provoked a veritable panic within the government, forcing it to move to repress the troubles, linguistic and otherwise.[47]

With the support of most of his Cabinet and the elected members of his party, Bertrand decided on what he hoped would be perceived as a middle-of-the-road course. He presented Bill 63, entitled An Act to Promote the French Language in Quebec,[48] which proposed to give all new arrivals in Quebec a knowledge of the French language. But the really important part of the new law, the one relevant to the St. Leonard affair, was the clause dealing with the language of instruction: it recognized the right of any Quebecker to enrol his or her child in an English-language school.

In general, English-speaking Quebeckers were satisfied with this new law. The Liberals, with the evident intention of embarrassing the Union Nationale, criticized the bill on the grounds that it did not really make French the "priority language" of Quebec.[49] As for the nationalists, many of whom were already supporting the fledgling Parti Québécois, they were furious at what they perceived as a "linguistic Munich," an ignominious surrender on the part of the Bertrand government, a powerful encouragement to the anglicization of Quebeckers. Immediately, they began urging repeal of the law. Thousands of demonstrators converged upon the National Assembly in Quebec City to express their opposition. Strikes erupted in the colleges and universities. When the next provincial elections were called, in 1970, the Union

Nationale was defeated handily by the Liberals, but the two-year-old Parti Québécois managed to garner one-quarter of the vote. It is difficult to judge the role of the language question in the Union Nationale's defeat, but the relative success of the Parti Québécois indicated that nationalist sentiment was rising.[50]

Now it was the turn of the Liberals to open Pandora's box. After the Gendron Commission finally published its report, in 1973, recommending strong measures in favour of French, they could no longer refrain from moving. Fearful of the rapidly improving fortunes of the Parti Québécois (which had obtained nearly one vote in three in the 1973 elections), the Liberals had to make proposals that would conserve the support of at least the less extreme nationalists. The nationalist camp was simply becoming too important to be neglected. Yet the Liberals also represented the non-French-speaking community in Quebec and business had considerable influence in the party. How could the Liberals hope to harmonize the rapidly polarizing positions on the language question?

Bill 22 was the Liberals' attempt to find a solution to the dilemma.[51] It clearly demonstrated their conviction that most French-speaking Quebeckers were now prepared to take strong measures to reinforce the position of the French language. Bill 22 thus proposed a series of measures designed to make French, at least to a greater degree, the language of work and of communication within Quebec. The means to bring this about were persuasive rather than coercive. More radically, though, the bill restricted access to schools in the English sector to anglophones and to allophones who had a sufficient knowledge of English, a level that was to be verified by tests. Moreover, a cap was placed on the size of enrolment in the English-language sector.

This measure showed that the Liberals were now willing to risk provoking the ire of the party's non-French-speaking supporters. Undoubtedly, they calculated that non-francophones, even though unhappy, constituted a captive electorate. After all, they had never backed the Union Nationale in the past and there was certainly no possibility of their supporting the independentist Parti Québécois.

But the Liberals gravely miscalculated the extent of anglophone discontent. A marathon radio program on the English-language station CFCF in Montreal brought 60 0000 Quebeckers, mostly anglophones, to sign a telegram-petition to Prime Minister Trudeau urging abolition of the law.[52]

Nationalists bitterly attacked Bill 22 because of numerous loopholes; they insisted that it would do little to bring immigrants into the French-language stream, and the statistics ultimately showed that they were right in this regard. Indeed, in 1976–77, the last year of operation of Bill 22, the percentage of allophone children attending English schools actually increased by 6.4 percent.[53] Still, the anglophone and allophone communities were even more adamant in their opposition to the law, particularly the stipulations regarding the language of education. When, in 1976, the Union Nationale, traditionally the voice of Quebec nationalism, made the sensational promise that, if elected, it would restore free choice of the language of schooling, large numbers of non-francophones rallied to it, deserting the now detested Liberal Party and its despised leader, Robert Bourassa.[54] For numerous other reasons unrelated to this paper, the Liberals lost ground while the Parti Québécois gained sufficient support to win the election and form the next government.

BILL 101: THE CHARTER OF THE FRENCH LANGUAGE

Contrary to the other two parties, the Parti Québécois had made no secret of its policy on language nor of the priority that it gave that question.[55] After all, the notion of an independent Quebec was predicated on the existence of a Quebec nation, of a separate identity, of a "personality at whose core is the fact that we speak French."[56] An independent Quebec would "make French the country's only official language," the party's 1971 program asserted. French would be the language of governmental institutions, it would be the working language of all enterprises, all new immigrants would be required to pass a French fluency test as a condition for obtaining a permanent visa or Quebec citizenship.[57] Since language was the fundamental value championed by the party, it was only natural that "Péquistes" be intensely concerned with the dangers faced by the French language in Quebec and committed to taking strong corrective measures. As befitted left-of-centre believers in a strongly interventionist government, laws would be adopted to solve linguistic problems.

Parti Québécois adherents were undoubtedly far more united on language policy than were the supporters of the two rival parties. Nevertheless, the Parti Québécois was on several occasions racked by acrimonious disputes concerning what rights or privileges, if any, would be accorded the province's English-speaking community.[58] For example, would there be a publicly financed English-language school sector? Radicals within the party who favoured unilingualism, many of whom had been members of the separatist Rassemblement pour l'indépendance nationale, wanted the demise of English schools; indeed, during the 1971 congress, party president René Lévesque had to threaten to resign in order to have his more moderate position prevail. Again, in February 1973, the party's executive had to take a harder line on public financing of English schools, agreeing to place a permanent ceiling on funding, in order to convince party members to accept simply the principle of the existence of schools for the English minority.[59]

The party program, on language as on all other questions, was defined with impressive democracy by elected delegates during frequent annual or biennial congresses; it certainly reflected the membership's aspirations, though generally tempered by the leadership's more moderate positions. It did not necessarily constitute a shrewd and sound appreciation of the Quebec context in general and of political realities in particular. Thus, after its election in 1976, the Parti Québécois quickly came to realize that designing a general policy was much easier than drawing up specific regulations and applying them to everyday situations. Like the other two parties, the Parti Québécois faced numerous constraints in dealing with language. Specifically, the need to take account of certain pressure made it impossible to build a Quebec as unilingually French as the party had originally intended.

Shortly after its arrival in power, the Parti Québécois government issued a White Paper detailing the language policy that it intended to implement.[60] This policy was soon set out in proposed legislation, the symbolically numbered Bill 1. The bill proposed vigorous measures to make French the language of the workplace and backed these up with threats of fines and other penalties for noncompliance. It also proposed that, generally, only French could appear on signs in public and that hitherto English-language institutions would have to communicate with the government and among themselves in French. The English-speaking school sector was to be maintained but, in most cases, only children with at least one parent who had had his or her primary schooling in Quebec in the English language were eligible. It was clear that the English sector was doomed to atrophy.

Reaction of Quebec's anglophones was uniformly negative, although, contrarily to what they had said of the Liberals, they could not pretend that the Parti Québécois had abandoned them.[61] English-speaking Quebeckers had shown only negligible support for the Parti Québécois, the party of separatism.[62] On language, the party's platform had always been quite clear — and quite unacceptable from the point of view of the English-speaking minority.[63]

In particular, business circles denounced certain aspects of Bill 1 linked to the language of the workplace. Essentially, they maintained that the law's requirements would increase costs and put Quebec enterprises at a comparative disadvantage in relation to firms elsewhere in

North America. They also contended that the law gave too much power to workers and unions. Finally, the clauses that severely limited enrolment in English-language schools caused deep concern: would recruiting efforts and transfers from outside the province not be hampered?

Certainly the Parti Québécois numbered few adherents in the business world. Business thus had to make special efforts to make its weight felt once the Parti Québécois came into office. In many respects, its remonstrances were successful in that the modified version of Bill 1, called Bill 101 (in particular, its final version) took heed of business criticism. Of course, the Parti Québécois could not, even had it so wished, have abandoned the key stipulations of its language project; closely surveyed by the party's membership, the government had to remain within bounds. On the other hand, the Parti Québécois could not afford to alienate irreparably the business world. A referendum on sovereignty-association had to be held during its first mandate in office and it was reasonable to assume that if Quebec's economy floundered during this period, the electors would spurn the project.

Even with the amendments, anglophone business clearly did not like the law. Many enterprises, particularly head offices, left Quebec, often blaming the language legislation. Sun Life was a noisy and well-publicized example of this exodus. Yet it is very difficult to evaluate the actual causes of these departures. For some, higher Quebec taxes were the important issue. For others, militant unionism made Quebec a difficult place in which to do business. For still others, it was important to be where the action was, and that meant moving west, to Toronto, or to Alberta during the oil boom of the late 1970s.

The Parti Québécois was thus forced to moderate its language legislation and to apply it less rigorously than might otherwise have been the case. For example, head offices and research centres were exempted from the law's provisions. Professionals who had no contact with the public would not have to pass a test of French proficiency.[64] Moreover, it was common knowledge that hundreds of students were illegally enrolled in the English Protestant schools; while denouncing the situation frequently, the government preferred that the law be flouted rather than use force to expel these students.[65]

The courts ultimately constituted an additional constraint. They declared unconstitutional certain sections of the language legislation, thus weakening Bill 101.[66] Since Quebec remains a part of Canada, the Supreme Court of Canada is the court of last appeal, a situation that the Parti Québécois did not foresee or did not want to imagine in the heady days of 1977. In addition, the new Canadian Constitution, adopted without Quebec's consent in 1982, contains certain language guarantees with which Quebec is not in agreement but which nevertheless apply.

One new element that could well have an impact on the language question is the return to power, in December 1985, of the Liberals under their reincarnated leader, Robert Bourassa. The party has again become the advocate of the English-speaking minority, which counts four ministers in the provincial Cabinet. Yet interestingly — and this is surely an indication of the very considerable evolution that Quebec has undergone in matters of language since the early 1970s — the Liberals have indicated that, while they may make certain concessions and adjust Bill 101 to make it more flexible, they will not abrogate the law. Among the modifications envisaged should be mentioned the softening of the requirement that signs be in French only. Public opinion polls show an increasing percentage of Quebeckers willing to accept bilingualism on signs.[67] Still, it is apparent that Quebec has adapted to the law and that the law has changed Quebec. More than half of all allophone children are now enrolled in schools in the French sector.[68] The proportion of workers who say they work in French has increased significantly.[69] Enterprises under French control now furnish more than 60 percent of all jobs in Quebec, up from 47 percent in 1960.[70] Even the English-speaking minority, which has undergone a veritable revolution since 1970, seems able to live with the law.[71] It was inevitable that the changes that occurred in Quebec in the early 1960s would eventually have an impact on language, a highly emotional issue. Within the federal government and the English-speaking provinces, these changes have certainly had some effect. The proportion of French-speakers in the federal civil service has increased and now approaches the proportion of francophones in the total population.[72] French-language services have become more widely available. Bilingualism has become more popular among Canada's English-speaking population.[73] Still, a command of English remains a virtual necessity for francophones outside Quebec, since, with some exceptions, the concentrations of French-speaking population are insufficient to allow daily activities, notably work, to be carried out in French. It is thus not surprising that assimilation takes a large toll among the French-speaking minorities and that even the awakening of the federal government, and at least some provincial governments, to the French fact does not seem to have stemmed linguistic losses.

The Quebec case is very different, since that province has always had a strong French-speaking majority that controls the provincial government. Nevertheless, until very recently, the English-speaking minority in Quebec has wielded enormous economic power (and to a somewhat lesser extent still does)[74] and, in addition, has benefited immensely from the prestige accruing to speakers of Canada's and North America's major language. The Quiet Revolution of the early 1960s made francophones aware of a linguistic disequilibrium that disadvantaged them.[75] But it was inevitable that any attempt to modify fundamentally the balance between the two languages in Quebec would provoke bitter disputes between the majority and the minority.

Three political parties faced the challenge of enhancing the status of the French language within Quebec and of improving opportunities for francophones. Each party's actions in this regard were affected by particular constraints. For the two old parties, the Liberals and the Union Nationale, the language issue caused internecine strife within party ranks as well as considerable harm at the polls. In particular, the Liberals had to deal with the fact that their supporters included virtually the entire non-francophone minority, a group whose conception of Quebec society was markedly different from that of most francophones.

The Parti Québécois, as we have seen, proceeded differently. Far from trying to shy away from the issue and to seek some middle ground that would not alienate important factions, the party placed language reform in the forefront of its program and it hoped that its promise of a strong stand in favour of the French language would generate support among a majority of French-speaking Quebeckers. That hope proved realistic enough, although, once in power, the Parti Québécois could no longer ignore key sectors of opinion that had opposed its language policy.

What does the future bode for the French language in Quebec? The heroic exploits of the knights of language are now fading rapidly into the past. There are many indications that the younger generation of Quebeckers, those who did not fight the battles of the 1960s and 1970s, believe that the question has been permanently resolved and that French is now secure in the province.[76] This phenomenon is perhaps an indication of the relative success of Bill 101 in changing the face of Quebec. Other observers, perhaps more perspicacious, see continued dangers for the French language, regardless of the language legislation. The Conseil de la langue française, charged with advising the government on matters of language, affirms that French has still not become the "normal, habitual language of work, of teaching, of communications, of commerce and business."[77] The English language continues to surround and to penetrate Quebec. Communications, and notably cable television, have made English-language stations more numerous for most subscribers than French-language stations.[78] American culture and cultural practices will undoubtedly have a growing impact on Quebec as an open society. In addition, the tremendous advances of computer science since the late 1970s, a phenomenon entirely unforeseen by the writers of Bill 101, have been largely in English, whether it be manufacturers' manuals or software. Indeed, the three offices concerned with the application of Bill 101 see the francization of this sector as the major challenge of the near future.[79]

Other problems, though having no relation to Bill 101, certainly affect the future of the French language in Quebec. Education critics have decried poor teaching of French in schools.[80] Even business leaders have protested against graduates' insufficient mastery of the French language. Finally, demographic projections for Quebec indicate that the province's population will begin to diminish shortly after the year 2000. Declining births (the Quebec fertility rate now stands at 1.42, considerably below the Canadian average of 1.68), minimal immigration from foreign countries, and, since the mid-1970s, a negative balance in population exchanges with other Canadian provinces explain this phenomenon, the repercussions of which could be dramatic.[81]

Language legislation in Canada, and particularly in Quebec, has undoubtedly had significant effects. Still, it appears certain that legislation alone cannot solve the major challenges that the French language must face if it is to maintain what has been acquired over the past twenty years.

NOTES

1. The secret instructions accompanying the Quebec Act of 1774 are eloquent in this regard. For historian Hilda Neatby, the act and the instructions taken together signified "gentle but steady and determined anglicization." See her *Quebec: The Revolutionary Age, 1760–1791* (Toronto: McClelland and Stewart, 1966), 139.

2. Historian Fernand Ouellet calculates the birth rate at a very respectable 50 to 55 per thousand during the century following the Conquest. See *Histoire économique et sociale du Québec, 1760–1850* (Montréal: Fides, 1966), 142, 197, 468.

3. In 1851, 75.2 percent of Quebec's population was French-speaking. By 1901, this figure had climbed to 80.3 percent: *Annuaire du Québec, 1968–1969* (Québec: Bureau de la Statistique du Québec, 1968), 179.

4. For a generally good study of English–French relations in the nineteenth century, see A.I. Silver, *The French-Canadian Idea of Confederation, 1864–1900* (Toronto: University of Toronto Press, 1982). On the Manitoba Schools Question, Paul Crunican's *Priests and Politicians: Manitoba Schools and the Election of 1869* (Toronto: University of Toronto Press, 1974) is excellent. As for Ontario's attempts to suppress French-language education, consult Robert Choquette, *Language and Religion: A History of English–French Conflict in Ontario* (Ottawa: University of Ottawa Press, 1975).

5. The Royal Commission on Bilingualism and Biculturalism, in an oft-quoted and abundantly discussed table, showed that French Canadians in Quebec placed twelfth among fourteen ethnic groups by average labour income of male salary- and wage-earners in 1961. Those of British origin placed first, at a level 55 percent higher than that of the French. Even bilingualism did not appear a significant economic asset. Looking specifically at language, unilingual anglophones were at the top of the ladder, well ahead of bilingual francophones: *Report*, Book 3: *The Work World* (Ottawa: Queen's Printer, 1969), 22–24. It should be mentioned, though, that by the 1980s the French had achieved virtual economic parity with the British in Canada: Jac-André Boulet and Laval Lavallée, *L'évolution des disparités linguistiques de revenus de travail au Canada de 1970 à 1980* (Ottawa: Conseil économique du Canada, October 1983).

6. Canadians whose mother tongue (i.e., the first language learned and still understood) was French accounted for 28.1 percent of the population in 1961, and for 25.7 percent in 1981: Statistics Canada, 1961 and 1981 censuses and tables furnished in *Language and Society* 9 (Spring 1983): 20–21. Also, 24.6 percent of Canadians told government census-takers in 1981 that the language they most often spoke at home was French. This question, more indicative of the actual strength of the French language in Canada, was first asked in 1971.

7. Royal Commission on Bilingualism and Biculturalism, *Report*, Book 1: *The Official Languages* (Ottawa: Queen's Printer, 1967), 173.

8. Daniel Johnson, premier of Quebec from 1966 to 1968, promoted the Two Nations concept. In this regard, he asserted: "French Canadians seek to identify themselves with the State of Quebec, the only state in which they can claim to be masters of their destiny, the only one that they can utilize to promote the development of their community." On the other hand, English Canadians tend, for their part, to "consider Ottawa as their national state": Daniel Johnson, *Égalité ou indépendance* (Montréal: Éditions Renaissance, 1965), 24, 50.

 9. S.C. 1969, c. 54, "An Act respecting the status of the official languages of Canada." The text and comments may be found in Commissioner of Official Languages, *First Annual Report, 1970–1971* (Ottawa: Information Canada, 1971), 105–14 and 1–11.

10. Sections 16 to 23 of the Constitution Act, 1982, specify language rights.

11. Commissioner of Official Languages, *Annual Report 1984* (Ottawa: Minister of Supply and Services Canada, 1985), preface.

12. This figure, however, represents a mere 5.5 percent of the total population of Canada's most populous province; francophones tend to be concentrated in the eastern and northern portions of the province.

13. Such is the case of Manitoba, now obliged by the Supreme Court to translate its laws into French. The francophones of that province proposed that, instead of translating thousands of laws, many of them inoperative, the provincial government offer certain services in French. In 1984, after having accepted the proposition, the government yielded to widespread anglophone opposition and backed down from its commitment.

14. Task Force on Canadian Unity, *A Future Together: Observations and Recommendations* (Ottawa: Minister of Supply and Services Canada, 1979), 51.

15. Statistics Canada, 1981 census, and tables furnished in Robert Bourbeau, "Canada's Language Transfer Phenomenon," *Language and Society* 11 (Autumn 1983): 14–22.

16. The most recent Statistics Canada report affirms that the French have maintained their positions, in relative terms, only in Quebec (figures quoted in *La Presse*, 26 janvier 1985).

17. Bourbeau, "Canada's Language Transfer Phenomenon," 15.

18. This phenomenon was first convincingly documented by Richard J. Joy in *Languages in Conflict* (Toronto: McClelland and Stewart, Carleton Library no. 61, 1972). Davidson Dunton, co-chairman of the Royal Commission on Bilingualism and Biculturalism, has remarked on the popularity of the "two unilingualisms" solutions to the Canadian language question: "The Muddy Waters of Bilingualism," *Language and Society* 1 (Autumn 1979): 7.

19. See Richard Jones, *Duplessis and the Union Nationale Administration* (Ottawa: Canadian Historical Association, booklet no. 35, 1983), and reprinted in this volume [*Quebec since 1945: Selected Readings*].

20. This era has recently been chronicled by political scientist Dale C. Thomson in *Jean Lesage and the Quiet Revolution* (Toronto: Macmillan of Canada, 1984).

21. "Masters in our own house" was the theme of the Liberal election campaign in 1962. The major issue of the campaign was the nationalization of the private electrical power companies (*Manifeste du parti libéral du Québec*, 1962, 1).

22. For example, Hubert Guindon, "Social Unrest, Social Class, and Quebec's Bureaucratic Revolution," *Queen's Quarterly* 71, 2 (Summer 1964): 150–62; Roch Denis, *Luttes de classes et question nationale au Québec, 1948–1968* (Montréal: Presses Socialistes Internationales, 1979).

23. The expression is from Université de Montréal sociologist Guy Rocher, *Le Québec en mutation* (Montréal: Éditions Hurtubise-HMH, 1973).

24. The titles of some of the separatist books published in these years are revealing: Raymond Barbeau, *Le Québec est-il une colonie?* (Montréal: Les Éditions de l'Homme, 1962); Raymond Barbeau, *La libération économique du Québec* (Montréal: Les Éditions de l'Homme, 1963); Andrew D'Allemagne, *Le colonialisme au Québec* (Montréal: Les Éditions R-B, 1966).

25. The major independentist group of the early 1960s, the Rassemblement pour l'indépendance nationale, vigorously denounced bilingualism and objected to any legislative recognition of rights for Quebec's English-speaking linguistic minority (*Programme du R.I.N.*, octobre 1962, 2).

26. Université Laval sociologist Fernand Dumont was one of those asking this question. See "Y a-t-il un avenir pour l'homme canadien-français?" in *La vigile du Québec* (Montréal: Éditions Hurtubise-HMH, 1971), 57–76.

27. "Programme d'immigration au service d'une politique raciste," editorial, *Le Devoir*, 7 octobre 1947, 1.

28. *Annuaire du Québec 1968–1969*, 255.

29. The percentage of New Canadians enrolled in French schools fell from 52 in 1931–32 to 25 in 1962–63, then to 11 by 1972–73: Gary Caldwell, "Assimilation and the Demographic Future of Quebec," in *Quebec's Language Policies: Background and Response*, ed. John R. Mallea (Québec: Centre international de recherche sur le bilinguisme, Presses de l'Université Laval, 1977), 57.

30. Jacques Henripin saw Montreal as being between 53 and 60 percent French-speaking by 2000, a decline of between 6 and 13 percent, in "Quebec and the Demographic Dilemma of French-Canadian Society," *Quebec's Language Policies*, 43, 48.

31. *Programme politique du Parti libéral du Québec*, 1960, 2.

32. *Québec en marche: Le programme politique du Parti libéral du Québec*, 1966, 5.

33. The best history of the party is Herbert F. Quinn's *The Union Nationale: Quebec Nationalism from Duplessis to Lévesque,* 2nd ed. (Toronto: University of Toronto Press, 1979).

34. *Objectifs 1966 de l'Union Nationale, un programme d'action pour une jeune nation. Québec d'abord,* 3.

35. Of the nearly 90 000 members of the Parti Québécois in 1971, nearly 40 percent belonged to the liberal professions, including a very large number of teachers, nearly 25 percent were white-collar workers, mainly office employees and service workers, and 15 percent were students: *Le Parti québécois en bref* (Montréal: Les Éditions du Parti québécois, 1971), 21.

36. Jean-Marc Léger, "Il faut créer dix, vingt, cinquante St-Léonard," *Le Devoir,* 4 septembre 1968.

37. "Allophone," in the Canadian context, is the term used to describe persons whose mother tongue is neither English nor French.

38. Since 1968, Quebec's unicameral legislature has been called the "National Assembly," an appellation of obvious symbolic value. The other Canadian provinces use the term "Legislative Assembly."

39. From Toronto, a *Globe and Mail* editorial denounced what it saw as "cultural protectionism": "Turning Back the Clock," 2 Sept. 1968.

40. See, for example, Johnson's speech at the first meeting of the Constitutional Conference in Ottawa in February, 1968. Constitutional Conference, First Meeting, *Proceedings* (Ottawa: Queen's Printer, 1968), 53–71.

41. Text of press conference quoted in Paul Gros d'Aillon, *Daniel Johnson, l'égalité avant l'indépendance* (Montréal: Les Éditions internationales Stanké, 1979), 230–34.

42. This was the interpretation of journalists, and even Bertrand admitted that there did seem to be a coincidence ("Des groupes francophones protestent: le bill sur les droits scolaires sera présenté aujourd'hui," *Le Devoir,* 26 novembre 1968). The election theme in the district of Notre-Dame-de-Grâce, an English-speaking constituency in Montreal, was "Remember St. Leonard" (*The Montreal Star,* editorial, 20 Nov. 1968).

43. This is the interpretation of Jérôme Proulx, a Union Nationale deputy, in his book, *Le panier de crabes* (Montréal: Éditions Parti Pris, 1971), 111–24. Journalists agreed ("Le bill sur les droits scolaires: l'opposition du caucus fait reculer Bertrand," *Le Devoir,* 27 novembre 1968, headline; Vincent Prince, "Le bill Bertrand renvoyé à un Comité," editorial, *Le Devoir,* 14 décembre 1968).

44. Order in council no. 3958, 9 Dec. 1968, quoted in Commission of Inquiry on the Position of the French Language and on Language Rights in Quebec, *Report: The Position of the French Language in Quebec; II: Language Rights* (Montréal, 1972), v.

45. Robert J. Macdonald, "In Search of a Language Policy: Francophone Reactions to Bill 85 and 63," in *Quebec's Language Policies,* 219–42.

46. Pierre Laporte's speech in *Débats de l'Assemblée nationale du Québec,* 10 octobre 1969, 3152.

47. Proulx, *Le panier de crabes,* 152–53.

48. The bill closely resembled Bill 85, presented a year earlier and withdrawn.

49. Opposition Leader Jean Lesage's speech in *Débats de l'Assemblée nationale du Québec,* 28 octobre 1969, 3376–78.

50. In the opinion of Jérôme Proulx, who resigned as a Union Nationale deputy to vote against Bill 63, the law destroyed the party. See *Le panier de crabes,* 153–54 and 193–94. A poll done for the Quebec City daily, *Le Soleil,* showed that the Union Nationale's stand on the language of education won it no support among anglophones, 71.9 percent of whom proposed to vote for the Liberals while only 9.4 percent preferred the Union Nationale (*Le Soleil,* 18 avril 1970, 12). Other polling, done by political scientist Peter Regenstreif, showed that at least a small majority of Quebeckers were satisfied with the government's record on language while large majorities were dissatisfied with its record on issues like strikes, taxes, and unemployment. Quoted in Vincent Lemieux, Marcel Gilbert, and André Blais, *Une élection de réalignement: l'élection générale du 29 avril 1970 au Québec* (Montréal: Éditions du Jour, 1970), 86.

51. Official Language Act, Statutes of Quebec, 1974, c. 6.

52. William Tetley, "The English and Language Legislation: A Personal History," in *The English of Quebec: From Majority to Minority Status,* ed. Gary Caldwell and Eric Waddell (Québec: Institut québécois de recherche sur la culture, 1982), 381–97. Tetley was an anglophone minister in the Bourassa cabinet that adopted Bill 22. For an informative study of anglophone opinion, see Michael B. Stein, "Bill 22 and the Non-francophone Population in Quebec: A Case Study of Minority Group Attitudes on Language Legislation," in *Quebec's Language Policies,* 243–65.

53. Michel Paillé, "The Impact of Language Policies on Enrolment in Public Schools in Quebec," in *Contribution à la démolinguistique du Québec* (Québec: Conseil de la langue française, avril 1985), 139–40; Claude St. Germain, *La situation linguistique dans les écoles primaires et secondaires, 1971–72 à 1978–79* (Québec: Conseil de la langue française, 1979), 12, 24.

54. Quinn, *The Union Nationale,* 279–80.

55. The party's "political action program," adopted during its third congress in February 1971, specifically promised to mount a campaign to fight for the repeal of Bill 63 (Parti Québécois, *Le programme—l'action politique—les status et règlements, édition 1971*, 35).

56. René Lévesque, *Option Québec* (Montréal: Les Éditions de l'Homme, 1968), 19.

57. Parti Québécois, *Le programme*, 21.

58. For Vera Murray, the Parti Québécois, even while in opposition, was rife with tension on virtually all aspects of its ideology. She sees the battles as pitting a "technocratic" wing, more moderate, emphasizing efficiency and planning, and controlling the party's executive, against a more radical "participationist" wing, representing a minority of the party's members, but very vigorous and noisy in the defence of its left-wing social-democratic positions: *Le Parti Québécois, de la fondation à la prise du pouvoir* (Montréal: Éditions Hurtubise-HMH, 1976), 29–30.

59. *Le Devoir*, 26 février 1973.

60. Camille Laurin, *La politique québécoise de la langue française* (Québec: Éditeur officiel, 1977).

61. Many anglophone organizations and firms testified during government hearings on Bill 1 (Assemblée nationale, Journal des Débats, Commission permanente de l'éducation, des affaires culturelles et des communications, *Délibérations*, juin–juillet 1977). One anglophone pressure group, the Positive Action Committee, sarcastically commented on the bill: "The anglophone collectivity has a place in Quebec on the condition that it is invisible and silent and progressively diminishes in number" (Alison d'Anglejan, "Language Planning in Quebec: An Historical Overview and Future Trends," in *Conflict and Language Planning in Quebec*, ed. Richard Y. Bourhis (Clevedon, England: Multilingual Matters Ltd., 1984), 29–52.

62. Only 9.5 percent of non-francophones proposed to support the Parti Québécois in 1976; 22 percent intended to vote for the Union Nationale and its policy of "free choice"; 40 percent refused to answer, proposed to abstain, or did not know which party they would support (poll figures quoted in André Bernard, *Québec élections 1976* [Montréal: Éditions Hurtubise-HMH, 1976]), 49.

63. Anglophone reactions are analyzed in Nadia Assimopoulous and Michel Laferrière, *Législation et perceptions ethniques: une étude du contenu de la presse anglaise de Montréal au vote de la loi 101* (Montréal: Office de la langue française, 1980).

64. These adaptations are examined in William D. Coleman, "From Bill 22 to Bill 101: The Politics of Language under the Parti Québécois," *Canadian Journal of Political Science* 14, 3 (Sept. 1981): 459–85, and reprinted in this volume [that is, *Quebec since 1945: Selected Readings*]; also in William D. Coleman, "A Comparative Study of Language Policy in Quebec: A Political Economy Approach," in *The Politics of Canadian Public Policy*, ed. Michael M. Atkinson and Marsha A. Chandler (Toronto: University of Toronto Press, 1983), 21–42.

65. Claude Ryan, minister of education in the new Bourassa Liberal government (elected on 2 December 1985), stated that he would prefer to settle the problem of the estimated 1800 "illegals" on a case-by-case basis (*Le Devoir*, 28 et 29 janvier 1986). The government decided nevertheless on a general amnesty, decried by critics because it rewarded those who disobeyed the law.

66. Gilles Rhéaume, president of two nationalist organizations, the Société Saint-Jean Baptiste de Montréal and the Mouvement national des Québécois, declared that the courts had riddled Bill 101 with so many holes that it was beginning to look like a piece of Swiss cheese (*The Gazette*, 5 Jan. 1985).

67. In 1979, fewer than one of three francophone Quebeckers thought that English should be allowed on public signs. A 1981 poll showed that two in three French-speaking Montrealers agreed with bilingualism on signs. By 1984, 80 percent of francophone Quebeckers disagreed with the French unilingualism imposed by the sign stipulation in Bill 101 (Commissioner of Official Languages, *Annual Report 1984*, 37). 1985 polls conducted by the Centre de Recherches sur l'Opinion publique showed similar findings (*La Presse*, 20 janvier and 27 avril 1985).

68. The figure increased from 30 percent in 1976–77 to 57 percent in 1984–85 (Michel Paillé, "Conséquences des politiques linguistiques québécoises sur les effectifs scolaires selon la langue d'enseignement," *Le Devoir*, 29 mai 1985).

69. Numerous surveys have been conducted on this question. The Gendron Commission prepared a lengthy study of the question as it stood in the early 1970s. Sixty-four percent of francophones declared that they worked almost solely in French (Commission d'enquête sur la situation de la langue française et sur les droits linguistiques au Québec, *Rapport*, Livre 1: *La langue de travail* (Quebec, décembre 1972, 16–19)). According to recent findings, 70 percent of francophones now work only in French, and another 20 percent generally in French ("A Linguistic Scarecrow," editorial, *The Gazette*, 9 Jan. 1985).

70. André Raynauld and François Vaillancourt, *L'appartenance des entreprises: le cas du Québec en 1978* (Montréal: Office de la langue française, 1985).

71. One-half of Quebec's anglophones (two-thirds of those under 30) are bilingual. The population of Anglo-Quebeckers, however, declined by 10 percent during the 1970s because of significant out-migration. Not

surprisingly, research has shown that anglophones who left tended to speak only English while anglophones who remained tended to be bilingual (Statistics Canada, *Language in Canada*, quoted in *The Gazette* and *Le Devoir*, 26 Jan. 1985).

72. Commissioner of Official Languages, *Annual Report* 1984, 60. However, over half of all francophone employees are in non-officer positions, including clerks, secretaries, and similar occupations.

73. Fifteen percent of Canadians class themselves as bilingual. Between 1971 and 1981, their number grew at double the rate of population increase. Only 7.6 percent of English Canadians are bilingual as compared with 36.2 percent of French Canadians. Considering only the English-speaking provinces, 5.4 percent of the English speak French while 78.9 percent of the French know English. Quebec boasts by far the highest proportion of bilinguals: Statistics Canada, *Language in Canada* (Ottawa: Supply and Services Canada, Jan. 1985). French immersion programs in the English-speaking provinces have recently become extremely popular (Commissioner of Official Languages, *Annual Report* 1984, 25–29).

74. Sixty-nine percent of managers in Quebec, in the public and private sectors, are now French-speaking. French-speaking managers even have a slight majority in English-Canadian and in foreign firms established in the province. Arnaud Sales, *Décideurs et gestionnaires; étude sur la direction et l'encadrement des secteurs privé et public* (Québec: Éditeur officiel, 1985), 177–202.

75. Language situations in which dominance is not based on demographic supremacy can easily produce social tensions. Such has been the case in Quebec. See Pierre E. Laporte, "Status Language Planning in Quebec: An Evaluation," in *Conflict and Language Planning in Quebec*, 57.

76. Polls conducted by the Conseil de la langue française, one of the organisms created by Bill 101, showed, in the opinion of the Conseil, that the young live "with the peacefulness of security brought about by the French language Charter." (Quoted in *The Gazette*, 22 April 1985.) The Conseil expressed shock when 40 percent of high school students queried affirmed that "living in French" was not necessary for their personal development! (*La situation linguistique actuelle* [Québec, Conseil de la langue française, janvier 1985], 27.)

77. *La situation linguistique actuelle*, 18.

78. A study commissioned by the Conseil showed that francophones spend about one-third of their television time watching English-language stations. Ibid., 12.

79. Jean-Pierre Proulx, "La question linguistique: la révolution informatique constitue le défi de l'heure," *Le Devoir*, 12 décembre 1985.

80. "Un constat de piètre qualité: l'apprentissage de la langue maternelle à l'école," *Le Soleil*, 17 janvier 1985; "L'apprentissage de la langue maternelle est en crise," *Le Devoir*, 16 janvier 1985.

81. Assemblée nationale du Québec, Commission parlementaire de la culture, *Le Québec à la croisée des chemins démographiques*, septembre 1985; Albert Juneau, "La défaite des berceaux," *Le Devoir*, 7 juin 1985; Jean-Claude Leclerc, "L'effondrement démographique: le réveil risque d'être tardif," *Le Devoir*, 8 novembre 1985; Georges Mathews, "La crise démographique au Québec," *Le Devoir*, 18 and 19 novembre 1985.

Article Thirty-Five

Québec-Canada's Constitutional Dossier

Alain-G. Gagnon

To begin with, Québec is not a province like the others. Adequately accounting for such a political reality necessitates an adapted analytical focus. As such, we employ the notion of the Québec state as a political nation inscribed within a multinational whole and as a historic region in order to highlight Québec's specificity, rather than simply treating Québec as a province, a subordinate government or a political grouping. The latter expressions appear to us as misleading considering the manner in which a large majority of Québecers perceive and define themselves.[1]

There are many ways to address Québec-Canada dynamics in the area of federal-provincial relations. Some researchers have opted for a legal approach . . . while others have chosen to proceed with the study of fiscal federalism (e.g., the Seguin Commission on fiscal imbalance in Canada[2]). The present text will privilege the historical-institutional dimensions of federal-provincial relations with the aim of providing a more encompassing portrait, allowing for a perspective that more effectively accounts for the evolution of power relations between orders of government as well as within the partisan system. We will proceed in three periods: (1) the first period will consider the historical foundations and the establishment of the first constitutional order; (2) the second period is one of transition and covers the years from 1960 to 1982; and (3) the third period extends from 1982, the year of constitutional repatriation without the consent of Québec, to the present time, stressing the rupture with the established constitutional order and the emergence of a new political order.

HISTORICAL FOUNDATIONS AND THE EMERGENCE OF THE FIRST CONSTITUTIONAL ORDER

The founding events of a political community are viewed rarely with unanimity. Nevertheless, in the case of Québec it is relatively easy to locate the important dates in which various interpretations are formed according to different political stands. We can identify, up to the 1960s, no less than four fundamental moments: (1) the Conquest of 1759–60 followed by the Surrender of 1763; (2) the Québec Act of 1774; (3) the Rebellions of 1837–1838 followed by the Act of Union in 1840; and (4) the Confederation of 1867. Each of these moments marked the development of Québec's political culture in a notable manner. Indeed, contemporary authors often hark back to them or follow up on them, but rarely are they dismissed.

The great episodes of the Conquest and of the Surrender have frequently been reviewed in analyses centred on Québec-Canada relations. The clashing interpretations advanced respectively by the contentions of those in the *École de Montreal* and the *École de Québec* and, closer to us, in the production of the Radio-Canada televised series titled *Canada: A People's History*, or still further in the exchanges between Gérard Bouchard and John Saul[3] demonstrate the political consequences of targeting one or the other of these two events.

The Québec Act of 1774 constitutes a fundamental moment whose repercussions continue to this day. Some analysts have evoked the desire of Great Britain to prevent an extension to the former French and Catholic possession of its military conflicts with the Americans, who sought to emancipate themselves from their colonizers. Other analysts have advanced more nuanced interpretations, recalling with interest that the passage of the Québec Act would constitute the first imperial statute that recognized a colony's own formal constitution.[4]

In this context, those who identified themselves as *les Canadiens*, and their elites, found themselves with the recognition, on the one hand, of the right to exercise their faith and to use the French language, while on the other, to obtain the re-establishment of the seigneurial regime, the tithe and the use of common law. Indeed, the Québec Act represents an interpretive document whose importance for following generations cannot be ignored.

The relevance of the Québec Act on the legitimacy of Québec's demands within the Canadian federation is in many regards proportional to the significance of the Royal Proclamation of 1763 on the status of Aboriginal nations. At the very least, it probably served to incite the authors of the preliminary report of the Royal Commission on Aboriginal Peoples to establish, in 1995, parallels between the claims of these nations and those of the Québec nation within Canada as a whole.

The events surrounding the rebellions of Lower Canada as well as the Act of Union of 1840 marked the imagination of French Canadians at the time. Moreover, the emergence of republican and liberal ideas in Québec can also be attributed to this period. Nevertheless, the year 1840 does not represent a memorable year for French Canadians as it signified the forced merger of Upper and Lower Canada without the institution of responsible government; it was not until 1848 that this political victory was attained.

It was with the advent of the Union of the two Canadas that French Canadians turned resolutely towards the Church, which provided them with protection and marked the infancy stage of an agreed consociational formula.[5]

In founding the Canadian Confederation in 1867, or what can be designated as the first constitutional order, French and English Canadians agreed on the main tenets of a power-sharing formula. Despite periodic modifications, this constitutional order would continue until repatriation in 1981.

Three interpretations came to the fore during this period: the creation of Canada was interpreted either as an imperial statute, as an agreement between the founding provinces, or as a pact between English Canadians and French Canadians. In Québec, the interpretation that has dominated all debates is centered on dualism, which has given rise to a rich literature concerning constitutional matters. For example, the work of Judge Thomas-Jean-Jacques Loranger, at the start of the 1880s,[6] deserves attention to the extent that it established links to the Québec Act of 1774, and for providing interpretive boundaries with regard to Québec-Canada relations. The main premises of Judge Loranger are summarized in the preliminary report of the Royal Commission on Aboriginal Peoples in 1993:

1. The confederation of the British Provinces was the result of a compact entered into by the provinces and the United Kingdom.
2. The provinces entered into the federal Union with their corporate identity, former constitutions, and all their legislative powers intact. A portion of these powers was ceded to the federal Parliament, to exercise them in common interest of the provinces. The powers not ceded were retained by the provincial legislatures, which continued to act within their own sphere according to their former constitutions, under certain modifications of form established by the federal compact.
3. Far from having been conferred upon them by the federal government, the powers of the provinces are the residue of their former colonial powers. The federal government is the creation of the provinces, the result of their association and of their compact.[7]

Judge Loranger supported his contentions on the basis of continuity in constitutional matters, and reminds us that it is not permissible for political actors to ignore treaties, agreements, and conventions in the elaboration of constitutional reforms. The influence of interpretations advanced by Judge Loranger in the elaboration of Québec's constitutional positions can also be read between the lines in the report of the Royal Commission of Inquiry on Constitutional Problems, the Tremblay Report, which was released by the government of Québec in 1956. The Tremblay report emphasized the notions of provincial autonomy in fiscal and financial domains, coordination between the two orders of government, and the principle of subsidiarity. The report recommended that Québec, as a member-state of the Canadian confederation, is fully responsible for the development of its culture. The Tremblay report allowed for the actualization of the conceptual contentions of Judge Loranger in matters of provincial autonomy, while representing a major source of inspiration for the architects of the Quiet Revolution at a time where a vast program of reforms on the cultural, economic, and social levels were to be elaborated, with the aim of reducing the rift that was developing between Québec and Ontario in particular.

FROM THE QUIET REVOLUTION TO REPATRIATION IN 1982: A PERIOD OF TRANSITION

The start of the 1960s was marked by an impressive political fervour in Québec: the arrival to power of the Liberals of Jean Lesage, the appearance of several third parties, state interventionism, the affirmation of civil society, the rise of the trade union movement and, to limit ourselves to these examples, the first expressions of the Front de Liberation du Québec. Social and political actors sought to redress the structural inequities to which Québec had been subjected over the years and provided Québecers with a context of choice that permitted their affirmation on cultural, political, social, and economic levels.

At the very beginning of the period, the government of Québec attempted to make alliances with the provincial capitals. Moreover, through the initiatives of Premier Jean Lesage, the provincial Premiers began to meet annually with a view to presenting a common front when confronted with unilateral actions by Ottawa in areas of competence that are exclusive to the provinces.

On the constitutional plane, and in response to Québec's demands, the minority Liberal government of Lester B. Pearson decided in 1963 to set up the Laurendeau-Dunton Commission on bilingualism and biculturalism, which provided real meaning to the principle of equality between the two founding peoples.[8] In this context of great fervour, the government of Québec, in concert with the other member-states of the federation, sought to elaborate propositions with the aim of arriving at negotiated agreements with the federal government. This had the particular effect of increasing the frequency of federal-provincial meetings, expanding the range of questions addressed at such encounters and promoting the creation of ministerial committees charged with studying disputed issues.

Subsequently, and inspired by the autonomist doctrine of Judge Loranger, Paul Gérin-Lajoie proposed the external extension of Québec's internal jurisdictions.[9] Québec invested in the international arena and began to establish relations with international organizations and foreign governments, provoking serious conflicts with Ottawa. The government of Québec recognized that foreign policy was a federal jurisdiction, yet argued for its right to act in this domain in cases that were relevant to its own exclusive fields. This approach was particularly effective from 1964–1966, a period in which Québec concluded several agreements related to education, youth, and cultural affairs. Québec's initiatives, combined with efforts in concert with other provincial governments, served to increase the pressure for constitutional reform.

At the time, the establishment of an amending formula constituted a major problem that obstructed constitutional reform. During the Liberal tenure of Jean Lesage (1960–1966), two amending formulas were proposed in Québec, and then rejected. In 1961, Lesage refused the formula proposed by the federal Minister of Justice at the time, Davie Fulton, because the federal government refused to limit the powers that it assumed in 1949, powers that permitted the federal government to unilaterally amend the Constitution in fields of exclusive federal competence. Moreover, Ottawa refused to grant Québec a voice with regard to reforms to central institutions such as the monarchy, the Senate, and the Supreme Court.

In January 1966, the Fulton-Favreau formula, which at the outset was received favourably by all provincial Premiers at the federal-provincial conference of October 1964, would undergo a similar fate with Québec withdrawing its support. This formula would have required the approval of the federal government and all other provincial governments for provisions respecting the division of powers, the use of both official languages, denominational rights in education and representation in the House of Commons. Other provisions respecting the monarchy and Senate representation could be amended by Ottawa with the concurrence of two-thirds of the provinces comprising more than 50 per cent of the Canadian population. Upon reflection, an amending formula based on unanimity was opposed in Québec because it could threaten the possibility of obtaining intergovernmental agreements on culturally sensitive issues, such as language policy, and could discourage any transfer of powers from the federal to the provincial order. With the aim of providing the system with a measure of flexibility, Québec also envisaged a clause regarding delegation of powers that would permit member-states of the federation and Ottawa to delegate, respectively, and under precise conditions, given responsibilities. As it stood, the consent of four provinces and the federal Parliament was necessary, which in effect prevented any bilateral agreement between Québec and Ottawa. The principle of dualism had been supplanted.

The central issue for Québec, however, was not the amending formula, but rather the overhaul of the constitution and a new division of powers.[10] Faced with the prospect of a provincial election, Lesage could not consent to proposals that would run against growing nationalist and autonomist sentiments in the province. Lesage refused to consider repatriation or an amending formula unless this was combined with a clear definition of Québec's powers and responsibilities, as well as the protection of the French language and culture. He thus established the framework that would guide the demands by future Québec governments in discussions concerning constitutional reform.

Afraid of being outflanked by Daniel Johnson of the *Union National* and pressured by the progressive wing within his party, Lesage abandoned any discourse on the equality of provinces in favour of a particular status for Québec. While Lesage was strengthening his autonomist discourse, he also sought to influence decisions of the federal government. In the 1966 Québec budget, the government went so far as to suggest that the province should participate directly in areas of exclusive federal jurisdiction, by participating in the development and execution of fiscal, monetary, and trade policies. The federal government rejected this proposition.

The Lesage government was resolute in pushing for reform, ready to risk an acrimonious relationship with Ottawa if this could enhance Québec's economic and political power and status. In 1964 the Québec government was granted control of its own public pension plan, which gave the province greater fiscal autonomy and allowed for new initiatives without authorization from Ottawa. The Québec pension plan constituted a major gain as it assisted in building the most impressive and durable public investment pool in Canada, the Caisse de dépôt et placement, the gem of Québec's financial institutions. At the time, the federal government attempted unsuccessfully to convince other provinces to follow Québec's lead, so that the latter would not appear to have obtained de facto special status.

The Union Nationale defeated the Liberals in 1966 with the slogan "Equality or independence" and would adopt the same approach with regard to federal-provincial relations, with a greater emphasis initially on nationalist discourse. By making reference to the binational character of Canada and by advancing a project based on distinct status, Premier Daniel Johnson conducted Québec to a new level. Johnson would later rely on his interpretation during the Confederation of Tomorrow Conference in the autumn of 1967, which was convened on the request of the Ontario Premier, John Robarts, who sought a solution to the Canadian malaise. Johnson wanted to obtain firm support from his colleagues, for a commitment recognizing Québec's right to a particular responsibility that would permit Québec to ensure the promotion of French-Canadian culture.

The position adopted by Johnson, and subsequently Jean-Jacques Bertrand (1968–70), tended to concur with the *Report of the Royal Commission of Inquiry on Constitutional Problems* (the Tremblay Commission 1953–1956) that the division of powers and revenues between the provinces and federal government should be based on the Québec interpretation of the British North America Act (BNAA) of 1867. In this perspective, the Union Nationale demanded limits on federal government transfer payments to individuals through pan-Canadian social programs, and complete federal withdrawal if these were run on a shared-cost basis.

Pursuing his demand for constitutional reform, and benefiting from the momentum provided by the Royal Commission of Bilingualism and Biculturalism (the Laurendeau-Dunton Commission 1963–1969), Johnson envisaged a binational solution to Canada's constitutional problems. His proposal was founded on an interpretation of the BNAA as a pact between two founding peoples. The Union Nationale, under Maurice Duplessis, in power in Québec from 1936–1939 and from 1944–1959, had already attempted to protect the division of powers of 1867 from federal encroachment. Under Johnson, the party asked for additional powers to protect francophones within Québec and to some extent those living outside of the province. These modifications were seen to be commensurate with Québec's responsibilities as the primary protector of the French-speaking community in Canada.

Despite constitutional differences, several issues were resolved during the second half of the 1960s. For example, several deals were made with Ottawa on tax revenues, and an opting-out formula was implemented. In addition, Québec started to play an important role in *la francophonie*, while an informal agreement with the federal government allowed Québec to expand the small immigration bureau established during Lesage's mandate into a legitimate department. This departure from established practice paved the way for asymmetrical federalism.

The selection of Pierre Trudeau as leader of the federal Liberal Party in April 1968 and his subsequent election as Prime Minister of Canada in June of that year would change the stakes significantly. His project of constitutional reform lead to much wrangling with the various Québec governments that would follow and, finally, to the repatriation of the constitution in spite of unanimous disagreement by the parties represented in Québec's National Assembly.

Upon his arrival, Pierre Trudeau refused to accord to Québec anything that he was not ready to concede to other member-states of the federation. This did not prevent Johnson from defending the premise that programs such as family allowances, pensions, social assistance, health services, and manpower training were the sole responsibility of the provinces. For Johnson, it was clear that the distinct character of Québec warranted bilateral arrangements between Québec and Ottawa that were not contingent upon the federal government's relations with other provinces. The spending power of the federal government was perceived as having a negative effect on the maintenance of federalism since it did not respect a watertight division of powers between the two orders of government.

Under successive governments, Québec and Ottawa did reach more formal agreements that broadened the province's responsibilities in the areas of immigration and, to a lesser extent, international relations. It should be stressed, however, that neither Ottawa nor the other provinces agreed to constitutional entrenchment of Québec's rights in these domains, conceding only the possibility of making administrative arrangements that are nothing more than reversible deals.

During the 1970s, the Québec government continued its search for greater autonomy by urging that it be given additional powers and the necessary revenues for its exercise. It is in this context that Robert Bourassa, Premier of Québec from 1970–76 and from 1984–93, developed the objectives of profitable federalism, cultural sovereignty, and later, shared sovereignty. It must be noted that Bourassa's priority was not for the entrenchment of Québec's national aspirations in the Canadian Constitution; rather, he sought a revision of the federal system that would assign Québec the requisite powers and resources needed for an affirmation of the bicultural character of Canada. At the Victoria Conference in 1971, political analysts believed that the constitutional debate would be successfully resolved under Bourassa, but the nationalist opposition forces in Québec forced him to retreat, and the agreement was never ratified. The reason given for this reversal was the imprecision of the text, particularly Article 94A, which outlined responsibilities for pensions and other social programs. For Québec, 94A was said to be a test of the extent to which its constitutional partners were willing to push for a significant change in the sharing of powers. Moreover, there was intense political pressure in Québec regarding the proposed amending formula that would have given a veto to Québec, Ontario, to the Western provinces collectively, and one to the Eastern provinces. For Québec, this signalled a vision of Canada without regard for dualism. The package deal proposed by Ottawa failed to guarantee to Québec control over cultural and social policies.

Negotiations resumed in 1975 with the federal government's suggestion that the issue of the division of powers be set aside in favour of a simple patriation with an amending formula. This implied that any discussion of a new division of powers would be the subject of future multilateral and bilateral bargaining among Québec, the other provinces, and the federal government. Ottawa recognized that in modifying the federal sharing of powers, the protection and promotion of linguistic and cultural concerns were of primary interest to Québec, and this was presented at the time as the recognition of Québec's demand for "special status."[11]

In effect, the federal government did not want to give further ammunition to the Parti Québécois, which was rapidly gaining in popularity among the Québec electorate. Québec then made public that it was prepared to accept this approach provided that its linguistic and cultural concerns were entrenched in the Constitution.[12] In exchange for patriation, Bourassa asked that the following provisions be included in a new Constitution: the right for Québec to veto future constitutional amendments; control of policies in the fields of education and culture in the province; the right to opt out of federal programs with compensation; a more important role in immigration, especially aspects dealing with selection and integration of immigrants into Québec society; and limits of the federal government's declaratory and spending powers in areas of provincial jurisdiction.

The federal initiative was accompanied by a threat of unilateral patriation by Ottawa, without the consent of the provinces, prompting the Premier of Québec to call an early election in the fall of 1976. The PQ assumed power on 15 November 1976 with a program of sovereignty-association. Under René Lévesque, the PQ government was committed to acquiring full political sovereignty, accompanied by an economic association (later replaced by the notion of economic union) between Québec and the rest of Canada. The election of an autonomist government under Lévesque in Québec did not change the federal government's inclination to push for the patriation of the Constitution with an amending formula.

In the meantime, the Pepin-Robarts Task Force had received a mandate from the government of Pierre Trudeau to work towards "the elaboration of the means aimed at the reinforcement of Canadian unity."[13] In Pierre Trudeau's estimation, this entailed a centralization of powers to Ottawa. The conclusions of the Pepin-Robarts report rested on three elements: the existence of different regions, the predominance of two cultures, and equality of the two orders of government. The main thrust of the proposed changes was the institutionalization of asymmetrical federalism, which implies that all provinces are not equal, nor are they the same. While avoiding a *de jure* special status for Québec, Québec's special relationship with the rest of Canada was said to be *de facto,* recognized in the arrangements that had been offered to all provinces but in which Québec had been the only participant. The Québec Pension Plan is the most potent example. This recognition of special status and asymmetry was extended to language, with the contention that each province had the right to determine provincial language policy.

Major institutional innovations included proposals for reforming the Senate, an expanded Supreme Court, and the abolition of certain antiquated federal powers, such as the powers of disallowance and reservation. The task force proposed the replacement of the Senate by a Council of the Federation entirely composed of delegates nominated by the provinces. Moreover, seats based on proportional representation would be added to the House of Commons in order to obtain a more equitable representation of political parties. In the area of justice, expanding and dividing the Supreme Court into specialized "benches" designed to address deficiencies in the ability of the courts to rule in various jurisdictions was also among the proposals. Finally, concurrency was proposed for federal declaratory, spending, and emergency powers. In an attempt to reconcile western alienation and Québec nationalism, the task force tackled the issues of provincial autonomy, provincial control over language policy, representation of provincial interests in Ottawa, as well as the status of Québec within the federation.

Failing to deliver the report desired by Trudeau, the task force nevertheless permitted the federal authorities to gain precious time by giving the federal government the possibility of engaging itself simultaneously in the elaboration of its reform project, an initiative set aside during the Québec election in November 1976. Ottawa could then kill two birds with one stone. On the one hand, the political strategists let it be believed that reconciliation could be possible in response to the expectations of the member-states of the federation and, on the other, they were preparing their intended reply by elaborating Bill C-60: A Time for Action. The origins of a Plan A and Plan B approach were emerging.[14]

In 1978, Ottawa introduced Bill C-60, the Constitutional Amendment Bill, containing terms very similar to those of the 1971 Victoria formula. The Bill included intrastate modifications that would strengthen provincial representation at the federal level, as well as a Charter of Rights and Freedoms (which was conceived at the time as an "opt-in" arrangement for the provinces!). According to Bill C-60, these transformations would have involved replacing the Senate with a House of the Federation, with half of its proposed 118 members selected by provincial assemblies and the other half selected by the House of Commons. This would have been accompanied by an entrenched representation of Québec in the Supreme Court, with the right to name three judges. In addition, the ability of the House of the Federation to veto changes to language legislation could be reduced to a 60 day suspensive veto, but could be overturned with the support of two-thirds of the House of Commons.[15]

In a reference decision in 1979, the Supreme Court of Canada ruled that the Parliament of Canada was not empowered to modify itself in a manner that might affect the provinces. The Court argued that despite the power of amendment in Section 91(1), the House of the Federation, in substituting for the Senate, was affecting an institution that was of interest to the provinces.[16]

The Québec government showed no interest in this new initiative, as it was in the process of preparing its own White Paper, *Québec-Canada: A New Deal* (1979), which argued for the formation of "two communities" where nine provinces would reconstitute Canada and the tenth, that is Québec, would exist as a separate state, on a political level, but would remain tied to Canada in the form of a new economic union. From Québec's perspective, the sovereignty-association option had the advantage of dealing directly with the enduring issue of duality, whereas in the rest of the country it was perceived as ignoring the emerging equality of provinces principle, increasingly popular among less populated provinces outside central Canada.

In May 1979, Canada elected its first Conservative government since 1968. Prime Minister Joe Clark was more disposed than Trudeau towards an acceptance of decentralized federalism, expressed in the conception of Canada as a "community of communities," which was favourable to more harmonious Québec-Canada relations. At the time, Canada was experiencing both a debilitating economic recession and a continuing constitutional crisis. Despite the change in the federal position, the Québec government under René Lévesque remained committed to holding a referendum on sovereignty-association. Then, unexpectedly, the cards were re-shuffled. The Conservative minority government was forced to call an election and the Trudeau Liberals returned to power in February 1980 with a renewed desire to crush the "separatists" and demonstrated little interest in finding solutions to Québec's claims.

During the 1980 referendum campaign, Trudeau challenged Québec "independentists" and sent his Québec-based ministers to campaign for the "No" forces. The Trudeau Liberals had promised that defeat of the referendum would not be interpreted as an endorsement of the status quo, promising to elaborate policies that would respond to Québec's special needs and concerns. Many supporters of this option during the referendum campaign were made to believe that renewed federalism meant an official recognition of Québec as a distinct society/people, and that new powers commensurate with this position would be given to Québec. One will remember that federalists of different persuasions had rallied around Pierre Elliott Trudeau to defeat Québec's claim for sovereignty-association as a new option. Québec's federal MPs, in an ultimate attempt to convince Québecers to vote against the PQ's proposal for independence, claimed that they were putting their seats on the line. This was generally believed to demonstrate the genuine desire of the federal government to accommodate Québec culturally and linguistically.

In 1981, the federal government repatriated the constitution without the consent of Québec. Instead of being granted special recognition, Québec was weakened by the federal order. The move was repudiated in Québec by both federalists and nationalists active on the provincial political scene, including those federalists who sided with Trudeau in May 1980. These federalists felt a sense of betrayal. Trudeau's victory turned sour as opinion leaders who once fought for the federalist cause (such as Claude Ryan, Robert Bourassa, and the business community at large) called for corrective measures to be implemented rapidly in order to keep Canada together.

This episode reveals that the federal government, contrary to what it had promised during the referendum campaign of May 1980, had interpreted the results favouring the federalist option (40 per cent for the "yes" option) as an indication that Québecers desired to remain within the federation, rather than as a mandate for its renewal. Ottawa's stance towards Québec became uncompromising since the so-called "separatists" were deemed to be disorganized and demoralized. Trudeau challenged provincialism and decentralization as outdated principles, and proposed a centralist vision. The PQ was in disarray, the Québec Liberal Party had fought a tough campaign against independence along with Ottawa, the Trudeau Liberals had a majority government, the state of the economy was abysmal, and a neo-liberal ideology was gaining support.

Trudeau lost no time after the referendum and planned a constitutional conference for September 1980. Afraid of a possible unilateral move by Ottawa if talks failed, Québec was busy forging alliances with other provinces. The federal government persisted by introducing, on 2 October 1980, a "Proposed Resolution for Address to Her Majesty the Queen Respecting the Constitution of Canada." Québec and seven other provinces — the Gang of Eight — opposed such action, preparing reference cases in the Québec, Manitoba, and Newfoundland Courts of Appeal that proved disappointing for the provincial forces. Ultimately, the case reached the Supreme Court of Canada, which reached a majority decision. Richard Simeon and Ian Robinson summarize the decision as follows:

> [I]t would be legal for Parliament to act without provincial consent, but that this would still be unconstitutional since it would breach an established convention of substantial provincial consent. . . . Provinces had been warned that if they continued to delay action, Ottawa might

move. The only way out was to return to the intergovernmental table. But now there was a critical difference: the convention, said the Court, did not mean unanimity; it required only "substantial consent." Two provinces was clearly not "substantial consent," but one province could no longer stop the process. The groundwork for a settlement without Québec had been laid.[17]

Taking advantage of these circumstances, a constitutional conference was called by Trudeau for November 1981. With the support of the Québec National Assembly and seven provincial Premiers (Ontario and New Brunswick excepted), Premier Lévesque expressed opposition to the central government's plans to reform and patriate the constitution unilaterally. Initially, and strategically, Lévesque agreed to the principle of provincial equality. At the same time, he continued to oppose patriation in the absence of agreement on an amending formula and a new division of powers, demanded that Québec be recognized as a culturally and linguistically distinct society, and asked for the responsibilities and resources that this implied. In return for Québec's acceptance of the equality of provinces notion, the premiers accepted Québec's veto right.

Opposing any form of special status, Trudeau isolated Québec. On 5 November 1981, in the absence of Premier Lévesque, the other premiers agreed to patriation and the entrenchment of a Charter of Rights and Freedoms. With agreement came their preferred amending formula[18] and the right to opt out of the secondary provisions of the Charter. The opting-out (or "notwithstanding") clause ensured the western premiers' support of the package deal. Québec was isolated, with no other course of action but to make use of the notwithstanding clause, which it did systematically until the election of the Québec Liberals in December 1985. The decision to patriate with an entrenched Charter of Rights and Freedoms proved to be a major assault on Québec's vision of federalism in an environment that was growing increasingly hostile to any protective measures. According to most centralist federalists, time would heal everything.[19]

This period of transition that began in the early 1960s with the firm desire to have Québec included as a fundamental element of the Canadian federation proceeds on a note of exclusion, isolation, and the refusal of recognition. During this time, the Canadian constitutional order has been reconsidered without Québec's demands being satisfied.

THE ESTABLISHMENT OF A NEW CONSTITUTIONAL ORDER: 1982 TO THE PRESENT

The imposition of a new constitutional order in 1982 constitutes a break with continuity and disregards the dualist vision as a defining element of the Canadian federation. According to the political philosopher James Tully, the imposition of this new constitutional order has resulted in a situation in which Québec is not free within the Canadian federation for at least three reasons:

1. Other member states of the federation can impose constitutional amendments without its consent;
2. The content of the amending formula, introduced in 1982, renders it virtually impossible, in practice, to amend the Constitution so that Québec be recognized as a nation;

To these two reasons, Tully adds a third following the decision in August 1998 by the Supreme Court on the right of Québec to secede:

3. The Court maintains that phase two of the negotiations, initiated by the attainment of a clear majority in a referendum, subject to a clear question, must be framed in terms of the present amending formula. Therefore, due to the first reason mentioned above,

Québec is not bound by this amending formula. Moreover, since Québec's right to initiate constitutional changes is impeded in practice, this phase of negotiations would conclude in an impasse and according to the Court itself, this injustice would legitimize Québec's position of claiming the right to secede unilaterally. Finally, every demand of recognition as a nation . . . implies as a corollary a demand for an amendment to the present amending formula.[20]

The fact that Québec is bound to the present amending formula, which it contests, implies in fact that its rights to propose constitutional changes are not recognized and that its sense of liberty has been unquestionably persecuted. A more in-depth discussion of the decision of the Supreme Court will be provided below.

The Constitution of 1982 has thus resulted in a reduction of democratic space by denying Québec a central place in the Canadian federation. This provided some motivation for the Conservatives of Brian Mulroney, following an election victory in September 1984, to identify a new path to repatriation and reintegrate Québec into the constitutional family with "honour and enthusiasm." Responding to this policy with friendly overtures, René Lévesque decided to re-enter the constitutional fray and spoke of the new situation as representing a "beau risque" for Québec.[21] In May 1985, Lévesque presented the new federal Prime Minister with a "Draft Agreement on the Constitution"[22] that embodied 22 claims made by Québec to settle the constitutional crisis.

These propositions would essentially be re-visited in the constitutional position adopted by Robert Bourassa upon his election victory in Québec in December 1985. The differences were more a question of degree than of kind. The *Péquiste* project, therefore, would serve as a point of departure for the Liberals in the negotiations that followed.[23] It must be noted that between 1981 and 1985, Lévesque, having lost the referendum in May 1980, negotiated from a position of weakness. This changed somewhat when Bourassa, a bona fide federalist, returned as Premier of Québec. The Québec Liberals limited their bottom-line demands to five, as a minimal condition to return to the negotiating table: (1) the explicit recognition of Québec as a distinct society; (2) increased power to Québec in immigration regarding recruitment, administration, and integration of new arrivals; (3) appointment of three Supreme Court judges with expertise in Québec civil law; (4) containment of the federal spending power, and; (5) a full veto for Québec on any new modifications to be made to the Canadian constitution.

The Meech Lake proposals (1987–1990) attempted to deal with most of these claims but failed due, on the one hand, to a lack of openness to difference on the part of the Canadian partners, and on the other, to a reform process (amending formula) that ignored Québec's view of Canadian dualism, as a principal founding partner of the Canadian federation. For Ottawa, the Meech Lake Accord reflected a constant preoccupation with uniformity as an operational principle of Canadian federalism, except for the distinct society clause. By providing all the other provinces that which had been granted to Québec, Ottawa could remove any impression of giving Québec a special status. In turn, the federal government would have obtained a major concession from Québec, as it was willing to recognize for the first time the federal spending power in spheres of exclusive provincial jurisdiction. In Québec, the federal spending power has always been viewed as a federal intrusion, and its acceptance by the Québec government led to great disenchantment among autonomists and nationalists. In the rest of Canada, many observers believed that the distinct society clause would seriously weaken the federal government, for the reason that those provinces choosing not to participate in pan-Canadian programs would be afforded the possibility of opting out with full financial compensation.

As the Meech Lake negotiations began, other interests organized with the aim of defeating Québec's vision of federalism. In the process, Québec's claims became secondary and were depicted as a threat to the rights of First Nations, the equality of provinces and the universality of social programs. The provincial elections of Manitoba, New Brunswick, and Newfoundland provided a platform for leaders to appeal to anti-Québec sentiments. This signalled the failure of the Meech Lake Accord.

Following the failure of the Meech Lake Accord in June 1990, the government of Québec no longer had a mandate to negotiate its reinsertion into the Canadian federation. This resulted in the Québec Liberal party's elaboration of a new policy platform (the Allaire Report) and convinced the Québec government to set up the Commission on the Political and Constitutional Future of Québec (the Bélanger-Campeau Commission). The mandate of this Commission was for a new definition of the political and constitutional arrangements that determined the status of Québec and its relations with other member-states of the federation. This constitutes a unique moment in Canadian history. A province, through its governing party and with the full backing of the official opposition, decided to assess the appropriateness of its continued association with the rest of the country of which it was a founding member, reviving the 1981 unanimity that had condemned unilateral patriation of the BNA Act without Québec's consent.

Following the tabling of the Bélanger-Campeau Report that recommended the setting up of two special National Assembly committees, Bill-150 was enacted to confirm such a proposal. The Québec government intended to maintain pressure on the other governments (provincial and federal) with these two public forums, by forcing a confrontation with the questions of renewed federalism and sovereignty on a daily basis. As a result, the Commission asked that a referendum on the future of Québec in Canada be held no later than 26 October 1992.

In an attempt to regain the initiative, on 24 September 1991, Ottawa released a discussion paper to propose, against all expectations, a restructured federation along the lines of a centralized economic model, and set up a joint Parliamentary Committee (Castonguay-Dobbie, and later Dobbie-Beaudoin) to once more examine the perennial issue of Québec's relations with the rest of Canada.

Contrary to all expectations, the federal government and the nine anglophone provinces reached a consensus on 7 July 1992. The essence of the deal was later confirmed in the 28 August 1992 Consensus Report on the Constitution (Charlottetown Accord). Far from recognizing Québec's distinct status in Canada, and proceeding towards a devolution of powers, the agreement proposed an increase of powers for the central government through the constitutionalization of its spending power, and the strengthening of federal institutions. Instead of transferring powers to the provinces, as has been demanded by Québec, the Charlottetown Accord proposed to make room for the provinces in the Senate and to consolidate the powers of the federal government to intervene in spheres of exclusive provincial jurisdiction. The Accord also included a "Canada clause" that gave equal weight to the distinct society clause, the equality of provinces principle, and the obligation for Canadians and their governments to promote Québec's anglophone minority. Moreover, a major section of the proposed accord dealt with Aboriginal rights to self-government.

The Accord was soundly defeated in Québec (56.7 per cent), as it was in Manitoba (61.6 per cent), in Saskatchewan (55.3 per cent), in Alberta (60.2 per cent), in British Columbia (68.3 per cent), in Nova Scotia (51.3 per cent) and in the Yukon (56.3 per cent). In addition, the Accord was rejected by Aboriginal communities throughout the country, to the great disappointment of the Chief of the Assembly of First Nations, Ovide Mercredi, whose leadership was shaken.

The defeat of the Charlottetown Accord constituted an unprecedented dismissal of the political class, as Canadians throughout the country said No to a package deal cobbled behind closed doors. Defeat also represented a major setback for Robert Bourassa who, according to his closest constitutional advisors, had "caved in" as he failed to defend Québec's traditional demands and political *acquis*. The Québec Premier did not secure even the five minimal conditions of the Meech Lake proposals that were to be met before Québec would agree to re-enter formal constitutional negotiations. In short, Québec had made no gains in the sharing of powers, and saw the centralization of power as being further ensconced, since the federal government could negotiate five-year reversible deals with individual provinces. Moreover, Ottawa confirmed and potentially reinforced its capabilities of intervention in areas of exclusive provincial jurisdiction. It is in this context that the more nationalist wing of the Québec Liberal Party would leave the party to form, under the leadership of Jean Allaire and later Mario Dumont, the *Action Démocratique du Québec*.

The consequences of the failure of the Charlottetown Accord were major for the federal Conservatives in that, having almost achieved reform earlier in their mandate, they were virtually wiped off the map in the 25 October 1993 elections. Québecers also voted in large numbers for the Bloc Québecois, as the party made impressive inroads by winning 54 of the 75 seats in Québec to form Her Majesty's Loyal Opposition in Ottawa. A nationalist party from Québec now occupied a strategic place within the House of Commons itself and could more effectively push for Québec's demands. The victory of the Parti Québecois in the 12 September 1994 election followed, and Jacques Parizeau, strengthened by the presence of the Bloc as an ally of Québec in Ottawa, pursued his intentions in favour of Québec sovereignty.

On the federal side, the governing party of Jean Chrétien proceeded, as though the national question in Québec was of interest to no one, to engage in a major reform project in the area of social programs. The best way to achieve this end was to significantly cut the lifeblood of the provinces, accomplished in February 1995 by the ratification of Bill C-76 that cut transfers to the provinces by a third, by six billion dollars over two years, in the field of health.[24]

It is in this context that a project of sovereignty, based on an economic and eventually a political partnership, was proposed as a solution to deal with the constitutional impasse in terms of Québec's position within the federation. The second referendum in 15 years was called on 30 October 1995, asking Québecers to determine their political future. Unlike the outcome of the 1980 referendum, which saw the No forces gain nearly 60 per cent of the vote, this campaign resulted in 50.6 per cent for the No camp. Moreover, 49.4 per cent of Québecers endorsed the option of sovereignty-partnership with a view to establishing a new political entity in Québec free to negotiate a new economic and political union with its partners.[25] A slim margin of 54,288 votes separated the two camps, and the referendum signalled somewhat of a victory for democracy, as 94 per cent of registered voters exercised their right to vote.

Reticent as always to any form of accommodation with regards to Québec, Prime Minister Chrétien preferred to maintain the constitutional status quo. In justifying such inertia, Chrétien referred to the notion that citizens were "fed up" with constitutional issues and that their immediate concerns related to more pressing matters of unemployment and the economy. With a certain urgency, and mostly to give the impression that it understood Québec's demands for political recognition, the Chrétien government adopted, by a simple statute, a resolution affirming the distinct character of Québec society within Canada, on December 11, 1995. Furthermore, on 2 February 1996, the federal government added a new obstacle to constitutional reform by superimposing a regional veto right to four territorial groups, consisting of Québec, Ontario, Western Canada, and the Atlantic provinces, onto the provisions already in the Canadian Constitution.[26] These veto rights are not guaranteed constitutionally, as they could be withdrawn following the adoption of a parliamentary statute.

In the same spirit, Ottawa and the Canadian provinces drafted the Calgary Declaration[27] on 14 February 1997, after public consultation among the Canadian population, and reiterated certain principles on which Canadian unity would be based. Having recognized the unique character of Québec society among a large array of conditions so as to undermine its significance, the signatories rejected all forms of asymmetrical federalism and agreed to prioritize one of the jurisdictions exclusive to the provinces, the performance of social programs. Moreover, they agreed that the declaration constitutes a framework for public consultation meant to reinforce the Canadian federation. The door was open for Ottawa to engage Canadians in a project for a social union, a project that had been in the works since the Charlottetown Accord.

The federal regime, notwithstanding a brief period of hesitation under the government of the federal Conservatives from 1984–1993, continued its assault on any form of provincial autonomy and chose to reinforce the new constitutional order of 1982 by establishing the rules of the game on its own. The re-election of a majority Liberal government in 1997, as well as in 2000, would contribute to making the task easier. The approach was simple: if the provinces did not collaborate in the direction desired by Ottawa, their transfers would be cut. The re-election of a sovereigntist majority government in Québec in 1998 did not put an end to the constitutional debates. Moreover, the fact that the provincial Liberals under the leadership of Jean Charest fell short of winning the 1998 election, yet still managed to garner more votes than the Parti Québecois, significantly limited the power of the governing party.

More recent years have been characterized by confrontations between Québec and the federal government. With a strong electoral victory in 1997, the Chrétien government engaged in a full frontal assault on Québec's right to secede. The responses obtained following the Reference case regarding the secession of Québec were not entirely expected by the federal government. Attempting to re-establish the principle of continuity in constitutional discourse, the Supreme Court recognized, as the very basis of the Canadian federation, four main principles: (1) federalism, (2) democracy, (3) constitutionalism and the primacy of law, and (4) the respect for minorities. The Supreme Court underlined, in Sections 84 and 85 of its ruling, that a constitutional modification could permit a province to secede. The Court contends in paragraph 87 that "the results of a referendum have no direct role or legal effect in our constitutional scheme,

> [but] . . . it would confer legitimacy on the efforts of the government of Québec to initiate the Constitution's amendment process in order to secede by constitutional means."[28]

If the repatriation of the Constitution in 1982 undermined Québec's liberty of action, as James Tully contends, the Court Ruling allows for some corrective measures. Paragraph 88 constitutes the Gordian knot,

> The clear repudiation by the people of Québec of the existing constitutional order would confer legitimacy on demands for secession, and place an obligation on the other provinces and the federal government to acknowledge and respect that expression of democratic will by entering into negotiations and conducting them in accordance with the underlying constitutional principles . . .

The ruling of the Supreme Court allows for the possibility of relations between Québec and Canada to be more open, for the re-vitalization to some extent of the democratic foundations of the Canadian federation, and paves the way for a possible return to the principle of continuity. The Court stresses that the obligation to negotiate with Québec remains an inalienable right. In paragraph 92, the ruling contends, with some interest, that

> The rights of other provinces and the federal government cannot deny the right of the government of Québec to pursue secession, should a clear majority of the people of Québec choose that goal, so long as in doing so, Québec respects the rights of others.

Contrary to repatriation in 1982, which discredited the Supreme Court in the eyes of many Québecers, the Reference Regarding the Secession of Québec has to some extent restored its credibility. James Tully concurs,

> The condition of liberty of a multinational society rests on the fact that its members remain free to initiate discussions and negotiations with regards to possible amending formulas to the structure of recognition in place and, as a corollary, the other members have the *obligation* to respond to those legitimate demands. A member that seeks recognition as a nation (in a form that is itself open to objection) is free to the extent that the possibilities for discussions, negotiations and amendments are not impeded, in practice, by arbitrary constraints. The Constitution of a society that endures such obstructions can be likened to a strait-jacket or a structure of domination. This situation of an absence of liberty is revealed, in Canada, as much by the case of Québec as that of the First Nations.[29]

What is the situation in Canada? Both the Aboriginal nations and the Québec nation are confronted with situations of domination. The repatriation of the Constitution has led Québec into an era of subjection in terms of its political liberty and the imposition of a new constitutional order.

Without delving deeply into the Clarity Bill (C-20) . . . it is worth noting that we are under an imposition of arbitrary measures by the federal government. This law, to some extent, undercuts the Ruling of the Supreme Court with regards to Québec's right to secede and undermines any desire for constitutional negotiations that Québec may want to pursue.

The re-election of the federal Liberals in the autumn of 2000 and the selection of Bernard Landry to replace Lucien Bouchard as leader of the Québec government in May 2001 did not bode well for any rapprochement between Québec and Canada in the near future. Moreover, while Québec persists in demonstrating that Canadian federalism is a façade, Ottawa continues to undermine the federal condition[30] pertaining to the non-subordination of powers by substituting for them a set of principles that do not take account of Canadian diversity, by imposing an increasing amount of constraining and homogenizing public policies, thus rendering any significant reforms to the federation illusory. Truly helpful reforms would respond to the fundamental expectations of Quebecers with regard to their diversity and would affirm a legitimate context for real choice, which would be supported comprehensively by Quebecers.

CONCLUSION

The federal elections in autumn 2000 have not provided any reason for optimism with regard to the re-establishment of constitutional peace in Canada. The Liberals of Jean Chrétien, having succeeded in securing a majority government for the third consecutive time, feel little urgency in proceeding towards constitutional modifications that would accommodate Québec's demands. It is, therefore, no great surprise that the federal ministers reacted to the recent political program of the Québec Liberal Party, Un projet pour le Québec. Affirmation, autonomie et leadership (2001) with a simple mention that this party did not exercise power in Québec, therefore it did not merit any commentary.

The Canadian condition reduces Québec to merely a province like the others within the federation, which is far from corresponding to the image that Québec projects for itself here as well as on the international scene. Rupturing the founding constitutional order, Québec-Canada relations after repatriation in 1982 have entered a phase of non-recognition and the impoverishing of democratic practices. The ruling of the Supreme Court concerning Québec's right to secede served to widen the realm of the possible, only to be confined and limited by the federal government, which evidently sought to impede the holding of a fundamental debate on the future of the federation.

By constantly ignoring constitutional conventions and denying the existence of the Québec nation, the potential of the government to forge a symbol of identity and to mobilize politically remains doubtful. In short, the Canadian federal experience is not worth pursuing unless the member-states are free to adhere to the federation and all structures of domination are condemned.

NOTES

1. The comments of Andrée Lajoie were very useful in the recasting of this text.
2. See the Commission sur le déséquilibre fiscal, *Pour un nouveau partage des moyens financiers au Canada* (Commission Séguin) (Québec: Bibliothèque nationale du Québec, 2002).
3. See Gérard Bouchard, "La vision siamoise de John Saul," *Le Devoir*, 15 and 17 Jan. 2000; John Saul, "Il n'y a pas de peuple conquis," *Le Devoir*, 22 and 24 Jan. 2000.
4. Hilda Neatby, *The Québec Act: Protest and Policy* (Scarborough: Prentice Hall, 1972); Philip Lawson, *The Imperial Challenge: Québec and Britain in the Age of the American Revolution* (Montreal: McGill-Queen's University Press, 1989).
5. Garth Stevenson, *Community Besieged: The Anglophone Minority and the Politics of Québec* (Montreal: McGill-Queen's University Press, 1999), ch. 2.
6. Thomas-Jean-Jacques Loranger, *Lettres sur l'interprétation de la constitution fédérale: premiere lettre* (Québec: Imprimerie A. Côté et Cie, 1883).
7. Royal Commission on Aboriginal Peoples (RCAP), *Partners in Confederation: Aboriginal Peoples, Self-Government and the Constitution* (Ottawa: Minister of Supply and Services, 1993), 22–23.
8. Every federal party has at one time or another in that decade recognized the concept of two founding peoples as a fundamental principle of the federation. This recognition, however, would vary in significance in the decades that followed.
9. The doctrine recognized and defended the right of provinces to negotiate agreements with international actors or organizations in their fields of jurisdiction.
10. Ironically, Québec accepted the principle of unanimity in 1980 in a last-ditch effort to block the repatriation project proposed by Ottawa.
11. Garth Stevenson, *Unfulfilled Union: Canadian Federalism and National Unity* (Toronto: Gage, 1982), 210.
12. Pierre Elliott Trudeau, "1976 Correspondence to all Provincial Premiers," in Peter Meekison, ed., *Canadian Federalism: Myth or Reality* (Toronto: Methuen, 1977), 140–67.
13. The Task Force on Canadian Unity, *Se retrouver. Observations et recommandations*, vol. 1 (Pepin-Robarts Report) (Ottawa: Official Editor, 1979), 143. Author's translation.
14. This consists of two approaches aimed at "resolving once and for all" the question of Québec: a conciliatory approach and a coercive one following the victory of the PQ in 1994 and the results obtained (nearly 50 per cent of the votes) during the referendum in 1995. We can refer with much interest to the work of the jurist Daniel Turp, notably his work, *La nation bâillonnée: le plan B ou l'offensive d'Ottawa contre le Québec* (Montreal: VLB éditeur, 2000).
15. Douglas Verney, *Three Civilizations, Two Cultures, One State, Canada's Political Traditions* (Durham: Duke University Press, 1986), 367.
16. According to Douglas Verney, the Court supported its decision with the federal White Paper, published in 1965, which recognized the "role of the provinces, even for modifications touching questions that were not exclusive to jurisdictions of the provinces." Author's translation, Verney, *Three Civilizations*, 367.
17. Richard Simeon and Ian Robinson; *State, Society and the Development of Canadian Federalism* (Toronto: University of Toronto Press, 1990), 278.
18. The principal amending formula provided for constitutional changes to be undertaken with the support of seven provinces covering 50 per cent of the Canadian population. The reform of the amending formula was subject to unanimity. This situation was imposed on Québec, which from that moment on had to abide by rules adopted by others, losing all liberty of action in this area.
19. If one is to believe the events that surrounded the celebrations organized by the federal government to mark 20 years of repatriation, in April 2002, federal strategists have not yet regretted their actions, even though the referendum of October 1995 could potentially have represented a fateful moment for the country.

20. James Tully, "Liberté et dévoilement dans les sociétés plurinationales," *Globe*, 2, 2 (1999): 31–32. Author's translation. Also, for a larger analysis, see James Tully, "Introduction," in Alain-G. Gagnon and James Tully, eds., *Multinational Democracies* (Cambridge: Cambridge University Press, 2001) 1–33.

21. For a recent political analysis, see Michel Vastel, "La Charte a 20 ans: Des promesses plusieurs fois repudiées," *Le Soleil*, 17 April 2002, A-6.

22. This document was largely inspired by a document prepared by the Ministry of Intergovernmental Affairs during the first mandate of the PQ government. See *Les positions constitutionnelles du Québec sur le partage des pouvoirs (1960–76)* (Québec: Éditeur officiel du Québec, 1978). For document updated to March 2001, see www.mce.gouv.qc.ca.

23. Before arriving to power, the provincial Liberals had prepared a series of documents that discussed questions for which compromises would have to be negotiated. See *Une nouvelle constitution canadienne*, (1980), also known as the Livre Beige, *Un nouveau leadership pour le Québec*, (1983), and *Maîtriser l'avenir* (1985).

24. See Alain-G. Gagnon and Hugh Segal, "Introduction," in *The Canadian Social Union Without Québec; 8 Critical Analyses* (Montreal: Institute for Research on Public Policy, 2000).

25. Alain-G. Gagnon and Guy Lachapelle, "Québec Confronts Canada: Two Competing Societal Projects Searching for Legitimacy," *Publius*, 26, 3, (1996): 177–91.

26. This indicated to specialists on the issue that the constitutional path had been closed. See Robert Dutrisac, "Une camisole de force," *Le Devoir*, 14 April 2002, G-7.

27. http://www.ccu-cuc.ca/fran/dossiers/calgary.html.

28. *Reference re Secession of Québec*, 2 S.C.R., 1998.

29. James Tully "Liberté et dévoilement dans les sociétés plurinationales," 30. Author's translation.

30. Donald Smiley *The Federal Condition in Canada* (Toronto: McGraw-Hill, 1987).

Topic Fifteen

Entering the 21st Century

The Canadarm2 (Space Station Remote Manipulator System) is a critical component of the orbiting International Space Station.

As Canada enters the 21st century, it faces a number of challenges whose origins extend back into the 19th and 20th centuries. History helps to understand how we got to this point in time; it is hoped history also provides some guidelines for the future.

The following three articles deal with three current issues certain to continue as major concerns into the 21st century. In "Aboriginal Peoples in the Twenty-first Century: A Plea for Realism," political scientist Alan C. Cairns provides a tempered discussion on how Aboriginal and non-Aboriginal peoples might live together in the future. In the first half of the paper, he looks at the historical evolution of Aboriginal and non-Aboriginal relations in Canada as context for studying the current situation, emphasizing that the White Paper of 1969 unintentionally inaugurated a new era in terms of the federal government's approach to Aboriginal peoples. A policy of paternalism gave way to a new era in which the federal government recognized Aboriginal rights. Cairns sees this paradigm shift as the Canadian equivalent of the end of colonialism in the overseas territories of the former European empires. The transition was marked by the substitution of the concept of Indians as "wards of the state" to be governed by others as evident in Section 91 (24) of the British North America Act of 1867 with that of "aboriginal peoples of Canada" in Section 35(2) of The Constitution Act of 1982 with their own rights, including the right to self-government. The transition is also evident in the important change in terminology from "Indians" to "First Nations" as the form of identification. He notes, however, that the term "First Nations" should not be construed to mean independence but rather the recognition of an autonomous people *within* Canada. Cairns argues that this new status offers two roads to the future: self-government through reserves, and the urban route. He explores both alternatives and the implications for Aboriginal and non-Aboriginal Canadians.

Political scientist Reg Whitaker looks at Canadian politics at the end of the 20th century and the implication for the new millennium in "Canadian Politics at the End of the Millennium: Old Dreams, New Nightmares." He begins by sketching out the familiar pattern of Canadian politics from 1867 to the 1990s with three ideologies — conservatism, liberalism, and socialism — represented by three parties, the Conservatives that dominated from 1867 to 1896, the Liberals that dominated the 20th century, and the New Democratic Party that emerged in the 1930s. But in the Canada of the 1990s, he argues, the old familiar narrative has undergone dramatic change, due to a number of new forces. He focuses on two of these forces: "(1) the economic challenges summed up in the issues of 'globalization' and the 'fiscal' or 'debt' crisis of the state; and (2) the challenge that the threat of Quebec separation poses to the fundamental nature of the Canadian political community."

The issue of Canadian sovereignty and security in the Canadian North is the subject of political scientist Rob Huebert's article, "Climate Change and Canadian Sovereignty in the Northwest Passage." Huebert argues that global warming especially in the polar North has serious implications for Canadian control of the Northwest Passage. He explores the implications in terms of the traditional historical argument, the attempt to enclose the Canadian Arctic Archipelago by straight baselines, and the claim that the Inuit's use of the ice in the waterway for their livelihood is the equivalent of claiming the land. The greatest challenge to Canadian sovereignty in the North today comes from the United States, Huebert claims — just as it was at the time of Confederation with the threat of American annexation of British North America.

What is the nature of the paradigm shift with regards to First Nations that occurred since the White Paper of 1969, and what is its impact on Aboriginal and non-Aboriginal relations in Canada in the 21st century? Reg Whitaker also talks about a paradigm shift in Canadian politics in the 1990s. In what ways has Canadian politics changed dramatically on the eve of the 21st century? How does global warming in the Arctic affect Canadian–American relations, and thus go to the heart of the issue of Canadian sovereignty and a Canadian identity in North America?

Recent surveys of the history of First Nations in Canada include Olive Patricia Dickason, *Canada's First Nations: A History of Founding Peoples from Earliest Times*, 3rd ed. (Don Mills, ON: Oxford University Press, 2002), and Arthur J. Ray, *I Have Lived Here since the World Began: An Illustrated History of Canada's Native People* (Toronto: Key Porter, 1996). Edward S. Rogers and Donald B. Smith, eds., *Aboriginal Ontario* (Toronto: Dundurn Press, 1994), looks at the history of the First Nations in Ontario.

For a review of Canadian Indian policy in the early 20th century see E. Brian Titley, *A Narrow Vision: Duncan Campbell Scott and the Administration of Indian Affairs in Canada* (Vancouver: University of British Columbia Press, 1986). Two important summaries of federal Indian policy can be found in Ian A.L. Getty and Antoine S. Lussier, eds., *As Long as the Sun Shines and Water Flows* (Vancouver: University of British Columbia Press, 1983); George F.G. Stanley, "As Long as the Sun Shines and Water Flows: An Historical Comment," pp. 1–26; and John L. Tobias, "Protection, Civilization, Assimilation: An Outline History of Canada's Indian Policy," pp. 39–55. J.R. Miller provides a complete account in *Skyscrapers Hide the Heavens: A History of Indian-White Relations in Canada*, 3rd ed. (Toronto: University of Toronto Press, 2000); see also Noel Dyck, *What Is the Indian "Problem"? Tutelage and Resistance in Canadian Indian Administration* (St. John's: Institute of Social and Economic Research, Memorial University of Newfoundland, 1991). Still valuable for the First Nations' perspective is Harold Cardinal, *The Unjust Society: The Tragedy of Canada's Indians*, 2nd ed. (Vancouver: Douglas and McIntyre, 2002).

For First Nations politics in the last 35 years, consult Sally M. Weaver, *Making Canadian Indian Policy: The Hidden Agenda, 1968–1970* (Toronto: University of Toronto Press, 1981); and J. Rick Ponting, ed., *Arduous Journey: Canadian Indians and Decolonization* (Toronto: McClelland & Stewart, 1986). On First Nations self-government see John H. Hylton, ed., *Aboriginal Self-Government in Canada*, 2nd ed. (Saskatoon: Purich Publishing, 1999); and Dan Smith, *The Seventh Fire: The Struggle for Aboriginal Government* (Toronto: Key Porter, 1993). An excellent source book on First Nations rights is Bradford W. Morse, ed., *Aboriginal Peoples and the Law: Indian, Métis and Inuit Rights in Canada*, rev. 1st ed. (Ottawa: Carleton University Press, 1989).

Very useful for Canadian–First Nations relations is John Bird, Lorraine Land, and Murray Macadam, eds., *Nation to Nation: Aboriginal Sovereignty and the Future of Canada* (Toronto: Irwin, 2002). Two recent contributions to the subject by political scientists are C. Cairns, *Citizens Plus: Aboriginal Peoples and the Canadian State* (Vancouver: University of British Columbia Press, 2000), and Tom Flanagan, *First Nations? Second Thoughts* (Montreal/Kingston: McGill-Queen's University Press, 2000).

On contemporary politics, see Hugh G. Thorburn and Alain Whitehorn, eds., *Party Politics in Canada*, 8th ed. (Toronto: Prentice-Hall, 2001). Excellent journalistic accounts of the Trudeau years are Stephen Clarkson and Christina McCall, *Trudeau and Our Times*, vol. 1, *The Magnificient Obsession*; vol. 2, *The Heroic Delusion* (Toronto: McClelland and Stewart, 1990, 1994); and Christina McCall Newman, *Grits: An Intimate Portrait of the Liberal Party* (Toronto: Macmillan, 1982). A variety of opinions, generally highly favourable, of Trudeau can be found in Andrew Cohen and J.L. Granatstein, eds., *Trudeau's Shadow: The Life and Legacy of Pierre Elliott Trudeau* (Toronto: Random House, 1998). Two books offer a critical dissection of the Mulroney government: Brooke Jeffrey, *Breaking Faith: The Mulroney Legacy of Deceit, Destruction and Disunity* (Toronto: Key Porter, 1992); and Linda McQuaig, *The Quick and the Dead: Brian Mulroney, Big Business and the Seduction of Canada* (Toronto: Viking, 1991). Laurence Martin looks at Jean Chrétien's years as prime minister in *Iron Man* (Toronto: Viking Canada, 2003). On the reform party, see Trevor Harrison, *Of Passionate Intensity: Right-Wing Populism and the Reform Party of Canada* (Toronto: University of Toronto Press, 1995); and Preston Manning,

Think Big (Toronto: McClelland and Stewart, 2002). The Bloc Québecois is discussed in Manon Cornellier, *The Bloc* (Toronto: James Lorimer, 1995); and Laurence Martin, *The Antagonist: Lucien Bouchard and the Politics of Delusion* (Toronto: Viking, 1997). Works on the Canadian left include John Richards, Robert Cairns, and Larry Pratt, eds., *Social Democracy without Illusions: Renewal of the Canadian Left* (Toronto: McClelland & Stewart, 1991); Alan Whithorn, *Canadian Socialism: Essays on the CCF-NDP* (Toronto: Oxford University Press, 1992); Ian McLeod, *Under Seige: The Federal NDP in the Nineties* (Toronto: James Lorimer, 1994); and James Laxer, *In Search of a New Left: Canadian Politics after the Neoconservative Assault* (Toronto: Penguin Books, 1996). Good studies on federal–provincial relations include David Milne, *Tug of War: Ottawa and the Provinces under Trudeau and Mulroney* (Toronto: James Lorimer, 1986); Garth Stevenson, *Unfilled Union: Canadian Federalism and National Unity*, 3rd ed. (Toronto: Gage, 1989); and Richard Simeon and Ian Robinson, *State, Society, and the Development of Federalism* (Toronto: University of Toronto Press, 1990). On constitutional developments, see David Milne, *The Canadian Constitution: From Patriation to Meech Lake*, new ed. (Toronto: James Lorimer, 1989).

Historical studies on the North include two volumes by Morris Zaslow: *The Opening of the Canadian North, 1870–1914* (Toronto: McClelland & Stewart, 1971), and *The Northward Expansion of Canada, 1914–1967* (Toronto: McClelland & Stewart, 1988). A good overview is William R. Morrison's *True North: The Yukon and Northwest Territories* (Toronto: Oxford University Press, 1998). Post–World War II developments in the North are reviewed in Shelagh D. Grant, *Sovereignty or Security: Government Policy in the Canadian North, 1936–1950* (Vancouver: University of British Columbia Press, 1988); Robert Page, *Northern Development: The Canadian Dilemma* (Toronto: McClelland & Stewart, 1996); and John David Hamilton, *Arctic Revolution: Social Change in the Northwest Territories, 1935–1994* (Toronto: Dundurn Press, 1994).

WEBLINKS

Delgamuukw v. British Columbia
http://www.lexum.umontreal.ca/csc-scc/en/pub/1997/vol3/html/1997scr3_1010.html
The complete Supreme Court of Canada ruling regarding the case of *Delgamuukw v. British Columbia*, which among other effects greatly strengthened the use of First Nations oral history as evidence in the Canadian legal system.

Aboriginal Canada Portal
http://www.aboriginalcanada.gc.ca
This portal links to dozens of aboriginal organizations in Canada, including the Assembly of First Nations, the Métis National Council, and the Inuit Tapiriit Kanatami.

ParlVU
http://parlvu.parl.gc.ca/parlvuen-ca
Live webcast of the Parliament of Canada and parliamentary committee meetings.

CSIS: Climate Change
http://www.csis-scrs.gc.ca/eng/comment/com86_e.html
A Canadian Security Intelligence Service publication regarding the likely causes and effects of climate change on Canada and the world.

North American Free Trade Agreement
http://www.dfait-maeci.gc.ca/nafta-alena/agree-en.asp
The complete text of the North American Free Trade Agreement (NAFTA).

Article Thirty-Six

Aboriginal Peoples in the Twenty-First Century: A Plea for Realism

Alan C. Cairns

I do not expect the arguments in this paper, especially those in the last half, to convince all who read or heard this presentation. In fact, if I fail to convince you, I may have succeeded in the much more important task of contributing to a discussion. The Aboriginal policy field has too many converts and too few discussions in which we listen to each other. Converts and discussion have an uneasy relationship: basically, each is the other's most feared opponent. At the turn of the century, converts and ideologies can look after themselves; discussion, however, needs help. Hence the following pages.

This paper has a single objective — to clarify the debate about how Aboriginal and non-Aboriginal peoples are to live together in the future. We cannot be successfully forward-looking, however, without understanding the past that has shaped us. The first half of the paper, accordingly, focusing as it does largely on the last half of the century, establishes how we got to 'now.' Now is defined as the post-1969 White Paper (Canada 1969) era, in which, I argue, there are two roads to the future — the self-government route based on Aboriginal nations and the urban route.

This is the era of Aboriginal nationalism; of Oka; of the Royal Commission on Aboriginal Peoples (RCAP); of major advances by Aboriginal peoples in the *Constitution Act*, 1982; of a huge increase in the number of Aboriginal post-secondary graduates; of the dramatic growth of the urban Aboriginal population; of the dawning recognition that Aboriginal communities, especially First Nations, are not going to disappear as believers in assimilation once thought; of the birth of Nunavut (1999); and of many other developments, most of which would have been inconceivable fifty years ago. This background underlines the reality that ours is a new era — that indeed we are creating a new Canada — and that we desperately need more understanding if we are to avoid major policy errors.

Of the many issues needing attention, I have selected the coexistence of the two roads to the future mentioned above. The last half of the paper, grandiosely subheaded "a plea for realism," tries to disentangle the issues posed by this apparent choice, to stick-handle through the claims of both the advocates and opponents of each route. I conclude that the debate is poorly conducted and that both roads will be with us for the foreseeable future. We need more information and analysis and less ideology if we are to make progress in one of the most politicized and conflict-filled policy areas on our agenda. (The paper focuses disproportionately on status Indians because neither Inuit nor Métis [with only eight small settlements in northern Alberta] confront the choice between the urban and the self-government route to the same degree.)

FROM PATERNALISM TO ABORIGINAL NATIONALISM

No dialogue between Indians and the federal government preceded the release of that government's 1969 White Paper which proposed ending the separate status of Indian people and their assimilation into Canadian society. This act of paternalism was repudiated by the organized

Source: *The Canadian Distinctiveness into the XXIst Century*, University of Ottawa Press, 2003. © University of Ottawa Press, 2003. Reprinted by permission of the University of Ottawa Press.

opposition of Indian peoples, led by the Indian Chiefs of Alberta (Indian Chiefs of Alberta 1970). The subsequent withdrawal of the White Paper was more than the defeat of a particular policy initiative. The historic federal policy of assimilation was in ruins. Since then, it has been generally assumed that Indian communities would survive as such — that they would have a distinct, ongoing communal existence in Canada (Weaver 1990). Thirty years after the White Paper's defeat, Canadians are still grappling with that new reality.

Since then, the federal government has lost or given up its leadership role. Initially, it appeared that the policy of assimilation had been cast in the dustbin of discarded experiments. For the first decade after the White Paper's withdrawal, the relevant actors repositioned themselves behind the vague consensus that assimilation, at least as a conscious policy, was dead, and that the emerging policy question was how Indian peoples — as peoples — or, as the terminology evolved, as nations — should be fitted into the Canadian constitutional order. In the period leading up to the *Constitution Act, 1982*, Inuit and Métis emerged and made independent claims for recognition and self-government. This foreshadowed the new constitutional category "Aboriginal Peoples of Canada," defined in the *Constitution Act, 1982*, s. 35(2), as including Indian, Inuit, and Métis.

Increasingly, initiatives in the broad field of Aboriginal policy came from Aboriginal organizations, particularly the National Indian Brotherhood, later renamed the Assembly of First Nations, which spoke for the legal status Indian population living on reserves. Its voice, and that of other Aboriginal organizations, was strengthened by a fortuitous convergence of factors.

The federal government policy of funding the major Aboriginal organizations — which commenced in the early 1970s, on the premise that the poverty, small populations, and geographical diffusion of Aboriginal peoples would otherwise marginalize them in democratic politics — gave them not only a voice but ultimately a unique status among the claimants for government attention. They quickly came to be much more than the standard interest group speaking for a particular clientele or cause. As the major Aboriginal associations acquired confidence, they decisively distanced themselves from the proliferating ethnic associations which represented the ethnocultural communities gathered under the official policy of multiculturalism. They represented not ethnic minorities, but nations.

The nation label gained sustenance from the opening up of the Constitution in response to Francophone nationalism in Québec, particularly following the victory of the Parti Québécois in the 1976 provincial election. This placed the question of Canada's future on the bargaining table. What kind of people were Canadians? What revised institutional arrangements and constitutional reforms were appropriate for a country increasingly separated from Europe, with an immigration policy that was transforming the face of major metropolitan centres, one that confronted a Québec nationalist challenge to its very survival, and one with indigenous peoples no longer willing to accept their marginalization? The opening up of the Constitution was quickly seen as providing an arena in which Aboriginal peoples could advance their claims for recognition, self-government, and an end to their stigmatized marginalization.

Trudeau's assertion "Everything is up for grabs" was a direct response to a reinvigorated, assertive Québec nationalism. Aboriginal peoples successfully inserted themselves into constitutional politics and made major gains in the Constitution Act, 1982. Simultaneously, their self-description as nations gathered momentum. The National Indian Brotherhood renamed itself the Assembly of First Nations. The 1983 Penner Committee, with its ringing advocacy of self-government for Indian peoples in its report, systematically employed the term nation in a clear response to the messages of Indian spokespersons who appeared before it (Canada 1983). The language of nationalism clearly added symbolic legitimacy to claims for recognition and special treatment.

This was evident in the four Aboriginal constitutional conferences, 1983 to 1987 (Schwartz 1986), primarily focusing on the inherent right of self-government. The conferences gave additional proof of, and stimulus to, the emerging distinct status of Aboriginal peoples. Aboriginal associations participated almost as bargaining equals of the federal and provincial governments on the other side of the table. Their goal was to carve out a separate category of constitutional space for the implementation of the inherent right of self-government. No other interest groups that flourished in democratic, pluralistic politics, whether representing women, disabled persons, Italian Canadians, or others, were given similar recognition.

The rhetoric surrounding the concept of nation became the standard terminology used to identify Aboriginal peoples. Indians became 'First Nations' in a clear attempt to gain historical priority and a stronger legitimacy than that of the two founding nations of French and English newcomers. The Métis also employed the self-identifying, status-raising label of nation as, to a lesser extent, did the Inuit. Perhaps, however, the most decisive indication of the status-enhancing capacity of the nation terminology was the dramatic diffusion of such self-labelling among Indian bands themselves. By 1999, about 30 per cent of over 600 Indian bands had added nation to their official name. Most of them had populations well under one thousand people (Canada 1985, 1990, 1999).

The language of nationalism changes the nature of Aboriginal policy discussions. The term nation easily, almost automatically, leads to a justification for an ongoing future existence, and therefore for the policy tools to achieve that goal. Nation attracts the supportive attention of prominent political theorists — Will Kymlicka, Sam LaSelva, Charles Taylor, Jim Tully — in a way that the term 'villages' would not. They add a certain philosophical legitimacy to Aboriginal nationalism and to the consequences that logically attach to that labelling. Nation, inevitably and desirably in the eyes of its proponents, stresses an internal within-group solidarity, while stressing the 'otherness' of the non-Aboriginal majority.

This otherness is reinforced by the widespread employment of the language of colonialism to describe the history of Aboriginal/non-Aboriginal relations from which an escape is sought. The colonial analogy is a dramatic reminder that the relation of indigenous people to the Canadian majority from the last half of the nineteenth century to the present has *always* been massively influenced by international trends — particularly the world of empire and of its ending. In the former, when a handful of European states ruled much of humanity, the wardship status of Indian peoples — their marginalization — their subjection to the demands of a majority confident of its own cultural superiority — did not have to be argued in terms of first principles — it was simply assumed. Canadian rule over indigenous peoples — most dramatically in the case of status Indians — was simply a spillover from the larger world of empire outside Canada.

The implicit international support in the imperial era for wardship for Indians, for their exclusion from the franchise until 1960, for leaving Inuit (then Eskimo) isolated and forgotten, and for the marginalization of the Métis, evaporated when empire ended. When the British left India, the French handed over power in Senegal, the Dutch lost control of Indonesia, and the Portuguese finally succumbed to exhaustion and retreated from Angola and Mozambique, the message flowing across Canadian borders no longer justified hierarchy with Aboriginal peoples at the base, whether hierarchy was conceived in cultural or racial terms.

The international system was no longer a club of white states. The Commonwealth — now a multicultural, multiracial association — contrasted dramatically with the older view of the white dominions as Britain overseas. The United Nations was transformed into a multiracial institution, with European states in a minority, after the collapse of European empires and the emergence of more than a hundred new states. The United Nations launched a crusade against colonialism and racism that inevitably challenged the legitimacy of white leadership over indigenous peoples in settler colonies — even if that leadership was dressed up in the language of trusteeship and guardianship.

We can argue, therefore, that the emergence of Aboriginal nationalism was overdetermined. It fed on the opening up of the Canadian Constitution; on the demise of European empires and the subsequent transformations in the international system; on the funding of Aboriginal associations by the federal government; on the defeat of the White Paper; and on the contagious, world-wide diffusion of nationalism among indigenous peoples. The simultaneous emergence of indigenous nationalism in Australia (Aborigines) and New Zealand (Maori) as well as in Canada, underlines the international forces at work. Those wishing to understand Aboriginal nationalism in Canada, accordingly, must look outward beyond domestic, within-Canada causes to embrace changes in the international environment. To look inwardly only at our domestic selves blinds us to the fact that indigenous peoples around the globe learn and borrow from each other. There is, in other words, an indigenous international.

The colonial analogy drawn from the international arena and the widespread diffusion of the label nation were appropriate yet, at the same time, potentially misleading. Colonialism was clearly a reasonable description of the system of alien rule and the displacement of Indian peoples onto reserves, thought of as schools for their civilization. It was somewhat less appropriate for Inuit and Métis, in that they were not subject to a separate administrative system, nor subjected to the same degree of cultural assault as Indians. On the other hand, they too were marginalized, defined as backward, and not considered to be full, ordinary citizens.

Colonialism, however, is also misleading. The end of colonialism in yesterday's world of the demise of the European empires resulted in independence. The new flag of a new country was raised, and the international community acquired a new member. The ending of colonialism in Canada, however, does not usher in independence but requires a rapprochement with the majority — the working out of arrangements that combine self-government where land-based Aboriginal communities exist with membership in the Canadian community of citizens. Colonialism focuses attention on the self-rule dimension, but it positively deflects attention from the rapprochement dimension, which requires a positive collaboration with yesterday's oppressor. Therefore, it contributes to a misunderstanding of the requirements of a workable reconciliation.

Nation is also Janus-faced. It is status-raising for those who employ it. It speaks to a positive sense of belonging and to a people's desire for a continuing future existence. For peoples whose difference has been reinforced by their treatment by the majority society, the attribution of nation is a logical if not inevitable response to their situation, especially for land-based communities. The term nation, however, can be misleading. Nation is a potent word that presupposes population sizes and self-government capacities that are beyond small populations of several hundred or several thousand people. The accompanying nation-to-nation theme, the key concept in the analysis of the RCAP report (Canada 1996), also misleads as it inevitably conjured up an image of Canada as an international system. It suggests autonomous, discrete actors bargaining the terms of their separate coexistence. If, however, "within Canada" means anything, the reality is that a part is rearranging its relationship with the whole of which it is a part. In other words, when federal and provincial governments are bargaining their future relations with an Aboriginal nation in a land claims/self-government negotiation for example, the members of the latter group are also and simultaneously represented as citizens by the federal and provincial governments. If this is not so, the whole system of voting and elections in federal and provincial politics and the receipt of standard federal and provincial services are based on a misunderstanding — an assertion that would find minimal support.

It is possible, and perhaps probable, that the leading players in public discussions realize that the language of colonialism, of nation, and of nation-to-nation in the Canadian context does not carry the same meaning and consequences in Canada as it did in Algeria or Kenya. There may be a tacit understanding on both sides of the table that these terms — colonialism, nation, and nation-to-nation — have a more limited, restricted meaning than the full sense of the words suggests. Even so, their use adds a potential element of confusion to our attempts to work out our relations with each other. The increasingly common description of Canada as a multinational country normally fails to mention that the Québec nation is some 7,000 times larger than the average Aboriginal nation proposed by the RCAP. Further, the RCAP figures — average nation size of 5,000–7,000 people — are not a current reality, but a goal that can only be achieved by aggregating small bands into larger units, a goal certain to generate considerable resistance. We cannot think clearly if we forget such realities.

Nor can we think clearly if we overlook the constitutional changes and judicial decisions that have provided indigenous peoples with constitutional support for their aspirations. The Constitution Act, 1982, declared that "The existing aboriginal and treaty rights of the aboriginal peoples of Canada are hereby recognized and affirmed," and "In this Act 'aboriginal peoples of Canada' includes the Indian, Inuit and Métis peoples of Canada," (s. 35(1) and (2)). This constitutional affirmation was, in effect, a repudiation of the original British North America Act, 1867, which in s. 91(24) simply treated Indians as a subject of federal jurisdiction, indicating that their constitutional recognition had nothing to do with their rights, but simply with which government had authority over them. Section 91(24) presupposed wards who, for their own sake, had to be governed by others. Section 35(1), by contrast, identified the rights of peoples that are to be recognized and affirmed. Section 35(2) created a new constitutional category, "aboriginal peoples of Canada," which inevitably generated pressures from the least favoured member of the category — the Métis — who achieved a constitutional recognition in 1982 they had long sought — access to state-provided, positive benefits, available to status Indian peoples. The move from s. 91(24) (1867) to s. 35 (1982), from wards to rights holders, was the domestic equivalent of the end of colonialism in the overseas territories of the former European empires. That domestic equivalent, of course, falls short of independence. The new status to which it leads is to be "within Canada."

The courts, which historically had played a limited role in affirming Aboriginal rights, made important contributions in the post-White Paper decades. Two decisions — Calder (1973) (*Calder v. AG BC*, [1973] SCR 313) and Delgamuukw (1997) (*Delgamuukw v. BC*, [1997] 3 SCR 1010) — underline the judicial contribution, which can be followed in more detail in any of the standard case books in Canadian constitutional law. In Calder, the Supreme Court dismissed an application by the Nishga (now Nisga'a) Indians of northwestern British Columbia for formal recognition of their Aboriginal title based on their immemorial occupation of the land. Six of the seven judges, however, recognized the concept of Aboriginal title, three of whom suggested that their Aboriginal title had not been extinguished. Subsequently, the Trudeau government announced a land claims policy, which is the origin of the modern land claims settlements already completed and of the many negotiations, especially in British Columbia, that are now underway.

In *Delgamuukw*, the Supreme Court confirmed that Aboriginal title existed in British Columbia and that it constitutes a right to the land itself, not just to traditional uses such as hunting. The Court also held that oral history should be included in the evidence legitimately before the Court. Both of these strands of *Delgamuukw* have profoundly transformed the treaty process in British Columbia by dramatically enhancing the bargaining resources of First Nations negotiators.

THE PERVASIVE IMPACT OF NATIONALISM

The emergence of Aboriginal nationalism and the response to it are highlighted in some of the key events of the past decade and a half listed below. This brief and elementary listing — all that space limitations allow — is neither exhaustive nor faithful to the complexities behind the events, but it will serve to underline the temper of the present era.

- The role of Elijah Harper in preventing debate on the Meech Lake Accord in the Manitoba legislature, just as the three-year ratification clock was running out in 1990, was a crucial factor in the defeat of the accord. Harper's role, backed by enthusiastic First Nations support, symbolized the willingness of First Nations — if their own demands were not met — to defeat a major constitutional effort to bring Québec back into the constitutional family with, in Prime Minister Mulroney's words, honour and enthusiasm.
- The Oka crisis of 1990, as well as other, less dramatic, indicators of frustration and anger expressed in road blocks, occupations, and demonstrations, underlined the growing tension in Aboriginal/non-Aboriginal relations.
- The massive, five-volume report of the Royal Commission on Aboriginal Peoples, released in 1996, its policy recommendations and its governing nation-to-nation theme, confirmed that the status quo was not viable. The RCAP Report is a document of Aboriginal nationalism.
- The establishment of the BC Treaty Commission in 1993, following the century-long denial by British Columbia governments that Aboriginal title was a continuing reality, suggested that even the most obdurate provincial government could not prevail against the combination of politicized First Nations claims and a supportive Supreme Court jurisprudence of Aboriginal and treaty rights.
- The passage of the Nisga'a treaty in 2000, in spite of a deeply divisive debate in British Columbia, including a court challenge, suggested that Aboriginal nationalism could be accommodated within Canadian federalism.
- The emergence of Nunavut in 1999 as a quasi-province with an Inuit majority was an even more symbolic indication of the possibility of finding common ground. On the other hand, the confrontation between Québec and Aboriginal nationalism, particularly of the northern Cree and Inuit, over the territorial integrity of Québec should it secede from Canada, underlined the limits of compromise, and confirmed that Aboriginal nationalism would be a major player and a major complication if Canada was threatened with a split.
- Nationalism, defined as the unwillingness to forget, and the willingness to pursue claims for redress for past maltreatment was a supportive factor in the emergence into public attention of the history of sexual and physical abuse in residential schools and the pursuit of claims for compensation by thousands of former students. These claims, which threaten devastating financial impacts on the major churches involved in what a recent scholar described as *A National Crime* in his history of residential schools (Milloy 1999), only surfaced when yesterday's paternalism was displaced by assertive nationalism.

The recognition and accommodation of Aboriginal nationalism *within Canada* is one of the most difficult, high-priority tasks confronting Canadian policy-makers. "Within Canada" indicates that the goal is not only to recognize Aboriginal difference but also to generate a positive identification with, and participation in, the Canadian community of citizens. Aboriginal nationalism is not enough. It has to be supplemented by a shared citizenship with other Canadians if our living together is to go beyond a wary coexistence.

THE SPIRIT OF THE TIMES—THEN AND NOW

Cumulatively, the preceding suggest a profound transformation in the spirit of the times from the conventional assumptions of forty years ago; in different language, the self-consciousness of the major players has been transformed; their very identities differ; non-Aboriginals no longer assume an unchallenged authority to be in charge, while Aboriginal peoples sense the possibility that this time historical momentum may be on their side. Differently phrased, Aboriginal peoples now occupy the moral high ground once occupied by the majority society that had justified its former leadership role, by virtue of the superior civilization it was assumed to be spreading. These changes in mood, in temperament, in identity, in consciousness, in confidence, and in taken-for-granted assumptions about who was in charge, and about what a desirable future would look like are not easily pinned down, yet they are fundamental components of where we are.

This profound transformation is best illustrated by the fate of the rhetoric of assimilation. Formerly the trademark of the non-Aboriginal liberal/left progressives in the middle of the twentieth century, it recently re-emerged on the right end of the spectrum in the Reform party and its successor, the Canadian Alliance, as a reaction against the policy thrust toward special treatment and a constitutionalized third order of Aboriginal governments. Now, however, the liberal/left end of the spectrum passionately opposes the assimilation it formerly supported; it now sees that assimilation is an unacceptable expression of cultural arrogance and ethnocentrism.

Assimilation was formerly the policy of the progressives. The Saskatchewan Co-operative Commonwealth Federation (CCF) under Tommy Douglas and Woodrow Lloyd, 1944–64, was a passionate advocate of assimilation well before the 1969 White Paper (Pitsula 1994). Some of this was a spillover from Afro-American pressure to join the mainstream in the United States, a perspective that saw American blacks seeking to 'get in' as anticipating what Canadian Indians would seek when their Martin Luther King belatedly emerged. Assimilation also drew sustenance from the belief that industrial civilization was the great leveller of cultural difference. Anthropologists took it for granted that assimilation was both the inevitable and desirable goal toward which we were heading. (Loram and McIlwraith 1943). Against such a powerful tendency, resistance was seen as futile. More generally, of course, assimilation had been the historic policy of the Canadian state since Canada was founded.

Support for assimilation has now drifted to the right end of the political spectrum. Preston Manning (Manning 1992), Stockwell Day—now succeeded by Stephen Harper—have replaced Tommy Douglas. Mel Smith (Smith 1995), Tom Flanagan (Flanagan 2000), and others now defend in a very different political-intellectual climate the ideas that attracted Trudeau and the team which produced the White Paper (Canada 1969). The tone of contemporary advocates of assimilation is, of necessity, different from the tone of its supporters of thirty to fifty years ago. Yesterday's advocates wrote and spoke with the easy authority that history was on their side. Contemporary advocates are not so sure. They frequently assert that they write against an unsympathetic climate of political correctness that challenges their right to speak. Other authors have noted the inhibitions which attend speaking out against what they detect as a political consensus behind the overall thrust toward recognition and implementation of the inherent right of self-government (Cairns 2000: 14–16 for references).[1]

This is another example of the changing spirit of the times; forty years ago, in the Hawthorn report of the mid-sixties (Hawthorn 1966–67) and in the 1969 White Paper, treaties were considered of marginal importance. Trudeau, indeed, found it inconceivable that one section of society could have a treaty with another part of society, declaring that "we must all be equal under the laws and we must not sign treaties amongst ourselves" (Trudeau 1969).

Now, the RCAP report informs the reader that treaties are the key, the fundamental instrument for regulating relationships between Aboriginal and non-Aboriginal peoples (Cairns 2000:134–136 for a discussion).

Observing the erosion of yesterday's conventional wisdom too easily leads to a complacent arrogance among the supporters of today's conventional wisdom, convinced that they have arrived at truth. A much better lesson would be a reminder that we, too, will be seen, in hindsight, as yesterday's conventional wisdom.

SOME CHARACTERISTICS OF THE PRESENT DEBATE

The present dialogue or debate has the following characteristics. First, there is now a burgeoning literature. Any reasonably sized bookstore currently stocks a sizeable collegian of books under the rubric of Native studies. The media now devotes considerable attention to Aboriginal issues. The *National Post*, which gives extensive coverage to Aboriginal issues, vigorously and recurrently attacks special status and espouses assimilation. Aboriginal issues are one of the staples of Jeffrey Simpson, the leading national affairs columnist for the *Globe and Mail* (Simpson 1998; 1999; 2000). Polar positions are now expressed in the national party system. The Reform and the Canadian Alliance analysis of the Aboriginal policy area closely mirror the assumptions behind the 1969 White Paper (Reform Party of Canada 1995; Cairns 2000: 72).

Second, there are prominent Aboriginal participants in the public dialogue. They include the major national and provincial Aboriginal associations whose leaders are often skilled in getting media coverage. They conduct research and publish major position papers. They are joined by a small but growing cadre of Aboriginal scholars in law and other disciplines. Their work receives practical sustenance from Native studies departments, Native studies associations, and specialized journals of Native Studies. They have already made major contributions to our collective search for improved understanding. Their numbers and importance will increase with the dramatic increase in number of Aboriginal graduates of post-secondary institutions.

Third, there is now an extensive university-based community of scholars whose focus is Aboriginal issues. Research is not monolithic — contrast, for example, on the non-Aboriginal side the work of Jim Tully (Tully 1995) and Tom Flanagan (Flanagan 2000), or on the Aboriginal side John Borrows (Borrows 1999), Taiaiake Alfred (Alfred 1999), and Mary Ellen Turpel-Lafond who now sits on the bench of the Provincial Court of Saskatchewan (Turpel 1989–90).

Given the above welcome diversity, it remains true that the major contemporary academic contributions to the debate come from an influential cadre of university law professors, who have taken on the task of enlarging the constitutional space for Aboriginal self-government. Their goal is to provide a legal rationale for the maximum jurisdictional autonomy for the Aboriginal governments of the future. They are unquestionably the major academic contributors to public discourse. Their importance is magnified by the role of the courts in the evolution of Aboriginal rights. Their contributions are supplemented by political scientists, anthropologists, and historians. Each of these disciplines brings different strengths and weaknesses to Aboriginal studies and to Aboriginal policy.

The conclusion is irresistible that the dominant role of legal scholars is defining the issues at stake, in fleshing out a rights-based discourse, and in contributing to a leading role for the courts has contributed to Aboriginal gains. On the other hand, academic legal contributors in this policy area show little concern for Canadian citizenship as a uniting bond, or more generally, for what will hold us together, and show much less interest in the 50 per cent of the Aboriginal population in urban areas, whose concerns are less amenable to the language of rights.[2]

A PLEA FOR REALISM

It is perhaps inevitable that Canadians — be they Aboriginal and non-Aboriginal, citizens and scholars — disagree on where we should go. We still hear the voices of assimilators and their antithesis — those who describe our future as coexisting solitudes maintaining a possibly friendly possibly cool distance from one another. There is another slightly different divide between advocates of a nation-to-nation relationship — competing solidarities who engage in a domestic version of international relations — and others who stress the necessity, at least at one level of our relationship, of a common citizenship as the contemporary source of the empathy that makes us feel responsible for each other. Each of these divides and the rhetoric that sustains them could easily consume the remainder of these pages. It would be a worthwhile task to explore the plausibilities, the exaggerations, the kernels of truth, and the simplifications that attend each side of the above divides. Each divide, in its own way, is at the very centre of our present search for understanding.

I have decided to focus on a different divide, or contrast, in the remaining pages — one which deserves more attention that it has received. This discussion will turn on two roads to the future: that of Aboriginal peoples in landed communities on the path to self-government and that of urban Aboriginals. The pressure and temptation when confronting two roads is to assume the necessity of choosing one, to set the two roads as rivals, to imply that those who have not chosen 'our' road can only have done so because of some false consciousness which clouds their reasoning, to suggest that the urban Aboriginal is somehow betraying Aboriginality by subjecting him/herself to the perils of cultural contagion that will eat away at Aboriginal difference that should be cherished and protected, or to intimate that the travellers on the self-government road overestimate the possibility of cultural renewal and economic viability for small nations distanced from urban centres.

I prefer not to take sides, but rather to try to think my way through both of these routes to the future, on the premise that there are advantages and disadvantages to each. To condemn one or the other I view as an unhelpful ideological position at this stage of our understanding and evolution.

TWO ROADS TO THE FUTURE

We have more information and analysis now than ever before to inform our policy decisions. Formerly, non-Aboriginals dominated the policy discussions of Aboriginal issues. This was especially true for status Indians. By definition wards are, after all, objects of policy determined by paternal authorities, not participants in its making. For the last thirty years, in contrast, we have had a dialogue with extensive and growing Aboriginal participation. The scholarly community studying Aboriginal issues is now dramatically larger than even a quarter of a century ago. Non-Aboriginals still dominate the field, but scholarly contributions from Aboriginal academics are on the increase. Further, non-Aboriginal academics are aware that their scholarly authority no longer flows automatically from their skin colour. These are all positive developments. Nevertheless, I argue that our understanding is imperfect, that there are immense gaps in our knowledge, that ideology plays too prominent a role, and that the inevitable politicization of a field in which nationalism and the response to it is the dominant focus often gets in the way of realism.

Whether we speak of Aboriginal policy writ large to include Indians, Inuit, and Métis or focus only on the status Indian population — the largest of the constitutionally recognized "Aboriginal peoples"— the reality is that there are two roads to the future — the self-government road and the urban route. This is obvious from even a casual acquaintance with elementary demographic data — half of the Aboriginal people live in urban centres.[3]

Amazingly, the coexistence of these alternative futures, which should be thought of as contemporary, is consistently, if not almost systematically, overlooked or deprecated by those who have cast their votes either for the nation-government route and who see urban life as a distraction or a threat, or by those who see self-government as slowing down the desirable migration to the job opportunities of the city. I argue for acceptance of the coexistence of these two roads to the future, coupled with the belief that each road merits the attention of policy-makers and analysts.

My reasons are elementary. Both roads exist and, as noted above, have about the same number of travellers. Of the status Indian population 42 per cent live off reserve, and 58 per cent live either on reserve (54 per cent) or on crown (4 per cent) land (1996 figures, Canada 1997b: xiv). When Métis and Inuit are included, about half of the Aboriginal population overall is urban. Generally speaking, these two roads lead to different goals. The self-government option, especially when it is practised with competence and integrity, can be a valuable instrument for cultural retention and renewal. The urban option, by its very nature, is more attuned to participation in non-Aboriginal society, with the resultant probability of higher income, less unemployment, and so on. Neither of these goals deserves to be deprecated as such — to be defined as unworthy, as representing an irrational choice. To opt for urban life is not an act of betrayal. To remain in an Aboriginal community, in part because that is where 'home' is, is not to opt for the past.

The fact that both routes exist and that they serve different purposes suggests that they should not be judged by the same criteria. Cultural survival and the modernization of tradition may be the appropriate and priority criteria for judging self-governing nations. Economic opportunities and higher incomes and other pursuits congenial to urban living are the appropriate criteria for assessing Aboriginal urban life. When the RCAP Report foresaw a future in which Aboriginal peoples would be proportionally represented in such prestigious professions as "doctors . . . biotechnologists . . . computer specialists . . . professors, archaeologists and . . . other careers" (Canada 1996, 3: 501) it was not referring to options available in small rural nations. To compare small rural nations with urban settings in terms of their respective capacities to sustain such professions would be to cook the books in favour of urban life. Equally, however, to make cultural renewal the prime criterion for judging the relative merits of urban living and self-governing nations is to predetermine the outcome against the urban setting. Each road to the future should be judged in terms of criteria appropriate to its virtues. This does not mean that economic criteria are irrelevant to judging self-government, nor that cultural criteria have no place in judging the urban situation, but that their relative significance varies according to the setting.

Clarity is not helped by attaching scarce words to one or the other route. 'Assimilation,' brandished as an aggressive description of the consequences of urban living — sometimes of course by its non-Aboriginal supporters — stigmatizes Aboriginals in the city. Assimilation implies losing oneself in someone else's culture. Further, since assimilation was the official, historical policy of the Canadian state, to be accused of having been assimilated suggests succumbing to a policy initially premised on the inferiority of Indian cultures. Of course, assimilation rhetoric often presupposes that an Aboriginal identity can only survive if it manifests itself in vastly different behaviours and beliefs from those of the non-Aboriginal majority. This is simply simplistic social psychology. Identity divergence and cultural convergence are obviously compatible. Is this not what has happened among the Québec Francophone majority? Culturally, convergence of values with Anglophone Canada is well advanced compared to half a century ago. On the other hand, a nationalist identity is unquestionably stronger. This, however, is not to suggest that identity loss never occurs, or to deny that after several generations of intermarriage in urban settings, individuals may retain only a sliver of Aboriginal culture and be happy with what and who they have become. To say that this could never happen is a form of blindness. To assert that it will not be allowed to happen is to deny individual choice. However, my large point remains — a modernizing, urban Aboriginality is perfectly compatible with the retention of a strong Aboriginal identity.

Equally unhelpful are scarce words attached to the separate existence of Indian communities. In the assimilation era, reserves were pejoratively referred to as the Gulag Archipelago, as representative of apartheid, and as equivalent to displaced persons camps. More recently, given the drive to self-government, they have been criticized as making "race the constitutive factor of the political order" and as "based on a closed racial principle" (Flanagan 2000: 194). These are all rhetorical devices to foreclose debate. Indian communities, unlike provincial communities, will be closed communities in the minimum sense of controlling their own membership. To describe them as "race based" (Gibson 2000), however, is not helpful, given the high rate of intermarriage. Further, at the present time, only about 5 per cent of Indian bands employ "blood quantum" criteria for membership and they were reproved by RCAP (Canada 1996, 2 (1): 237–40).

The existence of two roads to the future constitutes the fundamental reality against which should be judged the adequacy of the distribution of attention, of research, and in general, of all attempts to throw light on where we are and might go. From nearly every perspective, the urban dimension of Aboriginality is relegated to secondary importance, when it is not completely ignored. The recurrent use of the colonial analogy contributes to the neglect of the urban situation. The language of nation fits poorly with urban Aboriginals; the possibilities for self-government are limited. Accordingly, since neither nation (as the actor to battle colonialism) nor significant powers of self-government (the purpose of the struggle) make as much sense in the urban setting, urban Aboriginals remain largely outside the purview of one of the most potent organizing labels in contemporary disclosure. They are, therefore, naturally overlooked. The leading role of the academic legal community includes paying scant attention to the urban situation, which, in truth, does not lend itself as readily to analysis in terms of Aboriginal rights. Further, the urban setting lacks a compelling, simplifying focus equal to the appeal of nationalism and self-government as self-evident good causes for scholars to support. The urban scene presents a host of discrete practical problems that resist consolidation under a single rubric.

Indeed, when the heady language of nationalism, of treaties, of inherent rights to self-government, and of nation-to-nation relations casts its aura over one route to the future — self-government and cultural renewal — the second, urban route, which can easily be portrayed negatively in terms of youth gangs, Aboriginal ghettos in the urban core, language loss, and high rates of intermarriage, can be seen as an embarrassment. Indeed, it may even be seen as the road that obviously should not have been taken.

The nation and self-government focus of academics simply duplicates the historical operational bias of the federal department of Indian Affairs which, in administering the Indian Act, 1985, concentrated overwhelmingly on reserve-based Indian communities. The focus on Indian land-based communities is reinforced by the fact that the strongest and most visible national Aboriginal organization, the Assembly of First Nations (AFN), rests squarely on the Indian bands/nations, whose status is governed by the Indian Act, 1985.

For nearly twenty years, the most visible Aboriginal leader has been the Grand Chief of the AFN.

The favourable bias toward Aboriginal (especially Indian) nations and their self-government is graphically underlined by the RCAP Report, that is dominated by the nation-to-nation theme, contrasted with what it portrays as a "rootless urban existence" (Canada 1996, 2 (2): 1023). This negative judgment of the urban situation supports the focus on nation and on self-government as its servant for the task of cultural renewal. Alternatively, the nation preference, supported by a global ethnic revival and by a colonial analysis that sees self-government as the culmination of the anti-colonial struggle, requires a negative view of urban Aboriginal life, seen as getting in the way of the movement of history.

From these perspectives, urban Aboriginal life is distinctly unpromising. Urban Aboriginals come from too many diverse nations to coalesce into a sharing, self-governing group even if they had a coherent land base, which they do not. Further, urban Aboriginal life is, by definition, the setting for increased cultural contact leading both to to cultural erosion and the diminishing use of native languages and traditional customs. From the cultural perspective, therefore, urban living is easily viewed as a threat, not as a promise, and those who choose it are seen by its critics as, in a sense, lost to the cause.

Further, especially in the major cities of western Canada, but not confined to them, the Aboriginal concentration in urban core areas has depressing ghetto characteristics. Crime, drug abuse, youth gangs, violence, and prostitution are widespread (LaPrairie 1995). Recent reports speak of normlessness; of a fractured social fabric; and "the emergence of Canada's first US-style slum" in Winnipeg, evident to even a "casual visitor," and becoming evident in "other Prairie cities" (Mendelson and Battle 1999: 25; National Association of Friendship Centres and the Law Commission of Canada 1999: 63–5).

In the absence of some countervailing evidence, the preceding passages would constitute an almost unanswerable condemnation of the urban route. There is, however, another side. The RCAP outlined numerous positive features of urban life. The employment situation is superior; incomes are markedly higher; urban Indian people have the highest life expectancy among Aboriginal peoples; various indicators of social breakdown are much higher for the on-reserve compared to the non-reserve population (Cairns 2000: chap. 4). As well, preliminary findings of the Department of Indian Affairs Research and Analysis Directorate, based on 1991 data, reported a marked advantage for off-reserve status Indians in terms of life expectancy, educational attainment, and per capital income. Life expectancy was 4.6 years longer and per capita income 50 per cent higher (Beavon and Cooke 1998). Evelyn Peters reported "a significant urban Aboriginal population earning a good income" of $40,000 or more in 1990 (Peters 1994: 28 and Table 15).

These trends feed on the truly dramatic increase in the number of Aboriginal post-secondary graduates. In the late 1950s, there were only a handful of Indian university students. In 1969, there were fewer than 800 Aboriginal post-secondary graduates. Now, more than 150,000 Aboriginal people have completed or are in post-secondary education (Borrows 1999: 75). There was an increase in the number of Inuit and Indian students enrolled in post-secondary institutions of nearly 750 per cent from the numbers in 1977–1978 to the more than 27,000 reported in 1999–2000 (Canada 1997a: 36 and 2001: 33).[4]

This dramatic educational expansion, and the urbanization to which it will contribute, will almost certainly increase the out-marriage rate (see also Clatworthy and Smith 1992: 36). In a recent study employing five-year data ending in December 1995, the overall out-marriage rate was 33 per cent, ranging from 22.8 per cent out-marriage on reserve to 57.4 per cent off-reserve. In general, the smaller the reserve population, the higher the out-marriage rate (Canada 1997b: 21–3).

It is implausible to assume not only that this educational explosion can be contained but also that most graduates can have satisfying lives and find meaningful employment in small-self-governing nations with a weak private sector. This remains largely true even if, by a process of consolidation, the average population of self-governing nations is raised to the viable level of 5,000–7,000, as advocated by the RCAP.

Further, as John Borrows argues, Aboriginal peoples should seek to influence the overall structure of the larger society through vigorous participation. For Borrows, to think of Indianness, or more broadly Aboriginality, as restricted to self-governing, small national communities is to be condemned to a limited and partial existence. Borrows argues, in effect, that the expression of a modernizing Aboriginality should be diffused throughout society in politics, culture, the professions, and so on. He denies that Aboriginality is a fixed thing; he is obviously open to a selective incorporation of values and practices of non-Aboriginal society. As he says, "Identity is constantly undergoing renegotiation. We are traditional, modern, and post-modern people" (Borrows 1999: 77). Accordingly, the self-governing component of Aboriginal futures, while important, is by itself not enough. Neither, however, is the urban route.

Hundreds (sixty to eighty if RCAP hopes for consolidation are realized — more if they are not) of small, self-governing native communities will be scattered across the land, wielding jurisdictions proportionate to their capacity and desire. They are not about to disappear in any foreseeable future. Aboriginal and treaty rights "recognized and affirmed" in the Constitution Act, 1982 s. 35(1), cannot be removed by anything short of a constitutional amendment, the pursuit of which would be an unthinkable act of constitutional aggression. The relocation of communities is not possible. Dispossession of lands and setting band members adrift is not a policy choice. A ruthless cutting of benefits to encourage exodus is neither humane nor an available option. Any expeditious attempt to wind down the existence of small, self-governing nations would arouse an opposition that could not be overcome in a democratic society. Such a policy cannot be implemented; even if it could, to do so would be undesirable. The result would be a rapid exodus to the city that would add many more individuals to the dark side of urban life and would exacerbate the developing Aboriginal urban crisis while adding few success stories.

If we eliminate the pipe dreams of assimilation advocates from the spectrum of available policies, we are left with about half the Aboriginal population living in small, self-governing communities: these communities are not going to go away. They are sustained not only by inertia and by the fact that they are home, but their survival is buttressed by Aboriginal and treaty rights. The powerful force of nationalism can be mobilized on their behalf. Although limited by small populations, the availability of self-government provides some leverage for Aboriginal peoples to shape the terms of interaction with the majority society.

Further, Canadians through their governments are now engaged in major efforts to respond to Indian land claims where Aboriginal title still exists — most visibly in British Columbia, but also in Québec and Atlantic Canada. Discussions are underway to enlarge the land and resource base of many First Nations. When the preceding efforts are coupled with various attempts to increase economic activity on Indian reserves, the continuing significance and presence of self-governing Aboriginal communities is one of the taken-for-granteds of the Canadian future.

Neither the self-government route nor the urban route is an easy road to an unblemished, positive future for Aboriginal peoples or for their relations with their non-Aboriginal neighbours. The urban route, as already indicated, holds out the disturbing possibility in several metropolitan centres of becoming a Canadian version of those American cities that have a black middle class coexisting with a black ghetto. The Canadian parallel of an urban Aboriginal middle class and an Aboriginal ghetto could undermine the civility and social stability of a number of Canada's major metropolitan centres.

There is no easy answer to this unhappy prospect. The present relative inattention to the chequered reality of urban Aboriginal life is, however, obviously damaging. Since it would be arrogant of me to make specific recommendations, that would almost inevitably be either obvious, platitudinous, or superficial, I will restrict myself to the observation that we have studies and a literature that is helpful. *Seen But Not Heard: Native People in the Inner City,* by LaPrairie, is an excellent analysis, replete with policy suggestions and references to the pertinent literature (LaPrairie 1994).

The route of self-governing nations, even if there were no more outstanding claims and if existing lands and resources were significantly supplemented, will not produce across-the-board successes — healthy, Aboriginal communities, functioning democratically, whose members have standards of living comparable with neighbouring non-Aboriginal communities. Most communities are small; many are isolated; and the politics of which are often dominated by kinship relations in circumstances where the public sector is large and the private sector weak. Conditions are therefore often not propitious for victories over poverty, anomie, and existing inequalities.

The RCAP Report launched a comprehensive package of proposals, too detailed to be listed here, to improve the quality of Aboriginal life in every major dimension. Achievement of these goals, the report argued, required an extensive reallocation of lands and resources, economic opportunity expenditures, major improvements in housing and community infrastructure, dramatically enhanced educational opportunities and attainments, including training 10,000 Aboriginal professionals in health and social services within ten years, and much more (Canada 1996, 5: 213).

The RCAP Report proposed a massive increase in annual public spending, rising to an additional $1.5 to $2 billion in year five, to be sustained over a number of years (Canada 1996, 5: 56). Elsewhere the report wrote of an investment of up two billion a year for twenty years (Canada 1996, 5: 60). This was defined as a "good investment for all Canadians" (Canada 1996, 5: 55), as after fifteen to twenty years the positive benefits of these expenditures would generate a net gain, that would benefit both Aboriginal people and other Canadians and their governments (Canada 1996, 5: 57). This cost-benefit analysis is surely at best somewhere between an educated guess and a leap of faith. Even assuming the translation of RCAP proposals into government policy, many Aboriginal nations will remain impoverished, welfare dependent, and anomic.

Canada does not have a clean slate. The legacy of history cannot be wished away. The present distribution of Aboriginal peoples in towns, cities, reserves, in Nunavut, and elsewhere is not going to be transformed by depopulating the reserves, or Nunavut, or Métis settlements in Alberta by a massive migration to urban settings. But it is equally the case that the urban Aboriginal presence is not a passing phase to be repudiated by a massive return to various homelands. Many Aboriginals in the city have no homelands or, it they do, have no desire to return. Both these realities will confront Canadians in any middle range future we care to visualize. There will always be movement of individuals back and forth for a multitude of reasons. Where self-government successes occur, those nations may receive a net inflow, if the would-be returnees are welcomed (Canada 1997b: 5). Conversely, if positive urban Aboriginal role models become more frequent, urban life may become more of a beacon — seen as a plausible choice to make.

The coexistence of alternative futures should be viewed positively. Since the two routes do not have the same advantages — cultural renewal may be more likely in self-governing contexts and economic gains for individuals more predictable in urban settings — each route acts as a check against the other. They are complementary rivals, especially for those who have homelands to which they can return.

In these circumstances, the task of the state is to encourage both successful adaptation of individuals to urban life and community success stories in self-governing nations.

POLICY FOR THE FUTURE

Sound future policy requires an evolving understanding of what is developing in two different contexts. A series of natural experiments is unfolding at this very moment. There are hundreds of nation-renewing experiments already, or soon to be, underway. What works and what does not, and why? Multiple experiments are underway in urban settings too, and their significance will surely deepen and more innovations will occur as more urban governments and politicians are seized of the complexities, the dangers, and the possibilities created by the urban Aboriginal population.

If, by constant monitoring, we were made aware of what works and what does not, we could facilitate the diffusion of successful practices among both Aboriginal and non-Aboriginal governments. Achievement of this goal will require independent monitoring bodies to examine and report on both roads to the future. Similar proposals have surfaced in previous inquiries. The Hawthorn Report of 1966–67 proposed an Indian Progress Agency with the task of "preparing an annual progress report on the condition of the Indian people of Canada" to include, *inter alia,* educational, legal, economic, and social data and analysis (Hawthorn 1966, 1: 402–3). The purpose was to improve the quality of policy-making and public discussion and hence, in general, to act as a constant reminder of what remains to be done.

Thirty years later, the RCAP proposed an independent Aboriginal Peoples Review Commission headed by an Aboriginal chief commissioner, with most of the other commissioners and staff also to be Aboriginal. The Commission's task would be to monitor and report annually on progress being made "to honour and implement existing treaties . . . in achieving self-government and providing an adequate lands and resource base for Aboriginal peoples . . . in improving the social and economic well-being for Aboriginal people; and . . . in honouring governments' commitments and implementing" RCAP recommendations (Canada 1996, 5: 19–20). The Commission's focus would be broad. It would include "the activities of provincial and territorial governments within its review" (Canada 1996, 5: 19). The essential task would be to act as a watchdog to see that non-Aboriginal governments do not slacken in their endeavours. Judging the performance of Aboriginal governments does not appear as part of its mandate, however, though some monitoring might indirectly be undertaken by RCAP's proposed Aboriginal Government Transition Centre, which would be assigned to various tasks to facilitate successful transitions to self-government (Canada 1996, 5: 167–69). The Transition Centre would presumably have only minimal, if any, interest in Aboriginal peoples in urban settings.

The proposal offered here is more complex than that proposed in either Hawthorn or the RCAP. The recommendation is for two monitoring agencies. Implicitly they would be providing annual material to facilitate the comparison between an urban route and a self-government route. Explicitly, they will provide ongoing commentary and analysis — in the one case on the probably hundreds of self-government experiments underway and in the other on the developing indicators of achievements and shortfalls in urban Aboriginal life.

Surely such an ongoing set of monitoring and analyzing reports would reduce the ideology that dominates contemporary discussion. How these agencies should be institutionalized and how their analyses should be disseminated to have maximum effect would have to be worked out. The proposal may seem threatening, even paternalistic, especially to self-governing nations. Relatively soon, and possibly even immediately, however, the staffs of these agencies will have Aboriginal majorities. This is not the time for specifics, but rather for throwing out an idea for public discussion. Those who resist the proposal should suggest alternative means by which we can profitably learn from the fact that we are in the early stages of major policy experiments in areas where our ignorance is vast. To reduce that ignorance is to reduce the cost it imposes on Aboriginal peoples. Some will deny that these are experiments and thus there is nothing to learn, but such claims are not believable. Others might argue that if self-government is an inherent right, the manner of its exercise should be immune from public scrutiny. Such a claim will only survive if evidence of misgovernment is rare or sporadic, which is implausible given the number of small nations potentially involved and the immense problems and temptations they will encounter.

Both routes — the self-government and the urban — place the Aboriginal future directly within Canada. Even the largest unit of self-government, Nunavut, is clearly fully within Canada and deeply dependent on external funding. This will be overwhelmingly true for First Nations. They cannot realistically isolate themselves from the provincial, territorial, and Canadian contexts in which they live. Only 5 per cent of the Indian bands — 30 out of 623 — have on reserve populations of more than 2,000; 405 of 623 bands have on reserve populations of less than 500. There are 111 bands with on reserve populations of less than one hundred (Indian and Northern Affairs Canada 1997: xvi). The RCAP reports that a "disproportionate number of Aboriginal people live in small, remote, and northern communities" (Canada 1996, 5: 39). The RCAP recognized that the jurisdictions they are capable of wielding are severely limited, so the commissioners recommended aggregating bands to produce an average size of 5,000 to 7,000 for the sixty to eighty nations they hoped would emerge. These are still small populations, with a limited capacity to deliver services. Their populations, therefore, will be heavily dependent on federal and provincial governments for many services; the services they will receive from their own governments can only be provided if their governments are recipients of large infusions of outside monies. This double dependence makes it imperative that individual members of self-governing nations be thought of as full Canadian citizens in the psychological and sociological sense of the term. It is for this reason that the Hawthorn Report of the mid-1960s coined the phrase "Citizens plus" as an appropriate description of the place of Indian peoples in Canadian society. (Inuit and Métis were outside Hawthorn's terms of reference.) If Aboriginal individuals and the communities where they live are seen as strangers proclaiming "we are not you," the danger arises that the majority will agree that "they are not us." We must constantly work towards a common citizenship to support the "we" group that sustains our responsibility for each other. This will provide the secure basis for pursuing the "plus" dimension of Aboriginal Canadians.

Recognition as members of the Canadian community of citizens is equally necessary for Aboriginals in the city. Intermingled with non-Aboriginal neighbours, with at best only limited self-government possibilities, their links to municipal, provincial, and federal government will be crucial to their quality of life.

In both cases, therefore, it is essential that Aboriginal people be thought of as fellow citizens. In contemporary, democratic Western societies, citizenship provides the bonds of solidarity. Empathy weakens when citizenship erodes. At a certain point in the erosion, we see each other as strangers, owing little to each other.

If this thesis is accepted, one responsibility of our governors and of the major Aboriginal organizations will be to work constantly for a reconciliation between Aboriginal nationalism and Canadian citizenship. This is also an appropriate, indeed urgent, responsibility for scholars who wish to influence the course of events. The RCAP, the most elaborate inquiry into indigenous peoples and their relation to the majority society ever undertaken, failed in this task. The idea and reality of Aboriginal nations and nationalism crowded out that of Canadian citizenship. Discussion of the former was fulsome, passionate, and repeated. Discussion of the latter — mention is perhaps more accurate — was infrequent and typically lukewarm, except when claims for equality apropos the receipt of services were made. Thus, the shared rule dimension of Canadian federalism — participation in the Canadian practice of self-government via elections and Parliament — was little more than an afterthought. Access of Aboriginal governments to section 36 equalization payments did not receive the standard justification that it is a response to our common shared citizenship; instead it was justified on the weak claim that we share an economy.

In other words, the RCAP, the most exhaustive inquiry ever undertaken of Aboriginal and non-Aboriginal relations in Canada, failed to ask the elementary question "What will hold us together?" and thus the RCAP failed to answer it. This is a mistake that should not be repeated.

CONCLUSION

Realism suggests the following:

- There are two roads to the future: the nation or self-government road and the urban route; both require the attention of policymakers.
- Both roads can be thought of as natural experiments that need to be carefully monitored so we can learn from success and avoid the needless repetition of policy errors. Accordingly, two monitoring, analyzing, reporting agencies should be established to reduce the number of gaps in our knowledge.
- Both roads are clearly within Canada. Canada is not just a box or container, but a political community bound together by a solidarity based on citizenship. Aboriginal peoples must be part of, not outside, that community. A nation-to-nation description of who we are is insufficient. Aboriginal nationhood and Canadian citizenship should not be seen as rivals, but as complementary patterns of belonging to a complex political order. If we recognize only our diversities, "we" will become an uncaring aggregation of solitudes.

NOTES

1. The politicization of this policy area generates unusually polemical scholarly debates, as well as exchanges between authors and reviewers that threaten civility.
2. An important research project remains to be undertaken to 1) identify the changing relation between Aboriginal peoples and those who study them, and 2) assess the shifting relative influence of various disciplines. The hegemony of law is less than a quarter of a century old. Such a study should also track the emergent, growing role of indigenous scholars in the major disciplines. In doing so, it should also note their distribution among the three categories of Aboriginal people — Indian, Inuit, and Métis.
3. As always, there are exceptions to a simple contrast between self-governing nations and urban life, where nation has limited salience. There are urban reserves and urban nations. Further, some, albeit limited options for self-government can be made available to urban Aboriginals. Nevertheless, the contrast between self-government for Aboriginal nations and an urban existence is sufficiently real to focus discussion around these two alternative visions of the future.
4. Aboriginal students in post-secondary programs are much more likely than other Canadians to select trade and non-university programs than university programs — 76 per cent to 24 per cent for registered Indians; 70 per cent to 30 per cent for other Aboriginal students, compared to 58 per cent to 42 per cent for other Canadians (1991 figures) (Santiago 1997: 14–16).

Article Thirty-Seven

Canadian Politics at the End of the Millennium: Old Dreams, New Nightmares

Reg Whitaker

THE POLITICS THAT USED TO BE . . .

Once upon a time, Canadian politics followed a simpler script than it does today. When Canadians wanted to understand the political world, familiar narratives, or stories, were available to make sense of things. These grand narratives about politics were called "liberalism," "conservatism," and "socialism."

Each of these political stories was identified with a corresponding political party: the Liberal Party, the Progressive Conservative Party, and the New Democratic Party (NDP). Each party, and its tradition, had roots deep in Canada's past. The Conservatives were the dominant party in the formative period of the Canadian Confederation in the late nineteenth century. Their chief rivals, the Liberals, took over for most of the twentieth century. The NDP was younger — it traced its origins back to the Great Depression of the 1930s — and even though it had never been more than a third party in the national Parliament, from time to time it had formed governments in four of the ten provinces.

The three grand narratives each tried to explain the political world to the citizens, most of whom were usually preoccupied with other things than politics. Conservatism (or Toryism, as it was often called) stressed the values of the past, tried and tested by history, and continuity. In Canada continuity meant respect for the British connection: the monarchy, the Empire, and the Commonwealth, and for the forms of British parliamentary government. It meant deference to authority, and to the traditional elites of Canadian society. It meant mistrust of America and things American. It meant a cautious, ordered approach to change, and a deep aversion to blueprints for social engineering. Conservatives tended to see the political community as an organic whole that could not bear too much radical surgery. Conservatism tended sometimes to be uncomfortable with the multiethnic and bilingual nature of the Canadian society that took shape in the twentieth century, preferring a more stable social hierarchy that privileged those of "British" origin, but not always.

Liberalism stressed continuity as well, but with greater openness. Liberals saw change as a normal phenomenon in the social and economic spheres, and believed that politics must accommodate changes in society. They were also more apt to stress the value of individual freedom, and looked to progress as the answer to problems of the distribution of resources. Liberals also came, over time, to look approvingly on a limited amount of government regulation and management of the private sector of the economy, both to ensure economic progress and to promote the increased use of equality in the unregulated capitalist market system's operations. Liberalism also stressed the positive value of cultural pluralism among the various ethnic groups in Canadian society, and between the two linguistic communities.

Socialism, or social democracy, saw the world of the liberals and conservatives as infected by unfair economic privilege. Social democracy wanted to extend the principles of political democracy, especially equality, to cover the economic order as well. Social democracy saw government as a positive instrument that could be used to alleviate the wrongs inflicted on the poor and the weak by the market economy. Progress was measured in the advances of social welfare programs. But social democracy did not envisage the public sector displacing the private sector, only balancing private economic power with measured government regulation.

For many decades, these three stories played off against each other in the political arena like an eternal triangle. It went like this: on the right of the spectrum, Toryism tended to be backward-looking and behind the times, and found it hard to catch up; in the centre, liberalism recognized that the real dynamic in political life was coming from the left (that is, from the social democrats). Liberals tended to steal the social democrats' ideas, while implementing them cautiously, with an eye to maintaining the confidence of the business community and not stirring up those sectors of the society that did not like rapid change.

The result was that liberalism (and Liberals) tended to dominate national political life. Canadians grew to think of themselves as different from their American neighbours — not so much because they were British and had a Queen (that was the Tory story that had played well in the nineteenth century, but that made less sense as the twentieth century wore on and Canada became less British both ethnically and culturally) — but because we did things differently from the Americans. Chief among these differences were our social safety net, our social programs, like medicare, and our national cultural institutions, which expressed our unique national character. All were achievements of liberalism, drawing inspiration from time to time for social democracy. There was something else that was uniquely Canadian: we had two languages and two cultural traditions, two great communities, English and French Canada. Liberalism understood this best, and much of the liberal narrative of politics was about accommodating these two communities together within Confederation. Liberals called this national unity and made it the centrepiece of their thinking on how Canada must be governed. The Liberal Party benefited from this approach for well over half the twentieth century by collaring the bulk of Quebec seats in one federal election after another, which was a major asset in that it allowed the party to maintain its ascendancy in national politics.

Internationally, Canada saw itself playing a modest but helpful role in the world, first as a loyal junior partner to Britain in two world wars, and then as a loyal junior partner to the United States in the Cold War. By serving our senior partners, Canada helped guarantee the prosperity and commercial opportunities that were important for maintaining domestic peace. Moreover, the existence of a common external threat (first the Nazis and then, for a much longer period, the Communists) helped cement consensus and cooperation at home: there was little difference between the great political narratives when it came to foreign and defence policy.

This was a politics of accommodation and consensus. Underlying it was the assumption that the benefits of capitalist growth could be redistributed judiciously to take the edge off the complaints of those who felt they were not getting their fair shake. Liberalism placated the working and lower-middle classes with social programs, and the middle class by making the benefits universal. Regions were placated by such devices as equalization payments to top up the revenues of poorer provinces and by introducing government programs like unemployment insurance, which would benefit specific regions, such as Atlantic Canada and rural Quebec.

Because the dominant liberalism was so centrist and so consensual, but also because the other two political narratives were so blunted by liberalism's success, Canadian politics was not characterized by a great deal of conflict, nor by very much ideology. Some even suggested there were very few principles. There was, however, a great deal of what politicians liked to call "pragmatism." This is a fancy word for the behaviour of political parties that consists of watching polls very closely and going hunting where the ducks are. Public policies had little to do with party philosophies, something to do with marketing, and a lot to do with whatever seemed at the time to offend the least number of voters and influential interest groups.

Above all, this was a system designed, organized, and run by political elites, through political patronage. Canada was a democracy, of course, but a democracy was too important to be entrusted to the people to run. Instead, every few years the people chose to entrust public affairs to particular elites at the federal and provincial levels of government. These elites would then wheel and deal among themselves, usually behind closed doors, work out the nation's business, and then present the results more or less as a *fait accompli* to a grateful, or occasionally ungrateful, population. Elite accommodation was especially prized with regard to relations between the two great communities, English and French Canada, since there was a strong suspicion that ordinary people in both communities would, if given half a chance, probably call each other names, or even tear each other apart, and generally do national unity no good. Better to let the elites from the two communities, wise and schooled in the need for accommodation, work things out. This principle also applied to relations between the provinces and the national government, and between the regions.

Democracy in Canada was filtered through pragmatism and consensus, and through the offices of the elites who were entrusted with the mechanics. If the people were really sovereign, this was best understood as "consumer sovereignty." Just as corporations provide goods and services to consumers, after first selling them through advertising on what it is that they will think they need to buy, so too parties provided voters with public policies, after coaching them on which policies were in their best interests. Nice work, if you can get it.

. . . AND THE POLITICS OF TODAY

But, that was then. In the Canada of the 1990s, a very great deal has changed. The old certainties, the comfortable expectations, have vanished. Almost everything seems to be up for grabs. The 1990s have so far witnessed a series of events that have had a deep and disturbing impact on the political fabric: the divisive referendum campaign on the Charlottetown constitutional accord in 1992, the cataclysmic general election of 1993, and the traumatic Quebec sovereignty referendum standoff in 1995. The party system has been radically altered; the nature of the political game has been transformed; and the most fundamental question of all, the integrity and survival of the political community itself, has been forcibly posed, with no clear answer yet forthcoming.

The old familiar political narratives, the stories that made sense of the public realm to generations of Canadians, are among the leading casualties of this upheaval. Two of these narratives, Toryism and socialism, are pretty much dead and buried — at least in anything remotely resembling their earlier form. Liberalism survives in the corridors of power, but many suspect that it now only does so as a mask worn by new forces that have little in common with their predecessors. New and unfamiliar political narratives nudge at the mainstream from the edges: capitalist "revolution," right-wing populism, identity politics, separatist nationalism. A Canadian Rip Van Winkle, awakening in the mid-1990s from a sleep begun in the mid-1950s, might be forgiven for thinking that he had been consigned to a madhouse.

None of this, of course, happened out of the blue. The grand narratives had been breaking down over many years. Take Toryism: as the old Anglo-Saxon British Canada declined, Toryism underwent deep change. First, in the late 1950s and early 1960s the prairie populist John Diefenbaker built a regional base in the West, widened the party to include immigrants and ethnics, but failed miserably in Quebec. Then in the 1980s the Quebecker, Brian Mulroney, divested

Toryism of all its ancient trappings (which Diefenbaker had tried to maintain), such as anti-Americanism, Canadian nationalism, and an attachment to the role of the state (or the Crown, as old-style Tories liked to say) in economic life. With Mulroney, Toryism became a narrative much like that of the U.S. Republican Party: government is bad; the private sector and unregulated market forces are good; and progress is best achieved by leaving the rich alone to make money, while the benefits of this prosperity "trickle down" to the lower orders.

Social democracy similarly failed: first, by having its programs stolen time and again by the Liberals, who took the credit; second, by taking much of the blame when economic conditions turned against these programs. Moreover, when social democrats did achieve office in various provinces, they soon showed that they had little or nothing distinctive to offer.

When the old narratives fail to make sense of the political order for many people, two things are likely to happen: first, the legitimacy of the political order begins to crumble in the minds of citizens who can no longer connect their personal interests with the workings of the public realm; and second, new narratives emerge to take the place of the old. In Canada today, both these things are taking place simultaneously. The result is a period of confusion and flux.

A number of deep structural changes lie beneath these surface movements. I would like to focus on two broad sets of challenges that are closely interrelated: (1) the economic challenges summed up in the issues of "globalization" and the "fiscal" or "debt" crisis of the state, and (2) the challenge that the threat of Quebec separation poses to the fundamental nature of the Canadian political community.

THE NATIONAL STATE UNDER DURESS

Everywhere in the Western world, people are questioning the continued viability of the national state. Europe is seeking to integrate its economy and its political and administrative machinery, and thereby reduce the traditional sovereignty of the states that make up Europe. In North America, we have moved from a Canada–U.S. Free Trade Agreement to a North American Free Trade Agreement that includes Mexico and that is eventually supposed to expand to include other states in the Western hemisphere. Economic globalization not only means continental and regional economic blocs, but also the dominance of multinational corporations and the free flow of capital in the form of investment without much concern for national boundaries. National states are told (and believe) that they must make their national economies "competitive" on a global scale, or sink. Protecting their own industries, and their own citizens, from the shocks of eternal competition, is no longer considered either desirable or even feasible.

With this change in outlook, a whole policy toolbox of the modern national state goes out the window. Following World War II, Western states, Canada included, undertook the responsibility for a number of matters that had previously been thought to be the preserve of the private sector. Above all, responsibility for full employment was shouldered by the state, along with a series of social programs designed both to take the edge off the inevitable dislocations and temporary downturns in a capitalist market economy, and to buy a reasonable degree of social peace between business and labour. Governments, it was believed by many policy makers (although perhaps not by many business people), had the tools to regulate monetary and fiscal policy so as to counteract the business cycle and to shelter national citizens from depressions. In other words, a kind of tacit social contract among workers, the corporations, and the state.

Beginning in the 1970s, national states had increasing difficulty operating this system. Large-scale, persistent unemployment became a feature of virtually all Western economies. Nowhere have governments shown the dimmest idea of how to deal with this long-term unemployment, or to understand its causes. Even aside from the lack of ideas, they were prevented from coping with this problem because they were at the same time handcuffed by a cumulative deficit and debt crisis stemming from years of borrowing to pay for their expenditures — a crisis often accompanied by strong inflationary pressures that made the cost of borrowing higher. More and more, current expenditures were being allocated to pay off interest charges on previous borrowing, and less and less could be set aside for current programs. Moreover, pressures from international investors were forcing governments to cut back their programs, reduce their size, and curtail their role in the economy. No one, except the United States, felt strong enough to stand up to these pressures, and the United States chose not to. Canada neither could nor would. Power to regulate and manage the economy has been moving steadily out of the hands of national governments and into a new and uncharted area of "global market forces."

By the mid-1990s, there was a virtual consensus across parties and regions and throughout levels of government in Canada that deficit reduction was not only a priority, but the only priority. Everything else had to be subordinated to the urgent imperative of balancing budgets. In the political mainstream, no dissent was voiced on this, and disagreement was heard only on how quickly, and by which means, the target should be achieved. In the old political narratives, social democracy might have been expected to oppose balanced budgets as a priority, because budget balancing meant overwhelming social spending and threatening long-standing social programs. Instead, social democratic provincial governments have generally accepted the prevalent deficit mania as an evil that must be addressed as the first order of business. Conservatives and liberals have enthusiastically joined in contests to determine who can slash and burn with the greatest efficiency and ruthlessness. In some cases, as in Alberta and Ontario, this has meant self-conscious "revolutions" from above, top-down coups in which governments target themselves in sweeping campaigns to drastically shrink the public sector through massive cutbacks, privatization, and deregulation. One of the curiosities of this thrust is that those who once called themselves conservatives now style themselves as revolutionaries who wish to bring about radical changes. Liberals tend to eschew the radical rhetoric of the born-again conservative revolutionaries, but set about when in office to accomplish the same goals with quieter efficiency. It is left to the remnants of the social democratic stream, now mostly out of political office, but in the trade unions and in social movements, to articulate a kind of visceral conservatism in opposing rapid, radical surgery to the fabric of the liberal welfare state built up over the years, and to represent the fruits of past struggles that had been taken, wrongly now it would seem, as entitlements, or social citizenship rights. The old narratives are now quite hopelessly muddled: Toryism once represented an attachment to a conception of society as an organic whole, bound together by mutual rights and responsibilities, and an aversion to reckless change in the name of social engineering. Now it is the social democrats who try to slow engines of transformation driven by conservatives ruthlessly imposing abstract blueprints on society.

The dramatic reversal in the role of government is not just a matter of economics. More importantly, it constitutes the abandonment of the social contract between citizens and the state. In return for their allegiance, citizens had expected certain benefits to flow down from their governments: principally, relatively full employment and a guaranteed safety net or social minimum. Government, in the liberal narrative of politics, was to concern itself with the equitable redistribution of the surplus produced by the capitalist economy. Liberal managers stabilized the economy and adjudicated who got what and how much they got. The 1990s are an unprecedented new era of *negative redistribution*: the focus is no longer on who receives the most, but on who loses the least. This is not simply a return to the days before the modern liberal welfare state, because now people have expectations of what government ought to provide, a sense of entitlement to benefits, and this sense of rights is now being forcibly rolled back. Instead of the provident, beneficent state of the immediate past, the state is seen more and more as an antagonist, taking away rather than giving, and dismantling familiar and comforting shelters. The level of conflict and mistrust between state and society is thus heightened, and confrontations between aggrieved groups and the forces of law and order grow more tense and uncivil.

But the conflict does not stop there: in an era of negative redistribution, social conflict between groups in the society rises. Conflict is seen as a zero-sum game. Each group seeks not only to limit the damage to its own interests, but often tends to blame other, competing groups for its misfortunes and to demand that others be forced to give up their "privileges" (which in their own case they tend to see not as privileges but as "rights"). Thus, immigrants and refugees, visible minorities, Aboriginal people, working women, and so on are scapegoated as the cause of unemployment, economic decline, crime, and other social ills.

This mixture of animosities is even more complicated than it might appear. Just as the resources available for redistribution began to disappear, the liberal welfare state was encouraging more claimants. Groups hitherto marginalized or excluded on the basis of gender, ethnicity, and race, for example, have been growing more assertive in pressing for an equitable share of the pie, and have sometimes been rewarded. An increasing number of programs aimed at helping specific groups have been implemented, and special "equity," or affirmative action, laws and programs have been instituted to redress imbalances from past discrimination. At the same time, an assertive "rights culture" has been promoting the pursuit of equity issues through the courts, using the Charter of Rights and Freedoms as a weapon in the struggle for advancing group interests. In fact, the record of achievement in both the legislative and judicial branches of government has been quite mixed, but the perception of other groups in the society who see their positions challenged by such actions is that aggressive minority interests have been making considerable advances — at their expense. Unfortunately, policies such as employment equity have been introduced at the same historical moment as the traditionally white-male working class, and now even sections of the once more secure middle-class white-collar sector, have been taking a savage beating in terms of permanently lost jobs, reduced earning power, and deep anxieties about the prospects for the next generation. This is a potent brew for producing resentment against "special interests," who are seen as gaining special advantages from afar from neutral state. Taxpayers, who see fewer and fewer benefits from their tax dollars coming back to themselves, wax indignant about others jumping ahead of them to the front of the queue on the basis of their gender, colour, ethnic origin, or other special traits.

Two different, and radically incompatible, political narratives have begun to emerge from this conflict: *identity politics* and *populism*.

THE POLITICS OF IDENTITY

Identity politics takes people's allegiance and attention away, in part at least, from the political community as a whole (the nation or the country), and redirects them toward some other, more limited, group identification. Often, although not always, this has represented a form of "biopolitics"— that is, the particular identification has focused on such biological characteristics as gender, race, and ethnicity. In the past, religion offered a more voluntaristic form of identity politics (in the nineteenth century, Catholic and Protestant were identities with considerable political significance in Canada), and today it seems to be making a comeback, especially with politicized evangelical sects and militant Islamic communities. Language, which has always been a powerful sign of group identification in this country, has in the past few decades become the focus of highly political movements. Sexual identity has also been politicized with gay rights groups. One can speak of identity politics coming to the fore when these groups in effect enter the political arena with demands that are specific to themselves alone: for instance, the emergence of feminism as a political force that cuts across party, as well as regional, lines. In this sense, the Canadian public realm has witnessed a proliferation of identity-politics movements in recent years.

The most successful example of identity politics (except for Quebec sovereignty, which will be looked at later) is the movement for Aboriginal self-government, which has gained some legitimacy. Of course, Aboriginal people have always had a special place because they were never fully integrated into Canadian society. They have signed treaties as nations with Canada, and many live on their own lands where forms of self-government are possible. Achieving viable self-government for Native people is still a very long way off, but successive governments have committed themselves to the principle, and public support for the idea appears to be considerable. Problems begin where Aboriginal claims are seen to intrude on other Canadians, as with land claims and special rights over fishing, which are seen as giving Native fishermen a commercial advantage over non-Native competition. These instances give rise to complaints about special treatment, a common reaction to identity politics.

The decline of the national state no doubt has something to do with the rise of identity politics. As the national state loses its ability and willingness to offer positive benefits to its citizens, there is some loss of identification with, and some weakening of the allegiance to, the national state, which has always been underpinned by a strong sense of national identity. The social contract that is now being broken tended in the past to override limited group identities, especially when the benefits were provided on a universal basis. As national identification weakens, it is perhaps not so surprising that people seek more limited identities and the more tangible forms of community that come from single-minded movements on behalf of clearly defined groups. This tendency was reinforced when cash-strapped, tight-fisted governments discovered that they could gain political mileage with minority groups by offering symbolic concessions to identity politics at little cost (like multicultural programs, employment equity laws, or allowing Sikh RCMP officers to wear turbans instead of the traditional Mountie hat). Conversely, governments wishing to eliminate universalism in social programs have sometimes found it expedient to concentrate resources on programs that target specific groups but cost less overall.

Identity movements may reflect in part a desire to push the promise of the liberal and social democratic narrative of politics through to its logical conclusion. Groups that have been denied the full benefits of the liberal society on the basis of prejudice and discrimination demand the righting of the imbalance. The state had promised equality for all: now is the time to deliver on that promise. Liberal politics seems to encourage such group demands. Liberalism avoids any overarching community conception of "the Good" in favour of people pursuing a plurality of "goods." This is called *pluralism*. In a pluralist polity there are no hard and fast rules whereby competing claims may be adjudicated. Instead the operating principle has been described, perhaps unkindly, as "the squeaky wheel gets the grease." Some of those who had previously been marginalized watched the political game to see how it was played, saw that the system responded to organized, focused, and politically effective demands with strategic concessions, and then set about to campaign systematically for such concessions.

Symbol and representation are also important in identity politics. Great stress has been laid on the number of women, visible minority group members and so on who have gained representation as members of the political elites and within the governing institutions. To the extent that identity politics is played out on a field of symbolic representation (although, to be sure, this is only part of the story), it has increasingly turned into the *politics of recognition*. The politics of recognition does not have anything to do with the pursuit of equality in the old liberal sense, according to which differences between groups will eventually disappear when artificial disabilities are removed. The old liberal dream was of a state that would ultimately be colour- and gender-blind, after all forms of discrimination had been rooted out. In the 1990s, groups have more and more demanded recognition and validation of their differences by the dominant society. For instance, the demands of some visible minorities have shifted from the elimination of racial discrimination to the recognition of the dignity and value of minority cultures (i.e., demands for black studies programs and Afro-North American curricula in the schools). Some in the majority have decried this as a new form of self-inflicted separatism or *apartheid*. Proponents assert that the dominant institutions are hardly colour-blind and reflect their own cultural and ethnic specificity. Minority individuals, they claim, can only "succeed" in this world at the cost of undermining their very cultural identity. Hence, the notion of a "multicultural" national community, in which the dominant culture is no longer privileged, arises. Critics of multiculturalism charge that it discriminates against the majority culture, thereby undermining the basis of a viable national community.

This debate highlights one of the characteristics of the politics of identity that has generated widespread social anxiety. Not only are groups demanding changes, either symbolic or substantive, that threaten to overturn established ways of life, thus contributing to the generalized anxiety of an era of uncontrolled change, but they seem also to threaten a *politics of fragmentation*. Although attempts to build coalitions of different identity groups (as with the women's movement and visible minorities) have been made sporadically, for the most part identity politics has tended toward self-interested action with little or no regard to solidarity with other groups. And sometimes, groups have come into direct competition with one another. It is noteworthy that identity politics has tended to avoid party political action, for this is a form of activity that demands working with others in alliances of convenience to seek mutual advantage and the kind of compromises on principle that horrify believers in the purity of the cause. Instead, the favoured form of action has been outside parties and parliaments, as advocacy and interest groups trying to influence government directly on policy. Here, purity and clean hands can be maintained in the face of either success or failure, as each group advances its position separately with regard only to its own interests and its own members' sense of identity. The fragmentation inherent in such approaches is most obvious when the judicial route is pursued to challenge laws passed by legislatures: group rights are trumps; winners in Charter of Rights cases take all, losers get nothing. When identity politics does enter the field of party politics, it often does so for single-issue campaigns, where ideological zealousness corrodes the fabric of party pragmatism. The best (or worst) example of this is the abortion issue. But campaigns for and against gay rights, or censorship either on moral or "political correctness" criteria, have also debilitated party discipline and weakened the civility of public life, since the latter depends on a sense of commonality and compromise that comes with shared values and reciprocal rights and obligations.

Identity politics is also self-limiting. Despite the conviction and fervour of activists, many Canadians are not prepared to see themselves primarily or exclusively in terms of a single identity, whether on the basis of gender, race, ethnicity, language, religion or sexual preference. Many indeed feel the pull of overlapping, sometimes conflicting identities. A woman, for instance, may find herself reacting politically as a woman in one instance, yet reacting as a Chinese Canadian, or a British Columbian, or simply as a taxpayer, in the next. Multiple identities are a feature of our pluralistic, fragmented society, but they do not make building political campaigns on single identities easy.

The great irony of the rise of identity politics is that it has coincided with the triumph of an economic model of public policy that is totally at odds with it. The era of negative redistribution could not offer a worse framework for claims for special treatment for particular groups. To the very considerable extent that there are genuine economic grievances behind group politics, they are likely to be frustrated in the current cold fiscal climate. And to the extent that group demands are met by purely symbolic gestures on the part of government, the very symbolism of concession creates reaction and backlash among other groups jealous of any sign of favouritism by the state. Ironically, it may well be that the most substantive achievement of identity politics has been to provoke a powerful new populist reaction that in many ways defines itself in reaction to the very idea of special treatment for particular groups.

THE NEW POPULISM

Populism, the idea that "the people" must take control of their lives away from the political and economic elites, is not a new theme in Canadian politics. Indeed it has for many years been a subtext of the other narratives of politics. For a time, from the 1920s through World War II, populism even challenged the old two-party system, with Farmer and Progressive movements that won office in a few provinces and briefly emerged as the second largest party in the federal Parliament. Later the challenge came from the CCF (the predecessor to the NDP) as the left-wing variant, and Social Credit as the right-wing variant. These movements posed real alternatives, both economic and political, to the existing order, but they failed to make any lasting impression on the political system. In the case of the CCF/NDP, the alternative remained a minor element of the dominant system, but without its original populist thrust. Populist themes surfaced from time to time with mainstream politicians, but they did not take the form of a new political movement or a new political narrative.

This has changed with the dramatic emergence of the Reform Party. There is a new populism in Canada that is wider than Reform, as such, but the latter best sums up its dominant characteristics. Reform combines a muscular right-wing economic and social agenda with a program for the democratization of the political system. Reform wants to radically reduce the size and role of the state in Canadian life, and allow the untrammelled market to make social choices previously regulated by politicians and bureaucrats. On this score, Reform is at one with the powerful forces of the corporate new Right who may have made deficit elimination and downsizing the public sector the leading priorities of public policy. Yet Reform's economic thrust comes from a different direction, from below rather than from above. In the Reform view, the state has been captured by the "special interests," which is to say, all the groups who have demanded and received the redistribution of tax dollars in the form of entitlements and special treatment. Against this, "the people" are rising up and insisting that government be returned to them. Eliminating the deficit is not just an economic necessity, it is politically and socially desirable as well: Canada must be rescued from the debilitating grip of "the special interests" and restored to "the people."

"The people" are presented in this new populist narrative as undifferentiated (*the* people) standing in vivid contrast to the limited, fragmented, self-centred identities of "the special interests." In populist rhetoric, the Canada of the liberal welfare state appears as a kind of Bosnia torn apart by warring factions: Quebec separatists, Aboriginal militants, feminists, immigrant and ethnic groups, trade unionists, ecologists, social activists, gay rights campaigners, and so on. The people, by contrast, have no interest but the public interest. In the populist self-image, the people are not divided by class, language, culture, race, gender, sexual preference, or any other "limited" identity. In the perception of their critics, the new populists are in fact predominantly male, white, upper-middle class, and have all the usual marks of what the critics see as privileged status. Critics charge that the new populism is really a backlash by privileged taxpayers against the just claims of the various underprivileged and marginalized groups.

This is not the place to adjudicate these contradictory claims. The most important point is that this is a new political debate, born out of the decay of the old political narratives. The new populism is not unlike a very old form of liberalism, with its emphasis on individualism, limited government, the free market, and a taxpayer democracy. But it is also reformulated in direct reaction to the merger of liberalism with social democracy in the form of the welfare state, the widening of rights, and the growth of social entitlements. The old liberalism was never a populist doctrine; indeed, it was a target of the populists of an earlier era. The new populism seeks to articulate a democratic appeal that will rally the people against an alliance of the bureaucrats and the special interests in the name of the community as a whole. More direct popular control of the political institutions (Reform wants more referenda on major public issues; free votes in parliament; and the right of dissatisfied constituents to recall their MPs) and a market-driven fiscal and monetary program are the twin means proposed.

A strong sense of resentment also drives the new populism. There is the resentment of salaried and small business people over paying high taxes to benefit state clients (for instance, so-called welfare bums). And there is the resentment of those who have been made themselves to feel excluded or marginalized because of their "politically incorrect" views. The rather stifling Ottawa-constructed "consensus" on national unity, over issues such as bilingualism, multiculturalism, and immigration often led in practice to bullying those opposed by labelling them racists or extremists, or by describing any opposition as divisive. There was a strong feeling in many quarters that the national media, for instance, kept views sceptical of these "sacred cows" out of the loop of acceptable public discourse. Powerful currents of opposition that were, however, present in public opinion were being bottled up, and this unhealthy situation could breed real political extremism if no legitimate channel of expression were found. The Reform Party systematically broke these taboos and thus opened up a wider and freer debate in Canadian society. It remains to be seen if, having broken the spell of artificial consensus, resentment will continue to fuel the populist fire. One thing is certain, however. The terms of political debate have been irrevocably altered by both the new populism and its leading vehicle, the Reform Party.

The contested ground concerns who can command the value of fairness. Fairness is something that most Canadians would like to see in their political system. The difficulty is in establishing exactly what constitutes fairness. The proponents of identity politics have no doubt that fairness demands restitution of past wrongs and redistribution of resources from privileged to underprivileged groups: in short, *fairness as equity*. The new populists, on the other hand, see special treatment for special interests as unfair, and prefer to have everyone treated on the same basis: in short, *fairness as equality*. Whatever the outcome of this debate, it must be said that at present the populists seem to hold the upper hand. The economic climate of negative redistribution is inhospitable, to say the least, to those demanding equity, while it positively reinforces the position of the new populists. Perhaps as a reflection and cause of this cruel reality, the political Left has never been more bereft of effective political representation than it is today. In the form of the Reform Party, on the other hand, right-wing populism has a dynamic new political mechanism with considerable growth potential. As an emergent political force, Reform is already wielding influence over the mainstream, just as the Left once wielded influence. The wind is definitely in the sails of the new populism.

HOW QUEBEC SEPARATISM DRIVES CANADIAN POLITICS

The Quebec sovereignty movement is the outstanding exception to the trend of identity politics not doing particularly well. The drive to make Quebec independent is now ensconced in power in Quebec City and as the official Opposition in Ottawa. The referendum on sovereignty in October 1995 failed only by a paper-thin margin. Few would deny that another referendum in the near future could very well succeed.

Separatist nationalism is the most developed form of identity politics. National identification of Quebeckers so overwhelms other crosscutting loyalties to the wider political community that sovereignists seek to secede from the federation altogether. This form of identity politics has proved so successful in Quebec, as it has not elsewhere, because Quebec francophones already have their own provincial state, with its own government, bureaucracy, police, and so on, where they form a majority. In addition, the French language forms a natural barrier demarcating a separate culture, historical experience, and national self-consciousness, and the provincial jurisdiction of Quebec demarcates an already semi-autonomous political and economic space. Together, language and provincial jurisdiction give Quebec the clear potential to become a separate national state.

Quebec identity politics has a paradoxical quality. From the outside — from the perspective of the rest of Canada — it appears as the ultimately divisive form of group identity to the potential exclusion of any wider Canadian loyalty. Yet viewed from within Quebec, nationalism has the power to subordinate other identities to the single identity of nationality. For instance, the feminist movement in Quebec has to a large extent become an element within the sovereignty movement. Class politics are also to a degree subordinated to sovereignist goals: the trade unions supported the Yes side in the referendum, while the PQ government tries, with some success, to get labour and capital working together on behalf of the Quebec nation. However, one significant exception to sovereignty's inclusionary power remains: it stops entirely short of drawing support from the Quebec anglophone, ethnic, and Aboriginal communities whose members are not only indifferent to the appeal of sovereignty, but also actively, passionately hostile. Despite efforts by the sovereignists to present Quebec sovereignty as a liberal, *civic nationalist* project, inclusive of all communities in Quebec, it is in practice almost entirely limited to the francophone community. Thus, whatever its professed aims, sovereignty turns out to be largely an *ethnic nationalist* project.

The challenge of separation has had far greater effects on the rest of Canada than are immediately apparent. The continuing challenge, which has been with us now for more than a generation, has helped shape Canadian politics, if only negatively and by way of reaction. The sovereignty movement has greatly hastened the decay of the old political narratives, which rested on popular deference to the political elites and their age-old mission to preserve national unity through accommodation behind closed doors. With the emergence of the Parti Québécois, and later the Bloc Québécois, it has become apparent that an important part of the Quebec political elite has given up playing the old game of elite accommodation with the rest of the country. Instead it was set about systematically to break the whole edifice of accommodation. If this were not threatening enough, the means the PQ has chosen to achieve sovereignty — referenda in 1980 and 1995 — have had an explosive impact on the Canadian political culture. Historically, the Canadian constitution has been an elite affair: the British North America Act of 1867 was never submitted to popular ratification, and the Constitution Act of 1982 was hammered out by first ministers behind closed doors. There is no provision for amendment of the constitution by popular vote. Quebec sovereignists have insisted, however, that a majority vote by the people of Quebec would be a sufficient basis for leaving Canada and forming a new country. This assertion of democratic legitimacy has had profound reverberations in the rest of Canada.

When challenged by a democratic sovereignty movement, the instinctive response of the Canadian political elites has been to try to desperately rejig the mechanisms of elite accommodation. Hence the elite scramble to "patriate" the constitution in 1981–82 after the first sovereignty referendum. Next came the Meech Lake Accord fiasco of the late 1980s when eleven first ministers, behind closed doors, arrived at a constitutional revision that would have formally recognized Quebec as a distinct society. This proved unsaleable to the public outside Quebec, which reacted strongly against the appearance of elite manipulation and the lack of any effective vehicle for democratic expression, as well as against the content of the Accord. After the final inglorious death of Meech, the elites set out with renewed vigour to cobble together the Charlottetown Accord, which attempted to respond not only to Quebec but to the demands of other Canadian groups, especially Aboriginal peoples, for constitutional recognition as well. Again, the process was largely elite-driven, but was submitted to a national referendum for ratification, where it was roundly defeated both in Quebec and in the rest of Canada. The death of Charlottetown was widely viewed as having created constitutional "gridlock," a situation which still seems in place even following the near-victory for the Yes side in the 1995 sovereignty referendum.

The lessons of the 1980s and 1990s are not only that constitutional change seems increasingly difficult to achieve. At a deeper level, the challenge of the sovereignty movement has accelerated the crisis in the rest of Canada of the old political narratives and the mechanisms of elite accommodation that underlay them. All the efforts of the elites to shore up national unity seem to have failed: fifteen years after sovereignty was rejected by 60 percent of Quebec voters, support has risen to close to 50 percent (and close to two out of three Quebec francophones). Worse, the methods chosen to fight separatism seem to have further alienated Canadians outside Quebec from their political institutions.

Meech and Charlottetown were stages in a progressive revolt of the masses in English-speaking Canada against their elites. The federal election of 1993, a year after Charlottetown, saw two parties, fixtures for generations at the centre of Canadian political life, swept off the board and replaced by two new parties. The displaced parties, especially the Conservatives (who had been a leading factor in Canadian politics from the earliest beginnings in the nineteenth century) were deeply associated with the old narratives. The new parties, the Bloc Québécois and the Reform Party, have brought with them new political narratives: the politics of identity and the new populism. Unlike their predecessors, they are driven less by pragmatism than by ideology, less by compromise than by principle. And they also represent the fissure of Canada into two quite different political communities. The Bloc runs only in Quebec; Reform, the real opposition in the rest of Canada, has no presence whatever in Quebec and no realistic hope of gaining any.

The long preoccupation with constitutional questions has thus forced the growth of new political narratives, and new parties to tell these stories. It has also subtly, and sometimes not so subtly, altered the tone of politics. Constitutional politics are about setting the rules of the political game. Ordinary politics are about playing the game under rules accepted by all the players. The old political narratives were essentially about ordinary politics, with the rules taken for granted. The convulsions of recent years, driven in the first instance by the challenge of Quebec sovereignty, but subsequently taking on their own dynamic in the rest of Canada, have tended to throw the rules into question. Thus, the Charlottetown Accord was arrived at not merely to meet Quebec's demands, but also to rewrite the rules of politics for all Canadians. Identity politics was given a major boost as leading groups representing Aboriginal, feminist, and ethnic constituencies sought to find places at the negotiating table and achieve constitutional recognition. This raises the stakes of the political game. In ordinary politics, today's winner can be tomorrow's loser, and vice versa; no issue is ever final or definitive, and thus compromise is encouraged. In constitutional politics, since the very rules of competition are at stake, it is a case of winner take all. Even if the constitutional issue, as such, has reached gridlock, the high-stakes, high-adrenaline style associated with constitutional policies has seeped into regular electoral politics — witness its carryover from the Charlottetown referendum to the 1993 general election.

CANADIAN POLITICS AT THE END OF THE MILLENNIUM

The Parliament of Canada after 1993 presents a schizophrenic spectacle. On the one hand, the Bloc Québécois, the ultimate expression of identity politics, stands astride Quebec confronting Reform, the party of the new populism. Each is strongly ideological and programmatic in their approach to politics, and each puts a high value on faithfulness to principle, and a negative value on compromise. Yet it is the Liberal Party that is actually in office: the quintessential government party, the party of no fixed principles, the party of endless accommodation and compromise, of pragmatism and cynical political marketing. And it is this Liberal Party that continues to bask in unprecedentedly high levels of public approval, levels never seen by Canadian governments for generations, levels unmatched by any other governing party in the Western world. Have we been exaggerating the rate and depth of change if, after all, the party that has dominated Canadian politics throughout most of the twentieth century continues to do so as the century draws to a close? Is the old narrative of liberalism really in decay, if its storytellers continue to preach from the seats of power?

I think the answer to this is paradoxical. The Liberals are succeeding as a party — so far — precisely because their old narrative has decayed. These new narratives, intransigent sovereignist zeal dominating Quebec and intransigent populism dominating the rest of Canada, offer no way out, no common or middle ground. The Liberals, although weak in Quebec, still manage to offer the pretense of being a national party. Even after near defeat in the 1995 referendum, they remain the only political vehicle capable of offering yet another constitutional gambit as a compromise to keep Quebec part of Canada. Reform has broken with the national unity consensus that infused all the established actors in the past and is quite prepared to contemplate a Canada without Quebec. With its insistence on the principle of the equality of the provinces, Reform (and indeed wide populist opinion in the rest of Canada that does not necessarily represent Reform supporters) will never agree to the kind of Meech-like compromises giving Quebec special status that may be inevitable if some deal is to be struck short of Quebec secession.

While this may seem like a Liberal strength, it is actually a weakness. If Quebec secedes, the Liberal Party will likely be destroyed, or at least severely damaged. Yet every move to avert this eventuality tends to undermine Liberal strength in the rest of Canada, given the prevalent populist mood of hostility to special treatment for any part of Canada. Trying to straddle a widening breach might seem like a heroic effort at first, but it could end in disaster.

As for the other part of the old liberal narrative, the economic and social content of liberalism, there is no longer any pretense of fidelity to past traditions. Always something of a chameleon, taking its colouration from its surroundings, the Liberal Party is now taking its economic and social directions from the Reform Party. It is the Liberals, not the former Conservative government with its windy rhetoric of deficit elimination, who have actually imposed a historic reversal on federal indebtedness, with a timetable for deficit reduction that has gained the approval of the international bond rating agencies. The devastating effects of deep cuts on social programs, most of them brought in by former Liberal governments, do not rebound politically on the Liberals, as they cleverly herd Reform MPs ahead of them like human shields. With the disappearance of the social democratic narrative, the Liberals sense that the dynamic of English Canadian politics is now coming from the Right, from the new populism, and they seek to co-opt this dynamic for their own political advantage — in good, time-tested Liberal fashion. Yet this appropriation also limits their capacity to articulate a compelling national federalist vision to counter the sovereignist dream in Quebec. It is hard to counter a dynamic sovereignist politics of national identity with a vision that seeks to downsize and dismantle the institutions of the federal state as too costly for taxpayers to maintain.

The old political narratives are indeed decaying. The new ones taking their place offer confrontation and conflict in place of compromise and pragmatism. With their adherence to high principles and ideological purity, they are heady and seductive at the level of rhetoric. In practice, they point toward jolting, radical adjustments to the existing order, and strains on the social and economic fabric of Canadian life that may be intense. The one party that has survived the debacle of the old order, the Liberal Party, has so far prospered by papering over the widening cracks, but it does so without its old familiar political narrative to guide it. The great unfinished business of Canadian politics is the writing of a new grand narrative that will make sense of the transformed landscape without simply abandoning it to doctrinaires armed with ideological blueprints.

Article Thirty-Eight

Climate Change and Canadian Sovereignty in the Northwest Passage

Rob Huebert

The most recent report from the Intergovernmental Panel on Climate Change (IPCC) reports that the Arctic region is especially sensitive to the dynamics of warming temperatures.[1] The most recent scientific evidence strongly suggests that the Arctic is experiencing warming at a rate greater than almost any other region of the globe. This is evidenced by the thickness of the ice cover; the occurrence of both the melting and freezing of the Arctic Ocean and its surrounding waterways; and from the samples of ice cores.[2] Observations made by northern Aboriginal peoples also lend credence to the evidence that the Arctic is warming up.[3] Insects have been reported much further north than is the norm. Changes in animal migration patterns have also been reported.[4] Both northern Aboriginal peoples and scientists have reported significant changes in the hunting patterns of predators such as the polar bear. For example, Ian Sterling, one of the world's leading experts on the North American polar bear has noted that the polar bear population inhabiting the Hudson Bay region has become smaller.[5] He attributes this to the earlier melting of the ice cover on Hudson Bay, which has made it more difficult for the bears to hunt seal. The Canadian Ice Services of Environment Canada has noted that the ice cover has decreased since the mid-1970s.[6] Satellite data show that the ice cover has steadily been decreasing.

THE PROBLEM: CLIMATE CHANGE AND THE ICE COVER

Not all scientists agree that climate change is the cause of these changes in the Arctic. Some researchers suggest that the ice is thinning because of fluctuations in wind patterns and not as a result of increased temperatures.[7] However, those who suggest that climate change and the

Source: Rob Huebert, "Climate Change and Canadian Sovereignty in the Northwest Passage," *ISUMA: Canadian Journal of Policy Research*, 2, 4 (Winter 2001): 86–94. Used with permission.

resulting impact of global warming have not occurred or have not affected ice levels in the Arctic are in the distinct minority. The consensus is that climate change increases average temperatures in the Arctic regions which, in turn, causes the ice cover to melt.

INCREASED INTEREST IN THE CANADIAN NORTH

There are limited signs of renewed interest in shipping through the Northwest Passage. At the end of the Cold War, ecotourist voyages began to enter the Passage, but only between five and ten partial or complete voyages a year. To date, only icebreakers or ice-strengthened vessels have made the voyage in this capacity, and the companies responsible have requested the Canadian government's permission. Every company that used these vessels to transit the Passage has requested the Canadian Government's permission. Most of these voyages have been without incident. However, in 1996, the *Hanseatic* went aground on a sand bar near Cambridge Bay.[8] Although only a minor oil leak occurred, the grounding was severe enough to require the vessel's complete evacuation as well as the removal of most of its stores to facilitate its removal from the sand bar.

In 1999, the first non-American passage for commercial shipping purposes took place when a Russian company sold a floating dry dock based in Vladivostok. Its new owners decided to move the dock to Bermuda. With the aid of a Russian icebreaker and an ocean-going tug, the dry dock was successfully towed through the Passage. This use of the Passage to avoid storms in the open ocean demonstrated its advantage for international shipping should the ice be reduced. The fact that the dry dock was then almost lost in a storm off Newfoundland seemed to confirm the benefits of sheltered waters of the Passage route.

Also in 1999, a Chinese research vessel visited Tuktoyaktuk. While the Canadian embassy in Beijing had been informed of the Chinese plan to send a vessel to the western Arctic, local Canadian authorities were not informed. Consequently, local officials were considerably surprised when the Chinese arrived in Tuktoyaktuk. The voyage of the Chinese vessel demonstrated the limited Canadian surveillance capabilities. Canadian officials did not learn of the vessel's entry into Canadian waters until it actually arrived.

The U.S. Navy has begun to examine the issue of conducting surface vessel operations in Arctic waters. In April 2001, the U.S. Navy organized a symposium on the subject. This strongly suggests that it perceives the possibility of an ice-free Arctic where it may be required to operate and has begun to give the subject serious thought.

New multilateral efforts to prepare for increased maritime traffic in the Arctic have also begun in the 1990s. An initiative of the Canadian Coast Guard led a group of Arctic coastal states and relevant international shipping companies to meet in 1993 to develop what is now known as the Polar Code.[9] The meetings were intended to develop a common set of international standards governing the construction and operation of vessels that would operate in Arctic waters. To a large degree, these talks represented the Canadian Coast Guard's effort to initiate discussions in anticipation of increased shipping in the region. Unfortunately, the United States State Department has attempted to derail the negotiations for reasons that are not clear. Substantial progress was made when the discussions involved officials from the various Coast Guards. However, as the talks began to lead to an agreement, the American State Department became involved, and several elements of the American position were altered, including initial acceptance of developing a mandatory agreement and accepting the inclusion of Antarctic shipping. Although the other participants have accepted the changes in the American position, the Americans have still been reluctant to advance the negotiations.

While each of these events by themselves can be dismissed as interesting but unimportant events, when considered as a whole they indicate an upward trend in interest in Canadian Arctic waters. Furthermore, it is expected that there will be an increase in activity associated with the development of oil and gas deposits in this region. All things considered, the Canadian Arctic is becoming busy, and as it becomes increasingly ice free, it will become even busier.

THE CANADIAN CLAIM

The melting of the ice that covers the Northwest Passage gives rise to questions about the impact this has on Canadian claims of sovereignty. There is no question about the status of the land territory that comprises the Canadian Arctic archipelago. All conflicting land claims were settled in the 1930s,[10] with the sole exception of a dispute over the ownership of a small island between Baffin Island and Greenland named Hans Island. The government of Denmark contests the Canadian claim of ownership. The only relevance of this claim is its impact on the determination of the maritime boundary line between Canada and Greenland in the Davis Strait. Canadian claims of sovereignty of its Arctic areas with respect to maritime boundaries have resulted in three disputes. Canada disagrees with both the United States and Denmark over the maritime boundaries that border Alaska and Greenland respectively. Neither dispute will be influenced by reduced ice conditions.

It is a third dispute, concerning Canada's claim over the international legal status of the Northwest Passage, which will be adversely affected by a reduction of ice cover in the Passage. The Canadian government's official position is that the Northwest Passage is Canadian historical internal waters. This means that Canada assumes full sovereignty over the waters and thereby asserts complete control over all activity within them. The Government of Canada's most comprehensive statement to this end was made by then Secretary of State for External Affairs, Joe Clark, in the House of Commons on September 10, 1985. In that declaration, he included the following statement:

> Canada's Sovereignty in the Arctic is indivisible. It embraces land, sea, and ice. It extends without interruption to the seaward-facing coasts of the Arctic Islands. These Islands are joined and not divided by the waters between them. They are bridged for most of the year by ice. From time immemorial Canada's Inuit people have used and occupied the ice as they have used and occupied the land.[11]

The Department of Foreign Affairs has not issued any further official statements regarding the Passage since 1985. Following the end of the Cold War, the department's main focus in the north has been the development of new international institutions. These include the Arctic Environmental Protection Strategy and the Arctic Council. Both bodies are important new developments, but their focus has been based almost exclusively on sustainable development.[12] In June 2000, the department issued a "new" Arctic foreign policy statement listing four main objectives. The second objective was to "assert and ensure the preservation of Canada's sovereignty in the North."[13] However, the document does not discuss how Canada will assert and enforce its sovereignty. The only statement on the topic is that the "public concern about sovereignty issues has waned" and that "globalization has also altered the exercise of state sovereignty, partly through the development of a web of legally binding multilateral agreements, informal agreements and institutions. "[14] There is no explanation or justification as to how these assessments are reached.

The department has had little to say about the impact of climate change on Canadian claims. One of the few comments on the subject was made by an official from the Legal Affairs

Bureau in a presentation in Whitehorse on March 19, 2001 regarding Canadian sovereignty in the Arctic. Much of his focus was on the impact of climate change. Although his discussion is not official policy, it nevertheless provides the most current understanding of the position of the Department of Foreign Affairs. He argued that Canadian sovereignty over the waterways of the Canadian Arctic did not depend on the ice cover of the region, but that Canada's view,

> then and now, is that since the 1880 deed transfer [of the Arctic archipelago from the U.K. to Canada], the waters of the Arctic Archipelago have been Canada's internal waters by virtue of historical title. These waters have been used by Inuit, now of Canada, since time immemorial. Canada has unqualified and uninterrupted sovereignty over the waters.[15]

The official also noted that Canada has not relied on the concept of "ice as land" to support its claim of sovereignty. This is due in part to the differences between pack ice and shelf ice. Pack ice is "dynamic and ever-changing" and is therefore "unsuitable for legal analysis as being dry land." Shelf ice, while potentially more useful in determining boundaries, is not particularly useful to Canadian claims in that the four main ice shelves of the Canadian Arctic are on the northern border of Baffin Island, and therefore, are not pertinent to the issue of the Northwest Passage. Thus, he concluded that "even if the ice were to melt, Canada's legal sovereignty would be unaffected."[16] In conclusion, he argues "[S]overeignty over the marine areas is based on law, not on the fact that waters in question frequently are covered by ice. The waters between the lands and the islands are the waters of Canada by virtue of historical waters."[17]

There are several problems with this line of argument that are unrelated to the issue of ice use. First, the claim that these waters are internal by virtue of historical title is in doubt. A study by one of the leading Canadian legal jurists, Donat Pharand, has demonstrated the weakness of the use of this line of argumentation. In his major study of the issue he concludes that "[i]t is highly doubtful that Canada could succeed in proving that the waters of the Canadian Arctic Archipelago are historical internal waters over which it has complete sovereignty."[18] Pharand supports this conclusion with two sets of arguments. First, the use of the legal concept of historical waters has diminished in recent years. It is unlikely that it would be persuasive in an international court. Second, the requirements for proving historical waters are exacting. These include "exclusive control and long usage by the claimant State as well as acquiescence by foreign States, particularly those clearly affected by the claim."[19] Pharand argues this has not been the case for Canadian Arctic waters. Canada has not dedicated the resources to demonstrate exclusive control, and the foreign States with an interest, i.e., the United States and the European Union, have not acquiesced. Although Canada may make a claim that the Arctic waters are historical waters, Pharand convincingly argues that this claim would likely not withstand an international challenge.

The Canadian foreign affairs official also argued that the Government of Canada's decision in 1986 to enclose the Canadian Arctic Archipelago by straight baselines ensures that the waters within the straight baselines are internal. The weakness of this argument lies in the timing of the Canadian declaration. Canada implemented straight baselines around the Arctic on January 1, 1986. However, in 1982, it had signed the United Nations Law of the Sea Convention (UNCLOS), in which article 8(2) states that a State cannot close an international strait by declaring straight baselines.[20] Therefore, the Canadian government's claim that drawing straight baselines gives it the international legal right to claim jurisdiction over international shipping in these waters is also unlikely to withstand an international challenge.

The Foreign Affairs official offered a strong argument that the condition of the ice is not an important element of the Canadian claim. However, this is not entirely true. As stated earlier, the September 10, 1985 statement by Joe Clark clearly connects ice conditions to sovereignty. The statement provides that the islands of the Arctic are "joined and not divided by the waters between them. They are bridged for most of the year by ice." The statement continues that "[f]rom time immemorial Canada's Inuit people have used and occupied the ice as they have used and occupied the land."[21] The intent of the Government of Canada in issuing this statement is clear. The ice cover makes the Northwest Passage unique by virtue of the inhabitation of the Inuit on the ice. Thus, the ice can be considered more as land than water. Following this logic, the Government is obviously making the case that international law as it pertains to international straits does not apply. Since this statement remains as the definitive statement on Canadian Arctic sovereignty, it is clear that any new statements to the contrary are not accurate.

The Canadian legal position has been challenged. Both the United States and the European Union have indicated that they do not accept Canadian claims of sovereignty over the waters of the Canadian Arctic archipelago. However, neither the United States nor the European Union pushed their challenge as long as ice conditions precluded any economically viable international shipping. This hesitation will likely diminish as the ice melts, and this is the crux of the problem facing Canada.

THE AMERICAN AND EUROPEAN POSITION

The United States and the European Union position is that, contrary to Canadian claims, the Northwest Passage is an international strait. The Americans in particular do not accept the argument that ice cover makes a difference for the international legal definition of an international strait. The Americans have always maintained that the International Court of Justice's ruling in the Strait of Corfu case is applicable for the Northwest Passage. In that case, the Court ruled that an international strait is a body of water that joins two international bodies of water, and has been used by international shipping.[22] The United States argues that the Northwest Passage joins two international bodies of water and has been used for international shipping, albeit a very small number of transits.

Historically, the United States has posed the greatest challenge to Canadian claims of sovereignty. In 1969 and in 1970, the *Manhattan*, on behalf of Humble Oil, transited the Northwest Passage without seeking the Government of Canada's permission. The *Manhattan* was an ice-strengthened super tanker which could transit the Northwest Passage only with the assistance of icebreakers, and even then, ice conditions made the voyage very difficult and expensive.[23] In 1985, the American icebreaker, *Polar Sea*, was sent through the Passage without the Canadian government's permission. Though not designed to challenge Canadian claims of sovereignty, the voyage led to a significant diplomatic dispute.[24] However, to maintain good American–Canadian relations, an agreement was reached regarding future transits by American icebreakers. The 1988 agreement on Arctic co-operation between the Government of the United States of America and the Government of Canada required the United States to request Canadian consent for any future transit of the Passage by American government icebreakers.[25] However, both governments agreed to disagree on the actual status of the Passage. When the agreement was reached, the United States had only two icebreakers capable of such a passage. Since then, the Americans have built one more icebreaker, which invoked the agreement to transit the Passage in 2000.

In addition to the United States, the United Kingdom, acting on behalf of the European Community, issued a diplomatic protest against Canadian efforts in 1985 to enclose its Arctic waters as internal waters by using straight baselines.[26] The Europeans have kept their protests low key, preferring to allow the Americans to take the more active position. But by issuing a demarche against the Canadian claim, they have given notice that they have not acquiesced to Canadian claims of sovereignty.

SIGNIFICANCE OF THE DISPUTE

The difference between the Canadian position and that of the United States and the European Union is in the issue of control. If the Passage is Canadian internal waters as maintained by Canada, Canada has sovereign control over any activity, both foreign and domestic, that occurs in those waters. On the other hand, if the Northwest Passage is an international strait, then Canada cannot unilaterally control international shipping in it. Therefore, Canada would be unable to deny passage to any vessel that meets international standards for environmental protection, crew training and safety procedures. As these standards are set by the International Maritime Organization (IMO), Canada cannot set different standards, especially those which impose more demanding requirements.

However, Canada could invoke more exacting environmental standards through the United Nations Law of the Sea Convention (UNCLOS). Article 234, the ice-covered waters clause, allows a State to pass legislation that exceeds international standards for any ice-covered waters within its 200-mile Exclusive Economic Zone (EEZ). The Canadian clause, as it is referred to since Canada was its main proponent, states

> Coastal States have the right to adopt and enforce non-discriminatory laws and regulations for the preservation, reduction and control of marine pollution from vessels in ice-covered areas within the limits of the exclusive economic zone, where particularly severe climatic conditions and the presence of ice covering such areas for most of the year create obstructions or exceptional hazards to navigation, and pollution of the marine environment could cause major harm to or irreversible disturbance of the ecological balance. Such laws and regulations shall have due regard to navigation and the protection and preservation of the marine environment based on the best available scientific evidence.[27]

It is important to note that the article does not give the coastal State the right to deny passage. Rather it bestows the right to the coastal State to pass its own domestic legislation for environmental protection rather than being bound by international standards. Such legislation can be more demanding than that of existing international agreements.

It is interesting that despite the fact that Canada drafted the clause and was originally a strong supporter of the entire Convention, it has not ratified the Convention.[28] The Government of Canada has stated that it accepts most of the Convention as customary international law. However, while it has continued to issue vague statements that it someday intends to ratify the Convention, there is no evidence as to when or if this will actually happen.

Although the issue of sovereignty invokes strong nationalistic feelings for Canadians, the reality is that after Canada and the United States signed the Arctic Cooperation Agreement in 1988, which controls the passage of American icebreakers, and continued to officially ignore the transit of American nuclear-powered submarines through Canadian northern waters, there was little incentive to revisit the issue. As long as ice conditions remained hazardous to commercial shipping, there was little incentive for any country, the United States included, to challenge the Canadian position. However, if ice conditions become less hazardous, then this situation changes drastically. The main attraction of the Northwest Passage is obvious. It substantially shortens the distance from Asia to the east coast of the United States and Europe. It is more than 8,000 kilometres shorter than the current route through the Panama Canal, and would significantly shorten the voyage for vessels that are too large to fit through the Canal and must sail around the Cape Horn. The voyage of the *Manhattan* demonstrated that the Passage can accommodate supertankers of at least 120,000 tons. The shorter distance means substantial savings for shipping companies, which translates into reduced costs for the products that are shipped. It is easy to see why an ice-free Northwest Passage, even for a limited time, would be of tremendous interest to major international shipping companies as well as the countries that avail themselves of their services.

It is impossible to know who will make the first challenge. While it is reasonable to suspect that it might be either an American or a European vessel, it could also be from another country. For example, Japan has shown considerable interest in Arctic navigation in the 1990s. It was a major partner in a multi-year million-dollar study of navigation through the Russian Northern Sea Route (also known as the Northeast Passage).[29] The Japanese also were interested in buying the Canadian ice-strengthened oil tanker, *Arctic*, when the Canadian government put it up for sale. Perhaps even more telling is the amount of money that the Japanese put into polar research and development that is now substantial and continues to increase.[30] While the Japanese have never issued a statement of their view of the status of the Northwest Passage, it is clear that they would gain if it became a functioning international strait. Oil from both Venezuela and the Gulf of Mexico would then be cheaper to ship to Japan.

CANADIAN EFFORTS TO ASSERT AND MAINTAIN SOVEREIGNTY

It would appear that Canada should be now giving serious thought to how it can best respond to the prospects of any future challenges. Unfortunately there is little indication that this is happening. Instead, it appears that the Government continues to downgrade its existing limited capabilities. The two main government agencies with important roles in the protection and maintenance of Canadian international interests in the Arctic are the Department of National Defence (DND) and the Canadian Coast Guard (CCG). Both are continuing to see their northern capabilities reduced.

While the Department of National Defence has begun to consider the impact of a diminished ice cover, budget cuts forced it to eliminate most of its activities devoted to northern sovereignty. The previous Commander of Northern Area initiated a working group of relevant federal and territorial departments, called the Arctic Security Interdepartmental Working Group, which has been meeting twice a year since May 1999. The group shares both information and concerns and has raised the issue of climate change several times. However, it has almost no resources of its own and can only act as a means of co-ordination and networking.

Also at the initiative of the former Commander of Northern Area, DND recently assessed its capabilities in the north. The assessment found that Canada had limited resources that could be used in the northern area, and that the cost of any equipment and programs to remedy this shortcoming would be extremely expensive. The department concluded that given its constrained budget, resources would be allocated to more immediate priorities. It did note that projects could be developed to improve surveillance capabilities if funding was available.[31]

Financial cutbacks to the department have resulted in the elimination of most programs that gave Canada a presence in the North. Northern deployments of naval assets to Canadian northern waters, termed NORPLOYS, ended in 1990. Northern sovereignty overflights by Canadian long-range patrol aircraft (CP-140/CPI40A Aurora and Arcturus) were reduced in 1995 to one overflight per year and will soon be totally eliminated. The recently acquired Victoria class submarines do not have the capability to operate in Arctic waters. In fact, none of the Canadian naval units can operate in northern waters due to their thin hulls and the risk of ice damage.

The one exception to the cutbacks is the recent expansion of the number of Ranger Patrols. The Canadian government is increasing the number of serving Rangers from 3,500 to 4,800 by 2008.[32] However, although the Rangers can assert a presence in the north, they are a militia unit comprising northern inhabitants who can travel a moderate distance with snowmobiles.

In short, the ability of the Department of Defence to demonstrate a presence in the North is severely limited. The recently concluded defence study does suggest that it may be possible to improve surveillance with future technological developments including High Frequency Surface Wave Radar, rapidly deployable undersea surveillance systems and the use of UAVs (unmanned aerial vehicles-drones). While each system would prove useful for surveillance and presence in the North, none is currently being considered for deployment and all are still in the research and development phase. These technologies are unlikely to be purchased anytime soon.

The Canadian Coast Guard has the greatest responsibility for monitoring the Arctic region. Recently moved from the Department of Transport to the Department of Fisheries and Oceans, the CCG operates a fleet of icebreakers in the Arctic, consisting of two heavy ice-breakers and three medium icebreakers. The most recent icebreaker, the *Henry Larsen* was added in 1987, but the fleet is heavily tasked and is ageing. A prolonged refit between 1988 and 1993 resulted in the extension of the operating life of the largest icebreaker, *Louis St. Laurent*. However, the vessel will soon be reaching the end of its operational life. There are no plans to build any new icebreakers in the immediate future.

Following the 1969–1970 voyage of the *Manhattan*, the Trudeau Government enacted the *Arctic Waters Pollution Prevention Act*,[33] creating a 100-mile environmental protection zone within Canadian Arctic waters. AWPPA regulations forbid the discharge of any fluids or solid wastes into the Arctic waters and set design requirements for vessels. Upon entering Canadian Arctic waters, vessels are requested to register through NORDREG, a voluntary, not manda-tory, reporting system operated by the coast guard that all vessels (Canadian and otherwise) are requested to use when operating in Canadian Arctic waters. While such a system works rea-sonably well when few vessels enter the Northwest Passage, it is clear that it will not work when the number of voyages increases due to ice reduction. Consideration has been given to make NORDREG mandatory, but there has been no further action on this front.

The voluntary nature of NORDREG poses an obvious challenge to Canada's commitment to its claims. If Canada is serious about its statements that the waters of the Arctic Archipelago are internal waters, then there should be no question about its ability to enforce its rules and requirements. Yet, by making the system voluntary, the message internationally is that Canada questions its own ability to enforce its claim.

Canada does not have the capability to demonstrate a meaningful presence in its Arctic waters. So long as ice conditions in the north do not change, then this is not a significant problem. However, as the ice melts, it will become a serious problem.

THE INTERNATIONALIZATION OF THE NORTHWEST PASSAGE

Would it really matter if Canada lost an international challenge to its claim of sovereignty? The Canadian government is on record as stating that it does support international shipping through the Passage as long as Canadian regulations are followed.[34] The issue, then, is the type of regulations to be followed. Canada could claim that regardless of the status of the Passage, it retains the right to pass environmental regulations based on article 234 of UNCLOS. The problem with this argument is that the Canadian Government has not ratified the Convention. Therefore, the question is whether Canada could claim the rights provided by the article without ratifying the Convention.

The Canadian Coast Guard's efforts to formulate a Polar Code to govern the construction and operation of shipping in Arctic waters are designed to ensure that any international rules will have significant Canadian input. Canada, along with Russia, has played a key role in devel-oping the technical requirements contained in the code.[35] On the other hand, these efforts may send the message that Canada expects to lose the ability to develop regulations unilater-ally. Thus, there are signs that a new regime for regulating the international system is developing beyond Canada's control. Such a regime is likely to leave Canada facing tremendous challenges if, and when, shipping develops.

First, traditional security problems of an international waterway will arise. An examination of waterways in southeast Asia indicates that increased shipping can result in increased smuggling and other associated crimes. The deserted coastlines of northern Canada could be used for a host of illegal activities such as drug and human smuggling. It is also likely that smuggling of other goods, such as diamonds and fresh water could also take place. To control such potential problems, Canada will have to improve its surveillance and policing capabilities substantially.

The spread of new and exotic diseases is also a potential problem. Crews of most vessels come from southern countries and may carry strains of diseases to which northern Canadians have a low tolerance or to which they have not been exposed. Thus the risk of a disease outbreak could increase as shipping increases.

Even if Canada implements strong environmental regulations, the probability of an accident will increase with the corresponding increase of ship traffic. As the *Exxon Valdez* accident demonstrated, the grounding of a large vessel in northern waters will produce an ecological disaster. Currently, Canada is ill-equipped for even a moderate grounding, as was clearly demonstrated in 1996 when the *Hanseatic* grounded off Cambridge Bay.[36] The *Hanseatic* was successfully evacuated due only to the favourable weather conditions and the availability of local commercial pilots and planes. It is doubtful the grounding could have been responded to as successfully in a more isolated location and with severe weather conditions.

The lifestyle of Canada's northern Aboriginal people will be substantially affected by international shipping. Traditional hunting and trapping will be severely dislocated by the twin impact of global warming and the passages of large vessels. The influx of large numbers of foreigners associated with the new shipping will also affect their traditional way of life. Opportunities for employment will be available, but only for northerners with the right skills.

Nevertheless, there are some advantages to the melting of the Northwest Passage. Singapore has demonstrated that with the proper planning, geographical location on an international strait can bring substantial economic benefits. Vessels transiting the Passage would require certain services that could be provided by Canadian settlements. For example, Tuktoyaktuk and Iqaluit could conceivably become important ports of call if their port facilities were substantially improved.

CONCLUSIONS

Will climate change result in the melting of the Northwest Passage for some parts of the year? Will international shipping interests then attempt to take advantage of the more benign conditions? Will the Canadian status regarding the Passage be challenged? Will Canada be prepared? The evidence for the first is mounting. The question that remains is how fast these changes will occur and when the Passage will become economically viable for shipping interests. It is logical that international shipping interests will wish to take advantage if and when this happens. Canada can expect to face a challenge when this occurs. It is becoming apparent that the Canadian position will probably not be successful given the current low levels of Canadian activity in the region. But even if Canadian claims of sovereignty are upheld, pressure to allow the passage of international shipping will remain. Regardless of the nature of the international status, it is clear that Canada will face tremendous challenges in adapting to the opening of the Passage. The challenge that now faces Canada is to become aware of these possibilities and to begin taking action to prepare for them.

NOTES

1. Intergovernmental Panel on Climate Change, *Climate Change 2001: The Scientific Basis. A Report of Working Group I of the Intergovernmental Panel on Climate Change* (2001), PP- 2.2.5–2.2.6. [http://www.ipcc.sh/].

2. O.M. Johannessen, E.V. Shalina and M.W. Miles, "Satellite Evidence for an Arctic Sea Ice Cover in Transformation," *Science*, Vol. 286 (1999), pp. 1937–39; D.A. Rothrock, Y. Yu, and G.A. Maykut, "Thinning of the Arctic Sea-Ice Cover," *Geophysical Research Letters*, Vol. 26, no. 23 (December 1999), pp. 3469–3472; and M.J. Serreze, J. Walsh, F. Chapin, T. Osterkamp, M. Dyurgerov, V. Romanovsky, W. Oechel, J. Morrison, T. Zhang and R.G. Berry, "Observational Evidence of Recent Changes in Northern High-Latitude Environment," *Climate Change*, Vol. 46 (2000), pp. 159–207.

3. S. McKibbon, "Inuit Elders Say the Arctic Climate is Changing," *Nunatsiaq News* (June 2, 2000).

4. R. Bowkett, "Clear Signs of Global Warming: Dandelions at the Arctic Circle," *Anglican Journal*, Vol. 123, no. 8 (October 1997), p. 7; M. Nichols and D. Huffam, "The Heat Is On: A Crisis Is in the Making as Canada Confronts Its Commitment to Drastically Reduce Greenhouse-Gas Emissions," *Maclean's* (February 21, 2000), p. 48

5. I. Stirling, "Running out of Ice?" *Natural History*, Vol. 109, no. 2 (March 2000), p. 92.

6. J. Falkingham, "Sea Ice in the Canadian Arctic in the 21st Century," (September 2000) (unpublished paper).

7. B. Webber, "Arctic Sea Ice Is Not Melting: New Research," *Canadian Press* (April 24, 2001).

8. F. McCague "High Arctic Grips a Cruise Ship: Hundreds Evacuate by Dinghies as Tugs Try to Free the *Hanseatic*," *Alberta Report*, Vol. 2, no. 40 (September 16, 1996), p. 15.

9. L. Brigham, "Commentary: An International Polar Navigation Code for the Twenty-First Century," *Polar Record*, Vol. 33, no. 187 (1997), p. 283.

10. E. Franckx, Maritime *Claims in the Arctic* (Dordrecht: Martinus Nijhoff Publishers, 1993), pp. 71–74.

11. External Affairs Canada, *Statements* and *Speeches*, "Policy on Canadian Sovereignty" (September 10, 1985).

12. R. Huebert, "New Directions in Circumpolar Cooperation: Canada, The Arctic Environmental Protection Strategy, and the Arctic Council," *Canadian Foreign Policy*, Vol. 5, no. 2 (Winter 1998), pp. 37–57.

13. Department of Foreign Affairs and International Trade, *The Northern Dimension of Canada's Foreign Policy* (n.d.), p. 2.

14. *Ibid.*, p.5.

15. M. Gaillard, Legal Affairs Bureau, Department of Foreign Affairs and International Trade, "Canada's Sovereignty in Changing Arctic Waters," (March 19, 2001), Whitehorse, Yukon.

16. *Ibid.*, p.4.

17. *Ibid.*, p. 5.

18. D. Pharand, *Canada's Arctic Waters in International Law* (Cambridge: Cambridge University Press, 1988), p. 251.

19. *Ibid.*

20. United Nations, The Law of the Sea, *United Nations Convention on the Law of the Sea with Index and Final Act of the Third United Nations Conference on the Law of the Sea (UNCLOS)* (New York: United Nations, 1983), p. 4.

21. *Op. cit.*, External Affairs, note 11 at p. 2.

22. *Corfu Channel Case* [1949] ICJ, Rep.4.

23. D. McRae, "The Negotiation of Article 234," in F. Griffiths (ed.), *Politics of the Northwest Passage* (Kingston and Montreal; McGill-Queen's University Press, 1987), pp. 98–114.

24. R. Huebert, "Polar Vision or Tunnel Vision: The Making of Canadian Arctic Waters Policy," *Marine Policy*, Vol. 19, no. 4 (1995), pp. 343–363.

25. *Agreement between the Government of the United States of America and the Government of Canada on Arctic Cooperation*, (January 11, 1988).

26. R. Huebert, "Steel Ice and Decision-Making. The Voyage of the Polar Sea and its Aftermath: The Making of Canadian Northern Foreign Policy," (Halifax: Dalhousie Unversity, 1993), p. 331. (Unpublished thesis).

27. *Op. cit., UNCLOS*, note 20 at p. 84.

28. Canada remains one of only a handful of countries that have not ratified the Convention. Currently 135 States have ratified. The few that have not are either landlocked and/or a developing State. The United States is the only other major country that has not ratified. United Nations, Ocean and Law of the Sea Home Page, "Convention and Implementing Agreement," July 31, 2001 [http://www.un.org/Depts/los/losconv1.htm].

29. INSROP, International Northern Sea Route Programme, June 1993–March 1994. [http:www.fni.no/insrop/#Overview].

30. Natural Sciences and Engineering Research Council of Canada (NSERC) and Social Sciences and Humanities Research Council of Canada (SSHRC), *From Crisis to Opportunity: Rebuilding Canada's Role in Northern Research*

2000: Final Report to NSERC and SSHRC from the Task Force on Northern Research (Ottawa: NSERC and SSHRC, 2000), p. 12; B. Wuethrich, "New Center Gives Japan an Arctic Toehold," *Science*, vol. 285 (September 17, 1999), p. 1827.

31. A. Mitrovica, "Military Admits It Can't Detect Arctic Intruders," *Globe and Mail* (March 17, 2001), p. A3.

32. DND, VCDS, "Reserves and Cadets: Canadian Rangers." [http://www.rangers.dnd.ca/rangers/intro_e.asp].

33. *Arctic Water Pollution Prevention Act* 1970 [R.S.C. 1985 (1st Supp.) C.2, (1st Supp.) S.1.]

34. The most recent statement by the Government of Canada on the issue of shipping in the Northwest Passage can be found in its response to the Special Committee of the Senate and House of Commons on Canada's International Relations (Hockin Simard Report). See Department of External Affairs, Canada's *International Relations: Response of the Government of Canada to the Report of the Special Joint Committee of the Senate and the House of Commons* (December 1986), p. 32.

35. L. Brigham, "Commentary: An International Polar Navigation Code for the Twenty-First Century," *Polar Record*, vol. 33, no. 187 (1997), p. 283.

36. *Op. cit.*, McCague, note 8 at p. 15.

CONTRIBUTORS

Jean Barman is a professor in the Department of Educational Studies at the University of British Columbia in Vancouver.

Carl Berger is retired from the Department of History at the University of Toronto where he taught Canadian history and is currently Professor Emeritus.

Nancy B. Bouchier teaches sport history in the faculty of Kinesiology at McMaster University.

Bettina Bradbury teaches in the History Department at York University and in Women's Studies, Glendon College, York University.

Craig Brown is retired. He taught Canadian history at the University of Toronto.

Phillip Buckner taught history at the University of New Brunswick. He is currently a Senior Research Fellow at the Institute of Commonwealth Studies, University of London.

Alan C. Cairns is Adjunct Professor of Political Science at the University of Waterloo and Professor Emeritus in the Political Science Department at the University of British Columbia, where he taught from 1960 to 1995.

Lara Campbell teaches Canadian history at Simon Fraser University in Vancouver, British Columbia.

J. Terry Copp teaches Canadian history at Wilfrid Laurier University in Waterloo, Ontario.

Stephen Davies teaches in the Department of History at the University of Ottawa.

A.A. den Otter teaches Canadian history at Memorial University in St. John's, Newfoundland.

Peter deLottinville is an archivist at the National Archives of Canada in Ottawa.

James Eayrs taught political science at the University of Toronto from 1955 to 1980 and at Dalhousie University in Halifax from 1980 until his retirement in 1991.

Alain-G. Gagnon is Professor in the Department of Political Science at the Université du Québec à Montréal where he holds the Canada Research Chair in Quebec and Canadian Studies.

J.L. Granatstein taught Canadian history at York University, Toronto from 1966 to 1995, and is Distinguished Research Professor of History Emeritus. He served as the Director and CEO of the Canadian War Museum (1998–2001).

John Harles teaches political science at Messiah College in Grantham, Pennsylvania.

Ronald G. Haycock is Professor of Military History and War Studies at the Royal Military College of Canada in Kingston, Ontario.

Craig Heron teaches social science and Canadian history at York University in Toronto.

Colin D. Howell teaches Canadian history at St. Mary's University in Halifax, Nova Scotia.

Rob Huebert teaches in the Department of Political Science, and at the Centre for Military and Strategic Studies, University of Calgary.

Richard Jones has retired from the Department of History at Université Laval.

Will Kymlicka is a Professor of Philosophy at Queen's University in Kingston, Ontario.

David Lee is a historian with Historical Services Branch, National Historic Sites Directorate, Parks Canada, Canadian Heritage in Hull, Quebec.

Helen Lenskyj is Professor in the Sociology and Equity Studies in Education Program at the Ontario Institute for Studies in Education at the University of Toronto.

Joseph Levitt (1920–1995) taught history at the University of Ottawa.

Robert A.J. McDonald teaches Canadian history at the University of British Columbia in Vancouver.

J.R. Miller is Canada Research Chair and Professor of History at the University of Saskatchewan in Saskatoon.

Howard Palmer (1946–1991) taught Canadian history at the University of Calgary.

John A. Rohr is Professor of Public Administration at the Centre for Public Administration and Policy at Virginia Polytechnic Institute and State University.

Peter H. Russell is retired from the Department of Political Economy at the University of Toronto.

Robert Rutherdale teaches in the Department of History and Philosophy at Algoma University College, Laurentian University, Sault Ste Marie, Ontario.

Myer Siemiatycki teaches politics at Ryerson Polytechnic University.

A. Blair Stonechild is Head of Indigenous Studies, First Nations University of Canada, in Regina.

Veronica Strong-Boag is a Canadian historian working in Women's Studies and Educational Studies at the University of British Columbia in Vancouver.

James Struthers teaches history and Canadian Studies at Trent University in Peterborough, Ontario.

James W. St.G. Walker teaches Canadian history at the University of Waterloo.

Reg Whitaker is Distinguished Research Professor Emeritus at York University, and currently teaches Political Science at the University of Victoria.

PHOTO CREDITS

INDEX